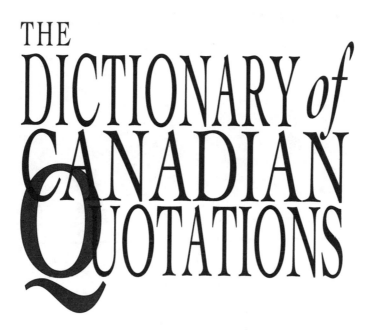

THE
DICTIONARY *of*
CANADIAN
QUOTATIONS

THE

DICTIONARY *of* CANADIAN QUOTATIONS

JOHN ROBERT COLOMBO

Stoddart

First published in 1991 by
Stoddart Publishing Co. Limited
34 Lesmill Road
Toronto, Canada
M3B 2T6

Canadian Cataloguing in Publication Data

Main entry under title:

The Dictionary of Canadian quotations

Includes index.
ISBN 0-7737-2515-6

1. Quotations, Canadian (English).*   2. Canada — Quotations,
maxims, etc.   I. Colombo, John Robert, 1936-

PN6081.D53 1991   C818'.02   C91-094814-3

Cover design: Brant Cowie/ArtPlus Limited
Typesetting: Tony Gordon Ltd.

Printed and bound in Canada

Introduction

A dictionary of quotations is a mosaic of meaningful, memorable remarks made about all subjects under the sun. A dictionary of Canadian quotations is a collection of such remarks so selected as to pay particular attention to a single people and their place in the world.

The Dictionary of Canadian Quotations is a national "quote book" and a completely new collection of quoted matter. It is based on no previous collection or selection prepared by the present compiler or by any other compiler. This quote book is a brand-new collection, a bright new mosaic.

It is also a book of surprises. It offers the reader or the user, whether a curious Canadian or a committed Canadianist, a large number of "quotable quotes" about a full range of subjects. Most aspects of modern life are illuminated, at least indirectly, somewhere in the pages of this book. The principles that govern the choice and selection of quotations are simply expressed. Canadians are quoted on all subjects; non-Canadians are quoted on this country and its people. Important and interesting observations made about all subjects are included; special prominence is given to characteristic remarks made by public figures on subjects of current public interest.

More than 6000 quotations originally written or spoken by about 2500 men and women are to be found in the pages of this book. The quotations are arranged by subject; there are more than 900 alphabetically arranged subject headings, and under each heading the quotations are arrayed, generally in chronological order, sometimes in thematic order. The sources of the quotations are given. The subject headings go from an entry on the letter *A* to an entry on the letters *Zzz*. There are a great many "see" and "see also" references; there is also an index of contributors which runs some 10,000 lines.

The Dictionary of Canadian Quotations is a work of popular reference. It is ideal for browsing and grazing, for borrowing ideas and burrowing into subjects. Indeed, it is a handy source of reference to current thinking about all manner of Canadian notions and expressions. It has been edited to meet the requirements of those who are in need of fresh ideas on familiar themes or are desirous of information on special topics, especially those of contemporary interest. The book is current and topical.

Unlike all earlier collections of quoted matter published in this country, this book is the result of brand-new research. With very few exceptions, quotations that have appeared in earlier quote books were not considered candidates for inclusion in this one. (The handful of quotations that do appear from earlier books are represented here by virtue of being freshly researched from newer sources.)

Perhaps half of the 6000 quotations refer to events and issues that have emerged since the 1970s; perhaps one-third refer to developments that have taken place since 1984, the year that Brian Mulroney was first elected Prime Minister of Canada. The book is about contemporary Canada. Yet its scope is not limited to current events; present-day historical research continues to alter our appreciation of the past and our approach to the present. The local weather keeps changing; so do our views about the national climate.

The major contributors to the present work happen to be the country's principal social commentators, yet attention has also been paid to the observations and remarks of commentators with local rather than national followings, to the findings of respected scholars, and to the expressions of opinion of men and women unknown to national, local, and specialist forums. An attempt has been made to represent all regions of the country. Indeed, an attempt has been made to globalize the undertaking — to see ourselves, if not *sub specie aeternitatis*, then at least *humanitatis*.

Today the very existence of the country is being called into question. Never before have the achievements and attitudes of Canadians in the past been so questioned. Changes in the world order and initiatives taken by successive neo-conservative administrations have brought Canadians face to face with foreign and domestic imperatives that are seemingly without number. A series of national debates has divided Canadians — debates on capital punishment, the availability of abortion, the Free Trade Agreement, the Meech Lake Constitutional Accord, provisions for Quebec as a "distinct society," federalism and separatism, the Oka crisis and native land claims, the downsizing of the federal and provincial public service, diminished equalization payments, deregulation, privatization of Crown corporations, the federal role in transportation and communications, foreign policy, immigration, drug use, national educational standards, the funding of research and development and the cultural industries, social welfare, medicare, provincial barriers, international competitiveness, etc. It is no wonder that Canadians have a reputation for navel gazing. After almost a century and a quarter of

Confederation, citizens across the country are re-examining, when not examining for the first time, the basis of national unity and the under-pinnings of their national identity, their sense of security, and their continued prosperity. The quotations in this book reflect this feeling that we are back to square one.

Public personalities, especially politicians, may love to have their words quoted, but they hate to have them quoted out of context. Yet words are always being taken out of their context. Who would wish to reproduce the entire context — an address to the Empire Club, say — to preserve a gem of a remark? Indeed, there is no quotation in this book that has not been separated from its oral or printed context. The quotation is the pearl; the context is the shell. It is necessary to pry open the shell to expose the pearl. Once removed from its cosy surroundings, the pearl-like quotation may be viewed "in the round," so to speak. So viewed, a quotation stands on its own. If it is an important or interesting remark, it not only stands on its own — it stands out. Many of the quotations in this book are most quotable indeed.

There are three different *types*, three different *kinds*, and three different *classes* of quotations.

The three different *types* of quoted matter are proverbs, aphorisms, and quotations proper. Proverbs, like "A stitch in time saves nine," are age old and anonymous. The proverb's country cousin is the proverbial expression ("Till hell freezes over"); its city cousin is graffiti ("Canada from Sea to Saw"). Proverbs and their cousins are general statements of popular wisdom. Although of unknown authorship, the provenance of some proverbs is known. Thomas Chandler Haliburton, the Nova Scotian judge and wit, is credited, like his Boston predecessor Benjamin Franklin, with originating or preserving a slew of proverbs and proverbial expres-sions that have become part and parcel of the English language. One proverb first recorded by Judge Haliburton goes like this: "A beautiful bird seldom sings."

Proverbs, for all their pith and power, are rough-hewn expressions of "the people." As such, they differ from aphorisms. An aphorism is a polished and pointed observation made by a man or woman at a given time and a particular place. An aphorism is the product not of the people but of one person's thought and expression. The aphorism partakes of the characteristics of the aphorist. Who other than Stephen Leacock would ever have written that a young twit "rode madly off in all direc-tions"? (The popularity of the remark is deserved, yet it took U.S.

President Theodore Roosevelt to draw it to national and thus international attention.) Aphorists of the calibre of Leacock — and his American predecessor Mark Twain and his American contemporary Will Rogers — have observed human nature closely, warmly, and characteristically.

The aphorism makes up in polish what it may lack in power. Yet neither polish nor power is characteristic of what is called the quotation proper. The quotation proper holds the stage and commands public attention because it gives current and characteristic expression to a present-day attitude. A quotation proper is a statement that tells us a lot about its subject matter but only a little about its speaker. An instance of a quotation proper is the remark made about the wealthy in this country by former Finance Minister Michael Wilson. "No matter how we define the term," he said, "Canada has an acute shortage of rich people."

While proverbs, aphorisms, and quotations proper are three different *types* of quoted matter, there are also three different *kinds* of quoted matter: historically important quotations, socially significant quotations, and psychologically relevant quotations. An historically important quotation (like Mackenzie King's formulation, "Conscription if necessary but not necessarily conscription") recalls an event or an era that has affected the lives of many people. A socially significant quotation (like Irving Layton's remark, "A Canadian is someone who keeps asking the question, 'What is a Canadian?'") is an aphorism about a society that summarizes an attitude characteristic of a time and place. A psychologically relevant quotation (like the remark of Wayne Gretzky, "I skate to where the puck is going to be, not where it's been") is an insight that functions more or less as a personal maxim. As well, quotations may combine these three characteristics. The importance of quotations generally lies in the fact that they illuminate subjects and topics of current or recurring interest and that they do so from the vantage point of history, society, or the individual.

Quotations may also be divided into three *classes*: familiar, characteristic, and informational. These features may be combined in any one quotation. The word *familiar* remains associated with the bookseller John Bartlett who is principally remembered as the compiler of *Bartlett's Familiar Quotations*. Bartlett used the word in a restricted sense. Passages of prose and poetry were familiar when they appeared in Greek, Latin, English, and American literatures and were cited by the educated person of the day, who was expected to be on nodding terms with them. The first edition of his celebrated *Familiar Quotations* appeared in 1855 (the same year as such poetical works as Longfellow's *The Song of Hiawatha* and Whitman's *Leaves of Grass*). Bartlett's compilation is now in its 15th (125th anniversary) edition; long ago it ceased to be a collection of familiar passages. Instead, like its British counterpart, *The Oxford Dictionary of Quotations* (1941; 3rd edition, 1979), it has become a storehouse of once-familiar prose and poetry — plus quips and quotes by celebrities, and with present-day catchphrases and advertising slogans.

In addition to familiar passages, there are *characteristic* remarks. These remarks are "chips off the old block"; they retain their association with their originators, who themselves bear familiar names. Once heard and hard to forget are remarks like C.D. Howe's rhetorical question "What's a million?" and Pierre Elliott Trudeau's disguised expletive "Fuddle duddle" and Brian Mulroney's boast (with respect to Meech Lake) about "the roll of the dice." Each is memorable and each brings its speaker immediately to mind.

Finally, there are quotations that are essentially *informational*. They share with the reader or listener a notion or a nugget of knowledge. The following little item from *Harper's* Index is a good instance of an informational quotation: "Number of Harlequin romances Americans bought last year, per hour: 7,191." The number of quotations that are essentially informational in the present collection is larger than might be expected.

Humorists, comedians, anonymous editorial writers, and unsung speech writers eventually receive credit for a good many *bon mots*. Accreditation often turns on geography. On the West Coast, a clever observation may as a matter of course be attributed to columnist Eric Nicol; on the Prairies, to Calgary newspaperman Bob Edwards; in Ontario, to Stephen Leacock, Wayne and Shuster, Don Harron, or Gary Lautens; in Quebec, to the cartoonist Aislin (if wicked enough); in the Maritimes to Judge Haliburton or Harry Bruce; on the Great Island, to Ray Guy (if sly enough). While Canadians work on a geographical basis, Americans arrange such things on a generational basis. If the remark was not made by Mark Twain, it was said by Will Rogers; if it is contemporary and clever, William Safire; if contemporary and convoluted, Yogi Berra. Such remarks often improve in the telling. (It was the humorist and author W.O. Mitchell who suggested that "if you tell a story three times, it's yours.") Repeated often enough, a story or a quotation becomes, in the words of the novelist Douglas Adams, "definitively inaccurate."

A good many of the pages in the present book are graced with the wit and wisdom of the man-of-letters Robertson Davies. Davies is a master aphorist and bookman. Referring to such compilations as *Bartlett's*

Familiar Quotations, he expressed the opinion that "there are hundreds of quotations in such books which I solemnly swear are not familiar to anyone." It is true that present-day familiarity with once-familiar expressions and quotations is not to be assumed. The message of the media seems to be that the "eternal present" is all that matters. The past is grist for the present. What has replaced the lost world of classical learning and traditional lore is a preoccupation with the contemporary lore of the pre-emptive present. While Canadian students may not recall or recognize the concluding lines of Earle Birney's poem *David*, they may know a verse or two of a song by Leonard Cohen or Rush.

It must be said that Canadians are not a quotable lot; nor are we quoted a lot, at least by foreign quote-masters. Only in the 1990s are the editors of the current editions of *Bartlett's Familiar Quotations* and *The Oxford Dictionary of Quotations* catching up with such eloquent speakers and writers as Marshall McLuhan and Pierre Elliott Trudeau, Northrop Frye and Robertson Davies. When their memorable remarks are added to the canon, the gentlemen themselves will join the columned, club-like chambers frequented by such earlier colleagues as Judge Haliburton, Bonar Law, Lord Beaverbrook, Sir William Osler, Stephen Leacock, and J. K. Galbraith.

The Dictionary of Canadian Quotations differs in many ways from the present compiler's earlier books of quotations — *Colombo's Canadian Quotations* (1974), *Colombo's Concise Canadian Quotations* (1976), and *Colombo's New Canadian Quotations* (1987). The "quotable quotes" in this new dictionary stress contemporary society and humanity, whereas the earlier books focused on culture and history. The present book is concerned with the importance of issue and place, and not directly with ideals and principles. Thus, this compilation is more a "random harvest" than a "cultivated crop." It takes its origin from a close examination of the news of the day, coupled with the ingrained habit of "determined browsing" along the throughways and pathways of one country's self-expressiveness.

The columns on these pages offer close to half a million words about Canada and about human nature. It is fair to ask, What do these words have to tell us about our past, our present, our future; about our problems, our preoccupations, and our potentials; about our weaknesses, our strains, and our strengths? What do these quotations have to tell us about being human beings in this time and in this place?

The words in this book are expressions of opinion, but they are also statements of facts and projections of attitudes; as such, they reveal unexpected possibilities and show surprising preferences of all sorts. Canada emerges from these pages as a varied country of people who have generated a wealth of ideas and insights. It might be said that if something exists somewhere in the world, its Canadian counterpart may be found almost anywhere in the vastness of the country where it will be virtually unknown to Canadians! We are cautious when it comes to curiosity; for too long we have taken the richness of the natural world around us for granted, and we have retained the notion (it may once have been more true for us than it is today) that brawn is as important as brain, that muscle does as much for one as mind, and that instincts need not be tempered with ideas.

Coral reefs grow larger and more labyrinthine over the years without the guidance of any "coral king"; so do the concerns of Canadians. Our Laocoön-like cares multiply in number and in numbing complexity at every corner. Quotation after quotation reveals the dimensions of such concerns and cares, a culture common to Canadians regardless of the languages they speak or the groups to which they belong or the regions that tax them. It is a common culture in the sense that Canadians have more in common one with another, no matter how they define themselves or where they live, than they have with the citizens of other countries, even other English-speaking countries in the Western world. There is a commonality of culture, with regional variations and voices, islands with somewhat similar cultures in an immense sea.

Everyone, from the hunter-gatherer to the urban cliff-dweller, has a culture; all he or she has to do is dig deep enough, socially and psychologically, to tap the mother lode. But cultural values and concerns, acquired habits and approaches, are not enough to ensure well-being, particularly in the late twentieth century, when so many of the world's cultures are at war between and even within themselves.

Cultural values have an importance of their own, but of the utmost importance are civilized values. Cultural values define what a group has in common. The culture that is truly civilized is the culture that takes into account not only the group but also the individual inside and outside that group. Every mature culture, while affirming collectivist considerations, makes elbow room for individualistic interests. But few cultures do little more than pay lip-service to the individual person. It is civilized values, as distinct from cultural values, that protect the individual and do more than pay lip-service to the rights and privileges of men and women. Such values assume freedom of speech, the rule of law, the right to order, a temperate people, a tempered bureaucracy, some social and intellectual ideals, the sense that one may and should live one's life as one wishes to live it, etc.

It is my belief that the quotations in this book collectively speak about both the culture and the civilization of contemporary Canada; they give voice to the conditions that must exist before this country becomes the most civilized part of the planet in which to live. Canada is a meaningful mosaic. It may some day become a memorable one.

I have always found that many hands make light work, so I am grateful to many people for their contributions to the present work.

My principal researcher, Alice M. Neal, made excellent use of the fine resources and facilities of both the Metropolitan Toronto Reference Library of the Toronto Public Library System and the John P. Robarts Reference Library of the University of Toronto. The librarians with these collections were unfailingly helpful. Specific assistance was rendered by Philip Singer of the Canadiana Collection of the North York Public Library System and by Michael Richardson of the same system's Armour Heights Branch. Thomas M. Paikeday of Mississauga, Ont., and Craig Ertl of Winnipeg, made measurable contributions. Queries were answered with equanimity by the librarians of *The Toronto Star*, *The Globe and Mail*, Cinémathèque Ontario, and the CBC Reference Library.

I remain indebted to Mel Hurtig of Hurtig Publishers Ltd. of Edmonton, the publisher of my earlier popular reference books. Normally I would acknowledge with pleasure the assistance received from two major governmental institutions, the Canada Council and the Department of the Secretary of State; but, truth to tell, officers of neither the Council's Explorations Program nor the Secretary of State's Canadian Studies Directorate would even entertain an application for subvention for this undertaking. Work had to proceed at considerable personal expense and at an impeded rate of progress. (Parenthetically, one cannot help but wonder about the *raison d'être* of these organizations.) The fact that the book appeared at all is a tribute to individual initiative and to the intervention of the private sector in the persons of Donald G. Bastian, Managing Editor, and Nelson Doucet, Vice-President, Stoddart Publishing Co. Limited, Toronto. They expressed timely and breathtaking enthusiasm for the project.

The manuscript has been edited with characteristic discernment and dispatch by Carlotta Lemieux of London, Ont. The above-mentioned Don Bastian gave me the benefit of his knowledge and experience. Naturally, I shoulder the sole responsibility for any errors of omission or commission. I remain eager to hear from readers who have comments to make. Write to me care of the publisher.

I wish to acknowledge, as well, the many contributions of Ruth Colombo, my wife, who is often quite quotable in her own right (especially on the subject of the rewards of authorship in this country — though not in these pages!). But I would be remiss if I failed to note the fact that the collection would never have appeared but for the sometimes wordy contributions of its contributors. At the same time I want to thank the men and women whose names appear below. Each person made a special contribution to the conception or the completion of this book:

Nelson Adams, Coach House Press, Toronto; Tom Atkinson, Toronto; Roz Austin, Legislative Librarian, Ontario Legislature, Queen's Park, Toronto; George Bain, Mahone Bay, N.S.; Dick Beddoes, Islington, Ont.; Frank C. Bentley, Toronto; Kamala Bhatia, Hamilton, Ont.; Joel Bonn, Magog, Que.; David L. Clink, North York, Ont.; John S. Crosbie, Toronto; Fred E. Crowe, Lonergan Research Institute of Regis College, Toronto; Don Currie, Toronto; James F. Doig, Wolfville, N.S.; William M. Duron, Toronto; Craig Ertl, Winnipeg; Edith Fowke, Scarborough, Ont.; Paul Grescoe, Vancouver; William Gough, Woodland Hills, Calif.; Cyril Greenland, Toronto; Sandra and Richard Gwyn, London, England; Anthony M. Hawke, Downsview; Bill Howell, Toronto; Brent Kearns, Toronto; M.T. Kelly, Toronto; William Kilbourn, Toronto; Michael Macklem, Ottawa; Alberto Manguel, Toronto; W. Edward Mann, Willowdale, Ont.; Joan Melvin, Deep River, Ont.; Thomas M. Paikeday, Mississauga, Ont.; Alan Rayburn, Ottawa; Budd Reilly, Scarborough, Ont.; Robin W. Rowland, Toronto; Anna Sandor, Woodland Hills, Calif.; James B. Simpson, Washington, D.C.; Milan and Judith Somborac, Collingwood, Ont.; Frank Spitzer, Toronto; Peter Warren, Winnipeg; Dorothy and Hugh Washburn, Panorama City, Calif.; Barbara and George Weider, Collingwood, Ont.; Andrew Weiner, Toronto; Dwight Whalen, Niagara Falls, Ont.; Betty Jane Wylie, MacTier, Ont.

A

See also EH?
ZED

It is a little-known fact that, besides the time-honoured use of A in its most obvious connotation of "first in line" as in "from A to Z" or in its Greek version "from alpha to omega," the letter also stands for stability, symmetry, feminine symbolism, and maybe even beauty, *i.e.,* if you can see eye to eye with Yves Saint Laurent's mid-1980s fancy for "skirts with high narrow waistbands spread out to A-line widths." If you can't, the A-line symbol has at least a utilitarian function — to keep some of us out of women's washrooms.

> THOMAS M. PAIKEDAY, lexicographer, compiler of *The Penguin Canadian Dictionary* (1990).

ABILITY

I am — I can.

> EDGAR KAISER, B.C. investor, chose these words for his personal maxim and for the motto of the Kaiser Foundation, quoted by Peter C. Newman in *Maclean's*, 7 March 1988.

ABORTION

See also BIRTH CONTROL
CONTRACEPTION

Is compulsory pregnancy ever justifiable?

> W. GIFFORD-JONES, physician, reversing the argument about abortion being justifiable, *On Being a Woman* (1971, 1973).

What's the magic about being able to kill a child just before it's born and not being able to kill it just after?

> OTTO LANG, Minister of Justice, expressing an opinion on the abortion issue, quoted by John Gray in *The Toronto Star*, 12 Aug. 1974.

At times we may be mistaken. But if we are to err, let it be on the side of life; for if we, instead, embrace death as our cause, we will debase our humanity and burden our souls.

> PERRIN BEATTY, M.P., speaking against the bill to widen the grounds for abortion, House of Commons, 28 Jan. 1975.

Obviously the justice of a society is well defined in terms of how it treats the weak.

And there is nothing human which is weaker than the foetus.

> GEORGE GRANT, philosopher, "Abortion and Rights" (1976), *Technology and Justice* (1986).

I am not pro-abortion any more than I am pro-appendectomy.

> HENRY MORGENTALER, medical doctor and leading proponent of "pro choice," quoted by Marq de Villiers in *Weekend Magazine*, 14 Sept. 1974.

How did you like my courageous silence on abortion?

> Attributed to BRIAN MULRONEY, Conservative leadership candidate, by William Walker in *The Toronto Star*, 17 Sept. 1988, who said the remark was made to an aide after Mulroney successfully skirted the issue during a leadership debate in 1984.

Despite the controversy over abortion, Canadian teenagers are nearly unanimous in maintaining that legal abortion should be a possibility under some circumstances. Specifically, close to 9 in 10 young people say that it should be possible for a woman who has been raped to obtain a legal abortion. There is no difference in attitudes between males and females. And, significantly, there is little difference between young Catholics and others.

> REGINALD W. BIBBY and DONALD C. POSTERSKI, sociologists, *The Emerging Generation: An Inside Look at Canada's Teenagers* (1985).

Despite the best efforts of the federal government to bury the question, abortion remains in the mid-1980's one of the most divisive issues in Canadian life. The struggle between those who wish to restrict and those who wish to extend access to abortion is fought out at every political level, from the election of hospital boards to the election of members of Parliament.

After having surveyed the history of the discussion of contraception and abortion in Canada from the 1880's to the 1980's it is difficult not to have a sense of *déjà vu* when observing the current conflict.

> ANGUS McLAREN and ARLENE TIGAR McLAREN, historian and sociologist, *The Bedroom and the State: The Changing Practices and Politics of Contraception and Abortion in Canada, 1880-1980* (1986).

I want to make my contribution to humanity so that there will be no more Auschwitzes. Children who are born wanted and are given love and attention will not build concentration camps.

> HENRY MORGENTALER, medical doctor and proponent of "pro choice," quoted by Chris Wood in *Maclean's*, 8 Feb. 1988.

Words of fire will surely be spoken in defence of the unborn person, and they will convert our hearts and minds. They must, or our society will perish.

> ANNE ROCHE MUGGERIDGE, writer and advocate of "pro life," on the ruling of the Supreme Court of Canada, 28 Jan. 1988, that the abortion law was unconstitutional, *The Globe and Mail*, 2 Feb. 1988.

The abortion debate. It's a wonder that we still describe it as such when neither side can bear to listen to the other's arguments and no one ever really wins.

> ANNE COLLINS, journalist, "Birth Enforcement," *Saturday Night*, Nov. 1989.

Until the true believers [the Roman Catholics who belong to the "pro life" group] graduate even to the level of religious faith (where doubt is always a partner), compromise on the abortion issue is a chimera. No political solution will soothe the souls of the true believers.

> ANNE COLLINS, journalist, "Birth Enforcement," *Saturday Night*, Nov. 1989.

What a dog begets is canine; what we beget is human.

> GEORGE GRANT, philosopher, discussing abortion, quoted by Robert Ready in the correspondence column, *The Globe and Mail*, 24 Nov. 1989.

ACADIANS

Eh bien, voilà. After more than two and a half centuries of separation, we find ourselves together again, Acadians and French of France. *Ah, Messieurs*, what hardships we have endured during those years! The Acadians, persecuted for so long in that territory of New France where Champlain founded . . . the first French settlement in Canada; the Acadians who were subsequently chased out, but who returned with courage and tenacity; the Acadians who, thanks to the miraculous fecundity and the admirable courage of their French mamas, now totalled three hundred and fifty thousand rather than two thousand as at the beginning, while the fantastic fidelity of their fathers resulted in their remaining, through their language, intellect, religion, and character, as French as ever.
> CHARLES DE GAULLE, French President, addressing a group of Acadians accorded official honours, Elysée Palace, Paris, Jan. 1968, to the dismay of the Canadian government, quoted by Dale C. Thomson in *Vive le Québec Libre* (1988).

We have our territory within us.
> ANTONINE MAILLET, Acadian author, quoted by Robert Duffy in *The Toronto Star*, 18 May 1980.

Then there's Hollywood. The face on the statue, smooth and beautiful and untouched by madness or years of wandering the wilderness, is that of Dolores Del Rio, the Mexican-born actress who completed the trinity by playing Evangeline in the 1929 movie, filmed nearby at Lake Catahoula. To thank the townspeople, the cast presented a statue of Evangeline-Emmeline that Miss Del Rio posed for. The actress, cynics said, saw a chance to have her beauty immortalized in something more durable than celluloid. If many citizens no longer know the name, they all know the face.
> WILLIAM LEAST HEAT MOON, native

American author and travel writer, *Blue Highways: A Journey into America* (1982). This is a description of the bronze statue of Evangeline erected over the burial place at St. Martinville, Louisiana, of Emmeline Labiche, the original Evangeline Bellefontaine. Another statue, which differs strikingly from the Cajun one, is the Canadian one erected in New Brunswick's Grand Pré National Park. It depicts the two ages of the Acadian heroine of Longfellow's poem — the young girl and the old woman.

The history of Acadia has never been written down as seen by its people. It's been written by historians from outside. These historians sometimes had reason not to write the truth, or didn't know the truth or didn't know the small things which become the big things, the inside story, what we in France call *la petite histoire.* History is made by the kings and the lords. But *la petite histoire* is made by the people.
> ANTONINE MAILLET, Acadian author, quoted by Isabel Vincent in *The Globe and Mail*, 24 June 1989.

ACHIEVEMENT
See also SUCCESS

Meanwhile, the meek are a long time inheriting the earth.
> BOB EDWARDS, publisher, *The Eye Opener*, 16 Sept. 1916.

A ship in harbour is safe, but that is not what ships are built for.
> PUNCH IMLACH, hockey coach, jotting in diary, quoted by Scott Young in *Heaven and Hell in the NHL: Punch Imlach's Own Story* (1982) written with Scott Young.

Probably because of our ancient, self-imposed status as a branch-plant country well back in the baggage train of the Anglo-Americans, we have come to regard achievements, other than by professional athletes and geriatrics, as somehow un-Canadian.
> CONRAD BLACK, newspaper proprietor

and columnist, "Why Does the Press Savage Success?" *The Globe and Mail's Report on Business Magazine*, March 1986.

Somewhere I picked up a card with that slogan and it instantly rang bells with me . . . You gotta wanna.
JIMMY PATTISON, capitalist, *Jimmy: An Autobiography* (1987) written with Paul Grescoe.

The greatest achievement of mankind was not the atom bomb, not the hydrogen bomb, but boredom. Sheer boredom.
IRVING LAYTON, poet, quoted by Philip Marchand in *The Toronto Star*, 16 Nov. 1989.

ACID RAIN
See also POLLUTION

There is a widespread perception that Americans really don't give a damn if we have any forests, any fish, or any lakes. The sense of an incredible selfishness on the part of the U.S. Government is going to have a fundamental effect on the way that Canadians think about the United States.
WILLIAM BLAIKIE, M.P., referring to the failure of the Reagan administration to comprehend the Canadian concern with American emissions of acid rain, quoted in *The New York Times*, 26 April 1987.

The one thing acid rain does not do is discriminate. It is despoiling your environment as inexorably as it is ours. It is damaging your environment from Michigan to Maine, and threatens marine life on the Eastern seaboard.
I ask you this: What would be said of a generation of North Americans that found a way to explore the stars, but allowed its lakes and forests to languish and die?
BRIAN MULRONEY, Prime Minister, addressing a joint sitting of the U.S. Congress, 27 April 1988, address carried in *The Toronto Star* the following day.

ACID RAIN IS RUINING MY GRAFFITI
Graffiti seen in Montreal, March 1989.

Acid rain is not an act of nature; it's the byproduct of industry, a man-made gift of death from the United States to Canada, from Great Britain to Norway, and from Germany's industrial heartland to its farthest reaches. We cannot defend against this deadly rain. Everywhere it falls, it destroys forests, lakes, agricultural lands, washing away human lives and the dreams on which they're built.
ANITA GORDON and DAVID SUZUKI, science broadcasters, *It's a Matter of Survival* (1990).

ACQUIRED IMMUNE DEFICIENCY SYNDROME
See AIDS

ACTION

Only action can testify to the validity of thoughts and emotions: action alone verifies the personality. It is the only authentic form of self-expression. *I act. Therefore I know who I am.*
STEPHEN VIZINCZEY, novelist, *An Innocent Millionaire* (1983).

ACTORS & ACTING
See also FILM
THEATRE

Don Harron is superb as the idiot.
Said to be a sentence from the review of Lorca's play *The Shoemaker's Prodigious Wife*, in which the youthful stage actor Don Harron played an eight-year-old boy; the review, by the late ROSE MACDONALD, apparently appeared in the *Toronto Telegram* in the 1940s. Quoted by Martha Harron in *Don Harron: A Parent Contradiction* (1988).

The best radio actor in the world.
ORSON WELLES, U.S. actor and director, referring to the versatile and well-loved actor John Drainie, recalled by Christopher Plummer in the 1970s, quoted by Bronwyn Drainie in *Living the Part: John*

Drainie and the Dilemma of Canadian Stardom (1988).

Ironically, although my father was the first of Canada's great actors, he was also probably one of the last who could devote himself exclusively to acting, who could make it to the top and stay there with no outside talent for producing, merchandising or promotion. He always saw his lack of entrepreneurial ability as a weakness, even though he would sneer quietly (in self-defence) at colleagues who were better self-promoters than he. And yet, if John Drainie represents something unique in Canada's performing community, it is that single-minded devotion to the art and craft and mystery of acting, entirely for its own sake. That is not weakness, it is strength. But it is not an adaptable kind of strength.

> BRONWYN DRAINIE, broadcaster and biographer, *Living the Part: John Drainie and the Dilemma of Canadian Stardom* (1988).

Why are you an actor? / Because you can't do anything else. / Like a glass shaped to hold water / You show the shapes of man's life and death / Only larger than life / So that all who see it / Will see it well.

> Poem composed by the theatre director JOHN HIRSCH and presented to Heath Lamberts when he graduated from the National Theatre School in the 1960s, reproduced in *The Free Press* (a publication of Canadian Stage), Fall 1988.

When the camera starts to roll, there is something of death about it.

> DONALD SUTHERLAND, actor, quoted by Lawrence O'Toole in *Maclean's*, 2 March 1981.

I'm a reserved Canadian.

> DAN AYKROYD, actor who specializes in madcap comedy, quoted by Jay Carr in *The Toronto Star*, 19 June 1988.

I wanted to do something with my life. I wanted to do something big. And I knew that the arena for doing it was not to be found in London, Ont.

KATE NELLIGAN, actress known as "Kate the Great," a native of London, Ont., quoted by Deirdre Kelly in *The Globe and Mail*, 27 Aug. 1988.

The essence of being a Canadian actor is being mistaken for somebody else.

> RICHARD MONETTE, actor, quoted by Ray Conlogue in *The Globe and Mail*, 9 Jan. 1988.

There are no stars in Canada. To have a star system you need the proper mechanics — an immense publicity industry, a public that wants stars, and a national point of view that encourages that idolizing. We have it in hockey, but practically nowhere else.

> R.H. THOMSON, actor, quoted in Dec. 1985 by Ed Gould in *Entertaining Canadians: Canada's International Stars 1900-1988* (1988).

Unlike Max I don't think I'm perrr-rrr-fect.

> MATT FREWER, actor, quoted by Jim Bawden in *The Toronto Star*, 7 Oct. 1987. Frewer is referring to his twin role on television which attracted a cult following: Edison Carter and Max Headroom in the TV series *Max Headroom* which was set "fifteen minutes in the future."

At any given moment the unemployment rate among Equity actors is estimated at 70 per cent.

> DAVID GARDNER, actor and theatre historian, "Acting," *The Oxford Companion to Canadian Theatre* (1989) edited by Eugene Benson and L.W. Conolly. At the time there were close to 9700 members of Canadian Actors' Equity.

Up to this point my height was the only thing I had in common with Alan Ladd.

> MICHAEL J. FOX, film star, comparing his fame and height with Alan Ladd's, quoted by Jamie Portman in *The Toronto Star*, 21 Nov. 1989.

When you're a short actor you stand on apple boxes, you walk on a ramp. When

you're a short *star* everybody else walks in a ditch.
> MICHAEL J. FOX, television and movie personality, who stands 5'5", quoted in *The Toronto Star*, 1 March 1991.

Having been as fortunate as I have and having a beautiful family and to be able to pretend I'm other people for a living, there's not much to be grumpy and lousy to people about. If I was a pipefitter, I might be a jerk. Who knows?
> MICHAEL J. FOX, actor, quoted by Luaine Lee in *The Winnipeg Free Press*, 8 March 1991.

It's only a job. If I want to, I can go back to welding.
> GRAHAM GREENE, native actor, one-time welder in Toronto, nominated for an Academy Award for his part in *Dances with Wolves*, quoted by Brian D. Johnson in *Maclean's*, 25 March 1991.

ADVENTURE

I would not know how to instill a taste for adventure in those who have not acquired it. (Anyway, who can ever prove the necessity for the gypsy life?)
> PIERRE ELLIOTT TRUDEAU, canoeist, "Exhaustion and Fulfilment: The Ascetic in a Canoe" (1944), *Wilderness Canada* (1970) edited by Borden Spears.

No. 1. Adventure equals Risk with Purpose. / No. 2. Satisfaction gained from a job is in inverse proportion to the money earned. / No. 3. Satisfaction equals service over income.
> Rules of thumb of ROBERT McCLURE, medical missionary, quoted by Munroe Scott in *McClure: Years of Challenge* (1979).

The larger the island of knowledge, the longer the shoreline of wonder.
> JOSEPH MacINNIS, undersea explorer, recollecting an adage, quoted by Donald Grant in *The Globe and Mail*, 8 Nov. 1986.

Canada has turned caution into an art form.
> RICK MORANIS, comic actor, quoted by Jay Scott in *The Globe and Mail*, 2 Jan. 1987.

ADVERTISING
See also BUSINESS

Early to bed, / Early to rise; / Never get tight, / And advertise.
> Ditty attributed (no doubt mischievously) to TIMOTHY EATON, the teetotalling Irish merchant who founded the T. Eaton Co. in Toronto in 1869, quoted by Diane Francis, address, Empire Club of Canada, Toronto, 1 Oct. 1986.

You just can't trust any judgement of anything these days. One wishes sometimes the world had not learned to write. It has led to such smart-Alec superficiality, every journalist trying to out-journal advertising, advertising, exploiting! Even plain decency has to be decorated with falsity — to push it down people's throats but they will gulp any indecency or dirt. Everything seems wrong. I suppose that is why we must go through these great upheavals, to stir the sediment settling at the bottom.
> EMILY CARR, artist, edited version of a letter sent to Humphrey Toms, 4 Dec. 1940, *Dear Nan: Letters of Emily Carr, Nan Cheney and Humphrey Toms* (1990) edited by Doreen Walker.

Ads are the cave art of the twentieth century.
> MARSHALL McLUHAN, media philosopher, *Culture Is Our Business* (1970).

Madison Avenue is a very powerful aggression against private consciousness. A demand that you yield your private consciousness to public manipulation.
> MARSHALL McLUHAN, media philosopher, interview, *Maclean's*, 7 March 1977.

How Modesty Has Made Me Canada's Best Advertising Man

Line of copy promoting the services of JERRY GOODIS, advertising executive and copywriter, *GOODIS: Shaking the Canadian Advertising Tree* (1991).

You see, advertising is a substitute for a salesperson, so it should be likeable. Who would buy from a salesperson who is rude, arrogant or insulting? People like to do business with people they like, therefore they respond to advertising created by people who like people.
    JERRY GOODIS, advertising executive, *GOODIS: Shaking the Canadian Advertising Tree* (1991).

My name is Alex Tilley and I am *not* afraid of Kryptonite.
    Line of copy in an advertisement attributed to ALEX TILLEY, founder of the adventure and sportswear line Tilley Endurables, *The Toronto Star*, 22 May 1988.

Guarantee? Extraordinary! Washing Instruction: "Give'em Hell"
    Wording on the label of some items sold by Tilley Endurables, 1980s.

Fresh Squeezed Glaciers / Clearly Canadian Sparkling Mineral Water in Wild Fruit Flavours
    Print advertisement for Adelma Mineral Waters, Quebec, Fall 1988.

Doing business without advertising is like winking at a pretty girl in the dark — you know what you're doing, but nobody else does.
    MURRAY KOFFLER, pharmacist and philanthropist, quoted by Frank Rasky in *Just a Simple Pharmacist: The Story of Murray Koffler, Builder of the Shoppers Drug Mart Empire* (1988).

Truth is the safest lie.
    MURRAY KOFFLER, pharmacist and philanthropist, quoted by Frank Rasky in *Just a Simple Pharmacist: The Story of Murray Koffler, Builder of the Shoppers Drug Mart Empire* (1988).

If commerce is the engine of our economy, then advertising is the spark. Responsible advertisers are the drivers who keep us on the right track, leading to a richer, more benevolent society.
    BRIAN PHILCOX, director, Canadian Advertising Foundation, quoted in *The Globe and Mail*, 16 Jan. 1989.

On est six million.
    Line from the Labatt advertising campaign created by advertising executive JACQUES BOUCHARD and quoted from *The Globe and Mail*, 28 Oct. 1989, where it is described as "a less than subtle appeal to nationalism." It translates "One is six million" and refers to the francophone population of Quebec.

Host: Today's skill-testing question is: What is more important to Molson Breweries? Is it re-cycling beer bottles or re-cycling beer workers? (Buzzer) Sorry, time's up. The answer is . . . BEER BOTTLES.
    Announcer: Molson workers only want what they already had — a job. No handouts, buyouts or payoffs. Just a job.
    Support the Molson workers. Don't buy Molson's, Coors, Fosters or Miller beers. Help us make Molson re-cycle beer workers — not just beer bottles. . . .
    Paid for by Local 304 Brewery Workers.
    Excerpt from the script for a radio commercial submitted to fifteen Ontario stations by Local 304, Brewery Worker (NUPGE) and rejected by all but two stations. The full text was published in *Now*, 28 Sept. 1989.

The Legend is Black.
    Popular campaign for Carling O'Keefe Breweries' Black Label Beer, launched June 1988, created by Paul Hains with the assistance of David Barbour and Robin Milward. It replaced the once-memorable campaign "Hey Mabel, Black Label!" of the 1950s.

It's just amazing how many companies suddenly want you to hold up their product after you've held up the Stanley Cup.

WAYNE GRETZKY, hockey personality and product endorser, *Gretzky: An Autobiography* (1990) written with Rick Reilly.

The only thing wrong with that slogan is that I didn't write it.
JERRY GOODIS, advertising executive with a flair for fine copy, commenting on another agency's slogan, *GOODIS: Shaking the Canadian Advertising Tree* (1991) written with Gene O'Keefe.

AGE
See also RETIREMENT
YOUTH

I think a *little* of whatever you like is the secret of keeping your interest, & yourself, alive and keen.
SIR CHARLES G.D. ROBERTS, poet and author, letter written in 1937, quoted by John Coldwell Adams in *Sir Charles God Damn: The Life of Sir Charles G.D. Roberts* (1986). In 1943, at the age of eighty-three, Sir Charles married a woman fifty years younger than himself, and promptly died.

I like a little bit of everything. A little bit of lovin', a little bit of drinkin', and a little bit of workin'. I watch out pretty carefully every day for banana peels.
MARGARET "MA" MURRAY, pioneer newspaperwoman, then in her early eighties, CBC Radio, 17 Oct. 1967.

You're too old now, my dear. / And I'm too old too, my dear. / Our faces are full of flaws. / The truth bites into our beauty.
ELIZABETH SMART, novelist and diarist, "My Life" (1951), *Autobiographies* (1987) edited by Christina Burridge.

I'm as old as my memory, and as young as my body.
JOANNE MacIVER, 17-year-old Orillia girl who in a hypnotic trance seemed to recall details of a previous incarnation, quoted by Jesse Stearn in *The Search for the Girl with the Blue Eyes* (1968).

While there's snow on the roof, it doesn't mean the fire has gone out in the furnace.
JOHN G. DIEFENBAKER, former Prime Minister, addressing celebrants in Ottawa on 17 Sept. 1975, the day before he turned eighty, quoted by Bruce Garvey in *The Toronto Star* the following day.

Of late I have searched diligently to discover the advantages of age, and there is, I have concluded, only one. It is that lovely women treat your approaches with understanding rather than with disdain.
JOHN KENNETH GALBRAITH, economist and author, "Recessional" (1975), *A View from the Stands of People, Politics, Military Power and the Arts* (1986) edited by Andrea D. Williams.

An unattractive smugness that some old ladies have — they seem suffused with self-congratulations.
The little papery old men, not. Aggression knocked out, they totter gratefully on.
ELIZABETH SMART, novelist and diarist, "Journal" (1982), *Autobiographies* (1987) edited by Christina Burridge.

When you are asked how old you are, the words can wrap themselves around your innermost fears and insecurities.
ROBERT F. MORGAN and JANE WILSON, authors, *Growing Younger: Adding Years to Your Life by Measuring and Controlling Your Body Age* (1982).

I'm interested in geriatrics because I'm going to be old someday, too.
ROBERT McCLURE, medical missionary, born in 1900, quoted by Christopher Donville in *The Globe and Mail*, 31 July 1987.

I have chosen the title as a declaration of war against the absurd tendency to divide life into three boxes: a first, in which one learns but does not work; a second, when one works but does not learn; and a third, in which one neither works nor learns. This has not been the story of my life.
HANS BLUMENFELD, architect-planner,

Life Begins at 65: The Not Entirely Candid Autobiography of a Drifter (1987).

When asked for the reasons for this unusual state of affairs, my answer is, "I am so full of venom that no virus can survive."
HANS BLUMENFELD, architect-planner, *Life Begins at 65: The Not Entirely Candid Autobiography of a Drifter* (1987). He is commenting on the excellent state of his health and his longevity (being born in 1892; he died in 1988).

It is my feeling that as we grow older we should become not less radical but more so. I do not, of course, mean this in any political-party sense, but in a willingness to struggle for those things in which we passionately believe. Social activism and the struggle for social justice are often thought of as natural activities of the young but not of the middle-aged or elderly. In fact, I don't think this was ever true. . . .
MARGARET LAURENCE, novelist, address, Trent University, Peterborough, Ont., 29 March 1983, quoted in the *The Globe and Mail*, 10 Jan. 1989.

If, as you grow older, you feel you are also growing stupider, do not worry. This is normal, and usually occurs around the time when your children, now grown, are discovering the opposite — they now see that you aren't nearly as stupid as they had believed when they were young teenagers. Take heart from that.
MARGARET LAURENCE, novelist, address at Trent University, 29 March 1983, quoted in *The Globe and Mail*, 10 Jan. 1989.

In such journeys, time is our ally, not our enemy. We can grow wise. As the arteries harden, the spirit can lighten. As the legs fail, the soul can take wing. Things do add up. Life does have shape and maybe even purpose. Or so it seems to me.
SYLVIA FRASER, author, *My Father's House: A Memoir of Incest and of Healing* (1987).

Maybe growing older is simply finding the terror in the familiar.
KEVIN LAND, playwright, CHCH-TV's *Turns*, 6 May 1989.

To grow older is to realize the universe is copernican, not ptolemaic, and that self and the loved one do not form the epicentre of the solar system.
EDWARD PHILLIPS, novelist, *Sunday Best* (1990).

AGRICULTURE
See also FARMING

If I may be pardoned for briefly delving, for the sake of clarity only, into mathematics, the farmer has learned that $O + A = RO^t$ (*Organization* plus *Action* equals *Results* in *Ottawa*).
LORNE T. MORGAN, economist, *The Permanent War or Homo the Sap* (1943).

One day, millions of acres of arable land in the Mackenzie Valley and the Yukon will be ploughed to grow grain and root crops. In time, each community in the north will be self-sufficient in fruit and vegetables, eggs, milk and a variety of nutritious foods.
SAM HALL, British correspondent, *The Fourth World: The Heritage of the Arctic and Its Destruction* (1987).

AIDS

I've got gay cancer. I'm going to die and so are you.
GAETAN DUGAS, Air Canada flight attendant and AIDS carrier, addressing his male sexual partners, quoted by Randy Shilts in *And the Band Played On: Politics, People and the AIDS Epidemic* (1987). Before his death in Quebec City in 1984, Dugas was identified only as "Patient X." Dugas boasted of infecting at least 2500 men across North America during the last decade of his life. AIDS is the acronym for Acquired Immune Deficiency Syndrome.

I want to have sex, but I don't want to die.

Wording of an educational videotape *Sex, Drugs and Aids*, noted with disapproval by B.C. Premier William Vander Zalm, 29 April 1987, quoted by Stephen Osborne and Mary Schendlinger in *Quotations from Chairman Zalm* (1988).

Canada is putting more money into eradicating harmless dandelions than it is in eradicating the AIDS virus.
JOSEPH CUMMINS, geneticist, quoted by Tim Tiner, *Now*, 11 Aug. 1988.

Condom is the operative word in my vocabulary now and I use it often.
BLUMA APPEL, socialite and Chairperson of the Canadian Foundation for AIDS Research (CanFAR), quoted by Jennifer David in "Sweet Charity," *Toronto Life Fashion*, Holiday Edition, 1989.

AIR

After the tragic fire in 1986 at the Chernobyl nuclear plant, radioisotopes were detected over Sweden within minutes and over Canada's Arctic in hours. It was a grim reminder that the air is a global commodity, a planetary system. No one nation has its own supply of air any more than any one of us has a private stock of it. The air of the Earth is finite and shared by all life forms.
ANITA GORDON and DAVID SUZUKI, science broadcasters, *It's a Matter of Survival* (1990).

AIR FORCE
See CANADIAN ARMED FORCES

AIR TRAVEL
See AVIATION

ALBERTA
See also EDMONTON
CALGARY

Albertans consider themselves a breed apart from other Canadians — and they certainly act that way.
STEPHEN BROOK, English travel writer,

Maple Leaf Rag: Travels across Canada (1987).

If it ain't Alberta, it ain't beef.
Wording on a billboard sponsored by the Alberta Cattle Commission, quoted in *The Toronto Star*, 30 Jan. 1988.

What if the Cretaceous extinctions hadn't wiped out the dinosaurs? What if the Alberta bigbrain had continued to evolve?
ROBERT T. BAKKER, U.S. paleontologist, discussing the Stenonychosaurus, the turkey-sized dinosaur with a brain as large as a modern bird's, fossils of which are found in Alberta, *The Dinosaur Heresies: New Themes Unlocking the Mystery of the Dinosaurs and Their Extinction* (1986).

The Born Against syndrome.
A reference to the sense of alienation experienced by Western Canadians with respect to the power bloc of Ontario and Quebec, noted by Ian Pearson in "Thou Shalt Not Ignore the West," *Saturday Night*, Dec. 1990.

The Edmonton Journal's cartoon showed Mr. Getty and his wife, Margaret, dining on a sumptuous dinner with wine. Mr. Getty laments, "The public expects me to divest this! Sell that! How am I supposed to put bread on this table!" Mrs. Getty replies: "Ask the servants to bring up another loaf, Don."
MIRO CERNETIG and PETER MOON, investigative journalists, *The Globe and Mail*, 28 Nov. 1990. The cartoon satirized Alberta Premier Don Getty, following public reaction to a series of articles which appeared in *The Globe and Mail* in which the two journalists quoted Getty as saying that since becoming premier his standard of living had dropped and that while in office he had invested in oil and gas properties because he had been forced to sell other assets to "put bread on the table." The remark attracted national attention and passed into Alberta lore. However, Getty produced transcripts of the interview that included the remark to show that his comment had been taken

out of context, and he argued that his actions broke no Alberta laws.

ALCOHOL
See also DRINKING

I am a prohibitionist. What I propose to prohibit is the reckless use of water.
> BOB EDWARDS, publisher, *The Eye Opener*, 17 March 1904.

Milk of the elderly.
> Descriptive epithet for alcohol used on occasion by the distinguished physician SIR WILLIAM OSLER, noted in *The Globe and Mail*, 13 Dec. 1988.

V.O.
> The initials "V.O." on the Seagram's label of the rye bottle stand for "Very Own" and not "Very Old," according to Stephen Birmingham in *The Rest of Us* (1984). The motto of Joseph E. Seagram was "Integrity, Craftsmanship, Tradition."

A few of our Year arranged to have a "night out." This began by sampling Canadian rye whisky which, to me, tasted like a mixture of molasses, senna and fire! I therefore handled it with Scots caution, otherwise I should not now be able to recollect the proceedings.
> J. MENZIES CAMPBELL, Toronto-trained Scottish dental historian, *Dentistry Then and Now* (1958; 3rd ed., 1981).

I was calling myself King Canada then — I didn't want any of those American boys knowing my real name — and I just told him he couldn't fool with me. He may be Al Capone, but I was King Canada. One mistake, I said, and your goose is cooked.
> BLAISE DIESBOURG, former bootlegger in the Thirties, interviewed at the age of ninety-one by Lynda Hurst in *The Toronto Star*, 31 July 1988.

The British humorist A.P. Herbert came to Toronto to address the Medico-Legal Society. On checking into the Royal York after a long journey, Herbert called room ser-

vice and ordered up a scotch and soda, only to learn that Ontario then banned the sale of liquor by the glass in hotel rooms. Fortunately someone from the society soon arrived with a 26 of whisky. Assured of its legality, Herbert had several drinks, all the while puzzling over a system that denied him one belt of spirits but not a full bottle. As he observed in his subsequent speech, "The parallel would seem to be that you cannot have an egg, I suppose, unless you buy a hen."
> DAVID MacDONALD, "Anecdotes," *The Toronto Star*, 10 Dec. 1988.

We were rather surprised that in Ontario we had to register at the local liquor store as alcoholics.
> ALEC GUINNESS, British actor, referring to the requirement that all purchases at the LCBO be registered, *Blessings in Disguise* (1985).

The Frenchman loves his native wine; / The German loves his beer; / The Englishman loves his 'alf and 'alf, / Because it brings good cheer. / The Irishman loves his "whiskey straight," / Because it gives him dizziness. / The Canadian has no choice at all, / So he drinks the whole damned business.
> KENNETH P. KIRKWOOD, author, diplomat, and versifier, *The Diplomat at Table: A Social and Anecdotal History through the Looking-Glass* (1974).

Americans are plagued with organized crime. We have provincial liquor boards.
> DAVE BROADFOOT, comedian, address, Empire Club of Canada, Toronto, 9 March 1978.

Take the prohibition years, for instance. If not for the good work undertaken at some personal risk by that celebrated Canadian altruist and Seagram's patriarch Sam Bronfman, a good many Americans would have been deprived of solace during those difficult years. Nobody could have been more eager than the obliging Bronfman

lads (Sam, Abe, Harry and Alan) to slake American thirst in style.
> MORDECAI RICHLER, novelist, "The Canadians Are Coming," *Signature*, April 1987.

It is absurd that throughout Canada no independent liquor stores are permitted. Consequently, prices are high and choice is poor.... Perhaps eventually the Canadians will treat their citizens as adults.
> STEPHEN BROOK, English travel writer, *Maple Leaf Rag: Travels across Canada* (1987).

ALPHABET

The magic of the phonetic alphabet is that it is more than a writing system; it is also a system for organizing information. Of all mankind's inventions, with the possible exception of language itself, nothing has proved more useful or led to more innovations than the alphabet.
> ROBERT K. LOGAN, physicist and educator, *The Alphabet Effect: The Impact of the Phonetic Alphabet on the Development of Western Civilization* (1986).

Canada, in Cyrillic characters, is sandwiched between Kenya and Cameroon.
> GREG GRANSDEN, correspondent, checking the card catalogue for Canadian authors at the Foreign Literature Library in Moscow, *The Globe and Mail*, 12 Jan. 1991.

AMBITION

Ambitious! I could laugh! Where is my ambition now? What does the word mean? What is it like to be ambitious? To feel that life is before you, a fair, unwritten white page where you may inscribe your name in letters of success? To feel that you have the wish and power to win your crown? To feel that the coming years are crowding to meet you and lay their largess at your feet? I *once* knew what it was to feel so!
> L. M. MONTGOMERY, author, journal entry, 30 June 1897, Belmont, P.E.I., *The Selected Journals of L.M. Montgomery: Volume I: 1889-1910* (1985) edited by Mary Rubio and Elizabeth Waterston.

If you want something badly enough, you will find a way to get it.
> JOHN KIM BELL, orchestra conductor and founder of the Canadian Native Arts Foundation, quoted on a poster distributed by the Kahnawake Social Services Resource Centre, Que., 1987.

Before you meet the handsome prince, you have got to kiss a lot of toads.
> Wording of a sign on the wall of the office of Susan Thompson, Birt Saddlery Co. Ltd., Winnipeg, Oct. 1989.

AMERICA
See also NORTH AMERICA
UNITED STATES
OF AMERICA

When I came down from Ku Su Terrace, in the East, / I had already arranged for a vessel to float on the sea: / And until now resentment lingers in my mind / That I did not succeed in exploring Fu Sang.
> Fu Sang may be a reference to North America, specifically to the coast and interior of British Columbia, which the Chinese Buddhist monk Huei Shan is said to have explored about A.D. 500. The verse was written by the ancient Chinese poet TU FU. "Poem of Fu Sang" (A.D. 726), translated by Florence Ayscouth, and quoted by Hendon Mason Harris in *The Asiatic Fathers of America* (c. 1980).

America has a new delicacy, a coarse, rank refinement.
> G. K. CHESTERTON, English essayist, *Charles Dickens* (1906).

The discovery of America was the occasion of the greatest outburst of cruelty and reckless greed known in history.
> JOSEPH CONRAD, Anglo-Polish novelist, "Geography and Some Explorers," *Last Essays* (1926).

American. Resident of the United States. The name has long irked those who think that *American* should cover anyone from North to South America; however, the practice is so deeply rooted that it is hard to imagine it changing.
> PAUL DICKSON, British writer, *What Do You Call a Person From . . . ? A Dictionary of Resident Names* (1990).

ANAGRAMS

ROBERT STANFIELD / ORNATE BRIEFS LTD.
> Anagram on the name of the former Conservative Party leader, whose family company manufactures Stanfield's "Unshrinkables," devised by Garry Newton of Medicine Hat, Alta., and quoted by Warren Clements in *The Globe and Mail*, 2 March 1991.

MICHAEL WILSON / WISH ALL INCOME
> Anagram on the name of the Finance Minister, devised by Murray Munn of Winnipeg and Sheila McGivern of Vancouver and quoted by Warren Clements in *The Globe and Mail*, 2 March 1991.

PIERRE TRUDEAU / I RUE DEPARTURE
> Anagram on the name of the former Liberal Prime Minister, devised by Joseph Cabra, of Islington, Ont., and quoted by Warren Clements in *The Globe and Mail*, 2 March 1991.

WILLIAM LYON MACKENZIE KING / AMAZINGLY, NO MEN KICK WILLIE
> Anagram on the name of the former Liberal Prime Minister, devised by James F. Doig of Wolfville, N.S., and quoted by Warren Clements in *The Globe and Mail*, 2 March 1991.

AGNES MACPHAIL / EACH GAL IS AN MP
> Anagram on the name of the Member of Parliament, who pioneered women's rights, devised by Glenda Bocknek of Toronto and quoted by Warren Clements in *The Globe and Mail*, 2 March 1991.

AUDREY McLAUGHLIN / MUCH LAUDING EARLY
> Anagram on the name of the NDP leader, devised by Marion Gilbert of London, Ont., and quoted by Warren Clements in *The Globe and Mail*, 2 March 1991.

SOCRED PREMIER WILLIAM VANDER ZALM / CRAZIER MALE MP LIVES IN DREAM WORLD; CRAZIER WINDMILL LOVERS ARE MADE MP
> Anagrams on the name of the B.C. Socred leader, devised by Patricia Bennett of Vernon, B.C., and quoted by Warren Clements in *The Globe and Mail*, 2 March 1991.

WENDY MESLEY / YE WED SLY MEN
> Anagram on the name of the CBC-TV commentator, wife of news anchor Peter Mansbridge, devised by Tim Bouma, Owen Sound, Ont., and quoted by Warren Clements in *The Globe and Mail*, 2 March 1991.

ANCESTORS

The neat thing about worshipping your ancestors is that you live your life knowing you too will become an ancestor one day.
> Comment of a character in the one-woman show *Afrika Solo* (1990) written by playwright DJANET SEARS.

ANGELS

To learn to talk with angels is really learning to talk with ourselves and with each other in new and profoundly deeper ways. It is learning how to communicate with our universe more openly and how to be more in tune with our role as co-creators and participate in its evolution.
> DOROTHY MACLEAN, medium, *To Hear the Angels Sing: An Odyssey of Co-Creation with the Devic Kingdom* (1980).

ANIMAL RIGHTS
See also ANIMALS

Animal liberation is human liberation! It's a concept often lost on all but the most reflective animal liberationists.
> VICKI MILLER, President, Toronto Humane Society, Editorial, *ARK II*, Summer 1986.

Where it's going to end I don't really know. I don't know whether the animal rights philosophy will extend itself beyond animals to plants and trees, to the planet itself.
> VICKI MILLER, President, Toronto Humane Society, quoted by Jack Cahill in *The Toronto Star*, 28 Dec. 1986.

It is important to know that every major breakthrough in the last hundred years in the medical labs has been achieved by the use of animals in laboratory experiments. That is what the animal rights movement is trying to stop, and very effectively in some cases.
> PIERRE BERTON, author and media personality, address, Ontario Fur Trade Association, Northern Ontario, 4 May 1990.

ANIMALS
See also ANIMAL RIGHTS
BEAVER
BIRDS
COWS
SEAL HUNT
WILDLIFE
WOLVES
ZOOS

But the Buffalo of the wild Plains is gone forever; and we who see those times in the glamour of romance can only bow the head and sadly say, "It had to be. He served his time, but now his time is passed."
> ERNEST THOMPSON SETON, naturalist and author, *Life Histories of Northern Animals* (1909).

Perhaps our species is the primitive stem of a new kind of animal, the intellectual qualities of which will differentiate and expand into another array of different and increasingly complex animals in the history of terrestrial life.
> DALE A. RUSSELL, paleontologist, "Fossil Animals," *The Canadian Encyclopedia* (1985).

It was now clear that neither God nor Darwinian selection produces and extinguishes species. Committees do.
> JOHN A. LIVINGSTON, naturalist, referring to the reclassification of the Ipswich sparrow as a subspecies and not a species following its apparent extinction, "Nature for the Sake of Nature," *Endangered Spaces: The Future for Canada's Wilderness* (1989) edited by Monte Hummel.

But the animals of the Burgess Shale are somehow even more satisfying in their adamantine factuality. We will argue forever about the meaning of life, but *Opabinia* either did or did not have five eyes — and we can't know for certain one way or the other. The animals of the Burgess Shale are the world's most important fossils, in part because they have revised our view of life, but also because they are objects of such exquisite beauty.
> STEPHEN JAY GOULD, biologist, discussing the unique, marine-animal fossils found in the Burgess Shale of B.C.'s Yoho National Park, *Wonderful Life: The Burgess Shale and the Nature of History* (1989).

ANNE OF GREEN GABLES

When I am asked if *Anne* herself is a "real person" I always answer "no" with an odd reluctance and an uncomfortable feeling of not telling the truth. For she is and always has been, from the moment I first thought of her, so real to me that I feel I am doing violence to something when I deny her an existence anywhere save in Dreamland.
> L. M. MONTGOMERY, author, journal entry, 27 Jan. 1911, Cavendish, P.E.I., *The Selected Journals of L.M. Montgomery: Volume II: 1910-1921* (1987) edited by Mary Rubio and Elizabeth Waterston. This is a

reference to Montgomery's childhood classic, *Anne of Green Gables* (1908) and its sequels.

ANTHEM, NATIONAL

Also I wrote an anthem for Canada, called *Anthem is as Anthem Does* but I haven't space to copy it out.
> CHRISTOPHER MORLEY, U.S. bookman, letter dated 5 Sept. 1946, concerning a visit to Toronto, quoted by David G. Pitt in *E.J. Pratt: The Master Years, 1927-1964* (1987).

We mumble for thee. Well, we admit it. We can't remember the words of "O Canada," either. This land is something to sing about, no doubt about it, but Canadians can't warble the national anthem worth a nickel. . . .
  It would be tempting to abandon "O Canada," in both official languages, if it weren't for the lack of an alternative. So, let's stick with the song we've got. Remember, there's something safe and pleasant about a country that can't remember the words to its national anthem.
> Editorial, *The Edmonton Journal*, 18 Sept. 1989.

ANTI-SEMITISM
See also JEWISH PEOPLE

It's noble to die a martyr's death for a cause; it is not a noble thing to be killed for the shape of one's nose.
> MAURICE EISENDRATH, Rabbi of the Holy Blossom Temple in Toronto, cited by Vincent Massey on 25 Oct. 1933 and quoted by Claude T. Bissell in *The Imperial Canadian: Vincent Massey in Office* (1986).

It would have taken a man in London who was both incautious and heroic to go counter to this formidable and dedicated bureaucracy. Vincent Massey was not such a man.
> CLAUDE T. BISSELL, biographer, *The Imperial Canadian: Vincent Massey in Office* (1986). The biographer is responding to

the charge that Vincent Massey, successively Canada's High Commissioner in London, its Ambassador in Washington, and its first native-born Governor General, was anti-semitic; apparently in private Massey blamed Canada's unwillingness to act on behalf of the world's stateless Jews in the late 1930s on the bureaucracy's "unholy triumvirate" (the phrase is that of Irving Abella and Harold Troper) of the Immigration Branch, the Cabinet, and the Department of External Affairs in opposing the admission to Canada of refugees in general and Jewish refugees in particular.

Duddy Kravitz Not Anti-Semitic
> Said to be the banner headline on an issue of *The Canadian Jewish News* in 1974, the year of the release of the film version of Mordecai Richler's novel *The Apprenticeship of Duddy Kravitz*. Noted by Martin Knelman in *Toronto Life*, Aug. 1989.

APATHY

Whenever I'm away from Canada, the thing I miss most is the apathy.
> MENDELSON JOE, performer and painter, quoted in *The Globe and Mail*, 31 Dec. 1987.

ARAB PEOPLE
See also OIL INDUSTRY

Arabs kill Jewish children; Jews kill Arab children. They are children; the noun is more important than the adjective.
> REUBEN SLONIM, rabbi and memoirist, *To Kill a Rabbi* (1987).

We are awed by the "real" Arab, the Bedouin tribespeople who have survived within an environment as hostile as that of our own Arctic, and who, again like our Inuit, yet have evolved a rich and intricate and pridefully independent lifestyle.
> RICHARD GWYN, correspondent, *The Toronto Star*, 16 Jan. 1991.

If there's one thing the West has indeed

learned about Islam, it's that the sacred and the secular are inseparable in Islamic terms. It is this sense of a coherent spiritual identity that is baffling to the West, which has come to regard culture and religious pluralism as divine doctrine, and committed itself to strict separation between church and state.

> JACK KAPICA, columnist, *The Globe and Mail*, 10 April 1991.

ARCHITECTURE

If I were asked by some stranger to North American culture to show him the most important religious building in Canada, I would take him to Toronto's Maple Leaf Gardens.

> WILLIAM KILBOURN, social historian, *Toronto Remembered: A Celebration of the City* (1984).

Doctors bury their mistakes; lawyers send theirs to jail; architects must cover theirs with ivy. Well, it takes a lot of ivy to cover a twenty-story building.

> JOHN C. PARKIN, architect, characteristic remark (recalling a similar remark attributed earlier to Frank Lloyd Wright), quoted by Michael Tenszen in *The Toronto Star*, 23 Nov. 1988.

But buildings, like animal skeletal bones, are the most intractable and immutable of things, and tend to remain even after the ideas have long gone.

> ARTHUR ERICKSON, architect, *Building with Words: Canadian Architects on Architecture* (1981) compiled by William Bernstein and Ruth Cawker.

For Everyone a Garden

> MOSHE SAFDIE, architect, Introduction (1987), *Beyond Habitat by 26 Years* (1970, 1987). "The idea of creating a humane and enriching work space for offices, and the preoccupation of designing public places that reinforce street life in the city, extrovert places, in contrast with the private introvert oases, were all on my mind."

If you're an optimist, you feel people will demand more and we'll get control of the environment. If you're a pessimist, you think the current trend will continue and Big Brother will wait around the corner, watching us in all these cell blocks.

I'm an optimist. I couldn't function as an architect if I wasn't.

> MOSHE SAFDIE, architect, quoted by Pearl Sheffy Gefen in *The Toronto Star*, 13 Nov. 1988.

The most beautiful house in the world is the one that you build for yourself.

> WITOLD RYBCZYNSKI, Montreal architect and author of *Home: A Short History of an Idea* and *The Most Beautiful House in the World*, quoted by Pamela Young in *Maclean's*, 19 June 1989.

If you're going to dream, why dream small?

> DOUGLAS CARDINAL, architect and designer of the Canadian Museum of Civilization in Hull, Que., quoted by Christopher Hume in *The Toronto Star*, 3 July 1989. One unnamed wit referred to the style selected by the Prairie architect for the CMC's exterior as "gopher baroque."

People ask me if I'm an artist or an architect. But I think they're the same.

> FRANK GEHRY, designer-architect, Toronto-born, Los Angeles-based, quoted by Christopher Hume in *The Toronto Star*, 4 Sept. 1987.

Anyone for Precambrian Modern?

> PETER C. NEWMAN, author, *Sometimes a Great Nation: Will Canada Belong to the 21st Century?* (1988).

ARCTIC
See also The NORTH

And their ordinary vent for them is a certain high hill in the North of *America*, whose people I can easily believe to be wholly descended of them, partly in regard of their colour, partly also in regard of the continuall use of Tobacco which the

Lunars use exceeding much, as living in a place abounding wonderfully with moysture, as also for the pleasure they take in it, and partly in some other respects, too long now to be rehearsed. Sometimes they mistake their aime, and fall upon Christendome, *Asia* or *Affricke*, marry that is but seldom.

> FRANCIS GODWIN, Anglican Bishop and satirist, *The Man in the Moone: Or a Discourse of a Voyage Thither . . .* (1683). In Godwin's 17th-century satire on the fabulous voyage, the inhabitants of the Moon (the Lunars or Lunatics) ship their criminally dangerous lunatics off to "a certain high hill" in the polar regions of the planet Earth. Thus the northern reaches of North America served as a lunatic asylum!

There is something unaccountably oppressive in this Arctic universe. The immensity of these regions, their dreariness, their silent immobility that appears like the stillness of the grave, have a strangely depressing effect. They weigh upon the mind, and bear it down like some fearful incubus, like that half-waking, half-dreaming, indistinct consciousness of weight upon the chest felt in the oppression of nightmare.

> JANUARIUS A. MacGAHAN, Irish-American war correspondent and member of the Pandora Expedition to the Eastern Arctic, *Under the Northern Lights* (1876).

Remember, then, as a sort of dream, that Doctor Kane of the Arctic Seas loved Maggie Fox of the spirit rappings.

> Request of ELISHA KENT KANE, the U.S. Naval physician, whose Arctic explorations are recalled in the naming of Kane Basin, N.W.T., from a letter he wrote before his death in Havana in 1857; it appears in *The Love-Life of Dr. Kane* (1866) and it was addressed to his *fiancée*, Margaret Fox, the spiritualist, or spirit-rapper, who was born in Canada West, now Ontario.

The state these Arctic Regions are kept in seems to me a declaration from Heaven that we are not wanted there.

> JOHN RUSKIN, English critic, letter written to Pauline Trevelyan in 1860, quoted by Stephen Brook in *Maple Leaf Rag: Travels across Canada* (1987).

Distances in the Arctic were not measured by miles or days but by the number of times you had to sleep.

> ARCHIE HUNTER, trader with the Hudson's Bay Company in the Far North, 1924-59, *Northern Traders: Caribou Hair in the Stew* (1983).

The Arctic is a world, not of Man, scarcely of beast, but of physical and geological and meteorological attributes only; it belongs to the universe of first creation, but not to the universe of last creation; of the First and Second Days, not of the Sixth Day.

> KENNETH P. KIRKWOOD, author and diplomat, "Arctic Intermezzo" (1940-43), *The Diplomat at Table: A Social and Anecdotal History through the Looking-Glass* (1974).

There are two kinds of Arctic problems, the imaginary and the real. Of the two, the imaginary are the more real.

> VILHJALMUR STEFANSSON, Arctic explorer, *The Arctic in Fact and Fable* (1945).

The Arctic is too important to be ignored. It is our heritage, and should be preserved for future generations. From now on, the Inuit, and the *qallunaat* must work together, as partners.

> SAM HALL, British correspondent, *The Fourth World: The Heritage of the Arctic and Its Destruction* (1987). *Qallunaat* means "white man" in Inuktitut.

This paper might have been subtitled "The enemy within," for during the last forty years the greatest practical threat to Canadian aspirations in the Arctic has been posed, curiously enough, by its formidable ally to the south, the United States of America.

> N.D. BANKS, law professor, "Forty Years

of Canadian Sovereignty Assertion in the Arctic, 1947-87," *Arctic*, Dec. 1987.

The passage is beaten.
Boast of the Arctic explorer JEFF MacINNIS at Pond Inlet, Baffin Island, N.W.T., 17 Aug. 1988. It took MacInnis (the son of undersea explorer Joseph MacInnis) three summers to do it, but he became the first person to navigate the North-West Passage powered solely by breeze and brawn. He covered a distance of 4000 kilometres/2500 miles in his eighteen-foot catamaran.

ARCTIC OX

To wear the arctic fox / you have to kill it. Wear / *qiviut* — the underwool of the arctic ox — / pulled off it like a sweater; / your coat is warm; your conscience, better.
Lines from the poem "The Arctic Ox (or Goat)" by the poet MARIANNE MOORE from her book *The Complete Poems of Marianne Moore* (1986) edited by Patricia C. Willis.

ARMY
See CANADIAN ARMED FORCES

ART & ARTISTS
See also CULTURE

We maintain that three-fourths of the Venuses and Aphrodites of the Louvre and Luxembourg are intolerable and indecent, for they are not goddesses, not women, or maidens, but nude female figures.
HUGH JOHNSTON, Montreal Methodist minister, *Toward the Sunrise: Sketches of Travel in Europe and the East* (1881).

Art persists by the same force that leads a man to do good, because it is true and beautiful to do so, and from no mercantile reason whatever, and thus art and religion are fed by the same translucent springs.
DUNCAN CAMPBELL SCOTT, poet and essayist, "The Mermaid Inn," 4 March 1893,

At the Mermaid Inn (1979) introduced by Barrie Davies.

We may hope, Sir, that the strong sun from our Prairies and the winds from our Northern Hills will not have disturbed unduly the classic repose of so historic a place.
VINCENT MASSEY, Canadian High Commissioner, speaking at the opening of an exhibition of Canadian painting at the Tate Gallery in London, England, 14 Oct. 1938. The passage is quoted by Claude T. Bissell who called it in *The Imperial Canadian: Vincent Massey in Office* (1986) "a good example of the style of dignified raillery of which he was a finished exponent."

No greater curse can befall a man than to be afflicted with artistic leanings in Canada.
FREDERICK PHILIP GROVE, novelist, quoted by Stan Obodiac in *My Experiences at a Canadian Authors' Convention* (1957).

I think it's about time for me to become popular.
HAROLD TOWN, artist and public figure, reacting to public adulation which took the form of a cover story in *Maclean's* in 1963, quoted by Robert Fulford in *Best Seat in the House: Memoirs of a Lucky Man* (1988), who added, "And quite soon, he was."

I have found that to consider art as an anti-environment or as a means of perceiving the hidden dimension of the environment, is exceedingly useful. Instead of explaining to people that art is something to be taken seriously because of some inherent superior quality, it makes more sense to point out that art has an indispensable function in cognition, and that men without art strongly tend to be automata, or somnambulists, imprisoned in a dream.
MARSHALL McLUHAN, media philosopher, letter dated 28 Jan. 1966, *Letters of Marshall McLuhan* (1987) edited by Matie

Molinaro, Corinne McLuhan, and William Toye.

Canada can accept some very advanced things in the arts and in the municipal government simply because we have no vested interests in any of the procedures that preceded these things elsewhere. Quebec is leap-frogging out of the 17th century into the 20th century. English Canada, relatively, is of 19th century origin and can only creep out of the 19th century into the 20th.

> MARSHALL McLUHAN, media philosopher, letter dated 6 Dec. 1966, *Letters of Marshall McLuhan* (1987) edited by Matie Molinaro, Corinne McLuhan, and William Toye.

I do hope that in your well-understood and natural desire to help your fellow Canadian artists you do not shut out the knowledge and influence of art from outside Canada. To do so, in the long run, would be a disservice.

> HENRY MOORE, sculptor, letter dated 23 Jan. 1974, quoted by Alan G. Wilkinson in *Henry Moore Remembered: The Collection at the Art Gallery of Ontario in Toronto* (1987). This was Moore's response to the request made by Michel Lambeth, chairman of the Toronto Chapter of Canadian Artists Representation, that the English artist withdraw his name from AGO's Moore Centre in favour of the Tom Thomson Wing.

We must not make bosses of our intellectuals. And we do them no good by letting them run the arts. Should they, when they read novels, find nothing in them but the endorsement of their opinions? Are we here on earth to play such games?

> SAUL BELLOW, Montreal-born novelist, Nobel Prize acceptance speech, Stockholm, Sweden, 12 Dec. 1976.

The Canada Council is not a give-away to others but an investment in ourselves.

> MAVOR MOORE, Chairman of the Canada Council, address, Empire Club of Canada, Toronto, 7 Feb. 1980.

If we do not now arrange to get to know each other better, to understand the rich variety of our differences and to rejoice in each other's triumphs instead of belittling them, we may haggle about oil or rewrite the constitution until we're blue in the face — but we will never have a country. Mutual understanding of this kind has always been best carried on through the creative arts and letters, whether "live" or as the "software" of modern communications. A nation which does not read or hear or watch its own artists is bent on severing its own lifeline.

> MAVOR MOORE, Chairman of the Canada Council, Foreword to *The Canada Council: 23rd Annual Report: 1979-1980* (1980).

Art can never be understood, but can only be seen as a kind of magic, the most profound and mysterious of all human activities.

> BILL REID, Haida artist, remark made in 1981, quoted by Martine J. Reid in "Silent Speakers," *The Spirit Sings: Artist Traditions of Canada's First Peoples* (1987).

Art experts are unfailingly opposed to Art for the simple reason that they are interested in Art — but Art is not interested in Art, Art is interested in life.

> STEPHEN VIZINCZEY, essayist, *Truth and Lies in Literature* (1986).

To me, the most important thing in a piece of art is the thought. Technique is totally secondary.

> ROBERT BATEMAN, wildlife artist, address, Empire Club of Canada, Toronto, 13 Nov. 1986.

Like every other form of art, literature is no more and nothing less than a matter of life and death. The only question worth asking about a story — or a poem, or a piece of sculpture, or a new concert hall — is, "Is it dead or alive?" If a work of the

imagination needs to be coaxed into life, it is better scrapped and forgotten.
MAVIS GALLANT, author, "What Is Style?" (1982), *Paris Notebooks: Essays and Reviews* (1986).

In this country the real artist will always live in relative obscurity or neglect, while the journalistic carnival goes on.
LOUIS DUDEK, aphorist, "Can. Lit. Notes," *The Bumper Book* (1986) edited by John Metcalf.

You can take a stand or you can take a fall.
Line from a song written and performed by the singer and painter MENDELSON JOE from his album *Fragile Man*, quoted by Roy MacGregor in *The Ottawa Citizen*, 8 Jan. 1987.

Artists, the real ones, the committed ones, have always sought, sometimes in ways prophetic and beyond their own times, to clarify and proclaim and enhance life, not to obscure and demean and destroy it. Even the so-called literature of despair is not really that at all. Despair is total silence, total withdrawal. Art, by its very nature of necessary expression, is an act of faith, an acknowledgement of the profound mystery at the core of life.
MARGARET LAURENCE, novelist, address, Trent University, Peterborough, Ont., 29 March 1983; quoted in *The Globe and Mail*, 10 Jan. 1989.

I look at art, question it, establish a dialogue with it. And I take a long time with the artist, because I am thinking in terms of fifteen or twenty years. I am serious about art because it recharges me, and gives me a better understanding of society, people. Because art is salvation, a great thing, like religion and law. Because art is the best, most challenging medicine for the mind.
CARMEN LAMANNA, art dealer, quoted in *The Globe and Mail*, 5 Sept. 1987.

My theory of esthetics is that good art is

what you like. I'm an artistic relativist, an anarchist that way.
SHEILA McCARTHY, filmmaker, quoted by Ron Graham in *The New York Times*, 8 Sept. 1987.

In the world of art, if you haven't got it, you've had it.
NICHOLAS GOLDSCHMIDT, orchestra conductor, quoted by Robertson Davies in *The Toronto Star*, 19 Sept. 1987.

I think everyone should do their utmost to see that this planet endures and also to try to help alleviate the suffering of their fellow human beings. In a certain sense the artist, perhaps, has even more of a duty to fulfill this obligation, first of all because he is to some extent in a position to be influential. Also, whether I like it or not, I often find myself playing in the presence of government people, although I haven't played for any of the supreme leaders of the world. I'm just as happy about that and would probably refuse invitations to play in either the Kremlin or the White House.
ANTON KUERTI, pianist, interviewed by Ulla Colgrass in *For the Love of Music* (1988).

But art can help us discover what money is for, while money can tell us nothing about what art is for.
ROBERT BRINGHURST, poet, "A Measure of Freedom," *The Globe and Mail*, 29 Oct. 1988.

Anyone who marries the spirit of his own generation will be a widow in the next.
LEONARD COHEN, poet and singer, "quoting a forgotten writer," according to Christopher Jones in *Now*, 5 Nov. 1988.

FAD = Famous And Dead / FOOF = Fine Old Ontario Family
Acronyms devised by CHARLES PACHTER, artist and diarist, 24 Sept. 1988.

My new work is a very Canadian form of self portrait — me describing myself in terms of what I am not.

GREG CURNOE, innovative artist and cultural nationalist, quoted by Deirdre Hanna in *Now*, 2 Nov. 1989.

ASTROLOGY

Astrology does not always make life easier to live, but it can make it much more meaningful. It can help you to take responsibility for yourself and for the various crises that we must face. Learning to deal with crises is essential for living a wholesome life.
> ROBIN ARMSTRONG, professional astrologer, *Robin Armstrong's Astrological Almanac: 1990* (1989).

ASTRONOMY
See also SPACE

Professional astronomical research consists mainly of coordinating the work of amateurs.
> T.B. PAWLICKI, author and theorist, *How You Can Explore Higher Dimensions of Space and Time* (1984).

As a boy the only profession I could ever imagine entering as an adult was astronomy. As a teenager the only form of literature that made sense was science fiction. As a young adult the only formal study I could contemplate was the science of space.
> RUSSELL McNEIL, science writer, *The Toronto Star*, 29 Jan. 1989.

ATHLETICS
See also SPORTS

Athletics has taught me so much about life that it's hard to know where to begin. One of the most important things that I have learned from athletics is the value of self-discipline.
> ELAINE TANNER, champion swimmer and Olympic champion, quoted in *The Globe and Mail*, 13 Nov. 1979.

ATLANTIC OCEAN

The Lord wants the pagan name of the Atlantic to be discarded and replaced by that of "Saul-Paul." If nations and navigators will adopt this glorious name, the ocean will be less stormy, says the Lord. Storms will cause fewer shipwrecks. And those who cross the ocean while commending themselves to the intercession of Saint Paul will suffer less seasickness.
> LOUIS RIEL, Métis leader and prophet, diary entry for 17-18 Oct. 1885, *The Diaries of Louis Riel* (1976) edited by Thomas Flanagan.

ATLANTIC PROVINCES
See also MARITIME PROVINCES
NEW BRUNSWICK
NEWFOUNDLAND
NOVA SCOTIA
PRINCE EDWARD ISLAND

The Islands of Nova Brunsland.
> The notion that there should be a political union of the four Atlantic provinces, a surprising proposal advanced by New Brunswick Premier Louis Robichaud at Charlottetown in 1964, led Prime Minister LESTER B. PEARSON to offer the above name for the new association, according to Della M.M. Stanley in *Louis Robichaud* (1984).

We need a new regional policy for Atlantic Canada, one that emboldens the four provinces to take their cue from the West European drive towards union and push the federal government — and the rest of the country — away from pork-barrel tokenism and towards hard-edged utilitarianism.
> JOHN FRASER, editor, "Diary," *Saturday Night*, Nov. 1989.

ATOMIC ENERGY
See also ENERGY
NUCLEAR ARMS
NUCLEAR ENERGY

The disintegration theory, advanced in explanation of the observations, has stood the test of time and has formed the basis of all subsequent developments. . . .

There is a saying that "it is the first step that counts," and it is clear that to McGill belongs whatever credit is due for the early ideas and experiments which opened up the way into the unknown that all subsequent investigators have followed.

SIR ERNEST RUTHERFORD, atomic scientist, letter written in 1932, assessing the importance of pioneering experimental and theoretical work undertaken with radioactivity in 1901-03 at the Macdonald Physics Building, McGill University, Montreal, quoted by Edgar A. Collard in *Montreal: The Days that Are No More* (1976).

In the greenstones east of McTavish Bay occur numerous interrupted stringers of calcspar, containing chalcopyrite, and the steep rocky shores which here present themselves to the lake are often stained with cobalt bloom and copper green.

JAMES MacINTOSH BELL, geologist, so described the rock formations on the south shore of Great Bear Lake, N.W.T. His careful description appeared in the Report of the Geological Survey of 1901. Gilbert A. LaBine, after examining the survey report at the Canadian Bureau of Mines in 1929, decided the description warranted a prospecting expedition. The gamble paid off. He discovered immense deposits of uranium on the shore of Great Bear Lake. Quoted by Pierre Berton in *The Mysterious North* (1956).

The study of atomic energy will never cease to be both fascinating and unpleasant at the same time.

BRUNO PONTECORVO, Italian-born atomic scientist, speaking to fellow scientist Bertrand Goldschmidt at the Montreal Lab in 1943, quoted by Margaret Gowing in *Britain and Atomic Energy: 1945-1952* (1964).

Tickling the dragon's tail.

This phrase, which refers to toying with

atomic energy, is attributed to LOUIS SLOTIN, atomic physicist and veteran of the Manhattan Project, and is repeated by Stewart Alsop and Ralph E. Lapp in "The Strange Death of Louis Slotin," *The Saturday Evening Post*, 6 March 1954.

Dr. Slotin was conducting a hands-on experiment with the critical mass of Uranium 235 at Los Alamos, N.M., 21 May 1946, when his screwdriver slipped and criticality was attained. With bare hands he disassembled the critical mass, and with his own body he shielded co-workers from lethal doses of radiation. He died of "radiation sickness" nine days later and was subsequently buried in a lead coffin in a Winnipeg cemetery.

I'm sorry I got you into this. I am afraid I have less than a fifty-fifty chance of living. I hope you have better than that.

LOUIS SLOTIN, atomic physicist, dying of atomic radiation in a hospital in Los Alamos, N.M., addressing an unnamed scientific co-worker who was also exposed to radiation but who survived, quoted by Stewart Alsop and Ralph E. Lapp in "The Strange Death of Louis Slotin," *The Saturday Evening Post*, 6 March 1954.

I woke up this morning / I counted my toes / My God, I had sixteen! / Start a demonstration / At your local hydro station.

Lyrics of "Radiation," a song written and performed by MARIE-LYNN HAMMOND, quoted by Ellen Schwartz in *Born a Woman: Seven Canadian Women Singer-Songwriters* (1988).

The seminal idea that led to the creation of the Candu reactor was conceived just before the outbreak of World War II in a Paris bathtub by Lew Kowarski, a Russian physicist then employed by Frédéric Joliot, the husband of Irène Curie and the son-in-law of Marie.

DAVID LEES, journalist, "Living in the Nuclear Shadow," *Toronto Life*, Nov. 1989. "Kowarski's plan, worked out with Joliot, was to suspend metallic bars of uranium, properly spaced, in a bath of heavy water so that the neutrons could stream from one bar to the other through the moderator. He had visualized the essence of the Candu reactor."

Like it or not, the Candu is an astonishing technological achievement. In 1987, when the Association of Consulting Engineers of Canada cited the top ten Canadian accomplishments, Candu made the list, along with the St. Lawrence Seaway, the Bombardier snowmobile and the Alouette satellite. It is the more remarkable in that it has been produced by the smallest of the five nations — the U.S., the U.S.S.R., Great Britain and France are the others — to have developed an indigenous reactor design. Each year when the trade magazine *Nuclear Engineering International* ranks the performance of the world's operating reactors, Candus make the list; seven of the top ten in both 1987 and 1988 were Candus.

> DAVID LEES, journalist, "Living in the Nuclear Shadow," *Toronto Life*, Nov. 1989.

ATTITUDES

I'm an optimist, and I'd better explain that because if you say you're an optimist people assume you're a simpleton. But I don't see how you can escape being an optimist when you consider the extraordinary things that man has done in the 30,000 years that he has been a recognizable human creature.

Extreme pessimism is a luxury that only the very young can afford. As you become older, pessimism becomes much more spiritually expensive, and you don't indulge in it unless you really are convinced of what you're saying. When you're a twenty-five-year-old it looks good to say that life is just a can of worms. When you're fifty-five it's not as funny. You've seen a few worms by that time.

> ROBERTSON DAVIES, man-of-letters, quoted by M.G. Lord in *Interview*, March 1989.

ATWOOD, MARGARET

Margaret Atwood will make one hell of an old lady. I'd like to be one of the young journalists who gather at her place on November 18, 2019, for her eightieth-birthday interview. I can't imagine what such people will want to ask her, but I can pretty well describe her answers — they'll be tart, aphoristic, defiant, confident.

> ROBERT FULFORD, cultural commentator, *Best Seat in the House: Memoirs of a Lucky Man* (1988).

As a small child, Margaret Atwood displayed the vivid imagination that has long since helped her to become one of the world's finest novelists. Not long ago her mother recalled a night when she squirmed into her pyjamas, eager for bed. "I'm telling myself a story," she explained, "and I can't wait to find out how it ends."

> DAVID MacDONALD, "Anecdotes," *The Toronto Star*, 16 April 1988.

Atwood is enroute to greater and greater recognition over the next four years. There are no major obstacles or immediate confrontations in her life in 1990. Her creative force is waxing amid greater demands for her time.

> ROBIN ARMSTRONG, professional astrologer, *Robin Armstrong's Astrological Almanac: 1990* (1989).

AUSTRALIA

Australia proved to be quite fascinating. . . . I was surprised to find the Australians to be more English than Canadians, and also more American than Canadians. They are a vivid, aggressive group who don't worry about the problem of a national identity.

> MARSHALL McLUHAN, media philosopher, letter dated 12 Aug. 1977, *Letters of Marshall McLuhan* (1987) edited by Matie Molinaro, Corinne McLuhan, and William Toye.

AUTHORITY

There is barely an area in our daily life untouched by authorities of one kind or another, instructing us on the use of both mind and body; we are subsumed by an army of specialists, hired to protect us from the hardening of our arteries and the softening of our minds.

> IRVINE SCHIFFER, psychoanalyst, *Charisma: A Psychoanalytic Look at Mass Society* (1973).

AUTOMOBILES
See also TRAVEL

But I don't know that I am wholly pleased with cars. Personally, I prefer a buggy with a nice lovable *living* horse. I occasionally remember with regret the old days — and moonlit nights — buggy driving.

Anyhow, I'm glad *my* courting days were over before the cars came!! There is no romance whatever in a car. A man can't safely drive it with one arm! And loitering is impossible.

> L.M. MONTGOMERY, author, letter of 26 Feb. 1919, quoted in *My Dear Mr. M.: Letters to G.B. MacMillan* (1980) edited by Francis W.P. Bolger and Elizabeth R. Epperly.

Our motor car is our supreme form of privacy when away from home.

> MARSHALL McLUHAN, media personality, address, Mohawk College, Hamilton, Ont., 17 May 1977.

If you're going to have a massive, embarrassing political failure, it should be something innovative. Besides, it got me on the *Today Show*. I was almost interviewed by Barbara Walters.

> RICHARD HATFIELD, New Brunswick Premier, remark made in Sept. 1980 concerning the fiasco of the Bricklin sportscar, quoted by Richard Starr in *Richard Hatfield: The Seventeen Year Saga* (1987).

The auto industry is perfect. It doesn't pollute, it never stops and it creates lots of jobs. They're laughing in Southern Ontario.

> BRIAN MULRONEY, Prime Minister, quoted by Michel Gratton in *"So, What Are the Boys Saying?": An Inside Look at Brian Mulroney in Power* (1987).

Canadian nationalists hoped that someday someone would make a distinctive Canadian car, like Sweden's Volvo, to meet Canadians' special needs (and until someone did many of them bought Volvos).

> MICHAEL BLISS, historian, *Northern Enterprise: Five Centuries of Canadian Business* (1987).

LET'S NOT MEET BY ACCIDENT

> Message on a bumpersticker spotted in Peterborough, Ont., Oct. 1989.

Hell must surely consist of driving for eternity along the 401, in a car that never needs refilling, with kidneys that never need draining.

> EDWARD PHILLIPS, novelist, referring to the Macdonald-Cartier Freeway (401), which goes from Windsor, Ont., to the Quebec border, *Sunday Best* (1990).

Perhaps the hardest question of all that we must face is whether, given the state of the world, there can be a future for the automobile.

> ANITA GORDON and DAVID SUZUKI, science broadcasters, *It's a Matter of Survival* (1990).

Keep your top down, your engine running, your foot on the gas, and your hand on the wheel.

> Philosophy of life of BILL SHERK, vintage auto enthusiast, *Old Autos*, 18 Feb, 1991.

AUTUMN
See SEASONS

AVIATION

See you in London.

> Last words uttered in public by JOHN ALCOCK on 14 June 1919, minutes before

the English pilot took off, with his co-pilot Arthur Whitten Brown, from St. John's, Nfld., for Clifden, Ireland. Quoted by John Fisher in *John Fisher Reports: An Anthology of Radio Scripts* (1949). The flight lasted 16 hours and 12 minutes. Eight years later Charles Lindbergh made the first solo non-stop flight across the Atlantic Ocean.

Away we went at 100 miles an hour and with amazing clearness the earth was visible below us at 2,500 feet. It was wonderful — simply wonderful. Next to falling in love for the first time, it is the greatest experience in life. A parable on wings — an allegory in the sky — the combination of a thousand thrills, of wonder, terror, rapture and triumph.
R.E. KNOWLES, columnist and interviewer, describing his impressions of an early airplane flight between Paris and London, quoted in his obituary in *The Toronto Star*, 15 Nov. 1946.

Exquisite in appearance, magnificent in design, but it won't fly.
JOHN G. DIEFENBAKER, Prime Minister, description of the Avro *Arrow* in 1959, according to Sean O'Sullivan in *Both My Houses* (1986) written with Rod McQueen.

Why do all international lines except Russia fly American planes?
GORDON SINCLAIR, broadcaster, "The Americans," broadcast of 5 June 1974, *Will Gordon Sinclair Please Sit Down* (1975).

Canadair was the worst-managed Canadian aircraft manufacturer; the better-managed one, de Havilland, also under government ownership, lost about $400 million in its own right. In the mid-1980s the only profitable Canadian manufacturer of complete aircraft was Fantasy Sky Productions Incorporated of Kitchener, Ontario, maker of the Labatt Blue and other hot-air balloons.
MICHAEL BLISS, historian, *Northern En-

terprise: Five Centuries of Canadian Business* (1987).

To me, climbing into a 747 has much of the same feeling as I used to get out of entering the St. Boniface basilica as a child. If God's presence could be imagined hovering once among echoing Gothic arches, why not somewhere among the hundred miles of wiring inside this mighty metal shell?
ROBERT HUNTER, activist and author, "A Small Tour in Germany," *On the Sky: Zen and the Art of International Freeloading* (1988).

Folks, we are a doomed flight today.
Sarcastic comment made by GEORGE MORWOOD, captain of Air Ontario's Flight 1363, minutes before the takeoff of the Fokker F-28 that abruptly ended in a crash that killed twenty-four people, including Morwood. A surviving passenger recalled the comment at the judicial inquiry, quoted by Michael Tenszen in *The Toronto Star*, 29 Sept. 1989.

Looking from my window one evening I saw a single steadily burning light in the dusk sky. It seemed to be motionless — Jupiter somehow magnified in the subarctic air, I thought, or perhaps a UFO? Silently it hung there against the darkening sky, and only very slowly majestically indeed, did it resolve itself into the form of a single small float-plane, bearing down on Yellowknife out of the north. Its light seemed so defiantly bright, the aircraft itself was so small, that when at last it landed with plumes of spray on the surface of the lake, I thought it a truly heroic image of Canada's northern adventure.
JAN MORRIS, Welsh-born travel writer, "Wild Blue-Yonder City," *Saturday Night*, Nov. 1989.

AWARDS & HONOURS

Well, I'm afraid I'm going to have to eat crow. I didn't like this play when it was performed on our network. I still don't like it. But thank you very much.

ERNEST BUSHNELL, CBC executive, acceptance speech at the 1944 Ohio Awards, Columbus, Ohio. Bushnell accepted the award on behalf of CBC Radio for the top drama as well as a special citation for the best submission in all categories of competition. He did so with respect to a single radio play: Andrew Allan's production of Len Peterson's *They're All Afraid* in the "Stage 44" series, despite attempts he had earlier made to block its production. Quoted by Bronwyn Drainie in *Living the Part: John Drainie and the Dilemma of Canadian Stardom* (1988).

Something really has to be accounted for. I have long been troubled by the cordiality of your attitudes towards me. Surely the capable and honest critic would not be tendered a banquet. He would be hated and reviled — possibly stoned. Wherein have I failed?
WILLIAM ARTHUR DEACON, veteran literary critic, address at retirement banquet in Toronto, 11 Jan. 1961, quoted by Clara Thomas and John Lennox in *William Arthur Deacon: A Canadian Literary Life* (1982).

I am dying by honourary degrees.
F.R. SCOTT, lawyer and poet, quip made to the present editor in 1965 after receiving yet another academic honour.

Shortly after he left Montreal in 1967 to work as an ordinary mission priest in West Africa, Paul-Emile Cardinal Léger won the $50,000 Royal Bank Award. Intending to spend it on lepers and handicapped children, he dutifully applied to his local bishop in Cameroon for permission to accept the money. Permission was granted. "If you refuse," the African prelate ruled, playfully, "it would be a cardinal sin."
DAVID MacDONALD, "Anecdotes," *The Toronto Star*, 29 Oct. 1988.

It's an American award given to a Canadian film about a Japanese adventurer on a Nepalese mountain.
F.R. (BUDGE) CRAWLEY, film producer, accepting the Academy Award for Best Foreign Film for *The Man Who Skied Down Everest* in Los Angeles, Calif., 29 March 1975 and reported the next day in *The Globe and Mail*.

I just thought you'ld like to know I've already got the only award that counts.
MILTON ACORN, poet, attending the awards ceremony in Ottawa and accepting the Governor General's Award for Poetry for 1975, informed the Governor General that he had earlier received "The People's Poet" award from fellow poets in Toronto in 1970.

The prize is an incident in life, but what an incident.
JOHN C. POLANYI, co-recipient of the Nobel Prize for Chemistry, awarded in Stockholm, Sweden, 10 Dec. 1986. Quoted by Stephen Strauss in *The Globe and Mail* the following day. At the banquet Polanyi said: "I know of no other place where princes assemble to pay homage to molecules."

When asked by a young student when the best time to win a Nobel Prize is, John C. Polanyi responded: "On your deathbed, because then it doesn't interrupt anything of colossal importance."
Adapted from a report by STEPHEN STRAUSS in *The Globe and Mail*, 12 Dec. 1987.

I think giving this computer to the last Luddite is ridiculous. It's like giving a Porsche to someone who just discovered the bicycle.
MICHAEL ONDAATJE, author, accepting a personal computer system at the Wang International Festival of Authors, Toronto, 23 Oct. 1988. Quoted by Jack Nagler in *Toronto Computes!*, Nov. 1988. The author is no Luddite but continues to write with a fountain pen.

In England, they call it Commander of the British Empire. Here, they're calling it Creator of Bargains Everywhere.

EDWIN MIRVISH, Toronto entrepreneur (known as "Honest Ed") and theatre owner, receiving the C.B.E. from Queen Elizabeth, quoted by Pearl Sheffy Gefen, *The Globe and Mail*, 29 July 1989.

I'm grateful to all my co-workers, my family, and my teachers — even my teachers back at West Hill.
I'll just go back to the lab and do more work. And just try to understand the thing I'm trying to understand.
SIDNEY ALTMAN addressed these words to the Canadian Press representative who contacted him at Yale University, New Haven, Conn., following the announcement that the Montreal-born Professor of Chemistry had just been named co-laureate of the 1989 Nobel Prize for Chemistry. Quoted by Jim Lesis in *The Toronto Star*, 13 Oct. 1989. Altman was a graduate of Montreal's West Hill High School.

For me, the greatest thing about the Junos is that everybody performs live. It's not like other award shows, where you have acts lipsynching or singing to a pre-recorded music track. The live acts at the Junos make it a real performance-oriented show.
PAUL SHAFFER, regular musical director of the TV show *Late Night With David Letterman* and special host of the 20th annual Juno Awards, quoted by Andrew Ryan in *TV Guide*, 2 March 1991.

BALLARD, HAROLD

The president and managing director, Harold E. Ballard, is back in office. The most famous building in Canada and the best-known hockey arena in the world once again knows his energetic leadership.

Saying it simply, the commander is back at the helm. Soon there will be new promotions, new concepts, and new directions sprouting from his great idea factory. Expect anything to happen now!

> Press release written by STAN OBODIAC, the chief publicist of Maple Leaf Gardens, referring to the release from Milhaven Penitentiary in 1974 of Harold E. Ballard, owner of the arena and the hockey club. Quoted by William Houston in *Ballard: A Portrait of Canada's Most Controversial Sports Figure* (1984).

Frum: Listen, I just go for the hearts and flowers, so I'm there Saturday night. . . .
Ballard: They shouldn't let females on the radio anyway. They're a joke. . . . You know where they're good. . . . You know where they're good, doncha? . . . You know where they're at their best, doncha? . . .

> The substance of the celebrated exchange between radio host Barbara Frum and Harold Ballard, owner of the Toronto Maple Leafs, on CBC Radio's *As It Happens*, 5 March 1979. Noted by Dick Beddoes in *Pal Hal: An Uninhibited, No-Holds-Barred Account of the Life and Times of Harold Ballard* (1989).

I'm going now.

> Dying words of outspoken sports personality HAROLD BALLARD at Wellesley Hospital, Toronto, 11 April 1990, quoted by Don Gillmor in "Love among the Ruins," *Saturday Night*, Sept. 1990.

BALLET
See DANCE

BALLOT
See also ELECTIONS

Universal suffrage necessitates universal education.

> ALFRED FITZPATRICK, Founder and Principal of Frontier College, *The University in Overalls: A Plea for Part-Time Study* (1920).

BANKS
See also FINANCE

Will there be any bankers in heaven? / Will there be any interest to pay? / Will there be any Liberals or Tories / To show us poor sinners the way?

> Verse of a ditty sung to the tune of "Red River Valley" and popular with farmers and labourers on the Prairies in the 1930s, as noted by Olenka Melnyk in *No Bankers in Heaven: Remembering the CCF* (1989).

Best wishes, Raymond Massey.

> "Massey was one of those rare stars who actually enjoyed signing autographs. On one occasion he signed a piece of paper which wandered back from his bank [and] said: 'Best wishes, Raymond Massey.'" Quoted by Ed Gould in *Entertaining Canadians: Canada's International Stars 1900-1988* (1988).

There must be some mistake. I'm a baker, not a banker.

> W. GARFIELD WESTON, Toronto-born baker in Britain, responding to the offer to become a bank director, the first non-Briton to be offered the distinction, quoted by John Picton in *The Toronto Star*, 1 Oct. 1989.

The easiest way to steal from a bank is to own one.

> ROBERT KORTHALS, President of the Toronto-Dominion Bank, quoted by Diane Francis in *Controlling Interest: Who Owns Canada?* (1986).

I would like to own half of a bank like this myself.

> ALEXEI KOSYGIN, Soviet President, examining the Annual Report of the Canadian Imperial Bank of Commerce with its President, Neil McKinnon, at the Kremlin, quoted by David MacDonald, "Anecdotes," *The Toronto Star*, 28 Jan. 1989.

The Canadian character is solid. Cautious and thrifty, Canadians are a nation of accountants. In Canada there are 6.4 million more savings accounts than there are people. Canadians are apparently the most heavily insured people in the world, and nothing gets them more aroused than talk of actuarial probabilities. Canadians don't like competition; discounts are considered flashy. Canadians are proud to pay list price.

> RICHARD STENGEL, U.S. journalist, "The Canadians," *Spy*, Feb. 1988.

The strange sight of a sod hut in the middle of the prairie open for business under a large Canadian Bank of Commerce sign astonished one visitor to pioneer Saskatchewan.

> WILLIAM KILBOURN, historian, "The Peaceable Kingdom Still," *Daedalus: Journal of the American Academy of Arts and Sciences*, "In Search of Canada," Fall 1988.

From 1981 to 1984, inclusive, Canada's seven largest banks made profits of $5.373 billion dollars and paid federal taxes on these profits at the rate of 1.34%. From 1980 to 1987, inclusive, Canada's banks made profits of over $7.64 billion and paid federal income taxes at the rate of 2.48%. These figures can only be described as appalling. . . . It is safe to say that the vast majority of bank tellers in Canada, including the lowest paid, paid a far higher rate of tax, throughout the entire decade of the 1980s, than the bank that he or she worked for.

> MEL HURTIG, publisher, Presentation to the Senate Standing Committee on Banking, Trade and Commerce, 26 July 1990.

Before going to the United States for my Guggenheim Fellowship I had to get a visa. The official at the American Embassy asked me for two references. Now without pride I offered, as the first, "the Rt. Hon. Arthur Meighen." "Who's he?" "The former Prime Minister of Canada." "Do you know a banker?" I told Meighen the story. He laughed and laughed.

> EUGENE FORSEY, constitutional authority, *A Life on the Fringe: The Memoirs of Eugene Forsey* (1990).

BARBADOS

One thing you do not know about me, and which I have been thinking of for the past few days: I have no real, true friends in this country, even after all these years; for those persons I hold dear are all in Barbados, or scattered throughout the other West Indian countries.

AUSTIN CLARKE, Barbadian-born novelist and Toronto resident since 1955, "A Stranger in a Strange Land," *The Globe and Mail*, 15 Aug. 1990.

BASEBALL

What bird symbolizes the Toronto Blue Jays baseball team?

TERRY JOHNSON, humorist, *Quick Quiz for Slow People* (1988).

No such obligation applies to the game of baseball, which Canadians embrace passionately. Unfortunately they are no good at it. True, the Toronto Blue Jays did extremely well during the months of my visit. . . . Why Canadians should be so frenetic fans of a team that contains not a single Canadian player is a mystery to me.

STEPHEN BROOK, English travel writer, *Maple Leaf Rag: Travels across Canada* (1987).

I have never worn an Expo's baseball cap. Not that I hate baseball, quite the opposite. But I think it is a bit silly to pay gold to U.S. muscle men to play ball in our name. But there is a chewing-gum streak in Montreal's nature; the National Baseball League is part of that streak; and we are part of that league.

But there is also the home-grown Ligue Nationale d'Improvisation, of which I am very proud, and which I like a lot more. It pits teams of brilliant young comedians who have borrowed all the gimmicks of Hockey Night in Canada against each other in matches of improvised comedy. That is a genial invention; there is a crackling, sparkling streak in Montreal's nature too.

Baseball and chewing gum are what meshed us into North America. Improvised comedy, developed here, has reached all other francophone markets overseas. That is the fun thing about Montreal.

JACQUES GODBOUT, author and filmmaker, *The Globe and Mail*, 6 Nov. 1989.

Industrial, agricultural and stone-age instincts are not automatically eradicated when not only the rules, but the very game itself is changed. We are no longer playing baseball: The game is now Jaialai and very few even know how to spell it.

FRANK OGDEN, futurologist, "Ogden's Fifteenth Law," *Dr. Tomorrow's Lessons from the Future* (June 1989).

BASKETBALL

Gym Naysmith wuz foolin round in a cherch basemint with a bullsbladder and a cuppla bushill baskit. He bloo up the bladder and put both them baskits at oppsit ends of that basemint. It wirked. He slamdunkt the wirld with sumthin noo, and them Massachewsuns new he wuz onto a good thing, but bein Yankys, they hadda thunk up sum improovmints. They thot the game wuz too Canjun, meein too slow.

DON HARRON, comedian, in the person of Charlie Farquharson, *Cum Buy the Farm* (1987).

BEARS

The artistic and philosophical evocation of the polar bear by Eskimo and pre-Eskimo cultures leads one to believe that their insight derives from a special affinity with the bear. To an extent, the Eskimo and the polar bear are alike, the lines of their successful adapation to the Arctic being parallel.

BARRY LOPEZ, naturalist, *Arctic Dreams: Imagination and Desire in a Northern Landscape* (1986).

What kind of bear was named for its grizzly appearance?

TERRY JOHNSON, humorist, *Quick Quiz for Slow People* (1988).

There's an old trapper's tale that says the best way to defend yourself against a polar bear attack is to shoot your buddy and run like hell.

Remark recalled by the Arctic adventurer JEFF MacINNIS in *Polar Passage: The Historic First Sail through the Northwest Passage* (1989) by Jeff MacInnis with Wade Rowland.

Most of the wastes are actually south of most of the rest of Canada and around the latitude of Antibes, although everyone acts with cheerful stoicism, as if there were polar bears round the next bend in the road: indeed there is a special train called the Polar Bear Express which runs all the way up to Moosonee, the latitude of Ilfracombe or Blankenberghe; they could as well call it the Mastodon Mail or the Giant Sloth Slow for all your chance of seeing its eponym from the observation car. This proves that climate is all in the mind, a thing to remember as Britain braces itself for its first tsunami.

ERIC KORN, columnist and antiquarian book dealer, *The Times Literary Supplement*, 15 June 1990.

BEAUTY
See also FASHION

The trouble with photographing beautiful women is that you never get into the dark room until after they've gone.

YOUSUF KARSH, portrait photographer, quoted in *The New York Daily Mirror*, 2 May 1963.

If you're fourteen and reading this, take solace: You probably look a lot better than you think. And *nobody* looks like Miss January.

MARGOT KIDDER, film actress, commenting on her photographic exposure in *Playboy*, March 1975.

My point is: You really don't need to go to Niagara Falls or the Rocky Mountains or Hawaii to see beauty. You have it right outside your back door. You are stumbling over it all the time, if you are tuned in and sensitive enough to nature. The amazing thing about nature is that you can walk fifty feet and get a totally different viewpoint, a totally different image.

ROBERT BATEMAN, wildlife artist, address, Empire Club of Canada, Toronto, 13 Nov. 1986.

A woman possessed of beauty is a woman possessed.

ROBIN SKELTON, man-of-letters, aphorism, May 1990.

BEAVER
See also ANIMALS

We believe that only the beavers had the right to build dams in our territory.

Resolution of the Cree bands whose lands in northwestern Quebec were threatened by the damming of rivers required by the James Bay hydro-development project, 1 July 1971, quoted by Roy MacGregor in *Chief: The Fearless Vision of Billy Diamond* (1989).

Were it not for a web-footed rodent and a haberdashery fad in eighteenth-century Europe, Minnesota might be a Canadian province today. The beaver, almost as much as the horse, helped shape the course of early American history.

WILLIAM LEAST HEAT MOON, native American writer and travel writer, *Blue Highways: A Journey into America* (1982).

When someone writes about *beavers*, one assumes that this person is a zoologist, works for a porno magazine, or is a Canadian.

REINHOLD AMAN, U.S. linguist, "What Is This Crime that Dare Not Speak Its Name?" *Maledicta*, No. 9, 1986-87.

What animal constructs beaver dams?

TERRY JOHNSON, humorist, *Quick Quiz for Slow People* (1988).

BEAVERBROOK, LORD

What's the news? . . . Good-bye-ee.
> LORD BEAVERBROOK, Canadian-born British press baron, characteristic expressions on the telephone, recalled by Robert Edwards, former editor of *The Daily Express*, in his memoirs, *Goodbye Fleet Street* (1988).

Our policy now can only be to sustain the fragments of what was once a glorious empire on which the sun never used to set and on which now it seldom rises.
> LORD BEAVERBROOK, press baron, interviewed on his 85th birthday, quoted in *The New York Times*, 25 May 1964.

I make my money in Britain, I spend it over here.
> Attributed to LORD BEAVERBROOK while in New Brunswick, where he spent his youthful years, by the historian A.L. Rowse and quoted by Harry Bruce in "Fredericton: Pampered Pet of Old New Brunswick," *Down Home: Notes of a Maritime Son* (1988).

In the nineteen sixties I went abroad more often, even crossing the Atlantic for the first and last time in my life. This of course was Max Beaverbrook's doing. As chancellor of the University of New Brunswick at Fredericton, Max spent a few weeks there every autumn, partly to stir up the professors and partly to strengthen the myth that one day he would retire to his "native province" (a fiction endorsed by the state legislature).
> A.J.P. TAYLOR, English historian and biographer, *A Personal History* (1983).

Lord Beaverbrook was at his very best when things were at their very worst.
> SIR WINSTON CHURCHILL, British wartime leader, recalling Lord Beaverbrook's years as Minister of Aircraft Production, quoted by Janet Aitken Kidd in *The Beaverbrook Girl: An Autobiography* (1987).

I am descended from eight or ten generations of agricultural labourers. Therefore I feel quite equal to the Cecil family, with this difference, that none of my ancestors stole church funds.
> Attributed to LORD BEAVERBROOK by David Cannadine in *The Decline and Fall of the British Aristocracy* (1991).

BEER
See also DRINKING

If you faced a long hungry period with nothing between you and starvation but a bit of barley and a pig, you'd be better off turning the barley into beer and letting the pig starve.
> JIM CAMERON, brewmaster, O'Keefe Brewery, Ottawa, quoted by Dave Brown in *The Ottawa Journal*, 14 Dec. 1968.

And it occurs to me that if I were aboard a rowboat floating in the middle of all the beer I've drunk in a lifetime, I'd never be able to see the shore.
> AL PURDY, poet, Preface, *The Collected Poems of Al Purdy* (1986) edited by Russell Brown.

It doesn't take long for even the most casual visitor to Canada to realize that a relatively small number of things lie at the heart of Canadian culture: The North. The weather. Not being Americans. Consensual politics. And Beer.
> H.S. BHABRA, columnist, "Torontonians," *The Toronto Star*, 5 Nov. 1988.

Q. Why is a Canadian making love in a canoe like American beer?
A. They're both fucking close to water.
> Joke noted by Val Sears, "Ottawa Notebook," *The Toronto Star*, 26 Nov. 1989.

Canadians think American beer is lemonade. Americans think our drinking laws came from Ulan Bator. Both are right.
> ALLAN FOTHERINGHAM, columnist, *Maclean's*, 3 July 1989.

The opportunities some Canadian companies find in the United States can produce

interesting anomalies. Moosehead, the New Brunswick beer that is the sixth most popular imported brand in America, is available in all 50 states but in only four of the 12 Canadian provinces and territories.
ANDREW H. MALCOLM, journalist, *The New York Times*, 28 Jan. 1990.

BELIEF

See also CATHOLICISM
CHRISTIANITY
DOUBT
GHOSTS
GOD
NEW AGE
PARAPSYCHOLOGY
PSYCHICAL RESEARCH
RELIGION
SPIRITUALISM
SUPERSTITION

In all of our studies of the brain, no mechanism has been discovered that can force the mind to think, or the individual to believe, anything. The mind continues free. This is a statement I have long considered. I have made every effort to disprove it, without success. The mind, I must conclude, is something more than a mechanism. It is, in a certain sense, above and beyond the brain, although it seems to depend upon brain action for its very existence. Yet it is free.
WILDER PENFIELD, neurosurgeon and essayist, "Science, the Arts, and the Spirit," *Second Thoughts: Science, the Arts, and the Spirit* (1970).

The parapsychologists admit they've come up with nothing concrete, but amid all that evidence, they keep hoping some might be valid. Well, maybe it is. And maybe there are eight tiny reindeer who can fly on Christmas Eve. There's an awful lot of evidence for the existence of Santa Claus, you know. The problem is that none of it happens to be very *good* evidence.
JAMES RANDI, conjuror and debunker of psychic claims, quoted by Bryan Johnson in *The Globe and Mail*, 13 April 1985.

We human beings tend to need to believe in something we cannot apprehend or understand — something greater and bigger than our meagre lives. Spirituality is part of our makeup.
LUCINDA VARDEY, author and apologist for Roman Catholicism, *Belonging: A Book for the Questioning Catholic Today* (1988).

It is easier to persuade a man to believe than to persuade him to think.
ROBIN SKELTON, man-of-letters, aphorism, May 1990.

I now *know* that our existence is infinitely more mysterious, more miraculous, and more complex than the average atheist and agnostic would suppose. Even rational science says that the hands before us, the pages we behold, and the chairs in which we sit are nothing but masses of tiny particles! If we truly understood that, we would not be so complacent about this mundane experience.
RON GRAHAM, journalist and author, *God's Dominion: A Sceptic's Quest* (1990).

BERMUDA

You can take the Group of Seven out of Canada, but you can't take Canada out of the Group of Seven. . . .
In 1932, painter J.E.H. MacDonald and wife Joan wintered in the Caribbean. There, the Group member kept a diary, from which we learn certain remarkable things. "Bermuda from the sea frequently resembles the shores of Lake Superior or Labrador," for example. And try this one: "The sea has a Lake Ontario blue." (Will Canada forgive those of her children who do not think of James Bay when gazing at the waters off Port of Spain?)
JOHN BENTLEY MAYS, cultural commentator, *The Globe and Mail*, 5 May 1988.

We are only twenty-six miles long and one mile wide. We have the highest average net income in the world, but we limit motor cars to only one per household and

the speed limit is twenty miles an hour. We are the only country in the world where you can see bank chairmen peddling to their offices on scooters. We exist just to serve all you nice Canadian and American tourists who come down and leave all those lovely dollars behind you. Frankly, we would all starve if you didn't. Some 80% of our income depends on tourism.
> SIR EDWIN LEATHER, Canadian-born Governor of Bermuda, address, 12 Dec. 1974.

BERTON, PIERRE

I once asked Wayne Gretzky if, having been so celebrated so early, he feared a later reaction — the same thing that happened to Berton. Wayne, bless his heart, said, "Is Pierre Berton a Canadian?"
> PETER GZOWSKI, host of CBC Radio's *Morningside*, commenting on the tendency of the media and the public to elevate and then denigrate public figures like Pierre Berton, *The Private Voice: A Journal of Reflections* (1988).

BIG FOOT
See SASQUATCH

BILINGUALISM
> *See also* CANADA
> FRENCH CANADA
> LANGUAGE
> LANGUAGE, FRENCH

No man, whether in Canada or elsewhere, should be looked upon as "well educated" today unless he is easily bilingual or multilingual. Such an education is so easy to achieve, especially in Canada!
> WILDER PENFIELD, neurosurgeon and essayist, Preface, *Second Thoughts: Science, the Arts, and the Spirit* (1970).

Tongue in cheek, I also suggested the use, to promote bilingualism, of some commercial slogans, popular at the time, "Does she or doesn't she" speak French? "The man of distinction" is bilingual. Bilingualism "for those who think young." And from

an ad for deodorants: Bilingualism, "It takes away the fear of being close!"
> JEAN-LUC PEPIN, Chairman of the Anti-Inflation Board, address, The Empire Club of Canada, Toronto, 14 Oct. 1976, quoting from an earlier speech dated 15 Jan. 1970.

All pro athletes are bilingual. They speak English and profanity.
> GORDIE HOWE, hockey personality, quoted by George Gamester in *The Toronto Star*, 27 May 1975.

English in Canada is not the language of the culture, it is the language of communication. French is both the language upon which the Québécois culture rests and the means of communication.
> RICHARD ROHMER, lawyer and author, address, Administrative Management Society, Toronto, quoted in *The Globe and Mail*, 24 March 1977.

The majority of Quebeckers are not bilingual. Just like you, most of them speak only one language. There are about five million francophones living in Quebec — and three-quarters of them speak only French. Think of it: About as many Quebeckers who speak only French as the combined total population of all three prairie provinces.
> PIERRE ELLIOTT TRUDEAU, Prime Minister, address to the Canadian Association of Broadcasters, Winnipeg, 18 April 1977, reported in *The Toronto Star* the following day.

Sometimes I wish we had never described the official languages policy as "bilingualism" — because the word apparently implies that our intent is for all Canadians to learn two languages. Such is not our intent at all.
> PIERRE ELLIOTT TRUDEAU, Prime Minister, address to the Canadian Association of Broadcasters, Winnipeg, 18 April 1977, reported in *The Toronto Star* the following day.

To choose such a Canada [a Canada based

on genuine acceptance of a newly dynamic, competitive and self-assertive French-speaking community, centred on but not confined to Quebec] does not mean that everyone will have to speak French. . . .

After all, the odds were much greater against those earlier Canadians who built from scratch this unexpected and even unlikely nation, a nation which, politically, socially and economically, is now one of the freest and most advanced in the world.

Where they built with their hands and their heads, conquering nature, devising vast transportation systems, we must now build with our hearts. We must now decide how we want to live together and better govern ourselves so that our children may live in a Canada which is truly united and truly itself.
>PIERRE ELLIOTT TRUDEAU, Prime Minister, address on national unity, 5 July 1977.

You say bilingual to an American and he thinks you're talking about a man who likes to wear women's clothing.
>DAVE BROADFOOT, comedian, address, Empire Club of Canada, Toronto, 9 March 1978.

As the French language is strengthened, the cultural insecurities that give rise to this attitude will diminish and hopefully be gone so that we can have the kind of minority freedoms and protections we all want.
>BRIAN MULRONEY, Prime Minister, referring to the francophones of Quebec who feel threatened by the overwhelming presence of anglophone North America, interviewed by Peter Gzowski on CBC Radio's *Morningside*, 22 Sept. 1989, quoted by Paul Koring in *The Globe and Mail* the following day.

ARRÊT / STOP
>Words on traffic signs seen in Quebec until the 1980s when the word "stop" stopped appearing. *Arrêt* appeared with accent in capital letters.

Maison Earle
OUV LUNDI
SAGO
OPEN MON
>Trilingual message on the sign on the front lawn of La Maison Earle House Restaurant, Wakefield, Que. "Ouv Lundi" is the French short form for "Ouverte Lundi" (Open Monday). "Sago" means "Welcome" in Mohawk. "Open Mon" is the short form for "Open Monday." In 1984, the Commission de Protection de la Langue Française initiated proceedings against the proprietor, Terry Jabour, for the illegal use of English on a public sign, in contravention of Bill 101, Quebec's language law. Eight years later Jabour was acquitted and Bill 101 was declared illegal.

Canadian teenagers are more accepting of bilingualism than adult Canadians in every region of the country. Some 70% indicate that they favour a policy of bilingualism that Canada should have English and French as its two official languages. This compares, for example, with only 55% of adults surveyed in 1980-81, and 49% surveyed in 1975.
>REGINALD W. BIBBY and DONALD C. POSTERSKI, sociologists, *The Emerging Generation: An Inside Look at Canada's Teenagers* (1985).

I believe that being "bilingual" is the best way to develop flexible and innovative thinking. Where did ancient Greek thought develop? Not on the mainland; all the "pre-Socratic" philosophers came from the colonies, where they probably were as fluent in the language of their neighbours, with whom they traded, as in their own.
>HANS BLUMENFELD, architect-planner, *Life Begins as 65: The Not Entirely Candid Autobiography of a Drifter* (1987).

If it's important, they'll say it in English.
>CLAIRE HOY, monolingual Toronto journalist, accompanying Prime Minister Mulroney on a junket to French-speaking Senegal, quoted by Michel Gratton in *"So,*

What Are the Boys Saying?": An Inside Look at Brian Mulroney in Power (1987).

Why on earth should a French Canadian expect to find a French-speaking clerk in a small British Columbia post office? Or why should a lost English-speaking soul insist on being served in English in a remote Beauce village?
> JACQUES FRANCOEUR, Publisher of Uni-Média Inc., contributor to *If I Were Prime Minister* (1987).

The federal Government has responded to Quebec nationalism by introducing bilingual menus in northern Saskatchewan.
> PIERRE-MARC JOHNSON, former Quebec Premier, address, Osgoode Hall, Toronto, quoted by Graham Fraser in *The Globe and Mail*, 28 March 1988.

I sensed a serious inequality. People who spoke two languages were shining shoes, and people who spoke one language owned the shoes that were being shined.
> RICHARD HATFIELD, former New Brunswick Premier, quoted by Silver Donald Cameron in *Language and Society*, Spring 1988.

We seem to think, in English Canada, that English is *the* world language. Somehow we've got it in our heads that learning another language is crippling, that it's a limitation. English Canadians must be the only people in the world who actually brag about not knowing another language.
> KEITH SPICER, former Commissioner of Official Languages, quoted by John Newlove in *Language and Society*, Spring 1988.

Bilingualism unites people; dualism divides them.
> PIERRE ELLIOTT TRUDEAU, former Prime Minister, Testimony to the Senate Submissions Group on the Meech Lake Constitutional Accord, *With a Bang, Not a Whimper: Pierre Trudeau Speaks Out* (1988) edited by Donald Johnston.

However, in France no one *expects* me to speak French, and they're more or less surprised when I do. In Quebec, it's *de rigueur* to *faire l'effort*. Making an idiot of yourself in the other official language appears to be one of the literary rituals shared by Anglophone and Francophone writers in this country.
> MARGARET ATWOOD, author, "Polyphonous Perverse," *Language and Literature*, Summer 1988.

In our situation, French is something you must work hard to acquire. English is something you catch, like the flu.
> NICOLE LEMAÎRE, francophone native of Sudbury, quoted by Benoît Aubin, *The Globe and Mail*, 27 Feb. 1989.

Canada is not remotely a bilingual, bicultural nation. It is an English-speaking society linked by historial accident to a province that is now clearly emerging as a European-style, French-speaking nation state.
> PETER BRIMELOW, journalist, *The Financial Post*, 6 June 1989.

I know so many people who speak only one language; to me, that's cultural poverty. . . . I find unilingualism sad.
> TOMSON HIGHWAY, miltilingual Cree playwright, interviewed by Ann Wilson in *Other Solitudes: Canadian Multicultural Fictions* (1990) edited by Linda Hutcheon and Marion Richmond.

This country will rise or fall on the bilingual nature of its character. What is Canada without it? There's no country; it's like an adjunct of the United States.
> BRIAN MULRONEY, Prime Minister, address in Kitchener, Ont., discussed in *The Globe and Mail*, 13 Feb. 1990.

What does a bilingual sign tell us? In very clear terms, it whispers in our ear: "You are not the only master in your own home."
> YVES BEAUCHEMIN, novelist, brief presented to the Bélanger-Campeau com-

mission on the future of Quebec, reproduced in *The Toronto Star*, 24 Dec. 1990.

Trading Mr. Trudeau's legacy for a "two-unilingualisms" policy would be a cruel betrayal of about three million Canadians who, by birth or choice, try to live in English in Quebec or French in the rest of Canada. That is more people than the combined populations of the Atlantic Provinces and the two territories. It is almost equal to the population of Israel, and a bigger fraction of the Canadian population than blacks are of the U.S. population.

A country that imposed on that many of its citizens what would be extreme mental cruelty at best, and "quiet genocide" at worst, would not deserve to survive.

> WILLIAM A. HYNES, journalist, criticizing the decentralizing and unilingual policies of the Conservatives, *The Globe and Mail*, 3 April 1991.

Robert Bourassa, Jacques Parizeau and Lucien Bouchard all speak fine English. Fortunes are spent on summer immersion programs for the heirs of the elite. Bill 101 is for the peasants.

> JOHN GRAY, playwright and composer, commenting on the fact that public opinion in Quebec is formed by bilingual leaders who wish to impose monolingualism on their followers through restrictive language laws like Bill 101, *The Globe and Mail*, 12 April 1991. "A bilingual managerial class vies for control over a unilingual labour force, wooing the North American marketplace. The neo-conservative Québécois. The Bombardier Péquistes, ready to take lunch with the world."

What do eastern Canadians think about bilingualism? Not much. That is to say, most of them don't think about bilingualism very much and, when they do think about it, they don't think much of it.

> JOHN DAFOE, columnist, "Western Attitudes: Growing Acceptance," *Language and Society* No. 34, Spring 1991.

BIRDS
See also CANADA GOOSE
LOON

We love birds. We love painting them, writing about and talking about them and listening to them, and attempting to learn something about them.

> J. FENWICK LANSDOWNE, wildlife artist, *Birds of the Northern Forest* (1966) with John A. Livingston.

One cardinal on a tree branch / outfitted like a lord. // You see how little it takes / to make my day.

> RAYMOND SOUSTER, poet, "Cutting It Short," *Asking for More* (1988).

BIRTH
See also BIRTH CONTROL

How early is "beginning"? From when is there a soul? / Do we discover living, or, somehow, are we told? / In sudden pain, in empty cold, in blinding light of day / We're given breath, and it takes our breath away.

> STAN ROGERS, singer and composer, "Delivery Delayed," *Between the Breaks . . . Live!* (Fogarty's Cove Music, 1979).

There was a man who never was. / This tragedy occurred because / His parents, being none too smart, / Were born two hundred years apart.

> DENNIS LEE, poet, "There Was a Man," *The Difficulty of Living on Other Planets* (1987).

BIRTH CONTROL
See also ABORTION
CONTRACEPTION

It is not birth control which needs to be taught to the people at large, whether high or low, but individual self control.

> E. CORA HIND, journalist, letter dated 28 April 1923, quoted by Angus McLaren and Arlene Tigar McLaren in *The Bedroom and the State: The Changing Practices and Politics of Contraception and Abortion in Canada, 1880-1980* (1986).

I have said, and still think, we must choose between birth control and revolution. We are raising too large a percentage of the dependent class and I do not blame them if they steal and fight before they starve.

> A.R. KAUFMAN, treasurer of the Eugenics Society of Canada, founder of the Parents' Information Bureau, and promoter of family planning, letter to the American essayist H.L.Mencken, 10 Aug. 1937, quoted by historian Angus McLean in *Our Own Master Race: Eugenics in Canada, 1885-1945* (1990).

Children have a right to be born with a reasonable chance to legitimately earn a living, but I fear that the percentage of those who can qualify for very little more than the permanently unemployed is rapidly increasing, and will constitute an unbearable relief burden, or become a menace to society.

> A.R. KAUFMAN, founder, Parents' Information Bureau, Bureau Bulletin (1938), quoted by Angus McLaren and Arlene Tigar McLaren in *The Bedroom and the State: The Changing Practices and Politics of Contraception and Abortion in Canada, 1880-1980* (1986).

When the husband uses contraceptives the wife may not seek sexual relations. Nor may she acquiesce in them, unless she is afraid of the very grave consequences that may attend her refusal, and provided that she totally rejects all attempts to give her total satisfaction.

> Two sentences from *Cours de Préparation du Mariage*, a Roman Catholic instruction manual for prospective husbands, issued by Action Catholique Canadienne, Service de Préparation au Mariage du Diocèse du Montréal, Ottawa, 1944. Reproduced by The Clio Collective (Micheline Dumont, Michèle Jean, Marie Lavigne, Jennifer Stoddart) in *Quebec Women: A History* (1987) translated by Roger Gannon and Rosalind Gill.

Everyone is guilty of an indictable offence and liable to two years' imprisonment who knowingly, without lawful excuse or justification, offers to sell, advertises, publishes an advertisement of or has for sale or disposal any medicine, drug or article intended or represented as a means of preventing conception or causing abortion.

> Section 179, Criminal Code of Canada, the law of the land from 1892 to 1969, quoted by The Clio Collective in *Canadian Women: A History* (1987).

I'm a Roman Catholic and I take a dim view of 2,500 celibates shuffling back and forth to Rome to discuss birth control and not one woman to raise a voice.

> LAURA SABIA, Chairperson, Ontario Advisory Council on the Status of Women, quoted by Lynda Hurst in *The Toronto Star*, 22 Aug. 1975.

By the year 2000 we're going to have six or seven billion people on earth. If this is doubled in the next two or three hundred years there won't be standing room. We're going to have to face the problem of birth control, or migrate to another planet.

> T.C. (TOMMY) DOUGLAS, socialist leader, *The Making of a Socialist: The Recollections of T.C. Douglas* (1982) edited by Lewis H. Thomas.

Speekin of witch, the breth controll habits is offal illoominate-in. Did you noe sevenny-too purrsent of Canajuns is on the pill, and 68 purrsent of them is wimmen?

> DON HARRON, comedian, in the person of Charlie Farquharson, *Cum Buy the Farm* (1987).

Be true to your religion. Go to mass every Sunday but practise birth control and get your abortions done in the United States or Ontario.

> From "Rules for Becoming a Québécois," the heading on a Letter to the Editor which was pseudonymously signed "J.M. St. John, Pierrefonds" and which appeared in the weekly *The Chronicle* (Pointe Claire, Que.), 13 April 1988. So

ill-received was the satire that the Saint-Jean-Baptiste Society and advertisers encouraged the publisher to disavow the sentiments expressed in the letter and apologize in paid advertisements in three other newspapers.

The time is past when people refer to lovemaking as "working for the sake of the country."
GÉRARD PELLETIER, former Cabinet Minister, "Quebec: Different but in Step with North America," *Daedalus: Journal of the American Academy of Arts and Sciences*, "In Search of Canada," Fall 1988.

Definition of Birth Control: Some form of the Canadian Shield.
Malapropism current in Ontario in March 1990.

BLACK, CONRAD

I like Conrad Black because he is the only person I have ever met who makes me feel positively "wet."
This remark was attributed to MARGARET THATCHER, the British Prime Minister and the personal friend of financier and publisher Conrad Black, by John Picton in *The Toronto Star*, 29 Nov. 1987. "Wet" is a term used by British Conservatives to disparage Liberals and leftists.

One day, despite his protestations, there may be a Lord Conrad of Black Ink.
DIANE FRANCIS, author and financial commentator, referring to "the capital K capitalist," *Controlling Interest: Who Owns Canada?* (1986).

I have a question for the Premier, who I am sure will be aware that the most symbolic representative of bloated capitalism at its worst, Conrad Black, the owner of Dominion Stores, skimmed off $62 million from the pension fund under the open eyes and ears of the government's pension commission.
BOB RAE, NDP leader and leader of the Opposition, addressing a question to Ontario Premier David Peterson concerning the status of the Dominion Stores' pension fund, Ontario Legislative Assembly, Toronto, 27 Jan. 1986.

Black turned out to be an extremely uncommon millionaire, not so much in the content of his conversation as in his manner. He was more theatrical than any other businessman of my acquaintance. His personality had a staged, directed feel to it. It was also oddly familiar. Where had I seen it before, a large, handsome man with a supercilious and condescending manner and a baroque vocabulary? Of course: Orson Welles in *Citizen Kane*. I was talking to Citizen Black.
ROBERT FULFORD, cultural commentator, *Best Seat in the House: Memoirs of a Lucky Man* (1988). Fulford was noting resemblances between Conrad Black, the Canadian financier and publisher, and Charles Foster Kane, Orson Welles's cinematic depiction of the American financier and publisher William Randolph Hearst.

. . . the not-so-local tycoon Conrad Black of Citizen Kane. I'm not convinced. We know from the start that Kane is a tragic figure, as we don't know yet of Black; to my mind, Fulford's account of him calls up a comic figure, Mr. Toad (of Toad Hall). The enthusiastic, childish vanity is unexpectedly endearing; here is another braggart. . . .
Anagnostes, "Briefly Noted," *The Idler*, No. 22, March-April 1989.

From an early age, Mr. Black has not suffered easily the occasions when his conduct has been critically appraised. This indicates that he is human.
DAVID OLIVE, journalist, "Conrad Black: Writ Large," *The Globe and Mail*, 24 Nov. 1990.

BLACKS

Some low fellows, they say, say to him, "Tom, why don't you make tracks for Can-

ada?" — "Ah, master trusted me, and I couldn't!"
> Words of uncle Tom, hero of HARRIET BEECHER STOWE's influential novel *Uncle Tom's Cabin; or, Life Among the Lowly* (1852). The figure of Uncle Tom was based on the life of Josiah Henson who erected his cabin near Chatham, Ont.

Who can speak the blessedness of that first day of freedom? Is not the *sense* of liberty a higher and a finer one than any of the other five?
> HARRIET BEECHER STOWE, New England author, *Uncle Tom's Cabin; or, Life Among the Lowly* (1852).

Africa is your home. Canada is not your home; it is too cold for you.
> STOKELY CARMICHAEL, former U.S. Black Panther leader who adopted the African name Kwame Ture, addressing an audience of blacks in Toronto, quoted by Eric Skelton in *The Globe and Mail*, 5 March 1990.

I don't think that even white Canadians consider themselves Canadians to the extent that Americans consider themselves Americans, and certainly, it seems to me obvious that the blacks in this country do not consider themselves Canadians to the same extent.
> AUSTIN CLARKE, novelist born in Barbados, interviewed by Marion Richmond in *Other Solitudes: Canadian Multicultural Fictions* (1990) edited by Linda Hutcheon and Marion Richmond.

BLOC QUÉBÉCOIS

For a year I have been working with the Bloc Québécois, and I affirm that the parliamentary motivations of the group are profoundly negative, and are only intended for the destruction of the country.
> GILBERT CHARTRAND, Quebec Member of Parliament, explaining his return to the fold after deserting the federal Conservative Party on 22 May 1990 for the Bloc Québécois, the group formed by former

Conservative ministers disenchanted with the rejection of the Meech Lake accord, quoted in an editorial, *The Globe and Mail*, 11 April 1991.

BOOKS
> *See also* CENSORSHIP
> LIBRARIES
> LITERATURE
> WRITERS
> WRITING

Come, see my books, and read with me, / And let us feast and talk together; / From care and strife, we shall be free, / And have no thoughts about the weather.
> Verse associated with the Albert Britnell Book Shop, a Toronto landmark since 1884, owned and operated by successive generations of the Britnell family, quoted by Stasia Evasuk, *The Toronto Star*, 13 May 1989.

Not "obsolete," but "obsolescent" is the term that applies to my analysis of the present status of the printed book. Obsolescence often precedes an extraordinary development in technology. The arrival of electric xerography certainly does not mean the end of the book, but rather a great enlargement of its scope and function.
> MARSHALL McLUHAN, communications theorist, letter dated 1 March 1966, *Letters of Marshall McLuhan* (1987) edited by Matie Molinaro, Corinne McLuhan, and William Toye.

Dedicated to the IBM 360-40 without which this book could not have been written.
> Unique dedication of *Space-Time Transients and Unusual Events* (1977) by its academic authors, MICHAEL A. PERSINGER and GYSLAINE F. LAFRENIÈRE.

The book is the world's most patient medium.
> NORTHROP FRYE, literary philosopher, NFB's documentary film *The Scholar in Society* (1984).

Children living in this country may grow up to be Canadians, but their imagination is nourished, not by Canadian books, but by books imported from Britain and the United States.

MICHAEL MACKLEM, publisher, "Seed Money," *The Bumper Book* (1986) edited by John Metcalf.

Three generalizations can be made about Canadian trade book editors: they tend to be young, they tend to be female, and they tend to be underpaid. (Speculation about the exact nature of the "linkage" between these three factors I leave to others more cynical than myself.)

DOUGLAS GIBSON, editor turned publisher, "Edited Any Good Books Lately?" *The Bumper Book* (1986) edited by John Metcalf.

When my glasses fell off the back of the loo and one of my lenses shattered on the tile floor, I was in the midst of a book tour, about to leave my hotel in Vancouver. Blinded by half, I proceeded on to Nanaimo by ferry. As the boat docked, I noticed a woman standing on the jetty, surrounded by a group of small children. As soon as she and her charges recognized me, they all began chanting together, "Up with Rumpole!" I continued on to the local bookstore. Here, standing in the queue, waiting to have a book signed, was a woman who instantly recognized my plight, for her husband was an oculist. She hustled me off to his office, where he examined the broken lens, and phoned ahead to a colleague in Victoria. By the time I arrived there, later that day, a new lens had been delivered to my hotel, all ready to pop into the frame. How kind Canadians are!

JOHN MORTIMER, English playwright and creator of the BBC-TV "Rumpole" series, quoted in *Saturday Night*, Dec. 1987.

If a Montreal author writes a book about Quebec, he calls it a book about Quebec. If a Toronto author writes a book about Toronto and Ottawa, he calls it a book about Canada.

GÉRARD PELLETIER, politician, address, Writers' Development Trust, Montreal, 1987, quoted by Mark Abley in *Saturday Night*, Feb. 1988.

Almost nobody reads *real* books any more except for writers themselves, and they don't count. I don't particularly try to sell my books to other writers, which is why I sell my books on a busy street with a mixed population and wear a provocative sign to arouse what little capacity for curiosity still exists in this world. I want to be available to anyone who's interested, and I don't care if they're not connected in any way to the book business. In fact, I *prefer* to sell to people who have no professional vested interest to read me.

CRAD KILODNEY, author, who hawks his publications at Toronto streetcorners, "How I Write Such Great Stories," unpublished Introduction to *Malignant Humours* (1988).

It is nice to have Ph.D. theses written about your turning-point novel. It is nicer to see that novel, in cheap paperback, on display in drugstores.

JOSEF SKVORECKY, novelist and essayist, "I Was Born in Náchod . . . " *Talkin' Moscow Blues* (1988) edited by Sam Solecki.

Why did I write a book? Because a publisher in Canada felt that if Jean Chrétien were to write a book it would be a good book and it would sell well. But if all the publishers originate in New York, nobody there would ever think of calling Chrétien to write a book.

In fact, my book was competing in Canada at the time with [Chrysler Corp. chair Lee] Iacocca's book, and I sold more books in Canada than Iacocca. But I did not sell one copy of my book in the United States. So just for fun I gave my book to a few friends in the States, and they could not understand it. "What is a Social Credit?"

they asked. "What the hell is a Réal Caouette?"

JEAN CHRÉTIEN, lawyer, former federal Cabinet Minister, and author, referring to his book of memoirs, *Straight from the Heart* (1985), written with Ron Graham, speaking at a press conference in Toronto in 1989, quoted by David Wilson in *Metropolis*, 2 Feb. 1989.

Canadians read American bestsellers when they want mystery, romance, glamour, sex, or violence. They read a Canadian bestseller when they want the history of the Canadian Pacific Railway.

ERIC NICOL and DAVE MORE, humorists, *The U.S. or Us: What's the Difference, Eh?* (1986).

A book is as individual as a fingerprint.

SYLVIA FRASER, novelist, interviewed by Alan Twigg in *Strong Voices: Conversations with Fifty Canadian Authors* (1988).

Certainly one of the signs of maturity in a country's literature is when all books do not have to aspire to be *War and Peace*.

ALAN TWIGG, interviewer, *Strong Voices: Conversations with Fifty Canadian Authors* (1988).

But I do write for people who delight in life and are curious about many aspects of it and are aware of its tragedy as well as its comedy but who do not adopt a sort of glum attitude which they think is realism.

ROBERTSON DAVIES, man-of-letters, interviewed by Robert Fulford in 1988, *Conversations with Robertson Davies* (1989) edited by J. Madison Davis.

In this country last year, more people caught AIDS than bought a Canadian book.

Scuttlebut noted by Susan Musgrave in *Great Musgrave* (1989) according to Dennis Kucherawy in *The Toronto Star*, 18 Nov. 1989.

My books do not appear in the old print format, just on computer discs . . . I believe that cold, static print is no competition for a dynamic combination of print, sound, colour and illustrations. The literati of the future will thus be forced to be able to absorb all this simultaneously.

FRANK OGDEN, futurologist known as "Dr. Tomorrow," letter to the present editor, 9 Dec. 1989. Ogden issues electronic texts — collectively known as *Lessons from the Future* — in the form of albums of computer discs; in the future they will be released in the CD-ROM format.

After Gutenberg came out with print, no one went back to the chisel.

FRANK OGDEN, futurologist, explaining why he offers his ideas on floppy discs rather than in printed books, quoted by Carolyn Myles in *The Washington Times*, 29 Jan. 1990.

A man sits alone with a book, the whole world around him grows silent, a voice so secret it can't be heard, just felt, is whispering to him and leading him deep into the world of the greatest wonder and power — his own imagination.

MORLEY CALLAGHAN, novelist "My Love for Miracles of the Imagination," *More than Words Can Say: Personal Perspectives on Literacy* (1990).

Number of Harlequin romances Americans bought last year, per hour: 7,191

Item from "Harper's Index," *Harper's*, Feb. 1990.

During the 1980s, for the first time, North Americans purchased more dictionaries than they did Bibles.

JOEL BONN, Montreal-based reading specialist and "dictophile" who has over 5000 dictionaries on the shelves of his personal library, *bon-mot*, 3 Feb. 1990.

Never wholly believe a book.

ROBIN SKELTON, man-of-letters, aphorism, May 1990.

Bob Tulk is the only Canadian writer whose works I've even seen in California supermarket shelves.

WILLIAM GOUGH, author and scriptwriter who was raised in Newfoundland and now resides in Los Angeles, private letter, 9 Aug. 1990. Gough is reacting to the incongruous sight of the bright yellow cover of Tulk's *Best Newfie Jokes* on the paperback book rack at Ralph's Supermarket, Woodland Hills, California. Gough wryly added: "Very few cultures can manage to make an industry of printing material about how stupid they are."

People don't buy my books to read, they buy them for Christmas for Aunt Hazel.
Attributed to PIERRE BERTON by Barry Broadfoot in *The Globe and Mail*, 8 Sept. 1990.

BORDER, CANADIAN-AMERICAN
See also CANADA
UNITED STATES
OF AMERICA

The geographical proximity of U.S. television to Canada has created five thousand miles of undefended boredom.
ERIC NICOL and DAVE MORE, humorists, *The U.S. or Us: What's the Difference, Eh?* (1986).

It's one of the longest straight lines in the world. A carpenter might have snapped a chalked line on a map of North America. A youngster might have slapped it down with a ruler and a Crayola. The damage this does to Canada's image among the family of nations is incalculable. Who can take a country seriously that lays down its boundary with such gross indifference? Until it's mussed up a bit all the way from Vancouver to the Lake of the Woods, we'll always be second or third rate.
RAY GUY, humorist, contributor to *If I Were Prime Minister* (1987).

I remember in Saskatchewan that the U.S.-Canada border was just a line of iron posts a mile apart. The real line was where the climate and topography changed.
WALLACE STEGNER, American-born au-

thor of *Wolf Willow* (1962), a memoir about growing up in Southern Saskatchewan, interviewed by Philip Marchand in *The Toronto Star*, 22 Aug. 1989.

The border controls, customs and immigration, American and Canadian alike, were regarded by all as an unnatural abrasion of the rights of man — and woman. So they were evaded as a matter of course.
JOHN KENNETH GALBRAITH, economist and author, "Canadian Customs," *Saturday Night*, Jan. 1987.

The Canadians are massed along the American border. Some 85 percent of all Canadians live within 100 miles of the U.S. — a four-day march, in other words, and only a few hours for motorized armour.
RICHARD STENGEL, U.S. journalist, "The Canadians," *Spy*, Feb. 1988.

Canada's 5000-mile borderline is unfortified and has the effect of keeping Canadians in a perpetual philosophic mood which nourishes flexibility in the absence of strong commitments or definite goals.
MARSHALL McLUHAN, media philosopher, and Bruce R. Powers, communications specialist, authors of *The Global Village: Transformations in World Life and Media in the 21st Century* (1989).

In photographs taken by satellite from outer space, the Canadian-American border on the prairies, the forty-ninth parallel, shows up with startling clarity. In southern Saskatchewan and Alberta there is grassland for cattle grazing, much of it on Indian reservations; in northern Montana, vast investment in irrigation projects has kept the land in wheat.
WILLIAM KILBOURN, historian, "The Peaceable Kingdom Still," *Daedalus: Journal of the American Academy of Arts and Sciences*, "In Search of Canada," Fall 1988.

The forty-ninth parallel actually comes fairly close to the drainage divide [Hudson Bay and the Gulf of Mexico], though the

Souris and Red rivers cross the border in Manitoba and Saskatchewan. South of the Cypress Hills, however, there is a sizable strip of Alberta and Saskatchewan that is drained by the Milk River, a tributary of the Missouri. Presumably, Spain once claimed this territory. Curently being pure W.O. Mitchell country, it shows no sign of this claim.
> F. KENNETH HARE, geographer, "Canada: The Land," *Daedalus: Journal of the American Academy of Arts and Sciences*, "In Search of Canada," Fall 1988.

Canadians who live near the border live in their nation's banana belt, the most temperate climate Canada offers. Americans on the border live in the deep north. Popular perceptions are flip-flopped in the border zone, for here Canada has sophisticated urban centres like Vancouver and Toronto and a dense network of roads and agriculture. The U.S. has mostly hardscrabble farms and vacation sites.
> PRIIT J. VESILIND, writer, "Common Ground, Different Dreams," *National Geographic*, March 1990.

This line — this imaginary line where the two white people couldn't get along — does not affect us. It goes above our heads.
> FRANCIS BOOTS, Mohawk resident of Cornwall Island, Ont., referring to the Canada-United States border, quoted by Priit J. Vesilind in *National Geographic*, March 1990.

BOURASSA, ROBERT

Cultural sovereignty within a profitable federalism.
> Slogan identified with Quebec Premier Robert Bourassa's first administration (1970-76), quoted by Léon Dion in *Quebec: The Unfinished Revolution* (1976) translated by Thérèse Romer.

Chien chaud.
> "Hot dog." Nickname for Quebec Premier Robert Bourassa, popularized by former

Prime Minister Pierre Elliott Trudeau, according to Dalton Camp in *The Toronto Star*, 24 Sept. 1989.

He's certainly a survivor. It's interesting that he's still there. The French don't like him; the English despise him and there he is. He's not a man I greatly admire and it's a mystery to me. He's not blessed physically. He doesn't seem to be punishingly intelligent. He's an outrageous liar, taking any political standpoint. But, there he is, and he goes on.
> MORDECAI RICHLER, author, quoted by Dennis Kucherawy, *Metropolis*, 16 Nov. 1989.

If he had a toothache he wouldn't go to the dentist, because it would hurt. He would nurse it until it developed into a full-fledged abscess and required root canal treatment.
> MORDECAI RICHLER, novelist, referring to Quebec Premier Robert Bourassa as "a federalist as long as it provides him with booty, but otherwise a crypto-separatist," address, Toronto, 27 Feb. 1990, quoted by Philip Marchand in *The Toronto Star* the following day.

BOXING

In North America now, the boxing situation provokes the image of a newly dug grave, the headstone freshly carved: "Killed by TV and the good life." . . . Hell, when the bell rings, the most interesting stuff has usually already happened.
> JIM CHRISTY, author, *Flesh & Blood: A Journey into the Heart of Boxing* (1990).

BRAZIL

How could I have imagined so surreal and seductive a world? One does not *like* the heat, yet its constancy, its all-surrounding-ness, is as fascinating as the smell of musk. Every moment is slow, as if under warm greenish water.
> P.K. PAGE, diarist and wife of the Canadian Ambassador to Brazil, first impres-

sion of Rio de Janeiro, 21 Jan. 1957, *Brazilian Journal* (1987).

Canada is the next Brazil.
Attributed to financial commentator DIANE FRANCIS by Richard Osler in "Richard's Day," *The Latest Morningside Papers* (1989) edited by Peter Gzowski.

BRITAIN
See BRITISH EMPIRE &
COMMONWEALTH
ENGLISH PEOPLE
IRISH PEOPLE
SCOTTISH PEOPLE
WELSH PEOPLE
UNITED KINGDOM

BRITISH COLUMBIA
See also VANCOUVER
VICTORIA

Those who are convicts, and those who ought to be.
Attributed to SIR ARTHUR EDWARD KENNEDY, last Royal Governor of Vancouver Island (1863-67), who thus described the class structure of the colony.

Were I an intending immigrant I would risk a good deal of discomfort to get on to land in British Columbia; and were I rich, with no attachments outside England, I would swiftly buy me a farm or a house in that country for the mere joy of it.
RUDYARD KIPLING, English author and world traveller, *Letters of Travel: 1892-1912* (1920).

The first almighty fact about British Columbia is mountains.
RODERICK HAIG-BROWN, author, "With Its Face to the West," *The Face of Canada* (1959).

Every province is the same. We become real Canadians in times of crisis, during a war or to offset an economic recession. Then we wake up to our Canadian identity. Here we lead a privileged life; we are able to golf, ski, sail, climb mountains, garden,

ten months every year. Philosophical discussion is not popular in B.C.
PADDY SHERMAN, editor of *The Vancouver Province*, quoted by Solange Chaput-Rolland in *My Country, Canada or Québec?* (1966).

Outside Calgary, we drove up into the Rockies. Finally we had crossed the plains. Now as we ran down the last miles into British Columbia it was as if nature ran riot after the almost existential bleakness of the prairies; the lushness and size of everything we saw seemed preposterously exaggerated. Our spirits lifted with the beauty of the place and its lush vegetation, huge waterfalls, deep black fjords and massive dark green pine forests.
BOB GELDOF, musician, crossing Canada by bus from Montreal to Vancouver in 1973, *Is That It?* (1986).

Valium West has a quality all its own.
ALLAN FOTHERINGHAM, columnist, *Malice in Blunderland or How the Grits Stole Christmas* (1982, 1983).

There is considerable unrest among teenagers regarding their preference in which province to live in. Whether the choice is to remain in the province where they presently live or to move to another part of Canada, the appeal of "Beautiful British Columbia" is unchallenged. Almost 80% of teens living in B.C. would like to remain right where they are. . . . Teenagers who want to move tend to look to B.C. It is the first choice of mobile-minded young people in every province except Prince Edward Island and Quebec, in which cases the preference is Ontario.
REGINALD W. BIBBY and DONALD C. POSTERSKI, sociologists, *The Emerging Generation: An Inside Look at Canada's Teenagers* (1985).

British Columbia may be beset by problems, economic and political, but it's an enjoyable corner of the world, far from the Presbyterian restraints of Ontario and the climatic constraints of the rest of Canada.

Its residents, though accused of apeing Californians, secretly aspire to be Tahitians.
STEPHEN BROOK, English travel writer, *Maple Leaf Rag: Travels across Canada* (1987).

People have no difficulty agreeing there is a Newfie culture. Or that Québec has a separate culture. But there are no generally observed definitions of what we have become in British Columbia.
ALAN TWIGG, journalist and interviewer, *Strong Voices: Conversations with Fifty Canadian Authors* (1988).

Our people tend to relate easier to the south than they do to the distant east.
WILLIAM VANDER ZALM, B.C. Premier, 24 March 1988, quoted by Stephen Osborne and Mary Schendlinger in *Quotations from Chairman Zalm* (1988).

BRITISH EMPIRE & COMMONWEALTH
See also EMPIRE

Benign Neglect (coined by the Earl of Durham in 1839 to describe England's treatment of Canada) is now used to mean, apparently, letting the underprivileged fight their own way up.
ANTHONY BURGESS, English man-of-letters, "Fair Speaking," *But Do Blondes Prefer Gentlemen: Homage to QWERT YUIOP and Other Writings* (1986). Lord Durham, in his celebrated Report on conditions in the Canadas following the Rebellions of 1837, wrote: "The time may have come when the issue of race could benefit from a period of benign neglect."

It is a question for consideration or division whether our North American Provinces are to be fought for or abandoned. There may be much to be said for the theory put forward by some, that our Colonies are an encumbrance and an expense, and that we should be better without them, but that is not the opinion of England, and it is not mine.
LORD PALMERSTON, Prime Minister of Great Britain, letter to the Colonial Secretary, dated 29 July 1864, quoted by Donald Creighton in *John A. Macdonald: The Young Politician* (1952).

Unquestionably it would be better for the British people to spend *hundreds of millions*, if necessary, in establishing a universal sway, mainly of intellectual and moral force, over the whole earth, rather than be compelled to spend *thousands of millions* in defending themselves from aggression, mainly by physical force, as it has latterly become manifest they may be required to do at any time.
HENRY WENTWORTH MONK, prophet, Manifesto issued in 1896, quoted by R.S. Lambert in *For the Time Is at Hand: An Account of the Prophesies of Henry Wentworth Monk of Ottawa, Friend of the Jews, and Pioneer of World Peace* (1947).

The Diamond Jubilee of Queen Victoria in 1897 also helped powerfully in the growth of imperial sentiment. Special Jubilee stamps were issued, containing a map of the world that was splashed with red wherever there were British possessions, with a proud declaration at the bottom of the stamp: "We hold a greater empire than has been." Who were the "we" who held this great empire? We Canadians? Of course not. But our Postmaster-General was identifying us with the British people who did hold it. I can remember, as a small boy of some eight years, collecting these stamps eagerly.
F.H. UNDERHILL, political scientist, *The Image of Confederation* (1964). The legend on the Jubilee stamps reads "We Hold a Vaster Empire than Has Been" and the wording has been attributed to the Postmaster-General Sir William Mulock.

Canada is the most puritanical part of the Empire and cherishes very much the Victorian standards in private life.
JOHN BUCHAN, Governor General Lord Tweedsmuir, conveying to Whitehall in 1936 the likely reaction of the Canadian

public to the impending abdication of Edward VIII, quoted by William Buchan in *John Buchan: A Memoir* (1982).

From the Atlantic to the Pacific, and from the tropics to the Arctic, lies a large part of the earth where there is no possibility of war between neighbours, whose peoples are wholly dedicated to the pursuits of peace, a pattern to all men of how civilized nations should live together.
> GEORGE VI, King, address to the British Empire delivered near the end of the Royal Tour, Halifax, N.S., 15 June 1939, quoted by Tom MacDonnell in *Daylight Upon Magic: The Royal Tour of Canada — 1939* (1989).

And the Empire too, / We can depend on you; / Freedom Remains, / These are the chains / Nothing can break. . . .
> Stirring lines from the patriotic song "There'll Always Be an England," composed by the English songwriting team of ROSS PARKER and HUGHIE CHARLES and first published in Toronto in 1939 prior to the outbreak of World War II. The words and music appear in the *Happy Gang Book of War Songs* (1941) compiled by Bert Pearl. The song anticipated the coming hostilities and the contribution to be made by the colonies and countries (like Canada) within the British Empire.

This is Singapore — is it in the Commonwealth?
> WILLIAM VANDER ZALM, B.C. Premier, preparing to meet dignitaries from Singapore, 18 July 1988, quoted by Stephen Osborne and Mary Schendlinger in *Quotations from Chairman Zalm* (1988).

Why in God's name are we afraid of our British North American roots? We are busy blasting away about multi-racialism and multiculturalism. Why can't one of the founding components of the nation assert with pride its own culture? You can't even use the phrase "British North American." You're considered a crackpot, a little old lady, a mental recessive, an anal retentive.

But the British North American traditions built the goddam country.
> SCOTT SYMONS, novelist and cultural commentator of British North American ancestry, interviewed in *The Idler*, No. 25, May-June 1990.

BRITISH PEOPLE
See BRITISH EMPIRE &
　　　COMMONWEALTH
　　ENGLISH PEOPLE
　　IRISH PEOPLE
　　SCOTTISH PEOPLE
　　WELSH PEOPLE
　　UNITED KINGDOM

BROADCASTING
See also CANADIAN BROADCASTING
　　　　CORPORATION
　　　NEWS
　　　RADIO
　　　TELEVISION

At present the majority of programs heard are from sources outside of Canada. It has been emphasized to us that the continued reception of these has a tendency to mould the minds of the young people in the home to ideals and opinions that are not Canadian. In a country of the vast geographical dimensions of Canada, broadcasting will undoubtedly become a great force in fostering national spirit and interpreting national citizenship.
> SIR JOHN AIRD, champion of public broadcasting, *Report of the Royal Commission on Radio Broadcasting* (1929), the so-called Aird Report.

The future of broadcasting rests with the individual who turns the dial.
> SIR HENRY THORNTON, pioneer of public broadcasting in the 1930s, recalled in an address to the Empire Club of Canada, Toronto, 10 Nov. 1977.

If time on the air can be bought for fifty dollars a minute for the expression of controversial opinion, then free air is just a sign outside a service station.
> LEONARD BROCKINGTON, first Chair-

man of the CBC, appearing before the regulatory commission in 1939, quoted in *The Globe and Mail*, 16 Sept. 1966. Another version of this statement, quoted by Herschel Hardin in *Closed Circuits* (1985), runs like this: "Freedom of speech is not for sale at fifty dollars a minute on the air."

You can't behave like Walter Cronkite if no one has ever taught you how.
ROBERT MacNEIL, Nova Scotia-born broadcaster, referring to his early training as an announcer for CBC Radio in Halifax in the early 1950s, *The Right Place at the Right Time* (1982).

Gentlemen, I admire you. I admire your proficiency, the perfection of your presentation. But I would like to ask you one question: In the final analysis, what will your organization do for humanity?
HARRY J. BOYLE, broadcaster and member of the CRTC, the broadcast regulatory commission, quoted by Val Clery in *The Canadian*, 15 Oct. 1975. The question was addressed to astonished lawyers presenting a brief on behalf of an applicant for a television franchise in 1968.

The dangers to both private and public broadcasting in Canada are Americanization by importation, by privatization, and by fiscal deprivation.
A.W. JOHNSON, President of the CBC in the 1970s, adapted from a remark quoted by Val Sears in *The Toronto Star*, 17 July 1988.

This is Prior Smith reporting from Toronto.
Identification of *The Canadian News*, which is a syndicated radio news service for Canadians vacationing in Florida carried twice a day, five days a week, by Florida stations but originating with the broadcaster PRIOR SMITH in Millbank, Ont. The program, 5.5 minutes in length, began in 1977, replacing an earlier news service called *Canada Calling* which had

originated in Fort Lauderdale about twenty years earlier.

Nobody calls me Mr. Kirck.
Characteristic remark on the desirability of informality in the media made by HARVEY KIRCK, CTV's news anchorman from 1963 to 1984. Kirck's memoirs, written with Wade Rowland, were titled *Nobody calls Me Mr. Kirck* (1985). Actually, his legal name was Krick, not Kirck. A glitch-ridden CTV news broadcast on 6 March 1975 was concluded with the following sign-off: "I'm Harvey Kirck, I think."

Radio is a "hot" medium and is indispensable when the issues get hot. TV is a fantasy medium, and has good reason to be called "cool."
MARSHALL McLUHAN, communications theorist, letter to Pierre Elliott Trudeau dated 16 April 1979, published in *Saturday Night*, Sept. 1987.

In general, Canadian programming is something we do because the law requires it, it's not *audience driven*. There isn't an enormous interest or belief that a Canadian show of a dramatic nature can attract a wide audience.
RICHARD NIELSEN, TV writer and producer, quoted by John Haslett Cuff in *The Globe and Mail*, 11 April 1987.

The trouble with Canadian radio was American radio. Powerful American stations had always covered Canada more thoroughly than home-grown transmitters.
MICHAEL BLISS, historian, referring to the strong radio broadcasting stations in the United States which transmitted their programs over immense areas of the continent, the situation in the 1920s before the formation of the American radio networks, *Northern Enterprise: Five Centuries of Canadian Business* (1987).

Canadians don't want more Canadian drama, they want better Canadian drama.
MICHAEL McCABE, spokesperson for the

Canadian Association of Broadcasters, quoted by Val Sears in *The Toronto Star*, 17 July 1988.

There is something in radio appropriate to the Canadian spirit. Canadians envy American materialism, yet stand a little aloof and critical. Less sure of their nationhood, Canadians have less need to parade their patriotism, less need for the national rituals that Americans crave; they are more individualistic and private, and radio is a private medium.

To be sure, television quickly became the dominant medium, but for historical and cultural reasons, radio meant more to Canada. It was the glue of modern Canadian feeling. Radio has held the nation together, while television is the medium of dissolution, of cultural absorption by the United States.

ROBERT MacNEIL, Nova Scotian-born writer and broadcaster, co-host of PBS's nightly *MacNeil-Lehrer NewsHour*, writing in his memoirs, *Wordstruck* (1989).

Thank you for this.

This is the wording of an all-purpose acknowledgement which hosts and news anchors of radio and television programs offer to interviewees and outside commentators for their contributions.

Apparently this form of acknowledgement was introduced by BARBARA FRUM when she was host of CBC Radio's *As It Happens*. She claims she does not use it as anchor of CBC-TV's *The Journal*, having dropped the succinct and useful sentence when other broadcasters took it up. "It's been taken away from me," she told Sid Adilman of *The Toronto Star*, 9 Jan. 1988. "I haven't said it since 1980. It's wonderful to be the founder of something."

Thanks for watching.

Regular signoff of PETER MANSBRIDGE, anchor on CBC-TV's *The Journal*. Quoted by Sid Adilman in *The Toronto Star*, 1 Jan. 1989.

Offering choices has always been an essential function of public broadcasting. Offering choices has also been central to the public regulation of private broadcasting. What local and regional cultures are to a nation, national cultures are to the international community. In the meltdown of globalization it is essential to offer programming that reflects the culture of one's own nation, that nourishes the pluralism of cultures and national values.

BERNARD OSTRY, Chairman, TVO, *The New York Times*, 31 Dec. 1989.

Broadcasting is fleeting — once you utter it, it's gone. In ten minutes it's winging its way around Mars.

REX LORING, veteran radio announcer, retiring after thirty-five years of service with CBC Radio, quoted by Helen Branswell in *The Globe and Mail*, 17 Aug. 1990.

BROTHERHOOD

I remember during the last war adopting as a kind of motto this phrase:

Last century made the world a neighbourhood, this century must make it a brotherhood.

The more I have studied history and economics, the more I have come to the conclusion that that is profoundly true. The choice is that or the deluge.

J.S. WOODSWORTH, CCF leader, casting the sole dissenting vote against Canada's declaration of war on Germany, House of Commons, 8 Sept. 1939.

BUDGETS

If Richard Six-pack Canadian was making $40,000 a year, spending $52,000 a year and was in hock for $120,000, he would be a financial goner. Yet this is exactly where Canada stands today.

RICHARD OSLER, investment adviser, "Richard's Day," *The Latest Morningside Papers* (1989) edited by Peter Gzowski.

These are my Michael Wilson shoes — low-down heel with no sole.

EDD ULUSCHAK, cartoonist, characteristic humorous remark, referring to Finance Minister Michael Wilson, 20 Feb. 1991.

BUFFALO

The buffalo / as they stand in a circle/ I join them.

Ojibwa poem, "Buffalo," *Songs of the Great Land* (1989) edited by John Robert Colombo.

BUREAUCRACY

An administrator in a bureaucratic world is a man who can feel big by merging his non-entity in an abstraction. A real person in touch with real things inspires terror in him.

MARSHALL McLUHAN, communications theorist, letter to Ezra Pound dated 22 June 1951, *Letters of Marshall McLuhan* (1987) edited by Matie Molinaro, Corinne McLuhan, and William Toye.

An efficient organization is one in which the accounting department knows the exact cost of every useless administrative procedure which they themselves have initiated.

E.W. STEACIE, scientist and administrator, *Science in Canada: Selections from the Speeches of E.W. Steacie* (1965) edited by J.D. Babbitt.

The harder bureaucrats work, the more damage they do.

FRANK STRONACH, corporate executive, address, Seneca College, Toronto, April 1987, quoted in *Sinc: An Inquiry into the Sinclair Stevens Investigation* (1987) by Jim Coyle, E. Kaye Fulton, Robert Hurst, and Margaret Polanyi.

BURGESS SHALE

Without hesitation or ambiguity, and fully mindful of such paleontological wonders as large dinosaurs and African ape-men, I state that the invertebrates of the Burgess Shale, found high in the Canadian Rockies in Yoho National Park, on the eastern border of British Columbia, are the world's most important animal fossils. Modern multicellular animals make their first uncontested appearance in the fossil record some 570 million years ago — and with a bang, not a protracted crescendo.

STEPHEN JAY GOULD, biologist, *Wonderful Life: The Burgess Shale and the Nature of History* (1989).

BUSINESS

See also ADVERTISING
CAPITALISM
DEVELOPERS
FREE TRADE
MULTINATIONALISM
TRADE & COMMERCE

My first wish is a continuance of the public's patronage — my highest ambition to deserve it.

Maxim of LEVI S. PARMLY, self-styled "Dentist and medical Electrician," *The Summum Bonum* (1815).

Timothy Eaton/*Robert Simpson* came from Ireland/*Scotland* to open a small shop in St. Mary's/*Newmarket* Ontario before he moved to Toronto in 1869/*1872* where he opened a small shop at/*near* the corner of Queen & Yonge.

JACK McLAREN, humorist, accounting for the parallel origins of the T. Eaton Co. Ltd. and The Robert Simpson Co. Ltd., *Let's All Hate Toronto* (1956).

Tell your story to [the] public — what you have and what you propose to sell — promise them not only bargains but that every article will be found just what it is guaranteed to be — use no deception in the smallest degree — no — nothing you cannot defend before God or man.

TIMOTHY EATON, founder of the T. Eaton Co. Ltd., handwritten statement of business principles dating from the 1870s.

Organize, Systematize, Capitalize, Advertise
> Business principles of EDGAR RANDOLPH PARKER, the dentist who in the 1920s advertised himself as "Painless" Parker, quoted by Ian Sclanders in *Maclean's*, 15 Dec. 1949.

I like a man who knows how to say yes.
> Remark attributed to W. GARFIELD WESTON, bakery and food executive, overheard at the 1971 annual meeting of George Weston Ltd., quoted by Charles Davies in *Bread Men: How the Westons Built an International Empire* (1987).

I hold no brief for private enterprise. But I have unshakeable faith in individual enterprise.
> C.L. BURTON, head of The Robert Simpson Co. Ltd., *A Sense of Urgency: Memoirs of a Canadian Merchant* (1952).

In management thirty years experience does not count for much if it merely means ten times three of the same experience.
> NEIL J. McKINNON, banker, quoted in *Public Utilities Fortnightly*, 4 Jan. 1968.

Montreal looks inward, faces east — across the Atlantic — to England and France, and dreams of the past; Toronto looks outward, faces south to the United States, and dreams of the future.
> PETER C. NEWMAN, author, *The Canadian Establishment: Volume One* (1975).

Once you go beyond two or three meals a day and something to keep you warm, all "necessities" are to a large degree man-created or artificial. If you want a tie and a haircut, these are man-made needs. Does anybody claim we should go back to prehistoric days when you needed only a hide to keep you warm and a roof over your head?
> JEAN DE GRANDPRÉ, President of Bell Canada, interviewed by Dean Walker in *A Case for the Enterprise System* (1975).

They say business is the law of the jungle. I think it's the law of life.
> ROY THOMSON, British press lord, quoted by Peter C. Newman in *The Canadian Establishment: Volume One* (1975).

If Canadians can feel that their business machine is working for them, that — more than any number of "O Canada's" — will generate a strong sense of Canada and proud identification with it.
> HEATHER MENZIES, journalist, *The Railroad's Not Enough: Canada Now* (1978).

If there is a hell, there must be a special pit reserved for nice, sweet, charming, intelligent secretaries who have spent their niceness, sweetness, charm and intelligence on covering up for their bosses.
> STEPHEN VIZINCZEY, novelist, *An Innocent Millionaire* (1983).

Politicians, unfortunately, seem congenitally blind to the inevitability — even the desirability — of periodic industrial fluctuations which let obsolescent technologies wither, while encouraging vibrant new technologies to develop and prosper. In ecology it's called the balance of nature; in politics, it's called corporate cruelty.
> TOM DAVEY, editor and columnist, *All the Views Fit to Print* (1985).

If you don't own the patents to the *ultimate* technology (no one anywhere really does anymore) and you don't have exclusive access to the source of low-cost money, the only factor that can give you a competitive edge is your people.
> EVA INNES, ROBERT L. PERRY, and JIM LYON, business journalists, *The Financial Post Selects the 100 Best Companies to Work for in Canada* (1986).

As a result of Canada's paper entrepreneurship, there are no Lee Iacoccas among Canada's corporate élite, much less technological geniuses like Stephen Jobs, who started Apple Computers. Most chief executive officers are lawyers, accountants, or stock market jockeys. . . . Small wonder that less money is spent on research and development here than is spent in Egypt. While foreign-owned enterprises are often blamed for doing insufficient research, the facts are that Canadian-owned firms are not doing much either.

DIANE FRANCIS, author, *Controlling Interest: Who Owns Canada?* (1986).

Right now, it is a hockey game with no referees in sight. Without new rules, we hurtle towards financial feudalism, with our children as economic serfs. It is feudalism or socialism. The choice is ours.

DIANE FRANCIS, author, *Controlling Interest: Who Owns Canada?* (1986).

If Canada became a country where reasonable profits could be made safely and honestly, industry and enterprise would flourish and tax revenues would increase as unemployment declined.

PETER WORTHINGTON, journalist, contributor to *If I Were Prime Minister* (1987) edited by Mel Hurtig.

We don't make folk heroes out of our entrepreneurs the way they do in the U.S. In the U.S., everybody wants to be an entrepreneur. In Canada, everybody wants to be a civil servant.

RUSSELL KNIGHT, Professor in the School of Business, University of Western Ontario, quoted by Jan Wong in *The Globe and Mail*, 17 Sept. 1987.

It was widely felt, probably accurately, that average Canadians were less interested in enterprise and risk-taking than Americans, less distrustful of authority and organizations, more interested in security and a quiet life. Perhaps the business bestsellers told the comparative story: *In Search of Excellence* in the United States, *The Best 100 Companies to Work for in Canada*.

MICHAEL BLISS, historian, *Northern Enterprise: Five Centuries of Canadian Business* (1987).

Small is terrifying but medium is beautiful.

SONIA JONES, founder of Peninsula Farms which produces Berry Best products, *It All Began with Daisy* (1987).

I believe *wanting to* is the most important quality a person can bring to business.

JIMMY PATTISON, company founder, *Jimmy: An Autobiography* (1987) written with Paul Grescoe.

And as for me, after a quarter of a century in business, after doing more than two hundred deals, after more success than I ever dreamed possible, I still wanna.

JIMMY PATTISON, company founder, *Jimmy: An Autobiography* (1987), written with Paul Grescoe.

If you don't inspect, then don't expect.

JOHN FRASER, CEO of Federal Industries, concerning natural curiosity and the need to know, quoted by Alexander Aird, Paul Nowack, and James Westcott in *Road to the Top: The Chief Executive Officer in Canada* (1988).

There's a great deal of prestige in being a businessman in this community: much less so in other parts of the world where I've lived. It's hard not to believe you're important when you're a businessman in Canada.

W. GALEN WESTON, corporate head, quoted by Stephen Brunt in *The Globe and Mail*, 13 Feb. 1988.

What I learned is that Canadians play softball, Americans play hardball, and the French play speedball. They do not enjoy outsiders having control.

WILLIAM TERON, Toronto-based developer, whose 1985 agreement with the French government to develop the Porte Maillot project fell through, quoted by Stevie Cameron in *The Globe and Mail*, 31 March 1988.

I consider myself a North American.

ROBERT CAMPEAU, corporate head, press conference, New York, 5 April 1988, quoted by Larry Welsh in *The Toronto Star* the following day.

In business you have to abide by the golden rule. Those with the gold make the rules.
JOHN GILLESPIE, business executive, quoted by Drew Fagan in *The Globe and Mail*, 3 May 1988.

The only job a Canadian can't have is the one running 3M Canada.
JOHN MYSER, President of 3M Canada Inc., quoted in *The Globe and Mail*, 29 Aug. 1988. Myser is an American citizen. A multinational firm, 3M rotates its division heads; the Canadian operation is a division, and the heads of all the divisions are Americans.

We have no particular interest in growing bigger. What drives us is usually the challenge, to be creative, to do something interesting. No successful businessman really has money in mind after a certain point. When we do something, we want to do it right. It's not monument building; it's more than that. The fact is, anyone who is able to do something well will want to do it until he is stopped by the force of time.
PAUL REICHMANN, one of the heads of Olympia & York Enterprises, quoted by Dianne Maley in *The Globe and Mail's Report on Business Magazine*, Dec. 1988.

I think of business as a book of great stories. The stories differ, but they all have the good guys and the bad guys fighting it out for high stakes.
RICHARD OSLER, investment adviser, "Richard's Day," *The Latest Morningside Papers* (1989) edited by Peter Gzowski.

The new alliance has the size and economies of scale to be low-cost producers, based in Canada, in competition around the world. All of that should give us the stable platforms we need to succeed.
MARSHALL (MICKEY) COHEN, business executive, referring to The Molson Companies Limited, address to the Metropol-

itan Toronto Board of Trade, 24 Jan. 1989, quoted in an editorial in *The Toronto Star*, 26 Jan. 1989.

Why should anyone be surprised at the fate of Quintette coal project in British Columbia . . . ?
It illustrates the three laws of northern and hinterland development, also known as the Dome Principles.
1. In remote areas, development benefits will be exaggerated by a factor of 10 and costs divided by the same amount.
2. The amount of hype before a project begins is inversely proportional to its economic viability.
3. Individual fantasies result in losses of public money.
JIM LOTZ, writer, "The Dome Principles," *The Globe and Mail's Report on Business Magazine*, Jan. 1989.

Poor Campeau. His debt plateau almost qualified him for status as a Third World country, which in the current climate of forgiveness might have solved his problems.
PETER C. NEWMAN, columnist, referring to Robert Campeau's retrenchment, *Maclean's*, 30 Oct. 1989.

Damn Your Lousy EXcuses
It takes guts to give your company an acronym like that. Especially when the Divisons you own are such veritable retailing organizations . . . like Club Monaco, Harry Rosen, Tip Top Tailors, Fairweather, Braemar, Steel, Thrifty's, Town & Country and Bi-Way to name a few.
Well, we're gutsy people. And that's why we have more fashion specialty stores than anyone else in North America. And we're growing.
Advertisement for Dylex Limited, *The Toronto Star*, 19 Oct. 1989. Dylex is an acronym for "Damn Your Lousy EXcuses."

The single most valuable skill in business . . . is the ability to make the right decisions most of the time.

CHARLES TEMPLETON, media personality, *Succeeding* (1989).

Canadians including the Reichmann family of Toronto, which owns the huge Olympia & York Real Estate Company, have acquired more than 25 million square feet of Manhattan office space, one square foot for each Canadian citizen.
ANDREW H. MALCOLM, journalist, *The New York Times*, 28 Jan. 1990.

Given our riches, our natural resources, our historical advantages and the fact we have never suffered occupation or a devastating war, where is our car? How come we can't produce something like the Hyundai or the Volvo?
MORDECAI RICHLER, novelist, address, Toronto, 27 Feb. 1990, quoted by Philip Marchand in *The Toronto Star* the following day.

When someone says "it is good business" you may be sure it is bad morality.
ROBIN SKELTON, man-of-letters, aphorism, May 1990.

CALGARY
See also ALBERTA

We, havin' pleasured ourselves considerable in the only genuine cowtown in Canada, namely Calgary, and havin' bin duly exposed to exceptional amounts of heartwarmin', tongue-loosin', back-slappin', neighbour-lovin' Western spirit, solemnly promise to communicate this here Calgary brand hospitality to all folks and critters who cross our trail thereafter, Honest Injun.
> The White Hatter Pledge of the Calgary Stampede quoted in *Time*, 5 Aug. 1974.

And what of Calgary itself? It has been said that the reason people in Calgary have such high ideals is that we are three thousand feet above sea level. True, our ideals are high, but why shouldn't they be? It is going to be one hell of a City once it's finally uncrated. People joke that the municipal bird is a construction crane, and that we need air traffic controllers to prevent mid-air collisions between them; but the excitement created by over two billion dollars in building permits last year cannot be denied. Cities made up exclusively of greedy, vulgar, hard-drinking, cigar-chewing, cowboy capitalist oil men do not win the right to host Olympic Games.
> RALPH KLEIN, Calgary Mayor, speech, Canadian Club, Burlington, Ont., 10 Feb. 1982. In passing, the controversial mayor paraphrased prairie journalist Bob Edwards and Montreal novelist Mordecai Richler.

The city of Calgary has more college educated citizens per capita than any other Canadian city.
> LINDA FRUM, journalist, *Linda Frum's Guide to Canadian Universities* (1987).

It's not that much different from the Ukraine.
> NIKOLAY GVOZD, artistic director of the Capella Banduristiv, initial reaction to Calgary, quoted by Brian Brennan in *The Calgary Herald*, 2 March 1988.

Official Host City for the Turn of the Century
> Calgary so designated itself in the aftermath of the Winter Olympics in March 1988.

Calgarian. Cowtowner, Stampeder.
> PAUL DICKSON, British writer, *What Do You Call a Person From . . . ? A Dictionary of Resident Names* (1990).

CALIFORNIA

California and the west coast leap-frogging from the 18th to the 20th century. Never had a 19th century. That's why they could have Hollywood. A 19th-century area like Chicago was too highly structured to accommodate a free-wheeling enterprise like Hollywood.
> MARSHALL McLUHAN, communications theorist, *Letters of Marshall McLuhan* (1987) edited by Matie Molinaro, Corinne McLuhan, and William Toye.

California! My friends all call you home, / And if you take away another, I'll be that much more alone. / Is it my fault that my kind are always drawn toward the sun / Like a child to home, whenever darkness comes?
> STAN ROGERS, singer and composer, "Gold," *Northwest Passage* (Fogarty's Cove Music, 1981).

After my first year I thought it was my divine right to have a Rolls-Royce, a tennis court, a Jacuzzi, a pool, and a Bel-Air mansion full of servants. It's easy to lose perspective here.
> MONICA PARKER, actress, Canadian-born, Los Angeles-based, quoted by Ron Graham in "Born Again in Babylon," *Saturday Night*, June 1983.

There are 600,000 Canadians living in southern California. I now know why they moved here — they all hate hockey.
> JACK KENT COOKE, expatriate Canadian business tycoon and owner of the then-disastrous Los Angeles Kings hockey club, quoted by Allan Fotheringham in *Maclean's*, 7 Nov. 1988.

One of the great symbols of the ultimate good life has become one of the first victims of our changing climate. Nearly everyone at some point must have dreamed of moving to Southern California and owning a kidney-shaped swimming pool.

Well, forget it. Most counties and cities in Southern California have now passed, or are in the process of passing, bylaws prohibiting the filling of those legendary swimming pools with water. I don't know about you, but to me that's the end of the Hollywood dream.
> BOB HUNTER, ecologist and columnist, "Water Shortage a Global Warning," *Metropolis*, 6 Sept. 1990.

CANADA

See also CANADA & THE
            UNITED STATES
          CANADIANISM
          CANADIANS
          DOMINION
          FRENCH CANADA

For many years Canada has held an obscure place among the countries of the globe. Our borders have been pictured as the abode of perpetual snows, and our people as indifferent, easy-going, indolent. But change is taking place.
> CHARLES R. TUTTLE, geologist, *Our North Land* (1885).

Canada has been the inspiration of my life. I have had before me as a pillar of fire by night and a pillar of cloud by day, a policy of true Canadianism, of moderation, of conciliation. . . . In all the difficulties, all the pains, and all the vicissitudes of our situation, let us always remember that love is better than hatred, and faith better than doubt, and let hope in our future destinies be the pillar of fire to guide us in our career.
> SIR WILFRID LAURIER, Prime Minister, quoted in an address delivered before the Empire Club of Canada, Toronto, 29 June 1983.

Of all the loveless, lifeless lands that writhe beneath the wrath of God, commend me to Canada! (I understand that the eastern cities, having known French culture, are comparatively habitable. Not having been there I cannot say.)
> ALEISTER CROWLEY, occultist and writer, May 1904, *The Confessions of Aleister Crowley: An Autohagiography* (1969)

edited by John Symonds and Kenneth Grant.

One nation, two cultures; one nationality, two races; one loyalty, two tongues, on this the Dominion of Canada is founded, on this the partnership rests by solemn contract, by mutual trust. And thus it must abide or perish.
GRAHAM SPRY, nationalist, "One Nation, Two Cultures," address, Canadian Club of Quebec, 17 Jan 1929, *The Canadian Nation*, Feb. 1929.

kenuk
This is the way the poet and literary personality EZRA POUND referred to Canuck or Canada in a letter dated 17 June 1951 to Marshall McLuhan, noted in *Letters of Marshall McLuhan* (1987) edited by Matie Molinaro, Corinne McLuhan, and William Toye.

Canada as a somewhat backward country enjoys many advantages. These become more evident as I encounter more advanced territories in the U.S.A. You could do a great deal of good for us all by making an inventory of particular advantages enjoyed by backward countries in the appraisal of advanced situations.
MARSHALL McLUHAN, communications theorist, letter to Peter Drucker, 6 Dec. 1966, *Letters of Marshall McLuhan* (1987) edited by Matie Molinaro, Corinne McLuhan, and William Toye.

One thinks of the Queen and cowboys. . . .
GORE VIDAL, U.S. novelist, image of Canada in 1969-70, quoted by Pierre Berton in *Hollywood's Canada: The Americanization of Our National Image* (1975).

Canada now, an imagined place / of strict decencies and the vast air, / where love might have prospered, and where / (as Dennis Lee would have it) we have failed.
DAVID HELWIG, poet and novelist, lines from "The Blue Feather: Four Poems from England," *The Best Name of Silence* (1972).

Toronto was a unique place in those days [1940s and 1950s]. Artistic perspectives were adjusted to a strong natural state of individuality. Everybody in Canada seemed to listen to what they enjoyed, and nobody could tell them what to like, or what was popular, or what was the In thing. Even today, it is very hard to brainwash a Canadian.
DUKE ELLINGTON, U.S. jazz performer, *Music Is My Mistress* (1973).

Today, when it takes little courage to be extreme, I am grateful that Canada has the courage to remain moderate. . . . As long as she remains aggressively moderate Canada will survive.
GEORGE JONAS, author, "In Praise of Moderation," *Maclean's*, Nov. 1974.

Canada is not a starting point, it's a goal
JEAN-CLAUDE FALARDEAU, political scientist, quoted in an address by Barney Danson, Empire Club of Canada, Toronto, 24 Nov. 1977.

Canada is a country so square that even the female impersonators are women.
Line from the screenplay of the film *Outrageous* (1977) written by RICHARD BENNER.

The excitement of Canada / The colour, smell, newness. Having a say. Being able to rush from the top of a pine tree on the mountain to a party at Government House. "You girls don't realize how lucky you are." Maple Sugar.
ELIZABETH SMART, novelist and diarist, "A Transatlantic Pursuit: My Affair with England (1978), *Autobiographies* (1987) edited by Christina Burridge.

Canada is not a national state in the usually accepted sense, but a mutable and often dynamic political continuum suited to the varied historical roots of its people and to the broken patterns of its geography. Any attempt to tidy it up into a centralized nation-state would bring its immediate disintegration.

GEORGE WOODCOCK, author, *The Canadians* (1979).

The huge advantage of Canada is its backwardness.
MARSHALL McLUHAN, communications theorist, quoted by Norman Snider in "Robertson Davies: The View from High Table," *The Bumper Book* (1986) edited by John Metcalf.

We peer so suspiciously at each other that we cannot see that we Canadians are standing on the mountaintop of human wealth, freedom and privilege.
PIERRE ELLIOTT TRUDEAU, Prime Minister, New Year's Message, published in *The Toronto Star*, 31 Dec. 1980.

This country is a land of small towns and big dreams.
Characteristic vision of Canada of Prime Minister BRIAN MULRONEY and noted in *The Calgary Herald*, 9 July 1984.

Canada, noun. A socialist protectorate full of nice people and clean streets, with no crime except teevee.
R.W. JACKSON, American writer, *The Diabolical Dictionary of Modern English* (1986).

Canada was formed by the last ice age, after which things slowed down.
ERIC NICOL and DAVE MORE, humorists, *The U.S. or Us: What's the Difference, Eh?* (1986).

There was more of it than I had seen, but what I had seen told me that the Canada I had grown up believing in no longer existed. . . . Canada remained an experiment, less bounded by irrevocable legacies than older societies. We were searching, economically and culturally, for more realistic possibilities than the ones envisaged seventy-five, or even twenty-five, years ago. In older countries the future was inherited, largely predetermined by the past. Here, if we had the will, we could still choose what we would become.

JOHN GALT, journalist and traveller, concluding lines, *Whistlestop: A Journey across Canada* (1987).

When I'm in Canada, I feel like this is what the world should be like.
JANE FONDA, film star, quoted in *Saturday Night*, Dec. 1987.

When I think of Canada I think of tonic water.
DUDLEY MOORE, comedian, quoted in *Saturday Night*, Dec. 1987.

I love it. It reminds me of Minnesota.
LONI ANDERSON, singer, quoted in *Saturday Night*, Dec. 1987.

The credo that has animated my work and my life is that Canada is the world's luckiest land — that to be a Canadian imposes obligations of thanksgiving not to take our individual freedoms and collective opportunities for granted. . . . I have always believed that although it may be absurd to advocate innovation and reform, it is far more absurd not even to try.
PETER C. NEWMAN, author, *Sometimes a Great Nation: Will Canada Belong to the 21st Century?* (1988).

After feeling for more than a century that being Canadian was a journey rather than a destination, we have arrived at last. We have attained a state of delicious grace which allows us to appreciate that what's important is not so much who we are but *that* we are — that sometimes a large nation can become a great one.
PETER C. NEWMAN, author, *Sometimes a Great Nation: Will Canada Belong to the 21st Century?* (1988).

I think there are tremendous virtues within the country and I personally am more at home with the somewhat reserved, quieter Canadian spirit than with the more energetic American spirit, and being Canadian I therefore understand the wish to preserve it. But I don't think that you necessarily preserve it by keeping those who didn't happen to be born here out of the country.

GLENN GOULD, pianist, interviewed by Ulla Colgrass in *For the Love of Music* (1988).

Canada is . . . the cry of the loon, Gretzky worship, rye and ginger in a paper cup, vinegar on the fires and . . . talking gas pumps.

NANCY WHITE, singer and satirist, Olympic Folk Festival, Calgary, quoted by Brian Brennan in *The Calgary Herald*, 2 March 1988.

Canada is an interesing place — the rest of the world thinks so, even if Canadians don't.

TERENCE M. GREEN, author, *Books in Canada*, April 1988.

But whatever outsiders may say to the detriment of Canada, we say much worse things ourselves. Indeed, in an early play of mine, I once said that Canada was not a country one loved, but a country one worried about, and to my dismay I now find that remark enshrined in a book of quotations.

ROBERTSON DAVIES, man-of-letters, Neil Gunn lecture, Edinburgh University, June 1988, published in *The Times Literary Supplement*, 30 Sept. 1988.

Even its name is a negative pun. In south German dialect, *Keine dah* ("nothing there") is pronounced "Kana dah." Portuguese explorers are supposed to have invented the name by saying *acada nada* ("nothing here"). In fact, *Kanata! Kanata!* (meaning something like "Yonder are our wigwams!") seem to have been the words spoken by Indians as they greeted Jacques Cartier in Stadacona in 1534.

WILLIAM KILBOURN, historian, "The Peaceable Kingdom Still," *Daedalus: Journal of the American Academy of Arts and Sciences*, "In Search of Canada," Fall 1988.

Why do we think we're a tiny population when we're three times bigger than Swe-

den? To whom are we comparing ourselves? Well, if you compare yourselves to a giant, you know what size you'll be — Gulliver found that out.

ADRIENNE CLARKSON, broadcaster, accepting an honorary degree, Dalhousie University, Halifax, 23 Oct. 1988.

Canadians and Americans share something very precious: a sense of the last frontier. The Canadian North has replaced the American West. That primeval woodland, that vast wilderness is there, from Banff to Newfoundland, giving all North Americans a spacial habitation Europeans do not know. For two centuries, at least, the frontier has taught us how to go out alone.

MARSHALL McLUHAN, communications theorist, and Bruce R. Powers, communications specialist, authors of *The Global Village: Transformations in World Life and Media in the 21st Century* (1989).

I have a sort of romantic sentiment about it. I think that Canada in a literary sense is a very Nordic country. It has its long winters and it has its Nordic glooms as well as its other passions. It has a very high readership ratio to the population by comparison with other nations. And publishing has just taken off here. . . . I had that sense of, maybe it's terribly dangerous to say it, of lost Europeans which I also had in the Soviet Union; of people with a tremendous cultural appetite and with a great intellectual reach.

JOHN LE CARRÉ, British espionage writer, interviewed in Toronto by Dennis Kucherawy in *Metropolis*, 15 June 1989.

I didn't realize how utterly pleasant it was to be here. I've come from New York, which is a warthog straight from hell. To sing my swan song here is very pleasant.

MARLON BRANDO, film star, on location in Toronto for twelve weeks shooting *The Freshman*, quoted by Murray Campbell in *The Globe and Mail*, 31 Aug. 1989.

It's going to be a great country when they finish unpacking it.

> ANDREW H. MALCOLM, Canadian correspondent for *The New York Times*, quoted by Geoffrey Stevens in *The Toronto Star*, 5 Nov. 1989.

I'm buying up maps of Canada — they may become collectors' items soon.

> EDD ULUSCHAK, cartoonist, Miller Features Syndicate, 18 July 1990.

It's cute. Nothing's happened here.

> Attributed to the New York author, satirist, and comic FRAN LIEBOWITZ in conversation, when asked about her impressions of Canada, following her appearance in Toronto on 28 July 1990.

There is in Canada, and about Canadians, a constant search for fairness, a receptiveness to honourable accommodation, of enabling the two principal language communities to flourish within the Canadian family.

> QUEEN ELIZABETH II, Canada Day address, Parliament Hill, Ottawa, 1 July 1990, quoted by David Vienneau in *The Toronto Star* the following day.

Canada has an aboriginal past, a bilingual present, and a multicultural future.

> GARY FILMON, Manitoba Premier, quoted by John Godfrey in *The Financial Post*, 13 July 1990.

In Canada I would like to see, the moment I descend from my plane, a snowman being pulled along by a seal, corresponding to an image from my childhood that persists to this day.

> MARIN SORESCU, Romanian poet, "Some Answers," *Symmetries: Selected Poems* (1982) translated from the Romanian by John Robert Colombo and Petronela Negosanu. The poet visited Canada for the first time in Oct. 1990, too early for a snowman, but he was presented with a soapstone carving of a seal.

The taste of Canada was too sour then for me to consider the more practical considerations of my pride.

> Line from the novel *Joanna* (1990) by the British author LISA ST. AUBIN DE TERÁN.

Let me be clear: Canada is not up for grabs. Either you have a country or you don't. You can't have it both ways. My country is Canada. I intend to strengthen it and I intend to keep it.

> BRIAN MULRONEY, Prime Minister, address, joint meeting of the Empire Club and the Canadian Club, Toronto, 12 Feb. 1991, printed in *The Toronto Star* the following day.

A country wasn't built by accountants. If we get obsessed with cost only, it may cost us the country.

> KEITH SPICER, Citizen's Forum on Canada's Future, appearing before a financial committee of the House of Commons, 21 March 1991, quoted in *The Globe and Mail* the following day.

CANADA & THE UNITED KINGDOM
See also UNITED KINGDOM

As far back as 1908 the Committee of Imperial Defence had decided that Britain should no longer contemplate defending Canada against the Americans.

> STEPHEN J. HARRIS, historian, *Canadian Brass: The Making of a Professional Army, 1860-1939* (1988).

Corn is what feeds millions, but it is the bread of literary rebuke. The Canadians are corny because of their environment but it makes them ill at ease in the Inns of Court & with people in nightclubs & they want to go back where limitless space will console them.

> ELIZABETH SMART, novelist and diarist, diary entry, 4 April 1945, *Autobiographies* (1987) edited by Christina Burridge.

A Canadian historian, Arthur Lower, said once that we Canadians love England but don't like Englishmen, and that we love

Americans but can't stand the United States.

ROBERTSON DAVIES, man-of-letters, Neil Gunn lecture, Edinburgh University, June 1988, published in *The Times Literary Supplement*, 30 Sept. 1988.

CANADA & THE UNITED STATES

See also UNITED STATES
OF AMERICA

Canada must be demolished — *Delenda est Carthago* — or we are undone!

WILLIAM LIVINGSTON, later first Revolutionary Governor of New Jersey, address made in 1756, quoted by Gwynne Dyer and Tina Viljoen, commentator and TV producer, *The Defence of Canada: In the Arms of the Empire* (1990).

By His Excellency / George Washington, Esquire, / Commander in Chief of the Army of the United Colonies of North-America. / To the Inhabitants of Canada. / Friends and Brethren, / The unnatural Contest between the English Colonies and Great-Britain, has now risen to such a Height, that Arms alone must decide it.... Come then, my Brethren, unite with us in an indissoluble Union, let us run together to the same Goal.

From a proclamation issued in French and English and distributed throughout Quebec by General (and future U.S.President) GEORGE WASHINGTON, Sept. 1775.

Art. 11. Canada acceding to this confederation, and joining in the measures of the United States, shall be admitted into, and entitled to all the advantages of this Union: but no other colony shall be admitted into the same, unless such admission be agreed to by nine States.

Article 11 (the so-called Canadian Article) of the Articles of Confederation, the name of the first constitution of the United States, drafted largely by JOHN DICKINSON of Pennsylvania, presented to Congress on 12 July 1776, adopted by Congress on 15 Nov. 1777, and accepted as the law of the land from 1781 to 1789, when it was superseded by the U.S. Constitution. Appendix, *The American's Guide: Comprising the Declaration of Independence, the Articles of Confederation, the Constitution of the United States . . .* (Philadelphia, 1843).

Presently friendly.

Estimate of the attitude of the United States towards Canada as prepared by Brigadier J. SUTHERLAND (BUSTER) BROWN, director of military operations and intelligence at Militia Headquarters, Ottawa, and principal author of Defence Scheme No. 1, 1921, which in the case of hostilities called for the Canadian Army to make a pre-emptive invasion of U.S. border states to gain time to allow the British to react, quoted by Stephen J. Harris in *Canadian Brass: The Making of a Professional Army, 1860-1939* (1988).

Canadians are a fine tribe of people. They are hardy — they got to be to live next to us.

WILL ROGERS, cowboy comedian, *The Best of Will Rogers* (1979) edited by Bryan B. Sterling.

The more I think over the whole situation, the more I believe . . . that the U.S. foreign policy at bottom is to bring Canada into as many situations affecting themselves as possible with a view to leading ultimately to the annexation of our two countries....

W. L. MACKENZIE KING, former Prime Minister, recording in his diary, 30 June 1950, his reactions to Canadian involvement in the Korean War, quoted by C.P. Stacey in *A Very Double Life: The Private World of Mackenzie King* (1976).

I am appalled by the Americanisation of Canada, especially in all the silly little things — I've just had a call to say a man has arrived to claim the typewriter.

J.B. PRIESTLEY, English author touring Canada, letter written to his wife Jacquetta Hawkes, Vancouver, 23 Feb.

1956, quoted by Vincent Brome in *J.B. Priestley* (1988).

This stone bears witness to the common purpose of two nations, whose frontiers are the frontiers of friendship, whose ways are the ways of freedom, and whose works are the works of peace.
> Inscription in bronze embedded in black granite on the International Friendship Memorial to mark the opening of the St. Lawrence Seaway and Power Project, dedicated by Queen Elizabeth II and U.S. Vice-President Richard M. Nixon, near Prescott, Ont., 27 June 1959.

Canada as a cultural DEW line, or distant early warning system, has a large untouched potential in relation to the U.S. . . . Yet we have no ultimate commitment to be American, or even to be Canadian. It is this detachment in action that would seem to give us our opportunity to share the creative process of the culture without any mere merging in it. This is what the jazz musicians mean by "real cool."
> MARSHALL McLUHAN, communications theorist, letter to Claude Bissell, 28 Jan. 1966, *Letters of Marshall McLuhan* (1987) edited by Matie Molinaro, Corinne McLuhan, and William Toye.

The only thing we are really sure of is that we are not Americans.
> PIERRE BERTON, author, "My Country," *Canada: Pictures of a Great Land* (1976) edited by Jürgen F. Goden and Hans Scherz.

The United States, thank God, had no plans for Canada at all. It never had and I trust never will have a Canadian policy.
> JOHN W. HOLMES, diplomat and author, *Canada: A Middle-Aged Power* (1976).

Canada and the United States are doomed by geography and history to friendship, irritation, co-operation, disputes, and, finally, a parallelism of outlook.
> HENRY KISSINGER, U.S. Security Adviser,

quoted by Geoffrey Stevens in *The Globe and Mail*, 20 Aug. 1976.

Certain truths seem to have to pass through the United States before being understood in Canada.
> RENÉ LÉVESQUE, Quebec Premier, press conference, Quebec City, 27 Jan. 1977. He was referring specifically to the widespread coverage in Canada of a nationally televised address he had delivered in New York. Prime Minister Trudeau took the same tack, speaking in New York to be heard in Toronto.

It is time we stopped thinking of our nearest neighbours as foreigners.
> RONALD REAGAN, former film actor, announcing his candidacy for the U.S. presidency, address, New York City, 13 Nov. 1979. This speech includes the first use of the phrase "A North American Accord."

We will also put to rest any doubt of those cynical enough to believe that the United States would seek to dominate any relationship among our three countries, or foolish enough to think that the governments and peoples of Canada and Mexico would ever permit such domination to occur.
> RONALD REAGAN, former film actor, announcing his candidacy for the U.S. presidency, address, New York City, 13 Nov. 1979.

No American who has chosen to leave the United States and take another citizenship will ever be a passionate nationalist anywhere, for what has turned us away from our own country is precisely that superpatriotism that has led to so many grievous mistakes both inside and outside the country. I will never be a super-Canadian, but in that I feel at home in a country which practises modesty and self-criticism regularly.
> JANE RULE, Canadian novelist of American birth, *The Globe and Mail*, 16 April 1980.

For some reason, a glaze passes over people's faces when you say Canada.
SONDRA GOTLIEB, columnist and wife of Canada's Ambassador in Washington, D.C., quoted in *The New York Times*, 8 July 1982.

Canada is not completely owned by the United States, and Canadians still have a freedom of choice, but there's a case to be made that Canada serves as a farm team for more American businesses than hockey and comedy. When the weak are weeded out and the strong emerge, there's often an American at the dressing-room door waving a dazzling contract.
RON GRAHAM, journalist, "Born Again in Babylon," *Saturday Night*, June 1983.

Canadians are often not really seen by Americans as *foreign*. We are neighbours, friends, cousins, fellow North Americans; we are Canadians, but we are not foreigners. When Peter Jennings was recently named anchor at ABC, Roone Arledge, head of ABC news and sports, was asked if there was a downside to having a non-U.S. citizen as anchorman of one of the three most influential news broadcasts in the country. I can't recall his precise words but they were something like "Well, you know, he's not really a foreigner, he's a Canadian." Well, this view of Canadians is an enormous and certainly unique compliment to us.
ALLAN GOTLIEB, Canadian Ambassador in Washington, D.C., address, Empire Club of Canada, Toronto, 10 Nov. 1983.

Living next door to the United States is like swimming with a whale. You risk being swallowed alive.
DAVID PETERSON, Ontario Premier, failing to better Trudeau's imagine of the elephant and the mouse, address, Empire Club of Canada, Toronto, 26 Sept. 1985.

We've always been the Great White North to Americans, even before the McKenzie Brothers invented the term. (Fleet Street improved on the phrase in the 1980s when, piqued by some cheekiness from the colonies, it dubbed Canada "The Great White Waste of Time.")
ALLAN FOTHERINGHAM, columnist, *Capitol Offences: Dr. Foth Meets Uncle Sam* (1986).

There can hardly have been a politically independent country that has survived semi-intact from such an onslaught of cultural dumping as the United States has unloaded on Canada: in movies, television, magazines, fads and fashions, sports and spoils. There are more Americans visiting Canada every year than the total Canadian population and they go home (mainly bearing salmon in their camper freezers and Kodak Instamatics worn to the frazzle) with the country left whole and unsullied, except for the cash registers. Rejoice, they are harmless and didn't catch anything from the water. We could have, as the cliché goes, worse neighbours. But let's keep them neighbours. At a safe distance.
ALLAN FOTHERINGHAM, columnist, *Capitol Offences: Dr. Foth Meets Uncle Sam* (1986).

When I would get worried is when the Americans do become interested in us. And I think of the countries they have become interested in, I think of Chile, I think of Iran, I think of Vietnam, I think of Grenada, I think of Nicaragua, and I think of Libya, so I say, Let's keep that ignorance flying.
ALLAN FOTHERINGHAM, columnist and author, address, Empire Club of Canada, Toronto, 16 Oct. 1986.

Geographically, Canada is smaller than the United States, unless we include the parts that don't count.
ERIC NICOL and DAVE MORE, humorists, *The U.S. or Us: What's the Difference, Eh?* (1986).

The received wisdom about my countrymen is that they are uniformly boring and understandably modest, the sorry inhabitants of a cultural and economic backwa-

ter, all their energy spent on fighting the frost. It has been given to few Americans, in high or low places, to grasp that Canadians, cunning beyond compare, have been infiltrating the upstart republic to the south for years. I hate to snitch on my own people, but if the present rate of penetration persists, we will soon all but totally control the American media, chemical and liquor industries, real estate, publishing and the images of high and popular culture.
> MORDECAI RICHLER, novelist, "The Canadians Are Coming," *Signature*, April 1987.

In public debates in Canada, the key words, those that determine the winner of the debate, are "equity" and "fairness"; in the U.S. the comparable determining words are "freedom" and "efficiency."
> RICHARD GWYN, correspondent, *Cultural Sovereignty: Myth or Reality? Proceedings of the 28th Annual Seminar on Canadian American Relations, University of Windsor, Windsor, 5-7 Nov. 1986* (1987) edited by James Chacko.

When we look at the Americans, we often do so to seek reassurance about our image of ourselves. Regrettably, when they look at us, they think of stereotypes — the 3M's — Mounties and Mountains and Molson's. They cannot fathom what we are driving at, especially when we talk of our national identity and express concerns about our culture and sovereignty.
> ALLAN GOTLIEB, Canadian Ambassador in Washington, D.C., address, Empire Club of Canada, Toronto, 9 April 1987.

Canada as a separate but dominated country has done about as well under the U.S. as women, worldwide, have done under men; about the only position they've ever adopted toward us, country to country, has been the missionary position, and we were not on the top. I guess that's why the national wisdom *vis-à-vis* Them has so often taken the form of lying still, keeping your mouth shut, and pretending you like it.

> MARGARET ATWOOD, author and cultural nationalist, testifying before the Parliamentary Committee on Free Trade, Fall 1987, *If You Love This Country: Facts and Feelings on Free Trade* (1987) edited by Laurier LaPierre.

The U.S. does not need to teach us its values: There is always a Canadian reader to do it for them.
> BERNARD OSTRY, television executive, address, Centre for American Studies, University of Western Ontario, London, Ont., quoted in *The Toronto Star*, 3 Oct. 1987.

Canada is a democratic country that worries more about the sinister influences of a democratic next-door neighbour than it does about the threat of a totalitarian neighbour next door on the other side.
> ANDREW H. MALCOLM, U.S. correspondent, "Northern Contradiction," *Saturday Night*, Dec. 1987.

The difference between Canadians and Americans is very simple. Americans assert themselves in the world as if they have a right to be there. They would never dream of asking, "Who do you think we are?" And yet that is the first question a Canadian will always ask.
> ERIC FISCHL, artist, quoted in *Saturday Night*, Dec. 1987.

Saying Uncle to Sam
> Chapter heading of *Friends in High Places: Politics and Patronage in the Mulroney Government* (1987) by the journalist CLAIRE HOY.

President Reagan has said that this deal represents the fulfillment of the American dream. I can understand that. Let the Americans dream, but we have our own dreams. We dream of an independent and a distinct nation north of the 49th parallel.
> JOHN TURNER, Liberal leader, referring to U.S. President Ronald Reagan's endorsing of the Free Trade Pact as the expres-

sion of "the American dream," address, 18 Dec. 1987.

Sherman woke up from a dream he couldn't remember, with his heart flailing away at his chest wall. It was the drinker's hour, that hour in the dead of night when drinkers and insomniacs suddenly wake up and know it's all over, his sleep dodge. He resisted the urge to look at the illuminated clock on the radio and the table beside the bed. He didn't want to know how many hours he would have to lie here fighting with this stranger, his heart, which was desperate to escape to some far far far far far far far far far Canada.

The nighttime thoughts of the young investment banker Sherman McCoy in the novel *The Bonfire of the Vanities* (1987) by the U.S. novelist and cultural commentator TOM WOLFE.

Among the mainstays of my faith is the notion that it is essential to preserve the relatively gentle society on *this* side of the 49th parallel. We must reject the seductive but fatal assumption at the source of the American way of life: the gospel that more is better and that progress, efficiency, and monetary gain should be the ultimate goals of human activity. It ain't necessarily so.

PETER C. NEWMAN, author, *Sometimes a Great Nation: Will Canada Belong to the 21st Century?* (1988).

American applauds with glee / the highest climber of the tree. // Englishman has half a mind / the tree is not the proper kind. // Canadian with tiny frown / takes an axe and chops it down.

ROBIN SKELTON, poet, verse on cultural differences, noted in *Memoirs of a Literary Blockhead* (1988).

Now they are slipping across the longest undefended border in the world and buying up U.S. companies, insinuating themselves into show business and the media. And like the pod people in *Invasion of the Body Snatchers*, they are virtually impossible to identify as they take control.

RICHARD STENGEL, journalist, writing tongue-in-cheek about the activities of Canadians in the United States, "The Canadians," *Spy*, Feb. 1988.

If Canadian society is gentler and less garish than American, it is also less competitive, individualistic, creative and, I suspect, less generous. Some of our famous compassion is traceable not to unlimited innate goodness of spirit, but to inhibition and the discreet national reinsurance policy that has arisen from an unjustified lack of national self-confidence.

CONRAD BLACK, capitalist and columnist, *The Globe and Mail's Report on Business Magazine*, 16 April 1988.

When I sought the leadership of my party, five years ago, I said that Canada and the United States were one another's best friend and greatest ally. Nothing in my experience in government — and we have known tensions and serious disagreement — has led me to revise my views about the profound value of an exemplary relationship between two of the world's great democracies.

BRIAN MULRONEY, Prime Minister, addressing a joint sitting of U.S. Congress, 27 April 1988, quoted in *The Toronto Star* the following day.

We're not married, thank heaven, but we are shacked up together.

Attributed to the diplomat and diarist CHARLIES RITCHIE by Robert MacNeil on CBC-TV, Sept. 1988.

George Bush wants a kinder, gentler country: It's called Canada.

Message on signs at a Liberal rally in St. John's, Nfld., referring to U.S. President George Bush and the Free Trade Agreement, 15 Nov. 1988, quoted by David Vienneau in *The Toronto Star* the following day.

Calvin Coolidge once said, "The chief business of the American people is business." But the business of Canada is *not* busi-

ness. It is figuring out how to survive as an independent entity next to the richest and most powerful nation in the history of what passes for civilization. It has done a fair-to-middling job of this for 121 years, and now the bean counters in the Tory countinghouse want to throw in the chips and tear down the border.
ALLAN FOTHERINGHAM, columnist, *Maclean's*, 14 Nov. 1988.

Americans cannot conceive of losing unless there's a conspiracy somewhere. Canadians, constrained by climate, distance and history, see no reason to expect victory.
J.M.S. CARELESS, historian, on national characteristics, quoted by Andrew H. Malcolm in *The New York Times*, 20 Nov. 1988.

There is anti-Americanism in Canada, but not enough to get you elected dogcatcher.
Attributed to Prime Minister BRIAN MULRONEY at the press conference at Baie-Comeau, Que., 22 Nov. 1988, called to celebrate the re-election of the Conservative Party the previous day. As more than one commentator noted on that occasion, dogcatchers are not elected in Canada but appointed.

Best friends or not, the U.S. sometimes acts like the bully on the block. Canadians derive many benefits from their proximity to the U.S., but they have to pay a price for it, too. How high a price remains negotiable, but economic, cultural and political sovereignty must be protected constantly or else be lost. The Loyalists knew that, the Fathers of Confederation knew it, and so, one hopes, do Canadians and their governments in the late 20th century.
J. L. GRANATSTEIN, historian, "Canada and the United States," *The Canadian Encyclopedia* (2nd ed., 1988).

Well, it doesn't take a Ph.D. in psychology to realize that Canadians' mock horror at the thought of becoming part of the United States actually masks a deep desire to do precisely that. They protest too much. Their lips say "no, no" but their eyes say "yes, yes."
MICHAEL KINSLEY, editor of *The New Republic*, *The Toronto Star*, 11 Dec. 1988.

Giant, genteel neighbor: "A camp for grown-ups"
Heading of a feature article on Canada published in the national daily tabloid newspaper *USA Today*, noted by Bob Hepburn in *The Toronto Star*, 30 Dec. 1988.

I didn't come to Canada to be a smart-ass American, and . . . most smart-ass Canadians tend to move to the United States.
Line spoken by an American-born teacher in Toronto from the novel *A Prayer for Owen Meany* (1989) by the U.S. author JOHN IRVING.

It's very American to have opinions as strong as your opinions. It's very Canadian to distrust strong opinions.
Line spoken by an American-born teacher in Toronto from the novel *A Prayer for Owen Meany* (1989) by the U.S. author JOHN IRVING.

C'est fine pour moi.
GEORGE BUSH, newly elected U.S. President, official visit to Canada, responding to Prime Minister Brian Mulroney's invitation for one last question at a press conference, Ottawa, 10 Feb. 1989.

One of the big differences between Americans and Canadians is politeness. The Americans says, "You a — —!" The Canadian says, "What are you, an a — —?"
DAVE BROADFOOT, comedian, quoted by Susan Kastner in *The Toronto Star*, 11 June 1989.

Canadians are the most smug people in the world. Americans are the most arrogant people in the world. That is why the world's longest undefended border separates them. Canadians secretly like the Americans being so arrogant because it enables them to be so smug.

ALLAN FOTHERINGHAM, columnist, *Maclean's*, 3 July 1989.

Like two trains that have moved thousands of miles along parallel railway tracks, they are far from where they started, but they are still separated.
SEYMOUR MARTIN LIPSET, U.S. sociologist, analogy for the differences between Canadians and Americans; comment at a press conference in Toronto, 11 Oct. 1989, announcing the results of a study sponsored by the Canadian-American Committee, reported in *The Globe and Mail* the following day.

Canadians are the world's oldest and most continuing un-Americans. They seek to defend the integrity of Canada against the United States by defining their own country as more humane, more democratic, more anti-imperialistic and more social democratic.
Attributed to SEYMOUR MARTIN LIPSET, U.S. sociologist, press conference in Toronto, 11 Oct. 1989, announcing the results of a study sponsored by the Canadian-American Committee, quoted by Carol Goar in *The Toronto Star*, 19 Oct. 1989.

As the border is gradually razed between inner and outer space, between the aggressive extroversion of the marketplace and the easy sociability of the home, North Americans will need another refuge, a place where nostalgia, for example, could serve as a link with the stability of times gone by. If a U.S. citizen so chose, Canada could become an enormous psychic theme park; something like a Hollywood set that simultaneously links the past with the present, the city with the wilderness. The Province of Quebec seems to have anticipated this role with its recent advertising slogan, "Foreign yet Near." The calculated ambivalence of the Canadian is a most efficient way of maintaining a low profile, as a receptive ground for other people's fantasies.
MARSHALL McLUHAN, communications

theorist, and Bruce R. Powers, communications specialist, authors of *The Global Village: Transformations in World Life and Media in the 21st Century* (1989).

Since the United States has become a world environment, Canada has become the anti-environment that renders the United States more acceptable and intelligible to many small countries of the world; anti-environments are indispensable for making an environment understandable.
MARSHALL McLUHAN, communications theorist, and Bruce R. Powers, communications specialist, authors of *The Global Village: Transformations in World Life and Media in the 21st Century* (1989).

Canada . . . ? That's another world.
Response of an employee of the Encino, California, branch of the U.S. Post Office upon being asked by Anna Sandor and William Gough the postal rate for mailing parcels to Canada, Christmas, 1989.

We are seen in some quarters as a solution in search of a problem. We seem a bit melancholy, even sour, about our lot in life as Canadians — a fate, incidentally, which others with real problems would envy. How ironic it is that others see Canadians in much more positive terms than we often see ourselves.
DEREK BURNEY, Canada's Ambassador to the United States, address, Empire Club of Canada, Toronto, 30 Nov. 1989.

Canada is the cedar chest of America. / And nobody can seem to figure out if / we're haunting their attic or / they're renting our basement apartment.
BILL HOWELL, poet, "Ring around the Moon," *Moonlight Saving Time* (1990).

Thirty years ago we had our noses pressed up against the American dream machine. But since the 1960s Canada has gained self-awareness. And here's the difference: We learn from your mistakes, and you don't learn from our successes.
MICHAEL ADAMS, Toronto-based opin-

ion pollster, quoted by Priit J. Vesilind in *National Geographic*, March 1990.

Viewed from the United States, the differences between Americans and Canadians may seem very minor. Viewed from Canada, they form the crux of an identity. To paraphrase Freud, Canadian identity is a national form of the narcissism of minor difference.
MICHAEL IGNATIEFF, historian, *The New York Times Book Review*, 13 May 1990.

I think the relationship is very strong. And I am determined not to take it for granted. I have found Brian Mulroney to be extraordinarily co-operative.
GEORGE BUSH, U.S. President, on the "special relationship" that exists between President Bush and Prime Minister Brian Mulroney, interviewed by Kevin Doyle and Hilary Mackenzie in *Maclean's*, 25 June 1990.

Throughout my childhood, Canada was always perceived as a more beautiful, unspoiled version of New Hampshire and Maine. We certainly had — I think most Americans had — no sense of any nationalistic differences.
JOHN IRVING, novelist raised in Exeter, N.H., quoted in *Maclean's*, 25 June 1990.

Should Canada and the United States become one country? Are they already one country culturally? I see it as a very basic conflict. It is the expectation of Canada's social system to look after the people who cannot take care of themselves. There is no such expectation in the United States. That is a huge difference between our two countries. And if our two countries were conceivably one day to merge, I do not think that Canada's social welfare system would prevail in the United States. I think that our lack of social consciousness would overrun this country and be rather widely embraced by this country in a hurry.
JOHN IRVING, novelist raised in Exeter, N.H., quoted in *Maclean's*, 25 June 1990.

Canada join the United States? Where would young Canadians run off to for adventure? Where would Americans run to escape?
PETER JENNINGS, Toronto-born ABC anchorman, *Maclean's*, 25 June 1990.

Besides, the Americans don't have to buy us: Brian Mulroney is leasing us out, week by increasing week.
ALLAN FOTHERINGHAM, columnist, *Maclean's*, 25 June 1990.

You're Invited to a / JULY 1 OOTING / and Uncle Sam's Not / If you say oot and aboot . . . and are tired of hearing your national anthem played only at hockey and baseball games . . . and believe Wayne Gretzky should be cannonized . . . and exchanged clean air, nationalized health care and your Bay Company credit Card for grid lock, med flies and goat cheese . . . then you're one of a million Canadians living in Southern California . . . and you're invited to Celebrate Canada Day, on July 1, from 1:30 to 8:30 p.m. at the Police Academy, Picnic Grounds, located at Elysian Park next to Dodger Stadium. Bring a box lunch — there will be games, entertainment, children's activities, exhibits, draws and prizes.
There's never been a better time to express your independence and recognize your Canadian heritage. For more information call. . . .
"Announcement," *The Hollywood Reporter*, 29 June 1990, drawing attention to the annual Canada Day Picnic held in Elysian Park, Los Angeles, California, sponsored by almost a dozen agencies and organizations including the Canadian Society of Southern California, Canadian Consulate General, Canada California Chamber of Commerce, and the provincial governments of Alberta, British Columbia, Ontario, and Quebec.

To pass from the United States to Canada or from Canada to the United States at any of the border crossings is certainly to enter a different world. But this is also true when one passes from Indiana to Kentucky, or Utah to Nevada; or, within Canada, from Ontario to the Maritime provinces of Nova Scotia and New Brunswick (I set aside the special case of Quebec); or within the countries of Europe, from the Côte d'Or to Provence, or the canton of Geneva to the Valais, or from Tuscany to the old Kingdom of Naples, or from Castile to Catalonia.

> J.M. CAMERON, historian, "The New Canadas," *The New York Review of Books*, 16 Aug. 1990.

Starting in the late sixties, our academic-bureaucratic-journalistic elite foisted upon us the replacement myth that Canada was a "more caring and compassionate" society than the U.S., by which they really mean more socialistic. All statistics, as well as personal experience, indicate that Canadians are not more generous than Americans.

> CONRAD BLACK, capitalist and columnist, "Enough Is Enough," *Saturday Night*, Sept. 1990.

In summary, our quest for an identity independent of the Americans has given us a prime rate five points above that of the United States; top tax rates almost twenty points higher; a sharply higher price index; a growing and proportionately much larger public-sector deficit despite the American defence burden; and only seventy per cent of the U.S. standard of living, despite the unique problems of the American black underclass. We are wedded to a redistribution of money between regions and individuals, which makes excessive taxation and public-sector solvency almost inevitable. In Gaullist terms, "We are crossing the desert."

> CONRAD BLACK, capitalist and columnist, "Enough Is Enough," *Saturday Night*, Sept. 1990.

With all our troops in the Middle East, am I the only one worrying about a sneak attack from Canada?

> JAY LENO, U.S. stand-up comedian, re-

mark made during the Gulf Crisis, quoted in "Just What Was Said" in *The Globe and Mail*, 18 Sept. 1990.

It wouldn't take the 10,000 soldiers of the U.S. 10th Mountain light infantry division at Fort Drum, just 80 miles south of Ottawa, more than a few hours to seize the Ottawa area and topple the Canadian government. We can assume that Fort Drum's official assignment sheet doesn't include an "invade Canada" entry; but what if, for the sake of argument, it did?

> Project Ploughshares for the Citizens' Inquiry into Peace and Security, *What Makes Canada Secure: Background Document for the Citizens' Inquiry into Peace and Security in Canada* (1991).

CANADA DAY
See HOLIDAYS

CANADA GOOSE

I saw another memorable sight. My ears advised me of it before my eyes noticed it. From overhead came the most thrilling music in the bird world — the honking of the wild geese. Looking up, I saw about sixty Common Geese flying over the creek. . . .

It is said that Canada Geese, unlike wild duck and most other birds, usually mate for life. Their marriage is a contract entered into and faithfully preserved "until death do us part." It is even claimed that the partnership, in effect, remains binding beyond death and that when either member of it dies the survivor does not pair again.

> MALCOLM MacDONALD, British High Commissioner in Ottawa, *The Birds of Brewery Creek* (1947).

And let us squarely face the dinosaurness of birds and the birdness of the Dinosauria. When the Canada geese honk their way northward, we can say: "The dinosaurs are migrating, it must be spring!"

> ROBERT T. BAKKER, paleontologist, proponent of the theory that dinosaurs were

warm-blooded beasts like present-day birds, which are their sole descendants, *Heresies: New Theories Unlocking the Mysteries of the Dinosaurs and Their Extinction* (1986).

CANADIAN ARMED FORCES
See also DEFENCE
WAR

The military has always been more loyal to Canada than the Canadian government has been loyal to its military.
> PETER WORTHINGTON, journalist who fought in World War II and whose father was a general in the Canadian Army, address, Empire Club of Canada, Toronto, 11 Oct. 1984.

The publicity material alludes to Canada with a sneer: "Who has more submarines than the Canadian Navy? West Edmonton Mall, of course."
> MARK ABLEY, traveller, commenting on advertising for the West Edmonton Mall; publicists for the giant mall had noted that its fleet of imitation submarines was larger than the naval arm of the Canadian Armed Forces, *Beyond Forget: Rediscovering the Prairies* (1986).

Specifically, I would like to see Canada leaving NATO and NORAD, expelling American military units from its soil, turning the armed forces into a corps devoted to cleaning up and preserving the environment, and diverting the vast sums earmarked for replacing obsolete weaponry to two important peaceful purposes: rebuilding our shipping services and our merchant marine so that our products would sail to the world in Canadian ships; and devoting a much higher proportion of the community's wealth to foreign aid, aimed at achieving a situation where the just anger of poor people would no longer remain as a threat to the world's peace.
> GEORGE WOODCOCK, author, contributor to *If I Were Prime Minister* (1987) edited by Mel Hurtig.

Now what? Every year, fewer Canadians are left to remember what is involved in war. No member of the Canadian Forces today fought in the Second World War, and only a few are left who served in Korea. Almost none of Canada's servicemen and women have ever heard a shot fired in anger.
Does that make them and their countrymen eager to test themselves against the other side, whoever that may be?
> J.L. GRANATSTEIN, historian, *The Globe and Mail*, 19 Aug. 1989.

CANADIAN BROADCASTING CORPORATION
See also BROADCASTING
NEWS

I would rather be on the governing board of the Canadian Radio Corporation than on the board of the greatest university in the world, for radio is the greatest university. Everyone belongs to it — and no one can be excluded because they have not passed.
> NELLIE L. McCLUNG, author and member of the board of governors of the early CBC, interview in 1937, quoted by Candace Savage in *Our Nell: A Scrapbook Biography of Nellie L. McClung* (1979).

A proscenium arch across the country.
> J. FRANK WILLIS, broadcaster, commenting on the national role of CBC Radio in the 1940s and 1950s, quoted by Bronwyn Drainie in *Living the Part: John Drainie and the Dilemma of Canadian Stardom* (1988).

The Voice of a Nation, / A View of the World
> Theme of CBC-TV's *25th Anniversary Special,* produced by STAN JACOBSON, 2 Oct. 1977.

Patrick Watson was right. The CBC is the only organization in the world where the milk rises to the top.
> ALLAN FOTHERINGHAM, columnist, quoting Patrick Watson, CBC-trained independent broadcaster, subsequently

appointed CBC Chairman, *Maclean's*, 4 Sept. 1978.

Amidst the myriad of other available voices, I believe that Canadians, now as when public broadcasting was first created in Canada, want at least one clear strong Canadian voice, from coast to coast, on the air waves of their own country.

PIERRE JUNEAU, CBC President, address, Faculty of Law, University of Toronto, 27 Feb. 1985.

The dispassionate objectivity of CBC radio newscasts, rivalled only by that of the BBC, makes it possible for a Canadian to be recognized as an intellectual without his having to learn to read.

ERIC NICOL and DAVE MORE, humorists, *The U.S. or Us: What's the Difference, Eh?* (1986).

Technology is rendering geography meaningless and endangering sovereignty. Satellites have become cultural border-busters. The sad truth is that the new technology has made Canada today a culturally occupied country. If it weren't for the programming of the CBC, we would have practically nothing Canadian on the air in prime time except for news and sports.

KNOWLTON NASH, television executive, *Prime Time at Ten: Behind-the-Camera Battles of Canadian TV Journalism* (1987).

The CBC spends more than a billion dollars a year, mostly taxpayers' money. That works out to about nine cents a day per Canadian, around one-third of the cost of a daily newspaper and certainly much cheaper than a bus fare.

KNOWLTON NASH, television executive, *Prime Time at Ten: Behind-the-Camera Battles of Canadian TV Journalism* (1987).

It must be recognized that the basic move to curtail subsidies to the CBC is a move in the right direction. Unfortunately, the government has not gone far enough and,

in our view, has missed a sterling opportunity to do something truly constructive.

WALTER BLOCK and MICHAEL WALKER, economists with the Fraser Institute, *Lexicon of Economic Thought* (1989).

I wish the CBC would become more elitist than it is, give up the struggle of competing with American networks, and become a PBS kind of station. And aside from presenting the news and hockey and baseball, it should be doing strictly high-quality drama and trying to sell it to the U.S. and England and Australia, instead of doing these imitation sitcoms and soap operas. They have other responsibilities that I believe are very serious. In the North, where distances are so immense and they have no entertainment whatsoever, the CBC has a different role. It's a muddled office they try to fill.

MORDECAI RICHLER, novelist, quoted by Don Gillmor in *Quill & Quire*, July 1989.

The Royal Canadian Air Farce had the best joke so far about the new CBC appointments. They said Patrick Watson had been hired to restore excellence in programming and reaffirm the country's faith in public broadcasting. The other guy, they said, was hired to make sure Watson doesn't have the money to do it.

BRONWYN DRAINIE, cultural commentator, *The Globe and Mail*, 14 Oct. 1989. She was referring to the appointment of the broadcaster Patrick Watson as CBC Chairman and Gérard Veilleux, former Secretary of the Treasury Board, as CBC President.

I called it Radio Iraq. I don't know why we didn't ship it to Baghdad. Both countries would have been ahead.

JOHN CRISPO, political economist, testifying before a CRTC hearing on funding of the CBC and criticizing the Corporation's coverage of the Gulf War, quoted upon his subsequent (and controversial) appointment to the Corporation's Board of Governors by Michael Valpy in *The Globe and Mail*, 4 April 1991.

CANADIAN PACIFIC RAILWAY
See RAILWAYS

CANADIANISM
See also CANADA

Mr. Chairman, I yield to no man the essential and significant abc's of my Canadianism — by ancestry, birth and commitment.
H. ALLAN LEAL, Q.C., address, Empire Club of Canada, Toronto, 18 Jan. 1977.

We're called upon to reflect on the meaning of what it is to be a Canadian and it's hard to find the usual and common characteristics of historical nations. Certainly we're not united by any particular geography: there are no natural boundaries or very few natural boundaries which define our country. We're not all of us linked by a common history. Many Canadians — almost a third of them — have a very recent history as Canadians. They come with their traditions, their hopes and their beliefs from many parts of the world. And we're not united by one race, one ethnic origin — we're not even united by one language.
PIERRE ELLIOTT TRUDEAU, Prime Minister, remarks at a Citizenship Ceremony, Ottawa, 15 Feb. 1977.

The effort to forestall the Canadian Content regulations failed: in January 1971, the CRTC rules became reality. Mention of the CanCon rules still produces — all these years later — glazed looks, exasperated sighs, and mutters of discontent on all sides. At the close of 1988, the president of one Canadian record company angrily wondered out loud why he was part of a deregulation going to Ottawa to demand that FM radio stations meet a 30 percent Canadian Content standard (the figure set for AM stations). Too often, he pointed out, Canadian radio stations met their CanCon requirements at 10:00 at night or early on Sunday mornings in special programs colloquially known in the radio business as "Beaver hours"; Canadian records were not programmed at peak drive-time listening hours; and the 30 percent requirement for AM radio was seen as a maximum to be reached, and never as a minimum to be exceeded.
RICHARD FLOHIL, popular music promoter, "The Biz,"quoted by Peter Goddard and Philip Kamin, editors of *Shakin' All Over: The Rock'N'Roll Years in Canada* (1989).

CANADIANS
See also CANADA
IDENTITY, NATIONAL

Above Everything, We Are Canadian.
Inscription on a scroll held by the life-size statue of SIR GEORGE-ÉTIENNE CARTIER in Jeanne-Mance Park, Montreal, quoted by Keith Hyde and Michael Bradshaw in *Leisure Ways*, Feb. 1989.

You hestitate. The trees are entangled with menace. / The voyage is perilous into the dark interior. / But then your hands go to the thwarts. You smile. And so / I watch you vanish in a wood of heroes, / Wild Hamlet with the features of Horatio.
DOUGLAS LePAN, poet, concluding stanza of the poem "Coureurs de Bois" (1948), *Weathering It: Complete Poems 1948-1987* (1987).

He played a very good game of bridge, golf and tennis; he was an officer in the reserve army of peacetime, he had no interest whatever in any of the arts or in ideas as such; he was unshakably decent, honest, hard-working, and unimaginative. He was typically Canadian.
Description of a character in the novel *Earth and High Heaven* (1944) by the author GWETHALYN GRAHAM.

It was awful. . . . Not that he was any of the things my mother said — he wasn't hateful, or cruel, or cold-hearted, or neurotic. But he seemed to be . . . I don't know . . . a Canadian.
Line of speech from *The War Between the*

Tates (1974), a novel by the U.S. author ALISON LURIE. The long-lost relative turns out to be "a middle-aged Canadian businessman, with a large wife and three small children . . . not very successful or well-educated. He didn't read much. He liked watching hockey, and camping."

The Canadians knew themselves to be strangers in their own land, without being at home anywhere else.
Remark made by a character in the novel *World of Wonders* (1975) by the author ROBERTSON DAVIES.

Who is a Canadian? Well, the political answer is that he is an American who avoided Revolution.
NORTHROP FRYE, literary philosopher, CBC-TV's *Journey without Arrival*, quoted in *The Globe and Mail*, 6 April 1976.

A Canadian is a D.P. with seniority.
DAVE BROADFOOT, comedian, address, Empire Club of Canada, Toronto, 9 March 1978. The term "D.P." for "Displaced Person" fell out of favour in the 1960s.

Some say, "Cast your bread upon the water, and it will return to you one hundred fold." A Canadian says, "What am I going to do with a hundred loaves of wet bread?" And yet if you tell a Canadian he's apathetic, he'll answer, "Who cares?"
DAVE BROADFOOT, comedian, address, Empire Club of Canada, Toronto, 9 March 1978.

The feeling of being a Canadian, that individual feeling, the one we must cultivate, the feeling of being loyal to something which is bigger than the province or the city that we happen to live in or the neighbourhood, that feeling must be based on a protection of the basic rights of a citizen, of the access of that citizen to a fair share of the abundance of wealth in this country and to the richness and diversity of its laws.
EDWARD SCHREYER, Governor General,

Speech from the Throne, House of Commons, 16 April 1980.

Canadians are very good second-bests.
Characteristic remark of the historian ARTHUR LOWER, quoted in his obituary by Alan Barnes in *The Toronto Star*, 8 Jan. 1988.

The energy of Canadian niceness, like the force of Canadian ennui, can be disconcerting to the foreigner.
JAN MORRIS, Welsh travel writer, "Too Nice for Words," *Saturday Night*, Feb. 1988.

It's too late for me to become Canadian, but I can understand the urge to be Canadian.
ANTHONY BURGESS, man-of-letters, remark made in Toronto, 12 May 1988, quoted by H.J. Kirchhoff in *The Globe and Mail*, 13 May 1988.

In today's world, only one person in every 200 is a Canadian.
MARGARET CATLEY-CARLSON, President of CIDA, "Aid: A Canadian Vocation," *Daedalus: Journal of the American Academy of Arts and Sciences*, "In Search of Canada," Fall 1988.

Canadians *want* to be thought boring.
MILES KINGSTON, British humorist, writing in *The Independent*, quoted by Richard Gwyn in *The Toronto Star*, 13 Nov. 1988.

Q. Why does a Canadian cross the road?
A. To get to the middle.
Joke noted by Val Sears, "Ottawa Notebook," *The Toronto Star*, 26 Nov. 1989.

In the welter of statistics about selected ethnic origins (singular or multiple) in the last census, one finding was often overlooked. Of the 25,309,330 people living in Canada in 1986, only 69,065 declared themselves to be Canadians.
CHARLOTTE GRAY, journalist, "Speaking in Tongues," *Saturday Night*, Dec. 1989.

He told the story of the Maritime fisherman carrying a pail of lobsters up from the wharf. Another fisherman warns him that the lobsters might escape because there's no lid on the pail. "Oh, no," says the first fisherman. "These are Canadian lobsters, boys. As soon as one makes it to the top, the others will drag him down."

> Story told by DEREK BURNEY, Canada's Ambassador to the United States, address, Empire Club of Canada, Toronto, 30 Nov. 1989, according to Jim Wilkes in *The Toronto Star*, 1 Dec. 1989.

It's ironic that Canadians, who have been fighting the stereotype of being hewers of wood and drawers of water, should select as their symbol the original hewer of wood and, well, dammer of water. America has the majestic eagle, the Soviet Union the mighty bear. Great Britain gives equal time to ferocious lions and stubborn bulldogs; Frenchmen line up behind a comely and capable-looking Amazon called Liberty. . . . We chose a rat.

> ARTHUR BLACK, broadcaster and humorist, "Our Symbol — The Rat," *That Old Black Magic* (1989).

The basic fact is Canadians, regardless of what language they speak, are a comparatively talented people, in a very rich territory. The geopolitical aspect is exceptional and enviable compared with all but a few countries of the world. We'll succeed if we can realign our political institutions so that Canadians do not live from year to year under the threat of the country cracking up.

> CONRAD BLACK, publisher, quoted by Diane Francis in *Maclean's*, 23 July 1990.

Defeat is the reason we are all foregathered on the best piece of real estate left on the globe.

> JOHN FRASER, editor and columnist, "Diary," *Saturday Night*, Sept. 1990.

CANOES

Paddle your own canoe.

Proverbial expression, which may well be of Canadian origin, that refers to individual effort and responsibility. "A French example is *Pas de lieu Rhône que nous*, which it is hardly necessary to explain makes no sense in French at all, although every word be true Gallic, but by a similar process of reading reveals the proverbial advice 'Paddle your own canoe.'" W.S. Walsh in *Hand-Book of Literary Curiosities* (1892) as quoted by Tony Augarde in *The Oxford Guide to Word Games* (1984).

To see a Birch Canoe managed with that inexpressible ease & composure which is the characteristic of an Indian is the prettiest sight imaginable. A man usually paddles at one end of it & a woman at the other but in smooth water little exertion is wanting & they sit quietly as if to take the air. The Canoe appears to move as if by clockwork. I always wish to conduct a Canoe myself when I see them manage it with such dexterity & grace. A European usually looks awkward & in a bustle compared with the Indians' quiet skill in a Canoe.

> ELIZABETH SIMCOE, diarist and wife of Governor John Graves Simcoe, diary entry, York (Toronto), 14 Sept. 1793, *Mrs. Simcoe's Diary* (1965) edited by Mary Quayle Innis.

The features of big lake travel — the vastness, the few constraints in finding shelter or campsites, and above all the potential peril from the power of big waves and high winds — are guarantees of its solitude, so precious to canoeists. In these days when the rivers are becoming crowded with rafts and canoes, the surest way to be alone with the elements is to travel great lakes, of which Canada has such riches.

> ERIC W. MORSE, historian and canoeist, *Freshwater Saga: Memoirs of a Lifetime of Wilderness Canoeing in Canada* (1987).

I think canoe trips are a bit like childbirth — better remembered than lived through.

> ARTHUR BLACK, broadcaster and hu-

morist, "Our Feathered Janitors," *That Old Black Magic* (1989).

CANUCK

This is a difficult term to typify because it is clearly derogatory and offensive in some cases but not so in others. In eastern Canada and northern New England it is seen as a racial slur by French-Canadians. In western Canada it is used, among other things, as a nickname for a hockey team: the Vancouver Canucks.

> PAUL DICKSON, British writer, *What Do You Call a Person From . . . ? A Dictionary of Resident Names* (1990). Dickinson goes on to note that *The Associated Press Stylebook and Libel Manual* regards the term as a "derogatory racial label" and cautions writers to "avoid the word except in formal names (the Vancouver Canucks . . .) or in quoted matter."

CAPE BRETON ISLAND
See also NOVA SCOTIA

I have travelled around the globe. I have seen the Canadian and the American Rockies, the Andes and the Alps and the Highlands of Scotland; but for simple beauty, Cape Breton Island outrivals them all.

> ALEXANDER GRAHAM BELL, inventor, resident of Cape Breton Island, N.S., quoted by Wes Rataushk in *Silver Highway: A Celebration of the Trans-Canada Highway* (1988).

Nineteen years ago I discovered Cape Breton when I was looking for a place I could afford to take my kids in the summer. I took the map of Nova Scotia and drove to the place with the fewest roads. I figured it would be isolated and I was right. It was years before anyone in the community figured out that I was a celebrity. A couple of years ago I was visiting my neighbour, a farmer who has since passed away. I was in his kitchen buying some cheese. His wife had just bought a piano and she asked me if I would play. He said to her, "Don't ask him to play the piano.

When I go to his house, he doesn't ask me to milk the cows." I thought that was one of the smartest things I had ever heard anyone say. And I didn't play that piano.

> PHILIP GLASS, U.S. composer, quoted in *Saturday Night*, Dec. 1987.

A Cape Breton fishing village is a way of life, a confrontation with the elements, not a tourist attraction.

> STEPHEN BROOK, English travel writer, *Maple Leaf Rag: Travels across Canada* (1987).

Home is Cape Breton, and I'm here to stay.

> RITA MacNEIL, singer and composer and resident of Big Pond, Cape Breton Island, N.S., quoted by Ann Finlayson in *Maclean's*, 7 Nov. 1988.

Cape Breton, Nova Scotia, is a scenic place. Every summer, Canadian tourists descend by the thousands to camp along its beaches and hike its winding trails. There are souvenir shops everywhere, and the gifts they carry — tartan tams, bright plaid ties, bagpiper key chains — proudly advertise the island's Scottish ancestry.

But the tourists seldom stop at Inverness, an old mining town on the western edge of the island. The coal mines began closing in the 1950s, and today Inverness is a desolate place plagued by unemployment and alcoholism. It's easy to buy a six-pack of beer here, but impossible to go to a library or see a movie.

> DEBORAH SOLOMON, U.S. art critic, writing about Richard Serra, American sculptor and sometime resident of Inverness, *The New York Times Magazine*, 15 Oct. 1989.

CAPITAL PUNISHMENT
See also CRIME

They'll never hang me. I'm too rich.

> TONY FRANK, Montreal mobster and murderer, protesting his wealth and not his innocence on the way to the gallows in the 1920s, noted by Eugene Forsey in *A*

Life on the Fringe: The Memoirs of Eugene Forsey (1990). Despite Frank's fate, it was popularly held during the first half of this century (at least until the abolition of capital punishment in 1976) that "nobody with $40,000 was ever hanged in Canada."

CAPITALISM
See also BUSINESS
FREE ENTERPRISE
LABOUR
UNIONS

Economic expansion accompanied by widespread suffering and injustice is not desirable social progress. A society motivated by the drive for private gain and special privilege is basically immoral.
"Winnipeg Manifesto: 1956 Winnipeg Declaration of Principles of the Co-operative Commonwealth Federation," reproduced in *The Decline and Fall of a Good Idea: CCF-NDP Manifestoes 1932 to 1969* (1974) introduced by Michael S. Cross.

To those who object that capitalism is "rooted in human nature," we answer: Possibly, but so was cannibalism. We no longer eat each other. A civilization is within our reach in which we shall no longer exploit each other.
EUGENE FORSEY, constitutional authority, "The Nature of the Canadian Economy," *Social Planning for Canada* (1932).

Capitalism must be replaced by socialism, by national planning of investment, and by the public ownerships of the means of production in the interests of the Canadian people as a whole.
"The Waffle Manifesto: For an Independent Socialist Canada" (1969) reprinted in *The Canadian Forum*, Dec. 1989.

There is not now an independent Canadian capitalism and any lingering pretensions on the part of Canadian businessmen to independence lack credibility.
"The Waffle Manifesto: For an Independent Socialist Canada" (1969) reprinted in *The Canadian Forum*, Dec. 1989.

If market forces operate in the absolute, I am happy to depend on my own teeth and claws. If they are to be modified, I hope that such modifications afford me an advantage, or at least do not impair my competitive capacity.
JOHN J. SHEPHERD, Nordicity Group Ltd., "Government Aid to Industry: A Private Sector Perspective" (1983), *Government and Enterprise in Canada* (1985) edited by K.J. Rea and Nelson Wiseman.

Capitalism is more a tacit acknowledgement of human behaviour than a formal political doctrine. Essentially pragmatic, it has no written constitution to sustain it, nor ideologies which restrict it. But it works. In a million ways it harnesses the dynamics of human potential, from the motivation of old ladies renting out rooms to mighty conglomerates seeking oil in Venezuela, or the hostile waters of Antarctica.
TOM DAVEY, editor and columnist, *All the Views Fit to Print* (1985).

The decline of America since the Second World War, in favour not of a rising Soviet Empire or the Third World, but of advanced capitalism in East Asia and Western Europe, is the greatest political revolution of our times.
JAMES LAXER, political scientist, *Decline of the Superpowers* (1987). Laxer argues this came about because "the United States has rejected the notion of an 'industrial strategy,' of an approach which combines private enterprise with public sector intervention."

It's wonderful to go from Dundas Street to Buckingham Palace, but what is really wonderful is to be lucky enough to live in a country where this is possible. There are many places in the world where, no matter how hard you work or what talents you have, you can't elevate yourself.
EDWIN MIRVISH, businessman and theatre proprietor, raised on Dundas Street in Toronto, upon being made Commander of the British Empire at Buckingham Pal-

ace in London, quoted by Pearl Sheffy Gefen in *The Globe and Mail*, 29 July 1989.

Greed is essential to the proper functioning of our economic system. Of course, we don't call it greed in polite company. On the supply side, we call it hustle or ambition or push-and-shove. On the demand side, we call it consumerism or, playfully, "shop till you drop."

WILLIAM A. DIMMA, corporate executive, address at York University, Toronto, quoted by Michael Valpy in *The Globe and Mail*, 29 Nov. 1989.

Capitalism's ability to "deliver the goods" economically has been much exaggerated. As a political system, it fails miserably to address the ordinary needs and demands of its citizens. As a moral system, it utterly fails to enlist people's will to a shared freedom, to justice, to equality, to community, or to love. If the best democratic socialism can offer is "a little more of this and a little more of that," we might as well pack our bags and call it a day.

BOB RAE, NDP leader, address, "A Socialist's Manifesto," *The Globe and Mail*, 1 Oct. 1990.

CARIBBEAN ISLANDS

A few years ago there was talk on Parliament Hill of annexing the Turks-Caicos Islands as our eleventh province. Do you know where the Turks-Caicos Islands are? They are the last week's pearls in a necklace called the Bahama Islands stretching languorously down into the Caribbean just north of Cuba and Haiti. Ottawa decided to curb any talk of such annexation. Wisely, I think. The Turks-Caicos are just tiny little buttons of coral, quite incapable of supporting twenty-five million snow-spooked Northerns each winter.

ARTHUR BLACK, broadcaster, "Winter," *Basic Black: The Wit and Whimsy of Arthur Black* (1981).

The Atlantic Provinces have a long history of trade (fish for rum and sugar) with the Caribbean. Halifax is closer to Kingston than to Vancouver, and the Bank of Nova Scotia opened a branch in Jamaica's capital before it had one in Toronto. The Commonwealth Caribbean is special for Canadians — it may be the only place on earth where Americans are asked what province they come from.

MARGARET CATLEY-CARLSON, President of CIDA, "Aid: A Canadian Vocation," *Daedalus: Journal of the American Academy of Arts and Sciences*, "In Search of Canada," Fall 1988.

CARIBOU

I seldom grow fat / eating this grey moss.

Ojibwa poem, "Caribou's Song," *Songs of the Great Land* (1989) edited by John Robert Colombo.

CARTOON ART
See COMIC ART

CATHOLICISM
See also BELIEF

I had some bitter seasons. I remember that when I was about ten I got into my head that the Catholic church was the only right one and that outside its pale all were heretics doomed to penal fires! I got these ideas out of a sample copy of a newspaper called "The Catholic World" which had been sent to the postmaster. Its statements were so dogmatic that they impressed me as authoritative. How I suffered because of this! It seems both funny and pitiful to me now. But it was real and inexorable then. And I was so miserably *alone.*

L. M. MONTGOMERY, author, journal entry, 7 Oct. 1897, Cavendish, P.E.I., *The Selected Journals of L.M. Montgomery: Volume I: 1889-1910* (1985) edited by Mary Rubio and Elizabeth Waterston.

The story of the Jesuit missionaries to Canada is not only a great act in the national drama . . . it is a saga of the human race.

E.J. PRATT, poet, address, 21 Nov. 1940, quoted by David G. Pitt in *E.J. Pratt: The Master Years, 1927-1964* (1987).

So it is that the profound and penetrating influence of liberal, Hegelian, Marxist, and romantic theories of history have been met by a firmer affirmation of the organic structure and functions of the Church, by a long series of social encyclicals, by calls to Catholic action, by a fuller advertence to collective responsibility, and by a deep and widespread interest in the doctrine of the Mystical Body.

BERNARD J.F. LONERGAN, Jesuit philosopher, *Insight: A Study of Human Understanding* (2nd ed., 1958).

The Devil can't stand a good Catholic girl / That's the kind he likes to tempt the most / So remember when you're dancing close / To leave room for the Holy Ghost.

MARIE-LYNN HAMMOND, songwriter and performer, "Leave Room for the Holy Ghost," quoted by Ellen Schwartz in *Born a Woman: Seven Canadian Women Singer-Songwriters* (1988).

The French won't take over and neither will the Pope, although he's not the menace he used to be.

PIERRE ELLIOTT TRUDEAU, Prime Minister, remark made at an Ottawa press conference, 25 Nov. 1976, quoted by Hugh Winsor in *The Globe and Mail* the following day.

Kneeling to receive Communion is not a criminal offence.

Ruling of the Supreme Court of Canada against the arrest of Roman Catholics in Nova Scotia for "disturbing the solemnity of a church service" by refusing to follow the new directive to stand while receiving the Eucharist, reported 30 Sept. 1985 and reproduced by James B. Simpson in *Simpson's Contemporary Quotations* (1988).

In a 1908 declaration, Pope Pius X mentioned the special link between the French-Canadian people who went forth into the New World and the man who went into the wilderness to prepare for the coming of Christ.

PATRICIA POIRIER, journalist, explaining the special regard held by the Quebec people for St. John the Baptist, *The Globe and Mail*, 23 June 1990.

CBC
See CANADIAN BROADCASTING CORPORATION

CCF
See NEW DEMOCRATIC PARTY

CENSORSHIP
See also BOOKS
NEWS
OBSCENITY
PORNOGRAPHY

The Bishop of Caps, who resides in this village, came to wait on Col. Simcoe. He is a man more esteemed for his learning than his Religion, being once accused of having Voltaire's works in his library, he replied, "Les meilleurs medicins tiennent les poisons en leur boutique."

ELIZABETH SIMCOE, diarist and wife of Governor John Graves Simcoe, diary entry, Quebec City, 8 June 1792, *Mrs. Simcoe's Diary* (1965) edited by Mary Quayle Innis.

Vile literature is secretly and widely circulated in Canada, literature of a character calculated to undermine the morals of the people, and entail the most disastrous consequences on society. Improper and obscene, or semi-obscene literature is imported into this country and openly sold. Drugs and instruments for procuring abortion and for kindred purposes are advertised secretly and are sold by agents, and this abuse cannot very readily be reached by the law as it now stands.

JOHN CHARLTON, M.P. for North Norfolk, address delivered in the House of Commons in 1892, as quoted by Angus McLaren and Arlene Tigar McLaren in *The*

Bedroom and the State: The Changing Practices and Politics of Contraception and Abortion in Canada, 1880-1980 (1986) who noted, "No one countered Charlton's sensational assertions."

Not all banned books are great. Some are trivial, and would die soon anyway — the sooner if not honoured by the public executioner. The death-rate of books is terrific. Our duty is to promote circulation of the best, not to go on lynching parties for trash.
>WILLIAM ARTHUR DEACON, literary critic, "Sh-h-h . . . Here Comes the Censor!" (1940), reprinted by Clara Thomas and John Lennox in *William Arthur Deacon: A Canadian Literary Life* (1982).

Literature, we say, is conscious mythology; it creates an autonomous world that gives us an imaginative perspective on the actual one. The only way to forestall the work of criticism is through censorship, which has the same relation to criticism that lynching has to justice.
>NORTHROP FRYE, literary critic, quoted by Richard Kostelanetz, "The Literature Professors' Literature Professor," *The Michigan Quarterly Review*, Fall 1978.

It is usually better to permit a piece of trash than to suppress a work of art.
>A. ALAN BOROVOY, General Counsel, Canadian Civil Liberties Assocation, *When Freedoms Collide: A Case for Our Civil Liberties* (1988).

Canada's main contribution to the Rushdie affair was a joke making the rounds that romance publisher Harlequin would be "putting out his next novel, *The Satanic Nurses*."
>BEVERLEY SLOPEN, book columnist, reporting gossip from the Frankfurt Book Fair concerning the Iranian death threat on Salman Rushdie for writing *The Satanic Verses*, *The Toronto Star*, 28 Oct. 1989.

If you aim for the Marquis de Sade you hit Margaret Laurence very time.
>Comment on censorship attributed to the novelist MARIAN ENGEL on CBC Radio's *Morningside*, 2 April 1991.

CENTRAL CANADA
See ONTARIO
QUEBEC

CHANCE

Tails never turns up. It's as if everyone's using two-headed coins.
>Comment of a character in the play *The Half of It* by JOHN KRIZANC, included in *Twenty Years at Play* (1990) edited by Jerry Wasserman.

CHANGE

In times of panic, chaos or rapid change, the bizarre becomes acceptable.
>FRANK OGDEN, futurologist, "Ogden's Ninth Law," *Dr. Tomorrow's Lessons from the Future* (Oct. 1988).

We do not promote real change until we see the ways in which we are the victimizers. We *must* see this and I think the unifying thing for all our babel of voices in North America would be for us to join forces as the victimizers that we are in relation to the Third World, in relation to the ecology and all of these things.
>JOY KOGAWA, author, interviewed by Magdalene Redekop, *The Canadian Forum*, Nov. 1989.

The Chinese have a sophisticated understanding of the crisis of change. In their written character symbol for "crisis," they combine the images of "danger" and "hidden opportunity." This expresses a philosophy that change, though dangerous, also holds the promise of new opportunities.
>FRANK FEATHER, futurologist, *G-Forces: Reinventing the World — The 35 Global Forces Restructuring Our World* (1989).

I want to cause what an Inuit acquaintance of mine once described as "constructive damage to the status quo."
> GÉRARD VEILLEUX, CBC President, principal author of the CBC's statement of purpose called "Mission, Values, Goals, and Objectives," *The Toronto Star*, 11 Oct. 1990.

CHARACTER

Character, like a photograph, develops in darkness.
> YOUSUF KARSH, portrait photographer, quoted in *Parade*, 3 Dec. 1978.

CHARITY
See also PHILANTHROPY

The less worldly philanthropists . . . often gave anonymously and without publicity. The extreme of philanthropic bad taste was reached in 1914 with the naming of Timothy Eaton Memorial Church in Toronto.
> MICHAEL BLISS, historian, discussing well-publicized philanthropic acts, including the naming of what has come to be called "Timothy Eaton & All Saints," *Northern Enterprise: Five Centuries of Canadian Business* (1987).

CHARLOTTETOWN
See also PRINCE EDWARD ISLAND

The Cradle of Confederation
> Epithetical reference to Charlottetown, P.E.I., which in 1864 hosted the first of the conferences that led three years later to the Confederation of the Dominion of Canada.

CHARTER OF RIGHTS
See also CONSTITUTION

The Charter reflects how the dialogue over rights has escaped beyond the boundaries of the traditional English-French duality. The political battle over the Charter fully engaged the women's movement, the ethnic communities of Canada, the disabled, and the aboriginal people. Thus, it signified a major broadening of the field of human and civil rights in Canada and in this way brought the constitutional, indeed the entire political, framework into greater conformity with the far more pluralistic and heterogeneous society that Canada has become.
> LLOYD AXWORTHY, M.P., "The Federal System — An Uncertain Path," *Daedalus: Journal of the American Academy of Arts and Sciences*, "In Search of Canada," Fall 1988. The Charter of Rights and Freedoms is part of the Constitution Act of 1982. Axworthy refers to the "Charter generation" of Canadians who demand new laws legislating equality and further enlightened programs and, generally, greater public entitlement.

CHILD ABUSE
See also CHILDREN

How we, as a society, respond to these deaths is a measure of our humanity.
> CYRIL GREENLAND, psychiatric social worker, *Preventing CAN Deaths: An International Study of Deaths Due to Child Abuse and Neglect* (1987).

CHILDREN
See also CHILD ABUSE

Through this, and other observations, I arrived at the little equation I hold to be true: an unhappy childhood can result in good; a happy childhood cannot but result in good.
> PATRICIA JOUDRY, playwright, . . . *And the Children Played* (1975).

The fetus can see, hear, experience, taste and, on a primitive level, even learn *in utero* (that is, in the uterus — before birth). Most importantly, he can *feel* — not with an adult's sophistication, but feel nonetheless.
> THOMAS VERNY, psychiatrist, *The Secret Life of the Unborn Child* (1981) written with John Kelly.

The challenge facing Canadian adults can be summed up in the succinct line on a plaque hanging in a school principal's office: "We give our children roots — and wings."

REGINALD W. BIBBY and DONALD C. POSTERSKI, sociologists, *The Emerging Generation: An Inside Look at Canada's Teenagers* (1985).

In recent decades, Quebec has made French the language of the public service and of the workplace. It has offered $4,500 in baby bonuses for each baby born to families that already have two children, to raise the birth rate from 1.47 births per woman of child-bearing age.

Editorial, *The Globe and Mail*, 7 Nov. 1989.

A child isn't a man, you can always get another man.

Comment of a character in the play *Under the Skin* by playwright BETTY LAMBERT, included in *Twenty Years at Play* (1990) edited by Jerry Wasserman.

Teenagers! Tired of Being Hassled by Your Stupid Parents? Act Now! Move Out, Get a Job, Pay Your Own Bills . . . While You Still Know *Everything*. (Sponsored by the Parents, Grandparents and Great-Grandparents of America and Canada.)

Photocopy lore in circulation at Centennial College, Scarborough, Ont., Aug. 1990.

CHINESE PEOPLE

Not a Chinaman's chance.

This expression is said to be of Canadian origin, dating back to the importation of Chinese labourers to work on the CPR in the 1880s. Specifically, it relates to the fact that Chinese were given the task of laying the explosive charges, a job that had a high turnover.

I have always yearned to go to Gold Mountain. / But instead it was hell, full of hardships. / I was detained in a prison and tears rolled down my cheeks. / My wife at home is longing for my letter, / Who can foretell when I will be able to return home? / I cannot sleep because my heart is filled with hate. / When I think of the foreign barbarians / My anger will rise sky high. / They put me in jail and make me suffer this misery. / I will moan until the early dawn, / But who will console me here?

Lines said to be carved in Mandarin Chinese in the wall of an immigration building in Victoria, B.C., 1919, quoted by Richard Thomas Wright in *In a Strange Land: A Pictorial Record of the Chinese in Canada 1788-1923* (1988).

In the Mandarin language, the printed characters for peace may be translated as "rice in the mouth" and "a roof over your head." The People's Republic of China was furnishing both to its people . . . [yet] there is a third meaning to the Chinese character for peace — two hearts beating together in understanding, friendship, harmony, and love.

LOIS WILSON, Christian activist, quoting in part the etymology for the Chinese word for "peace" offered by a Chinese friend, *Turning the World Upside Down: A Memoir* (1989).

I still don't understand how one billion Chinese manage to get along, living upside down like that.

ARTHUR BLACK, broadcaster and humorist, "Kinky Sects," *That Old Black Magic* (1989).

CHRÉTIEN, JEAN

In 1990 Mr. Chrétien will make his move towards power. He will become more vocal about stopping Meech Lake. The question is: are his efforts too little, too late? I do not think so. Chrétien is not yet ready to roll over and die. He has a major struggle ahead over the next three years, after which he is in an excellent position to win an election. If he captures the leadership of the Liberal Party, he will control it with great strength.

ROBIN ARMSTRONG, professional astrologer, *Robin Armstrong's Astrological Almanac: 1990* (1989).

Yesterday's man.
JEAN CHRÉTIEN was characterized as "yesterday's man" in 1988-90 by Conservative critics and fellow Liberal leadership contenders like Paul Martin Jr. and Sheila Copps. They dismissed Chrétien as someone who offered only yesterday's tired answers to today's pressing problems. Apparently Chrétien's extensive parliamentary experience, and his stint as Trudeau's Minister of Finance, was a handicap. Chrétien was elected Liberal leader in Calgary on 23 June 1990, at which time his supporters quipped, "Yesterday's man . . . tomorrow's leader."

Chrétien is completely disconnected from the new Quebec, and Trudeau is living on another planet. I remember telling my friends in Toronto that the election of Pierre Trudeau was the worst mistake English Canada ever made; the choice of Jean Chrétien will be the last mistake.
SERGE SAUCIER, founder with Claude Castonguay of the Quebec-based Association in Favour of Meech Lake, quoted by Peter C. Newman in *Maclean's*, 13 Aug. 1990.

CHRISTIANITY
See also BELIEF
CATHOLICISM

1. Thou shalt not have more Gods but me.
2. Before no idol bow thy knee.
3. Take not the name of God in vain:
4. Nor dare the sabbath day profane.
5. Give both thy parents honour due.
6. Take heed that thou no murder do.
7. Abstain from words and deeds unclean:
8. Nor steal, though thou art poor and mean.
9. Nor make a wilful lie, nor love it:
10. What is thy neighbour's, dare not covet.
The Ten Commandments in rhyme, *Collection of Hymns for the Use of Native Christians of the Iroquois, To Which are Added a Few Hymns in the Chippeway Tongue: Translated by Peter Jones* (1827), quoted by Donald B. Smith in *Sacred Feathers: The Reverend Peter Jones (Kahkewaquonaby) & the Mississauga Indians* (1987).

To bridge the Jewish-Christian gulf which Hitler has succeeded in creating is a task of incalculable importance, and at a Jewish-Christian colloquium prior to the events of May 1967 I attempted a hesitant step in that direction. I said there that if every Christian in Hitler's Europe had followed the example of the King of Denmark and decided to put on the yellow star, there would today be neither confusion nor despair in the church, nor talk of the death of God. I said with every emphasis at my command that, as a Jew after Auschwitz, I did not and could not speak as a judge, but only as a witness.
EMIL FACKENHEIM, philosopher, "Jews and Christians after Auschwitz" (1978), *The Jewish Thought of Emily Fackenheim: A Reader* (1987) edited by Michael L. Morgan.

CHRISTMAS
See HOLIDAYS

CHURCH
See BELIEF

CITIES & TOWNS
See also PLACES

See also the following cities with entries of their own: CALGARY, CHARLOTTETOWN, EDMONTON, FREDERICTON, HALIFAX, MONTREAL, NIAGARA FALLS, OTTAWA, QUEBEC CITY, REGINA, SAINT JOHN, ST. JOHN'S, TORONTO, VANCOUVER, VICTORIA, WHITEHORSE, WINNIPEG, YELLOWKNIFE

For Canada, by and large, is still a nation of small towns. Toronto, for all its sprawling size, has a small-town psychology. So, when it comes down to it, does Montreal; in this city we still have a great deal of the intimate small-town knowledge of life which New York and London lack. It has made us shrewder than we realize.

> HUGH MacLENNAN, essayist and novelist, "If You Drop a Stone . . . ," *The Other Side of Hugh MacLennan* (1978).

Calgary, Edmonton and Vancouver are surely the three most interesting cities in Canada. Every one of them is full of people trying to define a new version of urban. At the core of that new version there's going to have to be a new definition of the male/female relationship.

> ROBERT KROETSCH, novelist, interviewed by Alan Twigg in *Strong Voices: Conversations with Fifty Canadian Authors* (1988).

If there is anything worse than a second-city complex, which Chicago has, it's two cities which have a second-city complex about each other.

> ROGER EBERT, film personality, discussing the rivalry between Montreal and Toronto, hosts of the competing Montreal World Film Festival and Toronto's Festival of Festivals, appearing on the TV's *David Letterman Show*, quoted by Stephen Godfrey in *The Globe and Mail*, 20 Sept. 1989.

If Toronto is Canada's most important metropolis and Montreal its most complex, then Vancouver is certainly the city with the brightest future.

> ALAN F.J. ARTIBISE, planning consultant, "Canada as an Urban Nation," *Daedalus: Journal of the American Academy of Arts and Sciences*, "In Search of Canada," Fall 1988.

I do not care how many blocks there are in a city, for I am interested in the city block by block.

> DAVID WARREN, editor and columnist, "Notebook," *The Idler*, No. 28, March-April 1990.

If Toronto serves in North America as a model for good planning, with safe neighbourhoods and an active downtown core, this is as much a result of good luck and competent city administration as of the efforts of planners.

> EDWARD RELPH, geographer, *The Toronto Guide: The City / Metro / The Region* (Annual Conference, Association of American Geographers, Toronto, April 1990).

In Ontario almost all town halls, etc., face south; why? Is this custom more widespread?

> EDWARD RELPH, geographer, *The Toronto Guide: The City/Metro/The Region* (Annual Conference, Association of American Geographers, Toronto, April 1990).

CIVILIZATION

At present it casts the shadow of a Frankenstein monster; our creature, it may yet make us its creature and wreck both us and itself. Is it because this great civilization, like Frankenstein's monster, is soulless?

> MARY MAXWELL, a.k.a. Ruhíyyíh Khánum, leading member of the Bahá'í Faith, referring to Western civilization, *Prescription for Living* (1950). Maxwell, born in Montreal, is a leading figure in the faith.

CLARK, JOE

Certainly he's living proof that power is not always an aphrodisiac.

> CHARLOTTE GRAY, journalist, *Saturday Night*, July 1989.

CLASS, SOCIAL
See also The ESTABLISHMENT
SOCIETY

Indeed, Canada has a deep-rooted suspicion of class-based systems of any kind. Private schools are a minor part of the educational picture, private universities are nonexistent, and public transportation is all single-class, with the exception of the airlines (why?). Canada may not be a classless society, but Canadians are strongly attached to the belief that it is.

ROBERT G. EVANS, economist and health-care specialist, "'We'll Take Care of It for You': Health Care in the Canadian Community," *Daedalus: Journal of the American Academy of Arts and Sciences*, "In Search of Canada," Fall 1988.

In contrast to the American melting pot, Canada has been described as a vertical mosaic: a minuscule Anglo-Celtic elite at the top, supplemented in recent times by even smaller French-Canadian and Jewish elites, with, in descending order on the social totem pole, other English and French Canadians, Northern Europeans who assimilated quickly, Eastern and Southern Europeans, Asians, Latin Americans, blacks, and at the bottom, the aboriginals.

WILLIAM KILBOURN, historian, "The Peaceable Kingdom Still," *Daedalus: Journal of the American Academy of Arts and Sciences*, "In Search of Canada," Fall 1988.

CLIMATE
See also WEATHER

In climate, Canada is one big cold front, waiting to descend on the States and ruin the crops. Temperatures are colder because they come from Celsius, a miserable place in the Yukon.

ERIC NICOL and DAVE MORE, humorists, *The U.S. or Us: What's the Difference, Eh?* (1986).

I'm shaped by the Canadian climate and ecology, as I think we all will be. Ultimately that's the thing that will give the real character of the country. We will, of course, be influenced by different peoples, but in the end we'll be shaped by living in this cold climate and coming to terms with it.

R. MURRAY SCHAFER, composer, interviewed by Ulla Colgrass in *For the Love of Music* (1988).

CLOTHES
See FASHION

CLOUDS

Don't you ever, you up in the sky / don't you ever get tired / of having the clouds between you and us?

Clayoquot poem, "Sun," *Songs of the Great Land* (1989) edited by John Robert Colombo.

COLLEGES & UNIVERSITIES
See also EDUCATION

And I believe that the function of a university is to be counter-technical, subversive, iconoclastic; that it sets out to shatter assumptions and prejudices. A university can provide a kind of shock-treatment: it may annihilate a person and force him to make himself over into what he is, in the dawning knowledge of what he is not, and of what life is.

GEORGE WHALLEY, educator, address at Rothesay College School, Rothesay, N.B., 1959, *George Whalley: Remembrances* (1989) edited by Michael D. Moore.

Instead of going to college, go to work.

GORDON SHRUM, physicist and educator, address, B.C. School Trustees Association, Penticton, Oct. 1966, *An Autobiography* (1986) written with Peter Stursberg, edited by Clive Cocking.

While I am getting my B.A., I should be learning the rest of the alphabet.

Characteristic remark heard in the halls of Rochdale College, Toronto's alternative university in the 1960s, noted by David Sharpe in *Rochdale: The Runaway College* (1987).

The story is told of an absent-minded professor who lived on Toronto Island. One morning, he rushed down to dockside and saw the ferry about two feet out from the dock. He flung his briefcase aboard and, with a heroic leap, landed on board in a heap. Looking up with a benign smile, he gasped: "I made it." To which one of the hands replied: "Yes, sir, but why didn't you wait until we docked?"

> H. IAN MACDONALD, President, York University, address, Empire Club of Canada, Toronto, 17 April 1975.

TUKU

> Message on a T-shirt in the late 1970s, referring to the so-called University of Tuktoyaktut, seen in Calgary and Edmonton, according to Jim Lyon in *Dome: The Rise and Fall of the House that Jack Built* (1983).

If Canadian universities are underfunded so badly that they can no longer function effectively, Canada would disappear overnight from modern history and become again what it was at first, a blank area of natural resources to be exploited by more advanced countries. This is not empty rhetoric: it is a veritable fact, though I should not care to become known as the person who verified it.

> NORTHROP FRYE, literary critic, address, Empire Club of Canada, Toronto, 19 Jan. 1984.

Canadian schools are subject to brain drain. Luckily, the drain backs up often enough to maintain the level of American professors.

> ERIC NICOL and DAVE MORE, humorists, *The U.S. or Us: What's the Difference, Eh?* (1986).

Typically, students have to choose between large schools with good professors but no friends, or small schools with lots of friends but bad professors.

> LINDA FRUM, journalist, *Linda Frum's Guide to Canadian Universities* (1987).

The reason universities are so full of knowledge is that the students come with so much and they leave with so little.

> MARSHALL McLUHAN, communications theorist, quoted by Fred Thompson in "Monday Night Sessions," *Antigonish Review*, Summer-Autumn 1988. Thompson

noted: "An immediate burst of laughter revealed that many people had been caught off guard. They knew it was funny, but they didn't know why and McLuhan wasn't about to tell them. He was merely pushing people to discover the hidden ground which surrounded them. He hadn't invented the joke, he had merely uncovered it."

I don't know what universities are for if not the ferment of ideas and the expression of advocacy.

> STEPHEN LEWIS, public figure, Distinguished Visitor at the University of Toronto, quoted in *UC: University College Alumni Magazine*, Fall 1988.

One was from Vancouver Island, where a collector of malapropisms recalls a blimpish acquaintance of his, sipping pink gin on the verandah of a tennis club and gazing out on the well-wooded campus of the University of Victoria. "Ah," he murmured, "the groves of macadmia."

> DAVID MacDONALD, journalist, "Anecdotes," *The Toronto Star*, 10 Dec. 1988.

COLOMBIA

As I sit in my Toronto home, I am 2,740 miles south of the northern tip of Ellesmere Island, Canada's northernmost land for all practical purposes. If I swivel my chair and look directly south, there, a bit over the horizon but the same distance away, is Bogotá, the capital of Colombia. The District of Columbia, in contrast, is a mere hour's travel by jet.

> F. KENNETH HARE, geographer, "Canada: The Land," *Daedalus: Journal of the American Academy of Arts and Sciences*, "In Search of Canada," Fall, 1988.

COLONIALISM
See also BRITISH EMPIRE & COMMONWEALTH

To live in English Canada is, like it or not, to absorb the profound insecurity and the profounder mimicry of a colonized nation.

I often have to battle a British colonialism within myself, a quality from which most of Canada has escaped; but escape has led it only to a grovelling dependence on the U.S.A. "When you get right down to it," according to the afternoon's Winnipeg *Free Press*, "the most important Canadian TV people could be the handful of executives who visit California in May to decide what imports you'll see on the screens in the coming months and years."

MARK ABLEY, traveller, *Beyond Forget: Rediscovering the Prairies* (1986).

COMEDY

I'm the tall one.

FRANK SHUSTER, comedian, distinguishing himself from his partner Johnny Wayne (the short one), quoted by Ed Gould in *Entertaining Canadians: Canada's International Stars 1900-1988* (1988).

If I wanted to be controversial, I'd become a terrorist.

JOHNNY WAYNE, comedian, remark made in 1986, quoted by Bill Brioux in *TV Guide*, 25 Aug. 1990.

COMIC ART

It is clear that in many cases parents have no idea of the effect the reading of this muck — for that is what it is — can have on the minds of children. I cannot say too strongly that I think these two unfortunate boys have been strongly influenced by what they have been reading. I would like to see a concerted effort to wipe out this horrible and weird literature with which children are filling their heads.

A.W. McCLELLAN, Crown Prosecutor, Juvenile Court, Dawson Creek, Y.T., speaking in 1948 at the trial of two juvenile boys, quoted by the psychiatrist Fredric Wertham in *Seduction of the Innocent* (1953). Earlier that year the boys, aged thirteen and eleven, stole a rifle from a parked car and shot and killed a local farmer for no discernible reason — other than the fact (determined by the Department of Health and Welfare) that they were voracious readers of crime comics. "Although the number of comic books in Canada is infinitely smaller than in the United States, the problem was recognized there with far more seriousness," claimed Wertham, a foe of violence in comic books. He makes an appearance (via archival footage) in Ron Cohen's documentary film *Comic Book Confidential* (1988).

Comics, like TV, reinforced the notion that Canada was a backwater. In fact, comics were a welcome escape from our own culture's seeming dullness. Life in America, we just knew, was more exciting. Superman might visit his Fortress of Solitude in our Arctic from time to time, but never Toronto or Montreal, let alone Halifax where I lived.

JOHN BELL, researcher, "Yes, There Are Canadian Comics," *Canuck Comics* (1986) edited by John Bell.

Herman goes into an ice cream store, and they've got over a thousand flavours. So he says, "Gimme a vanilla," and the guy gives him a cone of thick, black ice cream with hair sticking out! So Herman says, "That's not vanilla," and the guy says, "Oh, I thought you said gorilla!" I got hundreds of letters from people who said they couldn't stop laughing at that one. That makes you feel good.

JIM UNGER, one-time cartoonist for the *Mississauga Times*, creator of the cartoon character Herman, recalling his favourite Herman cartoon, quoted in Coles *Booktalk*, Christmas 1990.

COMIC BOOKS & STRIPS
See COMIC ART

COMMERCE
See BUSINESS

COMMONWEALTH
See BRITISH EMPIRE &
      COMMONWEALTH

COMMUNICATIONS
See also BROADCASTING
TELEPHONE

Bliss was it in that dawn to be alive . . . [the] story goes back to the 1960s and the beginnings of the great decade of liberation. The scene is Toronto, for a brief period the intellectual centre of the world. There, a new theory was born, the theory of the primacy of communication in the structuring of human cultures and the human mind. In fact the origins of this theory may be sought ten years earlier in the work of the Toronto economist Harold Innis, *The Bias of Communication* (1951), but it was only in 1962-3 that three simultaneous publications presented a coherent picture of the views of the "Toronto School." They were [Eric A.] Havelock's *Preface to Plato*, *The Gutenberg Galaxy* by Marshall McLuhan, and an extended article by Jack Goody and Ian Watt called "The Consequences of Literacy."

Although each work offered its own modifications and developments, the basic theory appeared simple and universal: the most fundamental factor in the cultural progress of man was change in the modes of communication. The crucial question is not what is transmitted but how it is transmitted — in the famous slogan of McLuhan, the Medium is the Message.
> OSWYN MURRAY, Oxford historian, referring to the Toronto School of Communications in a review of recent publications in the field of communications theory which paid particular attention to the relationship between orality and literacy, *The Times Literary Supplement*, 16 June 1989.

Electronic reality compels us to live mythically and in depth, in a world of symbolic resonances, voices of the past, vibrations of an apocalyptic future, rushing through the vacuum of a meaningless present.
> FRANK ZINGRONE, communications theorist, "Communications and a New Humanism," *In Search: The Canadian Communications Quarterly*, Winter 1981.

In Canada, we've got a bizarre track record of producing the very technology that comes back to haunt us. We're the nation that's been the leader in satellite technology, yet it's that technology that is undermining the integrity and economic viability of the Canadian system, because there's never been sufficient funding for the software.
> TOM McPHAIL, communications studies, University of Calgary, quoted by Paul McLaughlin in *TV Guide*, 13 Nov. 1982.

Teleconferencing and conference calls are poor substitutes for handshakes.
> F. KENNETH HARE, geographer, "Canada: The Land," *Daedalus: Journal of the American Academy of Arts and Sciences*, "In Search of Canada," Fall 1988.

Today, the whole world is becoming a satellite dish, where everything that is knowable is known instantly and collectively. Nothing can be hidden.
> FRANK FEATHER, futurologist, *G-Forces: Reinventing the World — The 35 Global Forces Restructuring Our World* (1989).

As a community we should look at what the new technologies of message-forming and -transmitting do to our own real world of technology and democracy. This is why I have a sense of urgency to map the real world of technology, so we might see how in our social imagination the near is disadvantaged over the far. We should also understand that this does not have to be so.
> URSULA FRANKLIN, scientist, *The Real World of Technology* (1990), as excerpted in *The Canadian Forum*, July-Aug. 1990.

COMMUNISM
See also SOVIET UNION

You can't defect from hell to paradise.
> SVETLANA GOUZENKO, widow of Soviet defector Igor Gouzenko, explaining that in 1945 what the Gouzenko family did was

escape — not defect, quoted by John Picton in *The Toronto Star*, 5 Feb. 1989.

Even if communism were temporarily victorious it doesn't carry with it such a hopeless teleology of tyranny — even if tyrannical in its present phase — as did Nazism. In short anything [that] is a revolution must keep moving or it doesn't revolute: by its very nature it contains within it the seeds of its own destruction, so by 1989, say, everything ought to be hunky dory, all of which certainly doesn't make it any easier to live in 1950.
MALCOLM LOWRY, British-Canadian novelist, letter about the consequences of the Cold War written to a Canadian friend, Dec. 1950, quoted by Gordon Bowker in "Letters," *The Times Literary Supplement*, 29 June 1990. Bowker sees this passage as a prophetic anticipation of the collapse of communism through its internal contradictions four decades in the future.

Communism can be felt. . . . Any definition would prevent the application of the law.
Attributed to Quebec Premier MAURICE DUPLESSIS in passing the Act Respecting Communistic Propaganda (the infamous Padlock Act) when it was pointed out to him that the Act included no definition of Communism, according to Eugene Forsey in *A Life on the Fringe: The Memoirs of Eugene Forsey* (1990).

Stalinist communism is dead. The dogmatic, totalitarian state is deader. But we don't know what kind of new totalitarianism will arise or how it will adjust and evolve. So you can't say communism is completely dead.
FRANKLYN GRIFFITHS, academic, University of Toronto, quoted in *The Toronto Star*, 30 Sept. 1989.

Communists will have a long time roaming in the wilderness until they find their place again. But I wouldn't rule them out. The problems of history are not over. Boredom is not the future. In a world of turmoil and change there'll be openings for social movements and ideas. They won't vanish and we don't know where a changing communism will fit in with them. But we won't go back to the old style Stalinist communism. That's dead.
FRANKLYN GRIFFITHS, academic, University of Toronto, quoted in *The Toronto Star*, 30 Sept. 1989.

The fall of the Berlin Wall is the most important event in history since the invention of television.
DERRICK DE KERCKHOVE, communications specialist, quoted in *Metropolis*, 21 Dec. 1989.

I've never seen a Communist in my life. I've seen totalitarian governments, but I've never seen a Communist.
STANISLAW TYMINSKI, dark-horse candidate in the Polish presidential election, defeated by Lech Walesa on 10 Dec. 1990, quoted in *Maclean's*, 10 Dec. 1990. Tyminski left his native Poland and made his fortune in computers in Mississauga, Ont., and in cable television in Iquitos, Peru. He is the author of record of the Polish-language, book-length capitalist manifesto *The Sacred Dogs* (1990) co-written by Polish correspondent Robert Samsel.

COMMUNITY

It is not the individual but the group that transforms the culture. The group does so by its concern for excellence, by its ability to wait and let issues mature, by its persevering efforts to understand, by its discernment for what is at once simple and profound, by its demand for the first-rate and its horror of mere destructiveness.
BERNARD J.F. LONERGAN, Jesuit philosopher, *A Second Collection: Papers by Bernard J.F. Lonergan, S.J.* (1954).

Most regions are communities in name rather than reality. An effective community is a process, an ongoing collection of interactions and continuous relationships.

MICHAEL LINTON, founder of the Local Employment Trading System (LET-System) in B.C.'s Comox Valley in 1983, "Local Currencies," *Edges*, July-Sept. 1988.

Yet the human community is losing something essential, and nearly everyone senses it. It is something that won't sit still for quantification, still less for qualification. But losing it is making some of us very, very uneasy.

BRIAN FAWCETT, cultural commentator, *Public Eye: An Investigation into the Disappearance of the World* (1990).

COMPETITIVENESS

You are competitive if you can sell your product when your currency is strong. You are competitive when you can increase your profits and real wages at the same time.

TOM ATKINSON, executive, Hay Management Consultants, *obiter dicta*, defining competitiveness in business, 3 Dec. 1989.

COMPLIMENTS

You know that pretty girl that sits over there in the corner? Well, the fellow who sits behind her isn't all that bad.

TED REEVE, veteran newspaperman at *The Toronto Telegram*, drawing a colleague's attention to Andrew MacFarlane, then a novice reporter, who recalled the compliment in his collection of columns, *It Seemed Like a Good Idea at the Time* (1983).

COMPUTERS

The phrase "the computer does not impose" misleads, because it abstracts the computer from the destiny that was required for its making. Common sense may tell us that the computer is an instrument, but it is an instrument from within the destiny which does "impose" itself upon us, and therefore the computer *does* impose.

GEORGE GRANT, philosopher, "Thinking about Technology," *Technology and Justice* (1986).

The computer coupled to a printer converts every schoolchild into a publisher and reinforces the notion of writing as a communications activity rather than a dreadful and empty school exercise.

ROBERT K. LOGAN, physicist and educator, *The Alphabet Effect: The Impact of the Phonetic Alphabet on the Development of Western Civilization* (1986).

One of the things I really do want to spend some money on is setting up the Great Canadian Software Bank. This is a pet scheme I've had for years, under which we would buy universal Canadian rights to all kinds of computer software. We would then make it available to all Canadians free of charge. . . . The Software Bank would give them a resource base that would allow them to generate their own jobs.

DIAN COHEN, economist, contributor to *If I Were Prime Minister* (1987).

We are beginning to develop a very strange confusion between computer reality and reality reality. Some people would say that in the end there is no difference.

A.K. DEWDNEY, computer scientist and "Computer Recreations" columnist for *Scientific American*, quoted by Stephen Strauss in *The Globe and Mail*, 6 Feb. 1988.

In the last age you learned the old three "R's". Now learn the new three R's: Ram, Rom & Run. The next lesson will be the three C's: Conflict, Crisis, Change. Kindergarten has just opened.

FRANK OGDEN, futurologist, "Ogden's Twelfth Law," *Dr. Tomorrow's Lessons from the Future* (June 1989).

No one needs a word processor if he has an efficient secretary.

ROBERTSON DAVIES, man-of-letters, address, Ontario Science Centre, Toronto,

26 Nov. 1989, quoted by Tracey Tyler in *The Toronto Star* the next day. Davies happily added, "I am a technomoron."

The world already has 5-billion of the finest "computers" that will ever be developed — human brains. During the past hour, 12,000 children have been born around the world, and every one of them has a potential intelligence greater than any genius alive today.

FRANK FEATHER, futurologist, *G-Forces: Reinventing the World — The 35 Global Forces Restructuring Our World* (1989).

To use a computer — even a relatively home-spun one like mine — is to recognize the limitations of the genre. The difference between a computer and the human mind is the difference between a filing cabinet and a garden.

ARTHUR BLACK, broadcaster and humorist, "It'll Never Replace the Ballpoint," *That Old Black Magic* (1989).

CONFEDERATION
See also CANADA
DOMINION

The few members who watched the British North America Act of 1867 in its speedy passage through parliament could scarcely conceal their excruciating boredom; and after the ordeal was over, they turned with lively zeal and manifest relief to the great national problem of the tax on dogs.

DONALD CREIGHTON, historian, "The Victorians and the Empire" (1937), *Towards the Discovery of Canada: Selected Essays* (1972).

Henceforth we shall rank among the Nations.

Characteristically ebullient boast of SIR GEORGE-ÉTIENNE CARTIER, Father of Confederation, prior to the proclamation of the British North America Act of 1867.

We come to Your Majesty, who have given us liberty, to give us unity, that we may preserve and perpetuate our freedom.

THOMAS D'ARCY McGEE "visualized the Fathers of Confederation approaching Queen Victoria and addressing her in the florid oratory of the day," noted by John Conway, "An 'Adapted Organic Tradition,'" *Daedalus: Journal of the American Academy of Arts and Sciences*, "In Search of Canada," Fall 1988.

Died! Last night at twelve o'clock, the free and enlightened Province of Nova Scotia. Deceased was the off-spring of old English stock, and promised to prove an honour and a support to her parents in their declining years. Her death was occasioned by unnatural treatment at the hands of some of her ungrateful sons.

Editorial, *The Halifax Morning Chronicle*, 1 July 1867, referring to the absorption of Nova Scotia into the newly formed Dominion of Canada, quoted by W.L. Morton in *The Critical Years: The Union of British North America 1857-1873* (1964).

We shall like to remember, when Confederation has stood the test of time, how beautiful the day was when it began.

Editorial, *Le Journal des Trois-Rivières*, 1 July 1867.

The deconfederation of Canada began with the unbuilding of the transcontinental railway, a feat of engineering rivalling the *Titanic*.

ERIC NICOL, humorist, *Canada Cancelled Because of Lack of Interest* (1977) illustrated by Peter Whalley.

Canada is seen by some as a confederation of shopping centres.

Attributed to Prime Minister PIERRE ELLIOTT TRUDEAU in a reference to the view expressed by the provincial premiers anxious to protect their rights against federal incursions, 18 April 1981.

Confederation was started by a group of Confederate soldiers who were sore losers.

ERIC NICOL and DAVE MORE, humorists, *The U.S. or Us: What's the Difference, Eh?* (1986).

The Canadian Dominion came into being on 1 July 1867 with Sun 8CN51-0-UR 8CN39, and the Moon 28GE51.
Astrological information required for casting the horoscope of the Dominion of Canada offered by Michael Baigent, Nicholas Campion, and Charles Havey, astrologers and authors of *Mundane Astrology: The Astrology of Nations, Groups and Organizations* (1984).

After that, nothing really happened [in Canadian history] until 1867. That was the year the British North America Act created the Dominion of Canada out of four weak and divided colonies. Canada was born with a stroke of a pen: Canadians did not fight for their independence, they signed for it.
RICHARD STENGEL, journalist, "The Canadians," *Spy*, Feb. 1988.

I feel that directly in front of us lies a primary need for what I shall call Reconfederation, and which I think of essentially as providing a cultural skeleton for the country that fits its present conditions. Without a cultural Reconfederation there can be only continued political tinkering of the most futile kind.
NORTHROP FRYE, literary critic, address, Social Sciences and Humanities Research Council, Toronto, Fall 1990, printed in *The Globe and Mail*, 15 April 1991.

CONQUEST OF 1759

See QUEBEC, CONQUEST OF

CONSCRIPTION

Conscription if necessary, but not necessarily conscription.
This familiar verbal formulation was employed by Prime Minister MACKENZIE KING in the House of Commons with respect to the Conscription Crisis during World War II. Mackenzie King's formulation is frequently cited as an instance of the Prime Minister's penchant for "doubletalk" or "doublethink." Yet the formulation possesses both the precision of a definition and the elasticity of an expression that recommends it as a model for formulas which attempt to deal with the needs of the moment in terms of future necessities.
It is now believed that the origin of the formulation is a passage in an unsigned editorial titled "Mr. King on Conscription" which appeared in *The Toronto Star*, 11 June 1942. The anonymous editorial writer argued as follows: "But the government says enough are coming forward; that enough may continue to come forward, and that conscription for overseas duty, which it is willing to impose if necessary, may never be necessary at all."
According to the writer David MacDonald, the wording of this passage struck the right note with J.S. (Jack) Pickersgill of the Prime Minister's Office who drew it to the attention of Mackenzie King who agreed that the editorial aptly expressed the government's position on the plebiscite which sought to release the government from its commitment to the principle of voluntary rather than mandatory enlistment.
Thereupon Mackenzie King addressed the House of Commons, 7 July 1942, on behalf of the National Resources Mobilization Act: "If, in reference to the very difficult question of service overseas, anyone can conceive of a policy which is better calculated to serve the national interest than the one the government has formulated, and which is clearly and concisely expressed in the words: 'Not necessarily conscription, but conscription if necessary,' I shall be first to advocate its acceptance. . . . Those who oppose on other grounds do not differ fundamentally with the policy of the government with respect to service overseas: 'Not necessarily conscription but conscription if necessary.'"

CONSCIENCE

The good conscience of the wicked rests on the villainies they refrain from committing.
> Thought of Mark in the novel *An Innocent Millionaire* (1983) by the author STEPHEN VIZINCZEY.

In my experience, the more self-righteous people are, the less troubled they are by conscience.
> Remark made by a character in the novel *Memory Board* (1987) by the author JANE RULE.

I believe that there is within each of us some small, strong and even eternal point of our being that is beyond compromise. More than we know, this enables us to engage in authentic compromise with generosity of spirit and clarity of heart. I cannot prove to you that this is so. What we can do is to act on this belief, put it into practice, and make it more so.
> MARY JO LEDDY, social activist, "Where to Draw the Line?" *The Globe and Mail*, 3 July 1990.

CONSERVATION

I have spent a lifetime in conservation affairs and have gradually but inescapably been convinced that up until the present time all we conservationists have been able to achieve is fight a delaying action.
> JOHN A. LIVINGSTON, naturalist, *One Cosmic Instant: A Natural History of Human Arrogance* (1973).

The term *Conserver Society* itself was used for the first time in Report No. 19, *National Resource Policy Issues in Canada* (January 1973). This report contained a wide variety of recommendations regarding both policy and the need for new institutions specifically designed to protect and control resources development. . . . Finally, the term "conserver society" occurs in the recommendation . . . "that Canadians as individuals, and their governments, insti-tutions, and industries, begin the transition from a consumer society preoccupied with resource exploitation to a conserver society engaged in more constructive endeavours. Ideally, Canada could provide the leadership necessary to work toward more equitable distribution of the benefits of natural resources to all mankind."
> *Canada as a Conserver Society: Resource Uncertainties and the Need for New Technologies*, The Science Council of Canada, Report No. 27, Sept. 1977.

The concept of a Conserver Society arises from a deep concern for the future, and the realization that decisions taken today, in such areas as energy and resources, may have irreversible and possibly destructive impacts in the medium to long term.

The necessity for a Conserver Society follows from our perception of the world as a finite host to humanity, and from our recognition of increasing global independence.
> This brief definition of the concept of the "Conserver Society" was developed in March 1975 by the Committee established for that purpose by the Science Council of Canada. *Canada as a Conserver Society: Resource Uncertainties and the Need for New Technologies*, The Science Council of Canada, Report No. 27, Sept. 1977.

Who would believe, who would believe now, that just about thirty years ago C.D. Howe wanted to tear down the Parliamentary Library and the East Block on Parliament Hill and build modern steel and glass structures in their place? He would have done it if Mike Pearson hadn't stopped him.
> PIERRE BERTON, author, Chairman, Heritage Canada Foundation, address, Empire Club of Canada, Toronto, 11 Feb. 1982.

The future is R's.
> Slogan used on television in Ontario in Fall 1990 for the Blue Box recycling program sponsored by OMMRI: Corpora-

tions in Support of Recycling. OMMRI stands for Ontario Multi-Material Recycling Incorporated, established in Toronto in 1986, which introduced the Blue Box curbside collection system. The three R's are Recycling, Reduction, and Reuse.

CONSERVATIVE PARTY
See also POLITICS

When that time comes, time has come for a change; but in the very nature of things a Conservative does not believe in change for the sake of change, nor does he believe that it is essential to make a change merely because you may alter a name. I think most of us believe with Tennyson: That man's the true Conservative / Who lops the moulder'd branch away.
> R.B. BENNETT, Prime Minister, House of Commons, 13 May 1931.

The Conservative is not the guardian of a cemetery but the custodian of an orchard, wisely pruning the dead branches but always nourishing the roots without which the trees cannot live.
> GRATTAN O'LEARY, newspaperman and Senator, quoted by Norman DePoe in *The Toronto Star*, 30 April 1977.

Anyone who can bring the Conservative Party together can bring the country together.
> JOE CLARK, Conservative leader, quoted by Dalton Camp in *Points of Departure* (1979).

Ruled by Mulroney's branch-plant instincts, Canada is relinquishing its hard-won status as a medium power gained in two world wars and settling for the role of a satellite nation. Influenced by his propensity to placate and accommodate, the country is regressing from its stance as a critical and independent nation back into the neo-colonial past. The lessons of the journey from working class to branch-plant president are that, above all, the orders come from elsewhere. The lessons of the mediator, misplaced in a political context, are not to resolve issues with clarity but to attempt to strike a compromise among irreconcilable contradictions. When a leader lacks a commitment to well-defined national standards and values, the result is an increasing lack of coherence in national purpose. The lesson of the corporation is that there is no collective value more important than the bottom line. Under Brian Mulroney some Canadians may become richer, but Canada itself is in danger of losing its soul.
> NORMAN SNIDER, journalist, "The Fixer," *Saturday Night*, Nov. 1988.

The day Canada's Conservative party changed its name to the *Progressive* Conservative party, it publicly acknowledged its philosophical weakness and its willingness to play prostitution politics. With that one stroke, it could abandon any true conservative vision of the world and do battle solely on the basis of out-promising the Liberals; two political parties hugging the centre to death from different sides.
> WILLIAM D. GAIRDNER, academic and businessman, *The Trouble with Canada* (1990).

CONSERVATISM

The impossibility of conservatism in our era is the impossibility of Canada.
> GEORGE GRANT, philosopher, *Lament for a Nation* (1965).

To describe the movement which has so deeply affected Canada as "neo-conservative" risks dignifying the phenomenon intellectually more than is justified. While neo-conservatism was an important force in Britain and the United States, in Canada it was a hand-me-down, a set of broad concepts, slogans and generalizations, which added up to a licence for greed and social irresponsibility.
> JAMES LAXER, political economist, York University, criticizing the right-wing policies of the Conservative government, *The Toronto Star*, 3 April 1991.

CONSTITUTION
See also CHARTER OF RIGHTS

We should have no certainty or stability, unless the entire constitution were to become a Canadian constitution, binding on all future legislatures, and incapable of being altered save by a process which derives its validity from the will of the people alone.
> F. R. SCOTT, constitutional authority, "The Redistribution of Imperial Sovereignty" (1950), *Essays on the Constitution: Aspects of Canadian Law and Politics* (1977).

Since the end of the French régime, Canada has known five constitutions. After 112 years, devising a sixth one should not be such a traumatic experience.
> PIERRE-MARC JOHNSON, Quebec Minister of Labour, address, Empire Club of Canada, Toronto, 25 Oct. 1979. He identified them: Royal Proclamation (1763), Quebec Act (1774), Constitutional Act (1791), Act of Union (1841), BNA Act (1867). (The sixth came in 1982: the Constitution Act.)

A century and thirteen years ago, a group of remarkable people launched a remarkable endeavour. They created a country.
It is a long and painstaking process, building a country to match a dream. But just as each generation has made the sacrifices so each has repeated the rewards. Every generation of Canadians has given more than it has taken.
Now it is our time to repay our inheritance. Our duty is clear: It is to complete the foundations of our independence and of our freedom.
> PIERRE ELLIOTT TRUDEAU, Prime Minister, advising the provincial premiers of the federal government's intention of patriating the BNA Act and entrenching in it a Charter of Rights, with or without provincial approval, press conference, Ottawa, 2 Oct. 1980, published in *The Toronto Star* the following day.

I speak as a Canadian. I would like their Lordships to realize that the bill now before them runs contrary to the provisions of the international covenant on civil and political rights.
> MARTIN WOLF, Canadian actor and artist and long-time resident in Britain, speaking out from the visitor's gallery during a debate in the British House of Lords on the Canada Bill concerned with the patriation of the BNA Act, Feb. 1982, quoted by Jeffrey Simpson and Ged Martin in *The Canadian Guide to Britain: England* (1985).

I wish simply that the bringing home of our Constitution marks the end of a long winter, the breaking up of the ice jams and the beginning of a new spring. What we are celebrating today is not so much the completion of our task, but the renewal of our hope — not so much an ending, but a fresh beginning.
> PIERRE ELLIOTT TRUDEAU, Prime Minister, address, Patriation Ceremony, Ottawa, 17 April 1982.

The Government of Quebec decided that it wasn't enough. It decided not to participate in this ceremony, celebrating Canada's full independence. I know that many Quebecers feel themselves pulled in two directions by that decision. But one need look only at the results of the referendum in May, 1980, to realize how strong is the attachment to Canada among the people of Quebec. By definition, the silent majority does not make a lot of noise; it is content to make history.
> PIERRE ELLIOTT TRUDEAU, Prime Minister, address, Patriation Ceremony, Ottawa, 17 April 1982.

Today I have proclaimed this new Constitution — one that is truly Canadian at last. There could be no better monument for me, as Queen of Canada, to declare again my unbounded confidence in the future of this wonderful country.
May God bless and keep you all.
> ELIZABETH II, Queen of Canada, address,

Patriation Ceremony, Ottawa, 17 April 1982.

The Charter of Rights and Freedoms is a much more Americanizing act than free trade. The free-trade agreement is just that . . . I don't think it makes the same institutional differences in relations between the state and the individual.
SEYMOUR MARTIN LIPSET, U.S. sociologist, press conference in Toronto on 11 Oct. 1989, announcing the results of a study sponsored by the Canadian-American Committee, reported in *The Globe and Mail* the following day.

The "notwithstanding" clause should be revoked. No country can function when its highest courts, adjudicating the most vital questions of civil rights, are subject to revision and revocation by provincial legislatures. While that preposterous clause remains. . . .
CONRAD BLACK, capitalist and columnist, "Enough Is Enough," *Saturday Night*, Sept. 1990.

This rubbish about the British North America Act's being "foreign" and "imposed" still keeps cropping up. . . . It goes well, of course, with the nonsense that the Constitution Act of 1982 gave us "a new Constitution." In fact what it has given us is the old Constitution with knobs on: very important knobs — the Charter of Rights and Freedoms, five constitutional amending formulas, and some extra power for the provinces over natural resources, but still just knobs. Most of the Act of 1867 remains untouched, and the Act of 1982 lists no less than twenty-four Acts or Orders that are part of our written Constitution.
EUGENE FORSEY, constitutional authority, *A Life on the Fringe: The Memoirs of Eugene Forsey* (1990).

Like it or not, we have begun a process of "reconfederation." A radically different Canada will emerge. Reconfederation may produce a Canada that still includes Quebec. If so, it will be a much looser federation in which provincial governments assume many of the powers that have been exercised by the federal government.
GEOFFREY STEVENS, columnist, *The Toronto Star*, 3 Feb. 1991.

CONSUMERISM

Perhaps only in North America every man feels entitled to a motor car, but in Asia hundreds of millions of people do not expect to eat and be free.
LESTER B. PEARSON, diplomat, Nobel Peace Prize Lecture, Oslo, Norway, 11 Dec. 1957. The text is taken from *The Four Faces of Peace and the International Outlook* (1964) edited by Sherleigh G. Pierson.

Consumers have been told that they can only be ripped off if they are greedy or have larceny in their souls. What a rationale for the player who holds a stacked deck of cards, and then cheats the vulnerable, withholds information, and blames the victim.
LYNNE GORDON, consumer advocate, *Consumer Handbook* (1975).

By bringing men together primarily as buyers and sellers of each other, by enshrining profitability and material gain in place of humanity and spiritual growth, capitalism has always been inherently alienating.
"The Waffle Manifesto: For an Independent Socialist Canada" (1969) reprinted in *The Canadian Forum*, Dec. 1989.

Every buying decision sends a message to a supplier about his particular product or service. There's a nationwide daily referendum on everything that's offered for sale.
DEAN WALKER, journalist, *A Case for the Enterprise System* (1975).

But what is new in this century is a powerful system of mass media interlocked with a technological and economic

agenda that now threatens the entire planet. The paradox we face is that our lifestyle of luxury and "progress" — promulgated through the media over this century — increasingly reveals itself to be the prescription for planetary suicide.
JOYCE NELSON, social and cultural critic, *Sultans of Sleaze: Public Relations and the Media* (1989).

What is being asked of us in the name of survival is nothing less than to take a new measure of what it means to be human, to face the future stripped of the cloak of materialism.
ANITA GORDON and DAVID SUZUKI, science broadcasters, *It's a Matter of Survival* (1990).

Consumer society is not an artificial and catastrophic social invention. It is a culture with its own systemic properties. And we are not devouring beasts who treat with the devil. We are creatures who depend on the meanings contained in the material world.
GRANT McCRACKEN, curator, Institute of Contemporary Culture, Royal Ontario Museum, *The Globe and Mail*, 29 Oct. 1990.

CONTINENTALISM
See also FREE TRADE

I cannot see any possible reason to annex Canada. We do not want to have more people in the United States; what we want is to try and improve the mob we have now. And Canada couldn't help us out; they couldn't even learn us English — they speak it just as bad as we do.
WILL ROGERS, cowboy comedian, *The Best of Will Rogers* (1979) edited by Bryan B. Sterling.

We considered three options: (1) maintenance of the status quo; (2) closer integration with the United States; and (3) strengthening of the economy and other aspects of national life in order to secure our independence. The decision was taken to adopt the Third Option . . . specific policies and programs that will reduce Canadian vulnerability to the magnetic pull of the U.S.
ALLAN MacEACHEN, External Affairs Minister, referring to Prime Minister Trudeau's initiative to seek a "contractual link" with the European Community, quoted by Barry Conn Hughes in *The Canadian Magazine*, 21 June 1975.

CONTRACEPTION
See also ABORTION
BIRTH CONTROL

Not until the 1930's was the provision of birth control methods and information recognized by the courts as possibly serving the public good. Not until 1969 was the use of contraceptive devices made legal and abortion, under specific conditions, permitted. Canadian laws allowing easier access to birth control and abortion were slower to emerge and generally more restrictive than those of countries like England and the United States.
ANGUS McLAREN and ARLENE TIGAR McLAREN, historian and sociologist, *The Bedroom and the State: The Changing Practices and Politics of Contraception and Abortion in Canada, 1880-1980* (1986).

CONVERSATION

There's a fine line between being an artist of conversation, and having a big mouth.
Comment of a character in the play *The Idler* by playwright IAN WEIR, included in *Twenty Years at Play* (1990) edited by Jerry Wasserman.

COOKING
See FOOD & DRINK

CO-OPERATIVES

Fisherman: I understand you are making good Catholics of all those Nova Scotia fishermen.
Tompkins: God help us, man, can you tell me any Catholic way of canning lobsters?

Exchange between a Nova Scotia fisherman and Father JAMES TOMPKINS, one of the founders of the co-operative Antigonish Movement, quoted by J.R. Kidd in "The Social Gospel and Adult Education in Canada," *The Social Gospel in Canada* (1975) edited by Richard Allen.

We must create the kind of society in which man will be free to free his soul.
M.M. COADY, priest and one of the founders of the the co-operative Antigonish Movement, quoted by Harvey (Pablo) Steele in *Agent for Change: The Story of Pablo Steele* (1973) as told to Gary MacEoin.

One man cannot accomplish everything but by symbolic action he can incite others to do things.
PAUL-ÉMILE LÉGER, Cardinal and missionary in Africa, advertisement in *The Globe and Mail*, 27 May 1978, for *Lives: Cardinal Léger*, Global Television Network, 28 May 1978.

If competitive individualism is the mark of America, then the cooperation of groups within large institutional structures expresses an essential Canadian value.
WILLIAM KILBOURN, historian, "The Peaceable Kingdom Still," *Daedalus: Journal of the American Academy of Arts and Sciences*, "In Search of Canada," Fall 1988.

At 30 below, there are no self-made men (or women, much less children). A rugged individualist won't last till spring if things go wrong. But if people have the ability to cooperate, they can survive. Nature gives an annual, compulsory seminar in dependence and responsibility.
MARGARET CATLEY-CARLSON, President of CIDA, "Aid: A Canadian Vocation," *Daedalus: Journal of the American Academy of Arts and Sciences*, "In Search of Canada," Fall 1988.

COPYRIGHT

I saw the Plains of Abraham, and the spot where the lamented Wolfe stood when he made the memorable remark that he would rather be the author of Gray's "Elegy" than take Quebec. But why did he say so rash a thing? It was because he supposed there was going to be international copyright. Otherwise there would be no money in it.
MARK TWAIN, author, addressing a banquet held in his honour, Montreal, 8 Dec. 1881. The American humorist, lobbying for copyright reform, resided for some months in Montreal to secure Canadian and hence British Empire protection for his books. At the time unscrupulous Toronto publishers were pirating the American editions of his books.

Copyright laws and attempts to protect intellectual property are becoming obsolete. Individual intellectual property rights will become absurd once collective knowledge is shared in a single electronic global brain, accessible to all.
FRANK FEATHER, futurologist, *G-Forces: Reinventing the World — The 35 Global Forces Restructuring Our World* (1989).

CORPORATIONS

The mesh of the corporate web gets tighter and tighter. We do not view this as a good thing, though all reports indicate that corporate globalization currently views sustainable oligopoly as five to seven giant corporations in any single sector.
BREWSTER KNEEN, food system analyst, coining the phrase "sustainable oligopoly," *The Ram's Horn*, Jan. 1989.

CORRUPTION
See also CRIME
PATRONAGE

Sugar is the oil for political machines: / Without it all the gears would never mesh / A man must have a weakness / For a certain kind of sweetness / Be it soothing to the spirit or the flesh.
"A kind of distorted vaudeville song" sung by SIR JOHN A. MACDONALD in the

opera *Louis Riel*, premiered in Toronto on 23 Sept. 1967, libretto by Mavor Moore, music by Harry Somers.

You never know when constituents may drop in on a weekend.
MAURICE DUPLESSIS, Quebec Premier, referring to the drawer which contained $60,000 in ready cash, quoted by David MacDonald, "Anecdotes," *The Toronto Star*, 22 Oct. 1988.

In any case, it's only puritans from outside Quebec who worry about little things like that.
ROBERT BOURASSA, Quebec Premier, referring to widespread coverage outside the province of the Cliche Commission's report of corruption in the province's construction industry, Quebec City, 9 May 1975.

COUNTRY
See LAND
NATIONALISM

As the world changes, not only plants and animals, but cultures won't survive. There's no society that has lasted more than 500 years, because they can't change as everything around them changes.
FRANK OGDEN, futurologist, quoted by Nancy Spiller in *American Way*, 1 Sept. 1989.

Countries can't do what they're set up to do. They can't protect borders from immigrants, they can't protect citizens from terrorists, they can't protect their currency or their jobs.
FRANK OGDEN, futurologist, quoted by Nancy Spiller in *American Way*, 1 Sept. 1989.

COURAGE

I look down on people who just give up and become vegetables. You must always have enough courage to tell yourself that you can be important for someone else.

MICHEL TREMBLAY, playwright, quoted by Donald Smith in *Voices of Deliverance: Interviews with Quebec and Acadian Writers* (1986) translated by Donald Smith.

COWS

Nothing increases the value of a cow so much and so quickly as to get killed by a CNR train.
DONALD GORDON, President of the CNR (1950-66), quoted by Robert McKenzie in *The Toronto Star*, 4 Oct. 1966.

The Western world's desire for beef has doubled the cattle population in the past 40 years. There is now one cow for every four humans on the planet.
ANITA GORDON and DAVID SUZUKI, science broadcasters, *It's a Matter of Survival* (1990).

CRAFTS
See also ART & ARTISTS

Joy is a well-made object.
BILL REID, Haida carver, quoted by Nicholas Jennings in *Maclean's*, 16 Oct. 1989.

CREATION

The big puzzel is wat happin jist before yer Bang. Wut kinda four-play wuz goin on before that first Fired-ball started everythin goin like gang-bussers? Nuthin. But that's no anser. Nuthin is sumthin yuh find in a emty hole, and ther wernt nuthing there fer ther to be a hole in.

Nuthin is no kind of a answer to the riddel of Cremation, but funny enuff a hole jist mite be.
DON HARRON, humorist, writing in dialect, *Charlie Farquharson's Unyverse* (1990).

CREATIVITY

Successful creation is nothing more than putting a lot of mistakes together in a way that works. An artist becomes professional when he learns how to sell mistakes.

T.B. PAWLICKI, author and theorist, *How You Can Explore Higher Dimensions of Space and Time* (1984).

Put down whatever floats up from your unconscious. Put it all down. Every bit is the truth, but the whole thing, the final thing you create is a lie — a magic lie.

W.O. MITCHELL, author, quoted in *The Toronto Star*, 21 Oct. 1989.

CREDIT CARDS

While you can buy virtually anything by credit card from symphony concerts to holidays in Spain, you need cash or a cheque up front to renew your driver's licence or auto licence plate. With the same credit card, you can of course order the most expensive meal, complete with wine — in a town you have never visited before from a maître d' whose name you cannot pronounce. Credit cards enable you to buy Alka-Seltzer in Alberta, quiche in Quebec, suits in Saskatchewan and tires in Toronto — but you absolutely must pay cash to buy a five dollar bottle of plonk at a liquor store three blocks from your home in any province in Canada.

TOM DAVEY, editor and columnist, *Environmental Science & Engineering*, Oct. 1988.

CRIME

See also CAPITAL PUNISHMENT
CORRUPTION
JUSTICE & INJUSTICE
LAW
MURDER
PATRONAGE
POLICE

The Board of Trustees of the Toronto General Hospital recently named its Department of Psychiatry The D. Campbell Meyers Memorial Department of Psychiatry. D. Campbell Meyers introduced neuropsychiatry into the hospital during the 1890s

and founded there in May, 1906, the first psychiatric general hospital unit in Canada.

Press release, Toronto General Hospital, referring to D. CAMPBELL MEYERS (1863-1927), the distinguished Canadian psychiatrist who will always be remembered for the use made of his name ("Meyers, Toronto") by fellow physician Sir Arthur Conan Doyle in his novel *The Hound of the Baskervilles* (1902).

The speciality of a Sherlock Holmes is the everyday routine of a woodsman. Observation and deduction are part and parcel of his daily existence. He literally reads as he runs. The floor of the forest is his page.

H. HESKETH PRICHARD, British author of mysteries, *November Joe: Detective of the Woods* (1913). Prichard devoted a book to the tales of November Joe, a backwoods detective employed by the Quebec government. As Hugh Greene explained in *More Rivals of Sherlock Holmes* (1971): "So in Hesketh Prichard's book the methods of Baker Street are practised in the Quebec woods."

Am I a criminal because I violate a law which people do not want?

ROCCO PERRI, Hamilton bootlegger, remark made in 1922, quoted by James Dubro and Robin F. Rowland in *King of the Mob* (1988).

All I can say is, that judge is pretty darned liberal with another man's time.

NORMAN (RED) RYAN, lapsed bank robber, upon being sentenced to twenty-five years of imprisonment, quoted by John Dalrymple in *Liberty*, Dec. 1956.

The Mafia was preparing a cement overcoat for me.

PACIFIQUE (PAX) PLANTE, Montreal crime-fighter in the 1940s and 1950s, who retired and lived in seclusion in Mexico, quoted in *The Canadian Star Weekly*, 29 Nov. 1968.

I'm no hood! And I don't like to be called a hood. I'm a thief.
> ALVIN KARPIS, bank robber nicknamed "Creepy" who was once called Public Enemy No. One by the FBI, served twenty-five years in Alcatraz before being deported back to his native Canada in 1968, quoted by Carl Sifakis in *A Catalogue of Crime* (1979).

The dream of a crook is a man with a dream.
> STEPHEN VIZINCZEY, novelist, *An Innocent Millionaire* (1983).

If the Mafia exists in Montreal, it's probably like the Knights of Columbus.
> ARMAND COURVILLE, Montreal meat wholesaler and witness at the Quebec Police Commission Inquiry into organized crime, quoted by *The Globe and Mail*, 27 May 1975.

You need not say anything. You have nothing to hope from any promise or favour and nothing to fear from any threat whether or not you say anything. Anything you do say may be used as evidence. Do you understand the caution?
> Wording of the caution on the statement form of a Canadian police officer making an arrest, as reproduced by Frederick E. Jarman in *In Pursuit of Justice: Issues in Canadian Law* (1976).

Nevertheless, two-thirds (in certain cases up to five-sixths) of the actual time any prisoner spends in jail is determined by the bureaucracy of the parole system. When a judge sentences someone to nine years in prison, he will in fact only dispose of the next three years of that person's life. The other six years will be in the hands of prison and parole officers.
> EDWARD L. GREENSPAN, lawyer, *Greenspan: The Case for the Defence* (1987) written with George Jonas.

A crime may not be the whole story of any human life. Which one of us would like to be defined solely by the worst thing we have ever done. . . . That's why every cli-

ent is my kind of client, and every crime is my kind of crime.
> EDWARD L. GREENSPAN, lawyer, *Greenspan: The Case for the Defence* (1987) written with George Jonas.

That the violent crime rate of the Canadian metropolis is only 10 to 20 percent of that of the American (murders average 70 a year in Toronto but 700 in Detroit) is more than a matter of strict gun control in Canada and the lack of it in the United States. It is a matter of the two societies differing in their attitudes toward authority.
> WILLIAM KILBOURN, historian, "The Peaceable Kingdom Still," *Daedalus: Journal of the American Academy of Arts and Sciences*, "In Search of Canada," Fall 1988.

If you can't do the time, don't do the crime.
> EARL WORK, sales motivator, recalling a prison maxim, Nov. 1989.

So you amass $3 million from crime, and can keep it out of the clutches of the authorities, you can be fined up to $4 million. You won't pay the fine? Off to jail you go, for no more than ten years. If you keep your nose clean in jail, you will be a free man in about three years.
Quite an attractive proposition.
> DOUGLAS GAIR, essayist, "Crime Pays," *The Idler*, Jan.-Feb. 1990.

I act stupid.
> VIC COTRONI, Montreal mobster and Mafia don, giving the reason for his success in dealing with people, quoted by Peter Edwards in *Blood Brothers: How Canada's Most Powerful Mafia Family Runs Its Business* (1990).

If I'm such a bad criminal, why am I still walking around free?
> VIC COTRONI, Montreal mobster and Mafia don, quoted by Peter Edwards in *Blood Brothers: How Canada's Most Powerful Mafia Family Runs Its Business* (1990).

CRITICS & CRITICISM

See also DANCE
LITERATURE
MUSIC

Remember this, that the greatest number of sticks and stones are found under the good apple trees.
> Proverbial wisdom recalled by the merchant TIMOTHY EATON as quoted by Joy L. Santink in *Timothy Eaton and the Rise of His Department Store* (1990).

No literature worthy of preservation has anything to fear from criticism, no matter how misdirected; and only an unhealthy sense of inferiority would prompt a reply to the wholesale condemnation, which has been often heard in recent years.
> WILLIAM ARTHUR DEACON, literary critic, "Literature in Canada — in Its Centenary Year" (1929), reprinted by Clara Thomas and John Lennox in *William Arthur Deacon: A Canadian Literary Life* (1982).

I am a man before I am a critic and a nationalist before I am an artist.
> WILLIAM ARTHUR DEACON, literary critic, letter to John Mitchell, 12 Dec. 1933, reprinted by Clara Thomas and John Lennox in *William Arthur Deacon: A Canadian Literary Life* (1982).

Nathan Cohen has announced that his new play, *Blue Is for Mourning*, which opened this week at Jupiter Theatre in Toronto, is to be the first of a trilogy. Let us hope he will reconsider this terrible threat.
> LISTER SINCLAIR, radio personality, reviewing on CBC Radio's *Critically Speaking* the 1952 premiere of Nathan Cohen's one (and only) theatrical play. Quoted by Bronwyn Drainie in *Living the Part: John Drainie and the Dilemma of Canadian Stardom* (1988). As Drainie noted, Sinclair was "one of Cohen's frequent victims" and the play was a shambles, a fact acknowledged by the playwright who

dubbed the entire experience "an unmitigated disaster."

The defenders were left in the unenviable position of always arriving on the scene a little breathlessly and a little late.
> BERNARD J.F. LONERGAN, Jesuit philosopher, referring to the defence of religion against attacks from science, *Insight: A Study of Human Understanding* (2nd ed., 1958).

The final absurdity of this situation [admiring revolutionaries and non-conformists] penetrated my consciousness while I was watching the *Pierre Berton Hour* on commercial TV. Berton was interviewing Jack Webster, a Vancouver radio man famous for his irreverence. At one point Berton stopped Webster so that the commercials could come on. Berton turned to the audience and said, with a straight face: "We'll have some more iconoclasm after these messages." (The next morning I hoped it had been a dream — but there it was in my notes.)
> ROBERT FULFORD, columnist and author, "Pop Art and Museum Culture" (1964), *Crisis at the Victory Burlesk* (1968).

Once upon a time I thought there was an old man with a grey beard somewhere who knew the truth, and if I was good enough, naturally he would tell me that this was it. That person doesn't exist, but that's who I write for. The great critic in the sky.
> MARGARET ATWOOD, novelist, interviewed by Graeme Gibson in 1972, *Margaret Atwood: Conversations* (1990) edited by Earl G. Ingersoll.

A barking dog is often more useful than a sleeping lion.
> ROY THOMSON, newspaper publisher, *After I was Sixty: A Chapter of Autobiography* (1975) by Lord Thomson of Fleet.

Pessimism is for lazy minds.
> JEAN DRAPEAU, Montreal Mayor, countering criticism that the success of the

Montreal Olympics was at too great a cost, quoted by Chris Allan in *Weekend Magazine*, 19 July 1975.

Sibelius once remarked that nobody had ever seen a statue of a critic. Statues of playwrights, on the other hand, are seen very frequently, and usually in theatres, where they belong.
ROBERTSON DAVIES, man-of-letters, Preface, *Question Time* (1975).

Criticism is to art what history is to action and philosophy is to wisdom: a verbal imitation.
NORTHROP FRYE, literary critic, quoted by Richard Kostelanetz, "The Literature Professors' Literature Professor," *The Michigan Quarterly Review*, Fall 1978.

If you can't stand the heat, get out of the kitchen and let *Maureen* do the cooking.
EDD ULUSCHAK, cartoonist, responding to Foreign Affairs Minister Joe Clark's complaint that editorial cartoonists were too hard on him, *The Edmonton Journal*, Jan. 1983.

Any journalist who has worked an overseas beat knows that the key to success will always be the local-boy-makes-good story. Assiduously I collected items with a positively Canadian slant. But I soon discovered that what Nathan — or perhaps what his top brass at the *Star* — liked even more than local boy makes good was local boy makes bad.
I couldn't help but think that there was a certain national masochism here. Canadians, so I perceived, took more sour delight in some poor kid falling on his or her all-Canadian ass in full view of that of a Canadian critic. It may be very nice, as Burns himself obviously an insecure Scot, put it in a poem to a louse, "To see ourselves as others see us!" but in aesthetic terms such a point of view remains something of an irrelevant luxury.
CLIVE BARNES, Anglo-American critic and reviewer, sometime contributor of articles to *The Toronto Star*, whose entertainment editor, Nathan Cohen, advocated international and not national standards, "Much Ado About Nothing," *Saturday Night*, Dec. 1987.

And in the past thirty years the Canadian theatre has been doing a lot of building. But Canada is not going to be helped by constantly seeking approval from big brother and mother, nor by constantly relying on other people's yardsticks to measure its own excellence. What Canadian art surely needs is the confidence of its own arrogance.
CLIVE BARNES, Anglo-American critic and reviewer, "Much Ado About Nothing," *Saturday Night*, Dec. 1987.

As you know, my detractors work night and day to advance my reputation. It is impossible to buy so invaluable a service!
MARSHALL McLUHAN, communications consultant, letter to Jonathan Miller, 22 April 1970, *Letters of Marshall McLuhan* (1987) edited by Matie Molinaro, Corinne McLuhan, and William Toye.

It is my own belief that when someone has exposed a plausible shortcoming or error in something I have written, extreme silence is by all odds the best strategy.
JOHN KENNETH GALBRAITH, economist and author, "Big Shots," *The New York Review of Books*, 12 May 1988.

The thin skin of a leader should not be able to impair the free speech of a critic.
A. ALAN BOROVOY, General Counsel, Canadian Civil Liberties Association, *When Freedoms Collide: A Case for Our Civil Liberties* (1988).

Long ago I learned this proverb: If you do something important, there will always be critics. If you don't like critics, don't do anything important.
MARJORIE MONTGOMERY BOWKER, retired family court judge, *On Guard for Thee: An Independent Analysis, Based on the Actual Text of the Canada-U.S. Free Trade Agreement* (1988).

Criticism is the story of our search for story. That's why criticism is *so* exciting. Not because it provides answers but because it is a version of story.

> ROBERT KROETSCH, author, quoted by Aritha van Herk in *The Globe and Mail*, 15 April 1989.

If the reader is giggling or moved to tears, that's the criticism that counts.

> W.O. MITCHELL, author, quoted by H.J. Kirchhoff in *The Globe and Mail*, 21 Oct. 1989.

THE CROWN

The Crown represents the basic political ideals which all Canadians share. It stands for the idea that individual people matter more than theories; that we are all subject to the rule of law. These ideals are guaranteed by a common loyalty, through the Sovereign, to community and country.

> QUEEN ELIZABETH II, address, 75th anniversary of the Saskatchewan Legislative Building, Regina, 16 Oct. 1987, quoted by D. Michael Jackson in *The Canadian Monarchy in Saskatchewan* (1989).

CUBA

If I had to sum up in two words what I saw in Cuba, I would say: morality and discipline. The idea of everyone having a place to live, something to eat, a job, education, and health are, I would call, the social morality of Cuba. And this was brought about by discipline. You couldn't just do what you wanted. To make this program work for everyone, you had to do what you were told.

> ROBERT (BOB) OGLE, Catholic priest and former M.P., *North/South Calling* (1987).

The old hierarchy has been swept away to be replaced by a new military hierarchy: that's the long and the short of the story of Cuba.

> ROBERT HUNTER, activist and author, *On the Sky: Zen and the Art of International Freeloading* (1988).

CULTURAL INDUSTRIES
See CULTURE

CULTURE
See also ARTS & ARTISTS
CRITICS & CRITICISM
DANCE
FILM
FOLKLORE
GROUP OF SEVEN
LITERATURE
MUSIC
MYTHOLOGY
PAINTING
THEATRE

The state of literature, the arts, and sciences, in Canada, can scarcely be said to be at a low ebb, because they have never been known to flow.

> JOHN LAMBERT, English traveller, *Travels through Lower Canada and the United States of North America, in the Years 1806, 1807, and 1808* (1810).

When Randolph commented on the lack of Canadian culture Churchill responded fiercely, "Cultured people are merely the glittering scum which floats upon the deep river of production."

> WINSTON CHURCHILL, British imperialist, addressing his son Randolph in British Columbia in 1929, quoted by Piers Brendon in *Winston Churchill: An Authentic Hero* (1984).

Canada on the whole, it could be said, is busy *decanadianizing* itself, without being quite ready to abandon the certain advantages of standing apart and politically remaining "Canadian." Though there is no money in art or for scholarship, people hopefully concern themselves with those things — though never facing up to the fact that without money you can no more have a culture than you can exploit a nickel mine. Such people like to forget where they are. So there grows up in the intellectual an unconscious taboo on what is "regional."

> WYNDHAM LEWIS, English artist and au-

thor, "Nature's Place in Canadian Culture" (1940-44), *Wyndham Lewis in Canada* (1971) edited by George Woodcock.

The thin crust between society and the chaotic forces born from human nature and human ingenuity has always been heaving, and often been cracking, under foot. The societies which have succeeded best in winning and maintaining the most nearly tolerable existences for their members have been those which have given very free scope to their poets, artists, philosophers, scholars, inventors, adventurers, and other rebels, critics and innovators.
J. BARTLET BREBNER, scholar, *Scholarship in Canada: The Function of Graduate Studies* (1945).

Modern culture is the culture that knows about other cultures. . . . Far more open than classicist culture, far better informed, far more discerning, it lacks the convictions of its predecessor, its clearcut norms, its elemental strength.
BERNARD J.F. LONERGAN, Jesuit philosopher, *A Second Collection: Papers by Bernard J.F. Lonergan, S.J.* (1954).

America has nothing to look forward to but ruin. Now it's Brazil's turn (and Canada's).
JEAN COCTEAU, French man-of-letters, diary entry for 1953, *Past Tense* (1990), as quoted by Douglas Fetherling in "Foreign Perceptions of Canadian Culture," *Canadian Notes & Queries*, No. 44, Spring 1991.

There are limits to Canada's powers of economic influence. Canada cannot forever ride on the crest of a wave of wheat but must rely increasingly for its position and its right to influence world opinion on the authority of its diplomats and civil servants, of its scholars and scientists, and of its artists and writers.
CLAUDE T. BISSELL, President, University of Toronto, "Canadian Education Today," *Contemporary Canada* (1968) edited by Richard H. Leach.

According to the federal Treasury Board

Secretariat the percentage of total government expenditure provided for all cultural activities, including recreation, sport, the CBC and the administration of the Department of the Secretary of State, etc., is 1.8%. Ten years ago, it was 1.8%. In the years between it never varied more than one-tenth of one percent.
BERNARD OSTRY, Secretary-General, National Museums of Canada, address, Canadian Museums Association, Ottawa, 9 Nov. 1976.

At bottom, culture is the way we imagine ourselves and our world. Men live by imagination. They live by the myths and dreams that relate them to their past and their own place and their fellow men. And if imagination, the heart of all art and invention, seems an airy and insubstantial thing to be occupying governments and bankers, let me remind you that money itself is not less imaginary than your own dreams. The most practical and material things in our lives begin with the imagination: every part of an automobile comes from the human mind: even the steel of which it is made is invented, does not occur in nature. *We not only live by imagination but we live together by imagination.* Canada itself, to the eye of the mind, is a Platonic entity, the idea of an idea; but to the eye of imagination it is our country, cities and rivers, and prairies and mountains, it is our people, our history and our destiny.
BERNARD OSTRY, Secretary-General, National Museums of Canada, address, Canadian Museums Association, Ottawa, 9 Nov. 1976.

We are in a fight for our soul, for our cultural heritage and for our nationhood. Without a culture there is no political survival and we are not a nation.
A.W. JOHNSON, CBC President, *Touchstone for the CBC*, June 1977.

The first concern of cultural policy will be with the liberation of creative imaginaton wherever it is found, with support to those with the gifts to take advantage of it for their art. A second concern will be with conservation of the Canadian heritage and environment. The Canadian heritage should be understood to include everything Canadians cherish, no matter from what source: it includes Beethoven as well as Claude Champagne, Mark Twain as well as Stephen Leacock, Rembrandt as well as Iskowitz, the whooping crane as well as the harp seal, the Ursuline Convent in Québec City as well as the Powder Magazine at Fort Anne. Our age is eclectic and, what is more, indigenous art has never flourished in isolation . . . a policy of cultural development does not close doors, it opens them.

BERNARD OSTRY, arts administrator, *The Cultural Connection: An Essay on Culture and Government Policy in Canada* (1978).

We know, for example, that our present material prosperity does not mean, in itself, that we are a great country. We know intuitively that we will become great only when we translate our force and knowledge into spiritual and artistic terms. Then, and only then, will it matter to mankind whether Canada has existed or not.

HUGH MacLENNAN, essayist and novelist, "If You Drop a Stone . . . ," *The Other Side of Hugh MacLennan* (1978).

Our culture needs scientists and technicians as it does cellists, poets and sculptors, because in every case the thing done is both intrinsically worth doing and a unique embodiment of truth. It is good for a sculptor to sculpt and good for us to see his sculpture. It is good for an engineer to plan and good for us to use the fruits of his planning. It is in beautiful activities that we are truly human.

LARKIN KERWIN, President, National Research Council, address, Empire Club of Canada, Toronto, 12 Nov. 1981.

Political and economic movements tend to expand and centralize; cultural ones tend to decentralize, to bring to articulateness smaller and smaller communities. One has to keep the contrast steadily in mind: if we hitch a political development to a cultural one, as in separatism, we get a kind of neo-fascism; if we hitch a cultural development to a political one, we get a pompous, bureaucratic pseudo-culture.

NORTHROP FRYE, literary critic, address, Empire Club of Canada, Toronto, 19 Jan. 1984.

I am not interested here in discussing the problem of Canada as a colony, except to say that it is true that Canadian culture is largely colonial, and that it is colonial *by choice*.

KENNETH SHERMAN, poet, "The Survival of *Survival*," *The Idler*, No. 5, June-July 1985.

As culturally cringing as Canadians can sometimes be (with due cause when one considers not only the pressures of Empire but the arrogant presence of the United States flexing its muscles down there just below the border), when it comes to the dreams of joy captured in comics of the Forties, they need not bow their heads.

HARLAN ELLISON, U.S. science-fiction author and fan of comics from Canada in the 1940s, "Dreams of Joy Recaptured," *Canuck Comics* (1986) edited by John Bell.

The only culture you want to preserve is bacterial. Real culture is something you strive to attain, not something you keep in a pickle jar.

LOUIS DUDEK, poet and aphorist, "Can. Lit. Notes," *The Bumper Book* (1986) edited by John Metcalf.

To cut a long story short, I estimate that about 6% of the [Canada] Council budget goes directly to artists to create the permanent works of art, which will, in the future, define our culture — 6% to those on whom the rest of the arts community depend! Is it really surprising that Canadians feel that they have no distinct artistic culture? And how did the perception that artists are freeloaders on the state ever begin?

MARTIN KEVAN, arts manager, "When You Cut Your Pie Please Save Me a Piece,"

The Bumper Book (1986) edited by John Metcalf.

I think Canadian culture is what Canadian artists want to do, period. I don't think it's more complicated than that.
PETER PEARSON, Executive-Director, Telefilm Canada, quoted by Edward Greenspon in *The Globe and Mail*, 30 Jan. 1987.

If we do not tell ourselves funny or satirical or tragic or ironic stories about ourselves, if the teller of tales in the corner does not sing our songs, speak our sorrows, narrate our wars, then we will not exist as a nation.
MARY JANE MILLER, academic, *Turn Up the Contrast: CBC Television Drama Since 1952* (1987).

I have often thought that the fragility we ascribe to Canadian culture is the natural result of alienated, self-conscious, contrived, hothouse cultivation. We spend too much time trying to produce blooms that will appeal to what we see as a superior, more civilized sensibility, and not enough time on the local flora and fauna. So we are left with a fragile bouquet that wilts in the natural environment.
JOHN GRAY, composer and performer, Introduction, *Local Boy Makes Good: Three Musicals* (1987).

The growing homogenization of the world's languages and cultures is not necessarily beneficial to humanity. Diverse languages and cultures provide different insights into reality. These different insights are at the heart of human resourcefulness, and resourcefulness is universally recognized as a key to human survival.
PETER ERNERK, President, Keewatin Inuit Association, contributor to *If I Were Prime Minister* (1987).

What is culture? I'm not sure Canadians are all that concerned by what is traded away in culture. Canadians are already pretty influenced by American culture, and they don't seem to mind it too much. I don't think there's much wrong with the marketplace determining what people want in culture.
WILLIAM VANDER ZALM, B.C. Premier, 27 April 1987, quoted by Stephen Osborne and Mary Schendlinger in *Quotations from Chairman Zalm* (1988).

When we send a symphony orchestra or a ballet company abroad, they make Canada known in an international world that is of the highest importance because it shows that we are part of the *internationale* of cultivated people, and that, in so far as international cultural exchange favours a climate of world peace, we are doing not at all badly.
ROBERTSON DAVIES, man-of-letters, Neil Gunn lecture, Edinburgh University, June 1988, printed in *The Times Literary Supplement*, 30 Sept. 1988.

I avoid the term "national culture" because it has been abused by people who think of culture as a commodity, separable from the rest of the national life. Culture is an ambience, a part of the air we breathe. That special ozone is now to be breathed in Canada, because it arises from the land itself — not a few acres of snow, but a country of immensely varied beauty of landscape and of season, including our lovely and dangerous winters.
ROBERTSON DAVIES, man-of-letters, Neil Gunn lecture, Edinburgh University, June 1988, printed in *The Times Literary Supplement*, 30 Sept. 1988.

I would say that there is some kind of culture anywhere in the country you go, and if I can't see it, I'm at fault. It's always there, even if it's just in the way a man picks up a piece of wood and starts to whittle it.
R. MURRAY SCHAFER, composer, interviewed by Ulla Colgrass in *For the Love of Music* (1988).

As we enter the competitive and unforgiving world of globalization, much larger resources will have to be allocated to culture. Only the prime minister has the power and influence to provide the leadership necessary to mobilize them. This is a national need. Our institutions cannot jog along on the existing budgets and resources. Sums that may be enough for present local, regional or even national needs become totally inadequate in the global marketplace.

> BERNARD OSTRY, television executive, quoted by Derrick de Kerckhove in *The Canadian Forum*, Oct. 1989.

Canadian culture is at the very front of the second rank.

> BARRY CALLAGHAN, man-of-letters, quoted by Susan Kastner in *The Toronto Star*, 29 Oct. 1989.

You've got to be careful about nationalism. I don't blindly support my country right or wrong, or believe that we must have one centralized culture. I'm not interested in being (culturally) isolated from other countries, but I do want to see this country survive.

> GREG CURNOE, artist and regionalist if not nationalist, quoted by Deirdre Hanna in *Now*, 2 Nov. 1989.

We put our own past treasures, like the best tea cups, permanently on the shelf, declaring them too fragile and too expensive to handle except on special occasions, such as the CBC's 50th anniversary blowout three years ago. For every day, we use the plastic glasses from the Texaco station, the cheap and easily available nostalgia of borrowed cultures.

> BRONWYN DRAINIE, arts columnist, *The Globe and Mail*, 4 Nov. 1989.

Culture is the backbone of society, politics merely its entertainment.

> ELEANOR KOLDOFSKY, Canadian recording pioneer, remark first made in the 1970s, recalled on 24 Nov. 1989.

Walk down the main streets of any of the older Canadian towns and the whole trajectory of our culture is there. What is inert is not the culture, but the Canadians. All we have to do is wake up and have a look at it and do something about it.

> SCOTT SYMONS, novelist and cultural

commentator, interviewed in *The Idler*, No. 25, May-June 1990.

Creative culture is infinitely porous — it absorbs influences from all over the world. That is what differentiates a genuine culture from nationalism. Nationalism is the parody of the reality of cultural identity.

> NORTHROP FRYE, literary critic, interview conducted by Carl Mollins, *Maclean's*, 4 Feb. 1991.

CURIOSITY

And I say to you that if you bring curiosity to your work it will cease to be merely a job and become a door through which you enter the best that life has to give you.

> ROBERTSON DAVIES, man-of-letters, acceptance speech, Trent University, Peterborough, Ont., quoted in *The Toronto Star*, 9 Nov. 1974.

Curiosity is part of the cement that holds society together.

> ROBERTSON DAVIES, man-of-letters, quoted in *The Globe and Mail*, 24 Dec. 1976.

Many Canadians seem to suffer from permafrost of the mind: neither curious nor contentious, they simply don't discuss such things, as if born and bred into such material comfort that they have never had to think about it.

> JOHN DYSON, English writer, "such things" extending beyond "issues of the Arctic," *The Hot Arctic* (1979).

CURLING

The sport at witch Canajuns generally end up nummer 1 in the wirld is yer Curlin. Canajuns has become the teem to beet in yer Sliver Brooms and yer Bryers. The wife and I likes to curl up togethr all winter with our own bumspeels, taking turns neelin down to git our rocks off wile the uther pardner brakes wind in front.

> DON HARRON, comedian, in the person of Charlie Farquharson, *Cum Buy the Farm* (1987).

DANCE
See also CULTURE

The citizens of Winnipeg support the company because it is fine and because the citizens are neither surfeited nor corrupted. They take joy in beautiful things.
AGNES DE MILLE, New York dance personality, visiting Winnipeg to view the Royal Winnipeg Ballet in 1963, quoted in *Canada Today/D'Aujourd'Hui*, June 1982.

Why here, of all places, should there be a ballet company?
CLIVE BARNES, dance critic of *The New York Times*, visiting Winnipeg to review the Royal Winnipeg Ballet in 1968, the continent's second-oldest professional ballet company, quoted by Robert Fulford in *An Introduction to the Arts in Canada* (1977).

Ballet on the prairies was only something in the memory of many Canadians who had come from Europe at the beginning of the century, a lingering dream of colour and movement almost lost in the years of achievement and hardship in a new country.
GWENETH LLOYD, co-founder of the Winnipeg Ballet Club, precursor of the Royal Winnipeg Ballet, quoted by Jan Henderson in "Women in Dance," *Communiqué*, May 1975.

We've been out conquering the world, but we haven't conquered Winnipeg. It's a challenge.
ARNOLD SPOHR, artistic director of the Royal Winnipeg Ballet whose international success was met with municipal and provincial inertia and indifference, quoted in *Maclean's*, 23 Oct. 1978.

We decided to walk up from the station to the hotel. We were crossing St. Catherine Street and blazing on the marquee of the Cinéma de Paris was my name in lights. It was a film I had made of dance some time before in Paris. For me, it was an intense experience and an omen. I knew Montreal would be my city.
LUDMILLA CHIRIAEFF, Latvian-born dancer who trained at the Bolshoi and danced with the Ballets Russes and in 1952 emigrated to Quebec where three years later in Montreal she founded Les Grands Ballets Canadiens, quoted by Jan Henderson in "Women in Dance," *Communiqué*, May 1975.

I've come to watch those two. They're stars, you know. They're real stars.

SOL HUROK, legendary New York-based theatrical impresario, indicating Karen Kain, then 21, and Frank Augustyn, 19, at the New York opening of Rudolph Nureyev's production of the National Ballet Company's *The Sleeping Beauty.* Quoted by John Fraser in *Kain & Augustyn* (1977), a photographic study by Christopher Darling.

When I was in Toronto I finally realized that if I let the opportunity of expanding my art in the West slip by it would haunt me always.

MIKHAIL BARYSHNIKOV, star of the Kirov Ballet, referring to his decision to defect while on tour with the Bolshoi Ballet in Toronto, 29 June 1974, quoted by John Fraser in *The Globe and Mail*, 6 July 1974.

Potlatch: A Strict Law Bids Us Dance

This is the full title of a 53-minute documentary film devoted to the ceremony of the potlatch, once banned, which continues to be practised by the Kwakiutl Indians of the West Coast. The film, produced by the U'mista Cultural Society in 1975, was directed by Dennis Wheeler and narrated by Gloria Cranmer Webster.

To dance is a wonderful thing. Life would not be whole without it.

LYNN SEYMOUR, Alberta-born prima ballerina, quoted in *The Observer* (London), 5 Oct. 1975.

On occasion — and this is extremely rare — there will be dead silence after a performance, like nobody can manage to make a sound. It's weird, very weird. It's performances like these which, unusual as they might be, keep you going to ballet.

FRANK AUGUSTYN, ballet dancer, quoted by Stephen Dale, *Random Scan*, Jan. 1978.

I skate the way I think Isadora Duncan danced. I'm trying to explore every facet of my personality. I'm criticized as flamboyant, arrogant, and melodramatic. I'm black and white. I'm yes and no. I try to live my life touching extremes.

TOLLER CRANSTON, free-form skater, quoted by Yousuf Karsh in *Karsh Canadians* (1978).

It is important to me to be dancing the way I would always wish to be remembered. That time is now.

VERONICA TENNANT, principal dancer with the National Ballet of Canada, retiring after a twenty-four year career, quoted by Deirdre Kelly in *The Globe and Mail*, 14 Oct. 1988.

All my life, I worked as hard as I could to attain as much as I could and grow as much as possible, without ever thinking about what the end result would be. I have been surprised over the years by the results, which are the ones I could never have really dreamed of. The way it has turned out has gone beyond what I expected, or what anyone else expected.

VERONICA TENNANT, principal dancer, quoted by Deirdre Kelly in *The Globe and Mail*, 4 Feb. 1989.

Women, as well as men, in all ages and in all places, have danced on the earth, danced the life dance, danced joy, danced grief, danced despair, and danced hope. Literally danced all these and more, and danced them figuratively and metaphorically, by their very lives.

MARGARET LAURENCE, novelist, *Dance on the Earth: A Memoir* (1989).

DARKNESS

On the basis of present-day primates, fear of darkness seems to be well founded. . . . One's helplessness is never so conspicuous as it is in darkness.

JOHN A. LIVINGSTON, naturalist, *One Cosmic Instant: A Natural History of Human Arrogance* (1973).

Darkness puts us in touch with certain "things" in us that otherwise will remain unknown and therefore untapped.

TIMOTHY FINDLEY, novelist, interviewed by Alan Twigg in *Strong Voices: Conversations with Fifty Canadian Authors* (1988).

DATING

Don't go out with a perfect stranger. Remember, no one is perfect.
> BETTY JANE WYLIE, author, *Beginnings: A Book for Widows* (1977, rev. 1988).

DAVIES, ROBERTSON

Most critics don't sufficiently recognize the melodrama and the morality in my work. A satirist is a disappointed idealist; I am rather a moralist. The moralist looks at life and says that certain courses of action lead to certain consequences — here are people who are pursuing a dead end path, people who have put themselves in chains.
> ROBERTSON DAVIES, man-of-letters, interviewed by Ann Saddlemyer in 1981, *Conversations with Robertson Davies* (1989) edited by J. Madison Davis.

When, on *Morningside*, I told Robertson Davies that a few days earlier in an interview with me Anthony Burgess had suggested he, Davies, be given the Nobel Prize for literature, he said, "Goodness gracious, I'm sure I don't deserve it."
> PETER GZOWSKI, host of CBC Radio's *Morningside*, writing in *The Private Voice: A Journal of Reflections* (1988). On that program, even earlier, on 20 Oct. 1985, Gzowski quoted Burgess, the English man-of-letters, as saying: "I consider him . . . Canada's first Nobel Prize man."

Davies I discovered when it was still possible to drop his name and have presumptively informed friends say, "Who is that?"
> JOHN KENNETH GALBRAITH, economist and author, *A View from the Stands of People, Politics, Military Power and the Arts* (1986) edited by Andrea D. Williams.

When I was president of PEN, I took a vow never to mention another writer. But I will say that you have one here whom I'm very impressed by: Robertson Davies. I met him in New York, and I couldn't believe that anybody that pompous could be that good a writer.
> NORMAN MAILER, author, former President of International PEN, attending the Festival of Festivals in Toronto, quoted in *The Globe and Mail*, 14 Sept. 1987.

Canada has one great novelist (Robertson Davies), which means it has one for every twenty-five million citizens — the world's highest ratio.
> GEORGE F. WILL, syndicated columnist based in Washington, D.C., *The Toronto Star*, 14 Jan. 1988.

It's about time Canada had a Nobel Prize for literature, and I think he's the man — he's managed to bring to the Canadian novel a kind of universal quality which I think is marvellous.
> ANTHONY BURGESS, English man-of-letters, discussing in Toronto one of his enthusiasms, the novels of Robertson Davies, quoted by James Marck in *Now*, 12 May 1988.

Some people like to hear the magic phrase, "Governor General's Award-winner". . . . You don't want too much respect. If you get too much respect, you turn into Robertson Davies.
> GEORGE BOWERING, author and two-time winner of the Governor General's Award, quoted by Philip Marchand in *The Toronto Star*, 16 Dec. 1989.

DAYCARE

Without adequate daycare, no working mother is really in a position to compete equally in the marketplace.
> SHEILA COPPS, politician and feminist, *Nobody's Baby: A Survival Guide to Politics* (1986).

When the federal government announced that there was no consensus on the issue of daycare, and that the only help they could give to the growing number of latch-key kids was to start another task force, were they thinking of the children?

SHEILA COPPS, politician and feminist, *Nobody's Baby: A Survival Guide to Politics* (1986).

DEATH

See also DYING WORDS

Death is not a phantom; she is a truth which I will meet and whose force I will feel. She stands ahead of me as certainly as the road on which I set my foot.

LOUIS RIEL, Métis leader and mystic, diary entry for 11 Aug. 1885, *The Diaries of Louis Riel* (1976) edited by Thomas Flanagan.

Dust to dust, ashes to ashes, / Into the tomb the Great Queen dashes.

Couplet from an inadvertently amusing elegiac verse on the death of Queen Victoria attributed to JAMES GAY, the self-styled "Poet Laureate of Canada." The attribution is undoubtedly incorrect — Canada's Gay died in 1891, England's Victoria in 1901. Yet both the sentiment and the style are characteristic of Gay, in his day the leading "good bad" poetaster of the Dominion.

Among all the flotsam and jetsam of news-paper and magazines stories I have read one that made a powerful impression on my mind. It was a short one in the March *Atlantic*, and dealt with the first experiences of a disembodied spirit after death. It appealed to the curiosity that is in us all regarding the future — a curiosity that can never be satisfied until we are dead — and perhaps not even then. But if not — there will be no curiosity.

L. M. MONTGOMERY, author, journal entry, 1 May 1899, *The Selected Journals of L.M. Montgomery: Volume I: 1889-1910* (1985) edited by Mary Rubio and Elizabeth Waterston.

In sleep too deep for dreams I'll lie, — / Till One shall knock, and bid me rise / To quest new ventures, fare new roads, / Essay new suns and vaster skies.

SIR CHARLES G.D. ROBERTS, poet, "The Vagrant of Time" (1927), *Selected Poetry and Critical Prose* (1974) edited by W.J. Keith.

No Catholic could ask for the death of anyone under any circumstances.

JOHN PENFOLD, Jesuit historian, advising E.J. Pratt who was then writing his epic poem *Brébeuf and His Brethren* (1940) that no Jesuit priest, not even one like Brébeuf who was facing the prospect of Iroquois torture, would ever ask to die, quoted by David G. Pitt in *E.J. Pratt: The Master Years, 1927-1964* (1987).

I should think there is nothing very bad about dying except for the people one has to leave and the things one hasn't had time to do. When the time comes, If I know what it's all about, I suppose I shall think, among other things, of the fish I haven't caught and the places I haven't fished.

RODERICK HAIG-BROWN, author and angler who died in 1976, *A River Never Sleeps* (1946).

The cost of living is seeing others die.

ABRAHAM L. FEINBERG, rabbi and author, *Storm the Gates of Jericho* (1964).

Do you know how people die? Vomiting.

MARGARET LAURENCE, author, remark made to the present editor in Toronto in 1965.

Death, the cliché assures us, is the great leveler; but it obviously levels some a great deal more than others.

ALDEN WHITMAN, Nova Scotia-born journalist who became the chief obituary writer of *The New York Times*, Introduction, *The Obituary Book* (1971).

One of the things that puzzles me is that so few people want to look at life as a totality and to recognize that death is no more extraordinary than birth.

ROBERTSON DAVIES, man-of-letters, interviewed by Tom Harpur in 1975, *Conversations with Robertson Davies* (1989) edited by J. Madison Davis.

There is a kind of glory in sudden death: to go down at the peak of one's powers with both achievement and potential untarnished, all flags flying. The light is snapped off before it has had a chance to dim or fade. One giant step into the next world. But O pity the survivors!
> BETTY JANE WYLIE, author, *Beginnings: A Book for Widows* (1977).

Suttee, the practice whereby the widow throws herself on her husband's funeral pyre, has been outlawed in India. They still practise a subtle form of it in Canada. You die by inches, of loneliness.
> BETTY JANE WYLIE, author, *Beginnings: A Book for Widows* (1977).

Before my husband died my two chief problems in life were (1) how to find more time to write, and (2) how to lose weight. Now they are much more basic: sex and money. I don't know whether they represent progress or not.
> BETTY JANE WYLIE, author, *Beginnings: A Book for Widows* (1977).

We are the 2,000th human generation to be haunted by the most fundamental of all of the questions that man can ask himself: "Why am I here? Why do I exist? Where did I come from, and what will become of me?"

We will be the last generation, though, not to know the answer.
> IAN CURRIE, author and past-life therapist, *You Cannot Die: The Incredible Findings of a Century of Research on Death* (1978).

It's getting so I know more people in the cemetery than on the street.
> Line attributed to the character Peggy in the play *A Place on Earth* (1982) by the author BETTY JANE WYLIE.

So, if this were indeed my Final Hour, these would be my words to you. I would not claim to pass on any secret of life, for there is none, or any wisdom except the passionate plea of caring.
> MARGARET LAURENCE, author, address, Trent University, Peterborough, Ont., 29 March 1983, quoted in *The Globe and Mail*, 10 Jan. 1989.

There's only a hyphen between me and death.
> AL PURDY, poet, "Homer's Poem" (1986), *The Collected Poems of Al Purdy* (1986) edited by Russell Brown.

A man should have the courtesy to outlive his wife.
> Thoughts of a male character in the novel *Memory Board* (1987) by JANE RULE.

In my final hour, the subject here will not be rage, but reconciliation. I think I have come to live entirely for that word.
> TIMOTHY FINDLEY, novelist, speaking at Trent University, Peterborough, Ont., 1987, quoted by Gillian Mackay in *Maclean's*, 8 Oct. 1990.

I won't die until the Leafs win the Stanley Cup.
> HAROLD BALLARD, owner of the Maple Leafs hockey team, remark made following successful cardiac surgery at the age of eighty-four, quoted by Jim Proudfoot in *The Toronto Star*, 26 July 1988. Ballard died two years later; the Leafs last won the coveted Cup in 1967.

It came as a small revelation to me that fear of death was not the only possible motive behind religious belief. Some people cling to it to make the idea of *life* tolerable.
> GEORGE FALUDY, Hungarian-born poet, *Notes from the Rainforest* (1988).

There is a gathering time, a growing time, and a bearing time, and Death may be any one of these.
> ROBIN SKELTON, man-of-letters, aphorism, May 1990.

We're put on this earth to celebrate. You give it everything you have. Everything. That includes your death. The greatest thing you can do is possess your own death so that when it comes it's given, not taken. Honour your own death.
SCOTT SYMONS, novelist and cultural commentator, interviewed in *The Idler*, No. 25, May-June 1990.

DEBT

I just want to borrow enough to get out of debt.
EDD ULUSCHAK, cartoonist, Southam Syndicate, 23 Oct. 1987.

DECENCY

I can never find enough good things to say about this decent country.
GEORGE FALUDY, Hungarian-born poet who settled in Toronto in 1968, quoted by Kristjana Gunnars in *The Globe and Mail*, 18 Aug. 1990.

DEFEAT
See FAILURE

DEFENCE
See also CANADIAN ARMED
FORCES
WAR

The distinction between offensive and defensive arms was a very simple one. If you were in front of them, they were offensive; if you were behind them, they were defensive.
LESTER B. PEARSON, former Prime Minister, Reith Lectures of 1969, quoted by Charles Lynch in *The Lynch Mob: Stringing Up Our Prime Ministers* (1988).

In the later part of the Diefenbaker years, Canadian defence policy was dominated by the three "N's" of NORAD, NATO and nuclear weapons.
KENNETH C. EYRE, military affairs specialist, "Forty Years of Military Activity in the Canadian North, 1947-87," *Arctic*, Dec. 1987.

Our defence budget . . . is one-sixth of the total budget. That's a lot of money — $1,800 million for defence. And it's a lot of money especially when you realize that it's accompanied by a great deal of uncertainty on the part of Canadians.
PIERRE ELLIOTT TRUDEAU, Prime Minister, address, Alberta Liberal Association, Calgary, 12 April 1969.

The only defence is peace.
THÉRÈSE CASGRAIN, President, Voice of Women, quoted by Kay Macpherson and Meg Sears in "The Voice of Women: A History," *Women in the Canadian Mosaic* (1976) edited by Gwen Matheson.

Whether in trade or defence or protection of our environment and natural resources, our two nations shall continue the unique relationship that has been the envy of the world, a relationship which enhanced the standard of living and the freedom of our people. Let us continue and let us move forward together.
RONALD REAGAN, U.S. President, address, Canadian Forces Base Uplands, Ottawa, 10 March 1981.

Canadian defence expenditures currently consume about 2 per cent of all goods and services consumed (GNP) in Canada, about 10 per cent of federal government spending, and about 40 per cent of federal discretionary spending.
ERNIE REGEHR, political-affairs co-ordinator of Project Ploughshares, *Arms Canada: The Deadly Business of Military Exports* (1987). The point being made is that military expenditures increase at the expense of social programs.

Weapons, and the money it takes to build them, have become the grunts and gestures of a primal international language.
ERNIE REGEHR, political-affairs co-ordinator of Project Ploughshares, *Arms Can-*

ada: The Deadly Business of Military Exports (1987).

Canada doesn't make anything that goes bang.

BARNEY DANSON, former Minister of National Defence, quoted by Ernie Regehr in *Arms Canada: The Deadly Business of Military Exports* (1987). Regehr referred to Danson as an arms-industry booster and denied the truth of the statement. This rationale for the country's defence industry seems to be a popular one in Ottawa. "There's very little produced here that goes bang in the night," maintained Ed Healey, Assistant Deputy Minister, Department of National Defence, as quoted by John Kohut in *The Globe and Mail*, 10 Oct. 1988.

Being an intimate partner in defence with the U.S.A. is not easy at the best of times. As I have already demonstrated, American defence strategies are more difficult to predict than those of the U.S.S.R. More seriously still, by and large they do not exist.

JOHN HASEK, defence observer, *The Disarming of Canada* (1987).

The unhappy truth is that Canada's military has so declined since the end of the Second World War that we would have trouble defending our borders from the modern equivalent of a Fenian attack let alone a serious military threat.

JOHN HASEK, defence observer, *The Disarming of Canada* (1987).

The NORAD Command and Control centre lies deep within a granite mountain in Colorado. Military personnel enter through thirty-ton blast doors. Twenty-four hours a day, Canadian and American crews scan all objects in orbit around the earth. Their job is to phone the president of the United States should a missile be observed.

ROBERT DEL TREDICI, photographer and author, describing the situation inside Cheyenne Mountain, *At Work in the Fields of the Bomb* (1987).

Canada is a country that can enjoy the umbrella benefits of massive defence spending by the United States while pinching the pennies on its own defence commitments.

ANDREW H. MALCOLM, U.S. correspondent, "Northern Contradiction," *Saturday Night*, Dec. 1987.

The appeal to military "solutions" to political conflict defies rationality. The objective is ostensibly security, but the result is overwhelmingly and unmistakably insecurity.

ERNIE REGEHR, political-affairs co-ordinator of Project Ploughshares, "New Approaches to Security," *The Road to Peace* (1988) edited by Ernie Regehr and Simon Rosenblum.

National defence policies should be based on defensive rather than offensive capabilities.

Key statement in the position paper of the International Affairs Committee of the Canadian Council of Churches, released 17 Feb. 1988.

The economic problem was that the war proved costly to the United States and beneficial to its industrial rivals. Canada, for example, became the largest per capita war exporter, enriching itself on the destruction of Indochina while deploring American brutality.

NOAM CHOMSKY, linguist and critic of American foreign policy, *The Culture of Terrorism* (1988).

Canada has traditionally been the biggest foreign supplier to the U.S. military, but it still accounts for only about 0.5 per cent of the total Pentagon spending.

JOHN KOHUT, journalist, *The Globe and Mail*, 10 Oct. 1988.

What again was it we were defending? Real estate? There won't be much left of any value. A way of life? No one will be around to persevere with the old ways. A set of beliefs, an ideology? It will mean little to the insects and reptiles that are expected to survive the radiation.

LESLEY CHOYCE, author, *December Six: The Halifax Solution — An Alternative to Nuclear War* (1988).

If you had to justify Canadian defence policy to an inquisitive visitor from Mars, the major difficulty would be to explain why we, almost alone among the countries of the Western Hemisphere, act as if we had a vital security frontier somewhere in central Europe. It is an extraordinary misapprehension, but it arises quite naturally from the history of Canadian defence policy.

GWYNNE DYER and TINA VILJOEN, commentator and TV producer, *The Defence of Canada: In the Arms of the Empire* (1990).

Independence requires the power, on our own, to hurt an aggressor. Until we acquire our own nuclear deterrent, we will be wards of our allies.

DAVID FRUM, essayist, "Why She Needs the Bomb," *The Idler*, May-June 1990.

$12,360,000,000 / Does it make you feel safe?

That's how much our government spent in 1990 on the military. It was supposed to buy us a sense of security. But some Canadians aren't so sure.

Project Ploughshares for the Citizens' Inquiry into Peace and Security, *What Makes Canada Secure: Background Document for the Citizens' Inquiry into Peace and Security in Canada* (1991).

Canadians are used to thinking that Canada's military spending is minor league, but it actually spends more on military forces than does the entire continent of South America.

Project Ploughshares for the Citizens' Inquiry into Peace and Security, *What Makes Canada Secure: Background Document for the Citizens' Inquiry into Peace and Security in Canada* (1991).

DEMOCRACY

A lawless and unprincipled rabble, consisting of the refuse of mankind, recently emancipated from the subordination that exists in an advanced state of society, and all equal in point of right and possession, compose, of course, a democracy of the most revolting kind.

JOHN HOWISON, traveller and writer, *Sketches of Upper Canada* (1821).

What do they offer you in exchange for the present order? Socialism, Communism, dictatorship. They are sowing the seeds of unrest everywhere. Right in this city such propaganda is being carried on and in the little out of the way places as well. And we know that throughout Canada this propaganda is being put forward by organizations from foreign lands that seek to destroy our institutions. And we ask every man and woman in this country to put the iron heel of ruthlessness against a thing of that kind.

R.B. BENNETT, Prime Minister, address in Toronto, reported in *The Globe & Empire*, 10 Nov. 1932, quoted by Norman Penner in *Canadian Communism: The Stalin Years and Beyond* (1988).

One thing is sure . . . democracy is doomed. This is our last election.

It is Fascism or Communism. We are at the crossroads . . . I take the road of Fascism.

CHARLES E. COUGHLIN, "the radio priest," interviewed by Dale Kramer in 1936, quoted by George Seldes in *The Great Quotations* (1960).

They're always talking about the rights of man, never the rights of God. It has become fashionable for priests to be activists. . . . I guess I was a pioneer.

CHARLES E. COUGHLIN, "the radio priest," interviewed in 1966, quoted in *The People's Almanac No. 1* (1976). Coughlin conducted his "ministry of the air" on "The Golden Hour" from 1926 to 1940 from the Shrine of the Little Flower,

Royal Oak, Michigan. He was a Quebec-born, fascist-minded Roman Catholic priest.

If we are to build a real democracy, our most serious attention will have to be given to the foundation. We must build from the bottom up and not from the top down. We must, in other words, build on the foundation of the average common man.
JAMES J. TOMPKINS, priest and co-op founder, address, Antigonish Co-operative Conference, 16 Aug 1938, quoted by George Boyle in *Father Tompkins of Nova Scotia* (1953).

Democracy is the only truly revolutionary creed because it alone recognizes that change is a constant factor in human affairs.
NORTHROP FRYE, literary critic, observation made in the 1960s, quoted by Paul Wilson, "Growing Up with Orwell," *The Idler*, No. 24, July-Aug. 1989.

The application of democracy sometimes gives me trouble. Democracy requires that you set up a lot of committees and commissions.
WILLIAM VANDER ZALM, B.C. Premier, 5 Sept. 1982, quoted by Stephen Osborne and Mary Schendlinger in *Quotations from Chairman Zalm* (1988).

It's better to be defeated by democracy's enemies than to survive only by coming to resemble them.
GEORGE JONAS, columnist, *Crocodiles in the Bathtub and Other Perils* (1987).

Democracy is no less susceptible to erosion from within than to invasion from without.
A. ALAN BOROVOY, General Counsel, Canadian Civil Liberties Association, *When Freedoms Collide: A Case for Our Civil Liberties* (1988).

I believe that the human being is infinitely corruptible and therefore in need of de-

mocracy. In this world, the fear of the worst is a more reliable incentive than the hope for the best.
A. ALAN BOROVOY, General Counsel, Canadian Civil Liberties Association, *When Freedoms Collide: A Case for Our Civil Liberties* (1988).

An idea strikes me: This, surely, is Greene's dream. For is there any other socialism with a human face, except social democracy? I feel at home at last. And I wonder: Is that dream closer to reality or to dream in various countries of the West today, whether they call themselves Swedish-type socialism or simply welfare states? Isn't our Canada closer to that dream than all those pompous autocracies of the Empire that once looked like humanity's future, but now definitely resemble humanity's past?
JOSEF SKVORECKY, novelist and essayist, discussing some notions of Graham Greene and how they could relate to Canada, *The Globe and Mail*, 10 Sept. 1988.

To a totalitarian, democracies may appear to exist in a state of permanent chaos. But if let alone, they never experience a terminal crisis. They are amazingly improvable and capable of reform. On the other hand, systems that feature planned economies and 99.99 per cent election results cannot be reformed. They can only collapse.
JOSEF ŠKVORECKY, essayist and novelist, on the end of the rule of the Communist Party in Czechoslovakia, *The Globe and Mail*, 11 Dec. 1989.

To be democratic is to disagree about what democracy is.
PATRICK WATSON, broadcaster, and Benjamin Barber, historian, *The Struggle for Democracy* (1988).

Democracy pits the power of the many against the power of the moneyed.
PHILIPPE DEANE GIGANTES, author and Senator, *The Road Ahead* (1990).

DENTISTRY

See also MEDICINE

The teeth are so important, in dividing our food, as well as in conversation, and are so highly ornamental, as to render it a postive duty, with every one, to study the causes which lead to their premature destruction. . . .
    Though many think it doubtful whether Dentists are beneficial or hurtful to the teeth, yet all will allow the necessity and importance of these useful and attractive ornaments.
    LEVI S. PARMLY, "Dentist and Medical Electrician," *The Summum Bonum* (1815). This booklet, issued in Montreal, is the first publication on the subject of dentistry to be published in Canada.

DEPRESSION

There, I feel better for that little outburst of discontent. After all, I'm passably contented. I suppose that into everybody's life there come days of depression and discouragement, when all things in life seem to lose savour. The sunniest day has its clouds; but one must not forget that the sun is there all the same.
    (Item: — If you are out in a pouring rain does it do you much good, or keep you dry, to remember that the sun is there, just the same?)
    L. M. MONTGOMERY, author, journal entry, 14 Jan. 1900, *The Selected Journals of L.M. Montgomery: Volume I: 1889-1910* (1985) edited by Mary Rubio and Elizabeth Waterston.

Always call long distance. Your distant friends can't do anything for you at that distance and won't feel so guilty. Also it costs you so much that you can't afford to dwell on your troubles at great length and distance too.
    BETTY JANE WYLIE, author, *obiter dictum*, 1990.

DEPRESSIONS, ECONOMIC

The bubble burst, the companies toppled. Canada, a country built on compromise, compromised again. We ended up with two roads — one too many — a private road that made money, a public road saddled with debt for which the taxpayers, not the bondholders, were charged. It's unnerving to realize that in the seven worst years of the Depression, Ottawa shovelled out more money to service the debt of the CNR than it did in relief payments to the dispossessed.
    PIERRE BERTON, author, *Maclean's*, 21 Aug. 1989.

In short, never before in the history of man has his economy functioned as it is functioning today; never before has that economy distributed the purchasing-power it is distributing today. Within ten short years the modern industrial and capitalist world has literally jumped from the depths of its greatest depression to the peak of its greatest prosperity. WHY? *Because the world was fortunate enough to blunder into war.*
    LORNE T. MORGAN, economist, *The Permanent War or Homo the Sap* (1943), a pamphlet issued by the Workers' Educational Association, Toronto.

BLACK MONDAY
    Banner heading on *The Toronto Star*, 20 Oct. 1987. The Dow Jones industrial average of 30 blue-chip stocks plunged 508.32 points or 22.6%. The TSE 300 — the composite index of 300 stocks — plummeted 407.2 points or 11.32%. The phrase "Black Monday" is associated with the beginning of the Great Depression, Monday, 28 Oct. 1929.

The first "Mini-Depression" of the current long-wave cycle was in 1981-83 and was dubbed the "Great Recession" by economists because it was the deepest recession since the 1930s.
    The second "Mini-Depression" is due to

occur from 1990 to the end of 1993, give or take one year. Because it will occur at the very bottom of the long-wave "Mega-Cycle," this "Mini-Depression" will be more severe in depth and duration than that of 1981-83.

FRANK FEATHER, futurologist, *G-Forces: Reinventing the World — The 35 Global Forces Restructuring Our World* (1989).

DESIGN

My view is that, properly practised, design is nothing if not a courageous adventure.

ARTHUR ERICKSON, architect, *The Architecture of Arthur Erickson* (1988).

DESIRE

See also SEX

I hunger so much / I even hunger for / a very old woman.

Blackfoot poem, "Man's Song," *Songs of the Great Land* (1989) edited by John Robert Colombo.

DESPAIR

In our present and threatening world, it is only too easy to feel hopeless and helpless, to withdraw into lethargy or a concern only with our own personal lives, forgetting that we are an integral part of all humanity everywhere. It is my profound belief that we must not yield to such a withdrawal.

MARGARET LAURENCE, novelist, Convocation Address, York University, June 1980, *Dance on the Earth: A Memoir* (1989).

DETERMINISM

Determinism is but one characterization of human existence. There are many others, and they are more enlightening. With respect to the determinist characterization, it is a travesty of empiricism to declare, as some too taken by science do, that when all is said and done, men are merely homeostatic machines. Appearances are otherwise, and here at least we may side with Wilde in the proposition that it is only shallow people who do not judge by appearances.

TED HONDERICH, philosopher and editor, *Essays on Freedom of Action* (1973).

DEVELOPERS

My life has exceeded even my own fantasies.

MORTIMER ZUCKERMAN, Montreal-born, McGill-educated, Boston-based property developer and publishing executive, proprietor of *The Atlantic Monthly* and *U.S. News & World Report*, quoted by Marci McDonald in *Maclean's*, 27 Jan. 1986.

Canadian developers are the biggest and best in the world, not because they are smarter than their U.S. counterparts, but because they have been saved from competing against one another by our orderly planning system.

DIANE FRANCIS, financial columnist, *Controlling Interest: Who Owns Canada?* (1986).

Place Ville Marie was the first and one of the finest monuments to the skills of property developers in Canada, men and companies who in the 1960s literally shaped the urban growth of half the continent. There was no better symbol of the new Canadian affluence than the successes of these developers. They supplied houses, shopping centres, office towers, and highrise apartments, and many combinations of these, to the inhabitants of one of the most thinly settled countries in the world, who, fortunately, for the developers, liked to cluster in cities.

MICHAEL BLISS, historian, *Northern Enterprise: Five Centuries of Canadian Business* (1987).

The only sustainable development is personal development.

PETER FITZGERALD-MOORE, geologist

and environmental consultant, lecture on sustainable growth and the Brundtland Report, University of Calgary, *University of Calgary Gazette*, 5 Feb. 1990.

Awaiting development! If there is any town on earth that would be the apple of any developer's eyes, it is St. Andrews, New Brunswick — St. Andrews By The Sea, to use the vulgar sobriquet wished upon it by earlier entrepreneurs.
JAN MORRIS, Anglo-Welsh travel writer, "New Brunswick," *Saturday Night*, May 1990.

Very bad for animals.
Reply of a Cree elder at Fort George (Chisasibi), Que., when asked how he felt about the LG-2 hydro-electric development project, quoted by Orest Slepokura in *The Globe and Mail*, 2 May 1990.

DEVIL

The devil is the unexamined side of life; it's unexamined but it's certainly not powerless.
ROBERTSON DAVIES, man-of-letters, interviewed by Tom Harpur in 1974, *Conversations with Robertson Davies* (1989) edited by J. Madison Davis.

DIEFENBAKER, JOHN G.

One Canada.
"'One Canada' was born on the prairie trails; in the fire and comradeship of World War I; in the section shacks of the railroad among immigrants with unpronounceable names; in the dreams of a new world free of prejudice and discrimination. It was a Canada where every citizen possessed the same rights of citizenship; where the heritage of all was preserved, even that of the majority; where every citizen enjoyed the same chance to get ahead, regardless of what part of the country he lived in, what his name might be, or where his parents had come from. It was a Canadianism respecting differences, not erecting them into

impassable barriers." So wrote political aide Thomas Van Dusen in *The Chief* (1968). The phrase "One Canada" is associated with Diefenbaker's successful federal election campaign, June 1957.

Nobody knows you called me, except you and me. I'm sitting in an automobile on Queen Street and nobody knows that you called me at all.
JOHN W. BASSETT, publisher of *The Toronto Telegram*, responding to a call on his early-model mobile car telephone while in Toronto; the call was placed by Prime Minister Diefenbaker from his office in Ottawa, ordering Bassett to drop NDPer Doug Fisher's political column for the duration of the 1962 election campaign then underway. Bassett agreed to do so and also to keep the call confidential, little knowing that their conversation was monitored and that tapes and transcripts would circulate for years, according to journalist Richard Cleroux in *Official Secrets: The Story behind the Canadian Security Intelligence Service* (1990).

Dief is the chief, Dief is the chief, / Dief will be the chief again. / Everybody's happy back in '57 / And nobody's happy since then. / There was law in the land, order in the home, / Swimmin' in the river back then, / And I know in my heart / That Dief will be the chief / And a dollar worth a dollar again.
One verse of "Dief Will Be the Chief Again" (1975) written by BOB BOSSIN and performed by The Stringband.

He behaved as if he subscribed to the Islamic idea of power: that a sovereign has the right to govern only until a stronger one topples his throne.
PETER C. NEWMAN, author, on former Prime Mister John G. Diefenbaker, quoted by Mel Hurtig in the Introduction to *If I Were Prime Minister* (1987).

In a very real sense, his life was Canada. Over eight decades, he spanned our history, from the ox cart on the prairies to the satellite in space. He shaped much of that history — all of it shaped him.

JOE CLARK, Prime Minister, eulogy on former Prime Minister John G. Diefenbaker, interred on the Regina campus of his *alma mater*, the University of Saskatchewan, 22 Aug. 1979, quoted by Garrett Wilson and Kevin Wilson in *Diefenbaker for the Defence* (1988).

Then Diefenbaker spoke: "I have nothing to add to what the Minister has said." And for the space of ten minutes or so he proceeded to prove it. It was rather like one of Ramsay MacDonald's later speeches: loud detonations in a dense fog.... He had indeed nothing to add; but he had subtracted a great deal.

EUGENE FORSEY, constitutional authority, *A Life on the Fringe: The Memoirs of Eugene Forsey* (1990).

DIET

The Greeks idealized the human body; we treat it as little better than an animated garbage can.

ROBERT G. JACKSON, M.D., *The Fattening Regime: A Manual for the Too-Thin* (1928, 3rd ed., 1936).

Fatness, not sex, is a taboo in our culture; and fatness has taken on evil and moral overtones.

MARION WOODMAN, analyst and author, *The Owl Was a Baker's Daughter: Obesity, Anorexia Nervosa and the Repressed Feminine* (1980).

In a variety of dramatic situations, Dr. Erik Paterson, of British Columbia, has employed with equally dramatic success the unexpected — albeit simple and safe — expedient of fasting. His prescription is, "Don't eat. Drink at least two quarts of water a day. Let's see what happens." A "cure" is what usually happens. Fasting is nature's most time-tested remedy for what ails you.

HUMPHRY OSMOND, psychiatrist, "Fasting for Anorexia Nervosa," *Predicting the Past: Memos on the Enticing Universe of Possibility* (1981) produced by Jerome Agel.

Most people I know feel that life would be complete if they could just lose ten pounds.

BETTY JANE WYLIE, author, *obiter dictum*, 1990.

Going without breakfast is like trying to drive to New York from Toronto without gas. Every fat person I know skips breakfast.

JANE BRODY, science and food writer for *The New York Times*, quoted by Marion Kane in *The Toronto Star*, 14 Nov. 1990.

DIFFICULTIES

It is not for the predictably difficult situations that you must brace yourself, but for the simple events that can undo you.

BETTY JANE WYLIE, author, *Beginnings: A Book for Widows* (1977).

DINOSAURS

Dinosaurs are a touchstone that separates the mentality of children from that of adults.

DALE A. RUSSELL, paleontologist, *An Odyssey in Time: The Dinosaurs of North America* (1989).

We are awestruck by *Tyrannosaurus*; we marvel at the feathers of *Archaeopteryx*; we revel in every scrap of fossil human bone from Africa. But none of these has taught us anywhere near as much about the nature of evolution as a little two-inch Cambrian oddball invertebrate named *Opabinia*.

STEPHEN JAY GOULD, biologist, discussing the weird-looking fossil of a five-eyed creature found in the Burgess Shale of B.C.'s Yoho National Park, *Wonderful Life: The Burgess Shale and the Nature of History* (1989).

DIPLOMACY

Diplomacy is letting someone else have your way.
> LESTER B. PEARSON, Prime Minister, quoted in *The Observer*, 18 March 1965.

I believe in intervention and personal responsibility. In fact, to me, diplomacy is getting what you want without actually going to war.
> ADRIENNE CLARKSON, Ontario's Agent-General in Paris, address, Empire Club of Canada, Toronto, 21 Nov. 1985.

We'd look at each other and say, "What are we supposed to do?" And Allan would say, "Don't ask me, I've never been an ambassador before."
> SONDRA GOTLIEB, wife of Allan Gotlieb, Canada's Ambassador to the United States, on their first days in Washington, quoted by Bob Hepburn in *The Toronto Star*, 5 April 1987.

DISABILITIES
See also HANDICAPS

My disability is that I cannot use my legs. My handicap is your negative perception of that disability, and thus of me.
> RICK HANSEN, wheelchair athlete and fund-raiser, *Rick Hansen: Man in Motion* (1987) by Rick Hansen and Jim Taylor.

Always, always I.Q.s. Always how intelligent people are. They forget the soul. To us there's no I.Q. Everything is done by soul. These peple here are daring to sit on the edge of their soul. They dare to go down in the soul. The Famous People Players was created by soul.
> DIANE DUPUY, founder of the Famous People Players, a puppet and light show employing the mentally handicapped, quoted by Catherine Dunphy in *The Toronto Star*, 27 Oct. 1988.

I am a child of the earth / I've been a vegetable since birth.
> Couplet from the poem "Vegetableism"

written by SIMON BRISENDEN, disability awareness lecturer, equal opportunities trainer, poet, and author of *Poems for Perfect People* (1988).

DISCOVERY
See also EXPLORATION

There is in insulin glory enough for all.
> Epigram to *The Discovery of Insulin* (1982) written by MICHAEL BLISS, where the sentence is attributed to Lewellys Barker. The last four words were used as the title of the CBC-TV production on the work of Dr. Frederick Banting premiered in Dec. 1990.

DISCRIMINATION
See also PREJUDICE

We have instituted laws which discriminate and we call them "reverse discrimination," based on the profoundly stupid and anti-libertarian notion that if you force private citizens to hire, house and socialize with those groups they dislike, you will eliminate racism.
> BARBARA AMIEL, columnist, address, Empire Club of Canada, Toronto, 4 Feb. 1982.

Discrimination is nothing more than an expression of preference . . . the right to discriminate is a desirable feature of free societies.
Suppose you, as an employer, were faced with two job applicants, each with a productivity level of $10.00 per hour. Assume that the male had to be paid $10.00, while the woman, thanks to the magic of "discrimination," need only be paid $6.50. Who would you choose? Unless you were an extreme sexist, you would hire the woman because you could make an additional profit of $3.50 per hour from her labour.
> WALTER BLOCK and MICHAEL WALKER, economists with the Fraser Institute, *Lexicon of Economic Thought* (1989).

DISEASE
See also HEALTH

Cancers are not rare diseases — 29% of us will develop some type of cancer in our lifetime and one in five of us will die of a cancer at present rates. More than half of all families will be affected by cancer.
> RICHARD HASSELBACH, physician, Preface, *Understanding Cancer: An Invaluable Book for Cancer Patients and Their Families* (1985) by Marilyn Dunlop.

Multiple sclerosis is a disease which has neither the common courtesy to be curable nor the common decency to be terminal.
> DAVID JORGENSON, MS sufferer, quoted by Adrian Cloete in *The Toronto Star*, 15 June 1988.

DISTINCT SOCIETY
See also MEECH LAKE ACCORD

No one can deny that Quebec is, culturally and sociologically, a distinct society. So is Newfoundland.
> EUGENE FORSEY, constitutional authority, *A Life on the Fringe: The Memoirs of Eugene Forsey* (1990).

The Accord is a quagmire of ambiguities. . . . The "distinct society" clause is just the old open-ended "special status" with a wig and false whiskers. . . . Quebec would have the powers of a nation plus the powers of a province. The rest of the country would be in a state of neo-colonialism, with Quebec as the imperial power.
> EUGENE FORSEY, constitutional authority, referring to the distinct society provision in the preamble to the Meech Lake Accord, *A Life on the Fringe: The Memoirs of Eugene Forsey* (1990)

Having recognized that Quebec is a distinct society, I say to my friends in Quebec I believe it is the responsibility of all of the citizens of Quebec to place Canada first and recognize that, like all of the other provinces, Quebec is second. . . . Canada must come first.
> CLYDE WELLS, Newfoundland Premier, after giving qualified assent to the Meech Lake Accord, Ottawa, quoted by Patrick Doyle in *The Toronto Star*, 10 June 1990.

We, the original people of this country, have inherited through the oral traditions of our forefathers . . . distinct original languages. Fifty-two of these original languages of Canada are now on the brink of extinction. Unlike you, we cannot retrieve these languages from our mother country. Our mother country is Canada. What we lose in Canada, we lose forever. We cannot let the voices of our forefathers be silenced forever.
> PHIL FONTAINE, leader of the Assembly of Manitoba Chiefs, letter to Robert Bourassa concerning the extension of the "distinct society" status to both Quebec and the native peoples, quoted in *The Globe and Mail*, 19 June 1990.

What we thought was as obvious as the nose on one's face is that aboriginal people are a distinct society, if anyone is, and we're a fundamental part of Canada. Everybody recognizes this except for eleven first ministers.
> GEORGES ERASMUS, National Chief, Assembly of First Nations, on native leaders' opposition to the passage of the Meech Lake Accord, quoted by Darcy Henton in *The Toronto Star*, 20 June 1990.

English Canada must clearly understand that Quebec is today and forever a distinct society, capable of ensuring its own development and destiny.
> ROBERT BOURASSA, Quebec Premier, responding to the collapse of the Meech Lake Constitutional Accord, 22 June 1990, quoted in *Maclean's*, 24 Dec. 1990.

Whereas Quebec constitutes a distinct society, free and able to assume its own destiny; whereas the reinforcement of the Canadian economic union has been shown to be beneficial to the interests of

Quebec and Canada; whereas the failure of the Meech Lake accord confirms the impasse of the present [form of] federalism; it is proposed. . . .

Preamble to a report called *A Quebec Free to Choose*, draft resolution proposed by the constitutional committee, headed by Jean Allard, of the Quebec Liberal Party for consideration at its policy convention, 8-10 March 1991, unofficial translation published in *The Globe and Mail*, 30 Jan. 1991.

DIVORCE
See also MARRIAGE

Accorn to yer laidist sensus, 2 marges in 5 in Canda now ends up in yer deevorce cort, the uther 3 appairntly is deetermin to fite it out to yer bitter end.

DON HARRON, comedian, in the person of Charlie Farquharson, *Cum Buy the Farm* (1987).

In the dim dark days before antisepsis, women often died in childbirth, so it was not uncommon for a man to outlive two or three wives. A man can still have two or three wives, but it's called divorce and it's much more messy and expensive.

BETTY JANE WYLIE, author, *Beginnings: A Book for Widows* (1977, rev. 1988).

In the last couple of decades . . . people often went back and forth to the divorce court the way a tongue returns to a sore tooth time and time again, just to see if it still hurts and finds that, in fact, it does.

MERLE SHAIN, essayist, *Courage My Love: A Book to Light an Honest Path* (1988).

DOCTORS
See MEDICINE

DOGS

A thousand incidents might be adduced to show that in the north there is little possibility of winter travel without dogs and little possibility of life without winter travel.

ERNEST THOMPSON SETON, naturalist and artist, *Arctic Prairies* (1911).

There is no "instinctive" man-dog bond. One need only notice how dogs are treated in most parts of the world today, both in non-industrialized and in "developed" societies.

JOHN A. LIVINGSTON, naturalist, *One Cosmic Instant: A Natural History of Human Arrogance* (1973).

DOMINION
See also CANADA
CONFEDERATION

In the opening phrases of the preamble to the act which brought our country into being, we find the following words:

Whereas the provinces of Canada, Nova Scotia and New Brunswick have expressed their desire to be federally united into one dominion —

So we find the words "Canada" and "Dominion" in the first three lines of that preamble. The suggestion in the bill before us today is that we eliminate one of those words and replace it by another. Madame Speaker, we are forgetting our history.

DONALD W. MUNRO, Member for Esquimalt-Saanich, House of Commons, 14 March 1975.

The assault on "Dominion" especially was characterized by bad law, bad history, bad logic; by chopping and changing, cringing, creeping, crawling (sometimes to Americans or other "foreigners," sometimes to "many good and loyal Canadians" — unspecified); by dodging, ducking, wriggling, squirming, backing and filling; by confusions (notably between the "name" of our country, which is Canada, and its "title," which is Dominion); by untruths and fairy tales. The perpetrators of this performance did almost all their work darkly, at dead of night, the sod with their bayonets turning.

EUGENE FORSEY, constitutional authority, *A Life on the Fringe: The Memoirs of Eugene Forsey* (1990).

DOUBT

See also BELIEF

There *may* be a baby in the bathwater.
> JAMES RANDI, conjuror and debunker, referring to the parapsychological claims made by psychics, faith-healers, etc., address in Toronto, 14 Nov. 1987.

For being Catholic is about doubting; doubt is very much a part of the questioning Catholic's life.
> LUCINDA VARDEY, author and Roman Catholic apologist, *Belonging: A Book for the Questioning Catholic Today* (1988).

Never believe what you cannot doubt.
> ROBIN SKELTON, man-of-letters, aphorism, May 1990.

DOUKHOBORS

A lot of strange immigrants from Russia had just been landed on the shores of the Dominion and the press had decided that their fate should be made a matter of interest to the world at large. They were escaping domestic persecution but it seems that on account of their religious tenets they had got into difficulties at once with the authorities of the land of refuge. It seems the Russians' destiny to suffer from lawlessness in servitude and to strive for lawlessness in their freedom.
> JOSEPH CONRAD excised this passage about the plight of the Doukhobors from the early draft of "Razumov" which grew into the major novel *Under Western Eyes* (1911). The narrator mentions receiving a letter from a niece who lives somewhere in Canada, according to Eloise Knapp Hay in *The Political Novels of Joseph Conrad* (1963).

DREAMS

You cannot harm me / you cannot harm / one who has dreamed a dream like mine.
> Ojibwa chant, first recorded in the 18th century, chosen by M.T. (Terry) Kelly as the epigraph for his novel *A Dream Like Mine* (1987).

I deal in bread and dreams.
> W. GARFIELD WESTON, baker and business executive, quoted by Stephen Brunt in *The Globe and Mail*, 13 Feb. 1988.

If you dream of taking a trip to Canada alone: You must endure a painful experience. / If you dream of taking a trip to Canada with others: You enjoy amusements too much. / If you dream of living in Canada: An enemy is seeking your ruin.
> These attempts at dream analysis are adapted from *Zolar's Encyclopaedia and Dictionary of Dreams* (1963). Zolar was the professional name of an American astrologer named Brice King who died in New York in 1976. Zolar published numerous astrological texts and was the inventor of the ten-cent horoscope vending machine.

Dreams were the original TV.
> Remark attributed to a young Cree from Alberta who found modern television wanting when measured against the traditional techniques of dream interpretation practised by the native people, quoted by Jack Horn, *Psychology Today*, March 1978.

If you build it, he will come.
> This line is associated with the short story "Shoeless Joe Jackson Comes to Iowa" (1980) by the Edmonton-born writer W.P. KINSELLA. The story, a fantasy, was expanded into a novel, *Shoeless Joe* (1982), and the novel was later filmed as *Field of Dreams*. A farmer in Iowa responds to an inner voice and builds a baseball field which magically attracts his father's idol, Shoeless Joe Jackson, who was wrongly disgraced in the 1919 White Sox scandal.

This country is made up of small towns and big dreams.
> BRIAN MULRONEY, Prime Minister, vision of Canada, quoted by William Walker

in *The Toronto Star*, 17 Sept. 1988. An early version of this remark appeared in *The Calgary Herald*, 9 July 1984.

Bless you, my son. May you and your team accomplish all your hopes and dreams and arrive home safely.
POPE JOHN PAUL II spoke these words to Rick Hansen, wheelchair athlete, during a papal audience at the Vatican in Nov. 1985. Quoted by Rick Hansen and Jim Taylor in *Rick Hansen: Man in Motion* (1987).

I believe that the roots of the imagination are physical roots, real roots.
ANNE HÉBERT, poet, interviewed by Donald Smith in *Voices of Deliverance: Interviews with Quebec and Acadian Writers* (1986) translated by Larry Shouldice.

You see, dreams do still come true.
RICK HANSEN, wheelchair athlete, originator of the Man in Motion world tour, addressing a crowd of 10,000 in Vancouver, upon completion of his fund-raising marathon, 22 May 1987, quoted by Tim Harper in *The Toronto Star* the following day. Between 21 March 1985 and 22 May 1987, Hansen toured 34 countries, travelling 40,000 kilometres/25,000 miles in his wheelchair to realize his dream to prove that the disabled are handicapped only in the eyes of others.

Listen and learn and find your dream. When you have found it, don't give up.
ALWYN MORRIS, champion canoeist, wording on a poster distributed in 1987 by the Kahnawake Social Services Resource Centre, Que. The poster shows Morris holding aloft an eagle feather, symbol of the native people, the act which drew attention to his people at the 1984 Summer Olympics in Los Angeles where he became the first native Canadian to win an Olympic gold medal. He won the gold in the 1000-metre, two-man kayak event; as well, he won a bronze in the 500-metre, two-man kayak event.

There's no such thing as the Canadian dream.
WILLIAM KILBOURN, historian, distinguishing the Canadian reality from the American dream, quoted by Stephen Brook in *Maple Leaf Rag: Travels across Canada* (1987).

It's a dream. It doesn't matter if you dream big. Big car, big house, big money. It's a dream. Big dreams cost the same as little ones. Might as well dream big.
ELLY DANICA, writer, *Don't: A Woman's Word* (1988).

Dreams cost more than they used to.
BETTY JANE WYLIE, author, *The Best Is Yet to Come: Planning Ahead for a Financially Secure Retirement* (1988).

Well, when I win THE BIGGEST BINGO IN THE WORLD. No! After I win THE BIGGEST BINGO IN THE WORLD, I will go shopping for a brand-new stove. In Toronto. At the Eaton Centre. A great big stove. The kind Madame Benoît has. The kind that has the three different compartments in the oven alone. I'll have the biggest stove on the reserve. I'll cook for all the children on the reserve. . . . Oh, when I win THE BIGGEST BINGO IN THE WORLD!
Speech of the Indian woman Veronique in *The Rez Sisters* (1988), a play in two acts written by TOMSON HIGHWAY.

Dreams are independent, spontaneous manifestations of the unconscious. Their message seldom coincides with the tendencies of the conscious mind.
DARYL SHARP, analyst and author, *The Survival Papers: Anatomy of a Midlife Crisis* (1988).

We never get to keep our dreams. But some of us are lucky enough to have the chance to chase them.
STUART McLEAN, radio commentator, CBC Radio's *Morningside*, 27 Nov. 1989.

I know you are faithful to the dreams and commitments of your youth. I am sure that you will allow me to be true to mine.

LUCIEN BOUCHARD, Cabinet Minister who resigned from the Conservative Party over possible changes to the Meech Lake Accord, letter of resignation addressed to Prime Minister Brian Mulroney, 22 May 1990, quoted by Alan Freeman in *The Globe and Mail* the following day.

But I think the humorist vision sees things in proportion because it sees them out of proportion. In other words the customary proportions of things are somehow all wrong. Perhaps that's why we have dreams to remind us every night that we've spent the previous day in a world of petrified nonsense.

NORTHROP FRYE, literary critic, Afterword, Robert Zend's *Daymares: Selected Fictions on Dreams and Time* (1991) edited by Brian Wyatt.

DRESS
See FASHION

DRINKING
See also ALCOHOL
BEER
FOOD & DRINK
WINE

Until about 1960 Toronto was little more than an overgrown small town — rather boring, British and puritanical. Naked toddlers on the beaches were considered sinful; pubs were dismal places with separate bars for "Men Only" and "Ladies and Escorts," the latter allowing men only if accompanied by a woman (the maximum ratio I can recall is six men to one woman).

EDWARD RELPH, geographer, *The Toronto Guide: The City/Metro/The Region* (Annual Conference, Association of American Geographers, Toronto, April 1990).

Actually, I drink to forget . . . the future!

EDD ULUSCHAK, cartoonist, *The Edmonton Journal*, 19 March 1983.

Most Canadians still think drinking is the stuff of comedy.

EDWARD PHILLIPS, novelist, *Sunday Best* (1990).

DRUG TRADE
See also MEDICINE
STEROIDS

And in the 1890s a Brockville, Ontario, druggist, George T. Fulford, discovered how to market a new patent medicine: use saturation newspaper advertising, stress signed personal testimonials, and coin a catchy slogan to promote a product to cure everything. The product, "Dr. Williams' Pink Pills for Pale People," was an advertising and commercial sensation around the world. Fulford, too, became a millionaire, and his great slogan, "Pink Pills for Pale People," was for many years one of the few Canadian expressions deemed memorable enough for inclusion in *The Oxford Dictionary of Quotations*.

MICHAEL BLISS, historian, *Northern Enterprise: Five Centuries of Canadian Business* (1987).

The ceremonial and religious uses of psychedelics are much older than their recreational uses and abuses. For most of their history, they have been mysterious, dangerous substances and must be treated respectfully.

HUMPHRY OSMOND, psychiatrist, "The Birth of 'Psychedelic,'" *Predicting the Past: Memos on the Enticing Universe of Possibility* (1981) produced by Jerome Agel.

Lysergic acid hits the spot. / Forty billion neurons, that's a lot.

MARSHALL McLUHAN, communications theorist, discussing with LSD guru Timothy Leary in New York in the mid-1960s various means to ensure the social acceptance of mind-expanding drugs, as reported by Leary in *Flashbacks: An Autobiography* (1983).

The fashionable Canadian drug habit, instead of cocaine, is to sniff *real* snow.

ERIC NICOL and DAVE MORE, humorists, *The U.S. or Us: What's the Difference, Eh?* (1986).

Either societies legalize harmful substances, as is the case with cigarettes and alcohol, or they put their policies where their politics are. Legalize or ostracize. That is the only choice.
DIANE FRANCIS, columnist, *Maclean's*, 12 Sept. 1988.

Once considered a victimless crime, drug abuse imposes a staggering burden on society — one that we simply cannot afford to carry. At one time, drug users were thought to belong to a fringe of the lower economic classes. Today, this is no longer the case. Up to two million Canadians regularly smoke, snort, shoot or swallow illegal drugs. Drug abuse has spread to all levels of society — from welfare recipients and high-school dropouts to factory workers, yuppies and the well-to-do.
VICTOR MALAREK, investigative reporter, *Merchants of Misery* (1989).

Morally and logically, there is no difference between allowing people to harm themselves drinking booze or smoking tobacco or allowing them to take drugs such as cocaine, heroin, marijuana or hashish.
PHILIPPE DEANE GIGANTES, author and Senator, *The Road Ahead* (1990).

DUPLESSIS, MAURICE

Rouge à Ottawa, Bleu à Quebec.
"Red in Ottawa, Blue in Quebec." This refers to the Liberal Party (red) and the Union Nationale Party (blue). "This slogan . . . was the order of the day, so that most English-speaking Liberals in Quebec naturally focussed their attention on matters federal. Duplessis had the province locked up." So wrote Jamie Swift in *Odd Man Out: The Life and Times of Eric Kierans* (1988) about the decades the Province of Quebec was run by Premier Maurice Duplessis, prior to the Quiet Revolution of the 1960s. Other characteristic

expressions of *La Grand Noirceur*, "the great darkness" (1936-39, 1944-59) of Duplessisism in Quebec are "centralizers" (Ottawa bureaucrats), "provincial autonomy," "encroachments" (federal initiatives), and "A vote for the Liberals is a vote for national extinction."

This bridge is as strong as the Union Nationale.
MAURICE DUPLESSIS, Quebec Premier, unveiling the Duplessis Bridge at Trois-Rivières, Que., 7 June 1948. The bridge collapsed just over six months later, 31 Jan. 1949.

Of the Canadian politicians I have met, the one who impressed me the most was M. Duplessis, for many years the Premier — almost dictator — of the Province of Quebec . . . he could even make very funny jokes in English, the final test of bilingualism.
CECIL H. KING, British press lord, who as Chairman of the Daily Mirror Newspapers made visits to Canada between the late 1930s and the late 1960s, *Strictly Personal: Some Memoirs of Cecil H. King* (1969)

I never married because I have a mistress, a most demanding, but a wonderful mistress — my Province of Quebec.
MAURICE DUPLESSIS, Quebec Premier, adapted from a remark recalled by Pierre Sévigny in *This Game of Politics* (1965).

DUTIES
See RESPONSIBILITY

DYING WORDS
See also DEATH

Do you mind shaking hands with me?
Final words of REGINALD BIRCHALL, murderer, addressed to the hangman, Woodstock, Ont., 14 Nov. 1890.

What a trouble I am, Mrs. Stuart.
Dying words of the poet ISABELLA VALANCY CRAWFORD, addressed to her landlady in a Toronto flat, 12 Feb. 1887,

quoted by Albert and Theresa Moritz in *The Oxford Illustrated Literary Guide to Canada* (1987).

Here lies one whose name was writ in hot water.

These are neither the dying words nor the epitaph of ROBERT ROSS, the Canadian-born companion of Oscar Wilde. Ross, who shared in the shame of his mentor, mockingly offered the quip for his epitaph. It is quoted as such by Richard Ellman in *Oscar Wilde* (1987) who explained that Oscar Wilde died in 1900 and nine years later his remains were interred beneath the impressive funerary monument in Père Lachaise, the famous cemetery in Paris. "When Ross died in 1918, his will directed that his own ashes be put into the tomb. This was done." The tomb bears a verse by Wilde which ends with these words: "And outcasts always mourn." Robert Ross is also the name of the main character in Timothy Findley's novel *The Wars* (1977).

The Harbour almost reached after a splendid voyage, with such companions all the way, and my boy awaiting me.

Last written words of SIR WILLIAM OSLER, distinguished physician and teacher, found written on a slip of paper shortly after his death at Oxford, England, 29 Dec. 1919. The reference to "my boy" conveys the sorrow he felt on the death of his son who was killed in action in 1917 during the First World War. In his diary he recorded his son's death, concluding, "Call no man happy till he dies."

Eight o'clock and after so much walking I have got here. Oh, to see the swans and the spring flowers, and to smell them. . . . Pray God nothing stops me tonight. . . . God bless my children and look after them.

ALMA RATTENBURY, Canadian-born English socialite accused but acquitted of complicity in the death of her architect husband R.J. Rattenbury, left this letter on the bank of the river near Bourne-mouth, England, in which she drowned herself, 4 June 1935. Quoted by Frank Jones in *The Toronto Star*, 19 March 1989.

Actors trade tricks back and forth, smart directors sometimes inspire actors to new approaches and techniques, but the wellspring of inspiration is life itself. Close, acute, constant observation of people, animals, birds in day-to-day life imparts a constant stream of true and exciting expression for the actor. . . .

Last written words of the actor JOHN DRAINIE from a letter left incomplete at the time of his death. It was intended for J. Keiller Mackay, head of the Ontario Arts Council which had established an actor's bursary in Drainie's name. The letter ended in mid-sentence and the actor died a few days later, on 30 Sept. 1966. Quoted by Bronwyn Drainie in *Living the Part: John Drainie and the Dilemma of Canadian Stardom* (1988).

Lovely, Mircha, lovely. She is a very gracious lady.

Last words of VINCENT MASSEY, former Governor General, as recorded by his biographer Claude T. Bissell in *The Imperial Canadian: Vincent Massey in Office* (1986). These words were spoken to his valet, Mircha, whose full name is Miroslav Stanjanovich, about a bouquet of flowers sent by the Queen Mother. Massey uttered the words in his London flat at 10:00 a.m., 30 Dec. 1967.

I've got to speak to Al. Get him down here. Tell him only I can fix Massey.

The dying words of corporate head J.A. (BUD) McDOUGALD as quoted by Peter C. Newman in *The Canadian Establishment: Volume One* (1976). McDougald was summoning Al Thornborough, an executive of Massey-Ferguson, which was about to go under, when he died in Toronto, March 1978.

Am I still here?

Question asked by the old Cheyenne chief OLD LODGE SKINS in the Hollywood film *Little Big Man* (1970). The part of the old Chief was played by native spokesperson Dan George. The question, spoken in the early morning, expresses the character's surprise that, despite the presence of forerunners, he had survived the night.

Eric went Brazil?

These are among the last words spoken by MARSHALL McLUHAN following his stroke on 26 Sept. 1979. They concern the substitute appearance of Eric McLuhan, his son and collaborator, at a conference on McLuhanism to be held days hence in São Paulo, Brazil. Quoted by Matie Armstrong Molinaro in "Marshalling McLuhan," *The Antigonish Review*, Summer-Autumn 1988.

This is my persistent nightmare: / I jump into a shallow river / My feet sink in mud to mid-calf, the top of my head just breaks the surface / It's November / Too soon for the ice to preserve me.

ROBERT BILLINGS, poet, "Epiphanies of the First Cold Day," a poem written in 1983. Three years later, in November, Billings waded into the Niagara River and was swept over the Horseshoe Falls. Ice

formed and it was not until the following June that his body was released.

During a lengthy career in social work and local politics, Ottawa's Charlotte Whitton was called a bulldog, a busybody and a one-woman gang. But there was another epithet, coined by *Time* magazine, that she treasured to her dying day. That day came in 1975, after a heart attack put her in hospital at the age of seventy-eight. When her sister Kay arrived there, a doctor warned that Miss Whitton's mind was wandering; she might not be coherent. Gently wakened, she smiled up at Kay. "Do you know what I was?" she whispered, smiling at the memory. "I was 'hell on wheels.'"

DAVID MacDONALD, "Anecdotes," *The Toronto Star*, 26 Nov. 1988.

Perhaps darkness is another kind of light. I hope so.

One of the last entries in the journal of CLAUDE JUTRA, filmmaker and victim of Alzheimer's Disease, written on 29 Oct. 1986, eleven days before he leapt to his death from Montreal's Jacques Cartier Bridge, 5 Nov. 1986. Quoted by Ann Charney in *Saturday Night*, May 1988.

EARTH
See also NATURE

O earth / for the strength / of my heart / I thank Thee // O cloud / for the blood / in my body / I thank Thee // O fire / for the shine / in my eyes / I thank Thee // O sun / for the life / you gave me / I thank Thee
> CHIEF DAN GEORGE, native spokesperson and poet, *My Heart Soars* (1974).

No accident of fate was ever more significant to Earth than its critical distance from the sun, allowing for the thread-thin range of 100° C. within which the existence of liquid water is possible.
> JOHN A. LIVINGSTON, naturalist, *One Cosmic Instant: A Natural History of Human Arrogance* (1973).

On land, inevitably surrounded by trees or buildings or hills, it is easy to forget the *size* of the world, but at sea, impossible to ignore. Once out in the ocean, the scale of everything changes as though you had entered a new dimension, a dominion of gigantic beings.
> DAVID McTAGGART, ecologist and activist, *Greenpeace III: Journey into the Bomb* (1978).

To go softly upon the Earth is to respect her, to love her. To violate the Earth is to violate Gaia. She is patient. She endures. She is slow to anger. For a time she may acquiesce in this violation, but in the end she will turn upon her tormentors and destroy them.
> Lines about Gaia, the personification of Earth, from the novel *The Gaian Expedient* (1985) by the author WAYLAND DREW.

We need no longer act as isolated units; we can serve and help the Earth itself. We can acquire a new sense of destiny.
> DOROTHY MACLEAN, medium, *To Hear the Angels Sing: An Odyssey of Co-Creation with the Devic Kingdom* (1980).

Once we reach the early decades of the 21st-Century, the frailty of our evolution on planet Earth will start to be perceived as a purely temporary stepping-stone to a cosmic future — once we will learn to understand and manage with our minds as we move out into the Universe and the galaxies in the centuries beyond.
> FRANK FEATHER, futurologist, *G-Forces: Reinventing the World — The 35 Global Forces Restructuring Our World* (1989).

Our responsibility above any other responsibility is to leave the Earth in such a state as generations to come can live and breathe and enjoy life. This is the decade where we do, or don't, fulfill that responsibility.

TOMSON HIGHWAY, playwright, quoted in *Metropolis*, 21 Dec. 1989.

It is home to the people of Mexico, home to the people of Greece and Turkey. It's home to Israelis and Arabs. It's home to the Vietnamese. It's home to the aboriginal people and the farmers of the Australian outback. It's home to the people of Japan. It's home to the peoples of the Caribbean. It's home to all of us. And it's our *only* home.

Concluding words of narration, to the accompaniment of the appropriate images taken by the astronauts aboard the Space Shuttle Missions, spoken by editor, writer, narrator TONI MYERS in *Blue Planet*.

Blue Planet, an IMAX(R) film, is a presentation of the Smithsonian Institution's National Air and Space Museum and the Lockheed Corporation, filmed in cooperation with the National Aeronautics and Space Administration. (c) MCMXC Smithsonian Institution/Lockheed Corporation. *Blue Planet* was produced by Imax Space Technology Inc., a subisidiary of Imax Systems Corporation of Toronto.

EAST & WEST

The values of East and West do not clash. They are supplementary and interchangeable; and it will be well for the world when this is fully realized, and there is free circulation of thought.

L. ADAMS BECK, novelist and orientalist, *The Story of Oriental Philosophy* (1928).

While we are Westernizing the East by our old technology, we are Easternizing ourselves by the new technology. TV is an orientalizing force, taking us all on an "inner trip" that blurs the old idea of private identity altogether.

MARSHALL McLUHAN, media philosopher, letter to Hubert Humphrey dated 9 Feb. 1967, *Letters of Marshall McLuhan* (1987) edited by Matie Molinaro, Corinne McLuhan, and William Toye.

If Canada is to succeed in what has been called "the Pacific Century," we must start "thinking Asia."

WILLIAM DALTON, officer, Hongkong Bank of Canada, *The Globe and Mail*, 12 May 1990.

EASTER
See HOLIDAYS

ECOLOGY
See also ENVIRONMENTALISM
GREENPEACE
NATURE

The Ark on Prince Edward Island attempts to do this. It combines into one solar- and wind-powered structure a household, resident greenhouse, a microfarm (including aquaculture), a vegetable greenhouse and tree nursery component, a small barn shop, a waste-purifying system, and a research laboratory. It is a first attempt to create symbiotic associations out of support functions normally separated in space and time. Unprecedented levels of integration between energy, food, and shelter systems have been attempted. As such, the Ark is a first effort at a new synthesis.

JOHN TODD et al., ecologists, describing the experimental Ark on Prince Edward Island, *Tomorrow Is Our Permanent Address: The Search for an Ecological Science of Design as Embodied in the Bioshelter* (1980).

In fact, the biblical promise has come true at last. Man had dominion over the earth. God grant that he may now learn to have dominion over himself.

DONALD A. CHANT and RALPH O. BRINKHURST, environmentalists, *This*

Good, Good Earth: Our Fight for Survival (1971).

I don't want to see this beautiful country trampled over or exploited or wrecked haphazardly. As you know, we regret that we made so many mistakes in the South. Well, we now have the chance to profit by those mistakes in the North.
PIERRE BERTON, author, address, Empire Club of Canada, Toronto, 11 Oct. 1973.

If "human ecology" is ever to emerge as a definable body of knowledge or area of investigation, it is far more likely to emerge from the humanities than from any of the hard or soft sciences. Man is a cultural animal. Culture created the power structure over nature, and only in culture is the blueprint for its dismantlement.
JOHN A. LIVINGSTON, naturalist, *One Cosmic Instant: A Natural History of Human Arrogance* (1973).

There is a limit to human activity, not only because there might not be enough to go around, but because of the severe and often irreversible effects that human intervention has on the ecosystem.
URSULA FRANKLIN, Professor of Metallurgy and Metals Science, University of Toronto, address, Empire Club of Canada, Toronto, 30 March 1978.

Henceforth, not only will you all be no-growth humans and glad of it, but you will also, whether you like it or not, be living in a no-growth society. As in a poker game some will win and some lose. In the past all countries have tried to fiddle the rules to win by new laws of financing, and some countries like Canada have been able to draw fresh cards in the form of natural resources, but in the future we should realize that only good cards and good playing will avail and that one should not be too confident that one will automatically win without really trying.
J. TUZO WILSON, Director, Ontario Science Centre, Toronto, address, Empire Club of Canada, 1 March 1979.

In North America we must, in fact, reclaim the heritage of the Continent, a heritage which we have almost destroyed. Whatever our backgrounds, we will not be truly American or Canadian or Mexican until we, like the native peoples, recognize the Earth as our mother, and show respect for every form, function and power of Nature.
DOROTHY MACLEAN, medium, *To Hear the Angels Sing: An Odyssey of Co-Creation with the Devic Kingdom* (1980).

Everywhere we go, we destroy the natural environment with wholesale insensitivity to its rhythms and balances. We are reconstructing the entire surface of this planet to suit our alien dimensions. The distress we stir on this Earth may be due to the fact we don't belong here.
T.B. PAWLICKI, writer and thinker, *How to Build a Flying Saucer and Other Proposals in Speculative Engineering* (1981).

Hummus: the peanut butter of the intelligentsia.
EDWARD PHILLIPS, novelist, *Buried on Sunday* (1986).

It's humbling to ponder the thought that if the natives of the Americas had been able to impose their beliefs on the first Europeans instead of vice versa, the entire Western world could have evolved harmoniously with nature.
GARY and JOANIE McGUFFIN, ecologists, *Where Rivers Run* (1988).

When the Iroquois made a decision, they said, "How does it affect seven generations in the future?"
JEREMY RIFKIN, U.S. bioethicist, quoted by Edward Tivnan in *The New York Times Magazine*, 16 Oct. 1988.

The world was not created for people only, but for purposes that far transcend the human race with its limited foresight and imagination; and therefore it behoves all conscious inhabitants of this superb planet to nurture it as a garden, maintaining it in health, beauty, and diversity for whatever glorious future its denizens may together share.

J. STAN ROWE, naturalist, "The Importance of Conserving Systems," *Endangered Spaces: The Future for Canada's Wilderness* (1989) edited by Monte Hummel.

My people are hunters and trappers who have occupied and taken care of the land since time immemorial. The Cree land is vast, and we use this land to survive. In a Cree community, a person defines himself through his knowledge of the ways of the land. He learns the ways of the animals. And yet, future generations will not have access to this way of life because of the environmental damage created by the hydroelectric projects in Northern Quebec.

MATTHEW COON COME, Grand Chief, Grand Council of the Crees, statement distributed by the Earthroots Coalition, June 1991.

There's an old saying which goes: Once the last tree is cut and the last river poisoned, you will find you cannot eat your money.

JOYCE McLEAN, writer, *The Globe and Mail*, 1 Nov. 1989.

The Ten Commandments, though still valid, are completely lacking in concern for our relationship to other species and to the Earth itself. They prohibit adultery, murder and lying, but say nothing about the rights of animals, plants, rivers, oceans, or forests. We need an eleventh commandment which says: Thou shalt not commit genocide, the killing of the planet.

TOM HARPUR, religion columnist, *The Toronto Star*, 12 Nov. 1989.

If in the next decade people could ask themselves "What does this look like from 10,000 miles up in the sky," then perhaps we could change our legacy of treating Earth and life as though we are whales in goldfish bowls and realize we're just ants in the desert.

BOBBY WISEMAN, musician, quoted in *Metropolis*, 21 Dec. 1989.

The planet does not need "saving." It has periodically been coming apart — only to be pasted together again — since the proverbial Garden of Eden. Fundamentally, the Earth is in orbit within a self-correcting stable-state environment — the solar system. Our responsibility is to help it self-correct, and I believe we have the ability to do so.

FRANK FEATHER, futurologist, *G-Forces: Reinventing the World — The 35 Global Forces Restructuring Our World* (1989).

Maybe a series of ecological accidents, St-Basil-le-Grand to a higher power, will create a cultural shock that might generate a conversion to a new social vision.

GREGORY BAUM, theologian, "Symposium," *The Canadian Forum*, Jan. 1990.

If the right side wins, this combat may become known to future generations as the Crusade that Rescued the Earth. If the wrong side wins — there will *be* no future generations.

FARLEY MOWAT, author and naturalist, Introduction, *Rescue the Earth! Conversations with the Green Crusaders* (1990).

More than any other time in history, the 1990s will be a turning point for human civilization. Not only are we facing ecological diasters that could affect our ability to survive, but the crisis is forcing us to reexamine the value system that has governed our lives for at least the past 2000 years.

ANITA GORDON and DAVID SUZUKI, science broadcasters, *It's a Matter of Survival* (1990).

ECONOMIC NATIONALISM

Annexation talk anywhere in Canada can only be safely interpreted in the light of history: it is heard whenever there is a period of hard times, and dies down as soon as confidence is restored.

> WILLIAM ARTHUR DEACON, literary critic, "The Bogey of Annexation" (1925), quoted by Clara Thomas and John Lennox in *William Arthur Deacon: A Canadian Literary Life* (1982).

Should I venture to suggest that the entire issue of American ownership of Canadian resources is a considerable red herring? If the United States is the Canadian environment in the electric information age, does not the property issue become irrelevant? Is not property, as such, the old environment upon which we focus in the rear-view mirror? The real environment of electric information remains like all new environments, invisible.

> MARSHALL McLUHAN, media philosopher, letter to Tom Easterbrook, 22 Feb. 1967, *Letters of Marshall McLuhan* (1987) edited by Matie Molinaro, Corinne McLuhan, and William Toye.

I want a Canada that is determined in its thinking to become both economically strong and economically independent. Surely it is time that Canadian resources were owned by Canadians, controlled by Canadians. Mr. Trudeau may want to put his priorty on bringing home the Constitution. The priority of my party in this campaign is to bring Canada home to Canadians.

> ED BROADBENT, NDP leader, address, Empire Club of Canada, Toronto, 11 May 1979.

The one sure prescription for the eventual failure of the Canadian experiment in nationality would be to create an ever-widening gap in standards of living between the two North American democracies.

> MICHAEL BLISS, historian, *Northern Enterprise: Five Centuries of Canadian Business* (1987).

Do we really want to be the Western world's Manchuria?

> DAVID CRANE, columnist, on the failure of policy-makers in resource-rich Canada to come to grips with the Japanese challenge, *The Toronto Star*, 6 April 1988.

Foreign investors are buying our country from under our feet. Do you believe the French government would allow Connaught to buy Institute Merieux? I wonder when Canadians will stop being the last Boy Scouts in the international marketplace.

> DAVID PETERSON, Ontario Premier, speech, *The Globe and Mail*, 10 Oct. 1989.

Today, Canada has a greater degree of foreign ownership than would be tolerated in any other developed nation in the world. While it is not yet back to the appalling levels of the late 1960s and early 1970s, it is not only now rapidly headed in that direction but it is certain to reach new record levels. . . . Canada's foreign indebtedness compared to GNP was only 18 per cent [in 1965]. Today it's 39 per cent.

> MEL HURTIG, publisher and nationalist, address, Carleton University, Ottawa, 23 Sept. 1989.

ECONOMICS

I am delighted to see the lines on which you are trying to promote sensible ideas in Canada.

> JOHN MAYNARD KEYNES, British economist and theorist, letter dated 12 Jan. 1932 to Gerry McGeer, lawyer, M.P., and later Mayor of Vancouver, quoted by David Ricardo Williams in *Mayor Gerry:*

The Remarkable Gerald Grattan McGeer (1986).

One of the greatest pieces of economic wisdom is to know what you do not know.
JOHN KENNETH GALBRAITH, economist and author, quoted in *Instant Quotation Dictionary* (1969) compiled by Donald O. Bolander, Dolores D. Varner, Gary B. Wright, and Stephanie H. Greene.

Economic life develops by grace of innovating; it expands by grace of import-replacing.
JANE JACOBS, urbanologist, *Cities and the Wealth of Nations* (1984).

In fact, I was reminded of a friend's remark — or maybe I should say a former friend — who told me that "economists were created to make astrologers look serious." We are in a very risky business.
MARIE-JOSÉE DROUIN, economist and executive director of the Hudson Institute, address, Empire Club of Canada, Toronto, 13 Feb. 1986.

The great contemporary economic mystery is how the West could be doing so well while doing so badly at creating jobs.
RICHARD GWYN, columnist, *The Toronto Star*, 14 Oct. 1987.

We have become a globally interdependent economy, but we have not established the instruments of governance needed to guide global economic policy. The system is on autopilot, desperately needing human intervention. It is in this vacuum that chaos threatens.
GUY DAUNCEY, author, *After the Crash: The Emergence of the Rainbow Economy* (1988).

If Economics Is Sovereign, There Is No Right and Wrong.
Title of a section of *Wrong End of the Rainbow: The Collapse of Free Enterprise in Canada* (1988) by ERIC KIERANS and WALTER STEWART.

An economist, as you know, is someone who is good at figures but doesn't have the personality to be an accountant.
ALLAN FOTHERINGHAM, columnist, *Maclean's*, 12 Dec. 1988.

Distression.
Word coined by economist CARL BEIGIE to describe the state of the world economy as it heads into a recession, *The Globe and Mail*, 16 Feb. 1990. The neologism combines two words, "distress" and "recession." Economists define a "recession" in terms of two quarters of economic contraction.

Economics is basically very simple. It is the science or the art whereby we devise a system to feed, house and clothe people and give them the necessities of life.
REMI J. DE ROO, Bishop of Victoria, quoting with approval the definition of Xabier Gorostiaga, a Jesuit economist working in Nicaragua, quoted by George Mortimore in *The Canadian Forum*, May 1990.

The cozy world of economics is a closed, isolated system in which the real cost of doing business on this planet, the cost to the environment in terms of depletion of non-renewable resources and pollution, has no place.
ANITA GORDON and DAVID SUZUKI, science broadcasters, *It's a Matter of Survival* (1990).

ECONOMY, CANADIAN
See also ECONOMICS

In developing strategies for economic recovery, we firmly believe that first priority must be given to the real victims of the current recession, namely — the unemployed, the welfare poor, the working poor — pensioners, native peoples, women, young people — and small farmers, fishermen, some factory workers, and some small business men and women. This option calls for economic policies which realize that the needs of the poor have priority over the wants of the rich;

that the rights of workers are more important than the maximization of profits; that the participation of marginalized groups takes precedence over the preservation of a system which excludes them.

REMI J. DE ROO, Bishop of Victoria, "Ethical Reflections on the Economic Crisis," an essay released in Ottawa on 5 Jan. 1983 by the Canadian Conference of Catholic Bishops' Episcopal Commission for Social Affairs.

Under conditions of "tough competition" in international markets for capital and trade, the poor majority of the world is especially vulnerable. With three-quarters of the world's population, for example, the poor nations of the South are already expected to survive on less than one-fifth of the world's income. Within Canada itself, the top 20% receive 42.5% of total personal income while the bottom 20% receive 4.1%. These patterns of domination and inequality are likely to further intensify as the "survival of the fittest" doctrine is applied more rigorously to the economic order.

REMI J. DE ROO, Bishop of Victoria, "Ethical Reflections on the Economic Crisis," an essay released in Ottawa on 5 Jan. 1983 by the Canadian Conference of Catholic Bishops' Episcopal Commission for Social Affairs.

What do the Bishops know? They're not economists.

Attributed to Prime Minister PIERRE ELLIOTT TRUDEAU upon learning that the Canadian Conference of Catholic Bishops on 5 Jan. 1983 had criticized the government's anti-inflation policy with respect to its effects on the working man.

It's finally happened — the country's being repossessed!

EDD ULUSCHAK, cartoonist, The Edmonton Journal, 12 Sept. 1985.

The myth of a grand, coherent National Policy was first promulgated by the Liberal scholar and civil servant, O.D. Skel-

ton, in the "General Economic History" volume he contributed to the Canada and Its Provinces series in 1913. It was perpetuated through several generations of standard economic history textbooks, most notably Esterbrook and Aitken's Canadian Economic History. One of the idea's implications was that governments had the capacity to plan grand, coherent nation-building programs.

MICHAEL BLISS, historian, Northern Enterprise: Five Centuries of Canadian Business (1987).

My economic agenda reflects my view that the number-one challenge confronting Canada is to become more competitive by becoming more efficient, innovative, and productive. Only by these means can Canada achieve full employment, grow rapidly, significantly increase its people's standard of living, and generate the wherewithal — without social friction — to do better for the disadvantaged and downtrodden within our midst.

JOHN CRISPO, political economist, contributor to If I Were Prime Minister (1987) edited by Mel Hurtig.

Canada is a country with five economic regions dedicated to the idea that if one region suffers, all must suffer. But if one region succeeds, the rest must suffer.

DAVE BROADFOOT, comedian, quoted by Isabel Vincent in The Globe and Mail, 30 June 1989.

A nation is more than bottom line. I am not underestimating the threat of our huge public debt, it's disturbing. But running a country is not like running a business. The business of business is money and profits, return, productivity. The business of politics is people.

JOHN TURNER, Liberal leader, Toronto address, 1 Nov. 1989, reported by David Vienneau in The Toronto Star the following day.

In short, it is our ability to maintain the competitiveness of our existing resource-based industries, while enhancing industries that produce high-value-added, tradeable goods and services, that really determines whether Canada prospers or becomes an economic backwater.

Among the nations of the world, Canada ranks eighth in terms of per capita wealth. We used to be second. In other words, our relative wealth has declined. That is a sign that our economy is failing.

> J. FRASER MUSTARD, President, Canadian Institute for Advanced Research, *The Globe and Mail*, 3 Feb. 1990.

We should talk about the real constitution of the country — which, of course, is the economy.

> BOB RAE, Ontario Premier, address, joint meeting of the Canadian Club and the Empire Club of Canada, 29 Oct. 1990, quoted by Derek Ferguson in *The Toronto Star* the following day.

If the new Canada does not live within its means, this nation will stumble backwards into the 21st century on its way to becoming a Third World economy like Argentina or Brazil.

> PRESTON MANNING, leader, Reform Party, quoted in *Maclean's*, 29 Oct. 1990.

EDITORS
See also PUBLISHING

The editors are well under thirty and intend to remain so.

> Editorial, *The Canadian Mercury*, Vol. 1, No. 1, Dec. 1928.

Nobody works in this business for the money. Being an editor is a luxury.

> ANNA PORTER, editor turned publisher, quoted by Margaret Mironowicz in *The Globe and Mail*, 21 April 1977.

Editing books is like bringing up children: you know what you want them to be like, but they do not necessarily turn out that way. You have to accept what you get and, as often as not, what you get is better than what you first wanted.

> KRISTJANA GUNNARS, editor, Introduction, *Unexpected Fictions: New Icelandic Canadian Writing* (1989).

EDMONTON
See also ALBERTA

This is the town that has grown enormously in the last few years — it is the town for the new oil wells — and it seems to me a horrible place. A stag dinner tonight at a club with a lot of business and similar types doesn't promise any delights. I've spent most of this morning talking to newspapermen, and dodging into the lav[atory] as I've suddenly got a touch of something like dysentery, probably due to the sudden changes of water and temperature.

> J.B. PRIESTLEY, English author touring Canada, letter written to his wife Jacquetta Hawkes, Edmonton, 23 April 1956, quoted by Vincent Brome in *J.B. Priestley* (1988).

I had accepted the job at Edmonton in order to return to Canada.... But I had not realized how far north Edmonton was. It was a raw city, vibrating with energy, but saddled with what I thought were enormous handicaps — a flat landscape relieved only by the river, mosquitoes as big as sparrows in the summer, and winters that were inhumanly cold.

> DAVID SUZUKI, budding scientist and later media personality, writing about joining the University of Alberta in 1962, *Metamorphosis: Stages in a Life* (1987).

These terrible high-rises & fearsome geometry — not the breathtaking arrogance of N.Y. skyscrapers — & the muddy (but dried mud) parking lots — & the dominance of cars & the endless flat pavements, wide uneventful roads.

It stands to reason, there *must* be a pulsing human life *somewhere*, here as elsewhere, there *must* be. Does it take place in their homes — visiting back & forth, tiny exchanges, boring each other for a purpose?

O where for me shall my salvation come,
from whence arise?

> ELIZABETH SMART, novelist and diarist,
> "Edmonton Journal" (1982), *Autobiographies* (1987) edited by Christina Burridge.

The sunsets, the sunrises, & one morning
a gigantic rainbow without rain or sun. But
the hideousness of the buildings, muddy
parking lots, trim, unwitty parkland
around the University. One day, I ventured
a few yards down the ravine looking for
mushrooms — & found some — & felt
happy to have twigs tearing my hair & a
whiff of the wilderness.

> ELIZABETH SMART, novelist and diarist,
> "Edmonton Journal" (1982), *Autobiographies* (1987) edited by Christina Burridge.

Edmonton, Edmonton.

The capital of Alberta is a city you come
from, not a place to visit, unless you happen to have relatives there or an interest
in an oil well nearby. On first glance, and
even on third, it seems not so much a city
as a jumble of a used-building lot, where
the spare office towers and box-shaped
apartment buildings and cinder-block motels discarded in the construction of real
cities have been abandoned to waste
alway in the cruel prairie winter. . . .

There is hardly a tree to be seen downtown, nothing to delight the eye on Jasper
Avenue. On 30-below-zero nights, grim religious zealots loom on street corners,
speaking in tongues, and intrepid streetwalkers in miniskirts rap on the windows
of cars that have stopped for traffic. There
isn't a first-class restaurant anywhere in
town. But, for all that, the city of 700,000
has a fascinating history.

> MORDECAI RICHLER, novelist and journalist, "King of the New Canada," *The New York Times Sports Magazine*, 29 Sept. 1985.

It was apt, I thought, that Gourmet World
should exist in the mall, for the man who
invented the concept of the global village — Marshall McLuhan — was a native
of Edmonton. (His father dealt in real estate.) At West Edmonton the global village
has become a smorgasbord for the pleasure of North America.

> MARK ABLEY, traveller and writer, *Beyond Forget: Rediscovering the Prairies* (1986).

I cannot believe myself what we have built.

> NADER GHERMEZIAN, one of the five
> Ghermezian brothers, developers of the
> West Edmonton Mall, speaking at its
> opening, quoted by Stephen Brook, English travel writer, *Maple Leaf Rag: Travels across Canada* (1987).

Edmonton is also, it must be said, about
the coldest city in Christendom. No one
knows the meaning of the word "cold" who
has not waited for a bus on a street corner
near the University of Alberta campus on
a windy and overcast evening in February.

> MECHTILD HOPPENRATH and CHARLES
> OBERDORF, writers, *First-Class Canada* (1987).

Edmonton isn't really the end of the
world — although you can see it from
there.

> RALPH KLEIN, Calgary Mayor, addressing
> the Olympic Writers Festival, quoted by
> Brian Brennan in *The Calgary Herald*, 2
> March 1988.

It has more commercial space per capita
than most cities in North America; it has
the largest physical size of any city in
Canada (roughly 670 square kilometres),
and it has the country's largest municipal
budget ($1.2 billion in 1989).

> KENNETH BAGNELL, editor, "Northern
> Light," *The Imperial Oil Review*, Winter
> 1989.

I don't want Edmonton to grow too big. If
it grows too big it might lose some of its
friendliness. People might not participate
as much. And you might not be able to see
the sky, and Edmonton is not Edmonton if
you can't see the sky.

> JOE SHOCTOR, benefactor and booster,
> quoted by Kenneth Bagnell in "Northern

Light," *The Imperial Oil Review*, Winter 1989.

The biggest difference between L.A. and Edmonton was that instead of people looking at me, I was looking at them.
> WAYNE GRETZKY, hockey personality, referring to his move from Edmonton to Los Angeles, *Gretzky: An Autobiography* (1990) written with Rick Reilly.

EDUCATION
See also COLLEGES & UNIVERSITIES
HUMANITIES
SCIENCE & SCIENTISTS
TEACHERS & TEACHING
TECHNOLOGY

By Education, I mean not the mere acquisition of certain arts, or of certain branches of knowledge, but that instruction and discipline which qualify and dispose the subjects of it for their appropriate duties and appointments in life, as Christians, as persons in business, and also as members of the civil community in which they live.
> EGERTON RYERSON, Superintendent of Education in Canada West (Ontario) in 1844-76, *System of Public Instruction for Upper Canada* (1846), quoted by J. George Hodgins, editor of *The Story of My Life by the Late Rev. Egerton Ryerson, D.D., LL.D.* (1883).

... that our province ... possessing the best educational system in the world....
> Key words from the *Report of the Ontario Commission to the World's Columbian Exposition, 1893* (Toronto, 1894), quoted by Gerald Killan in *David Boyle: From Artisan to Archaeologist* (1983). The notion that public education in Ontario was the best in the world was surprisingly influential.

The education of the masses should not go too far beyond mere reading, writing and arithmetic and the object-lessons here proposed. The injunction "educate the people" must not be misinterpreted, as it certainly is in far too many cases.

Education must be special to the calling of the individual, a truth which Lady Aberdeen is now trying hard to inculcate: servants, nurses, cooks must learn how to minister unto the wants of others. Too much grammar, literature, music, embroidery, conchology and the like, unfits the farmer's daughter for the duties of her husband's sphere in life. Collegiate, University tuition are ill adapted to the farmer's son, if he is to follow in the footsteps of his sire; though enough of chemistry to be imparted in a few object lessons and enough of botany are essential to his success in agri-, horti-, sylvi- and arboriculture. Let us beware of "too much education," there is a danger of overdoing the thing and thus causing or inciting our should-be agriculturalists to be dissatisfied with their parents' mode of livelihood.
> CHARLES BAILLARGÉ, Quebec educator, "Technical Education of the People in Untechnical Language," *Transactions of the Royal Society of Canada*, May 1894.

Education is not advanced by moving stones from Dan to Beersheba and back again.
> ALFRED FITZPATRICK, Founder and Principal of Frontier College, *The University in Overalls: A Plea for Part-Time Study* (1920).

Too long our education systems have been putting the cart before the horse. We started out with a book in our hands when we should have begun with a tool. The order should have been the tool first, then the book.
> ALFRED FITZPATRICK, Founder and Principal of Frontier College, *The University in Overalls: A Plea for Part-Time Study* (1920).

And if our diagnosis is correct then we are on the eve of a great mass movement in adult education, the like of which the world has never seen. The reform of society will come, not through the indoctrination of the young but from the intellectual conversion and convictions of the adult. If this be true, then adult education has an important function. It is the agency whose sole purpose is to provide the people with the vision without which they will indeed perish.

> PETER SANDIFORD, Professor of Educational Psychology, Ontario College of Education, 1935, quoted by J.R. Kidd in "The Social Gospel and Adult Education in Canada," *The Social Gospel in Canada* (1975) edited by Richard Allen.

Education is casting false pearls before real swine.

> Attributed to H.J. CODY, Anglican Canon and President of the University of Toronto in 1932-44.

We believe also in the mute, inglorious Miltons. It is the duty of Adult Education to make the *mute vocal*, and to make the *blind see*.

> JAMES J. TOMPKINS, adult educator, address at the Antigonish Co-operative Conference, 16 Aug. 1938, quoted by George Boyle in *Father Tompkins of Nova Scotia* (1953).

An educated person is not a past participle: education is a life-long process never finished. It is often said that undergraduate training does nothing more than define the limits of one's ignorance. It also shows us that, no matter how much a good instructor can help us, we are the only ones who can do the work: we have to teach ourselves.

> GEORGE WHALLEY, educator, address at Rothesay College School, Rothesay, N.B., 1959, *George Whalley: Remembrances* (1989) edited by Michael D. Moore.

The mark of an educated man is not in his boast that he has built his mountain of facts and stood on top of it, but in his admission that there may be other peaks in the same range with men on top of them, and that, though their views of the landscape may be different from his, they are none the less legitimate.

> E.J. PRATT, address, Memorial University, St. John's, Nfld., 8 Oct. 1952, quoted by

David G. Pitt in *E.J. Pratt: The Master Years, 1927-1964* (1987).

"The advantages of a classical education are two-fold; it enables us to look with contempt upon those who have not shared its advantages, and it fits us for places of emolument, both in this world and in the next."

> E.W. STEACIE, scientist, quoting (with wry disapproval) "the Prebendary of Durham," address, University of Western Ontario, 23 Oct. 1958, *Science in Canada: Selections from the Speeches of E.W. Steacie* (1965) edited by J.D. Babbitt.

The chief educational reform that is needed in Canada is to make all Canadians, from coast to coast, bilingual in French and English. At present Canada is not a bilingual country; it is a di-lingual one, for most Canadians speak only one of the two national langauges and refuse to learn the other. What an opportunity they have been missing!

> ARNOLD TOYNBEE, historian, "The Case for a Bilingual Canada," *Temper of the Times: An Anthology of Assorted Contemporary Literature* (1969) edited by Ralph Greenfield and Ronald Side.

There are three purposes of an education. These are to entertain an idea, to entertain a stranger, and to entertain yourself.

> Attributed to "an old educator in the early 1950s," CBC Radio, 24 March 1986.

Education is not something to make a man a lawyer, a doctor, an engineer or a priest. It is something to make him a man. The true education is not to give a man a standard of living, but a standard of life.

> GRATTAN O'LEARY, publisher and Senator, quoted by I. Norman Smith in *The Journal Men* (1974).

There are many ways forward for improving mathematics education in Canada. There is no doubt that the time is ripe to make a great leap forward. . . . However, one fact of overriding importance must be in the forefront of everyone's efforts: *To mathematize is to joy!* It is to exult more of the powers distinctive of our humanity.

> A.J. COLEMAN, G.D. EDWARDS, and K.P. BELTZNER, mathematicians, *Mathematical Sciences in Canada* (1975), Science Council of Canada, Background Study No. 38, also known as the Coleman Report.

The low level of mathematical literacy in Canada is one of the biggest obstacles preventing the more effective use of mathematics in developing technology, planning for the future, minimizing environmental and social impact, rationalizing transportation and communications, and improving public services.

> A.J. COLEMAN, G.D. EDWARDS, and K.P. BELTZNER, mathematicians, *Mathematical Sciences in Canada* (1975), Science Council of Canada, Background Study No. 38, also known as the Coleman Report.

Our children are unusual, of course. And so are yours. No child is usual until it has been through the school system.

> PATRICIA JOUDRY, playwright, . . . *And the Children Played* (1975).

We have educated ourselves into a world from which wonder, and the fear and dread and splendour and freedom of wonder, have been banished.

> ROBERTSON DAVIES, man-of-letters, interviewed by Alan Twigg in 1981, *Conversations with Robertson Davies* (1989) edited by J. Madison Davis.

I want our youth to dream as my generation could dream — of a bright and satisfying future in a rich and wonderful land. . . . The country can no longer tolerate a condition whereby the finishing of an education is a ticket to despair.

> JOHN TURNER, Liberal leader, address, 17 March 1984.

The major personal concern of Canadian young people — characterizing almost 70% of them — is what they are going to do when they finish school.

> REGINALD W. BIBBY and DONALD C. POSTERSKI, sociologists, *The Emerging Generation: An Inside Look at Canada's Teenagers* (1985).

Only about 15% of all high-school students — under 1 in 7 — actually attend university following graduation from high school. Most teenagers taste the pain of relinquishing their university education dream before they turn twenty.

> REGINALD W. BIBBY and DONALD C. POSTERSKI, sociologists, *The Emerging Generation: An Inside Look at Canada's Teenagers* (1985).

Both American and Canadian high schools restrict corporal punishment to what happens to the teachers.

> ERIC NICOL and DAVE MORE, humorists, *The U.S. or Us: What's the Difference, Eh?* (1986).

My strongest impression . . . is that, in terms of educational philosophy, the system has increasingly been running on empty.

> GEORGE RADWANSKI, journalist and educational consultant, *Ontario Study of the Relevance of Education and the Issue of Dropouts*, a report released 30 Nov. 1987.

Education does not automatically result from warehousing young people in schools for any given number of years. That's merely schooling. Education, in the real sense that is vital to our society and to individuals for the reasons outlined above, can only be discussed meaningfully in terms of *outcome* — in terms, that is, of the actual knowledge and skills acquired by students during the time they spend in school.

> GEORGE RADWANSKI, journalist and educational consultant, *Ontario Study of the Relevance of Education and the Issue of Dropouts*, a report released 30 Nov. 1987.

Universities that administer literacy tests find that, on average, 40 per cent of their first-year students fail.

LINDA FRUM, journalist, *Linda Frum's Guide to Canadian Universities* (1987).

If a student fails, the teacher fails.
HARRY GILES, founder of the Toronto French School, quoted by Judy Steed in *The Globe and Mail*, 10 Dec. 1988.

Perhaps that sums up the ultimate justification of a private school: it tests and stretches potential early, pushing students to discover that the hardest limits to overcome are those that are self-imposed.
PETER C. NEWMAN, author, *Sometimes a Great Nation: Will Canada Belong to the 21st Century?* (1988).

I think the greatest need we have in Canada is to spend considerably more money and time and attention on our education. We have to educate better; if we do, we should be able to stand up to anybody.
TREVOR EYTON, corporate executive, quoted by Alexander R. Aird, Paul Nowack, and James W. Westcott in *Road to the Top: The Chief Executive Officer in Canada* (1988).

Personally, I believe you could put a kid through high school in four months.
FRANK OGDEN, futurologist, characteristic remark, 1980s.

If schools were factories, we would have closed them ten years ago because they're not producing a saleable product. Kids can't get jobs because they don't know what's happening.
FRANK OGDEN, futurologist, quoted by Nancy Spiller in *American Way*, 1 Sept. 1989.

It's not how many degrees you have that counts. What really matters is how many good books you are reading during your lifetime.
JOEL BONN, Montreal-based reading specialist, *obiter dictum*, 3 Feb. 1990.

That horizontal tyranny clearly does not

suppress the mind — Saskatoon claims to have more Ph.D.s per capita than anywhere else in Canada.
JAN MORRIS, Anglo-Welsh traveller, "Suddenly Saskatoon," *Saturday Night*, July-Aug. 1990.

Education Needs Stressed
One of the most boring headlines of all time, according to journalist DICK CAMPBELL, CBC Radio, 4 Sept. 1990.

I first heard the phrase "learning a living" from the late Marshall McLuhan, one of Canada's seminal thinkers. He told me in 1957 that South Korea, Hong Kong, Singapore and India would vault over entire eras of technological development, go from the wooden plough to computerized tools and challenge the established Western industrialized countries through better elementary and secondary education. We now know that he was prophetic.
PHILIPPE DEANE GIGANTES, author and Senator, *The Road Ahead* (1990).

Old high school drop-outs do not fade away; they become security guards.
EDWARD PHILLIPS, novelist, *Sunday Best* (1990).

EFFICIENCY

One trouble with being efficient is that it makes everybody hate you so.
BOB EDWARDS, newspaperman, *The Eye Opener*, 18 March 1916.

EFFORT

Rise again, rise again — though your heart it be broken / And life about to end — / No matter what you've lost, be it a home, a love, a friend / Like the Mary Ellen Carter, rise again.
STAN ROGERS, singer and composer, "The Mary Ellen Carter" *Between the Breaks . . . Live!* (Fogarty's Cove Music, 1979).

EH?

At the metaphorical border of Customs and Immigration at Toronto International Airport I was startled to hear an immigration official say, upon checking my passport, "Vindicated at last, eh?" (The upturned "eh" is a species of linguistic dim-witticism to which Canadians are addicted.) I muttered, "You're too kind," and moved on. There were so many people lined up to get through the gates of Toronto one would think that the city fathers were offering free citizenship to the first 500 refugees who could answer a skill-testing question.
> QUENTIN CRISP and JOHN HOFSESS, English-born entertainer and Canadian-born author, *Manners from Heaven: A Divine Guide to Good Behaviour* (1984).

"Eh?" is heard all over the English-speaking world and it dates back to the Middle Ages, according to *The Oxford English Dictionary*. The *O.E.D.* records Oliver Goldsmith as saying, "Wasn't it lucky, eh?" in *She Stoops to Conquer* (1773). Also, "eh?" occurs nineteen times in *Moby Dick* (1851): "But flukes! man, what makes thee want to go whaling, eh?" These usages don't prove that Goldsmith and Melville were members of the Writers' Union of Canada. Utterances like "eh?" are the relics of the animal cries from which human speech arose. As instinctive utterances, they have more or less the same meanings in most cultures. If one tribe of people is more addicted to one of these interjections, it is solely a matter of cultural identity.
> THOMAS M. PAIKEDAY, lexicographer, private communication 1 March 1991, compiler of *The Penguin Canadian Dictionary* (1990).

ELECTIONS
See also POLITICS

If you buy a man to stay at home, you can always tell whether he has kept his bargain or not.
> Attributed to EDWARD BLAKE, Ontario Liberal in the 19th century, by Gordon Aiken in *The Backbencher: Trials and Tribulations of a Member of Parliament* (1974).

It's a landslide for Mr. Roosevelt and the votes aren't in yet from Canada.
> RICHARD J. DOYLE, newspaperman, *Hurly-Burly: A Time at The Globe* (1990). "I thought about listening to the 1940 results on my father's radio and hearing H.V. Kaltenborn say, 'It's a landslide for Mr. Roosevelt and the votes aren't in yet from Canada.'"

We support the CCF except at elections.
> JOSEPH E. ATKINSON, publisher of *The Toronto Star*, referring to the CCF, the forerunner of the NDP, quoted by Ross Harkness in *J.E. Atkinson of the Star* (1963).

I have given the matter the fullest consideration and having examined the problem from all its angles reached the conclusion that it was because I didn't get enough votes!
> HOWARD GREEN, former Conservative Cabinet Minister, replying to a reporter who asked him why he was defeated in the election of 1963, quoted by John G. Diefenbaker in *One Canada: Memoirs of the Right Honourable John G. Diefenbaker: The Tumultuous Years, 1962-1967* (1977).

Eat Better, Love More, Vote Whelan
> EUGENE WHELAN, Liberal Minister of Agriculture, called these words his quasi-slogan in the election campaign of 1972 in *Whelan: The Man in the Green Stetson* (1986) written by Whelan with Rick Archbold.

The Regressive Preservative Party swept all regions of Canada to achieve the most astounding political triumph ever recorded by Barbara Frum.
> Anonymous satire, "A Bland Election," *The Idler*, No. 1, Jan. 1985.

It doesn't seem to matter whether we vote the rascals out or not. Things always stay the same. During the 1984 election one disgruntled man remarked, "It doesn't matter who gets elected. We still end up with a government." My sentiments entirely.

> PAUL MALVERN, journalist, *Persuaders: Influence Peddling, Lobbying and Political Corruption in Canada* (1985).

It is totally antiquated. It is really a bit of a farce. Most elections mean another dictator for three or four years.

> WILLIAM VANDER ZALM, B.C. Premier, discussing British parliamentary democracy, 3 March 1986, quoted by Stephen Osborne and Mary Schendlinger in *Quotations from Chairman Zalm* (1988).

That's why my colleagues and I are calling for an election. Indeed, anything could happen. Canada might win!

> ED BROADBENT, NDP leader, objecting to the signing of the Free Trade Agreement, quoted in *The Financial Post*, 19 Oct. 1987.

The 4th of September 1984, when I was honoured to lead the Conservative Party to the greatest victory in the history of Canada, I got fifty per cent of the vote, which meant that at the height of my popularity, the greatest ever in Canadian history, electorally, half of the people were opposed to me that very day.

> BRIAN MULRONEY, Prime Minister, interview on Global TV, 25 Sept. 1987.

Advisor: Do not concede defeat until the Army vote has come in. It is counted last and can swing close seats.
Hatfield: It would have to be the Chinese Army!

> Dialogue between an unnamed political advisor and RICHARD HATFIELD, who was defeated in the election of 13 Oct. 1987 after serving for seventeen years as Premier of New Brunswick. Fleet Street dubbed Hatfield "Disco Dick" for his fancy ways.

Voter apathy is a big problem and it's getting bigger all the time. To make matters worse — nobody gives a shit.

> CHARLIE McKENZIE, past National Campaign Chairman and Concierge of the Parti Rhinoceros, address, Queen's University, Kingston, Ont., 18 Jan. 1987.

In any other country, if the government turned its back on its own history to such a profound degree, there would be a revolution. I say, let us not have a revolution, but let there at least be an election.

> MEL HURTIG, publisher and nationalist, on the "free-trade election," quoted by John F. Burns in *The New York Times*, 13 Dec. 1987.

I would be happy to call an election, but it might inconvenience some people in the House.

> BRIAN MULRONEY, Prime Minister, answering Opposition calls for an election date, House of Commons, 5 Oct. 1987.

I can see the headlines after the next election: "Liberals Sweep to Victory — Liberal Caucus Demands Recount."

> JOHN TURNER, Liberal leader, quoted in *The Montreal Gazette*, 16 May 1988.

Spending money is how you really vote in the world. You do it every day and it determines how the world works. It is more significant than how you cast your ballot. It is time that we use our own money in our own communities.

> MICHAEL LINTON, founder of the Local Employment Trading System (LET-System) in B.C.'s Comox Valley in 1983, "Local Currencies," *Edges*, July-Sept. 1988.

Okay, we've won. What do we do now?

> BRIAN MULRONEY, Prime Minister, to his Conservative staffers after his second landslide victory in the general election, quoted by William Walker in *The Toronto Star*, 17 Sept. 1988.

Every election is a contest between heritage and impulse, as the verities of the past compete with the risks of the future.

PETER C. NEWMAN, columnist, *Maclean's*, 5 Dec. 1988.

The only way for an incumbent to lose a debate is to eat a live rat on stage.
ALLAN GREGG, pollster, commenting on televised election debates, quoted by Lynda Hurst in *The Toronto Star*, 19 Aug. 1990.

Who ya gonna call? Gritbusters!
DAN AYKROYD, actor and star of *Ghostbusters* and its sequel, campaigning for Tory candidate John Goodchild in the Kingston, Ont., area during a provincial campaign, quoted in *The Globe and Mail*, 27 Aug. 1990.

There is no disgrace in getting knocked down. The only disgrace is in not getting up.
DAVID PETERSON, Ontario Premier, speech to Liberal Party supporters in London, Ont., after losing his seat and the election to the NDP, 13 Sept. 1990.

Traditional but outdated electoral procedures and new developments in the party structures both within and outside Parliament are opening the way to a quasi-totalitarianism which, for the lack of a better name, I would call five-year fascism.
GEORGE WOODCOCK, social commentator, referring to current Canadian electoral practices and procedures, the maximum period between elections being five years. "Five-Year Fascism." *The Canadian Forum*, Dec. 1990.

ELECTRICAL POWER
See also ENERGY
POWER

But the Crees . . . didn't even know about electricity — let alone Hydro-Québec. In fact, they had barely managed to coin a word for this creature called "electricity," using a phrase — "*nimischiiuskutaau*" — which, translated literally, means "the fire of thunder."

ROY MacGREGOR, biographer, *Chief: The Fearless Vision of Billy Diamond* (1989).

I say on behalf of the Government, that the water power all over the country should not in the future be made the sport and prey of capitalists and shall not be treated as anything else but a valuable asset of the people of Ontario, whose trustees this Government of the people are.
JAMES P. WHITNEY, Ontario Premier, campaign promise in 1905, quoted by Merrill Denison in *The People's Power* (1960).

The people's power.
The People's Power (1960) is the title of the popular history of Ontario Hydro written by MERRILL DENISON (by kerosene lamp at Bon Echo, Ont.). Credit for the title phrase goes to the playwright John Coulter who worked on that book and evolved the words "the people's power" from the the the motto on the Coat of Arms of the Ontario Hydro-Electric Power Commission which was established in 1906. The Latin motto runs *Dona naturae pro populo sunt* and was devised by the Chief Engineer A.S.L. Barnes in 1940. It translates "The Gifts of Nature Are for the People." The message "For the People" was spelled out in electric light bulbs across King Street in Berlin, Ont., on 11 Oct. 1910, when that community, later named Kitchener, became the first community in Canada to be illuminated by power from Niagara.

Gentlemen, with this hand, tried and true, this hand which has made this project complete, I now turn on the power.
JAMES P. WHITNEY, Ontario Premier, taking hold of the hand of the public-power enthusiast Sir Adam Beck and with it switching on electrical power from Niagara Falls to illuminate Berlin, Ont., 11 Oct. 1910, quoted by Joseph Schull in *Ontario since 1867* (1978).

Labrador power will light Broadway!
Slogan of Newfoundland Premier J.R.

(JOEY) SMALLWOOD with regard to the development of hydro-electric power in Labrador in the 1960s. As Harold Horwood explained in his biography *Joey* (1989): "BRINCO spent $17 million proving the power potential of the Churchill, then faced years of frustration trying to find a way to market it. In the beginning it seemed that the only likely markets were in New England and New York. This gave Joey one of his great slogans. 'Labrador power will light Broadway!' he told a New York audience, then repeated it all across the country."

If there was anything sinister about this, it was not in the Candu itself, but rather in our collective demands for its power. I had expected to come face-to-face with the evil god of all the machines, and here I was staring at a wall full of plumbing.
DAVID LEES, journalist, "Living in the Nuclear Shadow," *Toronto Life*, Nov. 1989. Lees is referring to the Candu reactor which supplies electricity to Canadians based on atomic energy.

If you had to fill up with electricity every few days, you'd think about it a lot more.
D.G. MacKENZIE, Executive Vice-President of Sunoco Inc., quoted in an advertisement for Ontario Hydro, *The Toronto Star*, 29 Dec. 1989.

Toronto's SkyDome stadium uses enough electricity to light Prince Edward Island.
Canadian Press news item, "Social Studies," *The Globe and Mail*, 13 July 1990.

ELEMENTS
See also AIR
EARTH
FIRE
WATER

We can't live for more than a few minutes without air, a few days without water, a few weeks without food. Yet we continue to destroy the very things that keep us alive and in the process rob our children of a future.

ANITA GORDON and DAVID SUZUKI, science broadcasters, *It's a Matter of Survival* (1990).

EMBLEMS
See also BEAVER
CANADA GOOSE
MAPLE LEAF
SYMBOLS

The Beaver is not a noble creature, and other nations choose animal totems that are renowned for bravery, intelligence, and a quality of incalculability. The Beaver is famous only for industry and a certain rodent-like persistence. If I were asked to propose an animal totem for Canada I should choose the Lynx — our Loup-cervier, the *Lynx canadensis*; it is a daring, wily, beautiful animal, swift and potentially ferocious, tenacious in defence of what is its own and never caught asleep. If you insist on moral qualities, it is notably clean and fights only in defence. You can eat a Beaver and many animals do so. There is no record of anyone ever eating a Lynx.
ROBERTSON DAVIES, man-of-letters, Preface, *Question Time* (1975). As medieval bestiaries note, the beaver, when pursued, emasculates itself to save its own life. Perhaps the lizard is more appropriate as it drops its tail and then regrows another.

Canada is one of the few countries that does not have some rapacious animal as its national animal. It has a constructive animal, the beaver, which will not even bite your finger unless it is backed into a corner. And practically every other national flag has its origins in battle, while the Canadian flag is a maple leaf. It almost symbolizes a pastoral idyll.
TOM WOLFE, U.S. author and cultural commentator, interviewed in *Maclean's*, 14 Dec. 1987.

EMIGRATION
See also IMMIGRANTS

Canada has resignedly exported men and women as well as fish and fur, lumber and wheat, minerals and manufactures. . . . Today, one-quarter of the Canadian stock which has remained in North America lives in the United States.

> J. BARTLET BREBNER, historian, *Scholarship in Canada: The Function of Graduate Studies* (1945).

Teenagers in our society are pro-Canadian. We have already seen that more than 50% regard "being a Canadian" as very important. Another 30% say that it is "somewhat important" to them. Given the hypothetical opportunity of living in any country, more than 60% say that they would choose Canada. . . . The influence and appeal of the U.S. is also evident. Approximately 15% of Canadian teenagers would prefer to move south. . . . The remaining 25% would exercise various options. Australia has come to have some mystique; 5% would like to live "down under." English and French cultural roots do not hold as much appeal. Only 3% wish they could live in England or France. An equal proportion would like to move to Switzerland.

> REGINALD W. BIBBY and DONALD C. POSTERSKI, sociologists, *The Emerging Generation: An Inside Look at Canada's Teenagers* (1985).

I like to live in countries which you can leave. Without anybody asking. I felt this the first time when I was crossing the bridge at Niagara Falls to enter the U.S. We didn't stop at Canadian customs. We only waved to the Canadians. I said, "That's good." That you can leave.

> GEORGE FALUDY, Hungarian-born poet, interviewed by Alan Twigg in *Strong Voices: Conversations with Fifty Canadian Authors* (1988).

EMOTIONS

Do not think, young sir, that I compliment or congratulate you on having a kind heart. On the contrary, happy is he — a thousand times happy — who possesses a heart of brass, since he is constrained to live among men.

> PHILIPPE-JOSEPH AUBERT DE GASPÉ, Quebec man-of-letters, *A Man of Sentiment: The Memoirs of Philippe-Joseph Aubert de Gaspé, 1786-1871* (1988), originally written in 1866, translated by Jane Brierley.

Passion is a bonfire that soon burns out but affection can last a lifetime.

> MARION HILLIARD, physician, "A Woman Doctor Looks at Life," *Chatelaine*, Feb. 1956.

Even the human heart is slightly left of centre.

> Attributed to NORTHROP FRYE in the 1960s by Paul Wilson, "Growing Up with Orwell," *The Idler*, No. 24, July-Aug. 1989.

As Linda Rapson observed, everyone has practical skills. All it takes is a flower, lemon squares, stroking, a hug. Easy stuff.

> JUNE CALLWOOD, writer, *Twelve Weeks in Spring* (1986).

Try to feel, in your heart's core, the reality of others. This is the most painful thing in the world, probably, and the most necessary. In times of personal adversity, know that you are not alone. Know that although in the eternal scheme of things you are small, you are also unique and irreplaceable, as are all your fellow humans everywhere in the world. Know that your commitment is above all to life itself.

> MARGARET LAURENCE, novelist, address, Trent University, Peterborough, Ont., 29 March 1983, quoted in *The Globe and Mail*, 10 Jan. 1989.

Emotions are what you have to cope with before you cope with money.

> BETTY JANE WYLIE and LYNNE MacFARLANE, authors, *Everywoman's Money Book* (1989).

EMPIRE

> *See also* BRITISH EMPIRE &
> COMMONWEALTH
> CANADA & THE UNITED
> KINGDOM
> IMPERIALISM

People of my age grew up British — as part of the British Empire. And now we have to figure out whether we're part of the "American Empire" or not. There hasn't been much time that we've just been ourselves.

> PETER GZOWSKI, broadcaster, quoted by Priit J. Vesilind in *National Geographic*, March 1990.

EMPLOYMENT

> *See also* LABOUR
> UNEMPLOYMENT

It may well be that within a few years, as atomic energy is made releasable and usable in industry, there won't be enough productive employment available for anything like all the people in the world. It may well be that this time can come within twenty years.

> G. BROCK CHISHOLM, psychiatrist and executive with the World Health Organization, White Memorial Lecture, Washington, D.C., Oct. 1945, published as *The Psychiatry of Enduring Peace and Social Progress* (1945).

We are going to re-energize the private sector in this country because that is the way new jobs are created.

> Some Hon. Members: Hear, hear!
> BRIAN MULRONEY, Prime Minister, House of Commons, Ottawa, 7 Nov. 1984.

Young people are sending two clear messages to the governments of this country. First, they want an opportunity for more input into society. They feel they have a contribution to make, and want the chance to make it. Second, they want jobs. Rightly or wrongly, they are going to expect the leaders of the country, namely governments, to come through. The fail-ure for such expectations to be realized will result in disenchantment of enormous proportions.

> REGINALD W. BIBBY and DONALD C. POSTERSKI, sociologists, *The Emerging Generation: An Inside Look at Canada's Teenagers* (1985).

Do our political leaders really have no ideas for expanding the crucial service industry beyond being friendly to fast-food chains and ensuring plenty of Mc-Jobs for young people?

> JOHN FRASER, editor, "Diary," *Saturday Night*, Nov. 1989.

Job-sharing, part-time employment, shorter working hours and earlier retirement may all sound impractical now, but they will eventually create full employment in the West by sharing the work.

> FRANK FEATHER, futurologist, *G-Forces: Reinventing the World — The 35 Global Forces Restructuring Our World* (1989).

Countries that make full employment the principal aim of their economic policy seem to outperform countries that do not.

> PHILIPPE DEANE GIGANTES, author and Senator, *The Road Ahead* (1990).

We don't like it when Canadians are unemployed. We're concerned when ten per cent of the population in this country are unemployed. But what about when ninety per cent of Native Canadians are unemployed? I don't think we have a solitary thing we should be celebrating, unless we are going to do something different in the future.

> GEORGES ERASMUS, National Chief, Assembly of First Nations, address in Ottawa, responding to an invitation to help plan government-sponsored events to celebrate 125 years of Confederation and the 500th anniversary of Columbus's discovery of America in 1992. Quoted in *The Canadian Forum*, Jan. 1990.

Jobs, jobs, jobs!

> Attributed to Prime Minister BRIAN MUL-

RONEY in the election campaign of 1984, according to William Walker in *The Toronto Star*, 17 Sept. 1988.

Ask anyone to quote something from Mulroney's many orations and the answer most will give is, "Jobs, jobs, jobs." In time, and as the world turns, even this may turn out to be improvident, but it is, whatever else, a quotation more likely to end up on bumper stickers than carved on tablets of stone.
    DALTON CAMP, columnist, *The Toronto Star*, 18 Feb. 1990.

ENERGY
        See also ATOMIC ENERGY
                    ELECTRICAL POWER
                    OIL INDUSTRY
                    SOLAR ENERGY

Energy is merely impatience.
    ROBIN SKELTON, man-of-letters, aphorism, May 1990.

ENGINEERING

Engineering still remains *The Invisible Profession* — which, when it is not being ignored, is often scorned. . . . It must be really heartwarming being an engineer — getting blamed for environmental policies shaped by government lawyers — then taking the blame for environmental neglect across the country.
    TOM DAVEY, editor and columnist, *Environmental Science & Engineering*, Dec. 1989.

ENGLISH CANADA

The English Canadian is a little like one of those land mines left over from the Second World War, which still turn up from time to time. No trouble if you don't kick it too hard. But like the mine we go off with a considerable bang if detonated. Left alone we tick quietly away, submerged and inoffensive.
    Thoughts of an English-speaking Mon-

trealer in the novel *Sunday's Child* (1981) written by EDWARD PHILLIPS.

Today, English Canada might be more correctly referred to as The Rest of Canada, or TROCANA.
    CHARLES PACHTER, artist and essayist, *The Globe and Mail*, 28 March 1991.

ENGLISH PEOPLE
        See also BRITISH EMPIRE &
                    COMMONWEALTH
                    UNITED KINGDOM

Keats might come out of the fog. People put ducks in parks & birdwatched & had subtle sorrows concealed in conventional understatements. Even dumb people with libraries of uncut books respected what they didn't even try to understand.
    ELIZABETH SMART, novelist and diarist, "A Transatlantic Pursuit (My Affair with England)" (1978), *Autobiographies* (1987) edited by Christina Burridge.

Now, what this country needs are Englishmen. They need Englishmen to guide, Englishmen to lead, Englishmen to advise, Englishmen to overcome the problems now besetting Canada, Englishmen to steer Canada along the road of righteousness to still waters and therein rest, for all the world to see and marvel and emulate. I'll wait for the cheers to subside and the crowd to resume their seats. Now, are you back comfortably in your chairs?
    BEN WICKS, humorist and cartoonist, address, Empire Club of Canada, Toronto, 9 Nov. 1978.

ENTREPRENEURSHIP

Communism is recognizing the drawbacks of its dictatorial inefficiency and bureaucratic structures. Capitalism is recognizing the social costs of competition and hierarchical structures. Both are recognizing that they must transform themselves as the new technology takes us to an information economy. Information is at once a social leveler (it is socialistic) and also an

instigator of innovation (it is entrepreneurial). Both communism and capitalism are dissolving into a new hybrid form of political economy: socialist entrepreneurialism.
FRANK FEATHER, futurologist, *G-Forces: Reinventing the World — The 35 Global Forces Restructuring Our World* (1989).

The genesis of entrepreneurship is recognizing opportunities beyond the reach of resources currently available to the entrepreneur. If adequate resources were available, there would be no need for entrepreneurship, because good managers could do the job. The unique appeal of entrepreneurs is based on how they identify opportunities and how they multiply the effectiveness of their scarce resources in exploiting the opportunities they see.
DONALD RUMBALL, business writer, *The Entrepreneurial Edge: Canada's Top Entrepreneurs Reveal the Secrets of Their Success* (1989).

After he came to Canada from Scotland . . . Alexander Graham Bell invented the telephone, arguably the greatest life-changing invention of the last century. And if the ancestors of Thomas Edison and Walt Disney had not chosen to move down to the United States from Canada, would we not also be claiming the light bulb and Mickey Mouse as our own? Intelligence, tenacity, brightness, creative thinking and entrepreneurial ability do not stop abruptly at the 49th parallel, as though the forest would kill them.
ALLAN GOULD, journalist and author, "Big Ideas Meet Small Business," *Imperial Oil Review*, Spring 1990.

ENVIRONMENTALISM
See also ECOLOGY

Anything which speeds up an environment around another environment destroys the environment it surrounds.
MARSHALL McLUHAN, communications theorist, addressing a committee of Toronto City Council, 1970, quoted by Edward Relph in *The Toronto Guide: The City/Metro/The Region* (Annual Conference, Association of American Geographers, Toronto, April 1990).

Recycling is the main means to reduce both the plundering and the poisoning of nature. It can, however, never be complete; its costs rise exponentially with the percentage of any material recycled. *The real limits of growth are the limits of recycling.*
HANS BLUMENFELD, architect-planner, *Life Begins at 65: The Not Entirely Candid Autobiography of a Drifter* (1987).

Among the serious problems facing industrial society, none is more acute than the deterioration of our environment.
BRIAN MULRONEY, Prime Minister, address at the 1988 international conference on global warming, quoted by Anita Gordon and David Suzuki *It's a Matter of Survival* (1990).

Canadians have an international reputation as peacekeepers. Why can't Canada be peacekeepers in terms of environment, too? Clean water is the life-blood of the planet.
GERALDINE KENNY-WALLACE, scientist, quoted by Janice Dineen in *The Toronto Star*, 4 Sept. 1988.

Whenever reporters interview me about the genesis of the President's Choice G.R.E.E.N products I can see in their eyes that they're expecting me to tell them how I experienced a "blinding light" conversion on the road to some ecological Damascus and they're always disappointed to hear that, unlike St. Paul's conversion, my conversion arose from what Adam Smith referred to as "enlightened self-interest." An enlightened self-interest that sprang from having seen examples around the world of industries and companies that were destroyed by their management's lack of response to their customers' growing concern for the environment.

DAVE NICHOL, President, Loblaw International Merchants, address, Summit on the Environment, Toronto, 11 Sept. 1989.

I would like to direct my remarks specifically at the North American business community because I firmly believe that environmental concerns constitute the biggest opportunities and conversely the biggest risks that business faces in the foreseeable future.
DAVE NICHOL, President, Loblaw International Merchants, Summit on the Environment, Toronto, 11 Sept. 1989.

With God either dead or held hostage by the Sunday morning TV hucksters, it is only the environmentalists who can convincingly speak to our fears and remind us that we had better mend our ways, renounce our aggressions, curb our lusts, look after the poor and treat our women as equals or face the consequences. And not in the hereafter, but in the here-and-now.
DAVID LEES, journalist, "Living in the Nuclear Shadow," *Toronto Life*, Nov. 1989.

The moment we realized that the environmental holocaust has nothing to do with good and evil but only with ambiguity, we began to lose hope. We went to sleep one night in Burlington and got up in the morning in Beirut.
DAVID LEES, journalist, "Living in the Nuclear Shadow," *Toronto Life*, Nov. 1989.

The environment is in a mess and the palliatives being advanced are on the order of shipping PCBs to Wales.
JOHN FRASER, editor, "Diary," *Saturday Night*, Nov. 1989.

The training of environmental engineers is no less rigorous than doctors or aeronautical technicians. . . . Yet repeatedly environmental decisions are based on the sayings — *soothsayings* might be a more appropriate word — of people with little formal training on the subjects.
TOM DAVEY, editor and columnist, *Environmental Science & Engineering*, Nov. 1989.

Then there's the ubiquitous spokespersons from Friends of the Earth and Energy Probe, and many other groups who seem to multiply like amoeba. Collectively they produce more negatives than Eastman Kodak. I don't know why they call themselves *friends* of the Earth — they behave more like lovers — passionately devoted, sincere in their love and highly suspicious of anyone whom they think might violate their beloved.
TOM DAVEY, editor and columnist, *Environmental Science & Engineering*, Dec. 1989.

The collapse of the global environment would be at least as disastrous as global war.
Project Ploughshares for the Citizens' Inquiry into Peace and Security, *What Makes Canada Secure: Background Document for the Citizens' Inquiry into Peace and Security in Canada* (1991).

EPITAPHS
See also DYING WORDS

By His Genius / Distant Lands Converse / And Men Sail / Unafraid Upon The Deep.
Epitaph on the memorial tablet at the grave of REGINALD A. FESSENDEN, Quebec-born radio pioneer, who died on 22 July 1932, St. Mark's Church, Bermuda.

To the World He Was a Boy / To Us He Was the World.
Epitaph of a young boy named STEVEN YUZ who died on 20 Feb. 1980. It expresses the grief of his parents, Yoram and Judith Yuz, quoted by Susan Kastner in *The Toronto Star*, 2 Oct. 1988.

He gave himself away.
Self-selected epitaph of artist and dealer JACK POLLOCK in *Dear M: Letters from a Gentleman of Excess* (1990?).

EQUALITY

We are living in a society in which this absurd contradiction of equality has crept in. There isn't equality, there never will be, and to pretend there is, is an insult.
> JON VICKERS, opera singer, interviewed by Ulla Colgrass in *For the Love of Music* (1988).

ERRORS

I have a fat file marked "Errors". . . . It is hard to say which does the most damage: lawyers ill-acquainted with history, historians ill-acquainted with law, or political scientists ill-acquainted with both.
> EUGENE FORSEY, constitutional authority, *A Life on the Fringe: The Memoirs of Eugene Forsey* (1990).

ESKIMO
See also INUIT

The word "eskimo" is an Algonkian word meaning "eaters of flesh" (literally "he eats it raw"), an allusion to the prodigious consumption of animal protein by the hunters of the far north. The Eskimos do not use this name but call themselves simply "the people" (*Inuit*).
> CHARLES BERLITZ, U.S. linguist, *Native Tongues* (1982).

ESPIONAGE
See also SECRECY

I have seen injustice, and it works.
> FRED POLAND, suspect held contrary to the principle of *habeas corpus*, letter to Prime Minister Mackenzie King and Justice Minister Louis St. Laurent, 12 March 1946, quoted by June Callwood in *Emma* (1984). Poland was acquitted one year later.

One can only hope that the Russians will not be such cads as to read the *Canada Gazette*.
> This ironic sentence comes from an editorial which is said to have appeared in *The London Free Press*. It refers to the fact that classified information on the DEW Line was appearing regularly in the *Canada Gazette*, which is an official organ of the government and the journal of public record. Quoted by J. Barber in *Good Fences Make Good Neighbours* (1958).

Two hours, two years, later Bond was lying in the warm cabin in Weathership Charlie listening dreamily to an early morning radio programme from Canada. Various parts of his body ached.
> IAN FLEMING, novelist, *Goldfinger* (1959). This popular novel, featuring James Bond, Secret Agent 007, concludes with Bond and Pussy Galore crashlanding a Stratocruiser off the coast of Labrador and taking refuge aboard an ocean station.

The material filched from the Soviet embassy by Mr. Gouzenko was finally investigated by a royal commission appointed for that purpose by the Canadian government; and its report is the most complete picture of Communist treachery that we possess. It is hardly necessary to say that it cast no discredit on the Soviet Union whatsoever.
> REBECCA WEST, British writer, referring to the Royal Commission (the Gouzenko Inquiry) headed by Robert Taschereau and R.L. Kellock which issued its first interim report on 2 March 1946, *The New Meaning of Treason* (1964).

As long as Americans value courage and freedom there will be a special place in our hearts, our minds, and our history books for the Man called Intrepid.
> Message from U.S. President RONALD REAGAN read at the official dinner in Ottawa tendered for Sir William Stephenson, World War II intelligence officer, dubbed "the Quiet Canadian" by the biographer Montgomery Hyde and later "the Man called Intrepid" by the journalist William Stevenson, quoted by David Stafford in "A Myth Called Intrepid," *Saturday Night*, Oct. 1989.

In twenty-five years the RCMP Security Service has caught only one illegal — one *real* spy. Not a hell of a lot to brag about, is it?

> IAN ADAMS, journalist and novelist, theme of *S: Portrait of a Spy: RCMP Intelligence — The Inside Story* (1977), the first book — fact or fiction — ever written about the RCMP's Security Service. The remark occurs in dialogue in the novel, and it was written before the Force, in Feb. 1978, revealed the identities of thirteen Soviet agents engaged in espionage work in Canada. Publication of the book occasioned a lively and expensive lawsuit.

I've come to understand that the most powerful fantasy figure in our society is the spy. There are many reasons for this. One is that in a time when we are conditioned more and more to believe that we have no control or responsibility for our own lives, the spy survives as a kind of anima, a fantasy figure who is licensed to plan and commit all those violent antisocial acts we would like to perform when we are threatened or oppressed by the stresses of this life. That spies can act with such freedom and sanction from the authorities under the guise that it is for the protection of us all, makes their world all the more exciting.

> IAN ADAMS, journalist and novelist, "Secrets and Myths," *The Writer and Human Rights* (1983) edited by the Toronto arts Group for Human Rights.

There could never be a national investigation into un-Canadian activities in Canada, because the very existence of the national state rests upon the agreement that there shall be many different versions of what it is to be Canadian and that no one version must ever be advocated to the exclusion of others.

> JOHN CONWAY, historian, "An 'Adapted Organic Tradition,'" *Daedalus: Journal of the American Academy of Arts and Sciences*, "In Search of Canada," Fall 1988.

THE ESTABLISHMENT
See also SOCIETY

Measured against other ruling groups that make up the Canadian social fabric — the political, religious and cultural elites — the business elite has been the slowest to adjust to the new social realities of Canada. The typical power broker is still white, male and nominally Christian. Most are living testimony to the notion that the spirit of capitalism is synonymous with the Protestant ethic. That's not all bad, of course, but other groups with equally laudable values are still underrepresented in the boardrooms where power and capital converge and, as in the case of women, some are not represented at all.

> JAMES FLEMING, journalist, "Who Counts (and Who Doesn't) in Corporate Canada," *The Globe and Mail's Report on Business Magazine*, Dec. 1988.

There's not much *status* in the *quo* any more.

> ALLAN GREGG, pollster, referring to the expanding role of partnership in public affairs, interviewed by Peter Gzowski on CBC Radio's *Morningside*, 1 Nov. 1990.

ETHICS
See also GOOD & EVIL

The history of ethics is a history of contradiction, not a history of progress.

> MICHAEL IGNATIEFF, author and television personality, "Is Nothing Sacred? The Ethics of Television," *Daedalus: Journal of the American Academy of Arts and Sciences*, "In Search of Canada," Fall 1988.

ETHNICITY
See also MULTICULTURALISM

In an age when loneliness, malaise and an overwhelming bigness assail us, our ethnic communities are sometimes no more than bits of driftwood to which a few people cling in the midst of a typhoon. What we need are lifeboats. What we need is Noah's ark.

JOY KOGAWA, author, *Cultures and Writers: A Cultural Dialogue of Ethnic Writers* (1983) edited by Yvonne Grabowski.

Those who are uncomfortable with the low status of the adjective *ethnic* now favour the term *multicultural*, as in "multicultural group" or "multiculturals." To the extent that ethnic groups become the creations of government rather than representations of the natural sentiment of those of the descent group, this usage, which seems a semantic monstrosity at first, may be sound usage.

ROBERT F. HARNEY, historian, "'So Great a Heritage as Ours': Immigration and the Survival of the Canadian Polity," *Daedalus: Journal of the American Academy of Arts and Sciences*, "In Search of Canada," Fall 1988.

No single ethnic group accounts for the majority of the Canadian people. This should be recognized as a fact of enormous significance.

FRANK McGILLY, author, School of Social Work, McGill University, *An Introduction to Canada's Public Social Services: Understanding Income and Health Programs* (1990).

EUGENICS

You know as well as I do that if we breed from the bottom instead of the top we are courting disaster. Any farmer has more sense when it comes to breeding animals.

A.R. KAUFMAN, treasurer of the Eugenics Society of Canada, founder of the Parents' Information Bureau, and promoter of family planning, letter to American philanthropist Charles Gamble, 21 July 1937, quoted by historian Angus McLean in *Our Own Master Race: Eugenics in Canada, 1885-1945* (1990).

EUROPE

See also EUROPEAN COMMUNITY

The Europe of Bach and Voltaire had changed from a community of nation-states into an economy obsessed with prosperity. Crawling through the barbed wire, one suddenly found oneself in the glittering corridors of Europe, Inc.

GEORGE GABORI, Hungarian-born journalist, *When Evils Were Most Free* (1981) translated by Eric Johnson with George Faludy.

Canada is an ocean away from Europe, but bound to you by both tradition and destiny.

JOE CLARK, Secretary of State, address, Conference on Security and Cooperation in Europe, Vienna, Austria, 5 Nov. 1986.

I am mystified by Canada's indifference to Europe. Our apathy is the more difficult to understand at a time when we have focused so much national angst on American influence on our country.

ALLAN GOTLIEB, former Canadian Ambassador to the U.S., address, quoted in *The Toronto Star*, 7 April 1989.

Any column datelined "London" can be relied on to argue that Canada should remain in Europe rather than retreat back, if not to an island like Australia, then to the open half of a continent occupied mostly, to our unending discomfort (and to our great advantage in other respects) by Americans.

We will never, of course, choose consciously to turn away from Europe. My case is that we cannot avoid making a choice: Either we develop a policy and program to involve ourselves actively in Europe, or, by continuing to do nothing, we elect by neglect to slide away off by ourselves among the ice-floes, and the Americans.

RICHARD GWYN, columnist and London-based correspondent, *The Toronto Star*, 27 Oct. 1989.

EUROPEAN COMMUNITY

See also EUROPE

The European Common Market will expand to include all European nations, including Russia and the east bloc countries. They will have what amounts to a common currency and free trade across all of their borders. Talks aimed at merging most aspects of government will begin. . . . Russia will join the European Common Market by 1992, and the other east bloc countries will all be members by 1995.

MAURICE B. COOKE, channeller, *The Aquarian Wave: A Prophetic Handbook for the 90s* (1990).

EVIL

See also GOOD & EVIL

I think it is absolutely necessary for a man to recognize and accept the evil in himself. If he does that he is in a position to make the evil work in a different way; the charges of psychological energy involved can be re-directed in not necessarily good paths, but at least in understood paths.

ROBERTSON DAVIES, man-of-letters, interviewed by Tom Harpur in 1974, *Conversations with Robertson Davies* (1989) edited by J. Madison Davis.

Giving the devil his due will always jostle the angels.

Attributed to a character in *The Evil that Men Do* (1978) by R. LANCE HILL.

EVOLUTION

Evolution involves perpetual exploration of new environmental opportunities. Life as a whole may be described as "opportunistic."

JOHN A. LIVINGSTON, naturalist, *One Cosmic Instant: A Natural History of Human Arrogance* (1973).

Will it be *Homo sapiens* — rather than the time-tested machinery of evolution — that writes the next chapter in the history of genes?

DAVID SUZUKI, scientist and broadcaster, and Peter Knudtson, writer and biologist, *Genethics: The Ethics of Engineering Life* (1988).

Over 500 million years ago, a jellyfish was a relatively complicated organism, but now a flying fish is a relatively complicated organism. In a comparison between a jellyfish and a flying fish, progress is obvious in the increased behavioural complexity of the latter, which is made possibly by a greater number of harmoniously functioning parts.

DALE A. RUSSELL, paleontologist, *An Odyssey in Time: The Dinosaurs of North America* (1989).

EXCELLENCE

You cannot be better than the moment in time in which you find yourself.

VIVIAN RAKOFF, psychiatrist, quoted by Jonathan Caro in *Canadian Doctor*, Nov. 1987.

EXECUTIVES

See also MANAGEMENT

An executive is the man who tries to give the impression of hurrying in the direction he is being pushed.

SIDNEY SMITH, academic and politician, quoted by Frank E. Archibald in *Mostly Maritimes* (1972).

Executives used to rise from the ranks of engineering, marketing, or the service departments, developing experience in responding to customers' needs. Increasingly, today's management comes from law, accountancy, finance, or "government affairs," in short, a new breed of *paper entrepreneurs*.

Private entrepreneurs who get rich from take-overs, or from reshuffling paper companies, instead of making steel, or stamping out hubcaps, justly incur the public's indictment that they are major contributors to North America's *de-industrialization*.

TOM DAVEY, editor and columnist, *All the Views Fit to Print* (1985).

We found it hard to believe the fact that so many of the CEOs had not really planned

to get the top job, but simply took one step at a time.
ALEXANDER R. AIRD, PAUL NOWACK, and JAMES W. WESTCOTT, journalists, *Road to the Top: The Chief Executive Officer in Canada* (1988).

EXERCISE

Walking is best with two.
BETTY JANE WYLIE, author, *Beginnings: A Book for Widows* (1977).

EXPERIENCE

A powerful experience is something to be glad you've had. If you can feel so much joy, ecstasy, delight, isn't it obvious you can feel their opposites: unhappiness, misery, pain? Would you prefer not to feel at all? Not to be *able* to feel? That's the only alternative. And some people settle for it. They block all feeling. They opt for a quiet passionless life.
ELIZABETH SMART, novelist and diarist, "How to Mend a Broken Heart" (1982), *Autobiographies* (1987) edited by Christina Burridge.

Experience is like knowledge; you can never erase it once you've lived it or learned it.
EVELYN LAU, memoirist, *Runaway: Diary of a Street Kid* (1989).

EXPLORATION
See also DISCOVERY

This lande being almost under the Pole arctike, is ioyned towarde the Weast to *Florida*, and to the Landes of *Perou.*...
ANDRÉ THEVET, 16th-century French historian, *The New Founde Worlde, or Antarctike, Wherin Is Contained Wonderful and Strange Things* ... (1568). The first printed reference to Canada in the English language appears in this translation of Thevet's original French version printed in 1558.

We had many great explorers in the Arctic.

I am a student of those early explorers, and I never fail to be amazed and impressed by the tremendous courage that it must have taken to sail in those vast Arctic reaches, never knowing where they were going, and when they got there they didn't know where they were! And, of course, like Christopher Columbus, when they got back they had no idea where they had been or what they had discovered. The people that lived there didn't know they were being discovered because they had no idea that they were lost!
STUART M. HODGSON, N.W.T. Commissioner, address, Empire Club of Canada, Toronto, 13 March 1975.

I always say it's like skiing. If you go off on your own in the fresh snow, you may have more fun, but if you stay in the tracks that are already there, you may go farther.
JAMES RICHARDSON, Minister of National Defence, on taking chances in business and in life, quoted by Marci McDonald in *Maclean's*, March 1975.

Only those who have had the experience can know what a sense of physical and spiritual excitement comes to one who turns his face away from men towards the unknown. In his small way he is doing what the great explorers have done before him, and his elation recaptures theirs.
A.R.M. LOWER, historian, quoted by Eric W. Morse in *Freshwater Saga: Memoirs of a Lifetime of Wilderness Canoeing in Canada* (1987).

Discovery comes from dialogue that starts with the sharing of ignorance.
MARSHALL McLUHAN, media philosopher, quoted in *The Antigonish Review*, Summer-Autumn 1988.

The great voyage of exploration of the next millennium is going to be the exploration of the spirit of man, not the exploration of galaxies or stars. We have been to the Moon and we didn't find anything we didn't know before. But when you plunge inward you find things that are

really exciting, and mankind is enlarged by this kind of knowledge.
> ROBERTSON DAVIES, man-of-letters, quoted by Bruce Ward in *The Ottawa Citizen*, 17 Sept. 1988.

Do we ever remember / that somewhere above the sky / in some child's dream perhaps / Jacques Cartier is still sailing, / always on his way and always / about to discover a new Canada.
> MIRIAM WADDINGTON, poet, "Jacques Cartier in Toronto," *Toronto Life*, Dec. 1988.

When I explore the sea, I also metaphorically try to explore my own inner ocean and plumb the mysterious depths of the human psyche.
> JOSEPH MacINNIS, marine scientist and undersea explorer, quoted by Frank Rasky in *Leisure Ways*, April 1990.

EXPOSITIONS

There are clear alternatives to Expo 86 and like-minded megaprojects for stimulating the provincial economy and improving its long-term growth prospects. These policies include increased public spending for productive services in education, forest management and renewal, and preventative social services. It is ironic that these are the very areas which have been curtailed by the government in order to help finance its megaproject stragegy.
> ROBERT ANDERSON and ELEANOR WACHTEL, journalists, *The Expo Story* (1986).

I admired Vancouver . . , and its American kissing-cousin Seattle. Both are in the grip of that post-Exposition blues when cities wake up and find themselves stuck with monorails going nowhere and edifices of unsuitably light-hearted architecture. It's like going to the office in party dress and paper hat, or keeping your Christmas decorations up till March.
> ERIC KORN, columnist, "Remainders," *The Times Literary Supplement*, 13 April 1990.

EXTERNAL AFFAIRS
See FOREIGN AFFAIRS
INTERNATIONALISM

F

FACTS

Documents and facts are intended to direct our prejudiced hearts but rarely provide direction by themselves. I have boxes and boxes of documents but what I need is vision and vision comes from relationships. Facts bereft of love direct us nowhere.

> JOY KOGAWA, author, interviewed by Magdalene Redekop, *The Canadian Forum*, Nov. 1989.

FAILURE
See also SUCCESS

So many people have told me how successful I have been; they think I have been a success because the successes are all they have seen. But the failures and disappointments they don't see. I had my share of these in the past; some of them were hard.

> ROBERTSON DAVIES, man-of-letters, interviewed by Gordon Roper in 1968, *Conversations with Robertson Davies* (1989) edited by J. Madison Davis.

Reverse in life causes you to take another route, to explore alternatives you might not have touched otherwise. You learn more from failure because failure hurts.

> JOHN TRENT, director of CBC-TV's ill-fated *Whiteoaks of Jalna* series, 18 March 1974.

It's harder to try again than it was to begin.

> STAN ROGERS, singer and composer, "Second Effort," *Turnaround* (Fogarty's Cove Music, 1978).

I don't believe it's a failure when you change jobs or partners. They may be mistakes, but they are building blocks for the future.

> LYNNE GORDON, feminist and author of *Working without a Net* (1986).

FAIRIES
See also GHOSTS

People may simply think we are all mad, but that is up to them. There are fairies at the bottom of your garden, you may be sure of that.

> DOROTHY MACLEAN, medium and secretary of the Findhorn Foundation, quoted by Mike Cowley in "There are Fairies at the Bottom of Your Garden," *Weekend Magazine*, 9 June 1973.

FAITH

See also BELIEF

If one is not to affirm reason at the expense of faith or faith at the expense of reason, one is called upon both to produce a synthesis that unites two orders of truth and to give evidence of a successful symbiosis of two principles of knowledge.
> BERNARD J.F. LONERGAN, Jesuit philosopher, *Insight: A Study of Human Understanding* (2nd ed., 1958).

Be careful. Your "leap of faith" may merely be a jump on the bandwagon.
> BERNARD BASKIN, rabbi, Temple Anshe Sholom, Hamilton, *obiter dictum*, 22 May 1990.

FALKLAND ISLANDS

The Kelpers love to tell about the Canadian family who emigrated to the Falklands in 1982. They feared nuclear war, and thought this distant British island might escape the fallout. Argentina invaded within weeks of their arrival.
> ALAN SHARPE, essayist, "A Falkland Islands Ramble," *The Idler*, No. 22, March-April 1989.

FALL

See SEASONS

FAME

For the first thirty years of my life I made the headlines; now I'm lucky to make the footnotes.
> F.R. SCOTT, lawyer and poet, observation made in 1974 when the "radical youth" was the "grand old man."

We kept going. The album was doing brilliantly in Canada, where we were now a big name. It was an odd experience to cross and re-cross the border between the two countries and go just as easily from being a hit band to a bunch of unknowns. Sometimes the distance between fame and obscurity was only forty miles.
> BOB GELDOF, Irish-born musician, commenting on the reception given in Canada and the United States for him and his band on their 1977 tour, *Is That It?* (1986).

Fame is when it's you who gets asked to write the introduction to one of the *Paris Review* series of interviews with famous writers.
> MARGARET ATWOOD, author, on the *coup* of being asked to contribute the introduction to the *Paris Review*'s collection of interviews with women writers, quoted by Judith Timson in *Maclean's*, 3 Oct. 1988.

I think if I had to do it all over again I'd rather just be rich. I don't think that fame is worth a tinker's damn because it's very intrusive and the more you have the more intrusive it is.
> DINI PETTY, TV personality, "Sweet City Woman," *Toronto Life*, Dec. 1988.

I'd probably be famous now if I wasn't such a great waitress.
> JANE SIBERRY, composer and singer, line from a song which recalls her work as a waitress in Toronto before her performing career blossomed, quoted by Ed Gould in *Entertaining Canadians: Canada's International Stars 1900-1988* (1988).

It is easier to be famous in America than anywhere else on earth.
> ROBIN SKELTON, poet and author, *The Memoirs of a Literary Blockhead* (1988).

Celebrities are people who set out to be celebrities. Aside from criminals and billionaires, the only people who get sustained public attention are those who want it.
> ROBERT FULFORD, cultural commentator, *Best Seat in the House: Memoirs of a Lucky Man* (1988).

Canada was famous for fifteen minutes. There has to be something wrong with that. When Andry Warhol said that some day everyone will be famous for fifteen minutes, he was talking about people, not entire countries. Canada is, by land mass, the second-largest country in the world. That should be good for at least half an hour.

> CALVIN TRILLIN, U.S. columnist and essayist, *The Toronto Star*, 2 Feb. 1989.

I get between two thousand and five thousand fan letters a month and we answer them all. Being famous runs me about $25,000 a year in stamps, coloured photos and a secretary to answer it all. . . . Coca-Cola give us all the pictures and envelopes for free or it would be twice that.

> WAYNE GRETZKY, hockey personality, *Gretzky: An Autobiography* (1990) written with Rick Reilly.

FAMILY

Property like incest holds the family together.

> HAROLD ADAMS INNIS, economic historian, *The Idea File of Harold Adams Innis* (1980) edited by William Christian.

The nuclear family, that means a wife, a husband, a child (and their marriage counsellor and possibly a divorce lawyer) is out. The extended family is back in.

> DON HARRON, comedian, address, Empire Club of Canada, Toronto, 10 April 1980.

REAL Women believes the family is the most important unit in society. Society has yet to develop a better method to care for the young, protect the weak and attend the elderly.

> C. GWENDOLYN LANDOLT, lawyer and founder in 1983 of REAL Women of Canada (Realistic, Equal, Active for Life), *The Globe and Mail*, 23 April 1987.

Happily divorced and living in Montreal with my daughter and her boyfriend. I have an older son who lives with his father, and another son who lives with his girlfriend, his girlfriend's mother and his girlfriend's mother's boyfriend. I also have a mother who lives with the maid, and a boyfriend who lives with one of his ex-wives and two children by a previous marriage. I don't write much as I don't have time.

> HELEN P. HOLDEN, author and Montreal bookseller, author's profile, *Who's Who in the Writers' Union of Canada: A Directory of Members* (1988).

Tolstoy said that all happy families are alike, but who ever said any family was happy?

> BETTY JANE WYLIE, author, *All in the Family: A Survival Guide for Living and Loving in a Changing World* (1988).

Nobody brings out your shortcomings more quickly than a member of your own family.

> EDWARD PHILLIPS, novelist, *Sunday Best* (1990).

FANTASY

For us, fantasy is just reality waiting for a technology to give it birth.

> FRANK ZINGRONE, communications theorist, "Communications and a New Humanism," *In Search: The Canadian Communications Quarterly*, Winter 1981.

FARMING
See also AGRICULTURE

The Canadian peasantry, feeling no religious constraint, are profligate, unamiable, and dishonest.

> JOHN HOWISON, traveller and writer, *Sketches of Upper Canada* (1821).

There are no happier nor more contented people in the world than the agricultural population of Canada.

> GOLDWIN SMITH, historian, quoted by Charles Edward Whitcombe in *The Canadian Farmer's Manual of Agriculture* (1874).

We're too adaptable, / That's what's wrong with us now, / There must be hidden charms / In North Canadian farms.

NOEL COWARD, English entertainer, "Back to Nature (Co-Optimists)," one verse of the song written in the 1920s, *The Lyrics* (1965).

Not that the poesy of ploughing is continuous. The length of the lines is determined by the headlands, it is broken into verses by each strike out, and, if you wish to continue the simile, into different poems by the different fields. Such a nuisance these breaks are! Why cannot one plough one long straight furrow for ever without these petty hindrances?

A.G. STREET, British writer who farmed in Manitoba prior to the Great War, *Farmer's Glory* (1934).

Some people tell us that there ain't no hell, / But they never farmed, so how can they tell?

SIR ARTHUR CHETWYND, President, recalling a ditty about farming by way of introducing a speaker, Empire Club, Toronto, 7 Nov. 1974.

Gopher: Neglected western cashcrop. The most plentiful species of livestock. Burrows help control the horse population.

"Pass for a Native: Learn These Terms," *The Easterners' Guide to Western Canada* (1985) edited by Ron Marken.

Between 1890 and 1911 Massey-Harris made 15 per cent of all the manufactured goods exported from Canada. The sun never set on fields where Massey-Harris binders were working.

MICHAEL BLISS, historian, *Northern Enterprise: Five Centuries of Canadian Business* (1987).

But always, the farmer, the land, the persistent west wind fiddling on the telephone wire, the towering formulations of cloud. The land. Their heritage. This is what it is all about. Nothing more. The earth and its people.

BARRY BROADFOOT, oral historian, *Next-Year Country: Voices of Prairie People* (1988).

Although we whites have no mythical time, no time before time, in this province, "the farm" is rapidly becoming that. Perhaps this is where the history of the Saskatchewan soul begins, and we are creating it every day in our Eden-like memories and in our "I remember when I was a kid on the farm/my grandfather's farm" stories, and in our desperate but so far losing struggle to hang onto the few family farms that are left.

SHARON BUTALA, author, "Time, Space and Light: Discovering the Saskatchewan Soul" (1988), *Best Canadian Essays 1989* (1989) edited by Douglas Fetherling.

The ideology of industrialization *reifies* farming just as it reifies food; that is, both food and farming become *things*, their subsequent value to be determined by The Market, not by whether they husband the land and feed the population. Descriptions of short-term productivity and narrowly conceived efficiency reveal very little about how the farm is really doing or how healthy the children are.

BREWSTER KNEEN, food system analyst, *From Land to Mouth: Understanding the Food System* (1989).

The farmer turns out to be only a *rentier*: the real means of production are the genes, chromosomes, and germplasm which are rented out to the farmer in the form of various genetic packages, like seed, cow, and herbicide. Were efficiency, and not control, the real interest of the owners of the means of production, then the genetic design and engineering department would pursue different goals.

BREWSTER KNEEN, food system analyst, *From Land to Mouth: Understanding the Food System* (1989).

FASHION
See also BEAUTY
STYLE, PERSONAL

Don't wear too many diamonds. They make eyes and teeth dull by comparison.

KIT COLEMAN, women's editor and correspondent, *Queen of Hearts* (1978) edited by Ted Ferguson.

When you dress well, you can go anywhere.
>ROY TASH, dean of newsreel photographers who was a sharp dresser, quoted by Wilfred List, *Liberty*, 16 Feb. 1946.

The best-dressed woman is inevitably a lady who you can't wait to see without her clothes on.
>HAROLD TOWN, artist and wit, *The Toronto Telegram*, 19 March 1970.

The miniskirt is a form of high rise.
>Attributed to MARSHALL McLUHAN by Jock Carroll in *The Toronto Star*, 25 July 1970.

The Not-Yet-Famous Tilley Hat. No-Iron. Won't Shrink at All. Prepare for Adventure. It floats, ties on, repels rain, won't shrink, lasts, and comes with a four-page owner's manual. My life or yours! Our Tilley "Endurables" now have a Lifetime (mine or yours) Guarantee.
>Advertising and guarantees on the "adventure cap" and other sports items designed, manufactured, and sold by Alex Tilley, President of Tilley Endurables Inc., Toronto. Quoted by Allan Gould in *The New Entrepreneurs: 80 Canadian Success Stories* (1986). Characteristic of his forceful yet florid prose is this line from his apparel catalogue in the early 1980s: "It's made of natural coloured 10 oz. U.S. cotton, solid British Brass grommets and this Canada's persnicketiness."

There's only one thing I'm scared of: growing too big.
>ALFRED SUNG, fashion designer, quoted by Joyce Carter in *The Globe and Mail*, 9 Sept. 1976.

FATE

"Field Marshal F.F. Fate." My reader will search in vain for any reference to such an officer in the official histories of World War II, the reason being that Field Marshal F.F. Fate did not, in fact, exist. His full name is Field Marshal Fickle Finger (of) Fate, and is strictly an invention used to personify the element of luck.
>C. SYDNEY FROST, veteran, *Once a Patricia: Memoirs of a Junior Infantry Officer in World War II* (1988).

FEAR

A common fear, however, which usually means a common foe, is also, regrettably, the strongest force bringing people together, but in opposition to something or someone.
>LESTER B. PEARSON, diplomat, Nobel Peace Prize Lecture, Oslo, Norway, 11 Dec. 1957. The text is taken from *The Four Faces of Peace and the International Outlook* (1964) edited by Sherleigh G. Pierson.

Ghosts and goblins may frighten the average five-year-old, and invasive creatures from outer space disturb his older sibs. Younger teenagers may titillate themselves with the idea of werewolves, the abominable snowman and Bigfoot. But the real fear of the average adult must be what lies in the deepest shadows of his own mind. It is the invasion from inner space, faces not quite seen, voices not quite heard. It is the stuff of nightmares.
>MARGARET MILLAR, Canadian-born crime novelist, "Introduction" (1983), *Beast in View* (1955, 1983).

The fears we cannot climb become our walls.
>NOAH BEN SHEA, author, *Jacob the Baker* (1989).

FEDERALISM
See also FEDERAL-PROVINCIAL RELATIONS

The politics of federalism are the politics of accommodation on the part of governments and, it needs to be said, of people.
>PIERRE ELLIOTT TRUDEAU, Prime Minis-

ter, First Ministers' Conference, Ottawa, 14 Dec. 1976, published in *The Globe and Mail* later that day.

What is federalism? It is a form of government where the exercise of sovereignty is divided between two levels of government so that each can legislate, tax and spend in areas of its jurisdiction concerning people within its territory. That is what federalism is.

PIERRE ELLIOTT TRUDEAU, former Prime Minister, testimony to the Senate Submissions Group on the Meech Lake Constitutional Accord, *With a Bang, Not a Whimper: Pierre Trudeau Speaks Out* (1988) edited by Donald Johnston.

One of the ironies of present-day Canada's federal system is that at a time when the demand to meet economic pressures at home and abroad would appear to call for a more concerted national effort, the capacity to mount such an effort is being fragmented and decentralized.

LLOYD AXWORTHY, M.P., "The Federal System — An Uncertain Path," *Daedalus: Journal of the American Academy of Arts and Sciences*, "In Search of Canada," Fall 1988.

We did not receive a mandate from the population to practise federalism on bended knee.

ROBERT BOURASSA, Quebec Premier, address, Quebec Liberal Party, Quebec City, 25 Feb. 1990, quoted by Rhéal Séguin in *The Globe and Mail* the following day.

Federalism is a philosophy rather than a system, a movement rather than a definition, an association rather than a union.

GIL RÉMILLARD, Quebec Minister of Interprovincial Affairs, accepting an honourary degree in France, quoted by Rhéal Séguin in *The Globe and Mail*, 15 May 1990.

But always, always, always, without exception remaining faithful to federalism because Canada is one whole federal na-

tion and all of us have a responsibility to do whatever is necessary to maintain that.

CLYDE WELLS, Newfoundland Premier, after giving qualified assent to the Meech Lake Accord, Ottawa, quoted by Patrick Doyle in *The Toronto Star*, 10 June 1990.

The federal government has little credibility in Quebec, Quebec enjoys little goodwill in the rest of Canada, and Canadian federalism is a beached whale.

CONRAD BLACK, capitalist and columnist, "Enough Is Enough," *Saturday Night*, Sept. 1990.

Those who reject federalism outright have the burden of proving that their alternative, that is to say, independence, will better encourage the economic, social and cultural growth of the people of Quebec. They must prove that independence or sovereignty will be superior to federalism in promoting values such as generosity, tolerance, social justice, cultural diversity, the rights of individuals and minorities.

JEAN CHRÉTIEN, Liberal leader, submission to the Bélanger-Campeau Commission on Quebec's Constitutional Future, 17 Dec. 1990, quoted in *The Globe and Mail* the following day.

If I were living in Quebec, I would be a strong federalist because I think of Quebec as a political unit and therefore a province like other provinces. On the other hand, I think that French-speaking Canada is a tremendous cultural force in its own right. And I think that a reunited Canada is the inevitable context for Quebec because of the tendency of the economy to unite.

NORTHROP FRYE, literary critic, interviewed by Carl Mollins, *Maclean's*, 4 Feb. 1991.

FEDERAL-PROVINCIAL RELATIONS
See also FEDERALISM
REGIONALISM

The longest and most carefully defended border in the world is between the government of Canada and the governments of each of the provinces. Canadians have a fascination with federal-provincial relations that most other nations reserve for religion or sex.

ROBERT G. EVANS, economist and health-care specialist, "'We'll Take Care of It for You': Health Care in the Canadian Community," *Daedalus: Journal of the American Academy of Arts and Sciences,* "In Search of Canada," Fall 1988.

We do seem to have a habit of electing governments with conflicting principles and objectives and of hoping that, between them, they will thrash out an acceptable compromise in areas of competing jurisdiction.

ROBERT G. EVANS, economist and health-care specialist, "'We'll Take Care of It for You': Health Care in the Canadian Community," *Daedalus: Journal of the American Academy of Arts and Sciences,* "In Search of Canada," Fall 1988.

During the past elections and political crises in Canada, nothing was more difficult to explain to newcomers than the fact that Prime Minister Pierre Elliott Trudeau was not over and above René Lévesque, the premier of Quebec Province, and that Jean Drapeau, the famous mayor of Montreal, was not under the other two.

MONIQUE BÉGIN, former politician, "Debates and Silences — Reflections of a Politician," *Daedalus: Journal of the American Academy of Arts and Sciences,* "In Search of Canada," Fall 1988.

FEELINGS
See EMOTIONS

FELLOWSHIP

An almost intimate sense of fellowship seems to characterize the city, as you may see from the long and homely obituary notices inserted by the bereaved in the *Star-Phoenix*: "She was an avid bowler all her life"; "eager youngsters would gather to hear his tales of experiences"; or "died

Tuesday aged 86 years, 7 months and 7 days."

JAN MORRIS, Anglo-Welsh traveller, "Suddenly Saskatoon," *Saturday Night,* July-Aug. 1990.

FEMINISM
See also MONTREAL MASSACRE
WOMEN

Q. What is the difference between the Prime Minister and myself? A. Madame, I cannot conceive.

Exchange between an angry suffragette and Prime Minister SIR JOHN A. MACDONALD, attributed by Grant MacEwan, "Women Win the Vote," *Grant MacEwan's West: Sketches from the Past* (1990).

Political mendacity could hardly go farther. I know nothing about the contest in Saskatoon, and have not interfered in it. Far from wanting to knock women out of politics I have spent the relevant part of my life in trying to knock women into politics. If the candidate for the presidency of the University of Saskatoon, or any candidate for anything anywhere, is a professed anti-Feminist I hope the electors will knock him out of politics. The cabled message quoted as sent by me is an invention. The inventor might well be knocked out of politics also.

GEORGE BERNARD SHAW, playwright, sent this message in a letter dated 23 Feb. 1948 in response to a student prank. Darrall S. (Duke) Collins, a student at the University of Saskatchewan in Saskatoon, ran for Student Council president on an anti-feminist platform to generate interest in the election campaign. He faked an endorsement from Shaw which ran, "You never will have a quiet world until you knock women out of politics. Carry on. G.B.S." When this was drawn to his attention, Shaw repudiated the hoax, rightly pointing out that he had long advocated "not only Women's Rights but Men's Rights, which were very seriously changed unintentionally into Men's Wrongs." Collins lost the election; forty years later he was an Administrative Judge in Victoria, B.C., according to Vivian Elliot, editor of *Dear Mr. Shaw: Selections from Bernard Shaw's Postbag* (1987).

The true liberation of women cannot take place without the liberation of men. Basically, the women's liberation movement is not only feminist in inspiration, it is also humanist. Let men and women look at one another honestly and try together to give society a new set of values. The challenge which we, both men and women, must meet is that of living for a peaceful revolution and not dying for a revolution that would be cruel and, ultimately, illusory.

> THÉRÈSE CASGRAIN, Quebec feminist, quoted by Fernande Saint-Marin in *Châtelaine*, Oct. 1960, and reproduced by the Clio Collective (Micheline Dumont, Michèle Jean, Marie Lavigne, Jennifer Stoddart) in *Quebec Women: A History* (1987) translated by Roger Gannon and Rosalind Gill.

All mass movements have a lunatic fringe, but women's lib seems to have a lunatic centre.

> JOHN RICH, physician and marriage counsellor, "Watching All the Liberated Girls Go by," *Chatelaine*, April 1971.

Well, my philosophy has always been, that until all of us have made it, none of us has made it.

> ROSEMARY BROWN, politician and feminist, "A New Kind of Power" (1973), *Women in the Canadian Mosaic* (1976) edited by Gwen Matheson.

Tell it like it is, sisters, tell it like it is. / Tell it like it is, sisters, tell it like it is. / Control of our bodies, control of our minds, / Control of our bodies, control of our lives.

> RITA MacNEIL, composer and singer, lyrics of a song, quoted by Myrna Kostash in *Her Own Woman: Profiles of Ten Canadian Women* (1975) by Myrna Kostash, Melinda McCracken, Valerie Miner, Erna Paris, and Heather Robertson.

Power doesn't have to wear pinstripe suits.

> MAUDE BARLOW, human-relations consultant, quoted by Doris Johnston in *The Sunday Herald*, 16 March 1986.

Woman is the ultimate. Mother Earth belongs to woman, not man. She carries the void.

> AGNES WHISTLING ELK, female Manitoba shaman, quoted by Lynne V. Andrews in *Star Woman: We Are Made from Stars and to the Stars We Must Return* (1986).

Copps: Is there a doctor in the House?

Crosbie: Just quieten down, baby. You bunch of poltroons can shout all you like. The Rat Pack can quieten down. The titmice can quieten down.

Copps: I am thirty-two years old, I am elected Member of Parliament from Hamilton East and I'm nobody's baby.

> Exchange between SHEILA COPPS, M.P., and Cabinet Minister JOHN CROSBIE in the House of Commons; it inspired the title of Copps's memoirs, *Nobody's Baby: A Survival Guide to Politics* (1986).

I am not ashamed of saying I am a feminist, that I fight for women. I make no apologies, just as a farmer would never dream of apologizing for promoting the interests of his group. Women make up an absolute majority in this country. Why should our interests be considered trivial? Why should we leave it to others to represent us, and to fight our battles?

> SHEILA COPPS, politician and feminist, *Nobody's Baby: A Survival Guide to Politics* (1986).

Equality for women is a terrible step down.

> DON HARRON, humorist, speaking in the guise of the comic character Valerie Rosedale, quoted by Martha Harron in *A Parent Contradiction* (1988).

If you think REAL Women are a bunch of little pansies and housewives having babies, you're wrong.

C. GWENDOLYN LANDOLT, lawyer and founder in 1983 of REAL Women of Canada (Realistic, Equal, Active for Life), quoted by Catherine Dunphy in *The Toronto Star*, 22 Feb. 1988.

The media, they've done so fine / Exploited our bodies and buried our minds / Follow their line and you're sure to be / Another brainwashed member of society.
RITA MacNEIL, composer and singer, song lyrics, quoted by Ellen Schwartz in *Born a Woman: Seven Canadian Women Singer-Songwriters* (1988).

Women have no surnames of their own. Their names are literally sirnames. Women only have one name that is ours, our first or given name.
MARGARET LAURENCE, novelist, *Dance on the Earth: A Memoir* (1989).

Be Warlike not Whorelike
Graffiti in the women's washroom, Harbourfront, Toronto, June 1989.

But my resistance to makeup is even more fundamental than that. I just hate it. I don't like what it stands for, I don't like how they make it, I don't like what it implies for women. I don't like anything about it, so I choose not to wear it.
K.D. LANG, country and western singer, quoted by Christopher Jones in *Now*, 26 Oct. 1989.

Yes means yes, no means it's too small.
Message on a sign prepared and displayed by female students who were tired of being harassed and threatened with date rape by male students at Queen's University, Kingston, Ont., noted by Orland French in *The Globe and Mail*, 11 Nov. 1989.

I can imagine myself not a Westerner, not white, having no wealth. What I *can't* imagine is not being a woman!
Statement issued by a Toronto women's inter-faith group in 1988 recalled by Lois Wilson in *Turning the World Upside Down: A Memoir* (1989).

In the next decade I would like to see women use our new power and resources to exert our right to be physically safe from men. We will never have equality if we are the only sex that cannot experience the darkness alone.
LAURA TRACHUK, human-rights lawyer, quoted in *Metropolis*, 21 Dec. 1989.

The Canadian male mind has difficulty with emotions. There now has to be an act of male liberation that can stand up to the screaming side of feminism. Feminism has done some wonderful things, but I think the steam, the trust behind it is largely spent.
SCOTT SYMONS, novelist and cultural commentator of British North American ancestry, interviewed in *The Idler*, No. 25, May-June 1990.

FENIAN WAR
See also WAR

They may tak' Canada, but they'll no tak' Zorra.
Defiant cry of the Highland Scots farmers, Township of Zorra, Oxford County, U.C. (Ont.), Fenian invasion, May 1866, Letters to the Editor, *The Globe and Mail*, 27 Feb. 1989.

FICTION
See also LITERATURE

Short stories are not about events but the people that events happen to.
W.D. VALGARDSON, fiction writer, quoted by W.P. Kinsella as interviewed by Alan Twigg in *Strong Voices: Conversations with Fifty Canadian Authors* (1988).

FILM
See also ACTORS & ACTING
AWARDS & HONOURS

IS THERE A MAN NAMED CHAFFIN OR

SOMETHING LIKE THAT IN YOUR COM-
PANY?

This is the text of one of the most important telegrams in the history of the movies. It was sent in 1913 by the Canadian-
born producer MACK SENNETT to Fred
Karno's music-hall troupe which was
touring the United States. Sennett had
seen the troupe perform two years earlier
at the American Music Hall and had remembered the routine of one English pan-
tomime comic in particular, recalling his
name as "Chaffin" and earmarking him for
possible use in his Keystone Kops. The
comic was Charles Chaplin, and this was
his *entrée* to the movies. Quoted by
Charles J. Maland in *Chaplin and American Culture: The Evolution of a Star Image*
(1989).

We never made sport of religion, politics,
race or mothers. A mother never gits hit
with a custard pie. Mothers-in-law — yes.
But mothers — never.
MACK SENNETT, Canadian-born producer of the Keystone Kops movie come-
dies and inventor of the custard-pie
routine, quoted on the subject of slap-
stick comedy in *The New York Times*, 6
Nov. 1960.

Hello, sucker!
Characteristic greeting of MARY LOUISE
GUINAN, known as Texas Guinan, Broadway and Hollywood personality who was
born in Toronto and died in Vancouver.
The vaudeville star and New York night-
club entertainer became nationally
known as "the female W.S. Hart" and "the
gun girl" in Hollywood Westerns of the
silent era, as noted in her obituary, *Variety*, 7 Nov. 1933. Remarks associated with
her stage career include "Give this little
girl a great big hand" and "She won't go
anywhere without her mother — but her
mother'll go anywhere."

The National Film Board will be the eyes
of Canada. It will, through a national use
of cinema, see Canada and see it whole —
its people and its purposes.

JOHN GRIERSON, first NFB Commissioner, address in 1940, quoted by Joyce
Nelson in *The Colonized Eye: Rethinking
the Grierson Legend* (1988).

What is the difference whether a film
comes from Hollywood or Timbuktu or
Saskatoon so long as it is about the life of
man as it is lived and dreamed in common
everywhere.
JOHN GRIERSON, NFB Commissioner, "A
Film Policy for Canada," *Canadian Affairs*,
14 June 1944.

The film becomes the universal imagination in actors; and Mickey Mouse *le Byron
de nos jours*.
A.M. KLEIN, poet, "Queen Mab and
Mickey Mouse" (1946), *Literary Essays
and Reviews* (1987) edited by Usher
Caplan and M.W. Steinberg.

The trouble might have something to do
with the Canadian filmmaker's lack of vulgarity. Canadians do not consider themselves authoritative.
ANDREW SARRIS, New York film critic of
the *auteur* school, discussing the lack of
audacity in Canadian feature films, interviewed by John K. Harrison in *Saturday
Night*, April 1976.

We go to see these films, not as a patriotic
duty, but because we want to see them.
After decades of deprivation, is it possible
that the dream of a movie mythology of
our own has finally come to pass?
MARTIN KNELMAN, critic, *This Is Where
We Came In: The Career and Character of
Canadian Film* (1977).

You have to let the camera do the acting.
CHRISTOPHER PLUMMER, stage and
screen actor, quoted by Herbert Whittaker in *The Globe and Mail*, 27 Sept. 1977.

Shakespeare, Cervantes and Tolstoy were
popular artists of their time. Suppose they
had been Canadians living now and writing for Canadian TV and film. Shakespeare
wouldn't get *Hamlet* past the CFDC — "too

Danish." Cervantes, who predicted that *Don Quixote* would sell eighteen million copies, would be turned down by the CBC because its Export Sales Department would reject his "projection of foreign earnings" as too optimistic. The National Film Board in all likelihood would purchase the rights to *War and Peace* in perpetuity but would never make the film for lack of money and because of objections from the Defence Department, thus ensuring that no one would ever see it.

RICHARD NIELSEN, independent film producer, "The Mermaid Inn," *The Globe and Mail*, 29 Oct. 1977.

The Golden Age of Canadian film is going to be tomorrow. All it takes is an act of faith.

WILLIAM MARSHALL, film producer, addressing the trade forum of Toronto's Festival of Festivals, 6 Sept. 1980, quoted by Rick Groen in *The Globe and Mail*, 8 Sept. 1980.

I'm honoured and flattered. But why don't you wait a few years.

CAROLE LAURE, actress, on learning that the sponsors of Peterborough's Canadian Images Film Festival wanted to honour her in 1984 with an eight-film retrospective, quoted by Ed Gould in *Entertaining Canadians: Canada's International Stars 1900-1988* (1988).

Let's deal with film for a moment, the most important art to emerge in the twentieth century. It is our truly international medium of communication. It has become a permanent part of the intellectual and aesthetic life of our civilization. Film has reached more peple in the first twenty years of its life than printing did in over two hundred years after its invention. Film has no boundary. It merges fact and fancy. A film is the sum total of the beliefs and principles of its maker. It has become our new literature.

NORMAN JEWISON, film director, address, Empire Club of Canada, Toronto, 5 April 1984.

It's a small field, Venereal Horror, but at least I'm king of it.

DAVID CRONENBERG, director of horror films, quoted by Neil Gaiman and Kim Newman in *Ghastly beyond Belief* (1985). Cronenberg was once dubbed "the Baron of Blood."

Make no mistake, the almost chemical effect with which a good motion picture alters the mood of its audience can be dissipated or destroyed if it is shown in the wrong physical setting. . . . The fun of movie-going includes more than just seeing the film. It is the subtle blending of a series of pleasurable stimuli — the initial anticipation, the feeling of elegance, the congeniality of the surroundings — these are what establishes the final satisfaction, the total experience.

GARTH DRABINSKY, CEO of Cineplex Odeon Corporation, address, Empire Club of Canada, Toronto, 23 Oct. 1986.

We are forever being told we are "a young and inexperienced country" and that we are finding our way. This has become a banal and tiresome statement, and should be discarded. Canada was born long before the movies were invented. They are the one art we could have made our own, as the Americans have done. There is nothing wrong with our film-makers and artists, only with our producers who, as Alexander Walker wrote when deploring the internationalists, "are part of a clique in search of the Holy grail of Hollywood." They will never find it, but they will ruin us in the search.

GERALD PRATLEY, film critic and curator, *Torn Sprockets: The Uncertain Projection of the Canadian Film* (1987).

Among the five thousand or so feature films made in Canada during the past eight years, successes have been few and far between, failures have been many and often, and few among the latter could be called noble. For this and many other reasons relating to Canada's social and economic situation, Canadians have come to believe that when some among them decide to enter film and television there is little expectation that they will succeed. Success in this instance will be measured not by how good a film or television program may be as a Canadian work in the definitive sense, but by how good they are at being American.

GERALD PRATLEY, film critic and curator, *Torn Sprockets: The Uncertain Projection of the Canadian Film* (1987).

For years I've been on the Academy Award's documentary selection committee and the work we see from Canada has a flair for ideas which is unique.

RAY BRADBURY, science-fiction author, quoted by Leonard Klady in *The Toronto Star*, 16 Jan. 1987.

Actually there were only a few people who knew I was Canadian, because I told most people I was from Bellingham, Washington.

YVONNE DE CARLO, Vancouver-born film star, referring to her early years in Hollywood, *Yvonne: An Autobiography* (1987) written with Doug Warren.

Canadians trying to make it in the film industry are viewed by the immigration authorities as not unlike illegal Mexican dishwashers. We are referred to as "icebacks."

DANIELLE CRITTENDEN, Toronto writer working in Hollywood, "Typist to the Stars," *The Idler*, No. 14, Sept.-Oct., 1987.

Darth Drabinsky
Humorous reference to film exhibitor GARTH DRABINSKY which puns on the villainous Darth Vader of *Star Wars*. Cineplex Odeon, Drabinsky's one-time empire, was dubbed either Cine-Bucks (for its record size and one-time profits) or Cineplex Odious (for its dependence on small screens and screen advertising). Noted in *The Globe and Mail*, 21 Dec. 1987.

Up until today, I've been moonstruck. Now I'm starstruck. I think it's a great honour.

Films are forever, and the stars are embedded forever, at least until the next earthquake.

NORMAN JEWISON, director, punning on the title of his film *Moonstruck* when he added his imprint to Hollywood's Walk of Fame, 14 Nov. 1988, quoted in *The Globe and Mail*, 16 Nov. 1988.

Feature films are the literature of our generation. They express the conscience of a country: Films are *forever*.

NORMAN JEWISON, director, quoted in *Maclean's*, 4 April 1988.

Hollywood is just Scarborough with millionaires.

DON HARRON, comedian, quoted by Martha Harron in *Don Harron: A Parent Contradiction* (1988).

Canadians are crazy. On the deepest level, they're the most loyal people in the world. No matter how well actors do in the United States, you can call them and say, "They want you to shovel squirrel dirt in a movie in Canada." And they'll say, "It's for Canada, I'll be there." They love being Canadians.

PAUL MAZURSKY, American film director, quoted by Ed Gould in *Entertaining Canadians: Canada's International Stars 1900-1988* (1988).

Acting has become a therapy for my very elaborate fantasy life.

HELEN SHAVER, actress, quoted by Ed Gould in *Entertaining Canadians: Canada's International Stars 1900-1988* (1988).

As they say, you can take the boy out of the country but you can't take the country out of the boy. In my case the country is Canada.

LESLIE NIELSEN, Regina-born actor, quoted by Ed Gould in *Entertaining Canadians: Canada's International Stars 1900-1988* (1988).

Financing a film in Canada is like trying to juggle a watermelon, a peach, and a pea at the same time. Just when you think you've got them all up in the air, the pea slips through your fingers.

TED KOTCHEFF, director, quoted by Ed Gould in *Entertaining Canadians: Canada's International Stars 1900-1988* (1988).

At the beginning of my career, I was an unknown, unemployed director; now, at the height of my career, I am a famous, unemployed director.

Attributed to CLAUDE JUTRA, director of *Mon Oncle Antoine*, based on a remark quoted by Ann Charney in *Saturday Night*, May 1988.

I have always wanted to make a good Canadian movie. I have not been able to find a talented piece, a screenplay that is right. I hope that ambition is fulfilled within ten years. A film made in Canada about something that Canadians really care about.

NORMAN JEWISON, director and producer, quoted by Ed Gould in *Entertaining Canadians: Canada's International Stars 1900-1988* (1988).

The problem is that subservient Canada would like to gain just a teensy bit of control over the film industry in this country that the United States — being the United States and Canada being Canada — controls. (It is mean and picky to object, of course, the United States having controlled our oil industry and tire industry and auto industry and Mulroney industry for so long — but we try.)

ALLAN FOTHERINGHAM, columnist, commenting on Ottawa's indecisive initiatives in film policy to guarantee the exhibition of Canadian-made feature films in American-owned motion-picture theatre chains, *Maclean's*, 30 Oct. 1989.

That is the way the real world operates. I am afraid no prime minister, no president, no Congress, no Parliament can force citizens to watch something they don't want to see. In this country, as in all others, the consumer is king.

JACK VALENTI, chairman of the Motion Picture Export Association of America, address, Empire Club of Canada, Toronto, 19 Oct. 1989, quoted in *The Toronto Star* the following day.

A great deal of Canadian chauvinist pride went untapped during the war years. If someone in a film said he was from Montreal, or Toronto, there was cheering in the theatre and foot-stomping. Or if, in a murky London fog, a soldier admitted to being a "Canuck," you wouldn't hear the rest of the scene for the whistling.

MARY PEATE, memoirist, recalling seeing British and American feature films in Montreal in the 1940s, *Girl in a Sloppy Joe Sweater: Life on the Canadian Home Front during World War Two* (1989).

In a civilized society, they would have done something about the fire laws, but in Quebec, they decided you couldn't go to the movies, except for an occasional children's show.

JUDITH CRIST, New York-based film critic who grew up in Toronto and Montreal, noting that Quebec movie theatres in the 1940s were closed to children under the age of sixteen because there had once been a theatre fire, quoted by Pearl Sheffy Gefen in *The Globe and Mail*, 9 Jan. 1989.

Pain is temporary. Film is forever.

MICHAEL J. FOX, film star, quoted by Jamie Portman in *The Toronto Star*, 21 Nov. 1989.

The last time I was in Canada was for a showing of *King Kong* at Montreal's Olympics. Ingrid Bergman was there and got very scared and there was such a hush when Kong was mowed down at the end. There always is.

FAY WRAY, movie personality born on a farm outside Cardston, Alta., who appeared in seventy-seven movies but most notably in *King Kong*, interviewed in Hollywood by Jim Bawden in *The Toronto Star*, 13 Jan. 1990.

Can you believe that Warren Beatty is half-Canadian — the top half.

> Attributed to film star Warren Beatty's sister SHIRLEY MacLAINE by Rick Groen in *The Globe and Mail*, 30 Dec. 1990.

I don't think there's one person in the world that I couldn't do a documentary about.

> ALANIS OBOMSAWIN, documentary filmmaker, quoted by Cameron Bailey in *Now*, 9 Aug. 1990.

At the Toronto film festival you're greeted by a warm welcome and a cold beer, which is the exact opposite of Cannes.

> IAIN JOHNSTONE, British journalist and film-festival correspondent, at the Toronto International Film Festival, quoted by Philip Marchand in *The Toronto Star*, 15 Sept. 1990.

FINANCE

See also BANKS
FINANCE, PERSONAL
INVESTMENTS
MONEY
TAXES
WEALTH

Our governments have brought under their control everything but their deficits.

> JOHN BULLOCH, President, Canadian Federation of Independent Business, address, Empire Club of Canada, Toronto, 23 Feb. 1978.

Ottawa's most worrisome failure was its inability to break its own and the country's addiction to $30 billion dollar a year deficits. . . . In Canada the government did rather worse: the deficit through 1986 was proportionately 50 per cent larger than Washington's. It had to be supported by an economy less diverse, self-sufficient, and resilient; and Canadians and their governors seemed less anxious than Americans to do anything at all about the problem.

> MICHAEL BLISS, historian, *Northern En-*

terprise: Five Centuries of Canadian Business (1987).

If Alexander Graham Bell had looked to Canadians for financing rather than to his American father-in-law, we might still be waiting for the telephone.

> JERRY S. WHITE, management consultant, *Intra-preneuring: The Secrets of Corporate Success in Canada* (1988).

Foreign-investment controls, by reserving Canadian assets to Canadian bidders, have let a handful of home-grown acquisitors buy up the country at fire-sale prices. Foreign airlines may not fly domestic routes: so two domestic airlines divide the market between them. Foreign ownership of newspapers is forbidden: so instead two domestic newspaper chains control nearly half of daily circulation. Five families control almost 500 of our companies. Of the world's ten richest multi-billionaires, two countries number three apiece among their citizens. The U.S. is one. Canada is the other.

> ANDREW COYNE, journalist, *Saturday Night*, July 1989.

Apart from minting more money than he can possibly spend, Robert Campeau's ultimate ambition is to make history. He may yet succeed by presiding over Canada's most spectacular bankruptcy — his own — but for now, he'll have to settle for a footnote.

> PETER C. NEWMAN, columnist, making reference to the forced refinancing of Campeau's American acquisitions, *Maclean's*, 30 Oct. 1989.

The financial district is characterised above ground by its skyscrapers and canyon streets, and below ground by a maze of tunnels lined with stores. (I call these the "cashacombs" but it doesn't seem to be a name which has caught on.)

> EDWARD RELPH, geographer, *The Toronto Guide: The City/Metro/The Region* (Annual Conference, Association of

American Geographers, Toronto, April 1990).

FINANCE, PERSONAL
See also FINANCE

Bottom lines are higher than they used to be.
> BETTY JANE WYLIE, author, *All in the Family: A Survival Guide for Living and Loving in a Changing World* (1988).

By strengthening the strong, we can help the weak.
> WILLIAM VANDER ZALM, British Columbia Premier, quoted in *The Vancouver Sun*, 3 July 1986.

FIRE

It's the fire in the head of man, / It's the fire in the heart of woman, / The element, oh so human, / That consumes the human condition.
> FRANK STEVEN, singer and composer, "The Fire," *Elemental Love* (Contemporary Music, 1976).

FIRST MINISTERS' CONFERENCES

Albertans and other devotees of the Triple-E Senate — Equal, Elected and Effective — should reflect on the fact that they have something like a Triple-E Senate in the evolving "executive federalism." The First Ministers' Conferences, now enshrined by custom (and in the Constitution, if Meech Lake passes), provide a chamber in which each province has only one representative, who is elected and who can join with other premiers to pressure Ontario.
> PHILIPPE DEANE GIGANTES, author and Senator, *The Road Ahead* (1990).

FISH & FISHING

The fisheries of Newfoundland are inexhaustible and are of more value to the Empire than all the silver mines of Peru ...
greater than the gold mines of Golgonda, there is none so rich.
> SIR FRANCIS BACON, English essayist, "Of Plantations" (1608), *The Essayes or Counsels* (1625).

Angling is the name given to fishing by people who can't fish.
> Attributed to STEPHEN LEACOCK by William Sherwood Fox in *Silken Lines and Silver Hooks: A Life-long Fisherman Recounts His Catch* (1954).

Nehru, my cod to thee.
> All credit for originating this pun, which plays on the line from the hymn which runs "Nearer, my God, to thee," should go to the newspaperman GEORGE BAIN, who made it the punch-line of the satiric skit he wrote for the 1954 National Press Gallery Dinner in Ottawa. In the skit, Prime Minister St. Laurent explains why Canada is sending large cargoes of salt cod to Prime Minister Nehru of India. Since then the line has been widely credited but seldom to its originator, George Bain.

After forty years, rivers remain places of enchantment and the fish that swim in them creatures of wonder. Some small share in this is the fisherman's real reward.
> RODERICK HAIG-BROWN, angler and author, "The Man Behind the Rod" (1961), *Writings and Reflections (1982)* edited by Valerie Haig-Brown.

The large majority of drowned canoe fishermen are found with their flies open.
> HAROLD TOWN and DAVID SILCOX, authors, explaining the drowning of master canoeist Tom Thomson, *The Silence and the Storm* (1977).

No white fish or trout here, we leave them alone. / The inspectors raise hell if we take any home. / What kind of fishermen can't eat his catch / Or call what he's taken his own?
> STAN ROGERS, singer and composer, "Tiny Fish for Japan," *From Fresh Water* (Cole Harbour Music, 1984).

Impersonal life in the cold body of a trout, / A promise of happiness in a line of light.

> M.T. (TERRY) KELLY, poet and novelist, "All We Have," *Country You Can't Walk In and Other Poems* (1984).

I have to say here that Canadian literature, coast to coast, is literally squirming with fish. I could have done a whole anthology of fish stories alone. Seems they're as important in the minds of writers as they are in those of government negotiators, a rare overlap.

> MARGARET ATWOOD, author and editor, *The CanLit Foodbook: From Pen to Palate — A Collection of Tasty Literary Fare* (1987).

When the East Wind blows, the fish won't bite, / South Wind they bite least; / West Wind blow de bait right in their mouth, / North Wind they bite best.

> "That's the gospel according to JOE LAVALLY, a legendary Cree fishing guide who worked the Algonquin Park area of Ontario years ago. Lousy poetry . . . but great fishing lore," according to Arthur Black in *Back to Black: Comic Sketches* (1987).

To be a good fisherman, you have to be able to think like a fish.

> EDITH IGLAUER, essayist, *Fishing with John* (1988).

Sealing was dirty, dangerous, paid little, and offered its greatest reward in being able, simply, to return home again — alive.

> WILLIAM GOUGH, author, *The Art of David Blackwood* (1988).

Canada must be a very beautiful country. There must be excellent rivers for fishing. Canada must be extraordinary for trout and for salmon.

> MILOVAN DJILAS, Yugoslav dissident author and avid fisherman who has never visited Canada or fished in Canadian waters, quoted by Alan Ferguson in Belgrade in *The Toronto Star*, 20 Oct. 1990.

The animals of the Burgess Shale are holy objects — in the unconventional sense that this word conveys in some cultures. We do not place them on pedestals and worship from afar. We climb mountains and dynamite hillsides to find them. We quarry them, split them, carve them, draw them, and dissect them, struggling to wrest their secrets. We vilify and curse them for their damnable intransigence. They are grubby little creatures of a sea floor 530 million years old, but we greet them with awe because they are the Old Ones, and they are trying to tell us something.

> STEPHEN JAY GOULD, biologist, discussing the marine animal life found in the Burgess Shale of B.C.'s Yoho National Park, *Wonderful Life: The Burgess Shale and the Nature of History* (1989).

FITNESS
See also HEALTH

Exercise is the closest thing to an anti-aging and anti-disease pill.

> JOSEPH LEVY, physician, quoted by Leslie Holbrook and George Merry, *Improving with Age: How to Enjoy Your Senior Years* (1985).

Jog to the rear of the bus. If you're like most Canadians, it'll be the only *real* exercise you'll get today. *Don't run for the bus.* The shape you're in, you might not make it. *Swim, ski, jog.* Do something to get yourself in shape. Then run for the bus.

> Text of a television commercial prepared for ParticipAction, the federal government's fitness program, quoted by Wilfred List in *The Globe and Mail*, 29 Jan. 1988.

Now for the first time there is a natural way to improve our fitness and health without exercises by utilizing a natural mechanism that exercises the entire body and counters the number one cause of man's aches and pains. . . . What then is the Mitzvah Principle? My observation and study of good working bodies among the nomadic Bedouin of the deep Sinai desert led me to identify an interplay of forces acting between the pelvis and spine which activates a natural defence and corrective mechanism of the body. I named this interplay the Mitzvah Principle from the biblical Hebrew word "Mitzvah" meaning a good deed which in turn brings good to the doer. The interplay ripples the spine in an upward motion with every move and step we take, reinforcing the body's balance with gravity.

> M. COHEN-NEHEMIAH, founder, Mitzvah Technique Centre, Toronto, lecture, 18th World Congress of Natural Medicines, Havana, Cuba, April 1990.

FLAG
See also EMBLEMS

American students start the school day by pledging allegiance to the flag. The only time a Canadian student puts his hand over his heart is when he is trying to find his pulse.

> ERIC NICOL and DAVE MORE, humorists, *The U.S. or Us: What's the Difference, Eh?* (1986).

There flies a city flag in which (devised as it was for a visit by the British royal family in 1939) the fleur-de-lis occupies only one-quarter, the others being filled by a rose, a thistle, and a shamrock.

> JAN MORRIS, Welsh travel writer, describing the flag of the City of Montreal, "The Battle for Montreal," *Saturday Night*, July 1988.

I felt it should be bicultural, with symbols — both British and French — to remind us of the origins of our nation. Instead, what we have is not even multi-cultural or agricultural; it is silvicultural.

> EUGENE FORSEY, constitutional authority, referring to the Maple Leaf flag, *A Life on the Fringe: The Memoirs of Eugene Forsey* (1990).

One wind moves many flags.

> ROBERT PRIEST, poet, aphorism, March 1990.

FLORIDA

In general, even as tourists, Canadians are lively and adventurous travellers. (One does not count the snowbirds who have made Florida an extraterritorial province of Canada.)

> KILDARE DOBBS, travel writer, Preface, *Away from Home: Canadian Writers in Exotic Places* (1985).

How can you hate a place where you can play tennis thirteen months a year.

> ALLAN FOTHERINGHAM, columnist, referring to Florida, *Maclean's*, 28 March 1988.

Florida can be explained, defined, encapsulated, summarized, characterized, wrung out and hung up to dry in one short sentence: The only thing Florida has going for it is the Canadian winter.

> JOEY SLINGER, columnist and essayist, "Retreat of the Birds," *The Saturday Night Traveller* (1990) edited by George Galt.

FLOWERS
See also GARDENS

When you sail far across the wide ocean, / May you never forget those bright hours / That we spent on the banks of the river / In the evenings among prairie flowers!

> Final verse of the folksong "The Red River Valley," *Folk Songs of Canada* (1954) edited by Edith Fowke and Richard Johnston.

The national flower of Canada? Ogilvie Flour, of course.

> Attributed to railway builder SIR WILLIAM VAN HORNE when speaking to Alexander Ogilvie, Senator and a founder of Ogilvie Flour Mills, quoted by Janice Tyrwhitt in *The Mill* (1976) by William Fox and Bill Brooks.

Every flower is shouting at us of our common divinity, of our transcendent selves. We know it unconsciously. Our paradises have been gardens. We "say it with flowers." Our symbolic pictures of the universe, our mandalas, are flower designs. But now flowers are saying, with a new intensity, "Look, don't think; look directly at us and see God."

DOROTHY MACLEAN, medium, *To Hear the Angels Sing: An Odyssey of Co-Creation with the Devic Kingdom* (1980).

FOLKLORE
See also MYTHOLOGY

Canadian culture as it exists today ought not to be described as a mosaic, but rather as a bipartite tapestry with decorative embroidery or a jumble of separate pieces loosely attached to one another with their distinct colours and designs being only a superficial layer on top of a more substantial base — in other words, a jigsaw puzzle. This description matches the prevailing attitude towards minority-cultural traditions, demonstrated by action, though generally not by belief.

CAROLE HENDERSON CARPENTER, folklorist, *Many Voices: A Study of Folklore Activities in Canada and Their Role in Canadian Culture* (1979).

A . . . rumour of a poisonous snake attack scared many people away from Montreal's Botanical Garden in the summer of 1983. The park has long been a popular spot for wedding photographs when the flowers are in bloom, and the rumour that summer told of a bride who was bitten by a poisonous viper that had been lurking in the foliage. Garden officials and wedding photographers did their best to set the record straight, pointing out that no poisonous snakes live in Canada, but many wedding parties sought less worrisome backdrops for their pictures anyway. While the snake-in-the-coat story seems to draw on Freudian imagery and lurking subconscious fears, Montreal's wedding snake is closer to a modern retelling of the story of Adam and Eve.

HAL MORGAN and KERRY TUCKER, American researchers, relating the story of the shopper who was bitten by a baby cobra nesting in the sleeve of a fur coat she was trying on in a downtown department store, *More Rumour!* (1987).

When a reader in Yellowknife, Northwest Territories, wrote offering to be my listening post for urban legends up there, I thought, "Sure, ha ha; urban and suburban folklore can't possibly get that far into the wilds." A week later, he sent me notes on a couple of good ones he had just heard in Yellowknife. When I got a similar call from Whitehorse up in the Yukon, I listened.

JAN HAROLD BRUNVAND, folklorist at the University of Utah, *Curses! Broiled Again! The Hottest Urban Legends Going* (1989).

FOOD & DRINK
See also ALCOHOL

I inform thee that I intend to eat thee.

Thompson Indian poem, initial line, "Prayer to the Sunflower-Root," *Songs of the Great Land* (1989) edited by John Robert Colombo.

Take the scrapings from the driest outside corner of a very stale piece of cold roast beef, add to it lumps of rancid fat, then garnish all with long human hairs and short hairs of dogs and oxen and you have a fair imitation of common pemmican.

H.M. ROBINSON, author, description of pemmican, the mainstay of the Métis, *The Great Fur Land* (1892), as cited by Peter C. Newman in *Empire of the Bay: An Illustrated History of the Hudson's Bay Company* (1989).

Space is lacking here to go in detail into the abominations of Canadian cookery. With the most bountiful supply of provisions the culinary art is wholly neglected, and scarcely understood at all.

EZRA HURLBURT STAFFORD, physician and crank, "Social and Personal Measures for the Control and Limitation of Insanity," *The Dominion Medical Monthly and Ontario Medical Journal*, March 1898.

My candies are made in the morning and sold in the afternoon.
> Sign in the window of Rogers Chocolates, Victoria, 1890s, quoted by Michael Kluckner in *Victoria: The Way It Was* (1986).

It is an easy matter to learn to like entirely natural goods, because it is natural to like them.
> ROBERT G. JACKSON, M.D., *The Fattening Regime: A Manual for the Too-Thin* (1928, 3rd ed., 1936).

Lord grant us capacity / Longevity, elasticity, / Avoiding obesity. / Amen.
> Grace before meals, attributed to E.J. PRATT in 1956, recalled by Charles Comfort, quoted by David G. Pitt in *E.J. Pratt: The Master Years, 1927-1964* (1987).

Ashes to ashes, and dust to dust — but, in the meantime, blintzes are a *must.*
> Yiddish proverb translated by the poet A.M. Klein, *Literary Essays and Reviews* (1987) edited by Usher Caplan and M.W. Steinberg.

If you eat better, you love more.
> EUGENE WHELAN, Minister of Agriculture, address in Calgary, quoted in *The Toronto Star*, 19 Nov. 1976.

Apple pie without cheese / Is like the kiss without the squeeze.
> Couplet recalled by former Ontario Premier T.L. (TOM) KENNEDY who repeated it to encourage the sale of such Ontario farm produce as cheese and apples, quoted by Norman Webster in *The Globe and Mail*, 28 Nov. 1977.

Myself, I go on eating, as I go on breathing. / But I hope these two acts are all that tie me in this life / to those men and women who for now decide who starves.
> TOM WAYMAN, poet, "Kitchen Poem," *Free Time* (1977).

Anything expands to fit the space allowed for it, unless it's rice, which always gets carried away.
> BETTY JANE WYLIE, author, *Encore: The Leftovers Cookbook* (1979).

Sugar is an environmental hazard of great potency. Much more must be learned about it. What is known is decidedly disquieting.
> HUMPHRY OSMOND, psychiatrist, "How Unsweet It Is," *Predicting the Past: Memos on the Enticing Universe of Possibility* (1981) produced by Jerome Agel.

"A loaf of bread, a jug of wine, and thou" — add cheese, and you've got me for life.
> BETTY JANE WYLIE, author, *Betty Jane Wylie's Cheese Cookbook* (1984).

Winston. Host to the Stars.
> This slogan appears stamped in gold on the leather cover of the menu at Winston's. The Toronto dining establishment was founded as Winston's Theatre Grill by Oscar Berceller in 1938. Since 1966 it has continued, as Winston's, under the direction of John Arena, its clientelle coming from corporate finance rather than the theatre crowd. Quoted by Herbert Whittaker and Arnold Edinborough in *Winston's: The Life and Times of a Great Restaurant* (1988).

In this land of the musk-ox, the beaver, and the moose, there is no musk-ox or beaver or moose meat to be had. The man behind the counter at the meat store is little more than a butcher. The remains of cows and sheep and pigs are all he has to sell.
> BRUCE McCALL, satirist, "In the New Canada, Living Is a Way of Life," *The New Yorker*, 20 May 1985.

If you want good service avoid restaurants with red checked tablecloths.
> EDWARD PHILLIPS, novelist, *Buried on Sunday* (1986).

Whenever I have spoken at luncheons or banquets or done autographings in stores, women and men have told me they love reading my *Schmecks* books in bed. It has happened so often that I'm beginning to feel myself responsible for Canada's declining birth rate.

EDNA STAEBLER, specialist in Pennsylvania-Dutch cuisine, *Schmecks Appeal: More Mennonite Country Cooking* (1987). The earlier books are called *Food that Really Schmecks* and *More Food that Really Schmecks*.

Eating is our earliest metaphor, preceding our consciousness of gender difference, race, nationality, and language. We eat before we talk.

MARGARET ATWOOD, author and editor, *The CanLit Foodbook: From Pen to Palate — A Collection of Tasty Literary Fare* (1987).

After New York, Toronto must have the greatest contribution of restaurants of any North American city.

STEPHEN BROOK, English travel writer, *Maple Leaf Rag: Travels across Canada* (1987).

The customary toast before dinner is "Cheers," or "To Your Health," but most Canadians prefer the toast from the Inuit in the far reaches of Northern Canada. It is simply: "Chimo" . . . "Health."

PEGGY WHEDON and JOHN KIDNER, U.S. authors, *Dining in the Great Embassies Cookbook* (1987). The mixed Inuit-Indian word "chimo" means "cheers."

Anyway, as statistics show, coffee is a beverage of enormous centrality to the concept of Canadian consciousness. Indeed, it's arguable that coffee is the one thing that keeps us conscious as a people at all.

ERIKA RITTER, humorist, "Grounds for Discourse," *Ritter in Residence: A Comic Collection* (1987).

To order a meal from a menu is an act of faith: You don't get to see it or taste it before you order. You can try on a sweater, you can test drive a car. There is no trial period for food. Your only protection, once presented with a plate of food that is, in your opinion, inedible, is refusing to accept it. In fact, you are not legally bound to pay for a rejected plate.

CYNTHIA WINE, food specialist, "Dining Out, *The Toronto Star*, 19 Nov. 1988.

Two foods we know that everyone should avoid, however, are sugar and coffee, two North Americna favourites.

JAMES D'ADAMO, naturopath, *The D'Adamo Diet* (1989).

Our present industrial food system, pursuing the logic of distancing, has effectively alienated many people from an active relationship to food in any role other than that of consumers. Any restructuring of the food system will have to deal with and overcome this alienation. If universal accessibility means that everyone is entitled to adequate nutrition as a member of the society, then everyone also has to take some responsibility for the food system in the same way that they have to take responsibility for their health.

BREWSTER KNEEN, food system analyst, *From Land to Mouth: Understanding the Food System* (1989). The notion that there is a "food system" that embraces everything from agricultural input to wholesale and retail distribution has been pioneered by Brewster Kneen, the Toronto-based food system analyst, since Dec. 1985.

People do not normally submit to starvation just because no one has been around to market some product for them to consume.

BREWSTER KNEEN, food system analyst, *From Land to Mouth: Understanding the Food System* (1989).

You can't buy an electric kettle in the United States, for the simple reason that they don't drink tea.

ALLAN FOTHERINGHAM, columnist, *Maclean's*, 3 July 1989.

Chips and vinegar or *poutine*, butter tarts or *tourtière*, dim sum or bagels or chapati or baklava are *à votre choix*. Where else in the world is all this diversity so taken for granted?

CHARLES PACHTER, artist and essayist, *The Globe and Mail*, 28 March 1991.

Two rules have served me well for countless years. One is that all airline food is indigestibly alike. The other is that people who are learned and articulate about food are rarely, if ever, interesting on anything else.

JOHN KENNETH GALBRAITH, economist and author, quoted in *The Winnipeg Free Press*, 5 June 1990.

What we encountered most of, in the bilingual towns of the cupro-nickel belt, was *le poutine*. *Poutine* can be bought from *le chip-stand*, which is a feature, often the principal feature, of every tiny townlet. We met it only in its fast-food version, though there may be a domestic original of great ethnic deliciousness. In this phase, *poutine* is chips in a cardboard box of gravy. The gravy sits in the box for some time to absorb its flavours, like oak-matured sherry; then processed cheese is sprinkled over all. Simple as the components are, the effect is indescribable. The word isn't in the *OED*, not even the Supplement, though it is as common on the Anglo- as the Francophone bank of the Ottawa or Outaouais. It's as solid as can be along the Ottawa Waterway, yet there is a *poutine*-shaped void between *pou sto* (a teddy bear in an aqualung) and *poutnet* (a tartlet from the Auvergne). My respectable French dictionary has a similar gap between *poussoir* and *poutre*; and Gage's Canadian Dictionary doesn't help either. Can the word be a demented corruption of pouding? Of boudin? Of poteen? (Perhaps it was dutiable at one time and made by moonshire in clandestine stills.) It has a more than vaguely indecent sound, by no means inappropriate.

ERIC KORN, columnist and antiquarian book dealer, *The Times Literary Supplement*, 15 June 1990.

People commit suicide with their knives and forks.

Characteristic saying quoted in the obituary of ARNO KOEGLER, nauturopath from Waterloo County, Ont., who died at the age of 92, *The Globe and Mail*, 1 March 1991.

FOOD BANKS

In a city where everyone is scampering around buying jars of special mustard for the holidays, 36,000 kids is a lot of kids using food banks.

SUSAN PIGOTT, member of the Child Poverty Action Group, noting that thousands of Toronto children would spend Christmas in poverty, quoted in *The Globe and Mail*, 30 Dec. 1988.

We've got so much food in this country that soup kitchens in Montreal and Toronto can actually operate on the food that city restaurants *throw into the garbage* every day.

ARTHUR BLACK, broadcaster and humorist, "That's Not Fat — Just Christmas Calories," *That Old Black Magic* (1989).

Where else but Canada would you find a city like Toronto where 72,000 kids must turn to food banks each day for their meals yet city council spends four hours debating — before turning down the notion 9-8 — whether the city should be twinned with the Soviet city of Volgograd?

ROY MacGREGOR, columnist, *The Ottawa Citizen*, 10 April 1989.

Many of these weaknesses of the current North American version of capitalism don't require revelation by involved economic studies. The food banks next to the big banks are there for the ordinary, even uneducated, eye to see. So are the BMW's and the homeless in the streets.

JACK CAHILL, journalist, *The Toronto Star*, 17 Dec. 1989.

There are 625 McDonald's outlets nationwide; there are over 1,100 food banks and soup kitchens.

CAROLYN JACK, commentator, "Children

in Poverty," *The Canadian Forum*, Sept. 1990.

FOOD KITCHENS
See FOOD BANKS

FOOLS

An illiterate fool can be a useful fool, he can wash floors, but a fool with a doctorate is deadly. No amount of learning can cure stupidity and higher education positively fortifies it.
> STEPHEN VIZINCZEY, novelist, *An Innocent Millionaire* (1983).

Morrissey: I don't suffer fools.
Garrard: I do.
> Conversation between playwrights KIM MORRISSEY and JIM GARRARD, returning from the conference of the Playwrights Union of Canada, Montreal, 1988.

In my more jaundiced moments I have often said that Canada is a paradise for humbugs. If you have enough nerve, gall, rind, crust, you can palm yourself off on most of the population as a reincarnation of Socrates, Caruso, or Pope Innocent III. No one who knows anything about philosophy, or music, or the Catholic Church will be taken in, but the generality of people may be.
> EUGENE FORSEY, constitutional authority, *A Life on the Fringe: The Memoirs of Eugene Forsey* (1990).

FOOTBALL
See also SPORTS

I like our Canajun game better on accounta I allways luvs to see sumnthin go by air thats not gonna cost me 36 sents. Our game is menshun, by the wya, in yer Noo Testymint: "And it caim to pass." That's next to yer Qwarterbacks Creed: "It is more blested to handoff than to reseeve."
> DON HARRON, comedian, in the person of Charlie Farquharson, *Cum Buy the Farm* (1987).

You can fly from Montreal to Toronto during the last two minutes of an NFL game.
> TIM BURKE, sports columnist, *The Montreal Gazette*, 8 Dec. 1987.

How many quarters are in a football game?
> TERRY JOHNSON, humorist, *Quick Quiz for Slow People* (1988).

I'm saying now that I'll be at every home game. And I won't be sitting in any skybox; I'll be all over the stadium.
> JOHN CANDY, portly movie personality, quoted by Jim Proudfoot in *The Toronto Star*, 26 Feb. 1991. The remark was at the reception at Toronto's SkyDome to announce the purchase of the Toronto Argonauts Football Club by Bruce McNall, Wayne Gretzky, and John Candy. Sports journalists promptly dubbed the trio the Rich One, the Great One, and the Funny One.

FOREIGN AID
See also FOREIGN AFFAIRS

Just what kind of aid do we consent to give so consistently? Canada's official development assistance program is only middling in size, but broad in scope and varied in approach. Its budget this year is about U.S. $2.3 billion — one-half of one percent of Canada's GNP, or about two cents out of each dollar the federal government spends.
> MARGARET CATLEY-CARLSON, President of CIDA, "Aid: A Canadian Vocation," *Daedalus: Journal of the American Academy of Arts and Sciences*, "In Search of Canada," Fall 1988.

I believe Canadians are ready to contribute not a mere 0.45 percent of the GNP but as much as such countries as Norway (1.6 percent), the Netherlands (0.91 percent), Sweden (0.85 percent), and Denmark (0.73 percent) even if Canada would have to double its $2 billion annual contribution to do so.
> MONIQUE BÉGIN, former politician, "Debates and Silences — Reflections of a Pol-

itician," *Daedalus: Journal of the American Academy of Arts and Sciences*, "In Search of Canada," Fall 1988.

FOREIGN AFFAIRS
See also INTERNATIONALISM

Canada is a helpful fixer.
National role in international relations as defined by LESTER B. PEARSON, "mandarin" in the Department of External Affairs from the 1930s to the 1950s and Prime Minister from 1963 to 1968.

Canada has a role and ability to examine all world situations and to see the weak spots on all sides.
HARRISON SALISBURY, correspondent with *The New York Times*, address, Brandon, Man., 24 April 1980.

The barbarians are outside the walls and they are being fed by the Canadians.
BARBARA AMIEL, columnist and critic of current Canadian foreign-aid programs, address, Empire Club of Canada, Toronto, 4 Feb. 1982.

Foreign aid will "Newfoundlandize" the Third World. (Half of Newfoundland's income is "aid" from Ottawa.)
WILLIAM D. GAIRDNER, academic and businessman, *The Trouble with Canada* (1990).

Whenever a world crisis erupts, it's easy to spot the Canadian foreign minister: he's the man demanding a special session of the United Nations.
DAVID FRUM, essayist, "Why She Needs the Bomb," *The Idler*, May-June 1990.

Canada appears to be degenerating into an ungoverned federal state where regional/cultural/internal factors are taking precedence over most outside concerns, particularly concerns like Mexico which appear distant. It appears to outsiders that the Canadian Department of External Affairs spends more time analyzing Iraq

than Mexico, although Canada can do little about the former.
LEONARD WAVERMAN, economist, "A Canadian Vision of North American Economic Integration," *Continental Accord: North American Economic Integration* (1991) edited by Steven Globerman.

FOREIGN INVESTMENT
See also ECONOMIC NATIONALISM

Canada is a country that can both require foreign investment and complain about it at the same time, seeing no contradiction.
ANDREW H. MALCOLM, U.S. correspondent, "Northern Contradiction," *Saturday Night*, Dec. 1987.

The Foreign Investment Review Agency (FIRA), created in 1974, was replaced in June 1985 by Investment Canada, a government agency that has yet to reject a request for foreign investment in Canada.
MONIQUE BÉGIN, former politician, "Debates and Silences — Reflections of a Politician," *Daedalus: Journal of the American Academy of Arts and Sciences*, "In Search of Canada," Fall, 1988.

If we fail to invest in our own future we will be exporters of yesterday's product and importers of tomorrow's technology.
Attributed to Ontario Premier DAVID PETERSON in *The Globe and Mail*, 1 Jan. 1990.

Kenneth Thomson, the son of Lord Thomson, the Toronto newspaper magnate, owns 117 daily newspapers in the United States from Valdosta, Ga., to West Covina, Calif., plus dozens of trade publications. Another Toronto entrepreneur, Conrad Black, owns 54 American dailies. The Bank of Montreal owns Chicago's mammoth Harris Bank, which produces nearly a quarter of the parent bank's annual income, while Canada's Cineplex Odeon, the continent's second-largest theatre chain, controls 1,882 movie screens in the United States.

ANDREW H. MALCOLM, journalist, *The New York Times*, 28 Jan. 1990.

FOREIGN OWNERSHIP
See also ECONOMIC NATIONALISM

If Canadians keep borrowing to consume, it is possible that eventually the Japanese will own most of British Columbia, the Americans most of Ontario, the French most of Quebec, and the Europeans most of the Maritimes.

Adapted from a remark made by the economist CARL BEIGIE in an address to the Certified General Accounts Association of Ontario, Toronto, 9 Nov. 1989, as reported by George Brett in the *Toronto Star* the following day.

FORESTS
See also PULP & PAPER
TREES

There is no appearance of venerable antiquity in the Canadian woods. There are no ancient spreading oaks that might be called the patriarchs of the forest. A premature decay seems to be their doom. They are uprooted by the storm, and sink in their first maturity, to give place to a new generation that is ready to fill their places.

CATHARINE PARR TRAILL, pioneer writer, diary entry, 25 Oct. 1832, *The Backwoods of Canada: Being Letters from the Wife of an Emigrant Officer* (1836).

But now our lumbering is over and we are returning home, / To greet our wives and sweethearts and never more to roam, / To greet our friends and neighbours; we'll tell them not to go / To that forsaken G — D — place called Canaday I O.

Final verse of "Canaday I O," a lumberman's ballad, said to be composed by EPHRAIM BRALEY, a lumberman from Hudson, Maine, who hated lumbering in Quebec in 1854. Reproduced by Albert B. Friedman in his edition of *The Viking Book of Folk Ballads of the English-Speaking World* (1956, 1982).

They have never seen a tree or a forest, and it would be difficult to make an Eskimo understand what sort of thing a tree really is. They thought the wood was sent them by the good people of the under-world up through the sea.

JANUARIUS A. MacGAHAN, Irish-American adventurer and journalist, *Under the Northern Lights* (1876).

This morning I took a walk through the woods down to the spring — the loveliest spot. Oh, it was all so beautiful! The calm, fresh loveliness of the woods seemed to enter into my very spirit with voiceless harmony — the harmony of clear blue skies, mossy trees and gleaming snow. All the little fears and chafings shrank into nothing and vanished. Standing there beneath that endless blue dome, deep with the breathing of universal space, I felt as if all the world had a claim on my love — as if there were nothing of good I could not assimilate — no noble thought I could not re-echo. I put my arm around a lichened old spruce and laid my cheek against its rough side — it seemed like an old friend.

L. M. MONTGOMERY, author, journal entry, 16 March 1892, Park Corner, P.E.I., *The Selected Journals of L.M. Montgomery: Volume I: 1889-1910* (1985) edited by Mary Rubio and Elizabeth Waterston.

Smoke sometimes spreads for long distances. In 1950, forest fires in Canada made the sunsets similarly red in Europe; they created a haze that cut the daytime sunlight in half in Washington, D.C.

WILLIAM H. CALVIN, neurobiologist, *The River that Flows Uphill: A Journey from the Big Bang to the Big Brain* (1986).

Let's cut down the trees and create jobs.

WILLIAM VANDER ZALM, British Columbia Premier, quoted in *The Prince Rupert Daily News*, 10 July 1986.

The colonists lived in a world of wood. The pine forest was everywhere on the mainland; only Newfoundland had to make do with stunted trees poking up from the rock.

MICHAEL BLISS, historian, *Northern Enterprise: Five Centuries of Canadian Business* (1987).

They do not go into the forests to seek what they are, but to forget what they suspect themselves to be.... They do not ask the forests to speak to them. But the forests will speak if they can find a listener.

ROBERTSON DAVIES, man-of-letters, describing the unadventurousness of many contemporary Canadians, *The Lyre of Orpheus* (1988).

In Japan, I was amazed to find that over 50% of their solid waste is recycled: as our Federal Minister of the Environment recently pointed out, if we recycled paper at the same rate as the Japanese, we could save 80 million trees a year — an amount that equals the total annual logging production of Ontario.

DAVE NICHOL, President, Loblaw International Merchants, Summit on the Environment, Toronto, 11 Sept. 1989.

Once it took Haida Indians in the Queen Charlotte Islands more than a year to cut down a single giant cedar. When the Europeans arrived with the technological know-how — the two-man saw and steel ax — the task was shortened to a week. Today, one man with a portable chain saw can fell that tree in an hour.

ANITA GORDON and DAVID SUZUKI, science broadcasters, *It's a Matter of Survival* (1990).

What a piece of work is a man! In action how like an angel! And the only piece of man's handiwork that can be seen by the angels as they guard or at least regard the earth from geostationary orbit at 37 thousand kilometres is the great wound wrought in the temperate rain forests of Vancouver Island by MacMillan Bloedel and other logging companies. Or so at least British Columbians gloomily boast. Up there, where the Great Wall of China is

an invisible thread and the lights of Las Vegas the dimmest of sparks, Umbriel and Gabriel can see the plague spots, raw red against the green. They weep, presumably.

ERIC KORN, columnist, "Remainders," *The Times Literary Supplement*, 13 April 1990.

FOURTH WORLD
See also NATIVE PEOPLES

The genocide — not against one people, but against hundreds of different cultures — is not acknowledged. Fourth world leaders who do speak of genocide are regarded as wildly intemperate, in the grip of absurd rhetoric. The facts about what has been done to aboriginal peoples just do not seem to penetrate a twentieth-century consciousness.

HUGH BRODY, author, Introduction (1988), *Maps and Dreams: Indians and the British Columbia Frontier* (1981, 1988).

The original inhabitants of the Americas, Australasia and many other huge areas of the world have suffered an appalling and vicious colonialism. The surviving aboriginal societies, however, are not frozen in some archaic condition, but are our contemporaries.

HUGH BRODY, author, Introduction (1988), *Maps and Dreams: Indians and the British Columbia Frontier* (1981, 1988).

FRANCE
See also La FRANCOPHONIE
FRENCH CANADA
QUEBEC
ST. PIERRE & MIQUELON

We can be happy without Canada.

MADAME DE POMPADOUR to her lover Louis XV on learning that Quebec had fallen to the English in 1759, quoted by Nancy Mitford in *Madame de Pompadour* (1964).

Of course, the English are a very excellent people, a fact to which I am always proud to bear testimony, but it must be admitted that for cold common sense the French are very much their superiors.

Sentiment attributed to the main character, the fictional French detective Eugene Valmont, in "The Absent-Minded Coterie" in *The Triumphs of Eugene Valmont* (1906), a collection of mystery stories by ROBERT BARR.

It is hard to believe that there are people in Canada who dare criticize the French; if we were more like them in Canada we would be a nobler, a better race.

GEORGES P. VANIER, Canada's Ambassador to France and future Governor General, quoted by Robert Speaght in *Vanier: Soldier, Diplomat, and Governor General: A Biography* (1971).

If all the English Canadians who have prejudices against the French Canadians would go to Paris with all the French-Canadians there would be no more prejudices. And the same for the French-Canadians towards the English Canadians.

ROGER LEMELIN, novelist, writing a letter (in English) to his publishers, McClelland and Stewart Ltd., 15 Sept. 1950, quoted by Clara Thomas and John Lennox in *William Arthur Deacon: A Canadian Literary Life* (1982).

In his memoirs, de Gaulle has recorded an exchange that appears to have impressed him. Canada had a five thousand kilometre border with the United States, Mackenzie King told him, and that situation created an "often overwhelming proximity." It was also a member of the Commonwealth, and that, too, was "sometimes oppressive." Nevertheless, Canadians meant to act "with complete independence." Their ambition was to develop their enormous territory and resources. Accordingly, they had "no reason to clash with France in any of its areas of interest. On the contrary, everything made them want to support it within the limits of their interest and capability." De Gaulle responded in the same vein. The two world wars had demon-

strated the value of their alliance, he said, and, in time of peace, the French would doubtless have the occasion to take advantage of Canada's friendship. "What you have just said proves to me conclusively that France was right a thousand times over to come and sow civilization here." In a press conference before leaving Ottawa, de Gaulle repeated that message. Nothing separated the interests of the two countries, he declared, and they were "at the beginning of a vast development" in their relations.

Charles de Gaulle, paying his second visit to Canada, Aug. 1945, had these observations to make in the third volume of his memoirs and in an interview with *Le Droit*, according to DALE C. THOMSON in *Vive le Québec Libre* (1988).

I'll catch fish and you will cook them.

CHARLES DE GAULLE, French President, addressing Madame de Gaulle, outlining a contingency plan "to go to Canada for a period of rest" should he be unable to form an interim government following a key vote in the French Assembly, 19 Nov. 1945, as recalled by Canada's Ambassador to France Georges P. Vanier. Quoted by Dale C. Thomson in *Vive le Québec Libre* (1988).

When General de Gaulle had returned from North America in the spring, he had mentioned "the enormous potential of Quebec" and had asked Malraux to take an interest in it. And the very day the Quebecers arrived, he had raised the matter again in Cabinet and said, "Malraux, we have to do something about Quebec."

DALE C. THOMSON, historian, *Vive le Québec Libre* (1988), writing about the aftermath of the 1960 visit to Canada of French President Charles de Gaulle and its effect on culture minister André Malraux, who met in Paris with Quebec representatives who wished to establish a Maison du Québec in Paris.

We can develop our relations with Canada as it still exists. But, above all, we must establish special forms of cooperation with French Canada, and not allow what we do for and with it to be submerged in an arrangement involving the totality of the two Canadas. At any rate, French Canada will necessarily become a state and it is necessarily in that perspective that we must orient our actions.

CHARLES DE GAULLE, French President, memo to culture minister André Malraux, 4 Sept. 1963, quoted by Dale C. Thomson in *Vive le Québec Libre* (1988).

I have not come here to tell you what France offers you, but to tell you what France expects of you.

ANDRÉ MALRAUX, French culture minister, address in Montreal in Oct. 1963, paraphrasing an earlier remark employed by U.S. President John F. Kennedy. According to Dale C. Thomson in *Vive le Québec Libre* (1988), what Malraux and French President Charles de Gaulle had in mind was "that, within ten years, French Canadians would express their unique setting through great music and poetry. He made no secret of the fact that separatism held no attraction for him; clearly, it clashed with his universalist approach to life."

There is no question of my addressing a message to Canada or celebrating its "centennial." We can have good relations with the whole of Canada. We must have excellent ones with French Canada. But we have not to congratulate either the Canadians or ourselves for the creating of a "State" founded on our defeat in the past, and especially for the integration of a part of the French people into a British entity. At any rate, that entity has become very precarious.

CHARLES DE GAULLE, French President, private notation following the suggestion that congratulations be sent the Canadian government on the approaching Centennial of Confederation celebrations on 1 July 1967, quoted by Dale C. Thomson in *Vive le Québec Libre* (1988).

You really don't see me going over just to attend a fair.

CHARLES DE GAULLE, French President, remark to aides on receiving an official invitation on 13 Sept. 1966 to visit Ottawa, Expo 67 in Montreal, and other Canadian cities, quoted by Dale C. Thomson in *Vive le Québec Libre* (1988).

What about the cry *"Vive le Québec libre"*? It was not premeditated. Although he himself was highly intelligent and a rigorous thinker, de Gaulle believed that the masses had to be led by emotions and dreams, and he had great confidence in his ability to do that. While he knew the contents of the message he wanted to deliver, he had not identified the words or the occasion before he arrived. But he was certain that they would present themselves to him. They did, in the form of the RIN banners and the shouts from the crowd before Montreal City Hall. He had some doubts whether the situation was completely right, but had to seize the moment or appear to falter, or even worse, to lack courage. He had no choice but to go forward and pronounce the words. Did he know they were the slogan of the separatists? Probably, but he did not consider they had a monopoly on them. Was he carried away by his emotions? Possibly. . . . After the event, was he satisfied with what he had done? Following an initial hesitation, yes; although he would have handled the rest of his stay in Canada differently if he had had a choice . . . he would have softened the blow to Ottawa by assurances that he did not seek the break-up of Canada, and then would have expressed the hope that French and English Canadians could work out new arrangements to enable their harmonious and fruitful co-existence. He would have offered French assistance in making that possible. In short, was he favourable to the independence of Quebec? Yes, in some kind of common market or sovereignty-association relationship with the rest of Canada. And that was the objective he crossed the Atlantic to promote.

DALE C. THOMSON, historian, giving the rationale behind Charles de Gaulle's famous and infamous "Vive le Québec libre" speech in Montreal on 24 July 1967, quoted in *Vive le Québec Libre* (1988).

Forget your stereotypes of the French as a happy people fond of light wines and dancing. The French are a tough, hardheaded lot, who haven't changed since Caesar characterized them in his *Gallic Wars* as "short, stubborn with round heads." I might add that those round heads are filled with big gray brains, which they are taught to use at an early age in one of the finest and most democratic education systems in the world; and that they possess a collective will that is the positive aspect of their homogeneous society.

ADRIENNE CLARKSON, Ontario's Agent-General in Paris, address, Empire Club of Canada, Toronto, 21 Nov. 1985.

Only the French, who understand life's priorities, could have invented the bidet. After all, how else can you soak off your wine-labels when you travel?

TONY ASPLER, traveller and wine connoisseur, *bon-mot*, 14 Nov. 1987.

FRANCOPHONES

I always compare the Francophones, especially the Acadians, to salmon. You always have to swim against the current, all the time. At a certain point you get fed up. It's tiresome. You want to swim once in a while, just swim. But going upstream all the time, you get fed up. The only thing is that salmon is a better fish than any other. But who wants to be served on the other's plate. You want to live your life.

ANTONINE MAILLET, Acadian author, interviewed in *Language and Society*, Winter 1989.

LA FRANCOPHONIE

It is not utopian to dream of Canada as a meeting point for peoples and states of *la*

Francophonie, the Commonwealth and English-speaking America, each recognizing and benefiting from the specifics and diversity of the others. This would be the starting point for a vision of world civilization that would preserve the authenticity of cultures and safeguard their specificity against the threat of empty, anonymous universalism posed by the power of new technologies. Viewed in this context, *la Francophonie* would exemplify the importance of diversity and the need to defend the personalities of nations and individuals. This is one of the future's most important challenges.

NAIM KATTAN, author and arts administrator, *Language and Society*, Fall 1987.

It seems to me that the Francophone world is under siege, with Quebec as the first line of defence, and because Quebec knows this, it, more than any other country, is concerned about the heavy losses that the growing domination of the North American cultural and economic systems inflict on all the Francophone nations. Were Quebec to succumb to the avalanche of blows falling on it, our Francophone brothers-in-arms should realize that they themselves would be next in line.

LÉON DION, political scientist, "The Mystery of Quebec," *Daedalus: Journal of the American Academy of Arts and Sciences*, "In Search of Canada," Fall 1988.

What interests me now is international francophonie. We can't just huddle together as five million francophones in a corner of North America, we have to play our part with Belgium, with France, and with French Africa.

ROBERT CHARLEBOIS, chansonnier, quoted by Stephen Godfrey in *The Globe and Mail*, 26 June 1989.

FREDERICTON
See also NEW BRUNSWICK

Life to a man in Fredericton without the elms above him is unthinkable.

BRUCE HUTCHISON, newspaperman, *The*

Unknown Country: Canada and Her People (1942).

FREE ENTERPRISE

I was interested to read recently that, in a survey of Ontario university campuses, 82% of those students interviewed *disapproved* of "free enterprise" as it currently exists, although the vast majority approved of the *theory* of free enterprise. "We approve of free enterprise," they said, "but where is it?"

> GERALD E. PEARSON, President, Canadian Chamber of Commerce, address, Empire Club of Canada, Toronto, 1 April 1976.

We can ensure that national agencies reflect regional reality in this country. And I give you this commitment: We will end the system where the public sector treats the private sector as an enemy.

> JOE CLARK, Conservative leader, convention, Conservative Party, Quebec City, 4 Nov. 1977.

What I think we should push for is free society — not free enterprise.

> JOHN BULLOCH, President, Canadian Federation of Independent Business, quoted in an address at the Empire Club of Canada, Toronto, 23 Feb. 1978.

I know of no country that has retained liberal democracy and fundamental western values that does not have a mixed free-enterprise or modified capitalist system.

> JOHN CRISPO, political economist, address, Empire Club of Canada, 25 Jan. 1979.

FREE SPEECH

Commercial free speech simply means the right to inform the consumer of what's for sale. It is also the right of the consumer to be informed. At no time does an advertiser have licence to misinform. Let's not forget that advertising, along with all the other facets of marketing communication, is a deeply rooted part of our cultural heritage.

> BRIAN PHILCOX, Director, Canadian Advertising Foundation, address, *The Globe and Mail*, 16 Jan. 1989.

We strongly support free speech and we believe that *all* authors and publishers must support the following fundamental freedoms: freedom of thought, belief, opinion and expression, including freedom of the press and other media of communication. These fundamental freedoms are embodied in the Canadian Charter of Rights.

> Statement made by AVIE BENNETT, Chairman of McClelland and Stewart Inc., with respect to the statement of claim served on behalf of Conrad Black demanding the withdrawal of all copies of Ron Graham's book *God's Dominion* (1990), Newsletter of the Canadian Centre of International PEN, Dec. 1990.

FREE TRADE
See also TRADE & COMMERCE

Self-Government and Free Trade
> Motto on the copper halfpenny tokens issued for trade purposes by George and Simeon Davies and Henry Haszard, merchants on P.E.I., 1855 and 1857.

Responsible Government and Free Trade
> Motto on the copper tokens issued for trade purposes by Ralph Heaton & Co., Nfld., around 1860.

You have a great opportunity before you. Obtain reciprocity for us, and I venture to predict that you will be able to point to this hitherto-turbulent colony with satisfaction. . . . If free navigation and reciprocal trade with the Union be not secured for us, the worst, I fear, will come, and that at no distant day.

> LORD ELGIN, Governor General of the United Canadas, writing to the British Colonial Office in 1849, quoted by Edward

Banning in *The Globe and Mail*, 26 Nov. 1988.

In the course of the debates by which he introduced the National Policy, Sir John remarked that those who cared to be protected at all, wanted all the protection they could get. They were like the squaw who said of whisky, that "a little too much was just enough."
E.B. BIGGAR, biographer, *Anecdotal Life of Sir John Macdonald* (1891).

Veiled treason.
Phrase identified with the notion of free trade by Prime Minister SIR JOHN A. MAC-DONALD and the Conservative Party in the 1891 election campaign. In that election the Liberal Party favoured free trade, but Sir John made a successful appeal to the patriotism of the electorate.

I am sure that you could have nothing but contempt for any free people who measure their allegiance purely by commercial standards, and who, fearing to face the difficulties, which meet every nation, turn peddlers instead of protectors of their national birthright. Just as you had and have your croakers and cowards we have ours, but, Mr. Chairman, Canada is not for sale.
W. GEORGE BEERS, Montreal nationalist, sports enthusiast, and dentist, address, New York State Dental Society, Syracuse, N.Y., quoted by D.W. Gullet in *A History of Dentistry in Canada* (1971).

Canada, having once become the commercial and industrial vassal of the United States, would inevitably become the political vassal of that country and ultimately be absorbed.
SIR ROBERT BORDEN, Prime Minister, after his successful campaign against freer trade with the United States in 1911, quoted by *Maclean's*, 14 Nov. 1988.

Empire Free Trade is like liberty, something to be striven for. Men strive to be free. They never *wholly* succeed.
LORD BEAVERBROOK, press lord, ad-

vancing the notion that the British Empire should constitute a zone of free trade, and endorsing the United Empire Party, addressed in the depths of the Great Depression to his daughter, Janet Aitken Kidd, who quoted it in *The Beaverbrook Girl: An Autobiography* (1987).

It is a bitter commentary on our twentieth-century society that the very phrase "free trade" has come to have a hopelessly old-fashioned and unrealistic ring to it.
LESTER B. PEARSON, diplomat, Nobel Peace Prize Lecture, Oslo, Norway, 11 Dec. 1957. The text is taken from *The Four Faces of Peace and the International Outlook* (1964) edited by Sherleigh G. Pierson.

This country could not survive with a policy of unfettered free trade. I'm all in favour of eliminating unfair protectionism, where it exists. This is a separate country. We'd be swamped. We have in many ways a branch-plant economy in certain important sectors. All that would happen with that kind of concept would be the boys cranking up their plants throughout the United States in bad times and shutting their entire branch plants in Canada. It's bad enough as it is.
BRIAN MULRONEY, Conservative leader, addressing the journalist John Gray in June 1983, quoted by Claire Hoy in *Friends in High Places: Politics and Patronage in the Mulroney Government* (1987).

Well, we could never contemplate a situation where your dollar would be at a level that would be an inherent advantage that we felt was unfair.
Attributed to MALCOLM BALDRIGE, U.S. Secretary of Commerce in the Reagan administration, late in 1985, by Sinclair Stevens, former Cabinet Minister in the Mulroney administration, recalled during an interview conducted by Nate Laurie and Don Sellar and published in *The Toronto Star*, 2 Dec. 1990. Stevens maintained that there is a "gentleman's agreement" between the two nations that

the level of the Canadian dollar is to be kept high with respect to the American dollar and that this secret agreement was a precondition of the Free Trade Agreement. High interest rates maintain the high level of value and reduce Canada's international competitiveness. Spokespeople for the Mulroney administration immediately denied the truth of the charge.

The phrase "level playing field" is often linked to the other key American phrase, "everything on the table."
JAMES LAXER, political economist, *Leap of Faith: Free Trade and the Future of Canada* (1986).

Seems to me that the big mistake wuz bringin up them dam 2 words Free Traid in the firsplace. We wuz gittin along jist fine with Atey purrsent no tarfs, and the Yanks, as usual, ignoring us with their undivide attenshun.
DON HARRON, comedian, in the person of Charlie Farquharson, *Cum Buy the Farm* (1987).

The offishul Tory slowgo wuz "No Truckin Traid with Yanky Hanky Panky."
DON HARRON, comedian, in the person of Charlie Farquharson, *Cum Buy the Farm* (1987).

Is there such a thing as a free trader? I say "no" and I say it because I have never met one in my entire career. People may claim to be, but they are almost without exception people with a product that they can produce cheaply and want to export. These same individuals can change their tune just as quickly to that of protectionism when cheaper *imports* come from some other part of the world and threaten their lucrative businesses.
EUGENE WHELAN, former Agriculture Minister, "If the Elephant Rolls Over: Free Trade and Canadian Agriculture," *Canada Not for Sale: The Case Against Free Trade* (1987) introduced by Keith Davey.

It's terrific until the elephant twitches, and if it ever rolls over, you're a dead man.
BRIAN MULRONEY, contender for the Conservative leadership, discussing John Crosbie's advocacy of free trade during the 1983 campaign, quoted by Claire Hoy in *Friends in High Places: Politics and Patronage in the Mulroney Government* (1987).

Canada has struggled to become a separate nation with its own unique identity. Part of this identity is seen in our attempt to find creative solutions to regional disparities, cultural differences, and equality for all. We must not surrender our freedom to decide our own future.
MAUDE BARLOW, human-relations consultant, quoted in *The Toronto Star*, 6 March 1986.

A Canadian economy uncompetitive in costs and rife with underemployment and unemployment is a far greater risk to our political independence than is a comprehensive trade agreement with the United States.
DAVID M. CULVER, CEO, Alcan Aluminium Limited, address, Empire Club of Canada, Toronto, 17 April 1986.

In dividends . . . and in inter-corporate "service charges" alone, every hour of every day, twenty-four hours a day, seven days a week, fifty-two weeks of the year, $924,657 leaves Canada every single hour, to the U.S., to pay for the massive, unparalleled, unique amount of foreign domination of our economy that we have already. And if you add in interest payments, it's $1,529,680 every single hour of every single day.
MEL HURTIG, publisher and nationalist, address to the Council of Canadians, 19 Oct. 1986.

There is a lesson here. Reciprocity or customs union or free trade, whatever its name, is very much an emotional political issue and there seems little reason to believe that the 1980s have altered this fundamental fact. There are not very many lessons in history that stand out clearly; one that does, however, is that free trade between Canada and the United States has major political implications in Canada. Any political leader who forgets that does so at his peril.

> J. L. GRANATSTEIN, historian, "Free Trade: The History of an Issue," *The Future on the Table: Canada and the Free Trade Issue* (1987) edited by Michael D. Henderson.

Free trade with Canada is the single most important trade decision in the U.S. in this century.

> CLAYTON YEUTTER, U.S. Trade Representative, quoted by Mel Hurtig in an address to the Council of Canadians, Ottawa, 19 Oct. 1986.

Canada is a wonderful country. It hasn't got ten per cent of this continent's brains. It's got thirteen or fifteen per cent of them. Americans work hard, but Canadians work better. We will prosper in a free trade deal.

> PAUL REICHMANN, developer, quoted by Diane Francis in *Maclean's*, 19 Oct. 1987.

There will be no Canada within a generation if the Mulroney government is allowed to proceed with its plans.

> MEL HURTIG, publisher and Chairman of the Council of Canadians, appearing before the House of Commons Committee on External Affairs and International Trade, Ottawa, 17 Nov. 1987.

You can help screw Ontario. Support free trade.

> MORDECAI RICHLER, author and cultural commentator, making a tongue-in-cheek suggestion to help the Conservatives sell free trade to the other provinces, addressing the House of Commons Committee on External Affairs and International Trade, Ottawa, 17 Nov. 1987, reported in *The Toronto Star*, 15 Dec. 1987.

When I went up to Ottawa, / I met a man who sang tra-la. / "What did you do with the country today?" / "I gave it away to the U.S.A."

> DENNIS LEE, poet and versifier, "When I Went Up to Ottawa," *The Difficulty of Living on Other Planets* (1987).

In the end, free trade is *entirely* a question of culture, because it is a matter of the kind of society we and our descendants will inhabit as a result of the deal. Culture cannot be exempt, and neither can Canada.

> RICK SALUTIN, journalist and author, *The Globe and Mail*, 5 Nov. 1987.

Canada had to be competitive to survive even in its own market, where there was no hope whatever of keeping efficient foreigners indefinitely at bay. The country had to stop believing it could become a second United States — gargantuan in population, diversity, and wealth — and realize that its best hope was to emulate the Scandinavian countries in their relationship to Europe. Specialize, find and exploit comparative advantage, look outward, choose quality instead of quantity, let culture grow in the fresh air of economic freedom.

> MICHAEL BLISS, historian, presenting the argument supporting Free Trade offered by the Canadian Manufacturers' Association, *Northern Enterprise: Five Centuries of Canadian Business* (1987).

God only knows what we did, but I think we did something.

> PETER MURPHY, U.S. chief trade negotiator, announcing the free trade deal, quoted by Bob Hepburn in *The Toronto Star*, 30 Dec. 1987.

My favourite quote of the entire free trade controversy was an interjection during the House of Commons debate on April 28, 1987, about economic decision-making, when NDP financial critic Michael Cassidy exclaimed: "We are held back because of irresponsible decisions made in foreign

boardrooms — decisions which should have been made right here in Canada."
> PETER C. NEWMAN, author, *Sometimes a Great Nation: Will Canada Belong to the 21st Century?* (1988).

There are indeed no limits to what people can accomplish when they are free to follow their dreams. We're making that dream a reality. It is the American dream.
> RONALD REAGAN, U.S. President, speech, upon the signing of the Free Trade agreement, White House, Washington, D.C., 2 Jan. 1988.

Free Trade. Freer Trade. Enhanced Trade. Costly Trade. Free Raid.
> These are some of phrases, pro and con, associated with the drive of the second Mulroney administration (elected 21 Nov. 1988) to conclude a comprehensive free-trade arrangement between Canada and the United States. Frank Stronach of Magna International spoke of "fair enterprise." Other phrases of the day include "level playing field," "cultural industries," "leap of faith," "managed change," etc. Critics called it a "free raid" on Canada's resources. The Free Trade Agreement, finalized 28 Sept., become effective 1 Jan. 1989. It was instantly branded the Free Trade Disagreement.

Economic growth is now as much a matter of foreign policy as it is economic policy. We should build on the achievement of our free trade zone with Canada and work with our other neighbour, Mexico, to create a free trade zone of unprecedented size, a new North American compact. Protectionism simply benefits some industries at the expense of the rest of the economy. Protectionist measures would expose us to retaliation and an all-out trade war, which nobody can win.
> GEORGE BUSH, U.S. Vice-President, quoted in *Maclean's*, 7 March 1988.

Free / *Canada* / Trade / *Mulroney*
> Message on commercially sold T-shirts, Ottawa, March 1988.

In the process of debating what we might have to surrender, we discovered what we already had.
> PETER C. NEWMAN, author, *Sometimes a Great Nation: Will Canada Belong to the 21st Century?* (1988).

Those who claim Mulroney has given the national store away deserve to have their tongues plucked out with hot tongs, wielded by Mounties in red tunics.
> CONRAD BLACK, publisher and financier, quoted in *Actrascope*, Jan.-March 1988.

The Canadians don't understand what they have signed. In twenty years they will be sucked into the U.S. economy.
> Attributed to the U.S. trade ambassador CLAYTON YEUTTER in a speech, *Actrascope*, Jan.-March 1988.

To suggest that free trade with the United States is a solution to this basic structural defect is to teach swimming by throwing the candidate over Niagara Falls.
> WALTER PITMAN, educator, commenting on the lack of indigenous research and development, quoted in *The Globe and Mail*, 11 March 1988.

If we go ahead with Free Trade with the United States, and it really works, we should try it with the provinces of this country.
> Adapted from a remark made by the comic DON HARRON as quoted by Martha Harron in *Don Harron: A Parent Contradiction* (1988).

We will not only be harmonized, we will be homogenized, and we will be hosed.
> JOHN TURNER, Liberal leader, referring to the effects of free trade, quoted in *The Montreal Gazette*, 14 June 1988.

I deeply believe what is at risk is the very idea of Canada as it has come to be known. . . . This debate is really about whether what we would call the "Canadian way" or the "American way" will prevail in our country.

ED BROADBENT, NDP leader, quoted by Martin Cohn in *The Toronto Star*, 6 July 1988.

Well, it's more than a trade agreement, it's the Sale of Canada Act. . . . We have lowered barriers on the Canadian-American border so that eighty percent of the dollar value of the goods moving across that border go free of duty, free of tariff. So what we were really talking about was the remaining twenty percent. And for that remaining twenty percent, Mr. Mulroney gave away the store.
JOHN TURNER, Liberal leader, quoted in *The New York Times*, 7 Aug. 1988.

The free-trade agreement has no clothes.
This judgement is attributed to MARJORIE MONTGOMERY BOWKER, retired family-court judge, who spent six weeks studying the text of the Free Trade Agreement. The judgement was quoted in an editorial in *The Edmonton Journal*, 14 Sept. 1988. Alarmed with what she read, on 15 July 1988 she typed out a fifty-eight page analysis and critique of the Agreement and circulated it to interested parties and encouraged others to do the same. This act created a groundswell of interest in the text of the Agreement. In October the critique was published as *On Guard for Thee: An Independent Analysis Based on the Actual Text of The Canada-U.S. Free Trade Agreement* (1988). She concluded: "I began and ended my study as a supporter of free trade. I ended as an opponent of this particular Free Trade Agreement."

This is a moment future historians will cite as a landmark, a turning point in the forward march of trade, commerce and even civilization itself. . . . Free trade is an idea whose time has come.
RONALD REAGAN, U.S. President, signing the Free Trade bill in the Rose Garden of the White House, Washington, D.C., 28 Sept. 1988, quoted in *The Toronto Star* the following day. In the little speech he re-

ferred to Prime Minister Mulroney as "visionary" and as an "able ambassador."

I'm not going to let Mr. Mulroney destroy a great 120-year-old dream called Canada.
JOHN TURNER, Liberal leader, election rhetoric, quoted by Debra Black in *The Toronto Star*, 10 Oct. 1988.

In my recent oscillations between moderate pessimism and profound despair, I wonder how we can believe that money created the wealth of literature and culture that now forms our heritage. The richness of our collective unconscious has, ironically, never seemed as fruitful as now, when we seem to be ready to give it away.
ADRIENNE CLARKSON, broadcaster, accepting an honorary degree, Dalhousie University, Halifax, quoted in *The Toronto Star*, 23 Oct. 1988.

Any time, any time . . . I'll take you on any time. Flora and me! . . . I'll tell you what my mother would do with you! She'd wash your mouth out with soap!
BRIAN MULRONEY, Prime Minister, alongside Cabinet Minister Flora MacDonald, 28 Oct. 1988, responding to anti-free trade protester and hecklers, quoted by Joyce Nelson in *Sultans of Sleaze: Public Relations and the Media* (1989).

The business mind-set of the free trade boys charges that those of us who oppose the deal are arguing on emotional grounds. Right! For once they've got it right. If it weren't for emotion, there wouldn't be such an illogical thing as Canada. The whole concept doesn't make sense: 25 million people strung out in a narrow ribbon over some 5,000 miles with a population density less than that of Saudi Arabia. And with a northland, larger than India, speckled by fewer people than attend a baseball game in Yankee Stadium.
ALLAN FOTHERINGHAM, columnist, *Maclean's*, 14 Nov. 1988.

In some ways it should not be surprising that in the country of Marshall McLuhan,

Canadians have voted to expand the market-place of the Global Village. The new Canadian identity is global nationalism. It is Montreal Canadiens and Toronto Blue Jays nationalism. It is as Canadian as Bloomingdale's. It is McDonald's Canada. It is Team North America.

BARRY BROWN, Toronto journalist and commentator, *The Cleveland Plain-Dealer*, 15 Nov. 1988.

For Sale Canada: / Call 1-800-Mulroney / For a Stronger America, / Vote Mulroney.

Messages on signs spotted at a Liberal rally in St. John's, Nfld., 15 Nov. 1988, quoted by David Vienneau in *The Toronto Star* the following day.

Brian, take your leap of faith off the Calgary Tower.

Message on the placard carried by a protestor at the Conservative Party rally in Calgary, referring to Prime Minister Mulroney's suggestion that free trade called for "a leap of faith," quoted by Linda Diebel in *The Toronto Star*, 16 Nov. 1988.

Whatever little is left fluttering in the aftermath of this election, one thing is sure: the legacy of the trade debate will be a deeply divided country — the very thing Brian Mulroney once promised to repair.

MARGARET ATWOOD, author, "Free Traders Don't Eat Quiche," *The Globe and Mail*, 17 Nov. 1988.

I've come to love this country and its people and its beautiful environment, and my ego got the better of me. I thought, "If I can influence things, I should." I know the United States and you don't want to be like them."

But once you have no tariffs, you have increased rights of passage, and the next thing you know, you'll wake up one day with a nuclear crisis in the Yukon, which nobody ever told anybody about.

MARTIN SHEEN, U.S. actor, interviewed in Vancouver by Liam Lacey in *The Globe and Mail*, 19 Nov. 1988.

This is the fight of my life.

JOHN TURNER, Liberal leader, characteristic remark, quoted by Judy Steed in *The Globe and Mail*, 19 Nov. 1988.

Only donkeys don't change their minds.

BRIAN MULRONEY, Prime Minister, explaining how he could oppose free trade in 1983 and support it in 1988, quoted in *The Globe and Mail*, 21 Nov. 1988.

Mr. Turner, it [is] a document that is cancellable on six months' notice.

BRIAN MULRONEY, Prime Minister, televised leaders' debates, reported in *The Globe and Mail*, 21 Nov. 1988.

Don't cry for me, *Wall Street Journal*.

JOHN TURNER, Liberal leader, paraphrasing a hit song from the musical *Evita* in his response to Prime Minister Mulroney's reference to an editorial cartoon in *The Wall Street Journal* which likened Turner to Juan Peron who bankrupted Argentina, televised leaders' debates, reported in *The Globe and Mail*, 21 Nov. 1988.

You can't have growth in the garden without some death. Some flowers have to die for others to grow.

DAVID M. CULVER, CEO of Alcan Aluminium Limited, on free trade, quoted by Allan Fotheringham in *Maclean's*, 12 Dec. 1988.

When I was going down to New York to make my name in this dismal business, my mother took me aside — even though I was a grown man — and said, "Leonard, you be careful. Those people aren't like we are." And that's all I have to say about the free-trade issue.

LEONARD COHEN, poet and singer, quoted by Rick Groen in *The Globe and Mail*, 31 Dec. 1988.

Once the free trade agreement with the United States takes full effect, the next logical step will be to accept politically what has already happened economically — the integration of Canada into the United States. By the end of the 1990s, Puerto Rico will already have become the 51st state in the Union. And fulfilling a Canadian nationalist's worst nightmare, Canada may — if not by the year 2000, then soon thereafter — become the 52nd through the 55th states of the United States. Canada's western provinces — Alberta, Manitoba, Saskatchewan, British Columbia, the Yukon Territory, and the Northwest Territories — will be compacted into two states; Ontario and the eastern provinces — Newfoundland, Nova Scotia, New Brunswick, and Prince Edward Island — will combine into two more. Politically, the new American states will be evenly divided: the resource-rich, development-minded western states will join the Republican camp, while the urbanized eastern states will tend to vote Democratic. Quebec will at last receive its wish and become an independent nation, if in name only. Economically, it will remain wholly dependent on its neighbours for survival.

> MARVIN CETRON and OWEN DAVIES, forecaster and editor, *American Renaissance: Our Life at the Turn of the 21st Century* (1989), as excerpted in *The Toronto Star*, 26 Dec. 1989.

WASHINGTON (AP) July 1, 1993 — Governor Brian Mulroney told Congress today that with economic integration nearly complete between Canada and the United States, the Canadian monetary system can now be eliminated. The U.S. dollar will become Canada's only legal currency.

> Mock news story not released by Associated Press (AP) but circulated in a mailer released in Nov. 1989 by Maude Barlow, Chairperson, The Council of Canadians, who added: "Sound impossible? It's a lot closer than you think."

We are too close to see it clearly, but I believe the adoption of the Free Trade Agreement exorcises a strong negative factor in the Canadian psyche, a fear of the United States which, in turn, conceals a fear of coming to terms with our own potential and even of our greatness.

> ALLAN GOTLIEB, former Canadian Ambassador to the U.S., address, quoted in *The Toronto Star*, 7 April 1989.

What's wrong with Canada-U.S. free trade is that we should have signed an agreement with Japan instead, which would have had only one clause in it: for every engineer they send us, we send them seven lawyers.

> PETER C. NEWMAN, columnist, *Maclean's*, 26 June 1989.

Will it make us more competitive, or will it continue to let us act like Canadians?

> DAVE BROADFOOT, comedian, quoted by Isabel Vincent in *The Globe and Mail*, 30 June 1989.

Here in Canada, where most industries consist of only a few layers and fears of American dominance are part of the national birthright, the risks and benefits of that drive to create a free-trade zone from the Arctic Ocean to the Rio Grande are easier to pinpoint.

> BARNABY J. FEDER, correspondent, *The New York Times*, 8 Oct. 1989.

There are three people working on this [Agreement] at the U.S. trade representative's office and one at Commerce, compared to forty in Canada. Canada is ultimately going to gain more out of the treaty because they are paying more attention to it.

> TERESA TAYLOR, policy analyst for the Northeast-Midwest Congressional Coalition in Washington, D.C., quoted by Barnaby J. Feder in *The New York Times*, 8 Oct. 1989.

What could the Tories have been thinking about when they assured Canadians time and again that culture was protected? Did they mean that Canadians will be protected from the ravages of Canadian culture?

> MARJORIE NICHOLS, columnist, com-

menting on the Conservative position that the Free Trade Agreement will exempt cultural industries, quoted by Derrick de Kerckhove in *The Canadian Forum*, Oct. 1989.

It's not Free Trade itself that threatens the culture, it is what the agreement prevents us from doing, and how it ties us to American business rather than to American cultural practices.
DERRICK de KERCKHOVE, media analyst, "Control of the Collective Mind," *The Canadian Forum*, Oct. 1989.

Anti-free traders and pro-traders cannot have a dialogue because they refuse to agree about what each side means by "culture." Anti-free traders talk about the loss of cultural sovereignty. Pro-free traders pretend to know nothing about that. As Joyce Nelson has suggested, business people are not so much ruthless as rootless. They don't need a cultural identity; they don't have time for it, and it stands in the way of a corporate model.
DERRICK de KERCKHOVE, media analyst, "Control of the Collective Mind," *The Canadian Forum*, Oct. 1989.

I don't think it was a huge, imaginative departure on the part of Mulroney who is incapable of that sort of thing anyway. He's a slick politician. He panicked in view of the American Congress protectionist bills though. He was really more determined, I think, to protect what we have than to make huge gains.
We needed it much more than the United States. I think we went something like 100 people to the table, and they sent 10 who weren't busy at the main office. It was obvious they were getting a good deal.
MORDECAI RICHLER, author, quoted by Dennis Kucherawy, *Metropolis*, 16 Nov. 1989.

The commendable goal of promoting freer trade has led to a monstrous swindle, under which the Canadian government has ceded to the United States of America a large slice of the country's sovereignty over its economy and natural resources in exchange for advantages we already had, or were going to obtain in a few years anyway through the normal operation of the GATT.
Alas, by now it is clear that, barring a sharp and unlikely change of course, our Great Helmsman is indeed steering Canada toward peace and reconciliation — the kind to be found in the graveyards of the deep.
PIERRE ELLIOTT TRUDEAU, former Prime Minister, referring to Prime Minister Brian Mulroney as a "helmsman," "The Values of a Just Society," *Towards a Just Society: The Trudeau Years* (1990) edited by Thomas S. Axworthy and Pierre Elliott Trudeau, translated by Patricia Claxton.

You are really setting yourself up to being absorbed by the U.S. unless you develop insularities. Remember, Japan wouldn't be Japan if they allowed General Motors to buy Toyota, or if General Electric bought Mitsubishi. Mulroney seems to be more interested in north-south ties than east-west, given what he wants to do to the Canadian railway system.
RALPH NADER, U.S. consumer advocate, commenting on the Mulroney administration's Free Trade initiatives and curtailment of VIA Rail's operations, quoted by Howard Goldenthal in *Now*, 18 Jan. 1990.

Free trade is a global plan to let the multinationals have free rein. The interesting thing is that even the United States is suffering, because a lot of the industry is going to Mexico.
REMI J. DE ROO, Bishop of Victoria, quoted by George Mortimore in *The Canadian Forum*, May 1990.

There is not another mechanism devised by man that will have a more civilizing influence on the lives of nations than trade. Fair and freer trade.
BRIAN MULRONEY, Prime Minister, inter-

viewed by Kevin Doyle and Anthony Wilson-Smith, quoted in *Maclean's*, 25 June 1990.

Voters across the country made a choice to support the party that in turn supported the FTA. But institutional factors made the victory seem more decisive than it really was. Canada's parliamentary system elects MPs on a plurality basis, so that in most cases Tories were elected with less than 50 per cent of the votes; nationally, the Conservatives had the support of only 43 per cent of voters. In so far as both the Liberals and the NDP opposed the FTA, it might be said that the majority of Canadians, in fact, *voted against free trade*. But the parliamentary system operates on the basis of seats in the Commons, not votes in the hustings. The Tories, with 169 seats, have a clear majority. Moreover, the Liberal strategy of making free trade *the* issue of the campaign backfired to a degree, since by winning a majority, the Tories could claim an undisputed mandate to implement the deal.

ROBERT M. CAMPBELL and LESLIE A. PAL, political scientists, *The Real Worlds of Canadian Politics: Cases in Process and Policy* (1991).

Canadians fear their loss of sovereignty in a free trade agreement or its evolution to a customs union and a common market. But, the Canadian loss of sovereignty is more than offset by a much larger loss of sovereignty for the U.S. Sovereignty is a function of the ability to act unilaterally; common North American rules and institutions can greatly limit U.S. sovereignty (the sovereignty to hurt its neighbours).

LEONARD WAVERMAN, economist, "A Canadian Vision of North American Economic Integration," *Continental Accord: North American Economic Integration* (1991) edited by Steven Globerman.

There is no doubt that Canadian firms are adjusting to the free trade agreement. The problem is that too many are adjusting by leaving Canada.

CEDRIC RITCHIE, Chairman, Bank of Nova Scotia, address, annual meeting, Halifax, published in *The Toronto Star*, 20 Jan. 1991.

The Free Trade Act has established a new classification for Canadians which is not available to citizens of any other country. This classification, TC, is available for professional persons coming to perform occupations which are included on the schedule listed in Table No. 5.

DAN P. DANILOV, U.S. Attorney, *Immigrating to the U.S.A.: Who Is Allowed? What Is Required? How to Do It!* (5th edition, 1989). Listed in Table No. 5, "Schedule of TC Professions," are such professional categories as Accountants and Management Consultants. The author explained: "The United States – Canada Free Trade Agreement became effective January 1, 1989, and is intended to facilitate trade and travel between the two countries. . . . This Treaty provides that Canadians may now enter the United States in the E-1, Treaty Trader, and E-2, Treaty Investor, nonimmigrant classification. In addition, a new classification, TC (for Treaty Canada) has been established.

Canada and the U.S.A. will expand the free trade agreement to include a common currency, and Mexico will join the other two North American nations. Canada and the U.S.A. will initiate negotiations for a common currency.

MAURICE B. COOKE, channeller, *The Aquarian Wave: A Prophetic Handbook for the 90s* (1990).

FREE TRADE ZONES

What is obvious after twenty years of the Multinational Free Lunch is that EPZs and FTZs have primarily benefited the First World corporations involved and a small stratum of Third World elite. For the millions of others, the only things that have "trickled down" are greater oppression, disease, injury, pollution, and natural debt.

JOYCE NELSON, social and cultural critic, commenting on the proliferation of Export Processing Zones and Free Trade Zones in poor countries, *Sultans of Sleaze: Public Relations and the Media* (1989).

FREEDOM

The freedom of no one is safe unless the freedom of everyone is safe.

> Motto of the Canadian Civil Liberties Association, established in Toronto in 1964.

I must say, when I was arrested and charged with this crime, that I felt somewhat annoyed, but then I started to study the law and history books in order the better to prepare myself for my defence against this false accusation. I then began to consider that after all I had been thrust into rather illustrious company, for I found most of those who had led the fight for freedom had at some time or other been arrested and charged with uttering some opinions, and a great many had been thrown in jail, and I realized that this was what appeared to me to be a rear attack upon the forces of liberty.

> F.J. (FRED) DIXON, charged with seditious conspiracy in connection with the Winnipeg General Strike, address to the jury, Winnipeg, Feb. 13-14, 1920.

Freedom is a habit that must be kept alive by use.

> F.R. SCOTT, lawyer and poet, aphorism created in 1932, *Essays on the Constitution* (1977), as quoted by Margaret Laurence in *Dance on the Earth: A Memoir* (1989).

Freedom from moralities means freedom to observe, to think and behave sensibly, to the advantage of the person and of the group, free from outmoded types of loyalties and from the magic fears of our ancestors.

> G. BROCK CHISHOLM, psychiatrist, White Memorial Lecture, Washington, D.C., Oct. 1945, *The Psychiatry of Enduring Peace and Social Progress* (1945).

Only the tiniest fraction of mankind want freedom. All the rest want someone to tell them they are free.

> IRVING LAYTON, poet, *The Whole Bloody Bird (Obs, aphs & pomes)* (1969).

Our virtue, as a Canadian community, is precisely that there is not one single way of being a Canadian and no uniform way of expressing our identity. Most of us enjoy that freedom from uniformity. It has let some of us become a Maureen Forrester or a Bobby Orr. It has allowed others to raise good families quietly or to pursue other private goals. Political freedom is rare enough in the world, but the kind of social and cultural freedom which is the hallmark of Canada is even less common.

> JOE CLARK, Conservative leader, House of Commons, 18 Feb. 1977.

I am a Canadian, a free Canadian, / free to speak without fear, / free to worship God in my own way, / free to stand for what I think right, / free to oppose what I believe wrong, / free to choose those who shall govern my country. / This heritage of freedom I pledge to uphold / for myself and mankind.

> Pledge of the Canadian Bill of Rights as displayed in the Ukrainian Exhibit, Casa Loma, Toronto, 1978.

My freedom is my dearest possession. Men rightly die for it. But the question seldom asked is freedom to do what? At what point does my freedom transgress on yours, because fatally it must sooner or later.

> GERALD EMMETT CARDINAL CARTER, Archbishop of Toronto, address, Empire Club of Canada, Toronto, 6 Dec. 1979.

I am a wandering Jew. I always have my toothbrush handy. My allegiance is not to any piece of earth or particular set of rock outcroppings. My allegiance is to ideas, and most especially to the extraordinary idea of individual liberty. That idea is still there in the North American landscape, a landscape that I have come to love. But my suitcase is packed. I do not feel bound to any country or any popular will more than to my own conscience. I would leave here as easily as I would have left Germany when its people elected Hitler to power.

BARBARA AMIEL, columnist and author, *Confessions* (1980).

A sudden access of psychological freedom often turns from sheer excitement to deep panic.

W. EDWARD MANN and EDWARD HOFF-MAN, sociologist and psychologist, *The Man Who Dreamed of Tomorrow: A Conceptual Biography of Wilhelm Reich* (1980).

What happens if people vote democratically to become slaves? By definition, this is supposed to be impossible. But so various are human beings . . . that nothing is certain. . . . The questions remain: Can a democracy permit people to surrender their rights? Can it let others accept that surrender?

HUMPHRY OSMOND, psychiatrist, "Slavery: What If It Is Voluntary?" *Predicting the Past: Memos on the Enticing Universe of Possibilities* (1981) produced by Jerome Agel.

No matter how the nation's books are finally audited, one asset outweighs all the liabilities — Canadian society is as free as any ever known in the record of an always tormented world.

BRUCE HUTCHISON, newspaperman, *The Unfinished Country: To Canada with Love & Some Misgivings* (1985).

The most precious thing for an intellectual is to express himself freely, in print or in public. And that is taken away from intellectuals in dictatorships.

JOSEF SKVORECKY, Czech-born novelist, interviewed by Barbara Leckie in *So to Speak: Interviews with Canadian Writers* (1987) edited by Peter O'Brien.

A state that does not let people speak, write, associate, contact, travel, emigrate, participate in politics, acquire and dispose of property, engage in choices of residences, occupation or lifestyle is coercive, whatever its reasons.

GEORGE JONAS, columnist and author, *Crocodiles in the Bathtub and Other Perils* (1987).

It is no mere coincidence that an impoverished society breeds tyranny because beggars are not choosers. Without property and the right to use, augment and enjoy it, the individual may be effectively stripped of his livelihood and so disarmed of his will as to be incapable of effectively asserting or defending any human right.

MORRIS C. SHUMIATCHER, lawyer, "Property and the Canadian Charter of Rights and Freedoms," *Canadian Journal of Law and Jurisprudence*, July 1988.

The *area* of freedom is much greater in the West, but the difference is quantitative, not qualitative.

Having experience of both systems, I certainly prefer the tyranny of the market place — but only because its control over my affairs stops just there: in the market place.

GEORGE FALUDY, Hungarian-born poet, *Notes from the Rainforest* (1988).

Maybe that's what is crazy: to want to be free. A lot of people wouldn't cross the street for it.

GEORGE JONAS, Hungarian-born author, *A Passion Observed: The True Story of a Motorcycle Racer* (1989).

Global freedom is surely to be prized much more than individual freedom. It will represent freedom from the past: freedom from technological need, from work and economic want, from political nonparticipation, from nationalism, from weapons and war.

FRANK FEATHER, futurologist, *G-Forces: Reinventing the World — The 35 Global Forces Restructuring Our World* (1989).

FRENCH CANADA
See also QUEBEC

As to my opinion of the Canadians, I think there is nothing to fear from them, while we are in a state of prosperity, and nothing to hope from when in distress; I speak of the people at large; there are some among them who are guided by sentiments of honour, but the multitude is influenced only by hopes of gain, or fear of punishment.

> SIR GUY CARLETON, Governor, letter to Lord Sackville, 1776, concerning the French in Quebec, *Documents Relating to a Constitutional History of Canada: 1759-1828* (1907-35) edited by Adam Shortt and Sir Arthur Doughty.

A French Canadian if left to himself, and living on what his Master has, will rise very early, make a hearty meal, smoke his pipe, and lie down to sleep, and he will do little else through the day.

> DAVID THOMPSON, explorer, journal entry, 31 Dec. 1810, *David Thompson's Narrative of his Explorations in Western America, 1784-1812* (1916) edited by J.B. Tyrrell.

They have only one feeling — the French hate the English and would cut all their throats if they could — the English hate the French and only desire to ride rough shod over them.

> LORD SYDENHAM, Governor General, British North America, 13 March 1840, quoted by Gwynne Dyer and Tina Viljoen, commentator and TV producer, *The Defence of Canada: In the Arms of the Empire* (1990).

The habitant . . . knows no love stronger than that for the place where he was born, though giving him, in many cases, but a slender livelihood. In vain for him has the magnificent West been opened up, in vain for him have America and Europe been filled with accounts of prosperity in it. His dreams hover around his own fireside. His imagination is bounded by the fences round his farm. He asks no better lot than to live where his father lived, and to die where his father died.

> J. SHERIDAN HOGAN, author, *Canada: An Essay* (1855).

Can we not believe that in that supreme battle here, on the Plains of Abraham, when the fate of arms turned against us, can we not believe that it entered into the decrees of Providence that the two races, up to that time enemies, should henceforth live in peace and harmony, and henceforth should form one nation? Such was the inspired cause of Confederation.

> SIR WILFRID LAURIER, Prime Minister, address in Quebec City, 24 June 1889, *Wilfrid Laurier on the Platform: 1871-1890* (1890) edited by Ulric Barthe.

We should be French as the Americans are English. We should reserve and develop the instincts, the traditions and the intellectual powers which our origin has bequeathed to us; but we must centre our political allegiance and our national aspirations on Canadian soil.

> HENRI BOURASSA, publisher, "Le Patriotisme Canadien-Français" (1902), quoted by Joseph Levitt in *Henri Bourassa on Imperialism and Bi-culturalism, 1900-1918* (1970).

The *bonne entente* ("good will" or "cordial co-operation") movement attempted just after the First World War and through the 1920s to heal some of the widening fissures between English and French Canadians. The movement harboured business men and politicians whose vested interests were fairly obvious in innumerable after-dinner speeches of good will. The term became, and has remained, one of derision in nationalist circles in Quebec.

> SUSAN MANN TROFIMENKOFF, historian, *Abbé Groulx: Variations on a Nationalist Theme* (1973). Perhaps the *bonne entente* recalls, as well, the *entente cordiale*, the "friendly understanding" reached between Britain and France in 1904.

Whatever may be said, we are a little people who have never had much happiness to spare. At last there may come an hour in our life, a day of wholesome retaliation, when it will be possible for us to say to ourselves as others do: "I have a land of my own; I have a soul of my own; I have a future of my own."

LIONEL GROULX, Quebec nationalist, "Pourquoi nous sommes divisés," translated by G.O. Rothney, *French-Canadian Nationalism* (1969) edited by Ramsay Cook.

Canada wants to be herself, or, to be more accurate, each of the two Canadas wants to be herself. This is one thing on which French-speaking Canadians and English-speaking Canadians agree. French Canadians do not feel French; English-speaking Canadians do not feel British; and neither community feels American — not, at least, if "American" is equated with "United States."

ARNOLD TOYNBEE, historian, "The Case for a Bilingual Canada" (c. 1960), *Temper of the Times: An Anthology of Assorted Contemporary Literature* (1969) edited by Ralph Greenfield and Ronald Side.

Groulx is also credited with the policy of *La revênche des berceaux* — the Revenge of the Cradles, which meant it was the duty of French-Canadian women to breed as many children as their bodies could produce in order to gain for Quebec a political majority in Canada.

HUGH MacLENNAN, novelist and essayist, *The Toronto Star*, 18 May 1980.

We are what the geography of our country has made us. That is the main difference between ethnical groups. That is why, in a sense, we are nearer to English Canadians than to Frenchmen. After a month in Paris, which I loved with all my heart, I just the same got very lonesome for our trees, and the sight of the Laurentides and the horizon of Quebec. I felt lonesome for the Canadian sky so vast and so grandiose. In Paris, you have pieces of sky.

ROGER LEMELIN, novelist, writing a letter (in English) to his publishers, McClelland & Stewart Ltd., 15 Sept. 1950, quoted by Clara Thomas and John Lennox in *William Arthur Deacon: A Canadian Literary Life* (1982).

There are two miracles in Canadian history. The first is the survival of French Canada, and the second is the survival of Canada.

F.R. SCOTT, lawyer and poet, remark made in 1952, quoted by Ramsay Cook in *Canada and the French-Canadian Question* (1966).

It goes without saying that if, in the face of Anglo-Canadian nationalism, French Canadians retreat into their own nationalistic shell, they will condemn themselves to the same stagnation. And Canada will become a sterile soil for the minds of her people, a barren waste prey to every wandering host and conquering horde.

PIERRE ELLIOTT TRUDEAU, Prime Minister, "The Sorry Tale of French-Canadian Nationalism," *Trudeau and the French Canadians* (1968).

I had thought the French-Canadian thing was a joke. I thought they might say "merci" or something every now and again, but that would be the extent of it. It is very unsettling to arrive in North America and not understand anything. I said "s'il vous plaît" a few times.

BOB GELDOF, musician, flying into Montreal from Dublin in 1973, *Is That It?* (1986).

All my knowledge rests in my French-Canadianness and nowhere else.

JACK KEROUAC, novelist born in Lowell, Mass., of French-Canadian parents from Rivière-du-Loup, Que., undated remark probably from the early 1950s, quoted by Eric Waddell, organizer of a conference on Kerouac's life and work, Laval University, Quebec City, quoted in *The Toronto Star*, 22 Sept. 1987.

We are but a little people, one of the four or five in the world who ask themselves, before they go to sleep every night, "Will we still be here tomorrow?"
JEAN DRAPEAU, Montreal Mayor, address in Montreal, paraphrasing Canon Lionel Groulx, adapted from Richard Cleroux's coverage in *The Globe and Mail*, 10 Nov. 1978.

Above all, de Gaulle's place in history is assured as the great French leader who, whether right or wrong in his perspective and tactics, reached out to French Canada in a gesture of solidarity and affection.
DALE C. THOMSON, historian, *Vive le Québec Libre* (1988).

It's the French dimension of our national personality that constitutes the distinctive element of Canada. And that is why I am such a vigorous defender, not only of our privileged relationship with France, but also of *la francophonie* in Canada and its influence.
BRIAN MULRONEY, Prime Minister, quoted in the French newspaper *Le Figaro*, July 1989. Ron Goodman, the journalist who supplied the above translation of a key passage, devoted his "Ombudsman" column in *The Toronto Star* on 2 Sept. 1989 to a consideration of the implications of this remark. He noted the existence of its three distinct variations, each with its own particular meaning. The question remains: Did Mulroney call the French factor "a" or "the" distinct element of Canada?

We see political exchange all the time, but we (in French-speaking Canada) don't know much about English artists, except the big ones. English Canada doesn't even know who the big ones are in French Canada.
EDITH BUTLER, Acadian *chansonnière*,

quoted in *The Winnipeg Free Press*, 30 June 1990.

Marx remarked that anti-Semitism was the socialism of fools; a thoroughgoing enmity to French culture in Canada is the patriotism of fools.
J.M. CAMERON, historian, "The New Canadas," *The New York Review of Books*, 16 Aug. 1990.

French Canadians who live outside Quebec are still-warm corpses.
Attributed to author YVES BEAUCHEMIN, based on his presentation to the Bélanger-Campeau Commission on the Future of Quebec, according to *The Globe and Mail*, 30 Nov. 1990.

My great preoccupation is the difficulty of finding a consensus in English Canada, because English Canada as such does not exist. . . . How can we resolve this will of Quebec, which has always seen itself as a nation, and the other reality in Canada, just as legitimate, which sees Canada in terms of ten equal realities, not two nations. How do we reconcile that?
BENOÎT BOUCHARD, Minister of Industry, Science and Technology, interviewed by Graham Fraser in *The Globe and Mail*, 7 March 1991.

No one, however, has as yet come up with an acceptable alternative. Having myself been driven to employing the phrase "the rest of Canada," I have been compelled to find a useful expression to identify those who live there, which has produced "ROCs" — an acronym for "the rest of the Canadians." Thus, one could say: "If the Québécois want to separate, it will be okay with the ROCs."
Admitted, this is not to say satisfactory, but it does make the point that the English language can only be stretched so far, and finding the right words to describe Canada, without Quebec, is asking too much.

DALTON CAMP, columnist, *The Toronto Star*, 17 March 1991.

FRENCH LANGUAGE
See LANGUAGE: FRENCH

FRIENDSHIP

A waif upon the world's wide common, I expected nothing more than to drag out the remaining portion of my existence in those hard exertions of my public duties; how then shall I think of those beings who have rekindled the social spark, almost extinct, and have lighted up my heart again to friendship and esteem? It is as dew drops to the parched — as sunbeams through the prison gate — the key unlocking the barriers to society — the symbol that I have not *wholly* lost the affections of my countrymen.
    EDMUND KEAN, British actor, guest of honour at a public dinner in Montreal, 22 Aug. 1826, quoted by Raymund Fitzsimons in *Fire from Heaven* (1976). The tragedian played in Canadian cities in 1826, 1831, 1864, and 1865.

When a man is down his enemies stop kicking him and his friends begin.
    BOB EDWARDS, publisher, *The Eye Opener*, 15 May 1920.

I cannot describe or even conjure up in my mind the physical appearance of those who are closest to me. They have dropped so securely into my heart that I can't see them.
    BETTY JANE WYLIE, author, *No Two Alike* (1980).

Why do North Americans so often say, especially in reference to a more or less public figure, "He is a personal friend of mine"? Do they have any impersonal friends?

GEORGE FALUDY, Hungarian-born poet, *Notes from the Rainforest* (1988).

Old friends are like Krazy Glue.
    BETTY JANE WYLIE, author, *obiter dictum*, 1990.

FRONTIER

Every new frontier for mankind has become a new place to do battle.
    STANTON T. FRIEDMAN, scientist and UFO specialist, personal communication, 15 Jan. 1991.

FROST

The summer never thaws above the depth of what the following winter freezes.
    JAMES KNIGHT, factor, diary entry, 1710s, quoted by Peter C. Newman in *Empire of the Bay: An Illustrated History of the Hudson's Bay Company* (1989). Knight, administrator of York Factory, on the western shore of Hudson Bay, "penned the classic definition of another of the region's peculiarities, permafrost," noted Newman.

FRYE, NORTHROP

Read Blake or go to hell: that's my message to the modern world.
    Formulation of philosophy during his years as a divinity student by NORTHROP FRYE, as quoted in his obituary by Philip Marchand in *The Toronto Star*, 24 Jan. 1991.

Norrie is not struggling for his place in the sun. He is the sun.
    MARSHALL McLUHAN, media philosopher, paying tribute to a colleague at the University of Toronto, the literary philosopher Northrop Frye, quoted on the

jacket of the cloth edition of John Ayre's book *Northrop Frye: A Biography* (1989).

"You know what they say about him, Dad?" I quoted one of the Seniors. "In the first year you believe in God. In the second year you don't believe in God. In the third year you believe in Frye's God. In the fourth year you believe Frye is God."
Dad's laugh sounded very healthy.
JEAN LITTLE, author, recalling her course in Religious Knowledge taught by Northrop Frye at Victoria College, University of Toronto, in the 1950s, *Little by Little: A Writer's Education* (1987).

Oh, Frye has all the answers, he just doesn't seem to have any questions.
LOUIS DUDEK, poet and aphorist, "Can. Lit. Notes," *The Bumper Book* (1986) edited by John Metcalf.

More than any writer of this country, Northrop Frye has taught us how to see.
ELEANOR COOK, scholar, in "'A Seeing and Unseeing in the Eye': Canadian Literature and the Sense of Place," *Daedalus: Journal of the American Academy of Arts and Sciences*, "In Search of Canada," Fall 1988.

I don't know if there is a word for the kind of thing I am. I suppose "critic" comes closest, a critic who recognizes no boundaries.
NORTHROP FRYE, literary critic, interviewed late in 1990 by Carl Mollins, *Maclean's*, 4 Feb. 1991.

We all know the doggerel poem about critics: "Seeing an elephant, he exclaimed with a laugh, "What a wondrous thing is this giraffe." Perhaps one of his greatest gifts to writers was his lifelong work to ensure that if you created an elephant, it would never again be mistaken for a giraffe.
MARGARET ATWOOD, author, memorial tribute, quoted in *Vic Report*, Spring 1991.

As our personal future narrows, we become more aware of another dimension of time entirely, and may even catch glimpses of the powers and forces of a far greater creative design.
NORTHROP FRYE, literary critic, observation made in 1978, quoted by Albert C. Hamilton in *Vic Report*, Spring 1991.

Only Ulysses can bend the bow of Ulysses.
ROBERTSON DAVIES, man-of-letters, offering a response to the rhetorical question of whoever will "replace" Northrop Frye, the literary critic who died on 22 Jan. 1991, heard on CBC Radio's *The National* the following day.

The world is emptying.
TIMOTHY FINDLEY, novelist, memorial service, University of Toronto, 29 Jan. 1991, quoted by Philip Marchand in *The Toronto Star* the following day.

FUN

Party researchers have gone through all the Acts of Parliament, the Acts of all the provincial legislatures, and the Bylaws of every city, town, and hamlet across Canada. We have found that nowhere in any law passed since 1867 has the word "fun" ever been used. A Parti Rhinoceros government would rectify this without delay.
Platform (no. 8) of the Rhinoceros Party, quoted by Roy MacGregor in *The Ottawa Citizen*, 30 March 1988.

FUTURE
See also PREDICTION & PROPHECY
TIME

Oddly enough, in Mr. Speaker's room which I have the honour of inhabiting at present in Parliament Buildings, I picked out a book the other evening and read a couple of lines written in Mrs. Humphry Ward's journal of her impression of a journey right across Canada from sea to sea, taken in 1908: "So, in a swallow's flight from sea to sea, I saw the marvellous land wherein, perhaps, in a far, hidden future, lies the destiny of our race." That is a pregnant sentence. And one asks oneself, belonging to an old country, what preparation Canada is making for that day, what ideals she is keeping before herself; for by ideals alone a nation lives.

> STANLEY BALDWIN, Prime Minister of Great Britain, "To a Canadian Audience," Canadian Club of Ottawa, 15 Aug. 1932, *This Torch of Freedom: Speeches and Addresses* (1935). Mrs. Humphry Ward's novel was called *Canadian Born* (1908).

Coming into the second century is like passing through an open door. Beyond is the open country. There are no roads. They must be made. They can be made well or ill, and may be made to lead anywhere. There is talent enough if there is dedication enough. Craven fear must be left behind, and the best intelligence must be used, if the goal is to be worth reaching. Prophecy is futile; the possibilities are infinite.

> WILLIAM ARTHUR DEACON, literary critic, "The Bogey of Annexation" (1925), quoted by Clara Thomas and John Lennox in *William Arthur Deacon: A Canadian Literary Life* (1982).

Most forward-looking people have their heads turned sideways.

> HAROLD ADAMS INNIS, economic historian, *The Idea File of Harold Adams Innis* (1980) edited by William Christian.

Our master is the future.

> GEORGES-HENRI LÉVESQUE, political scientist, revising Lionel Groulx's earlier formulation "Our Master is the past," quoted by Lise Bissonnette in *The Globe and Mail*, 22 Oct. 1988.

Canada, as I have said, has no past, it has only a future.

> DONALD A. WOLLHEIM, U.S. science-fiction editor, "Whither Canadian Fantasy?" *Uncanny Tales*, Dec. 1942.

We have been building a Canadian nation for nearly two centuries. We were born old, born saying "No." French Canadians said "No" to the French revolution; United Empire Loyalists said "No" to the American revolution; our forebears said "No" to Papineau and Mackenzie when they wanted to introduce some democracy. We say "No" because so many ideas come from the south and if we say "Yes" too often we might wake up and find we are not so different. We are always looking back to the past, which means we say "No" to the future.

> F.H. UNDERHILL, political scientist, address, Couchiching Conference, 24 Feb. 1961, quoted in *The Toronto Telegram* the following day.

An idea about the future enters into the consciousness of people and will therefore determine the kind of life in which they live.

> GREGORY BAUM, theologian, quoted by David Quintner in *The Toronto Star*, 12 Nov. 1974.

And maybe it is time the metropolis listened to the voices on the frontier; time the metropolis realized it has something to learn from Old Crow and Hay River. Because what happens in the north will be of great importance to the future of our country.

> THOMAS BERGER, specialist in Northern affairs, address, Queen's University, Nov. 1975, quoted in an address, Empire Club of Toronto, 19 May 1977.

Only fools predict the future, particularly as the complex technological civilization totters to its apogee.

> GEORGE GRANT, philosopher, *The Globe and Mail*, 31 Dec. 1979.

Futurience
> The word *futurience* is defined by the futurologist FRANK FEATHER as "the actual experience of the future," noted by Wallace Immen in *The Globe and Mail*, 25 July 1980.

The global future of Canada will be based on how we bestir ourselves today. Inertia is a basic human failing and Canadians can be as lazy as anyone else on this planet. But we must begin to explore the future again in this country. We cannot rest on the achievements of the past. And this exploration of the future requires that we face trouble with courage; that we face disappointment with cheerfulness; and that when we triumph we triumph with humanity.

> FRANK FEATHER, President, Global Futures Network, address in Vancouver, *The Globe and Mail*, 4 Oct. 1982.

I think we should believe in that wonderful Inuit saying: "A long time ago in the future," which means something from long ago which will help us understand the future.

> JAMES HOUSTON, friend of the Inuit, quoted in *The Toronto Star*, 24 Nov. 1985.

But Canada remained an experiment, less bound by irrevocable legacies than older societies. We were searching, economically and culturally, for more realistic possibilities than the ones envisaged seventy-five, or even twenty-five, years ago. In older countries the future was inherited, largely predetermined by the past. Here, if we had the will, we could still choose what we would become.

> GEORGE GALT, traveller and author, *Whistlestop: A Journey across Canada* (1987).

Canadians must take heed of what they really are in terms of their past, and their northern land. Only then can they find, through their wholeness, the true path to their future.

> ROBERTSON DAVIES, man-of-letters, "Keeping Faith," *Saturday Night*, Jan. 1987.

Canadians, like their historians, have spent too much time remembering conflicts, crises, and failures. They forgot the great, quiet continuity of life in a vast and generous land. A cautious people learns from its past; a sensible people can face its future. Canadians, on the whole, are both.

> DESMOND MORTON, historian, "Strains of Affluence 1945-1987," *The Illustrated History of Canada* (1987) edited by Craig Brown.

Since the most ancient times, artists have passed on to succeeding generations the tales, the histories, the songs, the sagas, the skills of their trade. Can we conceive of a world in which there would be no succeeding generations? A world in which all the powerful works of the human imagination would be destroyed, would never again be seen or listened to or experienced? We must conceive that this is now a possibility, and one not too far in our uncertain future. We must not, as artists, or so I feel, stand by and passively allow this to happen.

> MARGARET LAURENCE, novelist, address, Trent University, Peterborough, Ont., 29 March 1983; quoted in *The Globe and Mail*, 10 Jan. 1989.

Travelling to the future is like any other trip. It is hard to know about the destination until you arrive.

> FRANK OGDEN, futurologist, "Ogden's Tenth Law," *Dr. Tomorrow's Lessons from the Future* (updated Oct. 1988).

It has been suggested that the best way to predict the future is to create it. Canada should put more attention to ensuring its future as a sovereign nation. The re-design of its educational system is a good first stop.

> WALTER PITMAN, educator, *The Globe and Mail*, 11 March 1988.

Science fiction is the only genre I've discovered which assumes there's going to be a future.

> SPIDER ROBINSON, author, speaking at the Calgary Olympics, quoted by Brian

Brennan in *The Calgary Herald*, 2 March 1988.

I have seen the future and it's here.
PETER GZOWSKI, media personality, referring to the fax machine and cellular telephone, CBC Radio's *Morningside*, 17 May 1988.

I really don't think of myself as a futurist. I'm just trying to make sense of contemporary reality. I think the world we live in is so hopelessly weird and complex that in order to come to terms with it, you need the tools that science fiction develops.
WILLIAM GIBSON, author, quoted by Victoria Hamburg in "The King of Cyberpunk," *Interview*, Jan. 1989.

Shamans have predicted that the native people will undergo a resurgence seven lifetimes after Columbus. That time has arrived.
I think what's happened to us Indian people at this point is that we are beginning to emerge as a stronger and more significant voice. We no longer see the necessity of continuing as an oppressed people; we see a bright future ahead of us.
TOMSON HIGHWAY, Cree playwright, adapted from comments reported by Robert Crew in *The Toronto Star*, 15 April 1989.

The 1990s could well be the most decisive decade in human history. What we do, or fail to do, will largely determine the future of life on our planet.
MAURICE STRONG, international consultant, quoted by Lynda Hurst in *The Toronto Star*, 9 Sept. 1989.

We must reinvent a future free of blinders so that we can choose from real options.
DAVID SUZUKI, scientist and author, *Inventing the Future* (1989).

We're coming up to the end of the century, our "out age." Out age. But the future is already here. The walls are coming down. The doors of perception are being cleansed before us.
B.W. POWE, literary critic, quoted in *Metropolis*, 21 Dec. 1989.

The future is not a spectator sport. As a geo-strategic planner, consulting futurist and businessman, one of my own slogans is "It's not what will happen, it's what you do about it". . . . We had better plan for it or suffer the consequences.
FRANK FEATHER, futurologist, *G-Forces: Reinventing the World — The 35 Global Forces Restructuring Our World* (1989).

The '90s will be the last hurrah of a dying culture, an exciting death spasm. The word "Canada" will describe little more than geography by the year 2000.
PATRICIA ROZEMA, film director, quoted in *Metropolis*, 21 Dec. 1989.

At some time in our distant past the human mind invented an abstract concept — *the future*. Of course the future doesn't exist, except as an idea, as the hypothetical extension of the present. However, by inventing a future, we created *choices* or *options* from which to select the best strategy to ensure our future well-being. That tactic has enabled us to survive to the present.
ANITA GORDON and DAVID SUZUKI, science broadcasters, *It's a Matter of Survival* (1990).

Look ahead, but do not peer.
ROBIN SKELTON, man-of-letters, aphorism, May 1990.

Maannamit.
This word is a proverbial expression. In Inuktitut, the language of the Inuit, it is said to signify "From now on, it is in the future."

GAMES & GAMBLING

"Did you ever play North-West Passage with me? . . . No, of course you didn't come my way!"

"It was the sort of game," he went on, "that every imaginative child plays all day. The idea was the discovery of a North-West Passage to school. The way to school was plain enough; the game consisted in finding some way that wasn't plain, starting off ten minutes early in some almost hopeless direction, and working my way round through unaccustomed streets to my new goal."

> H.G. WELLS, English author, "The Door in the Wall" (1906), *The Famous Short Stories of H.G. Wells* (1937).

Every American is entitled to Life, Liberty and the Pursuit of Trivia.

> Advertisement for the Trivial Pursuit board game, quoted by James B. Simpson in *Simpson's Contemporary Quotations* (1988).

P.S. My favourite Trivial Pursuit question is this: *Who invented Trivial Pursuit?* The answer, of course, is two Canadians, but nobody, not even masters of the game, can remember their names.

> BARRY CALLAGHAN, author, "Canadian Wry," *Punch*, Oct. 1985.

Losing by an inch was more intense than winning by a mile.

> BRIAN MOLONY, loan officer who defrauded the Canadian Imperial Bank of Commerce of $10.2 million in two years of compulsive gambling in Los Vegas, quoted by Gary Ross in *Stung: The Incredible Obsession of Brian Molony* (1987).

if he won / he won / if you won / it was only a game

> KIM MORRISSEY, lines from the poem "Dumont Was a Great Shot," *Batoche* (1989).

GARBAGE

In North America, every day, each person throws out almost 1800 grams (4 lb.) of waste. Over the course of a year, that's almost a ton of garbage a person.

> ANITA GORDON and DAVID SUZUKI, science broadcasters, *It's a Matter of Survival* (1990).

GARDENS

See also FLOWERS

It is very hard for people to accept that we share our world with the elementals. Yet, to those with higher senses, it is all very real. After all, early man could see these nature spirits, but we have become much too materially oriented, too sophisticated in that we have to look for proof everywhere. However, co-operation with the nature spirits will give excellent results. The love that you express for them through the plants will be returned many fold. And we have no doubts that if they are approached in the right way, they will use their powers to end pollution.

> DOROTHY MACLEAN, medium and secretary of the Findhorn Foundation, quoted by Mike Cowley in "There are Fairies at the Bottom of Your Garden," *Weekend Magazine*, 9 June 1973.

You don't catch folks who own lawns singing the praises of weeds and wilderness . . . because people with lawns know only too well how tenuous man's grip is on that fragile swatch of clearing that separates the driveway from the front walk.

> ARTHUR BLACK, broadcaster, "Dandelions," *Basic Black: The Wit and Whimsy of Arthur Black* (1981).

GAY RIGHTS

See HOMOSEXUALITY

GENETICS

DNA, the web which spins the spider.

> Definition of DNA offered by TREVOR SPENCER RINES, native of Burlington, Ont., in response to the request of science columnist Stephen Strauss for a six-word definition of DNA, "Getting a Handle on Explaining DNA," *The Globe and Mail*, 14 April 1990. Strauss explained the appeal of this definition: "That metaphor links structure with creation, with recreation and best of all it is unforgettable." Other

submissions from readers included the following: Life sentence, Living software, Database of life, Life-twine, Hard-wired Karma, Carbon original of life, Ataya-enraohwi (Huron disease spirit), etc.

Extreme left-wing people are afraid to find that intelligence, crime, happiness, extroversion, all these things probably have a genetic basis.

> J. PHILIPPE RUSHTON, controversial psychologist, University of Western Ontario, quoted by Howard Goldenthal in *Now*, 21 Feb. 1991.

I believe my research is compatible with almost any political system you can imagine, all the way from segregation-type ideas to a kind of laissez-faire capitalism, and the rights of the individual all the way up to strong intervention and affirmative action.

> J. PHILIPPE RUSHTON, controversial psychologist, University of Western Ontario, quoted by Howard Goldenthal in *Now*, 21 Feb. 1991.

GENIUS

He was that rarest of all beings in Canadian history, a genius — not a flawless and immaculate genius, but a genius whose characteristic weaknesses and imperfections, flaws of his upbringing and training, seem almost to heighten and intensify his special and unique brilliance.

> DONALD G. CREIGHTON, historian, tribute to the economic historian Harold Adams Innis, "A Special and Unique Brilliance" (1978), *The Passionate Observer: Selected Writings* (1980).

I wish I lived in a town where the streets and squares were named after great men instead of developers, mayors and trees. Why can't we have cities which honour genius at every corner? How could people aspire to anything but money when there is nothing in their surroundings to remind

them of the immortals who created things which do not lose their value with inflation.
STEPHEN VIZINCZEY, novelist, *In Praise of Older Women* (1965; rev. ed., 1990).

GEOGRAPHY
See also LAND

Thus I have fully completed the survey of this part of North America from sea to sea, and by almost innumerable astronomical observations have determined the positions of the mountains, lakes, and rivers, and other remarkable places on the northern part of this continent, the maps of all of which have been drawn, and laid down in geographical position, being now the work of twenty-seven years.
DAVID THOMPSON, explorer and surveyor, journal entry, 14 July 1811, Fort Astoria, *Travels in Western North America, 1784-1812* (1971) edited by Victor G. Hopwood. Thompson's "survey" was completed in the 1850s; he died in poverty, and it went unpublished for more than half a century.

Canada consists of 3,500,523 square miles mostly landscape. It is apparently intended for the home of a broad-minded people.
Aphorism associated with the Group of Seven, "The New Canadian Art," *The Daily Intelligencer* (Belleville, Ont.), 27 Sept. 1919.

Canada is an immense country, but it is not an easy country to know. Even under modern conditions, it is a long and expensive trip from St. John's to Vancouver, or from Windsor to Inuvik. The great differences of geography, history and economics within our country have produced a rich diversity of temperament, viewpoint and culture.
PIERRE ELLIOTT TRUDEAU, Prime Minister, introducing the Official Languages Act, House of Commons, 17 Oct. 1968.

All we have in this country is landscape.

M.T. (TERRY) KELLY, poet and novelist, "All We Have," *Country You Can't Walk In and Other Poems* (1984).

No European except for a Russian can ever take in the size of Canada except by travelling by train. A long plane journey gives some idea, particularly at night when the lights of cities are like rafts in what seems to be the emptiest and darkest of seas.
MAVIS GALLANT, author, Introduction to *The War Brides* (1978) edited by Joyce Hibbert.

In the Maritimes, drivers can't zoom along parallel lines from skyline to skyline. Instead, you snake from valley to forest to dykeland to sawed-off mountain. If your route follows a coast, you'd be smart to change all meetings over lunch into meetings over supper. Not counting the more than eleven hundred minor islands that lie off the Maritimes, the coastline of these provinces — which is even more intricate than the crocheted tablecloth I found in a box in the cupboard of The Parlour at The Place — stretches for 5240-odd miles, almost a thousand more than any surface route from St. John's, Newfoundland, to Victoria, British Columbia.
HARRY BRUCE, essayist, "The Land's Lousy — and Unforgettable," *Down Home: Notes of a Maritime Son* (1988).

Geographically speaking, the average Canadian, according to a weighted centre of gravity for the population, lives in Alpena, Michigan, two hundred miles north of Detroit.
WILLIAM KILBOURN, historian, "The Peaceable Kingdom Still," *Daedalus: Journal of the American Academy of Arts and Sciences*, "In Search of Canada," Fall 1988.

Canada is big — preposterously so. How can 26 million people lay convincing claim to sovereignty over 3.8 million square miles of a crowded planet?
F. KENNETH HARE, geographer, "Canada: The Land," *Daedalus: Journal of the Amer-*

ican Academy of Arts and Sciences, "In Search of Canada," Fall 1988.

If you head the same distance east from St. John's, you find yourself in Colonel Qaddafi's nest in Tripoli or somewhere just short of Moscow, depending on what tack you take. Either destination means that you will have spanned the Atlantic, plus the entire width of Europe. I repeat: such an extent is preposterous, in old-world terms. Can such a tiny scattering of people hold it together?

F. KENNETH HARE, geographer, relating an eastward extension to the westward extension from St. John's, Nfld., to Victoria, B.C., "Canada: The Land," *Daedalus: Journal of the American Academy of Arts and Sciences,* "In Search of Canada," Fall 1988.

One afternoon, by driving a few miles out to Cape Spear, I made myself for a moment the easternmost person in North America, and was chilled to think, as I stood there in the wind, that while at my back there was nothing but the ocean, before me there extended, almost as far as the imagination could conceive, the awful immensity of Canadian rock, forest, prairie, and mountain. St. John's is the edge of everywhere, the end and start of everything.

JAN MORRIS, travel writer, *Saturday Night,* March 1989.

Our miles and miles of miles and miles. . . .
Words evocative of the immense size of Canada, the second-largest country in the world, quoted by TONI ONLEY in *Onley's Arctic: Diaries and Paintings of the High Arctic* (1989).

GEOLOGY

It is contended, during a period of 210 m.y. [million years] a single great landmass divided and spread out to make up the configurations of the present continents. At the beginning of the Mesozoid a rift began to develop that became the Atlantic Ocean; in Tertiary time, about 60 m.y. ago,

a new rift was started that became the Indian Ocean, separating Africa, Australasia, Antarctica, and Asia from one another. If such enormous changes could occur in a comparatively short and recent (geologically speaking) interval of earth history, how many earlier movements may have happened in the preceding two or three billion years since the oldest rocks of the continental blocks began forming early in Precambrian time, at least 3,000 m.y. ago? The answer may be found within the rocks of the Canadian Shield, when we can read them.

MORRIS ZASLOW, geologist, *Reading the Rocks: The Story of the Geological Survey of Canada, 1842-1972* (1975).

The dinosaurs are indeed dead. The sight of their bronze skeletons in the darkened galleries of our museums seems to call us hauntingly. They too were wonderful, they are dead, and their death recalls to us something of the meaning of living. Their giant skeletons embody the abundance of a long-vanished world. The life of our planet has more than recovered from the forces that destroyed the world in which they lived. Yet, would we have survived had we been in their place?

DALE A. RUSSELL, paleontologist, *A Vanished World: The Dinosaurs of Western Canada* (1977).

And photographs of the Earth taken from space showed that the ancient cores of the continents, called *cratons,* were scarred with huge, shallow craters that had survived billions of years of weathering and scouring by glaciers. The oldest part of North America, the Canadian Shield, revealed to the eyes of satellites huge basins that had never been identified from the ground.

JOHN S. LEWIS and RUTH A. LEWIS, U.S. science-writing team, *Space Resources: Breaking the Bonds of Earth* (1987).

As for the kinds of creatures preserved in the Shales, the word *weird* only hints at a description of the oddities that have been

found. *Opabinia* was a critter with five eyes and a vacuum-cleaner-like appendage near the mouth. *Wiwaxia* was somewhat snail-like, but had a shell of spines and plates that it molted occasionally much like arthropods do today. The list goes on. There were many bizarre organisms that are unique to the time the Burgess Shales were formed. They died out soon afterward and left no descendants.
    ZEN FAULKES, biologist, "Getting Smart about Getting Smarts," *Skeptical Inquirier*, Spring 1991. Faulkes, a member of the Department of Biology, University of Victoria, is discussing the myriad life-forms that flourished just after the Cambrian explosion 570 million years ago and were caught in the Burgess Shales, Yoho National Park, B.C., discussed by Stephen Jay Gould in *Wonderful Life* (1989).

What the Dead Sea Scrolls are for the history of the early Church, the Burgess fossils are for the history of life on the planet.
    JIM SECORD, British geologist, commenting on the fossil-bearing Burgess Shale of the Rocky Mountains in a review of Stephen Jay Gould's *Wonderful Life: The Burgess Shale and the Nature of History* in *The Times Literary Supplement*, 4 May 1990.

GERMANY

I come from a country which is rather like Canada in one respect: Germany has never made a revolution. It is unlike Canada, however, in that it has a history of profound counter-revolution.
    HANS MAGNUS ENZENSBERGER, West German man-of-letters, "A Situation of Privilege," *The Writer and Human Rights* (1983) edited by the Toronto Arts Group for Human Rights.

GHOSTS
    See also BELIEF

Canada, I assert, is wretchedly under-monstered.

ROBERTSON DAVIES, man-of-letters, *Samuel Marchbanks' Almanack* (1967).

It is often pointed out that disembodied persons would be imperceptible, so that it would be impossible, even if there are any of them, for us to be aware of their presence.
    TERENCE PENELHUM, philosopher, *Survival and Disembodied Existence* (1970).

Ghosts and apparitions arise from unconscious psychological disturbances. This does not explain them away, but it does put them on a rather different footing than pretending that they come from the grave or something of that sort.
    ROBERTSON DAVIES, man-of-letters, interviewed by Terence M. Green in 1982, *Conversations with Robertson Davies* (1989) edited by J. Madison Davis.

Newfoundland has its fair share of ghosts, ghouls and other assorted characters from beyond although the spread of electricity and street lights seems to have cut seriously into the population.
    RAY GUY, humorist, "The Truth about Rum-Cats and Other Creatures from Beyond," *Ray Guy's Best* (1987).

There is nothing supernatural about ghosts. They are part of the world in which we live, and they follow laws which we are beginning to understand more fully as more and more research into parapsychology continues to be done.
    ROBIN SKELTON and JEAN KOZOCARI, practising witches and ghost-busters, *A Gathering of Ghosts: Hauntings and Exorcisms from the Personal Casebook of Robin Skelton and Jean Kozocari* (1989).

GIFTS & GIVING

Purest of gifts: / those that consist / only in giving.
    ALDEN NOWLAN, poet, "Purest of Gifts," *Bread, Wine and Salt* (1967).

GLOBAL VILLAGE

Forsdale: Marshall, you've often used the phrase *global village* in talking about the electric media.

McLuhan: It was just an accidental phrase that popped up. What it means, literally, is that, transmitted at the speed of light, all events on this planet are simultaneous. In the electric age of information, all events are simultaneous. There is no time or space separating events. Information and images bump against each other every day in massive quantities, and the resonance of this interfacing is like the babble of a village or tavern gossip session. The absence of space brings to mind the idea of a village. But actually, at the speed of light, the planet is not much bigger than this room we're in. In terms of time and the speed of the event that are now programmed, they hit each other so fast that even a village is too big a thing to use for a comparison. The acoustic or simultaneous space in which we now live is like a sphere whose centre is everywhere and whose margins are nowhere. Acoustic space cannot be cut into pieces, as visual space can. It is both compressed and indivisible.

Forsdale: If we live in a global village, does that mean that people are going to like each other?

McLuhan: Not likely, since proximity means there's more abrasiveness. Close quarters strain human tolerance.

Undated discussion between MARSHALL McLUHAN and LOUIS FORSDALE published in the McLuhan issue of *The Antigonish Review*, Summer-Autumn 1988.

We possess a village rather than a global mentality. Ironically, it was a Canadian, Marshall McLuhan, who in the 1960s coined the internationally known term *the global village*. In Canada, the focus has fallen on the word *village*, not the word *global*, for indeed peoples came here to live in a village peace.

GERALDINE A. KENNY-WALLACE and J. FRASER MUSTARD, scientists and spokespeople for science, "From Paradox to Paradigm: The Evolution of Science and Technology in Canada," *Daedalus: Journal of the American Academy of Arts and Sciences*, "In Search of Canada," Fall 1988.

In other words, we are increasingly witness to the transculturation of world affairs. Today, for example, a total of 400 satellites encircle the world. These "tom-toms" of the electronic global village will bring the world together as never before.

FRANK FEATHER, futurologist, *G-Forces: Reinventing the World — The 35 Global Forces Restructuring Our World* (1989).

GLOBALIZATION

Canada is involved in a race between political will and institutional inertia and international change. At the moment international change is winning, and the Canadian standard of living is falling. If Canada's future is to be as prosperous as its past, if Canada is not to be forever in a stage of immature development, the appropriate processes for making economic policy in a period of rapid change must be adopted and activated.

J. GILLIES, consultant, *Facing Reality: Consultation, Consensus and Making Economic Policy for the 21st Century* (1986), as cited by Geraldine A. Kenny-Wallace and J. Fraser Mustard in "From Paradox to Paradigm: The Evolution of Science and Technology in Canada," *Daedalus: Journal of the American Academy of Arts and Sciences*, "In Search of Canada," Fall 1988.

Unfortunately, the reality of the matter is that our national psychological defence system is rather lame at this point. TVOntario's chief executive officer, Bernard Ostry, says that we are the first victim of what other countries call "Canadianization," that is, a process in which a nation sets up the broadcasting system owned and run by and for its own citizens, only to find it a perfect carrier for American programming at bargain prices. We certainly could do a lot more to protect our media, even with the situation as it stands. We have no plan of defence. Maybe we should provide one.

> DERRICK DE KERCKHOVE, academic, "Control of the Collective Mind," *The Canadian Forum*, Oct. 1989.

GOD

See also BELIEF

Almighty Lord and eternal Father, there is more life in You than there is water in the Pacific Ocean.

> LOUIS RIEL, Métis leader and mystic, diary entry, June 1885, *The Diaries of Louis Riel* (1976) edited by Thomas Flanagan.

I took a day to search for God, / And found Him not. But as I trod / By rocky ledge, through woods untamed, / Just where one scarlet lily flamed, / I saw his footprint in the sod.

> BLISS CARMAN, poet, "Vestigia" (1921), *Later Poems* (1922).

How can one help but praise the power of God, who made a boy from St-Anicet a prince of the Church?

> PAUL-ÉMILE CARDINAL LÉGER, on becoming a Cardinal in 1953, quoted by Roy Bonisteel in *Man Alive: The Human Journey* (1983).

God . . . is love . . . and it is the overflowing of that love that creates and sustains and promotes this seething universe of mass and energy, of chemical process, of endlessly varied plant and animal life, of human intelligence and of human love.

> BERNARD J.F. LONERGAN, Jesuit philosopher, *A Second Collection: Papers by Bernard J.F. Lonergan, S.J.* (1954).

I have been speaking of the absence of God in modern culture. . . . But every absence is also a potential presence, not indeed in the sense that the past is to be restored, but in the sense that our creativity has to discover the future and our determination has to realize it.

> BERNARD J.F. LONERGAN, Jesuit philosopher, *A Second Collection: Papers by Bernard J.F. Lonergan, S.J.* (1954).

Either way, the idea of a god who intervenes in human affairs — and I say there is no such god and never was or will be — is a loser. Either god is indifferent to the sufferings of his people, or he is incapable of help. Take it either way you like, or find a middle course of your own. I see no answer to man's prayer, regardless of whether that prayer is to Allah, Buddha, Christ, or ABC, or go down to the bottom of a long list of deities to Zeus. Wherever the plea goes, it falls on deaf or uninterested ears.

> GORDON SINCLAIR, broadcaster and journalist, *Will the Real Gordon Sinclair Please Stand Up* (1966).

I can say that I do not think of God as a concept, but as an immediate and ever-present fact — an occasion for continuous dialogue.

> MARSHALL McLUHAN, media philosopher, letter to James Taylor, 15 Jan. 1969, responding to a questionnaire from the *United Church Observer* concerning beliefs and philosophy, *Letters of Marshall McLuhan* (1987) edited by Matie Molinaro, Corinne McLuhan, and William Toye.

Oh, great spirit, whose voice I hear in the winds, and whose breath gives life to the world, hear me. I come to you as one of your many children. I am small and weak. I need your strength and your wisdom. May I walk in beauty. Make my eyes ever behold the red and purple sunset. Make my hands respect the things that you have made and my ears sharp to hear your voice. Make me wise so that I may know the things you have taught your children, the lessons you have hidden in every leaf

and rock. Make me strong, not to be superior to my brothers, but to be able to fight my greatest enemy, myself. Make me ever ready to come to you with straight eyes, so that when life fades as the fading sunset, my spirit may come to you without shame.
> CHIEF DAN GEORGE, native leader, recited this self-composed prayer at the conclusion of the program devoted to him on CBC-TV's *Telescope*, 7 Sept. 1970.

As we begin to recognize God in every aspect of the world around us, that part of the world is redeemed, until ultimately the whole planet is redeemed.
> DOROTHY MACLEAN, medium, born in Guelph, Ont., one of the original founders of the Findhorn Community in Northern Scotland, quoted in *The Findhorn Garden* (1975) by The Findhorn Community with a Foreword by William Irwin Thompson.

O Supreme Builder of the Universe help us not to make the mistake of the builders of the first tower which you confounded.
> WILLIAM KURELEK, artist and religious zealot, proposed in 1975 that he engrave this prayer on a plaque to be installed in secret in a hidden chamber at the top of the CN Tower, which was under construction and was completed the following year. Quoted by Patricia Morley in *William Kurelek: A Biography* (1986).

We could say: God, *if he existed*, would have no attributes other than existence.
> JOHN LESLIE, philosopher, University of Guelph, "Efforts to Explain All Existence," *Mind*, April 1978.

I might never have another chance to interview God. I would like to know how you. . . .
> ROY BONISTEEL, host of CBC-TV's *Man Alive*, addressing the Dalai Lama in a filmed interview in Toronto in 1980. "That is as far as I got. His holiness began to giggle. . . ." *Man Alive: The Human Journey* (1983).

The phrase "God created man in His own image" does not make one particularly eager to meet Him.
> GEORGE FALUDY, Hungarian-born poet, *Notes from the Rainforest* (1988).

In 1981, a sudden public opinion movement whose exact strength and origin is hard to assess, made the cabinet and the Parliament add at the last minute a reference to God to the preamble of the new Constitution. This addition was made, but it did not commit anyone to much.
> MONIQUE BÉGIN, former politician, "Debates and Silences — Reflections of a Politician," *Daedalus: Journal of the American Academy of Arts and Sciences*, "In Search of Canada," Fall 1988.

I guess in *Gentle Sinners* I said something along the lines of "it's not whether one will have gods but which ones one worships." Often if we're too quick to dismiss the rituals of the past, we leave a kind of vacuum into which the behaviours that we substitute are not really adequate emotionally.
> W. D. VALGARDSON, novelist, quoting from his own prose, interviewed by Alan Twigg in *Strong Voices: Conversations with Fifty Canadian Authors* (1988).

I do not believe in some kind of a Creator. I believe in the Holy Spirit. I think there is an informing spirit in the whole of creation but I also believe we have some kind of free will.
> MARGARET LAURENCE, novelist, *Dance on the Earth: A Memoir* (1989).

Rasky: Does Northrop Frye talk to God?
Frye (pause, semi-smile): Yes.
> Intimate moment in a conversation between HARRY RASKY, documentary film producer, and NORTHROP FRYE, literary critic, *The Great Teacher: Northrop Frye*, CBC-TV, 25 Dec. 1989.

Twigg: You've written somewhere that you believe in God. . . .
Cohen: Because I've experienced the absolute.

Twigg: And the absolute is zero?

Cohen: It's a zero that is continually manifesting as one, two, three, four, five, six, seven, eight, nine, ten.

Twigg: A totality?

Cohen: It's the fundamental ground or field which is nothing, the still centre or whatever metaphor you use for it. It's neither dead nor alive. It is an indescribable energy. That's zero. It's so empty that myriads and myriads of forms rush in to fill it at every second.

> LEONARD COHEN, poet, and Alan Twigg, interviewer, *Strong Voices: Conversations with Fifty Canadian Authors* (1988).

GOLD

Should inflation come roaring back — and how else are governments to pay down the deficits they are accumulating in numbers that once were useful only for measuring distances in interstellar space — gold may well sell for thousands of dollars an ounce, but if it does that simply means gold will retain much of its value as paper money becomes worthless.

> KEN LEFOLII, journalist, *Claims: Adventures in the Gold Trade* (1987).

GOLF
See also SPORTS

Professional golfers are gypsies in polyester sportswear: conservative family men leading a radical, single man's lifestyle, they are independent businessmen whose offices are the fairways and greens of the world's top golf courses.

> PAUL McLAUGHLIN, journalist, *TV Guide*, 16 Aug. 1980.

Now I don't noe nuthin about this golfball game, I wooden noe witch end of yer caddy yuh grabs aholt of.

> DON HARRON, comedian, in the person of Charlie Farquharson, *Cum Buy the Farm* (1987).

It's one of those unintended conse-

quences of the game: You go out to make pars, and you make friends.

> LORNE RUBENSTEIN, golf columnist, *Links* (1990).

Golf encourages a dream state. It allows our minds and imaginations to roam. . . . Golf encourages reverie. To be part of golf is to come upon stories, to become a story, to tell stories.

> LORNE RUBENSTEIN, golf columnist, *Links* (1990).

GOOD & EVIL
See also RIGHT & WRONG

The virtues of those we dislike irritate us even more than their vices.

> IRVING LAYTON, poet, *The Whole Bloody Bird (obs, aphs & pomes)* (1969).

Putting aside the petty perspectives of good and evil means that there is nothing belonging to all human beings which need limit the building of the future. Oblivion of eternity is here.

> GEORGE GRANT, philosopher, "Nietzsche and the Ancients" (1979), *Technology and Justice* (1986).

For a good cause, wrongdoing is a virtue.

> NICHOLAS CATANOY, poet and aphorist, from "Notes on a Prison Wall (Fragment)," *Canadian Literature*, Summer 1989.

The devil doesn't make personal appearances.

> Comment of a character in a play included in *7 Stories* (1990) by playwright MORRIS PANYCH.

GOODS AND SERVICES TAX
See also TAXES

GST/TPS

> The GST (The Goods and Services Tax) or *la TPS (La Taxe sur les Produits et Services)*, a controversial surtax not unlike Europe's VAT (Value Added Tax), was imposed 1 Jan. 1991. Even before imposition it was dubbed "Grab, Snatch, and Take,"

"Gouge and Screw Tax," and the "Ghosts and Spirits Tax." When the Gulf War escalated, it was referred to as "Gulf Sur Tax" and "Get Saddam's Testicles" (from a T-sheet, Toronto, Jan. 1991).

A general tax on all goods and services, set at 9%, reset at 7%, was introduced by the Mulroney administration in Oct. 1989 and imposed on 1 Jan. 1991 to replace the MST (Manufacturers' Sales Tax), the long-standing wholesale tax on goods of 13.5%, as well as to raise revenue at least equivalent to the duties and excise taxes lost on goods imported from the United States through the imposition of Free Trade.

We're dealing with a cowardly government that is prepared to tax the democracy of print. The government is not willing to tax jumbo shrimp and caviar, but it will tax books and magazines. It's stunningly ludicrous.

JACQUELINE HUSHION, Executive Director, Canadian Book Publishers' Council, referring to the GST, the first tax ever levied on books, quoted by Isabel Vincent in *The Globe and Mail*, 25 Nov. 1989.

This goods and services tax is iniquitous, because it's once again forcing us to pay this deficit off the backs of the poor.

REMI J. DE ROO, Bishop of Victoria, quoted by George Mortimore in *The Canadian Forum*, May 1990.

I think that if governments are going to tax books, they ought to do more to breed readers. To lay a new burden on a fatigued and tottering industry seems to be the height of philistinism.

SAUL BELLOW, Lachine-born, Montreal-raised, Chicago-based author, referring to the GST, the first federal tax on reading matter, quoted by Stephen Godfrey in *The Globe and Mail*, 10 Nov. 1990.

If the Mulroney government had not passed Bill C-62, it would have lost everything. But in its desperation to Pass Bill C-62 at any cost, it lost whatever slender chance it had of re-election. Such are the hard realities of the real worlds of Canadian politics.

ROBERT M. CAMPBELL and LESLIE A. PAL, political scientists, *The Real Worlds of Canadian Politics: Cases in Process and Policy* (1991). Bill C-62 was given Royal Assent on 17 Dec. 1990, and the GST came into effect on 1 Jan. 1991.

GOSSIP

I have to keep on friendly terms with people in whose company I find not one spark of interest or congeniality — people who can talk nothing but gossip and not even entertainingly of that. For gossip is *sometimes* interesting, if it is skilfully and delicatedly handled; but when it is infused with misunderstanding and jealousy and spite — Good Lord, deliver us! It is dreadful to visit at a place where you have to say every word over to yourself before you utter it aloud to make sure it is harmless and won't involve you in mischief if reported elsewhere.

L. M. MONTGOMERY, author, journal entry, 5 June 1909, Cavendish, P.E.I., *The Selected Journals of L.M. Montgomery: Volume I: 1889-1910* (1985) edited by Mary Rubio and Elizabeth Waterston.

GOULD, GLENN

I resent the one-timeness, or the non-take-twoness, of the live concert experience.

GLENN GOULD, pianist who chose to be recalled as a recording artist rather than as a performing artist, quoted by Richard Kostelanetz in "Glenn Gould: Bach in the Electronic Age," *Esquire*, Nov. 1967.

GOVERNMENT
See also PARLIAMENT

There is no magic in government. After all, government is business, the people's business. Good government is therefore a matter of common sense.

LESLIE FROST, former Ontario Premier, quoted by Jonathan Manthorpe in *The*

*Power and the Tories: Ontario Politics —
1943 to the Present* (1974).

The acid test of freedom in a state is
whether power and office can pass peacefully from one political party to another.
"Her Majesty's Opposition" is just as necessary to free government as "Her
Majesty's Government." There is no need
to argue this point any more. People who
are still capable of believing in the freedom of citizens of the so-called "People's
Democracies" are too innocent for politics.
    F.H. UNDERHILL, political scientist, "Ca-
nadian Political Parties" (1957), *The Canadian Political Tradition: Basic Readings*
(1987) edited by R.S. Blair and J.T. Mc-
Leod.

Minority government can be not a "problem" but an opportunity, not a threat but
a promise. A government with a clear majority may go lickety-split in the wrong
direction. A government without a clear
majority is more likely to stop, look and
listen. I am not, of course, arguing that
minority government necessarily means
good government. I am simply arguing
that it does not necessarily mean bad government.
    F.H. UNDERHILL, political scientist, "Ca-
nadian Political Parties" (1957), *The Canadian Political Tradition: Basic Readings*
(1987) edited by R.S. Blair and J.T. Mc-
Leod.

Hands on. Arm's length.
    Familiar phrases which are used to con-
trast the relationship of the government
of the day to Crown corporations and
cultural agencies; "hands on" refers to
meddling, "arm's length" to independence.

Government offices seldom operate at the
vibrant pace of their counterparts in the
private sector. Usually a languorous ambience pervades, as though barbiturates
were being wafted through the ducts like
some invisible chemical Muzak.

TOM DAVEY, editor and columnist, *All the
Views Fit to Print* (1985).

World *government* as such is not, in my
view, either practicable or desirable. But
the evolution of a world *system* is an absolute imperative if civilized life is to continue. The United Nations is the essential
centrepiece of that system. If it did not
exist we would have to create it. Even
more today than when it was created, the
United Nations continues to reflect and
enshrine the hopes and aspirations of the
entire human family and the imperatives
for its future survival and well-being.
    MAURICE STRONG, former Executive Co-
ordinator, UN Office for Emergency Operations in Africa, *The Gaia Peace Atlas*
(1988) edited by Frank Barnaby.

Governments are becoming increasingly
irrelevant. They can no longer protect
their citizens against terrorism at home or
abroad, guard their borders against illegal
immigrants, defend their currency, their
technology or the jobs of their citizens.
And, they have failed to create a shield
against the environmental degradation
and vast cultural changes now sweeping
unhindered across their borders.
    FRANK OGDEN, futurologist, "Ogden's
Third Law," *Dr. Tomorrow's Lessons from
the Future* (updated Oct. 1988).

The question is not whether we need
global government but what form it
should take. The great weakness of the
present system is that it is state-centric.
The geo-centric vision of planetary government, where the greatest amount of
power would instead be vested in its
transnational global authority, is no
longer a utopian dream — it is an absolute
necessity.
    FRANK FEATHER, futurologist, *G-Forces:
Reinventing the World — The 35 Global
Forces Restructuring Our World* (1989).

The mandarins are the various deputy
ministers, assistant deputy ministers, and
high-level advisers who are the effective

leaders of individual government bureaucracies. At least 100 persons have deputy-minister status in the federal government, but a much smaller number actually run significant departments. A similar pattern prevails in the provinces.

> DAVID H. FLAHERTY, historian, "Who Rules Canada?" *Daedalus: Journal of the American Academy of Arts and Sciences,* "In Search of Canada," Fall 1988.

Moreoever, we have too many official holders of governmental power for the size of our country. One of the ten provinces, Prince Edward Island, has a panoply of public officeholders for a population of 127,000; there are 23 Canadian cities with larger populations than that.

> DAVID H. FLAHERTY, historian, "Who Rules Canada?" *Daedalus: Journal of the American Academy of Arts and Sciences,* "In Search of Canada," Fall 1988.

It's all right to act like a Fascist in America as long as you talk like a Christian.

> Comment of a character in the play *Dog and Crow* (1990) by playwright MICHAEL SPRINGATE.

Every little ruler / wants a 13th inch.

> ROBERT PRIEST, poet, aphorism, March 1990.

The fathers of the Canadian Confederation spoke of "peace, order, and good government," not of "life, liberty, and the pursuit of happiness." Peace, order, good government, these sound like goals that can be attained with diligence and prudence. Liberty and the pursuit of happiness are transcendental goals. It is as though the boredoms and frustrations of social life, inequality and exploitation, slavery and domination, all that seems to stand between us and the realization of the good society, can be overcome by a single liberating act. The pursuit of transcendental goals may breed violence, often rhetorical, sometimes physical.

> J.M. CAMERON, historian, "The New Can-

adas," *The New York Review of Books,* 16 Aug. 1990.

There are far too many overlapping jurisdictions in this country. Canadians are overgoverned.

> BRIAN MULRONEY, Prime Minister, address, joint meeting of the Empire Club and the Canadian Club, Toronto, 12 Feb. 1991, published in *The Toronto Star* the following day.

It is such a small world. Why does it cost so much to run it?

> HELEN STIMPSON, retired real-estate agent, characteristic remark, 7 March 1991.

I have just formulated Roberts' Law of Canadian Politics, whether federal or provincial: "Every government is worse than the last."

> RICHARD J. ROBERTS, Toronto contributor, Letters to the Editor, *The Globe and Mail,* 6 April 1991.

GOVERNOR GENERAL
See also MONARCHY
PARLIAMENT

There was an arch of cheeses — an arch of salt — an arch of wheels — an arch of hardware, stoves, pots and pans — an arch of sofas, chairs, and household furniture — an arch of ladders laden with firemen in their picturesque costumes — an arch of carriages — an arch of boats, a free trade arch, a protectionist arch — an arch of children, and last of all — an arch, no, not an arch, but rather a celestial rainbow — of lovely young ladies.

> LORD DUFFERIN, Governor General, address in Brockville, Ont., 1874, referring to the era's passion for ceremonial arches to mark royal and vice-regal passage, quoted by G. Stewart in *Canada under the Administration of the Earl of Dufferin* (1878).

They are but fleeting shadows and evanescent apparitions that haunt your history, but scarcely contribute a line to its pages. Should we leave behind us a single kindly memory, should our names hereafter mark a date, or identify a period, it is the most we can aspire to. Half a column of a biographical dictionary would suffice to exhibit the sum of our united achievements; so imperceptibly do we come and go, play our small part, and fade from off the scene.

> LORD DUFFERIN, Governor General, discussing the characteristics of the office, speech, 14 Feb. 1878, quoted by Jules Léger at the Annual Dinner, Canadian Press, Toronto, 1 May 1974.

Above him presided the Governor-General, who, in those days, was far from being a ceremonial cipher; representing both the Crown and the Prime Minister, he was the sole means of communication between the two governments, and thus wielded great power.

> ALISTAIR HORNE, biographer and historian, referring to the years in Canada immediately following World War I, *Macmillan: 1894-1956: Volume I of the Official Biography* (1988).

I don't for a moment flatter myself that I am a statesman or diplomat, but I don't think it makes too much difference if I bring to this job a high sense of responsibility.

> LORD ALEXANDER, Governor General, remark made shortly before being sworn in, 12 April 1946, quoted by John Cowan in *Canada's Governors-General 1867-1952* (1952).

I did have one other contact with Canada, but it was personal. Once at a countryside picnic in Pennsylvania where the Micheners of the world convened to celebrate the glories of their supposedly distinguished past, I met by accident my cousin the Right Honourable Roland Michener, the governor general of Canada, and we locals felt a bit puffed up.

> JAMES A. MICHENER, U.S. author, discussing both a meeting with D. Roland Michener, who served as Governor General in 1967-74, and the genesis of his novel set in the North, *Journey* (1988).

It is a great thing to be asked to symbolize a nation and its aspirations and to try to make the people of this country more conscious of their country.

> JEANNE SAUVÉ, Governor General, address, Empire Club of Canada, Toronto, 12 Nov. 1985.

Name Brian Mulroney governor general. While he had no qualifications to become prime minister — and it showed — he is eminently qualified to be G.G. He is bilingual. He dresses well. He has a smiling wife who walks one step behind him. He oozes unctuousness. He will not be missed in whatever it is he is now not doing.

> MEL WATKINS, political economist, contributor to *If I Were Prime Minister* (1987) edited by Mel Hurtig.

The governor-general holds what have been called Canada's great constitutional fire extinguishers — the powers, in an emergency, to dismiss a prime minister and dissolve Parliament. He or she also holds the constitutional rights of the head of state: the right to be consulted, the right to encourage, the right to warn.

> MICHAEL VALPY, columnist, *The Globe and Mail*, 13 Oct. 1989.

The Prime Minister, to excite the pulse, has announced that Ramon Hnatyshn, a defeated Tory candidate and therefore immediately eminently qualified for the job, will take over Rideau Hall in the new year. This follows a grand tradition. Vincent Massey was the first Canadian as governor general and Ed Schreyer was the first socialist gee-gee and Jeanne Sauvé was the first female one, and now we have the first one whose name can be neither spelled nor pronounced. He is from Saskatchewan, where all the great ones come from.

> ALLAN FOTHERINGHAM, columnist, *Maclean's*, 16 Oct. 1989. It is interesting to note that two other natives of Saskatche-

wan are Jeanne Sauvé — and Allan Fotheringham.

At some point in the next century or so, Canadians may well decide to weight the office of governor general with as much of the monarchical tradition as it can absorb and make its incumbent the real rather than the stand-in final authority for Canada.
 WILLIAM KILBOURN, historian, "The Peaceable Kingdom Still," *Daedalus: Journal of the American Academy of Arts and Sciences*, "In Search of Canada," Fall 1988.

GRAFFITI
 See also INSCRIPTIONS

There was a Canadian counterpart to Kilroy, a mythical Clem. His name was inscribed in every unlikely place in the army camps. At one command post, it drove the officer in charge to a point of extreme irritation. One morning he called out every single man in the camp to assemble, averred in strong language that the inscription must cease, dismissed them, and returned to his office — to find "Wot! No Clem?" inscribed on his desk.
 ROBERT REISNER, U.S. connoisseur of graffiti, *Graffiti: Two Thousand Years of Wall Writing* (1974).

OUR WALLS / OUR VOICE
 Graffiti painted on the side of a building, Toronto, Nov. 1988.

Scrap the Scummit
 Graffiti spotted in downtown Toronto, June 1990, left over from the Economic Summit, which opened in the city on 3 Feb. 1990.

GRAND CANAL PROJECT

The magnitude of the Grand Canal Project is some five times the size of the Apollo Moon Project, roughly 100 billion current dollars. It would taken ten years to construct and put into operation. . . . I believe that this project could provide the key to

a free trade agreement. . . . Do we have the courage and the imagination — yes, the audacity — to take on these two big projects, free trade and fresh water-sharing, at the same time?
 SIMON REISMAN, economist, "Canadian Trade at a Crossroads," Ontario Economic Council, 16-17 April 1985, quoted by James Laxer in *Leap of Faith: Free Trade and the Future of Canada* (1986).

GREAT BRITAIN
 See UNITED KINGDOM

GREAT LAKES

Where vast Ontario rolls his brineless tides, / And feeds the trackless forests on his sides, / Fair Cassia trembling hears the howling woods, / And trusts her tawny children to the floods.
 ERASMUS DARWIN, English scientist and poetaster, reference to the "Cassia-flowering plant" and to Lake Ontario, one of the five Great Lakes, *The Botanic Garden* (1791).

But I told that kid a hundred times, "Don't take the Lakes for granted. / They go from calm to a hundred knots so fast they seem enchanted." / But tonight some red-eyed Wiarton girl lies staring at the wall, / And her lover's gone into a white squall.
 STAN ROGERS, singer and composer, "White Squall," *From Fresh Water* (Cole Harbour Music, 1984).

"This must be the right lake," Champlain said eerily.
 A linguistic oddity known as the "Tom Swifty" contributed by ULRICH KRETSCHMAR, Washago, Ont., quoted by Warren Clements in *The Globe and Mail*, 16 March 1991.

GREATNESS

My own quest now has stretched for over half a lifetime. The search for greatness of spirit has compelled me to work harder — to strive for perfection, knowing it to be unattainable. My quest has brought me great joy when something close to my ideal has been attained. It has kept me young at heart, adventurous, forever seeking, and always aware that the heart and the mind are the true lens of the camera.

> YOUSUF KARSH, portrait photographer, *Karsh: A Fifty-Year Retrospective* (1983).

One must start early to become a great man.

> STEPHEN VIZINCZEY, novelist, *An Innocent Millionaire* (1983).

Everywhere greatness is recognized by acclamation, in Canada it comes by appointment.

> LOUIS DUDEK, aphorist, "Can. Lit. Notes," *The Bumper Book* (1986) edited by John Metcalf.

GREECE

At a young age I read all of Homer in the original. And a great deal of Greek literature. When I finally got to Greece, looking up the coast towards Athens, apart from the slight difference in ground cover, I could have been on some marvellous bay in Nova Scotia. What Homer was describing was exactly like the coast of Nova Scotia. It was the same kind of life. People going out to sea in small boats, people going off to war. Homer described what I knew better than any other writer.

> HUGH MacLENNAN, novelist, interviewed by Alan Twigg in *Strong Voices: Conversations with Fifty Canadian Authors* (1988).

GREENHOUSE EFFECT

The increase in temperature will mean that within the next few decades the oceans will rise by a metre, wiping out coastal areas and marshlands that are important breeding grounds for fish, or, if the West Antarctic Ice Shelf melts and drops into the sea, by as much as five to seven metres, in which case we'll be saying goodbye to Prince Edward Island, Lower Van-

couver, Florida, Bangladesh and the low countries of western Europe. The American and Canadian wheat belt will become a dust bowl, while the temperate growing zones, so important to agriculture, will shift north; when the ice cap melts, grain may grow again in Greenland, but not much will thrive in the thin soils of the Canadian and Russian tundra.

> DAVID LEES, journalist, "Living in the Nuclear Shadow," *Toronto Life*, Nov. 1989.

The wheat-growing season in Canada and the Soviet Union would lengthen and the more northern areas of these countries would be able to grow wheat for the first time . . . if the wheat belt shifted northwards, yields could increase by as much as 35% and more crop areas would be opened up . . . a carbon dioxide-enriched environment would improve crop productivity. . . . Therefore, the greenhouse effect would not necessarily impair, but could even enhance, our ability to feed ourselves — with plenty to spare.

> FRANK FEATHER, futurologist, *G-Forces: Reinventing the World — The 35 Global Forces Restructuring Our World* (1989).

What is alarming about greenhouse warming is not the increase in the past century but what is happening right now. Greenhouse-gas emissions — carbon dioxide, methane, and chlorofluorocarbons — are increasing so rapidly that it is "dead certain" when enough are released we will be into an era of unmanageable global change.

> ANITA GORDON and DAVID SUZUKI, science broadcasters, *It's a Matter of Survival* (1990).

GREENPEACE
See also ECOLOGY

Don't Make A Wave / It's Your Fault If Our Fault Goes

> Message on banners protesting the testing by the United States of a one-megaton nuclear bomb at Amchitka, one of the Aleutian Islands off the west coast of

Alaska, 2 Oct. 1969. The Don't Make A Wave Commitee became the Greenpeace Foundation. Quoted by Michael Brown and John May, journalists, *The Greenpeace Story* (1989).

You Can't Sink A Rainbow
Slogan associated with the public's response to the French security force's illegal undercover action of planting explosives aboard the Greenpeace protest vessel *Rainbow Warrior*, Auckland Harbour, N.Z., 10 July 1985. Quoted by Michael Brown and John May, journalists, *The Greenpeace Story* (1989).

From "God Save the Queen" to "God Save the Dolphins" in less than two decades. Greenpeace is truly Canadian Imperialism with real heart — a bleeding one at that.
ALLAN GOULD, satirist, *The Great Wiped Out North: or, When Sacred Cows Come Home to Roost* (1988).

GRETZKY, WAYNE
See also HOCKEY

Practise your backhand.
Advice given by hockey star GORDIE HOWE to a young but promising hockey hopeful, Wayne Gretzky, then aged eleven, in 1972, quoted by Al Strachan in *The Globe and Mail*, 16 Oct. 1989.

What if Wayne Gretzky's grandfather had decided not to emigrate from Russia?
Rhetorical question asked by hockey enthusiast PAUL QUARRINGTON in *Hometown Heroes: On the Road with Canada's National Hockey Team* (1988).

I feel I've gained more than I lost. I lost a record, but I gained a lot of friends.
GORDIE HOWE, veteran hockey player, reacting to the achievement of the hockey superstar Wayne Gretzky, who the previous evening, in a game played in Edmonton between the Edmonton Oilers, Gretzky's old team, and the Los Angeles Kings, his new team, exceeded Howe's record of 1850 career goals, quoted by Al

Strachan in *The Globe and Mail*, 16 Oct. 1989.

Wayne will get at least 3000 points before he's finished. When he's through, his record will last for a long time.
GORDIE HOWE, high-scoring hockey player, quoted by Al Strachan in *The Globe and Mail*, 16 Oct. 1989.

Gordie was saying something the other day that is true. The hardest thing about hockey is that the older you get, the more you love it. I've said many times that I enjoy it now more than when I was nineteen, when I first came in. I think part of the reason is that you know you're getting closer to the end. I love the game now more than ever.
WAYNE GRETZKY, Number 99, referring to veteran scorer Gordie Howe and their mutual love of the game, quoted by Al Strachan in *The Globe and Mail*, 16 Oct. 1989.

Q. How cold will it be this winter in Edmonton?
A. Minus 99.
Adapted from "Kakologia," *Maledicta: The International Journal of Verbal Aggression*, Volume X, 1988-89.

Hey, you're not the greats! *I* am the greatest! They call you The Great One, but only *I* am the greatest!
MUHAMMAD ALI, boxing personality, addressing Wayne Gretzky, recalled by Wayne Gretzky in *Gretzky: An Autobiography* (1990) written with Rick Reilly. Gretzky added, "No argument here, sir."

GRIEF

In grieving over the loss of another, what we are really doing is grieving over our loss of self, all the self that was invested in that person.
BETTY JANE WYLIE, author, *Beginnings: A Book for Widows* (1977).

Grief is death's way of telling us we aren't perfect.
> BETTY JANE WYLIE, author, *New Beginnings: Living through Loss and Grief* (1991).

Never stare at a man in tears, or turn away from a weeping woman.
> ROBIN SKELTON, man-of-letters, aphorism, May 1990.

GROUP OF SEVEN

The weather has been wet and cold all spring and the flies and mosquitoes much worse than I have seen them any day and fly dope doesn't have any effect on them. This however is the second warm day we have had this year and another day or so like this will finish them. Will send my winter sketches down in a day or two and have every intention of making some more but it has been almost impossible lately. Have done a great deal of paddling this spring and the fishing has been fine. Have done some guiding for fishing parties and will have some other trips this month and next with probably sketching in between.
> Excerpt from the last letter written by TOM THOMSON, the painter whose tragic death and vibrant vision inspired the work of the Group of Seven. The letter was addressed to J.M. MacCallum, the Toronto collector, and dated 7 July 1917, the day before he drowned in Canoe Lake, Algonquin Park, Ont. It is quoted by Peter Mellen in *The Group of Seven* (1970).

. . . for his head was full of savage scenes of great beauty and he had just started painting.
> WYNDHAM LEWIS, writer and painter, discussing Tom Thomson, "Nature's Place in Canadian Culture" (1940-44), *Wyndham Lewis in Canada* (1971) edited by George Woodcock.

New material demands new methods and new methods fling a challenge to old conventions. It is as impossible to depict the autumn pageantry of our northern woods with a lead pencil as it is to bind our young art with the conventions and methods of other climates and other ages.
> LAWREN HARRIS, a leading member of the Group of Seven, foreword to the second Group of Seven Catalogue Exhibition of Paintings, May 1921, reproduced by Peter Mellen in *The Group of Seven* (1970).

A word as to Canada. These pictures have all been executed in Canada during the past year. They express Canadian experience, and appeal to that experience in the onlooker. These are still pioneer days for artists and after the fashion of pioneers we believe whole-heartedly in the land. Some day we think that the land will return the compliment and believe in the artist, not as a nuisance or a luxury but as a real civilizing factor in national life.
> LAWREN HARRIS, a leading member of the Group of Seven, foreword to the second Group of Seven Catalogue Exhibition of Paintings, May 1921, reproduced by Peter Mellen in *The Group of Seven* (1970).

We argued that if a cow could stay in the drawing room, then why couldn't a bull moose?
> A.Y. JACKSON, painter, addressing the Empire Club of Canada, Toronto, 1925, mentioned in *The Toronto Star*, 27 Feb. 1925.

When the last cow is taken from the drawing room and the walls are alive with red maple, yellow birch, blue lakes and sparkling snow-scapes, I can hear the young modern painter up north say to his pal, "There's the trail that those old academic Johnnies, the Group of Seven, blazed."
> A.Y. JACKSON, painter, addressing the Empire Club of Canada, Toronto, 1925, mentioned in *The Toronto Star*, 27 Feb. 1925. The remark was followed by "laughter and applause."

Carmichael: How would you like to be a member of the Group?
Casson: That would be fine, Frank.
Carmichael: Well, you are one. We decided last night.

Exchange between FRANKLIN CAR-MICHAEL and A.J. CASSON in 1926 as recalled by Casson in *Saturday Night*, March 1986. He remembered his response to be "Gosh! That would be something, Frank," when asked "How'd you like to be a member?" according to Roy MacGregor in *The Canadian*, 28 May 1977.

THE GST

See GOODS & SERVICES TAX

GUILT

Guilt has the power to extract merciless sacrifices.
    CAROL SHIELDS, novelist, *Swann* (1987).

GULF WAR

See also WAR

Deficits have got nothing to do with the defence of freedom.
    BRIAN MULRONEY, Prime Minister, explaining that the cost of sending and maintaining Canadian troops in the Persian Gulf are supportable, 12 Nov. 1990, quoted by Susan Delacourt in *The Globe and Mail*, 15 Nov. 1990. He later noted that social programs would be cut to compensate for the costs.

The F-18 has not been built to deliver milk, and the troop is not the Red Cross.
    Attributed to Liberal leader JEAN CHRÉTIEN, address in Victoria, 6 Jan. 1991, carried on CBC-TV later that day.

Canada is a country that stands for decency and peace but we are also a country that stands for principles — respect for the law, freedom and human dignity.
    BRIAN MULRONEY, Prime Minister, House of Commons, 15 Jan. 1991.

Kuwait may seem a remote place geographically, and culturally, but so did Manchuria in 1931, Abyssinia in 1935, and Czechoslovakia in 1938.
    BRIAN MULRONEY, Prime Minister, comparing Iraq's occupation of Kuwait and

events that led to World War II, House of Commons, 15 Jan. 1991.

There's a general feeling of almost a physical illness. We are participating in a process that has launched a war and I never thought that would be under the job description of a member of Parliament.
    SHEILA COPPS, M.P., referring to parliamentary debate on the participation of Canadians in the war in the Persian Gulf, quoted by Geoffrey York in *The Globe and Mail*, 19 Jan. 1991.

This may be said to be a hell of a way to unite a country, but at least Canadians are unanimously in support of their men and women overseas and generally agreed upon the essential wickedness of the Iraqi regime.
    DALTON CAMP, columnist, on Canada's initial commitment of 2500 members of the armed forces to the Middle Eastern conflict, *The Toronto Star*, 23 Jan. 1991.

Instead of prefacing reports from the front with the familiar disclaimer "Subject to government reporting restrictions," the media should attach to all their war reports the warning: "Subject to the fact that we know none of the facts." That would leave the public a lot wiser.
    RICHARD GWYN, columnist, *The Toronto Star*, 3 March 1991.

I don't want to minimize the trauma of people getting killed, but our social programs are going to be the victims. Health programs, education programs, aboriginal programs — all the same people who are always the victims.
    AUDREY McLAUGHLIN, NDP leader, addressing the Manitoba NDP on the financial costs of the Gulf War, quoted by Donald Campbell in *The Winnipeg Free Press*, 17 Feb. 1991.

It's not all right to humiliate political prisoners, but it is all right to bomb cities, cut off their water supply and kill children. Frankly, give me a break.

MARGOT KIDDER, actress, addressing a press conference organized by the Campaign for Peace in the Middle East, referring to the Gulf War, New York, 21 Jan. 1991. Thereafter she was the subject of a headline ("Superman's Girl Defends Iraqis") and subjected to a nickname ("Baghdad Betty"). She called her own remark "the treasonous soundbite" in her memoir, "Confessions of 'Baghdad Betty,'" *The Nation*, 4 March 1991.

There is an immense consciousness of history here. Indeed, there is a greater consciousness of history than a readiness to try to remake history.

JOE CLARK, External Affairs Minister, discussing the ancient animosities of the Middle East at a news conference in Damascus, 11 March 1991, quoted by Richard Gwyn in *The Toronto Star* the following day. Clark's aphorism was variously reported. Rod Goodman weighed the differences in the versions in his column in *The Toronto Star*, 24 March 1991. It seems Clark said: "There is an enormous amount of history here and a great consciousness of history and almost more consciousness of history than there is a willingness to make history."

HABITS

Giving up a habit is consistent with loving yourself, seeing yourself as deserving the very best. Concentrating on your weaknesses will never help you to give up a habit.
JAMES D'ADAMO, naturopath, *The D'Adamo Diet* (1989).

HALIFAX
See also NOVA SCOTIA

Through those years this city of Halifax stood like a sentinel. It was the one spot where the Union Jack was never lowered. It waves now and will wave as long as there is a flag on the flagstaff in the world.
STANLEY BALDWIN, Prime Minister of Great Britain, speaking in Halifax, 18 Aug. 1927, quoted by Charles H. Mackintosh in *Chronicles of Canada's Diamond Jubilee* (1929). Haligonians remain loyal to British and Canadian institutions, but the Union Jack was lowered and the Maple Leaf was raised in 1965.

Heaven is my home doubtless. But Halifax is my haven.

BLISS CARMAN, poet, reception in Halifax in 1928, quoted by John Coldwell Adams in *Sir Charles God Damn* (1985).

In short, Halifax seems to us Canada's most humane city.
MECHTILD HOPPENRATH and CHARLES OBERDORF, authors, *First-Class Canada* (1987).

I have lived not only in Toronto but also in New York, London, Ottawa, and assorted smaller places in Ontario, New Brunswick, and California, and all of them had their attractions. But not one had the peculiar chemistry of charm and romance — the formula of physical drama and social intimacy — that makes Halifax the best town I've ever known. Haligonians share the secret, and the secret is the sea. They don't think about the ocean all the time, but it shapes the city's character, keeps its pride of history fresh, and makes its people closer to one another than city folk usually are.
HARRY BRUCE, essayist, "Halifax: The Best Town I've Ever Known," *Down Home: Notes of a Maritime Son* (1988).

HANDICAPS

It is one of the functions of heroic people to remind us that the happenstances of fate, however harsh, need not result in despair and demoralization.

HUMPHRY OSMOND, psychiatrist, "Inspiration," *Predicting the Past: Memos on the Enticing Universe of Possibility* (1981) produced by Jerome Agel.

At the time, I was just a kid who had been told she was different from the others, and being different was obviously something very bad. It would be years before I figured out that the word ["retard"] was a label people used to describe someone whom they consider less than normal. It would be years before I realized that "normal" was not quite the exalted state it was cracked up to be. It would be years before I realized that children use words like "freak" and "retard" to describe anyone who doesn't quite fit into their accepted pattern of appearance or behaviour; someone who is skinnier than the others, or fatter, even someone who chooses a black crayon for a drawing (rather than a red or blue one) and then has the nerve to colour outside the lines everyone else is following.

DIANE DUPUY, founder and director of the Famous People Players, *Dare to Dream: The Story of the Famous People Players* (1988) written with Liane Heller.

You broke the boy, / But you won't break the man . . . / Gonna be a man in motion. / All I need is a pair of wheels.

Theme song, "Man in Motion," words by JOHN PARR, music by David Foster based on his "Theme from St. Elmo's Fire," quoted by Rick Hansen in *Rick Hansen: Man in Motion* (1987) written with Jim Taylor.

Well, the circumference of the earth was 24,901.55 miles. That seemed an appropriate target and a good natural tie-in. With that as our guide we finalized a route based on political, geographical and climatic conditions to cover as many countries as possible.

RICK HANSEN, wheelchair athlete and fund-raiser, *Rick Hansen: Man in Motion* (1987) written with Jim Taylor. Hansen propelled himself on the Man in Motion world tour. Between March 1985 and May 1987, the Vancouver athlete covered some 40,000 kilometres — 24,901.55 miles — the distance around the world.

Life is the development of what you have, with an acceptance of the things you cannot change.

HUGH MacMILLAN, Director, Ontario Crippled Children's Centre, quoted by Adrian Cloete in *The Toronto Star*, 20 Feb. 1989.

But I sometimes think Canadians' favourite games are the Special Olympics for the handicapped. The closest thing to a national hero we have had in the 1980s is a cancer-ridden young man who tried to run across the country from ocean to ocean on one leg. Perhaps Terry Fox reminded us of all those wounded princes, heroines, animals, and anonymous ordinary folk in our literature who battled on defiantly though hurt beyond repair in body or mind, tenaciously refusing to submit to the exigencies of an apparently cruel universe and an inexorably hostile environment. These have run a streak of stoic iron through our soul and helped make us puritans, though it is a puritanism tempered by orgy.

WILLIAM KILBOURN, historian, "The Peaceable Kingdom Still," *Daedalus: Journal of the American Academy of Arts and Sciences*, "In Search of Canada," Fall 1988.

Most of us, if we are being honest, would prefer to get through the day without being confronted by the mentally handicapped. The vision of a human frame devoid of sensible consciousness strikes at primitive fears. It seems a form of living death.

> JOHN FRASER, author and editor, "Diary," *Saturday Night*, Nov. 1988.

HAPPINESS

There are many different happinesses — and we never have them all at once — because that would be perfect happiness and that is something the gods do not allow to mortals. We have some at one period of our lives and yet others at another. Perfect happiness I have never had — never will have. Yet there have been, after all, many wonderful and exquisite hours in my life.

> L.M. MONTGOMERY, author, diary, 13 March 1921, *The Selected Journals of L.M. Montgomery: Volume II: 1910-1921* (1987) edited by Mary Rubio and Elizabeth Waterston.

Happiness is not geometrical, but flows in from all sides wherever you look. If you are overwhelmed, you might as well relax in the whirl. It's winning. All you can learn is ecstatic surrender. Is it reprehensible alchemy to pleasure yourself with inevitable cataclysm? Do you call *that* expediency? To die, but to die with your eye on the need for submission? No, that's, as they say, God's will.

> ELIZABETH SMART, novelist and diarist, "My Life" (1951), *Autobiographies* (1987) edited by Christina Burridge.

Happiness is a certain degree of calm, a certain degree of having your feet firmly rooted in the ground, of being aware that however miserable things are at the moment that they're probably not going to be so bad after awhile, or possibly they may be going very well now, but you must keep your head because they're not going to be so good later. Happiness is a very deep and dispersed state. It's not a kind of excitement.

> ROBERTSON DAVIES, man-of-letters, interviewed by Paul Soles in 1972, *Conversations with Robertson Davies* (1989) edited by J. Madison Davis.

We wanted happiness for her above all, perhaps already intuiting the phrase that was to guide our thought: "Happiness first and all else follows."

> PATRICIA JOUDRY, playwright, . . . *And the Children Played* (1975). The playwright and her husband John Steele are wishing happiness for their daughter.

Things are just right once you realize they're never going to be just right.

> RICHARD J. NEEDHAM, newspaperman and aphorist, *The Globe and Mail*, 19 May 1975.

Happiness is a by-product which sneaks up on you, unsought, when you're busy at something else.

> BETTY JANE WYLIE, author, *Beginnings: A Book for Widows* (1977).

The famous story was with our manager. He sat me down one morning and said, "Frank, give me the bottom line. I know you guys love Canada, you enjoy being there, your families and friends are there, your roots are in Canada and all that" — and he knew he couldn't persuade us with money, because we've really never cared about the trappings — "but you come here, to the U.S., and your careers will flourish, they'll flower, you'll become truly international stars." He was trying desperately to think of something, and finally he came out with this line: "You know, Frank, there's more to life than happiness."

> FRANK SHUSTER, comedian, half of the comedy team of Wayne and Shuster, quoted by Jack McIver in *The Toronto Star*, 21 Sept. 1980.

Crying in times of loss is healing. But I try to stop as soon as possible, so I have the strength to face the happiness I suspect is lurking around the corner.

> LYNNE GORDON, broadcaster, author of *Working without a Net* (1986).

Happiness to me is not a word to describe a feeling in the present; nor is it a state I can or should feel entitled to in the future. Conditioned as I am not to feel happy, I tend to see the pursuit of happiness as an act of sin or selfishness. So when I am rewarded with a day of contentment or a day of achievement and have a sense of well-being, I feel guilty, feeling that the good feeling isn't something I am entitled to and is really only a calm stretch of water in the middle of a stormy sea.

> LUCINDA VARDEY, author, *Belonging: A Book for the Questioning Catholic Today* (1988).

To crawl out still further on a shaky limb, I'll even hazard this thought: Happiness is living solidly in the present reality while regarding it with some of the indulgence people usually reserve for fiction.

> GEORGE FALUDY, Hungarian-born poet, *Notes from the Rainforest* (1988).

Most men and women want to find happiness, but you don't *find* happiness any more than you *find* steel. You refine steel from the rough ore and you fashion happiness from life's opportunities.

> CHARLES TEMPLETON, media personality, *Succeeding* (1989).

HEALING
See also MEDICINE

For many years, accounts of cures among primitive peoples by medicine men, shamans and the like aroused little attention among psychiatrists. The development of modern psychotherapy has drawn attention to the mystery of the mechanism of psychological healing and shown how many of its details still puzzle us.

> HENRI ELLENBERGER, historian of psychiatry, *The Discovery of the Unconscious* (1970).

However, due to the folk belief that good health depends on the availability of doctors, diagnosis, drugs, and hospital beds, resistance to alternative models of child health and welfare must be anticipated.

> CYRIL GREENLAND, psychiatric social worker, *Preventing CAN Deaths: An International Study of Deaths Due to Child Abuse and Neglect* (1987).

HEALTH
See also HEALTH CARE
MEDICINE

One key to understanding what priority a country places on the health consequences of national defence and energy choices is the precision of its measurements of resultant health effects.

> ROSALIE BERTELL, anti-nuclear activist, *No Immediate Danger? Prognosis for a Radioactive Earth* (1985).

By selling inexpensive shoes in the Third World, the Bata Shoe Organization has probably done more for world health than a dozen Albert Schweitzers.

> KILDARE DOBBS, travel writer, *En Route*, June 1990.

You cannot heal where you cannot hurt.

> ROBIN SKELTON, man-of-letters, aphorism, May 1990.

HEALTH CARE
See also MEDICARE
MEDICINE

The poorer you are, the less healthy you are likely to be, over a shortened lifetime. This is one of the most neglected facts in Canadian health care.

> NICHOLAS REGUSH, columnist and author, *Condition Critical* (1987).

The Canadian system is socialized insurance, not socialized medicine. . . . The Canadian system gives governments control over the reimbursement function, not the delivery of care; it is a public health insurance system, not a public health service.

> ROBERT G. EVANS, economist and health-care specialist, "'We'll Take Care of It for You': Health Care in the Canadian

Community," *Daedalus: Journal of the American Academy of Arts and Sciences,* "In Search of Canada," Fall 1988.

The Canadian approach to funding health care may be markedly superior to the American on various objective and widely held criteria — many students of health care, including this one, believe that it is — and if so, the Canadian system is an important and rather rare collective achievement. Like beating the Russians at hockey, beating the Americans at anything is a source of considerable satisfaction.

The more basic point is simply that the Canadian health care system, precisely because it *is* different, responds to and reflects significant, if perhaps subtle, features of "Canadianness." It is one of the most convincing forms of evidence, perhaps *the* most convincing, that we are not Americans after all. (It may be difficult for non-Canadians, whether Americans or others, to appreciate what a relief that is.) But our approach differs from the various European health care systems as well, although we are closer to Europe than to the United States, and again the differences are indicative of underlying cultural values.

ROBERT G. EVANS, economist and health-care specialist, "'We'll Take Care of It for You': Health Care in the Canadian Community," *Daedalus: Journal of the American Academy of Arts and Sciences,* "In Search of Canada," Fall 1988.

Health care in Canada is free, because to charge the patient is to tax the sick.

ROBERT G. EVANS, economist and health-care specialist, "'We'll Take Care of It for You': Health Care in the Canadian Community," *Daedalus: Journal of the American Academy of Arts and Sciences,* "In Search of Canada," Fall 1988.

Canada's national health system is much admired by many in the United States, but you don't see American politicians rushing to pay for a similar service.

PETER JENNINGS, Toronto-born ABC anchorman, *Maclean's,* 25 June 1990.

Of all the benefits enjoyed by Canadians, health care is probably the most precious. Little wonder, as Canada has one of the most comprehensive health-care systems in the world. By comparison, universal access to health care in the United States is non-existent. In the United States, Medicare is available to persons over sixty-five and Medicaid for the poor (requiring a means test). For the vast majority of Americans, the choices are between expensive private health insurance (which Americans cannot afford) — paying their own medical expenses — or doing without medical care.

It has been said that Canada's program of health care is "a triumph of astute social planning and considerable will." They are both important. It is, however, very costly, absorbing 8.6% of the Gross National Product. The less-efficient American health-care system costs more: 10.6% per capita of the Gross National Product, and still leaves millions without public or private coverage.

MARJORIE MONTGOMERY BOWKER, retired family-court judge and critic of the Free Trade Agreement, *On Guard for Thee: An Independent Analysis Based on the Actual Text of The Canada-U.S. Free Trade Agreement* (1988).

HEART
See also EMOTIONS

One of these days I'm going to fly to the stars / And find out why they shine / I have a feeling that the reason they do / Is to light up that moonlight heart of mine.

CONNIE KALDOR, singer and songwriter, "Calais," quoted by Ellen Schwartz in *Born a Woman: Seven Canadian Women Singer-Songwriters* (1988).

HEAVEN

From what I've heard of the place, who in his right mind would ever want to get into Heaven even for a short visit.

GORDON SINCLAIR, media personality,

opinion expressed in 1971, quoted by Scott Young in *Gordon Sinclair: A Life . . . and Then Some* (1987).

Up at the top there's what used to be called Heaven with what used to be called God. Only now we've replaced Heaven with a kind of Utopian vision of what humanity could be if only. . . . Fill in the blank. The trouble with real life is once you try to implement Utopia, you end up with the Inferno. You end up pulling out a lot of fingernails from the people who don't agree with you.

> MARGARET ATWOOD, poet and novelist, interviewed by Alan Twigg in *Strong Voices: Conversations with Fifty Canadian Authors* (1988).

HERITAGE
See also TRADITION

It is the most unpoetical of lands; there is no scope for imagination, here all is new — the very soil seems newly formed; there is no hoary ancient grandeur in these woods, no recollections of former deeds connected with the country.

> CATHARINE PARR TRAILL, pioneer author, *The Backwoods of Canada* (1836).

So let us give you our definition of a heritage building. Any building that is structurally sound and for which an economically viable use can be found is a heritage building.

> PIERRE BERTON, Chairman, Heritage Canada Foundation, address, Empire Club of Canada, Toronto, 11 Feb. 1982.

The passion for roots — the mass pastime of family history — represses the sense of suffocation that family photographs can engender.

> MICHAEL IGNATIEFF, social commentator, descendant of White Russian exiles and Scottish Canadians, *The Russian Album* (1987).

It is no exaggeration to say that Quebecers, in their fascination with modernity, have made change into an end in itself. The result has been a crisis in the passing on of values. The problem is not that Quebecers no longer hold the heritage of their ancestors in the same veneration as in the past; it is that the generation which today controls all aspects of public life has lost its sense of heritage altogether.

> LÉON DION, political scientist, "The Mystery of Quebec," *Daedalus: Journal of the American Academy of Arts and Sciences*, "In Search of Canada," Fall 1988.

North York has no history — just a bunch of farmers.

> Remark made by a member of the Heritage Committee responsible for the maintenance of Gibson House, North York, Ont., 1990.

HEROES
See also LEADERSHIP

In his speech the present writer sorely wounded his pride by being guilty of an egregious slip of the tongue. In a fervent eulogy of Canada's heroic pioneers of both national origins he mispronounced the words, *nos grands héros*, so that they sounded like *nos grands zeros*; our great zeroes, our heroic ciphers!

> WILLIAM SHERWOOD FOX, former President of the University of Western Ontario, *Silken Lines and Silver Hooks: A Life-Long Fisherman Recounts His Catch* (1954).

Canadians do not like heroes, and so they do not have them. They do not even have great men in the accepted sense of the word.

> GEORGE WOODCOCK, author, *Canada and the Canadians* (1970).

Canadians do not only lack heroes. They lack a really heroic history. Consider what has taken place on Canadian soil.

> GEORGE WOODCOCK, author, *Canada and the Canadians* (1970).

As the economy dims, our heroes shine even brighter, casting their light on the dreary lives of all us unfortunates.

NORMAN JEWISON, film director, address, Empire Club of Canada, Toronto, 5 April 1984.

There is a deep well of hero-worship in any free country for anyone who can attain a position of power and still be accepted as a representative of "the little guy." He gets that acceptance because he dares to take runs at society's accepted values as well as at random targets of opportunity.
SCOTT YOUNG, author and biographer, *Gordon Sinclair: A Life . . . and Then Some* (1987).

A hero is someone who can surpass his own limitations to do the extraordinary. There's nothing real about a person who does only extraordinary things. It takes a real man to touch the real colours.
R.H. THOMSON, actor, creator of the TV roles of Charles A. Grant and Frederick G. Banting, quoted by Tony Atherton in *The Ottawa Citizen*, 15 Oct. 1988.

We don't need any more military heroics; we need heroes of peace.
FRANK FEATHER, futurologist, *G-Forces: Reinventing the World — The 35 Global Forces Restructuring Our World* (1989).

It is part of the civic genius — part of the Canadian genius, too — to reduce the heroic to the banal.
JAN MORRIS, Anglo-Welsh traveller, "Suddenly Saskatoon," *Saturday Night*, July-Aug. 1990.

Historical heroes, who inhabit the national psyche and feed the imagination of most peoples of the world, are sadly absent from Canadian life. The few exciting ones are apportioned to the two major linguistic groups and never fulfil a national mandate.
LAURIER LaPIERRE, historian and broadcaster, *1759: The Battle for Canada* (1990).

HISTORY & HISTORIANS
See also HISTORY, CANADIAN

We must somehow escape on the one hand from our obsession with the moment and on the other hand from our obsession with history. In freeing ourselves from time and attempting a balance between the demands of time and space we can develop conditions favourable to an interest in cultural activity.
HAROLD ADAMS INNIS, economic historian, "A Plea for Time" (1950), *The Bias of Communication* (1951).

History, like a menstruating woman, must periodically shed blood.
IRVING LAYTON, poet, letter dated 20 March 1968, *An Unlikely Affair: The Irving Layton-Dorothy Rath Correspondence* (1980).

The encounter between character and circumstance is essentially a story.
DONALD CREIGHTON, historian, "History and Literature" (1971), *Towards the Discovery of Canada: Selected Essays* (1972).

Historians who tread too closely on the heels of the present are likely to be kicked in the teeth. The dead have few to defend them; the living are easily aroused.
DESMOND MORTON, historian, *NDP: The Dream of Power* (1974).

The present study . . . is not a work of objectivity because it lacks the two prerequisites — ignorance and omniscience.
DESMOND MORTON, historian, discussing his own study, *NDP: The Dream of Power* (1974).

I am a historian and historians are supposed to believe that they can transport themselves in time to recapture experience swept away by the death of earlier generations. In even the most rigorously scientific history, there is a resurrectionary hope at work, a faith in the power of

imagination and empathy to vault the gulf of time.
>MICHAEL IGNATIEFF, social commentator, *The Russian Album* (1987).

History has less authority than memory, less legitimacy than tradition. History can never speak with the one voice that our need for belonging requires. It cannot heal the hurt of loss. Our knowledge of the past cannot satisfy our desire for the past. What we can know about the past and what we want from it are different things.
>MICHAEL IGNATIEFF, social commentator, *The Russian Album* (1987).

Mass makes history. In history we see the crowd, in art we see the face. In art, a single person is enough to animate a painting, a play, a movie, a book; but in history, the individual is important mainly as the symbol of mass.
>JAMES BACQUE, investigator, *Other Losses: An Investigation into the Mass Deaths of German Prisoners at the Hands of the French and Americans after World War II* (1989).

History for me is a whole steamer trunk full of stories.
>JACK HODGINS, novelist, quoted by H.J. Kirchhoff in *The Globe and Mail*, 27 Sept. 1990.

History teaches us that men behave wisely once they have exhausted all the alternatives.
>FRANK McKENNA, New Brunswick Premier, quoted by Tom Kierans in *The Globe and Mail's Report on Business Magazine*, Dec. 1990.

History is what the dead say to the living.
>AL PURDY, poet, quoted by Susan Walker in *The Toronto Star*, 13 Nov. 1990.

HISTORY, CANADIAN

See also HISTORY & HISTORIANS

Clerk: What is the use of all this quibbling, in this country, conquered by our arms, and which hasn't even a history?
Garneau: I shall write the history which you do not even know exists. You will see that our ancestors yielded only when outnumbered. There are defeats which are as glorious as victories.
>This exchange of opinion is said to have taken place between an unnamed English-language law clerk and the youthful lawyer and future historian FRANÇOIS-XAVIER GARNEAU in a law office in Quebec City in 1828; Garneau went on to chronicle the history of the Quebec people in such tomes as *History of Canada from the Time of Its Discovery till the Union Year 1840-41* (1862) translated by Andrew Bell.

Nothing can be of greater importance as a factor in the education of our youth than a good Canadian history for the use of the schools, in their education as future citizens particularly, as the mass which will before many years commence to form public opinion.
>DUNCAN CAMPBELL SCOTT, poet, "The Mermaid Inn," 28 Jan. 1893, *At the Mermaid Inn* (1979) edited by Barrie Davies.

Comparatively speaking, we Ontarians have no past, only yesterdays. True, there are chronicles of what the English and the French did to the Indians and to each other three hundred years ago. But our ancestors are all foreigners, immigrants, the earliest of whom arrived less than two centuries ago.
>MABEL DUNHAM, librarian and historian, *Grand River* (1945).

And we must associate ourselves not with a European past of a few hundred years or a few thousand years but with the past of our own country which is reckoned in millions of years.
>ROBERTSON DAVIES, man-of-letters, interviewed by Margaret Penman in 1975, *Conversations with Robertson Davies* (1989) edited by J. Madison Davis.

There's no blood in our history.
> PIERRE BERTON, author and media personality, interviewed by Alan Twigg in *Strong Voices: Conversations with Fifty Canadian Authors* (1988). The remark was made in the context of distinguishing between dramatic and documentary treatments of Canadian historical subjects.

I spent my entire life writing the history of a country that no longer exists.
> DONALD CREIGHTON, historian, quoted by Sandra Djwa in *The Politics of the Imagination: A Life of F.R. Scott* (1987).

Some people think that the history of Ontario is all 19th and 18th century. History is what happened two weeks ago.
> IAN E. WILSON, Ontario Provincial Archivist, quoted by Joe Serge in *The Toronto Star*, 10 Oct. 1988.

For much of the twentieth century, the writing of Canadian history has been a contest of denial. The liberal school of Arthur Lower and Frank Underhill sought to deny our British ties, and so emphasized our North American qualities. The conservative school of Donald Creighton and W.L. Morton sought to deny American influence, and so stressed the European link. Somewhere along the way, it was settled: henceforth, we would deny both, in favour of a fictitious, rootless Canadianism, whose guarantor would now be the state.
> ANDREW COYNE, journalist, *Saturday Night*, July 1989.

I still say the history of Canada is in shoeboxes under people's beds.
> JOYCE BEATON, social historian and former publisher of *Early Canadian Life*, quoted by Jeff Wilks in *The Muskoka Advance*, 28 Jan. 1990.

Canadians refuse to share a common history. And so history, the collective remembrance of moments past, is not an emotional act in this country. It is largely a political one.
> LAURIER LaPIERRE, historian and broadcaster, *1759: The Battle for Canada* (1990).

HOBBIES

You're lucky if you've laid in a store of gentle but effective palliatives — habits, hobbies. And if you haven't, now's the time to start. Anything from train-spotting to medieval history can come to your rescue! Botany or fungi-hunting, embroidery, modern painting, music from baroque to pop, collecting snuffboxes, first editions, stamps, matchboxes, Victory underwear — they can all take your mind off your broken heart, if only for a minute or two at a time.
> ELIZABETH SMART, novelist and diarist, "How to Mend a Broken Heart" (1982), *Autobiographies* (1987) edited by Christina Burridge.

HOCKEY
> *See also* BALLARD, HAROLD
> GRETZKY, WAYNE
> HOCKEY VIOLENCE
> SPORTS

There is pictorial evidence of a hockey-like game (Kalv) being played on ice in The Netherlands in the early 16th century. The game probably was first played in North America on Dec. 25, 1855, at Kingston, Ontario, Canada, but Halifax also lays claim to priority.
> DAVID A. BOEHM, editor, *Guinness Sports Record Book* (1989).

Your Imperial Oil hockey broadcast bringing you Foster Hewitt! (fanfare) "Hello, Canada, and hockey fans in the United States and Newfoundland."
> Opening of *Hockey Night in Canada*, the country's most popular program, first heard on national radio in 1931 and first seen on national television in 1952. The quoted line is the familiar salutation of the gravel-voiced sports broadcaster FOSTER HEWITT.

During one game I was shouting, "He shoots! He scores!" when my voice suddenly soared to a note so high that even a Metropolitan Opera soprano would have envied me. Quickly I apologetically remarked, "I almost blew a fuse on that one." Soon there arrived from widely scattered sources every type of fuse that man had devised.

FOSTER HEWITT, hockey broadcaster, *Hockey Night in Canada: The Maple Leafs' Story* (1953).

Les Canadiens sont là!
"The Canadiens are there!" This is the celebrated "battle cry" of the Montreal Canadiens. It recalls the refrain of an old Franco-Ontario folk song which runs: "Les canayens sont un peu là! / Ah! ah! les canayens sont un peu là!" (The Canadiens are always ready! / Ah! ah! The Canadiens are always ready!) The words and music appear in Edith Fowke's *Folklore of Canada* (1976).

"But it was in the early 1950s that *les Canadiens* really began to *sont là*," according to TRENT FRAYNE in *The Mad Men of Hockey* (1974). Anglo hockey fans had to make do with "Go, Habs, go!" which is based on the club's nickname, Habitants.

Every boy in Canada who owns a pair of skates hopes to play for Toronto when he grows up — and most of the good ones do!
CONN SMYTHE, hockey personality, quoted by Leslie Roberts in "Toronto," *The Saturday Evening Post*, 22 March 1952.

Fire on Ice
Evocative phrase associated with the game of hockey, especially with the "fire-wagon" style of play identified with the Montreal Canadiens between 1955 and 1985. The three words have been used by writers as book titles. *Fire on Ice: Hockey Superstars* (1974) was written by STAN FISCHLER, and SCOTT MORRISON wrote *Fire on Ice: Hockey's Greatest Series* (1987).

Da, da, Canada! / Nyet, nyet, Soviet!
Fans from Canada chanted these words (Yes, yes, Canada! / No, no, Soviet!) at the eight games in the Soviet-Canada series, 1972.

I no believe in pyramids; I no believe in any man upstairs. I just believe in the big fellow.
BORJE SALMING, Swedish-born defence-man with the Maple Leafs, with his limited command of English dismissing "pyramid power" and divine power and affirming his belief in himself, quoted by Frank Orr in *The Toronto Star*, 24 Dec. 1976.

Dreams really do come true, I thought to myself as I sat in the stands of Maple Leaf Gardens on that September day in 1973 when I first reported to the Toronto Maple Leafs. The building was dark, and I wanted to be alone, just to have time to think. It was an unbelievable feeling sitting there. I'd finally made it. There I was at the Gardens, about to begin playing for the Maple Leafs, the team I had cheered for like crazy as a kid. I sat there, realizing that everything I had dreamed about had come true.
LANNY McDONALD, hockey player, *Lanny* (1987) written with Steve Simmons.

Television ice hockey is a pestilence on a par with the hemlock looper and a pandemic of psoriasis combined.

It is a larger nuisance than the totalled efforts of municipal, provincial and federal governments and looms larger as a danger to the future of mankind than both baker's bread and the five-eighths-ounce jigger.

In short, it is nasty, boring, pernicious, deadening, silly, obnoxious, tedious and silly stuff.

It turns a large proportion of the population into gibbering idiots for six months of the year.
RAY GUY, humorist, "Breasting a Raging Tide of Madness," *That Far Greater Bay* (1976).

The National Hockey League is a business. Its business is entertainment. The entertainment it presents is sport.
JOHN A. ZIEGLER, Jr., President, National Hockey League, address, Empire Club of Canada, Toronto, 26 Jan. 1978.

Although European philosophers have argued for centuries about the purpose of life, in Canada this is well established. For any God-fearing young Canadian the ultimate reward is to be chosen for the NHL All-Star Game. If he later goes to Heaven, that is so much gravy.

> ERIC NICOL and DAVE MORE, humorists, *The Joy of Hockey* (1978).

How would you like a job where, every time you make a mistake, a big red light goes on and 18,000 people boo?

> Attributed to hockey player JACQUES PLANTE in 1985.

This is the only country in the world where, in thousands of gardens, tomato plants are held up with broken hockey sticks. This is a unique Canadian happening.

> ROBERT HARNEY, Director of the Multicultural History Society of Ontario, quoted by Joe Serge in *The Toronto Star*, 3 Aug. 1987.

Baseball can have its perfect dimensions, its undeniable drama, but hockey, for all its wrongs, still has the potential to deliver a momentary, flashing magic that is found in no other game we play.

> ROY MacGREGOR, columnist, *The Ottawa Citizen*, 21 April 1987.

Its funny, most peeples thinks of hocky as Canda's nashnul sport. It aint. Its La-Crotch, wich is now mostly plaid indores. It was thunk up by our abridgeinal peeples lookin fer sumthin to do with ther snowshoes wen they got all warp.

> DON HARRON, comedian, in the person of Charlie Farquharson, *Cum Buy the Farm* (1987).

I have many complicated notes about hockey, but at this point I can't make headnor-tail of them. I have also written this: *What matters to me about hockey is that to play it well requires both intelligence and skill, mind and body, and when a young man plays it well he is full of grace and glory.* That's not the kind of thing a sportswriter

writes. I'm not one. Neither am I a *rink-rat*. I am nothing more or less than me.

> PAUL QUARRINGTON, novelist and humorist as well as hockey enthusiast, *Hometown Heroes: On the Road with Canada's National Hockey Team* (1988).

Now back to you, Dick.

> Characteristic remark of DANNY GALLIVAN, Montreal Canadiens hockey broadcaster from 1952 to 1984, turning the microphone over to fellow broadcaster and sports personality Dick Irvin, *Now Back to You, Dick* (1988).

What sport does *Hockey Night in Canada* cover?

> TERRY JOHNSON, humorist, *Quick Quiz for Slow People* (1988).

Cannonading drives! Booming blasts! Scintillating saves. Negotiating contact with the puck! Spinnerama!

> A few of the neologisms associated with broadcaster DANNY GALLIVAN, "the loquacious lyricist of hockey" who covered Montreal Canadiens games from 1952 to 1984, some of which are noted by Brian McFarlane in *All New Hockey Quiz* (1989).

But I smile at the small-town myth for the harmless, happy days it gave me and God knows how many tens of thousands of others. Hockey, for most of us, was the first time — and so often the only time — we ever felt we truly mattered.

> KEN DRYDEN, sportsman, and Roy MacGregor, journalist, *Home Game* (1989).

The equipment that stayed up on the shelf has come down again. The boy becomes a man, the player a fan, a coach, a father, now a player again, and the game goes on.

> ROY MacGREGOR, journalist, and KEN DRYDEN, sportsman, *Home Game* (1989).

I love the self-discovery. Life off ice is so complicated, its outcomes smudged, its motivations rationalized and finessed, the picture you get of yourself so unclear. On the ice, you see your elemental self, whether you like it or not — do you try hard? do you quit? are you fair? are you selfish? do you give? are you willing to take risks? do you care too much or too little? do you fit in with a team on the ice, and off?

KEN DRYDEN, sportsman, and Roy Mac-Gregor, journalist, *Home Game* (1989).

Hockey is Canada's game. It may also be Canada's national theatre. On its frozen stage, each night the stuff of life is played out: ambition, hope, pride and fear, love and friendship, the fight for honour for city, team, each other, themselves. The puck flips one way, bounces another, and the players set out to control and direct it. It takes them where they never planned to go. It tests them. And in struggling to get it back, with the millions who watch in the arena or by television, the players find out who they really are. Like the bearpits in Shakespeare's time, we attend hockey games as our national theatre. It is a place where the monumental themes of Canadian life are played out — English and French, East and West, Canada and the U.S., Canada and the world, the timeless tensions of commerce and culture, our struggle to survive and civilize winter.

ROY MacGREGOR, journalist, and KEN DRYDEN, sportsman, *Home Game* (1989).

The Maple Leafs aren't playing this week so they aren't losing.

DICK BEDDOES, hockey personality, personal communication, 6 Feb. 1989.

Who wants to be Prime Minister if he can be Maple Leaf captain?

DICK BEDDOES, hockey personality, personal communication, 6 Feb. 1989.

Hockey is best described as warfare under wraps.

DICK BEDDOES, hockey personality, *Pal Hal: An Uninhibited, No-Holds-Barred Account of the Life and Times of Harold Ballard* (1989).

Americans could never, will never and cannot understand Shakespeare. They're far more fascinated with Cabbage Patch Dolls, the Hoola Hoop and the local hockey team, which is largely made up of Canadians. That's the best joke of all.

MARLON BRANDO, film star on location in Toronto, quoted by Murray Campbell in *The Globe and Mail*, 5 Sept. 1989.

Throughout the years ahead, just as in the past, NHL hockey will remain one of the most exciting team games, an awesome exhibition of strength, speed, endurance and finesse wherever it is played.

BRIAN McFARLANE, sports broadcaster, *One Hundred Years of Hockey* (1989).

Don is widely known as Grapes (if his last name were Grapes he'd likely be known as Cherry).

TRENT FRAYNE, sports columnist, writing about hockey broadcaster Don Cherry, *Maclean's*, 6 Nov. 1989.

Hockey is our winter ballet and in many ways our own national drama.

MORLEY CALLAGHAN, novelist, "The Game that Makes a Nation," *Riding on the Roar of the Crowd: A Hockey Anthology* (1989) edited by David Gowdey. Callaghan wrote glowingly about "our great northern ballet, the hockey game."

Canada is made up of half-failed hockey players — and half women — all of us involved in a shared delusion, whether in a church league in Toronto or the Wild Goose League in Saskatchewan.

DICK BEDDOES, sports personality, *Greatest Hockey Stories* (1990).

Okay. Drop the blessed puck. Maybe the Maple Leafs will win another Stanley Cup before the year 2018. Perhaps, too, the New York Rangers, who haven't won one since 1940. Doesn't matter who wins. If the game is good, we all win.

DICK BEDDOES, sports personality, *Greatest Hockey Stories* (1990).

Hockeywood
Title of the chapter in Wayne Gretzky's

Gretzky: An Autobiography (1990) written with Rick Reilly that deals with how he adjusted to life in Encino, California, after Edmonton, Alta. Gretzky credits the term to MIKE DOWNEY, columnist for *The Los Angeles Times.*

You know, I've held women and babies and jewels and money, but nothing will ever feel as good as holding that Cup.

WAYNE GRETZKY, hockey personality, referring to holding aloft the Stanley Cup, symbol of hockey supremacy, *Gretzky: An Autobiography* (1990) written with Rick Reilly.

HOCKEY VIOLENCE
See also HOCKEY

The Canadians were the inventors of the body check, the penalty bench, and the widespread view of fans that athletes who shirk bodily contact are pansies.

KARL ADOLF SCHERER, European hockey historian, quoted by Paul Quarrington in *Hometown Heroes: On the Road with Canada's National Hockey Team* (1988).

So don't tell me there's no hope for this game. The National Hockey League may have come to the conclusion that clutching and grabbing is as much a part of the game as scoring goals, they may have convinced themselves that violence is a necessary evil when it is necessary in no other sport, but hockey has not been destroyed by such persistent stupidity. Organized hockey may be out of control, greed may be too much in control — but when a game can still draw children to a raw outdoor rink in February there is reason to cheer.

ROY MacGREGOR, journalist, and KEN DRYDEN, sportsman, *Home Game* (1989).

You got to hit first.

BRIAN "SPINNER" SPENCER, Maple Leaf hockey player, quoted by Dick Beddoes in *The Toronto Star*, 14 Jan. 1989.

Violence in sports is father to violence in everyday life.

Sentence from the judgement of Ontario Provincial Court Judge SIDNEY HARRIS as recalled by Toronto District Court Judge Marie Corbett in upholding the assault conviction handed to NHL hockey player Dino Ciccarelli, quoted by Wendy Darroch in *The Toronto Star*, 30 Dec. 1989.

Intimidation's always going to be part of our game. I just don't know about standing back and watching two guys fight two or three times in a game.

WAYNE GRETZKY, hockey superstar, quoted by Eric Duhatschek in *The Toronto Star*, 22 Jan. 1991.

Hockey is the only team sport in the world that actually *encourages* fighting. I have no idea why we let it go on. The game itself is so fast, so exciting, so much fun to watch, why do we have to turn ice red so often? Why do the best shots in a game have to be on somebody's nose instead of somebody's net?

WAYNE GRETZKY, hockey personality, *Gretzky: An Autobiography* (1990) written with Rick Reilly.

HOLIDAYS

If you really are a writer, you are at it all the time. There are no holidays; you don't really want holidays.

ROBERTSON DAVIES, man-of-letters, interviewed by Gordon Roper in 1968, *Conversations with Robertson Davies* (1989) edited by J. Madison Davis.

Holidays are the greatest learning experience unknown to man.

FRANK OGDEN, futurologist, *obiter dictum*, 1983.

NEW YEAR'S DAY
When I go I'm going to take New Year's with me.

GUY LOMBARDO and his Royal Canadians orchestra ushered in the New Year from the ballroom of the Waldorf-Astoria in New York, first on radio and then on television from the 1930s to his death in 1977.

EASTER

Army recruit was asked by his superiors to list his religious affiliations. He wrote confidently, "C. and E." The officer in charge tore the paper in shreds and roared at him: "You mean C. of E., Church of England, idiot!" The recruit shook his head and retorted: "No, it's C. and E. — Christmas and Easter, sir."

TOM HARPUR, religion columnist, "Soul Hunger," *Always on Sunday* (1988).

VICTORIA DAY

Any nation that continues to celebrate Queen Victoria's birthday eighty-five years after the sour-duck breathed her last must hold in its psychic cupboard of toys any number of archaic baubles that can't help but render ineffective any emergent sense of a distinctly Canadian national identity.

STEPHEN BROOK, English travel writer, *Maple Leaf Rag: Travels across Canada* (1987).

CANADA DAY

Well, it's the day when people celebrate retaining their national identity by travelling to the U.S.A. to do their shopping.

PETER PERUGINI, Vancouver restaurateur, characterizing Canada Day (formerly Dominion Day), quoted in *Liberty*, Sept. 1963.

THANKSGIVING

Actually, you can't learn a lot about something like a free-trade agreement in a year. Even Canadians don't know everything that's in it. For instance, Canadians don't seem to realize that they're going to have to change their Thanksgiving Day. That's right. It's implied in the fine print.

The Canadians celebrate Thanksgiving in October, on what is our Columbus Day, and they don't celebrate Columbus Day at all. Canadians think that Christopher Columbus discovered the New World, but they don't care. Americans, particularly

Italian-Americans, care desperately.

If the economies of Canada and the United States become more or less one economy, we can't be celebrating two different Thanksgiving Days. Think of what would happen if a customer in Winnipeg phoned a widget supplier in Pennsylvania on what the Canadians thought was an ordinary November weekday and nobody answered; he might have to phone all the way to Japan. Picture the October afternoon when a Toronto branch manager wishes a New York colleague named Sal Provolini "Happy Turkey Day" and Provolini says, "If you pass another remark like that about Christopher Columbus, I'm going to come up there and rearrange your face."

CALVIN TRILLIN, contributor to *The New Yorker*, *The Toronto Star*, 2 Feb. 1989.

REMEMBRANCE DAY

Unlike troops returning from the First and Second World Wars, who received enthusiastic official receptions upon their arrival home, Canadian Forces on peacekeeping duty do not receive such a welcome back. It is quite a letdown for those who have been wounded or have risked their lives not to be granted some public recognition. On Remembrance Day we remember those killed in both world wars and in Korea. Why do we not also honour those killed on peacekeeping duty?

FRED GAFFEN, historian with the Canadian War Museum, Ottawa, *In the Eye of the Storm: A History of Canadian Peacekeeping* (1987).

CHRISTMAS

Sunday 25th, Christmas day. I went with Madame Báby at 5 in the morning to the Cathedral Church to see the illumination of the Altar, which to those who have not seen the highly-decorated Roman Catholic Church in Europe is worth seeing. The singing or chanting was solemn. The Church was crowded. I was wrapped up very much, and wore a kind of Calech lined with eiderdown, a very comfortable head-dress; but the cold was intense for the Roman Catholics will not admit of fires in their Churches lest the Pictures should be spoiled. I saw no fine pictures.

ELIZABETH SIMCOE, diarist and wife of Governor John Graves Simcoe, diary entry, Quebec City, 1791, *Mrs. Simcoe's Diary* (1965) edited by Mary Quayle Innis.

I wanted to say Merry Christmas and de-scribe the scene to you. There's thick white snow falling softly around the house and as far off as I can see. And the lights from our Christmas tree are spilling out the window onto the new snow. You know, it just doesn't get any better than this.

DONALD SUTHERLAND, actor, describ-ing life with his wife, actress Francine Racette, in Quebec's Eastern Townships, quoted by Bronwyn Drainie in *Living the Part: John Drainie and the Dilemma of Canadian Stardom* (1988).

Christmas takes place in the depth of our northern winter. It is a time of celebration of the birth of the inner Christ in each of us. The inner Christ is the light in the darkness, the spirit in the body, the eter-nal "I am" that makes possible uncondi-tional love and tolerance.

ALEXA PETRENKO, columnist, "Food for Thought," *Ontario's Common Ground Magazine*, Winter 1990.

HOLINESS

We no longer care about the lives of the saints, yet we long for a holiness of our own.

CAROL SHIELDS, novelist, *Swann* (1987).

HOLLYWOOD

See also CALIFORNIA
FILM

Usually overlooked in the celebration of "Canadians in Hollywood" is the disap-pointing fact that they do not represent a Canadian presence in American films: they are all required to be and play Ameri-cans, which they do very well, leaving us to ponder over whether this is due to their exceptional talent or simply points up the much debated issue of "there is little dif-ference" between Canadians and Ameri-cans.

GERALD PRATLEY, film archivist, "Holly-wood: 100 Years of Canadian Content," *Film News*, No. 19, 1987.

I like to call it Houlé-wood.

NORMAND HOULÉ, art director in televi-sion and films, born in Coaticook, Que., since 1948 a resident of Hollywood, quoted by Ron Graham in "Born Again in Babylon," *Saturday Night*, June 1983.

I wandered through the city wondering what to do. There was a romantic feeling about being unemployed in Hollywood. It is among the few places in the world where idleness can be construed as a tem-porary condition preceding greatness.

DANIELLE CRITTENDEN, Toronto writer working in Hollywood, "Typist to the Stars," *The Idler*, No. 14, Sept.-Oct., 1987.

What other country would spend $10,000 of taxpayers' money to send a government official to Hollywood to pick up an Oscar award for something he had absolutely nothing — repeat, *nothing* — to do with?

ROY MacGREGOR, columnist, *The Ottawa Citizen*, 10 April 1989. The government official was Communications Minister Marcel Masse who attended the 1989 Academy Awards ceremony and ac-cepted the special Oscar awarded to the National Film Board of Canada to mark its 50th anniversary.

THE JEWISH HOLOCAUST
See also JEWISH PEOPLE

I am not a brave man, but I am not a coward either.

Characteristic remark of CHARLES A. GRANT, Toronto-born businessman cred-ited with saving the lives of Jews in Vi-enna in 1938, as recalled in later years by his wife Eleanor Grant.

A Jew at Auschwitz was murdered because he was a Jew; a Christian was murdered only if he was a saint: but there are few saints among either Jews or Christians.
> EMIL FACKENHEIM, philosopher, "Jews and Christians after Auschwitz" (1978), *The Jewish Thought of Emil Fackenheim: A Reader* (1987) edited by Michael L. Morgan.

At Auschwitz, Jews came face to face with absolute evil. They were and still are singled out by it, but in the midst of it they bear an absolute commandment: *Jews are forbidden to grant posthumous victories to Hitler.* They are commanded to survive as Jews, lest the Jewish people perish. They are commanded to remember the victims of Auschwitz, lest their memory perish. They are forbidden to despair of man and his world, and to escape into either cynicism or otherworldliness, lest they cooperate in delivering the world over to the forces of Auschwitz. Finally, they are forbidden to despair of the God of Israel, lest Judaism perish.
> EMIL FACKENHEIM, philosopher, "Jewish Faith and the Holocaust: A Fragment" (1978), *The Jewish Thought of Emil Fackenheim: A Reader* (1987) edited by Michael L. Morgan.

Did Six Million Really Die?
> Title of a tract that tried to call into question the existence of the Jewish Holocaust, written and published by ERNST ZUNDEL, the German-born, Toronto-based publisher of hate literature who in 1985 was convicted of wilfully spreading false news likely to cause injury.

Innocence was no longer a possibility. The gates of whatever Eden our childhoods might have contained had clanged shut forever. We did not want to recognize, but we *had* to recognize, that humankind is indeed capable of an evil so all-encompassing that no words could possibly describe it. No mourning for those millions of murdered innocent people will ever be enough, will ever be complete.
> MARGARET LAURENCE, novelist, Convocation Address, York University, June 1980, *Dance on the Earth: A Memoir* (1989).

For instance, during the Holocaust, if only more people had said, "Where are all *my* friends and neighbours?" it might have helped.
> TIMOTHY FINDLEY, novelist, interviewed by Alan Twigg in *Strong Voices: Conversations with Fifty Canadian Authors* (1988).

It's a sad fact that Israel and Jewish education and all the other familiar buzzwords no longer serve to rally Jews behind the community. The Holocaust, though, works every time.
> SAMUEL BELZBERG, financier and backer of the Simon Wiesenthal Center in Los Angeles, quoted by Sheldon Teitelbaum and Tom Waldman, "The Unorthodox Rabbi," *The Los Angeles Times Magazine*, 15 July 1990.

HOME
See also HOUSING

I lived, hermit-like, in the woods, after the renowned example of Robinson Crusoe, passing my time, not unpleasantly, in healthy labour; building my house and cheering my solitude with the agreeable idea of bringing home my wife and little ones — to a home of my own making.
> MAJOR SAMUEL STRICKLAND, pioneer settler, *Twenty-Seven Years in Canada West; or, The Experience of an Early Settler* (1853) edited by Agnes Strickland.

A man's home is his hassle.
> AL BOLISKA, broadcaster, *The Maharishi Says . . .* (1968).

I've only circled back to find / Many changes made by time, / And many changes in my mind. / I was looking for a place called home.
> RITA MacNEIL, composer and singer, "A Place Called Home," quoted by Myrna Kostash in *Her Own Woman: Profiles of*

Ten Canadian Women (1975) by Myrna Kostash, Melinda McCracken, Valerie Miner, Erna Paris, and Heather Robertson.

Where we used to live / I merely reside
Line from a poem in *Something Might Happen* (1989) by the author BETTY JANE WYLIE.

HOMOSEXUALITY
See also SEX

But to the Indian, a homosexual is one of the most gifted persons there is. I think all shamans are homosexual or, anyway, bisexual.
NORVAL MORRISSEAU, native artist, "My Name Is Norval Morrisseau," *The Art of Norval Morrisseau* (1979) by Lister Sinclair and Jack Pollock.

The discriminating homosexual has far more appreciation of beautiful women than the macho moron who is constantly chinning himself on his own sexuality.
EDWARD PHILLIPS, novelist, *Buried on Sunday* (1986).

I think it is the first time that someone can write without any fear of being sued by my lawyers that I am gay.
LAURIER LaPIERRE, broadcaster, affirming his sexual orientation at a rally sponsored by Equality for Gays and Lesbians Everywhere, Parliament Hill, Ottawa, 4 March 1988, quoted in *The Toronto Star* the following day.

That would be something, Svend Robinson as minister of defence.
BRIAN MULRONEY, Prime Minister, slighting the courage of the NDPer Svend Robinson who earlier in 1988 became the first Member of Parliament to acknowledge publicly his homosexuality, quoted in *The Globe and Mail*, 21 Nov. 1988.

Sexual orientation is like being left-handed or right-handed or ambidextrous. There are a variety of sexual orientations: homo-

sexual, bisexual, heterosexual. These ought to be seen as a gift from God.
"Toward a Christian Understanding of Sexual Orientation, Lifestyles and Ministry," a report prepared by the National Co-ordinating Group of the United Church of Canada, released 4 March 1988. Quoted by André Picard in *The Globe and Mail* the following day.

In every school, one in ten males will be gay, and about one in twenty females will be lesbian.
SUE JOHANSON, sex counsellor, "On Being Gay," *Talk Sex: Sue Tells It Like It Is* (1988).

The homosexual man has the possibility in society to live an erotic life, period.
SCOTT SYMONS, novelist and cultural commentator, interviewed in *The Idler*, No. 25, May-June 1990.

HONESTY

I always kept before me the homely slogan of Sir James Whitney, who was the staunch and respected Premier of Ontario when I was a boy. "Bold enough to be honest, and honest enough to be bold." If I am remembered I hope that it will be as one who was bold enough to be honest in all things, and honest enough to be bold in all circumstances.
DONALD M. FLEMING, politician, *So Very Near: The Political Memoirs of the Honourable Donald M. Fleming — Volume 2, The Summit Years* (1985).

HONG KONG

The impact is real enough; Hong Kong is now our largest single source of immigrants. In 1988, Canada took in 24,588 people from Hong Kong, about twice as many as the U.S. and about three times as many as Australia accepted. And more are coming; in the frenzy of fear that followed the massacre in Tienanmen Square visa applications at the Canadian Commission office in Hong Kong reached 9,000 a day.

PAT CARNEY, journalist and politician, "The Golden Dragon," *Saturday Night*, Nov. 1989.

HOPE

Horace Walpole said of Italy, that it was "a land in which the memory saw more than the eye," and in Canada hope must play the part of memory.
ANNA BROWNELL JAMESON, traveller, *Winter Studies and Summer Rambles in Canada* (1838).

Hope can be so very cruel.
Remark made by a character in *The Taste of Fears* (1963), a crime novel by SARA WOODS.

In the heart must be wells invisible to the pathologist and anatomist from which we can draw hope, joy, and adventure.
JOEY SLINGER, columnist, *The Toronto Star*, 16 Oct. 1984.

We were trying to be a messenger, to let people know that no matter what the form of physical disability — loss of limb, blindness, cerebral palsy, paralysis — everyone has hopes and dreams. And that my dream of wheeling around the world was no more significant than the dream of someone trying to make the long journey from a hospital bed to an electric wheelchair and thus lead a more independent life.
RICK HANSEN, wheelchair athlete, *Rick Hansen: Man in Motion* (1987) written with Jim Taylor.

It is difficult to maintain hope in such a world, and yet I believe there must be hope. I want to proclaim my belief in the social gospel, as a Christian, a woman, a writer, a mother and a member of humanity, a sharer in a life that I believe in some way to be informed by the Holy Spirit.
MARGARET LAURENCE, novelist, Trent University, Peterborough, Ont., 29 March 1983; quoted in *The Globe and Mail*, 10 Jan. 1989.

Confidence is armoured, but hope runs naked.
ROBIN SKELTON, man-of-letters, aphorism, May 1990.

HORSES
See also RIDING

When the horse dies on the street the oats no longer pass through for the sparrows.
JOHN KENNETH GALBRAITH, economist and author, recording a Scottish saying and alluding to the "trickle down" theory of economics, quoted by Dave McIntosh in *When the Work's All Done This Fall: The Settling of the Land* (1989).

HOTELS

The room a dying poet took / at nightfall in a dead hotel / had both directories — the Book / of Heaven and the Book of Bell.
First verse of the poem "The Room" by the man-of-letters VLADIMIR NABOKOV, inspired by a guest room at the Park Plaza Hotel in Toronto, *The New Yorker*, 13 May 1950.

I have no illusions about hotels in this hemisphere; they are for conventions, not for the individual; for a thousand tight salesmen and not for the weary poet (or the weary poet's wife, says Véra). Slamming doors, shunting trains, the violent waterfalls of one's neighbour's toilet. Terrible.
VLADIMIR NABOKOV, Anglo-Russian novelist, letter to E.B. White written (on the letterhead of the Royal York Hotel, Toronto) in Oct. 1950, noted by Nabokov's biographer Brian Boyd. Boyd hazarded the opinion that the experience was "a catalyst" for the seduction scene of the novel *Lolita* (1955) which includes the following description: "Someone in a southern direction was extravagantly sick, almost coughing out his life with his liquor, and his toilet descended like a veritable Niagara, immediately beyond our bathroom. And finally when all the waterfalls had stopped. . . ." Boyd con-

cluded, "Nabokov appears to have built the Enchanted Hunters on the foundation of the Royal York: Toronto helped Nabokov to construct the climax of Humber's stalking of Lolita. Not, I suspect, something that the Royal York will use in its advertising. . . ."

HOUDE, CAMILLIEN

As long as we keep a good balance between prayer and sinning, I know my city is not going to sink into wickedness.
> CAMILLIEN HOUDE, Montreal Mayor, quoted by George Woodcock in *The Canadians* (1979).

I will erect not only urinals but also arsenals.
> CAMILLIEN HOUDE, Montreal Mayor, referring to his plan to open *vespasiennes* at Montreal thoroughfares, late 1940s.

I'll be happy to come back to Toronto to kick your balls off any time you want.
> CAMILLIEN HOUDE, Montreal Mayor, after attending to the ceremonial kick-off at a Grey Cup game in Toronto about 1946.

How many votes does the Queen have in St. Henri?
> CAMILLIEN HOUDE, Montreal Mayor, when accused in the 1950s of a slight to the Governor General, quoted by Leslie Roberts in *Saturday Night*, 7 June 1952.

I have the heart of the people.
> CAMILLIEN HOUDE, Montreal Mayor, as "Monsieur Montréal," according to *CBC Times*, 26 May 1962.

HOUSE OF COMMONS
See also PARLIAMENT

So long, trained seals!
> PIERRE ELLIOTT TRUDEAU, Prime Minister, concluding a press conference in Ottawa, 21 Oct. 1977, quoted in *The Toronto Star*, 22 Oct. 1977. The description was earlier used by René Lévesque in an address to the press in Montreal, 17 Oct.

1977. Before Lévesque, the description was used by George Drew, in reference to government members, during the Pipeline Debate, House of Commons, 15 May 1956.

Your Honour knows that there is no place for arguments in the House of Commons.
> ED BROADBENT, NDP leader, House of Commons, 29 Feb. 1988, as quoted by Pamela Chichinskas and Lynette Stokes in *The Leaders Speak!* (1988).

HOUSING
See also HOME

It is unfortunately true that a good many of us have no roof owing to the shortage of houses. The census now shows about 150,000,000 people in the United States with only housing accommodation for 100,000,000. There are 5,000,000 homeless people among us this Christmas time. It is only too true. I have myself seen them sitting around in the cabarets and palm rooms at two o'clock in the morning.
> STEPHEN LEACOCK, humorist, "Let Us Be Thankful: A Few Thoughts for Christmas" (1930s), *Reflections on the Yuletide Season* (1988).

Davey recalls another similarly hair-raising experience at the start of the 1974 campaign when Trudeau was introduced to a key group of new Liberal organizers at Toronto's Lichee Garden restaurant: "He came down there and it was really an incredibly awful performance. One of these guys said, 'I have a friend, Mr. Prime Minister, a kid who lives in Scarborough, who wants very much to buy a house and he just can't afford to, the prices are so terribly high. What will I say to him?' And I remember the prime minister saying: 'Tell him to move to Regina.' And it was just — God, it was just awful!"
> KEITH DAVEY, Senator, quoted by George Radwanski in *Trudeau* (1978).

A shortage of apartments? Bring in the rent controls which drive away the very people who build affordable housing. Abandon the mason's trowel in favour of the lawyer's brief; then create a huge secondary industry of rent control bureaucracies, replete with grants for tenants' groups.

This way enormous energies are directed, not towards increasing rental housing stock, but towards ensuring the tenant's rights are protected.

TOM DAVEY, editor and columnist, *Environmental Science & Engineering*, Aug. 1989.

The only way to live comfortably in an apartment building is to pretend you are the sole tenant.

EDWARD PHILLIPS, novelist, *Sunday Best* (1990).

In May of 1990 my colleagues and I built a demonstration house on the campus of McGill University, in downtown Montreal, to test a thesis of ours: if people thinking of changing houses could experience the advantages of high-quality, smaller, more flexible, and more adaptable houses, they might actually choose smaller rather than larger quarters.

WITOLD RYBCZYNSKI, architect, author, and proponent of the Grow House, "Living Smaller," *The Atlantic*, Feb. 1991.

HOWE, C.D.

"Gentlemen," he said in a room almost pulsing with animosity, "we all must realize that neither side has any monopoly on sons of bitches." Everyone burst out laughing, and the issue was soon settled.

C.D. HOWE, "minister of everything," handling a shipping dispute which led to an angry confrontation in Washington, D.C., noted by David MacDonald in "Anecdotes," 17 Dec. 1988.

HUDSON BAY

Henry Hudson had a large bay in northern Canada named after him. What is it called?

TERRY JOHNSON, humorist, *Quick Quiz for Slow People* (1988).

Rich as the trade to these parts have been or may be, the way of living is such that we can not reckon any man happy whose lot is cast upon this Bay . . . for that country is so prodigiously cold that nature is never impregnated by the sun; or, rather, her barren womb produces nothing for the subsistence of man.

JOHN OLDMIXON, antiquary, *The British Empire in America* (1708), as quoted by Peter C. Newman in *Empire of the Bay: An Illustrated History of the Hudson's Bay Company* (1989).

HUDSON'S BAY COMPANY

After some consideration, and much expectoration, he slowly replied: "Le'ss see, 'B.C.' in ancient history means 'Before Christ,' I b'lieve — 't least so the schoolmarm used to tell when I was to school — tharfore, I calc'late 'H.B.C.' to mean 'Here before Christ'; fur this 'tarnal location don't 'pear to've bin much overrun with strangers since that period."

R. BYRON JOHNSON, native of Victoria, B.C., explaining the meaning of the initials H.B.C. (for Hudson's Bay Company), which were emblazened on a flag flying above the fur fort, to an American vagabond, *Very Far West Indeed: A Few Rough Experiences on the North-West Pacific Coast* (1872).

The Hudson's Bay is not an ordinary commercial company, but a kind of kingdom by itself, and it needs statesmen to administer it.

JOHN BUCHAN, Governor General Lord Tweedsmuir, referring to the H.B.C., quoted by Peter C. Newman in *Empire of the Bay: An Illustrated History of the Hudson's Bay Company* (1989).

At the peak of its expansion it controlled nearly three million square miles of territory — nearly a twelfth of the earth's land

surface and an area ten times that of the Holy Roman Empire at its height.
> PETER C. NEWMAN, author, *Empire of the Bay: An Illustrated History of the Hudson's Bay Company* (1989). The author goes on to note that The Bay, which was founded in 1670, is "the oldest continuous commercial enterprise still in existence."

We never shoot our customers.
> "Company traders took great pride in their unofficial motto: 'We never shoot our customers,'" wrote PETER C. NEWMAN with reference to atrocity claims, *Maclean's*, 6 Aug. 1990.

HUMAN RIGHTS
See RIGHTS, HUMAN

HUMANITARIANISM

Every Individual can do something to make the world a better place to live in. One drop of water is part of the wave.
> DOROTHY LIVESAY, poet, quoted by Ken Adachi in *The Toronto Star*, 28 June 1987.

THE HUMANITIES

In the course of the last few years, I had noticed that knowledge of classical tongues and of the humanities existed in an inverse ratio with the penetration of communist ideas, which may have been why communists hastened to abolish the teaching of Latin in the grammar schools. . . . The most devoted, stubborn and biased supporters of the régime were middle-class people or intellectuals who had not studied Latin, while most of the communist writers or journalists occupying key positions had gone to technical schools.
> GEORGE FALUDY, Hungarian-born poet, *My Happy Days in Hell* (1962) translated by Kathleen Szasz.

HUMANITY
See also LIFE

My primary commitment is to humanity in which God is present.
> GREGORY BAUM, theologian, quoted by June Callwood in *The Globe and Mail*, 5 Aug. 1974.

There is no such thing as a superman, but it has always seemed to me there is such a thing as a subman.
> JOSEF SKVORECKY, novelist, *Emoke* (1977).

The individual is the leaf on the tree. The leaves fall but the tree endures. New leaves are born. This concept has been the mainstay of our species from time immemorial. Now the tree itself is threatened.
> MARGARET LAURENCE, novelist, address, Trent University, Peterborough, Ont., 29 March 1983; quoted in *The Globe and Mail*, 10 Jan. 1989.

To be authentically human is to centre one's life on the world God loves. It has always meant that, but today it is critical to do so. The creation God loves is sick unto death, and needs caretakers, lovers, gardeners, and partners who will work to preserve life rather than death, collective security rather than national security, rice in the mouth and a roof over the head rather than military and nuclear hardware.
> LOIS WILSON, Christian activist, *Turning the World Upside Down: A Memoir* (1989).

Our future lies in group survival and group success, not in individual achievement. We must understand that we share the planet with other species that we depend on to survive, that the destiny of all species is a shared one, because to extricate ourselves from the web of life is to perish.
> ANITA GORDON and DAVID SUZUKI, science broadcasters, *It's a Matter of Survival* (1990).

HUMOUR

See also LAUGHTER
LEACOCK, STEPHEN
MALAPROPISMS

The world has benefited largely by good-natured burlesques, and many a folly, which all the serious preaching in the world could not cure, has been driven from the stage of living realities by a joke.
WILLIAM FLEET, satirist, *How I Came to Be the Governor of the Island of Cacona with a Particular Account of My Administration of the Affairs of that Island Respectfully Dedicated to My Fellow Labourers by the Hon. Francis Thistleton, late Governor of the Island of Cacona* (Montreal, 1852)

Lord Mayor of London: If I smell your corsage will you blush?
Mayor of Ottawa: If I pull your chain will you flush?
This exchange is said to have taken place in Ottawa in the 1950s between the visiting Lord Mayor of London and CHARLOTTE WHITTON, the irrepressible Mayor of Ottawa. The English Mayor wore a symbolic chain of office around his neck; the Canadian Mayor, a rose pinned to her evening gown.

Qui verra, rira.
"Who sees it will laugh." Maxim of GRATIEN GÉLINAS who staged Montreal's annual one-man revue called *Les Fridolinades* beginning in 1948. Quoted by Matthew Fraser in *The Globe and Mail*, 27 Jan. 1987.

To be born with the gift of laughter makes life worthwhile. For humour is the mastery of misery.
JOHN D. ROBINS and MARGARET V. RAY, editors, *A Book of Canadian Humour* (1951).

Hilarity is excited by a union of opposites. The universe is a cosmic joke for His delight. Laughter is the voice of God — not Hebrew, Greek, Latin, or Sanskrit. You will hear the voice of God when you understand His cosmic joke.
T.B. PAWLICKI, author and theorist, *How You Can Explore Higher Dimensions of Space and Time* (1984).

Who buys coat hangers? They breed in your closet like rattlesnakes.
STUART McLEAN, broadcaster, quoted by Peter Gzowski in *The New Morningside Papers* (1987).

Two of my strongest feelings about Canadian history have been that it needed more humour and that a little more invention would make things a lot clearer.
MICHAEL BLISS, historian, endorsing *The House of Ontario: An Imaginary History* (1983) written by Royce MacGillivray. The note appeared in the publisher's catalogue for Fall-Winter 1987-88.

Lady Godiva was a Doukhobor.
SANDY STEWART, radio and television producer, recommending this as the title for a book of Canadian jokes, 17 Jan. 1988.

Wherever you go in the world, you just have to say you're Canadian and people laugh.
JOHN CANDY, Toronto-born comedian, quoted in *The Toronto Star*, 25 July 1988.

A sense of humour is one of the sexiest things there is.
MERLE SHAIN, author, interviewed by David Schatzky on CBC Radio, 14 Feb. 1989.

Nowadays if you're funny at anybody's expense they run to the UN and say, "I must have an ombudsman to protect me." You hardly dare have a shrewd perception about anybody. The only people you can abuse are WASPs. They're fair game.
ROBERTSON DAVIES, man-of-letters, interviewed by Alan Twigg in *Strong Voices: Conversations with Fifty Canadian Authors* (1988).

I often wondered why Canada never developed humour magazines like *Punch* or satirical publications like *Private Eye*. Now it is crystal clear. Nothing, absolutely nothing, could possibly be more hilarious than the verbatim transcripts in *Hansard*.

TOM DAVEY, editor and columnist, *Environmental Science & Engineering*, March 1991.

HUNGARY

Hungarians — and this is the first thing to understand about them — love a loser.

STEPHEN VIZINCZEY, Hungarian-born author, "Commentary on a Poem" (1976), *Truth and Lies in Literature: Essays and Reviews* (1986).

Every Hungarian is born with two acts of a play in his head. He spends the rest of his life working on the third.

JOHN HIRSCH, Hungarian-born director, quoted by Frank Rasky in *The Canadian Jewish News*, 10 Sept. 1987.

Self-analysis is not a Magyar strong point, and reflection in general seems to exert little appeal. Perhaps that is why the country has never produced a major philosopher and fewer minor ones than Denmark or Spain.

GEORGE FALUDY, Hungarian-born poet, *Notes from the Rainforest* (1988).

Canada is a peaceful country; here every day there is excitement. In each country, one longs a little for the other.

GEORGE FALUDY, Hungarian-born poet, one-time Toronto resident, Canadian citizen, living in Budapest, quoted by Ronald de Sousa in *The Globe and Mail*, 23 June 1990.

HUNGER
See also POVERTY

Heaven forbid that we, sheltered and fed, and considering this question at our own warm hearth, should audaciously set limits to any extremity of desperate distress!

CHARLES DICKENS, novelist and journalist, *Household Words: A Weekly Journal*, 2 Nov. 1854. The great novelist and master polemicist has prepared the reader that he will "set limits" by arguing that there are some acts that no Englishmen (especially no English gentlemen) would ever commit. Thus he attempted to refute the strong evidence that some members of the lost Franklin Expedition who were starving in the Arctic resorted to acts of cannibalism.

Hungry I was / and fed on fullness, / yet life was such / I knew but dullness. // Older I am / and yet am younger; / my life is full, / I feed on hunger.

BARKER FAIRLEY, poet and painter, "Hunger," *Poems of 1922 or Not Long After* (1972).

They say there was privation. But it is hard to starve when you can produce everything yourself except tea, sugar, and tobacco. In the "hard times" when people in St. John's could not earn enough to buy a pound of beans, some people in the outports had roast partridge to eat, and wild ducks and hares, lobsters, smoked salmon, herring roe, saddle of deer, lambs fattened on the salt marshes, dishes of steamed mussels, "cows butter," joints of beef and fresh eggs.

RAY GUY, humorist, commenting on Newfoundland outport life, "We Shall Undercome," *That Far Greater Bay* (1976).

When I give bread to the poor they call me a saint. When I ask why the poor are hungry, they call me a communist.

REMI J. DE ROO, Bishop of Victoria, observation made in 1976, quoted by June Callwood in *The Globe and Mail*, 20 Nov. 1987.

Why is the destructive course of industrial agriculture pursued as the only possible choice lying between us and starvation while millions go hungry?

> BREWSTER KNEEN, food system analyst, *From Land to Mouth: Understanding the Food System* (1989).

HUNTING

> *See also* ANIMALS
> SEAL HUNT

I will catch something. / Because I am a man.

> Montagnais-Naskapi poem, "We Will Go," *Songs of the Great Land* (1989) edited by John Robert Colombo.

In our time, however, it is difficult to understand why the pursuit of such wild game as remains continues to be carried on by North Americans of European descent, when the necessity no longer exists.

> JOHN A. LIVINGSTON, naturalist, *One Cosmic Instant: A Natural History of Human Arrogance* (1973).

I . . . take up my stupid little gun / I poke the nonsensical little bullet / into my silly little firing machine. / The disobedient little sights / of my childish weapon / are misaligned. / As it happens, my seemingly / useless, worthless little bullet / hits its true mark, / the uncounted, unaware, insignificant / little seal. / Reason to rejoice! / My worthless little gun knows how to kill a seal!

> WILLIAM KALLEO, Inuit poet, "My Stupid Little Gun," translated by Rose Pamack, reprinted in *Inuktitut* No. 70, 1989.

Americans have had only one reason to visit Canada: to enjoy the great outdoors by killing something.

> ERIC NICOL and DAVE MORE, humorists, *The U.S. or Us: What's the Difference, Eh?* (1986).

HYDRO

> *See* ELECTRICAL POWER

HYPOCRISY

> *See also* LIES

Hypocrisy is the vaseline of social intercourse.

> Graffiti, York University, Downsview, Ont., March 1990.

ICE

See also ICE AGE
ICEBERGS
SNOW

My dad would go out first, with a hatchet, to test the thickness of the ice. His words of wisdom on the subject of safe ice were these. . . . "One inch — no way. / Two inches — one may. / Three inches — small groups. / Four inches — okay."

> Traditional advice recalled by SUSAN PRYKE of Gravenhurst, Ont., and quoted by Peter Gzowski in *The New Morningside Papers* (1987).

Ice is meant, first, for hockey and, second, for keeping meat.

> Attributed to ROCH CARRIER, novelist, by Eleanor Cook in "'A Seeing and Unseeing in the Eye': Canadian Literature and the Sense of Place," *Daedalus: Journal of the American Academy of Arts and Sciences*, "In Search of Canada," Fall 1988.

ICE AGE

Finally, when the northern latitudes of the planet were engulfed by another ice age, Canadians were the last to know.

> ERIC NICOL, humorist, *Canada Cancelled Because of Lack of Interest* (1977), illustrated by Peter Whalley.

Ther wernt nothin fer to do, on accounta Canda wuz jist wun big rinka ice, and nobuddy yet had thunk up a Samboney.

> DON HARRON, comedian, in the person of Charlie Farquharson, *Cum Buy the Farm* (1987).

ICEBERGS

See also ICE

Fallen pieces of the moon . . . a mountainous architecture of ascetic contemplation.

> BARRY LOPEZ, naturalist, describing the appearance of icebergs in Davis Strait, N.W.T., *Arctic Dreams: Imagination and Desire in a Northern Landscape* (1986).

ICELANDIC PEOPLE

You have become a vital part of the Canadian people. I wish we had more of you. We can never have too many of you in Canada.

> JOHN BUCHAN, Governor General Lord Tweedsmuir, addressing an audience of Icelandic Canadians in Manitoba in 1936,

quoted by Ken Coates and Fred Mc-Guinness in *Manitoba: The Province and the People* (1987).

Of all the so-called ethnic groups — that is, those who are neither native, nor French, nor English in origin — none has a longer relationship with Canada than the Icelanders. The first white child born in North America was Snorri Thorfinnson, in Vinland, somewhere on the east coast of North America — perhaps Newfoundland — around the year 1004. His father was the Icelander Thorfinn Karlsefni, who was attempting to set up a permanent colony.
TOM OLESON, columnist, *The Winnipeg Free Press*, 5 Aug. 1989.

The Icelanders who came to Canada and America were, in fact, *released* from history. . . . In North America you were able, quite simply, to forget about your past if you wanted.
KRISTJANA GUNNARS, editor, Introduction, *Unexpected Fictions: New Icelandic Canadian Writing* (1989).

IDEAL

All nations have such a buried or uncreated ideal . . . and no nation has been more preoccupied with it than Canada.
NORTHROP FRYE, literary critic, *The Modern Century* (1967).

IDEALISM
See also IMAGINATION

Idealism is the only realism.
MATTHEW HALTON, CBC Radio correspondent, quoted by his daughter Kathleen Tynan in *The Life of Kenneth Tynan* (1987).

I think that there has to be an assumption that life is better than death, freedom better than slavery, happiness better than misery, equality better than exploitation, for all men everywhere without exception.
NORTHROP FRYE, literary philosopher,

letter, 17 April 1974, quoted by John Ayre in *Northrop Frye: A Biography* (1989).

I would renounce, therefore, the attempt to create heaven on earth, and focus instead on reducing the hell.
A. ALAN BOROVOY, General Counsel, Canadian Civil Liberties Association, *When Freedoms Collide: A Case for Our Civil Liberties* (1988).

Perhaps most importantly we have to come up with plans, programmes, and organizations that will harness the idealism of young Canadians who have been left to twiddle their thumbs for a generation or two.
JOHN FRASER, editor, "Diary," *Saturday Night*, Nov. 1989.

IDEAS
See also INTELLIGENCE

I am entirely a person who is concerned with the establishment of good international understanding. Therefore I am concerned with the floating of all ideas. I mean, I get as much from Gobineau as I get from Marx.
JOHN GRIERSON, first NFB Commissioner, referring to a proto-fascist and an early communist thinker, quoted by Gary Evans in *John Grierson and the NFB: The Politics of Wartime Propaganda* (1984).

The atom and the electron are just as much constructs as gravity, for no one has ever seen or handled either though it is now hard to realize that they are not facts (i.e., directly known phenomena).
D.O. HEBB, psychologist, "The Role of Neurological Ideas in Psychology," *Journal of Personality*, No. 20, 1951.

As a rule, the most dangerous ideas are not the ones which divide people, but those on which they agree.
STEPHEN VIZINCZEY, essayist, *The Rules of Chaos* (1969).

History demonstrates that the truly innovative ideas of the great have often been killed or fearfully distorted by zealous if well-meaning followers.

W. EDWARD MANN and EDWARD HOFF-MAN, sociologist and psychologist, *The Man Who Dreamed of Tomorrow: A Conceptual Biography of Wilhelm Reich* (1980).

The most lethal weapon in the world's arsenal is not the neutron bomb or chemical warfare but the human mind that devises such things and puts them to use.

MARGARET ATWOOD, author, "A Disneyland of the Soul," *The Writer and Human Rights* (1983) edited by the Toronto Arts Group for Human Rights.

Canadians have always had better taste than Americans. Like the British, they are more literary, more open to writing concerned with ideas.

RAY BRADBURY, science-fiction author, quoted by Leonard Klady in *The Toronto Star*, 16 Jan. 1987.

The most exciting world I know is the universe of the mind.

A. K. DEWDNEY, computer specialist called "the Swami of the Silicon Chip," quoted by Peter Stoler in *Time*, 27 April 1987.

Neoideophobia (a word of my coinage meaning "fear of new ideas") affects humans worldwide.

IAN STEVENSON, psychiatrist and psychical researcher, *Children Who Remember Previous Lives: A Question of Reincarnation* (1987).

For us, having a great idea is only the beginning. For a great idea to succeed in any fiercely competitive market, it must be presented with *truth, integrity, artistry*, and *memorability*.

JERRY GOODIS, advertising consultant, promotional publication entitled *We'll Meet You at the Barricades!* (1988).

An army of techno-peasants or millionaires can be created with the next new idea.

FRANK OGDEN, futurologist, "Ogden's Nineteenth Law," *Dr. Tomorrow's Lessons from the Future* (updated June 1989).

I had always assumed that the lack of interest [in ideas] I found among any psychoanalytic colleagues in Toronto was purely a product of the provincial nature of Canadian intellectual life.

JEFFREY MOUSSAEIF MASSON, critic of psychoanalysis who taught at the University of Toronto and was a non-medical candidate of the Toronto Psychoanalytic Society, *Final Analysis: The Making and Unmaking of a Psychoanalyst* (1991).

IDENTITY, NATIONAL

A great many, whom I met or observed, appeared to me to be the opposite of complacent. They were worried about themselves. They felt that, somehow, they ought to be having a better time. On a standard of living basis, they were all dressed up with nowhere to go.

They felt, I suspect, that they were duller than they ought to be. They were wondering if they were not too cautious, and yet had steeled themselves against being incautious.

J.B. PRIESTLEY, English writer on a tour of Canada, commenting on the suggestion that Canadian businessmen were "smug and complacent," "I Heard the Monotonous, Mournful Voices of Canadian Women" in *Liberty*, Aug. 1956.

A Canadian is lost when he asks himself what a Canadian is.

V.S. PRITCHETT, English essayist, remark made in 1964, *At Home and Abroad* (1989).

One of the derivations proposed for the word Canada is a Portuguese phrase meaning "nobody here." The etymology of the word Utopia is very similar, and perhaps the real Canada is an ideal with nobody in it. The Canada to which we really do owe loyalty is the Canada that we have failed to create.

NORTHROP FRYE, literary critic, *The Modern Century* (1967).

We have achieved the most amazing things, a few million people opening up half a continent. But we have not yet found a Canadian soul except in time of war.
LESTER B. PEARSON, Prime Minister, *Time*, 5 May 1967.

Canada is the only country in the world that has never had a national identity. In an age when all homogeneous nations are losing their identity images through rapid technological change, Canada alone can "keep it cool." We have never been committed to a single course or goal. This is now our greatest asset. The parallel is to be found in the recent need of the business world to switch from private enterprise to tribal conglomerates on the pattern of medieval dynastic marriages, another massive example of decentralism foisted upon us by electric speeds.
MARSHALL McLUHAN, communications theorist, letter to Pierre Elliott Trudeau, 2 Dec. 1968, *Letters of Marshall McLuhan* (1987) edited by Matie Molinaro, Corinne McLuhan, and William Toye.

We are a nation that is too big for simple symbols. Our preoccupation with the symbol of a single national identity has, in my judgment, obscured the great wealth we have in several local identities which are rich in themselves and which are skilled in getting along with others.
JOE CLARK, Conservative leader, address, Empire Club of Canada, Toronto, 19 April 1979.

Canada is, after all, a very big and diverse country, culturally divided, with bilingualism as a feeble cement purporting to hold together the English and French segments. In a way, a freak country, its economy closely integrated with America's, and entirely dependent on American nuclear arms for its defence, yet endlessly fretting about and seeking an identity of its own.

MALCOLM MUGGERIDGE, English author, "The Land that Time Forgot," *The Canadian*, 13 Oct. 1979.

What kind of identity is built on shivering in the cold?
MICHAEL BLISS, historian, commenting on the dispiriting influence of climate and landscape on nationalism, quoted by Stephen Brook in *Maple Leaf Rag: Travels across Canada* (1987).

National identity is indeed tenuous and exists primarily in terms of a contemplation of Canada's relation to its mighty neighbour, the United States. Regional identity, on the other hand, is far from weak. Canadians may indeed have a dimmed sense of national wholeness, but their sense of local rootedness is, if anything, overdeveloped.
STEPHEN BROOK, English travel writer, *Maple Leaf Rag: Travels across Canada* (1987).

Canada is in a psychological mess from which it can extract itself only by taking thought. Canada is not an extrovert country. . . . Until Canada wakes up, uses her excellent head, and adopts her true psychological direction, she will never be herself, but always a shadow of something else. She has nothing to lose, but her soul to gain.
ROBERTSON DAVIES, man-of-letters, "Keeping Faith," *Saturday Night*, Jan. 1987.

That's it. One by one, we can create the sum of our national identity. Canada is a collection of twenty-six million characters in search of an author.
PETER C. NEWMAN, author, *Sometimes a Great Nation: Will Canada Belong to the 21st Century?* (1988).

Telling Canada that she has a soul used to be rather like telling a stupid and unsophisticated girl that she was beautiful; she laughed coarsely, and kicked you on the shins. A great deal of persuasion was needed before she would pay attention to what you were saying, and stop calling you a fool.

ROBERTSON DAVIES, man-of-letters, Neil Gunn Lecture, Edinburgh University, June 1988, published in *The Times Literary Supplement*, 30 Sept. 1988.

No one wants to see his or her country forced into a kind of submerge, a kind of hibernation of identity. But Canadians are very famliar with the experience.

ROBIN MATHEWS, poet and teacher, *Canadian Identity: Major Forces Shaping the Life of a People* (1988).

The soul of the Canadian personality is supposed to be reticence. This is the country that has made "diffident" a bad word. Politeness is our second name. No one wishes to be pushy and those among us who are aggressive are assumed to be either Americans who have worked out their Vietnam draft-dodger angst or recent arrivals from Hong Kong. No one who is essentially Canadian, heart and brain, is supposed to aspire to anything.

ALLAN FOTHERINGHAM, columnist, *Maclean's*, 19 June 1989.

Not only in Quebec but in every region of the Dominion, such loyalty to the nation as abides hangs by the fraying threads of federal spending programmes. Canadian culture remains profoundly alien to its people; national symbols languish untended and unloved; political institutions command little interest or respect. Confederation, and with it almost four centuries of effort to create a separate existence in the North, is slowly sinking from view, to the vast indifference of its citizens.

ANDREW COYNE, journalist, *Saturday Night*, July 1989.

Today, when the old industrial hardware is obsolescent, we can see that the Canadian condition of low-profile identity and multiple borders approaches the ideal pattern of electronic living.

MARSHALL McLUHAN, communications theorist, and Bruce R. Powers, academic, authors of *The Global Village: Transforma-*

tions in World Life and Media in the 21st Century (1989).

National identity is the quintessential Canadian issue. Almost alone among modern developed countries, Canada has continued to debate its self-conception to the present day.

SEYMOUR MARTIN LIPSET, sociologist, *Continental Divide: The Values and Institutions of the United States and Canada* (1989).

The whole temper of life in Canada, its manners, its looks, its values, I think, are unmistakably Canadian. Few would deny that it is less exciting than the United States, but Americans often themselves concede that in many fundamental ways it is superior.

JAN MORRIS, Anglo-Welsh travel writer, Introduction, *City to City* (1990).

I think it deserves better of itself — more recognition of its own virtues, more readiness to blow its own trumpet, a little less becoming diffidence, a bit more vulgar swagger. Sometimes Canada's modesty touches me, but sometimes it makes me feel like giving it a kick in the seat of its ample pants, to get its adrenalin going.

JAN MORRIS, Anglo-Welsh travel writer, Introduction, *City to City* (1990). Morris wrote that "while it may not be the most thrilling of countries" Canada "has a genuine claim to be considered the best."

Canadians don't feel part of this country unless they're out of it. There's nothing to link a person from Winnipeg with someone from Quebec, unless they're in Venice together, sitting in St. Mark's Square drinking cappuccino. Suddenly you have something in common.

ROBERT LEPAGE, theatre director, quoted by Marianne Ackerman in "The Hectic Career of Robert Lepage," *Imperial Oil Review*, Winter 1990.

We've been searching for Canadian identity for several years now and we would greatly appreciate your assistance in finding it.

Letter sent by an unidentified Canadian correspondent to the fictional detective Sherlock Holmes, who in the fiction of Sir Arthur Conan Doyle resided at 221B Baker Street in London, England, noted by Tony Harries of the Abbey National Building Society who responds to such correspondence. According to columnist Isabel Vincent in *The Globe and Mail*, 8 Sept. 1990, Harries arranged for Holmes, who was amused, to reply "saying that identity is a state of mind."

Like Switzerland in 19th-century Europe, Canada must now preserve its identity by having many identities.

NORTHROP FRYE, literary critic, address, Social Sciences and Humanities Research Council, Toronto, Fall 1990, printed in *The Globe and Mail*, 15 April 1991.

But the real spirit of Canada is not measured in dollars, its strength is not measured in tons or bushels, nor is its influence measured in square kilometres. Canada lives in the hearts and minds of every Canadian.

BRIAN MULRONEY, Prime Minister, address, joint meeting of the Empire Club and the Canadian Club, Toronto, 12 Feb. 1991, published in *The Toronto Star* the following day.

IDEOLOGY

Falsehood is the final outcome of all ideologies. No ideology was ever born of true feelings.

JOSEF SKVORECKY, essayist and novelist, "Two Peas in a Pod" (1982), *Talkin' Moscow Blues* (1988) edited by Sam Solecki.

I made up my mind when I took the job that I wouldn't be ideologically precious.

STEPHEN LEWIS, former Ontario NDP leader, accepting the federal Conservative government's offer of the post of Am-

bassador to the United Nations (1984-88), *Maclean's*, 15 Feb. 1988.

We are still caught in what Tom Wolfe described as a 1960s neo-Marxist fog. In this one limited sense, Canada is a cultural backwater. It views events in the world the way it sees a faraway star — not as it actually is now, but rather as it was when its image began to travel light years ago. That is reinforced by our geography and self-sufficiency, which give Canada natural barriers against hard experience. The result is that we reflect the world as it was — but the world has been changing for the better and, regretfully, in that one sense Canada has not.

BARBARA AMIEL, columnist, *Maclean's*, 25 Sept. 1989.

But the experience illuminated for me — not for the first time — the degree to which we depend upon agencies we know little about to attend to affairs we don't understand. Issues that are already tortuously complex are further distorted by the insular arrogance of bureaucrats, the reductive sloganeering of professional critics, and the technological naïveté of the media. Inevitably, confronted by important decisions, we are thrown back upon our instincts and personal ideologies, not unlike primitives who come to terms with the forces around them through superstition.

DAVID LEES, journalist, "Living in the Nuclear Shadow," *Toronto Life*, Nov. 1989.

Every ism brings a schism.

ROBIN SKELTON, man-of-letters, aphorism, May 1990.

IGNORANCE

Letters from Damn Fools

Heading on a file folder used by STEPHEN LEACOCK and displayed at the Stephen Leacock Memorial Home, Orillia, Sept. 1987.

Our most stubborn assumptions are precisely those that remain unconscious: the biases that we bring to bear when we are judging each other's culture but which we ourselves are not aware of.

> MAVOR MOORE, former Chairman, Canada Council, *Cultures and Writers: A Cultural Dialogue of Ethnic Writers* (1983) edited by Yvonne Grabowski.

IMAGES & IMAGERY

Mr. Peterson, no slouch at the politics of symbolism himself, paid homage to a past master of the art at Thursday's unveiling. It was often said of Mr. Davis that "bland works," the premier recalled — but perhaps, he mused, the truth was that "It's *calling* yourself bland that works." Indeed. . . .

> GENE ALLEN, journalist, referring to Ontario Premier David Peterson with respect to the bland-on-purpose imagery of his predecessor William Davis, *The Globe and Mail*, 23 Oct. 1989.

IMAGINATION

See also IDEALISM

My problem in life has always been that my fantasies come true.

> PATRICIA JOUDRY, playwright, *. . . And the Children Played* (1975).

Once you commit yourself to "what if," anything is possible.

> BETTY JANE WYLIE, playwright, *Don't Just Stand There, Jiggle* (1980).

The question here is not whether the state has an imagination, but whether the writers *imagine* that the state has an imagination.

> PIERRE ELLIOTT TRUDEAU, former Prime Minister, addressing the 48th PEN Congress in New York, quoted by Jack Kapica in *The Globe and Mail*, 18 Jan. 1986.

It is precisely this failure of the imagination on the part of militarists and leaders that is so dangerous today, the failure to visualize what a nuclear holocaust would mean, the apparent inability to imagine the scorched and charred bodies of children . . . our children or children of Russian parents or parents anywhere, and to know, by an extension of imagination, that all children are our children.

> MARGARET LAURENCE, author, address, Trent University, Peterborough, Ont., 23 March 1983; quoted in *The Globe and Mail*, 10 Jan. 1989.

I believe that to change people's minds — and governments are people — we must not rely solely on economic or other arguments, but must create a sense of imagination.

> M.T. (TERRY) KELLY, novelist, accepting the Governor General's Award for Literature, Calgary, 1 Feb. 1988, quoted in *Books in Canada*, April 1988.

The basis of my approach as a teacher has always been that we participate in society by means of our imagination or the quality of our social vision. Our visions of what our society is, what it could be, and what it should be, are all structures of metaphor, because the metaphor is the unit of all imagination. Logical thinking in this field seldom does more than rationalize these metaphorical visions.

> NORTHROP FRYE, literary critic, address, Empire Club of Canada, Toronto, 19 Jan. 1984.

I might see a hideous concrete parking lot, but a kid can look at it and say, "What a lovely space in which to do incredible things."

> WILLIAM GIBSON, science-fiction author, quoted by Victoria Hamburg in "The King of Cyberpunk," *Interview*, Jan. 1989.

A country that can't imagine itself can't govern itself. It is also made uncomfortable by those who try to imagine it, which explains English Canada's schizophrenia towards "Canadian culture."

> MATT COHEN, novelist, "O Canada," *The Toronto Star*, 30 June 1990.

IMMIGRANTS
See also EMIGRATION
REFUGEES

They call it *America*. Each of the couples, after the common *involutions* and *evolutions*, successively whirls round in a circle, till all are in motion; and the dance seems intended to show how emigration catches till a whole neighbourhood is set afloat.
> JAMES BOSWELL, biographer, describing a game played by children in 18th-century England, *The Journal of a Tour to the Hebrides with Samuel Johnson, LL.D.* (1785).

Strong men were misunderstood, maligned; timid women hesitated on the threshold of public life. But they all heard the whisperings of the Great Spirit: "There is room for your thinkers, your men of vision, your lovers of freedom. Come, and I will make of you a great nation."
> MABEL DUNHAM, librarian and historian, *Grand River* (1945).

We are all immigrants in Canada, except the Indians and Eskimos, and no citizen's right can be greater than that of the least protected group.
> F.R. SCOTT, lawyer and poet, "The Deportation of the Japanese Canadians: An Open Letter to the Press" (1946), *Essays on the Constitution: Aspects of Canadian Law and Politics* (1977).

Of the place where we're going — Canada — I know nothing. There are vague outlines of half a continent, a sense of vast spaces and little habitation. . . . But to me, the word "Canada" has ominous echoes of the "Sahara."
> EVA HOFFMAN, Polish immigrant author, thoughts upon docking at Montreal in 1959, *Lost in Translation: A Life in a New Language* (1989).

A Canadian is an immigrant with seniority.
> Definition current in the 1960s and so noted by Cassandra Bruyns in *The Toronto Star*, 1 July 1982. "New Canadian"

was the label applied to immigrants to Canada from as early as 1900 to as late as 1967. The term "Displaced Persons" recalls the years of World War II; abbreviated to "D.P.," and then expanded to "Damn Polack," it became a derogatory description (though one that singer and actor Jan Rubes liked to maintain stood for "Delayed Pioneer"). Refugee status rather than immigrant status was claimed by the "Boat People," homeless Southeast Asian exiles of the 1970s. The "yacht people" are wealthy investors and their families who since the 1980s have been leaving Hong Kong for Canada, mainly Vancouver.

Canada is full of immigrants who hate immigration.
> Attributed to historian IRVING ABELLA by Matthew Behrens in *Now*, 1 Oct. 1987.

Bimeby we got sum noo inhibitants, but not frum Yerp, frum Azure. They cum over as soon as they got ther Bering Strait.
> DON HARRON, comedian, in the person of Charlie Farquharson, *Cum Buy the Farm* (1987).

A Secret Policy, Secretly Administered
> Heading of the chapter concerned with the federal government's immigration policies and procedures in *Double Standard: The Secret History of Canadian Immigration* (1987) by REG WHITAKER.

Be altered francophones. You'll have to contend with another even tougher bunch of immigrants who not only speak French but are bilingual and are not going to bow down to your constant whining and complaining. They may even start an English-language police-like watchdog group. Then where will you be?
> From "Rules for Becoming a Québécois," the heading on a Letter to the Editor, pseudonymously signed "J.M. St. John, Pierrefonds," which appeared in the weekly *The Chronicle* (Pointe Claire, Que.), 13 April 1988. So ill-received was the satire that the Saint-Jean-Baptiste So-

ciety and advertisers pressured the publisher to disavow the sentiments expressed in the letter and to place paid advertisements in three other area newspapers apologizing for publishing the satire.

In the past forty years, immigrants from the wider world have transformed the nation's appearance and personality beyond anything envisaged by its founders. In the coming decades, Canada's very survival depends upon more massive immigration — and on learning to construct a cohesive society out of many diverse communities that rival each other in size and ambitions.
BRUCE HUTCHISON, newspaperman, *Maclean's*, 11 July 1988.

Too many people in Canada forget that people crawl across minefields to get here.
IGNAT KANEFF, Bulgarian-born developer and founder of the Kaneff Group, quoted by Pat Brennan in *The Toronto Star*, 6 Feb. 1989.

I think one of the biggest mistakes made in this country was that it was so tough about immigration. We should have another 30 million more people here.
MORDECAI RICHLER, novelist, quoted by Don Gillmor in *Quill & Quire*, July 1989.

My own view is that we Canadians who came here first must accept our own share of the blame for emerging racial tensions. We have failed to identify and articulate our own values so that we could invite the newcomers either to conform or contribute their own concepts to them.
PAT CARNEY, journalist and politician, "The Golden Dragon," *Saturday Night*, Nov. 1989.

Hong Kong's brain drain is Canada's brain gain.
VICTOR LI, investor from Hong Kong who settled in Vancouver, quoted by Daniel Stoffman in *The Globe and Mail's Report on Business Magazine*, Nov. 1989.

Refugees are different from immigrants. While immigrants are pulled, refugees are pushed. Refugees do not want to leave their home country and flee only to avoid persecution. Refugees, at least initially, want to return once the danger subsides.
DAVID MATAS with ILANA SIMON, immigration lawyer and journalist, *Closing the Doors: The Failure of Refugee Protection* (1989).

I hope that Canada will continue to strive to be an open society, receiving "the alien" and all those who are desperately in need of succour and a new life, as the Judaic-Christian tradition dictates.
LOIS WILSON, Christian activist, *Turning the World Upside Down: A Memoir* (1989).

A Pole who immigrates to Argentina will be calling himself Argentine within five years, but a Pole who comes to Canada will continue to think of himself as being Polish.
MARILÚ MALLET, Chilean writer in Quebec, interviewed by Hugh Hazelton in *Other Solitudes: Canadian Multicultural Fictions* (1990) edited by Linda Hutcheon and Marion Richmond.

IMMORTALITY
See also TIME

In fifty years the mass of this vast multitude will be numbered amongst a bygone generation; and these stately works of art shall perish. What a worm am I amongst such a multitude! yet I am destined to immortality; have but a few years to live in a probationary state, but an eternity to exist!
EGERTON RYERSON, educator, Methodist minister, traveller not content with the Arc de Triomphe in Paris, *Story of My Life* (1884), as quoted by Eva-Marie Kröller in *Canadian Travellers in Europe, 1851-1900* (1987).

Eternal life, like life imprisonment, would be the cruellest punishment that could be inflicted on any living being.

JOHN A. LIVINGSTON, naturalist, *One Cosmic Instant: A Natural History of Human Arrogance* (1973).

Immortality is not really anyone's lifestyle.
BETTY JANE WYLIE, author, *New Beginnings: Living through Loss and Grief* (1991).

IMPERIALISM
See also BRITISH EMPIRE &
    COMMONWEALTH
    EMPIRE

At a time when it is a point of dispute, whether Canada or Guadalupe will prove the most valuable acquisition to this nation at the ensuing peace, it will not, perhaps, be thought unreasonable to enquire into the importance of the former. . . .
Opening remarks of an essay titled "The Importance of Canada Considered" published in *The Imperial Magazine, or, Complete Monthly Intelligencer*, Aug. 1760. Quoted by Michael Bliss in *Northern Enterprise: Five Centuries of Canadian Business* (1987).

A united Canada is of critical importance in pursuing a successful strategy against the reality of American imperialism. Quebec's history and aspirations must be allowed full expression and implementation in the conviction that new ties will emerge from the common perception of "two nations, one struggle."
"The Waffle Manifesto," a resolution to the Fifth Federal Convention of the New Democratic Party, Winnipeg, 28-31 Oct. 1969, quoted by Paul Fox in *Politics: Canada, Culture and Process* (3rd ed., 1970).

The American empire is a central reality for Canadians. It is an empire characterized by militarism abroad and racism at home. Canadian resources and diplomacy have been enlisted in support of that empire.
"The Waffle Manifesto: For an Independent Socialist Canada" (1969) reprinted in *The Canadian Forum*, Dec. 1989.

The fact is that I'm tired of being patronized by Americans, who are invited to our country and then have the presumption to tell us which attitudes are acceptable to them. The trouble is that imperial powers, whether British or American, find it next to impossible to slough off their supposed superiority. Immigrants from so-called minor nations don't behave in this sort of way when they come to Canada.
ROBIN MATHEWS, nationalist, quoted by Stephen Brook in *Maple Leaf Rag: Travels across Canada* (1987).

INCEST

Don't. I only know this word. This is the only word I have ever learned. Don't. I can not write with only this word. A woman's vocabulary: Don't.
ELLY DANICA, writer and incest survivor, *Don't: A Woman's Word* (1988).

INCOMES

DOCTORS FIRST, ARTISTS LAST ON LIST OF 1987 INCOMES
Headline on a news story from Canadian Press, released 19 Sept. 1987, based on a review of personal incomes released by Revenue Canada. The figures established the fact that "the average annual income of Canada's 37,000 doctors was $99,195 in 1987 — roughly seven times what artists and entertainers made that year. "Self-employed professionals, led by doctors, topped the Canadian pay scales in 1987, while the 21,000 self-employed entertainers and artists were at the bottom with an average income of $13,382." Apparently pensioners came out slightly ahead with an average income of $13,445, according to the summary provided by the editors of *Actrascope*, Fall 1989.

INDEPENDENCE

For to pursue independence seriously is to make visible the necessity of socialism in Canada.
"The Waffle Manifesto: For an Independent Socialist Canada" (1969) reprinted in *The Canadian Forum*, Dec. 1989.

Today, with the arrival of planetization, we are realizing how interdependent we are. We can no longer assume that the world is an open canvas on which we can happily paint our own designs. We live within a closed system where the repercussions of our activities come back to us.

> GUY DAUNCEY, author, *After the Crash: The Emergence of the Rainbow Economy* (1988).

It is no coincidence (and no cause for embarrassment) that Canada was, by more than half a century, the last major country in the Western Hemisphere to achieve independence. It would probably not have escaped absorption by the United States if it had become independent earlier.

> GWYNNE DYER and TINA VILJOEN, commentator and TV producer, *The Defence of Canada: In the Arms of the Empire* (1990).

INDIA

Ah, the man from the country of many bathtubs.

> MOHANDAS K. GANDHI, Indian leader, greeting the roving correspondent Gordon Sinclair in India in the mid-1930s, quoted by Scott Young in *Gordon Sinclair: A Life . . . and Then Some* (1987). It seems Mahatma Gandhi had once read a real-estate advertisement in a Canadian newspaper which described a Canadian home as having two bathtubs.

Up to May 1st this year Canada alone has given us a billion dollars. We are grateful for the credits and grants and particularly appreciate the fact that Canadian credits have been among the most liberal and most unencumbered that we have received, but as our economic base gains strength, our endeavour will be to earn our external resources through trade rather than aid.

> INDIRA GANDHI, Prime Minister of India, address, Empire Club of Canada, Toronto, 20 June 1973.

I was born in the Indian state of Kerala which is only three-fourths the size of Nova Scotia. It has a population slightly smaller than Canada's, a literacy rate higher than Canada's, a language and literature as old as English, more newspapers and larger circulations than those of Canadian dailies, and a Malayalam Lexicon that is probably next only to the great Oxford English Dictionary in size and scope.

I think what we need for becoming world class is not more money, but more imagination, initiative, originality, perseverance — and the determination to do better than the Americans.

> THOMAS M. PAIKEDAY, lexicographer and compiler of *The Penguin Canadian Dictionary*, the first dictionary with 100% Canadian content, private communication, 8 March 1990.

INDIANS
See also NATIVE PEOPLES

He order'd thee to be Born in *France*, with intent that thou shouldest believe what thou neither seest nor conceivest; and me he has caus'd to be Born a *Huron*, to the end that I should give credit to nothing but what I understand, and what my reason teaches me.

> BARON DE LAHONTAN, French traveller in New France, creating words about the deity for Adario, "A Conference or Dialogue between the Author and Adario, a Noted Man among the Savages," *New Voyages to North-America . . . from 1683 to 1694 . . . Done into English* (1703).

He would derive the Americans from the ancient Greeks, and these are his reasons: the Greeks have myths; some Americans have them too. The first Greeks went hunting; the Americans go, too. In the festivals of Greece there was dancing; there is dancing in America.

> VOLTAIRE, French writer, dismissing the early anthropological observations and ethnological theories of Joseph-François Lafitau, the French Jesuit who worked as a missionary in 1712 at today's Kahna-

wake, quoted by J.A.S. Evans in "The Sharp-eyed Jesuit," *The Idler*, No. 23, May-June 1989.

All are passing away, and the places which know them will soon know them no more.
W.B. WELLS, English traveller, *Canadiana: Containing Sketches of Upper Canada* (1837).

The Indian . . . does not become a good settler, he does not become an agriculturalist or a mechanic. He does become a drunkard and a debauchee, and his females and family follow the same course. He occupies valuable land, unprofitably to himself and injuriously to the country. He gives infinite trouble to the government.
LORD SYDENHAM, Governor, observation made in 1841, quoted by Roy MacGregor in *The Ottawa Citizen*, 23 Aug. 1988.

I have heard and read much of savages, and have since seen, during my long residence in the bush, somewhat of uncivilized life; but the Indian is one of Nature's gentlemen — he never says or does a rude or vulgar thing. The vicious, uneducated barbarians who form the surplus of overpopulous European countries, are far behind the wild man in delicacy of feeling or natural courtesy.
SUSANNA MOODIE, pioneer author, *Roughing It in the Bush; or, Forest Life in Canada* (1852).

The Spirit of God made me realize the extent of the rights which the Indian possesses to the land of the North-West. Yes, the extent of the Indian rights, the importance of the Indian cause are far above all other interests. People say the native stands on the edge of a chasm. It is not he who stands on the edge of the chasm; his claims are not false. They are just. The land question will soon be resolved, as it must, to his complete satisfaction. Every step the Indian takes is based upon a profound sense of fairness.
LOUIS RIEL, Métis leader, diary entry, 6 May 1876, *The Diaries of Louis Riel* (1976) edited by Thomas Flanagan.

The term person means an individual other than an Indian.
Section 12, Indian Act of 1880, as quoted by Roy MacGregor in *Chief: The Fearless Vision of Billy Diamond* (1989).

Yes, we Indians have lost many things. We have lost our lands, our forests, our game, our fish; we have lost our ancient religion, our ancient dress; some of the younger people have even lost their fathers' language and the legends and traditions of their ancestors. We cannot call those old things back to us; they will never come again. We may travel many days up the mountain trails, and look in the silent places for them. They are not there.
JOE CAPILANO, Squamish chief, quoted by Pauline Johnson in *Legends of Vancouver* (1911).

I want to get rid of the Indian problem. Our object is to continue until there is not a single Indian in Canada that has not been absorbed into the body politic, and there is no Indian question, and no Indian department.
DUNCAN CAMPBELL SCOTT, Deputy Superintendent of Indian Affairs, 1913-32, quoted by Georges Erasmus in *Drumbeat: Anger and Renewal in Indian Country* (1989) edited by Boyce Richardson.

I feel as an Indian, think as an Indian, all my ways are Indian, my heart is Indian. They, more than the whites, are to me, my people.
GREY OWL, author and naturalist, born Archibald Belaney, letter from Prince Albert National Park, Sask., 10 May 1935, *Dear Bill: The Correspondence of William Arthur Deacon* (1988) edited by John Lennox and Michèle Lacombe.

It is a strange anomaly that my wife who is nearly full-blood Indian, could not, when she married me, speak 10 words in any Indian language, even her own, & knew no more about bush life than a young miss from the sidewalk on Yonge Street. I, who was 3 parts white, was the better Indian. Civilization plays strange tricks on us.

GREY OWL, author and naturalist, born Archibald Belaney, referring to Anahareo, letter from Prince Albert National Park, Sask., 10 May 1935, *Dear Bill: The Correspondence of William Arthur Deacon* (1988) edited by John Lennox and Michèle Lacombe.

The first and foremost lesson that I learned from a field trip was that Indians are first of all people, individuals, human beings, and only secondarily Blackfoot Indians. By comparison with similarities, the differences, though undoubtedly there, seemed superficial.

ABRAHAM MASLOW, humanistic psychologist, describing his early field work as an anthropologist in 1933-37 with the Blackfoot at Gleichen, Alta., quoted by Edward Hoffman in *The Right to Be Human: A Biography of Abraham Maslow* (1988).

Lone Ranger: It looks like the end for us.
Tonto: What do you mean "us"?

This exchange between the Lone Ranger and Tonto took place when the Masked Rider of the Plains and his "faithful Indian companion" were surrounded by a band of hostile Indians. This joke does not appear in the scripts of *The Lone Ranger* — radio serials, comic books, movies, television programs — but it nevertheless made the rounds in the 1960s. The role of Tonto was created by JAY SILVERHEELS, the Mohawk athlete from Ontario's Six Nations Reserve. Tonto was always respectful of the Lone Ranger, addressing him as "*Kemo Sabe*." The words are said to mean "Faithful Friend" in some undisclosed Indian language, but could as well be a corruption of "*Quién sabe?*" — pidgin Spanish for "Don't understand."

Oh, God! Like the Thunderbird of old I shall rise again out of the sea; I shall grab the instruments of the white man's success — his education, his skills, and society. Before I follow the great Chiefs who have gone before us, oh Canada, I shall see these things come to pass.

CHIEF DAN GEORGE, native leader, B. C. Centennial address, Vancouver, 20 July 1971, quoted by T.C. McLuhan in *Touch the Earth: A Self-Portrait of Indian Existence* (1971).

It's in your hands. It's up to you to fight the white man. We cannot even talk to him. We raised you for this moment and you must now make the decision to stop this white man who has destroyed our land and brought us shame.

MALCOLM DIAMOND, elderly chief of Rupert House, addressing his son Billy Diamond, quoted by Roy MacGregor in *Chief: The Fearless Vision of Billy Diamond* (1989). Malcolm Diamond attempted to speak in Cree on behalf of the Indians of Quebec Association to protest personally to Quebec Premier Robert Bourassa the expropriation of Cree lands for the James Bay hydro-development scheme. They spoke in the Cabinet Room of the Government Building (known as "The Bunker") in Quebec City, Oct. 1972. But Bourassa said, "I cancelled my lunch to be with you," and departed, leaving Malcolm Diamond speechless. The Crees decided to seek redress through the courts, and in this way they were led by young Billy Diamond.

At the present time, there is not a great deal of creativity and vigour in the native nation; however, there are signs at the local level that a genuine red nationalism is beginning to emerge.

HOWARD ADAMS, native spokesperson, *Prison of Grass: Canada from a Native Point of View* (1975, rev. 1989).

There is a great tendency to continue the principle of Indian integration in which they are treated as just another contributing unit to the cultural mosaic of Canada. There is the feeling that if native people are given enough assistance they can compete as ordinary Canadians within the economic and political framework as it now exists.

The Indians in this country have never

accepted this view. Because of their original land rights, they feel they have an equity interest in resource development and a special degree of political autonomy within Canada. Without these two ingredients, no aboriginal people has ever escaped the valley of degradation, poverty and despair that occurs when faced with a technological society.

> JOHN WESLEY BEAVER, President, Churchill Falls (Labrador) Corporation Limited and Ojibwa spokesperson, address, Empire Club of Canada, Toronto, 4 Dec. 1975.

Being an Indian means being able to understand and live with this world in a very special way. It means living with the land, with the animals, with the birds and fish, as though they were your sisters and brothers. It means saying the land is an old friend and an old friend your father knew, your grandfather knew, indeed your people have always known.

> RICHARD NERYSOO, native of Fort McPherson, N.W.T., quoted by Thomas R. Berger in *Northern Frontier, Northern Homeland: The Report of the Mackenzie Valley Pipeline Inquiry* (1977).

Being part of Canada is something we did not choose. So for me to be proud to be part of this country would be only possible if the Dene Nation is recognized. And to be a nation, you have to have a land base.

> GEORGES ERASMUS, President, Indian Brotherhood of the N.W.T., quoted by Heather Menzies in *The Railroad's Not Enough: Canada Now* (1978).

It would seem that young people typically have limited hostility towards Indians, viewing them with negative imagery while at the same time believing they deserve a better fate in Canadian life.

> REGINALD W. BIBBY and DONALD C. POSTERSKI, sociologists, *The Emerging Generation: An Inside Look at Canada's Teenagers* (1985).

I say that I am a "so-called Indian" because like many citizens of the First Nations of Canada, I find the historical misnomer "Indian" to be a remnant of European imperialism and a pejorative term.

> GEORGES ERASMUS, National Chief of the First Nations, a contributor to *If I Were Prime Minister* (1987) edited by Mel Hurtig.

I would revise our policy with regard to native peoples and would move to end the reserve system. I would phase out paying Indians to stay in ghettos, which is what reserves are. I would start helping Indians to blend into Canadian society and end their isolation in apartheid-like "homelands." All could live where they wished and do as they wished — but not get handouts for doing it. Within a generation, Indians would become functioning first-class citizens.

> PETER WORTHINGTON, newspaperman, contributor to *If I Were Prime Minister* (1987) edited by Mel Hurtig.

White people work hard, start retirement savings plans, end work at age 65 and then live like Indians.

> Attributed to CLARE BRANT, psychiatrist of Mohawk ancestry, University of Western Ontario, in 1988.

Don't get your balls caught in a vise over an Indian.

> ROBERT ANDERSON, County Court Judge, advising a lawyer about dealings with the accused, Donald Marshall, a Micmac, at the Marshall inquiry in Halifax, quoted in *The Globe and Mail*, 6 Feb. 1988.

When Columbus landed, there wasn't one native person in a prison. There were no police, lawyers, or judges and no prison guards. We didn't need them because we didn't do bad things to each other or to our children. We treated our children like the spirit people they are.

> Adapted from a remark made by Ojibwa elder ART SOLOMON, interviewed by Millie Kirzner, *Now*, 31 March 1988.

I am distressed by the fact that one of the most common visual symbols within the Canadian urban psyche is that of an Indian drunk at every major street corner of every major Canadian city.
TOMSON HIGHWAY, Manitoba-born Cree, quoted by Robert Crew in *The Toronto Star*, 15 April 1989.

When I speak English I think from the head, but when I speak Cree I feel from the groin.
TOMSON HIGHWAY, native playwright, quoted by John Bemrose in *Maclean's*, 8 May 1989.

Christopher Columbus fell on his knees when his boat touched shore and then fell on the Indians. How can you say you have discovered a place when there are people greeting you from the shore?
LENNOX FARREL, Trinidad-born teacher in Toronto, addressing a forum on the upcoming 500th anniversary of Columbus's discovery of America, 13 Oct. 1989, reported in *The Toronto Star* the following day.

In the United States, I am a conductor who happens to be Indian. In Canada, I am an Indian who happens to be a conductor. I don't like that. It reflects that it is unusual, when it shouldn't be.
JOHN KIM BELL, conductor of native ancestry, quoted by Heather Robertson in *The Canadian Forum*, Oct. 1989.

O Great Spirit, help me never to judge another until I have walked two weeks in his moccasins.
Traditional Indian lore of unknown origin, doubtful provenance, and dubious authenticity which appears, in approximately this form, in *The Oxford Book of Prayer* (1988) edited by George Appleton.

Only last year (in November 1988), the U.S. Congress passed a declaration honouring the Iroquois Confederacy as a primary inspiration for the U.S. Constitution.
MICHAEL MITCHELL, Grand Chief, Mo-

hawk Council of Akwesasne, "An Unbroken Assertion of Sovereignty," *Drumbeat: Anger and Renewal in Indian Country* (1989) edited by Boyce Richardson.

Indians are the lively ghosts of Canadian history. They're always there, like the vegetation or the weather, but up to now, no one has taken their complaints or aspirations seriously. To be Indian in this country is to be dispossessed.
PETER C. NEWMAN, columnist, *Maclean's*, 6 Aug. 1990.

I'm just an ordinary Indian and I want to remain an ordinary Indian.
ELIJAH HARPER, Ojibwa-Cree and NDP Member of the Manitoba Legislative Assembly, noting the publicity attendant upon his stand in opposing the Meech Lake Accord, quoted by Gerald Flood in *The Winnipeg Free Press*, 16 June 1990.

A day-care centre surrounded by red tape, Indian Affairs has always been long on benevolence, but short on beneficence; for further details, ask any of the department's clientele.
DALTON CAMP, columnist, *The Toronto Star*, 5 Aug. 1990.

They have been treated less than justly. They have the right to be human and Indians. Their culture must be recognized as having integrity and must not be subverted.
DESMOND TUTU, Archbishop of Cape Town, South Africa, drawing some parallels between the plight of his fellow blacks in South Africa and the Indians of Canada, address, St. Paul's Anglican Church, Toronto, 12 Aug. 1990, quoted by Nicola Pulling in *The Globe and Mail* the following day.

Whereas people might want to draw invalid parallels between the situation here and in South Africa, one wants to say immediately that the aboriginal people are citizens of this country who can vote, but the vast majority of South Africans don't have the vote.

DESMOND TUTU, Archbishop of Cape Town, addressing a news conference on native issues in Toronto, 12 Aug. 1990, quoted in *Now*, 16 Aug. 1990.

You are there and yet you are not there.

DESMOND TUTU, Archbishop of Cape Town, noting the fact that the social institutions ignore the Indians in Canada as they do the blacks of his native South Africa, speaking at the Ojibwa community at Osnaburg, Ont., quoted by Geoffrey York in *The Globe and Mail*, 18 Aug. 1990.

One of the few social scientists who got as close as any outsider can to understanding the native culture was a University of Chicago anthropologist named Sol Tax. He spent much of his life with North American Indians and, when he had gathered all his research and analysed the results, came to this startling conclusion: "They seem to be waiting for us to go away."

That's it. Most Indians regard North American whites as temporary visitors to their nation, and not very welcome ones as that. They see themselves as the Palestinians of Canada, displaced within their own homeland, forced to live in enclaves under the rule of an illegitimate majority of newcomers.

PETER C. NEWMAN, columnist and author, *Maclean's*, 10 Sept. 1990.

We've gone from telling stories across the campfire to telling stories across the stage, and for me, across TV.

DREW HAYDEN TAYLOR, Ojibwa scriptwriter, quoted by Peter Kuitenbrouwer in *The Toronto Star*, 28 Oct. 1990.

It is impossible for me to live in a tent for the rest of my life, even though I was born in one; but I don't have any desire whatsoever to live in a tent for the rest of my life. It is nice enough for a couple of weeks in the summer, but I live in downtown Toronto, in a house with a microwave oven, and a piano and a washer and dryer.

TOMSON HIGHWAY, Cree playwright born in Northern Manitoba, interviewed by Ann Wilson in *Other Solitudes: Canadian Multicultural Fictions* (1990) edited by Linda Hutcheon and Marion Richmond.

We live in a world shaped by deductive reason. But that's simply the physical world. Our mental landscape, our spiritual lives, yearn for the inexplicable — we want something magical, miraculous, ridiculous.

DANIEL DAVID MOSES, native poet and playwright, contrasting the world view of the West with that of the aboriginal people, quoted by Jon Kaplan in *Now*, 23 May 1991.

INDIVIDUALISM

Over many years, I have worked so very hard to be original. Once you are original, you are different; once you are different, you are an individualist; once you are an individualist, you are alone.

STEWART JAMES, magician and inventor of magical effects, "On Originality," *Stewart James in Print: The First Fifty Years* (1989), created by Stewart James, edited by P. Howard Lyons and Allan Slaight, and illustrated by Joseph Schmidt.

Individual humans can do miraculous and extraordinary things. We are all inheritors of millions of years of human evolution. At the core of each of us is a unique set of lifelong relationships and a unique configuration of experience. There is no one else who can ever fill *your* role in the same way.

HUMPHRY OSMOND, psychiatrist, Introduction, *Predicting the Past: Memos on the Enticing Universe of Possibility* (1981) produced by Jerome Agel.

Our obsession with the individual and choice, our mosaic madness, is carrying considerable costs. It is affecting our everyday interactions, our most personal relationships, our institutional involvements. The madness is highly destructive, keeping us from experiencing the best possible quality of life, individually and collectively. But the recognition of its presence can mark the beginning of its demise. Social sanity is not beyond the realm of possibility.

REGINALD W. BIBBY, sociologist, *Mosaic Madness: The Poverty and Potential of Life in Canada* (1990).

INDONESIA

Unfortunately, Indonesia seems unable — or unwilling — to find a reasonable balance between order and overkill. As Islam moderates and modernizes, the rest of Indonesian society is also changing, and the colour of change is green. It is the colour of Islam, but it is also the colour of the army, the colour of forests, and the colour of money. The challenge is how to keep the green of Islam under control; how to cut down the green of the army before it takes control; how to re-green Indonesia's forests before they are completely cut down; how to weed out the corruption sparked by foreign greenbacks. A nation of nominal Muslims is coming of age in Indonesia. They want freedom, not fundamentalism, in their future.

MARTIN COHN, journalist, "Under Control," *Saturday Night*, Nov. 1989.

INDUSTRY
See also LABOUR

Canadian ownership is highest where technology levels are lowest. We have secured the commanding heights of the dying industries.

JOHN J. SHEPHERD, Vice-President, Science Council of Canada, "Uncertain Prospects: Canadian Manufacturing Industry, 1971-77" (Oct. 1977), a report of the SCC's Industrial Policies Committee.

We must create a society where change does not mean dramatic income loss, loss of self-esteem, the dark hole of poverty and helplessness that social and industrial change has come to mean to millions of workers since the Industrial Revolution.

BOB RAE, Ontario NDP leader, address,

"A Socialist's Manifesto," *The Globe and Mail*, 1 Oct. 1990.

INFLATION
See also ECONOMICS

Inflation is no more.

PIERRE ELLIOTT TRUDEAU, Prime Minister, quoted by John G. Diefenbaker in the House of Commons, 30 April 1975. "Two and a half years ago the Prime Minister (Mr. Trudeau) announced with great bravado — he was in this country — that he had great news for us."

No one in this House — and, I wager, no one in Canada — will forget the Prime Minister saying on national television, "Zap, you're frozen," trying to caricature a serious position put forward which he had condemned in 1974 and embraced in 1975 in an act of cynicism which has undermined the confidence of Canadians not just in this government but in the political process itself.
Some hon. Members: Hear, hear!
Some hon. Members: Zap!

JOE CLARK, Opposition leader, House of Commons, 1 Dec. 1976.

In 1970, we were fighting inflation with unemployment. In 1978, we are fighting unemployment with inflation.

BARRY MATHER, one-time Member of Parliament and journalist, observation made in July 1978.

It may be as well to remember that there has never yet been an inflation that wasn't followed by a deflation — permanent inflation beyond the capacity of the imagination or the mathematics of the mint.

KEN LEFOLII, journalist, *Claims: Adventures in the Gold Trade* (1987).

INFORMATION

One of the big effects of the speed of light, or the light of speed, is the tendency of everything to become software rather than hardware. The 19th century was an

age of hardware, the 20th century is that of software — that is, of information.
MARSHALL McLUHAN, communications theorist, address, Mohawk College, Hamilton, Ont., 17 May 1977.

Electronic information now encompasses the entire planet, forming another hidden borderline or frontier whose action has been to rob many countries of their former identities. In the case of the First World, the Fourth World of electronic information dims down nationalism and private identities, whereas in its encounter with the Third World of India, China, and Africa, the new electric information environment has the effect of depriving these people of their identities.
MARSHALL McLUHAN, communications theorist, and Bruce R. Powers, academic, authors of *The Global Village: Transformations in World Life and Media in the 21st Century* (1989).

I would try to get all Canadians to understand that in an information economy they have to think upside down. Money is kept in investments, where it earns interest. Information that is hoarded carries a negative interest rate: the longer you hoard it without acting on it, the less it's worth. This is a tough one and would take up a lot of my time.
DIAN COHEN, economist, contributor to *If I Were Prime Minister* (1987) edited by Mel Hurtig.

We're not withholding information. There are no details.
WILLIAM VANDER ZALM, B.C. Premier, *Quotations from Chairman Zalm* (1988) edited by Stephen Osborne and Mary Schendlinger.

The more shocking the message, the more information contained therein.
FRANK OGDEN, futurologist, "Ogden's Sixteenth Law," *Dr. Tomorrow's Lessons from the Future* (updated June 1989).

What is certain is that the future belongs to *we the people* — all armed with the power of new ideas in a world "globalized by information."
FRANK FEATHER, futurologist, *G-Forces: Reinventing the World — The 35 Global Forces Restructuring Our World* (1989).

Whitewash comes in many colours.
ROBERT PRIEST, poet, aphorism, March 1990.

Let me say data is like a bikini. What it reveals is interesting, what it conceals is often vital.
JANET HALLIWELL, President, Science Council of Canada, quoted by Stephen Strauss in *The Globe and Mail*, 11 March 1991.

INNOVATION

Great thinkers have seldom been honoured in their own time. From medieval scholars who faced the torture of the Inquisition for challenging the dogmas of their day to modern-day innovators who have endured professional censure or scientific excommunication, history shows that it is a mixed blessing to be far ahead of one's time.
W. EDWARD MANN and EDWARD HOFFMAN, sociologist and psychologist, *The Man Who Dreamed of Tomorrow: A Conceptual Biography of Wilhelm Reich* (1980).

INSCRIPTIONS
See also GRAFFITI

VEXATOR CANADIENSIS / THE TORMENTOR OF CANADA
This epithetical description of the English monarch, described as despotic, appears on the Vexator Canadiensis Tokens. These are among the strangest tokens issued anywhere. In 1825, the use of private tokens was outlawed in early Canada. These tokens, which were issued sometime after 1830 but backdated to 1811, resemble legitimate currency. VEXATOR is Latin for "Tormentor" and close to VENATOR (trapper).

UN SOUS
  There was an error in French on the first
  bank tokens issued in 1835. These copper
  tokens were issued by the Bank of Montreal. "The value was inscribed in French
  on the reverse, but was incorrectly expressed by the plural form SOUS rather
  than SOU," explained J.A. Haxby and R.C.
  Willey in Coins of Canada (1971). "This
  did not hinder their circulation at all for
  the error was taken by everyone as a
  guarantee of authenticity."

INSPIRATION

Some time, I think, / the perfect arrangement / of words will come / (though, even
as I write the word, / I doubt if I would like
perfection) / some time there will be / the
moment of illumination / (but aren't all
moments / moments of illumination?)
  ELIZABETH BREWSTER, poet, "Cloud
  Formations," *Entertaining Angels* (1988).

INSULTS

Pass me the tequila, Sheila, / And lie down
and love me again.
  Line of an old song quoted by Conservative Trade Minister John Crosbie and directed against Liberal Member Sheila
  Copps, at a Conservative gathering, Victoria, 27 February 1990, quoted in *The
  Toronto Star*, 1 March 1990. Reprimanded
  by Prime Minister Mulroney, Crosbie extended his apologies to Copps. This was
  offence No. 2. Offence No. 1 occurred five
  years earlier when Crosbie rose in the
  House of Commons and called Copps a
  "titmouse" and ordered her to "just quiet
  down, baby." Copps shot back: "I'm not
  his baby. And I'm no one's baby." This
  gave the feisty Copps the title for her
  memoirs, *Nobody's Baby* (1986).

INSURANCE

From 1980 to 1984 life insurance companies in Canada made total profits of $3.076
billion dollars, and paid federal income
taxes at the rate of 4.5%.

MEL HURTIG, publisher and nationalist,
presentation to the Senate Standing Committee on Banking, Trade and Commerce,
26 July 1990.

INTELLIGENCE
See also IDEAS
         THOUGHTS
         WISDOM

The visually oriented person is always
looking for connections rather than intervals. The gap or interval is where the action is. The connection is a hang-up.
  MARSHALL McLUHAN, communications
  theorist, letter to Emily Hahn, 17 March
  1970, *Letters of Marshall McLuhan* (1987)
  edited by Matie Molinaro, Corinne Mc-
  Luhan, and William Toye.

Fearful though I am of the havoc that will
be the inevitable result of continued selfishness and indifference, I am far from
despondent, for I believe in the human
quality of man's instincts and in the essential rational behaviour of which he is capable.
  PIERRE ELLIOTT TRUDEAU, Prime Minister, address, Mansion House, London, England, 13 March 1975.

I have experienced similar intense intellectual excitement perhaps a dozen times
during my career and have seen it frequently in others. I hope that each one of
you has had this experience at times during your careers, and frequently. But I wonder, and I am fearful. I do not think this
experience is as common as it once was
when there was a better balance between
training, education, and scholarship in
our universities.
  DONALD A. CHANT, Vice-President, University of Toronto, address, Empire Club
  of Canada, Toronto, 22 Jan. 1976.

Nothing so gives the illusion of intelligence as personal association with large
sums of money.
  JOHN KENNETH GALBRAITH, economist

and author, quoted by Charles Trueheart in *The Toronto Star*, 10 April 1988.

We are all functioning far below our upper intellectual reach. Throughout history, enterprising parents have increased their children's intelligence, by plan, to levels assessed as high as I.Q. 275. This is the level our brains are designed to work at.
SIDNEY LEDSON, reading and intelligence advancement specialist, news release, 23 March 1989.

Intelligent life may turn out to be a short-term evolutionary dead end. It has already had a cataclysmic effect on the rest of the biosphere.
BRIAN FAWCETT, cultural commentator, *Public Eye: An Investigation into the Disappearance of the World* (1990).

INTEREST RATES

It is a country that has one of the world's larger per capita national debts but frets more about interest rates in the United States.
ANDREW H. MALCOLM, U.S. correspondent, "Northern Contradiction," *Saturday Night*, Dec. 1987.

INTERNATIONALISM
See also FOREIGN AFFAIRS

Further than that, I should like to say this, that Canada is situated on the North American continent. Geographically and economically we are North American. To no small extent the attitude of our great neighbour must be a determining factor in our international relations. I cannot be accused of being overinclined to the Americans. I come from old United Empire Loyalist stock.
J.S. WOODSWORTH, CCF leader, casting the sole dissenting vote against Canada's declaration of war on Germany, House of Commons, 8 Sept. 1939.

If all these advantages were used not to affirm Canada as a state but to develop

Canada as a model-builder, then with the hindsight of history, the latter-day Solons, the creative institution-makers, the citizens who help recreate the world's image of itself might be recognized to have been citizens of Canada and Canada itself an "Athenian" variation on an Atlantic theme.
BARBARA WARD, British economist, "The First International Nation," *The Canadian Forum*, Oct. 1968.

Canada is still an international presence. . . . If we can find out why the *idea* rather than the *nation* of Canada can win a growing loyalty rather than commanding it, then, it seems to me, we shall have come very near to trapping that elusive creature, the Canadian Identity.
GEORGE WOODCOCK, author, *The Canadians* (1979).

Interdependence is the dominant fact of life in our era — that we are all responsible for each other's well-being, and that we must learn to live together or face the prospect of perishing together.
PIERRE ELLIOTT TRUDEAU, Prime Minister, Foreword, *Dangers & Options: The Matter of World Survival* (1982) by Willy Brandt.

Are Canadians Politically Naive?
The question should read: Are many Canadians politically naive? As much as I hate to hurt people's feelings, I am afraid I must answer yes. Unfortunately, many are.
JOSEF SKVORECKY, Czech-born novelist and essayist, "Are Canadians Politically Naive?" (1983), *Talkin' Moscow Blues* (1988) edited by Sam Solecki.

When the earth trembles near Naples, disaster strikes at Chernobyl, a mountain slides in Sicily, or a terrorist bomb explodes anywhere in Europe, Canadians are involved directly, personally.
JOE CLARK, Secretary of State, address, Vienna, Austria, Nov. 1986.

I became one of those people who are stuck here by circumstance, but who really belong someplace else, someplace more sensitive, more sophisticated, more international, yes, that's it, international, part of a world of the imagination, vastly more meaningful than wherever it is we happen to be, a world free of the messiness of the here and now, free of the pettiness of real people.

JOHN GRAY, composer and performer, Preface, *Local Boy Makes Good: Three Musicals* (1987).

Canadians, secure in the world because they don't feel the peculiarly American urge to cajole and bully the world into becoming a mirror image of itself, are relaxed and diffident. They do not need to be aggressive because they do not experience irrational fears of invasion from tiny Caribbean islands. Canadians are realists in the world, preferring to pour oil on troubled waters rather than to lay mines in them.

STEPHEN BROOK, English travel writer, *Maple Leaf Rag: Travels across Canada* (1987).

Why are so many Canadians willing to give up six bracing months of winter to venture south? It is, in most cases, merely a matter of an inherited sense of imperial mission. Or noblesse oblige, if you like.

MORDECAI RICHLER, novelist, commenting on the role of those Canadians who have "made it" in the United States, "The Canadians Are Coming," *Signature*, April 1987.

No one I know lives in the house where they grew up or even in the town or village where they once were children. Most of my friends live apart from their parents. Many were born in one country and now live in another. Others live in exile, forming their thoughts in a second language among strangers. I have friends whose family past was consumed in the concentration camps. They are orphans in time. This country has made migration, expatriation and exile the norm, rootedness the exception.

MICHAEL IGNATIEFF, historian and child of White Russian exiles and Scottish Canadians, opening lines of *The Russian Album* (1987).

The way stations on the road to this new internationalism were Armenia, Verdun, the Russian front, Auschwitz, Hiroshima, Vietnam, Cambodia, and Lebanon. A century of total war has made victims of us all, civilians and military, men, women, and children alike.

MICHAEL IGNATIEFF, author and television personality, "Is Nothing Sacred? The Ethics of Television," *Daedalus: Journal of the American Academy of Arts & Sciences*, "In Search of Canada," Fall 1988.

Illegal immigrants do not flee to places of no worth, nor do foreign companies voluntarily buy into dead ends. A country that recognized the envy with which so many outsiders viewed it should not be seeking to build barriers around itself but exploiting — economically, socially, and intellectually — its unbounded fortune.

JOHN FRASER, editor, "Diary," *Saturday Night*, Nov. 1989.

My country is the English language.

KILDARE DOBBS, travel writer, quoted by George Galt, editor of *The Saturday Night Traveller* (1990).

Peace, order, and good government have always been Canadian ideals, and we should work to make them global.

BOYCE RICHARDSON, author, *Time to Change: Canada's Place in a World in Crisis* (1990).

Canadians are particularly prone to think in simplistic terms about international affairs because the country has spent its entire history as a military appendage of either Britain or the United States.

GWYNNE DYER and TINA VILJOEN, commentator and TV producer, *The Defence of Canada: In the Arms of the Empire* (1990).

INTERVIEWS

See also NEWS

The first essential of an interviewer is to have a fine opinion of himself. There is no such joy to the interviewee as to find a man of magnitude interviewing him.

> R.E. KNOWLES, feature writer and interviewer for *The Toronto Star* in the 1930s, address to the Toronto Women's Press Club, quoted by Ross Harkness in *J.E. Atkinson of the Star* (1963).

That's why I pad my interviews with quotations. I enjoy getting paid for something Shakespeare wrote.

> R.E. KNOWLES, feature writer and interviewer for *The Toronto Star* in the 1930s, quoted by Roy Greenaway in *The News Game* (1966).

If I feel I have to hold my breath to ask a question, if it's instructive, then I don't ask. I want to hear what the person thinks, want to know the answer; but I won't cross the line if the question would be offensive.

> BARBARA FRUM, anchor of CBC-TV's *The Journal*, quoted by Sally Saddler in *TV Guide*, 24 March 1990.

I'd like to say it's pleasure to meet you, but I won't know that until I read what you write.

> STOMPIN' TOM CONNORS, singer and songwriter, addressing an interviewer, quoted by Mitch Potter in *The Toronto Star*, 27 May 1990.

INTUITION

No significant advance could have been made in civilizaton without intuition. No lasting work of art, no startling discovery, no wizardly piece of science, no delicious recipe, no successful business, no well-read child, no happy marriage could have been wrought without intuition.

> DANIEL CAPPON, physician and environmentalist, *Intuition: Harnessing the Hidden Power of the Mind* (1989).

INUIT

See also NATIVE PEOPLES

Let it be borne in mind, that where the Esquimaux can live, there the English seaman can live. We may yet hope to see the crews of the "Erebus" and "Terror" once more ready with a yarn about Christmas at the Pole, to help out a Christmas in England.

> CHARLES DICKENS and ROBERT McCORMICK, novelist and explorer, collaborators on an article called "Christmas in the Frozen Regions," *Household Words: A Weekly Journal*, 21 Dec. 1850.

We believe every savage to be in his heart covetous, treacherous, and cruel; and we have yet to learn what knowledge the white man — lost, houseless, shipless, apparently forgotten by his race, plainly famine-stricken, weak, frozen, helpless, and dying — has of the gentleness of Esquimaux nature.

> CHARLES DICKENS, novelist, author of an article on the Arctic published in *Household Words* in 1854, quoted by David Roberts in "Dickens and the Arctic," *Horizon*, Jan. 1980.

To judge by the legislation of the Pentateuch the ancient Semites appear to have passed through a course of moral evolution not unlike that which we can still detect in process among the Esquimaux of Baffin Land. Some of the old laws of Israel are clearly savage taboos of a familiar type thinly disguised as commands of the deity. This disguise is indeed a good deal more perfect in Palestine than in Baffin Land, but in substance it is the same. Among the Esquimaux, it is the will of Sedna; among the Israelites, it is the will of Jehovah.

> SIR JAMES G. FRAZER, social anthropologist and classical scholar, author of *The Golden Bough* (one-volume edition, 1922).

The ability to provide for a great number of people would seem to be the greatest glory to which an Eskimo can aspire.

When he becomes thoroughly civilized, this barbaric idea will of course be duly eradicated, and his ambition will then be to slaughter the greatest number.

> JANUARIUS A. MacGAHAN, Anglo-Irish correspondent and adventurer, *Under the Northern Lights* (1876).

My sincerest wish for our friends the Eskimo is that civilization may *never* reach them.

> ROALD AMUNDSEN, Arctic explorer, quoted by Pierre Berton in *The Mysterious North* (1956).

There are only very few Inuit, but millions of qallunaat, just like mosquitoes. It is something very special and wonderful to be an Inuk — they are like the snow geese. If an Inuk forgets his language and his Inuit ways, he will be nothing but just another mosquito.

> ABRAHAM OKPIK, Inuit spokesperson, "What It Means to Be an Inuk" (1960), reprinted in *Inuktitut* No. 70, 1989.

I envy them. They are the most enviable people in the world and they are fast disappearing and this breaks my heart.

> FARLEY MOWAT, writer, extolling the personal qualities of the Inuit, interviewed by Alexander Ross in *Maclean's*, March, 1968.

The Eskimo knife has hardly varied since the days of the first proto-Eskimos, four thousand years ago, and is basically little different from our own standard table knife. Eskimos, until very recently, would not use scissors: if offered a pair, they would separate the two blades for use as ordinary blades, to which they were accustomed.

> NIGEL DAVIES, British historian, *Voyages to the New World: Fact or Fantasy?* (1979).

In keeping with the teaching of the Second Vatican Council, they have striven with greater awareness to show you, as the Church earnestly desires, even greater respect for your patrimony, your language, and your customs. Christ himself has become Indian and Inuit in you, his members.

> POPE JOHN PAUL II, Pontiff, addressing a native delegation in Rome in 1984 and agreeing to make a second attempt to visit Fort Simpson, N.W.T., quoted by Ron Graham in *God's Dominion: A Sceptic's Quest* (1990).

What do the Inuit have to offer? Well, we have lived in harmony with our northern environment for thirty thousand years, while it has taken less than a thousand years for "Western" values to bring the entire planet's ecology to the brink of collapse. Perhaps a majority of Canadians will not realize that there are better ways of doing things — until more nuclear destruction, more toxic waste, more acid rain, more famine, more incurable diseases, and countless other miseries have taken their toll.

> PETER ERNERK, President of the Keewatin Inuit Association, former Member of the N.W.T. Legislative Assembly, contributor to *If I Were Prime Minister* (1987) edited by Mel Hurtig.

From Australia to the Americas, the image of the classic Eskimo is still that of Nanook of the North, the indomitable hunter clad in a sealskin anorak and polar-bear pants, his harpoon poised for the kill, his son lying happily with the husky puppies on the ice outside the family igloo. In the Arctic today, this vision is as ludicrous as that of Caesar, his toga flowing behind him, a bunch of grapes in one hand and a silver chalice in the other, striding through a traffic jam in Rome.

> SAM HALL, British correspondent, *The Fourth World: The Heritage of the Arctic and Its Destruction* (1987). Hall noted: "The transformation from Stone Age to Space Age began during World War Two."

The best thing for the Government of Canada to do to these Inuit is to establish one big apartment building in southern Ontario and move them all down there.

> Letter from an unnamed administrator with the Department of Indian and Northern Affairs noted by Charlie Watt, later

Senator Watt, quoted by Roy MacGregor in *Chief: The Fearless Vision of Billy Diamond* (1989).

If current trends continue, most of the Inuit living in the arctic in the year 2025 will be second-generation wards of the state, whose society, economy, and culture may have more in common with an urban slum than with the life their grandparents knew.

COLIN IRWIN, sociologist and author of *Lords of the Arctic: Wards of the State* (1988), a report prepared for the Department of National Health and Welfare, quoted in *Northern Perspectives*, Jan.-March 1989.

INVESTMENT

Canada has by far the greatest foreign domination of industry and resources of the twenty or so developed nations of the world: 99 percent of our tobacco industry is foreign owned, as is 92 percent of our automotive sector, 76 percent of our chemical industry, 78 percent of our electrical-apparatus industry, 84 percent of transportation, and 53 percent of our combined manufacturing and petroleum industries.

This is not foreign investment. This is foreign control. And most of it — almost three-quarters — is American.

MAUDE BARLOW, chairperson, Council of Canadians, *Parcel of Rogues: How Free Trade Is Failing Canada* (1990), as quoted in *The Canadian Forum*, Dec. 1990.

IRAQ
See GULF WAR

IRISH PEOPLE
See also BRITISH EMPIRE & COMMONWEALTH

I'm a Canadian by choice but an Irishman by profession.

SHEA DUFFIN, Irish-Canadian performer and impersonator of Brendan Behan, interview, CBC Radio, 24 Aug. 1989.

ISLANDS

Perhaps our children can sow the seeds in the sea and bring forth again the island that the world has been searching for since the dawn of history, the island that is both nature and human society restored to their original form, where there is no sovereignty and yet where all of us are kings.

NORTHROP FRYE, literary critic, final thoughts on Shakespeare's play *The Tempest*, in *Northrop Frye on Shakespeare* (1989) edited by Robert Sandler.

ISRAEL
See also JEWISH PEOPLE

Stand Up, O Jerusalem! That "the Land of Israel" may soon become like the Garden of Eden, and "The Joy of the Whole Earth" (as predicted) now that "The Federation of the World" and "Parliament of Man" has at last become an Imperative Necessity.

HENRY WENTWORTH MONK, prophet, Manifesto issued in 1896, quoted by R.S. Lambert in *For the Time Is at Hand: An Account of the Prophesies of Henry Wentworth Monk of Ottawa, Friend of the Jews, and Pioneer of World Peace* (1947).

My priorities are as follows: Torah or humanity, then Canada and Israel in equal portions.

REUBEN SLONIM, rabbi and author, *To Kill a Rabbi* (1987).

I was born on a Western prairie, but my heart is in the valley of Jezreel and in the mountains of Galilee. To the rest of the world, Zion is an ancient, distant soil; but to you and to me it is home.

REUBEN SLONIM, rabbi and author, finding common ground for the Palestinian Arab and the Israeli Jew, *To Kill a Rabbi* (1987).

But they continue to exist, inside and outside the boundaries of Israel established in 1948. Israel must find a way to live with them and with their Arab neighbours. At the time of my first visit I said pointedly, "Israel has a future only as a member of the Arab League."

HANS BLUMENFELD, architect-planner, referring to the Palestinian Arabs, *Life Begins at 65: The Not Entirely Candid Autobiography of a Drifter* (1987).

Israel stands alone as the only democratic system that works in an otherwise repressive region of the world. Its people are hardworking, educated and friendly — and its economy is just starting to mend, thanks, in part, to a free trade deal with the United States and ample help from Canadians and many others. But its leaders must come to terms with the desire of its Arab residents for a homeland of their own.

DIANE FRANCIS, columnist, *Maclean's*, 26 Sept. 1988.

They should put up a sign over passport control at Ben Gurion Airport that reads: "All logic stops here." This is the Middle East and it's a land of extremes.

LEON KOFFLER, Toronto-born resident of Tel Aviv, quoted by Helen Worthington in *The Toronto Star*, 5 April 1989.

There is a joke told frequently in Israel about how the Jews first received title to their strip of land on the eastern shore of the Mediterranean. Moses was a horrendous stutterer. After leading his people out of Egypt, he suggested they head for a roomy, resource-rich and trouble-free country called Canada. His newly freed followers, however, couldn't quite make out his instructions. They thought he said Canaan.

SHELDON TEITELBAUM, cultural commentator whose background links Montreal, Tel Aviv, and Los Angeles, "Continental Shifts," *The Los Angeles Times*, 17 July 1990.

ITALIAN PEOPLE

Deign to make all the Italians of the world eager right now for the foundation of a New Italy in the North-West.

LOUIS RIEL, Métis leader and mystic, diary entry, 19 Aug. 1885, *The Diaries of Louis Riel* (1976) edited by Thomas Flanagan.

Italy became my adopted home. I fell hopelessly in love with my curve of the Tiber. The best of old Rome was at my feet and there I am still planted — maple trees from Muskoka and all.

ROLOFF BENY, photographer, native of Medicine Hat, Alta., resident of Rome, Italy, from 1957 to his death in 1984, address, Empire Club of Canada, Toronto, 27 Oct. 1983.

Senator Peter Bosa recommended in a December 6, 1979 speech to the Senate that the government remedy the improper Anglicization of Caboto's name in Canadian toponomy so that, for example, the Cabot Trail would become the Caboto Trail.

ROBERT F. HARNEY, historian, referring to Giovanni Caboto (a.k.a. John Cabot), *Arrangiarsi: The Italian Immigration Experience in Canada* (1989) edited by Roberto Perin and Franco Sturino.

They are building Rome in one day in Toronto, and it will disappear in the snows.

PIER GIORGIO DI CICCO, poet, "Multicultural Blues," quoted by Kenneth Bagnell in *Canadese: A Portrait of the Italian Canadians* (1989).

On behalf of the government and people of Canada, I offer a full and unqualified apology for the wrongs done to our fellow Canadians of Italian origin during World War II.

BRIAN MULRONEY, Prime Minister, addressing the National Congress of Italian Canadians, Concord, Ont., 4 Nov. 1990, quoted by Jonathan Ferguson in *The Toronto Star* the following day. Some 700 Canadians of Italian background were deemed suspect and rounded up and sent to internment camps during World War II.

J

JAPANESE PEOPLE

Tears run down my cheek / Remembering your voice / Looking at the Canadian sunset.

> Translation of the Japanese-language refrain of the pop song "Love Letter from Canada" performed by the popular singer YOKO HATANAKA of Tokyo and a hit song in Tokyo in 1978-79.

Take a look at the Japanese. They have virtually no resources. All the Japanese really have going for them are ninety million over-achievers! Think what the Japanese would give for Canada's resources.

> ZOLTAN MERSZEI, CEO, Dow Chemical Company, address, Empire Club of Canada, Toronto, 16 Feb. 1978.

The story of the Japanese in Canada tells us something about universal corruption, universal greed, universal ignorance, blindness, and fear. We are at one with other countries of the world, dancing the same dance in our stained underwear.

> JOY KOGAWA, author, "The Enemy Within," *The Writer and Human Rights* (1983) edited by the Toronto Arts Group for Human Rights.

I was in Hiroshima, Japan, in the early 1970s. I landed in Tokyo, took the wrong train to Hiroshima, got into the wrong car on the wrong train for the trip, bumped my head on both exit and entrance of the train. . . . I didn't fit the country physically. Too tall. I kept hitting my head on something or other.

> AL PURDY, poet, Preface, *The Collected Poems of Al Purdy* (1986) edited by Russell Brown.

Close to three Japans would fit into Ontario, which has fewer people than Tokyo.

> ALLAN FOTHERINGHAM, columnist, *Capitol Offences: Dr. Foth Meets Uncle Sam* (1986).

My genes can be traced in a direct line to Japan. I am a pure-blooded member of the Japanese race. And whenever I go there, I am always astonished to see the power of that biological connection. In subways in Tokyo, I catch familiar glimpses of the eyes, hairline or smile of my Japanese relatives. Yet when those same people open their mouths to communicate, the vast cultural gulf that separates them from me becomes obvious: English is my language, Shakespeare is my literature, British his-

tory is what I learned and Beethoven is my music.
> DAVID SUZUKI, Vancouver-born scientist and media personality, *Metamorphosis: Stages in a Life* (1987).

Nearly half a century ago, in the crisis of wartime, the Government of Canada wrongfully incarcerated, seized the property, and disenfranchised thousands of citizens of Japanese ancestry.

We cannot change the past. But we must, as a nation, have the courage to face up to these historical facts.
> BRIAN MULRONEY, Prime Minister, offering the government's apology, accompanied by a comprehensive redress for the injustices committed against Japanese Canadians during World War II, House of Commons, 22 Sept. 1988.

Tokyo is the only city in the world that gets safer and cleaner as it gets bigger.
> RAYMOND MORIYAMA, architect, quoted by Robert Fulford in "Tokyo," *The Globe and Mail's Destinations*, Nov. 1989.

I also developed that night a theory, not watertight but useful, that I call the Reverse Generality. If a generality is more or less true in Canada, the opposite will likely be the case in Japan.
> ROBERT FULFORD, cultural commentator, "Tokyo," *The Globe and Mail's Destinations*, Nov. 1989.

Most Americans think Canadians are Japanese.
> Line of an advertisement in *Maclean's*, 27 Nov. 1989. The advertisement, promoting the magazine itself, was reporting on the findings of an opinion poll. Apparently when Americans were asked to identify their biggest trading partner, 69% said Japan; only 12% gave the correct answer, Canada.

Japan and Asia should be considered the Near West, not the Far East.
> Attributed to former Prime Minister PIERRE ELLIOTT TRUDEAU by executive

Mamoru Iwamoto in *The Globe and Mail's Destinations*, 3 Dec. 1990.

We feel very contrite about the unbearable sufferings and hardships brought upon the peoples of the Asia Pacific by the actions of the Japanese state. I expressed this formally to Prime Minister Mulroney. By saying that, I expressed my apology for the unbearable suffering and pain that was caused by the Japanese state against the Canadian people who experienced such sufferings.
> TOSHIKI KAIFU, Japan's Prime Minister, admitting guilt concerning treatment of Allied prisoners of war during World War II, press conference following his private meeting with Prime`Minister Mulroney, Tokyo, 28 May 1991, quoted by Edith Terry and Rudy Platiel in *The Globe and Mail* the following day.

JEWISH PEOPLE
> *See also* HOLOCAUST, THE JEWISH
> ISRAEL

Geyt, Yidelech, in der vayter velt; / In Kanade vet ir ferdinen gelt.
> Couplet from the Yiddish song titled "Song of the Gusgeyer" which translates "Go, dear Jews, into the wide world; / In Canada you will make your fortune." Quoted by Frank Rasky in *Just a Simple Pharmacist: The Story of Murray Koffler, Builder of the Shoppers Drug Mart Empire* (1988).

Oh the mental vacuum that is Canada. . . . There is terrible social cowardice, and all action here seems so furtive that one can only conclude that some unacknowledged guilt is behind it all. Canada needs about 2 million Jews to bring life to it.
> MARSHALL McLUHAN, communications theorist, letter to Wyndham Lewis, 13 Dec. 1944, *Letters of Marshall McLuhan* (1987) edited by Matie Molinaro, Corinne McLuhan, and William Toye. "Canada Needs More Jews" is the title of an article written by McLuhan in 1944 but never published. McLuhan argued, according

to biographer Philip Marchand in *Marshall McLuhan: The Medium and the Messenger* (1989), that Canada would benefit from Jewish energy, imagination, reverence for art, love of learning, and sense of community.

The novel — a Canadian work — turned out to be a beautifully written story but of no interest to me. A young Canadian man (Jewish) meets a young Canadian girl (gentile). They fall in love and what with her family's objection to him and his family's objection to her and the concerns of their friends and their inability to achieve reservations at a resort in the Laurentians, they have a hard time getting to a happy ending.
  GARSON KANIN, Hollywood scriptwriter and producer Samuel Goldwin's script adviser, *Hollywood* (1984). In the Spring of 1947, Goldwin had under option Gwethalyn Graham's novel *Earth and High Heaven*, but he never produced it, frequently referring to it as "a great story . . . 'The Highest Heaven.'"

Where the Jew thought of a pogrom annihilating him, now we all have the anxiety of an atom bomb or a hydrogen bomb annihilating us and where the Jew was concerned with the question of justice, what kind of justice? What kind of God will permit these things? Now everybody is concerned with that, in short everybody's become an existentialist but the Jew has been an existentialist all his life. So being a Jew gave me an enormous advantage because I was able to talk about things long before these things made an impact on the minds and hearts of others.
  IRVING LAYTON, poet, observations made in 1972, *Taking Sides: The Collected Social and Political Writings* (1977) edited by Howard Aster.

Why, I was asked, couldn't you have given the boy an Italian name?
  MORDECAI RICHLER, novelist, recalling a rhetorical question addressed to him by a member of the Montreal Jewish community upon the publication of *The Apprenticeship of Duddy Kravitz* (1959), address, Brock University, St. Catharines, 28 Nov. 1989, quoted by Shawn Berry in *The St. Catharines Standard* the following day.

"I have experienced anti-Semitism in public life in a very profound way," says Hier, harking back to his dinner with the Queen. Sitting at his table — Hier had ordered a kosher meal — was a kilt-clad Canadian admiral holding forth on the ethnicity he declared was ruining Canada. The admiral turned to Hier and said: "Take you, rabbi. Here we all are having dinner. And you have to eat differently."
  Hier turned to the admiral in disgust: "With all due respect, sir," Hier said, "if you are not embarrassed to sit amongst us wearing a skirt, I don't think I have to be embarrassed about what I choose to eat."
  Anecdote told by MARVIN HIER, the Orthodox rabbi who from 1962 led the Congregation Schara Tzedek in Vancouver and in 1977 founded the Simon Wiesenthal Center in Los Angeles, at a reception for Queen Elizabeth and Prince Philip in Victoria, quoted by Sheldon Teitelbaum and Tom Waldman, "The Unorthodox Rabbi," *The Los Angeles Times Magazine*, 15 July 1990.

Before we accuse the Jews, let us first accuse ourselves.
  JOHN BASSETT, publisher of *The Toronto Telegram*, quoted by Reuben Slonim in *To Kill a Rabbi* (1987).

The function of the rabbi is to sing songs, not the artificial and dainty melodies intended to please the decadent ears of the soft, the uncaring, the indifferent and the sufferers who use their pain to justify vindictiveness, for such a tune dies like tinkling notes in a hurricane. A rabbi must sing the songs of the people, so that the deaf ear of power may be touched and the hard heart of conventional living be moved. A rabbi must sing, above all else, of pity and justice and mercy.

REUBEN SLONIM, rabbi and memoirist, *To Kill a Rabbi* (1987).

For we are forbidden to turn present and future life into death, as the price of remembering death at Auschwitz. And we are equally forbidden to affirm present and future life, at the price of forgetting Auschwitz.
EMIL FACKENHEIM, philosopher, "The 614th Commandment" (1978), *The Jewish Thought of Emil Fackenheim: A Reader* (1987) edited by Michael L. Morgan. (This "commandment" is reproduced in italics in the original.)

A Jew today is one who except for an historical accident — Hitler's loss of the war — would have either been murdered or never been born. One makes this statement at a conference on Jewish identity. There is an awkward silence. And then the conference proceeds as if nothing had happened.
EMIL FACKENHEIM, philosopher, "The 614th Commandment" (1978), *The Jewish Thought of Emil Fackenheim: A Reader* (1987) edited by Michael L. Morgan.

I see the destruction of my country, the destruction of the Jewish community. . . . If the PQ forms the next government, it's going to be pure, absolute hell. . . . This is a fight. It's a war — absolute war. . . . If we turn our backs on the Liberals, it will be suicide. The moment the PQ gets in, folks, it's done. All over. . . .
I have a fantasy about holding the next Seagram's annual meeting and telling the shareholders it's the last one to be held in Montreal. If, God forbid, the PQ is elected, I will make that statement.
CHARLES BRONFMAN, Canadian corporate head, Seagram's, address, Allied Jewish Community Services Building, Montreal, delivered the night prior to the election of the Parti Québécois on 15 Nov. 1976. (The dire consequences never followed.) Quoted by Peter C. Newman in *Bronfman Dynasty: The Rothschilds of the New World* (1978).

My socialism stems from my Jewish background. I believe that one of the obligations of being a Jew, if you really follow the dictates of Judaism, is that you have to be exemplary. To be a Jew is to carry a greater share of moral responsibility. There should be at least a modicum of this principle in every Jewish home, and certainly no less in a Jewish state.
MIRIAM WADDINGTON, poet, quoted by Harry Gutkin with Mildred Gutkin in "The Poet as Landscape," *The Worst of Times/The Best of Times* (1987).

It is part of the Jewish faith to believe in struggle, to believe that there is a drive, a hunger towards improving the world and making it a better place. It is the struggle between idealism and realism. I see what is real, but I refuse to give into it!
SRUL IRVING GLICK, composer, *The Toronto Star*, 31 July 1988.

They take up too much space.
Remark made by the Montreal-based publisher and businessman PIERRE PÉLADEAU to a business associate concerning advertisements placed in his newspapers by Jewish clothing manufacturers, quoted in *L'Actualité*, April 1990.
Péladeau denied that the remark was an attack on the Jewish community and regretted that it was interpreted as racist. "*L'Actualité* quoted him as saying of Jews: 'They take up too much space.' He has also said that women 'often lack judgment' and that female executives use seduction to get what they want because they can't handle boardroom pressure." Barrie McKenna in *The Globe and Mail*, 24 April 1990.

I have great respect for the Jews, but they take too much space. I want us to help our people who are in much greater need of it.
Memo written by the Quebec publisher PIERRE PÉLADEAU to the editors of *Le Journal de Montréal* concerning the allocation of space for feature articles on Anglophone Jewish fashion designers, cited in an editorial in the *The Globe and Mail*, 25 April 1990.

In the city here ... there is no doubt that the fashion business is controlled by the Jewish people, English-speaking.

> Memo written by the Quebec publisher PIERRE PÉLADEAU to the editors of one of his publications, *Journal de Montréal*, when it launched its fashion section, according to *L'Actualité*, quoted by Patricia Poirier in *The Globe and Mail*, 27 April 1990.

I am disappointed in Canada. I have made it a policy not to visit countries with inadequate policies on war criminals. Canada is among them.

> SIMON WIESENTHAL, founder of the Jewish Documentation Centre in Vienna, letter to social activist Sol Littman. Littman read the text at the Toronto premiere of the feature film *Murderers among Us: The Simon Wiesenthal Story*, quoted by Stevie Cameron in *The Globe and Mail*, 8 June 1989.

In our ecumenical age so many non-Jews are fascinated by Jewish history and culture that even Jews are becoming curious about Judaism.

> BERNARD BASKIN, rabbi, Temple Anshe Sholom, Hamilton, *obiter dictum*, 22 May 1990.

There's One Word in Every Language that Evokes an Immediate Emotional Response / JEW

> Wording on a poster issued in May 1990 by the Institute for Jewish Learning, Toronto, drawing attention to "four-week courses in everything from Kashrut to Kant, Bible to Begin, Maimonides to Messiah."

JOHNSON, BEN

> *See also* OLYMPIC GAMES
> STEROIDS
> TRACK AND FIELD

The Fastest Man in the World

> Popular epithet for BEN JOHNSON, track and field star, who at the Goodwill Games in Moscow, 9 July 1986, set the world record for the 100-metre race at 9.95 seconds.

I was thinking about getting to the finishing line as soon as possible.

> BEN JOHNSON, champion sprinter, when asked at the press conference what he was thinking about when he set the world record of 9.83 seconds for the 100-metre dash, Rome, Italy, 30 Aug. 1987. According to James Christie, writing in *The Globe and Mail* the following day, Johnson said: "Maybe I can improve next year for the Olympics in Seoul."

I want to state clearly now that I have never knowingly taken illegal drugs nor have had illegal drugs administered to me. I have always believed, and I certainly believe now, that illegal drugs have no place in our society.... I'm innocent and I welcome the opportunity of proving it.

> BEN JOHNSON, sprinter, open letter to the people of Canada, carried by CP and published in *The Vancouver Sun*, 1 Oct. 1988. Johnson was accused of "uttering the most brazen lie in Canadian sports history." — John Barber, "Moving Target," *The Globe and Mail's Toronto Magazine*, April 1991. The scandal broke on 27 Sept. 1988.

I have never, ever knowingly taken illegal drugs, and I would never embarrass my family, my friends, my country, and the kids who love me.

> BEN JOHNSON, champion sprinter, press conference called after he was stripped of his Olympic gold medal, Toronto, 4 Oct. 1988, quoted by Joseph Hall in *The Toronto Star* the following day. Johnson subsequently admitted to the use of banned anabolic steroids.

I am sure I will be able to beat anyone — so long as other athletes are not taking drugs.

> BEN JOHNSON, sprinter, appearance on French television, quoted in *Maclean's*, 11 Dec. 1989.

If you don't take it, you won't make it.
>   Attributed to Dr. JAMIE ASTAPHAN, who
>   supplied steroids to runner Ben Johnson,
>   at the Dubin inquiry in 1989, quoted by
>   Rick Groen in *The Globe and Mail*, 30 Dec.
>   1990.

Q. Did you hear about the new Ben Johnson pantyhose?
A. It's guaranteed not to run for two years.
>   Adapted from "Kakologia," *Maledicta: The
>   International Journal of Verbal Aggression*,
>   Volume X, 1988-89.

Canadian Wins Gold Medal. / Jamaican-Canadian Accused of Steroid Use. / Jamaican Stripped of Gold Medal.
>   These three captions appear beneath
>   three identical drawings of sprinter Ben
>   Johnson in the editorial cartoon drawn
>   by FRANK EDWARDS which appeared in
>   *The Kingston Whig-Standard*, 28 Sept. 1988.
>   They graph the way Canadians "distanced" themselves from the runner.

Without doubt, without debate, without anyone coming close, the most famous Canadian of all time, worldwide, is an ex-gold medalist, an ex-world record holder, a cheat, now back from two years in the wilderness.
>   STEPHEN BRUNT, sports columnist, *The
>   Globe and Mail*, 29 Jan. 1991.

A perceptive reader points out that Dr. Norman Bethune — and not Johnson, as was suggested here earlier in the week — must be Canada's most famous product, since he's familiar to quite a few people here and just about everybody in the People's Republic of China. Point taken. But try to get a barroom debate going in Rio de Janeiro or Berlin or Kuala Lumpur about Dr. Bethune's bedside manner. You can do that anywhere, anytime about Johnson's running, which has to be the true test of fame.
>   STEPHEN BRUNT, sports columnist, *The
>   Globe and Mail*, 31 Jan. 1991.

JOURNALISM
See also NEWS

I would rather be editor of *The Globe* than governor of Canada.
>   GEORGE BROWN, Father of Confederation and founding editor of *The Globe* in
>   1844 which became *The Globe and Mail* in
>   1936, quoted by Richard J. Doyle in *Hurly-Burly: A Time at The Globe* (1990).

As long as you quoted your source you could publish the most outrageous hokum. News was not truth; it was what somebody *claimed* was truth, even though the phrases that somebody uttered were clearly balderdash. If it made a good story it went into print without qualification.
>   PIERRE BERTON, newspaperman and
>   author, referring to journalistic practices in the 1940s, *Starting Out: 1920-1947*
>   (1987).

Women are raped, watchmen taped, / Girls into slavery sold; / But you'll never read it in *The Globe and Mail*, / Unless it's below the fold.
>   Ditty sung by members of the Press Club
>   in the 1960s, concerning that newspaper's policy of downplaying sensational news, quoted by Val Sears in *Hello,
>   Sweetheart . . . Get Me Rewrite: Remembering the Great Newspaper Wars* (1988).

I just knew he wasn't an American!
>   LYNDON B. JOHNSON, U.S. President, response upon learning that Morley Safer,
>   who broke the story in Aug. 1965 on *CBS
>   Evening News* of how the U.S. Marines
>   levelled the Vietnam village of Cam Ne
>   was not a Communist but a Canadian,
>   quoted by Safer in *Flashbacks: On Returning to Vietnam* (1990).

Q. What makes a good reporter?
A. A good city editor.
>   KEITH DAVEY, Senator and Commissioner, *Report of the Special Senate Committee on Mass Media, Volume I: The
>   Uncertain Mirror* (1971).

In Canada, we have the worst political reporting in the free world. The Press Gallery, supposedly the cream of our journalists, are the most docile, lacklustre, subservient and regurgitative in the Western world.
> PETER WORTHINGTON, newspaperman, address, Empire Club of Canada, Toronto, 8 March 1979.

At *Maclean's*, the editors used to say, if there was no excuse to use the Queen on the cover, they could always get Gordie Howe.
> PETER GZOWSKI, journalist and broadcaster, *The Game of Our Lives* (1981).

I became a journalist, the only trade requiring no degree, papers or evidence of experience or ability. If you can do the job, you are a journalist. If you can't you are fired.
> GARRY MARCHANT, journalist, "Rio de Janeiro" (1974), *Away from Home: Canadian Writers in Exotic Places* (1985).

Mrs. Thatcher told me . . . she was impressed with Toronto, but not so much with some of our newspaper fellows. Like so many in the United Kingdom, she wondered at their lack of knowledge. I suggested that our journalists were not that bad.
> PAUL MARTIN, High Commissioner, entry for 9 Nov. 1975, *The London Diaries 1975-1979* (1988) edited by William R. Young.

The Canadian is a withdrawer from involvement. . . . We're the most politically illiterate people in any developed country in the world, and politically we are dull. . . . We go too far with political indifference.
> CHARLES LYNCH, columnist, quoted in *Meet the Media: Eight of Canada's Best-Known Journalists Talk with Robert Bullis* (1976).

When you're addressing an audience or writing for an audience you can get a wider bracket of people with a touch of entertainment or a bit of flair or preferably above all some humour in a rather humourless world.
> CHARLES LYNCH, columnist, explaining his brand of "personal" journalism, quoted in *Meet the Media: Eight of Canada's Best-Known Journalists Talk with Robert Bullis* (1976).

Where in the hell is Bain?
> Full text of a letter sent by Prime Minister PIERRE ELLIOTT TRUDEAU to *The Globe and Mail* when its featured columnist George Bain left the newspaper to contribute his column to *The Toronto Star*, quoted by Richard J. Doyle in *Hurly-Burly: A Time at The Globe* (1990).

Journalism is the *literature* of Canada.
> LOUIS DUDEK, aphorist, "Can. Lit. Notes," *The Bumper Book* (1986) edited by John Metcalf.

In fact, I don't know any good journalists who aren't as naive as three-year-olds (hence their unending capacity to be genuinely shocked by political duplicity) and as ruthless as Grandma Moses.
> JOHN FRASER, drama critic, foreign correspondent, and magazine editor, *Telling Tales* (1986).

But a press card is something of a passport; it gives a real-world person a privileged view of the unreal world without conferring citizenship.
> CHRISTIE BLATCHFORD, columnist, "Rules of the Game," *Spectator Sports* (1986).

What is left of the antagonistic prejudices of yesteryear is the Canadian media's unshakable predilection to destroy almost anyone who actually does anything.
> CONRAD BLACK, newspaper proprietor and columnist, "Why Does the Press Savage Success?" *The Globe and Mail's Report on Business Magazine*, March 1986.

There is no doubt that journalism is hasty, incomplete, sometimes inaccurate, occasionally misleading, and frequently flawed. It's an imperfect necessity.

KNOWLTON NASH, correspondent and news anchor, *Prime Time at Ten: Behind-the-Camera Battles of Canadian TV Journalism* (1987).

You know, I've had a dandy life, thank you. All I want on my tombstone now are the words: "He was a good reporter."

NORMAN DePOE, veteran newspaperman and broadcaster, quoted by Knowlton Nash in *Prime Time at Ten: Behind-the-Camera Battles of Canadian TV Journalism* (1987).

It is not realized that more than half the world is closed to the journalist these days although it is, in general, open to the businessman or even the tourist. Businessmen and tourists bring money. Journalists bring questions.

JACK CAHILL, correspondent, *Words on War* (1987).

Any politician making a career in the television age is always dicing with the adage "familiarity breeds contempt." Television, however, is not contemptuous about power. Towards the handful of offices that rules the modern world, it displays a degree of humility that contradicts the journalist's code of honour, that nothing is sacred.

MICHAEL IGNATIEFF, author and media personality, "The Ethics of Television," *Daedalus: Journal of the American Academy of Arts and Sciences*, "In Search of Canada," Fall 1988.

Even our titles came dangerously close to self-parody. . . . My own all-time favourite from this school, which I may well have written myself, appeared over an article by Sidney Katz, quite a nice piece of reporting on its own, but labelled, I'm afraid, "Canada's a nation of dental cripples."

PETER GZOWSKI, host of CBC Radio's *Morningside*, commenting on editorial practices at *Maclean's* in the 1950s, author of *The Private Voice: A Journal of Reflections* (1988).

What we have, to coin a phrase from contemporary jargon, is an imperial working press that aspires to be above the law.

CONRAD BLACK, capitalist and publisher, address, Annual Dinner, Canadian Press, 20 April 1988, reported in *The Globe and Mail* the following day.

Journalists as a group, unlike all other powerful groups, require some protection from themselves, and from their own excesses.

CONRAD BLACK, capitalist and publisher, address, Annual Dinner, Canadian Press, 20 April 1988, reported in *The Globe and Mail* the following day.

However, if a journalist's creed were being drawn up, the line, with minor amendments, would be worth stealing: "It is the responsibility of journalists to speak the truth (or as much of it as we can find out) and expose the lies (without prejudice)."

GEORGE BAIN, journalist and columnist, *Maclean's*, 21 Nov. 1988.

F = fairness; A = accuracy; C = clarity; T = thoroughness; S = simplicity.

TIM KOTCHEFF, CTV news vice-president, mnemonic, quoted in *Maclean's*, 3 Oct. 1988.

Two of the happiest days of my life were the day I started and the day I left.

E. GRAYDON CARTER, Canadian-born magazine editor and writer, on joining and then leaving the editorial department of *Time* in New York, prior to launching his own magazine, *Spy*, quoted by Henry Mietkiewicz in *The Toronto Star*, 26 Nov. 1988.

A good journalist is a member of nothing.

RICHARD J. DOYLE, publisher and Senator, quoted by Joey Slinger in *The Toronto Star*, 30 Nov. 1988.

His stock-in-trade is the really neat lead. My personal favourite, written thirty years ago about a suicide I came upon in Vancouver, read: "Gertrude Kringle, al-

ways a tidy girl, hanged herself in the closet today."
VAL SEARS, newspaperman, discussing the role of the feature writer and his "lead," *Hello, Sweetheart . . . Get Me Rewrite: Remembering the Great Newspaper Wars* (1988).

"*The Telegram* was one paper that came with the garbage already wrapped in it."
I lied. It wasn't garbage. It was the fragrant leavings of contemporary history.
VAL SEARS, newspaperman and former feature writer on *The Toronto Telegram*, author of *Hello, Sweetheart . . . Get Me Rewrite: Remembering the Great Newspaper Wars* (1988).

To be true is to be untamed but accurate.
JOHN BASSETT, newspaper publisher noted for his aggressive nature, quoted by Reuben Slonim in *To Kill a Rabbi* (1987).

Allan Fotheringham is the weekly communist for *Maclean's* magazine.
Typographical error in the tagline on Dr. Foth's syndicated column in *Canadian News*, a Florida publication, quoted by Gary Dunford in *The Toronto Sun*, 11 April 1990.

I have been on the road, away from home, for a quarter of a century. Canadians make good travellers. We make good foreign correspondents because we tend to see the world as it is, which is not always quite the way Washington believes that it is.
PETER JENNINGS, Toronto-born ABC anchorman, *Maclean's*, 25 June 1990.

In this business, you need a cast iron stomach and the ability to sleep anywhere.
JOE SCHLESINGER, CBC-TV foreign correspondent, quoted by Marc Dacey in *TV Guide*, 24 Nov. 1990.

JOY

The arch of sky and mightiness of storms / Have moved the spirit within me, / Till I am carried away / Trembling with joy.

UVAVNUK, Eskimo singer and shaman, quoted by Knud Rasmussen in *Across Arctic America: Narrative of the Fifth Thule Expedition* (1927).

JUDGEMENT

Greed overcomes good judgement.
PETER POCKLINGTON, sports and business personality, quoted by Peter Gzowski in *Saturday Night*, April 1982.

If we cease to judge this world, we may find ourselves, very quickly, in one which is infinitely worse.
MARGARET ATWOOD, author, "Witches" (1980), *Active Voice* (2nd ed., 1986) edited by W.H. New and W.E. Messenger.

JUSTICE & INJUSTICE
See also LAW

An Ogdensburgh Judge, recently passing sentence upon a convict, concluded his harangue with, "I banish you from the face of God's earth." The culprit stared at the Judge, and very naturally wondered in what part of the wild world he was going to fix his future residence. Sir Gravity replied, "I guess you may go to Canada or to the devil, but I banish you from the face of God's earth."
News item, *St. Catharines Standard*, 15 June 1837. Ogdensburgh is a small town in Upstate New York.

Future punishment, indeed! I am more concerned with present punishment. God knows we are all punished enough in this life for our misdeeds. Only — it seems to me that it is *weakness* that is punished — not *wickedness*. The weak suffer — the strong go free.
L.M. MONTGOMERY, author, diary, 2 June 1920, *The Selected Journals of L.M. Montgomery: Volume II: 1910-1921* (1987) edited by Mary Rubio and Elizabeth Waterston.

Our forefathers willed this country into being. Times, circumstance and pure will cemented us together in a unique national enterprise, and that enterprise, by flying in the face of all expectations, of all experiences, of all conventional wisdom, that enterprise provides the world with a lesson in fraternity.

This extraordinary undertaking is so advanced on the road to liberty, so advanced in the way of social justice and of prosperity, that to abandon it now would be to sin against the spirit, to sin against humanity.
> PIERRE ELLIOTT TRUDEAU, Prime Minister, address to the nation on the eve of the separatist electoral victory in Quebec, CBC-TV, 24 Nov. 1976, published in *The Globe and Mail* the following day.

Let me say, as forcibly as I can, that the Supreme Court of Canada is not a federal institution; it is a national institution and its members are under no federal allegiance merely because they were federally appointed. Just as there is no federal allegiance, there is no regional allegiance and no political allegiance.
> BORA LASKIN, Chief Justice of Canada, address, Empire Club of Canada, Toronto, 12 March 1981.

The true measure of the success of our society is the ideal we hold of justice and the effort we make to achieve that idea.
> JOHN CROSBIE, lawyer and Minister of Justice, address, Empire Club of Canada, Toronto, 24 Jan 1985.

Once we deny justice to any human life, then we are well on the road to the kind of thinking that impels a fascist dictatorship to the horrors of the death camp and the purge.
> GEORGE GRANT, philosopher, "Abortion and Rights" (1976), *Technology and Justice* (1986).

The Court is governed neither by the laws of nature nor by the laws of logic. Indeed, it is not even bound by the canons of consistency. So much depends upon the cosmic coincidence of which judges are sitting on which cases at any given time.

A. ALAN BOROVOY, General Counsel, Canadian Civil Liberties Association, *When Freedoms Collide: A Case for our Civil Liberties* (1988).

Anger wells up inside as I ask myself why go on overtaxing my strength with cross-country trips and seven-day work weeks, and I risk bankrupting my small law firm to help Canadian citizens whose government works against them.
> JOSEPH L. RAUH, Jr., Washington civil-rights attorney, letter to Prime Minister Brian Mulroney, 15 May 1986, quoted by Anne Collins in *In the Sleep Room: The Story of the CIA Brainwashing Experiments in Canada* (1988). Rauh was suing the Central Intelligence Agency on behalf of former patients at the Allan Memorial Institute in Montreal who served as guinea-pigs in secret CIA experiments. He never could understand the attitude of successive Canadian administrations which did nothing to assist him and his Canadian clients.

Forty years of inaction cannot be erased. What remains is one last chance to remedy a historical wrong. If Canada is not to have a permanent stain on its justice system, if we are not to rip the foundations of justice from beneath future generations, we, as a country, must waste no more time in bringing the remaining Nazi war criminals in Canada to justice.
> DAVID MATAS, civil-rights lawyer, Susan Charendoff, journalist, concluding words of *Justice Delayed: Nazi War Criminals in Canada* (1987).

If justice is fairness to all, then justice has not prevailed in Nova Scotia.
> Conclusion of the Commission Counsel for the Royal Commission on the Donald Marshall Jr. Prosecution, Sydney, N.S. Marshall, a 17-year-old Micmac, spent eleven years in prison for a 1971 murder he did not commit. Two RCMP investigations failed to absolve him. He was finally freed in 1982. The Commission reported its findings in Dec. 1988.

Is it enough to be merely fair? Couldn't we afford to be *more* than fair once in a while?

> GEORGE JONAS, columnist, *Crocodiles in the Bathtub and Other Perils* (1987). Jonas answered his own rhetorical question in the negative "because being better than fair is impossible, and in the end it leads to being worse."

There is no such thing as social justice. Like its bedfellow, the public interest, the pursuit of social justice has left in its wake the wreckage of individual justice. Unfortunately, many features of society have been moulded on the social justice principle: many aspects of labour relations legislation, so-called consumer protection, and social welfare legislation relating to unemployment insurance, old age pensions, and so on.

> WALTER BLOCK and MICHAEL WALKER, economists with the Fraser Institute, *Lexicon of Economic Thought* (1989).

My faith in the justice system began to erode as I grew up and saw the big businesses ripping off people by selling poorly produced products at high prices, resource companies gouging and raping the earth, governments producing nuclear arsenals capable of destroying life on earth many times over, pornographic magazines that normalized and glamourized rape, incest and sexual assult, and Indians being herded onto reservations to die. All these crimes against humanity and the earth are legal. They are protected and sanctioned by Parliament, the courts, the law and the police. This was all very wrong.

> ANN HANSEN, militant peace activist, "Direct Action: Ann Hansen's Statement to the Court," *Up and Doing: Canadian Women and Peace* (1989) edited by Janice Williamson and Deborah Gorham.

Never pray for justice, because you might get some.

> Thoughts of the narrator of the novel *Cat's Eye* (1988) by MARGARET ATWOOD.

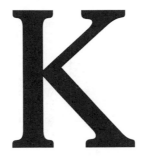

KINDNESS

But after expectation & excitement to be suddenly alone, endlessly, in this unreflecting apartment, or in my spacious office, hour after hour. And the kindness causes me more dismay — that one should need *kindness* seems wrong, a tinge of the insult, a feeling of being a chore. Pride is appalled.

> ELIZABETH SMART, novelist and diarist, "A Transatlantic Pursuit" (1978), *Autobiographies* (1987) edited by Christina Burridge.

KING, W.L. MACKENZIE

William Lyon Mackenzie King. / He never gives us a goddam thing.

> This couplet — a "press corps ditty" — refers to the taciturn and cautious Prime Minister who was the despair of the press corps during World War II. It was recited by Washington newsmen, according to Jonathan Daniels in *White House Witness: 1942-1945* (1975).

After they became fast friends, Mackenzie King liked to recall his first impression of Winston Churchill. It was in 1904, when the British politician made a lecture tour of Canada, and King took an immediate dislike to him — by one account, "a bumptious, conceited young jackanapes." Next time they met, four years later in London, Churchill was more subdued. "I made a frightful ass of myself on that trip," he conceded. "Well, Mr. Churchill, there were many Canadians who thought so," King replied in that famously roundabout way of his, "and I was one of them."

> DAVID MacDONALD, columnist, "Anecdotes," *The Toronto Star*, 27 May 1989.

When his wartime government was re-elected in 1945, Mackenzie King was defeated in his own riding of Prince Albert, Sask., because the so-called "soldier vote" from overseas went solidly against him. To rub it in, one veteran put up a sign he'd just brought home from Europe: "This town liberated by the Canadian Army."

> DAVID MacDONALD, columnist, "Anecdotes," *The Toronto Star*, 27 May 1989.

Thank you.

> King's dying words, said to be addressed to his nurse attendant, 22 July 1950, Kingsmere, Gatineau Park, Que.

KISSES
See also LOVE

Never trust a woman you cannot kiss.
ROBIN SKELTON, man-of-letters, aphorism, May 1990.

KLONDIKE GOLD RUSH

My background was historical. The ghosts of the gold rush walked the wooden sidewalks of the little town of Dawson City, and we lived with the memories of old men who had been young men and had gone over the trails and down the rivers.
PIERRE BERTON, author, reflecting on his childhood years spent in the Klondike region of the Yukon Territory, address, Empire Club of Canada, Toronto, 11 Oct. 1973.

KNOWLEDGE

The compiler of knowledge can never possess that sense of proportion, that balance, that caution which enables the original student to give correct impressions of the objects and scenes he describes. Hence the work of the compiler is little trustworthy in comparison with that of the original student.
W.F. GANONG, natural scientist and historian, "Notes on the Natural History and Physiography of New Brunswick," *Bulletins of the Natural History Society of New Brunswick*, No. XXI, Vol. V, Part I, 1903-7.

The very advance of knowledge brings a power over nature and over men too vast and terrifying to be entrusted to the good intentions of unconsciously biased minds.
BERNARD J.F. LONERGAN, Jesuit philosopher, *Insight: A Study of Human Understanding* (2nd ed., 1958).

To know the universe is to know yourself.

To know yourself is to journey to the end of the universe.
T.B. PAWLICKI, author and theorist, *How You Can Explore Higher Dimensions of Space and Time* (1984).

When time, land, space or the marketplace is uncharted, there are no maps, there are no rules. Hence no teachers, only rare knowledge navigators.
FRANK OGDEN, futurologist, "Ogden's Fourteenth Law," *Dr. Tomorrow's Lessons from the Future* (updated June 1989).

Nobody ever knows the whole of anything.
Thoughts of a character in ROBERTSON DAVIES's novel *What's Bred in the Bone* (1985).

All ignorance is motivated.
MARSHALL McLUHAN, communications theorist, quoted by Philip Marchand in *Marshall McLuhan: The Medium and the Messenger* (1989).

Most would subscribe to the proposition that what remains to be known is like an awesome chasm yawning below the tiny ledge of data upon which we stand, or like a boundless ocean of ignorance extending to the limits of a horizon we cannot see.
DALE A. RUSSELL, paleontologist, referring to man's knowledge of prehistoric lifeforms, *An Odyssey in Time: The Dinosaurs of North America* (1989).

The larger the island of knowledge, the longer the shoreline of wonder.
Favourite phrase of the marine scientist and undersea explorer JOSEPH MacINNIS, quoted by Frank Rasky in *Leisure Ways*, April 1990.

KUWAIT
See GULF WAR

LABOUR

See also CAPITALISM
INDUSTRY
UNEMPLOYMENT
UNIONS
WORK

One Penny Reward! / Ran away from the Subscriber on 16 April last, an indented apprentice to the Carpenter Trade, named Charles Golden, who is about 8 years of age. Whoever brings back the said runaway apprentice shall receive the above reward — and no more. / Emanuel Gaukel, Woolwich.

Advertisement which appeared in the German-language journal *Canada Museum* on 19 April 1836. Quoted by Isaac R. Horst in *Up the Conestogo* (1979). Woolwich is near Guelph, Ont.

Grass will grow, the river will reach the sea, the boy will become a man, and labour will come into its own.

F.J. (FRED) DIXON, charged with seditious conspiracy in connection with the Winnipeg General Strike, address to the jury, Winnipeg, Feb. 13-14, 1920.

There's no use being apologetic about labour's image. We are what we are, and no matter what we do employers and the media will never give us a good image.

JEAN-CLAUDE PARROT, President, Canadian Union of Postal Workers, facing a three-month jail sentence for failing to declare a 1978 strike invalid, quoted by John Deverell in *The Toronto Star*, 23 Dec. 1979.

LABRADOR

See also NEWFOUNDLAND

There was one Sebastian Gabato [Cabot], a Venetian, dwelling in Bristol, a man seen and expert in cosmography and navigation . . . he sailed — as he affirmed at his return, and made a chart thereof — very far westwards, with a quarter of the north, on the north side of Tierra de Labrador, until he came to the latitude of sixty-seven degrees and a half, finding the seas still open.

SIR FRANCIS BACON, essayist, *The History of the Reign of King Henry the Seventh* (1622), reproduced from the edition edited by Roger Lockyer in 1971.

Germany was so certain that she would be in a position to carry out her original plans by the winter of 1941, that Lord Haw-Haw, German Radio broadcast personality, was instructed to give a special discourse on Labrador. He told his listeners that Germany knew all the Canadian Government was doing at Goose Bay. He thanked them for their efforts, saying it would save Germany that much labour. He concluded by informing the Military Garrison at Rigolet that they would be cut off and starved to death before the spring of 1942. Rigolet is an isolated outpost on the coast at the entrance to Lake Melville, 113 miles from Goose Bay Airport. Lord Haw-Haw said he fully sympathized with these brave men and felt sorry they would have to suffer the slow lingering death by starvation.

Lord Haw-Haw was wrong — his Nazi masters were wrong.
> WILLIAM GUY CARR, Lt.-Cmdr., RCNR, *Checkmate in the North: The Axis Planned to Invade America* (1944).

Governor of Bras d'Or
> The only Governor Bras d'Or, Labrador, exists in the pages of the novel *Ada* (1969), written by the Anglo-Russian novelist VLADIMIR NABOKOV and set in some other dimension.

The time will come, is coming, when Labrador will secede. Newfoundland, now merely the Forgotten Province, will then be the non-existent province, alive in name only.
> Letter to the Editor, St. John's *Evening Telegram*, 9 Nov. 1976, quoted by Bren Walsh in *More than a Majority: The Story of Newfoundland's Confederation with Canada* (1985).

I am a fifth generation Newfoundlander, and I have said more than once, publicly and privately, that if there is any question of trying to seize Labrador every Newfoundlander in the world would rise to the defence of that boundary, and all the dead ones would rise from their graves and join us.
> EUGENE FORSEY, Senator, referring derisively to Quebec's designs on Labrador, address, Empire Club of Canada, Toronto, 28 April 1977.

Labrador is a land shrouded in mystery, if not water.
> JOHN McPHEE, essayist, "Briefly Noted," *The New Yorker*, 3 Oct. 1988. The reference was occasioned by the description in *Webster's New Geographical Dictionary*: "Labrador — large peninsula." The item caught the eye of the editors of *Spy*, who noted on Feb. 1989: "We called Labrador. Labrador said, 'Labrador is not a peninsula.'"

The whole thing gave me a feeling of time not passing, like in the afternoon when I'd seen the lake so clearly and imagined I'd heard voices from thousands of years ago. I'd felt like this before, in Northern Ontario, and in Labrador, watching the cliffs rise out of the ocean. Eloise's eyes were still. The inhuman light of Canada wasn't frightening. It was comforting.
> Thoughts of a character in the story "Eloise" in *Breath Dances between Them* (1991) by M.T. (TERRY) KELLY.

LAKES
> *See also* GREAT LAKES
> WATER

anyway it's hard to work up much enthusiasm / for large bodies of water / they tend to just lie there being inert
> AL PURDY, poet, "Home Thoughts," *The Collected Poems of Al Purdy* (1986) edited by Russell Brown.

I have always lived close to water. I love the tranquility of it. The great thing about going up to any lake is that there is really no clock. It's the most peaceful, relaxing way to unwind.
> BRIAN ORSER, Olympic figure skater, "Incredible Ontario," *Ontario: The Inside Story* (1990).

LAND
> *See also* GEOGRAPHY
> LAND CLAIMS

Good rich forest land can be bought within a day's journey of Toronto, the capital of

Upper Canada, with a population of 16,000, for twelve dollars per acre.
> WILLIAM THOMSON, traveller and writer, *A Tradesman's Travels, in the United States and Canada, in the Year 1840, 41, & 42* (1842).

This land ain't your land, this land ain't my land, / This All-Canadian, pie-in-the-sky-land; / Though we bemoan it, we'll never own it, / This land that's made for you and me; and me; and me; and me. . . .
> One verse of the lyrics of "This Land Is Whose Land" (1967) written by ALEC SOMERVILLE of The Brothers-in-Law. This is a parody version of "This Land Is Your Land," the words and music of which were written by Woody Guthrie in 1956 and adapted and performed by the Travellers in 1959.

Our people have a saying that the real owners of the land are not yet born.
> Traditional native saying, noted in *Native Land Settlements Newsletter* (Oxfam-Canada), Summer 1976.

So long as there is a single thread that links us to the ways of our grandfathers, our lives are strong. However thin and delicate that thread may be, it will support the weight of a stronger cord that will tie us securely to the land.
> GEORGE MANUEL, President of both the National Indian Brotherhood and the North American Indian Brotherhood, *The Fourth World* (1974) written with Michael Posluns.

There are those who find the wilderness exhilarating. I am not one of them. The expanses and vistas of Canada frustrate those who, like myself, often prefer the detail to the grand design. I relish virtuosity within confinement as much as, if not more than, the broad vivid brushstroke. Canada's mystique is its spaciousness, its northern emptiness. To me it is oppressive. You cannot bounce off the tundra: it receives no human imprint. It flattens my

spirits; others, fortunately, are able to soar.
> STEPHEN BROOK, English travel writer, *Maple Leaf Rag: Travels across Canada* (1987).

It starts with my life-long interest in Canada which began with a summer spent on Lake Muskoka in 1929. Canoeing into the wilderness north of there I caught a glimpse of the essential Canada: open, majestic, wild, challenging and filled with fine people and a commanding life. It was an unequalled introduction to the land of manifold beauties.
> JAMES A. MICHENER, U.S. author, discussing the genesis of his short novel *Journey* (1988), which takes place in the North.

I believe strongly that the land upon which one lives influences one's character, and our land has given us qualities that are more akin to the Scandinavian countries than any part of the United States except the New England states.
> ROBERTSON DAVIES, man-of-letters, Neil Gunn lecture, Edinburgh University, June 1988, printed in *The Times Literary Supplement*, 30 Sept. 1988.

Man enters the picture only as a small, insignificant figure, dwarfed by the immensity of the land. May the relationship always be so.
> PAT and ROSEMARIE KEOUGH, nature writers and photographers, *The Nahanni Portfolio* (1988).

We are claiming the land not by populating it but by polluting it.
> Remark adapted from *Walking the Line: Travels along the Canadian-American Border* (1989), by MARIAN BOTSFORD FRASER

LAND CLAIMS
See also LAND

If I were prime minister, therefore, I would want a very progressive aboriginal land rights policy. (Here, again, the government mistakenly calls this "land claims" by the Indians!) My policy would be aimed at facilitating the ability of First Nations to become self-reliant and self-governing. . . . There is enough land in Canada (which is the second-largest country in the world, with only about 25 million inhabitants) to satisfy legitimate and just aboriginal demands!

> GEORGES ERASMUS, National Chief of the Assembly of First Nations, contributor to *If I Were Prime Minister* (1987).

All across North America today First Nations share a common perception of what was then agreed: we would allow Europeans to stay among us and use a certain amount of our land, while in our own lands we would continue to exercise our own laws and maintain our own institutions and systems of government.

> GEORGES ERASMUS, National Chief, Assembly of First Nations, *Drumbeat: Anger and Renewal in Indian Country* (1989) edited by Boyce Richardson.

I don't feel proud that there are ranches in Canada that are bigger than ten or fifteen reserves put together. Do you? I don't feel good about the fact that Native people who have lived on land for thousands of years don't have any legal recognized aboriginal title to that land. Do you?

> GEORGES ERASMUS, National Chief, Assembly of First Nations, address in Ottawa, responding to an invitation to help plan government-sponsored events to celebrate 125 years of Confederation and the 500th anniversary of Columbus's discovery of America in 1992. Quoted in *The Canadian Forum*, Jan. 1990.

LANGUAGE

See also BILINGUALISM
LANGUAGE: ENGLISH
LANGUAGE: FRENCH
LANGUAGE ISSUE
SPEECH & SPEECHES
TRANSLATION

Nor were there any swear words. Parts of the body were simply parts of the body. If an Indian was angry, he might exclaim *Machi Manito* — bad spirit. Or he might refer to someone as *cocosh* — pig. But if he was really angry and he wanted to swear, the Indian had to revert to speaking English.

> HUGH MACKAY ROSS, H.B.C. trader, noting the lack of swear words among the Algonkian-speaking Ojibwa, *The Apprentice's Tale* (1986).

I don't speak either British or American, I speak Canadian. We have in fact changed the language and made it ours.

> MARGARET LAURENCE, novelist, quoted by Heather Menzies in *The Railroad's Not Enough: Canada Now* (1978).

It is obvious that social change would be reflected in changes of language but what interests me much more is the reverse possibility: that the teaching of language, and the structures of literature in which language is contained, may foster and encourage certain social changes.

> NORTHROP FRYE, literary critic, address, Empire Club of Canada, Toronto, 19 Jan. 1984.

In language, as in national character, Canadian identity often seems understated and unhistrionic beside the boisterous American giant across the border.

> ROBERT McCRUM, WILLIAM CRAN, and ROBERT MacNEIL, authors, *The Story of English* (1986).

The native people of half the Arctic, from Bering Strait to northern Greenland, speak nearly the same language. A linguistic continuity like this is not known anywhere else in the world. The mutual intelligibility of Eskimo dialects has facilitated the formation of a political body, the Inuit Circumpolar Conference, which now assists Alaskan, Canadian, and Greenlandic Eskimos in the settlement of land claims and in their pursuit of self-determination.

> BARRY LOPEZ, naturalist, *Arctic Dreams: Imagination and Desire in a Northern Landscape* (1986).

Just as the medium is the message for McLuhan, so for the lexicographer the meaning should be in the context, not in the definitions.

> THOMAS M. PAIKEDAY, lexicographer, referring to the practice of explanation by "collocation" rather than by definition, 18 Jan. 1987.

But for those of the generation I come from and the temperament I inhabit, the world will always divide itself into Those Who Loved Latin and Those Who Did Not. It's as good a way, *pace* Caesar and the partitioning of Gaul, to divide up the world as any.

> ERIKA RITTER, humorist, "Hot-Blooded Latin Lovers," *Ritter in Residence: A Comic Collection* (1987).

The greatest propaganda in the world is our mother tongue, that which we learn as children, and which we learn unconsciously. That shapes our perceptions for life. That is propaganda at its most extreme form.

> MARSHALL McLUHAN, media philosopher, quoted in *The Antigonish Review*, Summer-Autumn 1988.

Language expresses not only a person's identity but also that of the collectivity to which he or she belongs. In short, a language is inextricably linked with the particularity of a culture.

> LÉON DION, political scientist, "The Mystery of Quebec," *Daedalus: Journal of the American Academy of Arts and Sciences*, "In Search of Canada," Fall 1988.

It's no good looking like an Inuk if you can't speak like one.

> ABRAHAM OKPIK, Inuit spokesperson, "What It Means to Be an Inuk" (1960), reprinted in *Inuktitut* No. 70, 1989.

Are we going to celebrate the fact that our aboriginal languages are not considered important enough in this country to be regarded in any legal way? Are we going to celebrate the fact that there is not a single court in this country where if you speak in an indigenous language, you don't have any legal rights there, but you will be forced to speak in French and English?

> GEORGES ERASMUS, National Chief, Assembly of First Nations, address in Ottawa, responding to an invitation to help plan government-sponsored events to celebrate 125 years of Confederation and the 500th anniversary of Columbus's discovery of America in 1992. Quoted in *The Canadian Forum*, Jan. 1990.

LANGUAGE: ENGLISH
See also LANGUAGE

My brethren, I will hide nothing of my thoughts on this point: the heaviest tax resulting from the Conquest has been the necessity of knowing English. It is quite proper, I admit, that some people should acquire a knowledge of English, but of this tax let us not pay any more than is strictly necessary.

> LOUIS-FRANÇOIS LAFLÈCHE, Bishop of Trois-Rivières, address on Saint-Jean-Baptiste Day, 1866, quoted by Dominique Clift in *The Secret Kingdom: Interpretations of a Canadian Character* (1989).

By a parity of disparity an exclusively French village in the environs, where you may read on the sign-boards the ensigns of "forgeron," and "cafétier," and "maréchal ferrant," is called Mile-end. The oddest *mélange* I remember was in the case of a worthy Frenchman on the road to the Royal Mountain, who sold tea and sugar, and called his store "La Grocerie Royal." The terminology of "grocerie" suggesting a compromise between "épicier," on the one part, and "grocer" on the other, was, to say the least, ingenious.

> GEORGE AUGUSTUS SALA, British journalist and traveller, commenting on signs in Quebec's Eastern Townships and approaching Montreal's Mount Royal, *My Diary in America in the Midst of War* (1865).

My aunt was bitten by an ant in Ontario while she was singing Schubert's "Ave Maria."

GEORGE BERNARD SHAW, Anglo-Irish wit, employed this sentence to check the effectiveness of a phonetic alphabet, noted by Dan H. Laurence, editor, *Bernard Shaw: Collected Letters, Volume 4, 1926-1950* (1985).

At the same time, Mr. H. Walpole of Queen's University, Ontario, was able to put Basic on the map in Canada before going to Bogotá to make a start with some of the chief schools in Colombia.
C.K. OGDEN, English linguist and promoter of Basic English, referring to the years 1935-36, *Basic English: International Second Language* (rev. ed., 1968) edited by E.C. Graham.

What a lot of Frenchification is going on these days!
This includes the tendency to slew certain names around backasswards such as Radio Canada, Air Canada, Hotel Newfoundland, Hill Signal, Brook Corner, Current Swift and so on.
RAY GUY, humorist, "It Takes All Kinds," *That Far Greater Bay* (1976).

Considering the bombardment by American English from everywhere south of the 3000-mile border, it is remarkable that Canada's twenty-five million people should have preserved national characteristics as distinct as they are, and perhaps even more remarkable that the regional differences in Canadian English have not yet been snuffed out by the influence of American English.
ROBERT McCRUM, WILLIAM CRAN, and ROBERT MacNEIL, authors, *The Story of English* (1986).

Remembering the incidents of those years, I think, This is where I was first struck by words. This is where they made me more than a Canadian, an Englishman, or an American; or Scottish, or Irish, or German — all the things my forebears were. This is where I became what Joseph Brodsky calls a "citizen of the great English language."

ROBERT MacNEIL, broadcaster and language specialist, quoting the Russian poet and recalling his own schooling in Halifax in the 1930s, *Wordstruck: A Memoir* (1989).

LANGUAGE: FRENCH
See also LANGUAGE

Then, scratching away the frost from the pane, I saw by the roadside a horizontal bar of wood between two perpendiculars, very much like a gallows. It was not that emblem of civilization, but a sign-post, and thereon were painted in the two tongues the words, "Railway crossing — *Traverse du chemin de fer.*" From this I was enabled to realize the conception that we were now in the land of half-and-half — of about perhaps the most curious and bizarre medley of Franco-Anglicisms, or Anglo-Gallicisms, of conflicting speech, creed, manners, and customs, with which I was ever permitted to make acquaintance.
GEORGE AUGUSTUS SALA, British journalist and traveller, travelling by train from Vermont to Quebec, *My Diary in America in the Midst of War* (1865).

Laziness makes our language worse: / Even in the shortest discourse, / How few place words with proper thought, / And start and finish as they ought? // In the middle of good French prose / Unthinkingly some English goes: / Presently, indictment, impeachment, foreman, / Sheriff, writ, verdict, bill, roast beef, watchman.
Translation into English of French couplets written by the poet MICHEL BIBAUD and included in *Epîtres, Satires, Chansons, Epigrammes, et Autres Pièces de Vers* (1930),

"Now, Eugene, this is a subject on which Stanfield ought to be making a statement. Instead of that, he's taking a two-week immersion course in French." Then John's eyes started to shoot sparks and I said to myself: "Here comes one of the best." Sure enough, out it came: "Eugene, we Baptists

know all about immersion [pause], but we don't stay under for two weeks!"
EUGENE FORSEY, constitutional authority, quoting Prime Minister John G. Diefenbaker on Opposition leader Robert Stanfield, *A Life on the Fringe: The Memoirs of Eugene Forsey* (1990).

Canady French
This is Anglo-Russian novelist VLADIMIR NABOKOV's reference to the variety of French spoken by the Quebec of North America in his other-dimensional novel *Ada* (1969).

Français au verso.
This phrase (which translates "French on the other side") may well be the most familiar French phrase to anglophones. It appears, for instance, on boxes of breakfast cereals. The corresponding phrase for francophones is "English on the other side." Probably the most familiar single French word in English Canada is the one that appears on traffic signs — "Arrête" (Stop).

All in all, it would seem that the fact of speaking French irritates anglophones more than the fact of being French Canadian.
ANDRÉ LAURENDEAU, Quebec nationalist, diary entry for 1964, "A Québécois Journal," translated by Pat Smart, *The Canadian Forum*, Nov. 1990.

Covering the 1980 Winter Olympics at Lake Placid, N.Y., for viewers in France, the Paris-based television commentator announced: "*Il a shooté le puck.*" He was corrected by the Radio Canada commentator from Montreal who announced: "*Il a lancé la rondelle.*"
This story, said to be true, was first noted by an anglophone in Montreal in 1982.

Pro-French activists in Canada attack public signs of all sorts at night, repainting them in French. Street and highway signs saying STOP are relettered to read ARRETE — although "stop" is in the official

French dictionary, the sign painters consider the word too English.
CHARLES BERLITZ, linguist, *Native Tongues* (1982).

But all the legislation in the world cannot disguise the fact that even in the French-speaking parts of Canada, the reality of the English-speaking world is inescapable.
ROBERT McCRUM, WILLIAM CRAN, and ROBERT MacNEIL, authors, *The Story of English* (1986).

To be born Francophone is to inherit a major civilization and, most important of all, an infinitely rich language . . . a vast and universal heritage reaching to the four corners of the earth.
NAIM KATTAN, multilingual arts administrator, *Language & Society*, Fall 1987.

Indeed, the tavern is the only place in America where a French Canadian can speak his language freely.
JACQUES FERRON, author, "The Dead Cow in the Canyon," *Invisible Fictions: Contemporary Stories from Quebec* (1987) edited by Geoff Hancock.

Writers here in Quebec are well aware that French is living on borrowed time and that it is gradually degenerating.
LÉON DION, political scientist, "The Mystery of Quebec," *Daedalus: Journal of the American Academy of Arts and Sciences*, "In Search of Canada," Fall 1988. Dion went on to note: "As might be expected, the linguistic decline accompanies a crisis in culture everywhere."

The goal is not to convert North America to speaking French, since this continent is and will remain the preserve of English. The goal is, rather, to create an environment in Quebec in which French is the dominant mode of communication in the business world, even if this means dealing with Anglophone colleagues from outside in their own language. The idea, in short, is to set up a Francophone economic "unit" in Quebec. This is similar to what was done in the land forces with the creation of the twenty-second regiment and the Régiment de la Chaudière. These gave high-calibre officers a better chance of showing off their talents than in an Anglophone regiment.

LÉON DION, political scientist, "The Mystery of Quebec," *Daedalus: Journal of the American Academy of Arts and Sciences*, "In Search of Canada," Fall 1988.

Though you may cringe at your own linguistic ineptitude, there are compensations. I have a theory that inside each of us are a great many secret personalities, one for every language, waiting to get out. . . . When I speak French, however badly, however briefly, I'm allowed to encounter for a few moments, a few days, my secret French personality. I wave my hands around a lot more — due perhaps to vocabulary deficiencies — and my face starts moving about like rubber. I even shrug, something I never do in English. I experience a rush of freedom, partly because I'm not totally in charge of whatever I'm saying. Who knows what witticisms are emerging? Not me!

JAN MORRIS, Welsh travel writer, "The Battle for Montreal," *Saturday Night*, July 1988.

Next morning we watched the Quebec entry, *Et Patati et Patata*. The French jurors protested that they could understand neither the Canadian French dialogue nor the English subtitles. I raged at them and said: Christ, it's only eighteenth-century Norman.

Thoughts of the narrator who is attending a French film festival in ANTHONY BURGESS's novel *Earthly Powers* (1980).

Speak French only. However, let the French elite and your politicians send their children to American and English universities to become fluently bilingual thereby ensuring them top jobs anywhere in the world.

From "Rules for Becoming a Québécois," the heading on a Letter to the Editor,

pseudonymously signed "J.M. St. John, Pierrefonds," which appeared in the weekly *The Chronicle* (Pointe Claire, Que.), 13 April 1988. So ill-received was the satire that the Saint-Jean-Baptiste Society and advertisers encouraged the publisher to disavow the sentiments expressed in the letter and apologize in paid advertisements in three other newspapers.

The fear is rooted in a cultural insecurity that comes from the fact that in the province of Quebec there are, say, six million French Canadians in a — really not a country of 26 million — there are 6 million French Canadians in a continent of some 275 million English-speaking people. The protection of that small minority, its language and culture, is, as you know, a very difficult and challenging matter.

BRIAN MULRONEY, Prime Minister, interviewed by Peter Gzowski, host of CBC Radio's *Morningside*, 21 Sept. 1989, as published in *Language and Society*, Winter 1989.

The citizens of Quebec are so interested in speaking French that they may leave the Canadian federation just to do it. People in France are arguing about whether there should be a hyphen in "weekend" and people in Quebec are arguing about whether it's okay to arrest someone for putting an English word like "weekend" on a sign, hyphen or no hyphen. It's only a matter of time before anybody who wants to speak real French will have to go to Quebec.

CALVIN TRILLIN, contributor to *The New Yorker*, in *The Toronto Star*, 4 July 1990.

The public understands very well that I am still a Quebecer and a Francophone, even if I sing in English.

CÉLINE DION, chansonnière, declining the Félix prize as the best Anglophone artist for her English-language album *Unison*, quoted in *La Presse*, 22 Oct. 1990 as quoted by Danièle Noël in "Language in Quebec: A Historic Review," *Language and Society* No. 34, Spring 1991.

LANGUAGE ISSUE
See also LANGUAGE

Why should not the Canadian educational authorities in both the Canadian language groups invite a party of Swiss educationists to study the present systems of education in the two parts of Canada and to make recommendations for improving it?

> ARNOLD TOYNBEE, historian, "The Case for a Bilingual Canada," *Temper of the Times: An Anthology of Assorted Contemporary Literature* (1969) edited by Ralph Greenfield and Ronald Side.

I can remember René Lévesque telling me years ago about the shock of his first exposure to Montreal as a new arrival from the Gaspé when he discovered that the metropolis of Quebec was at heart an English-speaking city. English was heard everywhere but in the east end. The city even looked English. Eliminating English signs by legislation may seem absurd to the rest of North America but it is a matter of pride in Quebec. And I have always felt, as an English-speaking Montrealer, that we should respect that.

> PETER DESBARATS, journalist, address, Empire Club of Canada, Toronto, 7 Dec. 1978.

Education for Canada's Eskimo population has generally been offered in English. But recently French-speaking activists in Québec have strongly urged that the Eskimos be taught French as well, on the grounds that Canada has two official languages — English and French.

> CHARLES BERLITZ, linguist, *Native Tongues* (1982).

It was a polyglot street supposedly reduced to unilingual signage by the language law, but it would probably continue to have holdouts like the Slovenia Meat Market. In any case, the street would have polyglot undertones as far ahead as anyone could see. Boucherie Slovenia might appear superficially "francized" (a nasty bureaulogism introduced by Quebec officials to denote the rewriting of public signs in French), but the law could not put the butcher himself through its culture grinder. If the language police expected everyone in Montreal to act like a tenth-generation French-Canadian, they would have to cut out tongues.

> JOHN GALT, journalist and traveller, commenting on the application of Quebec's language legislation on Montreal street signs and sounds, *Whistlestop: a Journey across Canada* (1987).

And what is the interest of an elected Ontario politician in the language dispute in Quebec?

> ROBERT BOURASSA, Quebec Premier, questioning the relevance of reservations to the "distinct society" provisions expressed by Ontario Attorney-General Ian Scott who was advising Ontario Premier David Peterson at a Meech Lake meeting in Ottawa, 2 June 1987, quoted by Charlotte Gray, journalist, "Speaking in Tongues," *Saturday Night*, Dec. 1989.

For the first time in the history of Quebec, a premier went so far as to suspend civil liberties to protect and defend the French language, and you call that a half-measure.

> ROBERT BOURASSA, Quebec Premier, responding to criticism from francophones that he was not protecting the French language and from anglophones that he was not protecting civil liberties, quoted in *The Toronto Star*, 25 Sept. 1988.

I can't decide as an outsider whether the bill is needed or not. Neither can I make a judgment on that . . . in terms of the sociological reality. . . . It's not up to me to do it. It's up to the Province of Quebec.

> ED BROADBENT, NDP leader, avoiding comment on the dispute over Quebec's Bill 101, which prohibits English on public signs, during the televised election debates, quoted in *The Globe and Mail*, 21 Nov. 1988.

Governor General Georges Vanier once obtained a Karsh photograph of Pope John XXIII and sent it off to the Vatican to be autographed. There, because Vanier was the chief of state of an officially bilingual nation, Church officials spent some time debating whether the inscription should be in English or French. In the end, Pope John resorted to a typically "Canadian" compromise — he wrote in Latin.

> DAVID MacDONALD, "Anecdotes," *The Toronto Star*, 18 March 1989.

Progressive Conservative M.P.'s from the West are delighting each other with their new joke about Quebec's language policy: Premier Robert Bourassa dies, reaches the Pearly Gates and seeks admission into Heaven. After identifying himself, he is refused admission. He demands an explanation. St. Peter replies: Sorry, the new policy is French on the outside, English on the inside.

> News story, *The Globe and Mail*, 6 May 1989.

Canada's burgeoning language wars [are] childish. Future generations will laugh at our obsessions. We are not living through tragedy but farce. If this country flies apart from such matters, at least foreigners will find some comic relief in the plight of Canada.

> MORDECAI RICHLER, novelist, address, Toronto, 27 Feb. 1990, quoted by Philip Marchand in *The Toronto Star* the following day.

Cut the cake however you will, English is the language of success on this continent. Recent legislation which obliges immigrants to send their children to French language schools does not solve the problem but compounds it.

> MORDECAI RICHLER, novelist, address, Toronto, 27 Feb. 1990, quoted by Philip Marchand in *The Toronto Star* the following day.

It's not Bill 101 that threatens your culture, it's ABC, NBC — it's all the American culture.

> GILLES DUCEPPE, first separatist Member of Parliament, elected in the wake of the demise of the Meech Lake Accord in a Quebec by-election on 13 Aug. 1990, referring to English Canadian culture, quoted in *The Toronto Star* two days later.

Why French lingualism? Simply, because two cultures can't both bloom in the same linguistic space. Quebec, after all, isn't elastic. If English assumes more room, French will take up less. And if French takes up more, English has to assume less.

> YVES BEAUCHEMIN, novelist, brief presented to the Bélanger-Campeau commission on the future of Quebec, reproduced in *The Toronto Star*, 24 Dec. 1990.

There are two classes of Quebeckers who are fluently bilingual: the elite French who put their children into private U.S., British or Ontario schools, and the anglophones and allophones. There is a certain irony to this: the French intellectual and ruling class is fluently bilingual as well as separatist.

> ANDRÉ G. BORDELEAU, commentator, *The Globe and Mail*, 12 March 1991.

To summarize, one can therefore be a Francophone, a Canadian or a Quebecer today, and everyone can live in a "state" or a "country" and form a "people" or a "distinct society." What does this mean? That we are engaged in a war of synonyms, a dispute over words?

> DANIÈLE NOËL, sociolinguist, "Language in Quebec: A Historic Review," *Language and Society* No. 34, Spring 1991.

LAUGHTER
See also HUMOUR

A laugh is the reverse of a breakdown; it's a breakup.

> BERNARD SLADE, playwright, quoted by Tom Hedley in *The Canadian Magazine*, 26 July 1975.

Stay away from people you have never seen laugh. They're not only tedious, they're dangerous.

> ALLAN FOTHERINGHAM, columnist, *Maclean's*, 4 Sept. 1978.

LAURENTIAN SHIELD

The emptiness of the heart of Canada is a reflection of the barrenness of the Laurentian Shield. . . . It has been called the dead heart of Canada, and when today the cold of winter grips the surface, the image seems apt.

> F. KENNETH HARE, geographer, "Canada: The Land," *Daedalus: Journal of the American Academy of Arts and Sciences*, "In Search of Canada," Fall 1988.

LAW

    See also CRIME
             JUSTICE & INJUSTICE
             LAWYERS
             LIBERTIES, CIVIL
             RIGHTS, CIVIL

It is not burglary laws that keep most of us from theft. It is something out of which the burglary laws arose.

> STEPHEN LEACOCK, humorist and historian, "The Revision of Democracy," Presidential Address, *Papers and Proceedings of the Sixth Annual Meeting of the Canadian Political Science Association, 1934* (1934).

A will — scratched with a pocket knife on an auto fender — was probated by the Surrogate's Court, Saskatchewan, Canada, 1948.

> ROBERT L. RIPLEY, cartoonist and columnist, *Ripley's New Believe It or Not* (1950).

Facts in a court of law are what you can make the jury believe: no more, no less.

> Remark made by a character in *Malice Domestic* (1962), a crime novel by SARA WOODS.

The Space Age, even more than the Nuclear Age, seems to offer the dramatic possibility of an International Law of Positive Cooperation in place of the old International Law of Conflict.

> EDWARD McWHINNEY, law professor, *International Law and World Revolution* (1967).

We shall ensure that the laws passed by Parliament are worthy of respect. We shall also ensure that those laws are respected.

> PIERRE ELLIOTT TRUDEAU, Prime Minister, explaining the invoking of the War Measures Act during the October Crisis, CBC-TV, 16 Oct. 1970.

Canadian law makes it a crime to "alarm" Her Majesty the Queen.

> NIGEL NAPIER-ANDREWS, TV producer and writer, *This Is the Law? A Selection of Silly Laws from around the World* (1971).

The Constitution of Canada is the supreme law of Canada, and any law that is inconsistent with the provisions of the Constitution is, to the extent of the inconsistency, of no force or effect.

> *The Constitution Act, 1982*, Part VII, General, Section 52 (1).

People are driven to the law by intense pain or intense hate and are quite immune to practical considerations.

> STEPHEN VIZINCZEY, novelist, *An Innocent Millionaire* (1983).

I do not overrule decisions of a Judge of this Court. The judicial pecking order does not permit little peckers to overrule big peckers. It is the other way around.

> M.B. FUNDAK, Master, Alberta Court of Queen's Bench, South Side Woodwork (1979) Ltd. vs. R.C. Contracting Ltd., Decision, 10 Feb. 1988.

We are discovering our muted Miltons to be incipient Shakespeares. Judges are quoting Thomas Aquinas and writing like philosophers.

> MORRIS C. SHUMIATCHER, lawyer, "Discussion: Property Rights and Liberty," *Canadian Journal of Law and Jurisprudence*, July 1988.

A law simply tells you what should happen. It doesn't tell you what's going to happen.

> JOHN HUMPHREY, first Director of the UN's Division of Human Rights, quoted by

Ray E. Bennett in *The Globe and Mail,* 8 Dec. 1988.

Rules are like women, they are made to be violated.
Remark made during the course of a trial by Quebec Court Judge DENYS DIONNE, Longueuil, Que., 29 Jan. 1989, widely held to be inappropriate when discussed in the press, as noted by Rhéal Séguin in *The Globe and Mail,* 13 Feb. 1990.

The Supreme Court of Canada is 114 years old. For most of that time, it was, as the late chief justice Bora Laskin once put it, a "quiet court in an unquiet country."
GEOFFREY STEVENS, columnist, *The Toronto Star,* 27 Aug. 1989.

Follow principles, not laws.
ROBIN SKELTON, man-of-letters, aphorism, May 1990.

LAWYERS
See also LAW

The lawyers of Upper Canada will have an abundant harvest before them if nothing is done to cure this evil.
ROBERT GOURLAY, colonist and writer, commenting on careless and inaccurate boundary markers in Upper Canada in the early 19th century, *Statistical Account of Upper Canada Compiled with a View to a Grand System of Emigration* (1822).

Q.C. after a lawyer's name, denoting Queen's Counsel, actually means "my party's in power."
ALLAN FOTHERINGHAM, columnist, "Tort, Persiflage, Redundant & Weinstein" (1968), *Collected and Bound* (1972).

If a man were to give another an orange, he would say simply "have an orange." But if the transaction were entrusted to a lawyer, he would say, "I hereby give, grant, bargain and sell to you, all my right, title and interest in, of and to said orange, together with all its rind, skin, juice, pulp and pips and all rights and advantages therein with full power to bite, cut and eat of the same . . . etc., etc."
WALTER McGIBBON, lawyer, quoted by Henry Koch in *The Kitchener-Waterloo Record,* 24 Feb. 1979.

To state a lie firmly, categorically and with great authority, undeterred by the fact that all concerned know it to be a lie, is one of the principal activities defined by the term *practising law.*
STEPHEN VIZINCZEY, novelist, *An Innocent Millionaire* (1983).

I am not a lawyer. I have many other faults but that is not among them.
ED BROADBENT, NDP leader and former academic, House of Commons, 8 June 1987.

A lawyer can't turn away a client just because he's charged with an odious crime any more than a doctor can refuse to treat a patient just because he suffers from an odious illness.
EDWARD L. GREENSPAN, lawyer, *Greenspan: The Case for the Defence* (1987) written with George Jonas.

You've been my lawyer on earth and I'll be your lawyer in heaven.
Last words of the convicted murderer LEONARD JACKSON, before his execution in Toronto on 16 Dec. 1952, addressed to his lawyer Arthur Maloney, quoted by Val Sears in *Hello Sweetheart . . . Get Me Rewrite* (1988).

I will defend anyone only once.
ARTHUR MARTIN, criminal law lawyer, quoted by Val Sears in *Hello Sweetheart . . . Get Me Rewrite* (1988).

The only thing that outgrows a lawyer's earnings is his ego.
STUART MORRISON, publisher of *Canadian Lawyer,* quoted in *The Globe and Mail,* 30 Dec. 1988.

If women lawyers and women judges through differing perspectives on life can bring a new humanity to bear on the decision-making process, perhaps they *will* make a difference. Perhaps they will succeed in infusing the law with an understanding of what it means to be fully human.

> BERTHA WILSON, Justice, Supreme Court of Canada, lecture, Osgoode Hall Law School, York University, Toronto, 8 Feb. 1990.

Lawyers have to educate the public about the law. Hollywood and television in general haven't begun to scratch the surface of what our system's all about, that we have things like due process of law, the right to remain silent, proof on the prosecution beyond a reasonable doubt and the presumption of innocence. All these principles are more important than whether a particular person is or isn't guilty. If you want to see democracy in action, don't watch Question Period in the House of Commons; come to a criminal court.

> EDWARD L. GREENSPAN, criminal law lawyer, quoted by Rederick Jamer in *TV Guide*, 5 Jan. 1991.

LEADERSHIP
See also HEROES

"High muck-a-muck" does not mean "big chief" but is a more or less phonetic rendition of the Chinook Indian expression for "plenty of food." Apparently the first white visitors mistook the name of the feast for the title of the host.

> CHARLES BERLITZ, linguist, *Native Tongues* (1982).

The sheep are without shepherds: they are disoriented, bewildered, lost. Indeed what is true of the sheep, can also be true of the shepherds as well: they too can be disoriented, bewildered, lost.

> BERNARD J.F. LONERGAN, Jesuit philosopher, *A Second Collection: Papers by Bernard J.F. Lonergan, S.J.* (1954).

Leadership — that indeed is the question today. If we are led by people who accept sacrifice themselves before inflicting hardship on others; who practise the virtues of thrift, compassion and humility before exacting them from us; who respect Parliament and its institutions before castigating those who have walked the slippery road to defiance; who tell us the truth even when they think we don't want to hear it — if we have that kind of leadership, and have it we must, Canada may yet fulfill that most splendid promise of her youth.

> BRIAN MULRONEY, Montreal lawyer, address, Empire Club of Canada, Toronto, 15 Oct. 1975

The function of democratic leadership, it seems to me, is to respect the past, grasp the present, and enlarge the future.

> PETER C. NEWMAN, author, contributor to *If I Were Prime Minister* (1987) edited by Mel Hurtig.

Some say that "Nanabush" left this continent when the whiteman came. We believe he is still here among us — albeit a little worse for wear and tear — having assumed other guises. Without him — and without the spiritual health of this culture — the core of Indian culture would be gone forever.

> TOMSON HIGHWAY, native playwright, "A Note on Nanabush," *The Rez Sisters* (1988).

Great obstacles make great leaders.

> BILLY DIAMOND, Cree leader, quoted by Roy MacGregor in *Chief: The Fearless Vision of Billy Diamond* (1989).

Ironically, having now travelled so far along the road to nowhere, Canadians find themselves at the crossroads to anywhere. It's a nice, bracing location in political and social cartography, full of omens and possibilities, challenges and dangers. Just wait and see.

> JOHN FRASER, editor, "Diary," *Saturday Night*, Nov. 1989.

A good leader has to see the world through many eyes. That is my strength. I know what it is like to be poor and what it

is like to be comfortable. These are the worlds I want to pull together. There is nothing wrong about being a conciliator, a bridge builder.
> AUDREY McLAUGHLIN, NDP leader, quoted in *Maclean's*, 11 Dec. 1989.

The essence of leadership is making people feel good.
> Attributed to the politician JEAN CHRÉTIEN in 1984 by Edison Stewart in *The Toronto Star*, 24 Jan. 1990.

Leaders are dangerous / but the most dangerous people / are the followers
> ROBERT PRIEST, poet, aphorism, March 1990.

I come from a history of "I don't know, what do you think?"
> AUDREY McLAUGHLIN, NDP leader, referring to her consensual leadership style, quoted by Graham Fraser in *The Globe and Mail*, 1 Dec. 1990.

So the Canadians flounder and bicker on, with no charismatic leaders to inspire them into purpose, as their splendid country slowly loses its assurance and, I suspect, its self-respect.
> JAN MORRIS, Anglo-Welsh travel writer, *The Toronto Star*, 29 March 1990.

What this country needs is not more leadership, it is more partnership, more participation by the people in the decisions that affect their lives, and a major reform in our institutions, like Parliament and the political parties, that will provide for such participation.
> GEORGE WOODCOCK, author and social commentator, "Five-Year Fascism," *The Canadian Forum*, Dec. 1990.

Leaders who can transcend visionless coexistence will strike a responsive chord in the hearts of Canadians who are hungry for more significant goals and dreams.
> REGINALD W. BIBBY, sociologist, *Mosaic Madness: The Poverty and Potential of Life in Canada* (1990).

LEAGUE OF NATIONS

It is for the constitutional authorities of each Member to decide . . . in what degree the Member is bound to assure the execution of this obligation by employment of its military forces.
> This is the so-called Canadian Resolution on Article 10, League of Nations Assembly, 24 Sept. 1923, which permits each member country to determine the degree of its compliance with the general duty of maintaining the peace, quoted by Gwynne Dyer and Tina Viljoen, commentator and TV producer, *The Defence of Canada: In the Arms of the Empire* (1990). The authors note that the effect of Canada's interpretation of the League's resolution was to destroy the effectiveness of Article 10.

LEARNING
See also EDUCATION

A little learning is a boring thing.
> EDWARD PHILLIPS, novelist, *Sunday Best* (1990).

According to the experts, better than half the students of Canadian highschools, once they graduate, will never again read a book. Something is wrong somewhere.
> JOEL BONN, Montreal-based reading specialist, *obiter dictum*, 3 Feb. 1990.

LEGENDS
See also MYTHOLOGY

In spite of this reality, the legends persist — and why not! For they are indeed great yarns to be told and retold by the flickering light of camp-fires. To this day they are perpetuated in the numerous names that have been applied to features of the Nahanni landscape: Broken Skull River, Deadmen Valley, Sunblood Mountain, Hell Roaring Creek, the Funeral Range, the Headless Range, Death Lake, the Vampire Peaks.
> PAT and ROSEMARIE KEOUGH, nature writers and photographers, *The Nahanni*

Portfolio (1988). They are referring to the fact that legends persist that in the valley of the Nahanni River in the Northwest Territories there will be found a tropical valley populated by wild mountain men ruled over by a white queen.

Jacques Cartier, who built a reputation as a story-teller in his retirement, told several from the Indians: there was a people in the north who did not eat at all, and others with only one leg each. There were persistent reports of headless men too. . . .
> J.A.S. EVANS, classicist, *The Idler*, No. 23, May-June 1989.

LEISURE

The drive to overcome basic needs and achieve a leisure society results from two fundamental human traits: we are at once physically lazy and intellectually energetic.
> FRANK FEATHER, futurologist, *G-Forces: Reinventing the World — The 35 Global Forces Restructuring Our World* (1989).

LÉVESQUE, RENÉ
> *See also* PARTI QUÉBÉCOIS
> QUEBEC
> SEPARATISM

À la prochaine fois.
> RENÉ LÉVESQUE, Quebec Premier and Parti Québécois leader, announcing the results of the referendum of sovereignty-association (close to 60% against, 40% for), Paul Sauvé Arena, Montreal, 20 May 1980, recalled a decade later by Graham Fraser in *The Globe and Mail*, 19 May 1990. The French phrase means "Until next time."

He forced Canadians to come to terms with Quebec's place in Canada.
> JOHN TURNER, Liberal leader, on the late René Lévesque, quoted by John F. Burns in *The New York Times*, 3 Nov. 1987.

The memory of René Lévesque unites us all this weekend. For he revealed to Quebecers their inalienable right to decide their own destiny.
> From the text of the congratulatory telegram telexed by federal Environment Minister LUCIEN BOUCHARD, then in Paris, to be read by the Parti Québécois leader Jacques Parizeau at the opening of the party's national council meeting in Alma, Que., Bouchard's constituency, 19 May 1990. Quoted by Robert McKenzie in *The Toronto Star* the following day.

LIBEL & SLANDER

I only write books about dead people. They can't sue.
> PIERRE BERTON, media personality and author of historical tomes, quoted by George Galt in *Saturday Night*, Dec. 1988.

We need to insulate all discussions of public concern from libel — to allow free and robust public debate by all citizens.
> AUBREY E. GOLDEN, lawyer and commentator, "What to Do about Libel Chill," *The Canadian Forum*, Jan.-Feb. 1991.

No one likes to see reputations suffer needlessly, especially those of the innocent. However, less libel protection is the price we all need to pay to reduce self-censorship and discourage litigious bullies.
> AUBREY E. GOLDEN, lawyer and commentator, "What to Do about Libel Chill," *The Canadian Forum*, Jan.-Feb. 1991.

LIBERAL PARTY
> *See also* LIBERALISM
> POLITICS

You will be fine as long as you remember that the Liberal Party is a great big, heartless, headless machine.
> PAUL HELLYER, Liberal Cabinet Minister, quoted by Keith Davey in *The Rainmaker: A Passion for Politics* (1986).

The Liberals talk about a stable government but we don't know how bad the stable is going to smell.
> T.C. (TOMMY) DOUGLAS, NDP leader, re-

ferring to calls for "stable" — read majority Liberal — government, remark made 30 Oct. 1965, quoted by James B. Simpson in *Simpson's Contemporary Quotations* (1988).

A true Liberal is any politician, not in jail, who shows promise of restoring the Grits to their rightful place as the country's Governing Party.
> Adapted from a tongue-in-cheek observation made by PETER C. NEWMAN in *The Ottawa Citizen*, 17 Sept. 1988.

A Liberal is a Liberal is a Liberal, except in opposition when he sounds like a New Democrat.
> ED BROADBENT, NDP leader, *The Globe and Mail*, 30 June 1988.

In short, the six "isms" upon which the Liberal party has based its political life since 1968 are: centralism, elitism, official bilingualism, multiculturalism, egalitarianism, and nationalism.
> WILLIAM D. GAIRDNER, academic and businessman, *The Trouble with Canada* (1990).

LIBERALISM
See also LIBERAL PARTY

I am one of those who think that always and everywhere in human things there are abuses to be reformed, new horizons to be opened up, and new forces to be developed. The principle of liberalism is inherent in the very essence of our nature, in that desire of happiness with which we are born into the world, which pursues us throughout life, and which is never completely gratified on this side of the grave. We dream of good but never realize the best. Our means are limited but our nature is perfectible and we have the infinite for our arena.
> SIR WILFRID LAURIER, Prime Minister from 1896 to 1911, defining liberalism, quoted in *The Globe and Mail*, 3 March 1982.

LIBERTIES, CIVIL
See also RIGHTS, CIVIL

The same liberty that protects me also protects members of the Mafia.
> BARBARA AMIEL, columnist, address, Empire Club of Canada, Toronto, 4 Feb. 1982.

LIBERTY
See also FREEDOM

For myself, I have little enthusiasm for a species of liberty that can only profit vagabonds. My sympathies are all on the side of respectable men. Perhaps, in this independent age, it is an error in judgment on my part, but it is not given to everyone to feel the republican spirit that dominates our continent.

If my countrymen wish to retain the estimable reputation of *peuple gentilhomme* that they still possess, I strongly advise them above all not to hanker after that degree of liberty which our neighbours now enjoy.
> PHILIPPE-JOSEPH AUBERT DE GASPÉ, littérateur, *A Man of Sentiment: The Memoirs of Philippe-Joseph Aubert de Gaspé 1786-1871* (1988) translated by Jane Brierley.

LIBRARIES
See also BOOKS

I love libraries, but I will be damned if I will ever walk into a "Resource Centre."
> RICHARD NEEDHAM, columnist, *The Wit and Wisdom of Richard Needham* (1977).

For a well-rounded education, you could try curling up with good books and bad librarians.
> RICHARD NEEDHAM, columnist, *The Wit and Wisdom of Richard Needham* (1977).

I am constantly astounded to find references to the "fictional" detective Sherlock Holmes. I find that I am constantly coming to your defence and have had some run-ins with the local library authorities after

I removed all the stories of your adventures off the fiction shelves and placed them in "biographies" where they rightly belong.

Letter addressed to the fictional detective Sherlock Holmes at 221B Baker Street by BOB COGHILL, a resident of Willowdale, Ont., and an enthusiast for the detective stories of Sir Arthur Conan Doyle, *Letters to Sherlock Holmes* (1985) edited by Richard L. Green.

Yes. Yes. Yes. Know. Know. Know. / Say Yes to Knowledge. Get a Library Card.

Poster displayed in a Toronto library, February 1990.

LIES

See also HYPOCRISY
　　　　 TRUTH

"They say" is the biggest liar in Canada or any other country.

BOB EDWARDS, publisher, *The Eye Opener*, 22 Aug. 1903.

Better a noble lie than a miserable truth.

ROBERTSON DAVIES, man-of-letters, quoted by Alan Twigg in *For Openers: Conversations with Twenty-four Canadian Writers* (1981).

If hypocrisy is the tribute vice pays to virtue, marital lies are the tribute indifference pays to love.

STEPHEN VIZINCZEY, novelist, *An Innocent Millionaire* (1983).

Falsehood is the final outcome of all ideologies.

JOSEF SKVORECKY, novelist and essayist, "Two Peas in a Pod," *The Idler*, No. 10, Nov.-Dec. 1986.

The charm of falsehood is not that it distorts reality, but that it creates reality afresh.

CAROL SHIELDS, novelist, *Swann* (1987).

It gets easier to fool other people as you get older, but a lot harder to fool yourself.

EDWARD PHILLIPS, novelist, *Sunday Best* (1990).

LIEUTENANT-GOVERNOR

I don't want to be identified as an Icelander. I'm a Canadian, but I'm proud of my background.

GEORGE JOHNSON, Lieutenant-Governor of Manitoba, the first of Icelandic descent, quoted by John Lyons in *The Winnipeg Free Press*, 4 Dec. 1990.

LIFE

See also MANKIND
　　　　 MEN
　　　　 MEN & WOMEN
　　　　 PEOPLE
　　　　 WOMEN

We congratulate one another this day because we are still alive in this world.

"Address of Thanksgiving to the Powers of the Master of Life" (Green Corn Dance), "Seneca Fiction, Legends, and Myths" (Part 2), collected by J.N.B. Hewitt in 1896 on the Cattaraugus Reservation, N.Y., and translated by him. *Thirty-second Annual Report of the Bureau of American Ethnology to the Secretary of the Smithsonian Institution, 1910-1911* (1918).

The worst of it is, I don't think things will ever be much better. Life will just go on getting a little harder for me every year. I am practically alone in the world. Soon youth will be gone and I shall have to face a drab, solitary, struggling middle age. It is not a pleasant prospect.

L. M. MONTGOMERY, author, journal entry, 12 April 1903, *The Selected Journals of L.M. Montgomery: Volume I: 1889-1910* (1985) edited by Mary Rubio and Elizabeth Waterston.

To make men, not money, is the true object of life.

ALFRED FITZPATRICK, Founder and Principal of Frontier College, *The University in Overalls: A Plea for Part-Time Study* (1920).

Our life cannot be told in facts, don't you think, but in inner strivings and conflicts, very difficult to record.
GABRIELLE ROY, novelist, letter written from Encinitas, California, 11 March 1946, *Dear Bill: The Correspondence of William Arthur Deacon* (1988) edited by John Lennox and Michèle Lacombe.

The thing is to live life greatly.
ATHOL MURRAY, priest, quoted by Jack Gorman in *Père Murray and The Hounds* (1977).

Fate, I thought. Who is equal to it? For to be equal to fate is to be equal to the knowledge that everything we have done, achieved, endured and been proud and ashamed of is nothing.
HUGH MacLENNAN, author, thoughts of a character in the novel *The Watch that Ends the Night* (1958).

True greatness is like infinity, we cannot measure it.
STEPHEN VIZINCZEY, novelist and essayist, "One of the Very Few" (1968), *Truth & Lies in Literature: Essays & Reviews* (1986).

Life is something that happens to you while you're making other plans.
Remark attributed to a character in *Beyond This Point Are Monsters* (1970), a crime novel by MARGARET MILLAR. "This line, with a slight difference in wording, is associated with John Lennon of the Beatles," according to *The Mystery Lover's Book of Quotations* (1988) compiled by Jane E. Horning.

All lives are interesting; no one life is more interesting than another. Its fascination depends on how much is revealed, and in what manner.
MAVIS GALLANT, author, "Paul Léautaud" (1973), *Paris Notebooks: Essays and Reviews* (1986).

Something in the biosphere is drastically out of synchronization with everything else. That *something* is man.
JOHN A. LIVINGSTON, naturalist, *One Cosmic Instant: A Natural History of Human Arrogance* (1973).

We will first destroy all of the larger animals, either for meat or because they compete with us for space, together with those which may be intolerant of our activities because of their specific natural specializations. Extinction of nonhuman species, without replacement, will continue at an accelerating rate, until the only nonhuman living beings remaining will be those who are willing to share their squalor with us — rats, gutter curs, and parasites and micro-organisms which thrive in times of environmental dislocation.
JOHN A. LIVINGSTON, naturalist, *One Cosmic Instant: A Natural History of Human Arrogance* (1973).

It seems to me that the whole point of living is to become as human as possible; to learn to understand the world and to live in it; to be part of it; to learn to understand the animals, for they are our brothers and they have much to teach us. We are part of this world.
FRANK T'SELEIE, native chief, Fort Good Hope, N.W.T., statement to the Mackenzie Valley Pipeline Inquiry, quoted by Mel Watkins in *Dene Nation: The Colony Within* (1977).

The true world, of course, is life; but when Life becomes too real, and too earnest, we turn to the mirror of Life, either in dreams or in books.
KENNETH P. KIRKWOOD, author and diplomat, *The Diplomat at Table: A Social and Anecdotal History through the Looking-Glass* (1974).

We are worse than a people who mistrust art: we are a people who mistrust life.
ROBERTSON DAVIES, man-of-letters, "Canadian Nationalism in Arts and Science" (1975), *Transactions of the Royal Society of Canada*, Series IV, Volume XIII, 1975.

The decline and fall of everything is our daily bread.
SAUL BELLOW, Quebec-born author, Nobel Prize acceptance speech, Stockholm, 12 Dec. 1976.

It is not knowledge that truly enriches us; we need something more. If we are not bound by some conviction, conscious or unconscious, about the significance of life, we drift. It is not enough to know that kindliness is good and that cruelty is bad. Yet we do need the will to do good, and that lies within our power.
DOROTHY MACLEAN, medium, *To Hear the Angels Sing: An Odyssey of Co-Creation with the Devic Kingdom* (1980).

Yes, there is tragedy and unhappiness in this life, but there is also happiness and triumph and joy, and on balance, I think life is a joyful thing.
KNOWLTON NASH, anchor of CBC-TV's *The National*, quoted by Joan Sutton in *The Toronto Star*, 27 April 1981.

I can tell it's living, because it hurts.
Line attributed to the character Peggy in the play *A Place on Earth* (1982) by playwright BETTY JANE WYLIE.

There is no challenge in death: only defeat. There is no hope in destruction: only despair. Therefore, choose life — that we may live.
MORRIS C. SHUMIATCHER, lawyer, "The Good Death Maketh the Bad Life," *Annals of the Royal College of Physicians and Surgeons*, 3 May 1982.

We do not know *exactly* what life is all about. But the moment we lose our sensitivity for this central and mysterious question of our existence, our humanity is diminished.
JOSEF SKVORECKY, essayist and novelist, "I Was Born in Náchod . . . " (1984), *Talkin' Moscow Blues* (1988) edited by Sam Solecki.

I had the stubborn and stupid conviction that I ought to find the magical in real life.
MORLEY CALLAGHAN, novelist, CBC-TV, *First Person Singular*, 26 March 1986.

We were born too soon and will — or our offspring will — be thought of as mankind's last generation of children, mankind's last mortals.
JOHN CLUTE, science-fiction critic, "Being Earthbound," *Strokes: Essays and Reviews 1866-1986* (1988).

LIFE IS HARD, THEN YOU DIE
Message on a bumpersticker noted in the interior of Newfoundland in 1987 by Stephen Brook in *Maple Leaf Rag: Travels across Canada* (1987).

To exist is a gift.
GEORGE GRANT, philosopher, Appendix, *Technology and Justice* (1986).

In retrospect, I feel about my life the way some people feel about war. If you survive, then it becomes a good war.
SYLVIA FRASER, author and memoirist, *My Father's House: A Memoir of Incest and of Healing* (1987).

All of us are born into the second act of a tragedy-in-progress . . . but then spend the rest of our lives trying to figure out what went wrong in the first act.
SYLVIA FRASER, author and memoirist, *My Father's House: A Memoir of Incest and of Healing* (1987), quoted by Jill Johnston in *The New York Times Book Review*, 1 Oct. 1988.

Human life is fragile, easily snuffed out by a turn of the thermostat.
JOHN GRAY, playwright, Preface, *Local Boy Makes Good: Three Musicals* (1987).

If you're not annoying somebody, you're not really alive.
MARGARET ATWOOD, author, quoted by Judith Timson in *Maclean's*, 3 Oct. 1988.

You don't sit down and try to make sense of your life. The best thing to do is just regard it as "That's the way it was." Don't

ask me to make sense of it, to give a rational explanation which you will know is not
the truth at all. A rational explanation of a
man's life: nonsense!
> MORLEY CALLAGHAN, novelist, quoted
> by Dennis Kucherawy, *Metropolis*, 20 Oct.
> 1988.

Whoever it was up there who measured
the lengths of lives had one blind eye and
was all thumbs. No perception, none at all.
> JANE RULE, novelist, *After the Fire* (1989).

Living twice, maybe three times, is the
best revenge.
> Thoughts of the ubiquitous Solomon
> Gursky in MORDECAI RICHLER's novel
> *Solomon Gursky Was Here* (1989). This is
> a parody of the platitude "Living well is
> the best revenge."

As we used to say / in ancient Eygpt / Follow the heart / Love within us / and all
around us
> Characteristic ending of columns written
> by ALEXANDER BLAIR-EWART, publisher,
> *Dimensions: Toronto's New Age Monthly*,
> Jan. 1989.

People can earn a living by accident; but
learning to live is an art.
> EARL WORK, sales motivator, aphorism,
> Nov. 1989.

You're not here for a good time; you're
here for a long time.
> EARL WORK, sales motivator, discussing
> rehabilitation, Nov. 1989.

Only those who dare truly live.
> VICTOR DAVIS, champion swimmer,
> quoted by James Christie in *The Globe
> and Mail*, 13 Nov. 1989.

Knowing in our bones that life is the supreme gift, we can accept paradox. Life is
no longer broken into right and wrong,
light and dark, birth or death. Everything
is part of the awesome mystery.
> MARION WOODMAN, analyst and author,
> "Bedroom Thoughts," *The Ravaged Bride-
> groom: Masculinity in Women* (1990).

Go as long as you can in life without making up your mind about anything.
> ELWY YOST, television personality, re-
> calling a remark once made in 1948 by a
> professor at the University of Toronto,
> personal communication, 17 Jan. 1990.

I don't want glory but I want a sense of the
majesty of life, and for me that doesn't
come by having a halo. It comes in a pair
of passing eyes, or somebody smiling in an
extraordinary situation. Or somebody
who's brave enough to have tears in public, at the right moment. I have a sense
more of heroism than the hero; it's the
quality more than a single person.
> SCOTT SYMONS, novelist and cultural
> commentator, interviewed in *The Idler*,
> No. 25, May-June 1990.

LIGHT

I became convinced that how we see
things as a consequence of light is fundamental to the formation of human perception and imagination. In southern countries the earth is directly illuminated by
sun and the sky is dark, whereas in northern countries the sky is predominantly
white with light diffusing through cloud
cover and the earth is dark. Such different
lights must affect the psyche.
> ARTHUR ERICKSON, architect, *The Archi-
> tecture of Arthur Erickson* (1988).

LIMITS

The 20th century might be best thought of
as the century in which we have to learn
humanity's limitations.
> BOB RAE, Ontario Premier, writing in
> *What We Owe Each Other*, quoted by
> Nancy Logan in "Women on the Verge,"
> *Toronto Life Fashion*, March 1991.

LITERACY

The simple ability to read, write, and
count is essentially a passive acquire-
ment, a means of social adjustment. All
genuine teaching starts with this passive

literacy and then tries to transform it into an activity, reading with discrimination and writing with articulateness. Without this background, one may be able to read and write and still be functionally illiterate. It is discouraging for a student to find that he has reached university and is still totally unable to say what he thinks.

> NORTHROP FRYE, literary critic, address, Empire Club of Canada, Toronto, 19 Jan. 1984.

By the end of the 1990s if Canadian education continues to be run as it has been, most Canadian university graduates won't be able to read this sentence.

> LINDA FRUM, education critic, quoted in *Metropolis*, 21 Dec. 1989.

For there is no real polarity between books and life. Literature is a form and a way of life; it allows us to live more fully, intelligently, and honestly. And, of course, more joyfully, too. True literacy has more to do with the delights than the mechanics of reading. It is not a skill to be acquired once in a lifetime, but an art to be practised and polished one's whole life long.

> JANICE KULYK KEEFER, novelist, "Arks and Tunnels,"*More than Words Can Say: Personal Perspectives on Literacy* (1990).

The death of CanLit has another cause, as well. This is a nation not of illiterates but of ex-literates — supposedly educated people who haven't read a book since they escaped from school. Many of them are university graduates but they learn no love of the printed word. To see a forgettable American movie, these ex-literates will gladly spend a fortune on babysitters, parking, tickets and popcorn. But they'd never buy a Canadian novel for $24.95 — too expensive.

> CRAWFORD KILIAN, novelist and teacher, *The Globe and Mail*, 24 Feb. 1990.

LITERATURE

The point of literary history is not to articulate the memory of mankind by putting a mass of documents into an ordered and coherent narrative. Its documents are far better worth reading than any history of them could ever be. Its task is to reawaken and refresh our imaginative experience by showing us what unexplored riches of it lie within a certain area.

> NORTHROP FRYE, literary critic, "Nature Methodized" (1960), *Northrop Frye on Culture and Literature: A Collection of Review Essays* (1978) edited by Robert D. Denham.

A truly great book should be read in youth, again in maturity, and once more in old age, as a fine building should be seen by morning light, at noon, and by moonlight. We all read too much, too fast. I am taking the summer off to work slowly through several books that are due for a second reading.

> ROBERTSON DAVIES, man-of-letters, "Too Much, Too Fast" (1962), *The Enthusiasms of Robertson Davies* (1979) edited by Judith Skelton Grant.

There's only one story, the story of your life.

> NORTHROP FRYE, literary philosopher, remark made in May 1964 and recalled by NFB producer Tom Daly, quoted by John Ayre in *Northrop Frye: A Biography* (1989).

Criticism is the theory of literature, not a minor and non-essential element in its practice.

> NORTHROP FRYE, literary critic, *The Critical Path: An Essay on the Social Context of Literary Criticism* (1971).

Spend an hour or two every week reading one of the great religious texts of the past — the Upanishads, the Talmud, the Koran, the writings of Lao Tze, Confucius, Mencius, the New and the Old Testament — it will save you from superficiality and silliness, and it may help you when trouble comes.

LOUIS DUDEK, poet and professor, "Reality in the Arts and Education" (1971), *Technology and Culture: Six Lectures* (1979).

I don't think Canada is "better" than any other place, any more than I think Canadian literature is "better"; I live in one and read the other for a simple reason: they are mine, with all the sense of territory that implies. Refusing to acknowledge where you come from — and that must include the noodle man and his hostilities, the anti-nationalist lady and her doubts — is an act of amputation: you may become free floating, a citizen of the world (and in what other country is that an ambition?) but only at the cost of arms, legs or heart. By discovering your place you discover yourself.

MARGARET ATWOOD, novelist, "Travels Back," *Maclean's*, Jan. 1973.

And until a society or group is written about, it remain shapeless. An embarrassment somehow.

RUDY WIEBE, novelist, quoted by Suzanne Zwarun in *Maclean's*, 4 Sept. 1978.

SF is, then, a literary genre whose necessary and sufficient conditions are the presence and interaction of estrangement and cognition, and whose main formal device is an imaginative framework alternative to the author's empirical environment.

DARKO SUVIN, academic, *Metamorphosis of Science Fiction: On the Poetics and History of a Literary Genre* (1979).

Science fiction gives you a huge canvas: all of space, all of time, all forms of life.

ROBERT L. SAWYER, writer, *Books in Canada*, April 1988.

I wanted to scream out that if you had grown up in Canada, perhaps you'd realize that Jane Austen is every bit as foreign as Marquez. And if you'd grown up on the West Coast, you'd realize that all literatures were equally foreign.

JACK HODGINS, West Coast novelist, recalling a conversation with a visiting British poet and referring to English and Latin American literature, interviewed by Peter O'Brien in *So to Speak: Interviews with Canadian Writers* (1987).

Only critics, those great and good men, would wish any author to write in a way other than his own. As the Welsh proverb has it, we must sing with the voices God gave us.

ROBERTSON DAVIES, man-of-letters, *The Toronto Star*, 19 Sept. 1987.

A country's literature is a crystal ball into which its people may look to understand their past and their present, and to find some foretaste of their future.

ROBERTSON DAVIES, man-of-letters, Neil Gunn lecture, Edinburgh University, June 1988, published in *The Times Literary Supplement*, 30 Sept. 1988.

In any literary competition, vulgar pretension takes precedence over subtlety. If you want literary honours, abandon subtlety. Abandon taste. Go for the jugular of Popular Appeal, and rely upon the Stock Response.

ROBIN SKELTON, poet and author, *The Memoirs of a Literary Blockhead* (1988).

Two hundred years from now the Canadian public will catch up with me.

CRAD KILODNEY, maverick fiction writer, in conversation with Stuart McLean on CBC Radio's *Morningside*, 9 Jan. 1989.

The basis of all literature is oral performance, when thought turns into speech. You get more fluky insights when you talk than when you write. When you read a work you can see if a sentence is broken or if it flows. It's all part of Mitchell's messy method.

W.O. MITCHELL, author and story-teller, discussing his own method of composition, quoted by H.J. Kirchhoff in *The Globe and Mail*, 21 Oct. 1989.

My dream is still to win a lottery, move to the country and have a *pied-à-terre* in town, consult a bit and write full time. I still see myself as a writer who does this to make a living.

GREG GATENBY, poet and anthologist, artistic director of Harbourfront's series of literary readings and the International Festival of Authors, quoted by H.J. Kirchhoff in *The Globe and Mail*, 13 Oct. 1989.

When the Zulus have a Tolstoy, we shall read him.

SAUL BELLOW, Quebec-born novelist, quoted in "Forum," *Harper's*, Sept. 1989.

The British say, "Jolly good story!" The Canadians ask, "Can it happen here?" And the Americans say, "How much time have we got?"

MARGARET ATWOOD, author, commenting on the critical comments in the three countries of her novel *The Handmaid's Tale*, quoted by Sheldon Teitelbaum in *Cinefantastique*, March 1990.

Only the literary imagination can save us from the deadening influence of visual news and visual entertainment.

ROBERT FULFORD, essayist, quoted in *Soho Square III* (1991) edited by Alberto Manguel.

LITERATURE, CANADIAN

See also LITERATURE
WRITERS, CANADIAN

For I have always noticed that, whilst these gentry are constantly deploring the want of every kind of Colonial literature, and ascribing this circumstance to the system itself, they exercise all the influence they possess to render such literature impossible, by doing all in their

power to crush every effort (however feeble), which may be made to create it.

WILLIAM FLEET, satirist, *How I Came to Be the Governor of the Island of Cacona with a Particular Account of My Administration of the Affairs of that Island Respectfully Dedicated to My Fellow Labourers by the Hon. Francis Thistleton, late Governor of the Island of Cacona* (Montreal, 1852)

Evidently what is needed is more attention to be given to our Canadian writers in the schools and colleges. Why should the work of the classes in literature be confined to the English and American poets and our own be neglected? It is time our educationalists woke up to the fact that we have a literature well worthy of study. Perhaps that will come when more of the native-born begin to fill our professorial chairs.

Unsigned editorial, *The Canadian Magazine*, May 1907.

I do not think our literature is an expression of our national life as a whole. I think this is because we have only very recently — as time goes in the making of nations — had any real national life. Canada is only just finding herself. She has not yet fused her varying elements into a harmonious whole. Perhaps she will not do so until they are welded together by some great crisis of storm and stress. That is when a real national literature will be born. I do not believe that the great Canadian novel or poem will ever be written until we have had some kind of baptism by fire to purge away all our petty superficialities and lay bare the primal passions of humanity.

L. M. MONTGOMERY, author, passage written in 1910, recalled in a diary entry dated 27 Aug. 1919, *The Selected Journals of L.M. Montgomery: Volume II: 1910-1921* (1987) edited by Mary Rubio and Elizabeth Waterston.

[There was] a deep-seated belief that no novel written in or about Canada held any interest for English readers: "Lively, but

Canadian" was his comment on a novel he had liked but advised against.

PETER F. ALEXANDER, biographer, referring to the English bookman William Plomer who read literary submissions for Faber & Faber and other English publishers in the 1930s and 1940s, *William Plomer: A Biography* (1989), as quoted by Douglas Fetherling in "Foreign Perceptions of Canadian Culture," *Canadian Notes & Queries*, No. 44, Spring 1991.

I do not think that we have yet arrived, in writing, at a "Canadian consciousness." Thus far all we have had is a Canadian subconsciousness — made up of colonialism, Victorianism, etc.

A.M. KLEIN, poet and essayist, "Writing in Canada" (1946), *Literary Essays and Reviews* (1987) edited by Usher Caplan and M.W. Steinberg.

The literature emanating from Windsor, Ont. — you will agree with me — cannot be very different from that of Detroit, Mich. You may object, however: The literature of New Orleans will certainly be different from Windsor's. And I agree. As different as Windsor's from that of Dawson City, or Yamachiche, or Louisiana's from that of Oregon.

A.M. KLEIN, poet and essayist, "Writing in Canada" (1946), *Literary Essays and Reviews* (1987) edited by Usher Caplan and M.W. Steinberg.

In Paris, I had dinner with intellectuals and writers like François Mauriac, Jean Paulhan, Georges Duhamel, Charles Morgan, Jules Romains and many others. They talked only of themselves and did not ask me any questions about my books. Canada, for them, was very far. That was all.

ROGER LEMELIN, novelist, letter written in English and addressed to his publishers, McClelland & Stewart, 15 Sept. 1950, quoted by Clara Thomas and John Lennox in *William Arthur Deacon: A Canadian Literary Life* (1982).

The third period of Canadian literature will run from 1960 to 2000. Within the span

we shall get our 40 million population; we shall attain riches and power, and the self-confidence that goes with these things. That is the sort of soil out of which the great literatures have always come. It will be a lush time for reviewers also.

WILLIAM ARTHUR DEACON, literary critic, "The Reviewer" (1959), reprinted by Clara Thomas and John Lennox in *William Arthur Deacon: A Canadian Literary Life* (1982). Current estimates of Canada's population in the millennial year fall short of the 40 million figure; ditto its literature.

I contributed to a rising literary movement in Canada — a nation without a strong literary life is no shakes as a nation. I staked my life on it and I believe I won.

WILLIAM ARTHUR DEACON, retired literary critic, letter (among his last) to Lloyd Haines, 10 Dec. 1967, quoted by Clara Thomas and John Lennox in *William Arthur Deacon: A Canadian Literary Life* (1982).

I just got involved more or less gradually. But when I realized that Canada must be the only country in the world where high-school kids aren't taught their own literature, then I had to tell them and their teachers about it. I had to tell them what they're missing.

JAMES FOLEY, educator and enthusiast for Canadian literature who organized the first Canada Day in high schools at Port Colborne in the Spring of 1970, quoted by Al Purdy in *Weekend Magazine*, 15 June 1974.

I was asked in connection with *Fifth Business* to say what I was trying to do, and I said that I was trying to record the bizarre and passionate life of the Canadian people. Well, I was dropped on by some Canadian critics who said, There I was again, trying to make an effect and talking silly so that people would look at me and think what a fancy fellow I was.

ROBERTSON DAVIES, man-of-letters, interviewed by Silver Donald Cameron in

1971, *Conversations with Robertson Davies* (1989) edited by J. Madison Davis.

"In Canada," I said quietly, "all literature is, in effect, *samizdat*."
Spoken by the narrator of JOHN METCALF's novel *General Ludd* (1979). The point the narrator (and perhaps the author) is making is that the Canadian reading public is not reading serious Canadian books and that the publishers, reviewers, and arts administrators are doing little or nothing about it.

It is important for Canadian readers to encounter their own forests and waterways, their own towns and cities in literature. For people who have had to read mostly about other places, there is a sense of surprise and new reality in seeing their own world described and explored, put on the literary map. Only when Canada has a cultural identity can symbols such as the flag be meaningful. Literature is part of what makes a country not only a place to go but a place to come from.
JANE RULE, novelist, *The Globe and Mail*, 16 April 1980.

Whatever form Canadian writing may take, it has at its root an ineradicable introversion. . . . And it is not, I say with confidence, wanting in value as a literary attitude.
ROBERTSON DAVIES, man-of-letters, address, American Academy and Institute of Arts and Letters, New York, 15 May 1985.

Sixty or seventy years ago the kind of writing that was most popular with Canadians was represented by Stephen Leacock and Mazo de la Roche; thirty years later the popular writers were Hugh MacLennan and Morley Callaghan, and again, twenty years later, it was Pierre Berton and Arthur Hailey. Have we made progress, in discrimination and sensitivity to literary values? No, we have gone one step forward and two steps back.
LOUIS DUDEK, poet and aphorist, "Can.

Lit. Notes," *The Bumper Book* (1986) edited by John Metcalf.

If you want to read Richler in the original, read Saul Bellow.
LOUIS DUDEK, poet and aphorist, "Can. Lit. Notes," *The Bumper Book* (1986) edited by John Metcalf.

Yes, Canadian literature is forging ahead, but most of the writers are still as middling as ever.
LOUIS DUDEK, poet and aphorist, "Can. Lit. Notes," *The Bumper Book* (1986) edited by John Metcalf.

The problem with Canadian literature is that it is written in English and French. Canadians do not have a language entirely of their own; therefore, the fruits of their literary imagination have been, and always will be, willy-nilly, compared to the literatures of the cultures of the much older England and France and that of the much vaster U.S.A.
JOSEF SKVORECKY, Czech-born author, Foreword, *Ethos*, Autumn 1986.

If English-Canadian writing might be described as horizontal, based on an observing perception, Québécois writing is largely vertical, moving geometrically outward and inward.
GEOFF HANCOCK, editor, Introduction, *Invisible Fictions: Contemporary Stories from Quebec* (1987).

Literature in English other than British and American
Category that includes English-Canadian literature adopted by the Modern Language Association for its 1987 convention, noted by Eleanor Cook in "'A Seeing and Unseeing in the Eye': Canadian Literature and the Sense of Place," *Daedalus: Journal of the American Academy of Arts and Sciences*, "In Search of Canada," Fall 1988. As for French-Canadian literature, its category was "Literature in French outside of France."

The creation of the Jalna books is the most protracted single feat of literary invention in the brief history of Canadian literature.
ROBERTSON DAVIES, man-of-letters, quoted by Joan Givner in *Mazo de la Roche* (1989).

What I have to say is in my novels. The rest is gossip.
MORDECAI RICHLER, novelist, interviewed by Marlene Kadar in *Other Solitudes: Canadian Multicultural Fictions* (1990) edited by Linda Hutcheon and Marion Richmond.

I hold a master's degree in a nonexistent subject: Canadian literature. In a marginal way, CanLit still existed when I took my degree in 1972. But sometime during the eighties, CanLit faded away.
CRAWFORD KILIAN, novelist and teacher, *The Globe and Mail*, 24 Feb. 1990.

LONELINESS

Men and women suffer equally. The tragedy is not that they suffer, but that they suffer alone.
MARGARET LAURENCE, novelist, quoted by Sinclair Ross in *The Lamp at Noon* (1968).

Quebec has marvellous restaurants, wonderful shows, and cosier cafés than those of Paris. The Quebeckers have won on their home-ground a battle lost by all other Northerners: in the teeth of the English and spite of the snow, they have routed boredom.
FRÉDÉRIC BARREYRE, French commentator, *Quebec* (1987) with photographs by Pierre Toutain.

LOON
See also BIRDS

Among birds, for instance, I have found the loon's call to be the wildest, not in this area, where they are winterlings and haven't much to say for themselves, but farther north on their breeding grounds. Their call is one of utmost abandon, ecstasy, mad-

ness. Human beings have translated these sounds into words, but I must say they're a poor substitute for the real thing.
MARGARET MILLAR, mystery novelist, thoughts of a California-based character, *Spider Webs* (1986).

Untrue it is to term / The lonesome loon / For no one yet has known / A lake possessed of but one loon.
Last line of the poem "The Lonesome Loon" written by LOIS E. DARROCH and set to music by Leon Zuchert, sung at the Arts and Letters Club, 2 April 1990.

LOONIE

The happiest addition to our currency was unquestionably the loonie. Unlike the new bills, the $1 coin has the feel of something weighty and valuable. Made of a gold-coloured alloy, it might be an updated version of a piece of eight. Perhaps it should have been dubbed the doubloonie.
CHRISTOPHER HUME, art columnist, commenting on the introduction of a new design on the $50 bill, *The Toronto Star*, 13 Jan. 1990.

LOTTERIES
See GAMES & GAMBLING

LOVE
See also EMOTIONS
KISSES
LUST
MARRIAGE
MEN & WOMEN
PASSION
SEX

My lover looked like an eagle from the distance, but alas! / When he came nearer I saw that he was nothing but a buzzard.
Blackfoot poem, "Song of a Maiden Disappointed in Love," *Songs of the Great Land* (1989) edited by John Robert Colombo.

In politics I acknowledge but two parties, — those who hope and those who fear. In morals, but two parties, — those

who lie and those who speak the truth:
and all the world I divide into those who
love, and those who hate. This comprehensive arrangement saves me a vast deal
of trouble, and answers all my own purposes to admiration.
> ANNA BROWNELL JAMESON, pioneer
> traveller, *Winter Studies and Summer Ram-
> bles in Canada* (1838).

I believe that for *friendship* there should
be similarity; but for love there must be
dissimilarity.
> L.M. MONTGOMERY, author, letter of 1
> April 1907, *My Dear Mr. M.: Letters to G.B.
> MacMillan* (1980) edited by Francis W.P.
> Bolger and Elizabeth R. Epperly.

Remember that faith is better than doubt
and love is better than hate.
> SIR WILFRID LAURIER, Prime Minister, af-
> firmation characteristic of his last years.
> "In London, Ontario, I heard his last will
> and testament to the Young Liberals of
> Ontario," wrote Grattan O'Leary in *Recol-
> lections of People, Press and Politics* (1977).

I do not know if the world has lied / I have
lied / I do not know if the world has conspired against love / I have conspired
against love
> LEONARD COHEN, poet and singer,
> "What I'm Doing Here," *Selected Poems
> 1956-68* (1968).

Love is the terrible secret people are sus-
pected of unless they're married, then one
always suspects they don't.
> JANE RULE, novelist, quoted by Paul
> Grescoe in *The Canadian*, 4 Dec. 1976.

Happy lovers are not born, they learn to
outwit nature in some roundabout way.
> STEPHEN VIZINCZEY, novelist, *An Inno-
> cent Millionaire* (1983).

It's written in the scriptures. / It's written
there in blood. / I even heard the angels
declare it above. / There ain't no cure for
love.
> LEONARD COHEN, poet and singer, "Ain't

No Cure for Love," album *I'm Your Man*
(1988).

I LOVE LOVE / (Except between 6 and 9
p.m., when I'm studying, and Wednesdays
and Fridays, when I'm ironing or doing my
hair.
> Wording on a sign seen in Rochdale Col-
> lege, Toronto, in the 1960s, noted by
> David Sharpe in *Rochdale: The Runaway
> College* (1987).

Who could in a lifetime write down the
ways in which sexual love penetrates
every moment of our consciousness and is
never absent in any loving of the beautiful — present even when that love is universal?
> GEORGE GRANT, philosopher, "Faith and
> the Multiversity," *Technology and Justice*
> (1986).

To be loved is to be given great power.
> JANET AITKEN KIDD, Canadian-born
> daughter of Lord Beaverbrook, *The Bea-
> verbrook Girl: An Autobiography* (1987).

There is much goodness and kindness in
Newfoundland. And wisdom and gentle
simplicity, hospitality and love of others.
No more than elsewhere perhaps, but,
God witnessing, no less.
> RAY GUY, humorist, "Peace, Good Wife;
> We May Entertain Angels Unaware," *Ray
> Guy's Best* (1987).

You can blame it on the moon if you want
to / It really was big and bright / And though
it gave the whole show an exceptional
glow / It was you who lit up the night.
> SYLVIA TYSON, singer and composer,
> "Blame It On the Moon," quoted by Ellen
> Schwartz in *Born a Woman: Seven Cana-
> dian Women Singer-Songwriters* (1988).

One makes deals, or one can make love, of
this make what you will. A deal asks back
and love gives away, and a contract has to
be paid. But love never comes due, because once given away, it always comes
back to you.
> MERLE SHAIN, essayist, *Courage My Love:
> A Book to Light an Honest Path* (1988).

Telling someone you love him or her is like having a bath: it doesn't last and you have to do it every day.
> BETTY JANE WYLIE, author, *All in the Family: A Survival Guide for Living and Loving in a Changing World* (1988).

Old lovers go the way of old photographs, bleaching out gradually as in a slow bath of acid: first the moles and pimples, then the shadings, then the faces themselves, until nothing remains but the general outlines.
> Thoughts of the narrator of the novel *Cat's Eye* (1988) by MARGARET ATWOOD.

At twenty I wanted a man handsome, charming, witty, sophisticated, artistic — and a good dancer. Now the man I choose must be responsible, compassionate, honest, independent, generous-hearted . . . and must love women. That I now *choose* is an important difference. Literally and metaphorically, I do not wait for the phone to ring.
> FREDELLE BRUSER MAYNARD, memoirist, *The Tree of Life* (1988).

Love of neighbour in our moment of crisis must be extended to include the soil, the air, the running streams, and all creatures.
> TOM HARPUR, religion columnist, the *Toronto Star*, 12 Nov. 1989.

There is no evil so great / That love cannot accommodate.
> LEONARD GASPARINI, poet, "Inscription," *Ink from an Octopus* (1989).

Fantasy, need, habit: could these in combination actually be called love? The genuine feeling should certainly transcend such things, be ultimately altruistic and, yes, undying.
> JANE RULE, novelist, *After the Fire* (1989).

It requires less skill to love than to be loved.
> ROBIN SKELTON, man-of-letters, aphorism, May 1990.

LOYALTY & LOYALTIES
See also UNITED EMPIRE LOYALISTS

We grew up in an era that carried the official slogan: "Use it up, wear it out, make it do, or do without." Perhaps that accounts for our long-lasting loyalties.
> MARY PEATE, memoirist, recalling World War II slogans in Montreal, *Girl in a Sloppy Joe Sweater: Life on the Canadian Home Front during World War Two* (1989).

Loyalty that does not harm others, that lives within the law, that provides direction by the power of persuasion and moral force, not by compulsion or threat, is lasting loyalty. It will be renewed by each generation in search of commitment and security in a turbulent and insecure society.
> BRIAN A. GROSMAN, specialist in employment law, *Corporate Loyalty: A Trust Betrayed* (1988).

LUCK

It's far, far better to be lucky than to be good.
> Remark attributed to a character in *An Old-Fashioned Mystery* (1983), a crime novel attributed to RUNA FAIRLEIGH but edited and introduced by L.A. Morse.

LUST
See also LOVE

The first time I had hands laid on me in lust, and not in love, it took me a while to know the difference.
> BETTY JANE WYLIE, author, *Beginnings: A Book for Widows* (1977).

There's a lot to be said for simple lust, and not enough of it has been said by women.
> BETTY JANE WYLIE, author, *obiter dictum*, 1990.

Love is imagination; lust is energy.
> ROBIN SKELTON, man-of-letters, aphorism, May 1990.

M

MACDONALD, SIR JOHN A.

Touché, Taché.
> This riposte is attributed to SIR JOHN A.
> MACDONALD, Prime Minister, in con-
> versation with his worthy opponent,
> Alexandre-Antonin Taché, Bishop of St.
> Boniface, by the playwright John Coulter
> in *Riel: A Play in Two Parts* (1962).

Canada's "Old Tomorrow" lives today / In
unforgetting hearts, and nothing fears /
The long tomorrow of the coming years.
> Tribute in verse to "Old Tomorrow," the
> sobriquet for Sir John A. Macdonald em-
> ployed by the editors of *Punch* in the
> obituary notice in 1891, quoted by John
> Murray Gibbon in *Canadian Mosaic: The
> Making of a Northern Nation* (1938).

McLUHAN, MARSHALL
See also COMMUNICATIONS

I am an intellectual thug who has been
slowly accumulating a private arsenal
with every intention of using it. In a mind-
less age every insight takes on the character of a lethal weapon. Every man of good
will is the enemy of society.
> MARSHALL McLUHAN, media philoso-
> pher, letter to Ezra Pound, 22 June 1951,

Letters of Marshall McLuhan (1987) edited
by Matie Molinaro, Corinne McLuhan,
and William Toye.

The medium is the message.
> This now-famous formulation of the iden-
> tity of form and content was first used
> publicly by MARSHALL McLUHAN in his
> keynote address at the annual conven-
> tion of the National Association of Educa-
> tional Broadcasters, Omaha, Nebraska,
> 1958.
>
> "It was not the first time he had uttered
> these words — he had used them earlier
> that year, for example, in an address to a
> smaller gathering of broadcasters in Van-
> couver, B.C. But this was the first time he
> had used them before a truly influential
> forum, and it was to become a tag identi-
> fying him in the public mind." So ex-
> plained the biographer Philip Marchand
> in *Marshall McLuhan: The Medium and the
> Messenger* (1989). "It was simply one way
> of stating that all media . . . have effects
> on the human psyche quite apart from
> the explicit bits of information they might
> convey."

The Media
> First use of the term *the media* to refer to
> the total effect of newspapers, maga-

zines, books, radio, television, movies, video, etc., is attributed by Tom Wolfe, Jr., to MARSHALL McLUHAN who used the term in this sense as early as the mid-1950s. When McLuhan refered to *the media* — in the sense of "the print media" or "the electronic media" — he did so in the plural. By the mid-1960s, the term was widely used, sometimes as a plural noun, sometimes as a singular noun. *The Oxford English Dictionary* reproduces an American citation (noted by H.L. Mencken) for *a media* as a synonym for *a medium* as early as 1923, the same year *mass media* was recorded.

The Global Village
The notion that the world's multitude of parochial cultures and disconnected countries were being transformed into one planet-wide community characterized by interconnected needs and uniform services was pioneered and popularized by McLUHAN in the 1960s. According to biographer Philip Marchand writing in *Marshall McLuhan: The Medium and the Messenger* (1989), the germ of the idea grew from the following sentence from British author Wyndham Lewis's book *America and Cosmic Man* (1948): "The earth has become one big village, with telephones laid on from one end to the other, and air transport, both speedy and safe."

Seventy-five per cent of your material is new. A successful book cannot afford to be more than ten per cent new.
MARSHALL McLUHAN, communications theorist, quoting one of the unnamed editors of *Understanding Media: The Extensions of Man* (1964), cited by Richard Kostelanetz in "Marshall McLuhan: High Priest of the Electronic Village," *Master Minds* (1969).

McLuhan is doing for visual space what Freud did for sex.
JONATHAN MILLER, media personality, introducing Marshall McLuhan on BBC-TV, Feb. 1965, quoted by McLuhan in a letter to Harold Rosenberg, 1 March 1965, *Letters of Marshall McLuhan* (1987) edited by Matie Molinaro, Corinne McLuhan, and William Toye.

I'm the Only One Who Knows What the Hell Is Going On.
Title of a booklet on Marshall McLuhan's ideas compiled by BARRY DAY of the London-based advertising agency Lintas in 1967. This was a quotation that McLuhan afterward disclaimed, according to the editors of *Letters of Marshall McLuhan* (1987) edited by Matie Molinaro, Corinne McLuhan, and William Toye.

Marshall McLuhan, what are you doin'?
Tag line of actress GOLDIE HAWN on *Laugh-In* in the late 1960s, quoted by biographer Philip Marchand in *Marshall McLuhan: The Medium and the Messenger* (1989).

Most of what I have to say is secondhand, gathered however from esoteric sources.
MARSHALL McLUHAN, communications theorist, quoted by Richard Kostelanetz in "Marshall McLuhan: High Priest of the Electronic Village," *Master Minds* (1969).

Type is the prototype.
MARSHALL McLUHAN, communications theorist, characteristic observation concerning the effect of printing (moveable type) on human perception, quoted by Richard Kostelanetz in "Marshall McLuhan: High Priest of the Electronic Village," *Master Minds* (1969).

Some people read between the lines. I read between the pages.
Remark made in the 1970s by communications theorist MARSHALL McLUHAN to reading specialist Joel Bonn after taking Bonn's speed-reading course. McLuhan claimed that with a new book he always turned to page 69, read it, and then read the table of contents; if he decided to read the rest of the book, he read only left-hand pages, using his finger as a guide in the accepted speed-reading method.

I met another famous Torontonian, the late Marshall McLuhan, a few times. I liked him as a person, but I question his theories. He certainly had one of the best heads around, but he used it too often to stand on. His love of paradox vitiated his insights. It is not print, but speech, that is linear.

> HANS BLUMENFELD, architect-planner, *Life Begins at 65: The Not Entirely Candid Autobiography of a Drifter* (1987).

He was a great man. Much too great to be famous.

> EDWARD T. HALL, educator, commenting on Marshall McLuhan's contribution to culture and his status as a celebrity, quoted in *The Antigonish Review*, Summer-Autumn, 1988.

The best thing I ever heard said about McLuhan was by a professor named Kenneth Boulding.... He said McLuhan hits a very large nail not quite on the head. Not many people can do that. I'd be very happy if somebody said the same thing about us.

> ALVIN TOFFLER, futurologist, paraphrasing a remark by U.S. academic Kenneth Boulding, comparing the work of himself and his wife with that of McLuhan, quoted by Philip Marchand in *The Toronto Star*, 31 Oct. 1990.

For your information, let me ask you a question.

> MARSHALL McLUHAN, communications theorist, favourite conversational gambit, quoted by Philip Marchand in *Marshall McLuhan: The Medium and the Messenger* (1989).

Ashley, are you sure it's not too soon to go around parties saying, "What ever happened to Marshall McLuhan?"

> Caption to a cartoon in *The New Yorker*, 26 Sept. 1970, quoted by Philip Marchand in *Marshall McLuhan: The Medium and the Messenger* (1989).

MADNESS

The emotions of history, as of literature, are very rarely what in the light of psychiatry would be called normal. In a ruler the attributes of madness and of greatness were for many centuries in the popular mind interchangeable qualities. There is still some confusion upon this point.

> EZRA HURLBURT STAFFORD, physician and crank, "A Political Aspect of Mental Disease," *The Canadian Journal of Medicine and Surgery*, Vol. III, 1898.

They say madness is a hope denied.

> LEA HARPER, singer and songwriter, line from a lyric, reported in Dec. 1989.

MAGAZINES

Private Eye held on by its fingertips for years, and when it became comfortable it lost a little of its edge. I don't think Canadians should be too hard on themselves. Britain has, what, twice the population of Canada, yet only one *Private Eye*. The British adore self-mockery. Few other races share such a relish. We operated on telling the truth; and if we're not absolutely sure, but it sounds like the truth, we still print it. It doesn't always work.

> AUBERON WAUGH, one-time columnist for the British satiric magazine *Private Eye*, quoted by Michael Coren, "Canadian Satire," *The Toronto Star*, 25 Aug. 1990.

MAGIC

Sometimes the magic works, sometimes it doesn't.

> Admission of Old Lodge Skins, the Cheyenne chief whose part was created by Chief Dan George in the movie *Little Big Man* (1970).

I am a shamaness. I have been apprenticed for twelve years to a woman of knowledge whose name is Agnes Whistling Elk. She is an American Indian from Manitoba, Canada.

Many years ago I was initiated into the

Sisterhood of the Shields. The Sisterhood is comprised of forty-four women, each representing a different indigenous culture from somewhere in the world.
> LYNN V. ANDREWS, California-based New Age personality, author of *Crystal Woman: The Sisters of the Dreamtime* (1987). This "spiritual memoir" is one in a series which Andrews has written to describe or dramatize the alteration of consciousness that has followed her apprenticeship and initiation into "the Sisterhood of the Shields." Her mentor is Agnes Whistling Elk, who is presented as "a North American Indian from Manitoba, Canada," presumably a Cree medicinewoman from Northern Manitoba.

I hate to disappoint you, but I came up here on Air Canada. But I can't help thinking that the broomstick would be more ecologically sound.
> STARHAWK, California-based witch, born Miriam Simos, visiting Toronto for a talk, quoted by John Allemang in *The Globe and Mail*, 18 Sept. 1989.

MALAPROPISMS
See also HUMOUR

We're also fond of this quote from a corporal in the Royal Canadian Mounted Police, who was participating in a search for a missing child in Pender Harbour, Vancouver: "We have checked the area thoroughly," he told the Vancouver *Sun*, "and there is nothing to indicate that the child is actually lost, other than the fact that she is missing."
> BRUCE FELTON and MARK FOWLER, compilers, *Felton & Fowler's More Best, Worst, and Most Unusual* (1976).

After nine rounds of a slam-bang boxing match at Maple Leaf Gardens, radio commentator Chuck Murphy expected a strong finish: "Believe me, folks," he told his audience, "this is one close fight — a real cliff-dweller."

Noted by DAVID MacDONALD, "Anecdotes," *The Toronto Star*, 23 July 1988.

We all want to thank David Lam for his one-million-dollar anonymous gift that made this great project possible.
> MICHAEL (MIKE) HARCOURT, Vancouver Mayor, remark made at the official opening of the Dr. Sun Yat-sen Classical Chinese Garden, acknowledging the secret (and not so secret) contribution of the Hong Kong-born capitalist David Lam, quoted by Peter C. Newman in *Sometimes a Great Nation* (1988).

By strengthening the strong, we can help the weak.
> WILLIAM VANDER ZALM, B.C. Premier, remark made July 1986, quoted by Stephen Osborne and Mary Schendlinger in *Zalm Thought* (1988).

Kierans: Of course I have my own ox to grind here.
Camp: Ax to gore or ox to grind?
Kierans: Ax to grind, ox to grind. Okay. Okay.
> Slip of the tongue of ERIC KIERANS with response by Dalton Camp on CBC Radio's *Morningside*, noted by Jamie Swift in *Odd Man Out: The Life and Times of Eric Kierans* (1988).

I smell an axe to grind.
> DAVID HOMEL, novelist and journalist, remark made at a meeting in Ottawa, 28 Feb. 1989.

It's not the size of your caucus, it's how you use it.
> Attributed to the Cabinet Minister BARBARA McDOUGALL at a meeting of the Ontario members of the federal Conservative caucus, 4 June 1989.

Pharaoh forced the Hebrew slaves to make bread without straw. Moses led them to the Red Sea, where they made unleavened bread, which is bread made without any ingredients. Afterwards, Moses went up on Mount Cyanide to get the ten commandments. He died before he ever reached Canada.

> Malapropisms — genuine Grade VIII student bloopers — collected and assembled by RICHARD LEDERER and published in *Anguished English* (1988).

During the Middle Ages everybody was middle aged. Middle Evil society was made up of monks, lords, and surfs. After a revival of infantile commerce slowly creeped into Europe, merchants appeared. They roamed from town to town exposing themselves and organized big fairies in the countryside.

> Bloopers culled from students' history essays at the University of Alberta and McMaster University, quoted by Thomas M. Paikeday in *The Penguin Canadian Dictionary* (1990).

It is a hypothetical situation that does not exist. . . . Cheat fair! / Rightly or wrongly, you are quite wrong! / Canada is the greatest nation in this country. / I'm working all day this week.

> Malapropisms (a.k.a. "Lampys") attributed to master malapropist and former Toronto Mayor ALLAN LAMPORT in Oct.-Nov. 1990, hence too late for inclusion in *Quotations from Chairman Lamport* (1990) compiled by John Robert Colombo.

The ladies' meeting will be hell as usual next Wednesday.

> Misprint (which mistakes an "l" for a "d") on diocesan bulletin boards, from the office of Remi J. De Roo, Bishop of Victoria, noted by George Mortimore in *The Canadian Forum*, May 1990.

I'm not against abused women. I'm in favour of them 100 per cent.

> Malapropism committed by DOUG MANN, Niagara Falls regional councillor, arguing in council against increased funding for women's shelters, quoted by Carol Alaimo in *The St. Catharines Standard*, 6 Sept. 1990. His arguments were of no avail; the increased funding resolution was passed.

They see politicians feathering their own nests with their face in the trough.

> Mixed metaphor attributed to former Ontario Premier DAVID PETERSON, with respect to taxpayers' perceptions of politicians, noted by Jack White in *The Globe and Mail*, 6 Sept. 1990.

It hurts just as much to have a tooth extracted as it does to have it pulled out.

> Attributed to former Prime Minister JOHN G. DIEFENBAKER in *Maclean's*, 8 Oct. 1990.

You quietly made your points — loud and clear.

> Attributed to Albertan malapropist JOHN KUSHNER by Jack White in *The Globe and Mail*, 20 Oct. 1990.

Pain hurts.

> Attributed to BRIAN DORMER, resident of Norway House, Man., by Mike Vlasman, personal communication, 16 Feb. 1991.

MAN

See also MEN & WOMEN
MANKIND

He walks, he talks, he moves: but in the sight of God all his activities are no more than wretched sleep-walking.

> LOUIS RIEL, Métis leader and mystic, diary entry, 11 Aug. 1885, *The Diaries of Louis Riel* (1976) edited by Thomas Flanagan.

Man is, without doubt, the defacer, the destroyer. But spending at least the last three years in trying to understand the enemy has almost seduced me to his side.

> ELIZABETH SMART, novelist and diarist, entry for 12 Sept. 1936, *Necessary Secrets: The Journals of Elizabeth Smart* (1986) edited by Alice Van Wart.

The extinction of man is as certain as his existence. Extinction is certain for all species, faunas, planets and stars. Individual species, like individual beings, do not *matter* in the larger system of things. No indi-

vidual or species will be selected for immortality. We will be mourned by no one.
> JOHN A. LIVINGSTON, naturalist, *One Cosmic Instant: A Natural History of Human Arrogance* (1973).

Give a man an inch, and he thinks he's a ruler.
> DON HARRON, comedian, speaking as the matronly character Valerie Rosedale, quoted by Martha Harron in *A Parent Contradiction* (1988).

Maybe we have to get rid of the word *manhood*. It's done a lot of damage to both men and women. I don't know why, but I always associate the word manhood with killing.
> TIMOTHY FINDLEY, novelist, interviewed by Alan Twigg in *Strong Voices: Conversations with Fifty Canadian Authors* (1988).

The difference between men and boys is the price of their toys.
> Graffiti, hotel washroom, Montreal, June 1989.

MANAGEMENT
See also EXECUTIVES

1. What ought to be done.
2. How should it be done.
3. Who should do it.
4. Has it been done.
> These are "four things an executive should know," according to the publisher JOSEPH E. ATKINSON as quoted by Ross Harkness in *J.E. Atkinson of The Star* (1963).

MANITOBA
See also WINNIPEG

A Canadian province, Manitoba, is named for the Great Spirit of the Algonkians, Manitou — in other words, God.
> CHARLES BERLITZ, linguist, *Native Tongues* (1982). In truth, the Algonkian word *manitou* is closer in meaning to the English word "mystery" than it is to the English word "God."

The climate of Manitoba consists of seven months of Arctic winter and five months of cold weather.
> Remark attributed to "an American settler's guide" issued in 1883 which later that year caused the Department of Agriculture to issue a pamphlet titled *Canadian North-West, Climate and Productions: A Misrepresentation Exposed* (1883).

My native province has always seemed to me an unusual and fascinating place, possessed both of a history of great interest and of a deep sense of history.
> W.L. MORTON, historian, *Manitoba: A History* (1957).

Come and sit by my side if you love me, / Do not hasten to bid me adieu, / But remember the Red River Valley / And the girl who has loved you so true.
> Chorus of "The Red River Valley" (1870), *The Penguin Book of Canadian Folk Songs* (1973) edited by Edith Fowke, who noted: "This is probably the best known folk song on the Canadian prairies."

During all the years I lived on the West Coast I missed my home province of Manitoba most in September and October. Autumn is a subdued event in Vancouver. A few trees turn yellow or red and drop their leaves, but the prevailing colour — as it is all the year round — is green.
> CHRISTOPHER DAFOE, columnist, one-time Vancouver resident, *The Winnipeg Free Press*, 29 Sept. 1990.

I really believe our province is in the key position of North America and truly is the heart of the continent.
> ED RUSSENHOLT, CBC-TV weatherman in Manitoba from 1954 to 1962, quoted in his obituary by the Winnipeg columnist Gordon Sinclair in *The Winnipeg Free Press*, 5 Feb. 1991. He concluded each weather report with these words: "In the Red River Valley, the heart of the continent." He died at the age of 100 on 3 Feb. 1991.

MANKIND

See also LIFE

I have learned to look below the surface comedy of life into the tragedy underlying it. I have become *humanized* — no longer an isolated selfish unit, I have begun to feel myself *one with my kind* — to realize what someone has called "the infinite sadness of living," and to realize how much each of us has it in our power to increase or alleviate that sadness. I understand at last that "no man liveth to himself."
> L. M. MONTGOMERY, author, journal entry, 7 Oct. 1897, Cavendish, P.E.I., *The Selected Journals of L.M. Montgomery: Volume I: 1889-1910* (1985) edited by Mary Rubio and Elizabeth Waterston.

Try to have a vivid sense of the splendour of Human Life. Our miserable present conditions, our poverty and wealth with their attendant crimes and diseases, our morbid sex-conditions with their hideous fruit, our petty, silly, tedious lives — all these are quite unnecessary and out of date, and may be swept away as soon as we choose.
> FLORA MacDONALD DENISON, early feminist and transcendentalist, "To My Real Readers," *Sunset of Bon Echo*, April-May 1920.

Man is a marvellous being. However wonderful a nebula is, however perfect a crystal, however fascinating the core of an atom, they are neither as awe-inspiring nor as beautiful as man himself.
> MARY MAXWELL, a.k.a. Rúhíyyih Khánum, leading member of the Bahá'í Faith, referring to Western civilization, *Prescription for Living* (1950).

I feel terribly naked and isolated as a human being, feeling my species is going to die out through its own efforts. But if you can somehow learn to feel that you're *not* isolated, that we're part of a whole stream of life, then it's not so frightening. It ceases to be important whether we disappear as a species.
> FARLEY MOWAT, writer, interviewed by Alexander Ross in *Maclean's*, March, 1968.

The world has always had its doom criers, calamity howlers and pedlars of pessimism and now they are in full cry. But the human race is invincible and always has been. Deep down in the human spirit there is something eternal and you and I are part of it.
> GORDON SINCLAIR, journalist and broadcaster, *Will Gordon Sinclair Please Sit Down* (1975).

Whatever happens — although I didn't phrase it to myself in that way in those days — whatever happens anywhere in the macrocosm also happens in the microcosm, even though it may be written in smaller type in a sense. But whatever happens anywhere — in essence, the human experience — is universal.
> MARGARET LAURENCE, novelist, quoted by Heather Menzies in *The Railroad's Not Enough: Canada Now* (1978).

Everything alien is human to me.
> PHYLLIS GOTLIEB, poet and science-fiction writer, characteristic remark, a paraphrase of "Nothing human is alien to me" attributed to the Roman author Tacitus.

Through the senses and minds of mankind, a clod of earth talks of the millennia of its history, of the myriad invisible lives contained within it, of the manifold visible life that grows from it.
> DOROTHY MACLEAN, medium, *To Hear the Angels Sing: An Odyssey of Co-Creation with the Devic Kingdom* (1980).

In the purest Hindu tradition we can truly say that all nature is the family of man.
> HUBERT REEVES, Quebec-born astrophysicist and science popularizer in France, *Atoms of Silence* (1984), as quoted by Jamie Findlay in *Saturday Night*, Sept. 1987.

Human beings are in their essence needed beings, and when otherness has become

completely absent for us, we are hardly human beings at all.
GEORGE GRANT, philosopher, Appendix, *Technology and Justice* (1986).

One of the wonders of human nature is that most people are capable of fine behaviour in an emergency. . . . A genuine crisis — and death is the final and perhaps greatest testing time — releases the better being. For the individual who experiences it, it has the distinct feeling of growth; for the human tribe, it is a redemptive experience.
JUNE CALLWOOD, author and social activist, *Twelve Weeks in Spring* (1986).

In the 19th century, philosophers believed that the human being was infinitely perfectible and therefore worthy of democracy. On the basis of the 20th century, I believe that the human being is infinitely corruptible and therefore in need of democracy.
A. ALAN BOROVOY, General Counsel, Canadian Civil Liberties Association, *When Freedoms Collide: A Case for Our Civil Liberties* (1988).

I also feel sorry for us because not only are we a bad animal, but we're almost inevitably a doomed animal. Every species dies out. But our doom is here and now.
FARLEY MOWAT, naturalist and author, interviewed by Alan Twigg in *Strong Voices: Conversations with Fifty Canadian Authors* (1988).

Human brotherhood may be a myth, and a weak one at that, but it is the only myth that has yet to murder someone in its cause.
MICHAEL IGNATIEFF, author and television personality, "Is Nothing Sacred? The Ethics of Television," *Daedalus: Journal of the American Academy of Arts and Sciences*, "In Search of Canada," Fall 1988.

How dare we call our species *Homo sapiens*? The whales and dolphins, whom we are rapidly destroying, are surely superior in every way that counts.
MARGARET LAURENCE, novelist, *Dance on the Earth: A Memoir* (1989).

We are like yeast in a vat — mindlessly multiplying as we greedily devour a finite world. If we do not change our ways, we will perish as the yeasts perish — having exhausted our sustenance and poisoned ourselves in the lethal brew of our own wastes.
FARLEY MOWAT, naturalist and author, "L'Envoi," *Rescue the Earth! Conversations with the Green Crusaders* (1990).

And so, if you wish to ask the question of the ages — why do humans exist? — a major part of the answer, touching those aspects of the issue that science can treat at all, must be: because *Pikaia* survived the Burgess decimation.
STEPHEN JAY GOULD, biologist, discussing the implications of the fossil evidence of "*Pikaia*, the world's first known chordate," the earliest vertebrate, "the first recorded member of our immediate ancestor," found only in the Burgess Shale of B.C.'s Yoho National Park, *Wonderful Life: The Burgess Shale and the Nature of History* (1989). "*Pikaia* is the missing and final link in our story of contingency — the direct connection between Burgess decimation and eventual human evolution." The full name of the two-inch creature is *Pikaia gracilens*.

MANNERS

In sum: if manners present a particular difficulty in England it is how to leave people their privacy without seeming to shun them, and in America the difficulty is how to offer people your friendship without seeming to intrude.
QUENTIN CRISP and JOHN HOFSESS, English-born entertainer and Canadian-born author, *Manners from Heaven: A Divine Guide to Good Behaviour* (1984).

MANUFACTURING

See also INDUSTRY

The manufacturing we do possess is often controlled by non-Canadians; and while their control may be benign, it is inarguably out of our hands. We are a careful people. But paradoxically this timidity, this reluctance to make our own goods in our own factories, has become the path of recklessness. The riskiest thing we can do now is to balk at gambling on the new opportunities that science and technology have put into our hands.

> LARKIN KERWIN, President, National Research Council, address, Empire Club of Canada, Toronto, 12 Nov. 1981.

Made by Canadians.

> A study sponsored by the Conference Board of Canada recommended that the explanatory line "Made in Canada" on Canadian-manufactured products be replaced by the line "Made by Canadians." The study reported twenty-one product evaluations in eight countries. The findings of the researchers, Louise Heslop and Nicolas Papadopoulos of Carleton University, were reported by CP and carried by *The Globe and Mail*, 29 Nov. 1989.

We end up having the Canadian complaint. About half of Canadian manufacturing is foreign-owned, so Canadians don't get to compete for the top jobs. The best they can aspire to is CEO of a division.

> LESTER THUROW, management consultant, quoted by David Olive in *White Knights and Poison Pills: A Cynic's Dictionary of Business Jargon* (1990).

For example, why should we leave it to Finland to supply sophisticated pulp and paper machinery? Even worse, the Finns are beating us in the production of hockey sticks. It also seems obvious that Canadians should be world leaders in products designed to function in cold climates.

> CEDRIC RITCHIE, Chairman, Bank of Nova Scotia, address, annual meeting, Halifax,

published in *The Toronto Star*, 20 Jan. 1991.

Unless current trends are reversed, the number of Canadian factory jobs will follow the downward curve of agriculture, so that by 1999, fewer than 10 per cent of working Canadians will be employed in manufacturing. The Science Council of Japan dubbed Canada a Third World country with an artificially high standard of living back in 1986, and every available indicator since has continued to point downward.

> PETER C. NEWMAN, columnist, "Business Watch," *Maclean's*, 25 Feb. 1991.

MAPLE LEAF

Resolved: that all Native Canadians joining in the procession, whether identified with the National Societies or not, should wear the maple leaf as the emblem of the land of their birth.

> JAMES H. RICHARDSON, businessman and patriot, resolution adopted at the joint meeting of the National Societies, Toronto, 21 Aug. 1860, prior to the visit of the Prince of Wales, the date of the adoption of the maple leaf as the emblem for Canada.

We have given to the maple a prominence which was due to the birch.

> HAROLD ADAMS INNIS, political economist, *The Fur Trade in Canada* (1930).

The very symbol of Canada — the maple leaf — is being strangled by airborne pollution spewing from industry and car exhausts on both sides of the border.

> ANITA GORDON and DAVID SUZUKI, science broadcasters, *It's a Matter of Survival* (1990).

MAPLE SYRUP

He willed that there shall be growing forests in which there shall be certain trees from which (maple) sap shall habitually fall in its season. So, too, let us give thanks because there still grow here and there maple trees, for we still can look upon maple sugar.

"Address of Thanksgiving to the Powers of the Master of Life" (Green Corn Dance), "Seneca Fiction, Legends, and Myths" (Part 2), collected and translated by J.N.B. Hewitt in 1896 on the Cattaraugus Reservation, N.Y. *Thirty-second Annual Report of the Bureau of American Ethnology to the Secretary of the Smithsonian Institution, 1910-1911* (1918).

MAPS

A friend once told me that a large map of Canada on his office wall had the most southern bit of the nation, Pelee Island, at the floor and Ellesmere Island at the ceiling. He used it for a private survey, asking visitors to point out the farthest north they had been. Most were on their knees at once, with most of Canada above them.

YORKE EDWARDS, naturalist, "Wilderness Parks: A Concept with Conflicts," *Endangered Spaces: The Future for Canada's Wilderness* (1989) edited by Monte Hummel.

MARITIME PROVINCES

See also ATLANTIC PROVINCES
MARITIME UNION
NEW BRUNSWICK
NOVA SCOTIA
PRINCE EDWARD ISLAND

Others say that the line should strike across the narrow isthmus which runs between the Bays of Verte & Chignecto, & (by including the island of St. John's) sink the expanse of that abortion of a government.

EDWARD WINSLOW, colonist, letter to Ward Chipman, 26 April 1784, concerning the boundary between Nova Scotia and New Brunswick.

Let us be honest and modest, and not attempt too much, but go to the next World's Fair with what we have, and send, as we shall send, in pamphlet form, a fair, candid account, not too voluminous, of the Province, to show every man who may wish to emigrate, what sort of country this is. We do not pretend to rival the neighbouring States, but this we can say: that this country only began to be settled very many years after the old colonies; that we commenced with nothing in the wilderness, and all we have made has been made in little over a century. It has been said that the moose and caribou roamed through the forests a hundred years ago; and yet look what the efforts of man have done since that time!

JOSEPH HOWE, statesman, thoughts on the Maritime exhibit at the Paris Exhibition of 1854, *The Speeches and Public Letters of Joseph Howe* (1909) edited by J.A. Chisholm. These thoughts were occasioned by the following incident: "I came to two or three compartments having the names of New Brunswick and Nova Scotia painted in large letters above them, and beneath nothing at all. Then I bowed my head and thanked God that nobody knew me."

It is time for us to see ourselves under eastern eyes, in order to come to a better understanding of who we are, have been, and may become.

JANICE KULYK KEEFER, literary critic, *Under Eastern Eyes: A Critical Reading of Maritime Fiction* (1987). She is alluding to the better-known phrase "under western eyes" used for the title of a novel by Joseph Conrad.

Now we were all Down Home together. The term has many meanings. If a Maritimer says "Down Home" while sitting in a Toronto tavern, he could be talking of all the Maritimes, or Prince Edward Island, or a valley, cove, county, village, or the house where he grew up. Down-homer, in its gently derogatory sense, is also relative.

HARRY BRUCE, essayist, "Home for Christmas," *Down Home: Notes of a Maritime Son* (1988). He continues, discussing "Down Home" in terms of a "kind of neighbourhood," noting that it was in use in this sense in Nova Scotia in the 1920s.

On the map of Canada, the Maritimes look tiny, cosy, crowded with roads, ports, and villages. Knowledge that down-east settlement began in Shakespeare's time reinforces the idea that the entire region is like one of its own Historic Villages: a place to find much history in a few hours.
> HARRY BRUCE, essayist, "The Land's Lousy — and Unforgettable," *Down Home: Notes of a Maritime Son* (1988).

The Maritimes have one source that never fails them, however — beauty. Thousands are drawn to it each summer.
> F. KENNETH HARE, geographer, "Canada: The Land," *Daedalus: Journal of the American Academy of Arts and Sciences*, "In Search of Canada," Fall 1988.

MARITIME UNION

The old dream of Maritime Union therefore remains an old farce, and in the face of every argument to rationalize higher education, the Maritimes go right on funding no fewer than eighteen universities for a population not much better than greater Vancouver's.
> HARRY BRUCE, essayist, "Maritimers Are Like a Motorcycle Gang," *Down Home: Notes of a Maritime Son* (1988).

The Maritime provinces must begin to operate on the basis of a single economic unit. The time has come to create a single integrated market for over 1.3 million people and co-ordinate our strategic objectives so that we speak with a single voice at national and international levels.
> FRANK McKENNA, New Brunswick Premier, addressing the issue of co-operation among the three Maritime provinces, quoted by Deborah Jones in *The Globe and Mail*, 18 Sept. 1990. The notion was originally broached by J. R. Winter of Acadia University in *Maritime Union Study: Federal-Provincial Fiscal Relations and Maritime Union*, Aug. 1970.

MARKETING

In this country it's harder to buy something than to sell something.
> WILLIAM SEMEYN, West Coast business executive, characteristic remark first noted in Jan. 1991.

MARRIAGE
See also LOVE
 MEN & WOMEN

I wish I were a cloud / so I could stay / always in the air / and see my husband / all the time.
> British Columbian Indian poem, "Wife's Song," *Songs of the Great Land* (1989) edited by John Robert Colombo.

A Canadian is, in fact, a slave to his wife in the most extensive sense of that term. He is obliged to answer all her calls, to obey all her commands, and to execute all her commissions, without a murmur. No West-Indian slave-driver issues his mandates to the sable sons of Africa in a more authoritative tone than a Canadian fair one to him who is at once her Lord and Servant.
> EDWARD ALLEN TALBOT, colonist, *Five Year's Residence in the Canadas* (1824).

But while giving sex its due place I have laid stress on marriage as a life-long companionship in which two personalities join forces to face the many problems of life.
> ALFRED HENRY TYRER, Anglican minister and birth-control enthusiast, *Sex, Marriage and Birth Control: A Guide-book to Sex Health and a Satisfactory Sex Life in Marriage* (10th ed., 1936).

Next to actual disharmony in the matter of sex itself the question of money is the shoal in the sea of matrimony on which many wrecks occur.
> ALFRED HENRY TYRER, Anglican minister and birth-control enthusiast, *Sex, Marriage and Birth Control: A Guide-book to Sex Health and a Satisfactory Sex Life in Marriage* (10th ed., 1936).

The opportunity will never occur, but if I ever had the chance to become a wife, I'd pass it up.

I've seen too many wives. . . . Wives are people who have to match the other girls, eyelash for eyelash, curve for curve, without missing a wash day, garbage day, ironing day, or getting the kids off to school.

> ROBERT THOMAS ALLEN, essayist, "I'd Hate to Be a Wife," *Children, Wives & Other Wildlife* (1970).

The do-it-yourself divorce, / You have to be married of course. You study petitions, then draw up your own, / You don't need a lawyer, you do it alone. / You handle the case in court; / It's really an excellent sport. / And thirty-six dollars is all that it costs. / The do-it-yourself divorce.

> VERA JOHNSON, folksinger and composer, "The Do-It-Yourself Divorce," a popular song dating from the 1970s.

Twenty years of marriage spoil one for casual conversations.

> BETTY JANE WYLIE, author, *Beginnings: A Book for Widows* (1977, rev. 1988).

It used to be only mothers died young, mothers and babies. Now, husbands die.

> Line attributed to the character Peggy in the play *A Place on Earth* (1982) by the author BETTY JANE WYLIE.

In many ways, I was ahead of my time. I had decided to live my life according to my own ideas. I didn't want to get married — I hated marriage. I'm not at all "Women's Lib" but my friends had one goal, "get married," and to me that was not the only way to fulfil one. . . . I was the black sheep of my family and very proud of it.

> DENISE OUIMET, Quebec-born writer and second wife of French detective novelist Georges Simenon, quoted by Fentson S. Bresler in *The Mystery of Georges Simenon* (1983). Ouimet is the author of a biography, *Un Oiseau pour le Chat*, and a *roman à clef* about her life, *Le Phallus d'Or*, issued under the pseudonym "Odile Dissane." Simenon wrote a non-crime novel

about their relationship, *Trois Chambres à Manhattan*, which was filmed in France, and in his *Mémoires Intimes* he referred to their relationship with impatient contempt.

Marriage is a framework to preserve friendship. It is valuable because it gives much more room to develop than just living together. It provides a base from which a person can work at understanding himself and another person.

> ROBERTSON DAVIES, man-of-letters, interviewed by John Milton Harvard in 1984, *Conversations with Robertson Davies* (1989) edited by J. Madison Davis.

Dancing has always given me a special high. It releases the same kind of endorphins that others get from making love. My problem is that I married men who were good dancers, confusing their ability on the dance floor with their ability in bed. Now I just go dancing.

> LYNNE GORDON, feminist, remarks made at the Toronto launch of her memoirs, *Working without a Net* (1986).

We live in a Noah's Ark Society in which everything goes two by two, and you're all alone out here, treading water.

> BETTY JANE WYLIE, author, *Successfully Single* (1986).

Women who are foolhardy enough to marry a second time generally do so for companionship or a tax shelter.

> EDWARD PHILLIPS, novelist, *Buried on Sunday* (1986).

A neurotic collusion, I once read, occurs when the rocks in his head fit the holes in hers. That pretty well describes our marriage.

> FREDELLE BRUSER MAYNARD, memoirist, *The Tree of Life* (1988).

No one promises to love, honour and obey any more. At best, they promise to give it their best shot.

> MERLE SHAIN, essayist, *Courage, My*

Love: A Book to Light an Honest Path (1988).

Monogamy is the art of making someone feel special so that they can make you feel special too.
MERLE SHAIN, essayist, *Courage My Love: A Book to Light an Honest Path* (1988).

A marriage is really a nonstop conversation.
BETTY JANE WYLIE, author, *All in the Family: A Survival Guide for Living and Loving in a Changing World* (1988).

Marriage is to family what legs are to a table.
BETTY JANE WYLIE, author, *All in the Family: A Survival Guide for Living and Loving in a Changing World* (1988).

The solo bathroom is one of the biggest perks of being single.
BETTY JANE WYLIE, author, *obiter dictum*, 1990.

A wedding is the only theatrical presentation I can think of where the prompter stands up facing the audience and feeds lines to the principal players.
EDWARD PHILLIPS, novelist, *Sunday Best* (1990).

Thank God for bathrooms. Where would we be without them, eh? Those little private oases in the desert of eternal wedlock.
Comment of a character in a play included in *7 Stories* (1990) by playwright MORRIS PANYCH.

MATHEMATICS

Freud said biology is destiny. I say geometry is biology.
A.K. DEWDNEY, specialist in computer games, address, Toronto, Nov. 1988.

MATRIARCHY & PATRIARCHY

Patriarchy is like body odour; you are always the last one to know that you have it.
BRUCE KIDD, track and field star and sports historian, quoted by Laura Robinson in *The Globe and Mail*, 23 Aug. 1990.

MATURITY

A consenting adult cries in private, takes the pain, acknowledges it, praises the experience, blames nobody.
A consenting adult moves on.
ELIZABETH SMART, novelist and diarist, final lines of "How to Mend a Broken Heart" (Feb. 1982), *Autobiographies* (1987) edited by Christina Burridge.

One of the best things about growing old (or even growing up, for that matter) is the way one gradually learns to contemplate things without coveting them: to treat "life as a vehicle for contemplation and contemplation as a vehicle for joy," as a Spanish philosopher once put it.
GEORGE FALUDY, Hungarian-born poet, *Notes from the Rainforest* (1988).

Perhaps one of the surest signs of middle age is to realize you are far less interested in tailoring yourself to other people's expectations than in trying to live up to those you have set for yourself.
EDWARD PHILLIPS, novelist, *Sunday Best* (1990).

MEANING

Things matter. Nothing matters to that stone out there, but something matters to my dog, and things matter to you and me. There's a fundamental, ontological difference between living beings and non-living beings, that in some way or other, things matter to them. So you might say "mattering" instead of meaning. We are beings to whom things matter.
CHARLES TAYLOR, philosopher, inter-

viewed in *The Idler*, No. 26, Nov.-Dec. 1989.

I'm still searching for an answer to the question: What are people for?
JACK WEBSTER, journalist and broadcaster, *Webster!* (1990).

THE MEDIA
See also COMMUNICATIONS
McLUHAN, MARSHALL

There is the question of using hypnotism over the radio and television. While we do not have the slightest doubt that certain members of the audience could be thrown into the genuine trance by a hypnotist using such means of contact, the whole thing is impractical. The operator is too far removed from his various subjects and should anything go amiss the chances for trouble, including lawsuits, would be great.
G.H. ESTABROOKS, psychologist and authority on hypnotism, *Hypnotism* (1943, rev. 1957).

You either hear it or see it or you miss it.
R.S. LAMBERT, radio broadcaster and author, referring to the evanescence of events reported by "the electronic media" (radio and television) as distinct from their representation in the medium of print (newspapers, magazines, books, etc.), quoted in *The Globe and Mail*, 5 July 1956.

Whenever you are photographed, smile. Wave reassuringly. Radiate courage. Never complain or appear angry. It's okay if you come off as flamboyant and eccentric . . . you must be known for your smile.
MARSHALL McLUHAN, communications theorist, offering image-building advice to Timothy Leary who quoted the advice in *Flashbacks: An Autobiography* (1983).

I've always felt that the media are, in effect, an agent for the public in seeking out and providing information on what's happening, where, when and why.
KNOWLTON NASH, anchor of CBC-TV's

The National, address, Empire Club of Canada, Toronto, 26 June 1986.

As for the media, if they can't even tell the truth about the weather, how can they tell the truth about anything else?
LOUIS DUDEK, poet and aphorist, "Can. Lit. Notes," *The Bumper Book* (1986) edited by John Metcalf.

As Robert Fulford once told me, if print had been invented *after* radio and television, it would be regarded as a wildly innovative medium — compact, portable, requiring only a brain for use.
DAVID SUZUKI, scientist and media personality, *Metamorphosis: Stages in a Life* (1987).

Where British ministers try to manipulate the public by anonymously ingratiating themselves with the press, Canadian ministers and members of Parliament face a veritable unruly scrum of aggressive reporters who pressure and test and argue with them, using camera, microphone, and pen and pad to grill them on behalf of the public. Where in England the government tries to use the press to lead the public, in Canada the press forces the government to be accountable to the public. The scrum is a Canadian invention, and may be Canada's most important contribution to democratic freedom of information. By contrast, the presidential press conference so central to American public information is called at the pleasure of the president, and leaves little room for the combative style of the Ottawa scrum — a unique celebration of the fact that freedom of the press and the right of the people to know are one and the same.
PATRICK WATSON, broadcaster, and BENJAMIN BARBER, historian, *The Struggle for Democracy* (1988).

Our next guest, an extremely talented lady, has a fine voice and nice tits.
Caption on a caricature of radio and television host Peter Gzowski drawn by AISLIN (cartoonist Terry Mosher) and displayed by Aislin on the CBC-TV show

90 Minutes Live which was hosted by Gzowski. Aislin produced it in response to Gzowski's question, "Do you ever put your editors on the spot by giving them a controversial cartoon right at deadline?" The words were never spoken, of course, as Gzowski points out in *The Private Voice: A Journal of Reflections* (1988).

They [a set of four questions, which we call a tetrad] can be asked (and the answers checked) by anyone, anywhere, at any time, about any human artefact. The tetrad was found by asking, "What general, verifiable (that is, testable) statements can be made about all media?" We were surprised to find only four, here posed as questions:
* What does it enhance or intensify?
* What does it render obsolete or displace?
* What does it retrieve that was previously obsolesced?
* What does it produce or become when pressed to an extreme?
MARSHALL and ERIC McLUHAN, media philosophers, *Laws of Media: The New Science* (1988). The authors reduce these concepts to the following terms: Enhances, Reverses into, Retrieves, Obsolesces.

The state of our mass media should be a matter of concern to more Canadians, too. We must continue imaginatively to seek the right balance between cultural needs and economic realities.
MARY VIPOND, historian, *The Mass Media in Canada* (1989).

There was a time when people killed and died for the right to control their own minds individually. It was called the fight for tolerance in the years of the Reformation. Do we have to consider a media reformation to regain control of our collective mind? We value freedom more than anything else. The new freedom, the new tolerance issue is the right to have, maintain and protect access and control of the very means by which we make up this mind collectively and individually. Now, I'm not talking about how television *feeds* culture, but how it *is* culture.
DERRICK DE KERCKHOVE, academic, "Control of the Collective Mind," *The Canadian Forum*, Oct. 1989.

The melancholy fact is that for the mass media the expression of corporate values is the norm, while the expression of non-corporate values demonstrates lack of objectivity. It is thus that corporations have been able to use their economic power to become arbiters of most of what we see, hear, and do in Canada.
BOYCE RICHARDSON, journalist and filmmaker, "The Corporate Censor," *The Canadian Forum*, July-Aug. 1990.

Viewing or listening to television, radio, or videos is *shared experience carried out in private*.
URSULA FRANKLIN, scientist, *The Real World of Technology* (1990), as excerpted in *The Canadian Forum*, July-Aug. 1990.

MEDICAL RESEARCH
See also MEDICINE

On April 14th, 1921, I began working on this idea in the Physiological Labroatory of the University of Toronto. Professor Macleod allotted me Dr. Charles Best as an associate. Our first test was to tie the pancreatic ducts in a number of dogs. At the end of seven weeks these dogs were chloroformed.
FREDERICK BANTING, scientist, "Diabetes and Insulin," Nobel Lecture, Stockholm, 15 Sept. 1925. Banting meant by "this idea" the notion that "by ligating the duct and allowing time for the degeneration of the acinus cells, a means might be provided for obtaining an extract of the islet cells free from the destroying influence of trypsin and other pancreatic enzymes."

Insulin is not a cure for diabetics; it is a treatment. It enables the diabetic to burn sufficient carbohydrates, so that proteins and fats may be added to the diet in sufficient quantities to provide energy for the economic burdens of life.

> FREDERICK BANTING, scientist, concluding paragraph, "Diabetes and Insulin," Nobel Lecture, Stockholm, 15 Sept. 1925.

We should know on whose shoulders we stand.

> JASON A. HANNAH, physician who established the Hannah Institute for Research into a Study of the History of Medical and Related Services, quoted by Joan Hollobon in *The Globe and Mail*, 20 Jan. 1977.

MEDICAL SERVICES
See also HEALTH

The only area in Ontario in which nurses have an opportunity to fulfil their potential as health practitioners is north of the 60th parallel where doctors are rare.

> SHEILA COPPS, politician and feminist, *Nobody's Baby: A Survival Guide to Politics* (1986).

MEDICARE
See also HEALTH CARE

The Canadian environment is more stable and predictable precisely because its cost-control processes work relatively well. But in Canada, whatever has happened or may happen can be blamed on government and on the evils of "socialized medicine." Anxiety and dissatisfaction are easily, if not always accurately, focused and channeled collectively through the process of public negotiation. In the United States, it is harder for individual practitioners to find the villains, and still harder to identify an effective response. At the same time, it is easier to misinterpret the experience of other countries with more visible bargaining processes.

> ROBERT G. EVANS, et al., "Controlling Health Expenditures — The Canadian Reality," *The New England Journal of Medicine*, 2 March 1989.

Imagine owning a business where there are never any bad debts — and never any quarrels with customers about prices, whether the work done was necessary or whether it took too long to do. Imagine a business where you could direct your customers to use competitors only on your terms, get a commission by doing so and, at the same time, erect barriers to entry in your field. Sound like fiction? Welcome to medicine in Canada.

> DIANE FRANCIS, columnist, *Maclean's*, 26 March 1990.

Americans think medicare is a socialist menace. Canadians think the lack of an American medicare system is barbaric. One of the assessments is correct.

> ALLAN FOTHERINGHAM, columnist, *Maclean's*, 3 July 1989.

MEDICINE
See also DENTISTRY
DISABILITIES
DISEASE
FITNESS
HANDICAPS
HEALTH
MEDICAL RESEARCH
MEDICAL SERVICES
MEDICARE
PSYCHIATRY

Nature provides all cures for all illnesses. God would not put man on earth without such cures.

> JOSEPH LOGAN, elder of the Six Nations, quoted by Curtis Fuller in "Green Medicine," *Fate*, Feb. 1970.

Historically, modern dynamic psychotherapy derives from primitive medicine, and an uninterrupted continuity can be demonstrated between exorcism and magnetism, magnetism and hypnotism, and hypnotism and the modern dynamic schools.

> HENRI ELLENBERGER, historian of psychiatry, *The Discovery of the Unconscious* (1970).

I kept one basic principle in my mind. The less cutting you do, the less patching you have to do afterwards.
> FERDINAND WALDO DEMARA, impostor, quoted by Herma Silverstein and Caroline Arnold in *Hoaxes that Made Headlines* (1986). Demara, although neither physician nor surgeon, armed with the fraudulently obtained papers of Dr. Joseph Cyr, played the part of the Lieutenant-Surgeon aboard the RCN's *Cayuga* which was active during in the Korean War. Demara, as Cyr, pulled teeth, removed tonsils, and even extracted a bullet lodged near a patient's heart. Publicity led to his exposure.

A surgeon should have the eyes of a hawk, the heart of a lion, and the hands of a woman.
> CHRISTINA HILL, physician and surgeon, quoting a formulation dating back to the 15th century, medical convention, Halifax, quoted by Martin O'Malley in *Doctors* (1983).

But much of medicine is not traumatic surgery with an immediate operation under anesthesia that will fix the damaged limb; much of medicine is not the treatment of infections with antibiotics; much of medicine, just as much of psychiatry, is the day-to-day patchwork treatment of chronic, intractable, difficult conditions, the etiology of which is very often in doubt.
> VIVIAN RAKOFF, psychiatrist, quoted by Jonathan Caro in *The Canadian Doctor*, Nov. 1987.

MEDITATION

Whether meditating changed my life or whether I began to meditate because my life was changing is not really important — no doubt there is some truth in both.
> ALEXA PETRENKO, columnist, "Food for Thought," *Ontario's Common Ground Magazine*, Winter 1990.

MEECH LAKE ACCORD
See also DISTINCT SOCIETY
QUEBEC

In Quebec — and it is very obvious — there are wounds to be healed, worries to be calmed, enthusiasms to be rekindled, and bonds of trust to be established. The men and women of the province have undergone a collective trauma.
> BRIAN MULRONEY, Prime Minister, speech at the nomination meeting in his own riding, Sept-Iles, Que., 6 April 1984. With this speech, co-written with Lucien Bouchard, Mulroney moved to "bring Quebec into the Constitution" — as he expressed it "with honour and enthusiasm." Quoted by Graham Fraser in *The Globe and Mail* the following day.

Today has been a good day for Canada. Today's discussions have been marked by generosity and flexibility and, above all, the political will to find agreement in the spirit of compromise that characterizes the Canadian people.
> BRIAN MULRONEY, Prime Minister, announcing that the provincial premiers had reached an agreement to ratify at a later date the Meech Lake Accord, 30 April 1987, quoted in *The Globe and Mail*, 23 May 1990.

Quebec constitutes, within Canada, a distinct society.
> One of the key provisions of the Meech Lake Constitutional Accord, adopted for future provincial ratification at an all-ministers conference in Ottawa, 3 June 1987, was the recognition of Quebec as constituting a "distinct society." The Accord, by granting constitutional recognition of the distinctive character of the Province of Quebec, sought to provide for "two distinct societies (*deux nations*)" in Canada.

Canada is whole again . . . Quebec has joined the Canadian family.
> BRIAN MULRONEY, Prime Minister, speaking in the presence of the provincial premiers who had agreed on the wording

of the Meech Lake Accord, Meech Lake, 30 April 1987. Quoted by Charlotte Gray, journalist, "Speaking in Tongues," *Saturday Night*, Dec. 1989.

I protest this treason. The country is under attack from within.
MICHAEL CHARETTE, opponent of the Accord, from Mississauga, Ont., illegally entered the House of Commons through the Speaker's door, walked across the floor of the Commons, laid hands on the mace, and made the above protest, 1 July 1987, reported in *The Toronto Star* the following day. Charette was charged with causing a disturbance and petty trespass.

The governments of the Yukon and the Northwest Territories protested the provisions in the strongest terms. . . . Meech Lake reveals the Yukon's continuing vulnerability to federal politics and southern Canadian priorities. Once more the Yukon had been sacrificed to a greater Canadian ambition. It now seems that the Yukon Territory could well be doomed to the status of a permanent colony, denied even the ambition of constitutional evolution that sits at the base of the Canadian political tradition.
KEN S. COATES and WILLIAM R. MORRISON, historians, *Land of the Midnight Sun: A History of the Yukon* (1988).

It is a distinct society, and nobody is denying that. Nobody would probably even deny that, if you want, we can put it into a preamble somewhere. That might cause some pique with the Newfoundlanders, though, who only came into Canada in the lifetime of most of the people in this room. They could certainly say, "Well, why not us? Newfoundland and Labrador are a distinct society." There might be some dissatisfaction, but, at least, it would be doubtful that any legal confusion would arise. So you have distinct societies, some more distinct than others. I agree, if you like, that I am more distinct than Senator Marchand here — no, no, that's not right, he was distinct before I was!

PIERRE ELLIOTT TRUDEAU, former Prime Minister, Testimony to the Senate Submissions Group on the Meech Lake Constitutional Accord, *With a Bang, Not a Whimper: Pierre Trudeau Speaks Out* (1988) edited by Donald Johnston.

If the people of Canada want this accord, and that is not beyond the realm of possibility, then let that be part of the Constitution. I, for one, will be convinced that the Canada we know and love will be gone forever. But, then, Thucydides wrote that Themistocles' greatness lay in the fact that he realized Athens was not immortal. I think we have to realize that Canada is not immortal; but, if it is going to go, let it go with a bang rather than a whimper.
PIERRE ELLIOTT TRUDEAU, former Prime Minister, Testimony to the Senate Submissions Group on the Meech Lake Constitutional Accord, *With a Bang, Not a Whimper: Pierre Trudeau Speaks Out* (1988) edited by Donald Johnston.

We have made peace with Quebec by letting it believe that "distinct society" means Two Nations. If the courts hold that it does have that meaning, Canada is doomed. If they hold otherwise, Quebec will have been tricked, and the howls of protest will strengthen separatism. One way or another, Meech Lake may mean the peace of the grave for the Canada we know and love.
PIERRE ELLIOTT TRUDEAU, former Prime Minister, Testimony to the Senate Submissions Group on the Meech Lake Constitutional Accord, *With a Bang, Not a Whimper: Pierre Trudeau Speaks Out* (1988) edited by Donald Johnston.

Alas, only one eventuality hadn't been foreseen: that one day the government of Canada might fall into the hands of a weakling. It has now happened. And the Rt. Hon. Brian Mulroney, P.C., M.P., with the complicity of ten provincial premiers, has already entered into history as the author of a constitutional document which — if it is accepted by the people and their legislators — will render the Canadian state totally impotent.

That would destine it, given the dynamics of power, to eventually be governed by eunuchs.

> PIERRE ELLIOTT TRUDEAU, former Prime Minister, writing about the Meech Lake Accord, *The Globe and Mail*, 28 May 1987.

The real question to be asked is whether the French Canadians living in Quebec need a provincial government with more powers than the other provinces. I believe it is insulting for us to claim that we do.

> PIERRE ELLIOTT TRUDEAU, former Prime Minister, referring to the "distinct society" provisions of the Meech Lake Accord, *The Globe and Mail*, 28 May 1987.

The Meech Lake Accord is, in my opinion, one of the most splendid and powerful demonstrations of enlightened patriotism we have seen in this House since its history began. I am proud, and I feel sure my pride is shared by a very great majority of our fellow citizens.

> ROBERT BOURASSA, Quebec Premier, address in the National Assembly, 18 June 1987, reproduced by Donald Johnston, editor, *With a Bang, Not a Whimper: Pierre Trudeau Speaks Out* (1988).

It will be Meech Lake, nothing more, nothing less.

> ROBERT BOURASSA, Quebec Premier, addressing his fellow Premiers and the Prime Minister, Ottawa, 2 June 1987, quoted by Charlotte Gray, journalist, "Speaking in Tongues," *Saturday Night*, Dec. 1989.

Rest assured that in my family, Asa Meech will be remembered as a valiant Canadian settler and as a true hero, not as one after whom this distorted accord is called. I trust that the other nine provincial governments will eventually arrive at the same conclusion and reject this selfish and deliberate attempt to destroy the very fibre of our great country. The accord

should be named after its originator — it should be called the Mulroney Discord!... Although he may have demeaned my ancestor Asa Meech, it will be Mulroney's name that goes down in infamy.

> JOHN A. MEECH, Kingston, Ont., descendant of Asa Meech after whom Meech Lake was named, quoted in *The Toronto Star*, 26 June 1988.

It took some 120 years to reach an agreement of such importance. If not ratified, how long will it take to repeat that achievement? Quebec occupies a crucial and unique place in Canada's history, not only as a member of the Canadian federation but also as the bastion of one of the two great cultural expressions of the Canadian identity in North America.

> ROBERT BOURASSA, Quebec Premier, First Ministers' Conference, 9-10 Nov. 1989, quoted in *The Globe and Mail*, 14 April 1990.

I have no quarrel with acknowledging Quebec to be a distinct society. It is indeed a society that is distinctly different from any other province — although many people believe Newfoundland to be even more different than any other province.

> CLYDE WELLS, Newfoundland Premier, discussing the "distinct society" provision of the Accord, speech, Toronto, 4 Oct. 1989, quoted by Robert Sheppard in *The Globe and Mail* the following day.

There are tens of thousands of lakes besides Meech in the country.

> RONALD SUTHERLAND, columnist, conclusion of column on how the Accord is perceived by francophone students in Quebec's Eastern Townships, *The Globe and Mail*, 24 Oct. 1989.

Meech Lake is a win-win situation for French-Quebeckers. If the accord is ratified, Quebec grabs a new lot of fresh powers from Ottawa. If the accord fails, then Quebec is justified to look elsewhere, and move even further away from Canada.

PETER BLAIKIE, Montreal laywer and Accord critic, quoted in *The Globe and Mail*, 27 Oct. 1989.

All I want at the moment is that Quebec should not emerge from this sort of legal wrangle with the federal government on all fours, taking a kick in the pants, ashamed, cowering, beaten up, losing its feathers and saying: I love it.
JACQUES PARIZEAU, P.Q. leader, speaking at a press conference in Quebec City, referring to criticism of the Accord, quoted by Robert McKenzie in *The Toronto Star*, 3 Nov. 1989.

No matter whether we wind up being inside, outside, or just beside Canada, we will remain a distinct society anyway.
PIERRE FORTIER, former Quebec Minister of National Institutions, quoted in an editorial in *The Globe and Mail*, 7 Nov. 1989.

I am not rejecting Quebec. I am rejecting a Canada with a Class A province, a Class B province and eight Class C provinces.
CLYDE WELLS, Newfoundland Premier, First Ministers' Conference, Ottawa, 9 Nov. 1989, insisting on a renegotiation of the Meech Lake Accord with respect to the clause which grants Quebec the status of a "distinct society," reported in *The Toronto Star* the following day.

Such testing cannot be undertaken unless we accept, once and for all, the inevitable compromises, and unless the parties involved ratify their pact and do not let Canada drift into an unforeseeable future.
JEANNE SAUVÉ, Governor General, farewell speech to the nation, with its controversial reference to the Meech Lake "pact," Ottawa, 29 Dec. 1989, published in *The Toronto Star* the following day.

What the Meech Lake Accord ought to have shown us is that our whole process of constitutional amendment is wrong: out of date, undemocratic. The Constitution belongs to the people, not the politicians.

It is the people, not the politicians, who should decide what goes in, what stays in, what goes out.
EUGENE FORSEY, constitutional authority, *A Life on the Fringe: The Memoirs of Eugene Forsey* (1990).

We shall be very lucky if we escape a Canadian Munich — an agreement, or "accord," that would be hailed as a triumph of goodness, realism, moderation, and sweet reasonableness and might last no longer than the Munich agreement itself.
EUGENE FORSEY, constitutional authority, *A Life on the Fringe: The Memoirs of Eugene Forsey* (1990).

It all happened in secret one dark night, beside a pretty little lake in Quebec by the name of Meech. Canada has never been so divided as it has since that night.
PIERRE ELLIOTT TRUDEAU, former Prime Minister and critic of the Accord, "The Values of a Just Society," *Towards a Just Society: The Trudeau Years* (1990) edited by Thomas S. Axworthy and Pierre Elliott Trudeau, translated by Patricia Claxton.

The Meech Lake accord is a statement of love for Canada.
BRIAN MULRONEY, Prime Minister, addressing a Conservative rally, Chambly, Que., 2 Feb. 1990, quoted by Edison Stewart in *The Toronto Star* the following day.

Better a divorce, I think, than a marriage in name only. Canada is supposed to be a country, not a convenience store.
MORDECAI RICHLER, Quebec-based, English-language author, address in Toronto, 27 Feb. 1990, quoted by Julia Nunes in *The Globe and Mail* the following day.

We can acquiesce to Meech Lake out of fatigue and boredom, and God knows everybody is tired of it by now. We can acquiesce and thereby risk separation by stealth. Or we can say no to it, and risk the real thing. I think Trudeau's vision of Canada is worth fighting for after all. We must

say no to Meech Lake whatever the risks. Meech Lake is a junk bond. I'm sorry to sound so depressing, but I am depressed.
MORDECAI RICHLER, novelist, address, Toronto, 27 Feb. 1990, quoted by Philip Marchand in *The Toronto Star* the following day.

I expect to live long enough to see the day (unless Quebec becomes some sort of hyper-extended political appendage or something worse) when the phrase "distinct society" will be considered innocuous.
DALTON CAMP, political columnist, *The Toronto Star*, 28 Feb. 1990.

In a recent poll, fifty-four percent of Newfoundlanders favoured the Meech Accord, while only forty-six percent favoured the Honda Accord.
Joke current in Central Canada in March 1990.

As some people have been saying lately, "It's 'meech ado' about nothing."
BARBARA FRUM, broadcaster, CBC-TV's *The Journal*, 20 March 1990.

Nobody anticipated that governments would change, signatures would be repudiated, and all of a sudden a very simple, straightforward document of unity would become a catch-all for everybody's wishlist as governments changed across the country.
BRIAN MULRONEY, Prime Minister, responding to the resignation of Cabinet Minister Lucien Bouchard from the Conservative Party over the recommendation of the Charest commission that there be 23 changes to the Meech Lake Accord (which was originally signed on 30 April 1987), House of Commons, 22 May 1990, quoted by Susan Delacourt and Rhéal Séguin in *The Globe and Mail* the following day.

This country doesn't work any more. We have to remake it.
LUCIEN BOUCHARD, Cabinet Minister who resigned from the Conservative Party over possible changes to the Meech Lake Accord, press conference, Ottawa, 22 May 1990, quoted by Alan Freeman in *The Globe and Mail* the following day.

If you think this is a bluff, then I called my bluff. I quit the Cabinet.
LUCIEN BOUCHARD, Cabinet Minister, resigning from the Conservative Party over possible changes to the Meech Lake Accord and in the process employing unidiomatic English, press conference, Ottawa, 22 May 1990, quoted by Alan Freeman in *The Globe and Mail* the following day.

And while we were there a Québécois cabinet minister announced his resignation, for constitutional, patriotic and linguistic reasons. On television he was frank: "I decided to call my bluff." Could he have meant this, I wondered, and bought a copy of *La Presse*. "Moi, j'ai decidé de le caller, le bluff."
ERIC KORN, columnist and antiquarian book dealer, *The Times Literary Supplement*, 15 June 1990.

Normally polite Canadians have become uncivil in the extreme, and bitter.
ROBERT MacNEIL, co-host of PBS's Mac-Neil-Lehrer Report, noting one consequence of the Meech Lake controversy, quoted by John Lyons in *The Winnipeg Free Press*, 26 May 1990.

We have an aboriginal past and a multicultural future . . . not just the French-English duality that is seen as the fundamental characteristic.
GARY FILMON, Manitoba Premier, interviewed by Barbara Frum on CBC-TV's *The Journal*, 4 June 1990.

My own personal conviction is that what's in the Meech Lake accord is not the proper way to be generous to Quebec . . . and at the same time be fully faithful to the principles of federalism. And that's what's caused me to take this decision I've taken today.

The future of Canada may indeed be at stake. . . .
CLYDE WELLS, Newfoundland Premier, remarks made at the close of the First Ministers' Conference on changes to the Meech Lake Accord, Ottawa, 9 June 1990, carried in *The Globe and Mail*, 11 June 1990.

For Quebeckers, until now Canada was a legal country. Now it is a real one.
ROBERT BOURASSA, Quebec Premier, remark made at the close of the First Ministers' Conference on the Meech Lake Accord, Ottawa, 9 June 1990, quoted by Ross Howard in *The Globe and Mail*, 13 June 1990.

We all gave blood, but it flowed into the crucible called Canada.
DAVID PETERSON, Ontario Premier, remark made at the close of the First Ministers' Conference on the Meech Lake Accord, Ottawa, 9 June 1990, quoted by Ross Howard in *The Globe and Mail*, 13 June 1990.

It's unfair and it's the perpetuation of a double standard. Quebec has been here for 350 years, but we've been here for thousands of years.
PHIL FONTAINE, leader, Assembly of Manitoba Chiefs, commenting on the "distinct society" provision of the Accord, quoted by Geoffrey York in *The Globe and Mail*, 11 June 1990.

Right here, I told them when it would be. I told them a month ago when we were going to meet. It's like an election campaign; you count backward. I said, "That's the day we're going to roll the dice."
BRIAN MULRONEY, Prime Minister, interviewed at 24 Sussex Drive on 11 June 1990, explaining to reporters Susan Delacourt and Graham Fraser how one month earlier he and his advisers had gathered to map out the federal strategy to deal with the Meech Lake crisis and to set a First Ministers' meeting the first week of June, quoted in *The Globe and Mail*, 12 June 1990. He even added,

"That's the way it had to be done. You're asking me if I had any regrets? None whatsoever."
This is the origin of the notorious "roll the dice" remark which, more than any other phrase (except perhaps for the description of Quebec as a "distinct society"), brought about the demise of the Meech Lake Accord. When the boastful indiscretion drew editorial ire, public fire, and the wrath of at least two provincial premiers, Mulroney complained to *The Globe and Mail* that he had been misquoted. But the interview had been taped and the two journalists from the newspaper's Ottawa Bureau refused to "reinterpret" the Prime Minister's impolitic remark. Mulroney's eleventh-hour strategy failed and the reason for its failure was this heedless and needless indiscretion.
Later, Mulroney admitted regret — if not responsibility — to Barbara Frum on CBC-TV's *The Journal*, 29 June 1990: "If you're asking me . . . given the interpretations and the distortions that have been placed upon a few words in that, whether I could have chosen better words, yes."

I don't know exactly what it accomplished — we'll have to see in the future.
SHARON CARSTAIRS, Manitoba Liberal leader, on the still-uncertain fate of the Meech Lake Accord, quoted by W.A. Wilson in *The Winnipeg Free Press*, 12 June 1990.

I think (the Province of Manitoba) taught the other first ministers something about democracy and process. I think they have learned from us that non-partisanship and open hearings should be the way to proceed with constitutional amendments.
GARY FILMON, Manitoba Premier, on the Meech Lake process, quoted by Frances Russell in *The Winnipeg Free Press*, 13 June 1990.

There comes a time when you have to stand up, and in a sense this is an opportune time.
ELIJAH HARPER, Ojibwa-Cree and NDP

Member of the Manitoba Legislative Assembly, referring to his opposition to the Meech Lake Accord, quoted by Gerald Flood in *The Winnipeg Free Press*, 16 June 1990.

No, Mr. Speaker.

ELIJAH HARPER, M.L.A., addressing the Speaker in the Manitoba Legislative Assembly, 22 June 1990. The Ojibwa-Cree Member withheld the unanimity required for the Legislature to table and then ratify the Meech Lake Accord by its deadline the following day. "Never in Canadian history has a single word carried so much political weight," noted Pauline Comeau writing in *The Canadian Forum*, July-Aug. 1990.

Actually, Harper said "No, Mr. Speaker" a total of nine times between June 12 and June 22, stalling and eventually defeating the controversial Accord which had nothing to offer various minority and special-interest groups including the native peoples. Harper came to national attention and was wittily known as the "Cree de coeur."

I feel if I didn't make the decision I made, I would have regretted it for the rest of my life. I would have lost an opportunity to put forward the concerns of aboriginal people.

ELIJAH HARPER, Ojibwa-Cree and NDP Member of the Manitoba Legislative Assembly, who refused to permit the Legislature to discuss the Meech Lake Accord, quoted by Pauline Comeau in *The Winnipeg Free Press*, 16 June 1990.

We do not have a list of demands or an agenda of negotiations to suggest. We are not interested in negotiating. . . . The strategy here is to kill Meech Lake.

PHIL FONTAINE, leader, Assembly of Manitoba Chiefs, quoted by Pauline Comeau in *The Winnipeg Free Press*, 17 June 1990.

The terrible thing about the Meech Lake Accord and the way it has been promoted

is that it damages Canada whether we pass it or not.

PHILIPPE DEANE GIGANTES, author and Senator, *The Road Ahead* (1990).

Although we are poor people, we are very strong and we have won a moral victory for Canada.

ELIJAH HARPER, Ojibwa-Cree and NDP Member of the Manitoba Legislative Assembly, sole opponent of the Meech Lake Accord in the Legislature, quoted by Frances Russell in *The Winnipeg Free Press*, 20 June 1990.

When my grandchildren ask me where I was while Meech Lake went down the tubes, I'll tell them I was in traction, in intensive care, and in a coma. I even wish sometimes it were true.

DALTON CAMP, columnist, quoting an unidentified friend "who sees the country falling apart," *The Toronto Star*, 20 June 1990.

If Meech Lake passes, we get to keep Canada — awkward, ungainly, magnificent Canada.

BRIAN MULRONEY, Prime Minister, addressing the Newfoundland House of Assembly and encouraging its members to vote in favour of the consitutional accord, 21 June 1990, quoted by John Spears in *The Toronto Star* the following day.

Meech est mort — Vive le Québec souverain.

JACQUES PARIZEAU, Parti Québécois leader, to reporters on learning of the death of the Meech Lake Accord, 22 June 1990, quoted by Robert McKenzie in *The Toronto Star* the following day.

Canada has been ill-served by Brian Mulroney, who has played poker with our country. Every time Mulroney rolls the dice, Canada pays the price.

JEAN CHRÉTIEN, Liberal leadership contender, addressing the Liberal Leadership Convention, Calgary, 22 June 1990, quoted by Rosemary Speirs in *The Toronto Star* the following day.

What Canadians should do at this moment is take a break, take a good holiday. They should go to the beaches, travel in Quebec, travel in P.E.I. and avoid Lake Meech. It is not a good place to go at this time.
JEAN CHRÉTIEN, newly elected Liberal leader, addressing reporters following his election speech, Liberal Leadership Convention, Calgary Saddledome, 22 June 1990, quoted by Rosemary Speirs in *The Toronto Star* the following day. He was elected leader the day after the death of the Meech Lake Accord.

Since 1985 we've been asked what does Canada want and we are still waiting for their answer. English Canada must understand that, whatever we say or whatever we do, Quebec is today and will always be a distinct society that is free and capable of assuming its destiny and its development.
ROBERT BOURASSA, Quebec Premier, speaking in Quebec's National Assembly on the demise of the constitutional accord, 22 June 1990, quoted by Graham Fraser in *The Globe and Mail* the following day.

If you sell your soul, we'll treat you fairly.
CLYDE WELLS, Newfoundland Premier, describing the attitude of Senator Lowell Murray and Prime Minister Brian Mulroney when they attempted to pressure Premier Wells to conduct a free vote on the constitutional accord in the House of Assembly. Murray and Mulroney were trying to gain time to appeal to the Supreme Court of Canada to extend the deadline so that the Manitoba legislature could conduct its hearings. Quoted by John Spears in *The Toronto Star*, 23 June 1990.

There is no dishonour in having tried to overcome a serious threat to our unity. I would rather have failed trying to advance the cause of Canada's unity than to have simply played it safe, done nothing or criticized from the sidelines.
BRIAN MULRONEY, Prime Minister, televised address to the nation carried on CBC-TV on 23 June 1990, following the failure of the First Ministers to ratify the constitutional amendments, as quoted by Edison Stewart in *The Toronto Star*, 24 June 1990.

"Meech Lake is dead, Quebec is alive."
Wording on a placard carried through the streets of Montreal during the Saint-Jean-Baptiste Day parade, 24 June 1990, quoted by André Picard in *The Globe and Mail* the following day.

Meechcombers
Term newly minted to refer to those politicians and commentators who were traumatized by English Canada's unwillingness in June 1990 to ratify the Meech Lake Accord and who thereafter devoted much of their time to considering the consequences; first used (with an implied reference to CBC-TV's popular but cancelled program *Beachcombers*) by ERIC KIERANS on CBC Radio's *Morningside*, 4 Dec. 1990.

Although Meech Lake died and Jean Chrétien may very well be the next prime minister, the reality of Canadian political life is that the provinces will play an increasingly critical role at the national level of government — or in a vastly decentralized federation.
ROBERT M. CAMPBELL and LESLIE A. PAL, political scientists, *The Real Worlds of Canadian Politics: Cases in Process and Policy* (1991). The accord was "born" at the Mont-Gabriel conference on 9 May 1986, when Quebec declared its five basic conditions. It "died" in Winnipeg on 22 June 1990, when Elijah Harper said no in the Legislature for the ninth time, and Clyde Wells cancelled the Newfoundland Legislature's vote, 22 June 1990. Its formal "death" was the following day.

Elijah and Clyde, / Elijah and Clyde, / Stuck in their knives / And Canada died.

"I offer the following chant, soon to be a playground staple," wrote reader Robert G. Quinn, London, Ont., referring to Elijah Harper and Clyde Wells who stopped the Meech Lake Accord; Letters to the Editor, *The Globe and Mail*, 9 Feb. 1991.

Canada is not up for grabs. . . . Either you have a country or you don't. You can't have it both ways. . . . We have every intention of restructuring Canada. We have no intention of dismantling it.
BRIAN MULRONEY, Prime Minister, joint meeting, Empire Club and Canadian Club, Toronto, 12 Feb. 1991, quoted by Edison Stewart in *The Toronto Star* the following day.

In the last constitutional debate, the perfect became the enemy of the good. Had the same stringent tests of perfection been applied to the BNA Act as were applied to Meech Lake, the Fathers of Confederation might never have got Canada off the drawing board and on the way to nationhood. So in the next negotiation, let's ask what's practical. Let's ask what's doable and how to get it done.
BRIAN MULRONEY, Prime Minister, address, joint meeting of the Empire Club and the Canadian Club, Toronto, 12 Feb. 1991, published in *The Toronto Star* the following day.

That Was the Meech that Was
Title of a proposed television comedy show, noted by WARREN CLEMENTS in *The Globe and Mail*, 16 March 1991.

MEMORY

I've always said that when a person loses his memory, he's senile. A nation that loses its sense of history goes senile. That's why I think the memory should be kept active in the educational process; because of the continuity.
NORTHROP FRYE, literary critic, interviewed by Louise Brown and Bill Schiller in *The Toronto Star*, 10 May 1987.

Our memory of the past must be faithful to the future if it is to act as stimulus for the present.
NAIM KATTAN, author and arts administrator, *Language & Society*, Fall 1987.

Kierkegaard says only robbers and Gypsies never revisit the past. He's wrong. I revisit the past. And I'm a robber — of Ken's life. And a Gypsy: I live nowhere, a transatlantic migrant, happiest as a stranger in a Latin country. Robber, grave robber, user, usurer, used. Colleague, friend, victim, victimizer. Analyst, microscopist. Lover, dislover. Wife, daughter, mother. Still bound by hoops of steel.
KATHLEEN TYNAN, daughter of broadcaster Matthew Halton and widow and biographer of the critic and writer Kenneth Tynan, *The Life of Kenneth Tynan* (1987).

Memories are a mirage. There are some places that I would swear looked a certain way, but I go back to visit them, and I was wrong. I look at my notes and say, "How could I have written that?" Perhaps what is most important is simply what remains vivid.
LEON EDEL, literary critic, quoted by Stephen Godfrey in *The Globe and Mail*, 11 May 1989.

Memory is a form of hope.
TIMOTHY FINDLEY, novelist, *Inside Memory: Pages from a Writer's Notebook* (1990).

MEN
See also MEN & WOMEN

O men, let us beware of ourselves!
LOUIS RIEL, Métis leader and mystic, diary entry, 1 June 1884, *The Diaries of Louis Riel* (1976) edited by Thomas Flanagan.

Perfect young men don't get murdered, they don't even get born.
Remark attributed to a character in *Beyond This Point Are Monsters* (1970), a crime novel by MARGARET MILLAR.

MEN & WOMEN

See also LIFE
LOVE
MAN
MANKIND
MARRIAGE
SEX

If a lady treads on a banana skin and sprinkles herself all over the sidewalk, a man will gallantly gather up the pieces and help her to place herself together again. But if his own wife meets with a similar misfortune, he gives her a piece of his mind.
KIT COLEMAN, newspaperwoman and early feminist, *Kit Coleman: Queen of Hearts* (1978) edited by Ted Ferguson.

A man of the world accepts what a lady tells him, no matter how improbable.
Sentiment attributed to a character in "The Episode of the Mexican Seer" in *An African Millionaire* (1897), a collection of mystery stories by GRANT ALLEN.

Woman's most difficult task since the race began has been to humanize man in order to make civilized living with him possible.
Attributed to AGNES MACPHAIL, early feminist and federal M.P., 1940s.

In the eyes of the world, or at least of the society you live in, two take away one doesn't equal one. Most of the time it equals nothing.
BETTY JANE WYLIE, author, *Beginnings: A Book for Widows* (1977, rev. 1988).

Walk through any cemetery with tombstones in it dating from before the turn of the century and you will see the social change which has led to the situation of widows in North America today.
BETTY JANE WYLIE, author, *Beginnings: A Book for Widows* (1977, rev. 1988).

Women tell men things that men are not very likely to find out for themselves.
ROBERTSON DAVIES, man-of-letters, interviewed by Terence M. Green in 1982,

Conversations with Robertson Davies (1989) edited by J. Madison Davis.

Socially, individually, in every way but biologically, woman is made, not born. So, of course, is man. Each is a cultural artifact laboriously worked up, pieced together, written and rewritten as a kind of palimpsest.
SHEILA DELANY, scholar, *Writing Woman: Women Writers and Women in Literature, Medieval to Modern* (1983).

Men are no longer permitted to beat their wives — even when their wives deserve it.
ED HALIBURTON, one-time Nova Scotia Cabinet Minister and retired columnist, remark made in 1983 in his column in *The Halifax Chronicle-Herald*, roundly criticized by feminists, recalled in his obituary in *The Globe and Mail*, 15 March 1990.

I see what each sex is projecting onto the other and I wonder how we exist together on the same planet, let alone in the same household or the same bed.
MARION WOODMAN, analyst and author, *The Pregnant Virgin: A Process of Psychological Transformation* (1985).

It is not enough to change men. It is not enough to show them how to take the back seat gracefully. It will also be necessary to teach women how to occupy the driver's seat of a relationship without unease and resentment.
GEORGE JONAS, columnist, *Crocodiles in the Bathtub and Other Perils* (1987).

God is a man but the muses are women.
SHARON H. NELSON, poet, line from "Scream," *Celebrating Canadian Women: Prose and Poetry by and about Women* (1988) edited by Greta Hofmann Nemiroff.

Women collect grievances, hold grudges and change shape. They pass hard, legitimate judgements, unlike the purblind guesses of men, fogged with romanticism and ignorance and bias and wish. Women

know too much, they can neither be deceived nor trusted.
> Thoughts of the narrator of the novel *Cat's Eye* (1988) by MARGARET ATWOOD.

He wants to make love, then talk. I want to talk, then make love.
> MARION WOODMAN, analyst and author, "Bedroom Thoughts," *The Ravaged Bridegroom: Masculinity in Women* (1990).

One great thing about being a woman is I don't have to marry one.
> HELEN STIMPSON, retired real-estate agent, characteristic remark, 7 March 1991.

Men who like women rarely fall in love.
> ROBIN SKELTON, man-of-letters, aphorism, May 1990.

MENTAL ILLNESS
See also HEALTH

It is unfortunately still true that the outcomes of mental illness are still to a large extent determined by one's station in life.
> CYRIL GREENLAND, psychiatric social worker, interviewed by Sam Sussman in *Pioneers of Mental Health and Social Change: 1930-1989* (1989) by Djuwe Joe Blom and Sam Sussman.

MERCY

I am not merciful, but I am sorry.
> Thoughts of the narrator of the novel *Cat's Eye* (1988) by MARGARET ATWOOD.

MÉTIS
See INDIANS
RIEL, LOUIS

The original settlers of these river banks, they quickly became the most distinctive element in the battles for tenure and supremacy that followed the arrival of the Scottish (and a few Irish) crofters. "Métis," a word probably based on the Spanish "mestizo" (mixture), is an elusive term applying to anyone whose culture and genealogy combine the customs, living styles

and values of their roots, European and aboriginal.
> PETER C. NEWMAN, author, referring to the settlers on the banks of the Red River who were of mixed Indian-French ancestry, *Empire of the Bay: An Illustrated History of the Hudson's Bay Company* (1989).

METRIC SYSTEM

Metric will put us on a par with the United States, which will soon follow in our footsteps.
> JEAN-LUC PEPIN, Cabinet Minister in charge of conversion from the Imperial to the Metric system of measurement, prediction made in 1970, quoted by Charles Lynch in *The Lynch Mob* (1988).

MEXICO

The Maquiladora Industrial Program was begun by the Mexican government in the 1960s. It was and is based on a simple rule: non-manufactured materials may be imported from the United States tax free, manufactured in Mexico, and re-exported tax free. The only government charge is an American value-added tax on the imported manufactured goods, a minor cost.
> JOHN RALSTON SAUL, novelist and nationalist, address before a Parliamentary Committee on Free Trade, *If You Love This Country: Facts and Feelings on Free Trade* (1987) edited by Laurier LaPierre.

To prevent Mexico's economic and political system from collapse, the U.S. must cancel the debt and increasingly integrate Mexico into the "Amexicana" economy of America, Mexico and Canada. This integration will speed up if Mexico opens up to imports and foreign investment and, like Canada, signs a free trade deal with Washington.
> FRANK FEATHER, futurologist, *G-Forces: Reinventing the World — The 35 Global Forces Restructuring Our World* (1989).

In the past the Canadian horizon stopped

at the Rio Grande. Today, Canada's horizon seems to stop at Patagonia.

Adapted from a remark made by Mexican President CARLOS SALINAS DE GORTARI prior to Prime Minister Brian Mulroney's first official visit to Mexico, interviewed by Linda Hossie in *The Globe and Mail*, 15 March 1990.

Hence it is not an exaggeration to say that the signing of a free trade agreement with the United States and Canada will be the most important economic decision taken to date in Mexico, with implications for generations to come. An FTA will open the road toward greater economic integration in North America.

ROGELIO RAMIREZ DE LA O, Mexican economist, "A Mexican Vision of North American Economic Integration," *Continental Accord: North American Economic Integration* (1991) edited by Steven Globerman.

There's no way we can compete with wages of less than a dollar an hour. It's going to mean another vacuum cleaner taking jobs from Canada, and I don't know what jobs are going to replace them.

BOB WHITE, President, Canadian Auto Workers, responding to the federal government's decision to join the United States and Mexico in free trade negotiations, quoted by John Saunders and Madelaine Drohan in *The Globe and Mail*, 6 Feb. 1991.

MIDDLE CLASS

In fact, many things incline me to suspect that they, the middle class, neither rich enough to become decadent nor poor enough to become enfeebled, are the backbone of every society.

JOSEF SKVORECKY, essayist and novelist, "I Was Born in Náchod . . . " (1984), *Talkin' Moscow Blues* (1988) edited by Sam Solecki.

But no matter how much we liked Gilles Vigneault's songs vaunting his distant homeland on the Lower North Shore, we'd rather mow our lawns in suburbia, never even thinking of going back to our villages in the Gaspé or the Abitibi.

JACQUES GODBOUT, author and filmmaker, *The Globe and Mail*, 6 Nov. 1989.

MILITARISM

The American empire is held together through worldwide military alliances and by giant monopoly corporations. Canada's membership in the American alliance system and the ownership of the Canadian economy by American corporations precludes Canada's playing an independent role in the world. These bonds must be cut if corporate capitalism, and the social priorities it creates, is to be effectively challenged.

"The Waffle Manifesto: For an Independent Socialist Canada" (1969) reprinted in *The Canadian Forum*, Dec. 1989.

THE MILITARY

The entire annual cost of the proposed UN Action Plan to halt global desertification could be paid with just half of Canada's military budget. Canada's annual spending on ammunition and bombs alone — $325 million — would pay for the immunization of 30,000,000 children world-wide, saving as many as a million lives a year.

Project Ploughshares for the Citizens' Inquiry into Peace and Security, *What Makes Canada Secure: Background Document for the Citizens' Inquiry into Peace and Security in Canada* (1991).

MILLENNIUM

Yiciwekwaki nishenawishkan. / *Yiciwekwaki nishenawishkan.* / *Yiciwekwaki nishenawishkan.* / The end of the world, when I rattle.

Ojibwa poem, "Song to Bring about the End of the World," *Songs of the Great Land* (1989) edited by John Robert Colombo.

I think a very decisive, radical change is imminent, because in the psychological history of mankind there has been something which you can call a new revelation about every 2,000 years. The 2,000 years of Christianity, what might be called the Age of Pisces, is running out, and something will come to replace it; and perhaps to build upon it, as the Age of Pisces built upon the earlier, tremendous intellectual probing of the Greeks and also the extraordinary moral force and authority of the Hebrews. I think we are headed for something new.

> ROBERTSON DAVIES, man-of-letters, interviewed by Tom Harpur in 1981, *Conversations with Robertson Davies* (1989) edited by J. Madison Davis.

I don't think the world will come to an end. I just *can't* see the end of civilization. It's an idea which comes up in cycles. There's the Platonic millennium of two thousand years. I think that there will be a new age in 2001: people will be much gentler. This last millennium has brought in the idea of human well-being. How many hospitals were there when Christ was born? The turn of the century will be fascinating. I hope to be there.

> ROBERTSON DAVIES, man-of-letters, interviewed by John Milton Harvard in 1984, *Conversations with Robertson Davies* (1989) edited by J. Madison Davis.

MIND

Man has survived through thirty thousand years or so of existence, not because he was stronger than a lion or swifter than an antelope, but because of his mind. During the past four centuries since he discovered the experimental method, he has done more than survive. He has made himself the master of his fate.

> WILDER PENFIELD, neurosurgeon and author, "Science, the Arts, and the Spirit of Man," *Second Thoughts: Science, the Arts, and the Spirit of Man* (1970).

MINING

I believe this journey is the turning point. I hope to make money out of it as I made out of the South African trip at any rate we'll make enough to get out of fear for our future.

> FRANK HARRIS, English writer, describing his early life as a prospector, letter of 24 Sept. 1907, written from Cobalt, Ont., quoted by Philippa Pullar in *Frank Harris* (1975). Harris's trip was profitable and also supplied him with many experiences useful in his later fiction.

HAVE DISCOVERED THE GOLDEN POLE BEYOND DESCRIPTION. ANSWER MATHESON WEDNESDAY HAILEYBURY THURSDAY.

> Text of a telegram sent by a prospector describing a silver strike at Porcupine Lake, northwest of Cobalt, Ont., in 1909, which became known as the fabulous Dome mine, quoted by MICHAEL BLISS in *Northern Enterprise* (1987).

The ore goes to Tokyo, the profits to Toronto, the taxes to Ottawa, the jobs to Vancouver and we're left with a hole in the ground which, if the federal government gave permission, we could use as a garbage dump.

> DAVID KILGOUR, M.P., quoting an unnamed Yukon politician on mining prospects there, *The Globe and Mail*, 27 Sept. 1987.

MINORITIES

Where numbers warrant.

> Legalistic phrase from the Constitution Act, 1982, commonly heard in minority language disputes. It is found in a different form in the Canadian Charter of Rights and Freedoms, Schedule B, Part 1: 23(1)(a): " . . . applies wherever in the province the number of children of citizens who have such a right is sufficient to warrant the provision to them out of public funds of minority language instruction."

Sometimes, at international conferences, Canada is celebrated for what we are not. We are not a superpower, not an imperial power, not an aggressive nation. But we are a country deeply involved with the rights of minorities.

> JOE CLARK, Secretary of State, Third International Conference on Constitutional Law, Laval University, Quebec City, 8 March 1985.

If you're blind in Canada, chances are you're unemployed. If you're deaf, or physically or mentally disabled in any way, you're likely to be poor, badly housed, unemployed and on your own. If you're black, or a visible minority, chances are you're in a worse job, with lower pay, less recognition, and less opportunity than your white neighbour.

> BOB RAE, NDP leader, address, "A Socialist's Manifesto," *The Globe and Mail*, 1 Oct. 1990.

MISFORTUNES

No person can prevent misfortunes in life, but it shows true greatness of mind to bear them with sincerity.

> LEVI S. PARMLY, "Dentist and Medical Electrician," *The Summum Bonum* (1815).

MODERATION

Beyond a certain point, moderation is not only a virtue but an evolutionary necessity.

> JOHN A. LIVINGSTON, naturalist, *One Cosmic Instant: A Natural History of Human Arrogance* (1973).

Canada seems to impress non-Canadians as a moderate and reasonable country, potentially as happy a country to live in as the world affords.

> NORTHROP FRYE, literary critic, address, Social Sciences and Humanities Research Council, Toronto, Fall 1990, printed in *The Globe and Mail*, 15 April 1991.

MODERNITY

A century ago Canada was a nation in the world, but not wholly of it: the major cultural and political developments of Western Europe, still the main centre of the historical stage, were little known or understood in Canada. . . . Today, Canada is too much a part of the world to be thought of as a nation in it.

> NORTHROP FRYE, literary critic, *The Modern Century* (1967).

I never conceive why people want to be modern all the time. Being modern really means only now. There is only one instant of time.

> ROBERTSON DAVIES, man-of-letters, interviewed by Gordon Roper in 1968, *Conversations with Robertson Davies* (1989) edited by J. Madison Davis.

MONARCHY
> See also GOVERNOR GENERAL
> ROYAL FAMILY

Loyalty to the queen does not require a man to bow down to her manservant, or her maidservant — or her ass.

> Attributed to ALEXANDER MACKENZIE, second Prime Minister (1873-78), by Christopher Dafoe in *The Winnipeg Free Press*, 30 Sept. 1990.

Do you know what you're missing, you French-speaking Canadians? You are among the few Westerners who have not decapitated a king. You left France more than a century before the Revolution and the death of Louis XVI — and you fell under British authority more than a century after Cromwell's revolt and the execution of Charles I. You stand in need of an execution.

> HENRI MARROU, French historian, quoted by Gérard Pelletier in "Quebec: Different but in Step with North America," *Daedalus: Journal of the American Academy of Arts and Sciences*, "In Search of Canada," Fall 1988.

I like the Queen (though not as much as the Queen Mum), and am content to have her representative as a head of state. I like the ceremonies that spring from our royal tradition, too.

> PETER GZOWSKI, host of CBC Radio's *Morningside*, in *The Private Voice: A Journal of Reflections* (1988).

Once thought a *sine qua non* of Canadian distinctiveness, the Monarchy now survives as a plainly British institution not much modified by Canadian experience.

> GEORGE GALT, journalist, "Fantasy Kingdom," *Saturday Night*, Oct. 1989.

We have to make a decision about the Monarchy within the next ten years, and probably within the next five; or lose it. And if we lose the Crown, the capacity to survive of this nation is reduced by half.

> SCOTT SYMONS, novelist and cultural commentator, interviewed in *The Idler*, No. 25, May-June 1990.

MONEY
See also FINANCE
WEALTH

He pays twice who pays quickly.

> THOMAS WORKMAN, first President, Sun Life Assurance Company of Canada, Annual Report, 16 March 1888.

At the present rate of exchange, a Canadian with an income of one thousand dollars a year can live comfortably and enjoyably in Paris. If exchange were normal, the same Canadian would starve to death. Exchange is a wonderful thing.

> ERNEST HEMINGWAY, novelist and one-time reporter, *The Star Weekly*, 2 Feb. 1922.

I'd like to tell my young friend that money doesn't grow on gooseberry bushes.

> CHARLES A. DUNNING, Minister of Finance, to the young socialist T.C. (Tommy) Douglas prior to World War II,

as recalled by Douglas in *The Making of a Socialist* (1982).

Money costs too much.

> Remark attributed to Lew Archer, detective hero of the novel *The Goodbye Look* (1969) by ROSS MACDONALD.

When a thing is current, it creates currency.

> MARSHALL McLUHAN, communications theorist, quoted by Richard Kostelanetz, "Marshall McLuhan: High Priest of the Electronic Village," *Master Minds* (1969).

Money's a convenience. It lets me hire people to do things I'd be wasting my time at. I was underpaid for the first half of my life; I don't mind being overpaid for the second half.

> PIERRE BERTON, author and media personality, quoted by Gary Ross in *The Canadian Magazine*, 5 April 1975.

Money is all Canadians and North Americans think about, money, money, money. It doesn't interest me at all. When you look at the Eiffel Tower, what remains to think about? The honorarium Eiffel received or the structure he created?

> ROGER TAILLIBERT, Parisian architect who designed Montreal's Olympic Stadium, which escalated in cost from $60 to $600 million, remark made in 1976, quoted by Ruth Cawker and William Bernstein in *Contemporary Canadian Architecture: The Mainstream and Beyond* (1988).

Irish nationalists were blamed for a rumoured defacement of Canadian currency issued in 1954. Supposedly a devil's face had been slyly etched into Queen Elizabeth's hair and was printed in all denominations. This story was published as fact in the 1982 issue of *Parade* magazine, which revived the rumor after thirty years. A close examination of the actual bill shows that the public's vivid imagination was the moving force behind the "devil's face" — not any Irish nationalists.

HAL MORGAN and KERRY TUCKER, American researchers, *Rumor!* (1984).

I always judge a person by what he does with his money.
DAVID LAM, Hong Kong-born, West Coast capitalist, quoted by Peter C. Newman in *Sometimes a Great Nation* (1988).

Money is completely relative and it all depends on what you want to buy with it. I can't afford to buy the Blue Jays yet.
GEDDY LEE, leader of the popular rock group Rush, interviewed by Christopher Jones in *Now*, 3 March 1988.

Money has no personality.
NORMAN JEWISON, film director, *Maclean's*, 4 April 1988.

Money is really just an immaterial measure, like an inch, or a gallon, a pound or a degree. While there is certainly a limit on real resources — only so many tons of wheat, only so many feet of material, only so many hours in the day — there need never been a shortage of the measure. "Now you can't use inches today. There aren't any around, they are all being used somewhere else!" Yet this is precisely the situation in which we persist in regarding money.
MICHAEL LINTON, founder of the Local Employment Trading System (LET-System) in B.C.'s Comox Valley in 1983, "Local Currencies," *Edges*, July-Sept. 1988. Linton piloted the notion of "green dollars." "The unit of exchange, the green dollar, remains where it is generated, providing continual liquidity. The community's ultimate resource, the productive time of its members, need never be limited by lack of money."

Investors are individuals who bank on the climate; speculators gamble on the weather. Climates follow an established and predictable pattern; weather is notoriously temperamental and changeable.
CHRISTOPHER ONDAATJE, investor,

quoted by Peter C. Newman in *Maclean's*, 22 Aug. 1988.

Money talks, it is said, and it is time we started listening to it.
BETTY JANE WYLIE and LYNNE Mac-FARLANE, authors, *Everywoman's Money Book* (1989).

Where there's a will there's a relative.
Legal maxim of estate managers, noted in Montreal in Aug. 1990.

Sigh . . . another day — another 84.7 cents.
EDD ULUSCHAK, cartoonist, *The Sounder*, 9 Nov. 1990.

MONTREAL
See also QUEBEC

I found Montreal a highly interesting city, but not quite so picturesque a one as Quebec. It was not French enough for me, although I was hospitably received in a good many French houses; and the Archbishop of Montreal was so polite as to ask me to come and taste his hothouse grapes, of which his Grace cultivated no less than eighteen varieties. By the time that I had got to the twelfth, I am afraid that I meekly suggested that a small quantity of the juice of the grape in its fermented condition — that is to say, a glass of dry sherry — would not, under the circumstances, be unacceptable.
GEORGE AUGUSTUS SALA, English correspondent travelling throughout North America, visiting Montreal in early 1863, *The Life and Adventures of George Augustus Sala* (1895). He added: "Montreal, early in 1863, was full of British troops and fugitive Confederates. . . . I have said that Montreal was full of Confederates, ladies as well as gentlemen."

St. Urbain Street is in no way remarkable except that it is always very dirty. As every street in the city is in a more or less wretched condition about the first of

April, this street at that season of the year loses its sole claim to distinction.

ARTHUR CAMPBELL, novelist, *The Mystery of Martha Warne: A Tale of Montreal* (1881), as quoted by Eva-Marie Kröller in *Canadian Travellers in Europe, 1851-1900* (1987).

Before My departure, many souls warned Me not to travel to Montreal, saying, the majority of the inhabitants are Catholics, and are in the utmost fanaticism, that they are submerged in the sea of imitations, that they have not the capability to hearken to the call of the Kingdom of God, that the veil of bigotry has so covered the eyes that they have deprived themselves from beholding the signs of the most great guidance, and that the dogmas have taken possession of the hearts entirely, leaving no trace of reality. They asserted that should the Sun of Reality shine with perfect splendour throughout that Dominion, the dark, impenetrable clouds of superstitions have so enveloped the horizon that it would be utterly impossible for any one to behold its rays.

'ABDU'L-BAHÁ, Persian religious leader and living exemplar of the Bahá'í life, "Tablets to Canada from The Divine Plan," Haifa, Palestine, 21 Feb. 1917, reproduced in *'Abdu'l-Bahá in Canada* (1962).

The water shone and curved on great slabs of rock, spinning into foam at the Lachine Rapids, where it sucked and rumbled. On the other shore was Caughnawaga, where the Indians lived in shacks raised on stilts. Then came the burnt summer fields.

SAUL BELLOW, novelist, description of the outskirts of Montreal, *Herzog* (1964).

My life in Canada was partly frontier, partly Polish ghetto, partly the Middle Ages. . . . I've always been among foreigners and never considered myself a native of anything. . . . I was brought up in a polyglot community by parents who spoke many languages.

SAUL BELLOW, Lachine-born, Montreal-raised, Chicago-based author, quoted by Stephen Godfrey in *The Globe and Mail*, 10 Nov. 1990.

I have inadvertently brought about the production and installation of our own Taj Mahal as pure fallout of my love for you.

BUCKMINSTER FULLER, inventor of the Geodesic Dome, statement made to his wife of fifty years, referring to the Geodesic Dome of the American Pavilion, while touring Expo '67, 28 May 1967, quoted by Alden Hatch in *Buckminster Fuller at Home in the Universe* (1974).

Expo '67 is a show that revealed a great new star — the city of Montreal. And Canada has profited from the occasion to emerge in the eyes of the world as a young and determined country looking resolutely to the future.

MAURICE CHEVALIER, French actor and singer, *I Remember It Well* (1970).

Hello, I'm David Niven and I love Montreal.

DAVID NIVEN, film actor, parodying the standard celebrity gambit for the local media while on location in Montreal, quoted by Wayne Grigsby in *The Canadian*, 5 May 1979.

Montreal is the only Canadian city with 4:00 a.m. traffic jams.

ALLAN FOTHERINGHAM, columnist, *Malice in Blunderland or How the Grits Stole Christmas* (1982, 1983).

Montreal is back. To paraphrase someone or other, this may come as a surprise to some, who hadn't noticed that she was away. The sad truth is, however, that for about fifteen years following her fabulous world's fair in 1967, this was not an especially pleasant city to visit, particularly for Canadians from other parts of the country.

MECHTILD HOPPENRATH and CHARLES OBERDORF, travel writers, *First-Class Canada* (1987).

Wherever we live in the world, we all have a mental image of Montreal as the one big city of Canada that has defied homogenization — The One That Got Away. During the next few days, however, I found it to be rather more, or perhaps slightly less, than that. It is a city, I discovered, that does not quite go to plan.

> JAN MORRIS, Anglo-Welsh travel writer, "The Battle for Montreal," *Saturday Night*, July 1988.

Montreal is already the most interesting city in Canada, and for my money is rivalled in the United States, a nation of fathomlessly uninteresting cities, only by New York, Chicago, Boston, and Los Angeles.

> JAN MORRIS, Anglo-Welsh travel writer, "The Battle for Montreal," *Saturday Night*, July 1988.

It is above all an inconsolable city — it weeps still for that clash of distant powers which, two centuries ago, first tossed it from empire to empire, culture to culture. It has not, after all, Got Away.

> JAN MORRIS, Anglo-Welsh travel writer, "The Battle for Montreal," *Saturday Night*, July 1988.

Anglophones of Montreal are far less likely nowadays to belabour me with royalist sentiments, or recall their descent from the First Lord Sotheby or Parke-Bernet. They are not as shy as most other Canadians. They smile more easily, and perhaps cry more easily too. They are less *numb* than their cousins in Toronto or Vancouver: in short, not to put too fine a point upon it, they are more like the French.

> JAN MORRIS, Anglo-Welsh travel writer, "The Battle for Montreal," *Saturday Night*, July 1988.

Montreal is a strange city. It was built about 400 years ago on an ice-bound island in the St. Lawrence River by renegade Frenchmen who thought they had found the New World and would soon own it.

This has not come to pass — or at least not yet, according to the hard rockers who speak for the Free Speech Quebec Separatist Party who identify mainly with the I.R.A., Puerto Rican nationalists and the ghost of Chiang Kai-shek. But they say it will happen soon — that the long screw of history is still turning and the war is not over yet.

> HUNTER S. THOMPSON, "gonzo" journalist, "The Beast with Three Backs" (1985), *Generation of Swine: Tales of Shame and Degradation in the '80s* (1988).

Montreal — All nights are cold in Montreal. . . .

I left for the airport immediately, feeling lucky to get out of the country without being flogged.

> HUNTER S. THOMPSON, "gonzo" journalist, "The Beast with Three Backs" (1985), *Generation of Swine: Tales of Shame and Degradation in the '80s* (1988).

If Toronto is a sort of amalgam of New York and Chicago, Montreal can be understood as the best of Boston and New Orleans, a combination of old-world charm and modern technology.

> ALAN F.J. ARTIBISE, planning consultant, "Canada as an Urban Nation," *Daedalus: Journal of the American Academy of Arts and Sciences*, "In Search of Canada," Fall 1988.

It is its cosmopolitan nature that will ensure Montreal's future. I do not mean by that exotic restaurants, trendy boutiques or cafés; I mean a population that has come from all over the world, that accepts French as a natural fact, English as a convenient means of communication, and that will create a diversified culture grafted on a French-speaking tree.

> JACQUES GODBOUT, author and filmmaker, *The Globe and Mail*, 6 Nov. 1989.

The anglos of Montreal are easy to blame for Quebec's unhappiness, because Toronto sure as hell doesn't feel guilty about it.

> JACK KAPICA, Montreal-born, Toronto-based journalist and editor, *The Globe and Mail*, 19 May 1990.

Saint-Louis de Mile End
Name of a neighbourhood (now populated by Portuguese and Central American immigrants) in downtown Montreal.

The city's gift for communion, once religious and now cultural in the broadest
sense, is the thing visitors may be thinking
of when they say, as they so often do with
a wistfulness they can hardly explain, "I
love Montreal."
STEPHEN GODFREY, columnist, "Cross
Current," *The Globe and Mail*, 6 Aug. 1990.

MONTREAL MASSACRE
See also FEMINISM
WOMEN

You're all a bunch of feminists! . . . Women
to one side. You are all feminists, I hate
feminists.
Cry of the sometime student and mass
murderer MARC LÉPINE who donned
hunting garb and went on a rampage;
with a semi-automatic rifle he shot and
killed fourteen women students and
wounded twelve more on two floors of
the École Polytechnique, University of
Montreal, 4:30 p.m., 6 Dec. 1989; his cry
was reported the following day in *The
Globe and Mail*.

Fourteen women are dead for one reason:
they were women. Their male classmates
are still alive for one reason: they are men.
DIANE BRANSON, journalist, CBC Radio's
Morningside, 7 Dec. 1989, quoted by Lee
Lakeman in "The Montreal Massacre,"
This Magazine, March 1990.

As a female I have been in captivity since
I was born. I have been a political prisoner
since birth.
Part of the narrative of the video *Fourteen
Young Women in Montreal* (1990) written
and directed by LYNNE MOSS SHARMAN,
quoted by Cameron Bailey in *Now*, 22
Nov. 1990.

If those 14 students had lived to pursue
their careers, they would have repre-

sented one-half of one per cent of all
women engineers in Canada. That may not
sound like much, but when 14 people can
make a dent in the statistics, there is a
problem. The sad reality is that fewer than
3 per cent of all engineers are women.
LEIGH DAYTON, columnist, referring to
the massacre in Montreal which took
place on 6 Dec. 1989, *The Globe and Mail*,
13 Jan. 1990.

Feminism is caring about women and
wishing that they have an equal opportunity — an equal break. So I am a feminist,
a person who cares and wants to make a
difference.
MONIQUE FRIZE, occupant of the Women
in Engineering Chair, University of New
Brunswick, address at memorial service,
6 Dec. 1990, quoted by Michele
Landsberg in *The Toronto Star*, 8 March
1991.

MOON

I well remember, when I was a little boy,
being told by our aged people that I must
never point my finger at the moon, for, if I
did, she would consider it a great insult,
and instantly bite it off.
PETER JONES, Ojibwa Christian missionary, *History of the Ojibway Indians with
Especial Reference to Their Conversion to
Christianity* (1861).

Used to be a objeck in the sky before it
becum a vurb. Still seems well-hung up
there most nites.
DON HARRON, humorist, writing in dialect, *Charlie Farquharson's Unyverse*
(1990).

MOOSE
See also ANIMALS

Moosehead, moosehide, moosemeat — /
but there are other ways of looking at a
moose / than simply as an object to kill
and dismember.
DOUGLAS LePAN, poet, commencing
stanza of the poem "The Moose, or

Modes of Perception" (1948), *Weathering It: Complete Poems 1948-1987* (1987).

MORALITY
See also GOOD & EVIL

To me, morality is how you treat others.
GREGORY BAUM, priest and theologian, quoted by June Callwood in *The Globe and Mail*, 5 Aug. 1974.

Whether people are good or bad, useful or harmful, depends not on their moral principles or even their conscious aims, but on the strength of their imagination.
STEPHEN VIZINCZEY, novelist, *An Innocent Millionaire* (1983).

As soon as one is unhappy / one becomes moral.
NICHOLAS CATANOY, poet and aphorist, "Notes on a Prison Wall (Fragment)," *Canadian Literature*, Summer 1989.

Moral life is a struggle to see — a struggle against the desire to deny the testimony of one's own eyes and ears. The struggle to believe one's senses is at the heart of the process of moving from voyeurism to commitment.
MICHAEL IGNATIEFF, author and television personality, "Is Nothing Sacred? The Ethics of Television," *Daedalus: Journal of the American Academy of Arts and Sciences*, "In Search of Canada," Fall 1988.

MOSAIC
See also MULTICULTURALISM

We have never been a melting pot. The fact is we are more like a tossed salad. We are green, some of us are oily, and there's a little vinegar injected when you get up to Ottawa.
ARNOLD EDINBOROUGH, cultural commentator, quoted in *The New York Times*, 4 Aug. 1973.

If the prophet Ezekiel saw "wheels within wheels" as he looked toward the heavens, those looking toward Canada today see "mosaics within mosaics."
REGINALD W. BIBBY, sociologist, *Mosaic Madness: The Poverty and Potential of Life in Canada* (1990).

MOSQUITOES

I am too great / to be bitten / by those little mosquitoes / that are flying about.
Kwakiutl poem, "Boastful Chief," *Songs of the Great Land* (1989) edited by John Robert Colombo.

Here is now such swarms of a small sand flies that wee can hardly see the sun through them . . . they fly into our ears nose eyes mouth and down our throats as we be most sorely plagued with them. . . . Certainly these be the flyes that was sent as plagues to the Egyptians as caused a darkness over the land and brought such blotches and boils as broke out over them into sores.
JAMES KNIGHT, administrator of York Factory, western coast of Hudson Bay, diary entry, 11 Aug. 1717, quoted by Peter C. Newman in *Empire of the Bay: An Illustrated History of the Hudson's Bay Company* (1989).

MOTHERHOOD

I feel so sorry for us mothers — the last thing we ever intended was to turn into the Wicked Witch of the West.
BETTY JANE WYLIE, author, *No Two Alike* (1980).

It's my belief that between mothers and daughters there is a kind of blood-hyphen that is, finally, indissoluble.
CAROL SHIELDS, novelist, *Swann* (1987).

God gave mamas too much heart / And children that try to tear it apart / I know it doesn't seem fair / That I can't stop you from caring / And I just can't see / Why you got children like me.
CONNIE KALDOR, singer and songwriter, "God Made Mamas to Cry," quoted by

Ellen Schwartz in *Born a Woman: Seven Canadian Women Singer-Songwriters* (1988).

MOTION PICTURES
See FILM

MOTTO

"Not bad, eh?" could well be our national motto. Instead, of course, it is *A mari usque ad mare* — from sea unto sea. But even that, surely, is an understatement. Even a cursory survey of the map of this lovely land shows that it reaches not two but three oceans — from sea unto sea unto sea . . . *A mari usque ad mare et cetera.*
PETER GZOWSKI, host of CBC Radio's *Morningside, The Private Voice: A Journal of Reflections* (1988).

How happy, then, to find that this is really a motto we can all enjoy. *"Je me souviens"* is merely the first part of a phrase struck by Quebec architect Eugène Taché, which pays explicit tribute to both the province's English and French roots. The full phrase is *"Je me souviens que né sous le lys, je crois sous la rose,"* which means that "I remember that born under the (French fleur de) lys, I grow under the (English) rose." Grammatically, the principal clause being where it is, this would seem to place the emphasis on the growth under the rose. Even without getting prickly about it, it seems a tribute to both French and English roots.
STEPHEN GODFREY, columnist, *The Globe and Mail*, 24 Jan. 1991.

MOUNTAINS & MOUNTAINEERING
See also ROCKY MOUNTAINS

We climb for personal fulfillment. I hope people will understand what we are trying to achieve. We are rational people. Everest represents the ultimate accomplishment in this particular sport.
BILL MARCH, mountaineer, leader of the first Canadian expedition to attempt to

climb Mount Everest, quoted by Bruce Patterson in *The Toronto Star*, 18 July 1982.

We made it . . . we made it.
Boast of PETER SPEAR, manager of the Base Camp on the slope of Mount Everest, upon learning that the Canadian Everest Expedition, of which he was a member, had attained the peak. The Calgary climber Laurie Skreslet, accompanied by two sherpas, Sundare and Lhakpa Dorje, planted three flags — those of Canada, Nepal, and the Expedition — on the peak. After one hour spent at the summit of the Earth, they made their descent, 5 Oct. 1982. Quoted by Bruce Patterson and Larry Emrick in *The Toronto Star*, 5 Oct. 1982.

And our mountains are neither higher / nor more beautiful than the mountains / praised and loved by other nations
AL PURDY, poet, "Home Thoughts," *The Collected Poems of Al Purdy* (1986) edited by Russell Brown.

You do not know who you really are until you know what you can fully achieve. That is what makes living worthwhile. You had to be the best, period.
SHARON WOOD, mountaineer, member of the Canadian Everest Light Expedition, quoted in *Maclean's*, 29 Dec. 1986. She became the first North American woman to scale Everest, doing so with her companion Dwayne Congdon on 20 May 1986.

MOVIES
See FILM

MULRONEY, BRIAN

M (U L R) O N E Y
The last name of Brian Mulroney was doctored on campaign stickers to highlight the overspending of the Conservative Party in the 1984 general election, as noted by Claire Hoy in *Friends in High*

Places: Politics and Patronage in the Mulroney Government (1987).

No matter how you slice it, it's still Mulroney.
EDD ULUSCHAK, cartoonist, *The Edmonton Journal*, 19 April 1983.

Mal-Roney, Mieux-Roney
Puns on Brian Mulroney's last name in the French language, the meaning being "bad. . . ." or "so-so. . . ." In English, he was tagged "the boy from Baie-Comeau" and quickly dubbed as "Lyin' Brian."

Mal-Awney = "Cursed One"
It seems that in the Arabic language the name Mulroney sounds suspiciously like "Cursed One." "Most [Canadians] of Arab descent preferred to pronounce his name 'Mal-Awney' or 'Cursed One,'" Said Zafar observed in *The Globe and Mail*, 30 Jan. 1987.

You know me, and we'll do it together.
BRIAN MULRONEY, Conservative leader, speaking to the viewer on television commercials sponsored by the Conservative Party shown during the 1984 election campaign.

The eyes are Paul Newman blue. His hair has the swoop of the Robert Redford style and the voice the resonance of a Lorne Greene school of broadcasting. The jaw is by Gibraltar.
Description of Conservative leadership contender Brian Mulroney in *The Edmonton Journal*, as reported in *The New York Times*, 6 Sept. 1984.

I must respectfully say that I do not see how the Leader of the Opposition (Mr. Turner) can have the gall to criticize us for anything after having been with his colleagues in power for 20 years. As for us, we have only been in power for two months, but I can tell you this: Give us 20 years, and it is coming, and you will not recognize this country. Moreover, the whole area of federal-provincial relations will also be completely changed.
BRIAN MULRONEY, Prime Minister, House of Commons, Ottawa, first address as P.M., 7 Nov. 1984.

We seek an end to confrontation. We seek an end to division and conflict. We seek a new era of co-operation and understanding. . . . We believe that in this spirit of renewal and co-operation and in the search — and it is only a search — for a new consensus, we can and indeed we shall bring a new degree of prosperity to Canada and to Canadians.
BRIAN MULRONEY, Prime Minister, House of Commons, Ottawa, 7 Nov. 1984.

Brian Mulroney was, in short, a model comprador: a man who succeeded not from self-generated objectives but as an agent doing a job dictated by those who employed him and those who could fire him.
STEPHEN CLARKSON, political scientist, *Canada and the Reagan Challenge: Crisis and Adjustment, 1981-85* (1982; rev. ed., 1985). Here is how Clarkson defined a comprador: "Originally the native manager for a foreign establishment in China who served the interests of the company by acting as factotum and intermediary with the local population. In Canadian sociology, compradors are the senior executives of branch plants who follow the directives of their foreign headquarters."

The general impression you get is that our prime minister invited his boss home for dinner.
ERIC KIERANS, commentator, characterizing Prime Minister Mulroney's role *vis-à-vis* President Ronald Reagan at the so-called Shamrock Summit, Quebec City, March 1985, on CBC Radio's *Morningside*, quoted by Jamie Swift in *Odd Man Out: The Life and Times of Eric Kierans* (1988).

No, Brian Mulroney won't turn Canada into Ronald Reagan's 51st state, but

shouldn't somebody, someday, somehow?
  Editorial, *The Economist*, April 1985.

It's already the accepted wisdom that Mulroney will be in power a long time. Already, no one can remember anything he's said.
  BARRY CALLAGHAN, author and columnist, "Canadian Wry," *Punch*, Oct. 1985.

I am not denying anything I did not say.
  BRIAN MULRONEY, Prime Minister, Letter to the Editor, *The Globe and Mail*, 18 Sept. 1986, as recalled by Jack McLeod in *The Oxford Book of Canadian Political Anecdotes* (1988). The remark recalls how U.S. presidential press secretaries expressed concerns about "being misspoken" and "future deniability" and the remark of U.S. President Calvin Coolidge: "I have noticed that nothing I never said ever did me any harm."

His whole life has been built on subservience to American corporations. He's a company boy from a company town. But in this case, the town is Canada and the boy is the prime minister.
  SHEILA COPPS, politician and feminist, *Nobody's Baby: A Survival Guide to Politics* (1986).

To become a citizen of the U.S.A., all a Canadian has to do is cross the border and fill out a few forms. It is not very difficult and hundreds of thousands of Canadians have already done it. I don't know of anyone who is unhappy about that decision. I recommend it to our Prime Minister. I think he should cross the border, fill out the forms, and become a U.S. citizen, but I plead with him not to take me or you, my grandchildren, or our country with him. Let's just leave us alone. We will find a new Prime Minister, in time. But, please, can I deliver my heritage to my grandchildren and let them decide their own future?
  J.G. (JACK) McCLELLAND, publishing personality, *If You Love This Country: Facts and Feelings on Free Trade* (1987) edited by Laurier LaPierre.

Watching Mulroney, one got the feeling, as always, that beneath the plastic exterior of the studied politician there was an impenetrable layer of more plastic.
  CLAIRE HOY, journalist, *Friends in High Places: Politics and Patronage in the Mulroney Government* (1987).

So, what are the Boys saying?
  Attributed to Prime Minister MULRONEY by Michel Gratton in *"So, What Are the Boys Saying?" An Inside Look at Brian Mulroney in Power* (1987). Gratton explained the title of the book: "It was the Prime Minister's ritual way of saying hello, in person or on the phone, in English or in French; over the space of almost three years, I must have heard the phrase a million times. The Boys in question were the representatives of the nation's media, and, more specifically and most of the time, the learned correspondents of the Parliamentary Press Gallery. Some of the Boys, of course, were girls; all were embraced by that oft-repeated, all-purpose question."

I elected you the last time; it's up to you to elect me this time.
  Attributed to Prime Minister BRIAN MULRONEY, to the party caucus in anticipation of his second federal election, according to Val Sears in *The Toronto Star*, 1 March 1987.

The responses show that several foreign politicians are not well known in the U.S.A. In addition to being "unknown," politicians and other celebrities have not left a strong impression on our participants ("no opinion"). It is amazing how few Americans know the Prime Minister of Canada, Brian Mulroney, or have much of an opinion of him. In contrast, almost all Canadians consider him a *jerk*.
  REINHOLD AMAN, publisher of *Maledicta* and specialist in abusive language, "Results of Maledicta Poll 1988," *Maledicta: The International Journal of Verbal Aggression*, Volume X, 1988-89.

We have a prime minister today who's acting as a head waiter. "What do you guys in the provinces want? I'll give it to you." Mulroney likes to be loved. In politics you should try to be respected.

> JEAN CHRÉTIEN, former Cabinet Minister and Liberal leadership contender, speaking at a press conference, Toronto, 1989, quoted by David Wilson in *Metropolis*, 2 Feb. 1989.

Did we win?

> Attributed to British Prime Minister MARGARET THATCHER by Val Sears in *The Toronto Star*, 24 Oct. 1989. The remark, it is claimed, was made to fellow Conservative Prime Minister Mulroney following an important Canadian by-election.

A man of strong chin and weak mind who would be hard-pressed to be elected head of a local council in Britain.

> Unattributed description of Prime Minister Mulroney by an aide close to British Prime Minister Margaret Thatcher, published in *The Daily Express*, noted by Robert McKenzie in *The Toronto Star*, 24 Oct. 1989. Mulroney had criticized Thatcher's turnabout stand on sanctions against South Africa at the Commonwealth Conference.

Is there a law that prohibits a newspaper photographer from taking a picture of Mulroney with his mouth shut?

> ELEANOR KOLDOFSKY, Canadian recording pioneer, remark made on 24 Nov. 1989.

Canadians are fed up with a prime minister whose idea of regional development is to give the unemployed a train ticket to Toronto, and then cancel the train.

> JEAN CHRÉTIEN, Liberal leadership contender, Toronto forum, 28 Jan. 1990, quoted by Edison Stewart in *The Toronto Star* the following day.

This brings the discussion to the Prime Minister. It always does. Summoning John Buchanan to the Senate offers but one more illustration of Brian Mulroney's limitless compassion, his loyalty to his friends, which represent both an admirable virtue and a critical flaw, and while the Prime Minister has not always been fortunate in his choice of friends, none of them can say the same about him.

> DALTON CAMP, columnist and apologist for the federal Conservatives, *The Toronto Star*, 16 Sept. 1990. Fellow columnist Geoffrey Stevens characterized the Senate appointment of the Nova Scotia Premier in the following manner: "The unpopular appoints the unsuitable to force approval of the unacceptable."

We are going to have to ask ourselves an important question before the next federal election. "Hasn't George Bush been Prime Minister for long enough?"

> MARY JANE GIBSON, correspondent, Letters to the Editor, *The Globe and Mail*, 2 Feb. 1991.

Who in this room has not heard that Quebec was left out in 1982? It's been said by the Prime Minister. It's been said by the Premier of Quebec. . . . Until some sorcerer's apprentice came along some years later, the majority of Quebecers didn't feel left out.

> PIERRE ELLIOTT TRUDEAU, former Prime Minister, impromptu remarks referring to Prime Minister Brian Mulroney and whether or not Quebec was "left out" of the repatriated Constitution, made at the University of Toronto, 21 March 1991, quoted in *The Toronto Star* the following day.

The more he reminds Quebecers of their good fortune, the more the rest of Canada sees that province as "the spoiled child" of the federation.

> MIKE DUFFY, columnist and broadcaster, *The Toronto Sun*, 17 Feb. 1991.

MULTICULTURALISM

One Canada, one nation, my Canada, your Canada, cannot be a hyphenated Canada.

> JOHN G. DIEFENBAKER, M.P., maiden

speech in the House of Commons, noted in *One Canada: Memoirs of the Right Honourable John G. Diefenbaker: The Crusading Years, 1895-1956* (1975).

What I said in French was that we do not want to have in Canada a little France, a little England, a little Italy or a little Russia. We want in Canada a great country for all the people of Canada, for all the ethnic groups in our country. Through that channel we will achieve unity and we will reinforce our position in the whole world.

RÉAL CAOUETTE, Créditiste leader, speaking on the tabling of the Royal Commission Report on Bilingualism and Biculturalism, House of Commons, 8 Oct. 1971.

A dream is being realized. It has not yet obtained its final shape. Let us hope it will be as beautiful as the deep woods, the golden wheatfields and the Polar light up north over this young continent.

JOSEF SKVORECKY, Czech-born author and publisher, referring to the ethnic mix of Canadian students, "A City After My Own Heart" (1974), *Toronto Remembered: A Celebration of the City* (1984) edited by William Kilbourn.

History created this country from the meeting of two realities: the French and the English realities. Then these were enriched by the contribution of people from all parts of the world, but this coming together, this meeting, this encounter of realities, though at times difficult to accept, and hard to practise, this encounter has, itself, become the fabric of our life as a nation, the source of our individuality, the very cornerstone of our identity as a people.

PIERRE ELLIOTT TRUDEAU, Prime Minister, address on national radio and television in response to the election of a separatist government in Quebec, 24 Nov. 1976.

Multiculturalism, really, is folklore. It is a "red herring." The notion was devised to obscure "the Quebec business," "to give an impression that we are *all* ethnics and do not have to worry about special status for Quebec.

RENÉ LÉVESQUE, Quebec Premier, "Education in a Changing Society: A View from Québec," *Canadian Schools and Canadian Identity* (1977) edited by Alf Chaiton and Neil McDonald.

I was born and bred in this amazing land. I've always considered myself a Canadian, nothing more, nothing less, even though my parents were immigrants from Italy. How come that over the past ten or fifteen years we have all acquired a hyphen? We have allowed ourselves to become divided along the lines of ethnic origins, under the pretext of the "Great Mosaic." A dastardly deed has been perpetrated upon Canadians by politicians whose motto is "divide and rule." I, for one, refuse to be hyphenated. I am a Canadian, first and foremost. Don't hyphenate me.

LAURA SABIA, journalist and feminist, address, Empire Club of Canada, Toronto, 19 Oct. 1978.

Within fifty years, a moment in the sweep of history, our Canada has gone from aloofness, to tolerance, and beyond tolerance to respect for, indeed a deep desire for, the retention of the differentiations of our heritage and culture.

EDWARD SCHREYER, newly appointed Governor General, reply at the installation, House of Commons, 22 Jan. 1979.

Canada is where diversity comes together.

JOE CLARK, Prime Minister, address, Empire Club of Canada, Toronto, 14 Feb. 1980.

This charter shall be interpreted in a manner consistent with the preservation and enhancement of the multicultural heritage of Canadians.

The Constitution Act, 1982, Schedule B, Part 1, Section 27, Canadian Charter of Rights and Freedoms.

Some 50% of teens say that they favour the "mosaic" model for Canada . . . another 20% favour the "melting pot" model. . . . Most of the remaining 20% say that they have no preference either way. Only in Quebec do teenagers differ from the national norms. There, about 40% favour the mosaic and some 25% the melting pot. The main difference is that most of the rest (35%) say they have no preference.

> REGINALD W. BIBBY and DONALD C. POSTERSKI, sociologists, *The Emerging Generation: An Inside Look at Canada's Teenagers* (1985).

Song and dance is not enough.

> Remark concerning the need for more than the subsidy of minority groups made by an unidentified representative of the Ontario Coalition for Language Rights, *Minutes of Proceedings and Evidence of the Standing Committee on Multiculturalism*, 11 Dec. 1987, as cited by Robert F. Harney in "'So Great a Heritage as Ours': Immigration and the Survival of the Canadian Polity," *Daedalus: Journal of the American Academy of Arts and Sciences*, "In Search of Canada," Fall 1988.

Compared to some other parts of the globe where Urdu has found new homes in recent times, perhaps Canada is a more suitable place for building another new home on a relatively more solid ground. This harsh and beautiful land has never ceased to accommodate what can further enhance its beauty. And the Canadian cultural mosaic, symbolizing unity in diversity, has a charm of its own.

> W.A. SHAHEEN, Ottawa-based Urdu poet and editor, "Another Home?" *Across Continents: A Review of Urdu Language and Literature in Canada* (1988) edited by Wali Alam Shaheen, Anwar Nasim, and Izhar Mirza.

But in the next century, our descendants will have to manage and reconcile a multicultural society on a scale beyond our imagining.

Then will come the supreme test of Canada's realism, morality and genius. For, lacking sufficient numbers and the strength of unity, we cannot hope to possess half a continent in a crowded, desperate world. Nature will not forever tolerate a vacuum so huge and full of treasure. The alternatives decreed by history are inescapable. Canada must betray the grand dream of its founders or achieve its finest hour.

> BRUCE HUTCHISON, journalist, *Maclean's*, 11 July 1988.

Multiculturalism is keeping up with the MacDonalds, the Chartrands, the O'Haras, the Bondarchucks, the Changs, and the Singhs.

> ALLAN GOULD, satirist, *The Great Wiped Out North: or, When Sacred Cows Come Home to Roost* (1988).

A Canadian is a hyphen . . . we're diplomats by birth.

> JOY KOGAWA, novelist, interviewed by Magdalene Redekop in *Other Solitudes: Canadian Multicultural Fictions* (1990) edited by Linda Hutcheon and Marion Richmond.

Spending some time recently in Toronto, at the invitation of Canada's Ukrainian community, I couldn't help observing the neighbourhoods of that city — Ukrainian and Jewish neighbourhoods, Polish and Chinese ones, which together made up a sort of a precious alloy of differing nationalities and religions.

For me, a man from Central Europe in the last decade of the 20th century, this was a valuable lesson.

> ADAM MICHNIK, Polish dissident, "Notes on the Revolution," *The New York Times Magazine*, 11 March 1990.

What the hell does multiculturalism mean? We can't even get our own culture going; what are they talking about? How can it be "multi" when there isn't even one? I mean it's all wild. It's beautiful on paper, but its meaning is blank.

> SCOTT SYMONS, novelist and cultural

commentator, interviewed in *The Idler*, No. 25, May-June 1990.

In the morning, I go to the Korean *dépanneur* to buy the *Devoir* and *The Gazette*. Then I get my fresh *chala* at the European Kosher Bakery and say *bonjour* to my Greek neighbour.

This may or may not be your Canada, but it's my neighbourhood. And my neighbourhood is my country.
> MARIE-LOUISE GAY, author and illustrator, quoted in "O Canada," *The Toronto Star*, 30 June 1990.

There is no such thing as being an English-Canadian, for that matter. The English in Canada have been reduced to a visible minority. Roast beef has become an ethnic dish.
> VIVIAN RAKOFF, psychiatrist, quoted by Peter C. Newman in *Maclean's*, 2 July 1990.

Today, nearly half the children in Vancouver's school system have English as a second language. The city of Toronto, Canada's largest, routinely sends out property tax notices in six languages — English, French, Chinese, Italian, Greek and Portuguese.
> ANDREW H. MALCOLM, correspondent, *The New York Times*, 8 July 1990.

We have forgotten that one cannot forge a nation by encouraging separateness under the rubric of multiculturalism. A person's roots are a private matter, not a subject of public subsidy.
> BARBARA AMIEL, columnist, *Maclean's*, 10 Sept. 1990.

Multiculturalism, which was largely a self-conscious inability to require immigrants to assimilate, coupled with a cynical vote-buying exercise, was long and self-righteously held up as superior to the American melting pot. It is now finally being seriously questioned.
> CONRAD BLACK, capitalist and columnist, "Enough Is Enough," *Saturday Night*, Sept. 1990.

I know what multiculturalism means. It means the Scots own the banks and the Portuguese get to clean them.
> HERB DENTON, one-time Canadian correspondent for *The Washington Post*, quoted by Suanne Kelman in *The Globe and Mail*, 30 Oct. 1990.

Have we forgotten how far ahead of other countries we are in our commitment to living together with a comparative degree of tolerance? . . . Other countries cling to the cultural philosophy that monolithic is terrific. They make great places to visit but I wouldn't want to live there.
> CHARLES PACHTER, artist and essayist, *The Globe and Mail*, 28 March 1991.

MULTINATIONALISM
See also BUSINESS
ECONOMIC NATIONALISM

But multi-national firms are not simple profit maximizers. A multi-national corporation is a corporation which engages in foreign direct investment. It is the parent corporation which controls one or more incorporated subsidiaries and/or one or more unincorporated branches abroad.
> MEL WATKINS, political scientist, *Foreign Ownership and the Structure of Canadian Investment: Report of the Task Force on the Structure of Canadian Investment* (1968), commonly called "The Watkins Report."

American corporate capitalism is the dominant factor shaping Canadian society. In Canada, American economic control operates through the formidable medium of the multinational corporation. The Canadian corporate elite has opted for a junior partnership with these American enterprises. Canada has been reduced to a resource base and consumer market within the American empire.
> "The Waffle Manifesto: For an Indepen-

dent Socialist Canada" (1969) reprinted in *The Canadian Forum*, Dec. 1989.

The disappearance of any need for other than day-to-day management in Canada is particularly true in the auto industry, whose engineering, product design and product development are all done in Detroit. The president of Ford of Canada is thought to have a capital investment budget of $5,000 a year. Apart from managing the workers and selling the cars, there is nothing for an executive to do. This is what the British in India called the *subahdar* class — local officers whose job it was to manage local soldiers.
> JOHN RALSTON SAUL, social commentator, *The Globe and Mail's Report on Business Magazine*, Jan. 1988.

The earliest known branch factory in Canada was the Toronto plant of Allcock, Laight and Company, British manufacturers of needles and fishing tackle, established in 1854.
> MICHAEL BLISS, historian, *Northern Enterprise: Five Centuries of Canadian Business* (1987). In the 1960s the term "branch-plant economy" was widely used to describe Canadian dependency on foreign (especially American) business interests.

This last weekend, before a national election that will reset the fundamental political and economic directions of the second largest country in land size in the world, Canadians drove their Chevrolets, Plymouths and Fords to Sears stores, past the Holiday Inns and Midas Muffler shops. They ate lunch at McDonald's or Kentucky Fried Chicken and bought their groceries at Safeway. They took a pizza home from Domino's, brushed their teeth with Colgate toothpaste and laughed at *Saturday Night Live*. During commercial breaks in the National Football League games, many no doubt worried that the proposed Free Trade agreement with the United States could seriously threaten the so-called Canadian way of life.
> ANDREW H. MALCOLM, correspondent formerly based in Toronto, "Canada's Deeper Identity Not Made in the U.S.A.," *The New York Times*, 20 Nov. 1988.

Another of my concerns is the multinational corporations who are our new colonial powers. They operate above international and national laws. They dominate small countries, control prices and prop up corrupt governments. They avoid taxes at home and contribute miniscule amounts to the countries they exploit. But the worst aspect is that they grow rich while poor countries sink further into poverty.
> DORIS ANDERSON, writer, "Symposium," *The Canadian Forum*, Jan. 1990.

The multinationals, once seen as demons, may in fact be responsible for the peace of the world, because now everybody has a share in everybody else's prosperity.
> VIVIAN RAKOFF, psychiatrist, quoted by Peter C. Newman in *Maclean's*, 2 July 1990.

MURDER
See also CRIME

I'm like a carpenter who's discovered he has a knack for making coffins.
> ERIC WRIGHT, author of mystery novels, in conversation, Toronto, 23 Aug. 1987.

This is the mystery of our age: people get killed but there are no murderers.
> Line from *An Innocent Millionaire* (1983), a novel by STEPHEN VIZINCZEY.

Some part of us still believes that men should kill.
> ROBIN SKELTON, man-of-letters, aphorism, May 1990.

Human beings are the only creatures that kill from a distance.
> ROBIN SKELTON, man-of-letters, aphorism, May 1990.

MUSEUMS

Paralytic modesty is a common museum disease from Calgary to Halifax.

> SIR HENRY MIERS, museologist, commissioned by the Carnegie Corporation to report on the state of museums in Canada, after visiting 125 institutions in 1931, quoted by Lovat Dickson in *The Museum Makers: The Story of the Royal Ontario Museum* (1986).

Our future is optimistic. We should celebrate it. This national treasure house must welcome the people, teach them, inspire them, and send them away enlightened and optimistic that we are progressing as human individuals and as a nation.

> DOUGLAS J. CARDINAL, architect, "Museum of Man Proposal, 1983: From Earth Creatures to Star Creatures," *The Canadian Forum*, Oct. 1989. Cardinal won the competition to design the building in Hull to house the then-unrenamed National Museum of Canada. One critic described its curvy, low-lying exterior as "gopher baroque." The museum was ultimately named the Canadian Museum of Civilization, and officially opened on 29 June 1989. But critics of the exhibition policies of its director (who, it seems, had once visited Disneyland) dubbed it "the Canadian Confusion of Civilization."

Not far from Parliament is Ottawa's newest cultural monument, the National Museum of — well, no one is yet sure. Originally known as the National Museum of Man, the building is nameless until a special committee of experts (who else?) alights on a truly non-sexist name. Suggestions from the public include National Museum of Herstory and History, National Museum of Men, Women and Gays, and National Museum of Others, any one of which is sure to pull in the crowds.

> STEPHEN BROOK, English travel writer, *Maple Leaf Rag: Travels across Canada* (1987).

In some ways, Canada itself is a museum,

preserving many objects and cultural traits that over the years have disappeared from their homelands.

> GEORGE F. MacDONALD, director, Canadian Museum of Civilization, *Treasures of the Canadian Museum of Civilization* (1988).

This is the prototype, the museum for the Information Age. We intend to be the Super Bowl of cultural development in this country.... The whole museum is a television studio.

> GEORGE F. MacDONALD, director of the Canadian Museum of Civilization, Hull, Que., and the originator of its "Disneyland North" displays, quoted by David Lancashire in *Smithsonian*, March 1990.

MUSIC

See also ANTHEM, NATIONAL
MUSIC, POPULAR
MUSICIANS
OPERA
RECORD INDUSTRY
SONGS

Ettore Mazzoleni, then principal of the conservatory, phoned Guerrero to ask how young Malcolm was progressing after a year's work.

"I don't know," Guerrero is supposed to have replied. "I haven't heard him play yet. We spend all our time discussing painting and literature."

> Anecdote told by pianist MALCOLM TROUP, one-time pupil of the late Alberto Guerrero of the Toronto Conservatory of Music, noted by William Littler in *The Toronto Star*, 20 Oct. 1990.

I have met Canadians in many parts of the world but I have never met any who bragged about their music education, chamber music or anything else about musical achievements.

> YEHUDI MENUHIN, violinist, addressing the World Music Week Conference, Montreal, Oct. 1975, quoted in *Closed Circuit*, 15 Oct. 1975.

We yearn for our Mozarts, our Shakespeares and our Picassos. Nation-building is a matter of establishing links; and to the extent that the Great Artist is lacking, Canadians face the problem of a missing link.
Report of the Federal Cultural Policy Review Committee (1982). The passage elicited the following comment from R. MURRAY SCHAFER in On Canadian Music (1984): "In other words, if God had intended Canada to have a music, Mozart would have been born in Regina."

Having appeared in concerts in Toronto for the past fifty years or more, I am astounded by the contribution that the local artists have made to the advancement of the many cultural fields of music, opera, ballet, and drama.
ANDRÉS SEGOVIA, classical guitarist, Foreword, Recollections of a Violinist (1984) by Maurice Solway.

Composing is a lonely occupation, but I don't feel alone when my mind is immersed in the creation of a piece. The feeling of isolation is due to the situation in Canada, where serious music doesn't have a very high rating. Composers don't die of starvation here. They die of frustration.
JOHN WEINZWEIG, composer and teacher, quoted by Pearl Sheffy Gefen in The Globe and Mail, 24 Nov. 1989.

Our major orchestras are largely performing music of other cultures ... but Handel never watched TV, Mozart never travelled in a car nor Brahms in a plane. They wrote before the world was exposed to James Joyce, Sigmund Freud and Albert Einstein, before men landed on the moon. Composers today may look back, but we can't go back. The world is no longer beating to the tempo of a minuet.
JOHN WEINZWEIG, composer and teacher, quoted by Pearl Sheffy Gefen in The Globe and Mail, 24 Nov. 1989.

I find it laughable when I read the news about people being on strike for higher wages, lower working hours and greater security. At fifty-seven, I feel it would be very pleasant to earn at least the minimum wage.
MILTON BARNES, teacher and composer, "A Dog's Life for a Composer," The Toronto Star, 25 Nov. 1989.

Mission Impossible is an apt description for the life of anyone in Canada pursuing a career as a professional serious music composer.
MILTON BARNES, teacher and composer, "A Dog's Life for a Composer," The Toronto Star, 25 Nov. 1989.

What is the serious composer's position in Canada now? (Let's not fool ourselves for a moment into thinking that he might have a position elsewhere. Ask a European what he knows about Canadian music; first he'll look blank, then reply with the names Murray Schafer and Glenn Gould. Ask an American and all you'll get is a blank look.) The Canadian composer must go it alone.
CHRISTOPHER BUTTERFIELD, essayist, "Listening to Rain," The Idler, No. 19, Sept.-Oct. 1988.

MUSIC, POPULAR
See also MUSIC
MUSICIANS

Whatever else it may be, Presleyism is a cultural wasteland; it is less tenacious of life than poison ivy, spreading broadly but readily replaced. In the meantime, however, it is well nourished.
HUGH THOMSON and RALPH HICKLIN, cultural commentators, reacting in The Globe and Mail to Elvis Presley's performance at Toronto's Maple Leaf Gardens in 1957, quoted by Richard J. Doyle in Hurly-Burly: A Time at The Globe (1990).

"Elvis, you've got to call yourself 'Rock' or 'Jack' or something," I said. "Anything as long as it's not 'Elvis Presley.'"
Well, damn. You know what he told me? Elvis said, "I'm going to make more money

than all of you guys put together. And I'm going to make it with *my* name."

RONNIE HAWKINS and PETER GODDARD, performer and writer, *Ronnie Hawkins: Last of the Good Ol' Boys* (1989). This is a reference to the gratuitous advice given by the young Rompin' Ronnie Hawkins to another young rock-'n'-roll performer, Elvis Presley.

Four insouciant young men peering out from under superbangs, singing possibly, gyrating certainly, and in general having a whale of a time.

Typical sentence from the review of the Beatles performance at Maple Leaf Gardens in Sept. 1964, quoted by Richard J. Doyle in *Hurly-Burly: A Time at The Globe* (1990).

Jazz goes deeper; it is a psychological force, a beautiful force which gives me joy and pervades my whole emotional life. It is a source of never-ending pleasure, one of the things in my life which time has not spoiled for me. . . . I love that anonymous music. . . . Jazz, and everything it symbolizes, represents for me a key to all human striving.

JOSEF SKVORECKY, essayist and novelist, "An Interview in Prague" (1968), *Talkin' Moscow Blues* (1988) edited by Sam Solecki.

Toronto was a unique place in those days [the 1940s and 50s]. Artistic perspectives were adjusted to a strong natural state of individuality. Everybody in Canada seemed to listen to what they enjoyed, and nobody could tell them what to like, or what was popular, or what was the In Thing. Even today, it is very hard to brainwash a Canadian.

DUKE ELLINGTON, musician, *Music Is My Mistress* (1973).

When I first came to Canada, I had to say my backup boys were from Nashville or Memphis or somewhere — instead of Canadians, which is what they were. Club owners wouldn't book Canadian groups,

said they wouldn't draw. It's been a long, hard battle. This country's got everything but confidence.

Rompin' RONNIE HAWKINS, rock'n'roll personality, quoted by Jon Ruddy in *TV Guide*, 7 Nov. 1981.

There is this funny assumption, especially among professional musicians, that the fact that one is surrounded with wallpaper music is very harmful. I don't think it is harmful at all. I go into elevators that have it all the time, and when I go into restaurants it is usually there. Not only does it not bother me, but I have the ability to tune it out if I want to.

GLENN GOULD, pianist, interviewed by Ulla Colgrass in *For the Love of Music* (1988).

Muzak goes in one ear and out some other opening.

ANTON KUERTI, pianist, interviewed by Ulla Colgrass in *For the Love of Music* (1988).

Rompin' Ronnie is a legend in his spare time.

Said to be the message on the T-shirt worn by RONNIE HAWKINS, quoted by Ed Gould in *Entertaining Canadians: Canada's International Stars 1900-1988* (1988).

Sometimes my voice can make *me* cry.

LEONARD COHEN, poet and singer, quoted by Christopher Jones in *Now*, 3 Nov. 1988.

I'm afraid one day I'll wake up at forty years old and there won't be a single tune in my head.

DAVID FOSTER, songwriter, born in 1950, composer of such hits as "After the Love Is Gone," "The Theme from St. Elmo's Fire," "What a Feeling," and the 1988 Calgary Olympic's "Winter Games," quoted by Ed Gould in *Entertaining Canadians: Canada's International Stars 1900-1988* (1988).

I've had my boots made in Toronto since 1970. I design them and Master John makes them. You can say Canada's at my feet.

> CHUBBY CHECKER, performer, quoted by Rita Zekas in *The Toronto Star*, 18 Jan. 1988.

Singing in French is what makes me interesting, and I want to preserve it. In 1988, even singing in French in Montreal is a statement. I'm trying to preserve my soul and my roots even if I am not singing about snow and maple trees.

> MICHEL RIVARD, chansonnier, quoted by Stephen Godfrey in *The Globe and Mail*, 2 Dec. 1988.

I've had a really good career, but quite frankly I'd rather be a well-rounded human being than a well-rounded performer.

> ANNE MURRAY, singer, quoted by Bruce Blackadar in *The Toronto Star*, 8 Dec. 1988.

As a songwriter I write for people who don't have the ability to express themselves. Artists have the responsibility to speak for people.

> CONNIE KALDOR, singer and composer, quoted by Ellen Schwartz in *Born a Woman: Seven Canadian Women Singer-Songwriters* (1988).

I do what I want to do, and if I don't make it, that's o.k. When I'm on my deathbed I'll be able to say I did what I did from the heart and I'm proud of it.

> MARIE-LYNN HAMMOND, performer, quoted by Ellen Schwartz in *Born a Woman: Seven Canadian Women Singer-Songwriters* (1988).

I can say that in my entire career I've never played any bad places. Because wherever I was, there were always good people there.

> RITA MacNEIL, singer and performer, quoted by Chris Dafoe in *The Globe and Mail*, 5 Nov. 1988.

In my opinion she can sing a song as good as a song can be sung.

> RONNIE HAWKINS and PETER GODDARD, performer and writer, referring to Anne Murray, the popular Nova Scotia-born singer, *Ronnie Hawkins: Last of the Good Ol' Boys* (1989).

The ears and eyes of technology open to capture the responses of the audience and the players to the music, to the atmosphere, to each other. The panorama of faces alone mirrors a novel's worth of expression and emotion, intense, playful, concentrated, abandoned, pained, laughing, serious, and downright silly. . . . Hands perform, and hands respond. Hands gesture, and hands respond. A show of ears and eyes, a show of hearts and minds. A Show of Hands.

> NEIL PEART, acoustic and electronic percussion, member of the rock group Rush, liner notes for the video cassette *Rush: A Show of Hands* (1989).

Listen, Canada is a nice place to live if you're not an artist; but, from a career stand point, Canada only represents 5% of the world market share. So I don't waste a lot of time worrying about what Canada thinks of my ballads.

> DAN HILL, composer and performer, addressing a CBC interviewer who was suggesting "that Canadians had heard enough of your ballads after lyrics such as 'Sometimes when we touch / The honesty's too much. . . .'" Quoted by Peter Goddard and Philip Kamin, editors of *Shakin' All Over: The Rock 'N' Roll Years in Canada* (1989).

I'm living out my childhood fantasy and I've been able to make a living doing it. You can't beat that.

> IAN TYSON, singer and composer and rancher, quoted by Christopher Jones in *Now*, 9 Feb. 1989.

Now I want to be like Mitsou — *be* Mitsou — all over the world.

> MITSOU, singer and performer, aspiring

to translate Quebec success into global success, quoted by Kim Hughes in *Now*, 4 May 1989.

I wanted to develop the idea of torch *and* twang, that's what's inside me and it pretty much sums up the kind of music that interests me.
> K.D. LANG, country and western singer, describing her 1986 album *Angel with a Lariat*, quoted by Christopher Jones in *Now*, 26 Oct. 1989.

You look like a boy, dress like a girl, and sing like a bird.
> Tribute to k.d. lang, country and western singer, offered by ROY ACUFF of the Grand Ole Opry, quoted by Don Gillmor, *Saturday Night*, June 1990.

Now I don't want you behaving like normal restrained Canadians.
> MICK JAGGER, leader of the pop music group The Rolling Stones, playing a concert to a capacity audience at Toronto's SkyDome, 3 Dec. 1989, quoted by Craig MacInnis in *The Toronto Star* the following day.

In the old days the audiences made opera a background for eating, drinking, gambling and making love in the boxes of the theatre, and I must say I find it vastly preferable to what we get on the radio nowadays, like the Stones or the Bones or the Who, the Poo, whatever and that fellow with the huge mouth, and all those scruffy maniacs who jump up and down yelling and screaming. I think they're awful.
> ANNA RUSSELL, concert comedienne, endorsement for David W. Barber's *When the Fat Lady Sings* (1990).

I see the music as a gift, and I call it "the visit."
> LOREENA McKENNITT, singer and songwriter whose performances suggest Celtic, folk, and New Age influences, quoted by Ace Osmer in *Dimensions: Toronto's New Age Magazine*, April 1990.

The cows don't treat me any different.
> GEORGE FOX, country singer, alluding to his growing success as a recording artist, quoted by John Lyons in *The Winnipeg Free Press*, 14 May 1990.

After ten years of making records, I wanted to keep challenging myself, and you've got to have fun, that's the key. If you can make great rock records and have a laugh, that's the best part about being a musician.
> BRYAN ADAMS, rock singer, quoted by John Lyons in *The Winnipeg Free Press*, 12 May 1990.

Our parents were into Frank Sinatra and Rosemary Clooney and Perry Como — now I'm Perry Como.
> NEIL YOUNG, pop singer and composer, on being the "old kid on the block," quoted by Greg Pindera in *The Winnipeg Free Press*, 29 Nov. 1990.

I mean, I'm a rap artist, man — I can't sing. But here I am nominated for best male vocalist. That's great! It really shows how far rap has come in Canada.
> FRESH-WEST, rap performer, on being nominated for five Juno Awards in 1991, quoted by Mark Bastien in *The Winnipeg Free Press*, 8 Feb. 1991.

You can only cross Canada so many times. I hate that when people ask me if I'm selling out by going to the U.S. — that's not the point. But when people accuse me, I feel like saying, "This [Canadian music] is quality stuff. Let's show it to the rest of the world.
> SUE MEDLEY, Vancouver-based pop singer, quoted by Stephen Oslick in *The Winnipeg Free Press*, 23 March 1991.

MUSICIANS
See also MUSIC

One is left only to contemplate what would have happened to Russian music if Stalin, like Truman, had had a daughter who sang.

A.M. KLEIN, poet, "Sha! Sha! Shasta-kovitch!" (1948), *Literary Essays and Reviews* (1987) edited by Usher Caplan and M.W. Steinberg.

Little has been said yet about that magical box of wood and strings that made all my experiences possible — the violin. I believe this instrument strikes a sympathetic vibration in the human psyche. No other resembles the human voice so closely; no other is so capable of projecting human emotions. To me, the violin has served as a comfort in times of grief and an ally in times of joy.
MAURICE SOLWAY, violinist, *Recollections of a Violinist* (1984).

I think we do have a very lively musical life in Canada — I can't imagine what we need. Per capita, Toronto is probably second only to London in musical activity. Often it is the lack of performing space that restricts the number of performances.
ROBERT AITKEN, flutist, interviewed by Ulla Colgrass in *For the Love of Music* (1988).

Stop until you hear the birds again.
Direction from the score for "Music for Wilderness Lake" (1979), a naturalistic musical composition conceived by the innovative composer R. MURRAY SCHAFER, quoted by Ulla Colgrass in *For the Love of Music* (1988).

One of the wonderful things about being a musician is the combination of the intellectual, the physical and the spiritual, and it seems almost artificial not to enjoy the mechanical part at the same time as the musical.
ANTON KUERTI, pianist, interviewed by Ulla Colgrass in *For the Love of Music* (1988).

Because this work is, on first hearing, difficult, it will be played twice.
Program note written by the youthful GLENN GOULD for a Webern quartet in a concert arranged by the New Music Asso-

ciates in the early 1950s, quoted by Robert Fulford in *Best Seat in the House: Memoirs of a Lucky Man* (1988).

Another invitation that Gould scorned came from Jack Behrens, dean of the faculty of music at the University of Western Ontario, who had the marvelous idea of asking Gould to come on the day after his birthday and perform John Cage's 4'33", that celebrated oddity in which a pianist sits motionless before a piano throughout three silent movements of 33 seconds, 2 minutes 40 seconds, and 1 minute 20 seconds. The world's most famous non-performer was not amused.
OTTO FRIEDRICH, biographer, *Glenn Gould: A Life and Variations* (1989).

In order for a person to become a first-class international singer, he must first become a first-class human being.
GEORGE LONDON, Montreal-born opera singer and manager, philosophy of work formulated two years before his death in 1985, quoted by Ed Gould in *Entertaining Canadians: Canada's International Stars 1900-1988* (1988).

Temperament is to me an excuse for singers who don't know their parts or simply have bad manners.
MAUREEN FORRESTER, opera singer, interviewed by Ulla Colgrass in *For the Love of Music* (1988).

MYSTERIES

I prefer complexity to certainty, cheerful mysteries to sullen facts.
CLAUDE T. BISSELL, President, University of Toronto, "On University Discipline," address, Convocation Hall, University of Toronto, 1 Oct. 1969.

The fantastic is the real that most people want to ignore.
ROBERTSON DAVIES, novelist, interviewed by Harry Rasky on *The Magic Season of Robertson Davies*, CBC-TV, 27 Dec. 1990. Davies went on to discuss those

aspects of reality that are "inexplicable but inescapable."

The knowledge that you can have is inexhaustible, and what is inexhaustible is benevolent. The knowledge that you cannot have is of the riddles of birth and death, of our future destiny and the purposes of God. Here there is no knowledge, but illusions that restrict freedom and limit hope. Accept the mystery behind knowledge: it is not darkness but shadow.
    NORTHROP FRYE, literary critic, annual baccalaureate service. Metropolitan United Church, Toronto, 10 April 1988, quoted by Alexandra Johnston in *Vic Report*, Spring 1991.

MYSTICISM

Mysticism is just tomorrow's science, dreamed today.
    MARSHALL McLUHAN, communications theorist, quoted by Marilyn Ferguson in *The Aquarian Conspiracy: Personal and Social Transformation in the 1980s* (1980).

MYTHOLOGY
See also FOLKLORE

The thing about myths, of course, is that they seem to us to move naturally and inevitably, however strange and extraordinary they may seem. They're really the way things are. After all, we are human beings, and not creatures of infinite possibilities. And you do live much as other people have done in the past.
    ROBERTSON DAVIES, man-of-letters, interviewed by Gordon Roper in 1968, *Conversations with Robertson Davies* (1989) edited by J. Madison Davis.

Lake monster stories are primarily stories; i.e., discourses trying to find materiality through the misinterpretation of floating logs, bizarre waves, etc., and helped in the attempt by anomalic zoology and true occultism. But the top hat of scientism and the feather hat of neo-shamanism are both full of moths.
    MICHEL MEURGER, investigator, "Postscript to What 'Lake Monster Traditions' Means to Me" (1986), quoted by Bob Rickard in *Fortean Times*, Winter 1987.

Myths define a nation; they give it a name, an ethos. They delimit a nation.
    But myths can also limit a nation, if they are allowed to substitute for vision, if they become a retreat from challenge, if they become a refuge from reality.
    ALLAN GOTLIEB, Ambassador to the U.S., address, Empire Club of Canada, Toronto, 9 April 1987.

Sailors, lost on the oceans, become experts in spotting signs of land. Residents of the Sahara grow learned in the location of water. And Canadians are authorities on mythology. It is what we spectacularly lack and what we yearn to possess, what we fear may have eluded us and what we dream of finding or claiming.
    ROBERT FULFORD, cultural commentator, *Best Seat in the House: Memoirs of a Lucky Man* (1988).

Every nation rejoices in at least one epic moment from its past, as much myth as history — the Spanish Armada, the storming of the Bastille, the Boston tea party, the Long March, the Voortrek. Ours is unique, less violent but equally dramatic: the construction of a line of steel to unknown shores to create a nation. The covered wagon is not a Canadian symbol. Our immigrants invaded the West on the slatted seats of colonist cars.
    PIERRE BERTON, media personality and author of definitive popular histories of the Klondike Gold Rush and the construction of the CPR, *Maclean's*, 21 Aug. 1989.

Canadians do not even share myths — those imagined truths that find acceptance because they illuminate the soul and galvanize the national will.
    LAURIER LaPIERRE, historian and broadcaster, *1759: The Battle for Canada* (1990).

N

NAMES

See also NICKNAMES
PLACES

His Name is His Fortune / The Kwakiutl Indians of British Columbia pawn their names if they need money! Until the loan is repaid the borrower is nameless.
> ROBERT L. RIPLEY, columnist and cartoonist, *Ripley's New Believe It or Not!* (1950).

I wish Berlitz had added a favourite legend of mine about the origin of the name of my own country. Many years ago, it seems, on a Spanish explorer's map of North America, all that was marked on the undiscovered land above the St. Lawrence River was "*aqui esta nada.*" Eventually this was corrupted to read "Canada."
> MORDECAI RICHLER, "Journals" (1988), reviewing Charles Berlitz's *Native Tongues,* in *Broadsides: Reviews and Opinions* (1990).

If there are 250,000 unnamed lakes in Ontario alone, there is an even larger problem of toponomy in tracing the Canadian language.
> MARSHALL McLUHAN, media philosopher, and Bruce R. Powers, communica-

tions specialist, authors of *The Global Village: Transformations in World Life and Media in the 21st Century* (1989).

All are called Canadians, Ontarians, Torontonians. Right there, you have Indian names. There is an additional psychic magic that happens there, just as a result of that name. So I think that white culture in Canada is very much changing and transforming as a result of living with native culture; likewise Cree culture, native culture.
> TOMSON HIGHWAY, Cree playwright, interviewed by Ann Wilson in *Other Solitudes: Canadian Multicultural Fictions* (1990) edited by Linda Hutcheon and Marion Richmond.

NATION

A nation cannot be exalted intellectually, socially and morally, unless the great body of the people are raised intellectually, socially and morally — any more than a pyramid can be exalted without extending its base.
> HENRY WENTWORTH MONK, prophet, *A Simple Interpretation of the Revelation* (1857), quoted by R.S. Lambert in *For the Time Is at Hand: An Account of the Proph-*

esies of Henry Wentworth Monk of Ottawa, Friend of the Jews, and Pioneer of World Peace (1947).

NATIONAL ANTHEM
See ANTHEM, NATIONAL

NATIONAL FILM BOARD
See FILM

NATIONAL IDENTITY
See IDENTITY, NATIONAL

NATIONALISM
See also ECONOMIC NATIONALISM
IDENTITY, NATIONAL
INTERNATIONALISM
LOYALTY & LOYALTIES

Canada is free and freedom is nationality.
SIR WILFRID LAURIER, Prime Minister, quoted by Andrew Coyne in *Saturday Night*, July 1989.

The problem of man's aloneness on the face of the earth — is there a better milieu for its exposition than our wide grain-filled or snow-filled spaces? Man's relationship to his different fellow — a bilingual culture seems made to order for such a theme! The universal desire for adventure, conquest over nature — we who sit on the roof of the world ought to see further these possibilities than others. The new orientation of geography, an orientation which makes us neighbours to the hitherto remote, which emphasizes the oneness of this globe — the dialectic comes around full circle — is also ironically enough, a Canadian theme!
A.M. KLEIN, poet, "Writing in Canada" (1946), *Literary Essays and Reviews* (1987) edited by Usher Caplan and M.W. Steinberg.

When the all-embracing Canadian "identity" is felt to be threatened, the struggle for Canadian Nationalism is seen as something loyal and virtuous. Yet when the Québécois try to retain their identity through nationalism, through political in-dependence, the advocates of separatism are labelled "traitors."
RENÉ LÉVESQUE, Quebec Premier, "Education in a Changing Society: A View from Québec," *Canadian Schools and Canadian Identity* (1977) edited by Alf Chaiton and Neil McDonald.

The Mulroney challenge to Canada lies in its explicit and implicit "transnationalism." If the new government maintains its original commitment to continentalism, with mere gestures made in the direction of autonomy, the political struggle in Canada is likely to focus on defining the nature of the national interest.
STEPHEN CLARKSON, political scientist, *Canada and the Reagan Challenge: Crisis and Adjustment, 1981-85* (1982; rev. ed., 1985).

The debate today, in Canada, is not a debate about nationalism and internationalism. It is a debate between nationalism and continentalism. It is a debate about the very survival of Canada, about supporting multilateralism as opposed to supporting growing over-dependence.
MEL HURTIG, publisher and nationalist, address to the Second Annual Conference, Council of Canadians, Ottawa, 19 Oct. 1986.

The only panacea is pan-Canadianism of the kind that Lester Pearson and Pierre Trudeau sought. Pan-Canadian political strategies reinforce a united yet individuated country from coast to coast. It must be the goal of any prime minister to reinforce this pan-Canadianism while ensuring that we can play a unique role in the world's collective well-being.
SHEILA COPPS, M.P., contributor to *If I Were Prime Minister* (1987).

As I wandered about Canada I often asked what the following people would have in common if thrust into the same room and forced to make conversation: a Newfoundland fisherman, a Toronto banker, a Dene trapper, and a Vancouver restaurateur.

The answer, most people agreed, was not much. They could all talk about hockey, and perhaps they could debate the merits of rival beers, and they could certianly grumble about iniquitous Ottawa, but that would be it.

> STEPHEN BROOK, English travel writer, *Maple Leaf Rag: Travels across Canada* (1987).

Anxiety about Canada's identity is an expression of Canada's identity, as I learned in the late 1960s when I taught political philosophy at the University of Toronto.... One day I asked a class to define Canada's "national purpose." After an awkward pause, one student said: "Building the trans-Canadian railroad — that's all." When I said that surely there were other collective purposes, another student exclaimed: "You (Americans) took them all."

> GEORGE F. WILL, syndicated columnist based in Washington, referring to the Canadian Pacific Railway, *The Toronto Star*, 14 Jan. 1988.

But the state of Canada can never be a national state in anything other than name. When the state and its institutions refer to themselves as being national, the term always means something different in Quebec. Terms such as *the national interest* and *national objectives* are a source of constant annoyance to Quebecers. As for *binational state*, this term is hardly used any more; when it is, it too has a meaning that in Canada is different from what it is in Quebec.

> LÉON DION, political scientist, "The Mystery of Quebec," *Daedalus: Journal of the American Academy of Arts and Sciences*, "In Search of Canada," Fall 1988.

Maybe we've outlived the age of nation-states. This argument might make sense if the individual identity of nations were going to be sacrificed for some higher good, but in fact the sacrifice is merely for the commercial interest of corporations, without obligations to any community but their own shareholders.

> BERNARD OSTRY, Chairman, TVO, *The New York Times*, 31 Dec. 1989.

There is more to being a Canadian than simply being a resident of one province or a territory.

> CLYDE WELLS, Newfoundland Premier, after giving qualified assent to the Meech Lake Accord, Ottawa, quoted by Patrick Doyle in *The Toronto Star*, 10 June 1990.

Newfoundland's position ... has from the beginning placed the interest of the country first and the interest of Newfoundland second.

Now, I believe that is the responsibility of every province in this nation and, having recognized Quebec as a distinct society, I say to my friends in Quebec I believe it is the responsibility of all of the citizens of Quebec to put Canada first, and recognize that, like all of the other provinces, Quebec is second.

> CLYDE WELLS, Newfoundland Premier, remarks made at the close of the First Ministers' Conference on changes to the Meech Lake Accord, Ottawa, 9 June 1990, carried in *The Globe and Mail*, 11 June 1990.

The people of Canada want a citizenship that means holding shared values, and not merely a shared passport.

> JEAN CHRÉTIEN, contributor, *Towards a Just Society: The Trudeau Years* (1990) edited by Thomas S. Axworthy and Pierre Elliott Trudeau.

The definition of a country is people who create something in common that means something.

> BOB RAE, Ontario Premier, address, Queen's Park, 27 March 1991.

NATO
See NORTH ATLANTIC TREATY ORGANIZATION

NATIVE PEOPLES
See also INDIANS
INUIT

Should your blankets be torn / May your breezes be warm / May your treasures be what you find / May the burdens you bear / Like the boundaries be shared / May you leave something good behind / Would the sky and the land / Rise to your command / May your senses cut like the knife / Live in peace with the earth / As in death as in birth / May you prosper and have a good life.
> Translation of a verse "of a Native's wish to have a good life" to be recited with "a slow drum beat in the background" at Canadian summer camps, taken from *High above the Thundercloud* (1985), a camper's manual prepared by Jack Pearse, Bryce Taylor, John Jorgenson, and Jane McCutcheon.

Here ends all positive knowledge of her tribe, which she never narrated without tears.
> WILLIAM CORMACK, historian, describing the death of Shanawdithit, the last of the Beothuck, who died in 1829, quoted by James P. Howley in *The Beothucks or Red Indians* (1915).

It is not possible now to determine what will be the final influence of the aborigines on the generations of Canadians still to come. Doubtless all the tribes will disappear. Some will endure only a few years longer.
> DIAMOND JENNESS, anthropologist, *The Indians of Canada* (1932).

The alienated ones have a natural intuition of ecology, since they are the victims of its absence.
> MARSHALL McLUHAN, communications theorist, letter to Pierre Elliott Trudeau, 21 Sept. 1971, *Letters of Marshall McLuhan* (1987) edited by Matie Molinaro, Corinne McLuhan, and William Toye.

Deep in the glass and concrete of your world, you are stealing my soul, my spirit.
> FRANK T'SELEIE, Dene Chief, Fort Good Hope, N.W.T., addressing the Mackenzie Valley Pipeline Inquiry, 5 Aug. 1975, quoted by Mel Watkins in *Dene Nation: The Colony Within* (1977).

The real or half-real tribes which hover on the fringe of ancient geographies — Atavantes, Fenni, Parrossits or the dancing Spermatophagi — have their modern equivalents in the Bushman, the Shoshonean, the Eskimo and the Aboriginal.
> BRUCE CHATWIN, English travel writer, *The Songlines* (1987).

It's not the same as letting native people tell their own stories. Only the people who know the metaphors, the symbols, and the subtleties of the culture can tell the stories.
> LENORE KEESHIG-TOBIAS, Ojibwa storyteller, protesting the usurpation of native themes by non-natives, addressing a press conference called to launch a made-for-television movie about native education, quoted by Deirdre Kelly in *The Globe and Mail*, 16 Sept. 1989.

Native issues are almost never just native issues. Native issues are human issues.
> BUFFY SAINTE-MARIE, singer and native activist, quoted by Kim Hughes in *Now*, 2 Feb. 1989.

I don't think either the Indians of Canada or America expect that the white man is going to get back on the boat and return to Yugoslavia or Sweden or Denmark or wherever they came from. But I think it could be reasonable for them to expect, in this very loud political serenade where we constantly hear about democracy, that they should have a land of their own with their own laws, and some measure of continuing compensation for what happened to them.
> MARLON BRANDO, movie actor and advocate of native causes, interviewed on

location in Toronto, quoted by Murray Campbell in *The Globe and Mail*, 5 Sept. 1989.

You are the first citizens of this earth.
JOHN PAUL II, Pontiff, addressing a delegation of Quebec Cree at Vatican City headed by Billy Diamond, Nov. 1982, quoted by Roy MacGregor in *Chief: The Fearless Vision of Billy Diamond* (1989).

I never could bring myself to ask anyone if he was an aboriginal, though I am told the word is perfectly acceptable, and was thus reduced to the prissy interrogation: "Excuse me, but may I ask — are you a *Native Person*?"
JAN MORRIS, Anglo-Welsh travel writer, "Wild Blue-Yonder City," *Saturday Night*, Nov. 1989.

We are one of the last hunting-gathering cultures in North America, and just thirty years ago individual developments on our land dealt the final blow to our nomadic way of life.
DANIEL ASHINI, Innu spokesperson, "David Confronts Goliath: The Innu of Ungava versus the NATO Alliance," *Drumbeat: Anger and Renewal in Indian Country* (1989) edited by Boyce Richardson.

There are those who call our way of life "savage" and "primitive." These people know nothing about Innu culture. Is it "primitive" to place one's family above everything else, to show respect for the elderly, to raise children to be generous towards and considerate of others?
DANIEL ASHINI, Innu spokesperson, "David Confronts Goliath: The Innu of Ungava versus the NATO Alliance," *Drumbeat: Anger and Renewal in Indian Country* (1989) edited by Boyce Richardson.

To those who believe, / No explanation is necessary. / To those who do not believe, / No explanation is possible. / But we, the Native Aboriginal people of this land, / Are the first and still the best teachers about ecology / And about how to take care of our Earth Mother, / And all that lives on Her.
Poetic passage (slightly revised) which accompanied Four Directions, an exhibition of photographs taken by the photographer Greg Staats of the Six Nations Reserve, exhibited at the Native Canadian Centre, Toronto, quoted by Jim Poling in *The St. Catharines Standard*, 16 Dec. 1989.

As people of the First Nations of Canada we have a vision of the sort of country we want to live in and to build in collaboration with other Canadians. It is certainly not the sort of country we have now, one in which our people have been relegated to the lowest rung of the ladder of Canadian society; suffer the worst conditions of life, the lowest incomes, the poorest education and health; and can envision only the most depressing of futures for our children.
GEORGES ERASMUS, National Chief, Assembly of First Nations, *Drumbeat: Anger and Renewal in Indian Country* (1989) edited by Boyce Richardson.

In a word, western industrial societies have to learn to think more like Indians and less like Scrooge McDuck, or you can kiss your bottom line goodbye.
MARGARET ATWOOD, author, "Scrooge McDuck vs. the Trickster," *The Times Literary Supplement*, 16 March 1990.

We have heard those comments before. We have heard from leaders, from premiers who have promised to have constitutional conferences. We have heard those for the last few years, but aboriginal people have not been listened to.
ELIJAH HARPER, Ojibwa-Cree and NDP Member of the Manitoba Legislative Assembly, in an exchange with Premier Gary Filmon in the Legislature, quoted in *The Winnipeg Free Press*, 17 June 1990.

We are not Canadians and we are not Quebeckers, we are people of the First Nations.
GHISLAIN PICARD, native spokesperson and member of the Attikamek-Montagnais Council, Northern Quebec,

quoted by André Picard in *The Globe and Mail*, 21 July 1990.

NATURAL RESOURCES
See LAND
    NATURE
    WATER
    WILDLIFE

NATURE
See also ANIMALS
    ANIMAL RIGHTS
    BIRDS
    ECOLOGY
    POLLUTION
    WILDLIFE

I had always had a turn for carpentry, which now stood me in more good stead than the classical education I had received in England. The cultivated mind, however, will find charms in the rudest wilderness; and, though Nature was just now my book, I read her ample page with more pleasure for being conversant with the literature of my own and other lands.
> SAMUEL RICHARDSON, pioneer settler, *Twenty-Seven Years in Canada West; or, The Experience of an Early Settler* (1853) edited by Agnes Strickland.

It is evening while I am writing. The sun has got down behind the trees and their long, lazy shadows are falling over the lane and fields. Beyond, the brown hills are basking in an amber radiance underneath a pale aerial sky of rose and blue. The firs on the south hill are like burnished bronze and their long shadows are barring the hill meadows. Dear old world, you are very beautiful and I love you well.
> L. M. MONTGOMERY, author, journal entry, 1 May 1899, Cavendish, P.E.I., *The Selected Journals of L.M. Montgomery: Volume I: 1889-1910* (1985) edited by Mary Rubio and Elizabeth Waterston.

Civilisation says, "Nature belongs to man." The Indian says, "No, man belongs to nature."
> GREY OWL, naturalist and author, ad-dress at Norwich, England, reported 25 Dec. 1937, quoted by Donald B. Smith in *From the Land of Shadows: The Making of Grey Owl* (1990).

By the time modern man penetrated all the continents during the Pleistocene only 20,000 years ago, his "dominion" over nature was well established.
> JOHN A. LIVINGSTON, naturalist, *One Cosmic Instant: A Natural History of Human Arrogance* (1973).

We attempt to distinguish between plants and animals, but the harder we press our determination to differentiate between them, the fuzzier the distinction becomes. We attempt to distinguish between living and nonliving, and then we stumble on the virus. We attempt to distinguish between man and other living beings, when there is no distinction. Differentiation is the cruelest block to comprehension of the oneness of being.
> JOHN A. LIVINGSTON, naturalist, *One Cosmic Instant: A Natural History of Human Arrogance* (1973).

Above the water, the land and the trees is the sky. In the middle of winter the northern lights rise in great glowing shafts. From that beginning the sky can turn into almost any colour or shape, and if there are laws that govern the sky, they are still unknown.
> MATT COHEN, essayist and novelist, "The Country North of Kingston," *Ontario* (1983).

We have been conquering nature for two hundred years. Now we have to realize that we are beating it to death.
> HANS MARTIN, scientist, Environment Canada, concluding that the economic system is incapable of coping with acid rain and other environmental concerns, quoted in *The Globe and Mail*, 30 Dec. 1988.

Nature must be ridden, not driven.
> Maxim of the Arctic adventurer JEFF Mac-

INNIS from *Polar Passage: The Historic First Sail through the Northwest Passage* (1989) by Jeff MacInnis with Wade Rowland.

Today, our species alone has the power to affect the rest of the 30 million species on the planet.
ANITA GORDON and DAVID SUZUKI, science broadcasters, *It's a Matter of Survival* (1990).

NAVY
See CANADIAN ARMED FORCES

NDP
See NEW DEMOCRATIC PARTY

NEUTRALISM & NEUTRALITY

Canada's best protection would lie in neutrality, and its neutrality could be of a different and far more positive kind than the passive neutrality of the European countries that keep out of military alliances merely to save themselves from the perils of war. Canada's neutrality could be an active one, aimed not at keeping out of international problems but at resolving them peacefully and rationally.
GEORGE WOODCOCK, author, contributor to *If I Were Prime Minister* (1987) edited by Mel Hurtig.

Canadian territory should not be made available to any other country for the purpose of attacking or threatening a third country.
Project Ploughshares for the Citizens' Inquiry into Peace and Security, quoting a statement by Canadian church leaders, *What Makes Canada Secure: Background Document for the Citizens' Inquiry into Peace and Security in Canada* (1991).

Neutrality for Canada isn't a new idea, but sticking it on TV legitimizes it for a mass audience. To say that they [the CBC] were appalled at what we were saying only begins to scratch the surface. . . . According to the CBC, if we said, "Stay in NATO," it wasn't advocacy; if we said, "Get out," it was.
GWYNNE DYER, columnist and broadcaster, on the failure of the CBC to telecast the NFB documentary *Harder Than It Looks* (1987), quoted by Carolyn Dodds in *Saturday Night*, Aug. 1988.

NEW AGE
See also PREDICTION & PROPHECY

If our age is full of deep foreboding, still "only with the fall of twilight does Minerva's owl take wing."
BERNARD J.F. LONERGAN, Jesuit philosopher, *Collection* (1988).

Unquestionably there *are* energies and powers in the human mind as yet untapped by all but rare prophets and geniuses. We are not God (thank God!) but unless we are prepared to become the mature sons and daughters of God that the Bible speaks of we are destined to remain dependent, slavish imitations of what humans are ultimately all about.
TOM HARPUR, religion columnist, *The Toronto Star*, 14 Jan. 1990.

After 2,000 years of the laws of the Father and 2,000 years of the actions of the Son, it may be the turn of the Holy Ghost.
RON GRAHAM, journalist and author, *God's Dominion: A Sceptic's Quest* (1990).

NEW BRUNSWICK
See also FREDERICTON
SAINT JOHN

The Lord has not blessed New Brunswick with mountains.
LORD BEAVERBROOK, press lord and benefactor of New Brunswick, surveying the gentle autumn hills, quoted by William Kilbourn in "The Peaceable Kingdom Still," *Daedalus: Journal of the American Academy of Arts and Sciences*, "In Search of Canada," Fall 1988.

What I retained most forcefully from

[Prime Minister R.B.] Bennett's speech was that New Brunswickers could get rich by leaving. Much later I heard a distinguished judge in Regina put it another way: "The smart ones all come from New Brunswick, and the smarter they are, the quicker they come."
> CHARLES LYNCH, columnist and author, native of New Brunswick, *The Lynch Mob: Stringing Up Our Prime Ministers* (1988).

Even in New Brunswick, where island forests stretch across millions upon millions of acres, you can't get much more than a hundred miles from the sea. Most New Brunswickers live on salt-water bays, or tidal rivers, and even those herring-chokers in the uppermost forestlands are generally on rivers that they know run down to the ocean.
> HARRY BRUCE, essayist, "The Land's Lousy — and Unforgettable," *Down Home: Notes of a Maritime Son* (1988).

I'd already had some stories published, which is what allowed me to get away. And it's a good thing, too, because I was a wired New Yorker by that point. The farm took me far enough away from what you might call the global distractions of the '70s. In fact, when they impeached Nixon, I missed the whole damn thing — and I'm so glad I did.
> WILLIAM KOTZWINKLE, U.S. novelist, commenting on the years 1971-79 that he and his wife, the novelist Elizabeth Gundy, lived on a 200-acre farm near Fredericton, N.B., quoted by Henry Mietkiewicz in *The Toronto Star*, 10 June 1989.

Interviewer: We're sure glad you could make it here tonight, Mr. Premier.
Hatfield: No problem, I happened to be in New Brunswick today anyway.
> Comedy routine on CBC Radio's *Royal Canadian Air Farce*, featuring former New Brunswick Premier Richard Hatfield who favoured foreign travel while in office, quoted by Robert Sheppard in *The Globe and Mail*, 26 Sept. 1989.

As for [N.B. Premier Frank] McKenna, his contribution, whatever else, was a public relations triumph. Speaking to the nation — something New Brunswick premiers rarely get to do — from the theatre of the national press club, McKenna could say, "We should spike our guns with flowers." This should become a keeper for Colombo's book on Canadian quotations, even though, at any other moment, it would have been a clanger.
> DALTON CAMP, political columnist, writing about McKenna's contribution to the revision of the Meech Lake Accord, *The Toronto Star*, 25 March 1990.

If Quebec becomes independent it will be an outhouse like New Brunswick.
> According to the Canadian Press news service, JEAN CHRÉTIEN made this remark in 1976 when, as a federal Cabinet Minister, he was concerned about the effects on his native Quebec of the victory of the separatist Parti Québécois. The remark came to national attention fourteen years later when it was reported by CP and quoted by Patricia Poirier in *The Globe and Mail*, 28 Sept. 1990. The occasion was the announcement by Chrétien, the new Liberal leader, that he would contest a by-election in the New Brunswick riding of Beausejour, which he succeeded in winning on 10 Dec. 1990. Chrétien's staff, while denying that he made the remark in 1976, admitted that it had made the rounds at the time and had never been officially denied.

NEW DEMOCRATIC PARTY
See also POLITICAL PARTIES
POLITICS
SOCIALISM

The aim of the Co-operative Commonwealth Federation is the establishment in Canada by democratic means of a co-operative commonwealth in which the supply of human needs and enrichment of human life shall be the primary purpose of our society. Private profit and corporate power must be subordinated to social planning designed to achieve equality of opportunity and the highest possible living standards for all Canadians.

"Winnipeg Manifesto: 1956 Winnipeg Declaration of Principles of the Co-operative Commonwealth Federation," reproduced in *The Decline and Fall of a Good Idea: CCF-NDP Manifestoes 1932 to 1969* (1974) introduced by Michael S. Cross.

For years the people of British Columbia have been trying to elect a CCF government, but the British Columbia CCF has always managed to stop them!

T.C. (TOMMY) DOUGLAS, CCF leader, quoted by Eugene Forsey in *A Life on the Fringe: The Memoirs of Eugene Forsey* (1990).

Our aim as democratic socialists is to build an independent socialist Canada. Our aim as supporters of the New Democratic Party is to make it a truly socialist party.

"The Waffle Manifesto: For an Independent Socialist Canada" (1969) reprinted in *The Canadian Forum*, Dec. 1989.

The very name was an in-joke, a self-mocking spoof of political verbiage: Waffle.

"If I'm going to waffle, I'd rather waffle to the left than waffle to the right," someone said at Gerry Caplan's house, one weekend in 1969, when a manifesto for the New Democratic Party convention was being drawn up.

Was it Giles Endicott? James Laxer? Mr. Caplan?

Whoever the author was, it provoked a *Globe and Mail* editorial denouncing the document and baptizing it The Waffle Manifesto.

"It's such a lovely myth, one wouldn't want to clear it up," University of Toronto economist Mel Watkins chuckled recently when asked about the author of the remark.

GRAHAM FRASER, journalist, commenting on the short-lived Waffle group within the NDP which was devoted to economic nationalism, *The Globe and Mail*, 21 Nov. 1989.

It is true that absolute power corrupts absolutely; it is even truer that absolute lack of power can be more corrupting — witness the NDP in opposition, who have a certain power of influence without the power of implementation or accountability. Thus they can vigorously propose any policy without concern for cost or practicality.

PETER WORTHINGTON, journalist, contributor to *If I Were Prime Minister* (1987) edited by Mel Hurtig.

It's significant that I'm the first leader of the New Democratic Party who was born in Canada. Everybody knows where I'm coming from.

ED BROADBENT, NDP leader, quoted by Judy Steed in *Ed Broadbent: The Pursuit of Power* (1988).

The New Democratic Party (Canada's socialist party) has held power provincially in British Columbia, Saskatchewan, and Manitoba, and there now seems little doubt that it will in due course become the government in power in Ottawa.

JOHN CONWAY, historian, "An 'Adapted Organic Tradition,'" *Daedalus: Journal of the American Academy of Arts and Sciences*, "In Search of Canada," Fall 1988.

It is important that the NDP alternative exist. No one can measure the extent to which our efforts influenced, tempered and improved the Liberal and Tory governments that the voters chose in our stead. Nor can we underestimate the role of the NDP as the conscience and the gadfly of the political system.

ED FINN, first leader the NDP in Newfoundland, "So, Ye Want to Get Elected," *The Canadian Forum*, Nov. 1989.

Utopia must be our guide.

ED BROADBENT, NDP leader, announcing his decision to resign after 14 years as party leader on 28 Sept. 1989, quoted in *The Globe and Mail* the following day.

You don't need brains for this job, only physical stamina.
> Attributed to AUDREY McLAUGHLIN, newly elected NDP leader, Winnipeg convention, 2 Dec. 1989.

The New Democratic Party can, should and must become the green party of Canada, that is, a party thoroughly committed to a radical environmental policy and using all reasonable means at its disposal to advance it.
> LYNN McDONALD, former M.P., "Can the NDP Become the Green Party of Canada?" *The Canadian Forum*, Dec. 1989.

Winning the leadership of the NDP, unless the party holds the balance of power in Parliament, is like coming first in the Florida Grapfruit League. Out there in the real world it doesn't count.
> MORDECAI RICHLER, novelist and journalist, *Saturday Night*, April 1990.

The NDP simply assumes that freedom and wealth will always be here, just as children believe that money grows on trees or that Christmas is just around the corner.
> WILLIAM D. GAIRDNER, academic and businessman, *The Trouble with Canada* (1990).

The press club wits used to sneer that the cerebral socialist was "born in a log embassy" — the inference being that the son of respected diplomat Saul Rae somehow couldn't be sincere, considering his family background in Geneva and elsewhere.
> ALLAN FOTHERINGHAM, columnist, on Ontario's NDP Premier-elect Bob Rae, *Maclean's*, 17 Sept. 1990.

NEW FRANCE
See FRENCH CANADA
QUEBEC
QUEBEC, CONQUEST OF

NEW YEAR'S DAY
See HOLIDAYS

NEW YORK CITY

New York City is ground zero for the Canadian invasion. The Canadians here are led by an unlikely trio — Paul, Albert and Ralph Reichmann, three brothers from Toronto. Their company, Olympia & York, started buying commercial real estate in New York a decade ago, and it is now the largest commercial landlord in the city. It owns 24 million square feet of office space in New York, which is the equivalent of ten Empire State Buildings and — more frightening — almost exactly *one square foot per Canadian*.
> RICHARD STENGEL, journalist, "The Canadians," *Spy*, Feb. 1988.

What happens in New York if you bottom out, physically, professionally, emotionally? Every day I repeat this mantra: no buffer, just the gutter; no buffer, just the gutter.
> DAVID EDDIE, essayist, "Letter from New York," *The Idler*, No. 22, 1989.

NEWFIE JOKES

Once a simplistic image of a place or people gets set in the minds of mean people, the devil himself wouldn't budge it. Hence the persistent slanders that the Irish are lazy, Italians are cowardly, Poles are dumb, Jews are money-grubbing, Roman Catholics are priest-ridden, Newfies are goofy.
> RAY GUY, humorist, "Peace, Good Wife; We May Entertain Angels Unaware," *Ray Guy's Best* (1987).

With a Polish Pope and a Newfie finance minister, you mainlanders had better watch your jokes.
> JOHN CROSBIE, Newfoundland-born Minister of Finance from 1979 to 1980, quoted by Jeffrey Simpson in *Discipline of Power* (1980).

NEWFOUNDLAND
See also LABRADOR
ST. JOHN'S

Close to this commanding and historic spot Sir Humphrey Gilbert landed on the fifth day of August, 1583, and in taking possession of his new found land in the name of his sovereign Queen Elizabeth thereby founded Britain's overseas empire.
Wording on the plaque erected to commemorate Sir Humphrey Gilbert's landfall, Newfoundland War Memorial, St. John's, Nfld. The text was contributed by RUDYARD KIPLING.

What a remarkable Country is Newfoundland! A person might live to the end of his days and never cease to marvel and wonder, one way or another. There is no place else.
RAY GUY, humorist, "Catching Conners," *That Far Greater Bay* (1976).

Newfoundlanders fall into two classes, those who are St. John's men and those who are not. Townies and baymen. You're stamped at birth and not even an appeal to the Queen's Mercy (either Buckingham Palace or the Pearly Gates) can change it.
RAY GUY, humorist, "Country Comfort's a Penthouse in the City," *Ray Guy's Best* (1987).

For Newfoundlanders living by and upon it, the sea is the ultimate reality. They accept it as their master, for they know they will never master it. The sea is there. It is their destiny. It gives them life, and sometimes it gives them death.
FARLEY MOWAT, naturalist and author, *The New-Founde-Land* (1989).

So, with an average income of well over $6,400 a year, as of 1986, Newfoundlanders who . . . stay on the Rock can make a pretty good living, if they catch some fish on the side. If fishing is their main occupation, though, they've got big problems.
ALLAN GOULD, satirist, *The Great Wiped*

Out North; or, When Sacred Cows Come Home to Roost (1988).

Yet this is the man who single-handedly dragged a spirited, independent-minded, insular people, "kicking and scratching and screaming," to approximate Smallwood's own phrase, into confederation with Canada and who thereafter remained by the popular will as premier of Newfoundland for twenty-three years.
WILLIAM ROWE, novelist and reviewer, noting the pivotal role of Joseph Roberts Smallwood in Newfoundland's history during the course of a review of a biography of Smallwood by Harold Horwood in *The Toronto Star*, 7 Oct. 1989.

English Canada will have to choose between Quebec and Newfoundland.
Remark attributed to LUCIEN BOUCHARD, Environment Minister, news conference, Quebec City, 6 April 1990. Bouchard was expressing the frustration felt by the Quebec government and the Mulroney administration when Newfoundland Premier Clyde Wells withheld that province's approval of the Meech Lake Accord.
Bouchard's actual words were less provocative than the remark attributed to him. They were merely paraphrased — not quoted — in CP's coverage in *The Toronto Star* the following day: "And Prime Minister Brian Mulroney's Quebec lieutenant, Environment Minister Lucien Bouchard, says Canadians could be forced to choose between Quebec or Newfoundland. Asked which of the two he believes they would opt for, Bouchard said yesterday, 'It's pretty obvious. Canada without Quebec, I'm not sure what that would represent.'"

Rémillard: Canada can survive very well without Newfoundland.
Bouchard: We can imagine a situation where English Canada will have to choose between Quebec or Newfoundland.
Discussion between GIL RÉMILLARD, Quebec Minister of Intergovernmental Af-

fairs, and LUCIEN BOUCHARD, news conference, Quebec City, 6 April 1990, CP's coverage in *The Toronto Star* the following day.

Prime Minister Brian Mulroney, contacted by a CP reporter, was conciliatory: "Canada needs all of its component parts, including Newfoundland and Labrador."

The attributed version of the remark ("English Canada will have choose between Quebec and Newfounland"), never disavowed by the separatist-minded Bouchard, has passed into lore. It was quoted in this form in an editorial in *The Toronto Star*, 14 April 1990.

Newfoundland Premier Clyde Wells's response to Bouchard's remark was quoted by John Spears in *The Toronto Star*, 7 April 1990: "It's not a question of either Newfoundland or Quebec. It's a question of: Is what's in the Meech Lake accord the right thing for the future of the country, or is it not? If it is, let's do it. If it isn't, let's not do it."

Columnist Allan Fotheringham, writing in *Maclean's*, 30 April 1990, referred to Bouchard's remark as "the most stupid comment of the year."

Bouchard, an otherwise intelligent man who has been positioned in the newly sexy Environment portfolio by Mulroney in hopes he will be his francophone successor at 24 Sussex Drive, has an identity problem. Author of the brilliant statement that Canada may have to choose between Quebec and Newfoundland, he confesses that he is in the Ottawa cabinet to represent Quebec's interests. This is indeed quaint, since there is this old-fashioned theory extant that federal cabinet ministers, once appointed, are there to represent Ottawa's policies in Quebec — or Alberta, or wherever.
ALLAN FOTHERINGHAM, columnist, *Maclean's*, 30 April 1990.

The golden trough of Confederation.
Reference to Newfoundland which joined Confederation in 1949 made by "a prominent local entrepreneur" according to

John Fraser, "Diary," *Saturday Night*, Sept. 1990.

Canada Begins Right Here
Sign at the eastern terminus of the Trans-Canada Highway, Mile 0/Kilometre 0, City Hall, St. John's, Nfld. The western terminus is Victoria, B.C. The sign was reproduced in *The Globe and Mail*, 18 April 1990.

NEWS

See also CANADIAN BROADCASTING
CORPORATION
COMMUNICATIONS
JOURNALISM
MEDIA
NEWSPAPERS
RADIO
TELEVISION

If the Governor General shoots a photographer at a garden party, the party becomes secondary.
GILLIS PURCELL, General Manager of the Canadian Press news syndicate in the 1950s, quoted by Ted Ferguson in *The Review*, Spring 1989.

Where's Indonesia?
Attributed to RALPH ALLEN, journalist and editor, quoted by George Bain in "Never Ignore an Earthquake," *Canadian Newspapers: The Inside Story* (1980) edited by Walter Stewart. Allen directed this rhetorical question at Mark Gayn, Far Eastern correspondent for *The Toronto Star* in the 1960s, who claimed he had knowledge of an apprehended rebellion in Indonesia. Bain explained: "The intent seems to have been admonitory, for he went on to remind Gayn that the priorities of the Hong Kong bureau were: first, China; second, Vietnam; and third (and evidently a distant third), the rest of the known world...."

The press has to have hot quotes and sharp points of view. Real news is bad news. Since the press lives on advertising, and all advertising is good news, it takes a lot of bad news to sell all this good news. Even the good news of the gospel can only be sold by hellfire.

MARSHALL McLUHAN, communications theorist, letter to Pierre Elliott Trudeau, 24 Jan. 1969, *Letters of Marshall McLuhan* (1987) edited by Matie Molinaro, Corinne McLuhan, and William Toye.

Bad news concerns few, but good news can upset a whole culture.

MARSHALL McLUHAN, communications theorist, *War and Peace in the Global Village* (1968), as quoted by Philip Marchand in *Marshall McLuhan: The Medium and the Messenger* (1989).

The National also never misses an opportunity to bring some Toronto relevance to any international story: "The existence of God was verified today by Mount Palomar physicists . . . a spokesman for Bay Street denies the discovery will influence Monday's trading (cut to stock footage of Bay Street)."

"The Toronto Media," *The Westerners' Guide to Eastern Canada* (1985) edited by Don Gillmor.

What is connected with the universities is what is really happening: the political and economic charades also going on are what are called pseudo-events, created for and blown up by the news media to give us the illusion of living in history. The human lives behind these charades, of people losing their jobs or finding that they can no longer live on their pensions, certainly do not consist of pseudo-events. But they are not hot news items either.

NORTHROP FRYE, literary critic, address, Empire Club of Canada, Toronto, 19 Jan. 1984.

It is easy for Canadians to know what is an important event in their country: it is reported in *Time* magazine.

ERIC NICOL and DAVE MORE, humorists,

The U.S. or Us: What's the Difference, Eh? (1986).

In Canada, the press is addicted to creating news by the elevation and destruction of reputations. It is easier to manufacture news than to report it.

CONRAD BLACK, newspaper proprietor and columnist, "Why Does the Press Savage Success?" *The Globe and Mail's Report on Business Magazine*, March 1986.

When the rules of a genre are in such contradiction to the needs and intentions of those trying to make best use of it, there is a case for scrapping the genre altogether.

MICHAEL IGNATIEFF, author and media personality, discussing the limitations of television news coverage, "The Ethics of Television," *Daedalus: Journal of the American Academy of Arts and Sciences*, Fall, 1988.

News is a genre as much as fiction or drama: it is a regime of visual authority, a coercive organization of images according to a stopwatch.

MICHAEL IGNATIEFF, author and television personality, "Is Nothing Sacred? The Ethics of Television," *Daedalus: Journal of the American Academy of Arts and Sciences*, "In Search of Canada," Fall 1988.

Go into a big hotel and you might find forty-five channels on cable TV, of which perhaps half a dozen are Canadian, including junior ice hockey and the National News (known as "The Nash," and likely to start on these lines: "Good evening. Following an earthquake, the entire eastern seaboard of the United States has disappeared. Meanwhile, in Manitoba, new salmon-fishing regulations have come into effect").

SIMON HOGGART, Washington correspondent for *The Observer*, in *The Globe and Mail*, 9 Jan. 1990.

One writer back home had discussed on the radio how Canada always seems like an imaginary country whenever he travels outside its boundaries.

PAUL WEINBERG, columnist, writing from England during the Meech Lake discussions, "Citybeat," *Metropolis*, 19 July 1990.

NEWSPAPERS
See also NEWS

To Our Subscribers: The delay in the publication of the present number of the *Agriculturist* has been occasioned by unavoidable circumstances; among them may be mentioned our having to wait for the paper being manufactured.

Publisher's notice in the *Agriculturist*, Nov. 1852, a monthly publication issued in Upper Canada, quoted by Dave McIntosh in *When the Work's All Done This Fall: The Settling of the Land* (1989).

According to the latest figures issued by the Dominion Bureau of Statistics, over 90% of the world's newsprint is made in Canada. May God forgive us!

LEONARD BROCKINGTON, orator, quoted by Sir Edwin Leather, address, Empire Club of Canada, Toronto, 12 Dec. 1974.

I can't imagine any publishing company anywhere in the world that would be beyond our ability to acquire.

KENNETH THOMSON, proprietor of innumerable daily and weekly newspapers, urban and suburban, as well as magazine and book-publishing companies, quoted by John Picton in *The Toronto Star*, 1 Oct. 1989.

The role of a newspaper, as I see it, is to engage in the full and frank dissemination of news and opinion from the perspective of its values and particular view of society. It should report the news fairly and accurately, reflect all pertinent facts and opinions and not only what the official establishment thinks and says.

BELAND HONDERICH, publisher of *The Toronto Star* (1966-88), convocation address, Carleton University, Ottawa, 8 June 1989, reproduced in *The Toronto Star* the following day.

Great papers are produced by great editors, not great owners.

DAVID RADLER, president of Hollinger, Inc., new proprietor of *The Jerusalem Post*, assuring the editorial staff of the English-language newspaper published in Israel that it will be business as usual, quoted by Patrick Martin in *The Globe and Mail*, 13 Jan. 1990.

At a meeting of Southam fellows, I was asked if *The Globe* was still my favourite newspaper. I said it had to be; it is, as it was, the only paper that makes me angry every morning.

RICHARD J. DOYLE, newspaperman, *Hurly-Burly: A Time at The Globe* (1990).

Jerusalem New Tourist Mecca

Headline on a travel article about Israel recalled by journalist Dick Campbell, CBC Radio, 4 Sept. 1990.

NIAGARA FALLS

Nature will be Nature still, while palaces shall decay and fall in ruins. Yes, Niagara will be Niagara a thousand years hence! The rainbow, a wreath over her brow, shall continue as long as the sun, and the flowing of the river — while the work of art, however impregnable, shall in atoms fall!

GEORGE COPWAY, Ojibwa spokesperson, 1860s, quoted in *Network*, Feb.-March 1990.

There is one thing you do not see at Niagara — literature. With some difficulty, at a few of the museums, you may obtain an indifferent guide-book, and the Hamilton and U.S. newspapers are cried about by newsboys when the mail trains come in; but, beyond skimming through the telegrams, nobody reads at Niagara. You may lounge, you may loafe, you may saunter, you may moon, you may potter, you may eat lotuses, you may smoke, you may enjoy your *kef*, you may flirt, you may dance, you may drink; but you must not, or rather you cannot, study. There is a great open book before you, a book whose pages are infinite, whose lore is untold, and whose teaching is Eternal.

> GEORGE AUGUSTUS SALA, British journalist and traveller, *My Diary in America in the Midst of War* (1865).

They say that I am here to go over the falls, swim the rapids and dozens of other foolhardy exploits which can be performed only at the risk of one's life. I have taken great risks but that was earlier in my stage career. I am past that. . . . We're not here to flirt with the Fates.

> HARRY HOUDINI, magician and escape artist, explaining to a reporter from *The Niagara Falls Gazette* that he was attempting nothing dangerous while filming *The Man from Beyond* (1921), a feature-length film in which Houdini daringly rescues a damsel from the brink of the Falls; quoted by Dwight Whalen in *The Lady Who Conquered Niagara: The Annie Edson Taylor Story* (1990).

A mountain peak lit by the first light of dawn is superior to a slag heap in size and shape and design, but it is not conceited. Niagara Falls are unquestionably more impressive than the artifical cascade in Battersea Park, but they are singularly devoid of personal vanity.

> NOËL COWARD, theatrical personality, "Star Quality" (1951), *Star Quality: The Collected Stories of Noël Coward* (1987).

Someone said that if Niagara Falls were in Rhode Island, the English settlers would have pronounced it "Niffuls."

> WILLIAM LEAST HEAT MOON, native American writer and travel writer, *Blue Highways: A Journey into America* (1982).

I've seen the Grand Canyon in Arizona, Ayers Rock in Australia and some of the great natural sights in the world but I don't think that anything holds a candle to the magnificence, beauty and sheer power of Niagara Falls.

> EDWARD L. GREENSPAN, lawyer and native of Niagara Falls, Ont., "Incredible Ontario," *Ontario: The Inside Story* (1990).

Fame is fleeting, / Wealth unsure; / But Love and Niagara / Will both endure.

> Traditional verse quoted by Dwight Whalen in *Lover's Guide to Niagara* (1990).

Where is the boat that goes under the Falls? / At what time do you shut off the Falls? / Is Niagara Falls open after Labour Day? / I know we are in Ontario, but how do we get to Canada?

> Commonly asked questions compiled by the Niagara Falls Canada Visitor and Convention Bureau, *Niagara Parks Press: A Newsletter for and about Niagara Parks Employees*, Sept. 1990.

NOISE

Certainly, sound is the stuff of a city's vitality, but it is also a partner in the sensory storm that can make city life untenable. Let us bring quiet and repose to the city — while we still have quiet and repose enough to do so.

> GRANT McCRACKEN, curator, Royal Ontario Museum, *The Globe and Mail*, 13 July 1990.

NORAD

> *See* NORTH AMERICAN
> AEROSPACE DEFENCE
> COMMAND

THE NORTH

> *See also* ARCTIC
> NORTH POLE
> NORTH-WEST PASSAGE
> NORTHWEST TERRITORIES
> YUKON TERRITORY

The Canadian north stands as one of the greatest areas of real promise for humanity today. After this war, when we settle down to really take this planet in hand for humanity, Canada will first come into her greatness.

> DONALD A. WOLLHEIM, U.S. science-ficiton editor, "Whither Canadian Fantasy?" *Uncanny Tales*, Dec. 1942.

In years to come, those who have seen the North will never forget it. There will be a hankering to return to a land in which life somehow seems closer to the ideal life, that mystical life of the Golden Age, when the Earth was young and the spirit of Man was the spirit of Youth.

> DOUGLAS LEECHMAN, anthropologist, *Eskimo Summer* (1945).

The more I see of the country, the less I feel I know about it. There is a saying that after five years in the north every man is an expert; after ten years, a novice.

> PIERRE BERTON, author, *The Mysterious North* (1956, 1989).

If the north has a soul, it is here in this empty land which, harsh though it is, has a beauty that no man who has not lived there a lifetime can really understand.

> PIERRE BERTON, author, *The Mysterious North* (1956, 1989).

We are all shaped by our environment and it is a theory of mine that one of the things that makes us a distinctive people, and I am certain that we are different from any other people in the world, is the presence of this great northern wilderness bearing down on us. Ninety per cent of us live within 200 miles of the American border, but there is not one of us who is not aware of the presence of the North. Every foreign observer who has come here has made that point. André Siegfried, years ago, called it "a window out onto infinity."

> PIERRE BERTON, author, address, Empire Club of Canada, Toronto, 11 Oct. 1973.

Looking back over the years I probably could have done better in a material sense had I stayed on the Outside. But nowhere could I have enjoyed the variety and spice of life to be had during that time lived in the far reaches of the country. It spanned the primitive to the jet age.

It was a privilege to know it before civilization took over and put an end to what will be remembered by only a few and never experienced by anyone again.

> ARCHIE HUNTER, Hudson's Bay Company trader in the Far North, 1924-59, *Northern Traders: Caribou Hair in the Stew* (1983).

It is no coincidence that our national emblem is not a rising sun, a star, a hammer, a sickle, or a dragon, but a beaver and a maple leaf. Nor is it coincidence that there are more paintings of wilderness lakes, spruce bogs, and pine trees on more Canadian living-room walls than in any other nation on earth. We may scoff, we may deny, but the wilderness mystique is still a strong element of Canadian ethos.

> BLAIR FRASER, journalist, quoted by Bob Wenman in the House of Commons, 16 Dec. 1974.

The Canadian direction is true north; that way lies the interior that must be mapped. I believe we will see it in our lifetime.

> RUDY WIEBE, novelist, Introduction, *Stories from Pacific and Arctic Canada* (1974) edited by Andreas Schroeder and Rudy Wiebe.

I do not suggest that you should all go out and buy a parka and put on a pair of mukluks and come North, any more than I would suggest that all Northerners should suddenly come to Southern Canada. If all our people came down to watch a Grey Cup Game out at the CNE during the football seasons, the place would be depopulated, and by the same token if the audience that was watching one of those Grey Cup spectaculars suddenly decided to come North you would double our population in one fell swoop!

> STUART M. HODGSON, N.W.T. Commissioner, address, Empire Club of Canada, Toronto, 13 March 1975.

Maybe we have begun to realize that we have something to learn from those who have gone north from southern Canada to make the north their home. And maybe it is time the metropolis listened to the voices on the frontier, time the metropolis realized it has something to learn from Old Crow and Hay River. Because what happens in the north will be of great importance to the future of our country. It will tell what kind of people we are.

> THOMAS BERGER, head of the Berger Inquiry, lecture at Queen's University, Kingston, Ont., quoted by Martin O'Malley in *The Past and Future Land: An Account of the Berger Inquiry into the Mackenzie Valley Pipeline* (1976).

Make no mistake, the environmental issues at stake cannot be sloughed off. Remember, the north really is our last frontier: After we have passed this frontier, there is no other frontier beyond.

> THOMAS BERGER, head of the Berger Inquiry, address, Empire Club of Canada, Toronto, 19 May 1977.

Finally, when the northern latitudes of the planet were engulfed by another ice age, Canadians were the last to know.

> ERIC NICOL, humorist, *Canada Cancelled Because of Lack of Interest* (1977) illustrated by Peter Whalley.

The culture shock of going north is not leaving civilization behind, but finding it there when you arrive, after hours flying over large empty wilderness.

> HEATHER MENZIES, journalist, *The Railroad's Not Enough: Canada Now* (1978).

Well, the North is to Canada as the Outback is to Australia, and as the sea was to Melville, and as . . . let me see now, as Africa is, shall we say, to *Heart of Darkness*. It's the place where you go to find something out. It's the place of the unconscious. It's the place of the journey or the quest.

> MARGARET ATWOOD, novelist, interviewed by Jim Davidson in Melbourne, Australia, in 1978, *Margaret Atwood: Conversations* (1990) edited by Earl G. Ingersoll.

It's country you can't walk in. / The dance will break your legs.

> M.T. (TERRY) KELLY, poet and novelist, "Danse Macabre," *Country You Can't Walk In and Other Poems* (1984).

He talks of Canada's North — one and a quarter times larger than India with fewer people than attend a New York Yankees baseball game. . . . Our two northern territories are by themselves larger than West Germany, France, Britain, Italy, Egypt, Austria, Spain, Portugal, and all the New England and Middle Atlantic states put together.

> ALLAN FOTHERINGHAM, columnist, referring to the U.S. correspondent Andrew H. Malcolm, *Capitol Offences: Dr. Foth Meets Uncle Sam* (1986).

This is the land where airplanes track icebergs the size of Cleveland and polar bears fly down out of the stars.

> BARRY LOPEZ, naturalist, *Arctic Dreams: Imagination and Desire in a Northern Landscape* (1986).

This could have been a family reunion. But then the Arctic is like that. Hundreds, even thousands of miles, may separate communities, but since the total population is so minute it is hardly surprising that the entire Territories feels and acts more like a village than a sub-continent larger than India.

> STEPHEN BROOK, English travel writer, *Maple Leaf Rag: Travels across Canada* (1987).

The north focuses our anxieties. Turning to face north, we enter our own unconscious. Always, in retrospect, the journey north has the quality of dream.

> MARGARET ATWOOD, novelist, "True North," *Saturday Night*, Jan. 1987.

For a moment I was scared and very cold;

then I was ecstatic with my newfound freedom. Agnes directed me and we began to
fly with no effort except the outward vision of our intent. Before I knew what was
happening we were in the Far North. I
recognized the high pine trees and the
vast rolling tundra of Canada. I had forgotten about Santa Barbara, the dolphins,
and dreaming.

> LYNN V. ANDREWS, California-based au-
> thor, *Crystal Woman: The Sisters of the
> Dreamtime* (1987). Andrews has devoted
> a series of "spiritual memoirs" to describ-
> ing or dramatizing the effects of her initi-
> ation into "the Sisterhood of the Shields"
> as a disciple of Agnes Whistling Elk who
> is presented as "a North American Indian
> from Manitoba, Canada" who may or may
> not be a Cree medicine-woman from
> Northern Manitoba. In this passage she
> "flies" from Australia to the Canadian
> North.

I just finished writing an essay called "The
Country North of Canada." I heard an Ath-
abaskan guy two years ago say to me, "Oh,
you're travelling down into Canada." And
I knew what he meant, and part of it was
the language, an idiosyncratic way of putting it, but there's obviously more than
one Canada. He meant I was going down
into the city. I was going down into Winnipeg.

> HOWARD   NORMAN,   Vermont-based
> writer who sets much of his fiction in
> northern Canada, "A Direction of the
> Soul," *What*, Dec. 1989.

NORTH AMERICA
See also AMERICA
CANADA
MEXICO
NORTH & SOUTH
UNITED STATES OF
AMERICA

God does not like the present name of our
continent. It is not Americo who planted
the cross on the soil of the New World, but
Christopher Columbus. And the divine
will is that this continent be called "Beau-

tiful Columbia" in honour of the good
Christian and great man who discovered it.

> LOUIS RIEL, Métis leader and mystic,
> diary entry, 17-18 Oct. 1885, *The Diaries
> of Louis Riel* (1976) edited by Thomas
> Flanagan.

Praise be to God! I find these two great
American nations highly capable and advanced in all that appertains to progress
and civilization. These governments are
fair and equable. The motives and purposes of these people are lofty and inspiring.

> 'ABDU'L-BAHÁ, Persian religious leader
> and living exemplar of the Bahá'í life, ad-
> dress, St. James Methodist Church, Mon-
> treal, 5 Sept. 1912; quoted in *'Abdu'l-Bahá
> in Canada* (1962), a book issued by the
> National Spiritual Assembly of the
> Baha'ís of Canada to commemorate the
> fiftieth anniversary of the Persian reli-
> gious leader's visit to Canada.

It has been agreed that a Permanent Joint
Board of Defence shall be set up at once
by the two countries.

> Twenty-one of the 109 words of "The
> Ogdensburg Declaration, August 18,
> 1940," reproduced in *Historical Docu-
> ments of Canada: Volume V: The Arts of
> War and Peace, 1914-1945* (1972) edited
> by C.P. Stacey.

Among other important matters, the President and the Prime Minister discussed
measures by which the most prompt and
effective utilization might be made of the
productive facilities of North America for
the purposes both of local and hemisphere defence and of the assistance
which in addition to their own programs
both Canada and the United States are
rendering to Great Britain and the other
democracies.

> First of six paragraphs of "The Hyde Park
> Declaration, April 20, 1941," reproduced
> in *Historical Documents of Canada: Vol-
> ume V: The Arts of War and Peace, 1914-
> 1945* (1972) edited by C.P. Stacey. Stacey
> noted that, like "The Ogdensburg Decla-

ration," this declaration "was nothing more than a press release." Yet Prime Minister Mackenzie King regarded the two documents as "the two greatest landmarks of our wartime co-operation."

We are inescapably North American. In the long run our Canadian civilization will be a North American one. It is foolish to hope for anything else. If we are eventually to satisfy ourselves that we have at last achieved a Canadian identity, it will be only when we are satisfied that we have arrived at a better way of life than the Americans have. A better *American* way of life, not just a better way of life. Whether we have the capacity to reach that goal, nobody knows.
> F.H. UNDERHILL, political scientist, *The Image of Confederation* (1964).

The great community of the Americans cannot be complete without the participation of Canada.
> RICHARD M. NIXON, U.S. President, joint meeting of the Senate and the House of Commons, 14 April 1972.

That North America is a sick society seems to the author to be indisputable. The fact that many of the privileged among its ranks do not acknowledge it to be so is probably the most damning and serious indictment of all.
> JOHN CRISPO, political scientist, *The Public Right to Know: Accountability in the Secretive Society* (1975).

It isn't annexation by the United States we have to resist now; it is creeping continentalism, the incorporation of Canada by suction into an entity called North America.
> JOHN W. HOLMES, diplomat and author, *Canada: A Middle-Aged Power* (1976).

Together we will stand as an example. As we work to keep the spirit of co-operation fresh, we will continue to respect each other's sovereignty, recognize our distinct national interests, maintain our individual commitments to great self-sufficiency.

> RONALD REAGAN, U.S. President, address, state dinner, Ottawa, 10 March 1981, quoted in *The Globe and Mail* the following day.

"The United States of North America" has an ominous ring to it. Like Manifest Destiny.
> KEITH DAVEY, Senator, *The Rainmaker: A Passion for Politics* (1986).

Canadians who wish to be distinguished from Americans have asked that citizens of the neighbouring republic (the U.S.A.) be called Usasians. Or Statics. Neither name has caught on.
> ERIC NICOL and DAVE MORE, humorists, *The U.S. or Us: What's the Difference, Eh?* (1986).

Canadians and Americans are both North Americans — "co-tenants of the continent" in Opposition Leader John Turner's neat phrase. The continent shapes both of our characters; it makes us co-jointly a people accustomed to space, to newness, to the constancy of change.
> RICHARD GWYN, correspondent, address, *Cultural Sovereignty: Myth or Reality? Proceedings of the 28th Annual Seminar on Canadian-American Relations, University of Windsor, Windsor, 5-7 Nov. 1986* (1987) edited by James Chacko.

Whether or not Canadians have or have not achieved a better way of North American life is beside the point. The point instead is that Canadians have achieved a quite different way of North American life. It is our way, we invented it, nurtured it, refashioned it. I have not the slightest idea which — Canada's great civility, the United States' great creativity — is the better way of life. My certitude and thesis resides only in the fact that it is a quite different North American way of life.
> RICHARD GWYN, correspondent, address, *Cultural Sovereignty: Myth or Reality? Proceedings of the 28th Annual Seminar on Canadian-American Relations, University of Windsor, Windsor, 5-7 Nov. 1986* (1987) edited by James Chacko.

I'm not fully prepared to address it yet. I'm fundamentally not for protectionism. I'm for free trade, but fair trade. Some of these agreements have lent themselves to corporations profiting, but not workers working. I have an interest in forming a proper trade agreement with Mexico as well. One idea I've been promoting is a Pan-American energy alliance — Canada, Mexico, the United States, South America. A hemispheric energy policy for hemispheric energy security.

> JESSE JACKSON, U.S. Democrat, quoted in *Maclean's*, 7 March 1988.

NORTH AMERICAN AEROSPACE DEFENCE COMMAND

Canadian participation in the North American Aerospace Defence Command (NORAD) is neither necessary for, nor consistent with, the non-offensive peacetime management of Canadian territory.

> Project Ploughshares for the Citizens' Inquiry into Peace and Security, *What Makes Canada Secure: Background Document for the Citizens' Inquiry into Peace and Security in Canada* (1991).

NORTH & SOUTH

See also The NORTH

Our economies in the North are now dependent on the economies of the South.

> IVAN HEAD, director, International Development Research Centre, quoted by Judy Steed in *The Globe and Mail*, 28 May 1988.

NORTH ATLANTIC TREATY ORGANIZATION

I bear solemn witness to the fact that NATO heads of state and of government meet only to go through the tedious motions of reading speeches, drafted by others, with the principal objective of not rocking the boat.

> PIERRE ELLIOTT TRUDEAU, former Prime Minister, first major address on leaving office, accepting the Albert Einstein International Peace Prize, Washington, D.C., quoted in *The New York Times*, 14 Nov. 1984.

As a Canadian, can I feel guiltless? Certainly not. we could have pulled out of NATO, helped to unalign the world. We could have opened more doors in North America to Russia. Canadians could have become aggressive mediators between ideologies that we already straddled.

> LESLEY CHOYCE, author, *December Six: The Halifax Solution — An Alternative to Nuclear War* (1988).

Some of those bombs weigh over a thousand pounds, and they make huge craters in the ground; one we saw was over seven feet deep. They drop into rivers, and destroy beaver dams.

> BART BENASHUE, Innu hunter, reacting to the sight of a CFB/NATO bombing range in Labrador, traditional home of the Innu, threatened by low-level jet combat training flights, fall 1988; quoted by Daniel Ashini in "David Confronts Goliath: The Innu of Ungava versus the NATO Alliance," *Drumbeat: Anger and Renewal in Indian Country* (1989) edited by Boyce Richardson.

Few places contribute more to NATO's warmaking power than the industrial complex that stretches around the western edge of Lake Ontario from Oshawa to Rochester. The Russians will not be inclined to spare the northern two-thirds of the complex because it happens to fly a red and white flag instead of a red, white, and blue one.

> DAVID FRUM, essayist, "Why She Needs the Bomb," *The Idler*, May-June 1990.

Withdrawal is a much more realistic option than many people think. Contrary to common assertions, leaving NATO would enable Canada to reduce the size of its military forces. It would not cost Canada more money to "go it alone."

> Project Ploughshares for the Citizens' Inquiry into Peace and Security, *What*

Makes Canada Secure: Background Document for the Citizens' Inquiry into Peace and Security in Canada (1991).

NORTH POLE
See also The NORTH

At present I am reading *Farthest North* by [Norwegian explorer Fridtjof] Nansen. It reads like romance. . . . Nansen was exploring the fastnesses of the polar sea and getting nearer than any other man ever did to that mysterious bourne so many have tried to reach but never have reached. It would be rash to say that no one ever will. I certainly think someone will some day. There are few chances for immortality nowadays but this is one of them. Early remembrance is assured to the man who reaches the North Pole. It seems odd to think of it, too. It will do nobody any good. But it will satisfy human curiosity on that point and as it is human curiosity that has accomplished almost everything of value it deserves to be indulged in some of its whims.

L. M. MONTGOMERY, author, journal entry, 1 May 1900, Cavendish, P.E.I., *The Selected Journals of L.M. Montgomery: Volume I: 1889-1910* (1985) edited by Mary Rubio and Elizabeth Waterston.

Our presence at the North Pole was important, not only to science and technology. The North Pole Project confirmed that Canada has a capability to put small teams of divers anywhere below its Arctic Ocean. If these waters are truly Canadian, and their management our responsibility, then we must have the capability to operate above and below the ice.

JOSEPH MacINNIS, scientist and undersea explorer, address, Empire Club of Canada, Toronto, 26 Feb. 1976. The North Pole Project of the Arctic IV Expedition landed a team of scientists led by Dr. MacInnis at the North Pole. They remained "at the top of the world" for 63 hours in April 1974 where they performed the first dives beneath the Arctic ice.

I often think of the great play by Imre Madách, the nineteenth-century Hungarian poet and dramatist, *The Tragedy of Man*. It is based on the Faust legend and starts with Adam and Eve and finishes with the end of the world. The world gradually shrinks until finally life is possible only at the North Pole, and in a scene with Eskimos one asks the other why life is so difficult. The answer is "There are too many Eskimos and not enough seals." It has gone into the language as a catchphrase and sums up life in Budapest at that time very well: in other words, too many talents and not enough opportunities.

MIKLÓS RÓZSA, Hungarian-American composer, *Double Life* (1982, 1989).

This made me see the town in a different light again. When I next looked from my windows upon that stupendous wilderness, hazed in the morning by steam rising Arthurianly from the surface of the lake, radiant in the evening with the dim, pale glow of the Arctic sun — now in my romantic way I fancied the little city of Somba K'é truly returned to its sovereign origins, liberated from all interferences and embarrassments, as one of the capitals of a circumpolar federation, a federation of the top of the world. Its peoples would be bound by a common spirituality, and its envoys would assemble from their fishing settlements, their trappers' hamlets, their ice-camps and mining towns around the perimeter of the Arctic, at their symbolic apex, the North Pole itself. Why not? The bush pilots could find it.

JAN MORRIS, Anglo-Welsh travel writer, "Wild Blue-Yonder City," *Saturday Night*, Nov. 1989. Somba K'é is the Dene name for Yellowknife, N.W.T.

NORTH-WEST PASSAGE
See also The NORTH

There is nothing worth living for but to have one's name inscribed on the Arctic chart.

ALFRED, LORD TENNYSON, Poet-laureate of Great Britain, during the search for the Franklin Expedition, quoted by Pierre Berton in *The Arctic Grail: The Quest for the North West Passage and the North Pole, 1818-1909* (1988).

We might consider internationalizing the Northwest Passage in exchange for demilitarization of the Arctic.
WILLIAM THORSELL, journalist, contributor to *If I Were Prime Minister* (1987) edited by Mel Hurtig.

Ah, for just one time, I would take the Northwest Passage / To find the hand of Franklin reaching for the Beaufort Sea, / Tracing one warm line through a land so wide and savage, / And make a Northwest Passage to the sea. // How then am I so different from the first men through this way? / Like them I left a settled life, I threw it all away / To seek a Northwest Passage at the call of many men, / To find there but the road back home again.
STAN ROGERS, singer and composer, "Northwest Passage," *Northwest Passage* (Fogarty's Cove Music, 1981).

NORTHWEST TERRITORIES
See also The NORTH
YELLOWKNIFE

I need the Northwest Territories, although I feel no urgent desire to explore them, and when a foreign icebreaker questions Canadian sovereignty in the North, that icebreaker is, in a sense, invading my brains.
JOHN GRAY, composer and performer, Preface, *Local Boy Makes Good: Three Musicals* (1987).

NORWAY

A movie with Paul Muni called *Commandoes Strike at Dawn* was filmed on Vancouver Island, using Canadian soldiers, sailors, and airmen in supporting roles, but it was about the war in Norway. Vancouver Island's countryside was thought to closely resemble Norway's, even down to

the fjords. The hand-to-hand fighting was all done by commando-trained Canadian soldiers, who played both British and Germans (but not Canadians).
MARY PEATE, memoirist, recalling seeing British and American feature films in Montreal in the 1940s, *Girl in a Sloppy Joe Sweater: Life on the Canadian Home Front during World War Two* (1989)

NOSTALGIA

One cannot be certain whether man is the only animal capable of nostalgia, but having in mind his well-developed capacity for self-deception, one might suspect that he is.
JOHN A. LIVINGSTON, naturalist, *One Cosmic Instant: A Natural History of Human Arrogance* (1973).

Meanwhile, ensconce me in a Toronto penthouse with room service and all mod cons and I'll monger you reams of rustic nostalgia until the cows come home and the chickens to roost at the 28th storey.
RAY GUY, humorist, "Country Comfort's a Penthouse in the City," *Ray Guy's Best* (1987).

NOVA SCOTIA
See also CAPE BRETON ISLAND
HALIFAX
MARITIME PROVINCES

One thistle, stickant; one fisherman, hookant; and one Bluenose, drippant.
Tongue-in-cheek motto for the Province of Nova Scotia devised by actor and writer TOMMY TWEED for a play on CBC Radio's "Stage 50" series.

When *Nova Scotia* was first peopled, I remember a letter, published under the character of a New Planter, who related how much the climate put him in mind of Italy.
SAMUEL JOHNSON, English man-of-letters, *A Journey to the Western Islands of Scotland* (1985) edited by J.D. Fleeman. The letter in question, written by a settler

at Chebucto Harbour, appeared in *Gentlemen's Magazine*, Oct. 1749.

Nova Scotia is old and rugged and bears the scars of long battling with the cruel sea but her latch string is ever out for those who wish to know her byways and it is in the smaller places that visitors will get nearest her heart.
WILL R. BIRD, author, *Off-Trail in Nova Scotia* (1956).

Novelist Hugh MacLennan once swore he heard a Customs inspector in Halifax tell disembarking passengers, "Nova Scotians in Aisle A, aliens and Canadians in Aisle B."
HARRY BRUCE, essayist, "Maritimers are Like a Motorcycle Gang," *Down Home: Notes of a Maritime Son* (1988).

No part of Nova Scotia is more than thirty miles from the sea, and three-quarters of all bluenosers live within six miles of salt water.
HARRY BRUCE, essayist, "The Land's Lousy — and Unforgettable," *Down Home: Notes of a Maritime Son* (1988).

Walk through her green fields, go down to the sea / The fortune in your eyes is more like a dream / She's called Nova Scotia and she so makes you feel / You'll discover a treasure no other has seen.
RITA MacNEIL, performer, "She's Called Nova Scotia" (1986), quoted by Ellen Schwartz in *Born a Woman: Seven Canadian Women Singer-Songwriters* (1988).

They say that Nova Scotians spend the first twenty years of their lives trying to get away and all the rest of it trying to get back.
KELVIN OGILVIE, research chemist raised in Nova Scotia, quoted by Kelly Toughill in *The Toronto Star*, 15 April 1990.

You do a lot of dreaming when you live on a body of water like that. I would sit on the edge of the water and my mind would travel great distances. Eventually I figured

out that science was a way I could sail my own seas.
KELVIN OGILVIE, research chemist raised in Nova Scotia, quoted by Kelly Toughill in *The Toronto Star*, 15 April 1990.

NUCLEAR ARMS
See also NUCLEAR ENERGY
NUCLEAR WASTE

The hydrogen bomb is history's exclamation point. It ends an age-long sentence of manifest violence.
MARSHALL McLUHAN, communications theorist, quoted in *Instant Quotation Dictionary* (1969) compiled by Donald O. Bolander, Dolores D. Varner, Gary B. Wright, and Stephanie H. Greene.

The greatest danger of nuclear war . . . stems from the fatalism of those who believe that the actions required to avert disaster can only be taken after the meaning of a nuclear cataclysm has been made fully apparent — forged in the fire of the holocaust. This view denies the very elements in a civilization — such as human compassion and creativity — that make it worth saving.
JOHN C. POLANYI, scientist and peace activist, *The Dangers of Nuclear War* (1979).

I believe that the question of disarmament is the most pressing practical, moral and spiritual issue of our times.
MARGARET LAURENCE, novelist, Foreword, *Canada and the Nuclear Arms Race* (1983) edited by Ernie Regehr.

Human society now possesses the terrible ability to destroy all life on Earth and our planet itself. Can anyone who has ever marvelled at the miracle of creation — who has ever borne or fathered a beloved child, who has ever looked closely at a tree or a plant or a river — fail to feel concerned and indeed anguished, every single day, at this thought?
MARGARET LAURENCE, novelist, address, Trent University, Peterborough,

Ont., 29 March 1983; published in *The Globe and Mail*, 10 Jan. 1989.

In the event of a nuclear exchange, our capital city would be thirty minutes away from destruction by a modern ICBM. Canadian land and lives lie directly below the path of any polar strike between the superpowers. We are the second largest country in the world, with nearly ten million square kilometres, and all that would be a battleground if the catastrophe we are seeking to prevent in fact occurred.

JOE CLARK, Secretary of State, address in Vienna, Austria, 5 Nov. 1986.

No serious person today can be heard to argue that a war between combatants armed with hydrogen bombs could be justified as a means of settling national differences, because allowing such an event the differences would no longer be of the slightest interest.

JOHN C. POLANYI, scientist and peace activist, address, Empire Club of Canada, Toronto, 27 Nov. 1986.

I had known intellectually that the military never counted the costs in dollars and cents, but that afternoon it finally hit me that when it comes to building nuclear bombs, the military doesn't count the cost in human lives. And from that time on I really started to look for the people in every part of the nuclear weapons cycle, the hidden people, for whom World War III has already started. The military doesn't count the cost in human lives.

ROSALIE BERTELL, Grey Nun of the Sacred Heart and peace activist, quoted by Robert Del Tredici in *At Work in the Fields of the Bomb* (1987).

The greatest threat to Canada in our time is not a reassertion of Russian claims to Alaska with further threats to the Yukon and Whitehorse down to Edmonton. The greatest threat is of nuclear devastation by the superpowers — devastation of themselves and of all the countries, Canada being a prominent example, that lie in

between. I would like to see Canada as a strong voice of reason and calm in the face of this danger.

JOHN KENNETH GALBRAITH, author and economist, "Canadian Customs," *Saturday Night*, Jan. 1987.

So in the end it comes down to this: nuclear weapons are the world's biggest Rorschach ink-blot test. They are the perfect projection screen for the fears and illusions of nations, corporations, armies, and the employees of the world's industrial-military complex. What an incredible admission — all these weapons exist as a *psychological ploy*, a figment of our imagination, dispensing money, power, prestige, and dominance.

RICHARD HANDLER, writer, *Canadian Institute for International Peace and Security Magazine*, Spring 1987, quoted by Peter Gzowski in *The New Morningside Papers* (1987).

It would be an act unprecedented in human history for two nations with profound unresolved differences to agree to set aside a large portion of their weaponry. "Our differences remain," they would be saying, "but we shall, because we must, settle them without resort to such weapons."

JOHN C. POLANYI, scientist and peace activist, address, Governor General's Conference, Calgary, 30 May 1987.

How many people die every year for this program? If you count everybody from the uranium miners and millers and transport people to the ones that run the reactors, separate the plutonium, make the bombs and test them, and the people downwind, and the people that put up with the radioactive waste at every part of the cycle — how many deaths per year are required to build this number of nuclear weapons?

ROSALIE BERTELL, Grey Nun of Sacred Heart and peace activist, questioning the conventional wisdom of programs of nuclear preparedness during a briefing on nuclear warfare sponsored by the U.S.

State Department; quoted by Robert Del Tredici in *At Work in the Fields of the Bomb* (1987). "There was great silence on the stage, and everybody just looked at the person next to him as if to say, 'Who's going to answer that one?' Finally Paul Warnke came over very quickly to the microphone and he said, 'That's not our department.'"

As an immediate step, Canada should declare itself a nuclear-free zone and, like New Zealand, should prohibit any nation, not just the United States, from visiting or transiting our territory with nuclear-armed ships or aircraft. We should also refuse to be the testing ground for cruise missiles. And until nuclear reactors are assuredly accident-proof (and especially until a means of safely storing nuclear wastes throughout their lengthy half-life cycle has been found), we should place a moratorium on them.

DAVE BARRETT, politician, contributor to *If I Were Prime Minister* (1987) edited by Mel Hurtig.

A nuclear-weapon-free-zone is a defined geographic area within which the possession, deployment, storage, transit, manufacture, testing or other support of nuclear-weapons systems is prohibited.

ERNIE REGEHR, defence specialist and peace activist, "The Way Out: Canada as a Nuclear-Weapon-Free-Zone," *The Road to Peace* (1988) edited by Ernie Regehr and Simon Rosenblum.

It is safer to live in Costa Rica rather than in the United States, or in Finland rather than in the Soviet Union, except that Nuclear Winter is the great equalizer.

ANATOL RAPOPORT, psychologist and peace activist, address, University of Toronto, 20 Jan. 1988.

We were the first generation in the whole world to know that humankind had the power to destroy itself, all other creatures, and the planet on which we lived. Many of us have struggled against the awful, the unconscionable, nuclear arms race. We have not been prevented from going on, marrying, having our children, doing our life's work. Yet that shadow has, for us, always been there and will always be there.

MARGARET LAURENCE, novelist, *Dance on the Earth: A Memoir* (1989).

Let us pray that they [nuclear physicists] will restrain themselves from reaching out for the holy grail of experimental physics, the production of conditions like those which existed in our universe's earliest moments. While such conditions could superbly display the workings of a Theory of Everything whose formula could be written on a T-shirt, there might very soon be no one left alive to describe them.

JOHN LESLIE, philosopher, University of Guelph, "Risking the World's End," *Bulletin of the Canadian Nuclear Society*, May-June 1989.

The real world is hearing a message that is still only whispered within the confines of Pugwash — namely, that nuclear weapons are in the process of regulating not only nuclear war but war itself to the junk heap of history.

JOHN C. POLANYI, scientist and peace activist, address, Pugwash International Conference, reported in *The Globe and Mail*, 28 July 1989.

NUCLEAR ENERGY

Most of the uranium in North America, particularly in Canada, is on native lands; it's native people that are living with the consequences of uranium mining. They have sacrificed the native people of this country, of North America, for what they consider progress.

ADELE RATT, activist, "An Interview with Adele Ratt" (1986) conducted by Shari Dunnet, *Up and Doing: Canadian Women and Peace* (1989) edited by Janice Williamson and Deborah Gorham.

I've always been very interested in gap phenomenon, or field phenomenon. I think that's the magic of the technology of our century — the invisible forces which operate with no tangible effect, but which are very "heavy." Radiation is the same sort of thing — you can't see it, but it's very "heavy." Our generation has been brought up with a fear of this invisible enemy, or at least knowing that things invisible can affect you very deeply.

Which is not a fear that has been intrinsic to humans in the past.
> CHRISTOPHER DEWDNEY, poet, interviewed by Peter O'Brien in *So to Speak: Interviews with Canadian Writers* (1987).

NUCLEAR WASTE

Suppose our ancestors had discovered nuclear power in the middle ages, and had decided to bury their radioactive fuel. . . .
> MARJORIE LAMB, ecologist, *Two Minutes a Day for a Greener Planet* (1990).

OBSCENITY
See also CENSORSHIP

Obscenity laws are intrinsically unfair. The present clauses in the Criminal Code describe as criminally obscene a number of portrayals of sexuality in what the law calls an "undue" degree. It has taken our courts about thirty years to come to rough, uneven, mystic consensus about what "undue" means. Recently, Judge Stephen Borins startled that consensus by deciding, quote "the standard run-of-the-mill sexual intercourse," end quote, which he described as cunnilingus, oral and anal sex, and lesbianism, did not offend "community standards." Masturbation, however, does offend community standards except in Manitoba, where the Faculty of Medicine of the University of Manitoba was permitted, after an initial dispute with customs, to import a sex-therapist training film on masturbation.
> JUNE CALLWOOD, civil liberties advocate, address, Empire Club of Canada, Toronto, 2 Feb. 1984.

You may debate the merits of a malevolent obscenity; if someone calls your mother a whore, that's not a fit subject for debate.
> W. GUNTHER PLAUT, rabbi and author, quoted by A. Alan Borovoy in *The Globe and Mail*, 27 Feb. 1989.

OCEANS

And this is the longing, the distance between / an Atlantic memory and a Pacific dream.
> BILL HOWELL, poet, "Dancers in the Distance," *Moonlight Saving Time* (1990).

OCTOBER CRISIS
See also SEPARATISM

We're the FLQ!
> Cry of the two gunmen who kidnapped the British Trade Commissioner James Cross from his Westmount home in Montreal, 8:20 a.m., 5 Oct. 1970, quoted by Gail el Baroudi in *The Toronto Star*, 5 Oct. 1980.

Now Know Ye that WE, by and with the advice of Our Privy Council for Canada, do by this Our Proclamation proclaim and declare that apprehended insurrection exists and has existed as and from the fifteenth day of October, one thousand nine hundred and seventy.
> The War Measures Act was invoked by the Federal Government on 16 Oct. 1970, thereby suspending civil liberties. The

order was signed at 4:00 a.m. by Gérard Pelletier as Secretary of State who a decade later admitted he did so "with death in my soul." The Act was superseded by Bill C-181 — Public Order (Temporary Measures) Act, 3 Dec. 1970, which was allowed to lapse, reinstating civil liberties to Canada.

Notwithstanding these conditions — partly because of them — it has been demonstrated now to us by a few misguided persons just how fragile a democratic society can be, if democracy is not prepared to defend itself, and just how vulnerable to blackmail are tolerant, compassionate people.
PIERRE ELLIOTT TRUDEAU, Prime Minister, statement read on national television presenting the government's reasons for invoking the War Measures Act earlier that day, CBC-TV, 16 Oct. 1970.

Q. Who won?
A. I did. Pierre Laporte lost.
The question was asked by a reporter and answered by JAMES CROSS, the British consular official whose kidnapping by the FLQ sparked the October Crisis, CBC-TV, 26 Oct. 1975. The Quebec Minister Pierre Laporte was strangled by the FLQ.

I just wanted to talk and talk and talk.
JAMES CROSS, British consular official, reaction on being freed after fifty-nine days of captivity in Montreal in 1970, recalled eight years later and reported by Gerald Clark in *The Globe and Mail*, 6 Dec. 1978.

We have been one hundred times accused, one hundred times judged summarily, one hundred times convicted without appeal by the political machine in power.
JACQUES COSSETTE-TRUDEL and LOUISE LANCTÔT, two of the FLQ terrorists who kidnapped and held James Cross hostage, appealing for clemency and permission to return to Canada from their self-imposed exile in Cuba and then

France. Their self-serving open letter was published in *Le Devoir*, 3 Jan. 1978.

Maybe our hands are dirty. They probably are. But no one can have clean hands in the world, not the way it is.
FRANCIS SIMARD, FLQ terrorist, implicated in the kidnapping and murder of Pierre Laporte, exculpating himself, *Talking It Out: The October Crisis from Inside* (1987) translated by David Homel.

OIL INDUSTRY
See also ARAB PEOPLE

It was an oil boom. Maybe the world's first oil boom.
JAMES TUCK, archaeologist, quoted by Harry Thurston in "The Basque Connection," *Equinox*, Nov.-Dec. 1983. He is referring to the whale-oil industry established early in the 15th century by Spanish Basque whalers on the coast of Labrador.

To date, not one drop of oil has been sold from the Beaufort and commercial production this decade is questionable. But a lasting impression has remained with me after several visits to the Arctic, a feeling of inevitability that oil *will* be extracted from the North.
JIM LYON, author, *Dome: The Rise and Fall of the House that Jack Built* (1985).

Lord, Please Send Me Another Oil Boom and I Promise I Won't Piss It Away.
Message on a bumpersticker noted in Calgary, Dec. 1987.

No other major oil-producing country is also a food exporter, though Canada would count it as an exception if the Canadian oil producers were not captive suppliers to the U.S. market. America is the only industrial power that is also a major oil producer.
ELIOT JANEWAY, U.S. economist, *The Economics of Chaos: On Revitalizing the American Economy* (1989).

OKA STANDOFF
See also INDIANS

I ask the prime minister to show leadership and to tear down the barricades that are surrounding our brothers and sisters in Oka. Hopefully other Canadians will join in that call to tear down the barricades. We hope we have the support of all Canadian people.
> ELIJAH HARPER, NDP Member of the Manitoba Legislative Assembly, referring to the Winnipeg solidarity march of 22 July 1990 in support of the Mohawk standoff at Oka, Que., quoted by Kevin Rollason in *The Winnipeg Free Press*, 23 July 1990.

On 11 March 1990, Mohawks on the Kanesatake Reserve at Oka, Que., had erected a road blockade to draw attention to their 273-year-old land claim and the expansion of the Oka Golf Club. Mohawks, led by the armed and disguised Warrior band, then erected a blockade across the Mercier Bridge which links the South Shore to the Island of Montreal.

Before the crisis was resolved by the Canadian Army in September, jokes abounded:
Q. How do you get to the Mercier Bridge? A. Follow the arrows.
Q. What's the favourite game of Indians after bingo? A. Bridge.
Q. What two crises did Prime Minister Mulroney face in 1990? A. The Gulf Crisis (in Kuwait) and the Golf Crisis (at Oka).

We have a prime minister who, like Nero, fiddles while Rome burns. Is he waiting for the right time to roll the dice again?
> SHARON CARSTAIRS, Manitoba Liberal leader, recalling Prime Minister Brian Mulroney's infamous boast that all Meech Lake required was "a roll of the dice" and placing it in the context of the Mohawk Standoff at Oka, Que.; quoted by Kevin Rollason in *The Winnipeg Free Press*, 23 July 1990.

A criminal organization.

Phrase used by HARRY SWAIN, Deputy Minister of Indian Affairs, to refer to the Mohawk's Warrior Society, which at the time was leading a military-style operation in Quebec. The characterization occurred during a so-called background news briefing session held in Ottawa on 23 July 1990, according to Tim Harper in *The Toronto Star* the following day. The session was supposed to be "off the record" but the CBC identified Swain as the speaker. According to Geoffrey York in *The Globe and Mail*, 24 July 1990, Swain also said that the Mohawks were an "armed gang" who had "hijacked" the negotiations. Later Thomas Siddon, Minister of Indian Affairs, repudiated Swain's opinions.

According to Robert Matas, writing in *The Globe and Mail* on 1 Aug. 1990, Thomas Siddon, Minister of Indian Affairs, in Vancouver, 31 July, called the Mohawk activities at the Oka barricade "criminal" and then rephrased his comments, calling the activities "suspended violations of the law."

Although English Canada bears some responsibility for Quebec's rigid reaction, the current confrontation between the Mohawks and the provincial police is only the most recent sign that the tribunes of the Republic of Quebec may prove even worse governors of minorities than those of the English system have been to Quebec.
> HUGH GRAHAM, columnist, *The Globe and Mail*, 15 Aug. 1990.

Canada must be the only country in the world where sending in federal troops to replace police is considered a means of de-escalating tension. Actually, the decision by Quebec Premier Robert Bourassa to ask for, and that by Prime Minister Brian Mulroney to agree to, the use of the army at the Oka standoff is a commentary of sorts on how low things have sunk in the country we all used to think could be an example to the world of civilized behaviour.

FRED CLEVERLEY, columnist, *The Winnipeg Free Press*, 13 Aug. 1990.

If somebody wanted to play golf on my mother's grave, I'd be a little upset.
GRAHAM GREENE, Iroqouis actor from the Six Nations Reserve, referring to the misuse of native lands which sparked the Oka Crisis, quoted by John Lévesque in *The Hamilton Spectator*, 29 Nov. 1990.

Aboriginal resentment at the use of the army and police will increase, not abate. Aboriginal memory will now be shaped and deepened by the events at Oka. Every native child will learn to see Kanesatake and Kahnawake as moments of pride, defiance, dignity, and determination by men and women who are prepared to die for land and rights. Some of this is mythology, of course, but mythologies shield against despair. Other Canadians cannot afford to meet this deepened sense of memory and myth with the arrogant amnesia of victors.
ROBERT M. CAMPBELL and LESLIE A. PAL, political scientists, *The Real Worlds of Canadian Politics: Cases in Process and Policy* (1991). The Oka Crisis of 1990 lasted from March 11 to September 17 — a total of 77 days.

OLYMPIC GAMES
See also JOHNSON, BEN

Americans lost billions in Vietnam, while we had the Olympics right in Montreal.
DAVE BROADFOOT, comedian, address, Empire Club of Canada, Toronto, 9 March 1978.

Share the Flame
Motto of the Olympic Torch Relay, sponsored by Petro-Canada, which brought the Olympic torch over a circuitous route of 18,000 kilometres over 88 days from Halifax to Calgary in the winter of 1987-88. The XVth Olympic Winter Games were opened in Calgary on 13 Feb. 1988.

Can't you feel it?
Title of the theme song of the XVth Winter Olympics. It was "the musical question asked most frequently, but never answered, during the Olympics," observed Brian Brennan in *The Calgary Herald*, 2 March 1988.

I've had dreams about this night. I'm so happy!
ELIZABETH MANLEY, figure skater, winning a Silver Medal at the Calgary Olympics, quoted in *Maclean's*, 7 March 1988.

The Gold is for my mother, for everyone and for Canada.
BEN JOHNSON, runner, after winning the 100-metre race in 9.79 seconds, at the Summer Olympics in Seoul, South Korea, 23 Sept. 1988, quoted by James Christie in *The Globe and Mail* the following day.

Anyone can break my world record. But the Gold Medal is mine.
BEN JOHNSON, statement made hours before learning the results of a routine drug test at the Summer Olympics, quoted by Murray Campbell in *The Globe and Mail*, 26 Sept. 1988.

It's not the only thing in life to win a Gold Medal. I still have my parents. My family still loves me.
BEN JOHNSON, Gold Medallist at the Summer Olympics, stripped of his title and medal after testing positive for anabolic steroids, 27 Sept. 1988, quoted by Paul Hunter in *The Toronto Star* the following day.

If winning a gold medal in Olympic competition is the only achievement worthy of recognition, then everything is permissible in order to win. Such a proposition is completely unacceptable.
CHARLES DUBIN, Ontario Chief Justice, report on the use of drugs in sport, quoted in *The Toronto Star*, 27 June 1990.

ONTARIO
See also TORONTO

Do you wish for fruit culture? Why, half Ontario is an orchard.

Views of Members of the British Association and Others: Information for Intending Settlers (Ottawa, 1884), a promotional publication quoted by Dave McIntosh in *When the Work's All Done This Fall: The Settling of the Land* (1989).

Ontario is the hardest province to grasp. Partly because of its size and the diversities of its dimensions. And because it represents the standard against which the other regions measure their differences. And because for many, Ontario *is* Canada.
> HEATHER MENZIES, journalist, *The Railroad's Not Enough: Canada Now* (1978).

Is there any place you'd rather be?
> Campaign slogan of the Conservative Party of Ontario under Premier William Davis from 1971 to 1985.

What is good for the economy of Ontario is good, ultimately, for all of Canada.
> WILLIAM DAVIS, Ontario Premier, remark made in 1979, quoted by Gail Harvey and Roy MacGregor in *Poli-Graphs* (1989).

Will there be room for crickets and butterflies and milkweed in the new southern Ontario of superhighways and sprawling suburbia?
> J.A.S. EVANS, classicist, "The Road to Crieff," *The Idler*, No. 27, Jan.-Feb. 1990.

OPERA
See also MUSIC

With this production of *Elektra* the Canadian Opera Company introduces the projection of "surtitles" on the proscenium arch above the stage. The English surtitles were prepared by Sonya Friedman.
> Note from the program for the COC's production of Richard Strauss's *Elektra*, O'Keefe Centre, Toronto, 21 Jan. 1983. Surtitles were introduced to the world of opera by the Canadian Opera Company. They are now widely used for the simultaneous translation of foreign-language theatrical and musical productions of all sorts.

Only apathy can silence the opera.
> Line from the advertisement placed by Wood Gundy in *Arias* (1985), sponsored by the Canadian Opera Women's Committee, as recalled by Isabel Warren in the editorial in *Arias* (1990).

I find it hard to believe that the world's greatest opera company will be performing in a hockey rink, on the grounds of a country fair, in the wild west of Canada.
> ERWIN SWANGARD, President of the Pacific National Exhibition, referring to the ten performances in Aug. and Sept. 1986 of Milan's La Scala opera company at the Orpheum Theatre and the Coliseum in Vancouver; quoted by Stephen Godfrey in *The Globe and Mail*, 20 March 1986.

The activities of government allegedly in support of culture are nothing so much as an attempt to subvert the choices consumers have already made about what they want in the way of culture. The reality pokes through the charade when we realize that the elaborate sound and light shows quite standard at a modern rock concert and which make even the most elaborate opera seem puny by comparison require no subsidy but reap a substantial profit for the performers.
> WALTER BLOCK and MICHAEL WALKER, economists with the Fraser Institute, *Lexicon of Economic Thought* (1989).

OPINION POLLS

All I had to do was what Martin Goldfarb told me.
> PIERRE ELLIOTT TRUDEAU, Prime Minister, remark made following the successful 1974 election campaign, run along lines recommended by the public opinion organization of Martin Goldfarb; quoted by Geoffrey Barley in *Toronto Life*, Jan. 1979.

In a non-democratic society, he is the voice of the people.
> STEPHEN CLARKSON, political scientist, commenting on the influence of non-elected advisors like Martin Goldfarb and on the notion of "Government by Gold-

farb" (in John Diefenbaker's phrase); quoted by Geoffrey Barley in *Toronto Life*, Jan. 1979.

Thanks to the three "G'"s of Canadian politics — Gallup, Gregg and Goldfarb — the cart has moved so far ahead of the horse as far as leadership goes that true vision will come today only out of the eccentricity of the people themselves, which given the state of the "ordinary Canadian" seems unlikely indeed.
ROY MacGREGOR, journalist, "Essay," *The Ottawa Citizen*, 12 April 1986.

The latest poll shows sixty per cent of Canadians think the Liberals will win the next election. The other forty per cent are Liberals.
Attributed to JOHN TURNER, Liberal leader, annual dinner, National Press Gallery, Ottawa, May 1988.

I try not to use the word "psychographics." More simply, people have a shared psychology and shared beliefs.
ALLAN GREGG, Decima Research Ltd., quoted by Joyce Nelson in *Sultans of Sleaze: Public Relations and the Media* (1989).

I can envision a new game-show program, with a winning award of $100,000, to the single Canadian who can prove not to have been interviewed by anyone by July 1.
ALLAN FOTHERINGHAM, columnist, *Maclean's*, 31 Dec. 1991.

OPINIONS

When I want your opinion, I'll give it to you.
HAROLD BALLARD, owner of Maple Leaf Gardens, rejecting advice offered to him by General Manager Gerry McNamara, noted on 1 Aug. 1986; quoted by Allan Safarik in *Quotations from Chairman Ballard* (1989).

The real problem was to "create consent" for the government's position, by disseminating information through a programme

of "strategic and highly targeted media relations." They recommended setting up a SWAT (Special Words and Tactics) team, to ensure that the public gets the government story, in a form unrecognizable as propaganda.
BOYCE RICHARDSON, journalist, discussing advice given the federal government on the handling of native land claims, "Concealed Contempt," *The Canadian Forum*, Dec. 1989.

OPPORTUNITY

People say we're opportunistic, and I hope so. I think that's a compliment.
SAMUEL BELZBERG, corporate head and corporate raider, accepting the 1985 Businessman of the Year Award from the Vancouver Chamber of Commerce, quoted in *The Globe and Mail's Report on Business Magazine*, Sept. 1990.

Some day your ship will come in and, with your luck, you'll probably be at the airport.
Sign posted on the wall at a seaman's club in Vancouver, quoted by Robert Matas in *The Globe and Mail*, 11 Feb. 1991.

OPPOSITION
See also GOVERNMENT

To the vacuum that has been created has come a process of what might be called "extra-parliamentary" opposition. Provincial governments and the media have tended to become the new opposition. The resolution of differences goes on increasingly not within Parliament but through the media. We have been reduced to government by polls, by thirty-second news clips, and by advertisement.
MICHAEL PITFIELD, Senator, address, Empire Club of Canada, Toronto, 20 Oct. 1983.

ORDER & DISORDER

Infinity appears as a manageable dimension. It is the street outside that seems unreasonable.

MAVIS GALLANT, author, "Paris: The Taste of a New Age" (1981), *Paris Notebooks: Essays and Reviews* (1986).

OTTAWA

See also PARLIAMENT

I forget now where we went next; possibly Ottawa, which I loved. It was the fall, and the maple woods were beautiful. We stayed in a private house with a middle-aged admiral, a charming man who had a most lovely Alsatian dog. He used to take me out driving in a dog-cart through the maple trees.

AGATHA CHRISTIE, young wife and future writer, referring to her husband Archibald Christie and their brief stay in Ottawa on a round-the-world trip following World War I, *Agatha Christie: An Autobiography* (1977).

Ottawa is still a company town, but it is a company of which you are shareholders.

MICHAEL PITFIELD, Senator, address, Empire Club of Canada, Toronto, 20 Oct. 1983.

Ennui-on-the-Rideau.

Epithetical description of the capital in relation to the Rideau River offered by columnist ALLAN FOTHERINGHAM in *Malice in Blunderland or How the Grits Stole Christmas* (1982).

And then there is Disneyland on the Rideau. Dear Ottawa, the city that fun forgot.

ALLAN FOTHERINGHAM, columnist and author, address, Empire Club of Canada, Toronto, 16 Oct. 1986.

At least in my fancy the hush of the back country penetrates Ottawa even now: sometimes in the very centre of the city I seem to enter an abrupt inexplicable silence, broken not by the thrum of traffic but only by the swish of forest winds.

JAN MORRIS, Anglo-Welsh travel writer,

"Government Town," *Saturday Night*, Jan. 1987.

I have never understood why Queen Victoria chose a national capital filled with civil servants.

Attributed to WILLARD ESTEY, Justice of the Supreme Court, by Charles Lynch in *The Lynch Mob: Stringing Up Our Prime Ministers* (1988).

Outside, the deepening orange of the autumn sunshine was turning the green copper roofs of the turreted stone government buildings to a transient shimmering gold, and I reflected, watching from the windows, that I'd much liked this graceful city when I'd been here before. I was filled with a serene sense of peace and contentment, which I remembered a few times in the days lying ahead.

DICK FRANCIS, British crime novelist, reflecting on the beauty of Ottawa in the fall, *The Edge* (1988).

No wonder the Canadian political system shows such a strong tendency toward sycophancy the higher one rises. The only way to get applause in this town is to pay for it.

ROY MacGREGOR, columnist, *The Ottawa Citizen*, 3 June 1988.

The first thing that strikes me is the gorgeous setting. I am very impressed. How odd to find myself awed in Ottawa.

CHARLES PACHTER, artist, responding to the sights of Ottawa, *The Toronto Star*, 24 Sept. 1988. Pachter turned his response into a tongue-twister: "Odd it is how awed was I as I eyed Ottawa!"

Q. Why is C like Ottawa?
A. Because it is the capital of Canada.

Conundrum collected by A. Ross Eckler, "The Letter Conundrum," *Words Ways: The Journal of Recreational Linguistics*, Feb. 1991.

PACIFIC OCEAN

We came to a little rill whose current descends to the Pacific Ocean. May God in His Mercy give me to see where its waters flow into the ocean, and return in safety.
DAVID THOMPSON, geographer, crossing the Great Divide, c. 1799, *Travels in Western North America, 1784-1812* (1971) edited by Victor G. Hopwood.

God wants the Pacific Ocean to bear the name of the chief of the Apostles and to be called "the Simon-Peter."
LOUIS RIEL, Métis leader and mystic, diary entry 17-18 Oct. 1885, *The Diaries of Louis Riel* (1976) edited by Thomas Flanagan.

PACIFIC RIM

I thought, when I moved to the West Coast, I would feel Western. Instead I feel Eastern, Far Eastern.
GEORGE RYGA, Alberta-born playwright, resident of Summerland, B.C., observation made to the present editor, summer 1964.

Incidentally, a community that has accustomed itself to learning a second language for the purpose of carrying on business abroad, as Quebec has, will probably be in a better position to adapt to the new Pacific economic reality, inclusive of new languages, than the unilingual Anglo-Canadians.
DONALD S. MACDONALD, diplomat, "Three Perspectives on Canada's Future," *Daedalus: Journal of the American Academy of Arts and Sciences*, "In Search of Canada," Fall 1988.

If we are to become the bicoastal/tricoastal nation that shares the promised prosperity of the Pacific Century, our Asian trading partners should be convinced that Canada recognizes it no longer has its front door on the Atlantic and its back door on the Pacific. We need to acknowledge two front doors — one on each coast. Building our West Coast fleet is a direct and useful way to prove just that.
PETER C. NEWMAN, columnist and author, *Maclean's*, 3 Oct. 1988.

Today, Canada is seeking secure membership in the community vaguely and unhelpfully called the Pacific Rim. Vancouver has become the nation's leading port. There is a feeling abroad, almost unchanged since my childhood, that the Pa-

cific nations will come to dominate the world and that this is a community to which Canada must at all costs belong, constructively (and profitably).
> F. KENNETH HARE, geographer, "Canada: The Land," *Daedalus: Journal of the American Academy of Arts and Sciences*, "In Search of Canada," Fall 1988.

Almost unnoticed, the centre of gravity of the global economy shifted from the Atlantic Ocean to the Pacific Ocean. This occurred in 1986, when, for the first time in modern history, the volume of trade across the Pacific exceeded that across the Atlantic. Since then, the Pacific trading nations have continued to storm ahead.
> FRANK FEATHER, futurologist, *G-Forces: Reinventing the World — The 35 Global Forces Restructuring Our World* (1989).

PACIFICISM
> *See also* NEUTRALISM &
> NEUTRALITY

Pacifism, the naive or cowardly efforts to extricate ourselves from our common North American destiny in a world of powerful totalitarianism, is a guaranteed road to war.
> JOSEF SKVORECKY, essayist and novelist, "Are Canadians Politically Naive?" (1983), *Talkin' Moscow Blues* (1988) edited by Sam Solecki.

PAIN
> *See also* SUFFERING

Good God, how I suffered. I wonder how I lived through it! Things are changed for the better now. Pain, even the fiercest, wears itself out, even though its *effects* must endure to the end of time — and perhaps through all eternity, if such there be for us as sentient creatures. And so I, some way or other, have come up from the depths, and am not minded to go back to them.
> L. M. MONTGOMERY, author, journal entry, 4 April 1899, Cavendish, P.E.I., *The Selected Journals of L.M. Montgomery, Vol-*

ume I: 1889-1910 (1985) edited by Mary Rubio and Elizabeth Waterston.

You will produce a Pauline Julien too when you have been hurt.
> Adapted from a remark made by LISE PAYETTE, hostess of Radio Canada's *Appelez-moi Lise*, referring to the chansonnière who sings of the anguish of Quebec, quoted by James Quig in *Weekend Magazine*, 30 Oct. 1976.

I don't bleed. The pin stuck in my flesh leaves only the hole that proves I am dead.
> ELIZABETH SMART, novelist and diarist, entry for 22 Dec. 1950, *Necessary Secrets: The Journals of Elizabeth Smart* (1986) edited by Alice Van Wart.

Back pain is just a tension headache that has slipped down the back.
> JOHN V. BASMAJIAN, psychologist, quoted in *Time*, 14 July 1980.

My left knee is seventy-two years old, too, and it doesn't hurt.
> Line spoken by a character in the play *A Place on Earth* (1982) by the playwright BETTY JANE WYLIE.

People have a very low pain threshold, especially if it's someone else's pain. It gets to be a bore.
> Line spoken by a principal character in the play *Mark* (1979) by the playwright BETTY JANE WYLIE.

PAINTING
> *See also* ART
> GROUP OF SEVEN

Feel truly, all the rest is eyewash.
> JOHN LYMAN, painter, characteristic remark recorded in 1931, quoted in the catalogue *John Lyman* (1963).

At Emma Lake make no mistake / We're very pro we'd have you know. / Clement Greenberg told us so.
> Ditty published in *Canadian Art*, May-June 1963, in response to the art criticism

of Clement Greenberg who influenced a school of painters associated with the summer school at Emma Lake, Sask. The New York critic stressed professionalism and advocated "post-painterly abstraction."

I have a song to sing — the best way I know how. If only six people listen — that's enough. I'm lucky — the six who listened and liked it are pretty keen on quality, and nothing short of top quality at that.
JACK BUSH, painter, quoted by William Withrow in *Contemporary Canadian Painting* (1972).

I'd like to get down and look at them pictures of barns and outbuildings done by them fellas that used to paint by numbers — what they call yer grope of seven. Tom Thomson, Jack Jackson, John Johnson and Jim Jimson. Now that'd be the kinda culture I could take.
DON HARRON, humorist, appearing as the rural character Charlie Farquharson on a commercial promoting the Art Gallery of Ontario, CBC Radio on 26 Oct. 1974.

Emily Carr . . . a painting woman worked out in B.C. puttin swirls before pine.
DON HARRON, humorist, punning on the art of Emily Carr, *Debunk's Illustrated Guide to the Canadian Establishment* (1984).

Those who would become successful collectors must develop one skill very early in their collecting careers — the ability to see through dirt!
ROBERT McMICHAEL, art collector and gallery founder, *One Man's Obsession* (1986).

I'm painting trees right now because I'm stuck in the city! If I lived in the bush I'd probably paint diesels.
MENDELSON JOE, painter and singer, quoted by Roy MacGregor in *The Ottawa Citizen*, 8 Jan. 1987.

If you look at them you get healed.
Attributed to the native artist NORVAL MORRISSEAU with reference to the magical and curative properties of the imagery of his paintings, recalled by the Jasper-based collector Galal Helmy and quoted by John Masters in *The Toronto Star*, 10 Sept. 1988.

Painting is an experience that has been given form.
JACK SHADBOLT, painter, quoted by Christopher Hume in *The Toronto Star*, 17 Feb. 1990.

PAPER
See PULP & PAPER

PARAPSYCHOLOGY
See also BELIEF

When the Mandans undertake to make it rain, *they never fail to succeed*, for their ceremonies never stop until rain begins to fall.
GEORGE CATLIN, traveller, *Letters and Notes on the North American Indians* (1841).

We live in a world where in every country there are millions of people subject to illusions too numerous to be even classified.
SIMON NEWCOMB, Maritime-born scientist and first President of the American Society for Psychical Research, "Modern Occultism" (1909), *A Skeptic's Handbook of Parapsychology* (1985) edited by Paul Kurtz.

I believe our laws of physics are imperfect; that there are things happening around us that are inexplicable in our present state of knowledge; and that it is the duty of science to investigate these facts and either explain them away or enlarge its own boundaries to include them.
R.S. LAMBERT, author and psychical researcher, "Are You Sure There Are No Ghosts?" *Maclean's*, 1 Dec. 1953.

The world is wide and there is much in it, and the mind is deep. Psychical research for all that anyone can say to the contrary may be as necessary in terms of insight as any other study, and may, in the end be more harmless and edifying.
> A.R.G. OWEN, scientist and parapsychologist, and Victor Sims, newspaperman, *Science and the Spook: Eight Strange Cases of Haunting* (1971).

Anomalous experience.
> GRAHAM REED, psychologist, York University, is credited with the coinage of the term *anomalous experience* to refer to an experience that is so odd that it is taken to be paranormal in origin, in his academic study *The Psychology of Anomalous Experience* (1972, rev. ed. 1988).

Parapsychology is that branch of scientific inquiry which is currently addressing itself to . . . existential questions.
> HOWARD EISENBERG, physician and researcher, *Inner Spaces: Parapsychological Explorations of the Mind* (1977).

In fact, most of what parapsychology is related to would have to be considered right hemisphere.
> MARSHALL McLUHAN, media philosopher, address called "PSI in the Global Vilage: Toward the Post-Electronic Age," *Inner Life: Toronto's Aquarina Age Newsletter*, June-Aug. 1977.

Every psychic I know or have heard of is an absolute fraud.
> HENRY GORDON, magician and skeptic, *ExtraSensory Deception: ESP, Psychics, Shirley MacLaine, Ghosts, UFOs* (1987).

I am a congenital misfit. The cosmos blooped when I was made and where other men are glued with Krazy Glue to the time continuum, I'm connected with the time continuum with a very stretchable rubber band. That is why I can move forwards and backwards and outside and into parallel time.
> SWAMI NARAYANA, Mississauga-based psychic, quoted by Kaye Corbett in *The Toronto Sun*, 9 Jan. 1988.

There is a tiny psychic and a tiny skeptic in each one of us.
> JOHN ROBERT COLOMBO, author and editor, weighing reports of unexplained phenomena, quoted by Robin Rowland, *Now*, 25 Aug. 1988.

A century of parapsychological research has gone by, and the evidence for psi is no more convincing than it was a century ago.
> JAMES E. ALCOCK, psychologist and critic of parapsychological claims, *Science and Supernature: A Critical Appraisal of Parapsychology* (1990).

PARENTS
See also FAMILY

If you don't talk back to your parents they'll never learn anything.
> DON HARRON, comic, quoted by Martha Harron in *A Parent Contradiction* (1988).

If ever there was an oxymoron, it's the single parent.
> BETTY JANE WYLIE, author, *All in the Family: A Survival Guide for Living and Loving in a Changing World* (1988).

No one with children can remain completely virtuous.
> ROBIN SKELTON, man-of-letters, aphorism, May 1990.

PARIS
See also FRANCE

I must point out that on Blvd. Montparnasse one day after leaving Montreal, I felt more at home than in Montreal, a city which I have never liked because it has no real character, but an hybrid one. Difficult to explain: with these Frenchmen I felt like them and at the same time, very different. Our reactions, our language, our humour was the same, but they seem to lack the optimistic wisdom and youth I felt in myself when comparing it to them.

ROGER LEMELIN, novelist, writing a letter in English to his publishers, McClelland & Stewart, 15 Sept. 1950, quoted by Clara Thomas and John Lennox in *William Arthur Deacon: A Canadian Literary Life* (1982).

PARKS

National parks are maintained for all the people — for the ill, that they may be restored, for the well, that they may be fortified and inspired by the sunshine, the fresh air, the beauty, and all the other healing, ennobling, and inspiring agencies of Nature.

National Parks exist in order that every citizen of Canada may satisfy a craving for Nature and Nature's beauty; that we may absorb the poise and restfulness of the forests; that we may steep our souls in the brilliance of the wild flowers and the sublimity of the mountain peaks; that we may develop in ourselves the buoyancy, the joy, and the activity we see in the wild animals; that we may stock our minds with the raw material of intelligent optimism, great thoughts, noble ideas; that we may be made better, happier and healthier.
JAMES B. HARKIN, First Commissioner of National Parks (1911-36), *Welcome to National Parks* (Environment Canada, 1986).

One of the moments that gave me the greatest pleasure was flying over the beautiful fjords near Pangnirtung on Baffin Island. I was like a kid. I'd been there a few times before and had to tell everyone on the plane, "Look, look, you have to see this." I sat down next to my wife and said, "You love it, eh?" She said it was beautiful. I said, "I will make it a national park for you."
On Monday I went into my office and consulted with the Minister of Indian Affairs, who was me; I consulted with the Minister of Northern Affairs, who was me; I consulted with the Minister of Parks, who was me. And I took my pen, signed an agreement, and created a national park.
JEAN CHRÉTIEN, former Cabinet Minis-

ter, recalling his "six year, two-month, three day, and two-hour" tenure as Minister of Indian and Northern Affairs, speaking at a press conference in Toronto in 1989, quoted by David Wilson in *Metropolis*, 2 Feb. 1989.

In all this vast country our provincial and national parks have a common problem: parking.
F. KENNETH HARE, geographer, "Canada: The Land," *Daedalus: Journal of the American Academy of Arts and Sciences*, "In Search of Canada," Fall 1988.

As benchmarks, parks are living testimony both to what our planet was before it was civilized and to how our actions are degrading the world's natural ecosystems.
YORKE EDWARDS, naturalist, "Wilderness Parks: A Concept with Conflicts," *Endangered Spaces: The Future for Canada's Wilderness* (1989) edited by Monte Hummel.

PARLIAMENT
See also GOVERNMENT
HOUSE OF COMMONS
OTTAWA
PARLIAMENT HILL
SENATE

His Excellency the Governor General does not see fit to declare the causes of his summoning the present Parliament of Canada until the Speaker of the House of Commons shall have been chosen according to law.
Set speech delivered at the opening of each new Parliament by the Gentleman Usher of the Black Rod after knocking three times on the doors of the House of Commons, continuing a tradition of the British Parliament.

The day that Parliament becomes a slot machine into which you drop a slug and out comes legislation, freedom ends.
JOHN G. DIEFENBAKER, former Prime Minister, address, Canadian Club of Niag-

ara Falls, Ont., quoted in *The Niagara Falls Evening Review*, 25 Sept. 1964.

The best place in which to talk, if they want a forum, is, of course, Parliament. When they get home, when they get out of Parliament, when they are fifty yards from Parliament Hill, they are no longer honourable members, they are just nobodies.
PIERRE ELLIOTT TRUDEAU, Prime Minister, House of Commons, 25 July 1969.

Having no Hollywood, our politicians are our stars. Without soap operas, Parliament has become our own pitiful drama. Lacking sitcoms, Question Period has become the national laugh track.
ROY MacGREGOR, columnist, *The Ottawa Citizen*, 30 March 1988.

On Parliament Hill the sunlight is thick with the exhaust from the limousines waiting for the 39 cabinet ministers who are required to rule 26 million Canadians, while the Americans somehow can get along with 14 ministers to supervise 250 million.
ALLAN FOTHERINGHAM, columnist, *Maclean's*, 16 Oct. 1989.

PARLIAMENT HILL
See also OTTAWA

To experience Ottawa as a native it is imperative to first avoid the Parliament Buildings. A single trip illustrates the fact that not only do the natives stay away in droves, so do the Honourable Members. On a good day M.P.s are vastly outnumbered by Japanese tourists who, with the help of a visiting grade four class, could take over the reins of government without a shot fired.
"Ottawa at a Glance," *The Westerners' Guide to Eastern Canada* (1985) edited by Don Gillmor.

Parliament Hill is unsurrendered Algonquin land. And so is the entire watershed of the Ottawa River, which runs behind the Parliament buildings.

JEAN-MAURICE MATCHEWAN, Chief, Barriere Lake Indian Government, "Mitchikanibikonginik Algonquins of Barriere Lake: Our Long Battle to Create a Sustainable Future,"*Drumbeat: Anger and Renewal in Indian Country* (1989) edited by Boyce Richardson.

PARTI QUÉBÉCOIS
See also QUEBEC
SEPARATISM

The deep desire to cast off domination has often triumphed in the history of man, despite the power of the established order. Can this desire triumph at last in Quebec? That is my hope following the historic turning point of November 15, 1976.
PIERRE VALLIÈRES, former terrorist, referring to the election of the Parti Québécois, *The Assassination of Pierre Laporte: Behind the October '70 Scenario* (1977).

There's no need to tell you that I'm almost unable to comment on the extraordinary mark of confidence that has been expressed. I never thought I could be so proud of Quebeckers as I am tonight, the most beautiful and perhaps the biggest party in the history of Quebec.
RENÉ LÉVESQUE, P.Q. leader and Quebec Premier-elect, victory speech, Paul Sauvé Arena, Montreal, 15 Nov. 1976, quoted by Peter Lloyd in *The Toronto Star* the following day.

The first fact that we must acknowledge is that democracy is in good health in Quebec, and that is good news. . . . Quebeckers have chosen a new government; not a new country. . . . The stakes for Canadians are much more important and the question is this: Can Francophones of Quebec consider Canada as their country, or must they feel at home only in Quebec? . . . I believe that Canada cannot, indeed, that Canada must not survive by force. The country will only remain united — it should only remain united — if its citizens want to live together in one civil society.

> PIERRE ELLIOTT TRUDEAU, Prime Minister, address on national radio and television, responding to the election of Quebec's first separatist government, 15 Nov. 1976.

Love us and it won't happen. / Only worms can be cut in two and continue to survive. / The French won't take over and neither will the Pope, although he's not the menace he used to be.

> PIERRE ELLIOTT TRUDEAU, Prime Minister, sarcastic reactions to the P.Q. victory, press conference, Ottawa, 25 Nov. 1976, quoted by Hugh Winsor in *The Globe and Mail* the following day.

Never has a group of men and women carried such a load of hopes as this Government, and if we disappoint Quebeckers the whole collectivity will suffer. We have no right to fail.

> RENÉ LÉVESQUE, Quebec Premier, presenting his Cabinet, all francophone and all committed to separatism, National Assembly, Quebec City, 26 Nov. 1976, quoted by Richard Cleroux in *The Globe and Mail* the following day.

Equal to equal.

It's time to know what we want and say what we want, time for a new agreement between two peoples who are equal.

We will have thirty seconds in one day in the springtime to decide to open the future for Quebec.

> RENÉ LÉVESQUE, P.Q. leader, addressing a rally on the importance of the 1980 referendum of the issue of Quebec's independence, Montreal, 21 Oct. 1979, quoted in *The Globe and Mail* the following day. The Péquiste theme was "Starting Today, Tomorrow Belongs to Us."

Parti pour la souveraineté

> Slogan of the Parti Québécois for its 11th biennial convention in Quebec City in Jan. 1991, noted by Robert McKenzie in *The Toronto Star*, 24 Jan. 1991, who observes that the phrase is "a neat pun that

means both 'a party for sovereignty' and 'headed for sovereignty.'"

PARTIES, POLITICAL
See POLITICAL PARTIES

PASSION
See also EMOTIONS

You are passionate but you are not perfect. I know. I know. I am mad but I am not passionately seeking perfection. I am not seeking passion either.

> ELIZABETH SMART, novelist and diarist, "Notebook" (1943), *Autobiographies* (1987) edited by Christina Burridge.

An old barn catches on fire a whole lot faster than a new one.

> Observation made by Narcisse Mondoux, an elderly Quebec plumber, in GRATIEN GÉLINAS's play *The Passion of Narcisse Mondoux*, quoted by Stephen Godfrey in *The Globe and Mail*, 4 Feb. 1989.

PAST
See also HERITAGE
          TIME
          TRADITION

We have no castles, or keeps, or feudal mansions to connect us with the past of our country. We have no legendary lore to excite our wonder or to test our credulity.

> DAVID BOYLE, archaeologist, address, Canadian Institute, Niagara-on-the-Lake, Ont., 1890, quoted by Gerald Killan in *David Boyle: From Artisan to Archaeologist* (1983).

In Canada I know I'm not going to turn a corner and find a temple two thousand years old. Europe has given me so much in the way of beauty to photograph. But here the oldest object I'm likely to run into is a moose skull.

> ROLOFF BENY, photographer who was born in Medicine Hat, Sask., and chose to be a resident of Rome, Italy, quoted by Bruce Moss in *Weekend Magazine*, 11 July 1966.

If we have even a slight knowledge of the past we are aware that we can make happen what has never happened before, and we can have done to us what has never before been possible.

> GEORGE GRANT, philosopher, "Thinking about Technology" (1986), *Technology and Justice* (1986).

It is easy to grow up in North America without any sense of the past. In its trajectory towards the new, life rarely feels continuous or cyclical. It blasts off, and then each year drops away like the stages of a rocket.

> DANIELLE CRITTENDEN, writer, "Faces on the Other Side of the Planet," *The Idler*, No. 20, Nov.-Dec. 1988.

Political projections are always risky. However, it is clear that Canada has become a totally different country by liberating itself from the psychological weight of its own past.

> DOMINIQUE CLIFT, journalist and author, *The Secret Kingdom: Interpretations of a Canadian Character* (1989).

The past is still, for us, a place that is not yet safely settled.

> MICHAEL ONDAATJE, editor, Preface, *The Faber Book of Contemporary Canadian Stories* (1990).

The national understanding is woefully defective: we inhabit an almost entirely mythologized historical landscape, with only the vaguest comprehension of what has happened to us in the past and hardly any idea of why.

> GWYNNE DYER and TINA VILJOEN, commentator and TV producer, *The Defence of Canada: In the Arms of the Empire* (1990).

PATRIOTISM
See also NATIONALISM

PATRIAE PROFUIT / He Was Useful to His Country

> Inscription on the flat gray stone marking the resting place of Vincent Massey, Cemetery, St. Mark's Church, Port Hope, Ont. Massey, the first Canadian-born Governor General, died in London, England, on 30 Dec. 1967, on the eve of Canada's second century. Quoted by Claude T. Bissell in *The Imperial Canadian: Vincent Massey in Office* (1986).

Patriotism, to be sure, is the vulgar notion that my country is the best country because I live in it, but it is surely time for Canadians to shake off the constructions of their heritage, throw away the *fleur de lis* of Québec and the Union Jack of the Loyalist East, and relish to the full the honourable, unique, uncertain distinction of being, in invigoratingly various ways, Canadian.

> STEPHEN BROOK, English travel writer, *Maple Leaf Rag: Travels across Canada* (1987).

If a sculptor were to make a statue of a patriotic Canadian, he would depict somebody holding his breath and crossing his fingers. There has never been a time when Canada has not thought in terms of disintegration.

> NORTHROP FRYE, literary critic, interviewed by Carl Mollins, *Maclean's*, 4 Feb. 1991.

PATRONAGE
See also CORRUPTION

It has to be done . . . patriots can't be kept waiting: The machinery which works popular Government must be kept greased, or it'll go to pieces.

> WILLIAM FLEET, satirist, *How I Came to Be the Governor of the Island of Cacona with a Particular Account of My Administration of the Affairs of that Island Respectfully Dedicated to My Fellow Labourers by the Hon. Francis Thistleton, late Governor of the Island of Cacona* (Montreal, 1852)

Everything else being equal, no administraton was in the habit of preferring their opponents to their friends.

> SIR OLIVER MOWAT, Ontario Premier, re-

mark made on 4 May 1894, quoted by Jeffrey Simpson in *Spoils of Power: The Politics of Patronage* (1988).

As long as there are politicians who must get elected and governments that have favours to dispense, patronage will flourish. . . . The politician who distributes patronage carelessly may enhance his power in the short run, but in the end he will destroy himself. The sensible politician looks after his friends, but he takes care to look after the public interest, too.
GEOFFREY STEVENS, journalist, *Stanfield* (1973).

Let's face it, there's no whore like an old whore. If I'd been in Bryce's position, I'd have been right in there with my nose in the public trough like the rest of them.
BRIAN MULRONEY, Conservative leader, speaking confidentially about the appointment to a diplomatic post of Liberal Minister Bryce Mackasey, campaigning by plane, 15 July 1984, quoted by Claire Hoy in *Friends in High Places: Politics and Patronage in the Mulroney Government* (1987).

You had an option. You could have said, "No, I am not going to do it."
BRIAN MULRONEY, Conservative leader, attacking Prime Minister John Turner's eleventh-hour patronage appointments, leaders' debate on national television, 25 July 1984.

When I form a government, your faithful assistance will never be forgotten.
Sentence from a letter sent to a fundraiser immediately prior to the 1984 election by the Conservative leader Brian Mulroney, reproduced in *The Calgary Herald*, 1 Sept. 1984, according to Pamela Chichinskas and Lynette Stokes in *The Leaders Speak!* (1988).

The hint of patronage pleases many, but the granting of it pleases only one.
JEFFREY SIMPSON, journalist, *Spoils of Power: The Politics of Patronage* (1988).

Several Canadian governments have, through the Canada Council and the Secretariat of State for Multiculturalism, filled me with grateful astonishment by their unfashionable assumption that poets are better employed wielding pencils than selling them on the street in tin cups.
GEORGE FALUDY, Hungarian-born poet, expressing surprise and gratitude for arts grants, *Notes from the Rainforest* (1988).

PEACE
See also PEACEKEEPING
WAR

Among the many different concepts buried in greetings in various languages, perhaps one of the most unusual is expressed in the Mohawk greeting *Skennen kowa ken?* — "Does the great peace exist?" (a question still without an affirmative answer).
CHARLES BERLITZ, linguist, *Native Tongues* (1982). This is a reference to the Great Peace established ages ago among the Six Nations by Deganawida (or Dekanahwideh) and Hiawatha.

Deganawida told my people he had planted for them a Great Tree of Peace and all people who sought it out could live under its protection. Spreading out from the tree would be the White Roots of Peace. They would spread across the world and all nations would marvel and trace them back to their source and find peace under the Great Tree's shade. On the top of the tree Deganawida placed an eagle to stand on guard and give a warning whenever evil people approached to destroy the Great Peace.
CHIEF HA-HEE-HON, aged and blind Onondaga Chief of the Six Nations Reserve, Brantford, Ont., recalling the native tradition, quoted by Fred Bodsworth in *The Star Week Magazine*, 12 Sept. 1959.

George Washington admired our eagle, our Iroquois emblem. He asked to borrow it for the United States until they found one of their own. But the United States has not returned it yet. It is not their emblem and today the Tree of Peace has no guarding sentinel.

CHIEF HA-HEE-HON, aged and blind Onondaga Chief of the Six Nations Reserve, Brantford, Ont., recalling the native tradition, quoted by Fred Bodsworth in *The Star Week Magazine*, 12 Sept. 1959.

Peace and Freedom appear side by side. . . . Without freedom there can be no enduring peace, and without peace, no enduring freedom.

W.L. MACKENZIE KING, Prime Minister, address, unveiling of the National War Monument, Confederation Square, Ottawa, 21 May 1939, quoted by Tom MacDonnell in *Daylight upon Magic: The Royal Tour of Canada — 1939* (1989).

The children gathered their pennies and planted a rose garden and then held a fine ceremony in which they interchanged national flags and sang songs and that sort of thing; a beautiful incident. I take my place with the children.

J.S. WOODSWORTH, CCF leader, Methodist minister, life-long pacifist, and Member of Parliament, casting the sole dissenting vote on Canada's entry into World War II, House of Commons, 9 Sept. 1939.

Last night I had the strangest dream / I'd never dreamed before, / I dreamed the world had all agreed / To put an end to war.

ED McCURDY, folksinger and composer, opening lines of "The Strangest Dream" (1950), a protest folksong popular among members of the peace movement in the 1960s.

The grim fact, however, is that we prepare for war like precocious giants and for peace like retarded pygmies.

LESTER B. PEARSON, diplomat, Nobel Peace Prize Lecture, Oslo, Norway, 11 Dec. 1957. The text is taken from *The Four Faces of Peace and the International Outlook* (1964) edited by Sherleigh G. Pierson.

One can only conclude that the human race is hell-bent toward bankruptcy and suicide. This is incredible folly. I feel we ought to move vigorously and immediately to avert the catastrophe. I believe we can and must reach a workable accommodation with the Russians.

CYRUS EATON, peace activist, quoted by Miriam Chapin in *Contemporary Canada* (1959).

The maturity of the people is amazing when you consider Canada is so young. . . . Canada's attitudes with regard to Vietnam, China and NATO are very sensible.

Everything points to Canada as being one of the key countries in the new race for survival. We've had the arms race and the space race and the cold war — the time has come for the human race.

JOHN LENNON, former member of The Beatles, interviewed on his peace initiative in Toronto by Ritchie York in *The Globe and Mail*, 15 Dec. 1969. The city was papered with posters which read: "WAR IS OVER! if you want it / Happy Christmas from John & Yoko." The posters were designed to promote peace as well as a "world peace festival" scheduled for Mosport Raceway but never held.

Ev'rybody's talking about / Bagism, Shagism, Dragism, Madism, / Ragism, Tagism, / This-ism, that-ism, is-m, is-m, is-m. / All we are saying is give peace a chance. / All we are saying is give peace a chance.

Lines from the anti-war anthem "Give Peace a Chance" which was written and recorded by JOHN LENNON and YOKO ONO during their "bed-in for peace" conducted in their hotel room, Room 1742, Queen Elizabeth Hotel, Montreal, 30 May 1969. The lines were quoted by André Picard in *The Globe and Mail*, 1 Feb. 1991.

Lead me from death to life / From falsehood to truth / Lead me from despair to hope / From fear to trust / Lead me from hate to love / From war to peace / Let peace fill our heart / Our world our universe.

"World Peace Prayer" of Project Ploughshares, adapted from *Peace: A Dream Unfolding* (1986) edited by Penney Kome and Patrick Crean.

Our greatest enemies today are ignorance and indifference — not the human beings in other countries whose governments have the ability to launch their nuclear weapons. Perhaps the greatest promise of the peace movement is the way it crosses international borders and ideologies, overcoming ignorance by bringing people face to face.

PENNEY KOME and PATRICK CREAN, editors, *Peace: A Dream Unfolding* (1986).

Our two-track decision may also require, as the time for deployment comes closer, a "third rail" of high-level political energy to speed the course of agreement — a third rail through which might run the current of our broader political purpose, including our determination not to be intimidated.

PIERRE ELLIOTT TRUDEAU, Prime Minister, address, Conference on Strategies for Peace and Security in the Nuclear Age, University of Guelph, Ont., 27 Oct. 1983. During his final months in power, Trudeau promoted his personal peace initiative, contrasting NATO's "two-track" approach (deployment and negotiation) with his own "third-track" approach (confidence and communications).

Peace and security are not cold abstractions. Their purpose is to preserve the future of mankind, the growth of the human spirit, and the patrimony of our planet.

PIERRE ELLIOTT TRUDEAU, Prime Minister, address in Montreal, 13 Nov. 1983.

Let it be said of Canada, and of Canadians, that we saw the crisis, that we did act, that we took risks, that we were loyal to our friends and open with our adversaries, that we lived up to our ideals and that we have done what we could to lift the shadow of war.

PIERRE ELLIOTT TRUDEAU, Prime Minister, on his peace mission, House of Commons, 9 Feb. 1984.

The politicians, who once stated that war was too complex to be left to the generals, now act as though peace were too complex to be left to themselves.

PIERRE ELLIOTT TRUDEAU, former Prime Minister, address, Albert Einstein Peace Prize Foundation, Washington, D.C., 13 Nov. 1984.

We live peacefully together / That's the way we will survive / Don't have to kill each other to be free / You may mean something different / To every man alive / But Canada, you mean the world to me.

JOHN GRAY, composer and performer, "A Song for Canada," *Don Messer's Jubilee* (1985).

Canada has been called "the peaceable kingdom." It is the only nation on earth which has given up a nuclear arsenal and renounced the role of a nuclear force. It is the source of the "international peacekeeping force," and a leading one in regional conflict resolution. Canada is . . . one of the least threatening nations on earth.

C. DAVID CRENNA, editor, *Lifting the Shadow of War* (1987).

There is no winning move in the current chess game. We must have the courage to change the rules.

JOHN C. POLANYI, scientist and peace activist, quoted in *The Globe and Mail*, 19 June 1987.

We have a Department of Defence, but we do not have an equally prestigious Department of Peace. The very institution of such a department would signal to the public that we mean to take the promulgation of peace seriously.

W. GUNTHER PLAUT, senior scholar at the Holy Blossom Temple, Toronto, contributor to *If I Were Prime Minister* (1987) edited by Mel Hurtig.

All the ministries in the world today are ministries of defence.
> ANATOL RAPOPORT, psychologist and philosopher, address, University of Toronto, 20 Jan. 1988.

The planet is large enough for peace, but too small for war.
> WILLIAM BUNGE, geographer and critic of nuclearism, *Nuclear War Atlas* (1988).

I would prefer to live in peace but, when I looked around me, I couldn't find it anywhere. Everywhere I looked, the land was being destroyed, the Indians were victims of genocide, Third World peoples were oppressed and massacred, people lived in industrial wastelands and women were being raped and children molested. I could never live in peace, only quiet — the kind you find in cemeteries.
> ANN HANSEN, militant peace activist, "Direct Action: Ann Hansen's Statement to the Court," *Up and Doing: Canadian Women and Peace* (1989) edited by Janice Williamson and Deborah Gorham.

Not just peace / but a *just* peace.
> ROBERT PRIEST, poet, aphorism, March 1990.

PEACEKEEPING
See also PEACE

To ensure peace in the post-war era, we must be prepared to *police the world.* We must patrol the seas, and we must patrol the air. We must have military police in all aggressor nations and in the countries on which the aggressor nations imposed their will after conquest during the war.
   The men who do these duties must be carefully chosen. They must be ambassadors of good will as well as minions of the law.
> WILLIAM GUY CARR, Lt.-Cmdr., Royal Canadian Naval Reserve, *Checkmate in the*

North: The Axis Planned to Invade America (1944). This passage gives early and vigorous expression to postwar Canada's sole international initiative: peacekeeping operations.

We feel that if there is a description that could be given to nations — and that would be the peacemakers — then Canada obviously comes at the head of the list.
> KING HUSSEIN OF JORDAN addressing External Affairs Minister Allan MacEachen in Aqaba, quoted in *The Toronto Star*, 17 Jan. 1976.

PEARSON, LESTER B.

What can I say? For a time this evening, I wished I were back at the University of Toronto, teaching history.
> LESTER B. PEARSON, Liberal leader, facing the Conservative landslide victory in 1958, quoted by Peter Dempson in *Assignment Ottawa: Seventeen Years in the Press Gallery* (1968).

Treat those twin imposters, triumph and disaster, just the same.
> Rough translation of "the words . . . above a doorway at Oxford University, in England, where Pearson had studied as a young man," quoted by Lester B. Pearson the night in 1958 that his Liberal Party was routed by John G. Diefenbaker's Conservative Party, quoted by Peter Dempson in *Assignment Ottawa: Seventeen Years in the Press Gallery* (1968).

To excite the daring, test the strong, and give promise to the timid.
> A pledge attributed to LESTER B. PEARSON, Prime Minister, 1963-68.

In one of his personal papers Pearson had put down as his formula for life: "To deserve success is more important than to achieve it."
> JOHN ROBINSON BEAL, journalist, *The Pearson Phenomenon* (1964).

Lester Pearson was out of office and addressing a Liberal meeting in a room above a Chinese restaurant in downtown

Ottawa. When questions were invited, a questioner launched a question as convoluted and disoriented as I have ever heard, which went on and on like Tennyson's brook until he was finally persuaded by numerous and increasingly insistent shouts of "Question! question! question!" to finish up with: "My question is, 'Do you agree?'" Mr. Pearson's reply: "There may be something in what you say."
> Incident recalled by GARRETT J. O'NEILL of Ottawa in Letters to the Editor, *The Globe and Mail*, 19 Nov. 1988.

When Lester Pearson won the Nobel Peace Prize in 1957 for preventing World War III, he said, "Gee thanks." (A Pearsonian lisp embellishes this accurate story, but I am unable to master it.)
> PETER GZOWSKI, host of CBC Radio's *Morningside*, in *The Private Voice: A Journal of Reflections* (1988).

PENSIONS

At a job interview, a Canadian will ask about the pension plan before inquiring about the starting salary.
> RICHARD STENGEL, journalist, "The Canadians," *Spy*, Feb. 1988.

PEOPLE
See also LIFE
MANKIND

Yes, it *is* a truth — and a sad one. We do not love people for what is worthiest in them. We *admire* them for their good qualities, but we do not *love* them for them. Nay, worse, we often love them for what is positively unworthy.
> L. M. MONTGOMERY, author, journal entry, 5 Feb. 1911, Cavendish, P.E.I., *The Selected Journals of L.M. Montgomery: Volume II: 1910-1921* (Toronto) edited by Mary Rubio and Elizabeth Waterston.

It's the smallest, gentlest nobodys with the biggest dreams who are the only hope for this world.
> SUSAN COX, theatre personality, quoted

by Vit Wagner in *The Toronto Star*, 31 Dec. 1988.

I don't believe in self-improvement — except for other people.
> CRAD KILODNEY, author, original epigram, 16 Jan. 1989.

We're bigger than all of us.
> ROBERT PRIEST, poet, aphorism, March 1990.

PERFECTION

I don't think that perfection is possible or even, in psychological terms, desirable for human beings.
> ROBERTSON DAVIES, man-of-letters, interviewed by Tom Harpur in 1974, *Conversations with Robertson Davies* (1989) edited by J. Madison Davis.

To strive for perfection is to kill love because perfection does not recognize humanity.
> MARION WOODMAN, analyst and author, *Addition to Perfection: The Still Unravished Bride* (1982).

Fewer people survive perfection than survive reality.
> BETTY JANE WYLIE, author, *New Beginnings: Living through Loss and Grief* (1991).

PERSIAN GULF
See GULF WAR

PERSONALITIES

But where, I ask, are the large-town characters?
> ROY MacGREGOR, journalist, "Essay," *The Ottawa Citizen*, 12 April 1986.

Some Canadians say I'm a national institution, others say I should be put in one.
> LARRY ZOLF, commentator and author, quoted by Morton Ritts in *Maclean's*, 16 Oct. 1989. The interviewer concluded: "Chances are that Larry Zolf agrees — with both views."

PETS

See also ANIMALS

Do you have a cat? Then you have my sympathies.

Don't get me wrong. I like cats. I have one myself as a matter of fact. Actually, that statement is laughable. Nobody *has* a cat. Cats occasionally deign to let some benighted human wretch lavish free room and board on them. Cats will, from time to time, condescend to let a mere human hand stroke and fondle them. But nobody owns a cat. The very idea of fealty from a feline is ridiculous.

ARTHUR BLACK, broadcaster, *Back to Black: Comic Sketches* (1987).

ATTENTION / Chien Bizarre

Sign posted in front of a private, middle-income residence, Toronto, May 1990.

PHILANTHROPY

See also GIFTS & GIVING

Philanthropy plus 5%

Formula for investment by business interests in workers' housing, identified in *The City Below the Hill* (1986) by Sir Herbert B. Ames (1863-1954).

This is Lotta Hitschmanova of the Unitarian Service Committee . . . 56 Sparks St., Ottawa.

Once-familiar words heard on radio and television spoken by the Czech-born founder of the Unitarian Service Committee. She established the Ottawa-based service organization in 1945 and served as its executive director until 1982.

When you've inherited wealth, you don't feel that you have to spend money to impress anyone.

H.N.R. (HAL) JACKMAN, Toronto millionaire and philanthropist, quoted by John Picton in *The Toronto Star*, 1 Oct. 1989.

PHILOSOPHY

The philosophers of the Middle Ages demonstrated both that the earth did not exist and also that it was flat. Today they are still arguing about whether the world exists, but they no longer dispute about whether it is flat.

VILHJALMUR STEFANSSON, explorer and author, *The Standardization of Error* (1936).

For every philosopher, in every age, the first question must be: just what is philosophy?

FRANCIS SPARSHOTT, philosopher, "Speculation and Reflection," *Looking for Philosophy* (1972).

Indeed, the day was to come when Canadian scholars, defensive and self-denigrating about nearly everything else, said routinely to sceptical foreigners, "Well, we *do* have the Institute of Mediaeval Studies in Toronto, you know.

LESLIE ARMOUR and ELIZABETH TROTT, philosophers, *The Faces of Reason: An Essay on Philosophy and Culture in English Canada 1850-1950* (1981). The Pontificial Institute of Mediaeval Studies was established at St. Michael's College, University of Toronto, in 1929.

PHOTOGRAPHY

I said, "Forgive me, sir," and plucked the cigar out of his mouth. By the time I got back to my camera, he looked so belligerent he could have devoured me. It was at that instant that I took the photograph. The silence was deafening.

YOUSUF KARSH, portrait photographer, recalling how he took the inspired and inspiring "bulldog" photograph of British Prime Minister Winston S. Churchill, Speaker's Chambers, House of Commons, 30 Dec. 1941, *Karsh: A Fifty-Year Retrospective* (1983).

Fine images depend upon thinking about what you see and understanding what you feel about what you see. Fine images demand careful preparation. . . . There is no greater pleasure in photography than

achieving the image you set out to capture or create. . . . The joy of photography is the joy of self-discovery.
FREEMAN PATTERSON, photographer, *Photography for the Joy of It* (1977).

Great portraits are given, not taken.
JOHN REEVES, photographer, quoted by Robert Fulford in his Preface to Andrew Danson's *Unofficial Portraits* (1987).

A good photograph is not so much a work of art as a condensed experience. It is truth frozen in two dimensions — but partial truth.
ROBERT FULFORD, cultural commentator, Preface to Andrew Danson's *Unofficial Portraits* (1987).

Every photograph is like a thin slice of time, one moment in an infinite succession of moments, each made unique by incessant change. Change is the solid manifestation of the passage of time: without it we have no sense or measure of time.
VIRGIL MARTIN, photographer and historian whose specialty is "rephotography," revealing changes by placing side-by-side vintage and contemporary landscape photographs, *Changing Landscapes of Southern Ontario* (1988).

It takes two people to make a good photograph.
ARNAUD MAGGS, portrait photographer, quoted by Gail Harvey and Roy Mac-Gregor in *Poli-Graphs* (1989).

I began seeing the world as a storehouse of images: gusts of snow, the red face of the minister, the river ice melting. Opposing them, even mentally, gave me a feeling of competence I had never had. With a camera in my hands, I wasn't afraid of ridicule or of taking risks. It was almost, in fact, as if I became a different person.
DOUGLAS KIRKLAND, Toronto-born portrait photographer, *Light Years: Three Decades Photographing Among the Stars* (1989).

PHYSICS

Once we figure out how the dice are made, we may be able to figure out who is throwing them.
GRAEME ROSS, correspondent in Fredericton, N.B., rising to the challenge of defining "particle physics," quoted by Stephen Strauss in *The Globe and Mail*, 12 May 1990. Strauss added, "Mr. Ross captures both Godliness and the unpredictable physics of quantum mechanics in a single sentence."

PIONEERS
See also EXPLORATION

Out in B.C. I knew a couple of Englishmen who were batching and the only other people around were Indians. The first two years they was there they wouldn't have anything to do with the Indians because they was so dirty, and after that the Indians wouldn't have anything to do with them.
Speech of a character named Taylor in the three-act comedy *The Land of Promise* written by W. SOMERSET MAUGHAM and set in Tunbridge Wells and in Dyer and Prentice, Man., in the year 1912. "Perhaps *The Land of Promise* might still hold an audience," wrote Maugham in the Preface to his *Collected Plays* (1931). (The stage direction following Taylor's little speech runs: "He puts his fingers to his nose to indicate a nasty smell.")

This memorial was erected to the memory of men and women in this land throughout their generations, who braved the wilderness, maintained the settlements, performed the common task without praise or glory and were pioneers of political freedom and a system of responsible government which became the cornerstone of the British Commonwealth of Nations.
Inscription on the Pioneer Memorial Arch, Queen Victoria Park, Niagara Falls, unveiled by Prime Minister Mackenzie King in 1937 to honour the pioneers of Canada and to act as a "memento mori"

of those "charged with insurrection or treason and executed in 1838-1839" on the occasion of the centenary of the Rebellion of 1837. *Fifty-third Annual Report of the Niagara Parks Commission 1938 and 1939* (1940). The Arch was dismantled in 1968, giving profound meaning to the arch's Latin inscription: "Tempora mutantur nos et mutamur in illis."

Does it seem to you that I am talking about a nation of losers, of exiles and refugees? Modern Canada is a prosperous country, but the miseries of its earliest white inhabitants are bred in the bone, and cannot, even now, be rooted out of the flesh.
ROBERTSON DAVIES, man-of-letters, Neil Gunn lecture, Edinburgh University, June 1988, published in *The Times Literary Supplement*, 30 Sept. 1988.

PITY

Self-pity is a kind of permissive self-dramatization.
BETTY JANE WYLIE, author, *Beginnings: A Book for Widows* (1977).

For self-pity and self-deception are the two great destroyers. More lives, loves, money, happiness are lost through these two sneaky evils than anything else in the world. It's all your own fault. It's nobody's fault but your own. You wanted it. You got it. You're paying for it. *It's fair.*
ELIZABETH SMART, novelist and diarist, "How to Mend a Broken Heart" (Feb. 1982), *Autobiographies* (1987) edited by Christina Burridge.

Pity is never wholly free of contempt.
ROBIN SKELTON, man-of-letters, aphorism, May 1990.

PLACES
See also CITIES & TOWNS
COMMUNITY

The following cities have entries of their own:
CALGARY, CHARLOTTETOWN,

EDMONTON, FREDERICTON, HALIFAX, MONTREAL, NIAGARA FALLS, OTTAWA, QUEBEC CITY, REGINA, SAINT JOHN, ST. JOHN'S, TORONTO, VANCOUVER, VICTORIA, WHITEHORSE, WINNIPEG, YELLOWKNIFE

Strange, haunting and full of exciting sound are the names of Canada. Names full of our history, our achievements, our failures, our memories, the lost dreams of our youth, the splendid hope of our future.
BRUCE HUTCHISON, author, *The Unknown Country* (1942, 1948) as quoted by Penny Ham in *Place Names of Manitoba* (1980).

I said in an earlier article on Canadian literature that the Canadian problem of identity seemed to me primarily connected with locale, less a matter of "Who am I?" than of "Where is here?" Another friend, commenting on this, told me a story about a doctor from the south (that is, from one of the Canadian cities) travelling on the Arctic tundra with an Eskimo guide. A blizzard blew up, and they had to bivouac for the night. What with the cold, the storm, and the loneliness, the doctor panicked and began shouting, "We are lost!" The Eskimo looked at him thoughtfully and said, "We are not lost. We are here." A vast gulf between an indigenous and an immigrant mentality opened at that point. . . .
NORTHROP FRYE, literary critic, "Haunted by Lack of Ghosts: Some Patterns in the Imagery of Canadian Poetry," *The Canadian Imagination: Dimensions of a Literary Culture* (1977) edited by David Staines.

Some names alone stay with me, like a pocketful of coins from a crowd of nations that make up, in their jumbled combination, the currency of the prairies: Bruno and Valparaiso, Muenster and Carmel, Star City and Lac Vert . . . I stopped at none.
MARK ABLEY, traveller, *Beyond Forget: Rediscovering the Prairies* (1986).

Every region in Canada has a town people refer to as nowhere, whether it is Medicine Hat, Alberta, or Wawa, Ontario. It's a way people have of sublimating the feeling that their own town is nowhere, that they themselves are nowhere, that everything important is happening someplace else.
JOHN GRAY, composer and performer, Preface, *Local Boy Makes Good: Three Musicals* (1987).

A stray fragment of memory fluttered up to consciousness: Among themselves, American hobos called Canada "Big Lonely."
MARK ABLEY, traveller, *Beyond Forget: Rediscovering the Prairies* (1986).

Canada is a land of extraordinary place-names: the Indian names with their mysterious etymology, improbable names like Moose Jaw, anglicized French-Canadian names like Bien Fait, pronounced "bean-fate," names of sheer delight like Saskatoon and Saskatchewan.
ELEANOR COOK, scholar, in "'A Seeing and Unseeing in the Eye': Canadian Literature and the Sense of Place," *Daedalus: Journal of the American Academy of Arts and Sciences*, "In Search of Canada," Fall 1988.

To her ears, the sound of the word "Canada" had the same resonance as "Sahara." It connoted a strangeness and a vastness, everything that Poland was not. Canada was all contours and no content.
ALEXANDER W. SZEMBERG, essayist, referring to the resonances of the place name to a Polish-speaker, "What's in a Name?" *The Idler*, No. 25, Sept.-Oct. 1989.

Anywhere is everywhere so everywhere is anywhere.
Conundrum attributed to MARSHALL McLUHAN by Paul William Roberts in *Toronto Life*, Jan. 1999.

AKLAVIK, N.W.T.
No wonder the residents sometimes call Aklavik the Mudtropolis of the North.

PIERRE BERTON, author, referring to the northern community's terrain in summer, *The Mysterious North* (1956).

ALERT, N.W.T.
There is no place anything like this place, anywhere near this place, so this must be the place: Alert.
Sign outside Alert, N.W.T., the most northern permanent settlement in the world.

BANFF & LAKE LOUISE, ALTA.
After Ottawa we went to the Rockies, to Lake Louise and Banff. Lake Louise was for a long time my answer when I was asked which was the most beautiful place I had ever seen: — a great, long, blue lake, low mountains on either side, all of a most glorious shape, closing in with snow mountains at the end of it.
AGATHA CHRISTIE, mystery story writer, stopping off at Banff and Lake Louise on a round-the-world trip made in 1922, *An Autobiography* (1977).

BAIE-COMEAU, QUE.
When we want to know how to build a nation, we look to Baie-Comeau.
BRIAN MULRONEY, Prime Minister, address, 16 March 1988, *The Leaders Speak!* (1988) compiled by Pamela Chichinskas and Lynette Stokes.

BERING STRAIT, ALASKA
However, on the gradually accumulating evidence of stone tools found in the Yukon and in Alaska, and across the Bering Strait in Siberia, there has been for some time a credible inference that man came across the land-bridge more than 20,000 years ago. It would now appear that it was much earlier than that.
JOHN A. LIVINGSTON, naturalist, *One Cosmic Instant: A Natural History of Human Arrogance* (1973).

BROCKVILLE, ONT.
He told me about the St. Lawrence Seaway expansion, and the new city that they proposed to build at Brockville. This was

going to become the economic centre of Ontario.

CYRIL GREENLAND, psychiatric social worker, referring in 1957 to the offer of employment as a social worker in Ontario and the anticipated growth to the city of Brockville, Ont.; interviewed by Sam Sussman in *Pioneers of Mental Health and Social Change: 1930-1989* (1989) by Djuwe Joe Blom and Sam Sussman.

DAWSON CITY, Y.T.

Dawson City was full of ribbon clerks.

WILSON MIZENER, society personality, who "ended the 19th c. weighing gold and dealing faro in Dawson City saloons," according to Jim Christy in *Rough Road to the North* (1980).

BEAUPORT, QUE.

As the old Canadian saying goes, "A Beauport habitant is nobody's fool."

PHILIPPE-JOSEPH AUBERT de GASPÉ, man-of-letters, *A Man of Sentiment: The Memoirs of Philippe-Joseph Aubert de Gaspé 1786-1871* (1866) translated in 1988 by Jane Brierley.

BRACKEN, SASK.

The Best Wheat in the World Grown Here! Pop. 65.

Handpainted sign outside Bracken, Sask., noted by Mark Abley in *Beyond Forget: Rediscovering the Prairies* (1986). "Under the boast was a green sky; under the sky, a portrait of the community. It showed Bracken with a trio of grain elevators. Nowadays the village has but one."

CARDSTON, ALTA.

Well, there's a Fay Wray wishing well on the town's main street. And the good people shipped me the huge rock that says "wrayland" and was outside my father's ranch house. I gave it to my son and now a little bit of Alberta is in sunny California outside his home.

FAY WRAY, movie personality born on a farm outside Cardston, Alta., who appeared in seventy-seven movies but most notably in *King Kong*, interviewed by Jim Bawden in *The Toronto Star*, 13 Jan. 1990.

CAVENDISH, P.E.I.

Cavendish is looking very beautiful now, with bloomy mists purpling over its dark spruce hills and all the splendour of crimson and gold among its maples and birches. Cavendish is really the prettiest country place I've ever been in. It is a long, narrow settlement, bordering on and following the outline of the north shore, whose wonderful waters, ever changing in hue and sheen, now silvery gray, now shimmering blue, now darkly azure, now misty with moonrise or purple with sunsets, can be seen from any and every point.

L. M. MONTGOMERY, author, journal entry, 8 Oct. 1898, *The Selected Journals of L.M. Montgomery: Volume I: 1889-1910* (1985) edited by Mary Rubio and Elizabeth Waterston.

CHICOUTIMI, QUE.

Cadillac Capital of the World

Unofficial motto of Chicoutimi, Que., in the 1960s and 1970s. Chicoutimites preferred large and expensive American-made automobiles, especially Cadillacs. Noted in *The Globe and Mail*, 18 Oct. 1989.

CHURCHILL, MAN.

In all my life, I eventually decided, I had never seen such an odd little place. A town of the toughest individuals — many of whom are also tough-minded individualists — the modern Churchill is a government's creation, and it exists at the government's mercy. Its inhabitants — true believers in the north, its beauty, its way of life, its potential — seem to come from everywhere except the north. Hanging by its teeth onto Next Year Country, Churchill depends for its living on a threat to its residents: polar bears. The town defies generalization. it reminds me of nowhere else. It is a true original.

MARK ABLEY, traveller, *Beyond Forget: Rediscovering the Prairies* (1986).

CONSORT, ALTA.

Home of k.d. lang, Consort, Alberta.
> Sign on the outskirts of Consort, a town of fewer than 700 in east-central Alberta, quoted by Don Gillmor, *Saturday Night*, June 1990. The torch-and-twang singer was raised in Consort from 1962 to 1972, from her eighth to her eighteenth year.

DAWSON, Y.T.

I came from a very strange town, although I was not aware of that when I lived there. I don't suppose any of us really is. Dawson is unique; there is nothing like it anywhere in the world. But I did not know it was unique, and I must say until very recently I never thought of it in that way. Yet when I think of it now, I realize what a strange upbringing I had.
> PIERRE BERTON, author, address, Empire Club of Canada, Toronto, 11 Oct. 1973.

DOON, ONT.

After some years of restless wandering in quest of adequate media of expression in art . . . it came to me that among the nooks and scenes of this village nestling among the hills, I should find ample material to fix in some degree the infinite beauties that emanate from the mystery of sky and land.
> HOMER WATSON, painter and native of Doon, Ont., quoted by Muriel Miller in *Homer Watson: Man of Doon* (1938).

FORT MACLEOD, ALTA.

Fort Macleod is an outlying point and the men I know there can out-lie those of any district in the North-West.
> PATRICK JAMES NOWLAN, prairie lawyer, quoted by Grant MacEwan in "Paddy Was an Irishman," *Fifty Mighty Men* (1958). As Bob Edwards once explained, "All the best criminals go to Paddy Nolan."

GANDER, NFLD.

INDECENT ASSAULT ON PLANE: / CRITIC CHARGED, GIRL GOOSED OVER GANDER
> Possible headline imagined by Kenneth Tynan and reported by Kathleen Tynan in *The Life of Kenneth Tynan* (1987). The

drama critic, on a transatlantic flight from New York to London in 1958, while flying over Gander, Nfld., risked an assault charge when he began to fondle a female passenger who, to his relief, rather than resist, responded.

GRAND RIVER VALLEY, ONT.

There is scarcely a finer or more inviting section of country in North America than the Peninsula formed by Lake Ontario to the east, Lake Erie to the south and Lake Huron on the west, through the heart of which flows the Grand River.
> WILLIAM L. STONE, historian, *Life of Joseph Brant* (1845), quoted by Mabel Dunham in *Grand River* (1945).

GRAVENHURST, ONT.

It is a little town with the forbidding name of Gravenhurst, which Don instantly dubbed "Grave n' Hearse."
> MARTHA HARRON, author, explaining one of the puns of her father, the comedian Don Harron, in *Don Harron: A Parent Contradiction* (1988).

GUELPH, ONT.

I was well aware of the boding effect of a little solemnity on the minds of most men, especially of the unlettered.
> JOHN GALT, colonizer with the Canada Company, breaking open a bottle of champagne on a hilltop overlooking the site of the city of Guelph and giving the site the family name of King George IV, 23 April 1827.

The years of my childhood, spent at Summer Hill, developed my character, moulded my tastes, and coloured my point of view for life.
> ELINOR GLYN, English-born, California-based novelist and Hollywood scriptwriter who was raised on a farm at Summer Hill, near Guelph, Ont., *Romantic Adventure: Being the Autobiography of Elinor Glyn* (1936).

HAMILTON, ONT.

I suppose a person's hometown takes the

rap for how he felt about himself while growing up. I did not feel good about myself while growing up. I feel good about myself now. Therefore Hamilton becomes the measure of my discontent.
SYLVIA FRASER, novelist born in Hamilton, Ont., remarks made on 30 Sept. 1979.

Hamilton, Ontario, has a surprising number of cultural attractions. Perhaps not as many as Toronto — but at least you can get to them. It is an eminently livable city.
BERNARD BASKIN, rabbi, Temple Anshe Sholom, Hamilton, *obiter dictum*, 22 May 1990.

HEARNE, SASK.
The Voice of Hearne, Sask.
ALLAN FOTHERINGHAM, columnist and controversialist, self-described as "Dr. Foth" and (in an allusion to his place of birth) "The Voice of Hearne, Sask.," *Maclean's*, 6 Nov. 1989.

People from Hearne are called Hearnias. The town was so small we couldn't even afford a village idiot. Everyone had to take turns. (Eventually, however, I moved to British Columbia, which improved the I.Q. of both provinces.)
ALLAN FOTHERINGHAM, columnist, *Malice in Blunderland or How the Grits Stole Christmas* (1982).

HUDSON BAY
We should allow the Americans to use Hudson Bay as a sanctuary for their four submarines — provided that Washington agrees to scale down its retaliatory force and recognizes officially that we have undisputed sovereignty over our northern waters.
PHILIPPE DEANE GIGANTES, author and Senator, referring to U.S. atomic submarines, *The Road Ahead* (1990).

JAMES BAY
Objectively, unemotionally, one can state that the development of James Bay will set Quebec on a new road to progress. It is an undertaking which once again will furnish tangible proof of Quebec's vitality and spirit of enterprise, for the development of James Bay is the most daring project in Quebec's history. James Bay is the land of tomorrow.
Report of the James Bay Development Corporation, released in 1971, paving the way for Quebec Premier Robert Bourassa's "Project of the Century"; quoted by Roy MacGregor in *Chief: The Fearless Vision of Billy Diamond* (1989).

KINGSMERE, GATINEAU PARK, QUE.
I suppose I spend a good deal of time here. There is so much beauty and peace. It is good to have some familiar, well-loved place to spend time in, until one gets used to eternity.
PERCY J. PHILIP, Scots-born, Ottawa-based correspondent for *The New York Times*, maintaining he conversed with the ghost of the late W.L. Mackenzie King at Kingsmere, Gatineau Park, on a June evening in 1954, four years after the death of the spiritualist-minded Prime Minister. Philip published a number of accounts of this experience, the main one being "I Talked with Mackenzie King's Ghost," *Fate*, Oct. 1955.

KINGSTON, ONT.
The people of this Canadian paradise are more contented in their situation of life, than is common to observe in most places.
MICHAEL SMITH, traveller and writer, *A Geographical View of the Province of Upper Canada* (3rd ed., 1813).

KITCHENER, ONT.
I don't see any Yank divisions in the vicinity of Kitchener, and in spite of all that's going on now in the U.S. I am not worried about seeing one in the future. And that's one of the things I like about sweet Sister Canada and her Big Brother, with all his distasteful shortcomings.
JOSEF SKVORECKY, Czech-born author and publisher, commenting on the presence of Russian tanks in a city east of Prague and the absence of tanks in a city west of Toronto; "A City After My Own

Heart" (1974), *Toronto Remembered: A Celebration of the City* (1984) edited by William Kilbourn.

Too many Canadian places have prosaic imported names, saints' names, explorers' names, names inherited from Scottish estates, names like Windsor, Regina, or (God help us) Kitchener.
> JAN MORRIS, Anglo-Welsh traveller, "Suddenly Saskatoon," *Saturday Night*, July-Aug. 1990.

KUUJJUARAPIQ, QUE.
The Cree call it Whapmagoostui. The Inuit call it Kuujjuaraapik. French-Canadians call it Poste-de-la-Baleine. English-Canadians call it Great Whale Station. The mapmakers have settled on Kuujjuarapiq.
> ANDRÉ PICARD, journalist, discussing the names given a remote Quebec community on the eastern shore of Hudson Bay, *The Globe and Mail*, 17 March 1990.

LONDON, ONT.
London, Ontario, has a very active cultural scene that goes back to the 19th century and continues to the present. It's important that these things exist, and that we know they exist.
> CHRISTOPHER DEWDNEY, poet, introducing the work of fellow London artist Greg Curnoe, quoted by Deirdre Hanna in *Now*, 2 Nov. 1989.

To know London, Ontario, is to know that not much happens there. A medium-size city in a country full of medium-size cities, it is neither big enough to provide intrigue nor small enough to induce claustrophobia — it's the last place on earth to base a movie.
> DENIS SEGUIN, journalist, *Metropolis*, 22 March 1990. Seguin is referring to the feature film *Beautiful Dreams*, which is set in London in the summer of 1880 during the visit of the American poet Walt Whitman to the Canadian psychiatrist Dr. R.M. Bucke.

MACKENZIE VALLEY, Y.T.
I have seen the Great Mackenzie Valley and the fantastic sight of the Mackenzie Delta, one hundred and fifty miles of wriggling channels and little ponds. I have seen it from the air at sunset. Somebody once described it as a giant mirror splintered into ten thousand pieces shining up to you.
> PIERRE BERTON, author, address, Empire Club of Canada, Toronto, 11 Oct. 1973.

MARATHON, ONT.
Marathon is the sort of town that would have delighted Franz Kafka . . . because the bureaucratic structure and stratification of the town is emphasized by the kind of houses you find on various streets as you ascend from the harbour.
> GLENN GOULD, pianist, remark made in 1974 concerning the article "The Search for Petula Clark" (1967), *The Glenn Gould Reader* (1984) edited by Tim Page.

MEDICINE HAT, ALTA.
Bogart: This is not a ship — it's a *boat*.
Astor: In Medicine Hat we wouldn't know such things.
> Exchange between HUMPHREY BOGART and MARY ASTOR (who plays a naive young woman from Alberta) in the movie *Across the Pacific* (1942).

In Hollywood, about twenty years ago, I met Hedda Hopper, who was so influential she could make or break a career by just leaving a name *out* of her column. Later, she wrote, "All my life I've wanted to meet someone who actually came from Medicine Hat! Now one of my life's ambitions is realized!"
> ROLOFF BENY, photographer born in Medicine Hat, Alta., address, Empire Club of Canada, Toronto, 27 Oct. 1983.

LAKE MEMPHREMAGOG, QUE.
Memphremagog! ye hyperborean powers, what a name for a place in which to sing Christmas carols!
> GEORGE AUGUSTUS SALA, British journalist and traveller, concerning a winter's journey in the Eastern Townships, *My Diary in America in the Midst of War* (1865).

MONTMORENCY FALLS, QUE.

We made an excursion to a village on the banks of the St. Lawrence, called Indian Lorette; and thence proceeded to see the picturesque Falls of Montmorency, much smaller than those of Niagara, but, to my mind, surpassing them in beauty. Indian Lorette was one of the queerest half-French, half-Redskin townships that I met with in Canada. In some respects, when you alighted from your carriage, you seemed to have landed right in the middle of the eighteenth century.

GEORGE AUGUSTUS SALA, English correspondent, visiting Quebec City in mid-1864, *The Life and Adventures of George Augustus Sala* (1895).

MOOSE JAW, SASK.

I wanted to get out of England desperately. So after my basic training, I went. I was sent to the RCAF flight-training base at Moosejaw [*sic*], Saskatchewan, which is quite a place to be! That's where I discovered science fiction, in the magazine racks of the airbase cafeteria, and I've never looked back since!

J.G. BALLARD, science-ficiton writer, who enrolled with the RAF in the 1950s; remarks recorded in *Foundation*, No. 24, 1984.

According to another prairie legend — what is it about the west that breeds yarns? — tunnels run from Moose Jaw's capacious railway station to several of River Street's hotels. They date, it is said, from the epoch when Moose Jaw was a refuge for Al Capone, a Mecca for gamblers and opium smokers, a Jerusalem for pimps. (The Board of Trade, however, preferred to call the city "The Buckle of the Greatest Wheat Belt in the World.")

MARK ABLEY, traveller, *Beyond Forget: Rediscovering the Prairies* (1986).

MOOSE FACTORY, ONT.

But what a bore beside the lore / Of old Moose Factory!

DENNIS LEE, poet, "Homage to Moose Factory, Ont.," *Nicholas Knock and Other People* (1974).

NAHANNI RIVER

For the most part, the Nahanni Country remains a pristine wilderness. In a vanishing natural world, it survives in its primeval state, a legacy from that time before civilization.

PAT and ROSEMARIE KEOUGH, nature writers and photographers, *The Nahanni Portfolio* (1988).

NORANDA, QUE.

You might as well, you can't dance!

Characteristic expression, confined to the Noranda district, according to Jerry Smith, rector, St. Brice's Parish, North Bay, Ont., personal communication, 12 Feb. 1991.

ORILLIA, ONT.

I don't think you would like the accommodations as it is only a small town and no good hotels. There are some very nice boarding houses but about the only fare is lamb and beef. Please send me a dollar because there are a lot of little odds and ends I need. I will spend it cautiously. All the other boys have pocket money besides their regular allowance.

F. SCOTT FITZGERALD, future novelist, excerpt from earliest known letter, dated 18 July 1907, addressed to his mother, and posted from Camp Chatham, Orillia, Ont. *The Letters of F. Scott Fitzgerald* (1963) edited by Andrew Turnbull.

OSHAWA, ONT.

The city that "Moto-vates Canada" (the official slogan, not mine) is the birth-place of two famous Canadians. Ed Broadbent is one; the other was the winner of the Kentucky Derby, Northern Dancer. Both are treated with a detached, awed respect.

MICHAEL COREN, essayist and biographer, alluding to the fact that Oshawa's main employer is General Motors, "The Urban Peasant," *The Idler*, No. 23, May-June 1989.

OTTAWA VALLEY, ONT.

Who else but Joe Mufferaw?

Remark characteristic among the Ontario Irish of the Ottawa Valley whenever anonymous assistance is rendered; reference to the Valley's Paul Bunyan figure, 1920s.

PEGGY'S COVE, N.S.

I have read of the scenic splendours of the world, and I have sat and listened to people tell of them, who have visited them. A few I have seen. The semi-tropics, the desert, the Rocky Mountains, glorious Florida and California, the gigantic redwoods, the Grand Canyon — but all alone, on a separate page, in my memory book of beauty spots, I place all that I was able to drink into my being and paint upon the canvas of my heart, of Peggy's Cove. It's scenic unique!

GEORGE MATTHEW ADAMS, commentator, quoted by Will R. Bird in *Off-Trail in Nova Scotia* (1956).

PETERBOROUGH, ONT.

As the Canadian economy developed, Toronto had a number of advantages over Montreal that perhaps made its comparative progress a certainty. The most important of these advantages, I suggest, was Toronto's great good fortune in being located so close to such really productive municipalities as Peterborough.

MICHAEL BLISS, historian, "Better and Purer: The Peterborough Methodist Mafia and the Renaissance of Toronto," *Toronto Remembered: A Celebration of the City* (1984) edited by William Kilbourn.

PORT AUX BASQUES, NFLD.

Nobody has actually seen Port aux Basques for the past fifty years or so. We must take it as an article of faith it's there somewhere in deep fog.

RAY GUY, humorist, "Adventures of a Newfoundland Writer in Darkest Mainland," *Ray Guy's Best* (1987).

PORT RADIUM, N.W.T.

Port Radium, the mine that produced uranium for the early years of the nuclear age, is worked out. Even the name has vanished; it's now known as Echo Bay.

PIERRE BERTON, author, Postscript (1989), *The Mysterious North* (1956, 1989).

PORT SYDNEY, ONT.

Welcome to Port Sydney / The Home of . . . / 500 Nice People and One Old Grouch

Wording on a permanent sign on the highway outside Port Sydney, a village near Bracebridge, Ont., quoted by Helga Loverseed in *The Globe and Mail*, 10 Oct. 1990.

PRINCE ALBERT, SASK.

As Prince Albert goes, so goes the nation.

Characteristic remark of Prime Minister JOHN G. DIEFENBAKER. The Saskatchewan riding of Prince Albert elected three Prime Ministers, more than any other constituency: Sir Wilfrid Laurier, W.L. Mackenzie King, and John G. Diefenbaker.

ROBLIN LAKE, ONT.

And now there is a new thing on earth: a poetic cosmology focused concentrically around Roblin Lake, southeastern Ontario, Canada, North America, planet earth, all space and time. It does not invalidate visions of order centred elsewhere. But here is a muscular, roomy, and pervasive vision of coherence centred in our own here and now. Such a thing did not exist before.

DENNIS LEE, poet and critic, Afterword, *The Collected Poems of Al Purdy* (1986) edited by Russell Brown.

ST. ANDREWS, N.B.

To residents, of course, things are already not what they were — where are they, anywhere on earth? To the stranger's eye, though, St. Andrews seems enchantingly frozen in the patterns and postures of its past — a rare survival of quality in the age of trash.

JAN MORRIS, Anglo-Welsh travel writer, "New Brunswick," *Saturday Night*, May 1990.

SAINT JOHN, N.B.
[Donald] Sutherland's father was an air-raid warden and young Donny kept asking if the city was going to get an air-raid siren.

"No, son, we're not," his father explained. "We figure if the Nazis fly over, it'll probably be foggy and they'll never see us."

"But, Dad, what if the sky is clear?"

"Well, they'll still fly right by because they'll look down at Saint John, and they'll think they must have bombed it already."
> DONALD SUTHERLAND, the actor, was born in Saint John, N.B.; quoted by Bruce Ward in "People," *The Ottawa Citizen*, 13 Nov. 1988.

SALMON ARM, B.C.
Salmon Arm: A swim stroke developed by the Philosophy Department of Simon Fraser University. Widely copied in East Germany.
> "Pass for a Native: Learn These Terms," *The Easterners' Guide to Western Canada* (1985) edited by Ron Marken.

SARNIA, ONT.
The girl who shares this upstairs room / with a cat, a guitar and a chesterfield / left her native town, Sarnia, / because it was the end of the world.
> GEORGE JONAS, poet, "Greenwich Village," *Cities* (1973).

SASKATOON, SASK.
Arise, Saskatoon, Queen City of the North.
> JOHN NELSON LAKE, colonizer, naming the future prairie city of Saskatoon, diary entry, 20 Aug. 1882.

In the 1959 movie *A Connecticut Yankee in King Arthur's Court*, Bing Crosby finds himself flung back in time and facing a horrible execution, when, as I recall, he calculates that an eclipse of the sun is due momentarily. To the awe-struck medievals, he appears to invoke this phenomenon, and the magic words with which he does so are "SASKATOON, SASKATCHEWAN!"
> Noted in a Letter to the Editor contributed by Trevor S. Raymond, Georgetown, Ont., to *Saturday Night*, Nov. 1990.

Been hangin' 'round grain elevators, / Been learnin' 'bout food, / Been talkin' to soil farmers, / Been hangin' round, / This tune is home grown, / Don't come from Hong Kong. / This tune is home grown, / Don't come from Hong Kong.
> Lines from the third verse of "Running Back to Saskatoon" (1972), words by BURTON CUMMINGS and music by Kurt Winter, included in *All Star Canadian Song Book: Top Canadian Songs by Top Canadian Artists* (1972).

Saskawhere? Who'd want to move there?
> HAROLD BALLARD, hockey personality, remark made in Regina where he blocked Saskatoon's bid for a NHL franchise, *The Globe and Mail*, 14 Feb. 1983.

Saskatoon, Saskatchewan, seems to me the most thoroughly Canadian of Canadian cities, the least susceptible to outside stimulants or associations, the most organically itself and in many ways the most graphically illustrative of what we simplistic foreigners like to consider the Canadian character.
> JAN MORRIS, Anglo-Welsh traveller, "Suddenly Saskatoon," *Saturday Night*, July-Aug. 1990.

SAULT STE. MARIE
In Sault Ste. Marie, where they dig copper or nickel or something, there was a giant cent on top of a hill. The clouds were flat and grey and the bus crossed endless plains. . . . It was cornflake country gone to sleep for the winter.
> BOB GELDOF, musician, crossing Canada from Montreal to Vancouver by bus in 1973, mistaking Sault Ste. Marie for Sudbury, Ont., *Is That It?* (1986).

The last place I wanted to start out my professional hockey career was in Sault Ste. Marie. . . . Naturally, I was drafted by Sault Ste. Marie. It was 1977.
> WAYNE GRETZKY, hockey personality, *Gretzky: An Autobiography* (1990) written with Rick Reilly.

SUDBURY, ONT.

The girls are out to Bingo and the boys are gettin' stink-o; / We think no more of Inco on a Sudbury Saturday night.

Stompin' TOM CONNORS, composer and performer, first lines of "Sudbury Saturday Night," included by Bob Davis in *Singin' about Us* (1976).

The town is an environmental nightmare, an industrial combat zone that is so wasted and so ugly that it is widely known as "Sludgebury." For decades fumes from nickel-smelting operations poisoned the region so thoroughly that foliage for miles around the city simply died.

WILLIAM OSCAR JOHNSON, sports and travel writer, "Trans-Canada," *Sports Illustrated*, 27 Jan. 1988.

I think that a lot of people have a misconception about Sudbury — that it's still a "moon" city. There has been a tremendous amount of reforestation and land reclamation here over the years. It's really getting away from the one industry town.

ALEX BAUMANN, Olympic swimmer, contributor, "Incredible Ontario," *Ontario: The Inside Story* (1990).

Once described as "Canada's Pittsburgh without the orchestra," Sudbury now has its own symphony. . . .

PETER C. NEWMAN, columnist, *Maclean's*, 1 April 1991.

TEESWATER, ONT.

It is alleged that some years ago Dr. Gillies, when in Chicago, went to the railway station and asked a ticket agent to sell him a train ticket to Teeswater. The ticket agent said, "And where, may I ask, is Teeswater?" To which Dr. Gillies responded, "Do you mean to tell me that you don't know where Teeswater is? I am surprised because everyone in Teeswater knows where Chicago is!"

ROBERT L. ARMSTRONG, President, Empire Club, introducing Teeswater native James Gillies, M.P., Empire Club of Canada, Toronto, 25 Oct. 1973.

THULE

Thule, pronounced to rhyme with "cool," is in Greenland, in the Arctic. Thule, to rhyme with "newly," is in the Antarctic. This could matter quite a lot to anyone desirous of going to either place.

The word "Thule" is used in Canada to refer to the Fifth Thule Expedition led by Knud Rasmussen across the Canadian Arctic in the early 1920s. The word is also used to refer to the Eskimo culture described by Rasmussen. Its progenitor was the Dorest culture; its successor, the Inuit culture. Pronunciation was distinguished by E. Murray, 2 July 1982, *The Second Cuckoo: A Further Selection of Witty, Amusing and Memorable Letters to The Times* (1983) edited by Kenneth Gregory.

THUNDER BAY, ONT.

When one reaches Port Arthur one feels that one is at last in touch with ancient Canada, the Canada of Parkman, for when that great historian wished to describe the extreme edge of the human world in those days he speaks always of Thunder Bay. "The tribes were all up, from the Iroquois of the British Border to the wild Ojibbeways of Thunder Bay." This curve of Lake Superior is Thunder Bay, and up yonder on the wooded hill are the remains of the mission which was planted so long ago by the heroic Jesuit pioneers, who at the cost of their own lives, brought the first civilization into the wilderness.

SIR ARTHUR CONAN DOYLE, author and traveller, *Our Second American Adventure* (1923).

I'm seventy-five. I would have been seventy-six, but I spent a year in Thunder Bay.

RED SKELTON, comedian, aged 75, performing in Toronto, quoted by Rita Zekas in *The Toronto Star*, 17 March 1989.

TISDALE, SASK.

Welcome to Tisdale / Land of Rape and Honey

"Only in the middle of a weather-beaten sign beside a highway in eastern Saskatchewan does the old name stand on guard," wrote MARK ABLEY in *Beyond Forget: Rediscovering the Prairies* (1986), referring to "rape," which has since the 1960s been known as "canola."

VAL MARIE, SASK.
Folk wisdom from Ethel, a cashier in Val Marie: "Even in the Great Flood of Noah, Val Marie only got an inch."
MARK ABLEY, traveller, *Beyond Forget: Rediscovering the Prairies* (1986).

WHITE RIVER, ONT.
If you're adventurous enough to get off the train here in winter, wear everything you own.
WILLIAM COOS, traveller, author of a series of *Scenic Rail Guides*, quoted by William Oscar Johnson in *Sports Illustrated*, 27 Jan. 1988.

WINDSOR, ONT.
Assumption is a little bay of silence — a little backwater in a stagnant stream. Oh the mental vacuum that is Canada.
MARSHALL McLUHAN, media philosopher, referring to Assumption College which is now part of the University of Windsor, letter to Wyndham Lewis, 13 Dec. 1944, *Letters of Marshall McLuhan* (1987) edited by Matie Molinaro, Corinne McLuhan, and William Toye.

The other problem with Windsor is more topographical than spiritual: the city lies immediately to the *south* of Detroit, a fact that has utterly confused its Canadian population over the years. Still, tens of thousands of Windsorites continue to pour across the Detroit River every day, earning them the nickname "moistbacks."
ALLAN GOULD, satirist, *The Great Wiped Out North: or, When Sacred Cows Come Home to Roost* (1988).

YORKTON, SASK.
My roots are still here. I still think of myself as Canadian.
LEON EDEL, Yorkton-born literary critic and long-time resident of Hawaii, quoted in *The Toronto Star*, 12 Oct. 1982.

PLANNING

They are now working towards a solution which will dissatisfy everybody. That is the Canadian way of getting complete agreement.
TOMMY TWEED, actor and writer, "The Man from Number Ten," CBC Radio's "Stage 50" Series.

Every man for himself, as the elephant said while dancing among the chickens.
T.C. (TOMMY) DOUGLAS, NDP leader, election campaign of 1962, referring to free enterprise and socialism, quoted by Gad Horowitz in *Canadian Labour in Politics* (1968).

Now I am suspicious of these grand schemes. Ambitious planning does not guarantee an ambitious attack.
RICHARD SHARABURA, advertising consultant, *Shooting Your Way to $-Million: A Photographer's Strategy for Success* (1982).

PLAY

When people become too intense, too serious, they will have trouble in relating to any sort of social game or norm. Perhaps this is why jokes are so important. On one hand they tell us about where the problems and grievances are, and, at the same time, they provide the means of enduring these grievances by laughing at the problems.
MARSHALL McLUHAN, communications theorist, letter, 2 Feb. 1973, *Letters of Marshall McLuhan* (1987) edited by Matie Molinaro, Corinne McLuhan, and William Toye.

PLAYWRIGHTS
See also LITERATURE
THEATRE

I don't know of any good playwright who ever gave up writing because he couldn't make any money at it.
BILL GLASSCO, theatre director, quoted

by Jason Sherman in *The Toronto Star*, 4 Nov. 1989.

To be a playwright in this country, whether brand new or unproduced, is still to be completely marginalized, because theatre is still very peripheral. Even to stick to it for twenty years, to finally be recognized and receive multiple productions of a new play, is to reach the top of a very small heap.
> ROBERT WALLACE, playwright, quoted by Jason Sherman in *The Toronto Star*, 4 Nov. 1989

PLEASURES

In order that her creatures shall not be indifferent to her demands, nature has made the act of sexual intercourse a supreme physical pleasure of life.
> ALFRED HENRY TYRER, Anglican minister and birth-control enthusiast, *Sex, Marriage and Birth Control: A Guide-book to Sex Health and a Satisfactory Sex Life in Marriage* (10th ed., 1936).

POETRY & POETS
See also LITERATURE

I must get out of Canada if I am not to be married, have my hair smoothed down and work in a bank.
> FRANK PREWETT, Ontario-born poet who settled in England in 1919, *Selected Poems of Frank Prewett* (1988) edited by Bruce Meyer and Barry Callaghan.

Simply expressed, I write poetry only to reveal my civilization, my sensitivities, my craftsmanship. This, however, is not to be quoted.
> A.M. KLEIN, poet, letter to anthologist A.J.M. Smith, 21 Jan. 1943, *Literary Essays and Reviews* (1987) edited by Usher Caplan and M.W. Steinberg.

How are your gonads?
> E.J. PRATT, poet and professor, greeting fellow bard Irving Layton at the launching in Toronto in Sept. 1959 of Layton's collection *A Red Carpet for the Sun*; quoted by David G. Pitt in *E.J. Pratt: The Master Years, 1927-1964* (1987).

I am a genius who has written work that will survive with the best of Shakespeare, Wordsworth and Keats.
> IRVING LAYTON, poet, letter to *The Montreal Star*, 23 Oct. 1981, *Engagements: The Prose of Irving Layton* (1982).

The poet is someone life knocks on the head and makes ring like a tuning fork. The orchestra of life depends on that tuning fork.
> IRVING LAYTON, poet, seventieth birthday party celebration, Toronto, 12 March 1982, quoted in *The Globe and Mail* the following day.

A poet who appeals to both highbrow and lowbrow readers, like Chaplin in film, seems an impossibility in today's North America, except in the marginal field of nonsense verse.
> JOSEF SKVORECKY, essayist and novelist, "The Good Old Drinking Poet" (1984), *Talkin' Moscow Blues* (1988) edited by Sam Solecki.

Why doesn't anyone talk about Canadian writers? When I was in Canada I asked: What poets do you have? They answered: We have this poet, Pratt. The name didn't seem promising. There are two poems of his: one on the train that goes from Toronto to God-knows-where . . . (what can one expect from a railroad ode?). And the other is an extraordinary poem in which he speaks of a piece, a block of ice. I said: And then? "Well," they said, "other poets would have spoken of Canada's snowy woods, but he addresses himself directly to a block of ice — and that in itself is important". . . .
It surprised me that the United States, in New England, so near to the Canadian frontier, should have produced people such as Emerson, Melville, Henry James, and that next door Canada should have produced nothing, except, as Kipling said,

a country more orderly and essentially more civilized than the United States. Of course, having produced a civilization is having produced a great deal, but it isn't moving.

A civilized country is superior to a barbarian country, but it is not necessarily very interesting.
> JORGE LUIS BORGES, Argentine man-of-letters, interviewed in 1973 about the effects of an earlier visit to Canada; noted by María Esther Vázquez in *Borges, sus Días y su Tiempo* (1984).

A good poet is someone who manages, in a lifetime of standing out in thunderstorms, to be struck by lightning five or six times; a dozen or two dozen times and he is great.
> ROBIN SKELTON, poet, *The Poet's Calling* (1975).

Inner recesses of the mind are not at your beck and call. Perhaps there are small elves in the head, privileged guests living there and continually busy with their own affairs. The only connection the conscious mind has with them is when they permit a collaboration, which perhaps neither the conscious nor the unconscious was capable of alone.
> AL PURDY, poet, Preface, *The Collected Poems of Al Purdy* (1986) edited by Russell Brown.

A well-rounded poem is like a sphere. It is impossible to view it completely.
> JOHN V. HICKS, poet and writer, *Side Glances: Notes on the Writer's Craft* (1987).

How beautifully useless, / how deliciously defiant / a poem is!
> RAYMOND SOUSTER, poet, "Cutting It Short," *Asking for More* (1988).

I remember one of the first readings I ever attended. When the writer was in full flight, one of the reluctant sponsors of the reading came forward and interrupted, "Scuse me, uh, scuse me. Three-one Leafs!" How times change.

M.T. (TERRY) KELLY, novelist and poet, accepting the Governor General's Award for Literature, address published in *Books in Canada*, April 1988.

Music doesn't change the world. Why should poetry? All I can do is change an individual consciousness.
> PHYLLIS WEBB, poet, quoted by H.J. Kirchhoff in *The Globe and Mail*, 18 Feb. 1989.

Film today has taken the place of great poetry. There's no great poetry in our time. I just don't see much of a future for poetry.
> IRVING LAYTON, poet, quoted by Philip Marchand in *The Toronto Star*, 16 Nov. 1989.

Poetry, freedom. It is like air. You know you must have it only when it is taken away from you.
> GEORGE FALUDY, Hungarian-born poet, interviewed by Alan Twigg in *Strong Voices: Conversations with Fifty Canadian Authors* (1988).

The poet teaches with imagination and sympathy. You make a bonfire of your experiences to bring warmth and light to others in the darkness.
> IRVING LAYTON, poet, quoted by Susan Walker in *The Toronto Star*, 7 April 1990.

POLAND

Why doesn't my homeland look like yours?
> LECH WALESA, leader of the Polish trade union Solidarity, referring to the limited economic development of his native Poland compared with that of Canada, speaking at a meeting organized by the Canadian Labour Congress in Hamilton, Ont., 12 Nov. 1989, broadcast on CBC Radio later that day.

The Man from Nowhere
> Epithetical description from the Warsaw media of STANISLAW TYMINSKI, the Pol-

ish-born Canadian who arrived "from no-where" to contest Poland's presidential election, Nov.-Dec. 1990, giving Lech Walesa a run for his money in the first free election since World War II. It turned out that Tyminski made his fortune in computers in Mississauga, Ont., headed the Canadian Libertarian Party, had business interests in Peru, and nourished capitalistic aspirations for his native Poland in the post-Communist period.

POLICE
See also CRIME
ROYAL CANADIAN
MOUNTED POLICE

Remember too that most of the authority the policeman has is merely an extension of your own — if he was not providing the police service, you would have to provide it for yourself.
W.L. HIGGITT, RCMP Commissioner, address, Empire Club of Canada, Toronto, 29 Nov. 1973.

As for the Mounted Police, a few dozen of them managed to maintain law and order over half a continent. Where else in the world is the policeman something of a national symbol and a hero?
WILLIAM KILBOURN, historian, "The Peaceable Kingdom Still," *Daedalus: Journal of the American Academy of Arts and Sciences*, "In Search of Canada," Fall 1988.

The worst enemy of effective policing is the absence of public confidence.
MAX YALDEN, member, Canadian Human Rights Commission, speech, quoted by Commissioner Norman Inkster of the RCMP, McMaster University, Hamilton, Ont., 3 March 1990.

POLITICAL PARTIES
See also POLITICS

When people asked him why he had twice changed his party, his reply always was: "I change my party as I change my shirt, and for the same reason."

R.L. CALDER, Montreal Crown Prosecutor, his background being English, French, and Gaelic, his politics being Liberal, Conservative, and CCF; quoted by Eugene Forsey in *A Life on the Fringe: The Memoirs of Eugene Forsey* (1990). When asked whether he was French or English, he replied: "I am a prefiguration of the Canadian that is to be."

Without a strong national capitalist class behind them, Canadian governments, Liberal and Conservative, have functioned in the interests of international and particularly American capitalism, and have lacked the will to pursue even a modest strategy of economic independence.
"The Waffle Manifesto: For an Independent Socialist Canada" (1969) reprinted in *The Canadian Forum*, Dec. 1989.

None Dare Call Us Sheep / Nous ne sommes pas des moutons
Slogan and maxim of the Parti Rhinoceros/Rhinoceros Party, whose chief "concierge" at the party's Montreal-based "hindquarters" is CHARLIE McKENZIE, who refers to this important principle as the "Primal Promise" and the "Cornelius Factor," after the name of the rhino in the Granby Zoo. The satiric party's organizing meeting is known as the "Kitchen Table Conference," Longueuil, Que., Spring 1963.

The way Canada is run now, politicians must pledge loyalty to the party above all else. In this, Canada is unique among the democracies. Our party structure tolerates little deviation. Our political parties demand blind subservience that is matched only by the Nazi and Communist parties.
PETER WORTHINGTON, newspaperman, contributor to *If I Were Prime Minister* (1987) edited by Mel Hurtig.

I once tabulated the platform pledges of the three national parties over the past ten election campaigns. The promises they made were remarkably similar, varying only in their degree of distributing largess with the taxpayers' dollars: the Tories promised handouts to voters from birth to death; the Liberals, from womb to tomb; the Socialists, from erection to resurrection.

> PETER C. NEWMAN, author, *Sometimes a Great Nation: Will Canada Belong to the 21st Century?* (1988).

During more than a quarter-century of political reporting, I failed to discover any fundamental differences between Liberals and Conservatives — except, perhaps, that Liberals tend to fish from the sterns of rented rowboats while Tories prefer casting their lures off docks, encouraging the fish to come to them. (My research also revealed that Conservatives usually prefer twin beds, which may explain why there are more Liberals.)

> PETER C. NEWMAN, author, *Sometimes a Great Nation: Will Canada Belong to the 21st Century?* (1988).

The Grit cultural establishment likes irony and wit, because they're dry. The Tories were hairy, hopeless, and wild.

> SCOTT SYMONS, novelist and cultural commentator, interviewed in *The Idler*, No. 25, May-June 1990.

POLITICIANS
See also POLITICS

We Canadians are so frustrated by compromise in our daily lives that any man who dares stand up and say honestly what he thinks becomes famous overnight.

> ROGER LEMELIN, novelist and publisher, remark made in 1962, quoted by Jamie Swift in *Odd Man Out: The Life and Times of Eric Kierans* (1988).

I have always enjoyed being a politician. I think it is an honourable profession to pursue. And if politicians always keep their eyes on the human consequences of the changes they effect, politics can be an extraordinary way of changing the human condition for the better.

> STEPHEN LEWIS, M.P.P., address, Empire Club of Canada, Toronto, 26 Oct. 1978.

If I have committed any mistake it is in staying too close to absolute truths, rather than the conventional wisdom. A politician must take absolute truth and accommodate it to the facts around him.

> PIERRE ELLIOTT TRUDEAU, Prime Minister, quoted by Charles Lynch in *The Lynch Mob: Stringing Up Our Prime Ministers* (1988). Lynch added: "Every prime minister has had that struggle, but only Trudeau had the nerve to say it out loud."

Bill, I got a piece of advice for you. Please. Stay in the middle! Don't go too far to the right. Stay in the middle.

> BILL BENNETT, B.C. Premier, giving advice to his ultimate successor William Vander Zalm, quoted by Alan Twigg in *Vander Zalm: From Immigrant to Premier* (1986).

You need the stamina of a water buffalo, the hide of a rhino and the energy of a go-go dancer.

> STANLEY WATERS, retired General and Alberta's Senate nominee, commenting on the requirements of office, quoted by D'Arcy Jenish in *Maclean's*, 30 Oct. 1989.

The politician will be only too happy to abdicate in favour of his image, because the image will be so much more powerful than he could ever be.

> MARSHALL McLUHAN, communications theorist, quoted by Philip Marchand in *Marshall McLuhan: The Medium and the Messenger* (1989).

I was a socialist democrat; I was a pacifist, a Quaker; I was, in constitutional matters, as I still am, a John A. Macdonald Conservative (when I was in the Senate I used to say that I sat as a Pierre Trudeau Liberal because I was a John A. Macdonald Conservative, and it was not just a witticism).

> EUGENE FORSEY, political scientist and retired Senator, *A Life on the Fringe: The Memoirs of Eugene Forsey* (1990).

POLITICS

See also CONSERVATIVE PARTY
ELECTIONS
GOVERNMENT
LIBERAL PARTY
NEW DEMOCRATIC PARTY
PARLIAMENT
PARTI QUÉBÉCOIS
POLITICAL PARTIES
POLITICIANS
RHINOCEROS PARTY
SOCIAL CREDIT

Politics in its more primitive and vigorous manifestations is not a game or a sport, but a form of civil war, with only lethal weapons barred.
JOHN W. DAFOE, editor and publisher, *Clifford Sifton* (1931).

Politics in Canada has always been the art of making the necessary possible.
PETER C. NEWMAN, author, *Sometimes a Great Nation: Will Canada Belong to the 21st Century?* (1988).

Politics, as it turned out, lent itself admirably to storytelling. Where else can you find such a mix of greed, power, lust, conspiracy, sacrifice and secrecy?
VAL SEARS, newspaperman who turned from general feature-story writing in Toronto to political writing in Ottawa, *Hello Sweetheart . . . Get Me Rewrite: Remembering the Great Newspaper Wars* (1988).

Symbolism doesn't need to be defended. It can serve as an excuse for inaction. But it can also be a catalyst for action.
RICHARD GWYN, political correspondent, *The Toronto Star*, 3 Nov. 1989.

I communicate the kind of message that reflects the roots of the old CCF and New Democratic Party. I talk about the politics of the heart.
HOWARD McCURDY, M.P., quoted in *Maclean's*, 4 Dec. 1989.

We owe each other love, and the action that flows from that. We express that love

in deeds, in actions, in laws, institutions, entitlements.
BOB RAE, NDP leader, address, "A Socialist's Manifesto," *The Globe and Mail*, 1 Oct. 1990.

The "Me" Decade has ended. We could tell in the last few weeks [of the election campaign] that people wanted a more just society.
GARY DOER, Manitoba NDP leader, whose party went from 12 to 20 seats in the election on 11 Sept. 1990, quoted by George Nikides in *The Winnipeg Free Press* the following day.

Good government is the best answer to good politics.
JEFFREY SIMPSON, newspaper columnist and commentator, CBC-TV, 23 Sept. 1990.

In politics, madame, you need two things: friends, but above all an enemy.
BRIAN MULRONEY, Prime Minister, addressing a French-speaking reporter, following the by-election victory of Liberal leader Jean Chrétien on 10 Dec. 1990 at Beauséjour, N.S.; quoted by Graham Fraser in *The Globe and Mail*, 12 Dec. 1990.

POLLS

See OPINION POLLS

POLLUTION

See also NATURE

One of the earliest legislative enactments provided that the farmer who polluted a river with manure should pay a fine of $25 or else be imprisoned for two months.
W. FRASER RAE, author, referring to a statute passed in 1870 concerning the Red River Valley, *Newfoundland to Manitoba* (1881).

To learn from asbestos is to learn from the harshest of schoolmasters — tragedy.
Report of the Royal Commission on Matters of Health and Safety Arising from the Use of Asbestos in Ontario (1984), quoted by

Peter Edwards in *The Toronto Star*, 31 March 1990.

PCBs are going to be sent straight back to the SOBs who put them there in the first place.
> Platform of the Rhinoceros Party in the general election, quoted by Roy MacGregor in *The Toronto Star*, 10 Sept. 1988.

New York spends on garbage collection more than the whole world spends on the United Nations.
> Attributed to diplomat HUGH KEENLEYSIDE, in 1989, by Oline Luinenberg and Stephen Osborne in *The Little Pink Book: Quotations on Women* (1990).

The Don River used to run through the Don Valley, which was once one of the most beautiful valleys in all of Southern Ontario. Now the Don Valley Parkway runs through the Don Valley and the Don River hardly runs at all.
> ARTHUR BLACK, broadcaster and humorist, "The Not-So-Grand River," *That Old Black Magic* (1989).

There's an old, but effective saying: The solution to pollution is not dilution.
> DAVID POCH, counsel for Energy Probe, quoted in *The Globe and Mail*, 3 Nov. 1989.

The earth is four and a half million years old. But in the short space of recorded man — about 3000 years — we have almost managed to end civilization. First, with the nuclear bomb, and then through destruction of nature and our growing pollution of every space that we inhabit. In comparative terms, we have been on this planet less than the final few minutes in a whole year of time. Yet we have caused more damage than any other species and may soon make ourselves as defunct as the dinosaurs.
> DORIS ANDERSON, writer, "Symposium," *The Canadian Forum*, Jan. 1990.

Microchemophobia
> Neologism coined by PHILIP JONES, Professor of Engineering and Microbiology at the University of Toronto, writing in the *University of Toronto Bulletin*, quoted by Craig McInnes in *The Globe and Mail*, 7 July 1990. The new word refers to an unwarranted fear of trace levels of toxic chemicals.

We all contribute to the pollution load and we are all going to have to pay, one way or another — in the near future through increased taxes, and over the long haul through being forced to adjust to new processes, new habits, and changes in our way of life.
> ROY AITKEN, executive, Inco Limited, "Industry's Response," *Planet under Stress: The Challenge of Global Change* (1990) edited by Constance Mungall and Digby J. McLaren for the Royal Society of Canada.

I don't think it is enough for Jack to make millions on pollution and then Jill to make millions more cleaning it up.
> GEORGES ERASMUS, Chief of the Assembly of First Nations, remark made in 1990, noted by Oline Luinenberg and Stephen Osborne in *The Little Green Book: Quotations on the Environment* (1990).

POPULATION

The objective of Canada's immigration policy must be to enlarge the population of the country. It would be dangerous for a small population to attempt to hold so great a heritage as ours.
> W.L. MACKENZIE KING, Prime Minister, calling for a return to mass immigration, House of Commons, 1 May 1947; as quoted by Robert F. Harney in "'So Great a Heritage as Ours': Immigration and the Survival of the Canadian Polity," *Daedalus: Journal of the American Academy of Arts and Sciences*, "In Search of Canada," Fall 1988. At the time Canada had a population of 12 million, 50 percent from the British Isles and 30 percent from France.

There are sixty people per square mile in the United States, as opposed to only six per square mile in Canada.
ALLAN FOTHERINGHAM, columnist, *Capitol Offences: Dr. Foth Meets Uncle Sam* (1986).

At first glance, Canada seems thinly populated in a world overstuffed with five billion people. But people cannot live on space alone. Although Canada has productive lands and seas in many limited areas, on average most Canadian land has a very small capability to sustain human life in European style. That huge areas have such limited capacity is the harsh reality of an essentially granite-hard and polar-cold nation.
YORKE EDWARDS, naturalist, "Wilderness Parks: A Concept with Conflicts," *Endangered Spaces: The Future for Canada's Wilderness* (1989) edited by Monte Hummel.

By the middle of the 21st-Century, the world population "problem" will essentially have solved itself. We will all be living longer and healthier lives, with an extraordinarily increased quality of life worldwide and — rather than being viewed as a liability — people will have become their own greatest asset.
FRANK FEATHER, futurologist, *G-Forces: Reinventing the World — The 35 Global Forces Restructuring Our World* (1989).

PORNOGRAPHY

Vile literature is secretly and widely circulated in Canada, literature of a character calculated to undermine the morals of the people, and entail the most disastrous consequences on society. Improper and obscene, or semi-obscene literature is imported into this country and openly sold. Drugs and instruments for procuring abortion and for kindred purposes are advertised secretly and are sold by agents, and this abuse cannot very readily be reached by the law as it now stands.
JOHN CHARLTON, M.P. for North Norfolk,

address delivered in the House of Commons, 11 May 1892; as quoted by Angus McLaren and Arlene Tigar McLaren in *The Bedroom and the State: The Changing Practices and Politics of Contraception and Abortion in Canada, 1880-1980* (1986) who noted, "No one countered Charlton's sensational assertions."

What is wrong with Pornography is that it is a successful attempt to sell sex for more than it is worth.
QUENTIN CRISP and JOHN HOFSESS, English-born entertainer and Canadian-born author, *Manners from Heaven: A Divine Guide to Good Behaviour* (1984).

Nevertheless, only 12% of Canadian adults polled said that they regard pornography as a problem in their communities, with 59% seeing it either as a small problem or no problem at all.
REGINALD W. BIBBY and DONALD C. POSTERSKI, sociologists, *The Emerging Generation: An Inside Look at Canada's Teenagers* (1985).

The plan was to drive down over the border by Point Roberts, a town just inside the U.S. dedicated to loose drinking laws, porn movies and peepshows. The Canadians are strangely Victorian with regard to all three. Point Roberts does wonderful business.
BOB GELDOF, musician, on life in Vancouver in the mid-1970s, *Is That It?* (1986).

Tock about yer full frontals, goze on fer pages with everyone bear as a bird all over.
DON HARRON, comedian, in the person of Charlie Farquharson, *Cum Buy the Farm* (1987).

I work primarily as a prostitute, but I also do some work in porn, mostly in live sex and some photography. What a lot of porn workers would like to see is the right to exist, the right to work without being ostracized from society, the right to work without being charged and prosecuted.

We would like to see the obscenity laws taken away, and we'd like people to be able to make up their own minds about what they consider to be obscene.

VALERIE SCOTT, spokesperson for Canadian Organization for the Rights of Prostitutes (CORP), "Working Girls," in *Good Girls/Bad Girls: Sex Trade Workers and Feminists Face to Face* (1987) edited by Laurie Bell.

Our society has many intellectual difficulties in coming to terms with pornography; but this is not because the issue is a complicated one, rather because we are not very smart.

DAVID WARREN, editor and columnist, "Moral and Aesthetic Squalor," *The Idler*, 25 Sept.-Oct. 1989.

POST OFFICE

Meanwhile, I would ask one question of the post office: Why does it cost so much more to mail a letter in Canada, for much less service, than in the United States? As the gag goes, a letter in Canada costs 36 cents: 18 cents for delivery and 18 cents for storage!

JACQUES FRANCOEUR, President and Publisher of Uni-Média Inc., contributor to *If I Were Prime Minister* (1987) edited by Mel Hurtig.

No matter how efficient a postal service is, there will always be enough mistakes for people to remember. And no matter how good the service, it will never be good enough to match people's expectations.

DAVID STEWART-PATTERSON, journalist, *Post Mortem: Why Canada's Mail Won't Move* (1987).

Canada Post too gives new insights into waste treatment. For instance, biodegradability, the very basis of pulp and paper pollution abatement, can now be studied under controlled conditions as our letters inch (or centimetre) their way through the system. In fact, as so many letters and parcels disappear without a trace, it could well be that the Post Office has already

achieved total biodegradability — a process that has long eluded environmental scientists.

TOM DAVEY, editor and columnist, *Environmental Science & Engineering*, June-July 1990.

POSTAGE STAMPS

William, consider the humble stamp. It costs but a few pennies, but it has the ability to stick to one thing until it gets there.

Thoughts of a character in the novel *Going to the Dogs* (1987) by RUSSELL McRAE.

POVERTY
See also FOOD BANKS
HUNGER
THIRD WORLD

It seems to me that if we had a summit conference of women dedicated to the welfare of children all over the world, we might reach an understanding.

LOTTA DEMPSEY, columnist, *The Toronto Star*, 21 May 1960. This suggestion led social activist and feminist Kay Macpherson and others to convene just such a conference under the sponsorship of the Voice of Women; cited by Kay Macpherson in "The Voice of Women" (1986), *Up and Doing: Canadian Women and Peace* (1989) edited by Janice Williamson and Deborah Gorham.

In fact, as long as our economy is dominated by monopoly capitalism or any other form of such enterprise, and our society is permeated by values of personal gain, the primacy of private property and the protection of the wealthy, a great deal of poverty will be inevitable.

W. EDWARD MANN, sociologist, *Poverty and Social Policy in Canada* (1970).

The true cradle of confederation is Pointe Saint-Charles. It was the first industrial area in Canada and the source of a number

of empires — those of the Molsons, the Redpaths, the Ogilvies and others. These people based their power on the gross exploitation of natives and French and Irish Quebec workers. In 1981, less than fifty men living within one square mile of Montreal controlled more than half the wealth in Canada. That same year, one out of every four children born in the Point died before the age of two.
> DAVID FENNARIO, playwright, discussing the working-class Montreal district of Point Saint-Charles, quoted by Jon Kaplan in *Now*, 27 Oct. 1988.

Increasingly poverty in Canada has a female face. The feminization of poverty — the fact that three in five older single women, and 60 per cent of sole support mothers and their children are poor — is now a reality. And it is a disgrace in a country that is not only wealthy, but also espouses equality for all. As a result, we are witnessing the re-emergence of child poverty in Canada.
> MAUDE BARLOW, human-relations consultant, *The Ottawa Citizen*, 27 April 1988.

It has been predicted that by the year 2000 all the poor in the United States will be women and their children. What happens to men's children?
> BETTY JANE WYLIE and LYNNE Mac-FARLANE, authors, *Everywoman's Money Book* (1989).

Poverty isn't being broke; poverty is never having enough.
> BETTY JANE WYLIE and LYNNE Mac-FARLANE, authors, *Everywoman's Money Book* (1989).

We in Canada persist in hanging on to the myth that the [Third World] is all "over there," despite the burgeoning soup kitchens, the food banks, and the poverty in our own country.
> LOIS WILSON, Christian activist, *Turning the World Upside Down: A Memoir* (1989).

Christian theology rejects any deterministic understanding of the social process. Human history remains ever open to the new. Operative among people, especially among the poor and oppressed, is a spirit — the Spirit — that summons and empowers them to struggle against structures of injustice and replace them with structures that promote new life.
> GREGORY BAUM, theologian, "Symposium," *The Canadian Forum*, Jan. 1990.

We have a responsibility, not to ameliorate, but to eradicate poverty in this country by 2000.
> AUDREY McLAUGHLIN, NDP leader, quoted by Nick Martin in *The Winnipeg Free Press*, 31 Jan. 1990.

Headlines pass; breadlines continue.
> ROBIN SKELTON, man-of-letters, aphorism, May 1990.

Why don't the poor elect different governments? Because most of them aren't old enough to vote.
> CAROLYN JACK, commentator, "Children in Poverty," *The Canadian Forum*, Sept. 1990.

POWER
See also ELECTRICAL POWER
NUCLEAR POWER
SOLAR ENERGY

New Democrats must begin now to insist on the redistribution of power, and not simply welfare, in a socialist direction.
> "The Waffle Manifesto: For an Independent Socialist Canada" (1969) reprinted in *The Canadian Forum*, Dec. 1989.

Canada had taught me that your level of effectiveness increased in direct proportion to your level of power. The more people you knew, the more you could do.
> BOB GELDOF, Irish-born musician, on life in Vancouver writing for the *Georgia Strait* in the mid-1970s, *Is That It?* (1986).

The power of the invisible / is the visible.
> NICHOLAS CATANOY, poet and aphorist,

from "Notes on a Prison Wall (Fragment),"
Canadian Literature, Summer 1988.

The ability of small groups to stop an activity greatly exceeds the power of large groups to get something moving.
FRANK OGDEN, futurologist, "Ogden's Fourth Law," *Dr. Tomorrow's Lessons from the Future* (updated Oct. 1988).

Power is not real. It is an illusion maintained by the belief of the powerless that others hold it. For instance, Ottawa and Toronto believe that they are at the centre of things. Toronto is surer of this than Ottawa. In reality, every community believes *it* is the centre of the universe, but the rest of Canada does not support Cape Bretoners or Westerners in this delusion. However, people in Toronto have thousands of people elsewhere in Canada who willingly support them in their delusions. Because of this, we all give up a little of our power to Toronto and Ottawa. Places where money is accumulated or where decisions are made become powerful. These two elements — money and decision-making — help to define power.
ELIZABETH MAY, environmental activist, "Political Realities," *Endangered Spaces: The Future for Canada's Wilderness* (1989) edited by Monte Hummel.

The fault, I realized, is not with Hydro's engineers but with the fact that we have assigned to them the wrong task. Expecting Ontario Hydro, one of the most efficient and dedicated producers of power in the world, to teach us restraint in the use of power is like putting the liquor control board in charge of Alcoholics Anonymous.
DAVID LEES, journalist, "Living in the Nuclear Shadow," *Toronto Life*, Nov. 1989.

I believe, after all these years, that Canadians would chafe at the idea of living inside a superpower. We were never that comfortable living next door to one. Americans grow up imbued with a sense of power; Canadians grow up appreciating the value of influence. Canadians are more comfortable — and more often more effective — wielding influence.
PETER JENNINGS, Toronto-born ABC anchorman, *Maclean's*, 25 June 1990.

However, Canada is not, and has never been, a great power, and Canadians have thus been largely spared the excesses of national megalomania and paranoia to which the citizens of great powers usually fall victim.
GWYNNE DYER and TINA VILJOEN, commentator and TV producer, *The Defence of Canada: In the Arms of the Empire* (1990).

PRAIRIE PROVINCES

See also ALBERTA
MANITOBA
SASKATCHEWAN
The WEST

The Inhabitants of the Plains are so advantageously situated that they could live very happily independent of our assistance.
DUNCAN McGILLIVRAY, trapper, 1790s, quoted by A.S. Morton in *The Journal of Duncan McGillivray of the North West Company* (1929).

As for the ghastly monotony of the wilderness beyond them, through Calgary and Winnipeg right on to Toronto — words fortunately fail. The manners of the people are crude and offensive. They seem to resent the existence of civilized men; and show it by gratuitous insolence, which they mistake for a mask of manly independence. The whole country and its people are somehow cold and ill-favoured.
ALEISTER CROWLEY, occultist and traveller, impressions of the prairies in 1905-6, after finding even the Rockies wanting in effect, *The Confessions of Aleister Crowley: An Autohagiography* (1969) edited by John Symonds and Kenneth Grant.

From Calgary we went to Edmonton and from there to Regina and from there to Winnipeg. We stayed a day in each place, sleeping in our faithful private car. . . . All the towns are much the same, set in the middle of flat endless prairies, the "bald headed Prairie" indeed — interesting to those interested in wheat — but not otherwise.

AGATHA CHRISTIE, English mystery novelist, impressions of a trip made in 1922, quoted by Janet Morgan in her biography *Agatha Christie* (1984).

Moving from east to west the land / rises in successive giant steps / like prairie billiard tables / where players of sufficient stature / can't be found in the immediate vicinity

AL PURDY, poet, "Home Thoughts," *The Collected Poems of Al Purdy* (1986) edited by Russell Brown.

The depth, the uncompromising directness of the Prairies, is the traveller's only reward. Crossing this openness, one feels the appearance of a town on the horizon as an intrusion. I have driven through southern Manitoba and remember that the vision of Winnipeg at the end of the highway was a colossal disappointment. Another time, reaching Calgary from the south, its towers shining like those of the Emerald City of Oz, I had a sense of unreality; it seemed that while the dusty landscape I had come through possessed a taste and smell of its own, the Calgarian skyline was incorporeal, an impossible mirage.

ALBERTO MANGUEL, cultural commentator, "Prairie Zen," *The Globe and Mail's Destinations Magazine*, April 1988.

There is nothing remarkable or distinguished in admiring Niagara Falls or the Banff mountains; they are obviously admirable things. But a space that has the delicacy of not being loud, of not being adorned, in fact of hardly being at all, requires a different inspection. It demands an effort of both patience and imagination, like the abstract geometric mandalas used as instruments of contemplation in tantric yoga. In this sense, the Prairies are our most generous landscape because they highlight or explain nothing and allow us, instead, an unconditional freedom.

ALBERTO MANGUEL, cultural commentator, "Prairie Zen," *The Globe and Mail's Destinations*, April 1988.

The Prairie Provinces seem to most Canadians to be another natural region within the national framework. Again, however, it is often difficult to see any commonality of interest. As in the Maritimes, the mechanisms of collaboration exist. But political relationships are by no means close. I recall that one of the Prairie premiers, about twenty years ago, wrote to the Canadian Association of Geographers saying that he was surprised to hear us refer to the Prairie Provinces, as if they had much in common and were a natural grouping. In fact, he said, that was not the case. Alberta, Saskatchewan, and Manitoba have distinctive sets of special interests. It is the exception, not the rule, to find them in agreement.

F. KENNETH HARE, geographer, "Canada: The Land," *Daedalus: Journal of the American Academy of Arts and Sciences*, "In Search of Canada," Fall 1988.

The great North American prairie has a noble quality in its vast spaces and sensuous sparseness. A single tree becomes a monument in such a landscape; a house, a fortress; fences and roads and the ploughlines of the fields form an overlying, pervasive geometry.

ARTHUR ERICKSON, architect, *The Architecture of Arthur Erickson* (1988).

I was born and grew up / hereabouts / and for me this is / the most interesting country.

MARGARET LAURENCE, novelist and occasional poet, concluding lines of "Via Rail and Via Memory," *Dance on the Earth: A Memoir* (1989).

The grandeur of the place strikes me as unresolved, as if it too never quite achieves liftoff, but sinks back always under the sheer hugeness of everything.

JAN MORRIS, Anglo-Welsh traveller, commenting on "that infinite horizon" which lies over prairie cities, "Suddenly Saskatoon," *Saturday Night*, July-Aug. 1990.

PRAYER

O Great Spirit, whose voice I hear in the winds, and whose breath gives life to all the world, hear me. I am a man before you, one of your many children. I am small and weak, I need your strength and wisdoms. Let me walk in beauty and make my eyes ever behold the red and purple sunsets. Make my hands respect the things you have made, my ears sharp to hear your voice. Make me wise so that I may know the things you have taught my people, the lessons you have hidden in every leaf and rock. I seek strength, O Creator, not to be superior to my brothers, but to be able to fight my greatest enemy, myself. Make me ever ready to come to you with clean hand and straight eye, so that when life fades as the setting sunset, my spirit may come to you without shame.
> This is the text of the "Iroquois Prayer," a modern prayer with traditional elements, which is attributed to a chief or elder named WHITE CLOUD. There are many versions of the text, which is sometimes reproduced as prose and sometimes as free verse. This version, based on one in free verse form, was printed in Don Mills, Ont., in 1976.

Interviewer: Do you still find time to pray? Beaverbrook: Pray? Well, no. You see, I leave all that to the Moderator of the General Assembly of the Presbyterian Church in Canada.
> Exchange between an unidentified interviewer and LORD BEAVERBROOK, *The New York Herald Tribune*, 25 May 1964.

The very energy of asking for help from Christ, God, Allah, the angels, is a catalyst for change and is as strong as the strength of my belief.
> DOROTHY MACLEAN, medium, *To Hear the Angels Sing: An Odyssey of Co-Creation with the Devic Kingdom* (1980).

We're all like two-year-olds when it comes to prayer.
> BETTY JANE WYLIE, author, *No Two Alike* (1980).

In that midnight moment when the compass of our hearts points to vengeance and the will to ill, we have available to us the fiery weaponry of prayer. Whether we err or fail in our causes, we can abandon ourselves to the transforming and miraculous power of an utterly unlimited and terrifying love.
> JOY KOGAWA, novelist, "Is There a Just Cause?" (1983), *Up and Doing: Canadian Women and Peace* (1989) edited by Janice Williamson and Deborah Gorham.

Praying is a chance to come to terms with the good and evil inside yourself. It's not just trying to get something you want.
> ROBERTSON DAVIES, man-of-letters, interviewed by John Milton Harvard in 1984, *Conversations with Robertson Davies* (1989) edited by J. Madison Davis.

Clearly, you don't have to go to church to worship. But it can provide a fitting context. The sad thing is that so many people forget — or never realize — that they can do it anywhere.
> TOM HARPUR, religion columnist, "The Need for Worship," *Always on Sunday* (1988).

I think the state of prayer is a state of being. You don't have to be yapping at God, if He exists. It's a state of being that's first cousin to dance. Dance is prayer in motion. And eros is dance with touch. And sex is what you do if you don't succeed.
> SCOTT SYMONS, novelist and cultural commentator, interviewed in *The Idler*, No. 25, May-June 1990.

PREDICTION & PROPHECY

See also FUTURE
OPINION POLLS

I am the man who is called on earth by the name of Dekanahwideh, and I have just come from the west and am now going east for the purpose of propagating peace, so that the shedding of human blood might cease among you. . . .

I shall now build my canoe, for the time has come for me to set out on my mission in the world. Know that far away, on lake and many rivers, I go seeking the council smoke of nations beyond this lake, holding my course toward the sunrise. It is my business to stop the shedding of blood among human beings. . . .

It is I who came from the west and am going eastward and am called Dekanah-wideh in the world.

> Arrival and departure of Dekanahwideh, the semi-legendary founder of the Great Peace and the Six Nations Confederacy, speaking near the present site of Kingston, Ont., before embarking in his stone boat on the Great Lakes with the mission of establishing the Iroquois Confederacy. Quoted by Paul A.W. Wallace in *The White Roots of Peace* (1946). The words are derived from "The Traditional Narrative of the Origin of the Confederation of the Five Nations" adopted by the Council of Chiefs, Six Nations' Council of Grand River, Canada, 3 July 1900.

May not our mechanisms . . . be ultimately forced to admit that aerial flight is one of that great class of problems with which man can never cope, and give up all attempts to grapple with it? . . . The construction of an aerial vehicle which could carry even a single man from place to place at pleasure requires the discovery of some new metal or some new force. Even with such a discovery we could not expect one to do more than carry its own.

> SIMON NEWCOMB, Maritime-born scientist and astronomer, *The Independent*, 22 Oct. 1903, quoted by David Wallachinsky, Amy Wallace, and Irving Wallace in *The Book of Predictions* (1981). Two months later, on 17 Dec. 1903, the heavier-than-air flight was successfully demonstrated by the Wright Brothers.

The White Star, the Cunard and the Hamburg-American lines are not devoting their attention to the struggle for supremacy in obtaining the most luxurious appointments for their ships, but the time will soon come when the greatest and most appalling of all disasters at sea will be the result.

> CHARLES M. HAYES, President, Grand Trunk Railway, prediction made about steamship travel by a railway man who soon thereafter perished aboard the White Star's *Titanic*, 14 April 1912, as noted by George Behe in *Titanic: Psychic Warnings of a Tragedy* (1988).

Many things are yet to happen before others begin.

> Oracular pronouncement of Mr. Yahi-Bahi in "The Yahi-Bahi Oriental Society" in STEPHEN LEACOCK's satiric novel *Arcadian Adventures of the Idle Rich* (1914).

What about Canada? "Canada will be split up. It will divide. But the people won't feel it much."

> Prophecy made by the Russian psychic ZIMA (identified only as a college-educated "witch") in Moscow in July 1968, as recorded by Sheila Ostrander and Lynn Schroeder in *Psychic Discoveries behind the Iron Curtain* (1970). As the authors noted, "So far as Zima's predictions of international events are concerned, to be fair we should point out that they have less of the educated guess to them than they would if made by a Westerner. Soviets get infinitesimally little news about world events or even about the moves of their own country on the world stage."

At the end of the century, she said, Canada and Brazil will be among the most powerful countries because they'll have both food and energy.

Prediction made by JEANE DIXON, Washington-based seer and astrologer, as reported by Denis Brian in *Jeane Dixon: The Witnesses* (1976).

Your country, Canada, will become a different kind of union. It will become less cohesive than it is now and the provinces will be more independent of each other. This will be all for the good, however, as it will be the beginning of the northern hemisphere eventually becoming unified.

RUTH-ANN CAMPBELL, psychic, channelling her "spirit control," quoted by Joe Fisher in *The Toronto Sun*, 24 Feb. 1980.

North America will see many land changes. Alberta will become a paradise for archeologists as more prehistoric discoveries are made, such as the huge underwater river I predicted. The State of Washington will as well yield many prehistoric finds. There will be earthquakes in Alberta and Mount St. Helens is not finished spewing her rivers of black mud.... I feel over the next twenty years we will all have to accept the fact of other similar inhabited planets. People far more intelligent than this human race do exist. I feel this will come about due to scientific finds.

These observations are from a series of predictions made by NAJLA MADY, psychic and resident of St. Catharines, Ont., in her memoirs, *Simply Psychic* (1983).

I'd like to make a prediction of my own. The precogs will continue to flourish as they have for millennia and many people will continue to flock to psychics and continue to support the phony profession of precognition.

HENRY GORDON, magician and debunker of psychic claims, *ExtraSensory Deception: ESP, Psychics, Shirley MacLaine, Ghosts, UFOs* (1987).

If I dare make a prophecy, as a matter of fact, I would myself hazard an unpopular

guess that in fifty years' time Vancouver will be much as it is today, only less so.

JAN MORRIS, Anglo-Welsh travel writer, "Two Nice for Words," *Saturday Night*, Feb. 1988.

Her Britannic Majesty will be remembered as the last Queen of England and the Prince of Wales may never be crowned.

The incoming Conservative government shall abolish two obsolescent Canadian institutions: The Senate and the Post Office.

The overall success of free trade and its expansion into a world economic and political community will bring Brian Mulroney the Nobel Prize for Economics and assure the gentleman of being elected for a third term in office.

Predictions made by MAHA YOGI A.S. NARAYANA, known as Swami Narayana, "superpsychic," published in the newsletter of the Espon Corporation, Mississauga, Ont., 5 Oct. 1988.

I am predicting no unions by the year 2001. In Canada last year, 62% of all new jobs were created in the communications area and had five or less employees. Now you don't need to be a rocket trajectory scientist to figure out that in ten years we won't need any unions.

FRANK OGDEN, futurologist known as "Dr. Tomorrow," characteristic observation, 1980s.

Predictions have power: there is no rhetorical or propaganda device more powerful than prophecy. Predictions do not simply describe the world — they *act* on it.

MAX DUBLIN, sociologist, *FutureHype: The Tyranny of Prophecy* (1989).

Predicting the future has become so integral to the fabric of modern consciousness that few people feel compelled to question it, and fewer still feel the need to defend it. And yet, in surveying the landscape of modern prophecy, it was shocking to discover how much of what even our most respectable prophets have to say about the future is blatantly false, that is, either deeply flawed intellectually, or morally questionable, or both.

MAX DUBLIN, sociologist, *FutureHype: The Tyranny of Prophecy* (1989).

This decade is going to bring about almost unfathomable changes. Telecommunications are going to be virtually unrecognizable by the end of the '90s, and fibre-optics will have an amazing impact on our lives.

JAY INGRAM, host of CBC Radio's *Quirks and Quarks,* quoted in *Toronto Computes!,* March 1990.

In ten years we may begin to see electric cars on the market. The only reason we haven't seen them already is that, twenty years ago, we didn't foresee the problems we would cause by all these emissions. The big three car manufacturers just haven't felt the pressure to create non-fossil-fuel propelled cars as yet, but certainly with the kind of attention being paid to the environment, the pressure to come up with alternatives is building.

JAY INGRAM, host of CBC Radio's *Quirks and Quarks,* quoted in *Toronto Computes!,* March 1990.

You can't anticipate the unexpected.

Attributed to BRIAN DORMER, resident of Norway House, Man., by Mike Vlasman, personal communication, 16 Feb. 1991.

PREGNANCY
See also MOTHERHOOD

Certainly those that suffer, say from the pressure of unwanted pregnancy, will find it much, much easier to cope with the situation if they have a faith in Jesus Christ.

WILLIAM VANDER ZALM, British Columbia Premier, quoted by Keith Baldrey and Gary Mason in *Fantasyland* (1989).

I've gone through it four times and it's been a very enjoyable experience.

Attributed to B.C. Health Minister PETER DUECK, in 1988, by Oline Luinenberg and

Stephen Osborne in *The Little Pink Book: Quotations on Women* (1990).

PREJUDICE
See also DISCRIMINATION

The blue glasses of Prejudice spoils all colour-schemes.

Aphorism associated with the Group of Seven, "The New Canadian Art," *The Daily Intelligencer* (Belleville, Ont.), 27 Sept. 1919.

None is too many.

Attributed to an unnamed senior government official with the Department of Immigration who was explaining to journalists in early 1945 how many Jews would be allowed into Canada at the end of the Second World War. The remark — though not the sentiment — is erroneously attributed to F.C. BLAIR, Director of Immigration, who did write, in a letter to Undersecretary of State O.D. Skelton, 16 June 1939: "The line must be drawn somewhere." Noted by Irving Abella and Harold E. Troper in *None Is Too Many: Canada and the Jews of Europe, 1933-1948* (1982).

Usually the gentleman kisses the lady's hand but this time I'm going to reverse the procedure.

MARIAN ANDERSON, black American singer, kissing the hand of Oscar Berceller, Hungarian-born proprietor of Winston's Theatre Grill in Toronto in the early 1940s, who showed no discrimination on the basis of colour. In those days touring black entertainers were routinely refused admittance to hotels and service in hotel dining rooms and restaurants. Quoted by Herbert Whittaker and Arnold Edinborough in *Winston's: The Life and Times of a Great Restaurant* (1988).

The oldest paradox of prejudice is that it renders its victims simultaneously invisible and overexposed.

BHARATI MUKHERJEE, author born in India who lived in Canada and now lives in the United States, "An Invisible Woman," *Toronto Remembered: A Celebration of the City* (1984) edited by William Kilbourn.

I don't ask employers, for example, to *like* blacks or Jews or native people; I ask employers to *hire* the qualified members of these groups whether they like them or not.

A. ALAN BOROVOY, General Counsel, Canadian Civil Liberties Association, *When Freedoms Collide: A Case for Our Civil Liberties* (1988).

PREMIER

"Prime minister" translates into French as "premier ministre." That, in turn, translates back into English as "first minister."

Hence the compromise at federal-provincial conferences, where all heads of government, federal or provincial, are called first ministers, or *premiers ministres* in French.

Earlier in this century, the prime minister of Canada was called a premier, as was the prime minister of Britain. But gradually "premier" as a form of address applied to a national leader fell into disuse, first in London and later in Ottawa and the capitals of the other Commonwealth nations.

CHARLES LYNCH, columnist and author, *The Lynch Mob: Stringing Up Our Prime Ministers* (1988).

PRESENT
See also TIME

The present cannot be revealed to people until it has become yesterday.

MARSHALL McLUHAN, communications theorist, *War and Peace in the Global Village* (1968), as quoted by Philip Marchand in *Marshall McLuhan: The Medium and the Messenger* (1989).

The immediate is too important to leave for a moment.

ELIZABETH SMART, novelist and diarist,

"Journal 1982 (Edmonton)," *Autobiographies* (1987) edited by Christina Burridge.

PRIDE, NATIONAL

One is not supposed to be sentimental in Canada, least of all in generalization, but at a moment when almost everywhere in the world small nations are rediscovering themselves, I think it high time the Canadians resumed the practice of national pride. For myself I am not ashamed to say that I have grown to love their country, and would like to give it a figurative kick in the pants, to get its adrenalin going.

JAN MORRIS, Anglo-Welsh travel writer, *The Toronto Star*, 29 March 1990.

PRIME MINISTER

I am here because I am not particularly obnoxious to anybody.

Attributed to SIR JOHN ABBOTT, Prime Minister in 1891-92, quoted by Vincent Durant in *War Horse of Cumberland* (1985).

They think a prime minister has much power. He doesn't even have influence.

W.L. MACKENZIE KING, Prime Minister, a few months before his death, addressing Gordon Sinclair who quoted the remark in *Will Gordon Sinclair Please Sit Down* (1975).

Mackenzie King proved that a man could be Prime Minister for ever, John Diefenbaker proved that anyone could be Prime Minister, and Lester Pearson proved that we do not need a Prime Minister.

Attributed to T.C. (TOMMY) DOUGLAS, NDP leader, election campaign of 1966.

Can you imagine the American president having to lunch regularly with the premiers of Alberta and Newfoundland and deal with Quebec over breakfast in French?

JOHN W. HOLMES, diplomat and author, *Canada: A Middle-Aged Power* (1976).

This is a nation where somebody from a little corner of the foothills of Alberta, without much money behind him, can stand in equal opportunity with a millionaire's son to become prime minister of Canada.

> JOE CLARK, Prime Minister, address in Timmins, Ont., May 1979, quoted by Dalton Camp in *Points of Departure* (1979).

There ought to be a school for prime ministers so they can learn how to govern. Instead, they learn at public expense.

> VAL SEARS, newspaperman, quoted by Claire Hoy in *Friends in High Places: Politics and Patronage in the Mulroney Government* (1987).

Using this criterion [respect rather than the love and hate of the electorate], we have had only two great prime ministers: Sir John A. Macdonald and Sir Wilfrid Laurier. There have been four near-greats (Sir Robert Borden, Sir John Thompson, Lester Pearson, and Pierre Trudeau), four adequates (Alexander Mackenzie, R.B. Bennett, Arthur Meighen, and Louis St. Laurent), and four disasters (Sir John Abbott, Sir Mackenzie Bowell, Sir Charles Tupper, and John Diefenbaker).

> PETER C. NEWMAN, author, contributor to *If I Were Prime Minister* (1987) edited by Mel Hurtig.

There is a lot to be said for a prime minister concentrating on just keeping his head above water, without actually doing things. Politics, remember, is the art of the possible, and in Canadian politics not very much is ever possible.

> GEORGE BAIN, journalist, contributor to *If I Were Prime Minister* (1987).

Lester Pearson said it required the hide of a rhinoceros, the morals of St. Francis, the patience of Job, the wisdom of Solomon, the strength of Hercules, the leadership of Napoleon, the magnetism of a Beatle, and the subtlety of Machiavelli. And this was before saturation TV, the Charter of Rights and Freedoms, the resurgent Senate and the principle of total disclosure.

> CHARLES LYNCH, columnist and author, referring to the office of Prime Minister, *The Lynch Mob: Stringing Up Our Prime Ministers* (1988).

The next prime minister of Canada will be someone who had never been heard of yet.

> ALLAN FOTHERINGHAM, columnist, *Maclean's*, 19 June 1989.

Whatever the efforts of the opposition, a prime minister with an absolute majority in Canada has not been effectively challenged since the party rebellion that dislodged Sir John A. in 1873. Unless he commits some flagrantly criminal act, he remains immune and as absolute in his actions as he is in his majority.

> GEORGE WOODCOCK, author and social commentator, "Five-Year Fascism," *The Canadian Forum*, Dec. 1990.

PRINCE EDWARD ISLAND
See also CHARLOTTETOWN

How I love Cavendish! I love it for its beauty — I love it for its old associations, as I will never love any other spot on earth.

> L. M. MONTGOMERY, author, journal entry, 27 Jan. 1911, Cavendish, P.E.I., *The Selected Journals of L.M. Montgomery: Volume II, 1910-1921* (1987).

Is it the touch of austerity in the Island landscape that gives it its distinctive beauty? And whence comes this austerity? Is it from the fir and spruce? Or the glimpses of the sea? Or does it go deeper, to the very soul of the land? For lands have personalities, as have human beings.

> L.M. MONTGOMERY, author, letter of 13 Sept. 1913, *My Dear Mr. M.: Letters to G.B. MacMillan* (1980) edited by Francis W.P. Bolger and Elizabeth R. Epperly.

I have never been to Prince Edward Island, but I understand they have potatoes. I've never met a potato I didn't love.

ALLAN FOTHERINGHAM, columnist, *Maclean's*, Feb. 1978.

The smallest province, Prince Edward Island, is still almost twice as large as the smallest state, Rhode Island.
ALLAN FOTHERINGHAM, columnist, comparing sizes of Canadian provinces and American states, *Capitol Offences: Dr. Foth Meets Uncle Sam* (1986).

Prince Edward Island may well be the saddest province in Canada. It's not sad all the time, of course, and your typical Islander doesn't walk around looking as though a truck has just killed his favourite dog. But no other province is so tortured by the gap between a beautiful dream and a homely reality.
HARRY BRUCE, essayist, "The Seductive Myth of the Perfect Island," *Down Home: Notes of a Maritime Son* (1988). Bruce goes on to discuss the myth of "the island way of life" based on the notion that in the past "the Island's secret was self-sufficiency."

PRINCIPLES

When you have a philosophy, when you have a set of principles by which you live and upon which you can depend and which the party can run with, when you have principles, you don't have to have consultants, you don't have to have big meetings to tell you what it is that needs doing.
WILLIAM VANDER ZALM, B.C. Premier, address in Powell River, B.C., quoted by John Cruickshank in *The Globe and Mail*, 13 Feb. 1988.

PRISON

See also JUSTICE & INJUSTICE
PUNISHMENT

The imprisonment of those who hold unpopular opinions is the negation of democracy. While these men are in jail not one of us is really free. It was their turn yesterday. It may be ours tomorrow.

F.J. (FRED) DIXON, charged with seditious conspiracy in connection with the Winnipeg General Strike, Address to the Jury, Winnipeg, Feb. 13-14, 1920.

Once the shock of arrest subsides, it is a great relief in a Communist country to find yourself in a prison cell: Paradoxically you feel free at least to be yourself. Also there is the fact that many thousands share the same fate; and misery, after all, does love company.
GEORGE FALUDY, Hungarian-born poet, *Notes from the Rainforest* (1988).

Boredom, blood, tears, futility, that is what prison is all about. How uncanny that this description echoes words often spoken of life in the trenches of war.
JO-ANN MAYHEW, writer and inmate, "Corrections Is a Male Enterprise," *Journal of Prisoners on Prisons*, Summer 1988.

When a person begins to write, he also begins to read. I think art makes that one immeasurable leap where people can start to imagine their worlds are better.
STEPHEN REID, author who wrote his novel *Jackrabbit Parole* in Kingston Penitentiary, quoted by Dennis Kucherawy in *The Toronto Star*, 26 May 1990.

PRIVACY

See also SECRECY

The very peculiar feature of North Americans is that we go outside to be alone, and we go inside to be social. All the rest of mankind go outside to be social and inside to be alone. There's no privacy in the North American home.
MARSHALL McLUHAN, communications theorist, address, Mohawk College, Hamilton, Ont., 17 May 1977.

PRIVILEGE

It is a common error of the privileged to believe that their privileges exist for them and not *vice versa*. The only justification for privilege is that without it, indispensable things, such as civilization, cannot exist, since there is no one to take care of them.

> HUGH RUTHERFORD, essayist, "A School of Fallen Virtue," *The Idler*, No. 26, Nov.- Dec. 1989.

PROBLEMS

If you have enough problems, the major ones become indistinguishable from the minor ones and everything evens out in a nightmarish kind of way.

> PATRICIA JOUDRY, playwright, . . . *And the Children Played* (1975).

PROFESSIONALISM

It is a generally conceived notion that the profession adds dignity to the man. This idea is false; it is the man who dignifies the profession.

> C.P. LENNOX, dentist, *Canadian Journal of Dental Science*, Aug. 1870, quoted by D.W. Gullett in *A History of Dentistry in Canada* (1971).

Work hard, keep up with modern developments, give your client his dollar's worth, and enjoy the better things in life.

> Maxim of engineer and Nova Scotia land surveyor JAMES A.H. CHURCH who died in 1967, as quoted by James F. Doig in *A Life Worthwhile: A Biographical Sketch* (1991).

Only amateurs are confident.

> W.O. MITCHELL, writer, interviewed by Alan Twigg in *Strong Voices: Conversations with Fifty Canadian Authors* (1988).

PROFIT

The criterion that the most profitable pursuits are the most important ones causes the neglect of activities whose values cannot be measured by the standard of profitability. It is not accidental that housing, education, medical care, and public transportation are inadequately provided for by the present social system.

> "The Waffle Manifesto: For an Independent Socialist Canada" (1969) reprinted in *The Canadian Forum*, Dec. 1989.

I won't present that business is government by altruism. The name of the game *is* gain and profit and incentive. But hope for even more profit down the road keeps us going, keeps us digging, keeps us ploughing money back into the business.

> JERRY McAFEE, President of Gulf Oil Canada Limited, interviewed by Dean Walker in *A Case for the Enterprise System* (1975).

PROGRESS
See also CHANGE

We have been to the moon. Because of our very nature, we will be going to the stars. We cannot get there encumbered with superstitions and a limited vision of our potential. We must put childish things behind us.

> JAMES RANDI, Toronto-born conjuror and debunker of psychic claims, *The Faith Healers* (1987).

Whatever you do today, your children will do differently tomorrow, to show you how it should be done. This is the meaning of progress, I suppose: it skips a generation.

> BETTY JANE WYLIE, author, *All in the Family: A Survival Guide for Living and Loving in a Changing World* (1988).

I have come to believe sincerely that the facts of Western history (such as they are known) argue the presence of an almost-hidden group of people which has molded major patterns of human development, which has managed humanity at crisis points. We have been guided in our progress by a secret organization.

> MICHAEL BRADLEY, independent researcher, *Holy Grail across the Atlantic: The Secret History of Canadian Discovery and Exploration* (1988).

When one hears of progress one should ask for whom.

> ROBIN SKELTON, man-of-letters, aphorism, May 1990.

PROPAGANDA

Anything that asserts itself to be true is propaganda.
> ELWY YOST, television personality, recalling a remark once made in 1948 by a professor at the University of Toronto, personal communication, 17 Jan. 1990.

PROPHECY
See PREDICTION & PROPHECY

PROSTITUTION
See also SEX

There is more white slave trafficking in Hamilton than any other city its size in the whole of America — not Canada, but America.
> ERNEST BELL, evangelist, referring to Hamilton, Ont., *Fighting the Traffic in Young Girls or War on the White Slave Trade: A Complete and Detailed Account of the Shameless Traffic in Young Girls* (1911).

A prostitute is a realistic feminist as opposed to an idealistic, hypocritical, shadowy feminist who doesn't want to confront the facts of life, the facts of her own negotiating and trade-off in the marriage situation, the fact that the male is her brother and not the enemy and the fact that she's afraid of sex.
> VALERIE SCOTT, spokesperson for Canadian Organization for the Rights of Prostitutes (CORP), interviewed in *Good Girls/Bad Girls: Sex Trade Workers and Feminists Face to Face* (1987) edited by Laurie Bell.

We don't sell our bodies. Housewives do that. What we do is *rent* our bodies for sexual services
> VALERIE SCOTT, Toronto prostitute-by-choice, who prefers the term "whore," spokesperson for the Canadian Organization for the Rights of Prostitutes (CORP), quoted by Rosie DiManno in *The Toronto Star*, 27 Nov. 1989.

Has the collective libido of Niagara Falls changed?
> JOHN NUNZIATA, Member of Parliament, commenting on the decline of street prostitution in the tourist areas of Niagara Falls, Ont., quoted by Robert MacKenzie in *The Niagara Falls Review*, 10 Nov. 1989.

PROTEST
See also ECOLOGY
REBELLIONS

Politicians, take note. There is a power out there in suburbia, so far harnessed only to charity drives, campaigns and PTAs which, if ever properly brought to bear on the great problems of the day, will have an impact so great the result of its being detonated (like the Amchitka A-bomb test) cannot be predicted.
> ROBERT HUNTER, environmental and peace activist, noting the powerful potential of ordinary people, like the Vancouverites who established the Don't Make A Wave Committee to protest the U.S. bomb testing at Amchitka off the west coast of Alaska; the Committee became the Greenpeace Foundation; *The Vancouver Sun*, 2 Oct. 1969, quoted by Michael Brown and John May, journalists, *The Greenpeace Story* (1989).

As your neighbours, we consider your action in approving this test incomprehensible. . . . You are playing Russian roulette next door to where we live. We ask you, in the name of sanity and common sense, to stop it now.
> Part of the message on the telegram of protest addressed to the U.S. President in Washington, D.C., 4 Nov. 1971. The message bore the signatures of some 177,000 Canadians who deplored American plans for renewed atomic testing on the Aleutian Island of Amchitka. As noted in *The Vancouver Province*, 5 Nov. 1971, it took Western Union four days to relay the message, the longest telegram sent by Western Union in the United States.

Anyone who breaks the law to assert his

nationalism doesn't get much sympathy from me. I didn't feel like bringing up any case which would have caused Mr. Kosygin or Mr. Brezhnev to say, "Why should you put your revolutionaries in jail, and we not put ours?"
> PIERRE ELLIOTT TRUDEAU, Prime Minister, when questioned about his silence in Moscow on the subject of imprisoned Ukrainian nationalists in 1971; quoted by John Muggeridge, "The Impossible Country," *The Idler*, No. 14, Sept.-Oct. 1987.

I give my life in protest to the Canadian government for its treatment of Indian people for the past 100 years.
> Suicide note of NELSON SMALL LEGS JR., a native of Alberta, who in 1976 took his own life to protest the treatment of his people by the Department of Indian Affairs; quoted by Roy MacGregor in *The Ottawa Citizen*, 23 Aug. 1988.

PROVINCES

Much of the tension in this country has been created by the interference of the federal government into the jurisdiction of the provinces. This country is suffering from a disease which I call "overlapping jurisdictionalitis." And the provinces are just as guilty as the federal government. They are down the backs of all the municipalities.
> JOHN BULLOCH, President, Canadian Federation of Independent Business, address, Empire Club of Canada, Toronto, 23 Feb. 1989.

PSYCHIATRY
See also MEDICINE

I am sorry that Jones is planning to leave Toronto. We should be at a great loss without him in America.
> SIGMUND FREUD, founder of Psychoanalysis, letter to Carl Jung dated 2 April 1911. The Swiss psychiatrist replied: "Jones's intentions are news to me." At the time Ernest Jones, Freud's pupil and future biographer, was teaching at the University of Toronto. *The Freud/Jung Letters: The Correspondence between Sigmund Freud and C.G. Jung* (1988) translated by Ralph Manheim and R.F.C. Hull and edited by William McGuire.

A lady afterwards said that Europeans might dream of sleeping with their mothers but Canadians were different. Canadians, she said, respected their mothers even when they were asleep.
> ANTHONY BURGESS, novelist, *The End of the World News* (1983). This passage from the novel refers to the reaction of a lady who attended an address in Winnipeg on the subject of the Oedipus complex, delivered by Freud's disciple Ernest Jones.

There are no psychiatrists who minister to whole nations.
> ROBERTSON DAVIES, man-of-letters, quoted by Allan Gotlieb, address, Empire Club of Canada, Toronto, 9 April 1987.

Psychiatry is time consuming and the demand for psychiatry is not the reflection of some social frivolity. It is simply part of that expansion of expectation and the right to care which is probably the greatest achievement of our society.
> VIVIAN RAKOFF, psychiatrist, quoted by Jonathan Caro in *Canadian Doctor*, Nov. 1987.

Don't ever do anything to someone that you can't reverse.
> D. EWEN CAMERON, psychiatrist, maxim mentioned to the medical resident Ed Levinson while touring the wing of the Allan Memorial Institute in Montreal added in 1953, quoted by Don Gillmor in *I Swear by Apollo: Dr. Ewen Cameron and the CIA-Brainwashing Experiments* (1987).

Obviously, what has been achieved with respect to psychoneurotic patients can be extended to any field in which there is malfunction of the personality, whether within the area of psychiatry or not.
> D. EWEN CAMERON, physician and director of the Allan Memorial Institute in Mon-

treal, where "mind-control" experiments were documented in the 1950s, quoted by Harvey Weinstein in *A Father, a Son and the CIA* (1988).

How many more of us must die, before Canada does what is right and fulfills its many promises to help us?
> Open letter addressed to Prime Minister Brian Mulroney, dated 10 Dec. 1987, sent by the surviving victims of the "mind-control" experiments conducted in the 1950s at the Allan Memorial Institute in Montreal who sought redress from the Canadian government and assistance in their civil suit against the American government; quoted by Harvey Weinstein in *A Father, a Son and the CIA* (1988).

For a person who does not want to be locked up, it hurts no less if it is done by a psychiatrist who smiles than by a constable who growls.
> A. ALAN BOROVOY, General Counsel, Canadian Civil Liberties Association, *When Freedoms Collide: A Case for Our Civil Liberties* (1988).

PSYCHICAL RESEARCH
See also PARAPSYCHOLOGY

If the alleged phenomena are true I hold it to be unquestionable that they would be of more importance than any other in the science and philosophy of our time.
> G.J. ROMANES, Cambridge psychologist and zoologist, born in Kingston, Ont., writing on the subject of psychical research in 1881 to Sir William Barrett; quoted by Colin Wilson in his Introduction to the 1986 reprint of Barrett's book *Death-Bed Visions: The Psychical Experiences of the Dying* (1926).

PSYCHOLOGY

My argument is that it is only with the rubble of bad theories that we shall be able to build better ones, and that without theory of some kind, somewhere, psycho-

logical observation and description would at best be chaotic and meaningless.
> D.O. HEBB, psychologist, "The Role of Neurological Ideas in Psychology," *Journal of Personality*, No. 20, 1951.

PUBLIC INTEREST

Nobody behaves in the public interest unless it is in their own self-interest to do so.
> JOHN CRISPO, political economist, address, Empire Club of Canada, 25 Jan. 1979.

PUBLICITY

It was the 1960s and Toronto had opened up, with Yonge Street featuring strippers and topless go-go. One of the publicity types, only half in jest, suggested that an NDP rally should be led by a naked lady riding a horse down Yonge Street. Douglas considered this proposal carefully and finally said: "I think that would be a very good idea, it must have been years since the people of Toronto have seen a horse."
> MICHAEL BRADLEY, author, referring to "new-style" NDP fund-raising ventures and the discomfort they caused NDP leader T.C. (Tommy) Douglas, *Crisis of Clarity* (1985)

Ask me anything. You cannot embarrass me. Honestly. I'm a reporter's dream. . . . I love success and I love women, and I love exploring for gold. . . . Time will show me right.
> MURRAY PEZIM, Vancouver-based stock promoter, quoted by Ken MacQueen in *The Toronto Star*, 17 Sept. 1989.

PUBLISHING
See also BOOKS

Inspired typography . . . could give the world a means of visual communication that hurdles the barriers of race, religion, language, politics and economic and give the human race a common basis of communication and from this understanding and tolerance.

Words of the typographer and designer CARL DAIR which appear on the display in the history of printing exhibit at the Grimsby Museum, Grimsby, Ont. Born in Welland, Dair was an inspired printer and designer and teacher of design (one student was Allan Fleming). He designed Cartier, the first original Canadian typeface, in 1967, the year of his death.

In Canada, for the serious literary publisher with a reputation to maintain, it's not a question of losing money or not losing money. It's a question of how much money you lose and on what. The object of the game is to use the money at your disposal as efficiently as possible. The successful publisher is the one who achieves maximum results at minimum cost.

> MICHAEL MACKLEM, publisher, "Seed Money," *The Bumper Book* (1986) edited by John Metcalf.

The preliminary experience with word processing has been so positive that it is likely that the computer will be the inspiration for a new burst of literary activity similar to the one that accompanied the advent of the printing press.

> ROBERT K. LOGAN, physicist and educator, *The Alphabet Effect: The Impact of the Phonetic Alphabet on the Development of Western Civilization* (1986).

The paradox about publishing with a small press is that you have a lot more freedom to say what you want than you would with a big press, but nothing you say will have any impact on anyone or anything.

> CRAD KILODNEY, writer of fiction who hawks his publications at Toronto streetcorners, "How I Write Such Great Stories," unpublished introduction to *Malignant Humours* (1988).

Procrustes was an editor.

> ROBIN SKELTON, man-of-letters, aphorism, May 1990.

Canadian publishing is like diabetes. You can't cure it, but you can manage it.

> MALCOLM LESTER, publisher, on the demise of the firm Lester & Orpen Dennys, quoted by Roy MacSkimming in *The Globe and Mail*, 16 Jan. 1990.

PULP & PAPER

In Canada during the nineteenth century, mummy cloth was used in the manufacture of paper. Because the supply of rags for paper making proved inadequate, Canadian paper manufacturers imported thousands of mummies just for their wrappings. What happened to the bodies is not known.

> AIDAN COCKBURN, historian, Introduction, *Mummies, Disease, and Ancient Customs* (1980) edited by Aidan and Eve Cockburn. Cockburn is President of the Paleopathology Association and gives as his source for this claim A. Lucas's *Ancient Egyptian Materials and Industries* (4th ed., 1962).

Think of your own behaviour for a minute. You probably turned on a light when you woke this morning, you used hot water, you had something for breakfast that was either hot or cooked, and you undoubtedly used a forest product and probably took part of your journey there by car. If you did, you supported the forest industry as well as the mining and petroleum industries, you contributed to global warming and proportionately polluted your world far more than any pulp mill.

> ADAM ZIMMERMAN, Chairman of Noranda Forest Inc., address, Canadian Club, Toronto, quoted in *The Globe and Mail*, 22 Nov. 1989.

Canada, which supplies almost all the world's newsprint, cuts down 247,000 acres per year more trees than it replants.

> MARJORIE LAMB, ecologist, *Two Minutes a Day for a Greener Planet* (1990).

PUNISHMENT
See also PRISON

As a verse in the Bible says, "The wicked flee when no man pursueth," to which an older preacher used to add, "But they make better time if someone is after them."
F.R. SCOTT, lawyer and poet, letter written 13 Nov. 1973, quoted by Roy MacGregor in *Chief: The Fearless Vision of Billy Diamond* (1989).

Nothing is worse in prison than the consciousness of one's innocence.
NICHOLAS CATANOY, "Notes from a Prison Wall (Fragment)," *Canadian Literature*, Summer 1989.

QUEBEC

See also FRANCE
FRENCH CANADA
MONTREAL
PARTI QUÉBÉCOIS
QUEBEC, CONQUEST OF
QUEBEC & ENGLISH CANADA
QUEBEC CITY
Les QUÉBÉCOIS
QUIET REVOLUTION
SEPARATISM
SOVEREIGNTY, NATIONAL
SOVEREIGNTY-ASSOCIATION

This will sometime hence be a vast Empire, the seat of power & learning. Nature has refused them nothing; there will grow a people out of our little England, that will fill this vast space.
JAMES WOLFE, English general, musing on the future of Quebec, 11 Aug. 1758.

Aussie le Général Montcalm à Québec, tambien qu'il a perdu.
JACK KEROUAC, novelist of French-Canadian ancestry who occasionally wrote in the French of his childhood in Massachussets; quoted by Malcolm Reid in "Quixotic Quebec," *The Canadian Forum*, Dec. 1987.

Lower Canada — seemed to be as *little known* to the people of England, as the *deserts of Siberia*.
JOHN LAMBERT, English traveller, *Travels through Lower Canada and the United States of North America, in the years 1806, 1807, and 1808* (1810).

Uncorrupted as the French-Canadians are by the vices of a highly artificial state of society, as that which exists in Europe; blessed with a happy competency that supplies their few and unexaggerated wants, and removed by their comparative seclusion from the seductive and fatal influence of fashion and extravagance, they live in a state of pastoral and patriarchal purity of manners, sedulously attending to all the ordinances of their religion, that strongly engage in their favour the feelings and regard of all those who come in contact with them.
HENRY TUDOR, traveller and author, *Narrative of a Tour in North America* (1834).

It may well be that Wolfe's victory at Quebec not only made Canada safe for the British, at least for a time, but made the world safe for the American Revolution.
LESTER B. PEARSON, former Prime Minister, Reith Lectures of 1969, quoted by

Charles Lynch in *The Lynch Mob: Stringing Up Our Prime Ministers* (1988).

You see, I think of myself as living in a large rural house in one room. I love the whole house but it's that one room I'm completely at ease in. And that room is Quebec.
GABRIELLE ROY, novelist, quoted by David Cobb in *The Canadian*, 1 May 1976.

Quebec doesn't belong to Canada. It belongs to the United States.
LISE PAYETTE, television personality, quoted by James Quig in *Weekend Magazine*, 30 Oct. 1976.

You have to realize that this province will become as French as Ontario is English or at least as close as is humanly possible.
RENÉ LÉVESQUE, Quebec Premier, address in Montreal, quoted in *The Toronto Star*, 4 Oct. 1977.

Quebec, as a result, is a country, or community, or whatever you wish to call it, of cripples — spiritual cripples.
ROBERT SCULLY, columnist and literary editor of *Le Devoir*, "What It Means to Be French in Canada," *The Manchester Guardian*, 1 May 1977. This controversial article, originally commissioned by *The Washington Post*, was reprinted in *The Toronto Star*, 25 April 1977.

I am beginning to learn something about what is going on here. I know that Canada is divided into ten provinces and I have been out West where I felt as if I were in the United States. But Quebec seems more foreign to me, as though I were visiting a different country.
TENNESSEE WILLIAMS, playwright, interviewed by Lawrence Sabbath in *The Montreal Star*, 19 Nov. 1977. Williams was visiting Montreal for the production of Jean-Louis Roux's *Pièce à Deux*; "out West" refers to Toronto which, to many Americans, appears to be a mid-Western city.

Québec, then, is French, but it is not France; it is Canadian, but it is not Canada.
STEPHEN BROOK, English travel writer, *Maple Leaf Rag: Travels across Canada* (1987).

Yet Quebec's distinctiveness, I am proud to say, was probably served as well, if not better, through organs of culture like Radio Canada, the CBC, the Film Board and the Arts Council, all creations of the *federal* government, who rewarded quality of production, quality of French and quality of artistry, which was not always found in Quebec institutions.
PIERRE ELLIOTT TRUDEAU, former Prime Minister, Testimony to the Senate Submissions Group on the Meech Lake Constitutional Accord, *With a Bang, Not a Whimper: Pierre Trudeau Speaks Out* (1988) edited by Donald Johnston.

Historic residue.
"The British journalist (and later minister) RICHARD CROSSMAN described us as 'historic residue' when he reviewed Mason Wade's *The French Canadians* and declared that such a wreck was of no interest to him." So wrote Gérard Pelletier in "Quebec: Different but in Step with North America," *Daedalus: Journal of the American Academy of Arts and Sciences*, "In Search of Canada," Fall 1988.

There is no mystery surrounding Quebec. The only enigmatic element of a complex but perfectly logical evolution is the incredible tenacity demonstrated by a tiny group of people in keeping their language and culture alive against all odds.
GÉRARD PELLETIER, former Cabinet Minister, "Quebec: Different but in Step with North America," *Daedalus: Journal of the American Academy of Arts and Sciences*, "In Search of Canada," Fall 1988.

In all of Canada, however, Quebec alone is a self-contained community with a distinctive culture of sufficient unity to set it apart as a nation.
LÉON DION, political scientist, "The Mystery of Quebec," *Daedalus: Journal of the*

American Academy of Arts and Sciences, "In Search of Canada," Fall 1988.

I think this province will diminish in importance. They're not getting the vibrant immigrants. If you come from Portugal or Greece, you want your children to learn the language of success on this continent, which is English. They're just going to give this province a pass. The people with the most vitality and energy will be going to Ontario or out West.

MORDECAI RICHLER, novelist and resident of Quebec's Eastern Townships, quoted by Don Gillmor in *Quill & Quire,* July 1989.

Today, Quebec absorbs our attention. But the Quebec problem, after three decades in its acute form, is now stale. In many respects Estonia, after just two years of intense effort, is nearer today to neo-independence than Quebec is (although Estonians have to keep checking over their shoulders for tanks).

RICHARD GWYN, columnist, *The Toronto Star,* 4 Oct. 1989.

Until 1985, people were saying, "What does Quebec want?" We expressed Quebec's demands clearly. So, since 1985, the question is "What does Canada want?" We're still waiting for Canada's answer on this subject.

ROBERT BOURASSA, Quebec Premier, addressing the Quebec National Assembly following the death of the Meech Lake Accord, 22 June 1990, quoted by Robert McKenzie in *The Toronto Star* the following day. The two rhetorical questions were spoken in English.

CANADA-QUEBEC

Wording on plaques on desks occupied by officials representing Canada at international conferences in 1984, according to Claire Hoy in *Friends in High Places: Politics and Patronage in the Mulroney Government* (1987).

French-speaking Canada is a cultural reality of the highest importance; Quebec is a province like other provinces, and always will be; the more separatist its policies, the more inevitably provincial their characteristics.

NORTHROP FRYE, literary critic, address, Social Sciences and Humanities Research Council, Toronto, Fall 1990, printed in *The Globe and Mail,* 15 April 1991.

Quebec is not a province like the others, as all children learn before playing Atari or Nintendo.

JACQUES PARIZEAU, P.Q. leader, addressing a joint meeting of the Empire Club and the Canadian Club, Toronto, 11 Dec. 1990, quoted by Robert Sheppard in *The Globe and Mail* the following day.

We have a rendezvous with the future of Quebec.

ROBERT BOURASSA, Quebec Premier, address, Quebec Liberal Party convention, Montreal, 8 March 1991, quoted by Rhéal Séguin in *The Globe and Mail* the following day.

QUEBEC, CONQUEST OF

It is always easy to be on the negative side. If a man were now to deny that there is salt upon the table, you could not reduce him to an absurdity. Come, let us try this a little further. I deny that Canada is taken, and I can support my denial by pretty good arguments. The French are a much more numerous people than we; and it is not likely that they would allow us to take it. "But the ministry have assured us, in all the formality of *The Gazette,* that it is taken." — Very true. But the ministry have put us to an enormous expence by the war in America, and it is their interest to persuade us that we have got something for our money. — "But the fact is confirmed by thousands of men who were at the taking of it." — Ay, but these men have still more interest in deceiving us. They don't want that you should think the French have beat them, but that they have beat the French. Now suppose you should go over and find that it is really taken, that would only satisfy yourself; for when you come home we will not believe you. We will say, you have been bribed. — Yet, Sir, notwithstanding all these plausible objections, we have no doubt that Canada is really ours. Such is the weight of common testimony. How much stronger are the evidences of the Christian religion!

> JAMES BOSWELL, Scottish biographer, quoting Dr. Samuel Johnson on 14 July 1763 on the subject of reasonable certainty in uncertain matters, specifically "those who denied the truth of Christianity," and treating the Conquest of Quebec in 1759 as common knowledge; *Life of Johnson* (1791, 3rd ed., 1799).

Wolfe's monument has been completed. Lord Dalhousie, with equal good feeling and good taste, has united the names of the rival heroes Wolfe and Montcalm in the dedication of the pillar — a liberality of feeling that cannot but prove gratifying to the Canadian French, while it robs the English warrior of none of his glory.

> CATHARINE PARR TRAILL, pioneer author, *The Backwoods of Canada: Being Letters from the Wife of an Emigrant Officer* (1836).

The Plains of Abraham was not the parting of the ways. It was a reunion across centuries of history.

> GRAHAM SPRY, nationalist, "One Nation, Two Cultures," address, Canadian Club of Quebec, 17 Jan. 1929, published in *The Canadian Nation*, Feb. 1929.

At first Wolfe complained that he would rather write Gray's Elegy, but on being told that it had been written already (by Gray) he agreed to take Quebec. . . At this engagement the French had a very peculiar general with the unusual French name of Keep-calm.

On receiving a muffled report to the effect that Wolfe's men had captured Quebec, one of his aides-de-calm called out: "See! They fly!" "Who fly?" asked the Gen-

eral, and, on being assured that it was his own men who were flying, "Thank God!" said Keep-calm, with a sigh of satisfaction: "Now, I can fly in peace!"

> WALTER CARRUTHERS SELLAR and ROBERT JULIAN YEATMAN, English satirists, "Britain Muffles Through," *1066 and All That* (1930).

The real tragedy, the greatest wound inflicted on us, was that an entire continent slipped out of French hands in the eighteenth century. Ever since, we have been orphans who have only survived by withdrawing into our shell, increasingly concerned about our future as we emerge from it into the outside world. The separation from our mother country was the most traumatic aspect of our infancy as a people.

> LÉON DION, political scientist, "The Mystery of Quebec," *Daedalus: Journal of the American Academy of Arts and Sciences*, "In Search of Canada," Fall 1988.

"I, too, wish I had been able to wake up Montcalm and tell him the English were coming," I used to say in my speeches, "but I was not there."

> JEAN CHRÉTIEN, politician, *Straight from the Heart* (1985) written with Ron Graham.

THE DEATH OF WOLFE ON THE PLAINS OF ABRAHAM = On a path to fame, both he and his war foe fell

> Anagram attributed to the puzzler-constructor SAM WELLER in 1881 by O.V. Michaelsen in "Best Anagrams and Anti-grams," *Word Ways: The Journal of Recreational Linguistics*, Nov. 1990.

QUEBEC & ENGLISH CANADA
See also QUEBEC

Rivalry between French and English has done as much for this country as wheat. And I wouldn't want to see all of it ground down, blended, bleached, processed into

uniformity, wrapped in plastic, and sold as a substitute for real national development.
PETER DESBARATS, journalist, address, Empire Club of Canada, Toronto, 7 Dec. 1978.

If Quebec is weakened, then Canada is weakened. If Quebec is strong, then Canada is strong.
BRIAN MULRONEY, Prime Minister, speech, nomination meeting, Sept-Iles, Que., 6 April 1984.

My own feelings are ambivalent. When I think of Quebec, my homeland, my heart beats fast; when I think of Canada, my country, reason takes over. Yet in a sense Canada too is my homeland: my ancestors discovered, explored, and partially occupied it as far as the foothills of the Rockies, but they are somehow robbed of their great inheritance and gradually pushed back to Quebec, which they clung to and which they multiplied in. My emotional ties with Canada are thus weaker than they are with Quebec.
LÉON DION, political scientist, "The Mystery of Quebec," *Daedalus: Journal of the American Academy of Arts and Sciences*, "In Search of Canada," Fall 1988.

Canada without Quebec, what would that be? Canada can very well survive without Newfoundland. It's time for English Canada to start thinking about Canada.
GIL RÉMILLARD, Quebec Minister of Intergovernmental Affairs, quoted by Rhéal Séguin and André Picard in *The Globe and Mail*, 7 April 1990.

I will not try here to summarize the most recent developments — it would be too painful. We are like the couple, so much immersed in recrimination and pettiness, that they are getting to the point where their only way out is *divorce*. Divorce while living under the same roof, perhaps, because of the children and other considerations, but divorce all the same.
CLAUDE CASTONGUAY, one-time Liberal

politician and present-day Quebec corporate executive, address in Montreal, 20 Feb. 1990, quoted by Robert Sheppard in *The Globe and Mail* the following day.

TROC
Acronym for The Rest Of Canada (that is, Canada minus the Province of Quebec) in use by political advisers in Ottawa, Fall 1990, according to Eric Kierans on CBC Radio's *Morningside*, 4 Dec. 1990.

QUEBEC CITY
See also QUEBEC

There is my dear Quebec!
WILLA CATHER, U.S. novelist who went on to write *Shadows on the Rock* (1931), a novel set in Frontenac's Quebec, exclamation while sailing up the St. Lawrence River, recalled by Paul Martin in the diary entry for 22 Jan. 1978 in *The London Diaries 1975-1979* (1988) edited by William R. Young.

The Heights of Abraham are not particularly imposing: just a green slope and on top the Château Frontenac.
G. WILSON KNIGHT, English literary scholar who taught at the University of Toronto, *Atlantic Crossing: An Autobiographical Design* (1936).

Mr. Prime Minister, my visit to the old city of Quebec has recalled vividly to my mind that Canada is a nation founded on a union of two great races. The harmony of their equal partnership is an example to all mankind — an example everywhere in the world.
FRANKLIN DELANO ROOSEVELT, U.S. President, speaking in French, joint meeting of the Senate and the House of Commons, 25 Aug. 1943.

The only problem in Quebec is choosing the best restaurant.
BRIAN MULRONEY, Prime Minister, explaining why Quebec City was chosen to be the site of the so-called Shamrock

Summit which opened on St. Patrick's Day, 17 March 1985.

Québec City is no Paris, and that is its charm. It is unequivocally provincial.

STEPHEN BROOK, English travel writer, *Maple Leaf Rag: Travels across Canada* (1987).

UNESCO has classified Quebec City as a part of world heritage; but the only cosmopolitan crowd to be seen in this world-heritage capital city are the visiting tourists. In fact, it is just as if Quebec had been protected by some ethnic barrier, in much the same way the farmland was turned into a green belt by law.

JACQUES GODBOUT, author and filmmaker, *The Globe and Mail*, 6 Nov. 1989.

LES QUÉBÉCOIS
See also FRENCH CANADA

Always has our province been faithful to the crown of Britain; equally has it been faithful to traditions inherited from our forebears, to the pact of Confederation in 1867, and to that mission which British statesmen in 1791 confided to it — *to remain altogether French*. This past we cherish in our hearts and never shall we cease to consider the throne as the bulwark of our democratic institutions and our constitutional liberties.

MAURICE DUPLESSIS, Quebec Premier, address delivered before King George VI and Queen Elizabeth in Quebec City, 17 May 1939. The address was delivered in French except for the italicized words which were spoken in English, according to Tom MacDonnell in *Daylight upon Magic: The Royal Tour of Canada — 1939* (1989).

Do you know what a French Canadian is? A French Canadian is a spender.

JEAN LESAGE, Quebec Premier, remark made to Eric Kierans, according to Jamie Swift in *Odd Man Out: The Life and Times of Eric Kierans* (1988). "I need someone to collect the money," Lesage added, ap-

pointing Kierans the province's Minister of Revenue.

To make matters worse, the Quebeckers lack the two crucial features of states seeking a degree of independence: poverty and military oppressions. Most Quebeckers are well-off and enjoy the dual benefit of living under British law, with its respect for the individual, and of speaking the language of France where human rights were born. How curious it is! Two sources of liberty flowing into frustration.

FRÉDÉRIC BARREYRE, French commentator, *Quebec* (1987) with photographs by Pierre Toutain.

Be loyal to Quebec; don't buy anything Canadian. . . .

Go to Pittsburgh every weekend and smuggle your goods across the border. . . .

Be true to your religion, go to mass every Sunday and get your abortions done in the United States. . . .

Three of numerous so-called rules from a Letter to the Editor titled "Rules for Becoming Québécois" signed "J.M. St. John, Pierrefonds" and published in *The Chronicle* (Pointe Claire, Que.) on 13 April 1988. The response of groups like the Association of West Island Francophones and the threat of pressure from advertisers resulted in the publisher and editor of the Montreal weekly tabloid repudiating and apologizing for the publication of "Rules for Becoming Québécois." Paid letters of apology appeared in *La Presse*, *Le Soleil*, and *The Montreal Gazette*, according to *The Globe and Mail*, 24 June 1988.

It is a very long time since this was really Nouvelle France, and by now its Frenchness is all its own. Even its faces did not seem to me very French — many look half-Indian, and many more have been moulded, by the cruel winters and unforgiving wind-chill factors, into contours hardly recognizable as European.

JAN MORRIS, Anglo-Welsh travel writer, "The Battle for Montreal," *Saturday Night*, July 1988. Morris's observations were inspired by the faces seen on the streets of Montreal.

Il est choyé le francophone de Québec qui a eu la chance de connaître "les Anglais" et de s'en faire des amis, sans y perdre son âme! / Spoiled are *les Québécois* who have become acquainted with the English and have become their friends without losing their souls.
> GARY BELL, law student, *McGill Faculty of Law Year Book* (1988-89).

Our society had been characterized by a runaway birth rate for three centuries (on average, the French-speaking population of Canada doubled every twenty years with no significant arrival of immigrants). This birth rate was a principal reason for the survival of our people.
> GÉRARD PELLETIER, former Cabinet Minister, "Quebec: Different but in Step with North America," *Daedalus: Journal of the American Academy of Arts and Sciences*, "In Search of Canada," Fall 1988.

If the next generation of Québécois can reach a higher level of political maturity and overcome its fear of assimilation, the province — and Canada — will be free to achieve its greater potential. For this to happen, Québec must be "re-Canadianized" within the larger North American and global context.
> FRANK FEATHER, futurologist, *G-Forces: Reinventing the World — The 35 Global Forces Restructuring Our World* (1989).

It's pretty hard, you know, to have seven million people, one of the founding peoples, sitting on that snowbank over there, and say, "Isn't it wonderful? Aren't things terrific?" Well of course they're not terrific. It couldn't be otherwise.
> BRIAN MULRONEY, Prime Minister, commenting on the rejection of the Meech Lake Accord, speech, Becancour, Que., 27 Feb. 1990, quoted by Graham Fraser in *The Globe and Mail* the following day.

I want to assure the seven million people of Quebec, every last one of them, that nobody in the province of Newfoundland and Labrador is rejecting Quebec.
> CLYDE WELLS, Newfoundland Premier, after giving qualified assent to the Meech Lake Accord, Ottawa, quoted by Patrick Doyle in *The Toronto Star*, 10 June 1990.

QUEEN ELIZABETH
See also MONARCHY
ROYAL FAMILY

What the hell, she doesn't pay me, I pay her. Besides, what the hell position can a Queen play?
> HAROLD BALLARD, proprietor, Maple Leaf Gardens, justifying his decision to remove the portrait of Queen Elizabeth from the Gardens, quoted by William Houston in *Ballard* (1984).

QUIET REVOLUTION
See also QUEBEC

The Quiet Revolution
> The term "Quiet Revolution" was first used, according to the journalist Graham Fraser, by BRIAN UPTON, then a reporter with *The Toronto Telegram* and subsequently a bureaucrat with the federal government in Ottawa. It first appeared in the pages of the *Tely* in 1962 "or thereabouts," in English, and was subsequently translated into French and used by Premier Jean Lesage "and everybody else" to refer to the social changes in the province following the demise of Premier Maurice Duplessis and the defeat of the Union Nationale Party and everything that they represented. The French translation is *La Révolution Silencieuse.*

The more I see of Premier Lesage the more I appreciate the humility of General de Gaulle.
> J. R. (JOEY), SMALLWOOD, Newfoundland Premier, on the arrogance of Jean Lesage, Premier of Quebec from 1960 to 1966, quoted by Bren Walsh in *More than a Poor Majority: The Story of Newfoundland's Confederation with Canada* (1985).

QUOTATIONS

Everywhere Mencken has sought to catalogue only those sayings which are touched with some attic salt, or some tang of irony, or with the sour-sweetness of paradox. . . . We are doubtful, therefore, whether this book will add any harmony to the music of the spheres. But that it will add to the gaiety of nations cannot be denied.

> A.M. KLEIN, poet, *Literary Essays and Reviews* (1987) edited by Usher Caplan and M.W. Steinberg. The poet and *littérateur* was savouring the sweets-and-sours and all-sorts offered by H.L. Mencken in his *New Dictionary of Quotations* (1942). To Klein, the selections were "blushing platitudes . . . copy-book maxims" and the collection as a whole was "a borrowed verbal tuxedo." As for "this principle of selection," it was "the survival of the slickest."

The next-best thing to having uttered something memorable is to have been the person who recorded it for posterity.

> ANDREW MacFARLANE, newspaperman, "Somewhere South of Suburbia" (1963), *It Seemed Like a Good Idea at the Time* (1983).

Most of my writings consist of an attempt to translate aphorisms into continuous prose.

> NORTHROP FRYE, literary critic, quoted by Richard Kostelanetz, "The Literature Professors' Literature Professor," *The Michigan Quarterly Review*, Fall 1978.

Look it up in Colombo.

> LORNE PARTON, journalist, reviewing *Colombo's Canadian Quotations* (1974), recommending that these words be a "line for a future printing," *The Vancouver Province*, 22 Nov. 1974.

On the rare occasions when I didn't really like a person, I quoted them verbatim.

> JAY SCOTT, film critic, quoted by Paul McLaughlin in *How to Interview: The Art of Asking Questions* (2nd ed., 1990).

Can a person be misquoted even if we use the exact words? Yes, if we leave out nearby sentences that explain, modify or qualify the remark, or do not report facial expressions and gestures that might be important parts of the context. An ironic smile or a rolling of the eyes speaks volumes to the reporter, and these must be conveyed to the reader whenever they affect interpretation.

> J.A. McFARLANE and WARREN CLEMENTS, journalists, *The Globe and Mail Style Book* (1990).

Say *quotes* from the shortstop or the Prime Minister, but *quotations* from the Bible, Browning or Churchill.

> J.A. McFARLANE and WARREN CLEMENTS, journalists, distinguishing between the colloquial use of "quotes" and the formal use of "quotations," *The Globe and Mail Style Book* (1990).

The context belongs to the user. We are mere conduits of old voices, some of which are our own.

> FRANK ZINGRONE, communications specialist, commenting on the use of past words in present and future contexts, personal communication, 13 April 1991.

RACE & RACISM
See also PREJUDICE

The heart never knows the colour of the skin.
> CHIEF DAN GEORGE, native spokesperson, *My Heart Soars* (1974).

To cross an individual of a white race with an individual of a yellow race is to produce, in nine cases out of ten, a mongrel wastrel with the worst qualities of both races.
> A.W. NEILL, B.C. Member, House of Commons, 16 March 1927, quoted by David Suzuki in *Metamorphosis: Stages in a Life* (1987).

Let our slogan be for British Columbia: "No Japs from the Rockies to the seas."
> IAN MacKENZIE, federal Cabinet Minister, address, 18 Sept. 1944, quoted by David Suzuki in *Metamorphosis: Stages in a Life* (1987).

Racism [in Canada] is no less horrendous, no less systematic than in the United States. It is very clear you have an enormous problem.
> ANGELA DAVIS, U.S. social activist, Toronto address in the 1960s, recalled by Kelly Toughill on 26 Feb. 1988 and quoted in *The Toronto Star* the following day.

I have an essay somewhere entitled "Black Is Not a Colour." The "coloured peoples" are literally created by the white man. If there were no whites, there would be only people. Black is not in the colour spectrum at all, but is the interval between colours. White is all the colours at once, of course. One might say that the "white" peoples represent a maximum of miscegenations and that the coloured peoples are more "pure" and less mixed.
> MARSHALL McLUHAN, communications theorist, letter to Ashley Montague, 20 Jan. 1980, *Letters of Marshall McLuhan* (1987) edited by Matie Molinaro, Corinne McLuhan, and William Toye.

As a child, I was a direct victim of the effects of the braggadocio of geneticists early in this century. Of course, I only realized this long after I myself had become a geneticist. After Pearl Harbor, my family was stripped of all rights of Canadian citizenship for sharing genes that had come from the country of the enemy near the turn of the century.
> DAVID SUZUKI, scientist and author, *Inventing the Future* (1989).

Indeed, to talk of racism *in* Canadian immigration policy before 1978 is being overgenerous. Rather, we should talk of racism *as* Canadian immigration policy. Canada's immigration policy was guided by a bias against Asians, Jews and other minorities and in favour of Western Europeans.
DAVID MATAS with ILANA SIMON, immigration lawyer and journalist, *Closing the Doors: The Failure of Refugee Protection* (1989).

If you start to build walls around imagination, then you promote racism. Part of writing is to bring people of various cultures together. When you start focusing on differences, you have all sorts of excuses to have wars. After all, we all bleed the same colour.
DARLENE BARRY QUAIFE, writer, addressing the Writers' Union of Canada, Waterloo, Ont., quoted by Isabel Vincent in *The Globe and Mail*, 10 June 1989.

There is racism everywhere. What interests me is how governments, or people in authority, respond to acts of racism. This is related to how North American governments, and North Americans, perhaps, respond to the inevitable fact of the de-Europeanization of these countries.
BHARATI MUKHERJEE, Indian-born author and social commentator, quoted by H.J. Kirchhoff in *The Globe and Mail*, 19 Oct. 1989.

Canadians, even when they are racist, realize that it's not a nice thing to be.
NEIL BISSOONDATH, Trinidad-born novelist of East Indian origin, interviewed by Aruna Srivastava in *Other Solitudes: Canadian Multicultural Fictions* (1990) edited by Linda Hutcheon and Marion Richmond.

As we enter the last lap, we call on the people of Canada to gather and redouble their efforts and endeavours in support of our struggle.
NELSON MANDELA, black African leader, addressing an anti-apartheid rally in Queen's Park, Toronto, 18 June 1990, quoted by Walter Stefaniuk in *The Toronto Star* the following day.

RADIO
See also BROADCASTING
NEWS

This is VAS — The Voice of the Atlantic Seaboard.
Station identification of Guglielmo Marconi's radio transmitter at Table Head, near Glace Bay, N.S., which in the 1910s broadcast intermittent weather forecasts.

From the Lord Nelson Hotel in Halifax, Nova Scotia, this is radio station CHNS.
WILLIAM BORRETT, Army Major and founder of CHNS, "The Voice of Halifax: 960 on the Dial: First in Nova Scotia," licensed in 1925; quoted by Bill McNeil and Morris Wolfe in *Signing On: The Birth of Radio in Canada* (1982).

What is the issue? It is this: Shall the radio be subordinated to narrowly advertising purposes, or shall the Canadian people through their responsible instruments of government ensure that the fullest potentialities of this agency of communication be developed to serve the broadest Canadian purposes?
GRAHAM SPRY, enthusiast for public broadcasting, "The Canadian Broadcasting Issue," *The Canadian Forum*, April 1931.

Phil Harris: Mary Livingstone! As I live and breathe!
Mary Livingstone: Well! Phil Harris! Stop breathing. I want to *live* too!
Characteristic exchange on *The Jack Benny Show* on NBC in the 1940s between the bandleader Phil Harris, who played the lush, and the Canadian-born comedienne Mary Livingstone who was the wife — both on air and in life — of comedy master Jack Benny. Noted by Ed Gould in *Entertaining Canadians:*

Canada's International Stars 1900-1988
(1988).

Knock, knock. / Who's there? / It's the
Happy Gang! / Well, com'on in!
> Famous opening lines of CBC Radio's *The
> Happy Gang* which was heard from 1937
> to 1959. The nine-member group gave
> 4890 performances. Their motto, "Keep
> Happy with the Happy Gang," was set to
> music by their leader Bert Pearl, whom
> the Blood Indians named Chief Happy
> Voice in the Sky.

Radio was grown up last Sunday in Canada.
> JACK GOULD, radio critic for *The New
> York Times*, reviewing the CBC Stage pro-
> duction of Lister Sinclair's *A Play on
> Words* broadcast live on Sunday evening,
> 12 Nov. 1945.

Sleepily, I got to thinking about that
Golden Age of Radio. What was so golden
about it? I always notice that when people
celebrate that Golden Age, they dig up
programs to represent it that are not only
not golden, they're not even base metal.
To those of us who believed the public was
worthy of something better than soap-
opera, those are the programs we were
bucking against.

No age . . . I thought as I climbed between the sheets . . . no age is called
golden until it is long past. Any age is
mainly foot-slogging and twenty-five-hour
days. To survive, you need a good capacity to absorb disappointments.
> ANDREW ALLAN, veteran radio pro-
> ducer, "The Golden Age of Radio," *Andrew
> Allan: A Self-Portrait* (1974).

Good evening. This is James Bannerman.
> Characteristic   greeting   of   JAMES
> BANNERMAN, the veteran radio broad-
> caster and host of the weekly cultural
> program *CBC Wednesday Night* from 1950
> to his death in 1970.

There's no drinking here (which is probably as well, in my present state inside) and

not much of anything else except six radio
stations all churning out programmes indistinguishable from the usual idiotic
American radio. (I know because there's a
radio with a lot of knobs in my room and I
tried them all early this morning trying to
get some news and all I got was advertising
and rubbish.)
> J.B. PRIESTLEY, English author touring
> Canada, letter written to his wife
> Jacquetta Hawkes, Edmonton, 23 April
> 1956, quoted by Vincent Brome in *J.B.
> Priestley* (1988).

The little people out there in Vacuumland.
> Characteristic remark of ALLAN McFEE,
> self-styled "delightful host" of CBC
> Radio's *Eclectic Circus*, first heard in 1977,
> quoted by Ed Gould in *Entertaining Cana-
> dians: Canada's International Stars 1900-
> 1988* (1988).

It's tough work keeping the country safe
for democracy, ain't it?
> MARK STAROWICZ, CBC Radio producer,
> comment made to Patrick Martin and
> Bronwyn Drainie in 1980, concerning the
> ensuring of excellence in radio broad-
> casting; quoted by Bronwyn Drainie in
> *Living the Part: John Drainie and the Di-
> lemma of Canadian Stardom* (1988). She
> concluded: "It was a joke, delivered in
> Starowicz's usual George Raftian quack,
> but it carried the same message . . . Can-
> ada belonged to us, it was our responsi-
> bility. We were a small cabal of dedicated,
> energetic young journalists, convinced
> we were accomplishing something never
> before heard or seen in this country."
> Starowicz went on to produce CBC-TV's
> *The Journal*.

People ask me why I'm not a name drop-
per. After all, I meet a lot of celebrities. But
I can never remember their names!
> DAVID SCHATZKY, radio host and inter-
> viewer, remark made on 23 May 1987.

I long for the privacy of radio, with only a
few hundred thousand people listening.
> PETER GZOWSKI, host of CBC Radio's

Morningside, quoted by David Olive in *The Toronto Star*, 12 Nov. 1988.

But the task of the interviewer remains the same: to guide rather than to motivate. The subject paddles, the interviewer steers.
PETER GZOWSKI, host of CBC Radio's *Morningside*, writing in *The Private Voice: A Journal of Reflections* (1988).

Readio
Neologism: "a unique hybrid — not quite literature, not quite radio. 'Readio,' perhaps." The word was coined by arts reporter RICK GROEN, *The Globe and Mail*, 19 June 1990, to describe the compilations of contributions of regulars and listeners to CBC Radio's *Morningside* edited by its host Peter Gzowski.

And as always / this truth of North / this ether theatre / these shadows dancing / your mind's walls
BILL HOWELL, poet and radio producer, "How to Get Hear from There," *Moonlight Saving Time* (1990).

RAILWAYS
See also TRAVEL

All aboard for the West!
SIR GEORGE-ÉTIENNE CARTIER, Father of Confederation, stood up and shouted the above five words in the House of Commons, 1 June 1872, upon the passage of the Pacific Railway Act which charted the CPR.

This is *lovely, quite lovely*; I shall travel on this cowcatcher from summit to sea.
LADY AGNES MACDONALD, impulsive wife of Prime Minister Sir John A. Macdonald, who elected to travel, perched on the cowcatcher of the CPR's transcontinental train, from Laggan station in the Rockies for 600 miles, Summer 1886, quoted by Louis Reynolds in *Agnes: The Biography of Lady Macdonald* (1979).

The building of the C.P.R. [is] an exploit to which we look back now as the most mag-

nificent expression in our history of our national faith in ourselves.
F.H. UNDERHILL, historian, "Goldwin Smith" (1933), *In Search of Canadian Liberalism* (1960).

The construction of the Canadian Pacific, at the time the longest railway in the world, was one of the epic feats of nineteenth-century railway building, unmatched until Russia built the Trans-Siberian line at the end of the century. The transcontinental railway's importance to Canada was so fundamental that its history has been celebrated in song and story as a Canadian national epic.
MICHAEL BLISS, historian, *Northern Enterprise: Five Centuries of Canadian Business* (1987).

The Canadian love affair with railways, destined to last for more than three-quarters of a century, was part national dream, part nightmare.
MICHAEL BLISS, historian, *Northern Enterprise: Five Centuries of Canadian Business* (1987).

Nobody ever did anything worthwhile by pussyfooting.
Characteristic remark of DONALD GORDON, President of the CNR from 1950 to 1966, quoted in his obituary in *The Toronto Star*, 5 May 1969.

Canadian trains did not rush and rock. They pounded steadily along, every so often giving a warning blast on their sirens. I remember those sirens blowing in the icy darkness of winter nights in Ottawa, the most haunting sound, at once melancholy and stirring, like the mourning of some strange, sad beast.
WILLIAM BUCHAN, son of John Buchan, Governor General Lord Tweedsmuir, *A Memoir* (1982).

"I have a theory," he said, "that if we gave every kid in Canada a free ride coast-to-coast on this train at a given age — say 12 or 13 — we would change the nature of

this country. As it is, half the people in Canada don't know anything and don't want to know anything and never will know anything about this country except their own province."
> WILLIAM OSCAR JOHNSON, U.S. travel and sports writer, quoting an unnamed conductor aboard *The Canadian* west of Winnipeg, "Trans-Canada," *Sports Illustrated*, 27 Jan. 1988.

We'd like to thank you for travelling on VIA — where it's always our pleasure to take you for a ride.
> Recorded message, recalling those heard on flights, noted on U.S.-bound VIA passenger train, reported by Rosie DiManno in *The Toronto Star*, 27 Aug. 1989.

Most of us are in favour of the status Crow.
> DAVID PETERSON, Ontario Premier, punning in 1989 on the Crowsnest Pass Rates and *status quo*, quoted by Gail Harvey and Roy MacGregor in *Poli-Graphs* (1989).

The railway has held us together, spanning a bleak Precambrian desert, an angry ocean of plumed mountains, a chill wasteland of muskeg, to give us unity we could not otherwise have achieved.
> PIERRE BERTON, author and media personality, *Maclean's*, 21 Aug. 1989.

When the oil crisis strikes again, we will have to downgrade the buses and go back to the rails, as Calgary and Vancouver have already done. The euphemism is light rapid transit; but, light or heavy, a train is still a train, and the day will come when we will welcome it back as an old and trusted friend.
> PIERRE BERTON, author, *Maclean's*, 21 Aug. 1989.

If Paris was worth a mass, Craigellachie was worth a stop.
> PETER C. NEWMAN, columnist, referring to the failure of VIA Rail's management to allow *The Canadian* a sentimental stop at Craigellachie, B.C., where on 7 Nov. 1885

the "last spike" was driven home, *Maclean's*, 5 Feb. 1990

"Via Rail doesn't travel here any more," he said extraneously.
> A linguistic oddity known as the "Tom Swifty" contributed by Warren Ford, Owen Sound, Ont., quoted by Warren Clements in *The Globe and Mail*, 16 March 1991.

RAINBOW

You, whose day it is, / Make it beautiful. / Get out your rainbow colours / So it will be beautiful.
> Clayoquot poem, "Weather Song," *Songs of the Great Land* (1989) edited by John Robert Colombo.

RANCHING

You go out to Alberta, you stand in the foothills, surrounded by the greatest livestock the world has ever seen, and you ask, "What is Alberta giving Canada?" And the answer is blowing in the wind.
> DAVE BROADFOOT, comedian, address, Empire Club of Canada, Toronto, 9 March 1978.

RCMP
> *See* ROYAL CANADIAN MOUNTED POLICE

READING
> *See also* BOOKS

Blessings be on the inventors of the alphabet, pen and printing press! Life would be — to me at all events — a terrible thing without books. I cannot remember ever learning to read. I suppose there must have been a time when I took my first step into an enchanted world by learning that "A" was "A," but for any recollection of it, I might as well have been born with a capacity for reading just as for breathing or eating. It is fortunate, situated as I am, that I can read books over and over again with never failing interest and zest; otherwise I could never get enough reading matter to satisfy my voracious appetite.

L. M. MONTGOMERY, author, journal entry, 14 Jan. 1900, *The Selected Journals of L.M. Montgomery: Volume I: 1889-1910* (1985) edited by Mary Rubio and Elizabeth Waterston.

Lucky you if you have a habit of reading, for there's *always* a book you haven't read that can totally absorb you for hours: something new, or a classic, or, if you think your convalescence is going to be extra long, perhaps the complete works of an author you've always wanted to know better, read in chronological order, while time passes, and wounds heal.

ELIZABETH SMART, novelist and diarist, "How to Mend a Broken Heart" (1982), *Autobiographies* (1987) edited by Christina Burridge.

On a cold, wet Canadian winter night, there's nothing like crawling into bed with your laptop and curling up with a good disc.

FRANK OGDEN, futurologist known as "Dr. Tomorrow," characteristic observation, 1980s.

I strongly believe in "previewing." In reading dynamics, previewing is the principle that one reviews a work at high speed before one actually reads it. I always preview a book before I read it. I can honestly say that I have never read a book I didn't like.

JOEL BONN, director, Evelyn Wood Reading Dynamics Institute, *obiter dictum*, 3 Feb. 1990.

I once wrote an essay about books and reading named "A Call to the Clerisy," and I defined that unusual and almost obsolete word like this: "The clerisy are those who read for pleasure, but not for idleness; who read for pastime but not to kill time; who love books, but do not live by books." The clerisy are not professional critics or scholars, tirelessly assessing books, or bound by their work to read a lot of books that give them no pleasure. The clerisy are those who seek, and find, delight and enlargement of life in books. The clerisy are those for whom reading is a personal art.

ROBERTSON DAVIES, man-of-letters, personal statement about the pleasures of reading and book collecting, contributed to promotional material issued by the Folio Society, June 1990.

REALITY

Most of my world's not real. The real bits are rare and brief. . . . Oh! How incapable are we of sustained feeling and real life!

ELIZABETH SMART, novelist and diarist, entry, 29 April 1936, *Necessary Secrets: The Journals of Elizabeth Smart* (1986) edited by Alice Van Wart.

A world in which the presidency of the United States can be changed by one psychotic with a rifle is not real enough for an intelligent person to want to live in it.

NORTHROP FRYE, literary philosopher, observation in 1964, quoted by John Ayre in *Northrop Frye: A Biography* (1989).

One can only mirror reality by being at a distance from it.

ROBIN SKELTON, man-of-letters, aphorism, May 1990.

REASON

As in all human affairs, we run to extremes: property rights may be over-emphasized in one era; personal liberties may be over-emphasized in another. But human beings are basically reasonable creatures, and as the pendulum swings, we invariably leave the extremities and recover our balance for periods, albeit, some may seem short, in which we enjoy an equilibrium that assures our survival.

MORRIS C. SHUMIATCHER, lawyer, "Discussion: Property Rights and Liberty," *Canadian Journal of Law and Jurisprudence*, July 1988.

REBELLIONS

See also PROTEST

RIEL, LOUIS

Matthews: Sam. Sam, we lost.
Lount: No, Peter. We just haven't won yet.
  Dialogue between PETER MATTHEWS and SAMUEL LOUNT, rebels hanged for treason for their part in the Rebellion of 1837 in Upper Canada, reproduced from the stage play *1837: The Farmers' Revolt* (1975) by Rick Salutin.

Wait, I want to kill another Englishman.
  "Leaping into a trench, one young volunteer stared at the body of a defender who had fought to the end. He was a wrinkled, white-haired Métis of ninety-three named JOSEPH OUELLETTE, Dumont later recounted that he had pleaded with the old man to fall back. 'Several times I said to him, "Father, we have to retreat." And this simple man replied, "Wait, I want to kill another Englishman.""'" Ogden Tanner in *The Canadians: The Old West* (1977) with the editors of Time-Life Books. This occurred during the Battle of Batoche, 9-12 May 1885, which was well fought by Gabriel Dumont — and Joseph Ouellette.

RECESSION

As the ultimate obscenity was once to swearing, so the r-word is to Ottawa cabinet circles these days. . . . It will not cross the lips of the Prime Minister.
  LEW GLOIN, columnist, "Words," discussing the "r-word" — that is, "recession" — in *The Toronto Star*, 14 Oct. 1990.

RECORD INDUSTRY

See also MUSIC

Cut-Out Limbo.
  Succinct description of recordings which are no longer for sale because the record companies have failed to keep them in print, associated with Clyde Gilmour, host of CBC Radio's long-running program *Gilmour's Albums.*

The true recording artist, who really understands the values and implications of recording, is someone who is looking at the totality — sees it so clearly that it doesn't matter if you start with the middle note in the middle movement and work in either direction like a crab going back and forth. The mark of a true recording artist is an ability to be able to cut in at any moment in any work and say, "This works in a way that's only appropriate for this recording."
  GLENN GOULD, pianist, interviewed by Ulla Colgrass in *For the Love of Music* (1988).

The only reason we're doing vinyl on it at all is for the critics and for Canada, where there are lots of hippies and draft dodgers who still buy vinyl.
  WALT WILSON, executive, MCA Records, address, 31st annual meeting, National Association of Recording Merchandisers, explaining why some albums are released as CDs or cassettes and others as vinyl discs, quoted by Laurie Deans in *The Globe and Mail*, 17 March 1989.

So long for now.
  Characteristic signoff of CLYDE GILMOUR, host of CBC Radio's long-running *Gilmour's Albums*, quoted by Richard J. Doyle in *Hurly-Burly: A Time at The Globe* (1990).

RECYCLING

See also ENVIRONMENTALISM

The sky is blue and three-quarters of the universe appears blue to us and nobody complains.
  NYLE LUDOLPH, sanitation engineer, explaining why he authorized the use of the colour blue (rather than the green identified with conservationists) for the popular Blue Box Program for curbside recycling, private communication, 19 Dec. 1990. Ludolph is known as "the grandfather of recycling." The initial concept originated with Resource Integrations Systems of Toronto. Ludolph

authorized, on behalf of Laidlaw Waste Systems and Total Recycling Systems Ltd., the production of 200 corrugated, blue-coloured containers for trial use in Kitchener, Ont., in 1981. Each container was stencilled with the motto "We Recycle." Two years later, on 26 Sept. 1983, he authorized the distribution throughout that city of 34,000 boxes. By year's end the program was known as the Blue Box Program. Thereafter it spread across Canada and into the United States and the United Kingdom.

REFERENDUM

Obviously, there would have to be a referendum which the Parti Québécois proposes in order to get the decisive yes-or-no answer to the tired question: What does Quebec want? (This was precisely the procedure by which the only new province to join Confederation during our recent democratic past, Newfoundland, was consulted in 1948-49 about whether or not to opt in. So why not about opting out?)
RENÉ LÉVESQUE, Quebec Premier, "For an Independent Quebec" (1976), *The Globe and Mail*, 17 Nov. 1976. The Quebec Referendum on sovereignty-association, held in 1980, was dubbed the "renérendum" by L. Ian MacDonald, columnist with *The Montreal Gazette*.

I never thought I could be as proud to be a Quebecker and a Canadian as I am tonight.
PIERRE ELLIOTT TRUDEAU, Prime Minister, addressing the nation on the outcome of Quebec's referendum on sovereignty-association, 20 May 1980, quoted by Ramsay Cook in "'I Never Thought I Could Be as Proud . . .': The Trudeau-Lévesque Debate," *Towards a Just Society: The Trudeau Years* (1990) edited by Thomas S. Axworthy and Pierre Elliott Trudeau. The Prime Minister varied the words spoken by René Lévesque upon the election of the Parti Québécois, 15 Nov. 1976: "I

never thought I could be so proud of Quebeckers as I am tonight."

This is the year, I think, to hold a national referendum along these lines:
Do you authorize the governments of Canada and the provinces to negotiate a new distribution of constitutional responsibilities, consistent with the maintenance of a united Canada?
GEOFFREY STEVENS, columnist, *The Toronto Star*, 3 Feb. 1991.

REFORM
See also REBELLIONS

A good reformer keeps his eyes on the stars but his feet on the ground.
Adapted from a remark made by WILLIAM KASHTAN, long-time secretary of the Communist Party of Canada, noted by Jim Foster in *The Toronto Star*, 19 Jan. 1988. He retired as party leader after holding onto power for twenty-three years.

REFORM PARTY

The West Wants In
Early slogan of the Reform Party of Canada, established in May 1987 and led by Preston Manning who, at the party's convention in April 1991, announced that the western-based protest party would henceforth be a national party, noted by Jeffrey Simpson in *The Globe and Mail*, 11 April 1991.

REFUGEES
See also IMMIGRANTS

With virtually the total leadership of our society, including the leadership of all three major parties, religious leaders, professional leaders and virtually all the media supporting the increased figure of 50,000 sponsored refugees, the public support for that figure at best stood at 49%; the opposition was at least 37%. This occurred in spite of a total media emotional appeal to the heartstrings of Canadians.
HOWARD ADELMAN, philosopher and

spokesperson for Operation Lifeline which aided in 1979-80 in the settlement of the Boat People by families, organizatons, and the federal government. "Refugee Sponsorship and Backlash," *The Indochinese Refugee Movement: The Canadian Experience — Proceedings of a Conference in Toronto, October 19, 20 and 21, 1979* (1980) edited by Howard Adelman.

An elderly man in Kitchener raced up to me after I had addressed a crowd of three hundred, put his arms around me and hugged me, pronouncing, "Isn't it wonderful when a Mennonite can hug a Jew over sponsoring a Buddhist!"
HOWARD ADELMAN, philosopher and spokesman for Operation Lifeline, *Canada and the Indochinese Refugees* (1982).

Our tradition of sanctuary for refugees, begun with the "underground railroad" for escaping slaves, has been breached in the past and will be again if we forget how many Jews, fleeing to our gates from the Nazi terror in the prewar years, were locked out. Today, there are refugees from murderous regimes in Latin America, Asia, and Africa who seek our haven. As a multicultural society, we risk our soul if we lose compassion for the oppressed in any corner of the earth. Because we are the hope of a better world.
DAVE BARRETT, former B.C. Premier, contributor to *If I Were Prime Minister* (1987) edited by Mel Hurtig.

One in 324 Canadian citizens and landed immigrants today came here as a refugee, the highest proportion of any nation in the world.
WILLIAM KILBOURN, historian, "The Peaceable Kingdom Still," *Daedalus: Journal of the American Academy of Arts and Sciences*, "In Search of Canada," Fall 1988.

The word "refugee" is not used in the Bible, but the word "refuge" is frequently invoked to describe one of the main functions of religious communities. I covet for Canada the capacity to legislate equitably "refuge" for those who so desperately need sanctuary and hope.
LOIS WILSON, Christian activist, *Turning the World Upside Down: A Memoir* (1989).

Refugee claimants were actually alone among those seeking legal redress in Canada in having the right to a hearing, the right to know the case they had to meet, access to counsel, at initial stages, a meaningful appeal, and an explanation of the reasons for a judgement against them.
DAVID MATAS with ILANA SIMON, immigration lawyer and journalist, *Closing the Doors: The Failure of Refugee Protection* (1989).

Protecting refugees means helping people who need help and putting a generous face on Canada to the world. Denying protection to refugees means refusing to help the helpless and painting Canada as a cruel and mean-spirited nation. In the end, the judgement Canadians make about refugees is a judgement we make about ourselves.
DAVID MATAS with ILANA SIMON, immigration lawyer and journalist, *Closing the Doors: The Failure of Refugee Protection* (1989).

REGINA
See also SASKATCHEWAN

An unfortunate interruption of prairie space. . . . The best way to see Regina is through a double martini from 35,000 feet.
Sentiments attributed to the prairie-based painter RONALD BLOORE in the 1950s by Stephen Brook in *Maple Leaf Rag: Travels across Canada* (1987).

The pleasures of Regina are not immediately obvious. Its centre fails to cohere, its buildings are a graceless jumble, and its topography could hardly be flatter. Allowances, however, must be made.
MARK ABLEY, traveller, *Beyond Forget: Rediscovering the Prairies* (1986).

Regina rises from the prairies of Saskatchewan with a minimum of fuss.

PRIIT J. VESILIND, writer, "Common Ground, Different Dreams," *National Geographic*, March 1990.

REGIONALISM

See also FEDERALISM

We are, furthermore, a country of regions, whose right to *remain* as regions we hold dear. (I never did figure out what was wrong with Joe Clark's "community of communities.") If the economy goes sour in one part of the United States, the American belief is that its people can move elsewhere. When a part of Canada dries up, we think it's right to take part of our national pool of resources and pour it in so they can stay there.

PETER GZOWSKI, host of CBC Radio's *Morningside*, in *The Private Voice: A Journal of Reflections* (1988).

We are a country based on decent intervals, respectful solitudes and proper distances. Perhaps we have tried too hard for intimacy in recent years, and unwisely endangered the spaces that comfort us as peoples within the bosom of a single state. Perhaps we have tried too hard to escape our history in trying to assure our future.

WILLIAM THORSELL, columnist, *The Globe and Mail*, 23 Sept. 1989.

What Canada as a whole really needs is the bold vision of a New National Policy. Central to all must be the principle of fairness and equality of opportunity for the eight outer provinces generally that have worked so hard to strengthen the two inner ones — all too often at the expense of their own unrealized potential.

Canada needs a more compassionate vision that will provide a sense of common purpose for Canadians in every part of the country in order to re-energize a sense of unity that appears to be weakening. Greater unity is essential for us to survive as one country and one nation. Only a government with genuine respect for the outer regions of the country can inspire Canadians everywhere and make them feel fully equal partners in Confederation.

DAVID KILGOUR, Alberta M.P. and author, "Commentary," *The Toronto Star*, 28 Oct. 1989.

The focus is on our peripheral regions, which I call Outer Canada, including in the term virtually the entire country outside of Toronto-Montréal-Ottawa. Inner Canadians, more precisely, are a few thousand residents of Toronto's Old Forest Hill Village, the Bridle Path and upper Rosedale; Montréal's upper Westmount and sections of Outremont; and Ottawa's Rockcliffe Park and New Edinburgh. In short, they are those who by means of private wealth, position, and political clout have called most of the shots on national policy since Confederation. . . . Outer Canadians are the approximately eighteen million of us who live outside Toronto-Montréal-Ottawa.

DAVID KILGOUR, M.P., *Inside Outer Canada* (1990).

REGRET

Dancing through forgetting all / the things I was thinking through / instead of suddenly thinking about / simply dancing with you.

BILL HOWELL, poet, "What the Fiddles Never Forget," *Moonlight Saving Time* (1990).

REGULATION & DEREGULATION

The term "deregulation," then, is a misnomer, a myth. To be accurate, one should speak only of "reregulation." This latter term affords proper emphasis to government's role of apportioning and reapportioning relative rights and freedoms among contending interests.

ROBERT E. BABE, communications specialist, University of Ottawa, *Telecommunications in Canada: Technology, Industry, and Government* (1990).

RELATIONSHIPS

No one can get off scot-free, can *he*?
> BETTY JANE WYLIE, author, *obiter dictum*, 1990.

RELATIVITY

One man's precipice is another man's slope.
> BETTY JANE WYLIE, author, *No Two Alike* (1980).

RELIGION
See also BELIEF

Looking back on my past life I think I have had a rather peculiar spiritual experience. I am not "religiously inclined," as the phrase goes, but I have always possessed a deep *curiosity* about "things spiritual and eternal." I want to *find out* — to *know* and hence I am always poking and probing into creeds and religions, dead and alive, wanting to know for knowledge's sake what vital spark of immortal truth might be buried among all the verbiage and systems.
> L. M. MONTGOMERY, author, journal entry, 7 Oct. 1897, Cavendish, P.E.I., *The Selected Journals of L. M. Montgomery: Volume I: 1889-1910* (1985) edited by Mary Rubio and Elizabeth Waterston.

Likewise in the provinces of Canada, such as Newfoundland, Prince Edward Island, Nova Scotia, New Brunswick, Quebec, Ontario, Manitoba, Saskatchewan, Alberta, British Columbia, Ungava, Keewatin, Mackenzie, Yukon, and the Franklin Islands in the Arctic Circle — the believers of God must become self-sacrificing and like unto the candles of guidance become ignited in the provinces of Canada. Should they show forth such a magnanimity, it is assured that they will obtain universal divine confirmations, the heavenly cohorts will reinforce them uninterruptedly, and a most great victory will be obtained. Perchance, God willing, the call of the Kingdom may reach the ears of the Eskimos, the inhabitants of the Islands of Franklin in the north of Canada, as well as Greenland.
> 'ABDU'L-BAHÁ, Persian religious leader and living exemplar of the Bahá'í life, "Tablets to Canada from The Divine Plan," Haifa, Palestine, 5 April 1916, reproduced in *'Abdu'l-Bahá in Canada* (1962). Followers of the Bahá'í faith note that Newfoundland is granted the status of a province (it did not become one until thirty-three years later) and that there is an implicit prediction that the northern regions — Ungava, Keewatin, Mackenzie, Yukon, and the Franklin Islands — will in the fullness of time produce five separate provinces.

Within this phalanx, Canadians occupied a special place. The growth of (North) American missions in China is more astonishing when one realizes that almost one-quarter of British missionaries in 1919 (almost five hundred people) were in fact Canadians. Canada's contribution to the world missionary enterprise, like its contribution to the First World War, was larger than its share: it has been said that in proportion to their size and resources, the churches of Canada sponsored more missionaries than any other nation in Christendom.
> ALVYN J. AUSTIN, historian, *Saving China: Canadian Missionaries in the Middle Kingdom, 1888-1959* (1986).

WHEN HE CAME THERE WERE NO CHRISTIANS; WHEN HE DIED THERE WERE NO PAGANS
> Inscription on the tombstone of John Geddie, a Presbyterian missionary from Nova Scotia, who was killed and buried in his mission field in the New Hebrides, South Pacific; as noted by Alvyn J. Austin in *Saving China: Canadian Missionaries in the Middle Kingdom, 1888-1959* (1986).

Who is this man Jesus?
> Characteristic question of H.B. SHARMAN, Canadian-born Professor at Yenching University in Peking, China, founder of the Student Christian Movement's

Sharman method of Bible study; quoted by Alvyn J. Austin in *Saving China: Canadian Missionaries in the Middle Kingdom, 1888-1959* (1986).

In the Church, you know, there is a great heightening of every moment of experience, since every moment is played against a supernatural backdrop. Nothing can be humdrum in this scheme. Every least act of the mind has infinite significance.
MARSHALL McLUHAN, communications theorist, letter, 21 Jan. 1939, *Letters of Marshall McLuhan* (1987) edited by Matie Molinaro, Corinne McLuhan, and William Toye.

Religion may help people sleep more soundly, but, if it does, the reason for that has to be sought in man's waking state.
BERNARD J.F. LONERGAN, Jesuit philosopher, *A Second Collection: Papers by Bernard J.F. Lonergan, S.J.* (1954).

The church in Europe lost the workers in the nineteenth century; but would the church have lost the workers in the nineteenth century if she had not lost the intellectuals in the eighteenth?
BERNARD J.F. LONERGAN, Jesuit philosopher, *Understanding and Being: The Halifax Lectures on INSIGHT* (1990).

The core of both the Jewish and the Christian faiths is the belief that a God who is other than the world nevertheless enters into the world; that He enters into the world because He enters into the life of man.
EMIL FACKENHEIM, philosopher, "Martin Buber's Concept of Revelation" (1967), *The Jewish Thought of Emil Fackenheim: A Reader* (1987) edited by Michael L. Morgan.

I think that we're probably going to see the rise from the midst of all this queer, superstitious searching for something, a new religion. Perhaps not an entirely new religion, but at least a new form of religion.

ROBERTSON DAVIES, man-of-letters, interviewed by Louis Lague in 1976, *Conversations with Robertson Davies* (1989) edited by J. Madison Davis.

It's odd that the two poets in Canada who write obsessively about Jesus are Jews, while the others never mention him at all.
LOUIS DUDEK, aphorist, "Can. Lit. Notes," *The Bumper Book* (1986) edited by John Metcalf. The two poets are Irving Layton and Leonard Cohen.

When you're young, you discover sex. When you're older, you discover religion.
IRVING LAYTON, poet, quoted by Lucinda Vardy in *Belonging: A Book for the Questioning Catholic Today* (1988).

There are no lapsed Catholics after a Christmas concert by Pavarotti.
TIM BURKE, columnist, *The Montreal Gazette*, 8 Dec. 1987.

A sermon, in my own definition, is "a bridge that a preacher constructs between the Word of God in Scripture and the human situation in the personal and corporate lives of his people."
LEONARD GRIFFITH, preacher, *From Sunday to Sunday: Fifty Years in the Pulpit* (1987).

I'm not afraid of appearing too radical. The Church always has enough conservatives who are the brakes. But it doesn't always have enough radicals who are the spark plugs.
ROBERT McCLURE, retired medical missionary and former Moderator of the United Church of Canada, quoted by Christopher Donville in *The Globe and Mail*, 31 July 1987.

Today, I pray that the Holy Spirit will help you all find the just way so that Canada may be a model for the world in upholding the dignity of aboriginal peoples.
JOHN PAUL II, Pontiff, addressing a crowd of 5000 Dene, Fort Simpson, N.W.T., 20

Sept. 1987, quoted by Michael McAteer in *The Toronto Star* the following day.

If I could rewrite religious history I would, without a quiver of regret, eliminate Judaeo/Christian/Arabic/Moslem religions from the face of this planet.
FARLEY MOWAT, naturalist and author, interviewed by Alan Twigg in *Strong Voices: Conversations with Fifty Canadian Authors* (1988).

I rejoice that in my lifetime more and more Christian colleagues are discovering the riches of other faiths and are developing an awareness of other religions, not as threatening realities to be rejected, but as riches to be explored.
LOIS WILSON, Moderator of the United Church of Canada from 1980 to 1982, *Turning the World Upside Down: A Memoir* (1989).

Americans are much more religious than Canadians. Canadians are much more Catholic than Americans, though even Catholics don't go to church anymore.
ALLAN FOTHERINGHAM, columnist, *Maclean's*, 3 July 1989.

In a real world, the one outside the rarified atmosphere where Popes meet Archbishops of Canterbury, people no longer care whether somebody is an Anglican or a Roman Catholic. They already take it for granted that being a "believer" is more important than having a denominational name-tag any day of the week.
TOM HARPUR, religion columnist, *The Toronto Star*, 15 Oct. 1989.

They won't admit it, but it can't be stated too strongly or too often. The world's great religions, *as they are now*, are unable to cope with the almost overwhelming challenge presented by what we have done and are doing to devastate the Earth.
TOM HARPUR, religion columnist, *The Toronto Star*, 12 Nov. 1989.

The University of Toronto is a greater threat to Christianity than Bay Street, because Bay Street has sinners while the University of Toronto tends to produce agnostics.
ALOYSIUS AMBROZIC, Coadjutor Archbishop of Toronto, interviewed by Ron Graham in *God's Dominion: A Sceptic's Quest* (1990).

The majority of religions are merely diets.
ROBIN SKELTON, man-of-letters, aphorism, May 1990.

We are all priests of private religions.
ROBIN SKELTON, man-of-letters, aphorism, May 1990.

REMEMBRANCE DAY
See HOLIDAYS

RESEARCH & DEVELOPMENT

We have fallen well behind every other major developed country in the level at which we fund university research, and, indeed, the level at which we support research in government institutions as well.
DONALD A. CHANT, Vice-President, University of Toronto, address, Empire Club of Canada, Toronto, 22 Jan, 1976.

Canada is blessed with cheap power. Sometimes I think it may not have been so much of a blessing. It is like the rich man's son who never learns to work. We have been blessed with riches, but I am not sure that we have been the most intelligent stewards. The time to do something about it is now.
URSULA FRANKLIN, Professor of Metallurgy and Materials Science, University of Toronto, address, Empire Club of Canada, Toronto, 30 March 1978.

It has often happened in the sciences that a new discovery, even a new invention, seems to be of no immediate practical use. But fifty years later, it may turn out to be exactly what that science is then looking

for. Similarly, it has been noted many times that what poets have seen in any given period becomes what the whole world is doing fifty or a hundred years later.
NORTHROP FRYE, literary critic, address, Empire Club of Canada, Toronto, 19 Jan. 1984.

Yet Canada, abundantly rich in resources, is technologically poor. We act like a giant Kuwait! We have come to believe that we can dig it up, cut it down, or pump it out, endlessly.
DOUGLAS WRIGHT, President, University of Waterloo, address, Empire Club of Canada, Toronto, 28 Nov. 1985.

I was soon to discover the differences between Canada and the United States. My American peers, starting out as assistant professors like me, could expect their first grants in the $30,000 to $40,000 range. I was told that National Research Council of Canada grants begin at about $2,500!
DAVID SUZUKI, scientist and media personality, writing about his research work at the University of Alberta in 1962, *Metamorphosis: Stages in a Life* (1987).

In 1923, for instance, the problem of the discolouration of canned lobsters was solved through the investment by the council of $2,000. The fishing industry readily accepted the solution, which thereby prevented an annual loss of some $700,000, a sum equal to the entire cost of the National Research Council from its beginning to the time of its discovery. More recently, it was NRC laboratories that identified a new toxin in mussels that halted East Coast U.S. and Canada mussel sales temporarily in 1987.
GERALDINE A. KENNY-WALLACE and J. FRASER MUSTARD, scientists and spokespeople for science, "From Paradox to Paradigm: The Evolution of Science and Technology in Canada," *Daedalus: Journal of the American Academy of Arts and Sciences*, "In Search of Canada," Fall, 1988. The National Research Council (NRC), which goes back to an advisory

committee formed in 1916, was established in 1929.

It is interesting that the United States has not shown growth in innovation for at least a decade and now has a negative balance in trade in a number of advanced technologies.
GERALDINE A. KENNY-WALLACE and J. FRASER MUSTARD, scientists and spokespeople for science, "From Paradox to Paradigm: The Evolution of Science and Technology in Canada," *Daedalus: Journal of the American Academy of Arts and Sciences*, "In Search of Canada," Fall 1988.

Dr. Fred Aldrich, Director of Marine Biology, was a professor at Memorial University before moving to the laboratory at Logy Bay. He once set an exam question: "How would you set up a research program on the life history of the giant squid?" One bright young man wrote a four-word answer: "Show strong Liberal tendencies." Aldrich gave him full marks.
HAROLD HORWOOD, journalist and biographer, referring to the marine biology laboratory at Logy Bay, near St. John's, Nfld., and to the provincial Liberal government headed by Premier Joey Smallwood, in *Joey* (1989).

RESOURCES

While to open up these communications which have been so immensely beneficial to their commerce and industries, the Canadians have, by exaggerated representations, got from the mother-country resources which they were supposed unable to furnish themselves, they have yet been able to build imposing cities full of magnificent mansions, and at Montreal an hotel far exceeding in grandeur anything the mother-country could, at that time, show.
HERBERT SPENCER, British philosopher, recalling his visit to Montreal in 1882 and blandishments to invest in railways and

other industries, *An Autobiography* (1904).

It is high time that the great resources of nature be used not to make the few rich, but to make the many wise.
ALFRED FITZPATRICK, Founder and Principal of Frontier College, *The University in Overalls: A Plea for Part-Time Study* (1920).

There are finite limits to the non-renewable resources on which we depend so heavily, resources of fossil fuels, minerals, and all the rest. We are even pushing the finite limits of many of our so-called renewable resources: fish stocks are dwindling alarmingly, many of our forests are denuded and so on. And we have seen that there are finite limits to the capacity of the environment to absorb the waste materials and toxic substances with which we assault it in such incredible amounts. In short, we know that many kinds of growth must be limited in the very near future.
DONALD A. CHANT, Vice-President, University of Toronto, address, Empire Club of Canada, Toronto, 22 Jan, 1976.

Canada has real problems. We have been very successful at creating a fair and good society. But things have changed, and no one owes Canada a living. We have been a nation of real estate speculators for 100 years, sitting on a land mass which contained things the world wanted: trees, oil, copper and natural gas. Now there are alternative suppliers, and we still have this concept that we don't have to work very hard.
CLIFF HATCH JR., former CEO of Hiram Walker Resources Ltd. and now chief financial officer of Allied-Lyons PCL, quoted by Diane Francis in *Maclean's*, 9 May 1988.

Resources left in the ground are saved, not lost.
HUGH BRODY, author, *Maps and Dreams: Indians and the British Columbia Frontier* (1981, 1988).

The world does not lack resources; it lacks imagination about how to manage and allocate its resources.
FRANK FEATHER, futurologist, *G-Forces: Reinventing the World — The 35 Global Forces Restructuring Our World* (1989).

People. Seldom thought of like other resources, people may be our most valuable resource.
SUSAN A. McDANIEL, demographer, "People Pressure," *Planet under Stress: The Challenge of Global Change* (1990) edited by Constance Mungall and Digby J. McLaren for the Royal Society of Canada.

RESPECT

I am speaking to you as my fellow citizens. I am speaking to you of a deeper brotherhood than that of blood, of a fraternity of hope and of charity in the scriptural sense, for it the Canadian nation must survive, it will only survive in mutual respect and in love for one another.
PIERRE ELLIOTT TRUDEAU, Prime Minister, address on national radio and television in response to the election of a separatist government in Quebec, 24 Nov. 1976.

RESPONSIBILITY

So it is that modern man not only individually is responsible for the life he leads but also collectively as responsible for the world in which he leads it.
BERNARD J.F. LONERGAN, Jesuit philosopher, *A Second Collection: Papers by Bernard J.F. Lonergan, S.J.* (1954).

Only politicians and policemen have power. The rest of us have responsibilities.
PETER BENTLEY, business executive, quoted by Diane Francis in *Controlling Interest: Who Owns Canada?* (1986).

Citizens have an obligation to cry "fire" or "robbery," not an obligation to develop a private fire or police department.

ROSALIE BERTELL, anti-nuclear activist, Letters to the Editor, *Toronto Life*, Jan. 1990.

REST

See also RETIREMENT

The sun was setting in the west, / The birds were singing on ev'ry tree, / All nature seemed inclined for rest, / But still there was no rest for me.
Verse from the folksong "Nova Scotia Farewell" collected by Helen Creighton and included in *Traditional Songs from Nova Scotia* (1950).

RETIREMENT

See also AGE
REST

I know the day I'll retire but not the date. That'll be the day I die, and when that happens, they'll have to pile eight or nine tons of rocks on my grave to keep Joey down.
J.R. (JOEY) SMALLWOOD, former Newfoundland Premier, quoted by Frank Rasky in *The Toronto Star*, 24 Nov. 1979.

At sixty-four, you're still the best; / One year more, and then you're less / Than dust upon the floor.
STAN ROGERS, singer and composer, "The Last Watch," *From Fresh Water* (Cole Harbour Music, 1984).

You might as well count your nest eggs before they hatch.
BETTY JANE WYLIE, author, *The Best Is Yet to Come: Planning Ahead for a Financially Secure Retirement* (1988).

Few people give real thought to the possibility of being old and grey and full of sleep and nodding by the fire until they're cold and there's no firewood.
BETTY JANE WYLIE, author, *The Best Is Yet to Come: Planning Ahead for a Financially Secure Retirement* (1988).

A retired moderator of the United Church of Canada had once responded to a question on the subject of describing retiring as the putting on of a new set of tires. That was certainly the way I regarded my exit from electoral politics. I was free at last to explore the interests and opportunities opening up to me in education, international development and peace; free at last to stomp the country encouraging women to enter the political arena.
ROSEMARY BROWN, Jamaican-born feminist and public figure, *Being Brown: A Very Public Life* (1989).

When I was younger I used to worry about having enough money for my old age; now I worry about having enough old age for my money.
HELEN STIMPSON, retired real-estate agent, characteristic remark, 7 March 1991.

REVELATION

A divine revelation . . . is God's claim to have a say in the aims and purposes, the direction and development of human lives, human societies, human cultures, human history.
BERNARD J.F. LONERGAN, Jesuit philosopher, *A Second Collection: Papers by Bernard J.F. Lonergan, S.J.* (1954).

REVOLUTION

We Quebecers will never stage a revolution; we are incapable of staying awake for forty-eight hours in a row!
DANIEL JOHNSON, Quebec Premier in 1966-68, quoted by Gérard Pelletier in "Quebec: Different but in Step with North America," *Daedalus: Journal of the American Academy of Arts and Sciences*, "In Search of Canada," Fall 1988.

I, my generation, my nation, have been involuntarily through two revolutions, both of them socialist: one of the Right variety, one of the Left. Together they destroyed my peripheral vision.
JOSEF SVORECKY, essayist and novelist, "A Revolution Is Usually the Worst Solu-

tion," *The Writer and Human Rights* (1983) edited by the Toronto Arts Group for Human Rights.

I am reactionary because I believe there are certain traditional values that should not be forgotten, and if they are forgotten the results may be tragic.
JOSEF SKVORECKY, essayist and novelist, "An Interview in Toronto" (1983), *Talkin' Moscow Blues* (1988) edited by Sam Solecki.

When you don't have a country, wanting one becomes a revolutionary act. No one can change that.
FRANCIS SIMARD, member of the FLQ cell that kidnapped Pierre Laporte, *Talking It Out: The October Crisis from Inside* (1987) translated by David Homel.

They sentenced me to twenty years of boredom / For trying to change the system from within. / I'm coming now, I'm coming to reward them. / First we take Manhattan, then we take Berlin.
LEONARD COHEN, poet and singer, "First We Take Manhattan" from the 1988 album *I'm Your Man*.

Two nations, not one, came out of the American Revolution. Americans are descended from winners, Canadians, as their writers frequently reiterate, from losers.
SEYMOUR MARTIN LIPSET, U.S. sociologist, quoted by Carol Goar in *The Toronto Star*, 19 Oct. 1989.

RHINOCEROS PARTY
See also POLITICS

We cannot fool all of the people some of the time, or even some of the people all of the time — but if we can fool a majority of the people at election time, that's the time we need.
CHARLIE McKENZIE, "concierge," Rhinoceros Party, press conference, Montreal, reported in *The Globe and Mail*, 30 Sept. 1988.

Freedom of screech for Newfoundlanders. Reform schools for politicians. Replace chlorine in drinking water with steroids to make Canada the strongest country in the world. Eliminate all time zones; make the entire month of February a national holiday; establish a new national holiday in the month of February. Increase the speed of light to ease congestion in urban centres. Bottle acid rain and export it.

Place a supermailbox in front of everybody's home. Organize men's synchronized swimming teams. Fund a national dating service for seniors. As long as there's a Canada, there'll be a *Front Page Challenge*. The Rhinos have $6 million and .54 cents more than the federal Liberals. "We have 54 cents in the bank. The Liberals have been reported to be $6 million in debt."
Some planks in the platform of the Rhinoceros Party as presented by Charlie McKenzie, "concierge," Rhinoceros Party, press conference, Montreal, reported in *The Globe and Mail*, 30 Sept. 1988 and elsewhere. In the federal election of 1984, the Rhinos chalked up almost 99,200 votes.

RIDING
See also HORSES

One thing I didn't learn on the streets of Ottawa was how to ride a horse.
Attributed to LORNE GREENE, Ottawa-born star of the long-running television series *Bonanza* (1959-73).

RIEL, LOUIS

I remember seeing some of the Indians who had taken part in the Louis Riel Rebellion of 1885, also an old man produced every year at the Saskatoon Rodeo as "the man who captured Louis Riel." In fact, Riel surrendered himself.
JOHN PREBBLE, Anglo-Scots historian who was raised in Saskatchewan in the mid-1910s, quoted by Fredric Warburg in *All Authors Are Equal: The Publishing Life of Fredric Warburg 1936-1971* (1973).

No man in Canadian history suffered as many reversals of fortune during his life. He was, in turn, unofficial leader of his people, president of a provisional government, founder of the Province of Manitoba, fugitive in exile, member of Parliament, outlaw, leader of another provisional government, and prisoner.

> PIERRE ELLIOTT TRUDEAU, Prime Minister, address at the unveiling of the Louis Riel Monument, Regina, 2 Oct. 1969.

RIGHT & WRONG

See also GOOD & EVIL

One of us cannot be wrong.

> Attributed to the poet and singer LEONARD COHEN in the 1970s.

You can't go too far wrong if you believe that what you're doing is right.

> WILLIAM VANDER ZALM, British Columbia Premier, quoted in *The Vancouver Province*, 15 June 1988.

Error has no rights.

> GWYNNE DYER, correspondent and columnist, quoting his Catholic high school teachers in Newfoundland, *The Toronto Star*, 8 Jan. 1990.

RIGHTS

See RIGHT & WRONG
RIGHTS, ABORIGINAL
RIGHTS, CIVIL
RIGHTS, HUMAN

RIGHTS, ABORIGINAL

We pride ourselves too much on our sterling human-rights record. It is not so shining. If there is a common denominator in the history of the northern half of North America, it is the continuing inability to deal seriously with aboriginal rights. They are different from constitutional rights, and that gap in understanding constitutes the definitive and enduring Canadian tragedy — a tragedy perversely unifying our diverse geography, scattered population, linguistic incompatibility, and fractured drive towards some semblance of chartered order. The natives remain restless, and most of us continue unconcerned or irritated.

> JOHN FRASER, editor, "Diary," *Saturday Night*, Nov. 1989.

RIGHTS, CIVIL

Rights are rights are rights. There are no such things as inside rights and outside rights. No such things as rights for the talls and rights for the shorts. No such things as rights for the front and rights for the back or rights for East and rights for West. Rights are rights and always will be rights.

> CLIFFORD LINCOLN, Quebec Environment Minister, one of a handful of anglophone Members of the National Assembly, announcing his resignation from Cabinet following the decision of Quebec Premier Robert Bourassa to enact Bill 178 (which banned non-French signs outside but not inside commercial establishments), 20 Dec. 1988, quoted by Benoît Aubin in *The Globe and Mail* the following day.

Anglophones developed this wonderful sensitivity to individual rights only after they had secured collective rights for themselves over a vast empire.

> LAURENT PICARD, former head of Radio-Canada who teaches at McGill University, quoted in *The Globe and Mail*, 27 Oct. 1989.

French Canadians just don't have a great sensitivity to individual rights. They expect the government to take up where the church, and before that the king, had left, and take initiatives, make decisions for them.

> GRAEME DÉCARIE, Montreal historian, quoted in *The Globe and Mail*, 27 Oct. 1989.

Somehow, as dependence on the State has increased, a terrible and immoral chain-reaction has become established. . . . from *private* wants, to *public* needs, to *legal* rights, to moral *claims* against society. This is the destructive "rights illusion" at work in our society, and in the whole world.

> WILLIAM D. GAIRDNER, academic and businessman, *The Trouble with Canada* (1990).

RIGHTS, HUMAN

It turns out the achievement of 1948 was much greater than anybody would have dared to imagine at the time.

> JOHN HUMPHREY, constitutional expert, principal architect of the United Nation's Universal Declaration of Human Rights, adopted by the U.N. on 10 Dec. 1948. He was quoted at the U.N. in New York during a celebration to mark its fortieth anniversary, according to *The Toronto Star*, 9 Dec. 1988.

Nobody responsible can be innocent.

> Remark made by a character in the novel *Memory Board* (1987) by JANE RULE.

We will not make any real progress towards genuine fairness in our society until we recognize that creating gigantic bureaucracies under the banner of human rights does no-one much good.

> EDWARD HORE, commentator, *Saturday Night*, Sept. 1989.

RIVERS

See also WATER

Ever since then I have translated . . . every land with which I was connected into the speech of its rivers. . . . Canada I found most satisfying, with the superb trough of the St. Lawrence, the streams that radiate into Hudson's Bay from east, south and west, the gigantic Mackenzie seaming the North with its tributaries, and the fierce rivers that cut their way through the Rockies and the Coast range to the western sea.

> JOHN BUCHAN, Governor General Lord Tweedsmuir, *Memory Hold-the-Door* (1940).

ROCKY MOUNTAINS

See also MOUNTAINS & MOUNTAINEERING

The mountains last night seemed to be posing for the Detroit Photographic Company.

> WALLACE STEVENS, poet, Journal, 7 Aug. 1903, B.C., *Letters of Wallace Stevens* (1966) edited by Holly Stevens.

The Rockies have no majesty; they do not elevate the mind to contemplation of Almighty God any more than they warm the heart by seeming sentinels to watch over the habitations of one's fellow men.

> ALEISTER CROWLEY, English traveller and occultist, May 1904, *The Confessions of Aleister Crowley: An Autohagiography* (1969) edited by John Symonds and Kenneth Grant.

The sterile mountains which form the whole eastern border of British Columbia may well prove to be the treasure-chest of Canada, though the lid has been difficult to open. Whenever it has been opened a peep of something wonderful has been obtained.

> SIR ARTHUR CONAN DOYLE, author, *Our Second American Adventure* (1923).

A line of low distant hills broke the interminable plain which has extended with hardly a rising for 1,500 miles. Above them was, here and there, a peak of snow. Shades of Mayne Reid, they were the Rockies — my old familiar Rockies! Have I been here before? What an absurd question, when I lived here for about ten years of my life in all the hours of dreamland. What deeds have I not done among Redskins and trappers and grizzlies within their wilds! And here they were at last glimmering bright in the rising morning sun. At least, I have seen my dream mountains. Most boys never do.

> SIR ARTHUR CONAN DOYLE, author, recalling his youthful reading and his trip on the CPR in 1914, *Memories and Adventures* (1924).

When it's Springtime in the Rockies, / I am coming back to you, / Little sweetheart of the mountains, / With your bonny eyes of blue; / Once again I'll say "I love you," / While the birds sing all the day, / When it's Springtime in the Rockies, / In the Rockies, far away.

> Eight lines from the popular U.S. love song "When It's Springtime in the Rockies" (1929) with lyrics by MARY HALE WOOLSEY and music by Robert Sauer.

In time the Rockies may crumble, / Gibraltar may tumble, / They're only made of clay, / But our love is here to stay. / It's very clear / Our love is here to stay.

> Six lines from the popular U.S. love song "Love Is Here to Stay" (1938) with lyrics by IRA GERSHWIN and music by George Gershwin.

Westward still, to the mountains striding up from the United States clear through to the Arctic. A silent dispassionate force, unmoved by the seasons passing beneath them, they simply exist — Nature's mightiest challenge, to artists, geologists and adventurers.

> HEATHER MENZIES, journalist, *The Railroad's Not Enough: Canada Now* (1978).

If a globe were to be made 12 inches (30 cm) in diameter, with every detail of the earth's surface reproduced exactly to scale, the highest mountain in the Canadian Rockies would be represented by a bump roughly equal to the thickness of a single leaf of this book.

> VIRGIL MARTIN, photographic historian, *Changing Landscapes of Southern Ontario* (1988).

ROMANCE

I am the happiest man there has ever been in the world. . . .

> HAROLD MACMILLAN, future Prime Minister of the United Kingdom, letter written to Helen Macmillan, 27 Dec. 1919, quoted by Alistair Horne in *Macmillan: 1894-1956: Volume I of the Official Biography* (1988). Macmillan, a young unmarried diplomat, served the Governor General the Duke of Devonshire at Rideau Hall, Ottawa. The posting, a "permanent house-party" ten months long, inspired the above sentiment, as did his introduction to his future wife, Lady Dorothy Cavendish.

ROOTS

There's a feeling out there, especially after free trade, that if we don't find roots fast we're going to be uprooted.

> Stompin' TOM CONNORS, singer and composer, quoted in *Maclean's*, 14 May 1990.

ROYAL CANADIAN MOUNTED POLICE
See also CRIME
       POLICE

Devil child have forked tongue.

> Frequently parodied line spoken by an Indian played by the actor Victor Jory to the child actress Shirley Temple in the 1939 Hollywood movie *Susannah of the Mounties*.

In 1939 Shirley Temple sang and danced her way into the hearts of the Blackfoot in *Susannah of the Mounties* (William Seiter). While doing so she also managed to save Randolph Scott from being burned at the stake, kept the Blackfoot at peace with the Mounties, and acquired an Indian boyfriend.

> The plot of the Hollywood movie *Susannah of the Mounties* (1939) recounted by U.S. film historians RALPH E. FRIAR and NATASHA A. FRIAR in *The Only Good Indian . . . The Hollywood Gospel* (1972).

A pampered pet of the opera meets a rugged Canadian Mountie.

> Line from an original advertisement for the Broadway musical *Rose Marie* (1936) starring Jeanette MacDonald and Nelson Eddy. Quoted by Harry Purvis in *TV Guide*, 15 Sept. 1990.

A Mountie is assigned to break up a ring of Nazi saboteurs led by Colonel von Keller, the arrogant, vicious leader of a group which has landed by submarine on Hudson's Bay. The hero discredits himself with the Force in order to work his way into the spy ring. He uncovers a plot to blow up the critical Welland Canal.

> Synopsis of the movie *Northern Pursuit* (Warner Brothers, 1943), directed by Raoul Walsh and starring Errol and Julie Bishop, with Helmut Dantine (as the arrogant von Keller). The plot was based on Leslie T. White's novel *Five Thousand Trojan Horses* (1943). Quoted by Bernard A. Drew in *Lawmen in Scarlet: An Annotated Guide to Royal Canadian Mounted Police in Print and Performance* (1990).

Canada must be the only country in the world where a policeman is used as a national symbol; the Canadian contestant in Miss Universe contests invariably wears a cute Mountie uniform.

> MARGARET ATWOOD, author, *Survival: A Thematic Guide to Canadian Literature* (1972).

Our Centennial Year is fast drawing to a close and we are looking forward to meeting the challenges that lie ahead. In thinking of this year and of the way the people of Canada have come forward to honour us, I have asked myself, "Why do Canadians feel this way about the Force?" "Why have they taken us into their hearts?" I think I have the answer — *service. We have been serving Canada for one hundred years*.

> W.L. HIGGITT, RCMP Commissioner, address, Empire Club of Canada, Toronto, 29 Nov. 1973.

I never did like that emblim they have up on the wall "We always gits our man." Fur a change, they deserves to git the gurl. It's helthier.

> DON HARRON, humorist, *Charlie Farquharson's Jogfree of Canada, The Whirld and Other Places: A Pubic School Jogfree* (1974). The RCMP's official motto is "Maintiens le droit" or "Uphold the Right"; its unofficial motto, "We always get our man."

Our finest national spectacle consists of a group of police in red coats charging at nothing with spears.

> HAROLD TOWN, painter, commenting on the RCMP's Musical Ride, quoted by Peter C. Newman in *Sometimes a Great Nation* (1988).

We have the Mounties. They have the FBI. Can you imagine the FBI doing the Musical Ride?

> DAVE BROADFOOT, comedian, quoted by Vit Wagner in *The Toronto Star*, 29 June 1989.

The Mounties don't always get their man these days, being too busy appearing at inquiries about illegal wire-tapping, but they certainly used to.

> SIMON HOGGART, Washington correspondent for *The Observer*, in *The Globe and Mail*, 9 Jan. 1990.

Sikh And Ye Shall Find

> Proposal for a new motto for the Royal Canadian Mounted Police, to replace "Uphold the Right," following the decision of the Commissioner of the Force in February 1990 to relax the dress code to permit Sikh members to wear their traditional turbans.

ROYAL COMMISSIONS

A chance remark by somebody coming out of a bank or a supermarket might tell the man of the future a lot more about the 1970s than a whole shelf of Royal Commission reports.

> ANDREW ALLAN, radio producer, "On Writing Memoirs," *Andrew Allan: A Self-Portrait* (1974).

It is better to have shelved a royal commission than never to have enquired at all.

> Line from the *The Man from Number Ten*, a play for radio written by TOMMY TWEED and heard on CBC Stage in 1950.

In search of hyperbole, only a Canadian can say: "As Canadian as a Royal Commission"!

MARSHALL McLUHAN, communications theorist, and Bruce R. Powers, communications specialist, authors of *The Global Village: Transformations in World Life and Media in the 21st Century* (1989).

ROYAL FAMILY
See also QUEEN ELIZABETH
MONARCHY

Now I can have a permanent home among the people of the west, a place where I can come sometime and live a while.

EDWARD, PRINCE OF WALES, speaking in Winnipeg after the impulsive purchase of the Bedingfield Ranch hear High River, Alta., during his visit in 1923. He visited the newly named EP Ranch in 1924, 1927, 1941, and 1950, finally selling it in 1962. Although he acquired mineral rights with the land, he never did discover oil. The ranch was never a favourite of the Duchess of Windsor. Quoted by Robert M. Stamp in *Kings, Queens and Canadians* (1987).

How Kola . . . which, being interpreted, means, I come in peace, brother. . . . Goodbye brother, I'll be seeing you.

GREY OWL, naturalist and author, put out his hand to King George VI and touched him on the shoulder at a command performance for the Royal Family at Buckingham Palace in London, Fall 1936, as witnessed and described by Lovat Dickson in *Wilderness Man: The Strange Story of Grey Owl* (1973).

ROYAL TOUR

A Canadian war veteran, in hopes of settling an argument, asked the Queen whether she was Scottish or English. "Since we reached Quebec," she replied, "I've been a Canadian."

ROBERT M. STAMP, author, *Kings, Queens and Canadians: A Celebration of Canada's Infatuation with the British Royal Family*

(1987). The response was made during the Royal Visit of 1939 by Queen Elizabeth who is now styled the Queen Mother.

I think we must have seen everybody in Canada.

KING GEORGE VI, aboard the *Empress of Britain* off St. John's, completing the four-week Royal Tour (the first of a Dominion); quoted by Tom MacDonnell in *Daylight upon Magic: The Royal Tour of Canada — 1939* (1989).

The King, the Queen and Mr. King have now arrived at the city hall and Mr. Queen is on the steps to meet them. . . . The King is now shaking hands with Mr. Queen and now the Queen is shaking hands with Mr. Queen, and now Mr. King is shaking hands with Mr. Queen. . . . And now the King and Mr. Queen and the Queen and Mr. King are moving into the reception hall. . . . And now the King and Mr. Quing, I mean Mr. Keen and the Quing, I'm sorry, I mean, oh sh —.

Unidentified radio announcer's step-by-step coverage of the official reception accorded King George VI and Queen Elizabeth who were accompanied by Prime Minister Mackenzie King, Winnipeg, 24 May 1939, when they were greeted by (among others) Mayor John Queen. "Their arrival in fact became the occasion for a local radio announcer to perform the finest tongue-twisting moment of the tour — a rough transcript of which appeared the next day in *The Globe and Mail*"; quoted by Tom MacDonnell in *Daylight upon Magic: The Royal Tour of Canada — 1939* (1989).

By the smile of a Queen and the French words of a King, the English have conquered once more the cradle of New France.

OMER HÉROUX, commentator, writing in *Le Devoir* in 1939 about the Royal Visit of King George VI and Queen Elizabeth, quoted by Gwynne Dyer and Tina Viljoen, commentator and TV producer, *The De-*

fence of Canada: In the Arms of the Empire (1990).

I am more than pleased to be your host this evening, Your Royal Highness, as I was the guest of your family for four years until recently.
> CAMILLIEN HOUDE, long-time Montreal Mayor, greeting Princess Elizabeth and the Duke of Edinburgh on their Royal Visit to Canada in 1952, alluding to the years during World War II that he spent in prison because of his stand on the issue of conscription.

Oh, it's good to see you. I've just escaped from the Daughters of the American Revolution.
> PRINCE PHILIP, Duke of Edinburgh, addressing two ladies wearing pins identifying them as members of the Imperial Order Daughters of the Empire at a Halifax reception following a state visit to the United States for its Bicentennial; quoted by Thomas Coleman in *The Globe and Mail*, 14 July 1976.

In between, I was invited to participate in an exhibition in London called "Vestiges of Empire" where *Queen on Moose* made her English debut. A poster presented to Buckingham Palace was received with gracious aplomb by Sir Philip More, head of the Household, who commented, "Actually, it's rather a good likeness." "Of whom?" I asked. "Of them both!" he replied.

> CHARLES PACHTER, artist, famous and infamous both for his series of paintings and drawings of Queen Elizabeth astride a moose, address, Empire Club of Canada, Toronto, 19 March 1987.

No one at St. James's Palace would ever say in so many words that it's somewhat less of a privilege to have to cross the Atlantic periodically and wave at crowds, but one might reasonably speculate that the Prince of Wales may have at some time entertained such a thought.
> GEORGE GALT, journalist, "Fantasy Kingdom," *Saturday Night*, Oct. 1989.

By Appointment to Alfred the Great
> Simulated Royal warrant, one of the hallmarks of cartoons drawn by the versatile cartoonist LEN NORRIS, a mainstay of the editorial page of the *The Vancouver Sun* since 1950. Among other hallmarks are line drawings of Vancouver suburbia in the form of the village of Amblesnide and Tiddlycove.

RUSSIA
See also SOVIET UNION

I believe in the rather Jungian statement that North Americans will never deal in a successful way with the Russians until they deal with the Russians within themselves.
> W.D. VALGARDSON, novelist, interviewed by Alan Twigg in *Strong Voices: Conversations with Fifty Canadian Authors* (1988).

SACRED TRUST
See also HEALTH CARE
MEDICARE
SOCIAL PROGRAMS

Consider the prime minister's experience with the phrase "sacred trust." An inexperienced Brian Mulroney once referred to universality of social programmes in this way, and turned into a liar when he was forced to consider ending it. Had he refrained from hyperbole and merely termed universality "one of those commitments without which very serious questions about who we are must be asked," he would have been home free, and could have told that screeching grandmother at the protest rally to check her notes before getting all worked up. Mulroney wasn't lying when he placed universality in the empyrean; he probably just meant to say that he thought this universality thing was kind of neat. But by pinning it down with a word like "sacred," he closed the door on the chance to abolish it, and hasn't reopened the matter since.

> WIB EVERETT, social commentator, "Politicians Don't Lie," *The Idler*, No. 28, March-April 1990.

SAINT JOHN
See also NEW BRUNSWICK

Saint John. Saint Johner, but pronounced "Sinjohnner" according to a Canadian source, who says that the term is useful in distinguishing the Saint Johnners from the counterparts in St. John's, Newfoundland, who are known as "Noofi-johnners."

> PAUL DICKSON, British writer, *What Do You Call a Person From . . . ? A Dictionary of Resident Names* (1990).

ST. JOHN'S
See also NEWFOUNDLAND

Saint John's. St. Johnsians, but as Alan Rayburn pointed out in *Canadian Geographic* " . . . they are really better known as 'townies,' as opposed to 'baymen' who live in outpost communities."

> PAUL DICKSON, British writer, *What Do You Call a Person From . . . ? A Dictionary of Resident Names* (1990).

Thwack! Despite it all, the personality of St. John's, Newfoundland, hits you like a smack in the face with a dried cod, enthusiastically administered by its citizenry.

JAN MORRIS, Anglo-Welsh travel writer, *Saturday Night*, March 1989.

Such is the nature of this city: windy, fishy, anecdotal, proud, weather-beaten, quirky, obliging, ornery, and fun.
JAN MORRIS, Anglo-Welsh travel writer, *Saturday Night*, March 1989.

The point is that it's not so much a country as a clothesline, nearly 4,000 miles long. St. John's in Newfoundland is closer to Milan, Italy, than to Vancouver. Around 90 percent of the population lives within 300 miles of the U.S. border, which means that for most people, America is much nearer than their fellow citizens.
SIMON HOGGART, Washington correspondent for *The Observer*, in *The Globe and Mail*, 9 Jan. 1990.

ST. LAWRENCE RIVER

This lande was discovered by Iames Quartier, a Bryton, borne at S. Maloes, in the year 1535. . . . He sought out this unknowne countrie, untill he came to a great brode river, to the which they gave a name, in the whiche is founde very good fish, chiefly Salmons, and that great plentie.
ANDRÉ THEVET, French historian, referring to the voyage of Jacques Cartier, *The New Founde World, or Antarctike, wherin is contained Wonderful and Strange Things* . . . (1568).

The dream of the commercial empire of the St. Lawrence runs like an obsession through the whole of Canadian history; and men followed each other through life, planning and toiling to achieve it. The river was not only a great actuality: it was the central truth of a religion.
DONALD CREIGHTON, historian, *The Empire of the St. Lawrence, 1760-1850* (1937, 1956).

And although the bridges of Montreal are hideous one and all, the river they span is breathtakingly evocative, so lordly as it flows past Ile Ste-Hélène, so magnificently inconsolable when it rages through the rapids of Lachine — which are the true *raison d'être* of this city, and which in themselves, I presently came to think, adequately express its meaning.
JAN MORRIS, Anglo-Welsh travel writer, "The Battle for Montreal," *Saturday Night*, July 1988.

ST. PIERRE & MIQUELON

Then the matter of St. Pierre-Miquelon, St. John's own foreign-relations issue, is really a last irritant from the Seven Years' War, which ended in this very city 227 years ago. Though the islands are familiar enough to St. John's people (university students go there for French-language immersion courses), their presence somewhere over the southern horizon queerly haunted my thoughts in the city — so resolutely foreign still out there, so utterly separate, a department of France behaving, so close to Mayor Murphy's homely bailiwick, with such absolute damned Frenchness.
JAN MORRIS, Anglo-Welsh travel writer, referring to the St. John's Mayor and France's islands in the New World, *Saturday Night*, March 1989.

It is an outpost of socialism on our very own continent; it is subject to the authority of a government in which Communists play an active role. It lies squarely adjacent to the greatest trade route into the North American continent, with maritime access to the St. Lawrence River, the St. Lawrence Seaway and the Great Lakes, including our own Lake Michigan.
This object for our attention is St. Pierre and Miquelon, a French possession on Cabot Strait on the main approach to the Gulf of St. Lawrence.
JOHN KENNETH GALBRAITH, economist and author, "The St. Pierre Syndrome" (1982), *A View from the Stands of People, Politics, Military Power and the Arts* (1986) edited by Andrea D. Williams.

Canadians wonder who we are. We are French — not Canadian and especially not Quebeckers. We'll never join Canada. There's more distance between us than that water.
> MARC LEJEUNE, French citizen and resident of St. Pierre-Miquelon, quoted by Stephen Ward in *The Globe and Mail*, 26 Aug. 1989.

SAINTS

The patron saint of journalists, officially named by the church, is St. Francis de Sales. The traditional patron saint of editors is St. John Bosco. (The protector of computer-age journalists may well be St. Anthony of Padua, patron saint of searchers for lost articles.)
> J.A. McFARLANE and WARREN CLEMENTS, journalists, *The Globe and Mail Style Book* (1990).

SALESMANSHIP

The Greatest Good to the Greatest Number / Money Refunded if Goods are not Satisfactory / Canada's Greatest Store
> Advertising on the cover of the Fall and Winter Catalogue, No. 39, 1897-98, The T. Eaton Co. Limited, Toronto.

The sale begins when the customer says "No."
> Maxim of GEORGE METCALF, Loblaws executive, quoted by Charles Davies in *Bread Men: How the Westons Built an International Empire* (1987).

According to an anecdote that has become part of Bata folklore, two salesmen were sent overseas to explore the possibility of selling shoes in Africa. One of them cabled home: "Nobody wearing shoes. No market possibilities. Returning home soonest possible." The other one, a true Bata disciple, had a completely different reaction. "Everybody barefoot," he informed head office. "Tremendous sales opportunities."
> THOMAS J. BATA, world head of the Bata Shoe Company, discussing postwar sales,

Bata: Shoemaker to the World (1990) written with Sonja Sinclair.

SANITY

As an experience madness is terrific and in its lava I still find most of the things I write about.
> HUMPHRY OSMOND, psychiatrist, "A Good Man," *Predicting the Past: Memos on the Enticing Universe of Possibility* (1981) produced by Jerome Agel.

Canada has one of the highest rates of insanity in any civilized country and one reason might be that life in many places is so desperately dull.
> ROBERTSON DAVIES, man-of-letters, interviewed by Paul Soles in 1972, *Conversations with Robertson Davies* (1989) edited by J. Madison Davis.

SASKATCHEWAN
See also REGINA

Saskatchewan is the only place I'm tired of without ever having seen it.
> J.B. PRIESTLEY, English writer, quoted in Winnipeg prior to seeing the Prairies, "I Heard the Monotonous, Mournful Voices of Canadian Women," *Liberty*, Aug. 1956.

Imagine my delight when I received a copy of the first edition of this book inscribed by its author as "an instalment of interest on an old debt." His name being unknown to me, I hastened to ascertain whether his chair was at Oxford or Cambridge, Owen's or Edinburgh, Dublin or Birmingham. I learned that it was at Saskatoon, a place of which I had never heard, and that his university was that of Saskatchewan, which was connected in my imagination with ochred and feathered Indians rather than with a university apparently half a century ahead of Cambridge in science and of Oxford in common sense.
> GEORGE BERNARD SHAW, Anglo-Irish playwright and advocate of a phonetic alphabet, Preface to the 1948 edition of R.A. Wilson's *The Miraculous Birth of Language* (1937). Wilson was a Professor of

English at the University of Saskatchewan who embraced Shaw's pet notion of a new teaching alphabet.

I saw cowboys roping steers before I ever saw an aeroplane, and I knew the names of the Plains Tribes before I knew the names of the Kings of England. I saw Red River carts [over fifty years old] parked alongside Model-T Fords. Once I saw a Mounted Police Corporal ride into town to arrest the Chinese laundryman for murder. I dug arrow-heads out of slough-holes and traded them for apple-cores like Huck Finn. And after all that romantic nostalgia, it must be admitted that all I really wanted to do was to return to England.

> JOHN PREBBLE, Anglo-Scots historian who was raised in Saskatchewan in the mid-1910s, quoted by Fredric Warburg in *All Authors Are Equal: The Publishing Life of Fredric Warburg 1936-1971*(1973).

Saskatchewan, the Pampas area of the Argentine . . . portions of South Africa . . . these rich areas, with some portions of Montana and Nevada, must feed the world!

> Prophecy made in 1944 by EDGAR CAYCE, the so-called Sleeping Prophet, quoted by Mary Ellen Carter in *Edgar Cayce on Prophecy* (1968).

Where the hell is Saskatchewan and who is Emma Lake?

> Quip attributed to BARNETT NEWMAN when the New York abstract painter was invited to speak at the Emma Lake Artists Workshop in northern Saskatchewan in 1959; quoted by Liam Lacey in *The Globe and Mail*, 23 Oct. 1989.

Saskatoon seemed to me to be, not a *place*, but a sort of primeval background to the real world which consisted of *places*, certain points on the earth's surface where real things happened and real people lived: England, California, Egypt, Ontario. Saskatchewan was only a holding area where one waited impatiently till one was old enough to leave in order to enter the excitement of the real world.

> SHARON BUTALA, author, "Time, Space and Light: Discovering the Saskatchewan Soul" (1988), *Best Canadian Essays 1989* (1989) edited by Douglas Fetherling.

The Saskatchewan we all knew as children, the one that is embedded in our souls, is disappearing. We cannot save it entirely, but (through a device such as guaranteed annual income), if we could make it possible for people who want to live this way to return to small farms of perhaps a quarter section each, they might save our heritage. On small places it is possible to care for the land inch by inch and to return it to a more natural state, give it back its beauty, its productivity, and its peace.

> SHARON BUTALA, author, "Time, Space and Light: Discovering the Saskatchewan Soul" (1988), *Best Canadian Essays 1989* (1989) edited by Douglas Fetherling.

It just seemed to us that Saskatchewan is probably the mythic core of the country. It's the land of wide open spaces and winter and snow and ice and not many people.

> KEN DRYDEN and ROY MacGREGOR, authors of *Home Game: Hockey and Life in Canada* (1989), quoted by Philip Marchand in *The Toronto Star*, 7 Dec. 1989.

I'm a gypsy by nature. But I get a rush when I go to Saskatchewan or the land of my birth.

> JONI MITCHELL, Alberta-born singer, quoted by Stephen Ward in *The Winnipeg Free Press*, 11 Sept. 1990.

SASQUATCH

All too often researchers declare that either the North American Sasquatch (Bigfoot) exists or it is the best and most complicated hoax in history. In fact there is a strong possibility that both statements are partially true.

> MYRA SHACKLEY, British archaeologist,

Wildmen: Yeti, Sasquatch and the Neanderthal Enigma (1983).

What do you chaps want with me?
ALBERT OSTMAN, lumberjack who claimed he was captured and held captive for seven days by a family of sasquatches, Powell River, Vancouver Island, 1924, addressing his captors and receiving no reply, "A Chronology of Mysterious Happenings in History," *The People's Almanac No. 1* (1975).

I don't know if I am the world's most famous Bigfoot hunter, but I can tell you that I know more about this in an overall way than anybody in the world.
RENÉ DAHINDEN, Swiss-German Sasquatch-hunter, resident of British Columbia since 1953, interviewed by Danny Perez in *INFO Journal: The International Fortean Organization*, Sept. 1990.

When I was backpacking in Canada some years ago, I enquired about the Sasquatch at park headquarters in Alberta. "There are no Sasquatches in Alberta," a park official told me in a huffy voice. "They are a British Columbia problem!"
GEORGE EARLEY, American reviewer of Thomas Steenburg's book *The Sasquatch in Alberta* (1990), writing in *Fate*, May 1991.

SCANDAL

It has now reached the stage in Ottawa where no one, not even the opposition, can keep track of the mess.
It was so much easier back in the days when we had a prime minister who had no friends. We have now entered the era of the Generic Scandal, an all-pervading odour which covers everything under the thumb.
ROY MacGREGOR, columnist, referring to resignations of cabinet ministers over conflicts of interest, *The Ottawa Citizen*, 7 Feb. 1987.

I'm not down-hearted. It's my friends who need cheering up.
GUY FAVREAU, Justice Minister accused of scandal in 1965, quoted by Roy MacGregor in *The Ottawa Citizen*, 7 Feb. 1987.

SCANDINAVIA

Scandinavian and most north-European literature is tragic, gloomy, sordid — not that life is much different there from other countries, but the tense creative mind of the literary artist sees it so.
WILLIAM ARTHUR DEACON, literary critic, letter of 20 Nov. 1930, quoted by Clara Thomas and John Lennox in *William Arthur Deacon: A Canadian Literary Life* (1982).

SCHOLARSHIP
See also COLLEGES & UNIVERSITIES
RESEARCH &
DEVELOPMENT

A Rhodes Scholar is a young man with his future behind him.
This quip is attributed to former CNR President DONALD GORDON (as well as to many other prominent people) by Jack Cahill in reference to John Turner who in his youth held a Rhodes Scholarship, *John Turner: The Long Run* (1984).

SCIENCE & SCIENTISTS
See also EDUCATION
RESEARCH &
DEVELOPMENT
TECHNOLOGY

People have no leisure in a young country, except to quarrel.
J.H. LEFROY, scientist, lamenting the lack of a single scientific society in Toronto, letter to Sir W.J. Hooker, 20 Feb. 1852, quoted by Suzanne Zeller in *Inventing Canada: Early Victorian Science and the Idea of a Transcontinental Nation* (1987).

An infallible law exists with regard to all science and art, which, like that of the mutation of races and tongues, preserves the true or removes the imperfect, according to their development.

> W. GEORGE BEERS, dentist, address, Quebec Dental Society, Dec. 1870, quoted by D.W. Gullett in *A History of Dentistry in Canada* (1971).

Hypnotism may be a very dangerous thing in the hands of the unscrupulous, but so is the airplane, the rifle, the disease germ. Science wishes to know the facts. Once discovered, these truths are handed over to the public.

> GEORGE H. ESTABROOKS, psychologist, *Hypnotism* (1943, 1957).

The academic atmosphere, produced mainly by the humanities, is the only atmosphere in which pure science can flourish.

> E.W. STEACIE, scientist, address, University of Western Ontario, 1956, *Science in Canada: Selections from the Speeches of E.W. Steacie* (1965) edited by J.D. Babbitt.

Man has conquered outer space. He has not conquered himself. If he had, we would not be worrying today as much as we are about the destructive possibilities of scientific achievements.

> LESTER B. PEARSON, diplomat, Nobel Peace Prize Lecture, Oslo, Norway, 11 Dec. 1957. The text is taken from *The Four Faces of Peace and the International Outlook* (1964) edited by Sherleigh G. Pierson.

I think one could manage quite handsomely without knowing that 2 plus 2 equals 4. There are other matters, less easy to formulate, that we must know because if we lack them we die. "Without vision, the people perish."

> GEORGE WHALLEY, educator, address at Rothesay College School, Rothesay, N.B., 1959, *George Whalley: Remembrances* (1989) edited by Michael D. Moore.

A high standard of living is not, as such, a goal worth striving for unless a high standard of living includes a high standard of art, literature and science.

> GERHARD HERZBERG, scientist and Nobel laureate, quoted by David Spurgeon in *The Globe and Mail*, 3 Nov. 1971.

The point is rather that the quality of the man cannot be overlooked even in the most applied fields. When you see a Bobby Orr of science you let him develop his own style of play.

> F. RONALD HAYES, scientist, *The Chaining of Prometheus: Evolution of a Power Structure for Canadian Science* (1973).

Careful systematic testing of wrong but brilliant hypotheses can measurably increase human knowledge.

> W. EDWARD MANN, sociologist with a special interest in fringe groups and unconventional science, *Orgone, Reich and Eros: Wilhelm Reich's Theory of Life Energy* (1973).

A scientist has as much luck in communicating with the federal bureaucracy as you would have reciting Gaelic poetry to a deaf seagull.

> PETER LARKIN, scientist, Pacific Science Congress, Vancouver, 26 Aug. 1974, reported in *The Globe and Mail* the following day.

Science is like art. In both subjects you have to give people the freedom to be creative if you want to call yourself a civilized country. . . . Egalitarianism and good science don't go together. The very idea that everyone has a word in what research is to be done is the death of science. A team never has an idea. An individual does.

> GERHARD HERZBERG, scientist and Nobel laureate, quoted by David Spurgeon in *Weekend Magazine*, 10 Dec. 1977.

I do not suggest that there is no such thing as "pure science" — only that all human inventiveness is pure, whether of eye, head or hand.

> LARKIN KERWIN, President, National Re-

search Council, address, Empire Club of Canada, Toronto, 12 Nov. 1981.

In fact, what science is in the business of doing is showing that your latest ideas of the way the world is are wrong. Science is constantly modifying, changing or throwing out ideas.
DAVID SUZUKI, scientist and spokesperson, address, Empire Club of Canada, Toronto, 6 Dec. 1984.

I decided to follow a byway, rather than a highway. It is a procedure I have subsequently recommended to beginning scientists in this country, where research strategy is best modelled on that used by Wolfe at the Plains of Abraham. (British General James Wolfe defeated the French defending Quebec in 1759 after scaling a cliff for a surprise attack.)
JOHN C. POLANYI, scientist, address, Empire Club of Canada, Toronto, 27 Nov. 1986.

Nor can we afford to depend for scientific understanding exclusively on what is published abroad. To use science well, you must understand it well. To understand it well, you must do it well.
JOHN C. POLANYI, scientist, address, Empire Club of Canada, Toronto, 27 Nov. 1986.

The best part of science has always been in the *search*. The fun is in experimenting, designing new tricks and often getting totally unexpected results that lead in entirely new directions.
DAVID SUZUKI, scientist and broadcaster, *Metamorphosis: Stages in a Life* (1987).

Science is really in the business of disproving its current models or changing them to conform to new information. In essence, we are constantly proving our latest ideas are wrong.
DAVID SUZUKI, scientist and broadcaster, *Metamorphosis: Stages in a Life* (1987).

But there are so many things in this world that are magical — we call them magical or strange or incredible — that we have no scientific explanation for. And if we only had scientific explanations for things, what an impoverished world we would have.
RUDY WIEBE, novelist, interviewed by Thomas Gerry in *So to Speak: Interviews with Canadian Writers* (1987) edited by Peter O'Brien.

Winning with ideas is as rewarding as scoring goals. I've travelled all over this country and I've seen people with such good ideas. They need encouragement. This is the key to our future prosperity.
GERALDINE KENNY-WALLACE, Chairperson, Science Council of Canada, quoted by Janice Dineen in *The Toronto Star*, 4 Sept. 1988.

Science and technology are in themselves neither good nor evil. They are the product of human curiosity — the mind's relentless urge to explore, to know, to change. And that is a quality that we must always nourish.
DAVID SUZUKI, scientist and broadcaster, and Peter Knudtson, writer and biologist, *Genethics: The Ethics of Engineering Life* (1988)

In 1967, however, the study of black holes was revolutionized by Werner Israel, a Canadian scientist (who was born in Berlin, brought up in South Africa, and took his doctoral degree in Ireland). Israel showed that, according to general relativity, nonrotating black holes must be very simple; they were perfectly spherical, their size depended only on their mass, and any two such black holes with the same mass were identical.
STEPHEN W. HAWKING, theoretical physicist and cosmologist, *A Brief History of Time: From the Big Bang to Black Holes* (1988).

In the first place, the fruits of scientific inquiry are not necessarily facts. They are best described as tentative truths — unfinished ideas about nature's workings that are subjected to continuous criticism, modification and rejection by other researchers. In the second place, scientific explanations of the natural world are necessarily fragmentary. For science is condemned to see nature as a mosaic of arbitrarily defined, component parts.

> DAVID SUZUKI, scientist and broadcaster, and Peter Knudtson, writer and biologist, *Genethics: The Ethics of Engineering Life* (1988)

Creative scientists are typically independent thinkers, indifferent to formal religious organizations, nonconformists, strong achievers, given to insatiable curiosity, risk takers, often stubborn and hard to get along with, highly self-confident, loners except for a limited number of intellectual friendships, et cetera.

> W. EDWARD MANN, sociologist, *Vital Energy & Health: Dr. Wilhelm Reich's Revolutionary Discoveries and Supporting Evidence* (rev. ed., 1989).

Science has three faces. In the life of an individual, science can be a profession; in the search for truth, it is a method of furthering understanding; and in the world of social and economic interests, it rears its head as an unwieldly institution.

> GILLIAN KRANIAS, historian, "Women and the Changing Faces of Science," *Despite the Odds: Essays on Canadian Women and Science* (1990) edited by Marianne Gosztonyi Ainley.

The task of the future is to build knowledge and understanding among and between citizens and scientists, so that the distinction between the two groups vanishes — so that *both* become citizen scientists, potentially able to solve our problems together.

> URSULA FRANKLIN, metallurgist and spokesperson for the conserver society, "Reflections on Science and the Citizen," *Planet under Stress: The Challenge of Global Change* (1990) edited by Constance Mungall and Digby J. McLaren for the Royal Society of Canada.

We Canadians are disappointed all the time, that's why we're never out there in front. I don't want to encourage people to be any more disappointed than they already are. Instead, people should look at what happened with ganciclovir and realize that we need a culture that is more aware of the impact and value of scientific discoveries so that we can make things happen here, and then expect them to work.

> KELVIN OGILVIE, first chemist to synthesize ribonucleic acid (RNA), discoverer of ganciclovir, a drug to treat AIDS patients, quoted by Kelly Toughill in *The Toronto Star*, 15 April 1990.

"S&T" must, perforce, mean "steal and transfer."

> Attributed to CLIVE WILLIS, Vice-President, National Research Council, referring to Science & Technology, by Tim Harper in *The Toronto Star*, 12 July 1990.

Science will exhume the old notion of an all-pervasive Aether, and use it to explain physical reality in a more wholistic and less fragmented manner. The Aether will eventually be seen as a substrate accounting for all states of matter and fields of energy in the observable universe.

> MAURICE B. COOKE, channeller, *The Aquarian Wave: A Prophetic Handbook for the 90s* (1990).

SCOTTISH PEOPLE
See also BRITISH EMPIRE &
COMMONWEALTH
UNITED KINGDOM

Listen to me, as when ye heard our father / Sing long ago the song of other shores — / Listen to me, and then in chorus gather / All your deep voices, as ye pull your oars: / Fair these broad meads — these hoary woods are grand; // But we are exiles from our fathers' land.

> First verse with refrain of "Canadian Boat

Song" (from the Gaelic), *Blackwood's Edinburgh Magazine*, Sept. 1829, attributed to DAVID MACBETH MOIR.

[These Canadian Scots] were fiercely nationalistic, and their emotional nostalgia dominated my boyhood. I was impressed by images of blue mountains and black lochs, by all that Caledonia-stern-and-wild-fever of the Scots exile. Despite my parents' staunch Anglo-Saxon patriotism, I began to believe in Scotland as my homeland. I promised myself that I would visit Scotland some day, and Scotland in this sense was always the Highlands. I did not do so until I was twenty-two, and by a happy accident . . . it turned out to be all and more of what I had dreamed.
> JOHN PREBBLE, Scots historian, raised in Sutherland Township in Saskatchewan in the mid-1910s, quoted by Fredric Warburg in *All Authors are Equal: The Publishing Life of Fredric Warburg, 1936-1971* (1973).

The essential conditions of being a good regiment are to have achieved great things together, and to be determined on future achievement. May you who serve, and those who will follow you, continue to build upon our regiment's efficiency, loyalty, and devotion to duty, to the end that it will always be said: "This is the Toronto Scottish."
> QUEEN ELIZABETH THE QUEEN MOTHER, Colonel-in-Chief of the Toronto Scottish Regiment, address, Empire Club of Canada, Toronto, 26 June 1974.

McCanada
> A reference to the substantial influence of the Scots, the Gaels, and the Celtic people generally on this country, used by the novelist SCOTT SYMONS, *The Globe and Mail*, 23 April 1979.

SCULPTURE
See ART & ARTISTS

SEA
See also WATER

A mari usque ad mare
> This is the motto of the Dominion of Canada; the official translations of the Latin phrase into English and French are "From Sea to Sea" and "D'un océan à l'autre." The notion that Canada extends from sea to sea is repeated in the national anthem "O Canada"; the second and third verses of the English version by R. Stanley Weir of 1927 refer to the land extending "from East to Western Sea." Since Prime Minister John G. Diefenbaker's Northern Vision of the late 1950s, it has been fashionable to speak of Canada as a country extending "from sea to sea to sea" — from the Atlantic Ocean to the Pacific Ocean to the Arctic Ocean.
>
> The sea is "shining" south of the border. "America the Beautiful," the popular anthem of the United States, concludes with brotherhood being crowned "From sea to shining sea." There is, as well, a reference to "the sea" in "God Bless America," the unofficial U.S. anthem, which begins: "While the storm clouds gather / Far across the sea. . . ." The second verse includes these lines: "From the mountains to the prairies/ To the oceans white with foam. . . ."

SEAL HUNT
See also ANIMAL RIGHTS

In Europe, you call them Canadian assassins.
> BRIGITTE BARDOT, French movie star, referring to seal hunters at a press conference at Blanc Sablon, Labrador, Nfld., 19 March 1979; quoted by Robert Hunter in *Warriors of the Rainbow: A Chronicle of the Greenpeace Movement* (1979).

Canadians kill them all, / Each little baby seal pup, / That cannot run or swim, / They hit it with a spiked club, / Because they want its skin.
> Lyrics of a song protesting the annual seal hunt in Labrador sung to the tune of

"All Things Bright and Beautiful" by Greenpeace demonstrators in Trafalgar Square, London, according to *The Toronto Star*, 9 March 1980.

The catalogue of cruelty goes on and on. When I entered the field of animal welfare I had no idea there was so much to be done. When I resolved to end the bloody seal hunt I believed it to be the most outrageous cruelty to any living animals. Now, as new chapters of callous indifference to other living beings have become revealed to me, I wonder whether there is any end to it all. Then I look at what IFAW has accomplished in less than twenty years and I realize there is hope for the future.

BRIAN DAVIES, founder of the International Fund for Animal Welfare in 1969, *Red Ice: My Fight to Save the Seals* (1989).

I have no patience with Brigitte Bardot and her supporters in the animal rights movement. The ringed seal is not an endangered species. The Inuit of the Baffin coastline most certainly are.

PIERRE BERTON, author, Postscript (1989), *The Mysterious North* (1956, 1989).

CANADA'S GOVERNMENT WITHOUT PITY / "tolerates a Stone Age economy / in Newfoundland" / The Civilized World Urges Canada's Prime Minister Trudeau to find 4 weeks alternative employment for the 200 or so men who are brutalized as they beat baby seals to death at Canada's annual commercial Harp seal slaughter.

Message on a hoarding in plain view of Canada House, the office of the Canadian High Commission, Trafalgar Square, London, erected by the International Fund for Animal Welfare during its organization of the boycott of Canadian-made goods in Europe to protest the extent and the barbarity of the annual seal hunt, summer 1990.

SEASONS
See also WEATHER

Pity the poor creatures in warmer countries where the seasons never change. Where summer is eternal and they never know the pain of waiting and the joy at last when summer comes.

RAY GUY, humorist, "Catching Conners," *That Far Greater Bay* (1976).

The seasons came and went, gaining distinctive lustre in the extreme climate of Ontario. Each season was my favourite at the time: the white beauty of winter snow with its sporting games, the rushing abundance of spring, the heat and holidays of summer, and the flaming colours and smoky smells of autumn.

DOROTHY MACLEAN, medium, *To Hear the Angels Sing: An Odyssey of Co-Creation with the Devic Kingdom* (1980).

SPRING

As my eyes / search / the prairie / I feel / the summer / in spring.

Ojibwa poem, "A Song of Spring," *Songs of the Great Land* (1989) edited by John Robert Colombo.

There is a magic about the spring — some power that revives half-dead hopes and faiths and thrills numbed souls with the elixir of new life. There is no age in spring — everybody seems young and joyful. Care is in abeyance for a little while and hearts throb with the instinct of immortality.

L. M. MONTGOMERY, author, journal entry, 1 May 1899, *The Selected Journals of L.M. Montgomery: Volume I: 1889-1910* (1985) edited by Mary Rubio and Elizabeth Waterston.

I know of only one other season in one other country which compares in beauty with the Canadian fall. It is the English spring. The two seasons evoke different thoughts and emotions. The one cries "Hail!" and the other says "Farewell!" The one is concerned with birth and the other with death. One expresses joy and the other sorrow. Their moods contrast widely. But for sheer aesthetic beauty they are peers in perfection.

MALCOLM MacDONALD, British High

Commissioner in Ottawa, *The Bird of Brewery Creek* (1947).

But the Canadian spring is less rich than the English. Trees are thinner, bushes more wispy and separate, foliage a paler green. Islands float in the upper St. Lawrence with sun on the level, lake-like water, and pale-green mirage-like trees, a watery ethereal paradise, not of earth. And there is missing from the air that spring intoxication I have known in England and Persia.
G. WILSON KNIGHT, English literary scholar who taught at the University of Toronto, *Atlantic Crossing: An Autobiographical Design* (1936).

Ah, the sounds of spring — geese coughing overhead on their way North.
EDD ULUSCHAK, cartoonist, *The Edmonton Journal*, 12 April 1973.

SUMMER
There are two seasons in Newfoundland: August and Winter.
Traditional saying current in the 1980s.

There will be fireworks this weekend not because of some forgotten Queen, but because of remembered joy, because summer is here and we have suffered enough.
ROY MacGREGOR, columnist, *The Ottawa Citizen*, 16 May 1987.

The Canadian summer is a transitory joy, one so fleeting that even its difficulties are treasured. It is our secret time, the two or three or, with luck, four weeks when we believe we are our truest selves. It is our sweetest thought, one held in parentheses by the *opening up* and the *closing up*, the season beginning with sparklers and ending in embers, when suddenly, without warning, the seasons reverse. The leaves no longer shade but reveal; relief now is to be found inside rather than out, in fire rather than water. On an October morning so cold that the black lake steams, an outdoor toilet loses its July charm.
ROY MacGREGOR, columnist, "Another Kind of Place," *Canadian Living Magazine*, Aug. 1989.

AUTUMN
It is only here in large portions of Canada that wondrous *second wind*, the Indian summer, attains its amplitude and heavenly perfection, — the temperatures, the sunny haze; the mellow, rich, delicate, almost *flavoured* air: "Enough to live — enough to merely be."
WALT WHITMAN, poet, visiting Ontario and Quebec in July-Aug. 1880, *Walt Whitman in Canada* (1904) edited by W. Sloan Kennedy.

The summer is over now. It is October and autumn. We are having delightful fall days, misty and purple, with a pungent, mellow air and magnificent sunsets, followed by the rarest of golden twilights and moonlit nights floating in silver. Maple and birch are crimson and gold and the fields sun themselves in aftermaths. But it is autumn and beautiful as everything is, it is the beauty of decay — the sorrowful beauty of the end.
L. M. MONTGOMERY, author, journal entry, 7 Oct. 1899, *The Selected Journals of L.M. Montgomery: Volume I: 1889-1910* (1985) edited by Mary Rubio and Elizabeth Waterston.

The moment of supreme glory in the Canadian autumn, however, does not last long. In a few days it is past. Wind and rain strip the boughs of their frail leaves. The trees' fine raiment grows ever more scanty, dropping in brilliant oranges upon the ground. For a brief while the beauty lingers there. Scores of thousands of fallen leaves cover the earth with a deep carpet. No Persian rug woven by human hands can rival this fabric made by the Supreme Artist from dying leaves.
MALCOLM MacDONALD, British High Commissioner in Ottawa, *The Bird of Brewery Creek* (1947).

Though snowflakes fall upon my hair, / There's a touch of autumn in the air.
JOHN THOMAS McDONOUGH, playwright, concluding couplet of an unpublished sonnet on autumn, 1986.

WINTER

Oh Canadian love, Canadian love / it's either 40 below or it's 90 above/ and though it's hard to be yearning when you're freezing or burning / like the dollar we keep falling — in Canadian love.

> MARIE-LYNN HAMMOND, singer and songwriter, "Canadian Love" (1980), originally sung at the Mariposa Folk Festival in 1970.

Winter Canadians — all wear rubber overshoes. The overshoes are huge black galoshes with zippers. The pedestrians are hatless like at Sunday mass. The overshoes stick in the whitish-rust mush.

> ANDREI VOZNESENSKY, Russian poet, "North Country Passing," *Maclean's*, Dec. 1971.

In the part of Canada in which I live and over most of the country, there are only three months of the year when it almost definitely won't snow: June, July and August. Most of the time the snow stops in April and doesn't start until October or November. . . . Winter is the real season because it's the prevalent season in Canada.

> MARGARET ATWOOD, novelist, interviewed by Karla Hammond in 1978, *Margaret Atwood: Conversations* (1990) edited by Earl G. Ingersoll.

"Unnatural" is the key word. Winter is not natural. There's a perfectly good reason it is silent out there. Anything with legs or wings and two brain cells to rub together has left — that's why it's silent. Robins, Canada Geese, scarlet tanagers, canaries, monarch butterflies — do you hear them warbling about the eerie, haunting, silent unnatural beauty of a Canadian winter?

> ARTHUR BLACK, broadcaster, "Winter," *Basic Black: The Wit and Whimsy of Arthur Black* (1981).

I know, I know . . . there are songs and poems about the glory of winter. . . . Bing Crosby . . . "I'm Dreaming of a White Christmas." Sure. Why not? Bing Crosby lived in California. I'd daydream about a white Christmas too, if I was standing by a sand trap on the seventh hole of the Palm Springs Golf Course wondering whether to go with a wedgie or a mashie.

> ARTHUR BLACK, broadcaster, "Winter," *Basic Black: The Wit and Whimsy of Arthur Black* (1981).

I am told that the Inuit have some sixty words for snow . . . for different kinds of snow. That does not surprise me. They see a lot of it. I live considerably south of the tree line, but even I have seventeen words for snow — none of them useable in public.

> ARTHUR BLACK, broadcaster, "Winter," *Basic Black: The Wit and Whimsy of Arthur Black* (1981).

Winter, let's get divorced! / Your parting, truly, / holds little sorrow. // If you don't leave, / the spring thaw shall destroy you.

> Traditional Inuit poem from Labrador, "Labrador Inuit Poems" (1982), "Winter's Exodus," translated by Rose Pamack, reprinted in *Inuktitut* No. 70, 1989.

Cold breeds caution.

> ROBERTSON DAVIES, man-of-letters, alluding to national character as determined by land and elements, *Signature*, April 1987.

Nowhere is Canada's winter harsher than over the Laurentian Shield. Latitude for latitude — and Hudson's Bay marches alongside Britain and central and southern Scandinavia — this is the world's coldest place. Not merely frigid, but also windy, and along the southern and eastern margins very snowy as well. The summer is tantalizingly short. Growth goes on for two to four months before September sees the return of killing frost.

> F. KENNETH HARE, geographer, referring to gravel ridges or eskers, "Canada: The Land," *Daedalus: Journal of the American Academy of Arts and Sciences*, "In Search of Canada," Fall 1988.

Only the winter has the power to focus our minds on what we still share as Canadians . . . living to the *north* of the giant manufacturer of mass culture that is obliterating our consciousness of our own society.
MICHAEL VALPY, columnist, *The Globe and Mail*, 4 Dec. 1990.

SECRECY

It is a crime now in my country to talk about the government's crimes.
DAVID McTAGGART, activist with Greenpeace, referring to an Order-in-Council outlawing the release of any information about the involvement of the Canadian government in the uranium cartel, *Greenpeace III: Journey into the Bomb* (1978) written with Robert Hunter. In 1972 and 1973, McTaggart, backed by the Greenpeace Foundation and the Friends of the Earth, defied the French authorities by sailing into its self-declared nuclear zone in the South Pacific.

Canadian society is deficient, not in respect for law but in respect for liberty. And the fundamental function of secrecy in Canadian government practice is not concealment but the cultivation of docility. . . . What Official Secrets Acts do is legitimate the ignorance of the citizens and convince them that they have no right to know what their governors tell them it intends to conceal.
EDGAR Z. FRIEDENBERG, political scientist, *Deference to Authority: The Case of Canada* (1980).

Tradition and custom are often a greater impediment . . . than any Official Secrets Act which, in the Canadian setting, is more often invoked to camouflage the peccadilloes of politicians and mandarins than to protect legitimate state secrets.
JAMES BARROS, historian, *No Sense of Evil: Espionage, the Case of Herbert Norman* (1986).

Seven years ago Canada's Freedom of Information Act came into force. The act is badly misnamed. It is actually a secrecy Act, for it provides that no government document, no matter how old, shall be released to the public for the first time without being reviewed for its sensitivity. When in doubt, a National Archives reviewer consults the government department concerned.
JOHN BRYDEN, investigative reporter, *Deadly Allies: Canada's Secret War, 1937-1947* (1989).

SECURITY

The existing system is not properly called a security system — it is "the insecurity system," and around the world there is a serious search underway for alternatives to this armed anarchy. If there is one fundamental lesson to be learned from the world's repeated descent into warfare and the preparation for it, it is that nation states acting unilaterally are counterproductive to the pursuit of security. The unilateral pursuit of national security spells insecurity on a global scale.
ERNIE REGEHR, political-affairs co-ordinator of Project Ploughshares, "New Approaches to Security," *The Road to Peace* (1988) edited by Ernie Regehr and Simon Rosenblum.

On the issue of electronic bugging against domestic security threats, the Government of Canada has achieved something remarkable. It has made Ronald Reagan look like a civil libertarian.
A. ALAN BOROVOY, General Counsel, Canadian Civil Liberties Association, *When Freedoms Collide: A Case for our Civil Liberties* (1988).

[There's] a new civilian security service to be carved out of the remains of the old RCMP security service. It would be called the Canadian Security Intelligence Service (CSIS). People were told it would be pronounced "Cee-sus."
RICHARD CLEROUX, journalist, *Official Secrets: The Story behind the Canadian Security Intelligence Service* (1990).

In short, apart from burning down barns and roughing people up, CSIS can do legally everything that the RCMP used to do illegally.

RICHARD CLEROUX, journalist, *Official Secrets: The Story behind the Canadian Security Intelligence Service* (1990).

Nobody ever heard of CSIS targeting Oliver North's Contra war fund-raisers in Canada, but several left-wing and Latin American support groups have complained about CSIS intrusion in their activities. At one point, CSIS had only four people watching ultra right-wing political groups in Canada, and more than 400 watching left-wing groups. The argument at CSIS is that there are more people worth watching on the left side of the spectrum than on the right.

RICHARD CLEROUX, journalist, *Official Secrets: The Story behind the Canadian Security Intelligence Service* (1990).

Security is not about armies; it's about meeting human needs, now and in the future. Our security can only be achieved through global, collective action; it cannot be purchased with the insecurity of others.

Project Ploughshares for the Citizens' Inquiry into Peace and Security, *What Makes Canada Secure: Background Document for the Citizens' Inquiry into Peace and Security in Canada* (1991).

Security is mutual rather than competitive. Our security is enhanced by the security of others; it cannot be purchased with the insecurity of others.

Project Ploughshares for the Citizens' Inquiry into Peace and Security, *What Makes Canada Secure: Background Document for the Citizens' Inquiry into Peace and Security in Canada* (1991).

None of us is secure when any of us feels threatened.

BRIAN MULRONEY, Prime Minister, statement made on 12 Feb. 1990, quoted by Project Ploughshares, *What Makes Can-*ada Secure: Background Document for the Citizens' Inquiry into Peace and Security in Canada (1991).

SELF-KNOWLEDGE

In the main it is not by introspection but by reflecting on our living in common with others that we come to know ourselves.

BERNARD J.F. LONERGAN, Jesuit philosopher, quoted by Alec Lewis, editor of *The Quotable Quotations Book* (1981).

When I look at myself, I am very sad. When I compare myself, I am consoled.

LISE PAYETTE, Quebec broadcaster and feminist, quoted by Stephen Godfrey in *The Globe and Mail*, 7 April 1990.

SENATE
See also PARLIAMENT

The Senate, awful parallel, is formed by the same law as many valuable scientific discoveries are made — by the law of exclusion. Where a multitude of all sorts and conditions of men form a political body, it necessarily follows that in the course of years many of those who have enjoyed very respectable reputations, and have done great service to their confreres (and possibly even to the State at large) should slowly cease to be very useful. When the softening process mellows down to an unmistakable senility, the individual is usually elevated to the Senate Chamber. The Senate is the dement's Valhalla. The dement does not live in the present. He chews a cud of anachronisms, and like other ruminants enjoys for a second time, in the twilight of his honoured age, the fodder which delighted him in his pubescent morn. There is something inexpressibly moving in the slow and unexpected actions of an Upper House. A still and brooding wonder. A whispering gloom and pensive melancholy. A helpless tendency to wheezing and expectoration. A rhetorical partiality to tautology, and withal that habit of interfering in affairs of gravity, peculiar to the mentally collapsed. Possibly it would be considered indecent to disturb that which is already moribund, but the burden is great, and any idea of decency is only traditional, and not under any possibility scientific.

EZRA HURLBURT STAFFORD, physician and crank, "A Political Aspect of Mental Disease," *The Canadian Journal of Medicine and Surgery*, Volume III, 1898.

I have passed around a copy of the amendements to the shareholders, the directors, er, I mean the Senators.

SALTER HAYDEN, Senator and holder of directorships in twenty-three firms, slip of the tongue, Senate, 22 March 1975.

Under the BNA Act, the Senate was envisioned as a house of sober second thought. It has become a house of Frankenstein, with indexed pensions.

LAURA SABIA, journalist and feminist, address, Empire Club of Canada, Toronto, 19 Oct. 1978.

In essence, the question is: which of us, having a young family in a small house with an unfinished room, would — rather than redo the room for the family — pay the same amount to maintain it for advisers who come to stay from time to time. The answer is obvious. To knit the family closer together, we would finish the room. Yet, that is not what we have been prepared to do with the Senate.

The Senate is the unfinished room in our national house. We need it to build consensus in our family. The political, social, and economic development of our country is impeded because the Senate is not what it was meant to be. More than that, we need a reformed Senate for what it could be.

MICHAEL PITFIELD, Senator, address, Empire Club of Canada, Toronto, 20 Oct. 1983.

The Senate costs each Canadian just a few pennies a day. Indeed, His Honour Mr. Speaker Carbonneau recently pointed out that the Senate percentage of the national budget is .00026 percent. I think the people of Canada get much more than their money's worth.

KEITH DAVEY, Senator, *The Rainmaker: A Passion for Politics* (1986).

One certain thing is that I can't be accused of absenteeism! For in the last nine days I haven't left the Senate for one minute!

JACQUES HÉBERT, Senator, *21 Days* (1986) translated by Raymond Chamberlain. Senator Hébert staged a hunger strike from March 10 to 31, 1986, in the foyer of the Senate to draw attention to youth unemployment and to the cancellation of the Katimavik youth program which he had overseen.

Appoint Larry Zolf to the Senate, and just as he heaves himself with difficulty to his feet to make his maiden speech, abolish the Senate.

MEL WATKINS, political economist, contributor to *If I Were Prime Minister* (1987) edited by Mel Hurtig.

There is as much chance of having an elected Senate as there is of my becoming the Archbishop of Canterbury.

EUGENE FORSEY, constitutional authority and former Senator, submission to the Senate in 1987, quoted in *The Toronto Star*, 9 July 1987.

Anti-Senatism

Neologism first heard in Aug. 1988 in Toronto, a pun on "anti-Semitism," implying the need for Senate reform.

Vegetables. See Canadian Senate.

Entry in *The Great Wiped Out North: or, When Sacred Cows Come Home to Roost* (1988) by ALLAN GOULD.

The Triple E Senate

"Throughout his seven-year cross-country crusade for an elected, equal and effective (Triple E) Senate, Calgary-area grain farmer BERT BROWN has made hundreds of speeches and lobbied dozens of politicans. He has also encountered both scorn and skepticism. In 1983, recalls the founder of the 8,000-member Canadian Committee for a Triple E Senate, a reporter in Calgary bluntly told him that he was 'the most politically naive human being in Canada.'" D'Arcy Jenish in *Maclean's*, 30 Oct. 1989.

I see the Senate now as a comfortable little club. My mandate is to reform the place. An elected senator has moral authority.
STANLEY WATERS, retired Army General and nominee of the Alberta electorate for a summons to the Senate, quoted by D'Arcy Jenish in *Maclean's*, 30 Oct. 1989.

At the rate we are going under the Conservative government in Ottawa, if we are not careful we will end up with a Triple E Senate whether we like it or not. That will be when Canada has two senators in Washington.
KEN MILLIONS, correspondent in Edmonton, letter to the editor, *Maclean's*, 27 Nov. 1989.

A Senate acting as a House of Facts is essential, as an antidote for the poisoning of the democratic process by professional liars.
PHILIPPE DEANE GIGANTES, author and Senator, *The Road Ahead* (1990).

Apparently the collection of has-beens and never-weres has not understood the infallible pronouncements of the press. The Senate is clearly dead and damned. But, being dead, it still speaketh; being the tool of big interests, it stands up for the small man and ordinary citizen, the poor and him that hath no helper.
EUGENE FORSEY, political scientist and retired Senator, *A Life on the Fringe: The Memoirs of Eugene Forsey* (1990).

If their survival is contingent on the suppression of English, then they are suffering from something terminal.
MORDECAI RICHLER, Quebec-based, English-language author, address in Toronto, 27 Feb. 1990, quoted by Julia Nunes in *The Globe and Mail* the following day.

The Senate should have effective power to ensure the interests of residents of the less populous provinces and territories figure more prominently in national decision-making, reflect Canadian duality and strengthen the Government of Canada's capacity to govern on behalf of all citizens, while preserving the principle of the responsibility of the government to the House of Commons.
One provision of the First Ministers' Communique relating to the Meech Lake Accord, Ottawa, June 9, 1990, reproduced in *The Toronto Star*, 11 June 1990.

It's disgusting to think that a nation might self-destruct over the election of senators. What we've been witnessing is a comic spectacle on a grand scale.
MORLEY CALLAGHAN, author, quoted in "O Canada," *The Toronto Star*, 30 June 1990.

Unlike the Senate, which benefits from vacancies (a 100 per cent vacancy rate would arguably be a national benefit), a high court cannot function with an unfilled bench.
CONRAD BLACK, capitalist and columnist, "Enough Is Enough," *Saturday Night*, Sept. 1990.

The unpopular appoints the unsuitable to force approval of the unacceptable.
GEOFFREY STEVENS, columnist, referring to the appointment by an unpopular Prime Minister (Brian Mulroney) of an unsuitable candidate (Nova Scotia Premier John Buchanan whose administration was facing charges of corruption) to the Upper House to vote for the unacceptable (the controversial GST), *The Toronto Star*, 16 Sept. 1990.

It seems to me that a nation given to sober second thoughts would have taken steps to make the Senate democratic some years ago by making the office of senator elective. On the other hand, they might have arranged to have the "other place" closed down and the un-elected senators — Tory, Liberal and Independent — sent home.

CHRISTOPHER DAFOE, columnist, *The Winnipeg Free Press*, 30 Sept. 1990.

Today, there are fifty-four of them and the average age is likely fifty-something, over the hill, but on the hill. The country is safe, or as safe as ever.

DALTON CAMP, columnist, on Prime Minister Brian Mulroney's action of packing the Senate, *The Toronto Star*, 10 Oct. 1990.

SEPARATISM

See also LÉVESQUE, RENÉ
PARTI QUÉBÉCOIS
QUEBEC
SOVEREIGNTY-ASSOCIATION

Name me one country which became free entirely legally.

MARCEL CHAPUT, federal civil servant who was fired from a federal position for espousing the separatist cause in 1960, recalled by Peter C. Newman in *Maclean's*, 15 Oct. 1990.

Quebec won't separate, if we can live in Canada as a group. Unless Quebec can live in Canada as a group, we'll separate.

Two remarks — the first for English ears, the second for French ears — attributed to Quebec Premier DANIEL JOHNSON in the 1960s by Peter C. Newman in *Maclean's*, 15 Oct. 1990.

I'm against independence because if Quebec is ever independent you will lose all of your rights as an individual.

PIERRE ELLIOTT TRUDEAU, Minister of Justice, remark made in Paris in 1965 to the poet Gaston Miron, quoted by Rick Butler in *Quebec: The People Speak* (1978).

No government in Ontario could ever concede to Quebec half of what it demands without that government automatically destroying itself.

Remark made by a character in GRATIEN GÉLINAS's play *Yesterday, the Children Were Dancing* (1967) translated by Mavor Moore.

Q. Tell us, Mr. Lévesque, what institution is Quebec ready to leave in Ottawa's hands?
A. The Prime Minister's Office.

RENÉ LÉVESQUE, separatist, press conference in Ottawa in 1966, quoted by Peter Desbarats in *René: A Canadian in Search of a Country* (1977).

From the ground level in the square, the figure high above with the deep and vibrant voice seemed for an instant like some beneficient oracle come to deliver an inspired message. The crowd roared its approval. "This is what I have come to say to you this evening," he continued, "and to add that I will take away with me an unforgettable memory of this incredible meeting in Montreal. All France knows, sees and hears what goes on here, and I can tell you, it will be the better for it." Then, following his usual pattern, he shouted, "*Vive Montréal! Vive Québec!*" The separatists, brandishing their placards, chanted, "*France libre! Québec libre!*" and *Vive le Québec libre!*": challenging him to include their slogan as well. The crowd cheered them on. He had given them almost all they wanted to hear, they wanted to see if he would go all the way. The moment he had been looking for since before he left France had arrived. Besides, de Gaulle never avoided a challenge. "*Vive le Québec!*" he repeated, then after a pregnant pause, "*libre!*" It was done. The crowd was silent for a moment, unbelieving, then burst into wild applause. "*Vive le Canada français et vive la France!*" he added, almost as a postscript, and turned and disappeared inside the building.

CHARLES DE GAULLE, President of France, addressing the crowd gathered outside Montreal City Hall, 24 July 1967, described by Dale C. Thomson in *Vive le Québec Libre* (1988).

And Quebec? On 24 July, 1967, on a state visit to Canada, de Gaulle stood on a balcony and shouted: "*Vive le Québec Libre.*" The Cabinet of Lester Pearson announced that this was "unacceptable," and the General, cutting his visit short, flew to Paris at once. Surely Quebec was a mistake?

But he had a passion for it! The situation was unique enough. The bomb attacks were beginning. They gave one the feeling there should be a great drama in Quebec. In fact there was none and the Canadians arranged it among themselves. But the General was taken in by those who wanted help from us.

Interview with ANDRÉ MALRAUX, French statesman, adventurer, and apologist for General Charles de Gaulle, conducted by Bruce Chatwin, "André Malraux" (1974), *What Am I Doing Here?* (1989).

We belong to that little group of peoples . . . who share a particular kind of fate — a tragic fate. Their anxiety is not over whether they will be rich or unhappy, great or small, but over whether tomorrow they will see the dawn or disappear.

Montreal Mayor JEAN DRAPEAU quoted these sentiments of the Quebec nationalist Lionel Groulx in response to Charles de Gaulle's "Québec libre" speech earlier that day, quoted by Dale C. Thomson in *Vive le Québec Libre* (1988).

I do not suppose that he wishes to disrupt Canada, merely to underline and draw international attention to the Frenchness of French Canada. In that he has certainly succeeded as usual, and accomplished precisely what he intended in going there, nothing more and nothing less. It will be interesting to watch the reverberating effects of the emphasis he has given into the 1970s.

A.L. ROWSE, British historian, commenting on Charles de Gaulle's "Québec libre" speech in the correspondence columns of *The Times*, 12 Aug. 1967, reprinted in *The Second Cuckoo: A Further Selection of Witty, Amusing and Memorable Letters to The Times* (1983) edited by Kenneth Gregory.

Separatism a revolution? My eye. A counter-revolution; the national-socialist counter-revolution.

PIERRE ELLIOTT TRUDEAU, Prime Minister, "The Wigwam Complex," *Federalism and the French Canadians* (1968).

Newman: Is it true that there are separatists in French Production?
Lamy: Yes — one hundred percent. But don't worry. They're talented.

Conversation in fall 1970 between SYDNEY NEWMAN, newly appointed NFB Commissioner, and Assistant Commissioner (later Commissioner) ANDRÉ LAMY, quoted by D.B. Jones in *Movies and Memoranda: An Interpretive History of the National Film Board of Canada* (1981).

I myself have come to accept that every country in the world has become Coca-Colanized by U.S. movies and culture. A supermarket, whether it's in Montreal, Toronto, Paris, or Dallas, Texas, looks the same and sells the same Yankee products. To generalize broadly, I'd say that the mass of the six million people in Quebec are sick and tired of being the pain in the neck to the rest of Canada. If you're a pain in the neck, people simply give you an Aspirin — a mild sedative, like bilingualism — and tell you the pain will go away. What'll happen in the future? For most Quebeckers, it's hard to predict. We're like a coin that's being flipped. The coin is still in the air and nobody can tell on which side it will settle.

JACQUES GODBOUT, film producer and novelist, quoted by Frank Rasky in *The Toronto Star*, 14 April 1976.

A slogan for Premier-elect René Lévesque, "If at first you don't secede, try, try, try again."

RICHARD J. NEEDHAM, columnist, *The Globe and Mail*, 22 Nov. 1976.

We're not a minor people. We're maybe something like a great people. . . . I never thought I could be so proud of Quebeckers as I am tonight."
RENÉ LÉVESQUE, Parti Québécois leader, victory speech, Paul Sauvé Arena, 15 Nov. 1976, Montreal, quoted by Ramsay Cook in "'I Never Thought I Could Be as Proud . . .': The Trudeau-Lévesque Debate," *Towards a Just Society: The Trudeau Years* (1990) edited by Thomas S. Axworthy and Pierre Elliott Trudeau. Four years later Lévesque's words were recalled by Prime Minister Trudeau, when the referendum on sovereignty-association was defeated: "I never thought I could be as proud to be a Quebecker and a Canadian as I am tonight. . . ."

Lévesque: What I do in Quebec is none of your damn business.
Moores: What you are trying to do to Canada is my god-damn business.
Heated exchange between RENÉ LÉVESQUE, separatist-minded Quebec Premier, and FRANK MOORES, Newfoundland Premier, Ottawa, following the First Ministers' Conference, quoted by Richard Gwyn in *The Toronto Star*, 16 Dec. 1976.

And building on this foundation, it would lead this new "northern tier" to a future immeasurably richer and more stimulating than the 109-year-old bind in which two nations more often than not feel and act like Churchill's two scorpions in the same bottle.
RENÉ LÉVESQUE, Quebec Premier, "For an Independent Quebec" (1976), *The Globe and Mail*, 17 Nov. 1976.

You just cannot cut a country in two any more than you can cut a human being in two. If you do, you do not have two human beings; you have a corpse. You can cut a worm in two, I suppose, and have two worms, but a country like Canada is a very intricate society, and I don't believe you can divide it.

PIERRE ELLIOTT TRUDEAU, Prime Minister, press conference called in response to the electoral victory of the Parti Québécois, Ottawa, 25 Nov. 1976, published in *The Toronto Star* the following day. The remark is usually recalled in this form: "Only worms can be cut in two and continue to survive."

As I said before, don't be afraid, the French Canadians are not going to take over. You can say the Pope won't either but he is not as great a menace as he used to be. French Canadians are not going to take over the country even if they have a Prime Minister, Governor General, Speaker of the House, President of Air Canada, and so on. You are still good, you English Canadians are still good; you still have a lot of qualities. You still control a lot of money; you still have a lot of brains. Do not worry, love us, and if that happens, Quebeckers will not want to separate. Don't mind if you see Corn Flakes written in French.
PIERRE ELLIOTT TRUDEAU, Prime Minister, press conference called in response to the electoral victory of the Parti Québécois, Ottawa, 25 Nov. 1976, published in *The Toronto Star* the following day.

This is terrible. We won't be able to go to Montreal any more.
RICHARD HATFIELD, Nova Scotia Premier, later nicknamed "Disco Dick," reacting to the electoral victory of the Parti Québécois, quoted in *The Toronto Star*, 14 Oct. 1987.

No province has any legal right or power to secede from Canada. Secession would require an amendment to the British North America Act.
EUGENE FORSEY, Senator, *The Financial Post*, 4 Dec. 1976.

Whether we like it or not, it is written that on the blackboard of our history the Quebec independence movement is irreversible. Those who are not happy about it can move somewhere else. Others who don't think as we do are old and will soon disappear.

RENÉ LÉVESQUE, Quebec Premier, address, Economic Club, New York, Jan. 1977; quoted by Roger Lemelin in his address to the annual dinner of the Canadian Club, Toronto, 2 May 1979, reported in *The Globe and Mail* two days later.

We, on both sides of the Ottawa River, are condemned to be reasonable. Montreal and Toronto live, economically speaking, like each other's suburb.

JACQUES PARIZEAU, Quebec Minister of Finance, address, Empire Club of Canada, Toronto, 17 March 1977.

The answer to the question "Could Quebec legally and constitutionally secede?" is yes, provided all the other provinces consented, or nearly all the other provinces.

EUGENE FORSEY, Senator, address, Empire Club of Canada, Toronto, 28 April 1977.

When Rodrique Tremblay or René Lévesque suggest that Québec is in a similar position to the 100 countries who have gained independence since the Second World War, I tell him as a Quebecker that we need not be compared to Zaire, Uganda, Upper Volta, Togo, and so on.

JEAN CHRÉTIEN, Liberal leadership candidate, address in Montreal, 2 May 1977, published in *Canada's Third Option* (1987) edited by S.D. Berkowitz and Robert K. Logan.

Postcan

Name for Canada following the secession of Quebec, proposed at the Options Conference, University of Toronto, 14-15 Oct. 1977.

Let history say that both the Canadian people and the Quebec people got together and created common institutions related to their common interests. Let the future acknowledge that this did not solve all the problems of Canada, but it allowed two peoples to develop more freely, each according to its own will, its own priorities and its own identity, in a spirit of co-operation if not of outright cordiality.

PIERRE-MARC JOHNSON, Quebec Minister of Labour, address, Empire Club of Canada, Toronto, 25 Oct. 1979.

It is better to be master in your own house than a valet in Toronto or Vancouver.

CAMILLE LAURIN, Quebec Minister of Education, Quebec National Assembly, 13 March 1980, quoted in *The Globe and Mail* the following day.

All we need to know is this: is it in the interests of French-speaking Canadians to be a majority in a pluralist Quebec state, or a minority in a pluralist Canadian state? That is what the whole debate is about.

PIERRE ELLIOTT TRUDEAU, Prime Minister, *Le Devoir*, 17 July 1980. "Those are Trudeau's words, but [René] Lévesque could easily have uttered them. They agreed on the question; they disputed the answer." So wrote the historian Ramsay Cook in "'I Never Thought I Could Be as Proud . . .': The Trudeau-Lévesque Debate," *Towards a Just Society: The Trudeau Years* (1990) edited by Thomas S. Axworthy and Pierre Elliott Trudeau.

We have separatist movements, or incipient ones, everywhere from Newfoundland to Vancouver Island — although I often say to British Columbia separatists, "How can you separate when you never really joined?"

Everybody wants out, to some extent, except Ontario — and all the others seem to want Ontario out!

CHARLES LYNCH, columnist, address, Empire Club of Canada, Toronto, 9 April 1981.

So long as we have not achieved independence, it remains to be achieved.

GASTON MIRON, poet, quoted by Marc Raboy, editor, *Old Passions/New Visions: Social Movements and Political Activism in*

Quebec (1986) translated by Robert Chodos.

It wouldn't cause me any sleepless nights.
WILLIAM VANDER ZALM, B.C. Premier, pondering the implications of Quebec secession, 2 April 1983, quoted by Stephen Osborne and Mary Schendlinger in *Quotations from Chairman Zalm* (1988).

The question ultimately boils down to this: Do the people of Quebec need a state to themselves over which they have the maximum control possible before their claim of being a distinct society can become an indisputable fact?
My own view is that the political and constitutional status of Quebec is but a means to an end, albeit an indispensable means, if it is to realize the one goal from which it must never be diverted: to preserve and promote the French language as well as all other elements of our culture. This must take precedence over the preservation of English and Anglophone institutions.
LÉON DION, political scientist, "The Mystery of Quebec," *Daedalus: Journal of the American Academy of Arts and Sciences*, "In Search of Canada," Fall 1988.

Here again in Quebec, something of a "free spirit" towards the question of lifestyles that we have seen in our examination of values, sexuality, and beliefs is once more apparent. The Quebec teen attitude commonly seems to be, "Do what you yourself want." In the present instance it amounts to, "If you want to assimilate, do it; if you want to keep your heritage, do it." In either event, they are saying the people involved should be able to make the choice.
REGINALD W. BIBBY and DONALD C. POSTERSKI, sociologists, *The Emerging Generation: An Inside Look at Canada's Teenagers* (1985).

Unconsummated Divorce
Heading of the chapter on federal-provincial relations in STEPHEN BROOK's *Maple Leaf Rag: Travels across Canada* (1987).

I came early to the belief that every incident in Quebec's struggle for recognition of its distinct language and culture would one day be repeated in the southern United States, with Spanish in our country replacing the role of French in Canada. Canada thus became of vital interest, and I followed with a microscope the twists and turns of how this nation of two languages sought to apply intelligent answers to the problem.
JAMES A. MICHENER, U.S. author, discussing the genesis of his novel set in the Canadian North, *Journey* (1988).

M. Parizeau still talks of *Québec libre* in the high Gaullist way — of armies, of national currencies, of foreign treaties — but I speak to you by Merlin's oath that it will never come about, and that the force of this city's pride is fated to settle into permanent dispute, coming and going, flaring and subsiding, advancing and retreating and advancing again down the generations.
JAN MORRIS, Anglo-Welsh travel writer, "The Battle for Montreal," *Saturday Night*, July 1988.

It's never too late to pursue a dream. . . . It would be crazy to start from zero. We can start again from where we left off on May 20, 1980, and overcome together our fear — until the day we no longer will need a referendum.
GILLES VIGNEAULT, chansonnier, referring to the Quebec Referendum on sovereignty-association, quoted by Stephen Godfrey in *The Globe and Mail*, 17 Sept. 1988.

The biggest shock will be a major disruption in the bilingual nature of Canada. Forces of separatism rise again with great speed and potency. A great uneasiness will settle upon Canadian citizens.
ROBIN ARMSTRONG, professional astrologer, *Robin Armstrong's Astrological Almanac: 1990* (1989).

The opposition between the two communities remained strong. Soon, some people

started saying to Quebecers, "Look, you're a pain in the neck." And I think they were right. As far as Canada is concerned, Quebec is a pain in the neck. We cannot do our things without forcing the rest of Canada to do its things differently.
> JACQUES PARIZEAU, P.Q. leader, interviewed in *Maclean's*, 25 Sept. 1989.

The great bilingual Canada did not come to pass, nor did the great sovereign Quebec. The yearnings of each side were frustrated. Nothing happened. The slate is clean. We're back to square one. It's now a new trip with no more content than the one before.
> PIERRE BOURGAULT, independentist, *Moi, Je M'en Souviens* (1989); translated by Sinclair Robinson in *The Canadian Forum*, Nov. 1989.

The independentist dream was, and is, an internationalist dream, that of making Quebec a sovereign state able to deal as an equal with the other nations of the world, something that its provincial status prevents it from doing fully.
> PIERRE BOURGAULT, independentist, *Moi, Je M'en Souviens* (1989); translated by Sinclair Robinson in *The Canadian Forum*, Nov. 1989.

"A flower grows at its own pace and pulling it doesn't help it grow."

By that Claude Morin meant that independence would come of its own time, that it was pointless to get agitated, that nature has its own way and that it is better not to interfere too much.

That is how he always justified his wait-and-see policy, which allowed him to watch the train go by, while our opponents jumped on it.
> PIERRE BOURGAULT, independentist, *Moi, Je M'en Souviens* (1989); translated by Sinclair Robinson in *The Canadian Forum*, Nov. 1989.

I can understand the impatience with Quebec in the rest of Canada. And I really wish

we had a government of sufficient grit to say, "Okay, we're going to have a referendum with the real question. Do you want to stay or do you want to go? If you want to stay, there are certain civilities you have to observe." Most Quebecers are too conservative. Too many goodies come out of Ottawa.
> MORDECAI RICHLER, author, quoted by Dennis Kucherawy, *Metropolis*, 16 Nov. 1989.

I exist too.
> JACQUES PARIZEAU, Parti Québécois leader, stomping out of his scheduled news conference when he judged that the press was insufficiently represented, quoted by Robert Sheppard in *The Globe and Mail*, 21 Dec. 1989.

Separatism has already occurred. We are already separate.
> GILLES VIGNEAULT, chansonnier, radio interview, Vancouver, Winter 1990, quoted by John Gray in *The Globe and Mail*, 12 April 1991.

I remember Frank Scott telling me how one of these people had said: *"Nous allons arranger l'Ontario"* (We shall arrange Ontario); and I recall an article in *Le Devoir*, when the Afrikaners took control of the Union of South Africa, that looked forward to the day when the *Canadiens* would do the same for Canada.
> EUGENE FORSEY, constitutional authority, referring to the constitutional expert F.R. Scott and Quebec nationalists prior to the Quiet Revolution of the 1960s, *A Life on the Fringe: The Memoirs of Eugene Forsey* (1990).

As long as we allow ourselves to be fooled by this kind of legerdemain we shall be sitting ducks for every separatist or hemi-demi-semi separatist in the country.
> EUGENE FORSEY, constitutional authority, referring to purposeful confusion over the sociological and political meanings of the word *nation* in the two official

languages, *A Life on the Fringe: The Memoirs of Eugene Forsey* (1990).

When the First World War broke out, Sir Edward Grey, the British Foreign Secretary, said: "The lights are going out all over Europe." They did. I hope the lights are not now going out all over Canada.
EUGENE FORSEY, constitutional authority, *A Life on the Fringe: The Memoirs of Eugene Forsey* (1990).

Calling it national reconciliation, Prime Minister Mulroney has in fact been dismantling Canada for the benefit of the provinces. And under the noble pretext of satisfying Quebec, he has been fostering exactly the kind of dualism that is the stuff of the separatists' fondest dreams: an exclusively English-speaking Canada alongside an exclusively French-speaking Quebec.
PIERRE ELLIOTT TRUDEAU, former Prime Minister, "The Values of a Just Society," *Towards a Just Society: The Trudeau Years* (1990) edited by Thomas S. Axworthy and Pierre Elliott Trudeau, translated by Patricia Claxton.

Canada is not eternal. The United States is not eternal. Heaven knows, we know the Soviet Union is probably not eternal. Things change, but let's give the people a say.
PIERRE ELLIOTT TRUDEAU, former Prime Minister and critic of the Meech Lake Accord, Montreal, 20 March 1990, quoted by Patricia Poirier in *The Globe and Mail* the following day.

Is there any hope of *Ottawa* separating from the rest of Canada?
EDD ULUSCHAK, cartoonist, Miller Features Syndicate, 27 March 1990.

It's time to stop treating separatists with kid gloves. Separatists are traitors to Canada. They're no better than the racists and the bigots.
JOHN NUNZIATA, M.P. and Liberal leadership candidate, speaking at a leadership forum, where he attacked federal Environment Minister Lucien Bouchard, Halifax, 22 April 1990, quoted by Susan Delacourt in *The Globe and Mail* the following day.

The very idea that English Canada would debate whether Quebec was a distinct society, when it is really to us another country, is ridiculous.
PAUL PICHÉ, pop singer, quoted by Stephen Godfrey in *The Globe and Mail*, 19 May 1990.

Leaving one separatist to remark that "there are two questions that have to be answered about Quebec: just how federalist was René Lévesque, and just how separatist is Robert Bourassa?" The truth lies somewhere between the two answers. The distinction is a subtle one for most Canadians outside Quebec, and not easily understood. But it lies at the heart of much that is misunderstood about Quebec.
JACK KAPICA, Montreal-born, Toronto-based journalist and editor, *The Globe and Mail*, 19 May 1990.

Quebeckers must redefine the degree, the structures, and the conditions of their participation in Canada.
LUCIEN BOUCHARD, Cabinet Minister who resigned from the Conservative Party over possible changes to the Meech Lake Accord, letter of resignation addressed to Prime Minister Brian Mulroney, 22 May 1990, based on the CP text in *The Globe and Mail* the following day.

Only a Quebec state democratically invested with a clear mandate, based on the recovery of all its powers, will have the political authority needed to negotiate the Canadian association of tomorrow.
LUCIEN BOUCHARD, Cabinet Minister who resigned from the Conservative Party over possible changes to the Meech Lake Accord, letter of resignation addressed to Prime Minister Brian Mulroney, 22 May 1990, quoted in *The Toronto Star* the following day.

Whoever starts to negotiate on his knees is very likely to end up flat on his face.
LUCIEN BOUCHARD, Cabinet Minister who resigned from the Conservative Party over possible changes to the Meech Lake Accord, letter of resignation addressed to Prime Minister Brian Mulroney, 22 May 1990, quoted in *The Toronto Star* the following day.

There are things that need to be said. For one thing, the crux of the matter on language is that we should all join Quebec and separate together.
Stompin' TOM CONNORS, popular singer, addressing an interviewer, quoted by Mitch Potter in *The Toronto Star*, 27 May 1990.

Quebec may one day be able to survive without Canada but do we really want to survive without Quebec?
JAMES FLEMING, business columnist, *The Globe and Mail's Report on Business Magazine*, June 1990.

9 + 1 = 10
10 - 1 = 0
Numbers on a placard being waved by a federalist demonstrator outside the National Conference Centre, Ottawa, during deliberations of the First Ministers on the Meech Lake Accord, 7 June 1990.

And if Canada breaks up, what would become of those of us already down here? How will we triumphantly go on telling people that frozen food, Greenpeace, Michael J. Fox, the first transatlantic wireless message, the oldest newspaper, the world's longest covered bridge, Trivial Pursuit and Pablum were all Canadian.
Not to mention responsible government without revolution.
PETER JENNINGS, Toronto-born ABC anchorman, *Maclean's*, 25 June 1990.

Le Québec c'est mon vrai pays.
"Quebec is my real country." Wording on a placard carried through the streets of Montreal during the Saint-Jean-Baptiste Day parade, held on 25 June 1990, quoted by André Picard in *The Globe and Mail* the following day.

If this country does fragment, we will all be diminished, English and French, and this quarrelsome land will eventually split into a confusion of loopy little client-states. Whichever way it goes, I intend to remain in Quebec, though I don't fancy being a citizen of a state run by the likes of Lucien Bouchard, whom I take to be a menacing mix of demagogue and political opportunist.
MORDECAI RICHLER, novelist, quoted in "O Canada," *The Toronto Star*, 30 June 1990.

Our Real Country Is Quebec.
Sign carried on Canada Day in Hull, Que., quoted by Susan Delacourt in *The Globe and Mail*, 2 July 1990.

If they want to pull out with 15 per cent of the land, we'll let them go. Most of that 15 per cent is already polluted anyway.
MAX GROS-LOUIS, Grand Chief of the Huron Nation in Quebec, on Quebec's proposed separation from Canada, claiming ownership of most of the province; quoted by Darcy Henton in *The Winnipeg Free Press*, 28 July 1990.

The position of the native people is that the province belongs to the native people. Quebec cannot go out on its own and be separate. What Quebec should be talking about when it talks about separating is only the Montreal and Quebec City area and that's it.
BILLY DIAMOND, Cree chief, claiming Mohawk sovereignty over most of Quebec, quoted by Darcy Henton in *The Winnipeg Free Press*, 28 July 1990.

This will be the key debate of the 1990s: whether those of us who live outside Quebec can reinvent a country — not the Canada that was, but a Canada that could be.
PETER C. NEWMAN, columnist, *Maclean's*, 20 Aug. 1990.

Finally, there should be a secession mechanism. Any region or province that produces a sixty per cent referendum vote for secession, after having given six months' notice of the vote and full and fair rights to campaign to both sides of the issue, could assume its per-capita share of the national debt and go.

> CONRAD BLACK, capitalist and columnist, "Enough Is Enough," *Saturday Night*, Sept. 1990.

It is up to us to see that the word "Canada" (what a sickening conglomeration of syllables, don't you think?) becomes in all countries a synonym for placid stupidity.

> JEAN LAROSE, Quebec writer and separatist, *La Petite Noirceur* (1990), as quoted by Ken McGoogan in *The Toronto Star*, 21 Nov. 1990.

English Canada will not make concessions — and we are not even sure of that — unless it has a knife at its throat.

> LÉON DION, Professor of Law at Laval University, constitutional expert, and adviser to the Bourassa administration, appearing before the Bélanger-Campeau Commission on the Future of Quebec, 12 Dec. 1990, quoted by Rhéal Séguin in *The Globe and Mail* the following day.
>
> The knife in question is Quebec's threat that it will hold a referendum on independence. More forcefully worded is the account written by Philip Authier in *The Montreal Gazette*, 13 Dec. 1990: "English Canada won't give in until it has a knife at its throat. . . . If we come to the conclusion that Canada is not ready, not willing to negotiate something very serious with Quebec, then let's go straight to a referendum on independence."

For those who fear the future, whose confidence has been eroded by calls for regionalism, whose faith has been shaken by appeals to division, I propose a greater dream: a new Canada, emerging from the darkness of doubt and the dismay of lost opportunity; a new Canada, reconfederated, rebuilt and reborn, that will be modern, flexible and competitive, able to satisfy both the hopes of our newest immigrants and the pride of our founding peoples; a new Canada where all Canadians, French-speaking and English-speaking, come to admire one another for what we have achieved together and love Canada for the majestic contribution she has made to the cause of peace and justice throughout the world.

> BRIAN MULRONEY, Prime Minister, address, joint meeting of the Empire Club and the Canadian Club, Toronto, 12 Feb. 1991, published in *The Toronto Star* the following day.

What some people call "the rest of Canada" should understand is that Quebecers will never negotiate on their knees, and Quebecers should understand that "the rest of Canada" cannot be expected to negotiate "with a knife at its throat" — as a prominent Quebecer recently recommended.

> BRIAN MULRONEY, Prime Minister, address, joint meeting of the Empire Club and the Canadian Club, Toronto, 12 Feb. 1991, published in *The Toronto Star* the following day.

Today, I am saying just as frankly to Quebeckers: Beware the dream merchants, those who say that they can destroy a great country and then rebuild it effortlessly, who say they are able, all by themselves, to control the course of history. . . . Part-time countries make no sense.

> BRIAN MULRONEY, Prime Minister, address delivered in French, Chamber of Commerce, Quebec City, 13 Feb. 1991, translation reproduced in *The Globe and Mail* the following day.

They're specialists in division.

> BRIAN MULRONEY, Prime Minister, employing a new-found term for public figures who favour separatism or sovereignty-association, riding association speech, Baie-Comeau, Que., 15

March 1991 quoted in *The Globe and Mail* the following day.

Quebec has put on its coat in preparation to leave, but its boots are still in the closet.
    Attributed to Quebec columnist LYSIANE GAGNON by columnist David Olive in *The Globe and Mail*, 16 Feb. 1991.

Past injustices conceded, *il faut le dire*, Quebec has fared pretty well as part of Canada. As far as I can tell, no one has tried to stop les Québécois from being fruitful and multiplying and getting well paid for it, or preventing them from making superb films, writing great plays, cooking fabulous food, looking sexier, having more civilized liquor laws, capitalizing on their talents, exploiting the First Nations and the environment, or making silly xenophobic generalities about English Canada.
    CHARLES PACHTER, artist and essayist, *The Globe and Mail*, 28 March 1991.

Quebec's coming independence was the creation of Ottawa, not Quebec; of a government that promised and delivered decentralization, non-interventionist economics and an integrated North American marketplace.
    JOHN GRAY, playwright and composer, *The Globe and Mail*, 12 April 1991.

SERVICE
See also CHARITY

A nation like an individual to find itself must love itself in the service of others.
    W.L. MACKENZIE KING, Prime Minister, Confederation Address, Parliament Hill, 1 July 1927.

True service is unseen and unheard but never unnoticed.
    Advertisement of the Four Seasons Hotel and Resorts in the brochure of the Festival of Festivals: 13th Toronto International Film Festival, 8-17 Sept. 1988.

SETTLEMENT

After almost four centuries of continuous settlement, Canada still evokes images of an immense, unsettled Wilderness.
    ALAN F.J. ARTIBISE, planning consultant, "Canada as an Urban Nation," *Daedalus: Journal of the American Academy of Arts and Sciences*, "In Search of Canada," Fall 1988.

SEWAGE

The strong WASP influence in Upper Canada ensured that waste treatment in Canada reached a high state of technical excellence. The final effluents though were rather sterile, lacking the variety, colour, and exuberance of a truly great art form. The resulting sludges are somewhat bland and generally lacking in bouquet. Pathogens too would appear not to travel well in the receiving waters. In fact the situation might be compared to the Bolshoi Ballet, where perfection of technique has been achieved at the expense of artistic spontaneity!
    TOM DAVEY, editor and columnist, *Environmental Science & Engineering*, June-July 1990.

Environmental neglect is wide-spread across Canada, but no one does it with the élan and panache of *La Belle Province*. Ignoring the constraints imposed by formal treatment processes, the Québécois cleverly opted to harness the turbulence of the St. Lawrence River in a spontaneous, free-form, high-volume, raw-sewage discharge mode. Inevitably, some critics carp about ineffectual treatment; but all admit the Quebec effluent, like a good wine, retains its bouquet, that the effluent travels well, and that capital costs are negligible!
    TOM DAVEY, editor and columnist, *Environmental Science & Engineering*, June-July 1990.

SEX

See also HOMOSEXUALITY
LOVE
PORNOGRAPHY
PROSTITUTION
SEXUAL OFFENCES

Ooo-la-la. I'm contagious. I'm the French Bombshell who's never been to Par-ee. I'm no angel, let me tell you. Mae West could never keep up. My weakness was l'amour, toujours l'amour. 'Ello, beeg boy!
> Characteristic expressions on and off the stage and screen of FIFI D'ORSAY, the Montreal-born vaudevillan and Hollywood star (whose original name was Yvonne Lussier) known as "the French Bombshell" who specialized in playing silly and sexy French girls in the Thirties and Forties, according to Jim Bawden in *The Toronto Star*, 12 Feb. 1983.

The cumulative effect of the false religious teachings in regard to sex in the past has resulted in what may be called the tradition of reticence.
> ALFRED HENRY TYRER, Anglican minister and birth-control enthusiast, *Sex, Marriage and Birth Control: A Guide-book to Sex Health and a Satisfactory Sex Life in Marriage* (10th ed., 1936).

Concerning sexual excitement [when the wife knows that the husband is going to withdraw and ejaculate outside the vagina]: she may enjoy sexual excitement, even total satisfaction, that occurs during the time that sexual activity continues. But she may not seek to have her husband seek excitement for her if she had not experienced it.
> *Cours de Préparation au Mariage* (Action Catholique Canadienne, Service de Préparation au Mariage du Diocèse de Montréal, Ottawa, 1944), Roman Catholic instruction manual for prospective husbands. Reproduced by the Clio Collective (Micheline Dumont, Michèle Jean, Marie Lavigne, Jennifer Stoddart) in *Quebec Women: A History* (1987) translated by Roger Gannon and Rosalind Gill.

Buttocks and buttercups, / both have their devotees, / but I'm not one of them — / pick what you please!
> GEORGE WALTON, poet and physician, "Words, Words, Words," *The Wayward Queen* (1959).

A Canadian is somebody who talks sex but plays sports.
> Characteristic remark first recorded in 1968.

It amazes me that organs that piss / Can give human beings such perfect bliss.
> IRVING LAYTON, poet, *The Whole Bloody Bird (obs, aphs & pomes)* (1969).

May your cock continue life as a Canadian.
> American curse recalled by the novelist WILLIAM GASS in *On Being Blue* (1975).

. . . the twenty-minute gap, the abyss between the sexes.
> STEPHEN VIZINCZEY, novelist, *An Innocent Millionaire* (1983).

There are all kinds of ways of being unfaithful, not the worst of them with your body.
> BETTY JANE WYLIE, author, *All in the Family: A Survival Guide for Living and Loving in a Changing World* (1988).

Sex is part of life, an enormously important part, but it is not, I think, what a lot of people seem to imagine it to be. It is not an isolated area, and it is only an aspect of love in the much larger sense, the relationship between people. And not necessarily people of different sexes, or anything like that, but just the manifestation of our loneliness. This desire somehow to make contact with other living creatures: that is one way of putting it. It is not the only way, and it may not be the most important way.
> ROBERTSON DAVIES, man-of-letters, interviewed by Gordon Roper in 1968, *Conversations with Robertson Davies* (1989) edited by J. Madison Davis.

Personally, I never liked the thought of waking up in the morning and introducing my children to the man in bed beside me.

BETTY JANE WYLIE, author, *Beginnings: A Book for Widows* (1977, rev. 1988).

Sex that is not an evidence of a strong human tie is just like blowing your nose; it's not a celebration of a splendid relationship.
ROBERTSON DAVIES, man-of-letters, interviewed by Tom Harpur in 1974, *Conversations with Robertson Davies* (1989) edited by J. Madison Davis.

Half an hour of begging is not considered foreplay.
Wording on a sign in the back of an automobile noted in Ottawa in the 1980s.

The ideal companion in bed is a good book.
ROBERTSON DAVIES, man-of-letters, interviewed by Terence M. Green in 1982, *Conversations with Robertson Davies* (1989) edited by J. Madison Davis.

In the older beliefs sexual desire was one means through which love between human beings could abound; in our era love seems sometimes to be thought of as a means for the abounding of sexual enjoyment.
GEORGE GRANT, philosopher, "Faith and the Multiversity," *Technology and Justice* (1983).

It was drummed into me that I must never have sex with a man before I was married, and then the next day I was off to the studio where a very different set of rules prevailed — I must admit that it was lovely to be asked and even lovelier to say no . . . or yes.
DEANNA DURBIN, actress, interviewed in 1983 about her youthful years in Hollywood, quoted by Ronald Bergan in *Glamorous Musicals: Fifty Years of Hollywood's Ultimate Fantasy* (1984).

Canada imports more sex symbols than she exports. This despite the Canadian Development Corporation. Whatever it is

that the CDC has been developing, it doesn't steam your glasses.
ERIC NICOL and DAVE MORE, humorists, *The U.S. or Us: What's the Difference, Eh?* (1986).

Canadian women lust vicariously for American sex objects like Frank Sinatra, Paul Newman, and Neil Diamond, but at home they expect a man to come on like a grain elevator.
ERIC NICOL and DAVE MORE, humorists, *The U.S. or Us: What's the Difference, Eh?* (1986).

Canadian sex aids, such as the rubber nose for Inuit lovers, have limited appeal in the States. The inflatable doll made by a Canadian tire company failed to catch on because it had to be taken to a service station to be pumped up. And there were few takers for the vibrating bed that depended on a spin-dry cycle.
ERIC NICOL and DAVE MORE, humorists, *The U.S. or Us: What's the Difference, Eh?* (1986).

A woman generally becomes a blonde because there is no man in her life, or there is and he is younger.
EDWARD PHILLIPS, novelist, *Buried on Sunday* (1986).

Fer sex I jist ansered "Infreeqwint," and they ast me back if that wuz 1 word or 2.
DON HARRON, comedian, in the person of Charlie Farquharson, commenting on "our sensus," *Cum Buy the Farm* (1987).

Just as men in the Western world believe that the head is the seat of the soul, they are equally deluded in thinking that sexuality exists in the penis. Perhaps this explains our long-standing anxiety about its size and the current efforts to find the causes of sexual deviancy in the shaft of this frequently measured but highly overrated appendage.
CYRIL GREENLAND, psychiatric social worker, address, New York Academy of Sciences, 9 Jan. 1987.

First, a few samples from the realm of law. While trying to find similar legal definitions of illegal sexual practices in other English-speaking countries, I chanced upon two maximum punishments for *bestiality* and *buggery* in Canada: each crime is punished by "14 years imprisonment and whipping." (What kind of punishment is whipping, if the felon is a masochist?)

> REINHOLD AMAN, linguist, "What Is This Crime that Dare Not Speak Its Name?" *Maladicta* 19, 1987-88.

I like the parts that make me blush / Oh, you devil, you / . . . I like the parts that you write in French / And I'm not quite sure what you say.

> CONNIE KALDOR, songwriter and performer, "Love Letters," quoted by Ellen Schwartz in *Born a Woman: Seven Canadian Women Singer-Songwriters* (1988).

Give a man an inch and he thinks he's a ruler.

> DON HARRON, comedian, in the person of Valerie Rosedale, CBC Radio, 1 April 1988.

Sex (an irresistible force meeting an irresistible object) is simply too powerful a natural fact to deny by legislation, even in its more public manifestations, such as prostitution.

> WILLIAM THORSELL, columnist, *The Globe and Mail's Report on Business Magazine*, Feb. 1989.

BOYS WILL BE BOYS / BUT GIRLS WILL BE WOMEN

> Graffiti noted in Toronto, June 1989.

As for myself, I would like to see the locks come off sex. I would like to see a time when people regard sex as a need, in the same terms that they regard eating. To extend the food metaphor — just imagine that if, when you married, you promised that you would eat only with the person you married for the rest of your life, and that it would be disloyal and immoral to eat with someone else. Therefore, whether your mate is hungry or not, that person must eat with you or you can't eat. Follow that through and think of the tyranny of making somebody eat with you even if he isn't hungry. If he doesn't eat with you, you must go hungry. If he eats with you when he doesn't want to, so you can eat, he may find that sickening. Also, he's committed to eating the same kinds of food you eat. Resentment builds up on both sides. The sexual prohibitions have forced us into extremely unnatural and convoluted positions.

> SYLVIA FRASER, novelist, interviewed by Alan Twigg in *Strong Voices: Conversations with Fifty Canadian Authors* (1988).

Listening is one of the lesser-known skills that mistresses offer.

> BETTY JANE WYLIE, author, *All in the Family: A Survival Guide for Living and Loving in a Changing World* (1988).

A Canadian scandal is a hand in the till, not on the thigh.

> ROY MacGREGOR, columnist, *The Ottawa Citizen*, 29 March 1989.

A man comes along, sees a pair of hips and helps himself.

> MICHEL BOURASSA, judge of the court of the Northwest Territories, expressing the opinion that instances of sexual assault in the North are less violent than they are in the South because in the South "the dainty co-ed . . . gets jumped from behind," whereas in the North native women are drunk and passed out, as noted in *The Toronto Star*, 21 Dec. 1989.

He is a life-size demonstrator kit.

> Line from a poem in *Something Might Happen* (1989) by the author BETTY JANE WYLIE.

There is a line between sexuality and promiscuity, and the line is closer to celibacy than not.

> BETTY JANE WYLIE, author, *obiter dictum*, 1990.

STDs have become the conscience of us all.

> BETTY JANE WYLIE, author, referring to Sexually Transmitted Diseases, *obiter dictum*, 1990.

People aren't ashamed of the sex, they're ashamed of the fantasies.

> Comment of a character in the play *Dreaming and Duelling* by JOHN LAZARUS and JOA LAZARUS, included in *Twenty Years at Play* (1990) edited by Jerry Wasserman.

The way I see it, it's the responsibility of women to refuse to have sex until men start seeing hidden beauty. When guys start fantasizing about Mother Teresa, then we can talk.

> Comment of a character in the play *The Half of It* by JOHN KRIZANC, included in *Twenty Years at Play* (1990) edited by Jerry Wasserman.

More dreams are destroyed in bed than are ever found there.

> ROBIN SKELTON, man-of-letters, aphorism, May 1990.

Hammond's Law: Never sleep with anyone dumber than you. Hammond's Corollary: Unless you're at least 5000 miles from home and the alphabet is different.

> MARIE-LYNN HAMMOND, singer and songwriter, private communication, 10 Feb. 1991.

The most powerful word in the English language is . . . SEX.

It is probably the only word in the language that could be used in any advertising medium and people would automatically read, listen, or watch what was to follow.

> JERRY GOODIS, advertising executive, *GOODIS: Shaking the Canadian Advertising Tree* (1991) written with Gene O'Keefe.

SEXUAL OFFENCES

There is no one who automatically loses anything when a woman is pinched or otherwise harassed.

The pinching a secretary receives from her employer, while objectionable to many women, is not a coercive action. It is rather part of a package deal in which she agrees to accept the job and especially if she agrees to keep the job. The office is, after all, private property.

> WALTER BLOCK, economist with the Fraser Institute, unnamed book published in 1976, quoted in *Actrascope*, Summer 1989.

It is difficult to avoid concluding that many feminists believe that sex offenders should be severely punished, as if they were obstreperous children, in order to return them and the rest of mankind to some pre-existing state of innocence and harmony. Apart from the fact that retributive justice — giving the offender his just deserts — only increases the overall risks of interpersonal aggression, the danger is that in the process of scapegoating, the real causes of violence in our society will, once again, be concealed.

> CYRIL GREENLAND, psychiatric social worker, "The Treatment and Maltreatment of Sex Offenders: Ethical Issues," *Human Sexual Aggression* (Volume 528, 1989) edited by Robert A. Prentky and Vernon L. Quinsey.

The factor of gender can be germaine to the assessment of what is reasonable.

> Decision handed down by the Supreme Court of Canada, May 1990, in the case of Lynne Lavallée. The decision, drafted by Madame Justice BERTHA WILSON, dismissed the Crown's appeal. The Manitoba woman, charged with manslaughter after she shot and killed her abusive boy friend, was found not guilty by a Manitoba jury. The Supreme Court of Canada heard the case and accepted expert psychiatric testimony that abused women face special problems.

SHIPS & SAILING

See also TRAVEL

ROYAL WILLIAM, 363 tons, 36 men, John McDougall, master. Bound to London, British. Cargoe [*sic*]: 253 Chaldrons of coal, a

box of stuffed birds and six spars, produced of this Province. One box and one trunk, household furniture and a harp. All British and seven passengers.
> Contemporary description of the famous vessel *Royal William* which set sail from Halifax for London, 5 Aug. 1833, quoted by John M. Bassett in *Samuel Cunard* (1976).

It is the ship that stays afloat that gets to port.
> SIR SAMUEL CUNARD, shipbuilder, quoted by John S. Crosbie in *The Incredible Mrs. Chadwick: The Most Notorious Woman of Her Age* (1975).

The wood that can beat the *Bluenose* ain't been planted yet.
> ANGUS WALTERS, captain of the *Bluenose*, the last of the great clipper ships, launched in Lunenburg, N.S., in 1921, quoted by David MacDonald in "Unbeatable *Bluenose*," *Canada — This Land, These People: A Reader's Digest Collection* (1968). Oland's Brewery built the replica, *Bluenose II*, in 1963.

When does this place get to England?
> Celebrated quip of BEATRICE LILLIE, Canadian-born singer-comedienne, aboard the *Queen Mary* in the 1940s, quoted in *The New York Times*, 3 Sept. 1967.

Today, this Nation offers to mankind / This monument, when the passion in old foes / Is blest and sublimated and combined / To give Man's utmost for the best man knows.
> JOHN MASEFIELD, Poet Laureate of Great Britain, wrote an official ode on the opening of the St. Lawrence Seaway, quoted by William Ashworth in *The Late, Great Lakes: An Environmental History* (1986). The Dutch freighter *Prins Wilhelm George Frederich* was the first vessel to use the international waterway, 25 April 1959; officially the first vessel was the Royal Yacht *Britannia*, 26 June 1959.

SHOES
See also FOOTWEAR

Shoes tell you more about people and their history than any other artifact.
> SONJA BATA, collector of over 8,000 pairs of shoes, wife of Thomas J. Bata, quoted by Elaine Carey in *The Toronto Star*, 20 Oct. 1990.

SHOW BUSINESS

Familiarity with a good man does not breed contempt; but it takes away the burning desire to pay $1 to look at him.
> WILSON MacDONALD, poet and public performer, letter to William Arthur Deacon, 3 Feb. 1927, quoted by Clara Thomas and John Lennox in *William Arthur Deacon: A Canadian Literary Life* (1982).

Between shows Vallee recalled with a *Review* reporter his first trip to Canada when he was at the height of his fame. It was to Port Dover.
"The special train to Erie cost $500," says Vallee. "The ferry to Port Dover cost money, and we had just had built the first public address system ever used in Canada by a dance band. I was interviewed by a reporter who asked me what I thought of the girls in the hall — and I answered not so hot."
"That night because of the difference in Canadian hydro, the PA system burned out; the show was a flop for that reason, and we did not get paid our fee," says Vallee. "The pay-off was the next day when a headline appeared in a paper 'Rudy Vallee says Canadian girls are not so hot.' I hardly dared show my face in Canada again."
> RUDY VALLEE, U.S. popular singer, recalling his Canadian *début*, which occurred in the 1930s, interviewed by Harry Rustige in *The Niagara Falls Evening Review*, 31 May 1960.

Whoever planned Les's tour was a sadist — we played Canada in the dead of winter and Florida in August.

DORIS DAY, actress and singer, on the hazards of touring North America in the 1940s with Les Brown and His Band of Renown, quoted in *Doris Day: Her Own Story* (1975) written with A.E. Hotchner.

In Toronto — in Canada — it's frustrating sometimes to find that people ease up on ambition, that there isn't the same drive to make things happen. But while there isn't that sense of aggressive ambition here in Canada generally, there is, perhaps as a result, a sense of decency, a sense of fair play, that makes it one of the nicest places in the world.

AL WAXMAN, actor who works in Los Angeles and Toronto, quoted by John L.D. Keyes in *TV Guide*, 18 July 1987.

Hey, let's go and watch the people watching us.

MR. T., media personality, overheard addressing a female companion, Toronto's Festival of Festivals, 18 Sept. 1987.

It's not all that easy, you know. Becoming a woman can make a man out of you!

CRAIG RUSSELL, actor and female impersonator, quoted by Ed Gould in *Entertaining Canadians: Canada's International Stars 1900-1988* (1988).

You were a slob in Moose Jaw and you're still a slob over here!

Familiar line from BBC Radio's *Breakfast with Braden*, a popular morning program starring BERNARD BRADEN and his wife BARBARA KELLY, both Canadian-born, Braden coming from Moose Jaw, Sask. The line was spoken by Kelly impersonating a member of the audience. Quoted by Ed Gould in *Entertaining Canadians: Canada's International Stars 1900-1988* (1988).

This country lacks the audacity to adore.

WILLIAM HUTT, actor, quoted by Keith Garebian in *William Hutt: A Theatre Portrait* (1988).

Politics is a lot like show business. One

day you are a hero and the next, you are a zero.

RENÉ SIMARD, singer who achieved initial success as a teenager, quoted by Lisa Van Dusen in *Maclean's*, 12 Sept. 1988.

In my case, it was strictly a love of movies and a great imagination, and wanting to be the people on the screen. As all kids do. I was so obsessed with it, I would walk around as John Wayne for weeks after seeing him in a movie. Or get rough with some of the kids in the neighbourhood as Humphrey Bogart.

RICH LITTLE, Ottawa-born impressionist, describing how he developed his skills, quoted in *The Winnipeg Free Press*, 31 Dec. 1988.

It's always something.

Catchphrase familiar from SCTV's *Saturday Night Live* used by the fictitious news commentator called Roseanne Roseannadanna, the creation of comic GILDA RADNER, *It's Always Something* (1989).

I can't believe they pay me to talk!

SHIRLEY SOLOMON, talkative, thoughtful host of CTV's *Shirley Show*, remark made to inteviewer George Anthony in 1989.

I'd already been in showbusiness a good many years, but I never became really well known until I played Canada. . . . When I went back to the States they advertised me as the Canadian comedian.

RED SKELTON, American comedian who attributes much of his popularity to performing onstage in Toronto and Montreal through 1939, quoted by John Lyons in *The Winnipeg Free Press*, 17 Nov. 1989.

It's nice to work in Canada, but it's like the beef industry, you have to stretch out a bit.

GEORGE FOX, country singer, quoted by Karen Morrison in *The Western Producer's Western People Magazine*, 19 April 1990.

I come from a country where confidence means arrogance, and people are threat-

ened by that. They want you to be uncomfortable with [success] or filled with that inertia that happens to a brand new star. And I'm not. I'm so level-headed it's disgusting.
ALANNAH MYLES, rock performer, quoted by John Lyons in *The Winnipeg Free Press*, 5 May 1990.

We get 3,000 letters a week, a lot from Canada. One thing about Canadians, they don't mail me their electric bills and ask me to pay for them — like some Americans have — and don't send me dirty responses when I don't. I love that.
OPRAH WINFREY, talk-show host, quoted by John Lynons in *The Winnipeg Free Press*, 18 March 1991.

SIBERIA
See also SOVIET UNION

History will tell you that at one time the Russian forces were engaged by the Chukchi, that is a group of native people that are in far Siberia. Believe it or not, their comrades-in-arms, the North American Eskimos, crossed back over to Siberia to come to the aid of the Chukchi in turning back the invasion of the Russian people. Of course the onslaught kept coming on, and it was not until by the 17th century the Russians had reached the Pacific, they had colonized Alaska, and they had established posts as far down as just fifty miles north of San Francisco.
STUART M. HODGSON, N.W.T. Commissioner, address, Empire Club of Canada, Toronto, 13 March 1975.

SICKNESS
See MEDICINE

SIKHS

We have all seen or heard about the rash of letters and petitions relative to my position on the subject of the turban becoming an acceptable part of the RCMP uniform.
My concern is not for the few dedicated

racists who are opposed to anyone or anything different from themselves, but rather with what appears to be a significant portion of well-meaning, intelligent, and educated people who are among the opponents to the changes that a multiracial society inevitably brings. These people would say that they are not racist, nor bigotted or discriminatory — rather, they are concerned about the changes occurring to Canada, its traditions and its institutions. I am prepared to accept them at their word.
NORMAN INKSTER, RCMP Commissioner, address, McMaster University, Hamilton, Ont., 3 March 1990.

SILENCE
See also SOUNDS
MUSIC

I have often / regretted my words, / never my silence.
NICHOLAS CATANOY, poet and aphorist, from "Notes on a Prison Wall (Fragment)," *Canadian Literature*, Summer 1988.

Lying flat on your back on Ellesmere Island on rolling tundra without animals, without human trace, you can feel the silence stretching all the way to Asia.
BARRY LOPEZ, naturalist, *Arctic Dreams: Imagination and Desire in a Northern Landscape* (1986).

"This is magnificent. This is what I have been waiting for. I shall support you by any means in my power, even to the point of total silence" (which I thought might be the best gift I could give him).
Contents of a note written in French, and sent to Pierre Elliott Trudeau in 1968 when he was conducting his leadership campaign, by EUGENE FORSEY, constitutional authority, *A Life on the Fringe: The Memoirs of Eugene Forsey* (1990).

SIN

Of course we have original sin. It can be called anything else you like, but it is the same thing. The way people are when they are born is not civilized. Therefore, it is sinful, because that is what sin is — not conforming to what is expected of one when one is grown up — and so of course we will have sin in that sense always with us.

G. BROCK CHISHOLM, psychiatrist, White Memorial Lecture, Washington, D.C., 23 Oct., 1945, published as *The Psychiatry of Enduring Peace and Social Progress* (1945).

Our forefathers willed this country into being. Time, circumstance and pure will cemented us together in a unique national enterprise, and that enterprise, by flying in the face of all expectations, of all experiences, of all conventional wisdom, that enterprise provides the world with a lesson in fraternity.

This extraordinary undertaking is so advanced on the road to liberty, so advanced in the way of social justice and prosperity, that to abandon it now would be to sin against the spirit: to sin against humanity.

PIERRE ELLIOTT TRUDEAU, Prime Minister, address on national radio and television in response to the election of a separatist government in Quebec, 24 Nov. 1976.

Many people think that sin is just an acronym for their social insurance number.

BETTY JANE WYLIE, author, *All in the Family: A Survival Guide for Living and Loving in a Changing World* (1988).

Sin has become merely a kind of psychological concept, as if that made it unreal.

ROBERTSON DAVIES, man-of-letters, interviewed by Terence M. Green in 1982, *Conversations with Robertson Davies* (1989) edited by J. Madison Davis.

SKIING
See also SPORTS

Cross country skiing is basically jogging while wearing lumber.

ARTHUR BLACK, broadcaster, "Cross Country Skiing," *Basic Black: The Wit and Whimsy of Arthur Black* (1981).

Downhill racing is a sport which sometimes leaves competitors permanently maimed. On rare occasions, it is a killer. The knowledge is stored in every cell of every racer's brain.

KEN READ, champion skier, *White Circus: A Skiing Life with the Crazy Canucks* (1987) written with Matthew Fisher.

Not bad for a Canadian, eh?

STEVE PODBORSKI, champion skier, first North American male to win the World Cup downhill title, quoted by Joey Slinger in *The Toronto Star*, 12 Dec. 1989.

SKY

Around the sky / I walk; / a bird / I accompany.

Ojibwa poem, "Around the Sky," *Songs of the Great Land* (1989) edited by John Robert Colombo.

Get the habit of looking at the sky. It is the source of light and art.

Aphorism associated with the Group of Seven, "The New Canadian Art," *The Daily Intelligencer* (Belleville, Ont.), 27 Sept. 1919.

That sky over Canada is always smiling — unbridled nature spread to the very pole — the green sky of summer and the white sky of winter.

ANDREI VOZNESENSKY, Russian poet, "North Country Passing," *Maclean's*, Dec. 1971.

The horizon means open your eyes on the unknown. It connects earth and sky, sea and sky. It reminds you of your real height and dimension. The horizon is invitation.

NICOLE BROSSARD, poet, interviewed by Clea Notar in *So to Speak: Interviews with Canadian Writers* (1987) edited by Peter O'Brien.

SLAVERY

I'm on my way to Canada / Where everyone is free, / So Goodnight, Old Master, /
Don't chase after me.
"Slave song," *To Master — A Long Goodnight: The Story of "Uncle Tom," A Historical Narrative* (1946) by BRION GYSIN.

Here the slave found freedom. Before the
United States Civil War of 1861-65 Windsor
was an important terminal of the Underground Railway. Escaping from bondage,
thousands of fugitive slaves from the
South, men, women, and children landing
near this spot found in Canada friends,
freedom, protection under the British flag.
Wording on a plaque unveiled in 1930 by
the Historic Sites and Monuments Board
at Windsor, Ont., quoted by Brion Gysin
in *To Master — A Long Goodnight: The
Story of "Uncle Tom," A Historical Narrative* (1946). "In the town of Windsor today
there is a bronze plaque placed on the
wall of a building which stands near the
terminal of the old ferry crossing the Detroit River. It reads. . . ."

Once in Canada he was, indeed, as the
captain who had carried him there said, a
man, and considered so by all around him.
No longer a chattel slave, no longer a fugitive in fear of his life, he must prove to
himself and to the world that he was capable of making full use of his freedom.
BRION GYSIN, Franco-American writer,
*To Master — A Long Goodnight: The Story
of "Uncle Tom," A Historical Narrative*
(1946).

Canada is not merely a neighbour of Ne-
groes. Deep in our history of struggle for
freedom Canada was the North Star. The
Negro slave, denied education, dehuman-
ized, imprisoned on cruel plantations,
knew that far to the north a land existed
where a fugitive slave if he survived the
horrors of the journey could find freedom.
MARTIN LUTHER KING, Jr., U.S. civil liberties leader and black spokesperson,
CBC Radio's Massey Lectures, Nov.-Dec.

1967, published as *The Trumpet of Conscience* (1967).

SLEEP

Sleep can be a positive addiction.
BETTY JANE WYLIE, author, *Successfully
Single* (1986).

In fact, for most of human history the only
thing we've really known for certain about
sleep is that we need it — that trying to do
without it will drop us in our tracks in very
short order.
LYDIA DOTTO, author, *Asleep in the Fast
Lane: The Impact of Sleep on Work* (1990).

SMELL

We may *think* that we react with selective
sensibility to the smell of flowers, or food,
or sex, but these are the coarsest of responses. A dog's world of scent is a dimension which we have totally forgotten.
JOHN A. LIVINGSTON, naturalist, *One
Cosmic Instant: A Natural History of Human
Arrogance* (1973).

SMOKING

I can't quite twist my mind around the
logic of a society that persecutes people
who smoke a legal product from which the
government derives considerable tax revenue. As a non-smoker, I can't say that
cigarettes are any more or less irritating
than the noise pollution of Muzak or the
radiation from video display terminals.
Cigarettes must be less dangerous than
the daily bombardment of car, paint and
construction fumes or acid rain fallout.
BARBARA AMIEL, columnist, *Maclean's*,
12 Dec. 1988.

When it comes to the quality of life, not to
mention longevity, I am not at all certain
that cigarettes are deadlier on the whole
than cars.
GEORGE FALUDY, Hungarian-born poet,
Notes from the Rainforest (1988).

Imagine what would happen if someone "discovered" the cigarette today. "Gentlemen, I have a glorious new product. It stinks like hell, gives you headaches, and makes your eyes water. It is more addictive than heroin and causes throat cancers, lung cancer, emphysema, and heart disease. It's expensive, messy, a potential fire hazard, and possibly fatal to innocent bystanders. Now what am I bid?"

Not only would cigarettes not be accepted, authorities would probably throw the discoverer in the slammer, along with the rest of the drug pushers.

> ARTHUR BLACK, broadcaster and humorist, "Smoking Can Be Dangerous to Your Health," *That Old Black Magic* (1989).

I predict that ashtrays will become as obsolete as spitoons in our lifetime.

> ARTHUR BLACK, broadcaster and humorist, "Smoking Can Be Dangerous to Your Health," *That Old Black Magic* (1989).

Consider also tobacco. Health statistics show that 35,000 Canadians die each year as a result of smoking. They die painfully, horribly and very expensively. Yet governments allow the sale of tobacco and only demand that a small warning appear on cigarette packages. Revenues from the tax on tobacco sales are huge.

> PHILIPPE DEANE GIGANTES, author and Senator, *The Road Ahead* (1990).

The smoking of cigarettes will have virtually stopped by the year 2010, and the consumption of alcohol will become an antiquated habit clung to by only a few of the older generation.... By the year 2000, many large North American cities will have declared themselves smoke-free locations, banning outside and inside use of tobacco entirely except for private homes and designated "Smoke-rooms" in certain public buildings.

> MAURICE B. COOKE, channeller, *The Aquarian Wave: A Prophetic Handbook for the 90s* (1990).

SNAKES

No ancient fear is more deeply etched in our primate memory than the fear of snakes. A snake does not make himself visible until that last split-second when we are about to walk on him, and then we congeal with terror. It is a long, long memory which goes back to the time we were small animals and snakes were more common than they are today.

> JOHN A. LIVINGSTON, naturalist, *One Cosmic Instant: A Natural History of Human Arrogance* (1973).

SNOW
See also ICE

Terrible with snow.

> Epithetical description of the Arctic shores as known to the Greeks, who called the Arctic Ocean the Northern Ocean or the Hyperborean Sea at the time of PYTHEAS of Marseilles about 330 B.C., according to Barry Lopez in *Arctic Dreams: Imagination and Desire in a Northern Landscape* (1986).

Maybe you live somewhere that doesn't have snow in April; if so, I hope you appreciate it.

> Line from the novel *Time Pressure* (1987) by the novelist SPIDER ROBINSON who soon thereafter resettled from Halifax to Vancouver.

In the winter the beauty is even stronger. The Prairies eliminate the obviousness of a horizon and leave the traveller with the magnificence of an infinite blank page, land blending with sky. I have never understood "snow" to be a derogatory term.

> ALBERTO MANGUEL, editor and writer, "Prairie Zen," *The Globe and Mail's Destinations Magazine*, April 1988.

The Eskimos, I'm told, have seventeen different words for shades of *white*. This is even more than there are in *my* imagination.

> DIANA VREELAND, U.S. fashion personal-

ity, *D.V.: Diana Vreeland* (1984) edited by George Plimpton and Christopher Hemphill.

SOCIAL CREDIT
See also POLITICS

Alberta will kindle a world-wide torch.
Cable message sent by WILLIAM ABERH-ART, newly elected Premier of Alberta, to Hewlett Johnson, so-called Red Dean of Canterbury, when the Social Credit Party was swept into power, 22 Aug. 1935.

In the province of Alberta where the Social Credit Party had its original flowering, Bible Bill Aberhart used to conduct his campaigns in a most dramatic fashion. I am told by those who lived in Alberta in those days that when he addressed a public meeting he would have a huge cheque and a vast pen ready. He would call out, "Is there anyone out there who would like to come up and write a cheque for Alberta?" A young man would immediately run up — it was always the same young man — and write a cheque for $25 payable to every citizen in Alberta.
That young man rose through the ranks and later became premier of Alberta. When he arrived at that position of high eminence, however, the ink had run dry, and it was only the oil bubbling from the ground that allowed him to distribute largesse among the people in a conservative fashion.
A.C. ABBOTT, M.P., House of Commons, 11 July 1975. Abbott, the Liberal Member for Mississauga, Ont., was referring to Aberhart's successor as party leader and Premier, Ernest Manning.

Seventy-five per cent of those who voted for me don't expect any dividend, but hope for a just and honest government.
WILLIAM ABERHART, Alberta Premier, *The New York Times*, 1 Sept. 1935, quoted by John J. Barr in *The Dynasty: The Rise and Fall of Social Credit in Alberta* (1974).

What is Social Credit? Elect me and I'll find out.
MARGARET (MA) MURRAY, pioneer newspaper publisher and Social Credit candidate, campaign slogan in the early 1950s, quoted in *The Toronto Star*, 26 April 1981.

Try us out. You have nothing to lose.
RÉAL CAOUETTE, Créditiste leader, campaign oratory, quoted by Pierre Sévigny in *This Game of Politics* (1965).

All that is physically possible and desirable must be made financially possible. That's the beginning and end of Social Credit.
W.A.C. BENNETT, Social Crediter and former B.C. Premier, defining Social Credit, quoted by Ric Dolphin in *Maclean's*, 18 July 1988.

There is a bit of a Social Crediter in every Canadian.
ALAIN DUBUC, journalist, *La Presse*, 8 June 1988, quoted by Gilberte Côté-Mercier in *Michael: For the Triumph of the Immaculate*, Sept.-Oct. 1988.

SOCIAL DEMOCRACY

But most Canadians indicated, as they had for generations, that they wanted social democracy without social democrats.
DESMOND MORTON, historian, "Strains of Affluence 1945-1987," *The Illustrated History of Canada* (1987) edited by Craig Brown.

SOCIAL PROGRAMS
See also SACRED TRUST

What was good for Mackenzie King is not necessarily good for Canada today, to coin a phrase.
BRIAN MULRONEY, Prime Minister, attempting to justify the attempt in 1983 to de-index pensions and limit their universality, quoted by Claire Hoy in *Friends in High Places: Politics and Patronage in the Mulroney Government* (1987).

All our experience is in gearing society up. We have no experience at all in gearing one down.

URSULA FRANKLIN, scientist and specialist on the conserver society, address, Empire Club of Canada, Toronto, 30 March 1978.

Hard times have demonstrated how easily we sacrifice the care of the young, the old, the sick, and the helpless. The fragile state of social order and tolerance cannot withstand the pressures of mass unemployment and growing economic disparity. The smug assumptions of our peaceable kingdom depend more on recent prosperity than on our long-term history.

DESMOND MORTON and TERRY COPP, historians, *Working People* (rev. ed., 1984).

Our social safety-net — unemployment insurance (including, in this hostile climate, insurance against the perils of seasonal work), family allowances, universal old age pensions, maybe some day (certainly before the U.S.) a national day-care program — is the product of many factors: our history, our heritage, our need to huddle together against the cold. We are a scattered people, thinly spread across a forbidding landscape. There aren't enough of us to entice private capital to establish the institutions that, in other societies, define a nation and tie it together. So, instead, we've used public capital.

PETER GZOWSKI, host of CBC Radio's *Morningside*, in *The Private Voice: A Journal of Reflections* (1988).

I'm very optimistic about Canada. It may not have the largest military force or the biggest and fastest satellite, but it will, I think, be a wonderful country and it will continue to afford a quality and standard of living that will be envied by most of the world.

TREVOR EYTON, corporate head, quoted by Alexander R. Aird, Paul Nowack, and James W. Westcott, authors, *Road to the*

Top: The Chief Executive Officer in Canada (1988).

The countries who look after people the best compete the best and have far fewer social problems. Almost all the northern countries of Europe look after people better than we do with more generous maternity leave, child care, family benefits and less of a gap between the wages of men and women.

Canada should be modelling itself after them rather than the socially backward nation to our south.

DORIS ANDERSON, writer, "Symposium," *The Canadian Forum*, Jan. 1990.

Our "more caring and compassionate" society is really a giant levelling operation — the politics of envy compounded with a paralytic national feature of failure. In fiscal and constitutional terms, that fear is now very well founded and there is no international welfare system to care compassionately for mismanaged countries.

CONRAD BLACK, capitalist and columnist, "Enough Is Enough," *Saturday Night*, Sept. 1990.

A decent society provides a ladder up which all may climb and a net beneath which none may fall.

Anonymous formulation quoted by William D. Gairdner in *The Trouble with Canada* (1990).

SOCIALISM
See also NEW DEMOCRATIC PARTY

From a thousand hills a thousand rills gather into a mighty river which sweeps on to the ocean. An attempt to dam the Niagara, in the hope that it would never reach the sea, would be no more foolish than the attempt to dam labour from its resistless onward sweep towards its natural outlet — co-operative industry.

F.J. (FRED) DIXON, charged with seditious conspiracy in connection with the Winnipeg General Strike, address to the jury, Winnipeg, Feb. 13-14, 1920.

The main business of socialist parties is not to form governments but to change minds.
> Attributed to CARLYLE KING, socialist and teacher associated with the development of the CCF/NDP in western Canada.

We do not oppose the making of profit in all its forms; on the contrary, the profit motive, under proper control, is now and will be for a long time a most valuable stimulus to production. Not a single democratic socialist party anywhere plans to nationalize all forms of production, and in the privately owned sector the profit motive must continue.
> F.R. SCOTT, lawyer, address as National Chairman of the CCF in 1950, quoted by T.H. McLeod in *The Canadian Forum*, Nov. 1989.

The trouble with socialists is that they let their bleeding hearts go to their bloody heads.
> T.C. (TOMMY) DOUGLAS, CCF/NDP leader, quoted by J.L. Granatstein in *The Globe and Mail*, 16 July 1988.

Comradely greetings from the weakest socialist organization in the Western Hemisphere to the strongest one, the CCF of Canada. It is a comfort to have a big strong brother next door to me.
> Message from the American Social Democratic Federation, tabled at the CCF Convention in 1956, quoted by Gad Horowitz in *Canadian Labour in Politics* (1968).

In Canada, socialism is British, non-Marxist, and worldly; in the United States it is German, Marxist, and otherworldly.
> GAD HOROWITZ, political scientist, *Canadian Labour in Politics* (1968).

Socialism is a process and a programme. The process is the raising of socialist consciousness, the building of a mass base of socialists, and a strategy to make visible the limits of liberal capitalism.
> While the programme must evolve out of the process, its leading features seem

clear. Relevant instruments for bringing the Canadian economy under Canadian ownership and control for altering the priorities established by corporate capitalism are to hand.
> "The Waffle Manifesto: For an Independent Socialist Canada" (1969) reprinted in *The Canadian Forum*, Dec. 1989.

A socialist society must be one in which there is democratic control of all institutions which have a major effect on men's lives and where there is equal opportunity for creative non-exploitative self-development. It is now time to go beyond the welfare state.
> "The Waffle Manifesto: For an Independent Socialist Canada" (1969) reprinted in *The Canadian Forum*, Dec. 1989.

The major threat to Canadian survival today is American control of the Canadian economy. The major issue of our times is not national unity but national survival, and the fundamental threat is external, not internal.
> "The Waffle Manifesto: For an Independent Socialist Canada" (1969) reprinted in *The Canadian Forum*, Dec. 1989.

Socialist hordes.
> Phrase associated with B.C. Social Credit Premier W.A.C. BENNETT, quoted in *The Vancouver Province*, 22 Aug. 1972, as noted by Ivan Avakumovic in *Socialism in Canada: A Study of the CCF-NDP in Federal and Provincial Politics* (1978).

A reference to socialism isn't quite as alarming in Canada as it is in the States.
> JOHN KENNETH GALBRAITH, economist and author, quoted by Robert Lewis in *Maclean's*, 9 Feb. 1976.

As I said to Harrington, "You've got the thinkers and we've got the movement."
> ED BROADBENT, NDP leader, referring to a discusson with Michael Harrington of the Democratic Socialists of America, quoted by Judy Steed in *Ed Broadbent: The Pursuit of Power* (1988).

What virtually all Americans, and too many Canadians who deal in the international world of money, fail utterly to understand is that Canada is that political oddity, a socialist monarchy.

ROBERTSON DAVIES, man-of-letters, Neil Gunn lecture, Edinburgh University, June 1988, published in *The Times Literary Supplement*, 30 Sept. 1988.

If there is anything worse than a socialist it is a sanctimonious socialist.

BRIAN MULRONEY, Prime Minister, referring to NDP leader Ed Broadbent, *The Toronto Star*, 25 April 1985.

As for today's Messrs. Rae and Broadbent, they are splendid chaps, I know. But I, a descendant of a Grand Master of the Orange Lodge, ask you: What are we to make of socialists who are regularly upstaged by Catholic bishops?

MEL WATKINS, political economist, contributor to *If I Were Prime Minister* (1987). This is a reference to Bob Rae, Ontario NDP leader, and national NDP leader Ed Broadbent as well as to a report critical of the economic policies of the federal government written by Roman Catholic bishops led by Remi J. De Roo, Bishop of Victoria, B.C.

I'm a socialist, so I've learned patience.

STEPHEN LEWIS, UN Ambassador, quoted by Tim Tiner in *Now*, 7 July 1988.

Ed Broadbent / A dedicated socialist who means what he says. He doesn't believe in free enterprise. He doesn't believe in free trade. He's very, very scary.

Message conveyed by the National Citizens' Coalition in advertisements in newspapers across the country prior to the federal election of Nov. 1988.

Socialism is the wave of the future, precisely because it is the fulfillment of democracy. The old parties will continue to steal NDP policies, but they cannot steal the basic commitment which is the soul of the party.

DONALD C. MacDONALD, socialist, *The Happy Warrior: Political Memoirs* (1988).

Democratic socialism of the Canadian and Swedish kind has worked in that it has forced unbridled capitalism to the middle and we have come up with a kind of welfare capitalism or capitalism with a safety net. But even Canadian-style socialists may end up embracing the market because they will recognize that pluralism and giving people maximum opportunity is what they were really after in the first place.

PAUL MARANTZ, academic, University of British Columbia, quoted in *The Toronto Star*, 30 Sept. 1989.

You have no idea how wonderful it is for an American to hear Canadian socialists debate how to defend something we can hardly dream of having in the States.

MICHAEL HARRINGTON, American author and socialist, speaking to Ontario NDP leader Bob Rae, who quoted the remark in Harrington's obituary in *The Toronto Star*, 7 Aug. 1989.

At N.D.P. gatherings, there is no shyness about the word "socialism." To pronounce it is a kind of credential to prove oneself to be something (or not something else). We may well ask what the S-word now means, and whether the words "left" and "right" are now clear enough for the N.D.P. to be even divided along such lines.

GERALD OWEN, social commentator, "Class Struggle in the N.D.P.," *The Idler*, No. 17, Jan.-Feb. 1990.

In short, we must see socialism as embracing a creative tension between three realities: planning, democracy, and markets. If we ignore any of them, we are in trouble.

BOB RAE, NDP leader, address, "A Socialist's Manifesto," *The Globe and Mail*, 1 Oct. 1990.

Socialism is not a religion. It is no guarantor of personal spiritual happiness. It cannot protect us from all the tragedies of life.

Politics should not try to do too much. But it must do what it can.
> BOB RAE, NDP leader, address, "A Socialist's Manifesto," *The Globe and Mail*, 1 Oct. 1990.

SOCIETY
See also The ESTABLISHMENT
CLASS, SOCIAL

In the dead silence of the night you hear a distant but monotonous sound — Sir Gilbert Parker, climbing, climbing, climbing.
> BEATRICE WEBB, British socialist, diary entry in 1904, referring to the Canadian-born historical novelist, British Parliamentarian, and socialite, quoted by Carole Gerson in *A Purer Taste: The Writing and Reading of Fiction in English in 19th Century Canada* (1989).

We were located half way up the social ladder. Or half way down. It depends on which way you're looking.
> BEATRICE LILLIE, Canadian-born singer-comedienne, describing her humble beginnings in the 1910s in what she called "Orange Toronto," quoted by Donald Jones in *The Toronto Star*, 5 Aug. 1989.

Possibly it is true, as many non-WASPSs suggest, that we are hard to get along with. But then you must understand, our lives have been difficult. Running the world all these years has not been easy for us.
> ROBERT FULFORD, journalist, "On Being a WASP" (1968), *Crisis at the Victory Burlesk* (1968).

One of the things that has always puzzled me is that there is an identifiable class that *rules* Canada — the sociologists John Porter and Wallace Clement have documented what we've known for a long time — and it is class-conscious and becoming more entrenched. But there isn't an identifiable, let alone a class-conscious, class of the *ruled*. That's the NDP's dilemma now — how to convince people who live in a welfare state that they ought to want a socialist state.

> DAVID LEWIS, NDP leader, quoted by Christina Newman in *The Globe and Mail*, 10 June 1975.

In a truly responsible society, each individual has a responsibility to do his utmost to improve his own lot, and to contribute to the improvement of the society around him. Government's responsibility should be to provide a climate which fosters and rewards initiative at all levels of society.
> STEPHEN B. ROMAN, Chairman, Denison Mines Limited, address, Empire Club of Canada, Toronto, 16 Nov. 1978.

The four main villains in this loss of common sense in our society, the four horsemen of the modern apocalypse, are the politicians, the academics and intellectuals, the church and the media, not necessarily in that order. The masses, the people who work for a living, *have* common sense.
> PETER WORTHINGTON, newspaperman, address, Empire Club of Canada, Toronto, 8 March 1979.

Human communities are defined by a hierarchy of affluence and power in which those at the top have an interest in maintaining existing social relationships, while those at the bottom have an incentive for change.
> S.E.D. SHORTT, historian, Preface, *Victorian Lunacy: Richard M. Bucke and the Practice of Late Nineteenth-Century Psychiatry* (1986).

My own model of the ideal society is a libertarian and participatory one of a loose confederation of co-operative working groups and of neighbourhood associations coming together to administer their mutual interests, with co-operation and consensus rather than coercion and dominating principle, and with most of the action going on at the lower levels of the pyramid, where people's real interests lie, and very little left to be dealt with on a national level.

GEORGE WOODCOCK, author and social commentator, contributor to *If I Were Prime Minister* (1987) edited by Mel Hurtig.

For our society is changing. Once egg-shaped, with a large middle class, it is beginning to resemble a pear, with a small economic and social elite at the top, and a growing number of Canadians at the bottom facing reduced potential and fewer prospects.
MAUDE BARLOW, human-relations consultant, quoted in *The Ottawa Citizen*, 27 April 1988.

Saidye Bronfman: You've come a long way for a St. Urbain boy.
Mordecai Richler: And you've come a long way for a bootlegger's wife.
This exchange is said to have taken place between SAIDYE BRONFMAN, wife of the bootlegger-turned-distiller Sam Bronfman, and the author MORDECAI RICHLER at the Montreal premiere in 1973 of the movie *The Apprenticeship of Duddy Kravitz* based on his novel. Noted by Ed Gould in *Entertaining Canadians: Canada's International Stars 1900-1988* (1988).

For better and worse, Toronto became the only Canadian city where belonging to the local elite qualified one for cross-country status.
PETER C. NEWMAN, business columnist, "The Business of Change," *The 1980s: Maclean's Chronicles the Decade* (1989) edited by Kevin Doyle and Ann Johnston.

I love the natural environment of Canada. I'm not so pleased about the society, which is becoming increasingly vulgar, and hostile to quality. What we're involved in here is so marginal as to be almost invisible. That's why I like to go to Europe, where they still understand what quality means.
R. MURRAY SCHAFER, composer, quoted by Robert Everett-Green in *The Globe and Mail*, 16 Feb. 1991.

SOLAR ENERGY
See also ENERGY

In 1976, I was invited by . . . the New Alchemy Institute . . . to attend the official dedication by Canadian Prime Minister Pierre Trudeau of the Prince Edward Island Ark. The Ark is an experimental building, known as a bioshelter, combining the elements of a farm, a house, and, through its use of solar and wind power, an electrical generator. Its construction was approved by the provincial government of Prince Edward Island (one of the Maritime Provinces) as an alternative to a nuclear reactor, and on the day it opened it did indeed feed energy back into the island's power network. . . .
The entire south face of the Ark is covered in glass and solar panels. As I stood there, it caught the light of the sun and sky and was simply transformed into a building of light. It became ethereal, a temple of fire, and I felt myself transported into a place of rapture, a mythic realm where all the earth sang in a unity of joy. The Ark seemed to be the outpost of true planetary culture.
DAVID SPANGLER, U.S. speaker and writer about the New Age, *Emergence: The Rebirth of the Sacred* (1984). The Ark was designed to demonstrate the principles of ecological living and energy–saving on an island possessing no hydro-electric or nuclear-power generating stations of its own. It proved costly to maintain and is now abandoned.

I am a strong believer in the safe use of nuclear energy — really safe, because you don't do such things foolishly. If we don't experiment and utilize the new science, we will be the losers. I am worried about the kind of world in which everyone's grandchildren will be living, including my own. The Third World needs more and more of what energy resources there are, and we are going to run out of oil. Solar energy is a long way from being implementable economically. The most knowledgeable people in solar energy talk about the year 2025, and even then solar may produce ten percent of our needs — no more.

> LEO YAFFE, nuclear scientist and advocate of the peaceful use of the atom, "The Nuclear Chemist as a Man of Peace," *The Worst of Times / The Best of Times* (1987).

SOLITUDE

I have sometimes felt, to the point of suffocation, my people's bitter solitude in the universe.

> ANDRÉ LAURENDEAU, newspaperman, discussing conscription in Quebec, *La Crise de la Conscription* (1962), as quoted by Lise Bissonnette in *The Globe and Mail*, 19 Aug. 1989.

SONGS

See also MUSIC

Listen friends, / our neighbours, the birds, / are singing. / Pleasant are the sounds. / Let us sing with them. / Listen friends; / you will enjoy / the sounds *we* make.

> Ojibwa poem, "Singer's Song," *Songs of the Great Land* (1989) edited by John Robert Colombo.

When the words we want to use shoot up of themselves — we get a new song.

> ORPINGALIK, Inuit singer, quoted by Edmund Carpenter in "The Eskimo and His Art" (1970), *Canada: A Guide to the Peaceable Kingdom* (1970) edited by William Kilbourn.

Here, thus abandoned, I lie unrepenting, / And in the Saviour I have faith, unrelenting; / Oh, Holy Virgin, unfold your arms to me, / There would I lie for all eternity.

> JEAN CADIEUX, the legendary voyageur, is considered the composer of the lyrics of "Petit Rocher" ("Little Rock") also known as "La Complainte de Cadieux" ("The Lament of Cadieux"). He penned the song in his own blood on birchbark after seeing his family escape but suffering mortal wounds in the hands of the Iroquois on the Ottawa River in 1709.

I'm so young and you're so old / This my darling I've been told / I don't care just what they say / 'Cause forever I will pray / You and I will be as free / As the birds up in the trees / Oh please stay with me, Diana.

> PAUL ANKA, songwriter and performer, "Diana" (1957), an international hit song.

Four strong winds that blow lonely, / Seven seas that run high, / All those things that don't change come what may, / But our good times are all gone. And I'm bound for movin' on, / I'll look for you if I'm ever back this way.

> IAN TYSON, songwriter and singer, refrain of "Four Strong Winds" (1963), closely identified with Ian and Sylvia.

And you want to travel with her, / And you want to travel blind; / And you know that you can trust her, / For she's touched your perfect body with her mind.

> LEONARD COHEN, composer and singer, refrain of "Suzanne," introduced at the Newport and Mariposa folk festivals in 1967.

The city life / of flashing lights / busy streets / and fancy cars, / booze and drugs / and all the plugs . . . / I'm a star in New York / I'm a star in L.A.

> GENE WILLIAMS, lyricist, first verse of "From N.Y. to L.A." (1976), a disco version sung by Patsy Gallant of Gilles Vigneault's semi-anthem "Mon Pays.

If there has been any secret to my life, it is that I've loved every minute of my chosen career. I walk onto a stage and I know I'm going to have a good time, and the audience senses that joy.

> MAUREEN FORRESTER, opera singer, *Out of Character: A Memoir* (1986) written with Marci McDonald.

We are here to give forth emotions, ideas, thoughts. You know, the vocal cords lie in a very strange place, right here in the throat just a little bit above the heart, a little bit above the soul. I sincerely feel

that however you are feeling spiritually definitely affects the performance as a whole.
> TERESA STRATAS, opera singer, interviewed by Ulla Colgrass in *For the Love of Music* (1988).

Singing is the ultimate. It's a very emotional thing, very emotional to turn yourself inside out and ride each nuance and each note. It's what I live for.
> K.D. LANG, singer and songwriter, quoted in *The Winnipeg Free Press*, June 2, 1990.

It used to be — before the electronic media took over so strongly — that one of the ways people entertained themselves was by *entertaining themselves*. Families used to sit at the piano and sing together. But people got more and more plugged into television and computers, and music just got pushed aside.
> BRAM MORRISON, member of the Sharon, Lois, and Bram musical troup of children's entertainers, quoted by Barbara Wade Rose in "The Entertainers," *Imperial Oil Review*, Summer 1990.

SOPHISTICATION

Canadian reserve, I decided long ago, is a more impressive quality than New York sophistication.
> GEORGE FALUDY, Hungarian-born poet, *Reflections from a Rainforest* (1988).

SOULS
See also SPIRIT

Souls are not fashionable, at present. People will listen with wondering acquiescence to scientific talk of such invisible entities as are said to be everywhere and very important, but they shy away from talk of souls. Souls have a bad name in the world of atomic energy.
> ROBERTSON DAVIES, man-of-letters, *The Lyre of Orpheus* (1988).

SOUNDS
See also NOISE
SILENCE

The Arctic Ocean can seem utterly silent on a summer day to an observer standing far above. If you lowered a hydrophone, however, you would discover a sphere of "noise" that only spectrum analyzers and tape recorders could unravel.
> BARRY LOPEZ, naturalist, *Arctic Dreams: Imagination and Desire in a Northern Landscape* (1986).

SOUTH AFRICA

There will always be a light in the window for South Africa.
> Attributed to Prime Minister JOHN G. DIEFENBAKER by Secretary of State Joe Clark, Royal Commonwealth Society, London, 29 July 1985. Diefenbaker, at the 1961 Commonwealth Conference, to protest South Africa's apartheid policy, arranged for the country's expulsion from the Commonwealth.

You keep your Red Indians on reserves.
> P.W. BOTHA, President of the Republic of South Africa, to the correspondent Michael Valpy at a reception in Cape Town, recalled on Botha's retirement, by Valpy in *The Globe and Mail*, 16 Aug. 1989

I try to occupy the high moral ground so that the future leaders of South Africa will know where Canada stood.
> BRIAN MULRONEY, Prime Minister, explaining his government's opposition to the apartheid policy of the Republic of South Africa, which takes the form of maintaining limited trade embargoes, Commonwealth Conference, Kuala Lumpur, quoted by Val Sears in *The Toronto Star*, 24 Oct. 1989.

SOUTH AMERICA

Canadians have generally ignored Latin America, yet it may prove to be one of the most turbulent regions of the world over the next twenty-five years. Only one Canadian has been involved in peacekeeping there. It is earnestly hoped that he will remain the only one.

FRED GAFFEN, historian with the Canadian War Museum in Ottawa, *In the Eye of the Storm: A History of Canadian Peacekeeping* (1987). The sole Canadian peacekeeper in Latin America was Lt.-Col. P.A. Mayer, who served in the Dominican Republic in 1965-66.

The countries of South America will feel strong pressures to unite economically and otherwise as a result of widespread earthquake activity taking place with increasing severity during the 1990s. The resulting destruction and loss of life will infuse millions of people with feelings of brotherhood and a need to rescue those whose nations have been the most affected.

MAURICE B. COOKE, channeller, *The Aquarian Wave: A Prophetic Handbook for the 90s* (1990).

SOVEREIGNTY, NATIONAL

See also SOVEREIGNTY-ASSOCIATION

The most urgent issue for Canadians is the very survival of Canada. Anxiety is pervasive and the goal of great economic independence receives widespread support. But economic independence without socialism is a sham, and neither are meaningful without true participatory democracy.

"The Waffle Manifesto: For an Independent Socialist Canada" (1969) reprinted in *The Canadian Forum*, Dec. 1989.

We used to be a nation which set its own standards. . . . What happened to the sovereignty of our great country?

SHEILA COPPS, politician and feminist, *Nobody's Baby: A Survival Guide to Politics* (1986).

What we're talking about is sovereignty association between Canada and the U.S.; whether that's a cute phrase or not, that is exactly what we're talking about.

CARL BEIGIE, economist, former director of the C.D. Howe Institute, quoted by Mel Hurtig in an address to the Council of Canadians, Ottawa, 19 Oct. 1986.

I'm not sure I fully understand and I am not sure what it actually means. In many ways, it appears to be guises for protectionism.

PETER MURPHY, chief U.S. negotiator of Free Trade, professing suspicion or admitting confusion about cultural sovereignty, quoted by Derrick de Kerckhove in *The Canadian Forum*, Oct. 1989.

My own term for the phenomenon is "neo-independence." Traditional nation-states are losing sovereignty, either to the general forces of the global marketplace or to the specific rules imposed upon member states by the new economic groups — the European Community, the North American Free Trade Area.

In a parallel development, the cohesion of the Soviet empire is being eroded irreversibly by the collapse of the credibility of communism. Neo-independence thus is suddenly a practical, attainable step. . . . Neo-independence is an idea whose time has come. Its probable forms are unpredictable.

RICHARD GWYN, correspondent, *The Toronto Star*, 4 Oct. 1989.

Our interpretation of sovereignty is that one nation is sovereign; the other nation is sovereign; the tree is sovereign; the ocean is sovereign; the mountains are sovereign, and all work together to help each other and we form one earth, one unit.

ANDREW DELISLE, Mohawk observer, Parti Québécois convention, Quebec City, 27 Jan. 1991, quoted by Rhéal Séguin in *The Globe and Mail* the following day.

If you want to know who is going to change this country, go home and look in the mirror.
MAUDE BARLOW, Chairperson, Council of Canadians, address, Toronto, 25 May 1991.

SOVEREIGNTY-ASSOCIATION
See also QUEBEC
SEPARATISM
SOVEREIGNTY, NATIONAL

We have no wish to destroy. Our wish is to transform radically our union with the rest of Canada so that henceforth our relations may be conducted on a basis of complete equality. Sovereignty and association should therefore be achieved simultaneously and without rupture, after the people of Quebec have, through their decision in the referendum, given us a mandate to do so.
RENÉ LÉVESQUE, Quebec Premier, address, Quebec National Assembly, 10 Oct. 1978.

While I am on this subject, I would like to address myself to another cliché, that of the third option. Mr. Speaker, it has become somewhat fashionable to say: "I am not for the status quo, I am not for separatism, but there should be some compromise, a third option." I would simply like to warn my fellow-citizens not to fall in this trap, Mr. Speaker, because we never did invent this third option, the alternative to separatism and federalism — I am not saying status quo, but federalism. There is something called sovereignty assocation. . . . Now, Mr. Speaker, what is meant by this association? Are they trying to square the circle or what?
PIERRE ELLIOTT TRUDEAU, Prime Minister, House of Commons, 19 Oct. 1977.

In fact, sovereignty association implies by definition reshaping Canada. It can be a tremendous and valuable challenge for both our communities.
PIERRE-MARC JOHNSON, Quebec Minis-

ter of Labour, address, Empire Club of Canada, Toronto, 25 Oct. 1979.

Sovereignty does not go without association — they are inseparable.
The New Quebec-Canada Entente: A Proposition of the Quebec Government for an Agreement Between Equals — Sovereignty-Association (1979).

Sovereignty means the right to communicate freely with whomever we want, without being obliged to ask permission sometime almost like children who ask permission to pee at school.
RENÉ LÉVESQUE, Quebec Premier, Montreal rally, 21 Oct. 1979, quoted by William Johnson in *The Globe and Mail*, 29 Oct. 1979.

Un Québec independant dans un Canada uni!
YVON DESCHAMPS, comedian, defining an ideal state for Quebec within and without Canada, quoted by Richard Gwyn in *The Toronto Star*, 4 Oct. 1989. "An independent Quebec within a united Canada."

Un Québec souverain.
Cry heard at the post-election rally for the Parti Québécois, Repentigny, Que., 25 Sept. 1989, quoted by Graham Fraser in *The Globe and Mail* the following day. "A Sovereign Quebec."

I am a souvereignist because it does not make sense to spend half our time trying to prevent the rest of Canada from functioning normally, while in return, facing hurdles preventing us from functioning normally.
JACQUES PARIZEAU, P.Q. leader, quoted in *The Globe and Mail*, 27 Oct. 1989.

We can't say what might happen with Meech Lake, what kind of political superstructure could result. . . . I wasn't thinking of sovereignty-assocation, but I was evoking an economic superstructure like the European Common Market.
ROBERT BOURASSA, Quebec Premier, presenting industrialists in West Ger-

many with his new monetary and fiscal model for the relationship between Quebec and the rest of Canada, 29 Jan. 1990, quoted in *The Toronto Star* on 31 Jan. 1990 and on 1 Feb. 1990.

That's a wondrous label, because even if it sounds like simultaneous virginity and motherhood, it signifies anything we want it to mean.
PETER C. NEWMAN, columnist, *Maclean's*, 20 Aug. 1990.

If a Canadian *bonne entente* was really an offer, Quebec too would have to ask itself whether independence, with all its risks and renunciations, as well as exaltations of soul, were really preferable to "conditional federalism" with all its frustrations and uncertainties.
CONRAD BLACK, capitalist and columnist, "Enough Is Enough," *Saturday Night*, Sept. 1990.

Quebec should not imagine its departure would leave English Canadians hopeless, any more than English Canadians should imagine an independent Quebec would be a failure. In a sense both would enjoy a liberation, not the least from each other. But both would also lose an opportunity, and in an important way would have failed. Whatever happens, Canadians, French and English, will remain a reasonably talented people inhabiting a rich territory and enjoying brighter prospects than our current political institutions do. The world and posterity would rightly regard the dissolution of so promising a country and the squandering of so great an opportunity as a scandal and a profanation, but, if Canadians don't really wish to avoid that fate, it will eventually befall us. Whatever our destiny, it should be one we choose, not one imposed upon us by our own lassitude.
CONRAD BLACK, capitalist and columnist, "Enough Is Enough," *Saturday Night*, Sept. 1990.

The slogan of the federalist side during the 1980 referendum on sovereignty-association perfectly captured this divided loyalty: Le Québec, ma patrie; le Canada, mon pays. (Quebec, my homeland; Canada, my country.)
LYSIANE GAGNON, columnist, "Inside Quebec," *The Globe and Mail*, 16 Feb. 1991.

The truth is that sovereignty-association in any form is a horse that can't run. If Quebec insists on becoming a foreign country, we can negotiate that. It will not be easy. It will not be pleasant. It will impoverish us all, spiritually as well as materially. It will be a tragedy. But it can be done. But there is no way to negotiate dry water, boiling ice, sour sugar or stationary motion. Some people think that we should be willing to swallow any kind of nonsense in order to "preserve the unity of Canada."
I am not interested in a Canada that would be just a splash on the map, with a six-letter word scrawled across it. The only Canada I want to preserve is a Canada that can do something, for its own people, for the hungry two-thirds of the world, for the survival of the planet; not a phantom that can only watch helplessly as we all tumble down a steep place to destruction.
EUGENE FORSEY, constitutional expert, "No Surrender," *The Toronto Star*, 24 Feb. 1991.

Sovereignty may happen in Quebec. But if it happens, it will be tough, it will be painful, it will be hard!
BENOÎT BOUCHARD, Minister of Industry, Science, and Technology, interviewed in Montreal by Graham Fraser in *The Globe and Mail*, 7 March 1991.

SOVIET UNION
See also COMMUNISM

I thank you, Mr. Prime Minister, and ask you to convey my gratitude to the Government and people of Canada for their congratulations to the Soviet people, Government and Soviet Armed Forces on the occasion of the final victory over Germany. I congratulate you on this great victory.

JOSEPH STALIN, Soviet wartime leader and dictator, exchanging letters with Prime Minister Mackenzie King on the occasion of V-E Day; quoted by V. Makhotin in *USSR-Canada: Good-Neighbourly Co-operation* (1974) issued by the Novosti Press Agency Publishing House, Moscow.

Indeed, there was evidence of fresh East-West tension wherever one turned, as Ehrenburg himself found out when he paid a brief visit to Canada. The first question put to him was what did he think of the Soviet spy network, the first of the major postwar sensations of its kind, which had just been uncovered there? Ehrenburg gave a predictable answer: that the story had been blown up solely in order to poison East-West relations. All the same, he was profoundly depressed. For someone who had once hoped so ardently for East-West understanding, it was not pleasant to see an espionage scandal making nonsense of such hopes.

ANATOL GOLDBERG, U.S. commentator, describing the Russian writer Ilya Ehrenburg's reaction to the Gouzenko Affair during a postwar visit to Canada, *Ilya Ehrenburg: Writing, Politics and the Art of Survival* (1984).

Canada is not so strong as the United States, yet Canadians are not afraid of Red Army uniforms. If you wanted to send your famous Navy Band here, we would have no objection to their performing in their uniforms.

YEKATERINA FURTSEVA, first female member of the Politburo and Soviet Minister of Culture, concerning the U.S. State Department's refusal to permit the Red Army Chorus to perform in uniform on American soil, 10 June 1964; recalled by the American capitalist Armand Hammer in *Hammer* (1987) written with Neil Lyndon.

I did know about these demonstrations and this gave me much strength but I did not know their proportions until I arrived here. I was simply astonished by the level of fire.

VALENTYN MOROZ, Ukrainian nationalist, expressing gratitude upon his release from the Russian Gulag to Canadian Ukrainians and others who campaigned on his behalf, quoted by Victor Malarek in *The Globe and Mail*, 6 June 1979.

Siberia is in a sense a frontier, a great expanse with people of different tribal origins and in that sense I believe it is a place of discovery, a place where the future is being created, and my interest in it is probably due to the fact that in Canada we also have a frontier, which is to the north and northwest, where there are many people of different origins, where there is great potential and where the world of tomorrow has to be built.

PIERRE ELLIOTT TRUDEAU, former Prime Minister, visiting Siberia for personal and commercial reasons, speech made in Siberia, quoted by Sergei Ostroumov of Novosti Press Agency and carried by *The Toronto Star*, 27 July 1985.

The Soviet Union is bigger, but Canada is emptier, lonelier, lovelier, wilder, colder, leaner, cleaner, safer, duller, freer, saner, soberer, sweeter, neater.

WILLIAM OSCAR JOHNSON, U.S. travel and sports writer, "Trans Canada," *Sports Illustrated*, 27 Jan. 1988.

What took you so long?

MIKHAIL GORBACHEV, Soviet Premier, greeting Prime Minister Brian Mulroney at the Kremlin, Nov. 1989, quoted by Stephen Handelman in *The Toronto Star*, 18 May 1990. This was Mulroney's first official visit to the Soviet Union despite the fact that he had served as Prime Minister since 1984.

If we meet as rarely as now, with as much time between visits of the Canadian Prime Minister, I think this is inconsistent with the dynamics of the world and with the dyanmics of our friendship.

MIKHAIL GORBACHEV, Soviet President, addressing Prime Minister Brian Mulroney and commenting on the latter's tardiness in acknowledging the new spirit of glasnost and perestroika in the Soviet Union, Moscow, 20 Nov. 1989, quoted in *The Globe and Mail* three days later. Gorbachev and Mulroney first met in Moscow in 1985 at the funeral of Chernenko. Gorbachev and Prime Minister Trudeau met in Moscow in 1971. Gorbachev, as the youngest member of the Politburo, made his first visit to North America in May 1983 when he spent ten days in Canada, travelling (with Agriculture Minister Eugene Whelan) from Niagara Falls to Calgary.

History teaches us that tyrants, when covered, strike out. They start wars. Reason is abandoned, the old brain prevails over the new, atomic bomb or no atomic bomb.
JOSEF SKVORECKY, Czech-born essayist and novelist, Letter to the Editor, *The New York Review of Books*, 17 March 1987.

Alas, the glaring contradiction within Soviet society is that there are millions who have become so accustomed to lies and lying that they would go to any lengths to continue lying in the old way. The truth is feared.
Truth! *Pravda!* Russia has been the land of truthseekers, *pravdaiskateli*. Among the truthseekers were some of the greatest and noblest minds the country has produced. But perhaps truth was so diligently sought because it was, and still is, so rare.
SUZANNE ROSENBERG, native of Russia, student in Montreal, survivor of Soviet incarceration as an adult, *A Soviet Odyssey* (1988).

We are two large countries in the same geographical area, and there are many things we can decide together.
MIKHAIL S. GORBACHEV, Soviet President, quoted in Moscow by Stephen Handelman in *The Toronto Star*, 8 Nov. 1989.

We found we have a few of these left over.
ALEKSANDR YAKOVIEW, departing Soviet Ambassador in Ottawa, presenting an Olympic silver medal encased in lucite from the 1981 Moscow Olympic Games (which were boycotted by many Western countries) to Ivan Head, Trudeau's foreign policy adviser; quoted by Bill Keller in *The New York Times Magazine*, 19 Feb. 1989.

It's a day to feel proud of being Canadian.
GEORGE COHON, President of McDonald's Restaurants of Canada Ltd., opening the Soviet Union's first McDonald's outlet, Pushkin Square, Moscow, 31 Jan. 1990, quoted by Stephen Handelman in *The Toronto Star* later that day.

My family found out they were on the short list to be shot so we left. As a result of Stalin's actions I ended up in Canada. All my mother's family were sent away to the gulags in Siberia. Stalin's world is only breaking down now. There are millions of Canadians who can say they are here because of Stalin.
LUBOMIR MYKYTIUK, Toronto-based actor of Ukrainian background, quoted by Kevin Prokosh in *The Winnipeg Free Press*, 15 Feb. 1990. The actor played the part of the late Soviet dictator in the Manitoba Theatre Centre's production of David Pownell's play *Master Class*.

Our generation grew up believing that the real threat to prosperity and security came from beyond the Iron Curtain. With that curtain now in tatters, we see perhaps more clearly now that there are more threats, equally significant and in many ways more difficult to manage.
JOE CLARK, Minister of External Affairs, statement made on 26 April 1990, quoted by Project Ploughshares, *What Makes Canada Secure?* (1991), the background document for the Citizens' Inquiry into Peace and Security in Canada.

At this watershed in world history, the friendly feelings and creative aspirations of our two peoples can serve as the northern pillar of the bridge of confidence and security between East and West.

MIKHAIL GORBACHEV, Soviet President, speech about a demilitarized Arctic, made in Ottawa during a thirty-hour visit, quoted by Stephen Handelman in *The Toronto Star*, 2 June 1990.

I said to him, "May the Soviet Union and Canada divinely grow and supremely glow."

SRI CHINMOY, New York-based Hindu guru, addressing Soviet President Mikhail Gorbachev on his visit to Ottawa, 29 May 1990; quoted in *Maclean's*, 18 June 1990.

"You know what, Brian, you know what we gossip about Canada when we come over here?" "No." "We are absolutely mystified." I said, "About what?" "How 26 million people can produce such enormous wealth. We are absolutely flabbergasted at the enormity of your achievement." I suppose, when you think about it that way, here in Canada, 26 million people — less than one-tenth of the population of the Soviet Union — sitting at the G7 table.

BRIAN MULRONEY, Prime Minister, referring to his conversation with Soviet President Mikhail Gorbachev on his visit earlier that month; interviewed by Kevin Doyle and Anthony Wilson-Smith and quoted in *Maclean's*, 25 June 1990.

If Quebec and Canada can't solve their problems, I would have very little hope for all those people in Eastern Europe and the U.S.S.R. because here we are, clearly, a more sophisticated society politically.

CHRISTIAN DUFOUR, Quebec nationalist, "Québécois First," *The Idler*, 29 Aug. 1990.

SPACE

See also ASTRONOMY
UNIDENTIFIED FLYING
OBJECTS

The same as before — just the same — the long, magnificent delirious swoop of dizziness . . . the Great Circle . . . the swift path-

way to Arcturus. All as before but now infinitely more rapid. Never have I had such speed. Beyond the Moon and past the North Star in a twinkling, swooping in a long bright curve round the Pleiades. . . . Hello, there, old Betelgeuse, I'm off to the little blue star that points the way to the unknown. Forward into the untrodden.

JOHN DRAINIE, actor, reciting the emotional lines of the lead in *Mr. Arcularis*, CBC Radio's well-remembered "Stage 49" dramatization of Conrad Aiken's short story about an elderly man whose path to death takes him across the heavens.

Perhaps there is a hopeful possibility here in the conquest of outer space. Interplanetary activity may well give us planetary peace. Once we discover Martian space ships hovering over earth's air-space, we will all come together. "How dare they threaten us like this!" we shall shout, as one, at a really United Nations!

LESTER B. PEARSON, diplomat, Nobel Peace Prize Lecture, Oslo, Norway, 11 Dec. 1957. The text is taken from *The Four Faces of Peace and the International Outlook* (1964) edited by Sherleigh G. Pierson.

Gradually entering the world's consciousness, like a silent and rising tide within the human imagination, are those pictures taken from interstellar space, where our bright planet, Earth, full of life and light, hangs small, single, and alone in the cold void.

LESTER B. PEARSON, former Prime Minister, commenting on the Apollo lunar landing, 22 Oct. 1969.

Anik, the satellite, is a wonder. It is a big eye in the sky overlooking every Canadian.

NICHOLAS ARNATSIAQ, broadcaster in the N.W.T., "The Eye in the Sky" (1973), reprinted in *Inuktitut* No. 70, 1989.

Nicholas Knock was a venturesome boy, / He lived at Number Eight. / He went for walks in the universe / And generally got home late.

DENNIS LEE, poet, "Nicholas Knock," *Nicholas Knock and Other People* (1974).

Canadarm marks a new approach to space: we humans come there no longer as wary explorers, but to stay and build. This progression to the commercialization of space demands new ways of doing things. . . . Canada can be proud of its world leadership in this branch of robotics. We have a Canadian first, which is an achievement quite as beautiful as any other work of art.

LARKIN KERWIN, President, National Research Council, expressing national pride in the Remote Manipulator System (Canadarm) designed and built by NRC and Spar Aerospace for NASA's Space Shuttle, address, Empire Club of Canada, Toronto, 12 Nov. 1981.

Part of Canada's domestic satellite communications system, the *Anik B*, is already in place. *Anik C*, the second stage of a system designed to bring modern communications to the most remote corners of this vast commonwealth, should head spaceward sometime in 1982. Space development will be a mark of Canadian social and economic independence, as well as a method for tying together communications in a far-flung country with recurrent weather problems.

Prediction made by MICHAEL EDELHART in "Space: The New Frontier" in *The Omni Future Almanac* (1982) edited by Robert Weil.

Marc Garneau (in French): There is no one here to take your call. If you leave a message we will call you back.
Mission Control: *Parlez anglais.*

Conversation between the bilingual astronaut MARC GARNEAU and the unilingual operators at Mission Control in Houston, Texas, concerning answering a morning wake-up call aboard the Space Shuttle *Challenger*, 11 Oct. 1984; quoted in *Maclean's*, 22 Oct. 1984.

One realizes that one is very lucky to be a Canadian and to have as beautiful and vast a country as ours is.

MARC GARNEAU, astronaut, aboard the Space Shuttle *Challenger* 120 miles above Canada, quoted by Lydia Dotto in *Canada in Space* (1987).

With any luck, it will not be too long after the 500th anniversary of Columbus' discovery that humans will be able to look down on the continent he found — from a permanent home nearly 500 km above the earth.

LYDIA DOTTO, science writer, referring to the possible existence of an orbiting space station in the year 1992, *Canada in Space* (1987).

There's a little supernova in every one of us.

ROBERT GARRISON, astronomer, alluding to the discovery of Supernova Shelton 1987-A by the Chile-based Canadian astronomer Ian Shelton, quoted by Jack Miller in *The Toronto Star*, 22 Aug. 1987.

Dear God, have we infected the very stars with our fears and our hatreds?

RUDY WIEBE, novelist, on learning that particularly bright-looking stars in the heavens were in fact intelligence-gathering satellites, *Playing Dead: A Contemplation Concerning the Arctic* (1989).

Very probably we shall shortly be in a position to colonize our entire galaxy. Calculations suggest that such a process would take so short a time — a few million years only — that there is some problem in understanding why it has not already been carried out by extraterrestrials. Is it that there just are no extraterrestrial lives in our galaxy despite its containing sunlike stars in the hundreds of billions? Or is it that immensely many of those stars shine upon lives comparable to those of crocodiles or of stone age men, lives so nasty and brutish that their value might even be considered *negative*, while only twentieth century Earth bears a civiliza-

tion capable of curing toothache and of galactic colonization? Either way, galactic colonization could well seem a very strong moral duty.
JOHN LESLIE, philosopher, University of Guelph, Ont., "The Need to Generate Happy People," *Philosophia: Philosophical Quarterly of Israel*, May 1989.

One can't escape the sense that Voyager and its startling images of uninhabited worlds was giving us a warning: Keep your blue planet safe for biology because there is no haven elsewhere. There is beauty elsewhere but life only here.
STEPHEN STRAUSS, science reporter, covering the encounter of the Voyager 2 spacecraft and the planet Neptune, *The Globe and Mail*, 29 Aug. 1989.

Barring some spectacular breakthrough in the science of travel, Mars will be the last frontier for human settlement. People dream of flying faster than light to planets around far-off stars, to communicate with ETs.
But today's best science tells us we can't fly faster than light, our best telescopes can't guarantee there are any other planets out there, our best radios hear no sign that ETs exist. So when we stop dreaming and start planning, we see Mars as the farthest outpost we can ever really hope for.
JOHN MILLER, science columnist, pointing out that the "flying time" from Earth to Mars is 240 days each way, *The Toronto Star*, 8 Oct. 1989.

My hope, I suppose, is that the next generation can create a planet reshaped enough so it can qualify for admission to the cosmic kindergarten, and become part of the galactic neighbourhood.
STANTON T. FRIEDMAN, UFO researcher, quoted by John Spears in *The Toronto Star*, 24 Dec. 1989.

Thinking of all the unexpected natural catastrophes the Earth is heir to — from volcanic eruptions to earthquakes and tidal waves — I hope that people by the

year 2030 will not only take care of our planet but will also take heed of those other planets we will then be exploring in our solar system.
GERALDINE KENNY-WALLACE, physicist, chemist, and Chairperson, Science Council of Canada, "The Challenge of Environmental Peacemaking," *Planet under Stress: The Challenge of Global Change* (1990) edited by Constance Mungall and Digby J. McLaren for the Royal Society of Canada.

We live on a tiny planet orbiting an ordinary star on the periphery of a typical galaxy.
Observation of a character in the film *Jesus of Montreal* (1989), quoted by Rick Groen in *The Globe and Mail*, 30 Dec. 1990.

From an alien viewpoint, this must be a primitive society whose major activity is tribal welfare.
STANTON T. FRIEDMAN, scientist and UFO specialist, personal communication, 15 Jan. 1991.

SPAIN

One hundred days later the Canadian volunteers in Spain took the name "Mackenzie-Papineau Battalion." There are many Canadians who to this day never even heard of the "Mac-Paps," such was the curtain of obscurity draped at that time in the democracies over the cause of democracy. But the name lives in Spain, and when freedom comes to Spain it will be written on monuments.
MATTHEW HALTON, correspondent, "Ten Years to Alamein" (1944), quoted by Margaret Fairley in *Spirit of Canadian Democracy* (1945).

SPEECH & SPEECHES
See also LANGUAGE

I sketched a Connewaghna [Caughnawaga, Kahnawake] Indian today whose figure was quite antique. I have often observed (but never had more reason to do so than today) that when the Indians speak their air & action is more like that of Greek or Roman Orators than of Modern Nations. They have a great deal of impressive action, & look like the figures painted by the Old Masters.

ELIZABETH SIMCOE, diarist and wife of Governor John Graves Simcoe, diary entry, York (Toronto), 6 Jan. 1794, *Mrs. Simcoe's Diary* (1965) edited by Mary Quayle Innis.

Ladies and gentlemen: I am the obvious person to be speaking. I have looked up the word "obvious" in the dictionary and the definition is: "goes without saying." So that is what I propose to do.

SIR JULIAN BYNG, Governor General, "whereupon he left," according to John Raymond, "Worth Repeating," *The Globe and Mail*, 7 July 1989.

On the whole, and among the privileged, English-speaking Canadians were more conventional and literal-minded than the British. One soon learned, for instance, not to say in light mood the opposite of what one meant and expect the real meaning to get through. The nuances of British speech were absent.

DAVID WALKER, ADC to Governor General Lord Tweedsmuir, *Lean, Wind, Lean: A Few Times Remembered* (1985).

Most conversations are simply monologues delivered in the presence of a witness.

Remark made by a character in *The Weak-Eyed Bat* (1942), a crime novel written by MARGARET MILLAR.

If the gentleman who is so full of whys were as wise as he is full, he would return to that silence from which he ought never to have emerged.

LEONARD BROCKINGTON, noted orator and public figure, responding to a heckler who kept calling out "Why?" at a banquet in Red Deer, Alta., in the 1940s.

But anybody who did not know the language, or could not catch what they mumbled, might have imagined that they were referring briefly, but with infinite sadness, to incurable diseases that were afflicting them. And, indeed, you might say that they were, for this melancholy mumbling is an incurable disease for many Canadian males.

The women do not mumble, but the cadence of their voices, as a rule, is even sadder. Gay girls, with bright glances, often sound as if they had been hypnotized into enduring melancholy. Their voices do not fit their pretty faces at all; they should never have been wired for sound. Their speech is not downright ugly, as it often is in the Middle West, but it is monotonous and mournful, like a walk around Edmonton on a wet day.

J.B. PRIESTLEY, English writer on a tour of Canada, "I Heard the Monotonous, Mournful Voices of Canadian Women," *Liberty*, Aug. 1956.

Perhaps because of the voices, I often saw Canada as a huge, sad land, out of which everything could come except high spirits.

J.B. PRIESTLEY, English writer on a tour of Canada, "I Heard the Monotonous, Mournful Voices of Canadian Women," *Liberty*, Aug. 1956.

Almost anywhere in Nova Scotia some old timer can be found who will claim to be able to tell what county of the province any man comes from by listening to his speech.

H. REX WILSON, linguist, "Lunenburg Dutch: Fact and Folklore" (1958), *Canadian English: Origins and Structures* (1975) edited by J.K. Chambers.

Not long ago a Torontonian shopping in a large department store just across the border asked where he could find *chesterfields*. On following directions, he was somewhat dismayed to find himself at the cigar counter!

WALTER S. AVIS, linguist, "Speech Differences along the Ontario-United States Border" (1954), *Canadian English: Origins and Structures* (1975) edited by J.K. Chambers.

After seventeen years of teaching in the schools of British Columbia and eleven at a university, I have yet to find a student who can make intelligent use of vowel systems or pronunciation keys as they appear in most dictionaries.

> RICHARD H.C. MONK, linguist, observation made in 1967, quoted by Thomas M. Paikeday in an address, American Dialect Society, New Orleans, 30 Dec. 1988.

Thus, speakers of Canadian English are often identified by the speakers of adjoining dialects by their pronunciation of words like *wife* and *south*, which are usually mis-heard by speakers of General American as *weef* and *sooth*.

> J.K. CHAMBERS, linguist, "Canadian Raising," *Canadian English: Origins and Structures* (1975) edited by J.K. Chambers.

People need political and social leaders who can define policies, articulate problems, and express the aims and ideals of their society for those who cannot express them for themselves, though they may feel them very deeply. But the evidence is overwhelming that voters in a democracy want, and expect, bumble and burble from their leaders, and seem disturbed, if not upset, by the impact of articulate speech. Without exhaustive examination, I should guess that if we read Hansard we might have to go all the way back to Arthur Meighen to find a political leader who habitually used the language with skill and precision, and the correlation of his ability to speak with his success at the polls seems to me significant, like the similar correlation for Adlai Stevenson in the United States later.

> NORTHROP FRYE, literary critic, address, Empire Club of Canada, Toronto, 19 Jan. 1984.

There is a story, which I understand to be true, of a late colleague of mine, a professor of English who was private secretary to Prime Minister Mackenzie King during the war. In working on King's speeches, he inserted various quotations from Canadian poets, English and French, touched up clichés with a few metaphors, rounded out stock formulas with more concrete and lively language. These were regularly and routinely struck out. Eventually, the Prime Minister said: "Professor, the public memory for a picturesque phrase is very retentive."

> NORTHROP FRYE, literary critic, address, Empire Club of Canada, Toronto, 19 Jan. 1984.

The most obvious and distinctive feature of Canadian speech is probably its vowel sound, the dipthong *ou*. (Thus *out* rhymes with *boat*, so that a phrase like "out and about in a boat" emerges as "oat and aboat in a boat.") There is a deeply held belief that this trait comes from Scotland, but this is a myth.

> ROBERT McCRUM, WILLIAM CRAN, and ROBERT MacNEIL, authors, *The Story of English* (1986).

Your perfect accent was ruined / by a private school in Toronto.

> W. MARK SUTHERLAND, poet, "If These Quotes . . .," *Pursuing the Millennium* (1988).

To hear them addressing a public meeting is to experience them at their most depressing: oh, the long, slow, tuneless, humourless, saltless monotony of Canadian orthodoxy!

> JAN MORRIS, Anglo-Welsh travel writer, "Wild Blue-Yonder City," *Saturday Night*, Nov. 1989. This is a characterization of the rhetoric and speech patterns of bureaucrats and others on public occasions.

More than 2,000 people have walked out on my speeches.

> FRANK OGDEN, futurologist known as "Dr. Tomorrow," characteristic remark, 1980s.

If 10 percent of the audience has heard 10 percent of what I say, there's no charge.

FRANK OGDEN, futurologist known as "Dr. Tomorrow," quoted by Nancy Spiller in *American Way*, 1 Sept. 1989.

We can speak at a maximum rate of 480 phonemes per minute. The rate is far too slow for efficient communication. It is far too slow for the effective communication of information and ideas. We have a choice. We can become either speed talkers or speed readers.

JOEL BONN, Montreal-based reading specialist, *obiter dictum*, 3 Feb. 1990.

In this present Babbleonian Age, political rhetoric is largely ritual. Prime Ministers do not need speech writers to make them memorable but to keep them out of trouble.

DALTON CAMP, columnist, *The Toronto Star*, 18 Feb. 1990.

Anything said off the cuff has usually been written on it first.

ROBIN SKELTON, man-of-letters, aphorism, May 1990.

I'm going to break that world record. My vocal cords are at the peak of their beautiful maturity.

PHILIPPE DEANE GIGANTES, Senator, referring to his decision to deliver the world's longest fillibuster as part of the Liberal Party's plan to delay the key vote on the GST past the 1 Jan. 1991 deadline, quoted by Jonathan Ferguson in *The Toronto Star*, 7 Dec. 1990. To accomplish this, Gigantes spoke more than 43 hours, 41 minutes, a record set by a Texan politician. Earlier that week, Senator Joyce Fairbairn had spoken for 16.5 hours, setting the world record for the longest speech delivered by a female Parliamentarian.

SPIRIT
See also SOULS

In the New World, we find in the North American Red Men a race as much given

as the Celts are to a belief in various spirits like fairies. They believe that there are spirits in lakes, in rivers and in waterfalls, in rocks and trees, in the earth and in the air; and that these beings produce storms, droughts, good and bad harvest, abundance and scarcity of game, disease, and the varying fortunes of men.

W.Y. EVANS-WENTZ, American scholar, *The Fairy-Faith in Celtic Countries* (1911).

But when the nature of the energy that activates the mind is discovered (as I believe it will be), the time may yet come when scientists will be able to make a valid approach to a study of the nature of a spirit other than that of a man.

WILDER PENFIELD, neurosurgeon and author, *The Mystery of the Mind* (1975).

SPIRIT, NATIONAL

They wore the greyness as a protective outer garment. They did not murmur the national prayer: "O God, grant me mediocrity and comfort; protect me from the radiance of Thy light."

ROBERTSON DAVIES, man-of-letters, describing the conformity of contemporary Canadians, *The Lyre of Orpheus* (1988).

SPIRITUALISM
See also BELIEF

Spiritualism has taken a firm and deep hold upon the inhabitants of this country, and in some places exhibits a condition of progress little behind that of the States.

EMMA HARDINGE, British spiritualist also known as Mrs. Emma Hardinge-Britten, *Modern American Spiritualism: A Twenty Years' Record of the Communion between Earth and the World of Spirits* (1869). The Britten Memorial Church, a spiritualist congregation in Toronto, was named in her memory.

I much appreciate your kindness in suggesting that I might become a member of the International Institute for Psychical Research. At some later time, I would much appreciate this opportunity. For reasons which you will appreciate, it has seemed to me inadvisable to become too actively identified with Psychical Research work, pending the time that I may continue to hold my present position.

W.L. MACKENZIE KING, Prime Minister, letter dated 19 April 1938 in Ottawa and addressed to Nandor Fodor in New York who printed it in his book of reminiscences, *Between Two Worlds* (1964). Fodor, a psychiatrist and psychical researcher, was the founder of the above-mentioned Institute.

It was while I was in Britain during the war and word had reached us that a spiritualist, who had corresponded with King, was negotiating to publish his letters. I went down to London with another government lawyer and explained to her that Mr. King owned the copyright of every word that he had written and that if she even attempted to sell his property, we'd have her in court faster than you could say Ellen Terry.

As we came away into the blackout, I said to my companion, "I think we have struck a happy medium."

LEONARD BROCKINGTON, orator, referring to the attempt he made following the death of Mackenzie King in 1950 to "silence" the mediums in London whom the late Prime Minister had consulted; quoted by Richard J. Doyle in *Hurly-Burly: A Time at The Globe* (1990).

What you are going to see may be historic.

ARTHUR FORD, trance medium, addressing the television audience of the CTV Network show *Beyond Reason* which was videotaping a seance involving Ford and Episcopal Bishop James Pike, 17 Sept. 1967; quoted by Allen Spraggett *Arthur Ford: The Man Who Talked with the Devil* (1973).

It somehow never occurred to me that if Allen Spraggett's small hope worked out, it would draw national — indeed international — news coverage.

JAMES PIKE, Episcopal Bishop of California, expressing astonishment at the public reaction to the CTV Network show *Beyond Reason*, which showed Pike communicating through the mediumship of Arthur Ford with his dead son; quoted by Allen Spraggett in *The Bishop Pike Story* (1970).

There's a saying in psychic circles: "That's proof." The nervous circles say it over and over to each other in earnest, anxious tones, searching one another's eyes for confirmation. . . . The key word in Spiritualism is "proof." It's like a shot in the arm. You get it, you feel great, the next minute you need it again. The effect wears off in no time.

PATRICIA JOUDRY, playwright and medium who once believed she acted as George Bernard Shaw's spirit-amanuensis, *Spirit River to Angels' Roost: Religions I Have Loved and Left* (1977).

One evening in meditation I reached a powerful state of heightened consciousness, and I thought, now I'll contact one of those higher nature spirits. Since vegetables had been mentioned, I thought I might contact the spirit of some plant we were growing at Findhorn. I had always been fond of the garden pea which we had grown at home in Canada, and I could feel in sympathy in all ways with that plant. So I tried to focus on the essence of what the pea was to me and the love I felt for it. I got an immediate response in thought and feeling which I put into the following words:

I can speak to you, human. I am entirely directed by my work which is set out and molded and which I merely bring to fruition, yet you have come straight to my awareness. . . . While the vegetable kingdom holds no grudge against those it feeds, man takes what he can as a matter of course, giving no thanks. This makes us strangely hostile.

DOROTHY MACLEAN, medium, native of Guelph, Ont., was one of the three founders of the Findhorn Community in northern Scotland in 1962. She refers to the "essence" as a deva, Sanskrit for "shining one," and quotes the spirit (in italics) in her memoir *To Hear the Angels Sing* (1980).

Yes, I talk with angels, great Beings whose lives infuse and create all of Nature.
DOROTHY MACLEAN, medium, *To Hear the Angels Sing* (1980).

Humanity has always been attended by invisible beings.
JOE FISHER, journalist and psychic, *Hungry Ghosts* (1990).

SPIRITUALITY
See also BELIEF

It is in the nature of most men to crave a spiritual lightning rod, a protection against the caprice of accident, the convulsions of nature, the evil in other men's hearts.
MARY MAXWELL, a.k.a. Rúhíyyih Khánum, leading member of the Bahá'í Faith, *A Manual for Pioneers* (1974).

Try as one will to live a spiritual life, one still has a physical body that is comforted by human contact.
BETTY JANE WYLIE, author, *Beginnings: A Book for Widows* (1977, rev. 1988).

Few people, at least until recently, have stopped to wonder what has become of the sense of the sacred in Quebec. It has, unfortunately, all but disappeared: young people, in particular, search in vain for values to shape their personal development and end up looking elsewhere, chiefly to the United States. They have neither guidance nor criteria on which to base thier list of priorities, their life-styles, or their models.
LÉON DION, political scientist, "The Mystery of Quebec," *Daedalus: Journal of the American Academy of Arts and Sciences*, "In Search of Canada," Fall 1988.

Each person has his own spirituality, whether it's art or esotericism, or the extra-terrestrials. We haven't yet recov-

ered, in the Western World, from the disappearance of religion.
DENYS ARCAND, director, discussing his film *Jesus of Montreal*, quoted by Jay Scott in *The Globe and Mail*, 13 Sept. 1989.

And I've come to the conclusion that people who are living truly and have no interest in metaphysics are often doing a lot better than people who feel that they know all about the next world and are in direct contact with it.
JOE FISHER, author and specialist in reincarnation and channelling, quoted by Alexander Blair-Ewart in *Dimensions: Toronto's New Age Monthly*, April 1990.

SPORTS
See also ATHLETICS
BASEBALL
BASKETBALL
FISH & FISHING
FOOTBALL
GOLF
GRETZKY, WAYNE
HANDICAPS
HOCKEY
JOHNSON, BEN
OLYMPIC GAMES
RIDING
SKIING
SWIMMING
TRACK & FIELD

Sport is all hoke and hype, but I find it outrageous and wonderful.
DICK BEDDOES, sports personality, quoted by George Boddington in *Weekend Magazine*, 2 Aug. 1975.

Attends-moi, ce ne sera pas long.
GILLES VILLENEUVE, champion racing driver, characteristic remark, final words to his wife before his fatal crash, Louvaine, Belgium, 8 May 1982. "Wait for me, I won't be long." Quoted by Gerald Donaldson in *Gilles Villeneuve: The Life of the Legendary Racing Driver* (1989).

About 45% of Canadian young people maintain that sports is a source of "a great deal" of enjoyment. Predictably, sports is particularly important to males (57% vs. 32% for females). Six in 10 males and 3 in 10 females say they follow sports, while about 3 in 10 of either sex are frequent attenders of sports events.

REGINALD W. BIBBY and DONALD C. POSTERSKI, sociologists, *The Emerging Generation: An Inside Look at Canada's Teenagers* (1985).

High jumping has always been the easiest, most natural thing for me. I did it as others ran or climbed trees.

DEBBIE BRILL, track and field champion, *Jump* (1986) written with James Lawton.

When I started in track and field, there was no confusion about goals, no lure of money. I didn't think of money, because nobody did then. You did track and field because it was wonderful to do. It was something very deep inside you, something very personal. It was not something to barter.

DEBBIE BRILL, track and field champion, *Jump* (1986) written with James Lawton.

As David Murray would say, when confronted with questions about the apparently contradictory relationship among teammates: "Us? Rivals? Yeah, sure. For every two minutes every week we're enemies."

KEN READ, skier, *White Circus: A Skiing Life with the Crazy Canucks* (1987) written with Matthew Fisher.

But it's clear to me that few sports reporters or editors think they have any duty to make Canadians better informed about the accomplishments of their countrymen. They obviously feel that most Canadians are uninterested in non-professional athletic competition. But I think they're wrong. Given a fair chance, Canadians are.

KEN READ, skier, *White Circus: A Skiing Life with the Crazy Canucks* (1987) written with Matthew Fisher.

What other country allows teams composed entirely of foreigners, such as those who play for the Toronto Blue Jays and the Montreal Expos, to live in their land and get paid in foreign currency to compete against other foreigners? European, Asian, and South American countries restrict foreign players in hockey, basketball, volleyball, and baseball to two or three per team.

KEN READ, skier, *White Circus: A Skiing Life with the Crazy Canucks* (1987) written with Matthew Fisher.

Canadians can't play baseball because baseball is a summer game and Canada has no summer. Canadians should stick to their native sports, namely, hockey and pelt trapping.

JIMMY BRESLIN, U.S. sports columnist, commenting on the fact that singer Mary O'Dowd did not know the words of "O Canada" when she sang them at the Blue Jays-New York Yankees game in New York: quoted by Stephen Brook in *Maple Leaf Rag: Travels across Canada* (1987).

The athletic director is the guy who shows up when the team is winning.

TIM BURKE, columnist, *The Montreal Gazette*, 8 Dec. 1987.

Lawyer: Did you state publicly to the Canadian people, "I'm innocent and I never took any banned substances?"
Johnson: Yes, sir.
Lawyer: Those statements were not true?
Johnson: No, sir.

BEN JOHNSON, sprinter, answering questions at the Dubin Inquiry, quoted in *Maclean's*, 26 June 1989. Johnson later added: "I lied, and I was ashamed for my family and friends and the kids who looked up to me and the Canadian athletes who want to be in my position."

Sport seems specifically intended to exist separate from the rough and tumble of life where business is so squarely situated. The fact is, of course, without business, sport would still be on sandlots, in backyards, and on ponds, with very few players and even fewer spectators. It is business that has promoted and popularized sports and created its mass appeal.

> KEN DRYDEN and ROY MacGREGOR, sportsman and journalist, *Home Game* (1989).

For me, a game is first and last a contest with myself and it always has been.

> KEN DRYDEN and ROY MacGREGOR, sportsman and journalist, *Home Game* (1989).

There is no game as Canadian as lacrosse. Hockey is really an ice version of bandy, played by the English for years before it was adapted for Canada. Basketball was invented by a Canadian, but he invented it in the United States.

Lacrosse was the natives' game. Its origins are unclear, but it was played long before the Europeans arrived.

> WILLIAM HUMBER, sports history, "The Spirit of the Black Bear," *The Idler*, No. 24, July-Aug. 1989.

I love the competition. And it's such a great feeling when you win!

> HELEN KELESI, tennis player, quoted by C. Lee Crawford in *TV Guide*, 21 July 1990.

It is an axiom of sports that the legs go first. For sportswriters, it's the enthusiasm.

> TRENT FRAYNE, sportswriter, *The Tales of an Athletic Supporter* (1990).

All national and international sports federations will be disbanded and competitive "amateur" tournaments and spectacles beyond the civic level will be prohibited. The Olympic Games, in particular, will be discontinued on the grounds that they have become a hazard to public mental health and to the health of individual competitors.

> BRIAN FAWCETT, cultural commentator, listing a few of his many future-world strictures, *Public Eye: An Investigation into the Disappearance of the World* (1990).

I don't think anybody in this country speaks for the right-wing guy. The guy that gets up at 6:00 in the morning and works from 7:00 to 5:00 and pays the freight.

> DON (GRAPES) CHERRY, sports personality, accounting for his unique popularity, quoted by Craig MacInnis in *The Toronto Star*, 6 April 1991.

SPRING
See SEASONS

STATESMANSHIP

Diplomacy is simply politics exported.

> DON JAMIESON, Newfoundland politician, quoted by Robert Miller in *Maclean's*, 12 Dec. 1977.

Diplomacy is the art of postponing inevitable decisions for as long as possible.

> REUBEN SLONIM, rabbi and memoirist, *To Kill a Rabbi* (1987).

STEROIDS
See also DRUG TRADE
SPORTS

I said, "Sure, it's yours, take it back" because they can always take back the medal, but they can't take away my speed.

> BEN JOHNSON, track and field champion, on Italian television in Nov. 1988, quoted by Lynda Hurst in *The Toronto Star*, 31 Dec. 1988.

You don't go from 10.17 to 9.83 on Petro-Canada unleaded gas.

> JAMIE ASTAPHAN, physician who prescribed steroids to sprinter Ben Johnson, referring to the runner's performance time at the 1984 Olympics (which won him a bronze) and at the 1987 games in Stockholm (where he took the record as the world's fastest man). The remark was made before the Dubin Inquiry into the use of steroids and other drugs by professional athletes, 30 May 1989, quoted by Mary Hynes and Robert MacLeod in *The Globe and Mail* the following day.

Drugs and excellence do not mix. I'm for excellence.
ANDY HIGGINS, track and field coach, quoted by Bruce Kidd in "Today's Tradition Echoes the Past," *University of Toronto Magazine*, Winter 1989.

Drug testing in itself does not address the root problem. We must look beyond testing as the panacea that will cure this sickness in sport. While testing will always be necessary, we must ground the integrity of sport on the firmer base of fair play, ethics, and a sense of what is right.
CHARLES DUBIN, Ontario Chief Justice, report on the use of drugs in sport, quoted in *The Toronto Star*, 27 June 1990.

STOCK MARKET

BLACK MONDAY
Headline in *The Toronto Star*, Monday, 20 Oct. 1987. The wording recalled the earlier "black Monday," 28 Oct. 1929, which initiated the Great Depression.

The good thing about the crash is it made the bad stocks cost only half as much as they did before.
ADRIAN DU PLESSIS, floor trader turned whistleblower at the Vancouver Stock Exchange, quoted by Stevie Cameron in *The Globe and Mail*, 29 Oct. 1987.

Like most large North American cities, Vancouver has a serious garbage disposal problem, but this one is unique. The garbage is the Vancouver Stock Exchange. It is polluting much of the civilized world. . . . If anyone tries to peddle you anything listed on the Vancouver Stock exchange, hang up fast. There isn't any gold in Vancouver, but there's plenty of brass.
JOE QUEENAN, U.S. journalist, "Scam Capital of the World," *Forbes*, May 1989.

The market teaches you how to be an independent thinker. If you don't learn to think, the market will make you humble — and broke.
RICHARD OSLER, investment adviser, "Richard's Day," *The Latest Morningside Papers* (1989) edited by Peter Gzowski.

What's the thrill? It's being able to match yourself against the "market" — that funny amalgam of hopes and fears — and win. The key is to match your hope against someone else's fear, and their fear against your hope.
RICHARD OSLER, investment adviser, "Richard's Day," *The Latest Morningside Papers* (1989) edited by Peter Gzowski.

STORIES

I am constantly amazed by people who see themselves as very ordinary, who as I get to know them reveal incredible stories of their lives.
ROY McDONALD, diarist, *Living: A London Journal* (1978). McDonald, a Zen-like character, is the subject of Don Bell's literary work *Pocketman* (1979).

Everyone has a story to tell.
BARRY BROADFOOT, oral historian, quoted by Nancy J. White in *The Toronto Star*, 12 Nov. 1989.

I suppose history has taught me this: every person has an individual story. The stories have similar patterns, but each is unique and particular. . . . One of the beautiful things about telling stories is that you never tell them completely.
RUDY WIEBE, novelist, interviewed by Linda Hutcheon in *Other Solitudes: Canadian Multicultural Fictions* (1990) edited by Linda Hutcheon and Marion Richmond.

STRATFORD FESTIVAL
See also THEATRE

The instigator of this scheme was Mr. Tom Paterson [*sic*], a starry-eyed enthusiast of touching qualities who felt that as Stratford boasted a rather pedestrian statue of Shakespeare it should also perform his works.

ALEC GUINNESS, author, discussing Tom Patterson, founder of the Stratford Shakespearian Festival in 1953, *Blessings in Disguise* (1985).

Tom Patterson had seen opera in Italy.
TYRONE GUTHRIE, first artistic director of the Statford Festival, frequently repeated this remark to explain why, quite alone among the natives of Stratford, someone was committed to the arts. As Patterson later admitted: "He was, alas, quite mistaken. Indeed, I had never made it to Italy until many years after the Stratford Festival was established." Noted by Guthrie in *A Life in the Theatre* (1959).

Curtain: 8 o'clock, or One Hour after Train Arrival.
Notice of curtain time for that evening's play, mounted in a Nisson hut at forty degrees below zero, brought to Moosonee, Ont., by the touring Canadian Players, winter 1954.

Stratford was special. It was my home town. I wanted to see it done. And I did. But closing night of the first festival I was so broke I couldn't buy milk for the baby.
TOM PATTERSON, Festival founder, quoted by Lotta Dempsey in *The Toronto Star*, 18 June 1966.

One of the things at which Tyrone Guthrie certainly plugged away was pronunciation. For a long time, his large Canadian contingent of actors seemed unable to appreciate that the name "Buckingham," as in the Duke of Buckingham, must be pronounced in the English fashion, and not as "Bucking-HAM," the North American version. Finally he called the male members of the cast together. "I've had enough of Bucking-HAM," he was reported to have said. "Now just you listen to me. You're always talking about fucking 'em, aren't you? I'm told that you're always *doing* it. Well, this chap's name is Bucking'em. Got it?" From that moment on, their diction in this respect was faultless.

NICHOLAS MONSARRAT, novelist and one-time Ottawa resident, referring to Tyrone Guthrie, the Festival's first artistic director, *Life Is a Four-Letter Word: Volume II — Breaking Out* (1970).

Canadian actors, trained largely in the radio and in TV studios, accustomed to the extremely narrow limits which microphone and camera imposed, accustomed more to the intimate demands of modern naturalistic plays than to the wider imaginative and technical scope of great classics, do not readily lay their ears back and roar, cannot without self-consciousness make the broad and vehement gestures which match vehement declamation.
TYRONE GUTHRIE, director, quoted by Diana Valk in *Shylock for a Summer: The Story of One Year (1954-5) in the Life of Frederick Valk* (1958).

It is important, therefore, that Canadians should be able to express their own environment, not only for the artists themselves, not only for the community now, but for posterity.
TYRONE GUTHRIE, director, letter written from Ireland on 11 May 1952 to Dora Mavor Moore in Toronto, reproduced in *The Toronto Star*, 17 May 1971.

Canada is now potentially the richest nation in the world. Canadians know this; and know, further, that riches mean power and responsibility; that, if Canada is honourably to fulfill its destiny, it is not enough to be rich and powerful. Canada must not in the councils of the world use the cracked brash accents of millionaire adolescence, but must speak with maturity. To an extraordinary degree this theatrical project in a small provincial town symbolized Canada's desire for mature and, if possible, distinguished artistic expression.
TYRONE GUTHRIE, director, referring to the city of Stratford, Ont., and the Festival he helped to found, *A Life in the Theatre* (1959).

The answer was not clearly apparent in 1952. As a writer in the *Toronto Telegram* noted at the time, Stratford-upon-Avon, England, may have been synonymous with Shakespeare, but Stratford, Ontario, was synonymous with hockey. In our namesake in the Old Country, boards were *trod upon* by performers; in Canada's Stratford, they were something to be *knocked into.*

> TYRONE GUTHRIE, director, *A Life in the Theatre* (1959).

There can hardly be anyone in the Province of Ontario, perhaps even in the whole of Canada, who has not heard of Tom Patterson, the man who had the dream. If you live in a town called Stratford and are interested in theatre or public relations, it seems a fairly straight-forward dream to have had.

> JAMES MASON, actor who played the masked lead in *Oedipus Rex* in 1954, *Before I Forget: Autobiography and Drawings by James Mason* (1981). On the subject of Stratford's open stage, Mason wrote: "The auditorium was like a large round biscuit out of which one bite had been taken."

STRESS

See also MEDICINE

Hanson's Anti-Technostress Rule No. 1: Ask yourself — "Do I really need this?" Hanson's Anti-Technostress Rule No. 2: If you need it, keep the instructions.

> PETER G. HANSON, physician and author, *Stress for Success: Thriving on Stress at Work* (1989).

I'm going to come back to Canada. It's a place where you don't . . . well, very simply, it's a matter of stress, that new word that everybody throws around. Very little stress here.

> MARLON BRANDO, actor, filming on location outside Toronto, quoted by Murray Campbell in *The Globe and Mail*, 5 Sept. 1989.

What we all suffer from is a happiness gap and that's the real source of stress.

> BETTY JANE WYLIE, author, *obiter dictum*, 1990.

STRIKES

See also UNIONS

The sympathetic strike is the natural and logical sequence of organization. What more natural than that men who have interests in common should stand together in an emergency? A particular union or craft may be striking for a principle that is absolutely vital to every man in the industry, and just as the employers can down one single man, so they can down a single union unless all stand together. This is co-operation; it is brotherhood, and it is absolutely the same principle of sticking together that was employed in France.

> F.J. (FRED) DIXON, charged with seditious conspiracy in connection with the Winnipeg General Strike, address to the jury, Winnipeg, Feb. 13-14, 1920.

Gentlemen, if I have erred, I have erred in good company.

> WILLIAM PRITCHARD, worker and striker judged agitator, address to the jury, 23-24 March 1920, quoted by Norman Penner in *Winnipeg 1919: The Strikers' Own History of the Winnipeg General Strike* (1973).

I don't have to remind you of Canada's record in terms of industrial conflict. We are normally in the top five; we are seldom out of the top ten in the world league of strikes and lost time. The only country that we can't beat is Italy. We have tried! Even in 1976 when the Canadian Labour Congress called its day of protest, you all thought it was because they were protesting wage and price controls. I knew they wanted to lead the world league just once. But you can't beat the Italians. If they lose a soccer game they have a national strike.

> JOHN CRISPO, political economist, address, Empire Club of Canada, 25 Jan. 1979.

STUPIDITY

Earnestness is stupidity that went to college.
DANNY FINKLEMAN, comic and broadcaster, remark recalled by Michael Enright and quoted by Peter Gzowski in *The Private Voice: A Journal of Reflections* (1988).

Oh God, don't let me die stupid.
ROBERTSON DAVIES, man-of-letters noted for his wit and wisdom, heart-felt prayer, mentioned in *The Toronto Star*, 20 Oct. 1989.

STYLE, NATIONAL
See also FASHION

What we do should have a Canadian character. Nobody looks his best in somebody else's clothes.
VINCENT MASSEY, Governor General, observation recalled in his obituary, *Time*, 12 Jan. 1967.

While I was not present at any of their moments of triumph, I am reasonably certain that where a Greek would have said "Eureka!" or an American "Hot damn!", a Canadian would say only, "Not bad, eh?"
PETER GZOWSKI, host of CBC Radio's *Morningside*, in *The Private Voice: A Journal of Reflections* (1988).

In the end, I wanted the chancery to express an image of Canadian reserve and good manners, coupled with a characteristic gesture of openness and invitation, to affirm our similar heritages and at the same time project an element of freshness and forgivable naïveté.
ARTHUR ERICKSON, architect, discussing his design of the Canadian Chancery in Washington, D.C., *The Architecture of Arthur Erickson* (1988).

Canadians — and I am one and proudly so — are forever apologizing for themselves. It's as though being Canadian is the original sin. But it's a style, isn't it?
DONALD SUTHERLAND, actor, quoted by

Ed Gould in *Entertaining Canadians: Canada's Internatioanl Stars 1900-1988* (1988).

There is a bovine quality to Canada that at times I found acutely depressing. Cosy, acquiescent, quick to complain but slow to act, Canada can seem somnolent, as though sedated by the awesomeness of its landscape.
STEPHEN BROOK, English travel writer, *Maple Leaf Rag: Travels across Canada* (1987).

STYLE, PERSONAL
See also FASHION

It's like you never get a second chance to create a first impression.
WILLIAM VANDER ZALM, British Columbia Premier, quoted by Alan Twigg in *Vander Zalm: From Immigrant to Premier* (1986).

To me, the word consistency means I've remained true to my own standards.
JOHN C. PARKIN, architect, quoted in his obituary by Michael Tenszen in *The Toronto Star*, 23 Nov. 1988.

Constancy, sometimes confused with constipation, reigns.
ALLAN FOTHERINGHAM, columnist, *Maclean's*, 16 Oct. 1989.

Noble's all right. Noble does the dishes. Me, I go for assertive. Assertive has a maid.
Comment of a character in the play *The Half of It* by JOHN KRIZANC, included in *Twenty Years at Play* (1990) edited by Jerry Wasserman.

SUCCESS
See also ACHIEVEMENT
FAILURE
WINNING

You've got to meet success half-way. I wanted it to come all the way, so we never shook hands.
EMILY CARR, painter and writer, *Hun-*

dreds and Thousands: The Journals of Emily Carr (1966).

You must be what you are.
GORDON SINCLAIR, newspaperman and broadcaster, remark made in 1965, quoted by Scott Young in *Gordon Sinclair: A Life . . . and then Some* (1987).

Success is making a broken field run to snatch up snowboots, mitts, rucksacks of school books, fling them into the cupboard, and arrive at the door before the guests have to ring twice.
DORIS ANDERSON, columnist and feminist, referring to the lot of the housewife, *Chatelaine*, Feb. 1976.

But success is merely the ability to wrestle as much contentment and happiness out of life as can be got. When you see a very old but still sensible person who neither longs for nor fears death you see success. However it's accomplished.
RAY GUY, humorist, "We Shall Undercome," *That Far Greater Bay* (1976).

Nothing succeeds like successors.
WILDER PENFIELD, neurosurgeon and author, observation made on retirement from the Montreal Neurological Institute which he had founded, quoting his friend Alan Gregg, *No Man Alone: A Neurosurgeon's Life* (1977).

Success with yourself and in the inner life is the success that counts.
ROBERTSON DAVIES, man-of-letters, interviewed by Tom Harpur in 1981, *Conversations with Robertson Davies* (1989) edited by J. Madison Davis.

Dress British, look Irish, think Yiddish.
Formula for success of MURRAY KOFFLER, pharmacist and philanthropist, quoted by Frank Rasky in *Just a Simple Pharmacist: The Story of Murray Koffler, Builder of the Shoppers Drug Mart Empire* (1988).

The three keys to success are no money, no brains, and no education. It's all common sense and timing.

NELSON SKALBANIA, self-made millionaire, quoted by Patricia Chisholm in *Maclean's*, 3 April 1989.

There is a principle at the heart of life: Life is not what you find, it is what you create.
CHARLES TEMPLETON, jack of all trades, *Succeeding* (1989).

You are born with two things: existence and opportunity, and these are the raw materials out of which you can make a successful life.
CHARLES TEMPLETON, jack of all trades, *Succeeding* (1989).

My hunger to succeed must have been an anaesthetic for the fear that my chances of succeeding were only marginal.
DOUGLAS KIRKLAND, Toronto-born portrait photographer, *Light Years: Three Decades Photographing Among the Stars* (1989).

I was more certain of success when I was less certain of what I am doing.
Comment of a character in the play *Dog and Crow* (1990) by playwright MICHAEL SPRINGATE.

To succeed you don't need many thoughts, just a few infinitely repeated.
Comment of a character in the play *Dog and Crow* (1990) by playright MICHAEL SPRINGATE.

If you work very hard, and give life everything you've got, you may not quite make it.
ELWY YOST, television personality, characteristic remark, personal communication, 17 Jan. 1990.

Success is someone else's opinion.
ROBIN SKELTON, man-of-letters, aphorism, May 1990.

Nothing succeeds but success.
JOHN S. CROSBIE, pun collector, variation on the proverbial expression "Nothing succeeds like success," Aug. 1990.

SUFFERING
See also PAIN

It was a rich experience. Don't deny it. Don't denigrate it. Don't say If Only. *Suffer.* But plan pleasure. Small simple pleasure to eke out the hour.
> ELIZABETH SMART, novelist and diarist, "How to Mend a Broken Heart" (1982), *Autobiographies* (1987).

We cannot hear of all the crime in the world all the time, but there are particular sufferings that are calling us by name, and we must be answerable to those.
> JOY KOGAWA, author, quoted by Andrew Garrod in *Speaking for Myself: Canadian Writers in Interview* (1986).

A genuine crisis — and death is the final and perhaps greatest testing time — releases that better being. For the individual who experiences it, it has the distinct feeling of growth; for the human tribe, it is a redemptive experience.
> JUNE CALLWOOD, columnist and author, *Twelve Weeks in Spring* (1986).

Instead of suffering under Pontius Pilate, we suffer in emergency rooms of Canadian hospitals, where we are left to die.
> DENYS ARCAND, director, referring to his film *Jesus of Montreal*, remark quoted on 26 May 1989.

If we refuse to acknowledge the past, we conceal the nature of suffering, and therefore cannot understand demands in the present.
> HUGH BRODY, author, Introduction (1988), *Maps and Dreams: Indians and the British Columbia Frontier* (1981, 1988).

Whether it wishes or not, television has become the principal mediation between the suffering of strangers and the consciences of those in the world's few remaining zones of safety.
> MICHAEL IGNATIEFF, author and media personality, "The Ethics of Television," *Daedalus: Journal of the American Academy of Arts and Sciences*, "In Search of Canada," Fall 1988.

SUICIDE
See also DEATH
DYING WORDS

I have prayed for God's forgiveness if it is not too late.
> HERBERT NORMAN, diplomat and scholar, committed suicide in Cairo, Egypt, 4 April 1957. There were three suicide notes, two on his body (one for his wife and one for his fellow diplomats) and the third in his home. One of them said: "Illusion has been my besetting weakness, naïveté my chief flaw."

It's not the end of the world. Nothing is, except the end of the world.
> BETTY JANE WYLIE, author, *The Book of Matthew* (1984).

Suicide is *not* the ultimate survival technique!
> BETTY JANE WYLIE, author, *Successfully Single* (1986).

I identify with childhood, probably because mine was extraordinary. On the other hand, there were a lot of dark things underneath that I repressed. And the darkness emerged in the end.
> CLAUDE JUTRA, film director, commenting on the subject of his films and perhaps on his own eventual suicide, quoted in *TV Guide*, 26 Dec. 1987.

My name is Claude Jutra.
> Note (written in French) found on the body of the film director CLAUDE JUTRA, a victim of Alzheimer's. He disappeared on 5 Nov. 1986; his body was discovered in the St. Lawrence River at Cap-Santé, near Quebec City, 19 April 1987.

I have been unhappy for the past seven years.
> MARC LÉPINE, mass murderer, sentence from his handwritten suicide note found following the murder of fourteen female

students in Montreal, quoted by Greg Weston and Jack Aubry in *The Toronto Star*, 8 Feb. 1990.

SUMMER

See SEASONS

SUN

Our father, the Sun! / It is now time you were rising. I want to dance with you.
Blackfoot poem, "The Sun," *Songs of the Great Land* (1989) edited by John Robert Colombo.

SUPERNATURAL

See also BELIEF

Interest in "reality beyond the senses" is widespread. A careful analysis of the beliefs and practices of Canadian adults across the country has not revealed a tendency to abandon interest and involvement in things supranatural but simply a tendency to focus on *different kinds of supranatural phenomena*, in keeping with current cultural offerings. For example, older Canadians express more decisive beliefs in traditional Christian ideas — God, the divinity of Jesus, life after death — than do younger Canadian adults. Yet the latter, rather than abandoning the supernatural, are more inclined than the former to give credence to astrology, psychic phenomena, and communication with the dead.
REGINALD W. BIBBY and DONALD C. POSTERSKI, sociologists, *The Emerging Generation: An Inside Look at Canada's Teenagers* (1985).

SUPERSTITION

See also BELIEF

The real superstition is thinking that you can reject things unexamined.
ROBERTSON DAVIES, man-of-letters, interviewed by Terence M. Green in 1982, *Conversations with Robertson Davies* (1989) edited by J. Madison Davis.

And speaking of the 14th floor, I'd like to know why, if civilization has arrived on Planet Earth, elevators in high-rises do not have 13th floors designated as such.
CRAD KILODNEY, author, "How I Write Such Great Stories," alternative unpublished introduction to *Malignant Humours* (1988).

SURVIVAL, CULTURAL

This above all, to refuse to be a victim. Unless I can do that I can do nothing.
MARGARET ATWOOD, novelist, *Surfacing* (1972).

When I discovered the shape of the national tradition I was depressed . . . but I was exhilarated too: having bleak ground under your feet is better than having no ground at all.
MARGARET ATWOOD, novelist and cultural commentator, *Survival: A Thematic Guide to Canadian Literature* (1972).

I don't want to disappear.
Attributed to the Quebec comedian YVON DESCHAMPS by Martha Harron in *Don Harron: A Parent Contradiction* (1988).

In fact survival was the catchword, the cultural *mot-clé*, in Quebec for a long time — "survivance," just hanging on for dear life.
RENÉ LÉVESQUE, Quebec Premier, "Education in a Changing Society: A View from Québec," *Canadian Schools and Canadian Identity* (1977) edited by Alf Chaiton and Neil McDonald.

The key to surival is to adopt a strategy which turns your weakness into strength.
Comment of a character in the play *The Half of It* by JOHN KRIZANC, included in *Twenty Years at Play* (1990) edited by Jerry Wasserman.

SWEDISH PEOPLE

Sweden was a quite unexpected experience. If I had had any preconceptions, they would certainly have been outdone by the experience. My first feeling in Stockholm was: "Here is greatness consistent with human scale." The bounty of Sweden combines greatness and modesty, grandeur and playfulness, in the most unexpected ways.

MARSHALL McLUHAN, media philosopher, letter to King Carl Gustav of Sweden, 18 June 1974, *Letters of Marshall McLuhan* (1987) edited by Matie Molinaro, Corinne McLuhan, and William Toye.

I was very impressed with how the grain markets work in this country. It is easy to understand why so many Swedish farmers chose to abandon their stony patches for the rich Canadian Prairies when you see the dimensions of Canadian farming.

CARL XVI, King of Sweden, visiting Manitoba, quoted by Lisa Priest in *The Winnipeg Free Press*, 18 March 1988.

SWIMMING

See also SPORTS

I'd rather work with crippled kids than coach an Olympic champion.

GUS RYDER, swimming coach of Marilyn Bell and instructor of handicapped children, quoted by S.F. Wise and Douglas Fisher in *Canada's Sporting Heroes* (1974).

SWITZERLAND

Incidentally, I've always heard what a practical people the Swiss are — I finally understood these comments when I found out how they dispose of their mercury batteries. They collect them, and then dump them down an abandoned mine shaft — *in France!*

DAVE NICHOL, President, Loblaw International Merchants, Summit on the Environment, Toronto, 11 Sept. 1989.

SYMBOLS

The signal of Canada's arrival at adult status will be marked by its equitable and appropriate acknowledgement — without protest or undue allegiance — of all those mother-country symbols that mark the ethnic roots of its population.

IRVINE SCHIFFER, psychoanalyst, *Charisma: A Psychoanalytical Look at Mass Society* (1973).

Canada's national tree is the maple. Its animal is the beaver. Its sport is hockey. Its folk hero is the Mountie. Its musical instrument is the fiddle. Its gun is the shotgun. Its appliance is the heater.

Some people think Canada's vehicle is the train, or perhaps the snowmobile, but really it's the rowboat. We go forward, facing back. We can't see where we want to go, but we can see where we don't want to go.

JOHN GRAY, playwright and performer, contributor to *If You Love This Country: Facts and Feelings on Free Trade* (1987) edited by Laurier LaPierre.

SYMPATHY

And if self-pity keeps trying to sidle in, take action. So nobody helps you? Do you help them? Could you give them the sympathy you want to be given? Brace yourself and venture forth. It won't be hard to find somebody else with a broken heart to whom to give first aid, tea, sympathy, food, drink, a listening ear. Top marks if you can do this without (or as much without — I'm not suggesting you should try to be more than human) mentioning your own broken heart.

ELIZABETH SMART, novelist and diarist, "How to Mend a Broken Heart" (1982), *Autobiographies* (1987) edited by Christina Burridge.

TALENT

To spend money on everything but talent is the Canadian way.
> Remark attributed to TOM PATTERSON, the journalist who founded the Stratford Festival in 1953.

TAXES
See also FINANCE
GOODS & SERVICES TAX

Federal Income Tax Return (Simplified)
How much did you earn? $ ___.__
Send it in.
> Parody of the Income Tax Return produced by Revenue Canada (here called "Pillage Canada") reproduced by Jennifer J. Connor in "Parodies of Administrative Communications: Some Canadian Examples," *Culture and Tradition*, No. 10, 1986.

The Just Society — You tax people so heavily that they can't save up for their old age; then you grant them a pension which is (1) piddling to begin with and (2) eroded by taxes and (3) further eroded by inflation.
> RICHARD J. NEEDHAM, columnist, objecting to the economics of Trudeau's Just Society, *The Globe and Mail*, 18 Feb. 1972.

Why should Ontario pay for Quebec's fucking?
> GEORGE DREW, Ontario Premier, objecting to the proposed Family Allowance (or Baby Bonus) endorsed by Liberal leader Harry Nixon, quoted by Larry Zolf in *Saturday Night*, Dec. 1975.

Anyone who believes that Canada's only two official languages are English and French has never read the Income Tax Act.
> MARC DENHEZ, tax specialist, *Heritage Fights Back* (1978).

It is not possible in any democratic country in our time to urge forthright measures for the relief of the rich; that is thought politically too crude, even a trifle obscene. Some higher social purpose must be affirmed; incentives must be strengthened, incentive being the modern code word for returning more after-tax money to the affluent. That tax reduction was the real purpose of supply-side economics is now accepted by all whose detachment from concern for personal well-being allows a minimal clarity of view. That, of course, is not everyone. We must always respect the ability of the affluent to adjust economic belief to personal income enhancement.

JOHN KENNETH GALBRAITH, economist and author, address, Empire Club of Canada, Toronto, 3 Oct. 1983.

Is it consistent with equity to tax the man who works and saves as hard as the non-saver? Is it equity to tax the innovator, the entrepreneur, at the same rate as the drones in society?

W.O. TWAITS, Chairman, Imperial Oil, remark made in 1981, quoted by Jamie Swift in *Odd Man Out: The Life and Times of Eric Kierans* (1988).

In the spring of 1985, with Quebec's abandonment of its death and gift taxes, Canada became the only developed country without special taxes on the flow of wealth from one generation to another.

DIANE FRANCIS, financial writer, *Controlling Interest: Who Owns Canada?* (1986).

Canada has surprisingly low taxes. Indeed, when compared with the tax systems of twenty other western industrial nations, *Canada has the lowest overall tax on wealth*.

LINDA McQUAIG, journalist, *Behind Closed Doors* (1987).

But the realms where Canadians may demand freedom are restricted to moral matters; our governments do not bother their heads about morals, but they are firm in their insistence on controlling anything to do with money. Our country is only one among many that submit to hitherto undreamed-of burdens of taxation in order that gigantic sums may be spent on enterprises on which the ordinary citizen has only the vaguest understanding.

ROBERTSON DAVIES, man-of-letters, "Keeping Faith," *Saturday Night*, Jan. 1987.

The golden rule of Ottawa: It is more blessed to tax the many than to cut the few.

GEOFFREY STEVENS, commentator, *The Toronto Star*, 13 Aug. 1989.

There is a direct and absolute relationship between the amount of money a government takes from its people and the degree of power it exercises over their lives.

WILLIAM D. GAIRDNER, academic and businessman, *The Trouble with Canada* (1990).

In 1950 corporations and individuals each paid about half of the income tax collected in Canada. In 1989 individuals paid 88.1% of all income tax, and corporations only 11.9%.

MEL HURTIG, publisher, Presentation to the Senate Standing Committee on Banking, Trade and Commerce, 26 July 1990.

A fool and his money are soon taxed.

EDD ULUSCHAK, cartoonist, referring to Finance Minister Michael Wilson, "Woggles," Miller Features Syndicate, 16 Jan. 1990.

Between the Gulf War and the economy, I don't know if we should head for the bomb shelter or the tax shelter.

EDD ULUSCHAK, cartoonist, "Woggles," Miller Features Syndicate, 18 Dec. 1990.

Living in Canada is a very taxing experience.

EDD ULUSCHAK, cartoonist, *The Sounder*, 11 Jan. 1991.

TEACHERS & TEACHING
See also EDUCATION

The training of children is making a thousand neurotics for every one that psychiatrists can hope to help with psychotherapy. To produce a generation of mature citizens is the highest and most necessary job any country could undertake, and the reward in saving of misery and suffering would be colossal.

G. BROCK CHISHOLM, psychiatrist, White Memorial Lecture, Washington, D.C., Oct. 1945, published as *The Psychiatry of Enduring Peace and Social Progress* (1945).

It's the job of a teacher of the humanities to keep fighting for the liberalizing of the imagination, to encourage students to confront experience, to explore the shadows and the darkness, to distinguish evil from the portrayal of evil, and to meet the unexpected with tolerance.

NORTHROP FRYE, literary critic, "The Rear-View Mirror: Notes towards a Future," *Divisions on a Ground* (1978).

Some teachers make you wonder if you could pass Grade Four.

BETTY JANE WYLIE, author, *No Two Alike* (1980).

That which cannot be graded is rarely taught.

ROBIN SKELTON, man-of-letters, aphorism, May 1990.

When teachers disagree the student learns.

ROBIN SKELTON, man-of-letters, aphorism, May 1990.

The successful teacher today is really a coach. The good teacher is the guide on the side, not the sage on the stage.

NORMAN LEE, teacher in Winnipeg and one of twelve annual recipients of the Marshall McLuhan Distinguished Teacher Awards, quoted in a Maritime Life advertisement, *The Globe and Mail*, 13 June 1990.

We don't tell them how to be, we show them who we are.

KAHN-TINETA HORN, Mohawk activist, explaining the native way of raising children, quoted by Judy Steed in *The Toronto Star*, 11 Nov. 1990.

TEARS

First deal with your own tears; tomorrow do something about acid rain.

BETTY JANE WYLIE, author, *Successfully Single* (1986).

I'm working from morning till midnight / And weeping from midnight to dawn.

SYLVIA TYSON, performer, "Trucker's Cafe," quoted by Ellen Schwartz in *Born a Woman: Seven Canadian Women Singer-Songwriters* (1988).

TECHNOLOGY
See also SCIENCE & SCIENTISTS

Truly the epic of human genius in this century is its colossal mechanical contrivances. Two and three thousand years ago men wrote immortal poems. To-day they create marvellous inventions and bend the erstwhile undreamed-of forces of nature to their will. Which is the better, oh, ye gods of the Golden Age? After all, have we not lost as much as we have gained? The beautiful childhood of the world is gone forever. I believe its happiest days were in the dead-and-gone centuries of its song-singing, love-making, war-waging youth!

L. M. MONTGOMERY, author, journal entry, 23 Nov. 1901, Halifax, N.S., *The Selected Journals of L.M. Montgomery; Volume I: 1889-1910* (1985) edited by Mary Rubio and Elizabeth Waterston.

Wonder and fear are two bedfellows. There are many of us who are ever standing on the thresholds of workshops, looking and listening, never completely rid of the feeling that one day a spirit will enter and planet-strike the machines.

E.J. PRATT, poet, "Poetry and Science" (1947), quoted by David G. Pitt in *E.J. Pratt: The Master Years, 1927-1964* (1987).

Have you noticed that the word "escapism" has almost disappeared from the language? "Involvement" has taken its place. Under electric conditions there can be no escape.

MARSHALL McLUHAN, communications theorist, letter to Claude T. Bissell, 29 March 1967, *Letters of Marshall McLuhan* (1987) edited by Matie Molinaro, Corinne McLuhan, and William Toye.

I think electric technology is Orientalizing the entire Western world even while we are trying to westernize the Orient by old technology.

> MARSHALL McLUHAN, communications theorist, letter to William Jovanovich, 24 April 1967, *Letters of Marshall McLuhan* (1987) edited by Matie Molinaro, Corinne McLuhan, and William Toye.

The most recent development at the Centre for Culture and Technology is the completion of a study on "The Laws of the Media," which has led to the discovery that the most human thing about people is technology.

> MARSHALL McLUHAN, communications theorist, private communication, 30 April 1976.

At the speed of light, we become just an image. For example, when you are on the telephone, or on the radio or on TV, you do not have a body. You are just an image, minus a physical body.... What does it do to people? It has a profound effect on their ideas of themselves. I think it weakens the idea of private identity very much.

> MARSHALL McLUHAN, communications theorist, address, Mohawk College, Hamilton, Ont., 17 May 1977.

Instead of a traditional structure holding things together, you have each man holding his own gyroscope. Technology is sweeping away all meaningful relationships and replacing them with apparatus. We have to learn to live with this loss of relationship and humanize it.

> ROSS MACDONALD, crime novelist raised in Ontario, quoted by Raymond A. Sokolov, "The Art of Murder" (1971), as noted by Jerry Speir in *Ross Macdonald* (1978).

In the present day, technology proceeds for its own sake, not even for the human sake, in a succession of self-fulfilling prophecies. Technology makes something possible, then technology *must* go ahead and do it, regardless of necessity or consequence.

> JOHN A. LIVINGSTON, naturalist, *One Cosmic Instant: A Natural History of Human Arrogance* (1973).

By broadening our view, we change our lives and become more aware of life everywhere, even of the beauty in a rusted tin can. In fact, the power that is increasingly available through science and technology is an agent of change, because of its very vastness. We have to learn the responsible use of technology as an instrument of love. We can begin by caring for and appreciating our tools, our knives, pins or scissors.

> DOROTHY MACLEAN, medium, *To Hear the Angels Sing: An Odyssey of Co-Creation with the Devic Kingdom* (1980).

We are a nation rich in ideas. That Japan does so much with so little, and we so little with so much, is a question of national will. If we fail to exploit these current technological opportunities, or fail to develop new ones continually, we may still survive as woodcuts. But we must then be content with a woodcutter's wages.

> LARKIN KERWIN, President, National Research Council, address, Empire Club of Canada, Toronto, 12 Nov. 1981.

A point I've made for years — Friedman's Law — is that technological progress comes invariably from doing things differently in an unpredictable way. The future, technologically speaking, is not an extrapolation from the past. You have to change how you do things.

> STANTON T. FRIEDMAN, scientist and UFO researcher, quoted by Dennis Stacy in *UFO Report*, Winter 1981.

High-tech is not possible without whytech.

> HARRY ARTHURS, President, York University, Toronto, quoted by George Brett in *The Toronto Star*, 1 Oct. 1987.

Remote manipulator technology is destined to play an increasingly important role in space with the development of a permanently manned station and the wide range of commercial and scientific activities that will be associated with it. Indeed, Canada's major role in the coming era of permanent human habitation of space will centre on the use and furthur improvement of this technology.

LYDIA DOTTO, science writer, *Canada in Space* (1987).

History informs us very clearly that we can't depend on technology to keep coming up with solutions to social problems. Each new technology is accompanied by its own novel costs, and it is misguided to look to science to allow us to indulge ourselves without taking personal responsibility for the consequences. *Moderation* in our appetites is clearly the best rule to follow.

DAVID SUZUKI, scientist and broadcaster, *The Globe and Mail*, 1 Aug. 1987.

Technology has equipped our species with the mechanical equivalent of muscle power that now greatly exceeds that of any species that has ever lived. It has provided us with the resource base with which to multiply into the largest and most far-flung population of large mammals on earth. And a whole host of human activities — from commercial farming and forestry to the combustion of oil and coal — have altered the face of the planet in many ways that are easily visible from outer space.

DAVID SUZUKI, scientist and broadcaster, and Peter Knudtson, writer and biologist, *Genethics: The Ethics of Engineering Life* (1988)

In fact, Canada has been unique in its lack of interest in the nature of technology and its impact on each of us, to say nothing of the economy.

WALTER PITMAN, educator, *The Globe and Mail*, 11 March 1988.

Perhaps the New Canada is different from the Old Canada in only one important as-

pect. Old Canada had to invent everything and so created, on the spot, the instruments of its survival. The New Canada has the luxury of technology and so it tends to imitate. I'm not too certain the new nationalism will measure up.

LAURIER LaPIERRE, historian, reviewing Dominique Clift's *The Secret Kingdom: A Study of Canadian Character* (1989) in *Quill & Quire*, June 1989.

One must learn how to walk on quicksand and dance with electrons to thrive, not merely survive — or resign oneself to joining the "techno-peasants" of the future.

FRANK OGDEN, "Dr. Tomorrow," quoted in *Benchmarks*, Fall 1989.

It is far from coincidental that Canada and Canadians have been at the cutting edge of virtually every major technological innovation in this domain in the modern era. From the earlier inventions of Bell and Marconi to the more recent inventions in broadcast and satellite communications, Canadians have been at the centre of most of the breath-taking breakthroughs that have taken place in communication in the Twentieth Century.

D. PAUL SCHAFER, Director, World Culture Project, unpublished position paper "Canadian Cultural Sovereignty: Myth or Reality?" (1990).

The entire history of automobiles, airplanes, antibiotics, oral contraception, nuclear energy, computers, plastics, satellites and xerography is encompassed by the span of a single human life.

DAVID SUZUKI, scientist and broadcaster, interviewed in *Toronto Computes!*, March 1990.

In the real world of technology, I think, we would be well advised to question the authority of the images in the manner in which the Reformation questioned the authority of the Pope.

URSULA FRANKLIN, scientist, *The Real*

World of Technology (1990), as excerpted in *The Canadian Forum*, July-Aug. 1990.

There are thought to be about 1000 hi-tech firms operating in the Toronto region (compared with about 5000 in Silicon Valley in California).
EDWARD RELPH, geographer, *The Toronto Guide: The City/Metro/The Region* (Annual Conference, Association of American Geographers, Toronto, April 1990).

Technological progress almost invariably comes from doing things differently in an unpredictable way. The future, technologically speaking, is *not* an extrapolation of the past.
STANTON T. FRIEDMAN, scientist and UFO specialist, personal communication, 15 Jan. 1991.

TELEPHONE
See also COMMUNICATIONS

I had to answer the call of a very angry man. He wants to fight the government, to destroy buildings, and stir up hatred. I tried to persuade him to calm down, to come over and discuss matters peacefully. We must not use force when we want something, we must talk matters over calmly with the people whom we think are not on our side. The telephone is a most useful invention, we can discuss important matters, spread peace and love by persuading others as we talk. It was invented in Canada by Alexander Bell.
MOHANDAS K. GANDHI, Indian leader, addressing a group of school children about the newly installed telephone line in his quarters at Wardha, Central India, in 1935; as recalled by one of the school children, Kamala Bhatia, Mohawk College, Hamilton, Ont., in 1985.

The room a dying poet took / at nightfall in a dead hotel / had both directories — the Book / of Heaven and the Book of Bell. . . .
Lines from "The Room," a poem written by VLADIMIR NABOKOV about his room at the Park Plaza Hotel in Toronto in 1950 while guest lecturer at the University of Toronto, *The New Yorker*, 13 May 1950.

Not that I have ever enjoyed the telephone, my dear. It's like speaking through a keyhole.
Comment of a character in the play *Herringbone* by playwright TOM CONE, included in *Twenty Years at Play* (1990) edited by Jerry Wasserman.

TELEVISION
See also BROADCASTING
JOURNALISM
NEWS

It is coming, gentlemen, and we should be dealing with this question of radio broadcasting to keep the question of television well before us.
SIR JOHN AIRD, enthusiast for a public as well as a private broadcasting system, addressing a parliamentary radio committee in 1932.

The study of media begins with the observation of their effects. Effects cannot be observed by concepts or hypotheses as in conventional quantitative testing, for media are environments and inclusive processes, not products and packages. If the hot radio medium were turned off for a month in the oral cultures of the Near-East, there would be an instant cooling of the political climate. You cannot gnash your teeth on TV. If TV could be substituted, a mass revulsion for their "hot" attitudes would occur. The TV generation feels a revulsion for all centralist bureaucratic organization whether in education or politics, or in urban life.
MARSHALL McLUHAN, media philosopher, letter to *The Listener*, 11 Aug. 1971, *Letters of Marshall McLuhan* (1987) edited by Matie Molinaro, Corinne McLuhan, and William Toye.

Television is today as much a receptacle for the projection of a people's imagery as the moon used to be; it is seen as an instrument for the incitement of violence just as the moon, a celestial and "lunatic" scapegoat, was formerly believed to cause mankind's mental aberrations.

> IRVINE SCHIFFER, psychoanalyst, *Charisma: A Psychoanalytic Look at Mass Society* (1973).

Who will be responsible for putting Inuit content into television broadcasting? Who else but us! Inuit content can be meaningful and beautiful.

> NICHOLAS ARNATSIAQ, broadcaster in the N.W.T., "The Eye in the Sky" (1973), reprinted in *Inuktitut* No. 70, 1989.

The greatest difficulty in television is the need for condensation; it is a Procrustean bed in which not only the legs are trimmed off but also all else, except sometimes the head and the heart.

> JOHN KENNETH GALBRAITH, economist and author, "A Different Journey" (1977), *A View from the Stands of People, Politics, Military Power and the Arts* (1986) edited by Andrea D. Williams.

Television is bringing the outside inside, and bringing the aggressive states into the social states of the home.

> MARSHALL McLUHAN, media philosopher, address, Mohawk College, Hamilton, Ont., 17 May 1977.

When you see yourself on TV, as I have, you are innering and outering simultaneously.

> MARSHALL McLUHAN, media philosopher, quoted by Bruce R. Powers in the Preface to *The Global Village: Transformations in World Life and Media in the 21st Century* (1989) by Marshall McLuhan and Bruce R. Powers.

A Canadian Pay-TV approach would introduce a new dimension to Canadian broadcasting. Is it too bold, too impractical, to dare to think of a Canadian TV service, an *all-Canadian* TV service in Canada by 1980?

> STUART MacKAY, president of Selkirk Holdings Limited, addressing the Empire Club of Canada, Toronto, 10 Nov. 1977.

Monty Haul. Generous referee, who lets game characters survive and prosper; from TV personality MONTY HALL, in that this referee gives "gifts" to players.

> Definition of "Selected Terms Used by Fantasy Games" noted by Gary Alan Fine in *Shared Fantasy: Role-Playing Games as Social Worlds* (1983).

I'll tell you what I'm gonna do! I'll offer you fifty bucks for that! Is it a deal? Let's make a deal! I'll trade you what's in this box for that watch!

> Characteristic spiel of Monty Hall, host of the television show *Let's Make a Deal*, which has been called "probably the most successful game show in television history"; quoted by Harry Gutkin with Mildred Gutkin in "Monty Hall: America's Top Trader," *The Worst of Times / The Best of Times* (1987).

The power of television is its mass audience. I spent nine years in live television and found myself always struggling with network officials, advertising agency executives, and the sponsors themselves as to creative content of the programs. With hardly a single exception, their interests had nothing to do with responsibility to the viewer, with truth, with improving the artistic level of programming, with self-criticism.

Indeed, we witnessed the television industry in the United States actually become a mere extension of Madison Avenue and the advertising interests. CTV may have the glitz and hot American shows, but thank God for the CBC. I guess I had good training at the BBC and CBC, because in all those years of directing television, I never shot or was involved in one commercial.

> NORMAN JEWISON, film director, address, Empire Club of Canada, Toronto, 5 April 1984.

Television is not a visual medium. It is an acoustic medium.
> MARSHALL McLUHAN, media philosopher, *The Man and the Message*, CBC-TV, 18 Oct. 1984.

Cambodia: A Book for People Who Find Television Too Slow
> Title of a book of innovative fiction written by innovative author BRIAN FAWCETT and published in 1986.

A trapper living in the Mackenzie delta can turn on a television and watch a movie or instantaneous coverage of a sports event, with the result that Native people in some remote places on earth know more about what is happening in the Kremlin, the White House, or Hollywood than they do about what is happening in the headquarters of their own national organization.
> BRIAN MARACLE, native radio broadcaster, "New Expectations of Media in Canada's Evolving Native Communities," *Information/Crisis/Development*: News from the Third World (1986) edited by Peter Desbarats and John Southerst.

Endless pitches but no commercials; obvious fouls but no penalties; and if the audience grows weary of a character, they, not the producers, get the pleasure of throwing him out. . . . Television has been a hideous curse to the Canadian political system. *Hansard* should be read but not seen. Showbusiness has no business on the floor of the House of Commons. . . . The House of Commons has become an ongoing series for Canadian television viewers.
Lacking our own Hollywood, the televised proceedings serve as our soap opera, crime story, running ad, cartoon, consumers' report, nailbiting drama, tearjerker and welcome break from reality.
> ROY MacGREGOR, columnist, *The Ottawa Citizen*, 17 Oct. 1987.

If radio needed the full participation of the listener's imagination, live television required the complete suspension of the viewers' disbelief in order for them to connect with the drama through the maze of physical distractions that actor R.H. Thomson fondly refers to as "CBC clunky."
> BRONWYN DRAINIE, broadcaster and biographer, *Living the Part: John Drainie and the Dilemma of Canadian Stardom* (1988).

Watching TV ads is sitting in the corner watching all the lies go by. / The medium is no more the message than the Chivas Regal bottle is the whiskey.
> PATRICK O'FLAHERTY, literary critic, characteristic remarks, Jan. 1988.

Canadians, being natural outsiders, are adept at parody, the essential art form of our time. (Is that the Canadian influence?) Canadians [Loren] Michaels, [John] Candy, Eugene (SCTV) Levy and Rich Little all owe their success in America to making fun of American institutions. Moreover, when it comes to TV, they have an unfair advantage. Canada, with a population of less than 26 million, has eight full-time networks; thus, just about anyone in Canada who wants his own talk show can get one.
> RICHARD STENGEL, U.S. journalist, "The Canadians," *Spy*, Feb. 1988.

The medium's gaze is brief, intense, and promiscuous. The shelf life of the moral causes it makes its own is brutally short.
> MICHAEL IGNATIEFF, author and television personality, "Is Nothing Sacred? The Ethics of Television," *Daedalus: Journal of the American Academy of Arts & Sciences*, "In Search of Canada," Fall 1988.

At its best, television's morality is the morality of the war correspondent, the veteran who has heard all the recurring justifications for human cruelty advanced by the Left and the Right, and who learns in the end to pay attention only to the victims.
> MICHAEL IGNATIEFF, author and television personality, "Is Nothing Sacred? The Ethics of Television," *Daedalus: Journal of the American Academy of Arts & Sciences*, "In Search of Canada," Fall 1988.

If the dominant ethics in television today is that there are no good causes left — only victims of bad causes — there is no guarantee that the medium will not succumb to the next moral fashion. There is even a danger that television's healthy cynicism towards causes will topple into a shallow kind of misanthropy.

MICHAEL IGNATIEFF, author and television personality, "Is Nothing Sacred? The Ethics of Television," *Daedalus: Journal of the American Academy of Arts & Sciences*, "In Search of Canada," Fall 1988.

Over the next few years I was struck by the difference in tone between American and Canadian TV interview shows. Just about every televised interview I did in Canada had a suspicious edge to it; What kind of compromises had I made in order to succeed? Wasn't I embarrassed to be singing such personal songs? I was discovering that Canadians tended to be wary of success stories, especially Canadian success stories. They were skeptical, strangely disapproving of unabashed ambition. American TV was something else altogether. I wasn't interviewed so much as celebrated; each interviewer came armed with enough chart statistics about my latest record release to start up a PR firm.

DAN HILL, composer and performer, "Massaged by the Media," quoted by Peter Goddard and Philip Kamin, editors of *Shakin' All Over: The Rock'N'Roll Years in Canada* (1989).

What is then the all-important and pervasive function that television emulates in our brain? Imagination. TV is a technological and collective imagination at work, much more so than the film industry.

DERRICK de KERCKHOVE, academic, "Control of the Collective Mind," *The Canadian Forum*, Oct. 1989.

Television has now to live with computers which have begun to take it over and modify its market according to its own rules. In simple technical terms, computers, by improving recording and editing technol-

ogies and making them much cheaper, are putting television productions in the hands of smaller and smaller groups of interest. Now this has the two-fold advantage of decentralizing productions and promising a greater and better access to television production facilities to younger groups, for instance schools.

DERRICK de KERCKHOVE, academic, "Control of the Collective Mind," *The Canadian Forum*, Oct. 1989.

In a word, TV with computers doing the selection is TV with brains. For Canada, this means that ultimately decentralization may eventually liberate the local producer from the grip of the Hollywood majors.

DERRICK de KERCKHOVE, academic, "Control of the Collective Mind," *The Canadian Forum*, Oct. 1989.

While our thoughts are truly our own, television thinking is done for us by somebody else. It is a form of collective mind control.

And what is more, even as this new collective mind seeps into the sinks of our personal brains, it is diminishing and displacing two important support systems of psychology and identity, our past psychology, our past identity. It is displacing the old mythological resources of religious sensibility and the later cognitive responses of literacy. Though the media are no substitute for churches as means of social organization, that is what they are beginning to replace. For imagination, sensibility and mental processes, television and computers are beginning to exert as much power in our lives as once did the church.

DERRICK de KERCKHOVE, academic, "Control of the Collective Mind," *The Canadian Forum*, Oct. 1989.

Canadians, with more TV options than any viewers in the world, are living through a future Britain is only just becoming aware of; a multi-channel system simply expands product homogenization. It's up to public broadcasting services to create what I call "masterpiece TV," an alternative to mass-market programming. It's what makes TV an honourable medium.

> MICHAEL IGNATIEFF, author and TV personality, quoted by Greg Quill in *The Toronto Star*, 3 Oct. 1989.

At the same time, the pervasive influence of network and cabled U.S. television is probably the most underestimated development in modern Canadian history. Travel across Canada and turn on the television sets in Inuvik and Saskatoon, St. John's, and dozens of other communities across the nation, to satellite TV, direct from Detroit, and you will better understand how misplaced George Grant's faith was when he wrote, optimistically: "Most helpful is that among the young . . . the desire for independence is greater than for many generations."

> MEL HURTIG, publisher and nationalist, referring to the philosopher George Grant, address, Carleton University, Ottawa, 23 Sept. 1989.

Be you — that's who they invited. More important, that's what works.

> CHARLES TEMPLETON, media personality, tendering advice on how best to appear on TV, *Succeeding* (1989).

There is no real choice right now. There's just the same show on fifty channels. In the '90s there will be more personal vision and passion seen on the small screen.

> IVAN FECAN, program director, CBC-TV, quoted in *Metropolis*, 21 Dec. 1989.

"Narcissus Narcosis" was Marshall McLuhan's description of the media-induced stupor where audiences sit mindlessly before the tube, projecting themselves into the video mirror. Narcissus was the Greek god who fell in love with his reflection in a pool of water.

> WILSON BRYAN KEY, critic of subliminal images in advertising, *The Age of Manipulation: The Con in Confidence and the Sin in Sincere* (1989).

Television has become the activist's tutor. Along with the soap operas and the sports and the shrill evangelism it has provided a primer for quiet revolution.

> PIERRE BERTON, author, Preface (1989), *The Mysterious North* (1956, 1989).

In any conflict, it can now fairly be said, there are three sides — A, B and TV.

> ROY MacGREGOR, columnist, on how television shapes the news, *The Toronto Star*, 5 Sept. 1990.

We have handed over this most powerful medium to a foreign country. Nowhere else in the world has one country imported the total television output of another country.

> DENIS HARVEY, CBC-TV executive, addressing a conference in Toronto on international television issues, 31 Nov. 1990, quoted by Christopher Harris in *The Globe and Mail* the following day.

By the year 2010, 3-dimensional television will be developed, but will be abandoned in favour of a new kind of image-producing device, capable of projecting a 3-D holographic image suspended in free space.

> MAURICE B. COOKE, channeller, *The Aquarian Wave: A Prophetic Handbook for the 90s* (1990).

TENNIS

Tennis is not a game one automatically associates with Canada. The world's second-largest country is better known for its sports played in or near water in its various states: swimming, snow skiing, and ice skating or hockey. Those are the games in which Canadians have shown world-class, if not world-championship, skills.

Adopting a derivative, such as "tennis on ice," might be a sneaky shortcut, given the propensity of Candians to do well on frozen water.

> PETER USTINOV, entertainer, Foreword, *Advantage Canada: A Tennis Centenary* (1990) by Martin Kendrick.

TERRITORIES

See also NORTHWEST TERRITORIES
YUKON TERRITORY

The Yukon and the Northwest Territories are governed by regulations that do not have to be examined by Parliament and are not examined by Parliament, and the evidence of the past certainly has been that the regulatory bodies have considered any public discussion or critique of this system as both meddlesome and officious.

PIERRE BERTON, author, address, Empire Club of Canada, Toronto, 11 Oct. 1973.

TERRORISM

See also OCTOBER CRISIS

We live in a society of terrorized slaves, terrorized by the big bosses, Steinberg, Clark, Bronfman, Smith, Neopole, Timmins, Geoffrion, J.L. Lévesque, Hershorn, Thompson, Nesbitt, Desmarais, Kierans (next to these, Rémi Popol the Nightstick, Drapeau the Dog, the Simards' Simple Simon and Trudeau the Pansy are peanuts!).

We are terrorized by the Roman Capitalist Church, though this is less and less true today (who owns the square where the Stock Exchange was built?); terrorized by the payments owing to Household Finance, by the advertising of the grand masters of consumption, Eaton's, Simpson's, Morgan's, Steinberg's, General Motors.

Two paragraphs from the "FLQ Manifesto," 5 Oct. 1970, included by Marcel Rioux in Quebec in Question (1971).

To bow to the pressures of these kidnappers who demand that the prisoners be released would be not only an abdication of responsibility, it would lead to an increase in terrorist activities in Quebec. Should governments give in to this crude blackmail, we would be facing the breakdown of the legal system and its replacement by the law of the jungle.

PIERRE ELLIOTT TRUDEAU, Prime Minister, explaining the invoking of the War Measures Act during the October Crisis, CBC-TV, 16 Oct. 1970.

Canada remains one of the most wholesome and humane lands on this earth. If we stand firm, this current situation will soon pass. We will be able to say proudly, as we have for decades, that within Canada there is ample room for opposition and dissent, but none for intimidation and terror.

PIERRE ELLIOTT TRUDEAU, Prime Minister, explaining the invoking of the War Measures Act during the October Crisis, CBC-TV, 16 Oct. 1970.

The breakdown of international legality, characteristic of recent times, amounts to undeclared warfare and desperately weakens the political civilization we possess which was very costly to construct.

KENNETH TAYLOR, Consul General of Canada, New York, address, Empire Club of Canada, Toronto, 15 Jan. 1981.

Cry for Guatemala, with a corpse in every gate. / If I had a rocket launcher I would not hesitate.

BRUCE COCKBURN, composer and singer, "If I Had a Rocket Launcher," Stealing Fire (1984).

There are no "just solutions" to the terrorist's problem. His goals are as bloody and illegitimate as the means he employs to serve them. In fact, his means reveal his goals. (He may sincerely believe in them, of course; the fanatic is generally sincere.) If you want to evaluate something a person wants, if you want to know whether it is good or just, take a close look at how he goes about getting it. Nothing will tell you better.

GEORGE JONAS, columnist, Crocodiles in the Bathtub and Other Perils (1987).

There are many wrongs in the world, but none that could be righted by the terrorist's program. His program is what he does.

GEORGE JONAS, columnist, *Crocodiles in the Bathtub and Other Perils* (1987).

Wen I wuz a lad terrierism jist ment razin up a buncha puppies, and P.L.O. wuz sumthin our teecher put on the black-bored so us moniters wooden rub it off.

DON HARRON, comedian, in the person of Charlie Farquharson, *Cum Buy the Farm* (1987).

To have learnt from terror / to see one-self / as part of the enemy // Can be a reassurance / whatever it is / arises within us

PETER DALE SCOTT, poet, *Coming to Jakarta: A Poem about Terror* (1988).

Two years after three hundred and thirty-one people were murdered the Mounties who formed the Air-India Disaster Task Force were no closer to charging the culprits. For a party to mark the retirement of one task-force officer, they had circular crests created. The badges bore the RCMP insignia over the silhouette of a jumbo jet. A motto was emblazoned below: "Project Nightmare."

IAN MULGREW, journalist, referring to the act of sabotage that resulted in the Air India crash in 1985, *Unholy Terror: The Sikhs and International Terrorism* (1988).

What do you make of a country where they hijack a *bus*?

More to the point, what does it tell you about a country where the authorities manage somehow to lose this hijacked bus, where the police of one province can't be bothered calling the police in the next province over where the bus is heading, where they try to drive this bus across a *lawn* in the first week of April, where all ends peacefully and the hostages tell about how they joked and showed photographs of their families to fill in the time?

ROY MacGREGOR, columnist, referring to the bizarre highjacking of a bus that was taken to Parliament Hill, *The Ottawa Citizen*, 10 April 1989.

TEXAS

Texas is not my fault.

Line in a poem by PAULETTE JILES noted by Andreas Schroeder in an interview with Alan Twigg in *Strong Voices: Conversations with Fifty Canadian Authors* (1988).

THANKSGIVING
See HOLIDAYS

THEATRE
See also ACTORS & ACTING
AWARDS & HONOURS
CRITICS & CRITICISM
STRATFORD FESTIVAL

It only remains for the financial problems to be solved, and for the rising generation of Canadian writers and actors to resist the lure of Hollywood, New York, or London, and to establish, on their own soil and in their own fashion, a professional theatre which shall be as truly native as that of any other land.

PHYLLIS HARTNOLL, "Canada," *The Oxford Companion to Theatre* (2nd ed., 1957) edited by Phyllis Hartnoll.

It has been remarked that what the theatre needs is actors, not audiences. . . . This is an American remark about the American theatre. Perhaps it is true in its own reference. But here in Canada we appear to be caught in the truth of this statement in reverse. We have the actors and workers of the theatre, on our radio networks, and — as often as possible — on our stages. Our actors are in the habit of acting. It is to be hoped that those who make up our audiences will form the habit of coming to the theatre.

FLETCHER MARKLE, producer and director of the 1947 Toronto production of William Saroyan's *The Time of Your Life*, program note, quoted by Bronwyn Drainie in *Living the Part: John Drainie and the Dilemma of Canadian Stardom* (1988).

"Rise above it" was his catch-phrase for anything tiresome, undesirable or even disastrous, from undrinkable, tepid, canteen coffee, to toothache, or to the loss of all costumes and scenery on tour.

ALEC GUINNESS, British actor, describing the attitude of the director Tyrone Guthrie, *Blessings in Disguise* (1985).

I now had a big house and should have been able to make a respectable income, at least until I chose to spend half the year acting in a tent in Canada.

JAMES MASON, stage and screen actor who left his home in Hollywood in 1954 to star in the fledgling Stratford Shakespearian Festival's productions of *Oedipus Rex* and *Measure for Measure* being staged under a giant circus tent; quoted by Sheridan Morley in *Odd Man Out* (1989).

William Hutt: I'm doing *Private Lives* with my wife Zoe Caldwell.
Noël Coward: Mahvellous, dahling! You can't go wrong with the classics!

Fabled exchange between the Toronto-born actor WILLIAM HUTT and the English playwright and *bon vivant* NOËL COWARD in 1961 when Hutt was touring North America in Coward's play *Sail Away*; quoted by Ed Gould in *Entertaining Canadians: Canada's International Stars 1900-1988* (1988).

We want poets and critics and interpreters to use our stages. Let them speak softly, caustically, comically, dreamily, but let them speak. These people may well be among the playwrights. . . . When we hear their voices singing, and recognize them as our own, then the story of the true Canadian theatre will begin.

NATHAN COHEN, drama critic, "A Copy Theatre," *Century: 1867-1967* (1967) edited by John D. Harbron.

Things *have* changed. This can be seen if one compares conditions now with those of the twenties or thirties. Gone are those days of interminable and regular Farewell Tours by British artists; of Donald Wolfit and his company paddling their way across Canada like Mayfair voyageurs, of-

fering glittering bits of Shakespeare as barter to the nervous natives; of Little Theatres drearily discovering the easily discernible parts of Ibsen and Shaw; of endless music festivals and lectures; of Chautauqua and the Minneapolis Symphony for unwilling school kids; of boring stock companies, and elocutionists executing any poetry that came their way; of the last pale shadow of the Ballet Russe de Monte Carlo blowing across the land like the slipper-shod and doomed crew of a choreographic Flying Dutchman; of a continent's hitting its cultural apogee every Saturday afternoon when the Met came on the radio; of Manitoba-Moorish neighbourhood cinemas where one received, besides an awareness of how low the film art could sink, gifts of disastrous dinnerware designed to lure one back; of teachers' societies doing *Macbeth* and vice versa. All, thank God, are no longer with us. And our half-million regular-attending compatriots share our knowledge.

THOMAS HENDRY, theatre personality, "The Performing Arts," *The Canadians 1868-1967* (1967) edited by J.M. Careless and R. Craig Brown.

A good play ought to be one you can see more than once with pleasure. These plays which depend upon revulsion can only do it to you once.

ROBERTSON DAVIES, man-of-letters, interviewed by Gordon Roper in 1968, *Conversations with Robertson Davies* (1989) edited by J. Madison Davis.

The two great Canadian dramatists are Chekhov and Ibsen. The Ibsen and Chekhov situations can be paralleled in Canada twenty times over.

ROBERTSON DAVIES, man-of-letters, interviewed by Silver Donald Cameron in 1971, *Conversations with Robertson Davies* (1989) edited by J. Madison Davis.

Twigg: You once said Chekhov and Ibsen are our two great Canadian playwrights. Is that because they both explored self-satisfied small-mindedness?

Davies: Yes. And also because they explored a northern consciousness with an intensity that has not been equalled in Canada.

> ROBERTSON DAVIES, man-of-letters, interviewed by Alan Twigg in 1981, *Conversations with Robertson Davies* (1989) edited by J. Madison Davis.

All Shakespeare demands is two boards and a passion!

> Attributed to (among others) DORA MAVOR MOORE, theatre personality, quoted by Martha Harron in *Don Harron: A Parent Contradiction* (1988).

Now get this straight. Either you cut it out, or I'm going home.

> ZOE CALDWELL, actress, stepping out of the role of the Egyptian temptress in Shakespeare's play *Antony and Cleopatra*, during a production at the Stratford Festival which premiered in July 1967, to admonish young members of the student audience who were sniggering at her exposed breast during the scene with the asp, quoted by Ray Conlogue in *The Globe and Mail*, 10 Aug. 1990.

What are we going to do? / *Qu'est-ce qu'on va faire?*

> Final lines in English and French of the unemployed workers in the bilingual play *Balconville* (1979) by DAVID FENNARIO.

Plays survive in print, and can be judged by their texts. If poetry is what is lost in translation, theatre is what is lost with the performance.

> RONALD BRYDEN, theatre critic and teacher, Foreword, *Whittaker's Theatre: A Critic Looks at Stages in Canada and Thereabouts 1944-1975* (1985) edited by Ronald Bryden with Boyd Neil.

Like the curate's egg, Canadian theatre is good in parts.

> KEITH GAREBIAN, author, *The Bumper Book* (1986) edited by John Metcalf.

John Hirsch and I cannot be cast in the same play.

> JOHN NEVILLE, actor and artistic director, referring to fellow director noted for his artistic temperament, quoted by Robert A. Gaines in *John Neville Takes Command: The Story of the Stratford Shakespearean Festival in Production* (1987).

The Famous People Players would be like nothing that has ever been imagined in the theatre: a unique form of entertainment created by a unique group of performers. It would be more than a puppet show; it would be a black-light extravaganza of colour, movement, and music, brought to the stage by people who had spent their lives in the shadows. The company would be a way to bring these people out of the shadows, to change the world's perception of the mentally retarded.

> DIANE DUPUY, live puppet theatre founder and director, *Dare to Dream: The Story of the Famous People Players* (1988) written with Liane Heller.

Then, I pretended I was a fairy princess, Robin Hood, a great actress, or the Lone Ranger. It was down in that basement that I decided to become famous. Someday, I promised myself, everybody was going to applaud me. In that basement, I discovered that I could create a world of my own — a world of magic and dream — from my imagination. Everything could be transformed just by making up a story.

> DIANE DUPUY, live puppet theatre founder and director, *Dare to Dream: The Story of the Famous People Players* (1988) written with Liane Heller.

I write *a* vision of *a* writer of *a* situation, not *the* vision of *the* writer of *the* situation.

> MICHEL TREMBLAY, playwright, discussing his play *The Real World*, quoted by Robert Crew in *The Toronto Star*, 21 May 1988.

Theatre is the most human of the arts. It consists of people watching people becoming other people. This art of transformation is the essence of theatre, what is known as its "magic."

MIKE ALFREDS, director, program notes to Masterclass Theatre's production of *Blood Wedding*, Tarragon Theatre, Toronto, Sept. 1988.

I don't consider it entertainment when you have to pay attention to find out what's going on.

Letter addressed to the management of Toronto's Factory Theatre by an irate patron, *The Toronto Star*, 31 Dec. 1988.

You know what happens to you when you write a hit play in Canada? Nothing.

DAN NEEDLES, playwright, author of the "Wingfield" plays, quoted by Martin Hunger in *The Toronto Star*, 23 Sept. 1989.

I ran into a high school friend in Vancouver recently, and told him I was having a play produced. He said, "Oh, wonderful, I'll have to read the review." When I suggested that he actually go and see the play, he looked horrified, and said, "Oh, no, I couldn't do that. People my age rent videos and stay at home with baby."

SALLY CLARK, playwright, quoted by Jason Sherman in *The Toronto Star*, 4 Nov. 1989.

You know what theatre's best for? Showing pain. But nobody wants to see pain: not when they see it written all over the breakfast table every morning.

Comment of a character in the play *War Babies* by playwright MARGARET HOLLINGSWORTH, included in *Twenty Years at Play* (1990) edited by Jerry Wasserman.

Theatre artists (along with other stubborn survivalists) must more than ever before band together. Theatre critics must adopt a new responsibility of encouraging the public to go to theatre. For although Canadian theatre has taken exciting leaps within the last twenty years, that old adage "If there ain't no audience there ain't no show" says it all.

MARTHA ROSS, theatre director, quoted in *Metropolis*, 21 Dec. 1989.

There's something very attractive about creating works for a theatre, but also something repulsive. I find it harder and harder to believe in the theatre as a receptacle for serious art.

R. MURRAY SCHAFER, composer, quoted by Robert Everett-Green in *The Globe and Mail*, 16 Feb. 1991.

THEOLOGY

So too it may be that the contemporary crisis of human living and human values demands of the theologian, in addition to treatises on the unique and to treatises on the universal common to many instances, a treatise on the concrete universal that is mankind in the concrete and cumulative consequences of the acceptance or rejection of the message of the Gospel.

BERNARD J.F. LONERGAN, Jesuit philosopher, *Insight: A Study of Human Understanding* (2nd ed., 1958).

THIRD OPTION
See TRADE & COMMERCE

THIRD WORLD
See also HUNGER

The Prairie Provinces: Canada's Third World.

Title of a chapter of GEORGE WOODCOCK's study *The Canadians* (1979).

If to be part of the Third World is to be a hewer of wood and a supplier of food and natural products, the United States and Canada are, by a wide margin, the first of the Third World countries and should vote accordingly in the United Nations.

JOHN KENNETH GALBRAITH, economist and author, "The Multinational Corporation" (1978), *Annals of an Abiding Liberal* (1979).

We are a commodity exporter and a technology importer, which is the economic profile of every Third World nation. . . . Canada is the richest underdeveloped nation in the world.

> Attributed to the academic WILLIAM GRAHAM in an address reported in *The Globe and Mail*, 12 Nov. 1988.

In international affairs, the North-South conflict will take over from the East-West conflict and there will be all sorts of upheavals in the Third World and Latin America. But it's much less likely to take place under a banner of so-called Soviet-style communism. I don't think the people of the Third World now believe that the Soviet system has all the answers. They'll attempt to find the solutions in their own ways.

> PAUL MARANTZ, professor, University of British Columbia, Vancouver, quoted in *The Toronto Star*, 30 Sept. 1989.

Sharing many characteristics of the Third World, Canada mediates easily between the First and Third Worlds.

> MARSHALL McLUHAN, media philosopher, and Bruce R. Powers, communications specialist, authors of *The Global Village: Transformations in World Life and Media in the 21st Century* (1989).

This emerging Third World solidarity, as it continues to gather momentum, is the best hope that the developing world will be able to shake off both the Soviet Union and the United States — as with its colonizers before — and thereby allow its economies to prosper.

> FRANK FEATHER, futurologist, *G-Forces: Reinventing the World — The 35 Global Forces Restructuring Our World* (1989).

Have you noticed that if an anthropologist goes out and studies an ancient "third world" culture, and he finds knowledge or traditions way in advance of his own, he always ends up speculating on visitations from outer space.

> Comment of a character in the one-woman show *Afrika Solo* (1990) by playwright DJANET SEARS.

The native peoples of Canada have a living standard that belongs to the Third World, yet every day they rub shoulders with one of the richest and most leisured of modern societies.

> LISA HOBBS BIRNIE, author and journalist, *A Rock and a Hard Place: Inside Canada's Parole Board* (1990).

For the first time in history, we fortunate 20 percent of the world, we who use 80 percent of the planet's resources in pursuit of the good life, are being forced to face the fact that the Third World is part of an equation that will determine *our* survival on the Earth.

> ANITA GORDON and DAVID SUZUKI, science broadcasters, *It's a Matter of Survival* (1990).

Canada is well on the way to becoming an economic backwater. It will be the first time in history any nation has evolved backwards — from being a member of the First World to joining the Third.

> PETER C. NEWMAN, columnist, "Business Watch," *Maclean's*, 25 Feb. 1991.

THOMSON, ROY
See also NEWS

He moved to North Bay, named his shop Modern Electric, and began selling. "Name's Thomson — Call me Roy," the smiling fat man with the shiny, patched pants would introduce himself, as he hustled his goods, sold himself, angled for this or that deal, kited cheques, and made contacts. Modern Electric went down in the depression, but in 1931 Thomson had finagled his way into a licence to operate a local radio station and acquired some broken-down transmitting equipment. CFCH, North Bay, went on the air that March with a full fifty watts of power.

> MICHAEL BLISS, historian, recounting the hard work and hustle of Roy Thom-

son, *Northern Enterprise: Five Centuries of Canadian Business* (1987).

I just followed the same business principles that worked in Timmins and North Bay. I did the same things in Edinburgh and London as I did back here, except I added a few zeroes at the end.
ROY THOMSON, broadcaster and publisher who became Lord Thomson of Fleet, quoted by Roy MacSkimming in *The Toronto Star*, 16 July 1975.

If I have any advice to pass on, as a successful man, it is this: if one wants to be successful, one must think; one must think until it hurts.
ROY THOMSON, newspaper publisher, *After I Was Sixty: A Chapter of Autobiography* (1975) by Lord Thomson of Fleet.

Is it not true, then, that you had a licence to print money?
CHOU EN-LAI, Chinese leader, responding to Roy Thomson's suggestion that the Chinese borrow to buy modern newspaper equipment, *After I Was Sixty: A Chapter of Autobiography* (1975) by Lord Thomson of Fleet. Even in China they had heard Thomson's quip "A TV licence is a licence to print money."

And became Lord Thomson of Fleet, which should better have been named Fleetingly.
ALLAN FOTHERINGHAM, columnist, *Maclean's*, 7 Nov. 1988. Fotheringham, the self-styled Dr. Foth, no slouch with nicknames, dubbed Roy Thomson's son and heir, "young" Ken, "Lord Silverspoon."

He's richer than me, but then again he's six months older.
ROY THOMSON, publisher, hosting a lunch for the Anglo-American financier J. Paul Getty, both of whom were in their eighties; quoted by Diane Francis in *Controlling Interest: Who Owns Canada?* (1986).

I've always wanted to be a billionaire and never came close. God knows I'll never get there with my newspapers. But maybe this will give me my chance.
ROY THOMSON, publisher, agreeing to join the American oil executive Armand Hammer in a consortium to exploit North Sea oil in 1971; quoted by Hammer in his autobiography, *Hammer* (1987) written with Neil Lyndon.

To me, there was little resemblance between the two lords of Fleet. Father rotund, cherubic, eyes exaggerated by bifocals, always the salesman, the hustler. Son angular, fit, reserved, and attentive — the kind of man who would probably say "Thank you" as he stepped off automatic elevators.
Description of Kenneth Thomson by RICHARD J. DOYLE in *Hurly-Burly: A Time at The Globe* (1990).

THOUGHTS
See also INTELLIGENCE

Birds must fly, fish must swim, herbivorous animals must eat grasses and cereals, and man must observe and think freely.
G. BROCK CHISHOLM, psychiatrist, White Memorial Lecture, Washington, D.C., Oct. 1945, published as *The Psychiatry of Enduring Peace and Social Progress* (1945).

Thinking is work.
ROY THOMSON, newspaper publisher, *After I Was Sixty: A Chapter of Autobiography* (1975) by Lord Thomson of Fleet.

The ultimate building blocks of matter may well be, not neutrons or protons, but "conceptions."
HOWARD EISENBERG, physician and parapsychologist, remark made in 1989.

TIBET

Reporter: Why is the invasion of Kuwait by Iraq more problematic than the invasion of Tibet by China?
Dalai Lama: Because we have no oil.
Exchange at a press conference in To-

ronto, Sept.-Oct. 1990, between an un-named reporter and the DALAI LAMA, head of the Tibetan government-in-exile, occasioned by the unwillingness of Prime Minister Brian Mulroney to meet with the religious leader and Nobel-laureate peace activist; quoted by Alice Klein in *Now*, 4 Oct. 1990.

TIME

See also FUTURE
PAST
PREDICTION & PROPHECY
PRESENT

Having recently been working on that for-mulation that new technologies create new environments which mirror every-thing but the present, because they *are* the present. Is this not characteristic of the entire human past? Has not every age and every culture failed to see its own present while being fixated by the image of the preceding phase or situation?
MARSHALL McLUHAN, media philoso-pher, letter to Tom Easterbrook, 22 Feb. 1967, *Letters of Marshall McLuhan* (1987) edited by Matie Molinaro, Corinne Mc-Luhan, and William Toye.

Against the sustained tick of a watch, fic-tion takes the measure of a life, a season, a look exchanged, the turning point, de-sire as brief as a dream, the grief and terror that after childhood we cease to express. The lie, the book, the grief are without permanence. The watch continues to tick where the story stops.
MAVIS GALLANT, author, "What Is Style?" (1982), *Paris Notebooks: Essays and Re-views* (1986).

Time past and time future are both pres-ent in time present. We flesh out what we are with what we were; the better to be what we will be.
DONALD SUTHERLAND, film star, a "per-sonal note," according to Maria Topalovich in *A Pictorial History of the Canadian Film Awards* (1984).

What I regret most in my own life is the time I wasted when I was young. I have not wasted much since.
GORDON SHRUM, engineer and educator, *An Autobiography* (1986) written with Peter Stursberg, edited by Clive Cocking.

There is something ridiculous about our attitude towards time. People who would smile at the notion that Chilliwack, B.C., was the most important point in space do not hesitate to consider the point they themselves occupy in time the only one that really matters.
GEORGE FALUDY, Hungarian-born poet, *Notes from the Rainforest* (1988).

Our souls are marked by time; it is the substrate of our existence, so the healing of time is also the healing of our souls. Since our souls are marked by time, as long as we allow it to be fragmentary and incoherent, the passage of our souls through time will be meaningless and end in emptiness. Psyche is one of the Greek words for soul, and the word "healing" comes from a Teutonic root that means whole. Therefore the purpose of psycho-therapy is to try to make the soul whole again.
MAX DUBLIN, sociologist, "Dancing to the Tune of Time," *The Globe and Mail*, 29 Dec. 1989.

Time is not a line but a dimension, like the dimensions of space. If you can bend space you can bend time also, and if you knew enough and could move faster than light you could travel backwards in time and exist in two places at once.
MARGARET ATWOOD, novelist, *Cat's Eye* (1988).

You slip in and out of my present / Or am I slipping in and out of your past?
Line from a poem in *Something Might Hap-pen* (1989) by the author BETTY JANE WYLIE.

The beginning of the long dash, followed by 10 seconds of silence, indicates exactly one o'clock. . . .

Wording of "The National Research Council Time Signal," heard over CBC Radio, quoted by Russell McNeil in *The Toronto Star*, 17 Feb. 1991, who noted: "It may be Canada's longest-running if shortest radio program (as little as 15 seconds)."

TITLES

See AWARDS & HONOURS

TOLERANCE

In some countries today people are no longer free to enjoy the most innocent of all freedoms — tolerance — to be tolerant is to be disloyal. There is no middle ground.

MARY MAXWELL, a.k.a. Rúhíyyih Khánum, leading member of the Bahá'í Faith, *Success in Teaching* (1970).

TORONTO

See also ONTARIO

Toronto is also situated up a bay. . . . One of the most prominent objects in approaching this city is the Lunatic Asylum, and next, the extensive commons lying waste in front of it, though not quite so worthless to the world as the barracks and their occupants, also seen in the same view.

SOLON ROBINSON, traveller, "Sketches of Canada," *American Agriculturalist*, Oct. 1850.

Toronto is a fair matron with many children, whom she has planted out on either side and north of her as far as her great arms can stretch. She lies north and south, while her lips speak loving words to her offspring, and to her spouse, the County of York; when she rests she pillows her head on the pine-clad hills of sweet Rosedale, while her feet lave at pleasure in the blue waters of beautiful Lake Ontario.

Passage from the sentimental novel *A Romance of Toronto* (1888) by MRS. ANNIE GREGG SAVIGNY.

Toronto the Good
Epithet for the city associated with Toronto Mayor William Howland, a reformer who held office from 1886 to 1888, noted by Desmond Morton in *Mayor Howland: The Citizens' Candidate* (1973).

Toronto as a city carries out the idea of Canada as a country. It is a calculated crime both against the aspirations of the soul and the affections of the heart.

ALEISTER CROWLEY, occultist and writer, May 1904, *The Confessions of Aleister Crowley: An Autohagiography* (1969) edited by John Symonds and Kenneth Grant.

Toronto makes a Sunday in a Scotch village seem like a hashish dream!

ALEISTER CROWLEY, occultist and writer, "Art in America," *The English Review*, Nov. 1913.

Toronto on a Sunday morning — a beastly place.

Attributed to the American author JOHN DOS PASSOS in a letter written from Toronto in 1907, quoted by Albert and Theresa Moritz in *The Oxford Illustrated Literary Guide to Canada* (1987).

Toronto is a good city . . . so far as morality goes; and considering the five hundred old churches we have, I believe one of the Apostles won't be far from here when the Great Day comes.

Observation made about "Toronto the Good" by a taxi driver to his fare in the futuristic novel *Toronto in 1928 A.D.* (1908) written by FREDERICK NELSON.

We stopped for some hours at Toronto, and had time to renew our acquaintance with that magnificent city, which seems to have taken to giddy ways, for she has erected an enormous glittering sort of Coney Island place along the lake-side, which was in full swing as we passed, with many thousands of people on swings and switchbacks and other diversions. If money paid to the saloons diminished the family standard, then it seems to me that these profitless excitements must have the same effect; yet it must be admitted that the monotony of modern economic life does call for some stimulant, if it be only taken in reason.

SIR ARTHUR CONAN DOYLE, author and traveller, *Our Second American Adventure* (1923).

One feels at once in this city that vibrant sense of religious earnestness and fierce self-assertion which the dominant Catholic Church always brings with it. It is logical enough, for if your religion is really and literally true, then it must predominate over everything else. There is a good deal of virtue, however, in the "if."

SIR ARTHUR CONAN DOYLE, author and traveller, *Our Second American Adventure* (1923).

. . . a slow place, a dull place, where English snobbery met American vulgarity and each thrived on the other . . . a half-grown city, a nest of Methodists and Orangemen, of Puritans and Pharisees, who had not yet heard that Queen Victoria was dead.

Thoughts of a character in the novel *Jupiter Eight* (1938) by FRANCIS POLLOCK.

You know even in Toronto you can't dance, fly, play tennis, sail and lounge clad in a fountain pen.

EUGENIA WALCOTT, friend of the American black writer Jean Toomer, advising him to take on a non-writing vacation in Toronto, 23 May 1929, quoted by Cynthia Earl Kerman and Richard Eldrige in *The Lives of Jean Toomer: A Hunger for Wholeness* (1987).

City that suits Ron in toto.

Question in cryptic clue form by crossword puzzle creator TORQUEMADA (Edward Powys Mathers) of *The Observer* from 1926 to 1939, the answer being "Toronto." Noted by Tony Augarde in *The Oxford Guide to Word Games* (1984).

I never knew Toronto was disliked so much.

J.B. PRIESTLEY, English writer on a tour of Canada, "I Heard the Monotonous, Mournful Voices of Canadian Women," *Liberty*, Aug. 1956.

Instead of jail, Halban could merely be sent to Toronto for the duration of the war.

C.D. HOWE, Minister of Supply, addressing U.S. General Groves who wanted to reprimand the atomic scientist Hans von Halban of "The Montreal Lab" who in 1944-45 made an innocent but unauthorized trip to Paris to see Professor Joliot, known to be a Communist; quoted by Robert Bothwell in *Nucleus* (1988).

When [they] drove me in from the airport, I have to admit that I didn't recognize anything except the Royal York Hotel. Toronto is a sort of Brasilia — it seems to have sprung up all over on huge scale.

J.G. BALLARD, English writer making a return visit to Toronto, having first come to Canada in 1954 for pilot training as an RAF officer, seeing Quebec City, Montreal, and Toronto and spending nine months in Moose Jaw, Sask.; quoted by H.J. Kirchhoff in *The Globe and Mail*, 17 Oct. 1987.

Having completed the training in Glasgow, I decided to continue my studies across the Atlantic and chose Toronto because I realized that I should not be among entire strangers, due to this city's deeply rooted links with Scotland. How true that proved to be!

J. MENZIES CAMPBELL, Scottish dental historian, "Fifty Years Ago in Toronto" (1962), *Dentistry Then and Now* (1958, 3rd ed., 1981).

The people in Toronto, although no great beauties, seem healthier and better set-up than those in New York and Boston. Not so driven and not so cramped between big buildings and in narrow streets, they seem to be more good-natured, and they probably enjoy themselves more.

EDMUND WILSON, literary critic, recalling a visit in 1962, *Upstate: Records and Recollections of Northern United States* (1971).

As a relatively recent transplant from New York, I am frequently asked whether I find Toronto sufficiently exciting. I find it almost too exciting. The suspense is scary. Here is the most hopeful and healthy city in North America, still unmangled, still with options. . . . I am grateful at least to have enjoyed this great city before its destruction.
JANE JACOBS, writer and observer of urban life, upon moving from New York City to Toronto and buying a house situated on the edge of the proposed Spadina Expressway in 1970; quoted by Edward Relph in *The Toronto Guide: The City/Metro/The Region* (Annual Conference, Association of American Geographers, Toronto, April 1990).

When history looks at our city, I have but one wish, that it will see the greening of Toronto and say: There, there is where it turned.
DAVID CROMBIE, Toronto Mayor, inaugural address, Dec. 1974, quoted in *Time*, 23 June 1975.

Toronto, in short, is a city that works.
ANTHONY ASTRACHAN, U.S. correspondent, "A City that Works," *Harper's*, Dec. 1974.

I was born in this city. I was raised in this city. I went from this city to see nearly all of the world, and this is the place I want to live and die.
GORDON SINCLAIR, newspaperman and broadcasting personality, opening the CNE in Toronto, Aug. 1975, quoted by Scott Young in *Gordon Sinclair: A Life . . . and Then Some* (1987).

Toronto. The name still arouses feelings of deep resentment among many Canadians who live elsewhere in Canada. The word and the place Toronto continue to unify other Canadians as few things can.

MORRIS WOLFE and DOUGLAS DAYMOND, editors, Introduction, *Toronto Short Stories* (1977).

A favourite boast of local press agents is that it [Yonge Street] is, in fact, the longest street in the world. They arrive at this particular bit of propaganda by virtue of the fact that Yonge Street doesn't exactly end; it just sort of dissolves into the Ontario highway system, and it is possible to follow this road, north and west, for about twelve hundred miles (almost two thousand kilometres). Most of those miles traverse country that is absolutely haunting in its emptiness and bleakness and starkly magnificent beauty.
GLENN GOULD, pianist and television performer, "Toronto," *Cities: From the Television Series Conceived by John McGreevy* (1981).

The Big Lemon (as it is known in Western Canada). . . .
New designation for Toronto, apparently popular west of the Humber River, quoted by columnist Allan Fotheringham in *Malice in Blunderland or How the Grits Stole Christmas* (1982).

Mikhail Gorbachev told Eugene Whelan that Toronto was one of the most beautiful cities he'd ever seen by night and by day.
JOHN BENTLEY MAYS, cultural commentator, *The Globe and Mail*, 1 Aug. 1987. Mays is reporting on the recollections of Agricultural Minister Eugene Whelan who, in 1983, chaperoned Mikhail Gorbachev, then head of a Soviet agricultural mission, on his first trip to North America.

My particular favourite geography lesson was the junior at the University of California in Los Angeles who thought that Toronto must be in Italy.
BENJAMIN J. STEIN, scholar, "The Cheerful Ignorance of the Young in L.A." (1983), quoted by E.D. Hirsch, Jr., in *Cultural Literacy: What Every American Needs to Know* (1987). No doubt the junior con-

fused Toronto, Ontario, with Taranto in Calabria, Southern Italy — with some reason, as California place names come from all over the map and include both Ontario and La Cañada Flintridge.

If you're born in a city like London or Paris, you know you were born to one of the oldest cultures in the world. If you're born in a city like New York, you know you were born to be one of the kings of the world. But if you're born in Toronto — that's destiny.

> Remark attributed to the media personality MOSES ZNAIMER in 1984, Toronto's sesqui-centennial year.

As the twenty-first century dawns, if the world's cities are standing at all, there is every reason to believe that Toronto will still be the city that works, the city of hope, true to the meaning of its name in the Indian tongue, the name that means "abundance," an abundance for all its people to share.

> WILLIAM KILBOURN, historian, "Taking Power in the Seventies and What Happened After," *Toronto Remembered: A Celebration of the City* (1984) edited by William Kilbourn.

Even during this short visit it is clear to me that life has been very good to Toronto since I was last here. The dramatic changes in the Toronto skyline, I think, spell the message of success and prosperity, even to the most transient visitor and I congratulate you all on that success. . . . It's witness not only to the right policies but to the initiative and leadership of so many who are in this room today.

> MARGARET THATCHER, Prime Minister of Great Britain, address, Empire Club of Canada, Toronto, 27 Sept. 1984. Her previous visit was in 1975.

And I grew dizzy, and willed myself aloft above Toronto, for I had been reading much science fiction — and possibly for that reason the Shell Building and the streetcars and the sewers and the timid

innovations of plastic, all seemed suddenly insubstantial and on close view as imperfect and plywoody as a mockup of a new vacuum cleaner.

> JOHN CLUTE, science-fiction critic, "Being Earthbound; or Toronto Tale," *Strokes: Essays and Reviews 1966-1986* (1988).

This is Toronto the good; the good because it is a city where you can go about your business unmolested.

> Speech of a Mafia don played by the actor Dean Stockwell in the movie *Palais Royale* released in 1988.

There's even a certain confidence about the place. Visitors don't get asked, "So how do you like it here?" every five minutes anymore.

> MECHTILD HOPPENRATH and CHARLES OBERDORF, travel writers, *First-Class Canada* (1987).

Not bad, eh? (That's Toronto's favourite phrase: Not bad, eh?)

> MECHTILD HOPPENRATH and CHARLES OBERDORF, travel writers, *First-Class Canada* (1987).

In Toronto, the unexpected doesn't happen. The city is safe and reliable, and utterly predictable.

> STEPHEN BROOK, English travel writer, *Maple Leaf Rag: Travels across Canada* (1987).

It's all got to me. Pictures. Churches. Driving down the Arno in the early morning. Well, they called me back to the U.K. and they said, "Look here, Tapscott. We hear you're going bush in Florence. Only one thing for it. We're going to transfer you to Toronto."

"Bugger that for a lark!" I said. So I took early retirement.

> Speech of a British consular official named Tapscott who is thought to be "going native" in JOHN MORTIMER's comic novel *Summer's Lease* (1988).

Toronto is my second-favourite North American city after Buffalo.

Preference expressed by MARK PLUMMER, an Australian attorney and investigator, addressing the Ontario Skeptics in Toronto in 1986. At the time Plummer was based in Buffalo, N.Y., and was serving as chairperson of the Committee for the Scientific Investigation of Claims of the Paranormal.

Canada looks different from Toronto — it suddenly all looks like Toronto. There is nothing but Toronto.

LOUIS DUDEK, poet and aphorist, "Can. Lit. Notes," *The Bumper Book* (1986) edited by John Metcalf.

The question is: if Canadians don't have Toronto to kick around anymore — what in the world will hold this country together?

Not to worry. There's always Ottawa.

ARTHUR BLACK, broadcaster, *Back to Black: Comic Sketches* (1987).

Toronto . . . a kind of New York operated by the Swiss.

PETER USTINOV, actor and personality, quoted by John Bentley Mays in *The Globe and Mail*, 1 Aug. 1987.

But the city that works must be given credit for becoming something rarer — a city where most work.

PETER COOK, columnist, *The Globe and Mail*, 10 Sept. 1987. Cook was alluding to Anthony Astrachan's description in 1974 of Toronto as "a city that works."

Toronto remains a North American miracle, a city . . . without the decay, social squalor and unrest that characterizes so many U.S. cities, or Paris for that matter.

Editor, *Le Nouvel Observateur*, Paris, quoted in *The Financial Post*, 12 Oct. 1987, according to Alan F.J. Artibise, "Canada as an Urban Nation," *Daedalus: Journal of the American Academy of Arts and Sciences*, "In Search of Canada," Fall 1988.

I like to think that fifteen thousand years ago is only yesterday. And it is. The ice was a mile high on top of Toronto fifteen thousand years ago. That gives me a certain sense of being more at ease in this universe. With that thought behind me, I'm quite sure I'll be able to finish a new book.

HUGH MacLENNAN, novelist, interviewed by Alan Twigg in *Strong Voices: Conversations with Fifty Canadian Authors* (1988).

Only the largest centres can afford to build unique and innovative landmarks.

There is perhaps no better example of such a landmark than Toronto's CN Tower — a tower for the sake of a tower, and a concrete, science fiction counterpart to Monsieur Eiffel's pinnacle of steel.

VIRGIL MARTIN, photographic historian, *Changing Landscapes of Southern Ontario* (1988).

After so many years on the street I have drawn some conclusions. The population of Toronto breaks down as follows: 33% blobs, 33% snobs, 33% slobs, and 1% human.

CRAD KILODNEY, writer of fiction who hawks his publications in Toronto's streets, "How I Write Such Great Stories," alternate unpublished introduction to *Malignant Humours* (1988).

I spent the rest of the afternoon doing some shopping and walking and taxi-riding around, getting reacquainted with one of the most visually entertaining cities in the world. I'd found it architecturally exciting six years earlier, and it seemed to me now not less but more so, with glimpses of its slender tallest-in-the-world free-standing tower with the onion bulge near its top appearing tantalizingly between angular high-rises covered with black glass and gold. And they had built a whole new complex, Harbourfront, since I'd been there, a new face turned to Lake Ontario and the world.

Thoughts of the narrator of *The Edge* (1988), a crime novel set aboard a transcontinental train by English writer DICK FRANCIS.

But Canadians should stop being nervous and start counting their blessings, beginning with Toronto, which is a modern miracle — a city that has become better as it has become bigger.

GEORGE F. WILL, syndicated columnist based in Washington, D.C., and Toronto resident in the late 1960s, *The Toronto Star*, 14 Jan. 1988.

I just want people to understand Toronto for what it is — a world-class city with small-town civility.

ART EGGLETON, Toronto Mayor, referring specifically to Toronto's role as host of the Economic Summit, 19-21 June, 1988; quoted in *Maclean's*, 20 June 1988.

In 1969, when I opened this office, Toronto was still an impossible city. Now it's one of the exciting cities in North America.

ARTHUR ERICKSON, architect, noting the "ordered" and "civilized" nature of the city's life, quoted by Christopher Hume in *The Toronto Star*, 20 Sept. 1988.

I want Toronto to move energetically down the path of assuming world status, while preserving the very remarkable quality of life we have created. If we are going to play on the world stage we are going to have to change ourselves from a people of prose to a city of poetry, from the city that works to the city that lives.

JOE BERRIDGE, urban planner, quoted by Colin Vaughan in *The Globe and Mail's Toronto Magazine*, Oct. 1988.

If I were a traveller out of a Black Hole somewhere and had time only for a single metropolis before the rocket left again, I think I might well choose for my inspection the city of Toronto. There is no pretending that it is the most beautiful of towns. . . . It has hardly acquired the rich patina of antiquity, but in the last decades of the twentieth century it has become in many ways a microcosm of its time.

JAN MORRIS, Anglo-Welsh travel writer, Foreword, *Toronto: The Way It Was* (1988) by Michael Kluckner.

Try to walk out the door past it. Try to come along Spadina Avenue, see that goddamn Silver Dollar sign, hundreds of light bulbs in your face, and not be drawn in there. Have a few drinks. . . .

ELMORE LEONARD, crime novelist, *Killshot* (1989).

The Canadian trouble-spot I would keep an eye on is Toronto.

Through the '90s, I predict, Toronto will attempt to evolve, in law and in practice, into a city-state.

In fact, without Torontonians knowing it, Toronto is already a city-state rather than just a city. As city-states do, it earns its living, principally by trading either with the world, or among its own citizens, rather than by trading with the rest of Canada.

RICHARD GWYN, columnist, *The Toronto Star*, 4 Oct. 1989.

When Americans visit Toronto they can't help noticing how darn nice the place is. It's so . . . clean. Hollywood movie crews import their own garbage to make Toronto streets look more like the good old U.S.A. And if they leave the rubbish unguarded, the city sweeps it up.

RICK MARIN, television columnist for *The Washington Times* and former Torontonian, *The Globe and Mail*, 17 Nov. 1989.

Gotham Envy dates back to the late 1960s, when Toronto (pronounced Trawwna by the natives) latched onto the counter-culture movement and created a groovy simulacrum of Greenwich Village called Yorkville, now an elite shopping district.

As a full-blown collective neurosis, however, the phenomenon didn't take hold until the early 1980s. Political and economic circumstances combined with the decade's contagion of material green: "red" Pierre Trudeau was out, quasi-Reaganite Brian Mulroney was in. Almost overnight, Toronto became "T.O." Business boomed. Buildings got taller. Women kissed each other on the street. Men kissed each other on the lips. Suddenly, the city was swimming in cappuccino.

> RICK MARIN, television columnist for *The Washington Times* and former Torontonian, *The Globe and Mail*, 17 Nov. 1989.

Not content to be North America's most liveable — most pleasantly un-American — city, it prays for the day when some U.S. metropolis will want to call itself "the Toronto of the South."

But as Al Capone once said, "I don't even know what street Canada is on."

> RICK MARIN, television columnist for *The Washington Times* and former Torontonian, *The Globe and Mail*, 17 Nov. 1989.

The Vile Metropolis

> Epithet for Toronto by the novelist and one-time Toronto resident MARGARET LAURENCE in *Dance on the Earth: A Memoir* (1989).

A New Yorker cannot help finding Toronto a peaceful and well-kept place. That is what they find most striking. If they meant boring they would say so.

> MATT MURDOCH, journalist, *I.C.E. Magazine*, Issue No. 3, Holiday Season, 1989.

Toronto is where the Canadian West begins, where it is very easy to become a nameless wanderer.

> RUSSELL BANKS, American novelist, *Affliction* (1989).

We want our lake back, want to be able to swim in it. Want to feel we locate on one of the most beautiful lake systems in the world. *For most of us there simply is no lake there now!* Cut off by towers and cement. Surely our greatest mall, University Avenue, should have opened onto the lake, with parks spreading across the lakeshore.

> SCOTT SYMONS, novelist and cultural commentator, "Glitz City," *The Idler*, Nov.-Dec. 1989.

Is it crazy to compare Toronto with Venice? Two cities on the water. Venice, that Renaissance capital on the Adriatic, city of the Doges. It too was a money capital, commercial capital, a city of urgent entrepreneurs. And these men left us one of the most beautiful cities of all time. Why can't we think in such terms? Why not dare? We have the site, the history, the artists . . . and literally tons of money, one of the wealthiest cities in the world of all time!

> SCOTT SYMONS, novelist and cultural commentator, "Glitz City," *The Idler*, Nov.-Dec. 1989.

Truth is we're now both — cosmopolitan and small-town, high hick and neo-churl, with an ongoing lust for a murdered gentry, or at least a gentry plus brains.

> SCOTT SYMONS, novelist and cultural commentator, "Glitz City," *The Idler*, Nov.-Dec. 1989.

Toronto may well be the most multicultural city on Earth.

> This sentence appears in the City of Toronto's Olympic Bid Book, released 9 Jan. 1990. Its argument was that Toronto should host the XXVIth Olympic Games of 1996; they were awarded to Atlanta, Georgia. Two characteristics of Toronto's population were noted: Half the people in Metro were born outside Canada; one-third have backgrounds that are neither English nor French.

One of the things that I really like about Toronto is that it still has a liveable downtown. What I really love to do is just walk along the streets. There is a lot of architectural interest here. I believe that buildings are fossils of human events and reflect the significance of every city.

> MARGARET ATWOOD, author, contributor, "Incredible Ontario," *Ontario: The Inside Story* (1990).

Toronto is one of the great cosmopolitan cities and in my opinion, it's the city that really justifies the country. It's interesting to me that Toronto is now becoming a literary city in the way that London has been for years.

> MARGARET ATWOOD, author, contributor, "Incredible Ontario," *Ontario: The Inside Story* (1990).

Toronto is, in short, well integrated into the global economy of the late-20th century, and in that respect it has more in common (including inflated house prices) with New York, Los Angeles, London, Amsterdam, Hong Kong and Singapore than it does with most Canadian cities.

> EDWARD RELPH, geographer, *The Toronto Guide: The City/Metro/The Region* (Annual Conference, Association of American Geographers, Toronto, April 1990).

Movie makers . . . claim that Toronto can be used to conjure up the illusion of almost any northeastern North American city at any time in the last 150 years. Apparently parts of Toronto look more like early 20th-century Chicago than any extant districts there. Is this good? Or does it mean that there is no strong character here? Anyway, Toronto is the third-ranking movie and TV production centre in North America after L.A. and New York City (though perhaps declining). It also has the highest rate of per capita cinema attendance in North America.

> EDWARD RELPH, geographer, *The Toronto Guide: The City / Metro / The Region* (Annual Conference, Association of American Geographers, Toronto, April 1990).

It seems that Toronto can be made to look like almost anywhere in North America. I'm not sure whether this is a comment on its cosmopolitan character or its lack of a strong identity.

> EDWARD RELPH, geographer, *The Toronto Guide: The City/Metro/The Region* (Annual Conference, Association of American Geographers, Toronto, April 1990).

With imaginative municipal leadership, there might even be some thought of To-

ronto and its immediate environs functioning as a city-state, a Singapore of the West, but there would be none of the criteria of nationhood.

> CONRAD BLACK, capitalist and columnist, "Enough Is Enough," *Saturday Night*, Sept. 1990.

Metro is a creeping, crawling thing that tries to overlap everybody.

> JIM POTTICARY, Ottawa Regional Councillor, quoted by Jack Cahill in *The Toronto Star*, 7 Oct. 1990.

We can grow rich or we can grow poor. But we're going to grow.

> GARDNER CHURCH, Ontario deputy minister, Office of the Greater Toronto Area, quoted by Jack Cahill in *The Toronto Star*, 7 Oct. 1990.

The fascist state of Toronto.

> Characterization of Toronto by superstar MADONNA prior to her third "Blonde Ambition" performance at Toronto's Sky-Dome, 29 May 1990, when detectives from 52 Division and a crown attorney warned her performer's representatives that an act of simulated masturbation on stage would be the basis of a charge; caught on film in the 1991 documentary *Madonna: Truth or Dare*, quoted by Brian Gorman in *The Toronto Star*, 10 May 1991.

TOURISM
See also TRAVEL

Alienation is an essential part of the experience of travelling. It is the vision of estrangement that creates the world afresh.

> KILDARE DOBBS, travel writer, *Away from Home: Canadian Writers in Exotic Places* (1985).

"Friendly, familiar, foreign, and near." That was the old Canada. No such four glib adjectives could today limn this new Canada; or could they?

> BRUCE McCALL, satirist, "In the New Canada, Living Is a Way of Life," *The New Yorker,* 20 May 1985.

The difference between tourism and travel is that one's a business and the other's a way of life.

> SAM BLYTH, president of a personalized travel company, quoted by Susan Jones in *The Globe and Mail's Toronto Magazine*, July 1988.

Canada is one of the more expensive countries in the world for travelers, although the recent proliferation of budget accommodations such as hotels and campgrounds has made it possible to travel on an economy budget.

> PETER HOPKIRK and PATRICK O'LEARY, travel consultants, "An Introduction to Canada: The Civilized North America," *Fodor's Canada* (1978) edited by Robert C. Fisher and Leslie Brown.

People go to Spain for the sun and to France for the food, but they go to Canada for one reason only: To stay with their in-laws.

> MILES KINGSTON, British humour columnist, writing in *The Independent*, quoted by Richard Gwyn in *The Toronto Star*, 13 Nov. 1988.

Futurists have been predicting since the 1960s that tourism would become the largest industry in the world by the year 2000. Tourism is already the second largest industry in Toronto, for example, and became the second largest retail sales industry (after automobile sales) in North America in 1981.

> FRANK FEATHER, futurologist, *G-Forces: Reinventing the World — The 35 Global Forces Restructuring Our World* (1989).

Tourism is a kind of sanctioned stupidity. You walk stupidly about, ignorant of how to get where you're going, of how to ask — ignorant of how, in an alien culture, you look and sound to others.

> GARY ROSS, journalist, "Distant Intimacies," *The Saturday Night Traveller* (1990) edited by George Galt.

You ain't seen red until you've seen Canada in the Fall.

> Wording on an English-language billboard erected in the National Hotel in Moscow by Goliger's Travel of Toronto, noted by John Macdonald in *The Toronto Star*, 7 Oct. 1989.

Americans may love New York, but they have a passion for Canada.

> TOM HOCKIN, Minister of Tourism, summarizing the findings of a survey conducted into the preferences of U.S. travellers; it dismissed the image of Canada as "moose, mountains, and Mounties"; speech delivered at Fort Erie, Ont., 21 May 1990, quoted by Grace Beauchamp in *The Fort Erie Tribune* the following day.

TOYS

Little boys never grow up. Their toys just get more expensive.

> DON HARRON, humorist, speaking in the guise of the comic character Valerie Rosedale, quoted by Martha Harron in *A Parent Contradiction* (1988).

TRACK & FIELD
See also JOHNSON, BEN

Like all re-invented sports, walking cannot possibly be mastered without the top line in contemporary equipment: $100 shoes that go slower than $100 jogging shoes, stopwatches, shorts of a particular fabric, shirts with sarcastic racing stripes.

> ROY MacGREGOR, columnist, *The Ottawa Citizen*, 21 April 1987.

One hundred metres in 9.79 seconds, cheat or no cheat, creep or no creep, chemicals or no chemicals, endorsement-rich or penniless. That, any person, anywhere, can understand.

> STEPHEN BRUNT, sports columnist, commenting on the celebrity status of sprinter Ben Johnson, *The Globe and Mail*, 29 Jan. 1991.

TRADE & COMMERCE
See also FOREIGN AFFAIRS
FREE TRADE
INTERNATIONALISM

They buy more nor they sell, and eat more nor they raise.
> Remark attributed to Sam Slick, the fictional Yankee trader in the Maritimes created by the 19th-century satirist THOMAS CHANDLER HALIBURTON; quoted by William Arthur Deacon in "The Bogey of Annexation" (1925) reprinted by Clara Thomas and John Lennox in *William Arthur Deacon: A Canadian Literary Life* (1982).

It's better to trade bulls than bullets.
> Attributed to CYRUS EATON, Maritime-born capitalist and peace advocate, as a justification for selling a shipload of cattle to the Soviet Union at the height of the Cold War in the 1950s.

The basic aim of the [third] option would be, over time, to lessen the vulnerability of the Canadian economy to external factors, including, in particular, the impact of the United States and, in the process, to strengthen our capacity to advance basic Canadian goals and develop a more confident sense of national identity.
> MITCHELL SHARP, Finance Minister, "The Third Option," *International Perspective*, Aug. 1972. This article, part of a special issue called "Canada-U.S. Relations: Options for the Future" and issued by the Department of External Affairs, first uses the phrase "third option" for the federal trade initiative. Although Sharp signed the article, its authorship has been attributed to Klaus Goldschlag, later Ambassador to West Germany.

Trudeau: I will be speaking to the Prime Minister of Denmark and the Prime Minister of Luxembourg about the —
Stanfield: Missing link?
Trudeau: — contractual link. The hon. member is saying that it seems to be elusive. Perhaps he has not seen rather extensive reports which have been carried in the press to the effect that the commissioners' recommendation has been made to the commission, and the commission will be asking the council of ministers to authorize the beginning of negotiations with Canada. This, it seems to me, is very good progress indeed. Perhaps the hon. member does not understand it. I will try to explain it to him.
> Exchange between Prime Minister PIERRE ELLIOTT TRUDEAU and Conservative leader ROBERT STANFIELD in the House of Commons, 26 May 1975, concerning Trudeau's abortive attempt to establish a "contractual link" or "third option: for trade purposes between Canada and the European Common Market."

Nuther bad thing wat happen wuz yer Yerpeen Common Mark-up, to countervale all this . . .
And now the big Boogie is perteckshunism. I thot that wuz the cheef bizness of yer Mafiascos or yer Cosy Nostrils.
> DON HARRON, comedian, in the person of Charlie Farquharson, *Cum Buy the Farm* (1987).

The monetary value of that trade at present far exceeds the total of U.S. trade with both Japan and the European community. The province of Ontario alone is a larger American trading partner than Japan. And most goods and services cross the border free of any duty or restriction whatsoever.
> WILLIAM KILBOURN, historian, discussing "the heavy volume of trade between the two countries," "The Peaceable Kingdom Still," *Daedalus: Journal of the American Academy of Arts and Sciences*, "In Search of Canada," Fall 1988.

We can speak loudly and carry a big twig.
> JOHN CROSBIE, Trade Minister, referring to Canada's clout in trade disputes, quoted by John Raymond in *The Globe and Mail*, 13 June 1989.

Europe will emerge as the centrepiece of all international trade, against which everything else pales. The United States has been and is being progressively eclipsed.

STEPHEN LEWIS, former UN Ambassador, address in Toronto, 3 Oct. 1989, quoted by Bob Papoe in *The Toronto Star* the following day.

The reality of globalization is not that new frontiers — new lines to be pushed back or pierced — have suddenly appeared. What is happening is precisely the reverse: the lines are disappearing. Globalizaton is not so much our going out into the world; it is the world coming in and enveloping us. We are not dealing with *new* frontiers; we are dealing with *no* frontiers.

HELEN SINCLAIR, President, Canadian Bankers Association, address in Winnipeg, quoted in *The Globe and Mail*, 7 Nov. 1989.

Canada is like a womb with a view. We don't want to face the discomfort of the real world.

Adapted from a remark made by the economist CARL BEIGIE in an address to the Certified General Accounts Association of Ontario, Toronto, 9 Nov. 1989, as reported by George Brett in *The Toronto Star* the following day.

The nations that are most economically secure and successful in trade are West Germany, Sweden and Japan. All of them have several common elements. They stick to what they do well. They spend a lot of money and time on research and training the work force. And governments, business and unions work closely together.

DORIS ANDERSON, writer, "Symposium," *The Canadian Forum*, Jan. 1990.

America's biggest trading partner is Canada. Its trade with Ontario alone exceeds its trade with Japan. The nations have been moving toward an open market since the 1800s. Four-fifths of trade was free already.

PRIIT J. VESILIND, writer, "Common

Ground, Different Dreams," *National Geographic*, March 1990.

TRADITION
See also HERITAGE

Tradition can become a cage, when it takes my ability to think for myself, but without tradition I become the victim of present thinking. I need tradition to protect me from the omnipotence of the present.

ALOYSIUS AMBROZIC, Coadjutor Archbishop of Toronto, quoted by Ron Graham in *God's Dominion: A Sceptic's Quest* (1990).

TRAGEDY

Tragedy isn't getting something, or failing to get it: it's losing something you already have.

NICHOLAS CATANOY, poet and aphorist, "Notes on a Prison Wall (Fragment)," *Canadian Literature*, Summer 1989.

Marx says that when history repeats itself once it is tragedy but twice it is farce. Marx is wrong. Tragedy cannot be transmuted.

JOHN FRASER, columnist, "Diary," *Saturday Night*, Oct. 1989.

TRAINS
See RAILWAYS

TRANSLATION

English and French are not negative-positive images of each other, but entirely different instruments. The two languages cannot be made to work in the same way. A French sentence, transcribed exactly as it stands, means an English sentence with five words too many. The poise and tension of French, translated word for word, turns into a length of frayed elastic.

MAVIS GALLANT, author, "Limpid Pessimist: Marguerite Yourcenar" (1985), *Notebooks: Essays and Reviews* (1986).

Quite a few of my books have now been translated into French — some by Quebec translators, others by French-from-France ones. It always pleases me to see my work in French . . . but it also surprises me: my work in French seems, well, so *French*, and somehow more intellectual. Possibly this has been due to the excellence of my translators.

> MARGARET ATWOOD, novelist, "Polyphonous Perverse," *Language and Society*, Sept. 1988.

Mostly, I'm discovering that translating is an activity that involves playing with the *surface* level of meanings: kind of like standing in front of a mirror trying on different outfits until one finds the one that fits a particular mood and translates to the world the being within.

> PATRICIA SMART, translator, "Between the Two Cultures," *Language and Society*, Fall, 1989.

TRAVEL
See also AUTOMOBILES
AVIATION
RAILWAYS
SHIPS & SAILING
TOURISM

How I would love to travel and see all those old world lands and wonders. I wonder if I ever shall! England and Scotland first — then Italy and Greece — then Egypt and the Holy Land — but there, why not include the moon and have done with it? One is about as likely as the other. I expect the greater part of my travels will be on paper and I daresay that is much less trouble — and expense!

> L. M. MONTGOMERY, author, journal entry, 8 Oct. 1899, *The Selected Journals of L.M. Montgomery: Volume I: 1889-1910* (1985) edited by Mary Rubio and Elizabeth Waterston.

Just beyond the lake we passed the railway station of Crow's Nest, where a signboard and a neatly contrived parting of the stream in a trim flower-bed loudly proclaims "Great Divide." The whole thing is a fitting crown to Divine Nature — just like finding chewing gum for sale on the top of Mount Everest.

> PERCY GOMERY, motorist and travel writer, address, Vancouver Automobile Club, Feb. 1921, *A Motor Scamper 'Cross Canada: A Human-Interest Narrative of a Pathfinding Journey from Montreal to Vancouver* (1911).

We sailed in June 1948 in a Duchess liner of Canadian Pacific Steamships. The greatest travel system on earth, the CPR could still rightly call itself, but not for much longer. Both Empress ships were sunk in the war and had not been replaced. The rot of a proud institution was beginning.

> DAVID WALKER, ADC to Governor General Lord Tweedsmuir, *Lean, Wind, Lean: A Few Times Remembered* (1985).

All the Canadian hotels I stayed in were like machines — not bad machines, reasonably efficient and smooth running, but still machines. Nobody ever put a flower in my room or a message, hoping that everything was all right. I never exchanged a word with a manager or assistant-manager, never even saw one. . . . Arriving and registering at them is about as cosy and chummy as going to work in a steel mill.

> J.B. PRIESTLEY, English writer on a tour of Canada, "I Heard the Monotonous, Mournful Voices of Canadian Women," *Liberty*, Aug. 1956.

Canada is my fifty-ninth country.

> YEVGENY YEVTUSHENKO, well-travelled Russian poet, quoted by John Fraser in *The Globe and Mail*, 6 Dec. 1973.

I knew U.S. 1, stretching from the Canadian border to Key West, was capable of putting a man in an institution of one kind or another — at least it once was — but I hoped things had changed.
They hadn't.

> WILLIAM LEAST HEAT MOON, native American travel writer, referring to the U.S. 1 highway system, *Blue Highways: A Journey into America* (1982).

Americans on their way to Canada, it is joked, still strap skis to the roof racks in July, and the British can only place Canada on the map if they have relatives who live there.

STEPHEN BROOK, English travel writer, *Maple Leaf Rag: Travels across Canada* (1987).

It is astonishing to reflect, in parts of New Brunswick, that the piece of tortuous country lane you're driving on is the main road linking one part of the nation of Canada to the other. God willed it that way, I suppose, rather than political patronage entering into it.

RAY GUY, humorist, "Adventures of a Newfoundland Writer in Darkest Mainland," *Ray Guy's Best* (1987).

While working in both Barbados and Florida I became aware that Canadians are some of the best-informed travellers in the world, seeming always to know where they are going and what local custom and history have to offer.

JAMES A. MICHENER, bestselling author, discussing the genesis of his novel set in the North, Introduction, *Journey* (1988).

Is this my own journey or do I travel on someone else's.

Thoughts of a character in the novel *Daughters of Captain Cook* (1988) by LINDA SPALDING.

The best way to travel is to go where your feet take you, to arrive full of surprise.

BARRY CALLAGHAN, editor and traveller, Introduction, *Canadian Travellers in Italy* (1989).

The size of it, the emptiness, the challenges of ice and wilderness, the sense of power that has always been particularly conjured up by railways — these are what most people intuitively and immediately think of when they consider the idea of Canada.

JAN MORRIS, Anglo-Welsh travel writer, Introduction, *City to City* (1990).

It is our consuls who give Canadians "protection and assistance" — to use the official phrase — when they run into difficulties abroad. We now have around 350 consular officers in Canada's posts abroad, working in our embassies in foreign capitals, or at our consulates in large cities outside the capitals.

SIDNEY FREIFELD, retired foreign-service officer, *Undiplomatic Notes: Tales from the Canadian Foreign Service* (1990). Apparently Canadians make some 36 million trips abroad each year, "ranging from a day in New York City to a few months in Kabul or Katmandu. Assistance in some form can require our embassies and consulates in foreign countries to handle around 650,000 requests per annum."

TREES
See also FORESTS

I have seen giant redwoods with plaques on them stating that they are part of the primeval forest to be preserved forever for posterity, as this stand had been gifted for this purpose by so and so. And I look at the tip of these great trees and see that already they are dying — dying because man has created dams that keep back the yearly floods that nourish them, dying because of automobile pollution, or dying because the earth around them has been compacted by human feet.

DOROTHY MACLEAN, medium, *To Hear the Angels Sing: An Odyssey of Co-Creation with the Devic Kingdom* (1980).

Take away the trees but don't take away the rocks. The rocks don't grow back.

Attributed to A.J. CASSON, painter and last surviving member of the Group of Seven, quoted by David Lees in *Toronto Life*, Aug. 1988.

This land is special to us because we have come from nowhere else. We have found sites that our people have occupied, now covered by four feet of earth, campsites our ancestors were at 4,000 years ago. When we touch a tree, that tree is entwined with the earth that our ancestors walked on for 6,000 years. We can't kill the land because the future generations 6,000 years from now have a right to use it. They are descendants of all of you here. We have to stand up for this land.

> GARY POTTS, Chief of the Teme-Augama Anishnabai, leader of the native blockade on the Red Squirrel Road in Temagami, Ont., quoted by Ellie Kirzner in *Now*, 16 Nov. 1989.

Trees don't respond to a couple of Aspirin and a warm poultice. Foresters know that once you've interrupted a forest's cycle, the interruption can last for decades.

> ARTHUR BLACK, broadcaster and humorist, "My Maple: In Memoriam," *That Old Black Magic* (1989).

They have only one expression for trees: "Something that sticks up."

> JOHN ALLEMANG, journalist, referring to the Inuit and to the difficulty experienced by the Canadian Bible Society in translating the New Testament into Inuktitut, *The Globe and Mail*, 21 March 1990.

TROUBLE

Never sleep with anyone whose troubles are worse than your own.

> Advice given to Lew Archer, detective hero of *Black Money* (1966) by ROSS MAC-DONALD.

Do not face trouble; outface it.

> ROBIN SKELTON, man-of-letters, aphorism, May 1990.

TRUDEAU, PIERRE ELLIOTT

If all politicians were like Mr. Trudeau, there would be world peace. You people in Canada don't realize how lucky you are to have a man like Mr. Trudeau.

> JOHN LENNON, former Beatle, after he and his wife Yoko Ono conferred about the prospects for peace with Prime Minister Trudeau in the latter's office, Parlia-

ment Hill, Ottawa, Dec. 1969. Yoko added: "We're just enthralled meeting Mr. Trudeau, he is Beautiful People. It gives us great incentive seeing people like him in the Establishment."

You are immeasurably the greatest Prime Minister Canada has ever had, the first who has ever been equipped with an awareness of contemporary culture.

> MARSHALL McLUHAN, communications theorist, letter to Pierre Elliott Trudeau, 21 Sept. 1971, *Letters of Marshall McLuhan* (1987) edited by Matie Molinaro, Corinne McLuhan, and William Toye.

I prefer to confess my sins to the priest rather than to the press.

> PIERRE ELLIOTT TRUDEAU, Prime Minister, Nov. 1972, based on a remark noted by Paul Martin in *A Very Public Life: Volume II: So Many Worlds* (1985).

I don't want to hear any more of this negative talk. We're not going to allow the prime minister to descend to the grubby level of discussing unemployment. He's having a dialogue with the people about the Canadian identity.

> JAMES DAVEY, Prime Minister Trudeau's speech-writer, countering criticism that the Prime Minister's speeches lacked substance; quoted by Peter C. Newman in "Reflections on a Fall from Grace" (1972), *Home Country: People, Places, and Power Politics* (1973).

The present prime minister of Canada is the most fanatical anti-Quebec politician we have known in our history.

> PIERRE VALLIÈRES, former terrorist, *The Assassination of Pierre Laporte: Behind the October '70 Scenario* (1977) translated by Ralph Wells.

I am just one of many single parents who have to work.

> PIERRE ELLIOTT TRUDEAU, Prime Minister, campaign rhetoric following his separation from his wife Margaret, quoted in 1977 and noted by Paul Martin in *The*

London Diaries 1975-1979 (1988) edited by William R. Young.

The United States has its First Lady; Canada has its worst lady.
CRAIG RUSSELL, performer and female impersonator, referring to Margaret Trudeau, when in 1979 both were guests on a U.S. television talk show; recalled by Peter Gzowski on CBC Radio's *Morningside*, 1 Nov. 1990.

As a Liberal insider once put it: "Somebody is going to say some day, 'Will the real Mr. Trudeau please stand up,' and about fifty-eight people will rise.'"
GEORGE RADWANSKI, journalist and biographer, *Trudeau* (1978).

But the battle that brought him into politics — the struggle to dispel Quebec nationalism and replace it with full acceptance and involvement of French Canadians in Canada's national life — is now entering its most decisive phase, on terrain he himself has prepared. The outcome will determine Canada's fate and Pierre Elliott Trudeau's place in history.
GEORGE RADWANSKI, journalist and biographer, *Trudeau* (1978).

I want to assure all Canadians that wherever I am or whatever I do, I will continue to work and fight for our country.
PIERRE ELLIOTT TRUDEAU, Prime Minister, statement announcing his intention to resign as leader of the Liberal Party, news conference, Ottawa, 21 Nov. 1979.

Welcome to the 80s.
PIERRE ELLIOTT TRUDEAU, Prime Minister, television address, newly re-elected, referring to economic matters that would dominate the decade, 18 Feb. 1980.

For my part . . . I am a realist but, somehow, optimism always keeps breaking out.
PIERRE ELLIOTT TRUDEAU, Prime Minister, Convocation Address, Notre Dame University, South Bend, Indiana, 16 May 1982.

Trying to produce small talk when isolated with Trudeau at a stand-up cocktail reception has proved discomforting for the most accomplished social lioness. . . . "Isn't it a nice party?" doesn't seem quite appropriate, nor does "I enjoyed Kant's Categorical Imperative, didn't you?" Perhaps somewhere in between. But if you are lucky, someone will come to the rescue.
DON JOHNSTON, M.P., *Up the Hill* (1986).

The passionate Professor Trudeau of 1963 attacking the decision of Lester B. Pearson to accept nuclear weapons was a different man from the Prime Minister twenty years later who reluctantly conceded the need to test the Cruise missiles over the Canadian North. But as de Gaulle said in contrasting intellectuals with men in power, it is the statesman who takes risks, including moral ones.
THOMAS AXWORTHY, political scientist and author, Preface, *Lifting the Shadow of War* (1987) edited by C. David Crenna.

I went home, discussed it with the boys, put them to bed. I walked until midnight in the storm, then I went home and took a sauna for an hour and a half. It was all clear. I listened to my heart and saw if there were any signs of my destiny in the sky, and there were none — there were just snowflakes.
PIERRE ELLIOTT TRUDEAU, Prime Minister, announcing his decision to resign from office, press conference, Ottawa, 29 Feb. 1984, quoted by Graham Fraser in *The Globe and Mail* later that day. Trudeau announced his decision to retire from public during a leap year; the reference to "going for a walk in the snow" is recalled at four-year intervals. Before Leap Year 1984, associations with Feb. 29th were Sadie Hawkins' Day and the birthday of Henri (Pocket) Richard.

I don't promise that, on another sunny day, I won't go out and have another walk and think things over.
PIERRE ELLIOTT TRUDEAU, former

Prime Minister, remark made to a journalist, 8 March 1984.

Pierre Trudeau was, for many of us, the Canadian we would like to be — a bilingual, intellectual, clever, handsome fellow and a devil with women. A Canadian who never before existed except in the eye of God.
VAL SEARS, journalist, *The Toronto Star*, 6 April 1988.

But there he was, Pierre Trudeau, the most maddening, pleasing, perplexing, loved, hated, worshipped, vilified, vulgar, sophisticated, stubborn, passionate, obnoxious, arrogant, frivolous, brilliant politician this country has ever produced.
CLAIRE HOY, journalist, *Margin of Error: Pollsters and the Manipulation of Canadian Politics* (1989).

I've got mixed feelings about Trudeau, but he did have a notion of what he wanted this country to be. He was a very compelling political figure. In some ways he was very adolescent but he could be eloquent on occasion, and his notion of a bilingual country where civility ruled was one I could happily endorse.
MORDECAI RICHLER, novelist, quoted by Don Gillmor in *Quill & Quire*, July 1989.

It is not likely that Mr. Trudeau would return to politics; however, such a return cannot be ruled out. If angered enough, he could take a stand, and it would be possible for him (astrologically speaking) to win the next election. . . . He doesn't have to decide, but it remains an option — I give it a 20 per cent chance. It is a long shot.
ROBIN ARMSTRONG, professional astrologer, *Robin Armstrong's Astrological Almanac: 1990* (1989).

English Canada needs a strong central government; I recognize that. If I were an anglophone, I would think exactly like Trudeau.
LUCIEN BOUCHARD, Member of Parliament who left the Conservative Party to head the separatist group Bloc Québécois, quoted by Graham Fraser in *The Globe and Mail*, 3 Nov. 1990.

TRUST

Never rely on those who trust your judgement.
ROBIN SKELTON, man-of-letters, aphorism, May 1990.

TRUTH
See also LIES

But the history of hypnotism also shows us that, given time, the human mind will insist on the truth.
GEORGE H. ESTABROOKS, psychologist, *Hypnotism* (1943).

We need fear no sacredness. Truth has nothing to fear from the earnest and sincere research for truth. Anything that should survive will certainly survive the most searching light of intellectual examination.
G. BROCK CHISHOLM, psychiatrist, White Memorial Lecture, Washington, D.C., Oct. 1945, published as *The Psychiatry of Enduring Peace and Social Progress* (1945).

Truth I have no trouble with, it's the facts I get all screwed up.
FARLEY MOWAT, author, interviewed on CFRB, Toronto, 14 Dec. 1975.

It's easy to tell the truth about big things. It's the little things that trip you up.
BETTY JANE WYLIE, author of a collection of puppet plays, *Don't Just Stand There, Jiggle* (1980).

I believe it is better to learn what is probable about important matters than to be certain about trivial ones.
IAN STEVENSON, psychiatrist, *Children Who Remember Previous Lives: A Question of Reincarnation* (1987).

Only journalists are expected to deliver the whole truth, shining and incorruptible every day.

BORDEN SPEARS, newspaperman, quoted in *The Toronto Star*, 3 May 1987.

The truth is for those who deserve it.
MAX MAYNARD, artist, quoted by Fredelle Bruser Maynard in *The Tree of Life* (1988).

I've always said, half-jokingly, that I never let facts interfere with the truth.
FARLEY MOWAT, naturalist and author, interviewed by Alan Twigg in *Strong Voices: Conversations with Fifty Canadian Authors* (1988).

There are, so far as one knows, no truths of any sort accessible to the human intellect, only illusions and what we call facts — that two plus two equal four; that down is sometimes up; and that both philosophers and chickens occasionally lay eggs.
GEORGE FALUDY, Hungarian-born poet, *Notes from the Rainforest* (1988).

There are no skeletons in my closet — there are too many clothes.
MARILYN LASTMAN, wife of North York Mayor Mel Lastman and herself candidate for City Council, quoted by Leslie Scrivener in *The Toronto Star*, 16 Oct. 1988.

You may as well tell people the truth because they don't listen anyway.
EARL WORK, sales motivator, quoting "a friend from Prince Albert," Nov. 1989.

The moment anyone accepts an *objective reality*, an *eternal truth*, they have become vulnerable, manipulable, and eminently exploitable. They have ceased to function as an autonomous, creative, thinking individual, living in an integrated, interdependent world.
WILSON BRYAN KEY, psychologist and analyst of subliminal images in advertising, *The Age of Manipulation: The Con in Confidence and the Sin in Sincere* (1989).

Truth is not necessarily stranger than fiction, but coincidence can sometimes be.
EDWARD PHILLIPS, novelist, *Sunday Best* (1990).

Truth is plural.
ELWY YOST, television personality, characteristic remark, personal communication, 17 Jan. 1990.

Truth comes too late. The pages of history are crimson with the blood of idealists, iconoclasts, and prophets.
BERNARD BASKIN, rabbi, Temple Anshe Sholom, Hamilton, *obiter dictum*, 22 May 1990.

In the arts always tell the truth; it creates an aura of stunned confidence.
Attributed to arts administator and former intelligence officer PETER M. DWYER by Christopher Newton, artistic director, Shaw Festival, Niagara-on-the-Lake, Ont., 3 Aug. 1990.

TURNER, JOHN

I tell you this — there are more truck drivers in Canada than ballroom dancers.
BRIAN MULRONEY, Conservative leader, campaigning against Prime Minister John Turner, July 1984, quoted by Claire Hoy in *Friends in High Places: Politics and Patronage in the Mulroney Government* (1987). In 1958, at a well-publicized social gathering, the young John Turner danced with Princess Margaret; there is no record that Mulroney was ever a truck driver.

John Turner: Well, I have told you and told the Canadian people, Mr. Mulroney, that I had no option.
Brian Mulroney: You had an option, sir. You could have said, "I am not going to do it. This is wrong for Canada. And I am not going to ask Canadians to pay the price." You had an option, sir, to say no, and you chose to say yes, yes to the old attitudes and the old stories of the Liberal party.
John Turner: I had no option, I. . . .
Classic confrontation over the issue of

whether John Turner, as the incoming Prime Minister, had the right or responsibility to refuse to countenance the last-minute patronage appointments made by retiring Prime Minister Trudeau, which was grist for the mill of Conservative leader Brian Mulroney, national leaders' debate, CBC-TV, 25 July 1984.

I know more Liberals than any person alive.
JOHN TURNER, Liberal leader, quoted in *The Toronto Star*, 13 April 1986.

I'm not going to play politics on the floor of the House of Commons.
JOHN TURNER, Liberal leader, House of Commons, 1 Oct. 1987, quoted by Roy MacGregor in *The Ottawa Citizen* the following day.

I should have known in advance. The Prime Minister kept saying my Caucus was revolting. It's not that my Caucus wants to be led by Jesus Christ, just by somebody with the same initials.
JOHN TURNER, Liberal leader, referring to the revolt of his Caucus and the personal popularity of the former leadership contender Jean Chrétien, annual dinner, National Press Gallery, Ottawa, May 1988.

John Turner promises us all a better yesterday.
Remark attributed to the columnist JEFFREY SIMPSON by Peter C. Newman in *The Ottawa Citizen*, 17 Sept. 1988.

TWENTIETH CENTURY

The position which Canada now occupies in world affairs, a position which brings with it a sense of importance, strength, confidence — the twentieth century, as Laurier prophesied, may yet be ours. (Whatever that means.)
A.M. KLEIN, poet, "Writing in Canada" (1946), *Literary Essays and Reviews* (1987) edited by Usher Caplan and M.W. Steinberg. The allusion is to Sir Wilfrid

Laurier's famous remark of 1904: "The Twentieth Century belongs to Canada."

The real question is whether Canada will belong to the 21st century.
PETER C. NEWMAN, author, *Sometimes a Great Nation: Will Canada Belong to the 21st Century?* (1988).

Sir Wilfrid Laurier, Canada's prime minister in the early 1900s, was wrong about the 20th century belonging to Canada. But, in the final years of the American century, let Canadians enjoy the benefits of being an advanced modern state without the burdens and attendant guilt of an imperial past.
PETER JENNINGS, Toronto-born ABC anchorman, *Maclean's*, 25 June 1990.

As was the case with reciprocity, Laurier was wrong. Let's ensure that it will be the 21st century that belongs to Canada.
MEL HURTIG, publisher and nationalist, address, Fifth Anniversary Convention, Council of Canadians, Ottawa, 12 Oct. 1990.

TWO NATIONS

I thought of Durham's report on the state of Quebec when he arrived there after the Rebellion of 1837-38, and said he found two nations warring in the bosom of a single state. That would be the case in Canada, as applied to Canada as a whole, unless the whole question of conscription from now on is approached with the utmost care.
W.L. MACKENZIE KING, diary, referring to the conscription crisis, in 1942; quoted by Ramsay Cook in "The Triumph and Trials of Materialism 1900-1945," *The Illustrated History of Canada* (1987) edited by Craig Brown.

TWO SOLITUDES

Our old division into two solitudes now seems to me to have been a blessing in disguise. It makes uniformity impossible in Canada. What lacked in the past was love and mutual respect. What must come in the future — it is coming now, as a matter of fact — is affection and understanding.

HUGH MacLENNAN, novelist and essayist, "The Meaning of Canada," *Century 1867-1967*, 13 Feb. 1967. The phrase "two solitudes" was first used to refer to the solitude of two lovers by the German poet Rainer Maria Rilke in 1904. Montrealer Hugh MacLennan found it an apt and moving way to refer to the relationship between French Canadians and English Canadians in his novel *Two Solitudes* (1945).

But should Canada survive? Why should a country made up of two solitudes continue to exist? Would it not be more reasonable to divide Canada into two independent nations? There are many reasons why the Canadian duality should perdure as a political unity.

GREGORY BAUM, theologian, "A New Constitution for the Canadian Duality," *Canada's Third Option* (1987) edited by S.D. Berkowitz and Robert K. Logan.

U

UFOs

See UNIDENTIFIED FLYING
OBJECTS

UKRAINIAN PEOPLE

Ukrainians in Canada are not forced to
abandon their roots. . . . This is the message Canada must pioneer to the world.
VALENTYN MOROZ, Ukrainian dissident
and sometime Toronto resident, observation about life in Canada upon release
from the Gulag; quoted by David Miller
and Joe Serge in *The Toronto Star*, 9 June
1979.

How can you be in favour of a distinct
Ukraine and against a distinct Quebec?
ROBERT McKENZIE, journalist, posing a
rhetorical question, *The Toronto Star*, 5
Dec. 1989.

UNDERSTANDING

Insight is not any act of attention or memory, but the supervening act of understanding.
BERNARD J.F. LONERGAN, Jesuit philosopher, *Insight: A Study of Human Understanding* (1957).

If what we do not yet understand is like
what we do understand about life, then
the unknown will be challenging, interesting, and beautiful.
DALE A. RUSSELL, paleontologist, *An Odyssey in Time: The Dinosaurs of North
America* (1989).

UNEMPLOYMENT

See also LABOUR

The parliamentary secretary gave some
indication of that double standard when
he talked about the striking success this
government has had. . . . He referred to
pockets of unemployment. I suppose that
next the government will be telling us that
there is no unemployment, that it is just a
nasty rumour started by a lot of people
who are out of work.
ROB PARKER, M.P., House of Commons, 1
Dec. 1978.

I like to think of myself as a model citizen — unfortunately, I'm not a *working*
model.
EDD ULUSCHAK, cartoonist, *The Edmonton Jounral*, 16 March 1982.

People are unemployed not because they lack skills or they are unwilling to work, but simply because the money to employ them has drained away from the part of the world where they live.
MICHAEL LINTON, founder of the Local Employment Trading System (LET-System) in B.C.'s Comox Valley in 1983, "Local Currencies," *Edges*, July-Sept. 1988.

Just read the want ads.
TOM HOCKIN, Minister of State for Finance, addressing reporters following a speech to the Canadian Manufacturers' Association, Toronto, giving advice to the estimated 1400 brewery employees whose jobs would be eliminated over the next three years as part of the merger of Molson and Carling O'Keefe, quoted in *The Toronto Star*, 27 Jan. 1989.

The causal connecton between mental illness, crime, social problems and unemployment is now widely recognized. So that our first priority must be to reduce unemployment and the effects of poverty, rather than merely treating people who are depressed because they can't find jobs. Providing them with psychotherapy makes as much sense as spraying perfume on infected wounds.
CYRIL GREENLAND, psychiatric social worker, interviewed by Sam Sussman in *Pioneers of Mental Health and Social Change: 1930-1989* (1989) by Djuwe Joe Blom and Sam Sussman.

It is much cheaper for governments to subsidize a firm to hire an unemployed Canadian than pay him or her unemployment insurance or welfare.
PHILIPPE DEANE GIGANTES, author and Senator, *The Road Ahead* (1990).

If these people weren't unemployed, they'd be working today.
Attributed to Nova Scotia Premier ROGER BACON, commenting on the legion of unemployed, by Jack White in *The Globe and Mail*, 20 Oct. 1990.

UNGAVA

In trying to decide to which situation the government has shown the least sensitivity, one has a rich field of choice; but the heartless imposition of low-flying NATO planes over Innu lands in the Ungava peninsula is probably the winner. One could not find a better example anywhere of a government failing to represent the interests of its people.
BOYCE RICHARDSON, journalist, "Concealed Contempt," *The Canadian Forum*, Dec. 1989.

UNIDENTIFIED FLYING OBJECTS
See also SPACE

After well over fifty years of studying the sky, I fail to find any pattern of physical events which suggests that our atmosphere has been visited by an alien and intelligent life culture. I have the distinct impression that if or when this ever does occur, it will be much more self-evident than the cases now classified as UFOs.
PETER M. MILLMAN, astrophysicist, address, Canadian Association of Physical Transportation Management, Toronto, 12 March 1975.

Why have several hundred U.S. citizens claimed to have been abducted by UFOs, while only a handful of Canadians and Western Europeans have been? Do they find the bodies of U.S. citizens more interesting, or is it that we have more suggestible people and kooks in the U.S. than you people do?
PHILIP KLASS, U.S. critic of UFOs, press conference, Ontario Skeptics, Toronto, 14 Nov. 1987.

I was an early Kellogg's Cornflakes Tom Corbett Space Cadet, and have only taken to exploring Planet Earth as a feeble sub-stitute for genuine instantaneous interga-lactic teleportation, which I think is our destiny.

> ROBERT HUNTER, activist and author, "Better in the Bahamas," *On the Sky: Zen and the Art of International Freeloading* (1988).

By the year 2005, formal protocols will be in place to allow the earth to become a member of the galactic federation.

> MAURICE B. COOKE, channeller, *The Aquarian Wave: A Prophetic Handbook for the 90s* (1990).

UNION OF SOVIET SOCIALIST REPUBLICS
See SOVIET UNION

UNIONS
> *See also* CAPITALISM
> LABOUR
> STRIKES

Unionism undoubtedly is a good thing in some ways, but like strychnine, it must be taken in small doses.

> Editorial in an issue of *Industrial Canada* in 1909 published by the Canadian Manufacturers' Association, quoted by Michael Bliss in *Northern Enterprise* (1987).

I've had to fight finks and scabs and look out for my boys. It's a tough position and sometimes I haven't had time to be a gen-tleman. But I've done my job.

> HAL C. BANKS, President, International Seafarers' Union, convicted criminal, quoted by Peter Edwards in *Waterfront Warlord: The Life and Violent Times of Hal C. Banks* (1987).

Unions will survive in our society because, although they are heir to all the faults of humanity, they are also the creation of humanity's highest virtues. They will find men and women with the courage to rem-edy their faults and to realize new dreams. Through organization, working people will go on trying to realize the hopes that drew them or their ancestors to this country.

And if workers in their millions cannot build a better Canada, it can never be built.

> DESMOND MORTON and TERRY COPP, historians, *Working People* (rev. ed., 1984).

Men and women who have nothing to sell but their strength and their skill cannot afford to be divided. They will find, like their ancestors, that all human organiza-tions are imperfect. Unions will be con-demned as petty, short-sighted and some-times casual about the rights of their own members. Unions will protect their own shortcomings with a solidarity born of a sense of insecurity.

> DESMOND MORTON and TERRY COPP, historians, *Working People* (rev. ed., 1984).

Tommy McLean, longtime assistant direc-tor to George Burt in the Canadian Region, used to say that the only way to build a union in a plant is to have a strike. He came from the old school, which believed that people have to struggle together in order to understand unionism. I don't nec-essarily agree, but. . . .

> ROBERT (BOB) WHITE, President, Cana-dian Auto Workers, *Hard Bargains: My Life on the Line* (1987). Once at a union rally he saw somebody waving a banner which read "Better Red than White."

The trade union movement in Canada was founded to contribute to the realization of the legitimate aspirations of those who toil for a living, and it will not deviate from the pursuit of the cause of peace, freedom, and security for all peoples.

> SHIRLEY CARR, President, Canadian Lab-our Congress, contributor to *If I Were Prime Minister* (1987) edited by Mel Hurtig.

Any union leader from Glasgow or north-ern England who sought to come to to Canada, I would send back on the first Aeroflot plane — they've done enough

damage to Canadian unions and our economy over the years.
PETER WORTHINGTON, journalist, contributor to *If I Were Prime Minister* (1987) edited by Mel Hurtig.

UNITED EMPIRE LOYALISTS

Unity of the Empire, United Empire Loyalists
SIR GUY CARLETON, Order-in-Council, Quebec, 9 Nov. 1789. "Those Loyalists who have adhered to the Unity of the Empire: and joined the Royal Standard before the Treaty of Separation in the year 1783, and all their Children, and their Descendants, by either sex, are to be distinguished by the following Capitals affixed to their names 'U.E.' alluding to their great principle 'The Unity of the Empire.'"

In no country upon the face of the Globe, and at no period in the history of any country, has appeared a higher or purer order of patriotism, than is written upon the pages of the history of British America.... The U.E. Loyalists have been as a barrier of rock against which the waves of Republicanism have dashed in vain.
WILLIAM CANNIFF, historian, *History of the Settlement of Upper Canada* (1869).

They Sacrificed Everything Save Honour
Terse inscription on the cairn dedicated to the memory of the United Empire Loyalists, Tusket, Yarmouth County, N.S., unveiled in 1964. The words were chosen by the local historian Robert B. Blauveldt who is of U.E.L. descent.

The lesson of the Loyalists is that it is possible for people to make a new start, to integrate into a strange community and to be committed to a wider unity without in any way betraying the principles and aspirations of their predecessors.
PRINCE PHILIP, Duke of Edinburgh, addressing members of the United Empire Loyalist Association, Lennoxville, Que.,

20 May 1989, quoted by André Picard in *The Globe and Mail* two days later.

UNITED KINGDOM
See also BRITAIN
ENGLISH PEOPLE

Canada is a country which excites the imagination of the British people.
JAMES CALLAGHAN, Prime Minister of the United Kingdom, address, Empire Club of Canada, Toronto, 14 Sept. 1976.

For all these pleasures, Canadians here pay a considerable price. As soon as we pass through Heathrow Airport, we disappear.
RICHARD GWYN, British-born, Ottawa-based columnist, London-posted correspondent, *The Toronto Star*, 13 Nov. 1988.

The Land of the 3 M's
This is a reference to Canada, as seen in the United Kingdom as the land of Moose, Mountains, and Mounties. The catch phrase is associated with CURTIS BARLOW, cultural counsellor at Canada House, London, England. Quoted by Jamie Portman in *The Toronto Star*, 10 Nov. 1989.

It's hard for the British to picture the overwhelming American hegemony. Suppose you went into your local newsagent and eight out of ten titles were German. And in the book shop. And if nearly every radio station was in German. Cable TV means that viewers in, say, British Columbia, are more familiar with what's happening in Spokane, Washington, than in the community next door.
SIMON HOGGART, Washington correspondent for *The Observer*, in *The Globe and Mail*, 9 Jan. 1990.

UNITED NATIONS

We do now devote this tenth part of our wealth towards fitting Palestine to become that seat of government, and that capital for the world, as soon as all the great nations of Christendom shall agree to send their representatives there that henceforth we may have United Nations, and a general government responsible for general peace and order throughout the world.

This passage is widely believed to be the initial use of the words "United Nations" in the sense of a body for world government. There is no evidence that this usage, from a Manifesto issued by HENRY WENTWORTH MONK in 1880 in London, England, influenced the deliberations at San Francisco in 1945 when the UN was established. Noted by the biographer R.S. Lambert in Henry Wentworth Monk, prophet, *For the Time Is at Hand: An Account of the Prophesies of Henry Wentworth Monk of Ottawa, Friend of the Jews, and Pioneer of World Peace* (1947).

I would take Canada out of the Commonwealth, unless that body smartened up. As it is, I'd urge that the United Nations be moved from New York to, say, Uganda or Ulan Bator for a few years, since so many U.N. members seem to dislike America and the West. Perhaps it's Moscow's turn to host the U.N.?

PETER WORTHINGTON, journalist, contributor to *If I Were Prime Minister* (1987).

The only North American United Nations agency outside New York City — the International Civil Aviation Agency — is located in Montreal.

ALAN F.J. ARTIBISE, planning consultant, "Canada as an Urban Nation," *Daedalus: Journal of the American Academy of Arts and Sciences*, "In Search of Canada," Fall 1988.

UNITED STATES OF AMERICA

See also ALASKA
AMERICA
BORDER, CANADIAN-
AMERICAN
CALIFORNIA
CANADA & THE
UNITED STATES
FLORIDA
NEW YORK
WASHINGTON

It would be a strange thing if Six Nations of ignorant savages should be capable of forming a scheme for such a union, and be able to execute it in such a manner as that it has subsisted ages and appears indissoluble; and yet that a like union should be impracticable for ten or a dozen English colonies, to whom it is more necessary and must be more advantageous, and who cannot be supposed to want an equal understanding of their interests.

BENJAMIN FRANKLIN, American Founding Father, formally proposing a union of the American colonies and employing as an analogy the resilient Confederacy of the Six Nations, Albany Convention, 1754, quoted by Vincent H. Gaddis in *American Indian Myths and Mysteries* (1977).

The United States is the glory, jest, and terror of mankind.

JAMES M. MINIFIE, broadcaster, contributor to *The New Romans* (1968) edited by Al Purdy.

This Canadian thinks it is time to speak up for the Americans as the most generous and possibly the least appreciated people in all the earth.

GORDON SINCLAIR, newspaperman and broadcaster, *Let's Be Personal*, "Americans," CFRB, 5 June 1973, quoted by Scott Young in *Gordon Sinclair: A Life . . . and Then Some* (1987).

I can name to you 5,000 times when Americans raced to the help of other people in trouble. Can you name me one time when someone else raced to the Americans in trouble?

GORDON SINCLAIR, newspaperman and broadcaster, *Let's Be Personal*, "Americans," CFRB, 5 June 1973, quoted by Scott Young in *Gordon Sinclair: A Life . . . and Then Some* (1987).

The United States cannot permit itself to be vulnerable to the whims of a government that has acted less than responsibly toward us.

WALTER H. ANNENBERG, U.S. publisher of *TV Guide* and former U.S. Ambassador to Great Britain, expressing outrage that advertising in his publication lost its tax exempt status, quoted in *The Toronto Star*, 11 May 1977.

But most important of all, Americans never know whether their leaders are telling them the truth. Now, *we* don't have that problem!

DAVE BROADFOOT, comedian, address, Empire Club of Canada, Toronto, 1 March 1978.

A Canadian never feels more Canadian than when he is in the United States.

JOHN GRAY, playwright and performer, Preface to *Billy Bishop Goes to War* (1981) written with Eric Peterson.

The country that invented modern democracy is the modern democracy with the smallest percentage of its citizens practising it.

THOMAS AXWORTHY, public figure, Introduction, *Our American Cousins: The United States through Canadian Eyes* (1987).

The United States is a pluralistic, competitive, confrontational, litigious, turbulent society, almost totally absorbed in the extraordinarily difficult task of governing itself. Americans have little time and less inclination to look northward at all, let alone with manifest destiny on their minds. More than anything else, what most Americans would like best is to be left alone.

ALLAN GOTLIEB, Canadian Ambassador in Washington, address, Canadian Club of Ottawa, *The Globe and Mail*, 29 Oct. 1987.

Americans are generous to a fault: we sometimes behave as though it were a fault to be generous.

ROBERTSON DAVIES, man-of-letters, Neil Gunn lecture, Edinburgh University, June

1988, published in *The Times Literary Supplement*, 30 Sept. 1988.

Whether our future will be as crisis-ridden as the past depends greatly on whether the United States can live in a pluralistic world and cease to confront and fight most of the movements and developments that have emerged in the postwar era and have become more relevant since the irreversible collapse of Soviet and Chinese pretensions to lead international socialism.

GABRIEL KOLKO, political scientist, *Confronting the Third World: United States Foreign Policy, 1945-1980* (1988).

Question: What is the secret of American foreign policy?
Answer: Why did it never occur to Lucy to learn Spanish instead of mocking Ricky's accent?

DOUGLAS FETHERLING, cultural commentator, "Pop Culture: The Politics of Nostalgia," *The Whig-Standard Magazine*, 6 Feb. 1988.

In an era when Mexico seems to be annexing itself to the United States, one person at a time, and people with names like Dukakis are actually running for president, a merger with Canada would add millions of citizens with sturdy names like Mulroney and Turner, who speak English with hardly a trace of an accent, and whose native cuisine is virtually spice-free. Look for Canadian restaurants as the new food trend in New York.

MICHAEL KINSLEY, editor of *The New Republic* and columnist, *The Toronto Star*, 11 Dec. 1988.

Nations that dominate and bully lesser nations are always astonished when it is pointed out what they are in fact doing.

ALLAN FOTHERINGHAM, columnist, making special reference to the Hollywood film lobby in Ottawa, *Maclean's*, 30 Oct. 1989.

Sharing the American way, without commitment to American goals or responsibil-

ities, makes the Canadian intellectual detached and observant as an interpreter of the American destiny.
MARSHALL McLUHAN, media philosopher, and Bruce R. Powers, communications specialist, authors of *The Global Village: Transformations in World Life and Media in the 21st Century* (1989).

Percentage of the value of all foreign-owned U.S. real estate that is owned by Japanese companies: 15 / Percentage of the value of all foreign-owned U.S. real estate that is owned by Canadian companies: 26.
Item from "Harper's Index," *Harper's*, Feb. 1990.

The theory of American decline is bunk propagated by Euro-narcissists, faddish Nipponophiles, and the international soft Left, including its local espousers.
CONRAD BLACK, capitalist and columnist, "Enough Is Enough," *Saturday Night*, Sept. 1990.

English Canadian intellectuals see the United States as threatening; Québécois intellectuals see it as a land of liberty. I think there is enormous naïveté in both cases.
JACQUES GODBOUT, Quebec author, interviewed by Sherry Simon in *Other Solitudes: Canadian Multicultural Fictions* (1990) edited by Linda Hutcheon and Marion Richmond.

UNITY
See UNITY, NATIONAL

UNITY, NATIONAL
See also FEDERALISM

What really holds a nation together is not laws, nor economics, but adherence to those common experiences and common emotions loosely called its culture or tradition. Only the native can know in his bones what his own essence is and so express it that a fellow-native is able to

recognize his own thoughts and feelings. Let me write a nation's songs, said the wise man, and I care not who writes its laws.
WILLIAM ARTHUR DEACON, literary critic, letter to Carlton McNaught, 26 Dec. 1933, quoted by Clara Thomas and John Lennox in *William Arthur Deacon: A Canadian Literary Life* (1982).

Most people think of unity — the act of unifying a group of people — as a process of exclusion.
MARY MAXWELL, a.k.a. Rúhíyyih Khánum, leading member of the Bahá'í Faith, *A Manual for Pioneers* (1974).

I cannot admit that we have lost the will to stay together as the most favoured cluster of men and women on the face of the globe.
JOHN TURNER, former Finance Minister, address in Vancouver, 24 March 1977, quoted by Gerald Utting in *The Toronto Star* the following day.

At all these conferences all over the country, people are sitting around in rooms talking about national unity. "What is Canada after 100 years?" I'll tell you. Canada is ten *big* provinces and two vast wastelands — three if you count Ottawa.
DAVE BROADFOOT, comedian, address, Empire Club of Canada, Toronto, 9 March 1978.

We are divided by the Great Lakes, the great Prairies, the great Rocky Mountains, by two great languages, and eleven great governments.
BARRY MATHER, one-time Member of Parliament and journalist, observation made in July 1978.

Canadians probably do feel a quasi-mystical sense of unity when they consider their collective relation to the land, a feeling which can be shared by no other nation with the possible exception of the Russians, but on a more practical level political and cultural unity seems elusive.
STEPHEN BROOK, English travel writer,

Maple Leaf Rag: Travels across Canada (1987).

It is my fondest wish for this Canada Day that Canadians come together and remain together, rather than dwelling on the differences which might further divide them.
QUEEN ELIZABETH II, Canada Day address, Parliament Hill, Ottawa, 1 July 1990, quoted by Susan Delacourt in *The Globe and Mail* the following day.

UNIVERSE

I have always loved the moon. I suppose everybody does. We owe far more to the sun; in fact for all practical and essential purposes, we could get along quite as well without the moon altogether, while the loss of the sun would mean the extinction of our very lives. Yet nobody feels any particular affection for the sun. It is the moon we love. Her cold, silvery light irradiates the pages of old romance. Her never ceasing changes have all the charm of variety in a beautiful woman. There is no more exquisite sight in the universe than a young moon in a sunset sky. I have seen some new moons setting over dark hills that I shall remember in the halls of eternity.
L. M. MONTGOMERY, author, journal entry, 4 June 1909, Cavendish, P.E.I., *The Selected Journals of L.M. Montgomery: Volume I: 1889-1910* (1985) edited by Mary Rubio and Elizabeth Waterston.

It is no accident that the starry night stirs in us the most profound questions of origins, destinies and the ultimate meaning of it all. Humans are as much a part of the fabric of the cosmos as a moon rock, an ice particle in the rings of Saturn or an asteroid in a galaxy a billion light-years away. We are all star-stuff, assemblages of atoms cooked in the thermonuclear fires at the hearts of stars.
TERENCE DICKINSON, astronomer and author, *The Universe . . . and Beyond* (1986).

We are now becoming more aware of our links to the universe and are reaching out to the universe for knowledge. We are evolving from earth creatures to star creatures. Our minds now explore the worlds beyond, and we sense a destiny beyond this planet.
DOUGLAS CARDINAL, architect, "Museum of Man Proposal, 1983: From Earth Creatures to Star Creatures," *The Canadian Forum*, Oct. 1989.

UNIVERSITIES
See COLLEGES & UNIVERSITIES

U.S.S.R.
See SOVIET UNION

UTOPIA

The real utopia is a world not to see but to see by.
NORTHROP FRYE, literary critic, quoted by Lucinda Vardey in *Belonging: A Book for the Questioning Catholic Today* (1988).

It is better to be an Arcadian than a Utopian, to say, with the Viennese, "We look with confidence towards the past."
Editorial signed "Otiosus," *The Idler*, No. 18, July-Aug. 1988.

VACATIONS
See also TOURISM

Canadians . . . have no south of which they can speak warmly.
PRIIT J. VESILIND, writer, "Common Ground, Different Dreams," *National Geographic*, March 1990.

VALUES

We must now establish the basic principles, the basic values and beliefs which hold us together as Canadians so that beyond our regional loyalties there is a way of life and a system of values which make us proud of the country that has given us such freedom and such immeasurable joy.
PIERRE ELLIOTT TRUDEAU, Prime Minister, statement of affirmative values attached to the Canadian Charter of Rights and Freedoms, Constitution Act of 1982.

Yes, I bring a vision and a sense of values to an issue. However, I believe it is still an age of miracles, the glass is half full and the world is a wonderful place.
STUART McLEAN, radio journalist, quoted in *Metropolis*, 2 Nov. 1989.

The calculation of costs has replaced the estimation of values.
ROBIN SKELTON, man-of-letters, aphorism, May 1990.

Contemporary societies no longer debate the great philosophical questions or uphold a sense of values. And we cannot live without values. Art is precisely where new values are created, a place where we measure ourselves against the past to determine where we are going.
JOYCE ZEMANS, Director, The Canada Council, Statement, *The Canada Council: 33rd Annual Report* (1990).

VAMPIRES

The concept of the dead arising from their graves to feed upon the blood of the innocent and the beautiful is not a macabre but a voluptuous idea. The vampire works out his spell in the dark. He rises from the moist and damp earth in a glowing mist or black fog from the vaults that rest under cobwebs in the faint light of the dim radiance of a rising moon.
DEVANDRA P. VARMA, Professor of English, Dalhousie University, Halifax, scholar of Gothic literature and special-

ist in the legend of the vampire, quoted by Peter Underhill in *Exorcism!* (1990).

VANCOUVER
See also BRITISH COLUMBIA

Vancouver presents no interest to the casual visitor. It is severely Scotch. Its beauties lie in its surroundings.
> ALEISTER CROWLEY, occultist and traveller, May 1904, *The Confessions of Aleister Crowley: An Autohagiography* (1969) edited by John Symonds and Kenneth Grant.

Vancouver is lovely. There is no other word for it. High, snow-capped mountains dominate the town, and the land-locked, green-shored bay with its pellucid water makes a wonderful setting. The town, itself, is very American in appearance with its high buildings. Here also there can be no great expansion until western Canada is more populous, but sooner or later Vancouver will certainly be another San Francisco.
> SIR ARTHUR CONAN DOYLE, author and traveller, *Our Second American Adventure* (1923).

A lot of Imperialist ladies asked me to tea to meet schoolmasters from New Zealand and editors from Vancouver, and that was the dismalest business of all.
> Recollection of the fictional character Richard Hannay in the novel *The Thirty-nine Steps* (1915) by JOHN BUCHAN, future Governor General Lord Tweedsmuir.

I have never lost the inspiration of the picture of Vancouver that came to me so many years ago. It was the enthralment of the City of Destiny.
> G.G. (GERRY) McGEER, Vancouver Mayor, remark made upon his election, 12 Dec. 1934, quoted by David Ricardo Williams in *Mayor Gerry: The Remarkable Gerald Grattan McGeer* (1986).

Vancouver was a beautiful city set between the Rocky Mountains and the Pacific Ocean.
> BOB GELDOF, musician, crossing Canada from Montreal to Vancouver by bus in 1973, *Is That It?* (1986). Geldof wrote the song "The Neon Heart" about the red light area in Vancouver's Gastown district.

Vancouver enjoys one of the most splendid of all city settings — better than San Francisco's, because of all the greenness, better than Sydney's, because of the mountains all around, rivalled perhaps only by Rio and Hong Kong. It is almost as though the surroundings have been artificially landscaped, on the most colossal scale, and this necessarily gives the city an exhibition flavour, as if consciously on display.
> JAN MORRIS, Anglo-Welsh travel writer, "Too Nice for Words," *Saturday Night*, Feb. 1988. And as the popular historian James Morris, she noted in *Pax Britannica: The Climax of an Empire* (1968): "When I speak of the travellers who consider Stanley Park the most beautiful of all, emphatically among them I number myself."

Captain George Vancouver had a Canadian city named after him. Which city is it?
> TERRY JOHNSON, humorist, *Quick Quiz for Slow People* (1988).

But one need not parody, or even exaggerate, the pleasantness of Vancouver. This is, one might say, the last resort of pleasantness, and especially, I think pleasantness of a middle-class, middle-income, middle-aged Englishy kind.
> JAN MORRIS, Anglo-Welsh travel writer, "Too Nice for Words," *Saturday Night*, Feb. 1988.

Vancouver is lovely and lazy and famous and marginal.
> WILLIAM THORSELL, columnist, *The Globe and Mail's Report on Business Magazine*, Jan. 1989.

The day I realized that Vancouver is a resort more than a city, everything seemed to fall into place. You ask most people the best thing about Vancouver, and they say it's the ability to get away from it to the mountains, the sea, the parks. This is not a recipe for a throbbing urban environment.

> STEPHEN GODFREY, journalist, quoted by William Thorsell in *The Globe and Mail's Report on Business Magazine*, Jan. 1989.

Few take seriously the hysterical claims about Vancouver becoming an "Asian city." They know it will remain a Canadian city with, as always, many citizens of Asian background. The one big difference is that Vancouver will be a Pacific city in a Pacific century — in the centre of things from now on.

> DANIEL STOFFMAN, journalist, *The Globe and Mail's Report on Business Magazine*, Jan. 1989.

A previous mayor, Thomas J. Campbell, used to dream that the city would one day become a "New York of the Pacific." No one shares that dream now. Instead, Vancouver wants to be Canada's Zurich on the Pacific. That is why the province and city pushed Ottawa to designate the city as an international financial centre (IFC), so that international financial business conducted with non-residents would get a lower rate of taxation. Like Switzerland, Canada offers political stability; unlike the United States, it has never frozen anybody's assets or imposed exchange controls.

> DANIEL STOFFMAN, journalist, *The Globe and Mail's Report on Business Magazine*, Jan. 1989.

Like multiculturalism, Vancouver's livability has turned out to be not a frill but an attraction of major economic importance. This is new. Of course, it was always enjoyable to call up the relatives in Winnipeg on a Sunday in February and tell them the crocuses were out, the rain clouds had lifted and the mountains looked great. That's nice, they would say, but you can't eat the scenery. Now you can. In the age of computer, fax and jet lane, a service- or knowledge-based industry can be run from wherever its managers want to live.

A growing number of such businesses are setting up shop in Vancouver.

> DANIEL STOFFMAN, journalist, *The Globe and Mail's Report on Business Magazine*, Nov. 1989.

My father did not know geography very well. When I told him I was going to Vancouver, he thought I told him I was going to "Van-Cuba." He said, "What Jewish boy goes to a communist country?"

> MARVIN HIER, rabbi and founder of The Simon Wiesenthal Center in Los Angeles, explaining to his Polish-born father in New York's Lower East Side in 1962 that he had accepted the call of the Orthodox Congregation Schara Tzedek in Vancouver; quoted by Sheldon Teitelbaum and Tom Waldman, "The Unorthodox Rabbi," *The Los Angeles Times Magazine*, 15 July 1990.

VANCOUVER ISLAND

I have consecrated Vancouver Island in advance of your arrival. Many beautiful people with much light.

> RICHARD ALPERT, a.k.a. the yogi Ram Dass, letter with blessings addressed to the visiting American poet Robert Sward and awaiting him on arrival at Victoria, Vancouver Island, B.C., 1968, *Contemporary Authors Autobiography Series* (1990), Volume 13.

On the 16th Day of *June* 1703, a Boy on the Top-mast discovered Land. On the 17th we came in full View of a great Island or Continent, (for we knew not whether) on the South-side whereof was a small Neck of Land jutting out into the sea, and a Creek too shallow to hold a Ship of above one hundred Tuns.

> JONATHAN SWIFT, Anglo-Irish author, thus describes the first sight of Brobdingnag in *Travels into Several Remote Nations of the World* (1726), the work otherwise known as "Gulliver's Travels." Brobdingnag is the land where Captain Lemuel Gulliver encounters the giants. Swift locates it off the West Coast of

North America somewhat north of the conjectured Strait of Anian. It shares its geographical locale with Vancouver Island: "This vast Tract of Land to the North-west Parts of *America....*"

VANDER ZALM, WILLIAM

The answer, I suppose, is to be Bill Vander Slap, who, as far as anyone can determine, has never read a book and therefore cannot steal from anyone. There are gifts to being an original. However brief.
> ALLAN FOTHERINGHAM, columnist, referring to politicians like B.C. Premier William Vander Zalm who employ ghost writers and make use of the ideas of others for their speeches and their books, *Maclean's*, 28 Sept. 1987.

The things I say are probably what a lot of people are thinking.
> WILLIAM VANDER ZALM, B.C. Premier, 2 Dec. 1982, quoted by Stephen Osborne and Mary Schendlinger in *Quotations from Chairman Zalm* (1988).

I wish I could clone myself.
> WILLIAM VANDER ZALM, B.C. Premier, 5 Sept. 1986, quoted by Stephen Osborne and Mary Schendlinger in *Quotations from Chairman Zalm* (1988).

In the last two weeks it seems to have gone from Vandermania to Zalmnesia.
> Pun attributed to B.C. opposition leader MIKE HARCOURT, with reference to the resignation of B.C. Premier William Vander Zalm, CBC Radio, 17 April 1991.

VANITY

If there is a simple quality that is shared by all great men, it is vanity.
> YOUSUF KARSH, portrait photographer, *Cosmopolitan*, Dec. 1955.

Women are less vain then men. This has been my experience.
> YOUSUF KARSH, portrait photography, interviewed by Art Finley, radio, 26 Nov. 1976.

VARIETY

Genetic diversity, in both human and non-human species, is a precious planetary resource, and it is in our best interests to monitor and preserve that diversity.
> DAVID SUZUKI, scientist and broadcaster, and Peter Knudtson, writer and biologist, *Genethics: The Ethics of Engineering Life* (1988)

VEGETARIANISM

Wagner thought everyone should become vegetarian.... The lakes of the north of Canada, he wrote, are chock-full of vegetarian panthers and tigers. (This may have been true in Wagner's day. But there weren't any left last time I looked.)
> DAVID W. BARBER, opera commentator, quoting from an unnamed literary work by the German composer Richard Wagner, *When the Fat Lady Sings: Opera History as It Ought to Be Taught* (1990).

VENGEANCE

An eye for an eye leads only to more blindness.
> Thoughts of the narrator of the novel *Cat's Eye* (1988) by MARGARET ATWOOD.

VICE

A vice is merely a pleasure to which somebody has objected.
> ROBIN SKELTON, man-of-letters, aphorism, May 1990.

VICTIM

It's so much easier, I've discovered, to be a victim than it is to be responsible for being a victimizer that it's almost automatically chosen and one looks for those ways in which one is a victim.
> JOY KOGAWA, author, interviewed by Magdalene Redekop, *The Canadian Forum*, Nov. 1989.

VICTORIA
See also BRITISH COLUMBIA

There is no society for ladies, nor indeed for cultivated persons of any description.
D.G.F. MacDONALD, surveyor with the International Boundary Commission, *Lecture on British Columbia and Vancouver's Island* (1863).

When I remember that here I am as far from Ottawa, as Ottawa is from London, I realize something of the vastness of Canada. When I saw the broad plains, changed by pioneers to the uses of man, and the mighty mountain ranges through which they cut their roads, I began to understand the qualities of the Canadian people.
KING GEORGE VI, address, Victoria, B.C., 30 May 1939, quoted by Tom MacDonnell in *Daylight upon Magic: The Royal Tour of Canada — 1939* (1989).

God's Waiting Room
Epithetical description of Victoria, the capital of British Columbia, the retirement home of many Canadians, heard in 1965.

It never occurred to me there existed in this world an outpost of people who, more than two hundred years after the event, still regarded the dumping of tea into Boston Harbor as a criminal act, who believed Paul Revere to be "the enemy," and who, though they lived twenty miles from Seattle, felt an emotional bond with King George III (the crazy one) and Queen Elizabeth II.
ROBERT SWARD, American-born poet and teacher, resident of Victoria in 1968-79, *Contemporary Authors Autobiography Series* (1990), Volume 13.

VICTORIA DAY
See HOLIDAYS

VICTORY

He had tried: he had not won. But oh! what did it matter? He would die in humble circs: it did not matter. There would be no victory for Ginger Coffey, no victory big or little, for there, on the courthouse steps, he had learned the truth. Life was the victory, wasn't it? Going on was the victory.
BRIAN MOORE, novelist, *The Luck of Ginger Coffey* (1960).

VIETNAM WAR
See also WAR

In the barbarous war in Vietnam, Canada has supported the United States through its membership on the International Control Commission and through sales of arms and strategic resources to the American military-industrial complex.
"The Waffle Manifesto: For an Independent Socialist Canada" (1969) reprinted in *The Canadian Forum*, Dec. 1989.

John J. Rambo
The name Rambo has become a synonym for the tough, returned Viet vet. John J. Rambo is the name of the fictional veteran of the Green Berets; the character was created by DAVID MORRELL, the novelist, born in Kitchener, Ont., resident of the State of Iowa, in his violent novel *First Blood* (1972). Rambo was created by Sylvester Stallone in *Rambo: First Blood* (1982), directed by Ted Kotcheff, and in the sequels, which begin with *Rambo: First Blood, Part II* (1985) which was "novelized" by Morrell.
"Rambo is sent back to Vietnam to rescue some American prisoners — which he does, amidst much slaughter. The character's name became a household word when President Reagan saw fit to commend this second film in one of his speeches. 'Rambo' promptly entered the vocabulary of politicians and journalists the world over as a designation for Reagan himself, particulary when referring to his policy of overseas military intervention." — David Pringle in *Imaginary People: A Who's Who of Modern Fictional Characters* (1980).
"Reagan: 'In the spirit of *Rambo*, let me tell you, we're going to win this time.'

Sylvester Stallone, in *Rambo*: 'Do we get to win this time?'" — Allan Fotheringham in *Capitol Offences: Dr. Foth Meets Uncle Sam* (1986).

History may argue that the advance of Communism might have been stopped if the Indo-China wars had ended in American victory. This doesn't take into account the loss of human life during these last thirty years. My conscience is clear. As Canadian foreign minister I know that we did everything during the Pearson administration to help bring about a cease-fire. . . . Sometimes, I believe the war in Vietnam, now so universally condemned, may help to bring an end to the wasteful use of force by nations — never again will the United States, I am sure, make such rash judgments with such fateful consequences involving the waste of human life — war is an anachronism.
> PAUL MARTIN, High Commissioner in London, entry for 29 April 1975, *The London Diaries 1975-1979* (1988) edited by William R. Young.

If we learned nothing from Vietnam we should have learned how little helicopters, armies, weapons and those walls count if they are not backed by the spirit of determination and a belief among the people that they are fighting for a worthwhile cause.
> BARBARA AMIEL, columnist, address, Empire Club of Canada, Toronto, 4 Feb. 1982.

Saigon had seduced the French and almost ruined the Americans. It is a whore of a city that will one day corrupt even the Communists.
> JACK CAHILL, correspondent, *Words of War* (1987).

The profoundly unliberated walk as much as a thousand miles to liberate the equally unliberated, to kill them when necessary, and to kill perfect strangers who've flown thirteen thousand miles to do the same.
> MORLEY SAFER, Canadian-born television correspondent, *Flashbacks: On Returning to Vietnam* (1990).

VIOLENCE
See also HOCKEY VIOLENCE

There is no basic distinction between man and nature, no opposition. . . . For instance, the Chinook Indians in northwestern America will render the following sentence, "The evil man has killed the poor child," into "The wickedness of the man has killed the poorness of the child."
> CLAUDE LÉVI-STRAUSS, anthropologist, *La Pensée Sauvage* (1962), as quoted by Armaury de Reincourt in *The Eye of Shiva: Eastern Mysticism and Science* (1980).

I've tasted my blood too much / to abide what I was born to.
> MILTON ACORN, poet, last lines of the title poem of *I've Tasted My Blood* (1969).

You must not strike a woman except with a flower.
> PIERRE DECARY, Montreal judge, imposing a $650 fine on a man who slapped a woman during an argument over a game of golf. "When handing down that *obiter dictum*, Judge Decary may have been thinking of an annual midsummer rite in Nice, France, known as the Battle of Flowers, in which both the spectators and the participants in a lavish carnival parade spiritedly pelt each other with rose petals," explained Bruce Felton and Mark Fowler in *Felton & Fowler's More Best, Worst, and Most Unusual* (1976).

We may not all be guilty but, like it or not, we are certainly all responsible.
> NEIL BISSOONDATH, author, referring to the massacre of fourteen students in Montreal, quoted in *Metropolis*, 21 Dec. 1989.

From an evolutionary point of view, humans are "flight" animals, not "fight" animals.
> ROSALIE BERTELL, anti-nuclear activist, *No Immediate Danger? Prognosis for a Radioactive Earth* (1985).

English Canadians don't realize to what extent their political and cultural life is Americanized; outsiders can hardly see any difference. Certainly Canada is less violent, but there are less violent states too, like Vermont. English Canada is simply a non-violent American state.

JACQUES GODBOUT, Quebec author, interviewed by Sherry Simon in *Other Solitudes: Canadian Multicultural Fictions* (1990) edited by Linda Hutcheon and Marion Richmond.VIOLENCE

VIRTUES & VICES
See GOOD & EVIL

VISION

People are very, very hungry for some kind of contact with a greater world than the one which they can immediately perceive.

ROBERTSON DAVIES, man-of-letters, interviewed by Terence M. Green in 1982, *Conversations with Robertson Davies* (1989) edited by J. Madison Davis.

VOTES
See ELECTIONS

W

WAGES

There is only one consensus in this country. It is universal. It is held by everyone. And that is as follows: "Everybody else is overpaid, relative to me." Is there anybody in this room who thinks he is overpaid? If you put your hand up, two little people in white coats will come in and take you away, because you are certifiable.
JOHN CRISPO, political economist, address, Empire Club of Canada, 25 Jan. 1979.

WALES
See WELSH PEOPLE

WAR
See also CANADIAN ARMED FORCES
DEFENCE
FENIAN WAR
GULF WAR
PEACE
PEACEKEEPING
VIETNAM WAR
WAR DEAD
WAR OF 1812
WAR RESISTERS
WORLD WAR I
WORLD WAR II
WORLD WAR III

I know that truth is one of the first victims of war.
J.S. WOODSWORTH, CCF leader, casting the sole dissenting vote against Canada's declaration of war on Germany, House of Commons, 8 Sept. 1939.

If you were to ask any Canadian, "Do you *have* to go to war if England does?" he'd answer at once, "Oh, no." If you then said, "*Would* you go to war if England does?" he'd answer, "Oh, yes." And if you asked, "Why?" he would say, reflectively, "Well, you see, we'd *have* to."
STEPHEN LEACOCK, humorist, *Atlantic Monthly*, June 1939.

Surely the glamour has gone out of war. The thin but heroic red line of the nineteenth century is now the production line. The warrior is the man with a test tube or the one who pushes the nuclear button. This should have a salutary effect on man's emotions. A realization of the consequences that must follow if and when he does push the button, should have a salutary effect also on his reason.
LESTER B. PEARSON, diplomat, Nobel Peace Prize Lecture, Oslo, Norway, 11 Dec. 1957. The text is taken from *The Four Faces of Peace and the International Out-*

look (1964) edited by Sherleigh G. Pierson.

The war has dirtied the snow.
Last line of ROCH CARRIER's novel *La Guerre, Yes Sir!* (1970) translated by Sheila Fischman.

If you believe that military activity is like a sex drive, that it's a natural part of human nature, then we are going to continue fighting wars forever. But I don't subscribe to that.
GWYNNE DYER, military affairs specialist, quoted by Paul McLaughlin in *TV Guide*, 8 Oct. 1983.

It is a very nice place to live; there are no wars.
Unidentified Ukrainian farmer, then in his nineties, who lived close to Bird's Hill Park, near Winnipeg, quoted by Dian Cohen and Kristin Shannon in *The Next Canadian Economy* (1984).

Let it be said of Canada and of Canadians, that we saw the crisis; that we did act; that we took risks; that we were loyal to our friends and open with our adversaries; that we have lived up to our ideals; and that we have done what we could to lift the shadow of war.
PIERRE ELLIOTT TRUDEAU, Prime Minister, final address on his peace initiative, 9 Feb. 1984. "The words also serve as a fitting memorial to his own career," wrote Thomas S. Axworthy.

Warlike behaviour has been and is being cultivated and taught in most modern societies.
ROSALIE BERTELL, anti-nuclear activist, *No Immediate Danger? Prognosis for a Radioactive Earth* (1985).

Canada is one of the most fortunate of countries in that she has not had a battle on home ground for more than a century.
MARY BEACOCK FRYER, historian, *Battlefields of Canada* (1986).

The twentieth century has seen a quantum leap in the numbers of people who fell victim to such man-made catastrophes as war and revolution, numbing those who assemble previously unheard-of statistics of the dead.
MICHAEL R. MARRUS, historian, *The Holocaust in History* (1987).

Military responses to political conflict remain strangely compelling to human beings. More than five million soldiers for more than forty countries are currently fighting in about thirty-five wars.
ERNIE REGEHR, political-affairs co-ordinator of Project Ploughshares, "New Approaches to Security," *The Road to Peace* (1988) edited by Ernie Regehr and Simon Rosenblum.

In one respect, at least, the Russians are a lot like the Americans: afraid. We all have that in common, all of us in the target nations. Our politics may not necessarily mesh, but we do share the same emotions, the same desire to survive. All we need is better co-operation.
LESLEY CHOYCE, author, *December Six: The Halifax Solution — An Alternative to Nuclear War* (1988).

But Canada, along with New Zealand, South Africa and Australia, fought in someone else's wars for the relatively abstract reasons of justice and freedom. And Canada, alone among the Dominions, did not seek territorial acquisitions in the peace settlements.
There may be something noble in this. To fight for abstractions, to mobilize in defence of principles, is altruism of the highest order. Or, there might be something utterly foolish in a nation arming its manpower and going off to war for abstractions.
J.L. GRANATSTEIN, historian, *The Globe and Mail*, 19 Aug. 1989.

War has always had a high price, in money, in misery and in lives, but we shouldn't fool ourselves. We've gone on fighting wars all down our history because we were willing to pay the price; but in more and more of the world, as time goes on, we simply cannot afford to pay the price of war at all any more. There's nothing in the world that's worth blowing the whole world up for.

> GWYNNE DYER, military affairs analyst, quoted in an advertisement in *The Winnipeg Free Press* for his speech at the University of Winnipeg, 28 Feb. 1991.

WAR DEAD
See also WAR

The wind and the thunder, / They are the same everywhere, / What does it matter then, / If I die here in a strange land?

> Ojibwa poem, "Song of a Man About to Die," *Songs of the Great Land* (1989) edited by John Robert Colombo.

Thank you forever.

> Message written in English in the Book of Remembrance by a local Dutch visitor to the Canadian War Cemetery, Bergen-op-Zoom, Holland, noted by Douglas MacArthur in *The Globe and Mail*, 11 Nov. 1989.

To Canadians no place-names stir more heart-throbs than names such as Mons, Ypres, Passchendaele, St. Julien and Langemarck, and no day in the year means more than Poppy Day.

> JOHN MURRAY GIBBON, nationalist and publicist, *Canadian Mosaic: The Making of a Northern Nation* (1938).

The death and destruction unleashed by the Second World War was unparalleled. Those men and women who gave their lives might have written great books, discovered cures for disease, or, more likely, simply have lived out their days in peace in their native land. They lost the chance for a full life because of forces beyond their control, beyond their country's control — forces most of them comprehended only dimly.

> J.L. GRANATSTEIN and DESMOND MORTON, historians, *A Nation Forged in Fire: Canadians and the Second World War 1939-1945* (1989).

At least ten times as many Germans — undoubtedly 800,000, almost certainly more than 900,000, and quite probably over 1-million — died in the French and American camps as were killed in all the combat on the Western Front in northwest Europe from America's entry into the war in 1941 through April, 1945.

> JAMES BACQUE, journalist and author, "The Last Dirty Secret of World War Two," *Saturday Night*, Sept. 1989.

Not to be able to speak the truth about the American atrocity is an eerie echo of knowing nothing about the Nazi camps.

> JAMES BACQUE, investigator, *Other Losses: An Investigation into the Mass Deaths of German Prisoners at the Hands of the French and Americans after World War II* (1989).

WAR MEASURES ACT
See OCTOBER CRISIS

WAR OF 1812

Don't give up the ship, boys!

> This is the best-known quotation to grow out of either side of the War of 1812. It is attributed to JAMES LAWRENCE, according to *They Never Said It: A Book of Fake Quotes, Misquotes, and Misleading Attributions* (1989) edited by Paul F. Goller, Jr., and John George: "In June 1813, Captian James Lawrence, commander of the U.S. frigate *Chesapeake*, engaged the British frigate *Shannon* in battle and was mortally wounded. As he was being carried below, he was supposed to have cried, 'Don't give up the ship, boys,' and the words became a popular rallying cry in the U.S. Navy during the rest of the War of 1812. But what Lawrence actually said was more prolix: 'Tell the men to fire faster and not to give up the ship; fight

her till she sinks.' In the end, the British hauled down the *Chesapeake*'s flag."

During the War of 1812, which was basically a scrap between Britain and the United States over fur trading, the Americans marched into Ontario to pull the wretched inhabitants from under the British boot-heel. They were astounded to be met by a hail of gunfire, and retreated at speed. The event appears in every Canadian history book and not, so far as I know, in a single American one.

SIMON HOGGART, Washington correspondent for *The Observer*, in *The Globe and Mail*, 9 Jan. 1990.

Should I be the happy mortal destined to turn the scale of war, will you not rejoice, O my father? May Heaven be propitious, and smile on the cause of my country. But if we are destined to fall, may my fall be like Wolfe's — to sleep in the arms of victory.

ZEBULON PIKE, U.S. Brigadier-General, last letter addressed to his father, late April 1813. Gen. Pike's secret mission was to attack and destroy the defences of York (Toronto); he succeeded but was mortally wounded in the engagement, 27 April 1813. "Pike lived for several hours suffering terrible agony. When a captured British flag was brought to him, he motioned to have it placed under his head." Quoted by John Upton Terrell in *Zebulon Pike: The Life and Times of an Adventurer* (1968).

Did at great Risk peril & danger travelling on foot & partly in the Night by a circuitous route, through woods mountains, and enemys lines & Indian Encampments to give important intelligence of a mediated attack of the Americans upon our troops & by which circumstance has laid the foundation of a disease from which she has never recovered. . . .

LAURA SECORD's own account (written in the third person) of her celebrated trek of almost twenty miles at night from Queenston to De Cew's House to warn of an impending American attack in the Niagara Peninsula, June 1813. Her account was a petition, written for monetary and other considerations in 1840, addressed to the Lieutenant-Governor; it failed. Quoted by Ruth McKenzie in *Laura Secord: The Legend and the Lady* (1971).

Mr. Churchill inquired also why no big monument had been erected to Gen. Sir Roger H. Sheaffe who recaptured the heights from the Americans although a tall column had been placed on the height to honour Gen. Brock who lost his life in the attempt. It was explained to Mr. Churchill that a small marker had been erected by the Historic Sites and Monuments Board to honour Gen. Sheaffe. Mr. Churchill suggested that no large monument had been erected to commemorate Gen. Sheaffe's exploit because he wasn't killed.

News item concerning British wartime leader Winston Churchill and Brock's Monument at Queenston Heights in the Niagara Peninsula, *The Niagara Falls Evening Review*, 12 Aug. 1943.

WAR RESISTERS
See also WAR

Number of American draft resisters still living in Canada: 10,000.

"Anachronisms," *The Harper's Index Book* (1987) by Lewis H. Lapham, Michael Pollan, and Eric Etheridge.

Dan Quayle did not go to Canada and did not burn his draft card and he damn sure did not burn the American flag.

GEORGE BUSH, U.S. Vice-President, defending, as presidential candidate, the reputation of his embattled running mate, Senator Dan Quayle, who found "home service" with the Indiana National Guard during the years of the Vietnam War, Chicago address, 22 Aug. 1988, quoted in *The Toronto Star* the following day.

WASHINGTON, D.C.
See also UNITED STATES OF
AMERICA

The press is very powerful in Washington. It's the only permanent power in Washington; everything else is transient.
> SONDRA GOTLIEB, author and "wife of" the Canadian Ambassador in Washington, address, Empire Club of Canada, Toronto, 31 Oct. 1985.

The key to success in Washington is suck above, kick below.
> Attributed to writer SONDRA GOTLIEB, columnist, author, and wife of Canadian Ambassador in Washington, D.C., by Allan Fotheringham *Capitol Offences: Dr. Foth Meets Uncle Sam* (1986).

And Washington . . . this is a very small town, especially among the social/journalistic elite, since, because the black population is so predominant, the effective white population of the city is some two hundred thousand. It's like living in London, Ontario.
> ALLAN FOTHERINGHAM, columnist, *Capitol Offences: Dr. Foth Meets Uncle Sam* (1986).

In Washington, gossip is intelligence.
> ALLAN GOTLIEB, former Canadian Ambassador in Washington, quoted in *The Toronto Star*, 7 April 1989.

WATER
See also GREAT LAKES
NIAGARA FALLS

So, too, we give thanks because there are waters that flow as ordained, and because there are springs of water likewise, which are for our comfort as we go to-and-fro over the earth.
> "Address of Thanksgiving to the Powers of the Master of Life" (Green Corn Dance), "Seneca Fiction, Legends, and Myths" (Part 2), collected and translated by J.N.B. Hewitt in 1896, *Thirty-second Annual Report of the Bureau of American Ethnology to the Secretary of the Smithsonian Institution, 1910-1911* (1918).

It would surprise most Canadians, who think of the Prairies as a sterile Sahara, that it abounds with water. That would be Manitoba and one of the eerie experiences of our time is floating along the Red River, above Winnipeg up to Selkirk, in a huge paddle steamer on a spring evening, a live Prairie schooner in full flight.
> ALLAN FOTHERINGHAM, columnist, *Maclean's*, Feb. 1978.

Before being appointed as Canada's chief trade negotiator, Simon Reisman was personally associated with the Grand Canal Company as an economic adviser. The Grand Canal Company, as its name suggests, has been exploring the feasibility of feeding the fresh water from twenty rivers that empty into James Bay south into Lake Huron. From Lake Huron, the water would go through a continental grid system to feed the American Midwest and other parts of the United States with some of the flow going to western Canada.
> JAMES LAXER, political economist, *Leap of Faith: Free Trade and the Future of Canada* (1986).

Canada will only be able, in the long run, to say no to water export if it fills up its empty spaces with forty or fifty million people.
> ROY FAIBISH, broadcaster, quoted by Peter C. Newman in *Sometimes a Great Nation: Will Canada Belong to the 21st Century?* (1988).

One thing, David, never to forget, is never give away our water.
> WILLIAM DAVIS, former Ontario Premier, advising Ontario Premier David Peterson on the emotional impact of the water issue, quoted by William Walker in *The Toronto Star*, 30 June 1988.

But water is to Canadians as the Alps are to the Swiss — something that transcends the resource. It's so much a part of how Canadians see themselves. We're a land of rivers and lakes. Our history is built on it.
> DON GAMBLE, scientist, Rawson Academy of Aquatic Science in Ottawa, quoted by Priit J. Vesilind in *National Geographic*, March 1990.

Will our great-grandchildren be able to drink the water we used to hose down the dog?
> MARJORIE LAMB, ecologist, *Two Minutes a Day for a Greener Planet* (1990).

The Canadian Department of Fisheries and Oceans estimates that 14,000 lakes, stretching from Manitoba to Newfoundland, are already dead, and 150,000 more are at risk.
> ANITA GORDON and DAVID SUZUKI, science broadcasters, *It's a Matter of Survival* (1990).

WEALTH
See also MONEY

In the United States, and I think also in Canada, the voice of privilege is much louder and much more articulate than that of the people at large and tends to be mistaken for the voice of the masses.
> JOHN KENNETH GALBRAITH, economist and author, quoted by Robert Lewis in *Maclean's*, 9 Feb. 1976.

The rich don't have children; they have heirs.
> PETER C. NEWMAN, author, *The Establishment Man: A Portrait of Power* (1982).

I like both Main Street and Bay Street, and they both voted for our party.
> BRIAN MULRONEY, Prime Minister, House of Commons, Ottawa, 7 Nov. 1984.

Now I acknowledge that it would be just delightful if we could solve our fiscal problems by asking only rich people to carry the burden of restoring fiscal responsibil-

ity. But that brings us face to face with another one of those sobering realities.... No matter how we define the term, Canada has an acute shortage of rich people.... The economic assumptions underlying the budget's fiscal projections are as conservative as the budget is progressive.
> MICHAEL WILSON, Minister of Finance, referring to the newly tabled federal budget in his address to the annual meeting of the Canadian Economics Association, Montreal, 30 May 1985, reported in *The Globe and Mail* the following day. The CP reporter added, "Suppressed guffaws greeted Mr. Wilson's remark that 'Canada has an acute shortage of rich people.'"

We're not rich. We are merely guardians of wealth.
> ERIC MOLSON, head of the Molson Companies Ltd., referring to the Molson family fortune, quoted by Diane Francis in *Controlling Interest: Who Owns Canada?* (1986).

It remains a fact of life in Canada that it is easy to stay rich, but difficult to get rich.
> DIANE FRANCIS, financial writer, *Controlling Interest: Who Owns Canada?* (1986).

If the words "rich" and "poor" have become taboo, the reality of wealth and poverty in our country has not. We may not talk about it much any more, but an enormous gulf remains between the rich and the poor.
> LINDA McQUAIG, journalist, *Behind Closed Doors* (1987).

I have my own personal definition: Wealth is the ability to do whatever I want in life without compromising my standard of living. In other words, comfortable independence.
> GORDON PAPE, financial writer, *Building Wealth: Achieving Your Financial Goals* (1988).

Canada could easily become the richest country in the world. All we have to do is push up the Canadian dollar to about

$1.70 U.S. That is effectively what happened in Japan.
> ANDREW COYNE, essayist, "Seven Barroom Myths about Japan," *The Idler*, No. 22, March-April 1989.

For real wealth and real power in Canada, inherit it, marry it or forget it.
> WALTER STEWART, journalist, quoted by Stephen McHale in *The Globe and Mail*, 23 Jan. 1991.

WEAPONS

Missiles create budget deficits, but satellites are generators of economic wealth.
> FRANK FEATHER, futurologist, *G-Forces: Reinventing the World — The 35 Global Forces Restructuring Our World* (1989).

WEATHER
See also CLIMATE
SEASONS

I no longer wonder that the elegant arts are unknown here; the rigour of the climate suspends the very powers of the understanding.
> FRANCES BROOKE, early novelist, *The History of Emily Montague* (1769).

The weather belongs to us all, it doesn't cost us anything, and it's about one of the few possessions we can afford.
> MARGARET (MA) MURRAY, pioneer newspaperwoman, quoted in *The Vancouver Sun*, 2 Aug. 1962.

I want to thank God personally for the beautiful weather He has given us.
> PHILIP A. GAGLIARDI, B.C. Minister of Highways, speech delivered at the opening of the Trans-Canada Highway, Rogers Pass, B.C., 3 Sept. 1962.

Weather: Unsettled / Rain: Intermittent / Cloud: Occasional / Temperatures: Varying / Air: Light, getting dark toward evening / Wind: Multi-directional / Pressure: Constant from high to low and back again /

Seasonal Change: On and off / Forecast beyond 2000: Much the same.
> DON HARRON, comedian and author, parodying weather forecasting, *Charlie Farquharson's K-O-R-N Filled Allmynack* (1976).

Canadians love to sit in the dark trembling with fear at weather forecasts.
> ROBERT MORLEY, British actor, CBC-TV interview in 1972, quoted by Lorraine Monk in *Between Friends/Entre Amis* (1976).

Canadians are careful. We have two railroads, two airlines, two languages, and two temperatures.
> BARRY MATHER, journalist and former Parliamentarian, letter, 1 July 1979.

I am delighted to be here in the one part of Canada where the good weather goes northwards to the United States.
> RICHARD GWYN, correspondent, noting that Windsor, Ont., lies due south of Detroit, Michigan, *Cultural Sovereignty: Myth or Reality? Proceedings of the 28th Annual Seminar on Canadian-American Relations, University of Windsor, 5-7 Nov. 1986* (1987) edited by James Chacko.

I wouldn't say it's cold, but every year Winnipeg's athlete of the year is an ice fisherman.
> DALE TALLON, U.S. journalist, covering a hockey game played in Winnipeg between the Chicago Black Hawks and the Winnipeg Jets, *Sports Illustrated*, 22 Dec. 1986.

It was about 11:00 p.m., Central Standard Time (our story taking place within the boundaries of that particular time zone), and due to a cold front off the Rockies meeting up with a warm front off the Great Lakes there was heavy precipitation in the form of rain, winds gusting up to 40 miles per hour, and generally low visibility, or in other words, it was a dark and stormy night.
> MOSES MONTGOMERY, contestant from Winnipeg, entry in the 1990 Bulwer-Lytton Fiction Contest, conducted by

Scott Rice of San Jose State University, California; quoted in *The Toronto Star*, 7 July 1990.

WEIGHT
See DIET

WELFARE

After medicare, what is next on the womb-to-tomb welfare list? Well, there are legal-care, morticare, carcare, housecare, leisurecare, and endless other possibilities.
LUBOR J. ZINK, columnist, *The Toronto Telegram*, 26 July 1965.

We are responsible for each other, but we are not responsible to each other.
MICHAEL IGNATIEFF, essayist, *The Needs of Strangers* (1985).

More than 200,000 troubled youths under 18 years of age are defined in the Canadian Child Welfare Act as emotionally disturbed, delinquent, neglected, or abandoned and in need of the assistance of the state. Approximately 60,000 of these youths become crown wards and depend solely upon the state for their well-being.
MARTYN KENDRICK, journalist, *Nobody's Children: The Foster Care Crisis in Canada* (1990).

You show me a child that is moved to 10 different foster homes over a period of years and I'll show you a psychopath.
ELLIOT BARKER, President, Society for the Prevention of Cruelty to Children, quoted by Martyn Kendrick in *Nobody's Children: The Foster Care Crisis in Canada* (1990).

WELSH PEOPLE
See also UNITED KINGDOM

The Welsh are the only Celtic race who had the advantage of 500 years of Roman civilization.
ROBERTSON DAVIES, man-of-letters, quoted by Bruce Ward in *The Ottawa Citizen*, 17 Sept. 1988.

A Welshman is an Irishman who can't swim.
SHEA DUFFIN, Irish-Canadian impersonator of Brendan Behan, CBC Radio, 24 Aug. 1989.

WEST COAST

I travelled by sea via Victoria to Seattle. My principal observation is that the inhabitants of the Pacific coast have almost everything in common; original racial differences seem to matter little; I suppose because the great distance from the base makes them feel that they have burnt their boats. It would be quite impossible to distinguish a British Columbian from a Californian, while, on the other hand, the people of the coast differ very widely from anyone east of the Rockies. The point is important.
ALEISTER CROWLEY, occultist and traveller, observation made in 1917, *The Confessions of Aleister Crowley: An Autohagiography* (1969) edited by Julian Symonds and Kenneth Grant.

We need the West Coast. It is the psychological equivalent of a black satin negligée, the little luxury we allow ourselves when we're weary of wearing practical cotton pyjamas. It is the sandbox in the Canadian schoolyard. It is the escape valve for an entire country.
PAUL GRESCOE, journalist, "Coasting," *The Canadian Magazine*, 25 May 1975.

WEST INDIES
See also CARIBBEAN ISLANDS

If I'd stayed in Jamaica, I'd probably be a bum today.
BEN JOHNSON, sprinter, born in Jamaica in 1960, brought to Canada at the age of fourteen, quoted by James R. Christie in *Ben Johnson: The Fastest Man on Earth* (1988).

The present in Jamaica is omnipresent. The past or the future in any given location resides in the background.

JUDITH MERRIL, science-fiction personality, observation on Jamaica, Dec. 1989.

WESTERN PROVINCES
See also ALBERTA
BRITISH COLUMBIA
MANITOBA
PRAIRIE PROVINCES
SASKATCHEWAN
WEST COAST

I was learning to cherish the diversity of the west, its hidden swaths of tradition and perception, at a moment when they stand exposed to the advance of the continent's routines. All across the prairies the monoculture of a single language, like the botanical monoculture of wheat, continues to uproot thickets, reeds and forests that have formed part of the social landscape since white settlement began. It is, unfortunately, only a fragment of a worldwide trend.
MARK ABLEY, traveller, *Beyond Forget: Rediscovering the Prairies* (1986).

The west is simply a different culture. And the west is a different culture from the east mainly because it doesn't rain out there. These things really do shape lives. I often say I missed being a Canadian by an inch of rain. If there had been more rain my father would have stayed and we would have become Canadian citizens.
WALLACE STEGNER, U.S. author who was raised in southern Saskatchewan, quoted by Philip Marchand in *The Toronto Star*, 22 Aug. 1989.

Where the impulse in the U.S. is usually to define oneself as American, the Canadian . . . is always quoting his many sources. Our sense of region resists our national sense. I hear myself saying, I'm from *Western* Canada. Or, even beyond that — because I was born in Alberta and now live in Manitoba — people ask me, seriously, if I think of myself as an Albertan or Manitoban.
ROBERT KROETSCH, novelist, *The Lovely*

Treachery of Words: Essays New and Selected (1989).

There's no question there's a new reality (in Canada) and that new reality is in Western Canada. If there is going to be a bloc in Ontario and a bloc in Quebec, well they're going to find a big bloc in the West. We are going to spend less time talking about Quebec and French issues and more about Western Canadian issues.
GRANT DEVINE, Saskatchewan Premier, quoted by Donald Campbell in *The Winnipeg Free Press*, 13 Aug. 1990.

WHALES

Baby beluga in the deep blue sea, / Swim so wild and you swim so free. / Heaven above and the sea below, / And a little white whale on the go.
First verse of the popular children's song "Baby Beluga" written and sung by RAFFI, reproduced from Raffi's *Baby Beluga Book* (1983).

WHEAT
See also FARMING

Long before one reaches it one sees the mountainous wheat elevators in which much of the western harvest is stored until it can be shipped eastwards. They have been called the "Castles of Commerce," and from a distance they look like a combination of the great keep of a Norman fortress, with the pillars of Luxor built into it. There is one which is alone sufficient to hold the bread-supply of the whole population of the United Kingdom for five days.
SIR ARTHUR CONAN DOYLE, author and traveller, evoking the grain elevators at present-day Thunder Bay, *Our Second American Adventure* (1923).

Harvest: Annual ritual in which billions of dollars worth of machinery collects millions of dollars worth of wheat.
"Pass for a Native: Learn These Terms,"

The Easterners' Guide to Western Canada (1985) edited by Ron Marken.

WHITEHORSE
See also YUKON TERRITORY

What I like best about this place is its quality of life. Within five minutes I can be out of sight of any human habitation and take deep gulps of air devoid of any sense of contamination. Yet one can be in touch with the world via radio, newspapers and the Anik satellite. And thank heaven for FM radio.
   TED HARRISON, artist and resident of Whitehorse, Y.T., *The Globe and Mail*, 13 Jan. 1990.

WILDERNESS
See also ECOLOGY
The NORTH

There being no Towns nor Plantations in this Country, but two or three poor Forts to defend the factories, we thought we were at Liberty to place it where we pleas'd, and were loath to let our History open with the Description of so miserable a Wilderness.
   JOHN OLDMIXON, antiquary, dismissing the development of the Northwest by the Hudson's Bay Company, *The British Empire in America* (1708), as quoted by Peter C. Newman in *Empire of the Bay: An Illustrated History of the Hudson's Bay Company* (1989).

The Coopers made many trips together. In 1930 they set off for Canada with Lord Dudley and his young son Billy. It was a camping holiday deep in the country, sleeping on a bed of spruce branches, riding, fishing, canoeing. For Duff it was flies, fleas, indigestible food and a lack of hot water; for Diana the romance of open spaces, still waters, sunrise and sunset in the wild. Duff bore it nobly, but never were their differing views as to what constituted an ideal holiday more dramatically displayed.
   PHILIP ZIEGLER, biographer, referring to the English socialites Lady Diana and Duff Cooper who roughed it in the bush, *Diana Cooper: The Biography of Lady Diana Cooper* (1981).

I don't think you can live with the flat, metallic lakes, the brooding firs and pines, and the great expanses of gray rock that stretch all the way from Yellowknife to Labrador, with the naked birches and the rattling aspens, with the ghostly call of the loon and the haunting cry of the wolf, without being a very special kind of person.
   PIERRE BERTON, author, address, Empire Club of Canada, Toronto, 11 Oct. 1973.

CANOE
   Acronym for Child Acculturated North Of Eglinton — that is, north of Eglinton Avenue, at one time an effective boundary of the City of Toronto — devised by the artist CHARLES PACHTER, address, Empire Club of Canada, Toronto, 19 March 1987.

It is hard for some newcomers, for instance, to understand that the concept of space is very important to Canadians. We have a need for space and for wilderness uncontaminated by human settlements, and when you destroy that, you are destroying a myth.
   R. MURRAY SCHAFER, composer, interviewed by Ulla Colgrass in *For the Love of Music* (1988).

Many, perhaps most people, have a need for wilderness in some form, but the majority may never have the opportunity to experience the truly wild and remote places. For some of these men and women, it is enough that the promise remains. They take solace in the knowledge that these wild regions still exist and that perhaps one day they, too, or their children may awaken to find Grizzly bear tracks through their water-hole at dawn, see an eagle's feathers ruffle in the wind, and hear the howl of a wolf echo through the canyons at dusk.
   PAT and ROSEMARIE KEOUGH, nature

writers and photographers, *The Nahanni Portfolio* (1988).

Behind the weekend exodus to lakes and mountains, behind the loons on sweatshirts and adventure-travel brochures, are profound influences rooted in spacious, mysterious, and sometimes dangerous wilderness. Therefore, as we surrender our wild heritage, we surrender much of what distinguishes us as Canadians.
BRUCE LITTELJOHN, naturalist, "Wilderness and the Canadian Psyche," *Endangered Spaces: The Future for Canada's Wilderness* (1989) edited by Monte Hummel.

Whereas humankind is but one of millions of species sharing planet Earth and whereas the future of the Earth is severely threatened by the activities of this single species.... We the undersigned agree and urge: That governments, industries, environmental groups and individual Canadians commit themselves to a national effort to establish at least one representative protected area in each of the natural regions of Canada by the year 2000.
Excerpt from "Canadian Wilderness Charter," *Endangered Spaces: The Future for Canada's Wilderness* (1989) edited by Monte Hummel.

What's really interesting is that wherever we go we carry the lifestyle of Algonquin Park with us. It's ingrained in our spirits.
MICHAEL BUDMAN and DON GREEN, co-founders of Roots Canada, an idea that was conceived in Ontario's Algonquin Park, "Incredible Ontario," *Ontario: The Inside Story* (1990).

WILDLIFE
See also ANIMALS
ANIMAL RIGHTS
BIRDS
ECOLOGY
NATURE
WILDERNESS

We have only realized very late the importance of great truths — that the conservation of our game is as vital a subject for consideration and attention as is the conservation of any other of our natural resources.
ARTHUR MEIGHEN, Minister of the Interior, Ottawa address on "The Conservation of Game, Fur-bearing Animals, and Other Wild Life," quoted by Janet Foster in *Working for Wildlife: The Beginning of Preservation in Canada* (1978).

I am the grassland. Out of the abyss of a million years I have emerged. I have been a sea and a tropical jungle, the home of the coral and the dinosaur. I have been a sleeping giant under the masses of glacial ice and I have awakened. I am a part of a changing earth, but for centuries my constancy has been my silence.
Opening paragraph of a poetically written brief submitted by THELMA POIRIER, Killdeer, 13 May 1976, *Report of the Public Hearings Board on the Proposed Grasslands National Park* issued by the Saskatchewan Ministry of Tourism, 9 Aug. 1976.

One suspects that the simple reason for the growing interest in Canada is a deepening longing to go to those parts of the world where history and culture have to do with great forests, with birds in clear skies, with shining mountains, with untouched prairies. More and more people would like to go where humans have not yet destroyed the earth, and Canada is imagined to be one of those places.
DAVID PLANTE, U.S. novelist of French-Canadian ancestry, reviewing Mark Abley's *Beyond Forget* in *The Times Literary Supplement*, 15 April 1988.

WILL POWER

With God's help and guidance / 'Tis not the gales, but the set of the sails / That determines the way you go.
Inscription on the memorial to W. Garfield Weston (1898-1978), baker and busi-

ness executive, Mount Pleasant Cemetery, Toronto.

Strong as habit is, it hinges on a pivot and that pivot is will-power, the engine that every man is born with ready to his hand, to be hitched to a thousand tasks, is his will.
MARY MAXWELL, a.k.a. Rúhíyyih Khánum, leading member of the Bahá'í Faith, referring to Western civilization, *Prescription for Living* (1950).

WINE
See also FOOD & DRINK

Canadian wines? You're kidding. Look at any map; it is white above the border, which means there is snow in Canada. All they have is beer and whiskey.
WILLIAM E. MASSEE, oenologist and author of *Wines of America* (1974), quoted by Tony Aspler in *Vintage Canada* (1984).

Labrusca: A native North American vine species whose grapes have a "foxy" flavour and aroma. Very winter hardy and prolific. The best known are Concord and Niagara.
Foxy: The aroma and bouquet of Labrusca varieties like Concord. A grape juice smell which pervades the flavour as well.
Definitions of two terms associated with wine-making in the Niagara region of Ontario supplied by the oenologist Tony Aspler in *Vintage Canada* (1984).

Wine is my meat and potatoes.
TONY ASPLER, oenologist, intentional malapropism, in conversation, Toronto, 23 Aug. 1987.

My glass has been politicized. When I drink from a decent bottle of French red, I get a nagging twinge, telling me that every sip is souring the fortunes of the Ontario grape grower, that his livelihood is now as irretrievably lost as a cork pushed into the bottle.
JOHN MUGGERIDGE JR., journalist who sometimes uses the byline Malcolm

Stone, "The Wines of Ontario," *The Idler*, No. 18, July-Aug. 1988.

It's astonishing how many countries now produce good wine. The Indians make a decent champagne. Lebanese wine is superb. Chilean isn't bad. There's some nice Canadian wine, believe it or not, though I recommend you avoid at all costs something called "Cold Duck."
SIMON HOGGART, columnist, *Observer Magazine*, quoted in *The Globe and Mail*, 23 Oct. 1990.

Without wine there would be no worship.
ROBIN SKELTON, man-of-letters, aphorism, May 1990.

WINNING
See also SUCCESS

It's fun when you're winning.
JACQUES PLANT, hockey player, quoted by Chris Raible in *The Toronto Star*, 3 Nov. 1989.

A sportswriter learns early that the best stories are often told on the losers' side of the dressing room, where former victories lose their shine, and recent defeats turn rotten.
DICK BEDDOES, sports personality, *Greatest Hockey Stories* (1990).

WINNIPEG
See also MANITOBA

Winnipeg. The only thing I know about Winnipeg is that it doesn't quite rhyme with guinea-pig.
ROBIN SCOTT, British-born ADC to Governor General Lord Tweedsmuir, quoted by David Walker in *Lean, Wind, Lean: A Few Times Remembered* (1985).

A trip to Winnipeg, as flat and on the whole as small-minded as ever.
ANDRÉ LAURENDEAU, Quebec nationalist, diary entry for 1965, "A Québécois Journal," translated by Pat Smart, *The Canadian Forum*, Nov. 1990.

It's a place where you can try practically anything. It offers a fantastic challenge. It's a tempering place (in the sense that steel is tempered) because you have many difficulties to overcome. But those are good difficulties — good things to grapple with.

JOHN HIRSCH, cofounder of the Manitoba Theatre Centre, interviewed by Danny Finkleman in *Speaking of Winnipeg* (1974) edited by John Parr.

When I come back — no matter how many times I experience it — I cannot believe I grew up and lived in this flat world. Nowhere else have I experienced this way of being in space, looking out on a pingpong table at eye level. Anything that disturbs the contour is a kind of miracle. No matter where you're going you can *see* where you're going; that is very, very eerie.

JACK LUDWIG, Winnipeg-born novelist, interviewed by Terry Campbell in *Speaking of Winnipeg* (1974) edited by John Parr.

Toronto people are just as sure Winnipeg is in the West as Vancouver people are that it is in the East.

BARRY MATHER, journalist and one-time Parliamentarian, observation made in July 1978.

The first time I looked out over Moscow from my twelfth-storey room in the Intourist Hotel, I *liked* the place. Something about it reminded me of Winnipeg, the city of my birth.

Moscow in September reminded me of Winnipeg in April.

JIM COLEMAN, sports writer, *Hockey Is Our Game: Canada in the World of International Hockey* (1987).

Winnipeg is a prosperous and cultivated city that also embraces the largest Indian slum in North America. It's been there for years.

STEPHEN BROOK, English travel writer, *Maple Leaf Rag: Travels across Canada* (1987).

How can I explain the shock of being a little kid and one day realizing you are alive, which is nice, but on the downside you are in the middle of a fucking Winnipeg winter, and no one is going to come to rescue you and take you away to a habitable part of the world. You could be trapped here until you died, if you weren't careful.

ROBERT HUNTER, activist and author, "Better in the Bahamas," *On the Sky: Zen and the Art of International Freeloading* (1988).

North Winnipeg is a breeding ground for combatants.

DAVID STEINBERG, television personality and native of Winnipeg, quoted by Ed Gould in *Entertaining Canadians: Canada's International Stars 1900-1988* (1988).

I'd quickly discovered that the Westin Hotel was sitting over an entrance to a subterranean shopping mall that stretched like a rabbit warren in all directions. Shopping, in Canada, had largely gone underground to defeat the winter.

Thoughts of the narrator of *The Edge* (1988), a crime novel set aboard a transcontinental train and in cities along the way by English writer DICK FRANCIS.

Personally I've had some hilariously funny interviews with Hollywood people about this. They would set *Barometer Rising* somewhere other than Halifax. "Gotta be American. Boy meets girl in Paris, France. Okay. Boy meets girl in Winnipeg. Who cares?" That's a literal quotation.

HUGH MacLENNAN, novelist, interviewed by Alan Twigg in *Strong Voices: Conversations with Fifty Canadian Authors* (1988).

Winnipeg is a great city that ought to have been the national capital.

F. KENNETH HARE, geographer, "Canada: The Land," *Daedalus: Journal of the American Academy of Arts and Sciences*, "In Search of Canada," Fall 1988.

Viewed from the air, Winnipeg is like a city in the forest. Visitors to the city, who expect to see buildings and houses set on a flat and treeless plain, are pleasantly surprised by all the trees. People who live in high-rise apartments can enjoy the lush greens of summer and the gold, red, and brown of autumn spread out beneath them like a carpet.

> CHRISTOPHER DAFOE, columnist, *The Winnipeg Free Press*, 7 Oct. 1990.

WINTER

See ICE
SEASONS
SNOW

WISDOM

See also INTELLIGENCE
MATURITY

The caravans still journey from the heart of Asia, carrying merchandise more to be desired than gold or jewels.

> L. ADAMS BECK, novelist and orientalist, *The Story of Oriental Philosophy* (1928).

There are car accidents, fires, rivals, muggers, diseases, bitches, indifferences, weaknesses — disasters and devils of every kind are roaming around just waiting for their chance. Love can't be carefree. But hallelujah! some *moments* can.

> ELIZABETH SMART, novelist and diarist, "How to Mend a Broken Heart" (1982), *Autobiographies* (1987) edited by Christina Burridge.

Often the wisdom of the body clarifies the despair of the spirit.

> MARION WOODMAN, Jungian analyst and author, *Addition to Perfection: The Still Unravished Bride* (1982).

Things are nicely balanced in Canada; we've got cold, deep lakes and warm, shallow people.

> Aphorism coined by MARUS E. MALLON, author, resident of Deep River, Ont., Oct. 1990.

Mankind cannot be made wise and the world cannot be made sacred by legislation, yet nothing less than wisdom and consecration seem to be required for peace of mind and the survival of the planet. In that sense, religion is not an escapist fantasy: it is a realistic need.

> RON GRAHAM, journalist and author, *God's Dominion: A Sceptic's Quest* (1990).

WITCHCRAFT

There may be no witches in Canada, but there are witch-hunters.

> PERCY J. PHILIP, Ottawa correspondent for *The New York Times*, "My Conversation with Mackenzie King's Ghost," *Liberty*, Jan. 1955.

Witches were consulted in private, but their only public role was to be persecuted, or, as we say, "hunted."

> MARGARET ATWOOD, author, "Witches" (1980), *Active Voice* (2nd ed., 1986) edited by W.H. New and W.E. Messenger.

Witches, unite! You have nothing to lose but your brooms!

> Line attributed to a character Peggy in the play *A Place on Earth* (1982) by the playwright BETTY JANE WYLIE.

We are the only people who are still judged by the standards of Mother Goose and Walt Disney.

> JEAN KOZOCARI, witch, commenting on the popular image of witches and witchcraft today, quoted by Kevin Marron in *Witches, Pagans, & Magic in the New Age* (1989).

I am somewhat relieved to be able to say that in all my encounters with witches and magicians I did not ever feel that I had come under a spell or suffered a curse. I did, however, learn to respect magic, not as a supernatural force, but as a way of dealing with the world that exerts considerable influence on many people today.

> KEVIN MARRON, author, *Witches, Pagans, & Magic in the New Age* (1989).

Everyone has the right to be weird.
> CHARLES ARNOLD, clerical worker at Toronto's Humber College of Applied Arts and Technology, high priest and Elder of the Spendweick Coven, quoted by Ron Graham in *God's Dominion: A Sceptic's Quest* (1990). Wicca's two major holidays are Nov. 1 (Samhain) and May 1 (Belthane). An Ontario arbitration board ruled that Arnold was entitled to paid leave to celebrate these two holidays, thus establishing a precedent for the quasi-official recognition of Wicca as a religion.

Wicca is both the oldest of all religions and one of the youngest.
> ROBIN SKELTON, author and witch, *The Practice of Witchcraft* (1990).

WOLVES

There is no authentic report of wolves ever having killed a human being in the Canadian North; although there must have been times when the temptation was well-nigh irresistible.
> FARLEY MOWAT, author and naturalist, *Never Cry Wolf* (1963).

WOMEN

See also FEMINISM
LIFE
MANKIND
MEN & WOMEN

I told them that if I had a wife, and any one came to take her away, I would surely shoot him; Ah, that is the way you White Men, and our Neighbours the Nahathaways always talk and do, a Woman cannot be touched but you get hold of long Knives; What is a woman good for, she cannot hunt, she is only to Work and carry our things, and on no account whatever ought the ground to be made red with man's blood. Then the strong men take Women when they want them; Certainly the strong men have a right to the Women.
> DAVID THOMPSON, surveyor and explorer, conversing with a Chipewyan Indian, Reindeer Lake, *David Thompson's Narrative of His Explorations in Western America 1784-1812* (1916) edited by J.B. Tyrrell.

I have not often in my life met with contented and cheerful-minded women, but I never met with so many repining and discontented women as in Canada. I never met with *one* woman recently settled here who considered herself happy in her new home and country.
> ANNA BROWNELL JAMESON, writer and traveller, *Winter Studies and Summer Rambles in Canada* (1838).

Women ought to feel a glorious new pride in their sex, now that it is shown to be the main trunk of the tree of life. They ought to feel an unbounded hope and power in their ability to remake the race and to help manage it on better terms than ever before. And they ought also to burn with shame, deep scorching shame, at the pitiful limitations with which so many of them are still contented.
> FLORA MacDONALD DENISON, early feminist, "To My Real Readers," *Sunset of Bon Echo*, April-May 1920.

The world has suffered long from too much masculinity and not enough humanity.
> NELLIE L. McCLUNG, pioneer feminist, quoted in *Women in the Canadian Mosaic* (1976) edited by Gwen Matheson.

If there were enough women in Parliament, the Health Ministry would become more important than that of Finance.
> GORDON BATES, physician, founder of the Health League of Canada, remark made in 1941.

Whatever my sex, I'm no lady.
> Attributed to CHARLOTTE WHITTON, Ottawa Mayor, characteristic remark in the 1950s.

It is important for a woman to cultivate, with ever-increasing perfection, elegance

and beauty as well as the various household arts which, in our daily lives, carry on the finest French traditions. However, the fine arts, politics, education, science or social problems are today no longer the special preserve of the stronger sex; the accomplished woman should also know a little about everything, since her destiny and that of her children are tied to the fate of the world.
> FERNANDE SAINT-MARTIN, columnist, *Chatelaine*, Oct. 1960, reprinted by The Clio Collective (Micheline Dumont, Michèle Jean, Marie Lavigne, Jennifer Stoddart) in *Quebec Women: A History* (1987) translated by Roger Gannon and Rosalind Gill.

For generations, women have been relegated to the biological beat — bed, board and babies.
> LAURA SABIA, Chairperson, Ontario Advisory Council on the Status of Women, quoted by Lynda Hurst in *The Toronto Star*, 22 Aug. 1975.

Women make the best cooks and housewives and should be encouraged in that role.
> WILLIAM VANDER ZALM, British Columbia Premier, quoted in *The Vancouver Sun*, 23 March 1976.

Life conspires to keep a woman tangled in trifles.
> MARYON KANTAROFF, sculptor and feminist, quoted in *Women in the Canadian Mosaic* (1976) edited by Gwen Matheson.

I can never understand why women want to be equal. Why would they willingly accept a demotion?
> ALLAN FOTHERINGHAM, columnist, *Maclean's*, 4 Sept. 1978.

Until recently Canada has always had a male minister responsible for the status of women, a duty rotated among ministers since 1971. It made life miserable for the poor man appointed, particularly at international meetings. Inside Canada, nobody ever paid the slightest attention to this fact, with the exception of the male cabinet members who dreaded the prime minister's call.
> MONIQUE BÉGIN, former politician, "Debates and Silences — Reflections of a Politician," *Daedalus: Journal of the American Academy of Arts and Sciences*, "In Search of Canada," Fall 1988. The first female Minister responsible for the Status of Women was Judith Erola, Minister of State (Mines), then Minister of Consumer and Corporate Affairs, who was given the additional responsibility in Sept. 1981.

It is the law that all things must be born in woman, even things invented by men.
> Remarks attributed to a Cree shaman or medicine woman in northern Manitoba named AGNES WHISTLING ELK in Lynn V. Andrews's "spirit quest" book *Medicine Woman* (1981).

Woman's world, cooking and babies / Little girls with knowing eyes / Woman's world, caught in a circle / Smaller than truth and bigger than lies.
> SYLVIA TYSON, songwriter and singer, "Woman's World," quoted by Ellen Schwartz in *Born a Woman: Seven Canadian Women Singer-Songwriters* (1988).

Woman's place is in the house, and that's where she should go just as soon as she leaves the office.
> SHEILA COPPS, politician and feminist, *Nobody's Baby: A Survival Guide to Politics* (1986).

Women do not make up a homogeneous monolithic group that can be represented by only one ideology. No one organization can speak for all women any more than one organization can speak for all men. Before women can have equality with men, they must have equality among themselves — including tolerance and respect for differing points of view.
> C. GWENDOLYN LANDOLT, lawyer, activist, and founder of REAL Women of Canada, quoted in *The Globe and Mail*, 23

April 1987. Landolt was a founder of REAL Women in 1983. The acronym stands for Realistic, Equal, Active for Life.

To be born a woman, you quickly learn / Your body will be their first concern.
RITA MacNEIL, songwriter and singer, "Born a Woman," quoted by Ellen Schwartz in *Born a Woman: Seven Canadian Women Singer-Songwriters* (1988).

One woman's luxury is another woman's necessity, and it's important to know the difference, to you.
BETTY JANE WYLIE and LYNNE Mac-FARLANE, authors, *Everywoman's Money Book* (1989).

I can imagine myself not a Westerner, not white, having no wealth. What I *can't* imagine is not being a woman!
LOIS WILSON, Christian activist, *Turning the World Upside Down: A Memoir* (1989).

Comme Platon, je trouve les femmes plus intelligentes que les hommes parce que plus intuitives. Mais elles manquent souvent de jugement. Pour ce qui est de la séduction au travail, je ne suis pas contre. Mais elles doivent s'en servir dans l'intérêt de l'enterprise, et non pour se prouver qu'elles sont belles! Il faut que ce soit un plus pour Quebecor.
PIERRE PÉLADEAU, Quebec publisher, quoted by Jean Blouin in "Péladeau tout craché," *L'Actualité*, 15 April 1990. Péladeau's words on women and on prejudice were widely reproduced. A literal translation of his remarks on women from the article "Péladeau Through and Through" reads as follows: "Like Plato, I find women to be more intelligent than men because they are more intuitive. But they often lack judgement. Therefore they use seduction at work. I am not against this. But they ought to use seduction in the service of the enterprise and not to prove that they are beautiful! They ought to be more for Quebecor."

WONDER

A smile, a sexual experience, or an athletic achievement may give us a transcendent experience. With a sense of wonder, something in our environment uplifts our whole being, and we are more whole than before.
DOROTHY MACLEAN, medium, *To Hear the Angels Sing: An Odyssey of Co-Creation with the Devic Kingdom* (1980).

The purpose of art is the lifelong construction of a state of wonder.
GLENN GOULD, pianist, quoted by Lorraine Monk, Commencement Address, York University, Toronto, 6 Nov. 1982.

Yet even here I see a gift, for in place of my narrow, pragmatic world of cause and effect and matter moving to immutable laws, I have burst into an infinite world full of wonder. The whole mystery of the universe has my reverence. Nothing is sure but nothing can be dismissed. I pay attention.
SYLVIA FRASER, author, *My Father's House: A Memoir of Incest and of Healing* (1987).

A sense of wonder is in itself a religious feeling. But in so many people the sense of wonder gets lost. It gets scarred over. It's as though a tortoise shell has grown over it. People reach a stage where they're never surprised, never delighted. They're never suddenly aware of glorious freedom or splendour in their lives. However hard a life may be, I think for virtually all people this is possible.
ROBERTSON DAVIES, man-of-letters, interviewed by Alan Twigg in *Strong Voices: Conversations with Fifty Canadian Authors* (1988).

WORDS
See also NAMES

We need words to keep us human. Being human is an accomplishment like playing an instrument. It takes practice.

MICHAEL IGNATIEFF, essayist, *The Needs of Strangers* (1985).

More words are coined in saloons than in salons.
DICK BEDDOES, sports personality, *obiter dictum*, 21 May 1990.

Poor is the man who can't spell a word more than one way.
CLARKE WALLACE, writer, scriptwriter, and poor speller, characteristic remark, 18 Oct. 1990.

WORK
See also LABOUR

The greatest inconvenience in this country is want of servants, which are not to be got. The worst of people do you a favour if they merely wash dishes for twenty shillings a month.
ELIZABETH SIMCOE, diarist and wife of Governor John Graves Simcoe, letter Feb. 1793, *Mrs. Simcoe's Diary* (1965) edited by Mary Quayle Innis.

I ask you, are you going to repudiate your obligations? No. Then you are going to get down to real business; you are going to doff your broadcloth and don your overalls.
JOHN OLIVER, B.C. Premier, addressing a delegation from financially hard-pressed municipalities during World War I. The remark, becoming proverbial, was often simplified: "If you would meet your debts you must doff the broadcloth and don the overalls." Quoted by James Morton in *Honest John Oliver: The Life Story of the Honourable John Oliver, Premier of British Columbia, 1918-1927* (1933).

So long as Canadian economic activity is dominated by the corporate elite, and so long as workers' rights are confined within their present limits, corporate requirements for profit will continue to take precedence over human needs.
"The Waffle Manifesto: For an Independent Socialist Canada" (1969) reprinted in *The Canadian Forum*, Dec. 1989.

A man will die for a cause but only work for wages, my father used to say. I added these words: All causes eventually turn into work with wages.
DON CULLEN, actor and performer, characteristic remark, Nov. 1973.

If they don't have a shovel, they should get one, because otherwise we're going to give them one.
Attributed to WILLIAM VANDER ZALM, B.C. Minister of Human Resources, swearing-in ceremony, Victoria, 22 Dec. 1975, quoted by Alan Twigg in *Vander Zalm: From Immigrant to Premier* (1986).

We will eliminate unemployment in Newfoundland by creating hundreds of jobs for thousands of Newfoundlanders.
Attributed to Newfoundland Premier BRIAN PECKFORD by Knowlton Nash, address, Empire Club of Canada, Toronto, 26 June 1986.

Moonlighting becomes you.
BETTY JANE WYLIE, author, *The Best Is Yet to Come: Planning Ahead for a Financially Secure Retirement* (1988).

A literal translation from the Hebrew reads that on the seventh day, God "rested from all his work that God created to do." Commentators struggle with the meaning of the last two words. Ibn Ezra [a 12th-century commentator] says that in God's creation, the seeds were there for everything that will ever be. Thus God finished the world in six days and gave it to the people as the raw material "to do," to create with. In other words: "Here is the material, now you people take it and develop it."
PAUL REICHMANN, Olympia & York Investments and student of the Talmud, quoted by Dianne Maley in *The Globe and Mail's Report on Business Magazine*, Dec. 1988.

WORLD

The world is in order / The dead below / The living above
> Epigraph to the novel *Héloïse* (1980) by ANNE HÉBERT.

The Earth is a world-class planet.
> DAVID SCHATZKY, CBC Radio personality, mimicking the practice of some public figures (like Ontario Premier David Peterson) who lavishly described things and actions as "world class," 1 July 1986.

We the Unwilling / Led by the Unqualified / Have Been Doing the Unbelievable / For So Long With So Little / That We Now Attempt / The Impossible / With Nothing.
> Photocopy lore, Centennial College, Scarborough, Ont., Sept. 1990.

WORLD WAR I
See also WAR

Soldiers. The world regards you as a marvel.
> Farewell message of General SAM HUGHES to the departing Canadian Corps, 3 Oct. 1914, quoted by Desmond Morton and J.L. Granatstein in *Marching to Armageddon: Canadians and the Great War 1914-1919* (1989).

Langemarcke / St. Julien / Festubert / Givenchy / More are coming — / Will you be there? / Enlist!
> Message on a Canadian enlistment poster issued in 1917 to boost enlistment for the Great War. Reproduced in *The Poster in History* (1989) by Max Gallo.

There are people who say we should forget the war and cut out these "crazy military parades" and put an end to such nonsense . . . but I wonder how far it is wise for us to forget. Who made this nation? Who died? If these are things we must forget in the history of Canada, what are the things we should remember?
> SIR ARTHUR CURRIE, General during World War I, one of his last interviews, quoted by Donald Jones in *The Toronto Star*, 25 June 1988.

The troops with the worst reputation for acts of violence against prisoners were the Canadians (and later the Australians).
> ROBERT GRAVES, poet and author, *Goodbye to All That* (1929, 1958).

The Canadians are a queer crowd; they seem to think they are the best troops in France and that we have to get them to do our most difficult jobs. . . . They forget that the whole art of war is to gain your objective with as little loss as possible.
I was disappointed in them. At plain straight-forward fighting they are magnificent, but they are narrow-minded and lack soldierly instincts.
> BERNARD MONTGOMERY, officer in World War I, Field Marshal in World War II, letter to his mother written in 1917; quoted by Jeffery Williams in *The Long Left Flank: The Hard Fought Way to the Reich, 1944-1945* (1988). Monty (as he was later known) continued: "The Canadian troops were magnificent soldiers, but their leadership poor."

We have them on the run. That means we have to do it over again in another twenty-five years.
> ANDREW McNAUGHTON, General, referring to the advancing Canadian Corps and the retreating German Army in Belgium at the end of the Great War in 1918. The next world war broke out in 1939, four years earlier than the perceptive general predicted. Quoted by Desmond Morton and J.L. Granatstein in *Marching to Armageddon: Canadians and the Great War 1914-1919* (1989).

The Great War of 1914-1919 lies like a great angry scar across the history of Western civilization. At least thirteen million people died in the war, most of them young men. So did four old empires. A dozen newly sovereign states emerged, among them Canada.
> DESMOND MORTON and J.L. GRANAT-

STEIN, historians, in *Marching to Armageddon: Canadians and the Great War 1914-1919* (1989).

WORLD WAR II
See also WAR

We who wish to see the highest good of our fellow man must cooperate in every possible way toward that end. You, I believe, can do more than any man living today to help your own and other countries along the path to peace and progress. What [that] may come to mean to the world, no man can say.
W.L. MACKENZIE KING, Prime Minister, letter addressed to the Nazi dictator Adolf Hitler, 30 June 1937, the day following their meeting in Berlin, quoted by Erna Paris in *Jews: An Account of Their Experience in Canada* (1980).

There will be no war in Europe. The real villains in the piece are not Hitler etc but the Comintern, the free masons and the international operators who have their headquarters in Prague. Hitler is being backed by Chamberlain and Roosevelt (appearances to the contrary).
MARSHALL McLUHAN, communications theorist, letter to Elise McLuhan, 24 Sept. 1938, *Letters of Marshall McLuhan* (1987) edited by Matie Molinaro, Corinne McLuhan, and William Toye.

If any shooting is to be done the first people who should face the firing squad are those who have made money out of the war.
J.S. WOODSWORTH, CCF leader, explaining why he will cast the sole vote against Canadian participation in World War II, House of Commons, 8 Sept. 1939; quoted by Ivan Avakumovic in *Socialism in Canada: A Study of the CCF-NDP in Federal and Provincial Politics* (1978).

Out of the last war emerged their status, out of this one their stature.
VINCENT MASSEY, High Commissioner in London, Empire Day Broadcast, 3 July 1944, quoted by Claude T. Bissell in *The Imperial Canadian: Vincent Massey in Office* (1986). Bissell called this "a modest epigram." It refers specifically to the status of the Dominions as independent countries which followed World War I.

The children can't go without me. I can't leave the King, and of course the King won't go.
ELIZABETH THE QUEEN MOTHER, responding to the suggestion that her daughters by King George VI— the future Queen Elizabeth II and Princess Margaret — should be evacuated to Canada; noted in a letter, *The Times*, 19 Feb. 1952, *The Third Cuckoo: More Classic Letters to The Times 1900-1985* (1985) edited by Keith Gregory.

I could not help but reflect on how quickly the big three had carved up the world. Why were the Canadian and other participating governments in the Second World War not at Yalta? What right had the United States, Britain, and the Soviet Union to make fundamental decisions without us and the others? We, too, had made our sacrifice for the preservation of freedom in the common struggle against Hitler. Why weren't we?
PAUL MARTIN, High Commissioner in London, entry for 29 June 1975, *The London Diaries 1975-1979* (1988).

Why has there always been such a deafening silence in Canada about the 1st Canadian Corps and the Italian Campaign— no memorial observances, no recognition? The irony of the matter is that there is still one group who will never forget the Canadians — their prime antagonists, the German paratroop and panzer divisions.
C. SYDNEY FROST, veteran, *Once a Patricia: Memoirs of a Junior Infantry Officer in World War II* (1988).

Winston Churchill wrote his version of the Second World War in the sixties. God knows I admired him. But in the first four volumes of ninety thousand lines —I very carefully measured them — Canada got only fifty-three lines for her contribution. Of those, twenty-eight were in some letter to Mackenzie King about Newfoundland. Canada's contribution to that war was enormous! But the English couldn't have cared less.

HUGH MacLENNAN, novelist, interviewed by Alan Twigg in *Strong Voices: Conversations with Fifty Canadian Authors* (1988).

The nation had escaped the destruction that war had brought to most of the rest of the world. In fact, war had brought unparalleled prosperity to a country that in 1939 had been trapped in the Great Depression. A new Canada had emerged, forged in the fires of war.

J.L. GRANATSTEIN and DESMOND MORTON, historians, *A Nation Forged in Fire: Canadians and the Second World War 1939-1945* (1989).

And had they asked, "Was war hell, Mom?" I would have had to admit, "Not hell, exactly, but you could say that on the homefront 'War is heck.'"

MARY PEATE, memoirist and author, *Girl in a Sloppy Joe Sweater: Life on the Canadian Home Front during World War Two* (1989).

WORLD WAR III
See also WAR

Since the thesis here advanced is that *a permanent war is necessary to the successful operation of our present economic system*, we must consider the results of war on that economy as fully as possible. . . .

I advocate a scientific war, *every phase of which would be planned in advance, and which would be operated in strict conjunction with the business cycle.*

LORNE T. MORGAN, economist and satirist, *The Permanent War or Homo the Sap* (1943).

The people who definitely do not want to fight any more wars must promise annihilation to any nation which starts to fight and must be prepared immediately and ruthlessly to carry out that promise without parley or negotiation. This involves the continual upkeep of widely dispersed atomic rocket stations covering the whole world and a continual high pressure research program to discover even more efficient methods of killing to keep ahead of any possible competition. This must go on until we, all the people, are re-educated to be able to live in space together, until we are free to observe clearly and to think and behave sensibly.

G. BROCK CHISHOLM, psychiatrist, White Memorial Lecture, Washington, D.C., Oct. 1945, published as *The Psychiatry of Enduring Peace and Social Progress* (1945).

What we face now is not merely slaughter or genocide, but "omnicide," the obliteration of all humans and all living species.

PENNEY KOME and PATRICK CREAN, editors, Foreword, *Peace: A Dream Unfolding* (1986).

There may be survivors from a nuclear war, but there will be no winners.

GORDON SHRUM, engineer and educator, *An Autobiography* (1986) written with Peter Stursberg and edited by Clive Cocking.

I have three young children at home and I want to leave for them a world free of nuclear war. This would be the greatest gift all politicians could give to the children of the world.

BRIAN MULRONEY, Prime Minister, quoted by William Walker in *The Toronto Star*, 17 Sept. 1988.

Our survival mechanism is the imagination. If we can imagine what it will be like, we will be capable of action. We can't just brush it aside. We have to be very selfish about this. Breathe in how good it feels to still be alive, to still have a chance. You don't have to take up a life of perpetual anxiety. You just have to do every little bit you can to prevent the great tragedy.

LESLEY CHOYCE, author, *December Six: The Halifax Solution — An Alternative to Nuclear War* (1988).

Come World War III, the important question for Canada will in any case not be how many adequately equipped soldiers it has stationed in Norway or Alberta, but how many unradiated young men and women are left alive in, say, Fort Good Hope, Northwest Territories, and what books are in its public libraries.

GEORGE FALUDY, Hungarian-born poet, *Notes from the Rainforest* (1988).

If we keep troops in NATO, they will be involved in the fighting in the first few days of a European war, conventional or nuclear. Canada itself will certainly be a target in a major nuclear war, its air-space used by friend and foe, whether or not we are active allies of the United States or declared neutrals.

J.L. GRANATSTEIN, historian, *The Globe and Mail*, 19 Aug. 1989.

WORRY

Much of the misery of my life — just as much of the pleasure — has been caused by my habit of living everything over beforehand. It is never half as bad — or half as delightful — when it really comes.

L.M. MONTGOMERY, author, diary, 4 June 1920, *The Selected Journals of L.M. Montgomery: Volume II: 1910-1921* (1987) edited by Mary Rubio and Elizabeth Waterston.

WRITERS

See also ATWOOD, MARGARET
DAVIES, ROBERTSON
FRYE, NORTHROP
LITERATURE
WRITERS, CANADIAN
WRITING

Write out of your own experience; write simply. This is the law and the prophets

for an author who hopes to be read in the centuries to come.

WILLIAM ARTHUR DEACON, literary critic, "On Literary Immortality," *Pens and Pirates* (1923).

Always hire drunks, they don't last long but they're grateful for the work and don't ask for much money.

Attributed to JACK KENT COOKE, parsimonious publisher of *Liberty* and *Saturday Night* in the 1950s, millionaire capitalist in the 1960s, billionaire capitalist in the 1970s, quoted by Paul Stuewe in *The Storms Below: The Turbulent Life and Times of Hugh Garner* (1988).

Any writers I know spend a great deal of time consistently and evenly every day, every week, every month, lowering a bucket into themselves and everything that they have been. Whatever art illusion the writer creates, the bubble he blows simply has to grow out of the fact that he inhabits a certain place upon the skin of the earth and a certain point in time.

W.O. MITCHELL, writer, interviewed by Donald Cameron in *Conversations with Canadian Novelists* (1973).

Ask any writer about the ones-that-got-away and you'll hear sadder stories than any fisherman could ever tell.

BETTY JANE WYLIE, author of a collection of puppet plays, *Don't Just Stand There, Jiggle* (1980).

The writer, unless he is a mere word processor, retains three attitudes that power-made regimes cannot tolerate: a human imagination, in the many forms it may take; the power to communicate; and hope.

MARGARET ATWOOD, novelist, "A Disneyland of the Soul," *The Writer and Human Rights* (1983) edited by the Toronto Arts Group for Human Rights.

For some writers are less free today than writers were fifty or one hundred years ago, and even in the Western world, our liberty is threatened by a reactionary tide. All those writers who are part of the resistance in totalitarian countries are fighting for an ideal of liberty which they think we have here, but we cannot be wholly free until we have helped them attain it.

MARIE-CLAIRE BLAIS, "The Unending Struggle," *The Writer and Human Rights* (1983) edited by the Toronto Arts Group for Human Rights.

Perhaps the essence of a writer is a sensitive uncertainty. Not just about the value of what he is doing, but also about the value of all ready-made answers. . . . It is the inability to say the final word that is human. All else is delusion, often dangerous delusion. Endlösungen (final solutions), as we know by now, are all false. In the end they solve nothing. They only increase suffering and multiply work.

JOSEF SKVORECKY, essayist and novelist, "I Was Born in Náchod . . ." (1984), *Talkin' Moscow Blues* (1988) edited by Sam Solecki.

Reading, though, is the way to learn to write. Someone interested in writing should just read, without looking at all the structures and strategy of the writing. Writers can show you directions. We're all influenced by the people we read to one degree or another, and we shouldn't deny those influences. Other people show us what is possible.

CAROL SHIELDS, author, interviewed by Andrew Garrod in *Speaking for Myself: Canadian Writers in Interview* (1986).

I live the way I had been living but now I can afford it.

WILLIAM NOVAK, Canadian-born U.S.-based writer, referring to his success as a ghostwriter which took his annual income from $25,000 to "low six figures"; quoted by Garry Abrams in *The Toronto Star*, 19 Sept. 1987.

The theory I'm developing now is that the writer should be slightly afraid of what he's writing about. When the writer is in too much control, that excess will get communicated.

SUSAN MUSGRAVE, poet and essayist, interviewed by Alan Twigg in *Strong Voices: Conversations with Fifty Canadian Authors* (1988).

One of the facts of writing is that it's part of the entertainment business. Some writers may not be happy about that, but that's the way it is.

MATT COHEN, novelist, interviewed by Alan Twigg in *Strong Voices: Conversations with Fifty Canadian Authors* (1988).

I write to discover what I think. I don't think and then write. If you think and then write you often get propaganda.

W.D. VALGARDSON, novelist, interviewed by Alan Twigg in *Strong Voices: Conversations with Fifty Canadian Authors* (1988).

Every writer I've talked to has had this experience where they have suddenly been given permission to be Canadian.

W.D. VALGARDSON, novelist, interviewed by Alan Twigg in *Strong Voices: Conversations with Fifty Canadian Authors* (1988).

All writers are shy egomaniacs. That's why we read them, for insights and glimpses into the soul that they don't blurt out in the pub.

ALLAN FOTHERINGHAM, columnist, *Maclean's*, 12 Dec. 1988.

The glamour, romance, and respect that writers supposedly enjoy seem entirely mythical when you have to stand on the street with a sign around your neck and peddle books that you published yourself.

CRAD KILODNEY, fiction writer who hawks some of his publications on Toronto streets, "How I Write Such Great Stories," alternate unpublished introduction to *Malignant Humours* (1988).

There is a lot of money in Toronto and, thanks to the Great Gatenby, some of it is going to writers.

BLAKE MORRISON, British author, guest

at a literary reading at Harbourfront, or-ganized by Toronto poet and impresario Greg Gatenby, *The Times Literary Supple-ment*, 24 March 1989.

It would be tempting to predict the death of the printed word, but the best writers I've seen lately are a ten-year-old girl and a sixteen-year-old boy. There is something in the human spirit that doesn't want it to die.
PAUL QUARRINGTON, novelist, quoted in *Metropolis*, 21 Dec. 1989.

WRITERS, CANADIAN
See also WRITERS

In my candid opinion I was the best writer in America in the Thirties.
MORLEY CALLAGHAN, fiction writer, quoted by Philip Marchand, memorial ar-ticle, *The Toronto Star*, 26 Aug. 1990.

In the only address that I made, I said that I thought of the writers of this country as being members of a kind of tribe.... There is still that tremendous sense of belonging to a community. And we all need that sense of community.
MARGARET LAURENCE, novelist and act-ing chairperson of the Writers' Union of Canada formed in 1973, quoted by Alan Twigg in *For Openers: Conversations with 24 Canadian Writers* (1981).

Just beyond the mountains which form the other horizon of my world, Canada seems to hang like a glacier slowly moving down on me from its notch. I expect it to overtake me before I die, reminding me with its chill and weight that I belong to the north after all.
ROSS MACDONALD, crime novelist, "The Writer's Sense of Place," *South Dakota Review*, Autumn 1975, as quoted by Jerry Speir in *Ross Macdonald* (1978).

It is to my habits of procrastination in things academic that I owe my success as a writer, for if I had done scholarship true

justice, how would I ever have had time to write?
MARGARET ATWOOD, writer and former academic, "Witches" (1980), *Active Voice* (2nd ed., 1986) edited by W.H. New and W.E. Messenger.

To summarize, the plight of the ethnic writer is isolation: Isolation from the coun-try of origin, isolation from the wider pub-lic, from the media, the publishers, the libraries, the reviewers; isolation from practically everything that is important to a creative artist who wants to reach a public.
YVONNE GRABOWSKI, academic, *Cul-tures and Writers: A Cultural Dialogue of Ethnic Writers* (1983) edited by Yvonne Grabowski.

Writers are not a tribe. That is a com-pletely mistaken idea.
MAVIS GALLANT, author, interviewed by Debra Martens in *So to Speak: Interviews with Canadian Writers* (1987) edited by Peter O'Brien.

I didn't know at this time that there was such a thing as a Canadian writer. In fact, upon graduation I couldn't name with as-surance a single Canadian author, poet, composer, musician or artist. I had never played a Canadian song. If there was one lesson to be learned in Truro, if there was one area where my teachers and Elvis Pre-sley were in complete agreement, it was the knowledge that culture was something that comes from someplace else.
JOHN GRAY, composer and performer, Preface, *Local Boy Makes Good: Three Mu-sicals* (1987).

The typical Canadian novelist begins with a potential readership of 25 million. But those working in English automatically forefeit the one-third who do not read in English.
Half of what is left do not read at all. Nine-tenths of what is left do not read fiction. Three quarters of what is left do not read Canadian. Half of what is left are

juvenile readers. Half of what is left read romance.

The typical Canadian novelist, therefore, is usually related to each and every reader of the book in question, which conveniently will explain why Canadian Literature seems so obsessed with roots and madness and with a complete failure to be understood as a human being.

> ROY MacGREGOR, columnist, *The Ottawa Citizen*, 30 April 1987.

My whole secret is to try and make it read like a novel.

> PIERRE BERTON, author and media personality, referring to his writing style and even the physical appearance of the text and the book, interviewed by Alan Twigg in *Strong Voices: Conversations with Fifty Canadian Authors* (1988).

Canada is a country where the serious writers are hockey fans and readers of comic books. They don't play chess.

> LOUIS DUDEK, poet and aphorist, "Can. Lit. Notes," *The Bumper Book* (1986) edited by John Metcalf.

The grand total of all direct grants and subsidy assistance received from the federal treasury by *all* of Canada's approximately 9,000 professional and non-professional writers in 1988 was merely equivalent to what the federal government gave to Dome Petroleum for just over *30 working minutes* of its entire 1983 operating year. Canada, measured by its gross national product, earned that amount in just under *28 seconds* of a single working day.

> ANDREAS SCHROEDER, author and arts adviser, *Word for Word: The Business of Writing in Alberta* (1988).

Also, if you're a writer, it's attractive to find new territory. Again, when I wrote *Shame*, I had the sense of writing in almost virgin soil; nobody had been there. And that, I think, is a feeling a lot of Western writers can never have, because the world is so written about here; wherever you go, a hundred writers have been before. That's less so in Canada, and I've heard Canadian writers talk about the way in which Canadian literature is gradually building an imaginative map of the country. I think it's rather wonderful for the writer to be in a place where there is still a lot to be done. In England, you can't take a step without falling over somebody else's book, or somebody else's patch of ground. Every piece of London has blue plaques on it where writers used to live and which they have written about, so to be able to find a metropolis that had not been written about was a gift. It attracted me for reasons that have nothing to do with politics or race, to say look at this, it's an interesting rich world and it's right next door.

> SALMAN RUSHDIE, Anglo-Indian novelist, interviewed at Harbourfront's International Festival of Authors by Catherine Bush in *What*, Feb. 1989.

Somebody like me coming from Canada and teaching so many war veterans, I really didn't know how important Viet Nam was until I arrived here. So I've kept my stranger-in-a-strange-land kind of attitude right up to the present.

> DAVID MORRELL, novelist born in Kitchener, Ont., who lives in Iowa City, Iowa, creator of the character Rambo; quoted by Jim Bawden in *The Toronto Star*, 22 Jan. 1989.

It is highly unlikely that an American would write about a young lad from Saskatchewan.

> MARGARET ATWOOD, author, commenting on short fiction by Canadian authors included in her edition of *The Best American Short Stories* (1989), *Maclean's*, 4 Dec. 1989.

Maybe one of the problems with literature in Canada is that writers are known for their roles rather than their books.

> MATT COHEN, novelist, interviewed by Mervin Butovsky, in *Other Solitudes: Canadian Multicultural Fictions* (1990) edited

by Linda Hutcheon and Marion Richmond.

WRITING

See also WRITERS

The fascinating thing about writing is that it's a way of transforming the things you've experienced; it's like being able to live twice.
JACQUES GODBOUT, author and filmmaker, quoted by Donald Smith in *Voices of Deliverance: Interviews with Quebec and Acadian Writers* (1986) translated by Larry Shouldice.

A story is an emotion that has found a metaphor.
JOHN V. HICKS, poet and writer, *Side Glances: Notes on the Writer's Craft* (1987).

Regional writing in Canada is defined as any work done outside of Toronto.
Attributed to the Ottawa newspaper columnist ROY MacGREGOR in 1989.

I read the article twice and both times couldn't remember what I'd read 10 minutes later. The article, like so many newsmagazine cover stories, was so full of names, ages, polls, charts and statistics that it all became a blur. It was, to coin a word, *factful* rather than thoughtful. And it read as though it were written by a committee.
MORRIS WOLFE, columnist, coining a new word to describe a cover story in *Time*, in *The Globe and Mail*, 16 Dec. 1989.

The story is all. . . . . I think story, story, story all the time. . . . My stock-in-trade is confidentiality.
ARTHUR HAILEY, popular novelist, quoted by Meriké Weiler in *The Toronto Star*, 7 April 1990.

Words, sentences, books: so much more than simple pleasure, so much the very heart of life itself.
NEIL BISSOONDATH, author, "Choose a Book, Choose Another,"*More than Words Can Say: Personal Perspectives on Literacy* (1990).

If the pen is mightier than the sword, why isn't it a felony to carry a ball-point in your jacket pocket?
MICHAEL COREN, biographer, "Canadian Satire," *The Toronto Star*, 25 Aug. 1990.

X

Strangely enough, the letter *X* by itself crops up far more often than those words that begin with *X*. We see the letter *X* everywhere — on clock faces using Roman numerals, on pedestrian crossings, at the end of love letters, and even on ladies' undergarments (remember the brassière ad on television telling you to "cross your heart"?).

BILL SHERK, neologist, *Brave New Words* (1979). The word of Canadian coinage that Sherk found for the X section of his alphabetically arranged book was "Xian." It means "a passive and indifferent Christian," and was coined by the poet Irving Layton who made use of it in the Foreword to his book of poems *The Covenant* (1977).

YELLOWKNIFE
See also NORTHWEST TERRITORIES

But think of this: Yellowknife, capital of a region larger than India, is younger than I am — and good gracious, I am not all *that* old.
> JAN MORRIS, Anglo-born travel writer, "Wild Blue-Yonder City," *Saturday Night*, Nov. 1989.

Nevertheless the longer I stayed in Yellow-knife — the longer I stayed! A week in all! — the more it seemed to me like a town in an occupied territory, the Dene and Métis its subject people, the whites its overlords.
> JAN MORRIS, Anglo-born travel writer, "Wild Blue-Yonder City," *Saturday Night*, Nov. 1989.

Yellowknife is the key to the Canadian identity, the very bedrock of the Canadian consciousness. I shall demonstrate: Y.K. is the capital of the Northwest Territories. The Northwest Territories are the largest part of the Canadian North. The Canadian North is embedded in the national psyche. Therefore, Yellowknife is the capital of the national psyche.
> CLAIRE DEANE, essayist, "The Greenhouse Effect," *The Idler*, No. 22, 1989.

YOUTH
See also AGE

She'll look up to that weathered face / That loves hers, line for line, / To see that maiden shining in her eyes / And laugh at how her mirror tells her lies.
> STAN ROGERS, singer and composer, "Lies," *Northwest Passage* (1981).

Teenagers give evidence of believing in the Canadian Dream. They believe that individuals have the opportunity through hard work and education to be successful. They believe that, regardless of their own family experiences, marriage and children are major means to the happiness and love they have come to value. Most believe that their lives are best lived in Canada.
> REGINALD W. BIBBY and DONALD C. POSTERSKI, sociologists, *The Emerging Generation: An Inside Look at Canada's Teenagers* (1985).

It seems apparent that today's teenagers are "little adults." They are conforming to the norms they perceive around them.

Rather than being like sculptors who shape and create new forms, adolescents are more like sponges soaking up the prevailing standards in their environment.
REGINALD W. BIBBY and DONALD C. POSTERSKI, sociologists, *The Emerging Generation: An Inside Look at Canada's Teenagers* (1985).

At eighteen everyone has a right to be fatuous.
EDWARD PHILLIPS, novelist, *Buried on Sunday* (1986).

Young men exaggerate; old men pretend.
ROBIN SKELTON, man-of-letters, aphorism, May 1990.

There is very little people in their early twenties can tell me that I don't already know, except about computers.
EDWARD PHILLIPS, novelist, *Sunday Best* (1990).

It's the three I's — they think they're immortal, immune and infertile. I see it as a massive power trip. By breaking the rules, they're testing their own power.
MARY SUE McCARTHY, educationalist, discussing the attitude of today's youth, quoted by Janice Dineen in *The Toronto Star*, 18 May 1991.

YUKON TERRITORY
See also KLONDIKE GOLD RUSH
The NORTH
WHITEHORSE

O Solitude, where are the charms / That sages have seen in thy face? / Better dwell in the midst of alarms / Than reign in this horrible place.
ROBERT CAMPBELL, H.B.C. trader and poetaster, sojourner in the Yukon in the 1850s; quoted by Ken S. Coates and William R. Morrison in *Land of the Midnight Sun: A History of the Yukon* (1988).

This Is No Picnic / Working and living conditions on this job are as difficult as those encountered on any construction job ever done in the United States or foreign territory. Men hired for this job will be required to work and live under the most extreme conditions imaginable. Temperatures will range from ninety degrees above zero to seventy degrees below zero. Men will have to fight swamps, rivers, ice and cold. Mosquitoes, flies and gnats will not only be annoying but will cause bodily harm. If you are not prepared to work under these and similar conditions *Do Not Apply.*
Sign in the employment office of the Bechtel-Price-Callaghan company which built the Alaska Highway in 1942, quoted by Pierre Berton in *The Mysterious North* (1956).

It does not seem reasonable that the destiny of a territory as large as the Yukon should be finally determined by the few residents living there.
T. DUFF PATTULLO, B.C. Premier, native of the Klondike region, quoted by Ken S. Coates and William R. Morrison in *Land of the Midnight Sun: A History of the Yukon* (1988).

I lived in a house under a wooded hill, and I knew that from my back door, through that hill, all the way north across the Arctic Circle to the cold ocean there was nothing but trees, rivers and rocks — scarcely a human being and probably no white men at all. I lived with the wilderness; it was all around me; and I have no doubt, looking back at it, that this had a great effect on me.
PIERRE BERTON, author, reflecting on his childhood spent in the Yukon Territory, address, Empire Club of Canada, Toronto, 11 Oct. 1973.

The Yukon was probably the first region of North America to be settled by humans.
ERLING FRIIS-BAASTAD, journalist, referring to the Asiatic migrants who more than 10,000 years ago trekked across Beringia and Alaska to settle in the vicinity of Old Crow, Y.T., in *The Globe and Mail*, 17 Dec. 1988.

For anyone who's never been to the Yukon, I'm not even going to try to describe the scenery. Suffice to say that the Yukon, near as I can make out, is 207,000 square miles of suck-your-breath-out photo opportunity.

ARTHUR BLACK, broadcaster and humorist, "Meet You at the Corner of Klondike and Yukon," *That Old Black Magic* (1989).

The Magic and the Mystery

Legend chosen to appear on automobile licence plates issued in the Yukon Territory, replacing the image of the gold-panner and the emblem of the fireweed, noted by Ted Harrison in *The Globe and Mail*, 13 Jan. 1990.

Yukoners call areas beyond the territory "outside." My newspaper even capitalizes the word. But only in winter does a more profound meaning of that term come to mind. The real outside, the world beyond the gentle border of the sky, reasserts its power. We go inside, into our homes and offices and cozy corner tables in restaurants, to contemplate the outside — the edge of our world and the fringes of our imagination.

JOHN DUNN, journalist with the *Whitehorse Star*, "Contrasts," *The Globe and Mail*, 18 Dec. 1990.

ZED

We have built a society that both expresses what we are and *is* what we are. Saying "zed" rather than "zee" does not make us different.

RICHARD GWYN, journalist, *Cultural Sovereignty: Myth or Reality? Proceedings of the 28th Annual Seminar on Canadian-American Relations, University of Windsor, Windsor, 5-7 Nov. 1986* (1987) edited by James Chacko.

ZOOS
See also ANIMALS

Man's dominion over the beasts of the earth includes a responsibility to preserve them in their own habitat.

DON HEPWORTH, Chief Inspector, Ontario Humane Society, *Gorilla in the Garage . . . and Other Stories* (1987).

It's exploiting. I have the same feeling about all zoos. I have no use for zoos. When I become world dictator my first job is to go around carefully opening all the cells of all the zoos in the world. I say carefully because most of the animals have been locked up for a few years and may be a bit . . . unreliable.

FARLEY MOWAT, naturalist and author, interviewed by Alan Twigg in *Strong Voices: Conversations with Fifty Canadian Authors* (1988).

ZZZ

Till recently, lexicographers had closed off their dictionaries with such words as "zymosan" (*Webster's Collegiate*), "zymurgy" (*Webster's New World*), and "zyzzyva" (*American Heritage*), but it was left to the editors of the *New Oxford English Dictionary* to discover the genius of the English language — the one word which puts all lexicographers and their readers to perpetual sleep, "zzz." And they have appropriately defined it as "z recurring."

THOMAS M. PAIKEDAY, lexicographer, compiler of *The Penguin Canadian Dictionary* (1990).

INDEX